THE YEAR'S WORK IN MODERN LANGUAGE STUDIES

THE
YEAR'S WORK IN
MODERN LANGUAGE
STUDIES

GENERAL EDITOR
STEPHEN PARKINSON

SECTION EDITORS

LATIN, ROMANCE LINGUISTICS, FRENCH,
OCCITAN, SPANISH, CATALAN, PORTUGUESE,
GALICIAN, LATIN AMERICAN
STEPHEN PARKINSON, M.A., PH.D.
Lecturer in
Portuguese Language and Linguistics,
University of Oxford

ITALIAN, ROMANIAN, RHETO-ROMANCE
JOHN M. A. LINDON, M.A.
Professor of Italian Studies,
University College London

CELTIC
DAVID A. THORNE, M.A., PH.D.
Reader in Welsh,
University of Wales, Lampeter

GERMANIC
DAVID A. WELLS, M.A., PH.D.
Professor of German,
Birkbeck College, University of London

SLAVONIC
PETER J. MAYO, M.A., PH.D.
Formerly Senior Lecturer in
Russian and Slavonic Studies,
University of Sheffield

VOLUME 60
1998

MANEY PUBLISHING
for the
MODERN HUMANITIES RESEARCH ASSOCIATION
1999

The Year's Work in Modern Language Studies may be ordered from the Hon. Treasurer, MHRA, King's College London, Strand, London WC2R 2LS, England.

ISBN 1 902653 06 8

ISSN 0084–4152

Produced in Great Britain by
MANEY PUBLISHING
HUDSON ROAD   LEEDS LS9 7DL

CONTENTS

x *Contents*

ABBREVIATIONS

NAME INDEX   969

PREFACE

This volume surveys work, published in 1998, unless otherwise stated, in the fields of Romance, Celtic, Germanic, and Slavonic languages and literatures. Up-to-date information on *YWMLS*, including current contributors and abbreviations lists, is now available on the MHRA's WWW site (http://www.mhra.org.uk/YWMLS/).

The attention of users is drawn to the lists of abbreviations at the end of the volume. An asterisk before a title indicates that the item in question has not been seen by the contributor.

Many authors, editors, and publishers supply review copies and offprints of their publications. To these we and our contributors are grateful and we invite others to follow their example, especially in the case of work issuing from an unusual or unexpected source of publication. We would ask that, whenever possible, items for review be sent directly to the appropriate contributor rather than to one of the editors. However, items relating to a number of fields are best sent to one of the editors who will then take appropriate steps.

The compilation of a contribution to the volume, especially in the field of the major languages and periods of literature, is a substantial research task requiring wide-ranging and specialized knowledge of the subject besides a huge reading effort accompanied by the constant exercise of critical judgement. Our thanks are due both to the authors and to the many other individuals and institutions who have contributed in one way or another to the making of this volume. They include the various institutions that have made research grants to contributors, Peter Mayo, compiler of the name index, Lisa Barber, Editorial Assistant for the Latin, Romance Linguistics, French, Occitan, Hispanic, and Germanic sections, the secretarial staff of the Faculty of Modern Languages, Oxford University, and our printers, Maney Publishing, amongst whose staff we would single out Michael Gallico, Emma Lonsdale-Wells, and Liz Rosindale with whom, as ever, it has been a pleasure to collaborate.

12 December 1999   S.R.P., J.M.A.L., D.A.T., D.A.W, P.J.M.

1

LATIN

I. MEDIEVAL LATIN

By Christopher J. McDonough, *Professor of Classics, University of Toronto*

1. General

D. Howlett, 'Insular acrostics, Celtic Latin colophons', *CMCS*, 35:27–44, edits and translates five Latin hexameter poems, three by Laurentius and Vergilius, which give some indication of the quality of intellectual life in 7th-c. Insular centres. Mary Carruthers, *The Craft of Thought. Meditation, Rhetoric, and the Making of Images, 400–1200*, CUP, xvii + 399 pp., draws on late antique, Carolingian, and 12th-c. sources to study the imaging techniques of monastic meditation that influenced and were realized in medieval literature. Peter Stotz, *Formenlehre, Syntax und Stilistik* (Handbuch zur lateinischen Sprache des Mittelalters, 4), Munich, C. H. Beck, xxvi + 510 pp., comprehensively surveys with copious examples the lexicology and grammar of medieval Latin together with a section on style that covers the figures of periphrasis, pleonasm, rhyme, alliteration, and poeticisms in prose. P. Gatti, 'Sul *Glossarium Patavinum Anonymum*', *Maia*, 49, 1997:139–41, offers emendations to a dictionary of synonyms that is important for the didactic praxis of the Middle Ages. G. Wieland, 'Interpreting the interpretation: the polysemy of the Latin gloss', *JMLat*, 8:59–71, re-examines the various positions taken in the debate about the purpose of interlinear and marginal annotations in manuscripts and finds that the answer depends on the different perspectives afforded by the gloss's origin, transmission, implied audience, and purpose. M. Sammer, 'Zur Bedeutungsgeschichte des Basilisken im Abendland', *Euphorion*, 92:143–221, surveys ancient, late antique, and medieval accounts of the basilisk's birth and death contained in encyclopedic and scientific sources, before discussing the meanings attributed to it in Christian allegoresis and biblical exegesis. H. Lutterbach, 'Gleichgeschlechtliches sexuelles Verhalten. Ein Tabu zwischen Spätantike und früher Neuzeit', *HZ*, 267:281–311, argues on the basis of Leviticus and a wide range of theological writings that in the Judeo-Christian tradition there was no tolerance for same-sex relations. M. A. Valante, 'Reassessing the Irish "monastic town"', *IHS*, 121:1–18, examines the *Life of St Columba* and other hagiographic documents, including Cogitosus's

Vita Brigitae, in the course of arguing that Irish monasteries were not proto-urban. O. Phillips, 'From man to mongoose: Lucan's *psyllus* and Isidore's *suillus*', *MJ*, 33:15–20, traces the stages by which the reading *psyllus* in Dracontius, *De laudibus dei* 1.515, was corrupted to *suillus* in the Eugenius recension, from which Isidore inferred that the ichneumon was pig-like. *Roma, magistra mundi. Itineraria culturae medievalis*, ed. Jacqueline Hamesse, Louvain-la-Neuve, Fédération internationale des Instituts d'Études Médiévales, x + 1030 pp., includes: V. Brown, 'Homiletic setting and a new witness to Redaction I of the *Visio Sancti Pauli*: Funeral sermons in Beneventan script (Vat. Borghese 86)' (71–88), an edition of the anonymous apocalypse written in southern Italy; M. W. Herren, 'Irish biblical commentaries before 800' (391–407), which argues the case for the Irish origins of certain works; J. Hill, 'Aelfric, Gregory and the Carolingians' (409–23), a study of intertextuality based on four homilies by Aelfric and Gregory; A. G. Rigg, 'Walter Map, the shaggy dog story, and the *quaestio disputata*' (723–35), which suggests that certain of Map's stories parody or mock specific scholastic disputations.

2. ANGLO-SAXON ENGLAND

S. Rosser, 'Aethelthryth: a conventional saint?', *BJR*, 79.3, 1997:15–24, shows how Bede drew upon other royal women as a model for his treatment of the saint in the *Historia ecclesiastica*. S. Gwara, 'Glosses to Aldhelm's "Prosa de virginitate" and glossaries from the Anglo-Saxon golden age, ca. 670–800', *SM*, 38, 1997[1998]:561–645, divides the glossed MSS into three classes, and traces the transmission of the glosses based on identified hands, before he isolates and dates a common recension that may be contemporary with Aldhelm. N. G. Discenza, ' "Wise wealhstodas": the prologue to Sirach as a model for Alfred's preface to the *Pastoral Care*', *JEGP*, 97:488–99, shows how Alfred appropriated the thematic progression of the prologue to Sirach as a framework for his own writing, and emphasized the rhetorical strategies to reassure the audience of the legitimacy of the act of translation. D. F. Johnson, 'The fall of Lucifer in *Genesis A* and two Anglo-Latin royal charters', *ib.*, 500–21, discovers two Latin analogues for the narrative pattern and interpretation of the myth in *Genesis A*, common to which is the reading that all of physical creation came about to fill the void occasioned by the primal lapse of the rebel angels. C. A. Jones, '*Meatim sed et rustica*: Aelfric of Eynsham as a medieval Latin author', *JMLat*, 8:1–57, re-examines the Latin writings attributed to Aelfric and the assumptions about style and authorial method that have formed the basis for establishing the canon, analyses selected works, qualifies the prevailing view of his

Latinity and explores the implications of this revaluation for understanding his works. Id., 'The book of the liturgy in Anglo-Saxon England', *Speculum*, 73:659–702, examines the reception and uses of theoretical comment on the liturgy between *c.*800 and *c.*1100, the most influential of which were Isidore's *De ecclesiasticis officiis*, the Carolingian *expositiones missae* and the commentary of Amalarius of Metz.

3. THE CAROLINGIAN AND OTTONIAN PERIOD

D. R. Howlett, 'Miscouplings in couplets', *ALMA*, 55, 1997:271–76, edits and translates a poem entitled *In nomine Trinitatis*, which precedes the chapter headings to Isidore's *Origines* contained in Oxford, Queen's College, MS 320; Id., 'Singers' ratios in *Rauca Sonora*', *ib.*, 277–80, reproduces a text from Paris, BN, lat. 8069, fols 1^v–2^r, with a translation and analysis of the poem's structure based on the ratios of music theory. R. Jakobi, 'Notizen zu mittelalterlichen Klassikerkommentaren', *SM*, 38, 1997[1998]:305–15, tracks an *Achilleis* commentary to Northern France of the early 9th c., emends a commentary on Priscian's *Partitiones* and publishes Ovidian glosses. F. Mosetti Casaretto, 'L'"Epistola ad Grimaldum abbatem" di Ermenrico di Ellwangen: identità e destinazione, scopo, tipologia redazionale', *ib.*, 647–77, examines the work as both letter and epitome, addressed both to an indeterminate public and to a private individual. M. Giovini, 'Un intarsio Virgiliano: La morte di Lamberto di Spoleto nei *Gesta Berengarii Imperatoris*', *Maia*, 50:349–61, argues that the omnipresence of Vergil's language and style in *Gesta* 3.249–79 is a means of continuing a conceptual dialogue with the earlier texts and contexts.

4. THE ELEVENTH CENTURY

H. Meyer, ' "Intentio auctoris, utilitas libri". Wirkungsabsicht und Nutzen literarischer Werke nach Accessus-Prologen des 11. bis 13. Jahrhunderts', *FmSt*, 31, 1997:390–413, draws out the presuppositions underlying statements regarding intention and utility found in about 200 accessus to literary works, books of the Bible and legal texts, before he divides them into nine categories. A. A. Grotans, ' "Sih dir selbo lector." Cues for reading in tenth- and eleventh-century St. Gall', *Scriptorium*, 51, 1997:251–302, connects the lexical and graphic cues used in the schoolroom with two aspects of *lectio*, namely, the structural analysis and oral performance of texts. The *Encomium Emma Reginae*, ed. Alistair Campbell, CUP, lxix + 112 pp., reappears with a supplementary introduction by Simon Keynes, who supplies the historical context in which the work was written. M. Atherton, 'The image of the temple in the *Psychomachia* and late Anglo-Saxon literature', *BJR*, 79.3, 1997:263–85, compares the various images in illustrations and discusses the artistic and literary parallels in liturgical MSS and homiletic works. R. Gamberini, 'La modernità e il fallimento del *Ruodlieb*', *Maia*, 49, 1997:129–38, suggests that the author conceived the poem as a modern epic and locates its originality in the amalgam of elements assembled from different genres and from oral and popular culture, especially saga, and mime. V. B. Jordan, 'Chronology and discourse in the *Vita Aedwardi Regis*', *JMLat*, 8:122–55, offers a culturally-specific approach to a biography that has suffered from an anachronistic application of modern genre theory and argues that the text's formal prosimetric forms of discourse reflect the work's thematic design. E. Cownie, 'The cult of St Edmund in the eleventh and twelfth centuries. The language and communication of a medieval saint's cult', *NMi*, 99:177–97, examines Latin and vernacular sources to demonstrate the multi-media and multi-lingual strategies used to advance the cult by abbot Baldwin, which were designed to cross the language barrier between monks and the laity. J. Öberg, 'Gastgelehrter als literarische Zielscheibe um das Jahr 1000: Die Invektive Warners von Rouen gegen den Iren Moriuht', *MJ*, 33.2:21–43, offers his own edition of the poem in response to a recent edition.

5. THE TWELFTH CENTURY

Commedie Latine del XII e XIII secolo, ed. Ferruccio Bertini, Genoa U.P., 526 pp., contains new editions of the *Alda, Lidia, Rapularius II, De more medicorum*, and *De uxore cerdonis*, all accompanied by concise introductions and Italian translations, but only the *Lidia* is equipped with a splendid commentary by Isabella Gualandri and Giovanni Orlandi. Baudri de Bourgueil, *Poèmes*. Tome 1, ed. Jean-Yves Tilliette, Les Belles Lettres, lxv + 236 pp., supplies an historical and literary introduction to a collection preserved almost entirely in a single MS (Vatican Reg. lat. 1351), a readable French translation and concise notes. Adelard of Bath, *Conversations with his Nephew. On the Same and the Different, Questions on Natural Science and on Birds*, ed. and transl. Charles Burnett (Cambridge Medieval Classics, 9), CUP, lii + 287 pp., offers new Latin texts based on fresh collations of the MSS with facing English translations and brief notes. A. Wlosok, 'Illustrated Vergil manuscripts: reception and exegesis', *CJ*, 93:355–82, examines the interpretive significance of the illustrations and their influence on the reception of the epic's major characters by medieval mythographers (Isidore, Hrabanus Maurus and Theodulf), the *Aeneid* commentary attributed to Bernardus Silvestris, and John of Salisbury's *Policraticus*. C. Whitehead, 'Making a cloister of the soul in medieval religious treatises', *MAe*, 67 : 1–29, investigates the relationship between the allegorical cloister of the mind and the literal monastic cloister in Hugh of Fouilloy's *De claustro animae*, *Le Pèlerinage de la vie humaine*, and the ME *The Abbey of the Holy Ghost*, the last a translation of a vernacular prose treatise *Li Liure du cloistre de l'âme*. J. A. Allen, 'On the dating of Abailard's *Dialogus*: a reply to Mews', *Vivarium*, 36 : 135–51, argues for dating the work *c.*1142 on the basis of comparing its definition of sin with that contained in the *Ethica*. Th. Falmagne, 'Les Cisterciens et les nouvelles formes d'organisation des florilèges aux 12e et 13e siècles', *ALMA*, 55, 1997 : 73–176, discusses old and new forms of classical and medieval florilegia, alphabetic arrangement, and indexation, before he appends a list of unedited miscellanies. J. R. E. Bliese, 'Saint Cuthbert and war', *JMH*, 24 : 215–41, examines the rhetoric of several 12th-c. accounts of the saint's appearance to King Alfred at the battle of Eddington in 878, including the *Historia de sancto Cuthberto*, *Capitula de miraculis et translationibus sancti Cuthberti*, Symeon of Durham's *Historia ecclesiae Dunhelmensis*, William of Malmesbury's *Gesta regum Anglorum* and Aelred of Rievaulx's *Genealogia regum Anglorum*. P. Le Rider, 'Lions et dragons dans la littérature, de Pierre Damien à Chrétien de Troyes', *MA*, 104 : 9–52, detects oriental influence in the source used by Alexander Neckam, *DNR* 2. 148 (pp. 229–30W), who drew his account from a resumé of a vernacular text. A. Bisanti, 'Nota a Bernardo di Morlas, "De contemptu mundi" II 552', *SM*, 38 : 1997[1998] : 837–44, emends the name *Lydia* to *Livia*, rather than to *Laida*; Id., 'La figura di Sileno nell' "Altercatio Phyllidis et Flore" (*Carmina Burana* 92, 70–71)', *ib.*, 845–49, names Vergil *Ecl.* 6 and Ovid *Ars* 1, 543–47 as the sources of the poem's comic interlude. E. Wolff, 'Les *Carmina Burana*: plurilinguisme et poésie', *BGB*, 56, 1997 : 260–71, examines two categories of vernacular insertion into Latin texts and closely analyses the structures of *CB* 118 and 185. Alexander Neckam *Nouus Auianus*, ed. T. A.-P. Klein (Favolisti Latini Medievali e Umanistici, 7), Genoa, offers an edition based on a new collation of three MSS, and includes a concise introduction, German translation and brief notes on the six fables. D. Roth, 'Mittelalterliche Misogynie - ein Mythos? Die antiken *molestiae nuptiarum* im *Adversus Iovinianum* und ihre Rezeption in der lateinischen Literatur des 12. Jahrhunderts', *AKG*, 80 : 39–66, tracks the reception of *exempla* compiled from pagan literature by Jerome in Abelard's *Theologia Christiana* and the *Historia Calamitatum*, John of Salisbury's *Policraticus*, Walter Map's *Dissuasio Valerii*, Peter of Blois's *Epistola ad amicum*, and Hugo of Folieto's *De Nuptiis libri duo*, all texts which justify the ancient *dicta* on the grounds of their exemplarity and moral utility in urging rejection of marriage. M. Molina Sánchez, 'La *Aulularia* de Vital de Blois y el pensamiento filosófico medieval', *Maia*, 49, 1997:425–46, connects the philosophical and cultural world of the play with the school of Chartres and Bernardus Silvestris and concludes that the philosophical parody is not directed against the latter. Id., 'Algunas puntualizaciones sobre la *Aulularia* de Vital de Blois', *MedRom*, 32:190–208, explores the significance of the play's prologue, comments on the figure Euclion, and the presence of Lucretius in the text. S. Copello, 'Il *Micrologus* di Guido d'Arezzo', *Maia*, 49, 1997:447–57, analyses the contents and the artistic style of its prose. M. Meckler, 'Traditional teaching or modernist manifesto? Matthew of Vendôme's criticisms of ancient poetry in the *Ars versificatoria*', *JMLat*, 8:192–205, discovers from examining *Ars* 4.1–15 that Matthew's anti-classical criticism should be situated within the context of the authoritative tradition of the ancients. G. Giordanengo, 'La bibliothèque de Geoffroy de Vendôme (1093–1132)', *CCMe*, 41:105–25, identifies the volumes that belonged to the library of La Trinité of Vendôme during Geoffrey's tenure and concludes that patristic authors and scientific and medical works held a special interest for him. I. Marchesin, 'Les jongleurs dans les psautiers du haut moyen âge: nouvelles hypothèses sur la symbolique de l'histrion médiéval', *ib.*, 127–39, sketches the literary tradition of the morally suspect juggler, the antithesis of the good Christian, before she examines iconographic material that points to the symbolic function of the juggler, whose gestures could refer to human or to spiritual music. A. G. Rigg, 'Calchas, renegade and traitor: Dares and Joseph of Exeter', *NQ*, 243:176–78, traces the identification of Calchas as a Trojan back to Dares, before he suggests that Joseph artfully concealed Calchas's Trojan origins in order to reveal him later as a betrayer. T. E. Burman, '*Tafsīr* and translation: traditional Arabic Qur'ān exegesis and the Latin Qur'āns of Robert of Ketton and Mark of Toledo', *Speculum*, 73:703–32, argues for the superiority of Robert's translation, *Lex Mahumet*, over the more literal version of Mark, because the former tried to ensure that his paraphrase reflected what Muslims themselves thought to be the meaning of the Qur'ān, as shown by his incorporation of glosses and explanations from Arabic commentaries; C. W. Bynum, 'Metamorphosis, or Gerald and the werewolf', *ib.*, 987–1013, explores three discourses or genres that explicitly treat change from one thing to another, namely Ovidian poetry, theological discussions of miraculous change, and collections of marvels, especially those involving species transformation, before she examines werewolves in the works of Gerald of Wales and Gervais of Tilbury; V. A. Kolve, 'Ganymede/*Son of Getron*: medieval monasticism and the drama of same-sex desire', *ib.*, 1014–67, discusses the St. Nicholas play *Filius Getronis* to show how monastic communities attempted to confront and transcend the reality of homoerotic desire. F. W. Worstbrock, 'Zum Stand der Forschung über Warnerius von Basel', *MJ*, 33.2:45–54, contests recent claims that Warnerius came from a French-speaking area, that he composed the *Synodus* around the middle of the 12th c., and that he was the bishop of Langres from 1163–79. T. Gärtner, 'Die Eros-Exkurs in "De planctu Naturae" (VIII 247 – X 20) und seine Stellung im dichterischen Gesamtwerk des Alanus ab Insulis', *ib.*, 55–65, lists verbal correspondences to show that the excursus can only be fully understood by comparing the rhythmical poem, *Vix nodosum*, also written by Alan. B. Ruppel, 'Ein verschollenes Gedichte des 12. Jahrhunderts: Heinrichs von Huntingdon "De herbis" ', *FmSt*, 31, 1997:197–213, examines the authorship, date, and structure of a poem in London, BL, MS Sloane 3468, which he attributes to Henry, and from which he prints an excerpt. R. Fulton, ' "Quae est ista quae ascendit sicut aurora consurgens?": the Song of Songs as the *Historia* for the Office of the Assumption', *MedS*, 60:55–122, explains how and why verses from a biblical book were used to recall the biography of Mary and became a dialogic exchange between Christ and his mother. *Hildegard of Bingen. The Context of her Thought and Art*, ed. Charles Burnett and Peter Dronke, London, Warburg Institute, 234 pp., contains 13 essays that deal with Hildegard's intellectual background, the transmission of her manuscripts and the accompanying illuminations, and the novel aspects of her poetry and scientific pursuits. Siân Echard, *Arthurian Narrative in the Latin Tradition*, CUP, xi + 256 pp., examines the backgrounds and preoccupations of Geoffrey of Monmouth's *Historia regum Britanniae* and the *Vita Merlini*, as well as Arthurian episodes embedded in the writings of Gerald of Wales, Etienne de Rouen, Johannes de Hauvilla, Andreas Capellanus, Walter Map, Robert of Torigny, and John of Glastonbury.

6. THE THIRTEENTH CENTURY

Der 'Occultus Erfordensis' des Nicolaus von Bibra, ed. Christine Mundhenk, Weimar, Hermann Böhlaus Nachfolger, 1997, 395 pp., offers a critical edition, based on 12 MSS, of a rambling poem that documents an ecclesiastical dispute in Erfurt, complete with an informative introduction that describes the issues and personalities involved, a facing German translation and a brief commentary. L. Tewes, 'Der *Dialogus miraculorum* des Caesarius von Heisterbach. Beobachtungen zum Gliederungs-und Werkcharakter', *AKG*, 79, 1997:13–30, follows the reception of the work by historians and philologists over the last 150 years before he examines the work's theme, purpose, and the author's motivation. D. Vitali, 'Noch einmal zu Lat. *inossari*', *ALMA*, 55, 1997:281–82, adduces three examples of the verb from unpublished material and suggests that it was probably modelled on CL *incarnare*. S. Young, 'Donatus, bishop of Fiesole 829–76, and the cult of St Brigit in Italy', *CMCS*, 35:13–26, examines the account in the *Acta Sancti Andreae* in which Andreas's sister, Brigida, is summoned to Italy, and concludes that she was a double of Brigit of Kildare. G. Mombello, 'La "Confessio lupi, vulpis et asini" du ms. 0210 de l'Accademia delle Scienze de Turin', *Reinardus*, 11:118–29, identifies a MS of Italian origin unknown to previous editors of the *Poenitentiarius*, describes its composition and contents, reports 69 readings (many erroneous) that are unique to the MS, and discusses the text's reception in sermons and collections of *exempla*. M. Okubo, 'Le Château de la Dame: le symbolisme marial du château chez Robert Grosseteste', *Actes* (Rambures), 271–82, traces the allegorical development of the figure, based on Luke 10.38, in sermon literature, before she argues that it forms the focal point of the *Château d'amour*, where Grosseteste innovatively unites the science of optics and theology. M. G. Bajoni, 'Da Ausonio a Giovanni di Garlandia: un possibile percorso della *Rota Vergilii*', *Emerita*, 65, 1997:281–85, traces the origin of a medieval didactic device to a metaphor in Sidonius Apollinaris, *Ep.* 9.15.1. R. Schnell, 'The discourse on marriage in the Middle Ages', *Speculum*, 73:771–86, draws upon the sermon collection of the Dominican friar Peregrinus to show the contrast between the pragmatic treatment of the theme in a pastoral setting and the different perspective offered in academic texts. T. A.-P. Klein, ' "Arabs" siue "De dimidio et integro amico". Mittelalterliche Paraphrasendichtung am Beispiel der Petrus-Alfonsi-Rezeption im 13. und 14. Jahrhundert', *MJ*, 33.2:67–84, offers a second edition of an anonymous poem, uniquely preserved in Leipzig, UB, lat. 351, which versifies material from the *Disciplina clericalis* of Petrus Alfonsi. K. Harthun, 'Die lateinische Übersetzung der Gregoriuslegende Hartmanns von Aue. Zur These ihrer Relegendarisierung durch Arnold von Lübeck', *ib.*, 85–104, scrutinizes the literary-theoretical comments contained in the prologues of both the original and translation, before she discusses their generic differences.

7. THE FOURTEENTH AND FIFTEENTH CENTURIES

F. Eisermann, ' "Diversae et plurimae materiae in diversis capitulis". Der "Stimulus amoris" als literarisches Dokument', *FmSt*, 31, 1997:214–32, uses a popular work to explore the modalities of disseminating spiritual literature and finds from examining its reception that the *Stimulus amoris* functioned as an effective ascetic document in the reform movements. G. Porta, 'La symbolique des animaux dans les lettres de Cola di Rienzo', *Reinardus*, 11:175–84, finds that the symbolic interpretation of animals, inspired by apocalyptic literature, and the allegorical interpretation of history in which Cola favoured Livy, Sallust, Seneca, and above all Boethius, provide the intellectual contexts for Cola's polemic against the oppressors of Rome, Italy and the church. M. L. Colker, 'A previously unpublished history of the Trojans', *JMLat*, 8:80–121, edits the anonymous *Hystoria Troianorum* preserved in two MSS: Chantilly, Musée Condé, MS Condé 954, and London, BL, MS Burney 186. N. Cartlidge, 'Misogyny in a medieval university? The "Hoc contra malos" commentary on Walter Map's *Dissuasio Valerii*', *ib.*, 156–91, edits from Cambridge, St. John's College, MS E. 12 and Cambridge, Clare College, MS N. 2. 5, a moralizing commentary that transforms Map's bigotry against women into pious illustrations of prudent Christian conduct, and suggests that the commentator was attracted to the earlier work for its collection of classical anecdotes and rhetorical flair. A. Placanica, 'Bonifazio VIII, Timoteo Eluro e le trombe (Una leggenda sull'abdicazione di Celestino V)', *Maia*, 49, 1997:143–50, finds that the 6th-c. *Historia ecclesiastica* of Theodoros Anagnostes contains all the elements of the story concerning Celestine. S. Echard, 'With Carmen's help: Latin authorities in the *Confessio Amantis*', *SP*, 95:1–40, investigates the poet's decision to use Latin and its subsequent treatment in the MSS. M. Burns, 'Classicizing and medievalizing Chaucer: the sources for Pyramus' death-throes in the Legend of Good Women', *Neophilologus*, 81, 1997:637–47, demonstrates the poet's close dependence on Ovid's *Metamorphoses* and concludes that the use of Geoffrey of Monmouth's *Historia regum Britanniae* remains unproven. M. W. Musgrove, 'Cyclopean Latin: intertextual readings in Dante's *Eclogues* and Góngora's *Polifemo y Galatea*', *CML*, 18:125–36, demonstrates the continuity of controversies about style in the pastoral tradition. P. Herrera Roldán, 'Léxicos en la obra de S. Eulogio de Córdoba', *ALMA*, 55, 1997:35–72, offers a selection of neologisms to illustrate the continuing vitality of medieval Latin. D. Trotter, 'Some lexical gleanings from Anglo-French Gascony', *ZRP*, 114:53–72, illustrates the vital linguistic mix of French, Gascon, and Latin found in documents from Britain and Gascony. J. Pendergrass, 'Lettres, poèmes et débat scolaire de Germain Maciot, étudiant Parisien du XVe siècle Ms. latin 8659 de la Bibliothèque Nationale de France', *ALMA*, 55, 1997:177–270, edits works addressed by a student to his professors, including Bernard Roillet, with a detailed description of the MS and the student's literary models, who included Vergil, Ovid, Francesco Negri and Girolamo Balbi. R.-H. Steinmetz, 'Der "Libellus muliebri nequitia plenus". Eine ungedruckte lateinische Version der "Sieben weisen Meister" und ihre deutsche Übersetzung aus dem 15. Jahrhundert', *ZDA*, 126, 1997:397–446, offers parallel editions of a 14th-c. Latin text and a 15th-c. translation of it into German, the latter based on two MSS from St Florian and Vienna, followed by reflections on the significance of the two texts; D. Roth and R.-H. Steinmetz, 'Eine zweite Handschrift der "Allegatio septem sapientum" ("Libellus muliebri nequitia plenus")', *ib.*, 127:307–22, describe and analyse the contents of Munich, Bayerische Staatsbibliothek, Clm 22378 and its relationship with the German translation. A. E. Wright, 'Readers and wolves: late-medieval commentaries on the "De lupo et capite"', *JMLat*, 8:72–79, describes glosses from 15th-c. codices on the fables of the Anonymous Neveleti and notes how readers responded to the uncharacteristic features of the tale about a wolf and its discovery of a lifeless head. R. Kieckhefer, 'Convention and conversion: patterns in late medieval piety', *Church History*, 67:32–51, adduces the stories of Margaret Kempe, Richard Rolle, and Johannes Tauler to support the thesis that conversion was seen as a turning away from conventional devotionalism that was centred on specific objects, like the Eucharist and the saints. F. Mormando, 'Bernardino of Siena: "Great defender" or "merciless betrayer" of women?', *Italica*, 75:22–40, mines the writings relevant to Bernardino's teachings about women to find that he upheld the status quo in gender relations. D. Roth, 'Von der *dissuasio* zur *quaestio*. Die Transformation des Topos *An vir sapiens ducat uxorem* in Wittenwilers "Ehedebatte"', *Euphorion*, 91, 1997:377–96, documents the impact of the question, disseminated by Jerome's *Contra Iovinianum*, on several medieval Latin works before he turns to its appropriation by vernacular writers. P. Gilli, 'Le conflit entre le juriste et l'orateur d'après une lettre de Cosma Raimondi, humaniste italien en Avignon (c. 1431–1432)', *Rhetorica*, 16:259–86, edits from two MSS Cosma's letter denouncing the dominance of lawyers over students of the humanities. J. Simpson, 'The other book of Troy: Guido delle Colonne's *Historia destructionis Troiae* in fourteenth- and fifteenth-century England', *Speculum*, 73:397–423, emphasizes the anti-imperialistic tradition represented in three literary retellings of Guido's work, namely the anonymous Laud Troy Book, Lydgate's *Troy Book*, and John Clerk's *Destruction of Troy*; J. A. Burrow, 'Hoccleve's *Complaint* and Isidore of Seville again', *ib.*, 424–28, demonstrates that Hoccleve's English verse and Latin glosses derive from an epitome, not the full text, of Isidore's *Synonyma*, similar to the one contained in Oxford, Bodleian Library, MS Bodley 110. M. P. Rodríguez-Escalona, 'Canticum alphabeticum de mala muliere', *MJ*, 33.2:119–27, edits an anonymous rhythmical poem that was inspired by the Gregorian reform's insistence on chastity for religious. M. Asper, U. Kühne, and M. Pickavé, 'Petripauli Vergerii Iustinopolitani Comedia. Eine Neuedition des "Paulus"', *ib.*, 129–76, offer a critical edition of a comedy in the Terentian tradition, based on five MSS. M. Uguccione, 'A proposito dell' umanista feltrino Antonio da Romagno', *SM*, 39:397–447, re-examines the chronology of Antonio's life before he edits his correspondence with Ambrogio of Senigallia.

NEO-LATIN

POSTPONED

2
ROMANCE LANGUAGES

I. ROMANCE LINGUISTICS

By JOHN N. GREEN, *University of Bradford*

1. ACTA, FESTSCHRIFTEN

Thanks to a heroic editorial effort by Giovanni Ruffino, *Atti* (Palermo), I–VI, were released as a complete, elegant set in 1998, in time for the Brussels Congress; in addition to the usual intrasystemic studies, they give special prominence to the Middle Ages and to the linguistic and cultural matrix of the Mediterranean. *LSRL 26* and *LSRL 27*, both neat volumes characterized by efficient and self-effacing editing, assemble respectively 18 and 22 papers from the annual American Symposia, with a heavy preponderance of Minimalist/Optimalist syntax and very light leavening of phonology, the majority concentrating on French and Spanish, but with nods in the direction of more exotic comparative data (individual items are discussed below). By contrast, *RK 11*, the proceedings of the 1995 Giessen Colloquium, celebrates biodiversity in a whole gamut of new descriptive approaches on offer to Romance; splendid in principle, though the empirical data does get trampled in the rush of enthusiasm.

Wilmet Vol. opens with a friendly tribute by R. Martin, 'Marc Wilmet, de la patience philologique à l'intuition théorisante' (9–20), followed by a bibliography compiled by A.-R. Delbart (21–30) and 28 contributions mainly on French syntax and discourse. Similarly focused, *Blanche-Benveniste Vol.* includes a bibliography compiled by P. Swiggers (7–18) and 33 papers, mostly on methods for the description of authentic speech. *CFS*, 50, 1997[1998], ed. R. Amacker, marks its half centenary with a memorial to Louis J. Prieto, reprinting four of his less accessible articles alongside tributes and bibliographies. *TLP*, 35–36, ed. M. Bierbach et al., poignantly appears as a memorial to Manfred Höfler — the bibliography by B. von Gemmingen (11–18) and the 26, mostly lexicographical, articles having been planned as a *Festschrift*. Other periodical dedications include: *RRL*, 42.1–2, 1997[1998], for Sorin Stati; and *La Linguistique*, 34.2, ed. A. Lefebvre, for Henriette Walter — happily still very productive, as witnessed by the intentionally selective bibliography provided by her husband and collaborator Gérard (153–58). A retirement tribute, Germà Colón Domènech, *Estudis de filologia catalana i romànica*, ed. Antoni Ferrando and Josep Massot, València U.P., 1997, xxx + 508 pp., assembles 36 of C.'s papers, written or newly translated into (Valencian) Catalan, mixing erudite historical lexicology with open rebukes ('Mossarabomania' and 'En la trista actualitat') for over-enthusiastic etymology and glottopolitics.

2. GENERAL ROMANCE AND LATIN

Price, *Encyclopedia*, is a reliable, no-nonsense alphabetic reference manual, concentrating on external history and 'useful facts' such as speaker numbers and the sometimes bewildering names of non-standard varieties, with excellent coverage of Romance. An equally authoritative foil is available in Ramat, *Indo-European*, which consciously excludes Romance but has valuable overviews and sections on Greek, Latin, and Italic. In praise of linguistic deflation, Ž. Muljačić, 'Tertium datur. Per una nuova interpretazione della "genesi" delle lingue romanze', *Atti* (Palermo), v, 485–90, thankfully concludes that of the 40 Romance varieties aspiring to language status in 1970 less than half will achieve this goal. Behind the rather cryptic title of R. Posner's 'Romance linguistics in the nineties', *RPh*, 51:326–55, lies a review article on five volumes of symposium papers, which she finds professional but narrow — more linguistic than Romance — and perhaps too ephemeral to warrant permanent hard bindings (see *YWMLS*, 57:19, 58:15). Looking forward, W. Raible, 'Mögliche Partnerschaften', *ZFSL*, 108:258–63, speculates on how well Romance linguistics will adapt to a future of teamwork and research projects rather than lone scholars, and recommends seeking partnerships with practitioners of other disciplines, which he believes can be achieved without blurring distinctiveness.

A collection of papers by Giuliano Bonfante, **The Origins of the Romance Languages: Stages in the Development of Latin*, has been edited by Larissa Bonfante, Heidelberg, Winter, 1997. *Atti* (Palermo), vi, focuses on models for interpreting Medieval culture and texts, with a round table on codicology including A. Varvaro's rehabilitation of a neglected source of philological evidence, 'Elogio della copia' (785–96). Yvonne Cazal, *Les Voix du Peuple — Verbum Dei. Le bilinguisme latin — latin vulgaire au moyen âge*, Geneva, Droz, 336 pp., a careful study of the linguistic and literary attributes of the so-called 'épîtres farcies', 13th-c. texts predominantly in Church Latin but with OF interpolations, pays special attention to the *Ludus Paschalis* of Origny-Saint-Benoîte. *La transizione dal latino alle lingue romanze*, ed. József Herman, Tübingen, Niemeyer [viii +] 260 pp., assembles 14 well focused papers from a 1996 Venice colloquium, with a detailed prospectus by H., 'La chronologie de la transition' (5–26), and

R. Wright's 'Il latino: da madrelingua nativa a lingua straniera' (77–85), tracing stages in the reconceptualization of Latin as the significant other. No less significant, but alas too numerous for individual review are the 55 *Papers from the Seventh International Colloquium on Latin Linguistics* (IBS, 86), ed. Hannah Rosén, 1996, 735 pp., among which E. Coseriu, 'Latin et grec dans le latin dit "vulgaire"' (27–37) reports on a large-scale project to identify the full extent of Greek influence, much more pervasive than most Romanists realize and responsible for both lexical and syntactic calques and maybe even for such seismic shifts as the evolution of the definite articles. As I gave a warm welcome in these pages last year to Barbara Frank's *Inventaire systématique* (*YWMLS*, 59:24), it is only fair to point out that G. Roques, *RLiR*, 62:470–75, has deep reservations about definitions, choices of text and especially the dating and location of manuscripts; but he does hope that it will be a stimulus to scholarly research. More predictable was W. Mańczak's catalogue of putative 'Erreurs dans le *Lexikon der romanistischen Linguistik, II, 1*', *KN*, 44, 1997:179–88, since its contributors are not persuaded that Romance descends directly from Classical Latin, nor that lexico-statistical evidence (whose value no-one denies) is *sufficient* to undermine Wartburg's areo-genetic classification of Romance.

3. HISTORY OF ROMANCE LINGUISTICS

History of Linguistics. III: Renaissance and Early Modern Linguistics, ed. Giulio Lepschy, London, Longman, xxiv + 263 pp., contains essays by M. Tavoni on Western Europe with a subsection on comparative Romance (Dante, and the Hispanic tradition), and by R. Simone on the early modern period, including Port Royal, Condillac and Diderot. Vol. IV of the compendium is wholly taken up by Anna Morpurgo Davies's erudite account of *Nineteenth-Century Linguistics*, *ib.*, xxvi + 434 pp.; the thematic treatment of historicism and organicism is especially revealing. Baker, *Encyclopedia*, gives prominence to regional and country-specific traditions of translating, with good coverage of Latin and Romance, including A. Pym, 'Spanish tradition' (552–63), whose sharp image of Alfonso X counterbalances good editing skills with total political ineptitude. A. Quilis, 'La historiografía lingüística española', *RPh*, 51:475–83, welcomes *BICRES*, the monumental bibliography assembled by H.-J. Nied-erehe, adding material of his own on Nebrija and later authors. An interesting note by G. Graffi, 'L'interiezione tra i grammatici greci e i grammatici latini', *ILing*, 19, 1996[1997]:11–18, traces Priscian's ambivalence to an earlier dispute: the ancient Greek philosophers had regarded interjections as devoid of independent meaning and therefore incapable of constituting a grammatical category, whereas the more empirical approach of Carisius and Donatus had demonstrated that, whatever else, they could not be satisfactorily subsumed under adverbials.

The liveliness of the history section of the 1998 Brussels Congress is noted by G. Haßler, 'XXIIe congrès international', *BGS*, 8 : 298–301; we await with interest the matured products. Lively but painful is the *Vergangenheitsbewertigung* being experienced in Germany, judging by the predictably furious reactions stirred up by Nerlich's comments on Curtius (*YWMLS*, 59 : 27): J. Bem, A. Guyaux, C. Jacquemard–de Gemeaux, and E. J. Richards, 'Réponses à Michael Nerlich', *RF*, 110 : 478–90, defend their respective stances, with a counterattack by E. J. R. 'outing' a quite prominent Romanist [intentionally unnamed here] as a Nazi collaborator who probably had to seek the protection of Curtius after the War. The facts are unclear, and the motives murky. Meanwhile, an ill-informed piece by G. Berkenbusch and C. Bierbach purports to assess 'La filologia romànica alemanya i el seu interès per la llengua catalana', *TSC*, 13, 1997 : 123–47, praising the sociolinguistic work and political solidarity evident since the 1970s [see Colón's version, p. 14], but according only passing mention to Meyer-Lübke and his contemporaries, and dating the emergence of German *Romanistik* to the *end* of the 19th c. [*sic*, 123]. Less controversially, M. Décimo probes what happened 'Quand les romanistes, le docteur Alphonse Bos et Gaston Paris s'intéressaient à l'Île Maurice et à Charles Baissac', *Études Créoles*, 21 : 71–80; Bos, a ship's surgeon, medical scholar and amateur linguist, was invited by Paris to contribute a note on Mauritian and to review Baissac's new book of folk tales, which he did in *Romania* of 1881 and 1882, putting forward the then revolutionary idea that creole might be 'néo-français'. P. Swiggers and H. Seldeslachts continue their 'Documenta linguistica'. *Orbis*, 39, 1996–97[1998] : 159–79, with four short items involving Schuchardt in debates on language planning and the development of an international auxiliary language. A sympathetic evaluation by J.-P. Chambon, 'Aspects de l'œuvre linguistique de Georges Straka', *ib.*, 97–126, suggests that S.'s view of the chronology and actuation of phonetic change evolved greatly in his later life, from straightforwardly Neogrammarian to sociolinguistic; it remains valuable in bridging the gap between abstract and concrete approaches. C. Duarte i Montserrat, 'Joan Coromines (1905–1997)', *RPh*, 51 : 302–24, while acknowledging Catalan language and linguistics as the main beneficiaries of C.'s herculean labours, draws careful attention to the lesser-known toponomastic studies that may have been C.'s first love. A full necrological essay on 'Yakov Malkiel (1914–1998)', *La corónica*, 27 : 249–62, penned by his pupil S. N.

Dworkin, concludes — and who could disagree? — that an era has ended.

4. Phonology

Martínez-Gil, *Issues*, is a well balanced collection of 20 essays mainly on stress, prominence, and the status of imperatives, treated within optimality theory; readers must supply their own comparative inferences. Examining the resolution of uneven trochees in French and Italian, B. E. Bullock, 'The myth of equivalence: where two lights do not make a long', *LSRL 26*, 53–70, argues that while even trochees may be theoretically optimal, they simply do not occur in Romance. Similarly for H. Jacobs, 'Latin enclitic stress revisited', *LI*, 28, 1997:648–61, the uneven trochees produced in compounds with -QUE and -LIBET must not be overlooked (as in some recent treatments) but they do not inherently favour any particular theory. Two technical items by R. S. Gess, 'Alignment and sonority in the syllable structure of late Latin and Gallo-Romance', *LSRL 26*, 193–204, and 'Old French NoCoda effects from constraint interaction', *Probus*, 10:207–18, eschew the obvious — that optimality should automatically predict open final syllables — producing the same outcome by a conspiracy of lesser constraints.

RivL, 10.1, ed. J. I. Hualde, devoted to 'Metaphony and vowel harmony in Romance and beyond', includes a treatise by A. Calabrese, 'Metaphony revisited' (7–68), and other interesting items, most querying whether metaphony is a unitary process, and perhaps inevitably reaching diverse conclusions. M. L. Mazzola, 'Sullo sviluppo del vocalismo romanzo', *Atti* (Palermo), 1, 221–29, deals with problems of reconstructing syllable weight and accent. Seeking an explanation for the relative rarity of 'Los diptongos [i̯ą, u̯ą] en la Romania', *Verba*, 24, 1997:83–97, F. Sánchez Miret discards Schürr (1970; see also *YWMLS*, 34:24) in favour of a centennial Havet (1877), whose postulated trend towards irreversible stress shift in inherently unstable falling diphthongs now seems very plausible. Two virtual monographs repay attention: M. Benedetti, 'Dittonghi e geminazione consonantica in latino', *SSL*, 36, 1996[1998]:11–93, identifies a tendency even in Republican times for /-V:C-/ sequences to drift to /-VCC-/ under certain morphological and sociolinguistic conditions; and F. Guazzelli, 'Alle origini della sonorizzazione delle occlusive sorde intervocaliche', *ID*, 59, 1996[1998]:7–95, a careful examination of mainly Tuscan texts, establishes western dialect areas as the innovators, with frequent voicing in lexical items and personal names, but little in verb endings or toponyms. C. Hare, 'El fonema nasal palatal incial en las lenguas romances', *Atti* (Palermo), 1,

127–32, shows how borrowing from Amerindian languages has altered the phonotactics of Portuguese and Spanish, creating a small typological schism between them and Catalan. Brimming with useful comparative data but inconclusive, F. Jensen, 'On internal occlusive +*R* clusters in Romance', *Romania*, 116:524–33, notes that sparse examples hamper attempts to distil regular patterns: the voiced clusters are more problematic than the voiceless, with /-br-/ regular within each dialect but diverse overall, /-dr-/ a complete mess, and /-gr-/ little better but too scarce to lose sleep over.

5. MORPHOSYNTAX AND TYPOLOGY

A. Calabrese, 'Some remarks on the Latin case system and its development in Romance', *LSRL 26*, 71–126, treats case as a bundle of features governed by shifting constraints whose interaction can cause syncretism or null exponency; he posits three case types in Romance, Nom [+subject, +direct], Acc [−subject, +direct] and Gen [+possessor, −location]. In an updated version of word-and-paradigm morphology drawing on ideas of M. Selig (clarification of immanent relations and compensation), H. Werner links 'Artikelent-stehung und Verlust der Kasusflexion in der Romania', *ZRP*, 114:381–413. Naturalness in morphology cannot be equated with transparent mapping of form to meaning, according to M. Maiden, 'Towards an explanation of some morphological changes which "should never have happened"', *ICHL 13*, 241–54; perverse examples include the generalization of feminine plurals and gerunds in Italian and Romanian. In a painstaking study of 'Variation in the Romance infinitive', *TPS*, 96:1–61, A. Ledgeway dismisses Greek substrate influence as the explanation of the south Calabrian 'inflected' infinitive, proposing instead a 'macrocategory' admitting person and number but not tense marking, which would account for wider Romance manifestations. Meanwhile, C. J. Pountain, 'Person and voice in the Spanish infinitive', *BHS (L)*, 75:393–410, reflects on the rise and rise of a popular category with the pragmatic advantage of economy but the matching disadvantage of ambiguity. Finally, the uneven success of the -sc- infix as a conjugation marker is investigated by H. J. Wolf, 'Du latin aux langues romanes', *TLP*, 35–36:441–54, tentatively suggesting MACRESCĔRE as the leader word for the change — a lean source indeed.

Atti (Palermo), II, devoted to 'Morfologia e sintassi delle lingue romanze', includes a round table on grammatical categories con-vened by N. Vincent (877–933), together with many valuable monolingual contributions. Vol. I, on 'Grammatica storica delle lingue romanze', is more comparative in scope and likewise ends with a round table discussion (437–88), on new ways of analysing phonetic and morphological change, with contributions by G. Marotta (439–54) on non-linear explanations, by D. Wanner (471–81) on the elusiveness of diachronic change, and by R. Wright (483–86) on the sociolinguistics of monolingualism. Vol. I also contains: E. Blasco Ferrer, 'Variazione e cambiamento di strutture nella grammatica storica' (69–87), founding a new theory of dynamic reanalysis on variable features of Late Latin and early Italian; M. Maiden, 'La tesi di Reichenkron e l'origine delle desinenze -*i* e -*e* nel romanzo "orientale"' (173–86), refurbishing the older phonetic explanation; W. Mańczak, 'Les aires latérales ne sont pas plus archaïques que les aires centrales' (187–91), again using cognate lists to undermine Bartoli's norms; A. Nocentini, 'La formazione del future romanzo', (259–65), advancing a notion of conjunctural grammaticalization; and A. Ricós, 'Estudio contrastivo de la evolución de las construcciones pasivas' (291–305), offering useful statistics on Spanish and Catalan.

Indeed, it has been a good year for voice relations, tackled from various theoretical and descriptive angles. Leading the way are ten papers on *Transitivität und Diathese in romanischen Sprachen* (LA, 392), ed. Hans Geisler and Daniel Jacob, Tübingen, Niemeyer, [iv +] 173 pp., mainly dealing with Spanish, French and Italian. Stressing divergent reanalyses in Romance, M. M. Parry, 'The interpretation of the reflexive in Piedmontese', *TPS*, 96:63–116, illustrates the compatibility of passive and impersonal/thematic meanings where *se* is not a subject clitic. Parallel constructions lacking grammatical subjects but assuming human agency in Romanian and Spanish lead J. S. Turley to propose 'A prototype analysis of Spanish indeterminate reflexive constructions', *LSc*, 20:137–62 (see also *YWMLS*, 59:29); but a similar prototypical approach treating reflexivity as a voice leads J. D. Quesada, 'Transitivity, voice, and the middle Spanish *se* revisited', *RF*, 110:1–36, to argue tenaciously that *se* is not a passive but a middle. B. Wehr, 'Zur Beschreibung der SE-konstruktionen im Romanischen', *RK 11*, 127–48, splits off unaccusatives from true *se*-diathetics. Although this year's balance of opinion evidently favours subjectless impersonals, C. Dobrovie-Sorin, 'Construcţiile romanice cu *si* impersonal şi pasivizarea intranzitivelor (1)', *SCL*, 46, 1995[1998]:19–38, finds so many problems associated with Cinque's (GB) analysis of the two *si*-types as [±arg] that she opts for the traditional case distinction of nominative versus accusative *se*. Reflexives resemble intensifiers, according to G. Reb, 'Diachronie/synchronie: l'élaboration du système prédicatif des verbes pronominaux', *TrL*, 36:189–97, who is intrigued by their voice neutrality, placing them on the very cusp of (in-)transitivity. This particular

Gordian knot is cut by M. Cennamo, 'The loss of the voice dimension between Late Latin and Early Romance', *ICHL 13*, 77–100, proposing that 'voice' dissolved by the 4th c., most of its earlier functions being recreated through the interaction of three transitivity parameters: control, verb class, and animacy.

Mario Squartini, *Verbal Periphrases in Romance. Aspect, Actionality, and Grammaticalization*, Berlin, Mouton de Gruyter, xii + 370 pp., gives an authoritative survey of productive types and constraints, majoring on progressives and appealing to Bybee's notion of 'persistence' to account for their profusion in Ibero-Romance, where they are nevertheless limited to durative atelic senses. C. Schwarze, 'A lexical-functional analysis of Romance auxiliaries', *TL*, 24:83–105, advances the idea of non-predicate 'light' verbs composed of agreement features but not completely bleached of independent meaning — a conclusion reinforced by J. Feuillet, 'Typologie de "être" et phrases essives', Feuillet, *Actance*, 663–751, whose survey of existential, attributive and 'situative' uses convinces him that *be*-verbs are as meaningful as indispensable. J. Wüest, 'Zur Entstehung der analytischen Verbformen in den romanischen Sprachen', *Fest. Pfister*, II, 31–44, claims an early date for the first stirrings, but concedes that analytic perfects must have had a prolonged symbiosis with their synthetic counterparts. Refreshingly, C. Schapira, 'Grammaticalisation et hiérarchie', *TrL*, 36:175–88, is prepared to admit that, for such a pivotal process as auxiliarization, what researchers discover must depend to a large extent on their point of departure.

At last, the first three tomes of findings from the ambitious Eurotyp project have been published, a rich source of comparative data that brooks no parochialism and forces Romanists to look beyond the genetic family. Feuillet, *Actance*, kicks off with G. Lazard's crisp 'Définition des actants dans les langues d'Europe' (11–146!), and includes two interesting items by G. Bossong, 'Le marquage différentiel de l'objet' (193–258), and 'Eléments d'une typologie actancielle des langues romanes' (769–87), which succeeds in reformulating the familiar dichotomies of synthetic/analytic and SOV/SVO as shifts from centripetal morphology to centrifugal morphosyntax. Auwera, *Adverbial Constructions*, contains a thorough survey by P. Ramat and D. Ricca of 'Sentence adverbs' (187–275), with excellent summary tables and a four-way taxonomy: participant-oriented and event-oriented evaluatives, speech act adverbs, and modals. Siewierska, *Order*, eagerly awaited, is rather disappointing, despite a handy appendix by S. et al. of 'Twelve word order variables in the languages of Europe' (783–812) and the areal trends graphically revealed by M. S. Dryer, 'Aspects of word order in the languages of Europe' (283–319), whose computer maps make their typological points precisely by flouting the frontiers of Europe; the 'Overview of the main word order characteristics of Romance' by A. R. Arnaiz (47–73) is unfortunately pedestrian, largely restricted to the standard languages, and marred by strange assertions about dialects and speaker numbers. A single European *Sprachbund* is contemplated by T. Kuteva, 'Large linguistic areas in grammaticalization', *LSc*, 20:289–311, whose corpus-based study of auxiliary formation shows unmistakable evidence of convergent patterns. The 11 papers in Ramat, *Grammaticalization*, explore mechanisms, limitations, and the bi-directional shunts between grammar and lexicon, drawing widely on Romance for exemplification; A. Giacalone Ramat, 'Testing the boundaries' (107–27), probes where the lexeme-to-morpheme model fails. 'Can grammaticalization be explained invisible handedly?', *ICHL 13*, 191–200, asks J. Klausenburger; yes, it can even explain coherent Romance developments like right-branching and the HAB-ĒRE-futures, which Bybee and colleagues had denied. Even so, some processes are elusive and some apparent changes can go into reverse: C. J. Pountain, 'Learnèd syntax and the Romance languages', *TPS*, 96:159–201, illustrates the difficulty of distinguishing borrowing from influence, by extrapolating from a Spanish literary construction akin to the accusative and infinitive, though not a direct descendant, whose 16th-c. vogue and rapid decline seem due to disconcertingly similar linguistic factors, perhaps operating under different social conditions.

6. SYNTACTIC THEORY AND SEMANTICS

Esther Torrego, *The Dependencies of Objects*, Cambridge, Mass., MIT Press, 216 pp., treats the enigmatic Romance prepositional objects within Minimalist Case Theory, straying onto clitic doubling, object movement and causatives. Three related items, with relevance beyond their severe titles, may be found in *LSRL 27*: D. Arteaga, 'On null objects in Old French' (1–11), L. Zaring, 'Object shift in Old French' (319–32), and E. Raposo, 'Definite/zero alternations in Portuguese' (197–212), on Iberian topicalization and object omission. In a novel reconciliation of strange bedfellows, C. Schmitt, 'Lack of iteration: accusative clitic doubling, participial absolutes and *have* + agreeing participles', *Probus*, 10:243–300, proposes that clitic-doubled sequences are in fact identificational small clauses sharing a single theta role, whose incidence not only correlates inversely with strong determiners but is also heavily influenced by terminative versus durative aspect. C. Muller, 'La position des clitiques complé-ments des langues romanes actuelles', *TrL*, 36:47–58, emphasizes the

influence of secondary government (including subordination, negation and certain adverbials) in determining enclitic or proclitic order.
D. Heap, 'Optimalizing Iberian clitic sequences', *LSRL 26*, 227–48,
is politely dismissive of derivational, parametric or template-based
accounts of clitic placement, which have all failed to deal with non-
standard variants; a theory of interacting constraints with variable
ranking is far better. Clitics figure prominently in the eight contributions to Balari, *Romance*; witness S. Balari, 'Pronouns, variables and
extraction in HPSG' (151–217), and P. Monachesi, 'Decomposing
Italian clitics' (305–57), which dares to ask whether clitics form a
single category, *loro* being a lexical item and others behaving just like
inflectional affixes. *Déjà vu?* As if to confirm category hopping, V. M.
Longa, G. Lorenzo, and G. Rigau, 'Subject clitics and clitic recycling',
JL, 34:125–64, examine what happens when Iberian varieties run
out of morphs for locatives and existentials; some, like Catalan, are
well blessed, but others must keep recycling their old accusative
clitics. It gives a new meaning to sustainable development.

Maria Luisa Zubizarreta, *Prosody, Focus and Word Order*, Cambridge,
Mass., MIT Press, 232 pp., argues that syntax drives the phonology
of focus and sentential prominence, with minor differences in the
application of asymmetric c-command and head-to-argument links
accounting for seemingly major divergence between Romance and
Germanic. No less ingenious, Andrea Moro, *The Raising of Predicates.
Predicative Noun Phrases and the Theory of Clause Structure*, CUP, 1997,
x + 318 pp., unifies copular sentences and predicate raising, existentials and *ci*, quasi-copulas with *seem*, and unaccusativity, all by
substituting a left-branching structure for direct NP-embedding
below the clause node. Paul Rowlett, *Sentential Negation in French*,
OUP, xviii + 233 pp., recognizes negative markers, adverbs and
arguments (incidentally reviving the central tenet of Jespersen's
analysis; see *YWMLS*, 59:30), while the companion piece, 'A non-
overt negative operator in French', *Probus*, 10:185–206, proposes a
null operator alongside *pas* to account for the complex licensing
conditions of *ne*, so explaining some puzzling differences between
French and most other varieties of Romance. As if in echo, L. Silva-
Villar, 'Morphology and syntax of Romance imperatives', *ib.*,
115–38, distinguishes sharply between suppletive and true imperatives, of which only the latter have dedicated morphology; complex
interactions with plurality and negation parametrize Romance into
northern and southern subgroups. J. C. Castillo, 'A syntactic account
of perfective and possessive verb selection', *LSRL 26*, 159–74, is a
minimalist reworking of the old generative semantic analysis deriving
auxiliaries and possessives from abstract BE predicates, so denying
them main verb status. M. Suñer, 'Resumptive restrictive relatives',

Language, 74: 335–64, pinpoints the feature composition of the relative complementizer as the prime cause of linguistic diversity and notes a correlation between pied-piping and lexical relative pronouns; Romance resumptive constructions like *Compró una casa que sus abuelos solían vivir en ella*, so abhorred by purists, are seen as more efficient forms than their approved alternates. In 'Reference to kinds across languages', *Natural · Language Semantics*, 6: 339–405, G. Chierchia locates language groups along a continuum depending on whether they treat bare nominals as arguments or predicates; 'Romance' is placed at the predicate pole, but the data are all from standard Italian, which is not necessarily typical in its treatment of generics or proper names, Reinhard Meisterfeld, *Numerus und Nominalaspekt. Eine Studie zur romanischen Apprehension* (*ZRP*, Beiheft 293), viii + 147 pp., apparently takes a cognitive approach to the properties of nouns that permit enumeration — that is, more than the mere feature [± count]. A. E. Ojeda, 'A semantics for the counting numerals of Latin', *JS*, 14, 1997[1998]: 143–71, appeals to 'mereological model-theoretic semantics' to obfuscate his otherwise revealing analysis of the cardinal/collective pairs like DUO/BĪNĪ and TRES/TRĪNĪ, seen as denoting respectively individuation and partition.

7. LEXIS

Atti (Palermo), III, on 'Lessicologia e semantica delle lingue romanze', buzzes with activity, from etymology, through borrowing, to term banks and the challenges of computerizing major dictionaries; its associated round table, led by J.-P. Chambon and M. Sala (985–1022), asks whether a new pan-Romance etymological dictionary is desirable, even if feasible. Meyer-Lübke would be astonished. According to N. Felecan, 'La paronymie et l'attraction paronymique', *ib.*, 223–30, are probably universal processes, driven by formal criteria to risk homonymy, and at best reined in by semantics. C. Gruaz, 'Les variations sémantiques et formelles du mot français et d'autres langues romanes', *ib.*, 317–29, introduces EUROLEXIQUE, a research project to identify synchronic word families. A neat taxonomic schema for English borrowing into Romance, including pseudo-anglicisms, is set up by J. Gómez Capuz, 'Aportaciones a un estudio contrastivo de la influencia angloamericana' (269–81) — on which see also M. V. Calvi's 'Notas sobre la adopción de anglicismos en español y italiano', *LEA*, 20: 29–39, on contrasting attitudes. According to M. Lieber and F. Marri, 'Le maratone popolari', *Atti* (Palermo), III, 419–33, have spawned a new lexical field whose technical terms have diverged in sense from their apparent cognates in other sports such as cycling. F. Melka and M. C. Augusto, 'Les verbes français et portugais suivis d'une construction bénéficiaire du type: *pour/para/por* + NP', *ib.*, 485–97, apply Jackendoff's semantic structures to Romance, averring that his third category of intransitives requiring a beneficiary complement is (rather surprisingly) the largest. C. Mujdei, 'Structuration diachronique et système sémantique', *ib.*, 589–95, offers meteorology as a neat case study for the interaction of popular and scientific vocabulary: most weather terms are taken from Latin but every Romance language has its own subsystem and variants. I. Oancea and L. Vasilută consider 'Il superstrato culturale latino', *ib.*, 641–52, as the origin and explanation for a high register that is substantially shared across Romance. On cue, F. Fusco, 'Un latinismo paneuropeo nel lessico universitario', *IL*, 20, 1997 [1998]: 201–09, charts the success of NUMERUS CLAUSUS, except in Italy where *numero programmato* is being substituted owing to the unsavoury connotations of an anti-Jewish policy adopted in Tsarist Russia. Conversely, a rare instance of positive revaluing is offered by O. Lurati, 'Dal discorso repressivo al discorso mitico', *RLiR*, 62 : 5–19, who posits an origin in gypsy slang for *cuccagna/cucaña/cocagne*, originally designating a group of layabouts, later reinterpreted as those not needing to work and inhabiting the mythical land of milk and honey — indeed, an early instance of the leisure society.

Kurt Baldinger, *Etymologien 2* (*ZRP*, Beiheft 288), Tübingen, Niemeyer, xii + 666 pp., reprints B.'s substantial revisions and addenda to vols 21–23 of the *FEW*, in more accessible form and with updated bibliographies. In 'Die Doppelentwicklung als Prinzip für die romanische Etymologie', *Fest. Pfister*, I, 5–21, H. D. Bork proposes a model recognizing weak and strong causes (like sentential stress) of splits, crosses and blends where a doublet is not necessarily the result; while B. Müller, 'Fortleben inkognito', *ib.*, 195–99, untangles the (Old) Romance progeny of AFFERRE, in some cases wrongly attributed to (A)FERIRE. In a fascinating glimpse of social mores encoded in the lexicon, R. López Gregoris, 'Casarse en latín', *Emérita*, 66 : 95–103, shows that the dichotomy DUCĔRE : NUBĔRE, said of the man and woman, must be supplemented by SPONDĔRE, said of the bride's father who could afford a dowry, or COLLOCĀRE if he could not. A case study of TOLLĔRE and LEVĀRE by F.-J. Klein, 'Mehr als nur ein Argot-Phänomen', *ZRP*, 114 : 414–37, partly vindicates Meillet's idea of lexical contamination, while appealing to wider causes. Effervescent and often cyclic renewal characterizes words for 'grass snake', claims J.-P. Dalbera, 'Dimension diatopique, ressort motivationnel et étymologie', *QS*, 18.2, 1997[1998] : 195–214, tracing one line back to ORBU VERME replacing earlier *ORBITTU. A learned disquisition on poppies by E. Grab-Kempf, 'Zur Wortgeschichte von dial. sp., arag., kat., val., *ababol*, pg., *papoula*, *papoila*, sp., *amapola*, gal., *mapoula*, jud.

sp., *ḥanapoya*, marokk. jud. sp., *maḥapola'*, *ZRP*, 114:496–504, points eventually to a Mozarabic etymon with divergent phonological dissimilation. A tasty morsel by P. Blanchet, '*Calice, calisson, calzone, chausson* . . . e tutti quanti', *ib.*, 447–61, rejects the *FEW* proposal of a dissimilated variant of *canissoun* 'wicker tray' <*CANICCUM, favouring Greek καλάθιον 'basket', or better καλιτσούνια, extant in Crete as an Easter cake with similar ingredients.

J. C. Moreno Cabrera, 'On the relationships between grammaticalization and lexicalization', Ramat, *Grammaticalization*, 211–27, links the processes respectively to metaphor and metonymy, so explaining productive elliptical patterns like Sp. *la corneta, la trompeta* 'cornet, trumpet', *el corneta, el trompeta* 'cornet/trumpet player'. Forensic work on the suffix -ōsus leads V. Popovici, 'Héritage latin ou dérivation romane', *Atti* (Palermo), III, 703–15, to conclude that productivity can mask history, so that even a well attested Latin etymon is no more than a presumption of continuity; pattern congruity can be the deciding factor. D. Tomescu, 'Le suffixe latin -*aria* et sa continuité dans les langues romanes', *ib.*, I, 403–07, points to possible parallels in the development of -ALIA. The history of a further productive suffix is traced by H. J. Wolf, 'Sarde *pettorra, liporra*, le mérinos et le suffixe -INU', *RLiR*, 62:331–46, using the survival of dactylic stress on non-syncopated forms to argue against early merger of -ĪNU and -ĬNU, as proposed by J. L. Butler (*YWMLS*, 34:28). A modern corpus-based study by R. Veland of 'Les adverbes en *mente* dans trois langues romanes', *RF*, 110:427–44, reveals forms unacknowledged by any reference dictionary, a much higher incidence in running text than could be predicted from frequency dictionaries of the 1960s and 70s, and Italian rapidly catching up with Spanish, where the high usage of -*mente* still seems to be strongly correlated with register.

8. SOCIOLINGUISTICS AND DIALECTOLOGY

Atti (Palermo), V, is wholly devoted to 'Dialettologia, geolinguistica, sociolinguistica', while IV has a section shedding light on the 'Storia linguistica e culturale del Mediterraneo'. Holtus, *Lexikon*, VII, the penultimate of the series (*YWMLS*, 50:16, 51:20, 52:18, 53:12, 54:17, 56:33, 57:22, 58:16) deals chiefly with aspects of contact and migration, offering good coverage of creoles and lingua franca (601–79) and of what are rather quixotically dubbed 'artificial languages' (Old Occitan, Old Galician, and Franco-Italian, 680–756); but it was a mistake to juxtapose this substantial section with a much shorter one, on contrastive studies (six items, 757–873), classification and subgrouping (nine items, 873–1003) and typology (a mere three, counting generously, 1003–85) that is bound to look like an afterthought — a pity, when solid and authoritative contributions like those of Ž. Muljačić, 'Areale Gliederung der Romania' (873–92), G. Bossong, 'Typologie der romanischen Sprachen' (1003–19) and M. Metzeltin, 'Die romanischen Sprachen: eine Gesamtschau' (1040–85), are overshadowed by the sheer monumental comprehensiveness of the undertaking. Gustav Ineichen, *Arabisch-orientalische Sprachkontakte in der Romania* (RA, 41), 1997, viii + 109 pp., is a useful guide, intentionally limited to what nonspecialists must know in order to assess claims about Arabic loans or other forms of influence. Paleolithic contacts continue to exercise M. Alinei, 'La teoria della continuità', *RID*, 21, 1997[1998]:73–96, who argues for continuous transmission from the Paleolithic period onwards and inveighs against the 'invasionist dogma' that is putting such unnecessary strain on Romance scholarship.

N. Operstein asks 'Was lingua franca ever creolized?', *JPCL*, 13:377–80, and avers not, having weighed the trusty evidence of a previously overlooked 1545 farce *Zingana* by Gigio Artemio Giancarli; there was just too much instability and variation in speaker competence. Among numerous publications in creolistics, two important items command attention. J. H. McWhorter, 'Identifying the creole prototype', *Language* 74:788–818, alarmed by recent sympathetic debate on the Chaudenson–Mufwene hypothesis of creolization without pidginization or discontinuity, aims to vindicate 'creole' as a typological class, not a mere socio-historical convenience, by tracking features widely attested in Romance and other creoles which can only have arisen during a rapid phase of pidginization and then persisted into the stabilized creole. The culmination of a 20-year research programme, Claire Lefebvre's *Creole Genesis and the Acquisition of Grammar*, CUP, xviii + 461 pp., works systematically through the morphosyntax of Haitian Creole showing undeniable morph-for-morph correspondences with the putative substrate language, Fongbe, and proposing a parametric mechanism for relexification; it shifts the focus onto *adult* learners of colonial superstrates and looks much more convincing as a blockbusting monograph than as a series of well documented but inevitably tendentious individual articles (see, for instance, *YWMLS*, 58:28). How ironical, that creoles should become the testbed and possible vindication of stratigraphic theories explicitly developed for European Romance, where they are no longer fashionable or even respected.

II. FRENCH STUDIES*

LANGUAGE

By GLANVILLE PRICE,
University of Wales Aberystwyth

1. GENERAL AND BIBLIOGRAPHICAL

Seven years ago, we reported favourably (*YWMLS*, 53:25) on the first edition (1991) of Willy Bal et al., *Bibliographie sélective de linguistique française et romane*, in the 'Champs linguistiques' series (see also pp. 36 and 37 below). The 2nd edition, Louvain-la-Neuve, Duculot, 1997, 336 pp., really is, as the introduction claims, 'remaniée et amplifiée' (it is definitely not one of those publications where such terms as 'revue et augmentée' seem to mean little more than 'with a few corrections and an extra page or so'). The expansion here is real (up from 268 pp., so by some 25 per cent, and by about 30 per cent in the case of French), with a considerable number of post–1991 publications. A welcome new feature is the inclusion of 11 attractively produced colour maps.

Price, *Encyclopedia*, includes articles by the editor on 'Gallo-Romance languages' (188–89) and 'French' (167–77); see also pp. 44 and 45 below. Nicol C. W. Spence, *The Structure(s) of French*, Egham, Runnymede Books, 1996, 267 pp., is wide-ranging and readable; main sections on 'Phonology', 'Lexicology and Word-Formation' and 'Grammar' (mainly on syntax) are followed by supplementary chapters on 'Standard and Non-standard French' and 'The Spoken and Written Codes'. Achim Stein, **Einführung in die französische Sprachwissenschaft*, Stuttgart, Metzler, x + 222 pp. Henriette Walter, **Le français d'ici, de là, de là-bas*, La Hès, 416 pp. Marina Yaguello, *Petits faits de langue*, Seuil, 158 pp., consists of 24 lively essays covering points of pronunciation, grammar, lexicon, or style that are characteristic of the way the French language is evolving or else are subjects of controversy (among them the phonemic status of *-ng* as in *parking*, the pronunciation of the ambiguous *j'en veux plus*, and the hardy annual *Madame la Ministre* and the like).

Blanche-Benveniste Vol. is planned under the following headings: I, 'Méthodologie et théorisation' (I.A, 'Conceptualisations et procédures'; I.B, 'Les concepts confrontés aux données'; I.C, 'Diversités des approches et des données'); II, Description (II.A, 'Analyse et

* The place of publication of books is Paris unless otherwise stated.

argumentation en syntaxe'; II.B, 'Analyse sur corpus: la diversité des objets'), which has the effect of bringing together apparently heterogeneous papers while dividing those that, on a more conventional plan, would be more closely associated; however, those papers (a substantial majority) that fall within the scope of *YWMLS* are itemized below according to more usual categories.

Michel Pougeoise, *_Dictionnaire didactique de la langue française: grammaire, linguistique, rhétorique, narratologie, expression et stylistique_, Armand Colin, 1996, xi + 443 pp. Mario Rossi and Évelyne Peter-Defare, *_Les Lapsus, ou comment notre fourche a langué_, PUF, xii + 163 pp. Michel Rocard, *_Le Français: langue des droits de l'homme?_, Grigny (Rhône), Paroles d'aube, 64 pp.

TrL, 37, a thematic issue, 'Le lexique-grammaire', ed. Béatrice Lamiroy, consists (apart from one item on Korean) of items relating specifically to French: B. Lamiroy, 'Le lexique-grammaire. Essai de synthèse' (7–23), an overview of work published in the last 20 years; M. Gross, 'La fonction sémantique des verbes supports' (25–46), dealing particularly with *être*, *avoir*, and *faire*; J. Labelle, 'Lexique-grammaire comparés d'un français à l'autre' (47–70), on Parisian French, Quebec French, and their 'intersection' which is *le français commun*; M. Garrigues, 'La place de l'adjectif en français et sa formalisation dans un dictionnaire électronique' (91–107), based on the DELAS (*Dictionnaire électronique des mots simples du français*); J. Senellart, 'Reconnaissance automatique des entrées du lexique-grammaire des phrases figées' (109–25); M. Silberztein, 'Transducteurs pour le traitement automatique des textes' (127–43); J.-C. Chevalier, 'Lexique-grammaire et histoire de la linguistique. Un lexique-grammaire: *Lesclarcissement* de John Palsgrave 1530' (143–54); and C. Leclere, 'Travaux récents en lexique-grammaire' (155–86), which constitutes the 'Chronique de linguistique générale et française (X)'. *CPr* has brought out four more thematic issues: 28 (1997), 'La contextualisation de l'oral'; 29 (1997), 'Le système verbal selon Guillaume. Lectures critiques'; 30, 'Les opérations de thématisation en français'; 31, 'Linguistique et représentations'. Xavier Deniau, *_La Francophonie_ (Que sais-je?), PUF, 128 pp.

2. HISTORY OF GRAMMAR AND OF LINGUISTIC THEORY

H. Saw and J.-M. Dewaele in 'La naissance des premières grammaires françaises', *Cahiers AFLS*, 4 : 15–23, take a brief look at John Barton's *Donait françois* (*c.*1400), Palsgrave, Jacques Dubois, and Meigret. S. Monsonégo and O. Derniame examine the 'Vocabulaire de la syntaxe au XVe siècle d'après quelques documents français', *Demarolle Vol.*, 175–92. P. Swiggers, 'Terminologie et systématique de l'article chez les grammairiens français du seizième siècle', *TLP*, 35–36:409–25, is apparently part of an on-going study of the ideas and terminology of French 16th-c. grammarians. Colette Demaizière edits and translates Jacques Dubois's *Introduction à la langue française* and *Grammaire* (1531), Champion, 448 pp. *Problèmes de cohésion syntaxique: de 1550 à 1720*, ed. Janine Baudry and Philippe Caron, Limoges, PULIM, 312 pp., is a volume of conference proceedings.

After R. Godel's *Sources manuscrites du Cours de linguistique générale* (1958) and R. Engler's critical edition of the *Cours* (2 vols, 1968, 1974), a further important contribution to the analysis and exposition of Saussure's seminal theories is presented by Claudia Mejía, *La Linguistique diachronique: le projet saussurien* (Publs du Cercle Ferdinand de Saussure), Geneva, Droz, viii + 206 pp. Basing herself primarily on the students' notes published by Engler, M. probes Saussure's understanding of 'la linguistique diachronique' (the term is of his own coining), an aspect of his theory that, at his death, 'est resté [. . .] à l'état d'ébauche', and, moving on from that, to 'comprendre enfin la structure entière du projet saussurien d'une linguistique générale'. After a thorough study of a number of aspects of Saussure's thinking in so far as it can be documented, she leads us to the conclusion that, since 'un projet' is all that Saussure left us with, 'la linguistique diachronique est donc à faire et, avec l'étude de la transmission de la langue évolutive, ce sont les fondements de la sémiologie générale qui attendent d'être posées depuis la mort du maître'.

The contents of *CFS*, 50, 1997, largely fall outside the scope of *YWMLS*, but also include R. Engler, 'Bibliographie saussurienne, 6' (248–95) (covering the years 1990–97), an index to vols 1–50 of *CFS* by E. Fadda (299–336), a retrospective survey, 'Les *Cahiers Ferdinand de Saussure* des origines à nos jours', by R. Amacker, C.-A. Forel and A.-M. Fryba-Reber (341–54), and documents by Ch. Bally and A. Sechehaye relating to the origins and early days of the *Cahiers* (355–60).

CPr, 29, 1997, ed. Jacques Bres, is devoted to 'Le système verbal selon G. Guillaume. Lectures critiques', and includes: A.-R. Delbart and M. Wilmet, '*Imparfait* et *passé simple* chez Gustave Guillaume: un couple mal assorti' (15–31); D. O'Kelly, 'L'aspect en question(s)? Relecture de *Temps et verbe* de G. Guillaume' (33–58); J.-C. Chevalier, 'Symétrie et transcendance: le cas du futur hypothétique et le cas de l'aspect' (59–80); R. Lowe, 'Chronogenèse et schématisation: la représentation du temps d'univers et du temps d'événement aux chronogenèses indicative, quasi-nominale et subjonctive' (81–108); O. Soutet, 'La diachronie, "preuve" et épreuve de la théorie guillaumienne du verbe français' (109–33); P. Le Goffic, 'Temps, temps vécu, temps linguistique. A propos des conceptions de

G. Guillaume et de E. Minkowski' (135–55); J. Bres, 'Ascendance/
descendance; incidence/décadence; affaires de couples . . .' (157–83);
and M. Toussaint, 'Le sujet du temps' (185–203).

F. Gadet, 'Le "français avancé" à l'épreuve de ses données',
Blanche-Benveniste Vol., 59–68, is severely critical of H. Frei's *La
Grammaire des fautes* (1929). M. Schreiber, 'Ferdinand Brunot: *La pensée
et la langue*', *ZFSL*, 108:225–40, attempts a new evaluation in the light
of cognitive linguistics.

The stated aim of Anne Zribi-Hertz, *L'Anaphore et les pronoms: une
introduction à la syntaxe générative*, Villeneuve-d'Ascq, Presses Univ. du
Septentrion, 1996, 279 pp., is to familiarize French scholars and
students with the evolution, methodology, and terminology of
Chomskyan linguistics, and this it does with considerable success,
tracing the evolution of Chomsky's own thinking and bringing in also
that of others such as R. Langacker and R. Jackendoff. Examples are
taken mainly though not exclusively from French, there is a most
useful French–English glossary of technical terms, and each chapter
is accompanied by exercises and a key thereto. *Les Pronoms:
morphologie, syntaxe et typologie*, ed. Anne Zribi-Hertz, Vincennes U.P.,
1997, 286 pp.

3. HISTORY OF THE LANGUAGE

Glanville Price, *The French Language: Present and Past*, London, Grant &
Cutler, xix + 283 pp., is a slightly revised and updated edition of a
work that first appeared in 1971 (see *YWMLS*, 33:30). Michèle
Perret, *Introduction à l'histoire de la langue française*, SEDES, 192 pp.
Claude Hagège, *Le français, histoire d'un combat*, LGF, 188 pp., is a
series of ten broadcast talks.

4. TEXTS

Stephen Dorr, *Der älteste Astronomietraktat in französischer Sprache:
'L'Introductoire d'astronomie'. Édition und lexikalische Analyse* (*ZRP*, Beiheft
289), vii + 208 pp., devotes over half its space (pp. 85–200) to
comments on about 350 lexical items (including a few proper names),
with references to the relevant dictionaries (the *AND* yet again being
quite improperly referred to as 'Stone'). *RLiR*, 62.2, includes a
number of text-based linguistic studies: A. Eskénazi, 'Le complément
du comparatif d'inégalité dans *Guillaume de Dole*' (21–31); M. Plou-
zeau, 'Les mots en *quanqu*' dans les *Enfances de Doon de Mayance*: à
propos d'un article d'Albert Henry' (57–94) (for A. H.'s article, see
YWMLS, 58:33); and T. Matsumura, 'Les régionalismes dans *Jourdain
de Blaye en alexandrins*' (129–66). *TLP*, 35–36, also includes a number

of text-based articles, most of them of somewhat limited interest: J.-P. Chambon, 'La langue du *Sermon joyeux du mesnage* (Koopmans 19) est-elle vraiment "standardisée"?' (165–81), disputing the view that it is; J. Fennis on a number of terms based on *galère* in the work of Barras de la Penne (1650–1730) (191–209); C. Schmitt, 'Remarques sur le vocabulaire culinaire d'un enfant royal' (373–84), based on Jean Héroard's *Journal*; H. J. Schmitt, 'Le vocabulaire du *Journal (1675–1692)* du pasteur genevois Jacques Flournoy' (385–407). Constructions of the type *ne vault un bouton* and the like are the subject of R. Bellon, 'Le renforcement affectif de la négation par l'expression d'une valeur minimale dans *La Belle Hélène de Constantinople*', *Demarolle Vol.*, 105–18, and A. Planche, ' "Ne valoir une pomme, une bille, une cive. . .". L'expression concrète de la valeur nulle dans *Le Roman de la Rose* (partie Jean de Meun)', *ib.*, 119–32. C. Brucker considers '*Si/ainsi* en moyen français', *ib.*, 133–48, with particular reference to *Bérinus*.

5. PHONETICS AND PHONOLOGY

Anita Berit Hansen, *Les Voyelles nasales du français parisien moderne: aspects linguistiques, sociolinguistiques et perceptuels des changements en cours*, Copenhagen, Museum Tusculanum, 373 pp.; she also has a well documented and wide ranging article on 'Le nouveau [ə] prépausal dans le français parlé à Paris', *Fónagy Vol.*, 173–98. Mary-Annick Borel and Laurent Danon-Boileau, *Grammaire de l'intonation: l'exemple du français*, Gap, Ophrys, 231 pp.

6. ORTHOGRAPHY

Yannick Portebois, *Les Saisons de la langue: les écrivains et la réforme de l'orthographe de 1889 à 1914*, Champion, 576 pp. Rolande Causse, *La Langue française fait signe(s): lettres, accents, ponctuation*, Seuil, 256 pp. N. Andrieux-Reix, 'La lettre *z*. Esquisse d'une histoire dans les codes graphiques successifs du français', *Demarolle Vol.*, 87–99, offers a brief coverage from the *Eulalie* to the 1980s.

7. GRAMMAR

OLD AND MIDDLE FRENCH

Geneviève Joly, *Précis d'ancien français: morphologie, syntaxe*, Armand Colin, 429 pp., is thorough, clear and reliable; though there is no section on historical phonetics as such, detailed discussion of phonetic evolution is included *passim* in parts 1, 'Morphologie nominale', and 2, 'Morphologie verbale', while one notes with satisfaction that part

3, 'Syntaxe', accounts for nearly half of the book; inevitably, one might disagree with points of detail here and there but, in general, this is a book that can be commended without reservation. A. Lanly, 'Une forme verbale mal connue de la *Chanson de Roland*: *ainz* (v. 2667)', *Demarolle Vol.*, 101–04, argues persuasively that *ainz*, corrected to *aint*, is the 3 sg. pres. subjunctive of a rare verb *aner*, corresponding to *anar*, *andar(e)* in other Romance languages; his arguments for *aditare* as the etymon are less cogent.

Barbara S. Vance, *Syntactic Change in Medieval French: Verb-Second and Null Subjects*, Norwell, MA, Kluwer, 1997, x + 399 pp. L. Schøsler, 'La valence verbale et l'identification des membres valentiels', *Monfrin Vol.*, 527–54, makes out a good *prima facie* case, which would be well worth developing at much greater length, that, alongside the case system and word-order and throughout the period from Latin to modern French, 'la valence verbale était un facteur primordial pour l'identification des membres de la phrase'. L. Zaring, 'Object Shift in Old French', *LRSL 27*: 319–32, argues that, despite superficial differences, O[bject] S[hift] of pronominal *ce* in OFr and MidFr is akin to constructions found widely in Germanic languages. M. Herslund, 'Les prédicats verbo-nominaux en moyen français', *Monfrin Vol.*, 327–43, stresses the need to 'distinguer soigneusement entre incorporation et construction à PVN'.

B. Combettes, 'Évolution des progressions thématiques en moyen français', *Demarolle Vol.*, 149–73, draws examples from a number of prose texts, foremost among them Molinet's *Chroniques*. C. Marchello-Nizia, 'Dislocations en diachronie: archéologie d'un phénomène du "français oral"', *Blanche-Benveniste Vol.*, 327–37, traces the evolution in the status of the construction in Old and Middle French; while A. Valli writes 'A propos de "flottements" dans l'expression du sujet pronominal avant le XVIe siècle: réflexion sur la notion de variation en syntaxe', *ib.*, 371–80. A. Henry, '*Autel* et *autretel* en moyen français. Le crépuscule', *Romania*, 116: 289–315, is characteristically well documented and argued.

Stéphane Marcotte, *La Coordination des propositions subordonnées en moyen français* (PRF, 221), Geneva, Droz, 1997, 435 pp., is an important contribution to our knowledge and understanding of Middle French syntax, a field which, despite the increasing interest manifested in it in a number of major publications in recent decades, is still woefully understudied. Though written from a transformational theoretical standpoint, this volume is, as compared with all too many others written from a similar standpoint, relatively accessible to non-transformationalists who are prepared to devote to it the close and sustained attention it calls for. M.'s main preoccupation is the conditions in which, when two subordinate clauses are coordinated, the subordinating element and the subject are or are not repeated in the second. After a first part in which problems and methods are discussed, a second and more specific part, which constitutes the main body of the book, is devoted to 'La coordination des propositions adjectives' and covers principally relative clauses but also others introduced by *où, quand, comme* or *comment*.

Nathalie Fournier, *Grammaire du français classique*, Belin, 447 pp., is a much needed and particularly useful reference work. It falls into three main sections, 'La phrase', 'Les expressions référentielles', and 'Le verbe'. Each of the 18 chapters not only analyses and illustrates thoroughly and clearly its subject-matter but is completed by a section (sometimes running to several pages) of 'Observations des grammairiens et remarqueurs classiques' (primarily, but not exclusively, Maupas, Oudin, Vaugelas, Arnauld and Lancelot, Bouhours, Ménage).

Michel Pougeoise, *Dictionnaire de grammaire et des difficultés grammaticales*, Armand Colin, xii + 436 pp., covers both morphology and syntax; articles range from highly specific ones (such as the conjugation and limitations on the use of verbs like *clore* and *gémir* and a complete list of words having an *h aspiré*) to general ones on such topics as the article, aspect, conjugation, and the direct object; others cross over the border between syntax and semantics (e.g. expressions based on individual words such as *autant, peine, sans*); all in all, a compact but comprehensive and most useful reference work.

Dulcie Engel, George Evans, and Valerie Howells, *A French Grammar Workbook*, Oxford, Blackwell, ix + 220 pp., is a companion volume to Glanville Price's *Comprehensive French Grammar* (4th edn, 1993, see *YWMLS*, 55:50) and contains a range of exercises each constructed around a specific grammatical topic. Margaret Jubb and Annie Rouxeville, *French Grammar in Context: Analysis and Practice*, London, Arnold, 232 pp., consists of a collection of 28 texts, each chosen to illustrate a particular grammatical point and accompanied by explanatory notes and a variety of exercises.

Franck Neveu, **Études sur l'apposition. Aspects du détachement nominal et adjectival en français contemporain, dans un corpus de textes de J.-P. Sartre*, Champion, 288 pp. Picking up a problem that brings in both anaphora and the use of hypernyms versus hyponyms, A. Theissen, 'Quand est-ce qu'*un chien* devient *l'animal*?', *JFLS*, 8:221–39, has interesting *aperçus* but recognizes that there is work still to be done. G. Kleiber, 'Est-ce qu'un veau peut être rapide et tendre? Du comptable au massif', *RF*, 110:327–47, is characteristically well and interestingly argued.

TrL, 35, ed. Dominique Willems and Ludo Melis, a thematic issue devoted to 'Les objets: relations grammaticales et rôles sémantiques', includes: D. Gaatone, 'L'objet direct comme notion formelle dans la formulation des règles syntaxiques' (13–20); J. François, 'La passivité des objets: rôles prototypiques et transitivité' (21–37); M. Noailly, 'Les traces de l'actant objet dans l'emploi absolu' (39–47); A. Borillo, 'Quand le complément direct d'objet est un "lieu"' (51–65); D.Van de Velde, 'Cet obscur objet du désir. L'objet des verbes de sentiment' (67–78); M. Larjavaara, 'A quoi sert l'objet interne?' (79–88); B. Defrancq and D. Willems, '*Quelque chose*: un objet pas comme les autres' (91–102); V. Lagae, '*En* quantitatif: pronom lié à la fonction objet ou à une position?' (103–14); I. Baron, 'Objet effectué et constructions nominales' (115–25); B. Combettes, 'Évolution des caractéristiques de l'objet en français' (129–42); and G. Siouffi, 'L'"objet": le grand absent de la grammaire classique? (XVIe–XVIIe siècles)' (143–59).

TrL, 26, ed. A. Boone and M. Pierrard, is also a thematic issue, devoted to 'Les marqueurs de hiérarchie et la grammaticalisation'. The great majority of the 18 articles relate to French: L. Melis and P. Desmet, 'La grammaticalisation: réflexions sur la spécificité de la notion' (13–26); H. Bat-Zeev Shyldkrot, 'Grammaticalisation et évolution de la langue: théories et systèmes' (27–35); J. Garrido, 'Syntaxe de la phrase dans le discours' (37–46); K. Jonasson, 'Le déterminant démonstratif en français: un marqueur de quoi?' (59–70); D. Van Raemdonck, 'Les adverbiaux connecteurs: hiérarchiseurs entre lexicalisation et grammaticalisation' (71–84); C. Blanche-Benveniste, '*Une fois* dans la grammaire' (85–101); S. Michels, 'De la quantification à la cohérence textuelle: le cas de *aussi (bien)*' (103–13); C. Rossari, 'Analyse contrastive: grammaticalisation et sémantique des connecteurs' (115–26); M. Pierrard, '*Comme* "relatif à antécedent" en ancien français: grammaticalisation de la proforme indéfinie' (127–46); P. Blumenthal, '*Le fait que*: origine et combinatoire' (147–60); C. Schapira, 'Grammaticalisation et hiérarchie; auxiliaires, semi-auxiliaires et surauxiliaires' (175–88); M. Tabatchnik, 'Problème des marqueurs temporels: étude sémantico-grammaticale' (199–208); I. Bartning, 'Procédés de grammaticalisation dans l'acquisition des prédications verbales en français parlé' (223–34); and J.-M. Léard, '*Façon* et *manière*: noms abstraits et intégration des prédicats comme arguments' (235–45).

A. Boone discusses 'La pronominalisation des complétives objet direct', *Blanche-Benveniste Vol.*, 103–14; I. Choi-Jonin, 'Anaphore associative dans une prédication simple: le cas du complément *avec le nom*', *ib.*, 199–209, identifies a number of variations on the construction; C. Muller, 'La portée variable des constructions attributives', *ib.*, 239–47, shows that much work remains to be done on 'le type de relation sous-jacente structurant ces prédications'; likewise, D. Gaatone, 'Sur une construction de caractérisation en français', *ib.*, 211–19, on the conditions for the type *une affaire d'importance, de/d'une grande importance* and other similar but not identical uses of *de*, concludes that we are dealing with 'une construction extrêmement problématique' and that 'il reste encore tout à faire pour tenter de dégager un quelconque système derrière ce foisonnement de données'; L. Kupferman, '*Des*: pluriel de *du*?', *ib.*, 229–38, is uncontroversial but useful, as are also M. Yaguello, 'La réalisation zéro des clitiques objet dans les constructions di-transitives du français parlé', *ib.*, 267–74, and M. Blasco, 'La séquence clitique + pronom tonique en français: un cas de prolongement pronominal', *ib.*, 277–85. M. Salles, 'La construction converse *être un peu lent de la tête mais rapide des pieds*', *La Linguistique*, 34.1:121–36, discusses the distinction between the types *rapide des pieds* and the more widespread *blanc de peau*. I. Bartning proposes a 'Modèle intégré des syntagmes nominaux complexes en *de* — typologie d'interprétations et reprise anaphorique', *RF*, 110:165–84. D. Bouchard discusses 'The distribution and interpretation of adjectives in French: a consequence of Bare Phrase Structure', *Probus*, 10:139–83.

Borillo, *Variations*, includes, apart from two items on English and one on German, the following which relate solely or primarily to French: P. Le Goffic, 'Préalables morphologiques à l'étude du verbe français' (1–33); A.-M. Berthonneau and G. Kleiber, 'Imparfait, anaphore et inférences' (35–65); H. Irandoust, 'Épisodes, cadres de référence et interprétation temporelle: application à l'imparfait' (67–89); D. M. Engel, 'Combler le vide: le passé simple est-il important dans le système verbal?' (91–107); C. Vetters and M. Vuillaume, 'Comment peut-on ressusciter le passé?' (109–23); J. Bres, 'De l'alternance temporelle passé composé/présent en récit oral conversationnel' (125–61); H. Portine, 'Représentation textuelle et représentation géométrique du temps: le présent est-il un temps du passé?' (137–61); P. Laurendeau, 'Moment de l'énonciation, temps de l'énoncé et ordre de procès' (177–98); J.-J. Franckel and D. Paillard, 'Les emplois temporels des prépositions: le cas de *sur*' (199–211); S. Vogeleer and W. De Mulder, '*Quand* spécifique et point de vue' (213–33); A. Le Draoulec, 'La négation dans les subordonnées temporelles' (257–75); S. Aslanides Rousselet, 'Exprimer linguistiquement une relation entre deux événements: les connecteurs de la simultanéité en français' (277–92); and L. Abouda, 'Vers une localisation syntaxique des modes verbaux. Cas de la phrase indépendante' (293–322).

R. Posner, 'La morphologie "progressive" en français: aperçu historique', *La Linguistique*, 34.2 : 103–10, considers why a progressive construction of the type *être* + *-ant* has not been grammaticalized in French.

**'Être'* et *'avoir'*: *syntaxe, sémantique, typologie*, ed. Alain Rouveret, Vincennes U.P., 266 pp. Pierre Le Goffic, **Les Formes conjuguées du verbe français oral et écrit*, Gap, Ophrys, 133 pp. Louis Lalaire, **La Variation modale dans les subordonnées à temps fini du français moderne: approche syntaxique* (EH, XXI.195), x + 277 pp.

Uta Lausberg, **'Modale' Verba adiecta?* — *Funktionale Untersuchungen zu den französischen Verbalphrase der Charakterisierung*, Münster, Nodus, 1996, 319 pp.

The excellent 'Champs linguistiques' series (see also pp. 27 above and 37 below) now brings us David Gaatone, *Le Passif en français*, Louvain-la-Neuve, Duculot, 300 pp. Opening his introduction with the observation that 'il n'existe à ce jour aucune monographie tant soit peu exhaustive sur le passif en français', G. sets out to fill this surprising gap, and does so with considerable success. G. is, of course, aware that the range of the term 'passive' has sometimes been widely (and often unjustifiably) extended, and so, quite properly, defines his domain very precisely as that of *être* and a past participle, the latter being 'tout participe passé dont le support n'est pas le premier argument de son lexème verbal, et est raccordable à ce support par *être*, indépendamment du temps-aspect'. He then ranges widely in many different directions, bringing in such topics as, *inter alia*, the functions of the passive, problems specific to particular verbs, the 'impersonal' passive, constraints on the passive, 'le complément dit "d'agent"', passives with no corresponding active, and a variety of 'problematic passives'. This impressive book is clearly argued and well documented and illustrated throughout. P. Skårup discusses 'Les emplois de *être* + participe passé en français contemporain', *Blanche-Benveniste Vol.*, 257–65, with reference both to compound tenses and to the passive. R. Velan, 'Une construction dite ne pas exister en français moderne: le passif suivi d'un infinitif nu', *JFLS*, 8 : 97–113, argues that constructions of the type *elle a été entendue pleurer* may well be on the increase even in the written language. F. Drijkoningen takes 'A minimalist approach to past participle agreement in French', *RLFRU*, 17 : 40–56. V. Déprez discusses 'Semantic effects of agreement: the case of French past participle agreement', *Probus*, 10 : 1–65.

Borillo, *Aspect*, includes the following on French: Y. Keromnes, 'Aspect et anaphore' (1–19); C. Touratier, 'L'imparfait, temps du passé non marqué' (21–28); C. Marque-Pucheu, 'Contraintes sur le mode/temps et l'aspect induites par les adverbes' (107–26); R. Faiz and M. Gondran, 'Modélisation temporelle et granularité dans les textes juridiques' (141–56); and A. Borillo, 'Les adjectifs et l'aspect en français' (177–89). P.-A. Buvet and J.-H. Lim, 'Les déterminants nominaux aspectuels', *LInv*, 20, 1996:271–85, is specifically on French.

Annick Englebert, *L'Infinitif dit 'de narration'*, Louvain-la-Neuve, Duculot, 236 pp., another 'Champs linguistiques' volume (see p. 27 above), deals with what is otherwise known as the 'infinitif historique'. Paying due attention to the diachronic dimension and providing an extended analysis of earlier work in the field (in particular, that of L. Tesniere, G. Guillaume, G. Moignet, P. Barbaud, and J.-M. Léard), E. takes a fresh new look at the problem, leading to the conclusion that the widely held view that the construction in question is something of an archaism is totally without foundation. K. Peterson, 'L'absence de déterminant dans l'impératif nominal', *JFLS*, 8:209–19, contrasting nominal imperatives without and with a determiner (e.g. *Silence! Passeports!* as opposed to *La porte!, Un scalpel!*), is based on a very limited corpus (29 Tintin and Astérix books). Lise Lapierre, **Le Participe passé en français: sa syntaxe et ses fonctions dans le texte de spécialité*, Frankfurt, Lang, 179 pp.

A. Coveney, 'Awareness of linguistic constraints on variable *ne* omission', *JFLS*, 8:159–87, reports on an Intuitions Elicitation Test designed to explore the extent to which such an awareness exists both for native-speakers and for advanced learners. P. Rowlett, 'A non-overt negative operator in French', *Probus*, 10:185–206, seeks to identify in constructions in which *ne* functions without *pas* 'a phonologically null negative operator'. H. de Swart discusses 'La position de *ni* dans le système de la négation', *RLFRU*, 17:67–80.

Using French examples, K. Baschung, 'Le Contrôle revisité: y a-t-il une différence entre verbes "à contrôle" et verbes "à montée"?', *JFLS*, 8:1–27, proposes, within the framework of Head-driven Phrase Structure Grammar, 'un traitement alternatif du problème de la sélection du contrôleur'.

V. Lagae and C. Rouget, 'Quelques réflexions sur les relatives prédicatives', *Blanche-Benveniste Vol.*, 313–25, is on constructions of the type *il y a/j'ai X qui . . .* E. Moline discusses the construction '*C'est juste une fille comme toi et moi*: un exemple de relatives en *comme*. De la comparaison au prototype', *RevR*, 33:67–86.

J. van Baardewijk-Rességuier, 'Topoï et marqueurs: application à *bien*', *RLFRU*, 17:1–9, starts from the concept of *topos* 'tel qu'il a été exploité par [J.-C.] Anscombre et [O.] Ducrot'. M. Tuţescu discusses '*Alors* vs *sinon*: un cas d'antonymie discurso-argumentative', *RRL*, 42, 1997 [1998]:85–88.

Pierre Cadiot, *Les Prépositions abstraites du français*, Armand Colin, 1997, 295 pp., is a searching and interesting study of those prepositions that express a relationship other than a precisely definable local or temporal one. It ranges widely over the functions of, primarily, *à*, *de*, *pour*, *avec*, and *en*, but does not overlook others. Rigorous reflection on theoretical matters involving syntax, semantics, and pragmatics is blended with specific consideration of such problematic but basic topics as the use of *à* and *de* in binomials, the alternation between these same two prepositions with such verbs as *obliger*, *commencer*, *décider*, *se mêler*, and numerous others, the alternation between *de* and *avec* in various contexts (*pousser quelqu'un du/avec le coude, regarder quelqu'un d'un/ avec un oeil* + adjective, *entourer de/ avec*, etc.), the alternations *à/en* (*croire à/en*), *en/dans*, *de/en* (*un manteau de/en laine*), and the use of *en*, *dans*, *avec*, *par* and *à* with the noun *train*. Andrée Borillo, **L'Espace et son expression en français*, Gap, Ophrys, vi + 160 pp.

K. van den Eynde, P. Mertens, and P. Swiggers, 'Structuration segmentale et suprasegmentale en syntaxe. Vers un modèle intégrationniste de l'écrit et de l'oral', *Blanche-Benveniste Vol.*, 33–57, is of general applicability but is illustrated from French; M. Bilger, 'Le statut micro- et macrosyntaxique de *et*', *ib.*, 91–102, argues that *et* has two clearly distinct functions; O. Halmøy, '*Comme*: adverbe, conjonction [. . .] et préposition?', *ib.*, 221–28, claims that, since in certain contexts *comme* can enter into competition with *pour, en, de, en tant que*, *en guise de, en qualité de*, it has 'bien des allures de préposition'; M. Piot, 'L'adverbe conjonctif *seulement*', *ib.*, 249–56, looks at constructions in which *seulement* can or cannot behave in much the same manner as *mais*; and M. Savelli, 'Au gré du temps', *ib.*, 359–69, discusses the construction *plus [. . .], plus [. . .]*. M. Gross discusses 'Les formes *être Prép X* du français', *LInv*, 20, 1996:217–70. D. van de Velde discusses 'Un dispositif linguistique propre à faire entrer certaines activités dans des taxinomies: *faire* + *du* + *nom d'activité*', *RLiR*, 61:369–95.

CPr, 30, ed. Catherine Fuchs and Christiane Marchello-Nizia, is devoted to 'Les opérations de thématisation en français' and includes: S. Prévost, 'La notion de thème: flou terminologique et conceptuel' (13–35); P. Siblot, 'Nommer, c'est déjà prédiquer' (37–54); N. Fournier and C. Fuchs, 'Place du sujet nominal et opérations de thématisation' (55–88);A. Lacheret-Dujour, S. Ploux, and B. Victorri, 'Prosodie et thématisation en français parlé' (89–111); N. Le Querler, 'Le marquage syntaxique de la thématisation de l'objet dans *La Pluie d'été* de Marguerite Duras' (113–31); B. Combettes, 'Thématisation, topicalisation et éléments non référentiels: le cas de l'adjectif détaché' (133–59); and C. Marchello-Nizia, 'Dislocations en ancien français: thématisation ou rhématisation?' (161–78). Bernard Combettes, **Les Constructions détachées en français*, Gap, Ophrys, 143 pp. T. Etchegoyhen and G. Tsoulas, 'Thetic and categorical, attributive and referential. Towards an explanation of definiteness effects', *LRSL 27*, 81–95, refer to the 'mostly programmatic character' of their paper on the use of *il* in '*there*-insertion contexts' in French. B. Kampers-Manhe, '*Je veux que parte Paul.* A neglected construction', *ib.*, 129–41, argues that 'the postverbal subject construction in subjunctive clauses is not the same phenomenon as subject inversion in wh-clauses' and that 'it is closer to the existential *there* construction in English'.

C. Rossari and J. Jayez, '*Donc* et les consécutifs. Des systèmes de contraintes différentiels', *LInv*, 20, 1996:117–43, contrast the use of *donc* with that of *de ce fait, du coup* and *alors* as connectives, while R. Kozlowska-Heuchin proposes a 'Méthode d'analyse des connecteurs du français en vue d'un traitement automatique', *ib.*, 365–80. R. Veiland discusses '*Quand même* et *tout de même*: concessivité, synonymie, évolution', *RevR*, 33:217–47. T. Nyan, **Metalinguistic Operators with Reference to French*, Berne, Lang, 169 pp.

8. LEXICOGRAPHY

The *FEW* has reached fasc. 155, 1997, forming vol. 30, pp. 809–960, and fasc. 156, 1997, forming vol. 22, part 1, pp. 289–316. J.-P. Chauveau, 'Sur quelques emprunts supposés au breton', *TLP*, 35–36:183–90, disputes the *FEW*'s suggested Breton etyma for eight words. T. R. Wooldridge reviews 'Le lexique français du XVIe siècle dans le *GDFL* et le *FEW*', *ZRP*, 114:210–57. Kurt Baldinger, *Dictionnaire étymologique de l'ancien français*, Tübingen, Niemeyer, has reached fasc. H2, 92 pp. L. Bray, 'Lexicologie et néologie au XVIIe siècle', *TLP*, 35–36:149–64, discusses Italian neologisms in the first edition of the Academy's dictionary. M. Glatigny offers an 'Aperçu sur l'accueil fait dans les dictionnaires du XIXe siècle aux remarques normatives du *Dictionaire Critique* de Féraud', *ib.*, 257–74. **Le Dictionnaire de l'Académie française et la lexicographie institutionnelle européenne (Actes du colloque international, 17, 18 et 19 novembre 1994)*, ed. Bernard Quemada, Champion, 534 pp. M. Lindemann discusses 'Le Dictionnaire de l'Académie française de 1694 — les principes et la réalisation', *TLP*, 35–36:281–97. B. von Gemmingen reviews the first 50 years of 'Langenscheidt: la maison d'édition et ses dictionnaires bilingues français-allemand/allemand-français (1856–1906)', *ib.*, 223–56.

It is a pleasure to announce the appearance of a third edition, with additions and corrections, of Jacques Van Roey, Sylviane Granger, and Helen Swallow, *Dictionnaire des/ Dictionary of faux amis, français-anglais, English-French*, Paris and Brussels, Duculot, lxix + 794 pp., on the first edition of which we reported enthusiastically ten years ago (*YWMLS*, 50:34).

This year sees the appearance of two more volumes in the enterprising and in many cases highly original 'Dico' series published by Seuil (see, most recently, *YWMLS*, 59:47): Colette Guillemard, *Le Dico des mots de la couleur*, 474 pp., ranges astonishingly widely over names of colours and words and expressions relating to or deriving from names of colours, with subtle definitions and ample illustrations and comments; Claude Duneton, *Le Guide du français familier*, 604 pp., which opens with a 32-page essay, 'Le français familier, pourquoi?', is arranged according to concepts (from *abîmer*, which has the entries *bousiller*, *péter*, and *maganer*, to *yeux*, which gives *les mirettes* and *les châsses*); again, there are ample illustrations and comment (including origins and datings); comments 'en complément' identify words that seem to be on the way out and Canadianisms are marked by a marginal maple-leaf. We have frequently drawn attention in these surveys to volumes in the series 'Le Français retrouvé' published by Belin. Two new additions to the series are also among the most substantial and the most useful: if, as the title of Gabriel Otman, *Les Mots de la cyberculture*, 320 pp., suggests, it concentrates on computer science and information technology, other fields such as space exploration and advances in medical research are not overlooked — one finds in it numerous words or expressions that are not in even the most recent bilingual dictionaries (e.g. *cybernaute* 'net-surfer', *page d'accueil* 'home page', *relais de trame* 'frame relay'); Jean Tournier, *Les Mots anglais du français*, 588 pp., presents, in seven thematically classified chapters ('Sports et loisirs', 'Sciences humaines', 'La vie quotidienne', etc.) and with origins, dates, and definitions, some 3500 words (including false Anglicisms like *ball-trap*) ranging from *triforium* to *browser* and from *has-been* to *thatchérien*. Marion Spickenbom, **Belgizismen in französischen Wörterbüchern und Enzyklopädien seit Anfang dieses Jahrhunderts*, Münster, Nodus, 1996, 289 pp.

Marcel Lachiver, **Dictionnaire du monde rural: les mots du passé*, Fayard, 1766 pp. Pierre Rézeau, **Dictionnaire des noms de cépages en France: histoire et étymologie*, CNRS, 480 pp. Robert Galisson and Jean-Claude André, **Dictionnaire de noms de marques courants: essai de lexiculture ordinaire*, Didier-Érudition, 342 pp. Annie Mollard-Desfour, *Le Dictionnaire des mots et expressions de couleur du XXe siècle: le bleu*, CNRS, 257 pp. **Dictionnaire des medias*, ed. Francis Balle, Larousse-Bordas, 281 pp.

Julie de Bos, 'Quand tous les chemins mènent à Paris, ou l'ethnocentrisme des dictionnaires', *CLe*, 72:189–98, argues on the basis of five monolingual dictionaries that 'les dictionnaires hexagonaux demeurent axés sur leur culture' — maybe, but one would need a more thorough study than this to demonstrate it convincingly.

B. Courtois discusses 'Formes ambiguës de la langue française', *LInv*, 20, 1996 : 167–202, in terms of the problems they present for the elaboration of electronic dictionaries.

9. LEXICOLOGY

Conforming to the typical pattern of the genre, Marie-Noëlle Lamy, *The Cambridge French–English Thesaurus*, CUP, xii + 326 pp., presents the French language as a network of ideas under 142 headings (with in most cases from two to upwards of 25 subheadings), 44 of them grouped in a separate section entitled 'Conversational gambits'; there are frequent helpful indications as to the register and collocational range of the words and expressions listed; coverage is up to date and access is facilitated by both English and French word-indexes.

M. Lindeck, 'Le vocabulaire de l'aviation française', *ZFSL*, 108 : 1–7, makes comparisons with English, from which most of the relevant terms derive.

J. R. Smeets, 'Glanures lexicales', *Romania*, 116 : 3–33, presents a number of words, expressions, and meanings that he had not found in Old French dictionaries. A. Henry, *ib.*, 256–56, adds a note to his earlier article on *ester(c)* (see *YWMLS*, 59 : 47). E. W. Poe, 'Old Occitan/Old French *tifeignon*: its meaning and its etymology', *RPh*, 51 : 287–301, plausibly identifies it as a reflex of TIPINUM 'antimony'. J. C. Szirmai, '*Stephanin* ou la couleur de saint Étienne: essai d'explication sémantique', *RLiR*, 61 : 361–68, argues that the adjective *stephanin*, which is applied to pigeons in the *Bestiaire* of Guillaume le Clerc and which has puzzled various commentators, refers to the blood of St Stephen the protomartyr and so signifies 'red'. F. Möhren, 'Afr. *haraz*: un cas de cuisine lexicographique', *ib.*, 439–52, and G. Roques, 'Errements étymologiques: le cas de *haras* et de *haridelle*', *ib.*, 453–58, both draw attention to the pitfalls into which even wary etymologists may fall. P. Blanchet, '*Calice, calisson, calzone, chausson* [. . .] e tutti quanti: point sur une étymologie difficile entre métaphore et symbolique', *ZRP*, 114 : 447–61, considers that Greco-Latin CALICE is the most probable etymon, though Greek KALÀTHION is also a plausible contender. R. Arveiller, 'De quelques noms de plantes', *TLP*, 35–36 : 19–30, discusses *couille de prêtre, crête de coq/ de geline, oignon* + complement (*de bois, de chien*, etc.), *scorpioïde, scorpion*, and *vitriole*.

Monfrin Vol. includes a number of items on the vocabulary of Middle French (contributions in other fields are cited elsewhere in this survey): C. Buridant, 'Essai d'analyse du vocabulaire de la *Chronique* de Jean Le Fèvre' (81–134); M. C. Timelli, 'Le lexique français de la grammaire et de la syntaxe: créations du XIIIe au XVe siècle' (151–72); D. M. González Doreste, 'Notas para la creación del vocabulario scientifico en francés: neologismos en *Le Régime du corps* de Aldebrandin de Siena' (183–203); B. Dunn-Lardeau, 'La contribution de la *Légende dorée* (Lyon, 1476) à la lexicographie du moyen français' (225–37); A. M. Finoli, 'Les néologismes chez Nicole Oresme: remarques et réflexions' (239–47); M. J. Freeman, 'A fringueur, fringueur et demi: création verbale et phénomènes de société dans le Paris de Guillaume Coquillart' (249–68); U. Jokinen, 'L'épithète animalière en moyen français' (317–26); N. Margolis, 'Les terminaisons dangereuses: lyrisme, féminisme et humanisme néologiques chez Christine de Pizan' (381–404); B. Merrilees and J. Shaw, 'Innovation et création lexicales dans le *Glossarium gallico-latinum* (BN. lat. 7684)' (405–30); A. Rigamonti, 'Guillaume Cretin: la contribution d'un rhétoriqueur à l'enrichissement du français' (431–50); L. Rosier, 'L'interjection comme point nodal de la créativité lexicale: la particule sensible *aïe*' (451–60); B. Roy, 'Des angevinismes dans le *Pathelin?*' (461–78); A. Slerca, 'Octavien de Saint-Gelais traducteur de Virgile et d'Ovide, et la néologie' (555–68); and R. Van Deyck, 'Création verbale et valorisation sémique dans le *Testament* de François Villon' (637–48).

M. Sourdot, 'De l'hapax au Robert: les cheminements de la néologie', *La Linguistique*, 34.2:111–18, seeks to explain the progression of neologisms from the status of hapax to their recognition in dictionaries. Y. Y. Mathieu, G. Gross, and C. Fouquéré, 'Vers une extraction automatique de néologismes', *CLe*, 72:199–208, is based on a computerized analysis of *Le Monde* for 1993 and 'une version automatisée du [. . .] *TLF*'. J.-R. Klein, N. Lienart, and S. Ostyn, 'L'anglicisme et la presse. Enquête et analyse à travers quatre quotidiens français et belges', *RLiR*, 61:337–60, conclude very sensibly that 'le français "digère" beaucoup mieux ses emprunts que ne le laissent croire des fantasmes puristes allant parfois jusqu'à la xénophobie linguistique'. H. Geckeler reviews 'Les emprunts aller-retour français-anglais-français', *TLP*, 35–36:211–21.

Martine Temple, *Pour une sémantique des mots construits*, Villeneuve-d'Ascq, Presses Univ. du Septentrion, 1996, 373 pp., reviews critically first the approaches of a range of dictionaries, both traditional and others that 'se réclament explicitement d'une théorie linguistique', and then four different theories of lexical semantics, none of which strikes her as fully adequate to explain the 'comportement référentiel des mots construits'. A consideration of models of derivational morphology leads to the conclusion that the theoretical framework proposed by D. Corbin is the most likely to 'relayer les théories de sémantique lexicale pour servir de cadre à l'analyse sémantique des mots construits'. This theory is then tested empirically in two chapters that together count for over half of the substance of the volume and is shown to provide a satisfactory answer to the problem of 'mots construits' as set out in earlier chapters. Dany Amiot, *L'Antériorité temporelle dans la préfixation en français*, Villeneuve-d'Ascq, Presses Univ. du Septentrion, 1997, 339 pp., is a thorough, subtle, and rigorously planned study ranging over the fields of morphology, syntax, and semantics. A first part assesses the work of earlier scholars of varying theoretical persuasions, compares the values of Latin *prae-, ante-, pro-,* with those of French *pré-, anté-, pro-,* and sets out the bases of the corpus (six French dictionaries) on which the study is based. The body of the work is devoted to, first, an analysis of the 'Modalités de construction du sens des mots préfixés par *pré-, avant-, anté-* et *pro'* and, secondly, to the 'Attribution des valeurs "continue" et "discontinue" aux mots préfixés par *pré-, anté-* et *avant'* (it having been shown, not surprisingly perhaps, that 'les sens temporels (mais aussi spatiaux) construits par ce préfixe ne sont pas de vrais sens d'antériorité'). A. frequently acknowledges her indebtedness to the work of D. Corbin and A. Culioli. Yet another volume in the important series 'Sens et structures', to which Temple's and Amiot's books belong (and see also Zribi-Hertz, p. 30 above), is Françoise Kerleroux, *La Coupure invisible: études de syntaxe et de morphologie*, Villeneuve-d'Ascq, Presses Univ. du Septentrion, 1996, 408 pp. K.'s starting point is the problem of the categorization and labelling of forms that function as more than one part of speech (substantivized infinitives and adjectives, in particular). Many of these have traditionally been grouped under the heading of 'improper derivation'. Taking her inspiration from the work of J.-C. Milner (*Introduction à une science du langage*, 1989, and numerous articles), K. brings together the 'plan des positions syntaxiques, définies par leur occupabilité' and the 'plan des termes définis par le triplet des propriétés que sont la forme phonique, le sens lexical et l'appartenance catégorielle'. The 'coupure invisible' of the title is the distinction that can be recognized only structurally between two or more superficially identical forms (*une rose odorante, des joues roses, le rose de ses joues,* but also homonyms arising from the morphological rules of the language, *la marche à pied, il marche*). An introductory chapter ranging widely over general considerations (including borderline cases and paradoxical cases) is followed by others devoted respectively to substantivized infinitives in modern French, substantivized adjectives, and 'noms déverbaux non-affixés' (type *la réclame, la bouffe*), and another providing an 'Analyse de la notion de dérivation impropre'. Although much of the contents of this book could be applied to other languages, the focus of attention throughout is French. H. Constantin de Chancy, 'Les célibataires sont-ils seuls?', *CLe*, 72:97–126, applies the model of polylectal grammar to an examination of the opposition between *marié* and *célibataire* in contemporary French.

P. Rézeau, 'Le suffixe *-ouille* en français de France', *TLP*, 35–36:345–62, is abundantly documented. A. Berrendonner, 'Aspects pragmatiques de la dérivation morphologique', *Blanche-Benveniste Vol.*, 23–31, reflects on the light cast on derivational procedures by aberrant forms in spoken and written French; Y.-C. Mourin, 'La flexion du verbe français à l'oral: morphématique ou analogie?', *ib.*, 69–78, argues that formations of the type *ils jou(z)ent* (Quebec French) can be accounted for 'sans avoir à postuler d'unités morphologiques plus petites que le mot'.

10. ONOMASTICS

Paul Fabre, *Les Noms de personnes en France* (Que sais-je?), PUF, 127 pp., replaces P. Lebel's 1946 volume in the series; the new volume covers Gaulish, Latin, and Germanic names used in what is now France as well as, primarily, the history, typology and sources of specifically French names together with (modern) Germanic, Flemish, Breton, Basque, and Jewish names.

11. SEMANTICS

Vincent Nyckees, *La Sémantique, Belin, 365 pp., is illustrated from French.

12. DIALECTS AND REGIONAL FRENCH

Jean-Pierre Chambon, Pierre Rézeau and Éliane Schneider, **Mélanges sur les variétés du français de France d'hier et d'aujourd'hui*, 2, Klincksieck, 1997, 266 pp. A. Lodge follows up his earlier studies of the spoken French of Paris with 'Vers une histoire du dialecte urbain de Paris', *RLiR*, 62:95–128. Price, *Encylopedia*, includes articles by the editor on the linguistic situation of Belgium (32–34, with a map), 'Walloon' (487–88), 'Picard' (356–57), 'Channel Islands French' (84–85), 'Alderney French (Auregnais)' (8), 'Guernsey French (Guernesais)' (224), 'Jersey French (Jèrriais)' (276–77), and 'Sark French (Sercquiais)' (408).

Louis Remacle, **Étymologie et phonétique wallonnes (questions diverses)*, Liège U.P., 1997, 262 pp. The *Atlas linguistique de la Wallonie* has reached *vol. 15, *Le corps humain et les maladies* (2ᵉ partie), ed. Marie-Guy Boutier, Liège U. P., 1997, 401 pp., while Fernand Carton and Maurice Lebègue, **Atlas linguistique et ethnographique picard* continues with *vol. 2, *Le Temps, la maison, l'homme, animaux et plantes sauvages*, *morphologie*, CNRS, 1997, 308 pp. M.-G. Boutier, 'Sur la pratique de la localisation implicite dans le *Dictionnaire de l'Ouest-wallon* d'Arille Carlier', *TLP*, 35–36: 129–47, shows that apparently non-localized forms in the dictionary are in fact implicitly localized. F. J. Hausmann discusses ' "Droit dans mes bottes." Les belgicismes locutionnels', *ib.*, 275–80. Timothy Pooley, **Chtimi: the Urban Vernaculars of Northern France*, Clevedon, Multilingual Matters, 1996, viii + 318 pp. Gaston Vasseur, **Dictionnaire des parlers picards du Vimeu, Somme*, Fontenay-sous-Bois, SIDES, 816 pp. J. Lanier, '*On* suivi du pluriel', *Demarolle Vol.*, 223–37, shows that the construction in question 'caractérise Metz et la région messine immédiate'. Michèle Schortz, **Le Parler de Senneville-sur-Fécamp* (SRU, 55), 278 pp.

This year has seen the appearance of three more volumes in the series of dictionaries of regional French published by Bonneton (see *YWMLS*, 55:62 and references thereat and 57:46): the dictionary counting for the greater part of George Lebouc, *Le belge dans tous ses états: dictionnaire de belgicismes, grammaire et prononciation*, 159 pp., is more or less limited to definitions with or without examples but is preceded by a substantial essay, 'Des belgicismes bien vivants', and followed by two brief appendices on, respectively, pronunciation and morphology and syntax; Claudine Fréchet and Jean-Baptiste Martin, *Dictionnaire du français régional de l'Ain: Bresse, Bugey, Dombes*, 160 pp., is more ambitious, listing some 2000 words with not only definitions and examples but indications as to vitality (e.g. 'Usuel à partir de 60 ans, connu au-dessous') and/or geographical spread, and etymology; René Lepelley and Catherine Bougy, **Expressions familières de Normandie*, 160 pp.

Robert Deguillaume, **Dictionnaire français-gallo, gallo-français*, Saint-Cast-Le Guildo, R. Deguillaume, 415 pp. **Vitalité des parlers de l'Ouest et du Canada francophone à la fin du XXe siècle (Actes du VIe Colloque international de dialectologie et de littérature du domaine d'oïl occidental)*, ed. Francis Manzano, Rennes U.P., 1997, 451 pp.

André Thibault, **Dictionnaire suisse romand: particularités lexicales du français contemporain*, Carouge, Zoé, 1997, 854 pp.

J.-P. Montreuil, 'Vestigial trochees in oïl dialects', *LSRL 27*, 183–95, argues that the best synchronic account of Norman, Gallo and Lorrain cognates of *dure*, *mère*, etc., is provided if we postulate the existence of vestigial trochees in which 'the weak member of the trochee is not [. . .] manifested'.

13. ANGLO-NORMAN

Price, *Encylopedia*, includes an article by D. A. Trotter on 'Anglo-Norman' (8–10). The editor-in-chief of the *Anglo-Norman Dictionary*,

W. Rothwell, 'Anglo-Norman at the (green)grocer's', *FS*, 52:1–16, again points to the weaknesses of dictionaries of French or English that pay insufficient heed to the evidence provided by Anglo-Norman and argues further that the elaboration of adequate dictionaries of Old or Middle French and, indeed, of Old Occitan, depends on 'a large-scale attack on all forms of non-literary documents still awaiting attention in France'. Likewise, although restricting himself in general to a consideration of words in A-, one of Rothwell's co-editors, D. A. Trotter, 'Les néologismes de l'anglo-français et le *FEW*', *Monfrin Vol.*, 577–35, is able to argue persuasively that 'il est temps enfin d'incorporer les fruits des recherches anglo-normandes dans le *FEW*'. Pointing out that 'for linguistic purposes, the documentary evidence of three hundred years of Anglo-French occupation of Gascony has been largely ignored', Id., 'Some lexical gleanings from Anglo-French Gascony', *ZRP*, 114:53–72, discusses some 90 arguably Anglo-French words or senses from unpublished documents written in Gascony or from Britain to Gascony. W. Rothwell, 'Arrivals and departures: the adoption of French terminology into Middle English', *ESt*, 79:144–65, effectively demonstrates *inter alia* how unsound are the views that there was extensive creolization in medieval England and that the arrival of Eleanor of Provence as Henry III's wife in 1236 led to 'a wholesale enrichment of the Middle English lexis from Central French sources'. Considering both the sole manuscript and the only and 'seriously flawed' edition of a 15th-c. text, Id., 'The place of *Femina* in Anglo-Norman studies', *SN*, 70:55–82, demonstrates that both scribal and editorial errors are such that the text cannot be used for lexicographical purposes unless supported by other evidence.

14. FRENCH IN NORTH AMERICA

Léandre Bergeron, *Dictionnaire de la langue québécoise*, Montreal, Typo, 572 pp.

Gaston Cholette, *L'Action internationale du Québec en matière linguistique; coopération avec la France et la francophonie de 1961 à 1995*, Sainte-Foy, Laval U.P., 1997, 197 pp. Jean Forest, *Chronologie du québécois*, Montreal, Triptyque, 378 pp. Diane Lamonde, *Le maquignon et son joual: l'aménagement du français québécois*, Montreal, Liber, 16 pp.

P. Martin, 'Dynamique vocalique en français du Québec', *La Linguistique*, 34.2:67–76, discusses low and mid-oral vowels, in terms of archiphonemes, phonemes, and allophones. D. Uritescu, 'L'effacement du /l/ en québécois et le type morphologique du français', *RLiR*, 61:397–437, deals with the loss both of postvocalic /l/ in the subject personal pronouns and of prevocalic /l/ in object pronouns and articles, and seeks an explanation in the agglutinating tendency of French.

K. J. Rottet, 'Clause subordination structures in language decline', *JFLS*, 8:63–95, draws on evidence from a Cajun French community. *Dictionnaire historique du français québécois: monographies lexicographiques de québécismes*, ed. Claude Poirier, Sainte-Foy, Laval U.P., lx + 640 pp. L. Wolf, 'Les emprunts à l'anglo-américain dans le français populaire rural du Canada', *TLP*, 35–36:455–65, modestly presented as an 'essai d'une première vue d'ensemble', is of much greater significance than R. Wooldridge, 'Coquetel lexical: vocabulaire des boissons américaines d'après un article de l'*Art vivant* (1926) et un livre de recettes (1900)', *ib.*, 467–78.

15. FRENCH IN AFRICA

Alternances codiques et français parlé en Afrique, ed. A. Queffélec, Aix-en-Provence, Univ. de Provence, 380 pp., publishes the proceedings of a conference held at Aix in 1995. *Francophonies africaines*, ed. André Batiana and Gisèle Prignitz, Rouen U.P., 128 pp. Claude Frey, *Le français au Burundi*, Vanves, EDICEF-AUPELF, 1996, 233 pp.

16. FRENCH CREOLES

Dictionary of Louisiana Creole, ed. Albert Valdman et al., Bloomington, Indiana U.P., 672 pp. L. Caid discusses 'Les marqueurs du passé et de l'accompli en créole réunionnais', Borillo, *Aspect*, 51–73. C. Lefebvre investigates 'Relexification in creole genesis: the case of demonstrative terms in Haitian Creole', *JPCL*, 12, 1997:181–201, while V. Déprez and M.-T. Vinet study 'Predicative constructions and functional categories in Haitian Creole', *ib.*, 203–35.

17. SPECIAL REGISTERS

S. Marcotte offers some 'Prolégomènes à l'étude syntaxique de la langue du droit médiéval français', *RLiR*, 62:347–75. M. Boulton discusses 'Le langage de la dévotion affective en moyen français', *Monfrin Vol.*, 53–63, on the basis of three texts relating to the Passion of Christ or the Transfiguration. Teresa Jaroszewska, *Le Vocabulaire du théâtre de la Renaissance en France (1540–1585): Contribution à l'histoire du lexique théâtral*, Lodz U.P., 1997, 301 pp. Boris Seguin and Frédéric Teillard, *Les Céfras parlent aux Français: chronique de la langue des cités*, Seuil, 227 pp. Pierre Merle, *Le Dico du français qui se cause*, Toulouse, Milan, 256 pp. Philippe Pierre-Adolphe, Rex Mamoud, and Georges-Olivier Tzanos, *Tchatche de banlieue: suivi de L'Argot de la police*, Mille et une nuits, 128 pp. G. Petit offers an 'Approche lexicale et sémantique du vocabulaire familier', *CLe*, 72:5–40; F. Antoine, 'Des mots et des oms: verlan, troncation et recyclage formel dans l'argot contemporain', *ib.*, 41–70. Pierre Merle, **L'Argot du foot*, Boulevard du jean, 79 pp.

18. SOCIOLINGUISTICS

Rodney Ball, *The French-Speaking World: A Practical Introduction to Sociolinguistic Issues*, London, Routledge, 1997, xvi + 228 pp., is original in its conception and generally well planned. It ranges over such topics as French as a world language, French in Switzerland, Belgium, Canada, selected former colonies and protectorates, regional languages, and regional forms of French in France itself, creoles, the use of French by immigrants, situational and social variation, current innovatory tendencies, and the role of the state and the Academy. Each chapter provides a certain amount of documentation (this could have been expanded to advantage), well devised exercises, and suggestions for further reading. N. Armstrong, 'La variation sociolinguistique dans le lexique français', *ZRP*, 114:462–95, studies some 430 pairs of the types *se balader* (fam.)/*se promener*, *bourré* (pop.)/*ivre*, *connerie* (vulg.)/*bêtise*; and Id., 'The sociolinguistic gender pattern in French: a comparison of two linguistic levels', *JFLS*, 8:139–58, examines, on the basis of a corpus of the speech of girls aged 11–12, rates of development at the levels of pronunciation and discourse and suggests reasons for difference in their communicative competence at the two levels.

19. PRAGMATICS

A. Culioli, ' "*Non, mais des fois!*" ', *Blanche-Benveniste Vol.*, 115–21, comments towards the end of his article that the reaction of some will be to say 'beaucoup de bruit pour rien (ou pour peu)' — which is precisely the expression that had come independently to my mind. M. Monville-Burston and L. R. Waugh discuss 'Lexicon, genre and local discourse organisation: French speech act verbs and journalistic texts', *JFLS*, 8:45–62. C. Tatillon, 'Un genre bien à elles', *La Linguistique*, 34.1:107–12, reflects on the controversy caused by three ministers who wish to be addressed as 'Madame la ministre'.

20. CONTRASTIVE STUDIES

Agnès Celle, **Étude contrastive du futur français et de ses réalisations en anglais*, Gap, Ophrys, 1997, 235 pp. Lucie Hoarau, **Étude contrastive* *de la coordination en français et en anglais*, Gap, Ophrys, 1997, 220 pp. H. Chuquet discusses 'La notion de point de vue en analyse contrastive anglais–français', *JFLS*, 8:29–43. S. Fleischman, 'Des jumeaux du discours', *La Linguistique*, 34.2:31–47, compares the discourse markers *like* (taken to be characteristic of the American English of the younger generations — but it is well established in British English) and *genre*.

EARLY MEDIEVAL LITERATURE

By A. E. Cobby, *University of Cambridge*, and
Finn E. Sinclair, *University of Cambridge*

1. GENERAL

Jens N. Faaborg, *Les Enfants dans la littérature française du moyen âge*
(Études romanes, 39), Copenhagen, Museum Tusculanum Press,
1997, 512 pp., is a vast bank of textual extracts, classified to indicate
the place, representation, and treatment of the child in medieval
literature, with quotations from other scholars but minimal original
comment. *A Dictionary of Medieval Heroes: Characters in Medieval Narrative
Traditions and their Afterlife in Literature, Theatre and the Visual Arts*, ed.
Willem P. Gerritsen and Anthony G. van Melle, trans. Tanis Guest,
Woodbridge, Boydell, vii + 336 pp., traces the fortunes of over 80
characters, giving the context of the first (or a selected) manifestation,
a survey of later medieval and any post-medieval versions, the state
of scholarly research, and other material which varies between
entries. There is an introduction on transmission of the legends, an
index of all characters referred to, and brief bibliographies. Jacqueline
de Weever, *Sheba's Daughters: Whitening and Demonizing the Saracen
Woman in Medieval French Epic* (GRLH, 2077), xxxvii + 253 pp.,
examines the portrayal of the Saracen woman in the epics of the High
Middle Ages (1150–1350), with particular emphasis on the ideological
nature of physical representation. The description of alterity becomes
problematic, as the Saracen woman either is assimilated to the
western aesthetic norm and depicted as white, or becomes the black
representative of death and destruction. In 'Paul Zumthor: errance et
transgressions dans une destinée d'historien', *EsC*, 38.1:104–16,
Y. Bonnefoy offers a poet's reflections on Z.'s understanding of
orality, vocality and performance. W. Calin, 'Makers of the Middle
Ages: Ernst Robert Curtius', *Ménard Vol.*, 199–209, defends C.,
stressing the humanist side of his early work, his valorizing of literary
studies, and his modernity, and discusses the significance of the *topos*
for medieval and post-medieval criticism. Y. G. Lepage, 'La tradition
éditoriale d'œuvres majeures: de la *Chanson de Roland* au *Testament* de
Villon', *Demarolle Vol.*, 39–51, surveys editions of the *Chanson de Roland*,
Chrétien de Troyes and Villon, and their methods, concluding with a
look ahead to editions desirable in the future. F. Vielliard, 'Le
manuscrit avant l'auteur: diffusion et conservation de la littérature
médiévale en ancien français (XIIe–XIIIe siècles)', *TLit*, 11:39–53,
studies the circumstances of production of early Fr. literary MSS and

of their preservation during the Middle Ages. G. Bianciotto, *'De quelques phénix médiévaux', *Shimmura Vol.*, 1–20.

H. Akkari, ' "Moult grant duel demener" ou le rituel de la mort', Bertrand, *Geste*, 13–24, studies the topos of mourning in a range of texts dating from the 11th to the 14th c., concluding that this differs in form and intensity according to whether it is expressed by men or women. Renate Blumenfeld-Kosinski, *Reading Myth: Classical Mythology and its Interpretation in Medieval French Literature*, Stanford U.P., 1997, 314 pp. *New Medieval Literatures*, i, ed. Rita Copeland et al., OUP, 1997, 240 pp. *New Medieval Literatures*, ii, ed. Rita Copeland et al., OUP, 282 pp. *Joan M. Ferrante, *To the Glory of her Sex: Women's Roles in the Composition of Medieval Texts*, Bloomington, Indiana U.P., 1997, 295 pp. *New approaches to medieval textuality*, ed. Mikle Dave Ledgerwood, Bern, Lang, 151 pp. *Ásdís R. Magnúsdóttir, *La Voix du cor: la relique de Roncevaux et l'origine d'un motif dans la littérature du Moyen Age (XIIe–XIVe siècles)*, Amsterdam–Atlanta, GA, Rodopi, 432 pp. M. Perret, 'Typologie des fins dans les œuvres de fiction', *PRIS-MA*, 14 : 155–74, points to the explicit nature of closure in the majority of medieval texts. Lack of this is more common in cyclical works and early *romans d'antiquité*, but this is not sufficent to indicate the existence of an aesthetic of non-closure. K. Pratt, 'Reading epic through romance: the *Roland* and the *Roman de Thèbes*', *Fest. Emden*, 101–27, examines the extent to which the romance's dialogue with the *matière de France* provides insights into generic transformation and the reception and potential meanings of the Oxford *Roland* and the tradition of Roncevaux.

2. EPIC

GENERAL. R. Colliot, 'De la gestuelle de quelques dames épiques et autres', Bertrand, *Geste*, 591–603, uses a range of mostly epic texts to build a picture of female gestures, which are mostly brief but significant, sometimes strange, and often bring a romance dimension on the artistic level to epic women who on the narrative level conform to the contemporary stereotype of weak, emotional, secondary beings. J.-P. Martin, 'Un espace en marge: l'image de la Hongrie dans quelques chansons de geste', *Géographie*, 109–24, concludes after surveying many *chansons de geste* that Hungary in them is a symbolic fiction, marginal and ambiguous, a place apart and an intermediate zone between East and West, the pagan and the Christian, the imperial past and the pagan past. P. Noble, 'Military leadership in the Old French epic', *Fest. Emden*, 171–91, compares the heroes of the *Chanson de Roland*, the *Chanson de Guillaume* and *Raoul de Cambrai* with contemporary military leaders to ascertain what is meant by leadership. Birth, courage, physical strength, and skill, Christian faith, a righteous cause and the power to inspire troops are central qualities of the literary heroes, while the real-life leaders are more aware of tactics and strategy. †C. Smith, 'On Spanish ballads and French epics', *ib.*, 297–311, is a *summa* of what is known about the relationship between these two literary forms, and stresses the position of Spain as a setting for many *chansons de geste* and its role in preserving epic material both in MSS and in oral tradition.

ROLAND AND CHARLEMAGNE.　*Le Pèlerinage de Charlemagne*, ed. Glyn S. Burgess (British Rencesvals Publications, 2), Edinburgh, Société Rencesvals British Branch, lvii + 70 pp., is a student edition with a facing line-by-line translation into English, a substantial introduction and bibliography, notes and an index of proper names. A previously unpublished fragment has independently been edited twice this year, by A. Kerr, 'The Sées fragments of *Gui de Bourgogne* and *Anseïs de Cartage*', *Fest. Emden*, 193–32, and R. Mori, 'L'*Anseïs de Carthage* nel frammento di Sées', *Melli Vol.*, 543–53, a second fragment being included by Kerr. Kerr's is a semi-diplomatic edition with critical apparatus, Mori gives a more critical text. Each has a solid introduction. Some readings are radically divergent, and reconstructions of the missing parts of each line differ. P. E. Bennett, 'Ganelon's false message: a critical false perspective?', *Fest. Emden*, 149–69, surveys critical approaches to the episode in the *Roland* and concludes that they rely on 20th-c. misconceptions about the form and function of a letter in the medieval context. A. Corbellari, 'Traduire ou ne pas traduire: le dilemme de Bédier. A propos de la traduction de la *Chanson de Roland*', *VR*, 56, 1997:63–82, compares B.'s translation with modern ones to establish the nature of his language, and finds it a *langue* of his own, neither OF nor Modern Fr., which B. uses both here and in his *Tristan* translation. H. Diament, 'Deux toponymes mystérieux de la *Chanson de Roland*: *Seinz* et *Besençun*, clefs pour la sémantique territoriale du mot *France* au XIe siècle', *Mandach Vol.*, 9–28, discusses the meanings of 'France' in the *Roland*, its semantics being in transition at the time, and concludes that it embraces Picardy and Normandy at their 1080 borders but not all the Capetian royal domain. He interprets 'Seinz' as a cluster of places named Sains in Picardy, and reads 'Besençun' as 'Besentun', namely Bazentin (Somme). Y. Greub, 'Les recherches pré-bédieriennes sur le stemma du *Roland*: tentative de classement', *RLaR*, 102:147–66, is a detailed study of stemmas and methods. J. Subrenat, 'De la paix de Vienne au drame de Roncevaux', *Fest. Emden*, 1–9, shows how the content of *Girart de Vienne* opens the way to new developments in the later *Roland* versions, notably that of the Paris MS. C. Zemmour, 'Principaux vocables et statuts actantiels anatomiques dans la *Chanson de Roland*: réflexions sur une symbolique du geste du moyen âge (du début de la *Chanson* à la mort de Roland, vv. 1 à 2396)', Bertrand, *Geste*, 571–87, studies parts of the body from a semantic and a gestural viewpoint, minutely classifying gestures and postures. J. Simpson, 'All's fair in love and war: conflicts and continuities in *Anseïs de Carthage*', *Fest. Emden*, 129–48, shows how sexual and military conquests are intertwined as Anseïs's military achievements are foregrounded, and how echoes of the *Roland* present the later text as a reappraising sequel to the latter. M. le Person, 'Le rire et le sourire dans *La Destruction de Rome* et *Fierabras*', *Ménard Vol.*, 897–915, finds moments of comic relief even in these serious works, and identifies an ideological function of laughter, enabling ridicule of the enemy. A. de Mandach, 'Les textes et festivals du *Fierabras* en Ibérie et en Amérique latine: plaidoyer en faveur de la littérature orale, épine dorsale des chansons épiques mondiales', *Melli Vol.*, 471–75, describes the survival and adaptations of the Fr. legend in performance. J. Subrenat, 'Monde chrétien, monde sarrasin, dans la *Chanson des Saisnes* de Jehan Bodel', *Mandach Vol.*, 65–76, is a close textual study, finding typical Christian epic details applied to the Franks and Saracen details to the Saxons, in a manner faithful to the spirit of the *chanson de geste* but with added subtlety. J.-C. Vallecalle, '*Fortitudo* et *stultitia*: remarques sur le personnage d'Estout dans les chansons de geste', *Ménard Vol.*, 1423–34, surveys the development of the character Estout de Langres, from being a simply brave companion of Roland in the *Chanson de Roland*, through separating from him in *Gui de Bourgogne*, until for the Franco-Italian poets he becomes both more central and more extravagant, an old-style fighter out of place in a civilized world. P. Skårup, 'Traductions norroises de textes français: un aperçu', *RLaR*, 102:3–6, provides an introductory overview for an issue of *RLaR* partly devoted to such translations. It includes: J. Kjær, '*Karlamagnús saga*: la Saga de Charlemagne' (7–23), a description of the branches of the *Saga* and their OF sources, the MS tradition and transmission, modern editions and translations, and a study of the five branches containing close imitations of the OF in the light of the handling of religion, courtliness and the figure of the king in the *Saga* as a whole, so as to bring out the mentality of the collection; and P. Skårup, '*Flóvents saga* et la chanson française de *Floovent neveu de Constantin*' (45–55), who argues that *Flóvents saga* is not an imitation of the extant *Floovant*, but a translation or adaptation of another, lost text, probably of the 12th c., of which he also finds a version in the 14th c. Italian prose *Fioravante*.

GUILLAUME D'ORANGE AND THE GARIN CYCLE. N. Andrieux-Reix, 'De l'honneur du monde à la gloire du ciel: Guillaume ermite au désert', *Ménard Vol.*, 37–49, focuses on the conflict between the heroic and the saintly moralities to show how the hermit episode in the cyclic MSS marks the accomplishment both of Guillaume's final aspiration and of the cyclical design. E. A. Heinemann, 'Patterns of narrative and poetic organisation in the kernel William cycle', *Fest. Emden*, 249–67, analyses various aspects of metrics and *laisse* composition in *La Prise d'Orange, Le Couronnement de Louis* and *Le Charroi de Nîmes*. D. Hüe, 'Brèves remarques sur l'écu de Guillaume', *Mandach Vol.*, 115–33, argues that Guillaume's shield in *Aliscans* is a symbol of military and supernatural power which, by being destroyed, gives way to the Christian spirit. C. Lachet, 'Échos signifiants dans la composition d'*Aliscans*', *Ménard Vol.*, 783–97, studies in detail a network of echoes and correspondences which he finds in *Aliscans*, and sees in it evidence that this is a carefully constructed text. A. Moisan, 'Du tinel à l'épée, ou le lent apprentissage du métier des armes chez *Rainouart au Tinel*', Bertrand, *Geste*, 429–41, traces the development of Rainouart from *tinel*-wielder to swordsman in the *Chanson de Guillaume, Aliscans, La Bataille Loquifer*, and *Le Moniage Rainouart I*, and so shows his growth in chivalry as he fights against his destiny. M. Ott, 'Les songes d'Aymeri dans *La Mort Aymeri de Narbonne*', *Demarolle Vol.*, 241–62, shows how Aymeri's dreams reinforce the coherence of the poem by announcing events, and suggests that the dreams and their interpretation refer to a problem left unsolved, the succession of Narbonne.

EPICS OF REVOLT. M. J. Ailes, 'Deux fragments inconnus de *Maugis d'Aigremont*', *Romania*, 116:415–30, publishes two binding fragments from the second half of the 12th c., found in the London PRO, containing 276 lines of *Maugis d'Aigremont* in a version tending to conform to that of MS *C*. A. Labbé has published many articles on epics of revolt. 'Enchantement et subversion dans *Girart de Roussillon* et *Renaut de Montauban*', *Chant et enchantement*, 121–55, brings out the ambivalent status of Fouchier and Maugis as magicians and thieves, subversive, transfunctional characters who reveal the trifunctional world order. 'Le dit et le non-dit des gestes: à propos de quelques pratiques de Maugis dans *Renaut de Montauban*', Bertrand, *Geste*, 293–317, continues that article by analysing the means by which enchantment takes place in *Renaut de Montauban*, finding that only a few of the available devices are used and that a single reading is not possible. 'Le miracle comme clotûre du récit épique: *Girart de Roussillon* et *Renaut de Montauban*', *PRIS-MA*, 14:135–54, turns to the Christian marvellous, showing how miracles close both texts while opening the epic to hagiography, though their relation to what precedes differs. In 'Lumières au ciel de Bourgogne: l'écriture du miracle dans *Girart de Roussillon*', *Bulletin de la Société des Fouilles Archéologiques et des Monuments*

Historiques de l'Yonne, 15:63–78, L. offers a close analysis of two miracles, the storm at Vaubenton and the vision at Vézelay. 'Le château au péril du songe: le rêve de Clarisse dans *Renaut de Montauban*', *Actes* (Rambures), 195–207, argues that Clarisse's dream, in which the reassuring image of Montauban is overturned, is exceptional in content and in formulation, which is linked to the dreamer's being a woman. 'Renaut et ses frères: une complicité de sourire', *Ménard Vol.*, 769–81, studies the solidarity between the four brothers, and the dimming of their individuality, which are brought to completion by the adjunction of Maugis. Finally in 'La croix, l'épée et la flamme: autour de l'incendie d'Origny dans *Raoul de Cambrai*', *Feu et Lumière*, I, 121–57, L. turns to *Raoul de Cambrai* to discuss the symbolic purpose of the many fires in the poem, their ideological meaning and narrative function; the fire at Origny, to which all the others refer, has a unique emotional charge. J. J. Duggan, 'L'épisode d'Aupais dans *Girart de Roussillon*', *Fest. Emden*, 11–23, is an analysis of the episode to show the otherworldly origins of Aupais. D. Kullmann, 'Kirchliche Lehren in *Girart de Roussillon*', *Melli Vol.*, 403–17, finds clear evidence that the poet not only had a clerical education but was also consciously bringing in specific church teachings which were the subject of contemporary theological discussion. R. Lafont, '*Girart de Roussillon*: un texte occitan', *Mandach Vol.*, 29–50, argues by close study of rhymes that the version in MS *O* betrays the *oïlisation* of an Occ. text. He proposes a four-stage development of the historical and textual elements and defends the thesis of bipartite composition. D. Rieger, ' "E trait sos meillors omes ab un consel": émotion, mise en scène et "consilium" féodale dans *Girart de Roussillon*', *ZRP*, 114:628–50, studies the council scenes in *Girart de Roussillon* from the point of view of ritualized verbal exchange contrasted with the real or apparent spontaneity of emotional reactions. M. Pagano, 'Ancora qualche noterella sulle versioni D et L del *Renaut de Montauban*', *Melli Vol.*, 623–33, compares passages in the two versions to show the workings of *amplificatio*. J. Subrenat, 'Renaut de Montauban en Terre-Sainte: une refléxion épique sur le pèlerinage de Jérusalem dans la chanson des *Quatre Fils Aymon*', *Brault Vol.*, 223–38, finds in Renaut's pious end the influence both of crusade epics and of older traditions, and suggests that the similarities between *Renaut de Montauban* and the *Chanson de Jérusalem* are not due to chance. J. Belam, 'Ogier le Danois: making use of a legend', *Fest. Emden*, 25–40, outlines the development of Ogier's character and legend, arguing that *La Chevalerie Ogier* owes little to pre-existing sources and that its most important theme is the danger to the individual and the community of isolation from society. N. Cazauran, 'Retour de "faërie": *Ogier le Danois* deux cents ans après', *Ménard Vol.*, 311–24, discusses the evolution of the Ogier legend from the decasyllabic continuation of *La Chevalerie Ogier* via the alexandrine version through to the incunable prose of 1496, focusing on *faërie* in the person of Morgan. M. Ailes, 'Traitors and rebels: the *Geste de Maience*', *Fest. Emden*, 41–68, traces the development and fusion of the originally distinct lineages of Ganelon and the rebels, through to the eventual disintegration of the union.

OTHER EPICS. F. Suard, 'Héros et action épiques dans la *Chanson d'Antioche*', *Melli Vol.*, 763–77, focuses on the tension between a globalizing outlook or panoramic view, and a fragmented composition or narrative fresco, and wonders whether the *remanieur*, with his aim of showing the expedition as the celebration of a Christian people, may not have given an epic transformation to earlier, already composite material. E. J. Mickel, '*Enfances Godefroi*: the making of popular history', *Romania*, 116: 148–69, looks at the historical development of Lotharingia as a backdrop for the fictional history, as an aid to understanding the contradiction between the Godfrey family's Carolingian background and their loyalty to the Empire. D. Boutet, '*Jehan de Lanson* et les traditions normandes du motif des funérailles feintes', *Ménard Vol.*, 173–84, examines the appearances of this folklore motif in a variety of texts with a Norman connection, and concludes that the author shared a culture with, and remembered the dreams of, the Normans of southern Italy, whence he obtained it.

3. ROMANCE

GENERAL. C. Brucker, 'Aventure, discours et structure dans le roman médiévale au XIIIe et XIVe siècles', *Ménard Vol.*, 227–47, studies the depiction and role of adventure and its place in the discourse, *récit*, and structure of a range of romances, concluding that the modern definition of 'adventure' became more evident during the 13th and 14th centuries. David Rollo, **Historical Fabrication, Ethnic Fable and French Romance in Twelfth-Century England*, FFM, 335 pp. Beate Schmolke-Hasselmann, *The Evolution of Arthurian Romance: the Verse Tradition from Chrétien to Froissart*, trans. Margaret and Roger Middleton, CUP, xlix + 322 pp., draws on, and redefines, the work of earlier German scholars in a study which provides an important contribution to reception history and genre history. A useful introduction provides an overview of the evolution of Old French Arthurian literary studies. The text then focuses in particular on the response to Chrétien in later epigonal romances. R. T. Pickens, 'Transmission et *translatio*: mouvement textuel et variance', *FrF*, 23: 133–45, considers the problematic nature of textual *mouvance* and *variance* with reference to the CD-ROM Project *Charrette*, concluding that these features did not stem from transmission alone, but were an integral part of contemporary literary culture. Romaine Wolf-Bonvin, *Textus. De la tradition latine à l'esthétique du roman médiéval. Le Bel Inconnu, Amadas et Ydoine*, Champion, 1997, 409 pp. R. Baudry, 'Et l'absence, éloquente, de geste . . .', Bertrand, *Geste*, 43–50, considers the significance of the absence of gesture, illustrating that the vision or memory of the beloved and the intrusion of the divine are both sources of the same paralysing ecstasy. C. Bouillot, 'Gestes et pudeur dans les romans courtois du XIIIe siècle', *ib.*, 111–23, examines the implications of a prudish veiling of the body and emotions in the romance; the author is seen as haunted by the ever-present regard of the reader as other. J. Cerquiglini-Toulet, 'Une parole muette: le rire amoureux au moyen âge', *Ménard Vol.*, 325–36, points to the prevalence of the smiling heroine as a topos of medieval romance, *lai*, and lyric. She concludes that this suggests a capacity to relate to the outside world, but that the enigmatic nature of the smile signals the enigmatic nature of woman. A. Berthelot, 'Magiciennes et enchanteurs: comment apprivoisier l'autre faé', *Chant et enchantement*, 105–20, traces the evolution of the term 'faé' from oral tales to the written *matière de Bretagne*. The alterity of the supernatural is reduced through the systematic demonization, banalization, or rationalization of its manifestations in 13th-c. literature. N. J. Lacy, 'Coutumes, merveilles, aventures', *ib.*, 157–69, concentrates on the significance and function of the 'coutume' as a means of generating narrative, linking this with the power of enchantment and the topos of adventure used as structuring devices. F. Wolfzettel, 'Die Frau im Turm: zu einem märchenhaften Motiv in der altfranzösischen Literatur', *Fest. Birkhan*, 330–59, gives an overview of the use of motif in romance and *lai*, pointing to the phallic nature of the tower, and its implicit link with incest narrative.

CHRÉTIEN DE TROYES. A. S. Laranjinha, 'L'ironie comme principe structurant chez Chrétien de Troyes', *CCMe*, 41 : 175–82, studies the use of irony in relation to the interlacing of narrative themes and as a marker of the fundamental ambiguity which Chrétien manifests towards the notions of authority and writing. E. Baumgartner, 'La musique pervertit les mœurs', *Ménard Vol.*, 75–89, links the lack of a musician-hero in Chrétien's romances with the connection between musicians and devils and enchantment in other contemporary romances. C. B. G. Waddington, 'L'imaginaire celte et le renverse-ment de l'ordre féodal chez Chrétien de Troyes', *Mandach Vol.*, 221–30, posits that Chrétien purposely allocates a space to the Celtic imaginary in his work, without assimilating it to the the courtly ethic. J. Merceron, 'De la "mauvaise humeur" du sénéchal Keu: Chrétien de Troyes, littérature et psychologie', *CCMe*, 41 : 17–34, offers a new interpretation of Keu's character, analysing this in the context of the physiological theory of humours, which influenced Keu's decline from his original heroic status. L. Löfstedt, 'Chrétien de Troyes et le Décret de Gratien', *NMi*, 49:5–16, traces the links between Chrétien's romances and Gratian's *Decretum*, pointing to the influence of canon law on *Erec et Enide* and *Le Conte du Graal* in particular. P. Le Rider, 'L'Episode de l'épervier dans *Erec et Enide*', *Romania*, 116:368–93, points to the dramatic importance of this episode as a means of valorizing and qualifying Enide as the opposite of a *fée*. F. Wolfzettel, '*Cligès*, roman "épiphanique"', *ib.*, 1489–1507, studies the bipartite structure of *Cligès*, suggesting that the opposition of Byzantium and the Arthurian world stems from a dialectic which sets history against non-history in a search for epiphanic truth. L. D. Wolfgang, 'The manuscripts of the *Chevalier de la Charrette (Lancelot)* of Chrétien de Troyes. Preliminary remarks to a new edition: the case of ms. E', *Ménard Vol.*, 1477–88, compares MS. E, the 'worst' and most reworked of the *Lancelot* MSS, to MS. C, the 'best' of them, concluding that the effect of the scribal *remaniement* is to 'prosify' the poetic text. P. G. Beltrami, 'Appunti di lavoro da una tradizione poetica del *Chevalier da la Charrete*', *Melli Vol.*, 69–86, underscores the link between the rationalization of the *merveilleux* and the shift from verse to prose during the 13th c., with particular reference to the *Charrete* and its later translations. P. Le Rider, 'Lions et dragons dans la littérature, de Pierre Damien à Chrétien de Troyes', *MA*, 104:9–52, examines the allegorical nature of the lion, as wounded, or as battling with the dragon/serpent, suggesting that the *Chevalier au Lion* avoids such allegorization and is more obviously influenced by the *Chanson des Chétifs* than by the romance of *Gilles de Chin*. P. Bretel, 'La conversion de Perceval. Lecture de l'épisode de l'ermite dans *Le Conte du Graal* de Chrétien de Troyes', *IL*, 50:3–12, sees this as the point which marks the synthesis of adventure and spiritual and moral qualities for the hero, and which has far-reaching importance for the further development of Arthurian literature. D. Buschinger, 'Le mythe de l'au-delà celtique dans *Le Conte du Graal* de Chrétien de Troyes et le *Parzival* de Wolfram von Eschenbach', *Demarolle Vol.*, 295–311, reads the mythical tradition of *Parzival* against that of the *Conte*, concluding that the German version presents a more realistic tale, in which the mythical elements are reduced, or transformed into the *merveilleux*. M. de Combarieu du Grès, 'Perceval et les péchés de la langue', *Littératures*, 39:5–29, concentrates on the positive or negative value given to language and silence in a text produced at the point of the cultural juxtaposition of literature and orality. T. Amazawa, 'La devineuse du nom de Perceval', *Ménard Vol.*, 33–36, displaces the divination of the name from Perceval or the narrator, to the *pucelle*, claiming that only she can act as guarantor of its authenticity. R. Baudry, 'Châteaux-frères et châteaux-fées de l'autre monde dans *Le Conte du Graal*, *Actes* (Rambures), 261–69, compares aspects of the Grail castle visited by Perceval, and of that visited by Gauvain. J.-C. Lozac'Hmeur, 'Le forgeron, le roi-pêcheur et la libération des eaux ou l'arrière-plan mythologique d'une légende', *Ménard Vol.*, 917–31, links *Le Conte du Graal* with Iranian and Irish legends, underscoring the mythical origins of the narrative. P. Maninchedda, 'I nemici immemori: Perceval e Gauvain nel *Conte du Graal*', *Melli Vol.*, 477–92, explores the symmetry between the two protagonists in relation to the themes of quest, memory, and origins. J.-J. Vincensini, 'Impatience et impotence. L'étrangeté des rois du château du Graal dans *Le Conte du Graal*', *Romania*, 116:112–30, considers the importance of the themes and structures uniting characters in order to point to the mythical nature of the narrative.

OTHER ARTHURIAN. J.-G. Gouttebroze, 'J'ai deux amours... Guinglain entre épouse et maîtresse', *CCMe*, 41:55–63, studies the diametric and symbolic opposition of the two female characters in Renaut de Beaujeu's *Li Biaus Desconneüs*; the one representing Eros and the pleasure principle, the other society and the reality principle. M.-N. Toury, '*Le Bel Inconnu*, un roman de l'ironie', *Ménard Vol.*, 1399–1407, points to the ambiguity of a text which privileges lyric form, yet uses parodic irony to reveal the hypocrisy of *fin'amors*. H. Braet, '*Le Bel Inconnu* ou les délices de l'incertitude', *Demarolle Vol.*, 275–83, links the ambivalence of the hero's identity and his lack of decision with the author's interweaving of different genres, which creates an intrinsic narrative uncertainty. D. Maddox, 'Les armoires de l'*Inconnu*', *Ménard Vol.*, 933–42, examines the use of heraldic arms in the context of *Le Bel Inconnu*, where they serve to valorize the hero, but also testify to the contemporary fascination for a naissant form of cultural representation.

K. Busby, ' "Estrangement se merveilla". L'Autre dans les *Continuations* de *Perceval*', *Ménard Vol.*, 279–97, contrasts the general integration of the *merveilleux* into the Arthurian world with the perplexity and disorientation which it provokes in *Perceval*, arguing that Chrétien's continuators understood and perpetuated this depiction. A. Saly, 'Le *Perlesvaus* et Gerbert de Montreuil', *ib.*, 1163–82, argues that the simplified form of the *Continuation* marks its anteriority. F. Dubost, 'Les nuits magnétiques du *Perlesvaus*', *ib.*, 429–46, points to the difference between nocturnal and diurnal adventure; night being the site of fascinating, horrifying, and erotic encounters, in which tension is created between the love object and the religious object.

*Lancelot du Lac, Vol. III, ed. François Mosès (Coll. Lettres Gothiques), Livre de Poche, 351 pp. F. Suard, 'Bohort de Gaunes, image et héraut de Lancelot', *Ménard Vol.*, 1297–1317, traces the

parallels between Bohort and Lancelot, arguing that the story of Bohort functions as a metanarrative, offering commentary on Lancelot's itinerary and perpetuating his memory. F. Wolfzettel, 'L'Autre dans le *Lancelot du Lac*', *Fest. Ertzdorff*, 327–38, studies the triangular relationship between Lancelot, Guinevere, and Galahad, in which transgressive love has an inassimilable alterity. R. Hyatte, 'Praise and subversion of romance ethos in the prose *Lancelot*', *Neophilologus*, 82 : 11–18, considers the problematic nature of reader-reponse to a work which shifts between glorification and censure of the chivalric romance ethos personified by the heroes. E. Kennedy, 'Structures d'entrelacement contrastantes dans le *Lancelot en prose* et le *Perlesvaus*', *Ménard Vol.*, 745–57, links the difference in narrative structure with the contrast in textual motivation: the *Lancelot* is presented as true, while the *Perlesvaus* is divinely inspired. *Jean-René Valette, *La Poétique du merveilleux dans le "Lancelot en prose"*, Champion, 544 pp. Kathryn Karczewska, *Prophecy and the Quest for the Holy Grail: Critiquing Knowledge in the Vulgate Cycle*, Bern, Lang, 279 pp.

J.-P. Ponceau, 'L'Auteur de *L'Estoire del Saint Graal* et celui de *La Queste del Saint Graal* sont vraisemblablement distincts', *Ménard Vol.*, 1043–56, maps the disparities and contradictions between the two romances, concluding that the author of the *Queste* drew on episodes from the *Estoire*. M. Stanesco, 'Parole autoritaire et "accord des semblances" dans *La Queste del Saint Graal*', *ib.*, 1267–79, examines the doubling and fragmentation of narrative through the use of *translatio*: the textual gloss represents a collective voice which contrasts with its less authoritarian use in the *Perlesvaus*.

D. Delcourt, 'La verité dans *La Mort le roi Artu*. Couverture, détours, et labyrinthe', *MedRom*, 22 : 16–60, views the *Mort* as a 'roman-labyrinthe', in which the secular is opposed to the spiritual; the way of error to the way of truth. F. Suard, 'Hasard et nécessité dans *La Mort le roi Artu*', *Mandach Vol.*, 281–94, considers the inter-relation of necessity, chance and passion and their influence on the tragic destiny of the text's characters. B. Guidot, 'Le bonheur dans *La Mort le roi Artu*', *Ménard Vol.*, 585–600, posits that the destruction of the Arthurian world is accompanied by a quest for pleasure, in which hedonistic pleasure is opposed to a moral and religious form of joy. A. Planche, 'Les mots de la mort et du malheur dans *La Mort le roi Artu*', *Mandach Vol.*, 269–80, provides a lexical study of the terms relating to death, evil, and dishonour; terms which reveal the disintegration of Arthur's court. J. Maurice, 'Le château dans *La Mort le roi Artu*', *Actes* (Rambures), 251–59, gives a socio-historical signific-ance to the literary representation of the château, in which the aristocracy is invested with a political importance contrary to the cultural marginalization which threatened it. M.-O. Bodnheimer, 'Le

Château de Morgane, monde réel et monde enchanté dans *La Mort le roi Artu*', *ib.*, 241–49, suggests that although the château presents an ambivalent image, its description is based on architectural realism, which grounds the narrative in a universe of truth. F. Mora, 'L'Accident de chasse de Lancelot dans *La Mort le roi Artu*: jeux du narrateur et jeux de destin', *Ménard Vol.*, 1007–18, notes the symbolic link between the accusation of Guinevere and Lancelot's hunting accident. Both episodes provoke a sudden deviation of narrative and refer back to the couple's sexual misdemeanours.

TRISTAN AND ISEUT. Norris J. Lacy, *Early French Tristan Poems*, 2 vols, Cambridge, Brewer, offers an introduction, edition, English translation and notes for a range of works, including Béroul, Thomas, *Les Folies Tristan*, and Marie de France's *Chevrefeuille*. J.-M. Pastre, 'Tristan et la magie du geste', Bertrand, *Geste*, 463–86, gives an overview of the mythical and magical tradition in *Tristan*, pointing to its evolution from a divine to a warrior trait. V. P. Bertolucci, 'L'arpa d'Isotta: variazioni testuali e figurative', *Ménard Vol.*, 101–19, gives an overview of the importance of the harp as a motif which links together Tristan and Yseut. G. J. Brault, 'L'Amer, l'amor, la mer: la scène des aveux dans le *Tristan* de Thomas à la lumière du fragment de Carlisle', *ib.*, 215–26, considers the importance of the Carlisle fragment in its portrayal of the declaration of love and the play on words which this entails. T. Hunt, 'Béroul's *Tristan*: the discovery of the lovers in the forest', *Fest. Emden*, 233–48, illustrates the sophistication of Béroul's poetic technique, particularly in regard to the insoluble ambiguity of visual signs. P. Walter, 'La tête coupée du Morrois (Béroul, v. 1658–1749)', *Mandach Vol.*, 245–55, is an etymological study of the naming of forest and characters which reveals the mythical scheme fundamental to the Tristan legend. S. Sasaki, '*Anel* et *seel*: de Béroul et du *Lancelot* au roman de *Tristan en prose*', *Ménard Vol.*, 1203–12, views the use of rings and seals as privileged objects which underscore the sense and structure of a narrative.

Le Roman de Tristan en prose, Vol. XI, ed. Laurence Harf-Lancner, Geneva, Droz, 1997, 352 pp. H. Legros, 'La "Folie Tristan" dans le *Tristan en prose*: aboutissement de traditions antérieures et réécriture', *Ménard Vol.*, 869–78, points to the originality of the treatment of Tristan's madness here. Rather than involving a loss of chivalric quality, madness acts as a purifying experience which privileges prowess and adventure. L. Harf-Lancner, ' "Une seule chair, un seul cœur, une seule âme". La mort des amants dans le *Tristan en prose*', *ib.*, 613–28, contrasts the death of the lovers with that of alternative versions, concluding that the prose offers a glorification of passionate love which opposes the ideal of the Grail. F. Plet, 'Le nom de l'Autre: le géant et le fou dans *Le Roman de Tristan en prose*', *Littératures*, 38 : 5–17,

studies the distinction between the named and the unnamed representatives of Otherness, and points to the new tendency to assimilate
and eradicate difference. G. Roussineau, 'Remarques sur les relations
entre la *Suite de Merlin* et sa continuation et le *Tristan en prose*', *Ménard
Vol.*, 1149–62, considers the chronological and narrative relationship
between the texts, concluding that the *Suite* justifies and exploits the
narrative details of *Tristan*. J. Subrenat, 'Tristan sur les chemins du
Graal', *ib.*, 1319–28, suggests that although spiritual search is not a
major preoccupation for Tristan, his integration into the Grail Quest
is intrinsically linked to his destiny as a tragic lover.

ROMANS D'ANTIQUITÉ. *Catherine Gaullier-Bougassas, *Les Romans
d'Alexandre. Aux frontières de l'épique et du romanesque*, Champion, 580 pp.
*Martin Gosman, *La Légende d'Alexandre le Grand dans la littérature
française du 12e siècle. Une réécriture permanente*, Amsterdam–Atlanta, GA,
Rodopi, 1997, 395 pp. M. Gosman, ' "Touzjor vesquirent d'armes,
itel fu lor labor": L'aventure épique dans le Roman d'Alexandre',
Mandach Vol., 85–98, studies the epic motivation of the *Alexandre* in the
context of received ideals of courage and sacrifice. F. Suard,
'Quelques aspects de l'écriture épique dans le *Roman d'Alexandre*
d'Alexandre de Paris', *Fest. Emden*, 85–100, analyses the stylistic
proximity between the *Alexandre* and epic, revealing the poet's skill in
creating a transitional form of narrative. G. Zaganelli, 'Alessandro
Magno, Tristano, Cligès e una camicia tessuta sui Tamigi', *Melli Vol.*,
897–909, concentrates on the poetic construction of the *Roman
d'Alexandre*, pointing to links with the Tristan narrative and *Cligès*,
both known to the author. U. Mölk, 'A propos de quelques passages
difficiles de l'*Alexandre* d'Alberic', *Ménard Vol.*, 985–91, discusses the
problems of interpretation and translation in respect of the first and
fourth *laisses* of the poem.

D. Kelly, 'Horace et le *Roman de Troie* de Benoît de Sainte-Maure',
Ménard Vol., 723–31, considers the problems encountered by Béroul
in the transition from Latin to vernacular text, and studies the
implications of this for narratorial intervention. A. Petit, 'Le
"Planctus" d'Ysmaine dans le manuscrit P du *Roman de Thèbes*', *ib.*,
1019–28, studies this episode in MS P as revealing the originality of
the redaction and of the shift from an evocation of the power and
horror of death (found in earlier redactions) to a more lyrical form of
description.

OTHER ROMANCES. R. T. Pickens, ' "Vassalage" épique et
courtoisie romanesque dans le *Roman de Brut*', *Mandach Vol.*, 165–200,
views the form of *courtoisie* which appears in Wace's *Brut* as investing
epic 'vasselage' with qualities which transcend those of the epic code
of honour, thus paving the way for the development of *fin'amors*.
J. Gilbert, 'The practice of gender in *Aucassin et Nicolette*', *FMLS*, 33,

1997:215–28, questions the validity of reading the narrative as a straightforward case of gender role reversal, arguing that each character's relation to gender norms is fragmented and ambivalent, while gender only forms one aspect of the power structures shaping the romance. M.-L. Chênerie, 'La dénomination des personnages féminins dans les romans de Hue de Rotelande', *Ménard Vol.*, 347–59, links the anonymity of female characters with the opposition between the known and unknown, the individual and stereotype, and points to the misogynistic tone which dominates Hue's romances. *Jean Renart and the Art of Romance: Essays on Guillaume de Dole*, ed. Nancy Vine Durling, Florida U.P., 1997, 240 pp., comprises a series of articles divided between the sections 'Text and Context', 'The Language of the Lyric and the Language of Romance', and 'Music and Perform-ance'. A. Gier, 'L'Anneau et le miroir: *Le Lai de l'ombre* à la lumière de Narcisse', *RF*, 110:445–55, points to the ironic treatment of the episode between the lovers in the *Lai*, which disavows both the egocentrism of the *Narcissus* and the exaggerated idealism of *fin'amors*. L. Louison, 'Mimétisme et sémantisme des gestes dans *L'Escoufle*, vers 502–669', Bertrand, *Geste*, 383–99, considers the use of gesture to produce meaning and and realism, but also note its ambiguous and potentially deceptive nature. P. Simons and P. Eley, 'A subtext and its subversion: the variant endings to *Partonopeus de Blois*', *Neophilologus*, 82:181–97, points to MS A as presenting the version closest to the original, but also points to the political sub-text of the romance. B. N. Sargent-Baur, 'La structure temporelle de la *Manekine* de Philippe de Rémi', *Romania*, 116:131–47, summarises the romance, emphasizing its internal chronology and pointing to the importance of the liturgical calendar within this. Id., 'Echos de Chrétien de Troyes dans les romans de Philippe de Rémi', *Ménard Vol.*, 1193–201, compares specific passages by the two authors, indicating parallel episodes and verbal echoes. C. Harvey, 'Courtly discourse and folklore in *La Manekine*', *Papers* (ICLS 8), 395–403, shows how the author skilfully combines elements from courtly ideology with key motifs from folklore. A. Soler, '*Jehan et Blonde* de Philippe de Rémi: l'amour contrarié et l'affirmation d'un héros nouveau', *Francofonia*, 34:69–91, plots the thematic and formal innovations of the *roman d'aventure*, particularly in regard to the construction of the love-narrative and its protagonists. J.-L. Leclanche, 'Deux notes sur les témoins manuscrits du *Dolopathos* d'Herbert', *Ménard Vol.*, 849–63, examines the distribu-tion of ornamental capitals in the three principle manuscripts. B. Levy, ' "Honor" et "honneur". Le rôle du château-foyer dans deux romans lignagers anglo-normands', *Actes* (Rambures), 297–308, argues that the image of the château is integrated into the fiction of the 'roman lignager', yet it also serves to illustrate the real desires and fears of the contemporary Anglo-Norman aristocracy.

LAIS. C. Alvar, 'A propósito del marco de los lais narrativos', *Ménard Vol.*, 15–31, lists the significant features which help to define *lais* as a genre, with particular reference to those of Marie de France. M. S. Beretta, 'L'usignolo nello scrigno. Poesia come *remembrance* nei *Lais* di Maria di Francia', *Melli Vol.*, 753–62,, relates the symbolic role of the nightingale in *Laüstic* to that of poetry itself as a form of remembrance. P. E. Bennett, 'Marie de France, lectrice de Gaimar? Le Cas d'*Equitan*', *ib.*, 87–102, contends that *Equitan* has a deceptive simplicity; in reality it confounds two different systems of moral absolutes, those of Christianity and *fin'amors*, and can be thematically linked to Gaimar's text. H. Braet, 'Marie de France, poète du visuel?', *Ménard Vol.*, 185–94, points to Marie's economy of writing. Lack of descriptive detail and individuality of character are seen as producing greater audience identification. R. Bruseçan, 'Le *Lai du lecheur* et la tradition du lai plaisant', *ib.*, 249–65, classifies this as a 'lai plaisant'; a metanarrative which synthesizes *lai* and *fabliau* traits. R. Dubuis, 'Les XII joies de Marie', *ib.*, 447–63, examines the use of the term 'joie' in Marie's attributed works, arguing that this is fundamental to the *Lais*. J. Eccles, 'Feminist criticism and the lay of *Lanval*', *RoN*, 38:281–86, questions the validity of applying feminist criticism to *Lanval* on the grounds that no gender bias exists in the text: the Fairy Mistress and Guinevere both present strong female characters, one positive, one negative. S. K. Gertz, 'Echoes and reflections of enigmatic beauty in Ovid and Marie de France', *Speculum*, 73:372–96, compares Narcissus and Guigemar in an examination of the relation between language, creation, and beauty. G. Gros, 'Où l'on devient Bisclavret. Etude sur le site de la métamorphose (Marie de France, *Bisclavret*, vers 89–96)', *Ménard Vol.*, 573–83, compares the symbolic nature of the chapel in *Bisclavret* with that in Béroul's *Tristan*, pointing to the problematic nature of the relationship between religion and the *merveilleux*. J. Larmat, 'Les héroïnes des *Lais* de Marie de France', *ib.*, 839–47, traces the idealized traits shared by the female protagonists, contrasting these with the realistic lack of freedom for women depicted by Marie. M. Mikhaëlova, 'L'Espace dans les *Lais* de Marie de France', *CCMe*, 40, 1997:145–57, equates the organization of physical space in the *Lais* with Marie's skilful deployment of a 'rhetoric of space' which creates an openness of meaning in the text. J. Ribard, 'Le Symbolisme dans les *Lais* de Marie de France', *Ménard Vol.*, 1099–1108, signals the importance of 'verité' and 'remembrance' in a text which emphasises 'sens' over 'matière'.

4. Religious Writings

G. S. Burgess, 'La souffrance et le repos dans *Le Voyage de saint Brendan* par Benedeit', *Ménard Vol.*, 267–77, examines the role and vocabulary of suffering, linking this with trust in God and resistance to temptation. Gautier de Coinci, **Le Miracle de Théophile ou comment Théophile vint à la pénitence*, ed. Annette Garnier, Champion, 240 pp. M. Eusei, 'Le due conclusioni del *Saint Alexis*', *Ménard Vol.*, 485–91, studies the incompatible nature of strophes 109–10 and 122–25 of MS. L (Hildesheim), arguing that these are drawn from two different earlier versions. Françoise Laurent, **Plaire et Edifier. Les récits hagiographiques composés en Angleterre aux XIIe et XIIIe siècles*, Champion, 632 pp. J.-P. Perrot, 'Figures du temps et logiques de l'imagination en hagiographie médiévale', *RHS*, 251:57–72, proposes that hagiography contributed to the emergence of a sense of self through its privileging of a dialectic between a consciousness and unconsciousness of temporality. P. Walter, 'Hagiographie médiévale et mythologie préchrétien. L'Exemple de saint Martin', *ib.*, 43–55, calls for a re-evaluation of the links between hagiography and myth, particularly evident in the case of St. Martin, linked by Walter with Merlin.

5. Other Genres

LYRIC. '*Prions en chantant': Devotional Songs of the Trouvères*, ed. and trans. Marcia Jenneth Epstein, Toronto U.P., 1997, xi + 340 pp., is an edition of 61 songs, with modern English translations and, when available, the music. The introduction sets them in their literary, musical, sociological, and doctrinal context; the edition is a compromise between a full scholarly edition and a performing text. Christine Jacob-Hugon, **L'Œuvre jongleresque de Jean Bodel: l'art de séduire un public* (Bibliothèque du moyen âge, 10), Paris–Brussels, De Boeck, 363 pp. The title of A. Brasseur, 'La poésie des adieux: les *Congés* de Jean Bodel, essai de mise en français moderne', *Ménard Vol.*, 195–213, is self-explanatory. X. Deflorenne, 'L'intervalle, plainte du ladre: lectures des *Congés* de Jean Bodel par le biais de la plainte funèbre', *LR*, 51, 1997:223–41, compares the *Congés* to the *plainte funèbre* from the structural, formal, and thematic points of view, and finds in the former a funerary intention, a desire to be remembered, but also the expression of concern for Bodel's future material support and for his salvation. Susan E. Bécam, *Rhyme in Gace Brulé's Lyric: Formal and Semantic Interplay* (StH, 34), NY, Lang, ix + 230 pp., is a statistical and stylistic study of rhyme words. Introductory chapters on statistics and on rhyme-word associations are followed by others organized by

theme, in each of which the author considers the semantic implications of repeated rhymes and shows how rhyme expresses thematic
continuity and rhetorical discontinuity. A final chapter analyses one
poem to show how identical rhyme words can express opposing
thoughts. M. Tyssens, 'Lectures des chansons de Chrétien', *Ménard
Vol.*, 1409–22, surveys work done on 'D'amors qui m'a tolu a moi'
and 'Amors, tençon et bataille', and brings out the kinship between
the two texts. *Le canzoni di Eustache le Peintre*, ed. Maria Luisa Gambini
(Biblioteca della Ricerca, Medio Evo di Francia, 6), Fasano, Schena,
1997, 337 pp. J. T. E. Thomas, 'Une chanson de Richard de
Fournival: "La dame ou la demoiselle?" (R. 759)', *Melli Vol.*, 779–95,
offers a critical edition with introduction, translation, and commentary. R. Crespo, 'R. 1278 (Richard de Fournival)', *Romania*,
116:394–414, is a critical edition based on MS *a*. Id., 'Due congetture
fuorvianti: R. 1541 (Richard de Fournival), v. 15 e v. 26', *CN*,
58:91–100, discusses readings by Lepage and others of these
contentious lines. W. C. Jordan, '"Amen!" Cinq fois "Amen!" Les
chansons de la croisade égyptienne de saint Louis, une source
négligée d'opinion royaliste', *Médiévales*, 34:79–90, studies three
anonymous songs as evidence of royalist sentiments before and after
the failed expedition of 1250, and uses the musical setting of one of
them to evaluate the impact of failure on Louis.

ROMAN DE RENART. Kenneth Varty, *The Roman de Renart: a Guide to
Scholarly Work*, Lanham, Md.–London, Scarecrow, ix + 181 pp., is a
critical bibliography of MSS, scholarly editions, facsimiles, translations, adaptations, readers, critical studies, and reviews of the *Roman
de Renart* proper, up to mid 1997. There are indexes of branches,
subjects, and scholars. Id., 'Le motif littéraire du baron régent et
traître dans l'*Historia Regum Britanniae*, le *Roman de Brut*, *La Mort le Roi
Artu*, et la branche x (*Renart Empereur*) du *Roman de Renart*', *Ménard Vol.*,
1435–43, quotes and summarizes occurrences of the motif, dates
Renart Empereur to 1235–40 on the grounds of its parodic inversion of
the motif as found in the *Mort Artu*, and suggests that the targets of the
author's mockery include the *Roman de Renart* itself. Id., *'La
pénétration du *Roman de Renart* en Angleterre au moyen âge: les
témoignages iconographiques', *Shimmura Vol.*, 93–99. R. Bellon, 'Du
temps que les bestes parloient: à propos de la création des animaux
dans le *Roman de Renart*', *RTUG*, 55:21–33, analyses the creation
scene, compares it with Genesis and finds apocryphal elements, for
which he identifies possible sources in a wide range of ancient and
medieval texts. Id., ' "Ouvrir la bouche", "fermer les yeux":
remarques sur l'emploi de ces motifs dans le *Roman de Renart* et
quelques-uns de ses avant-textes latins', Bertrand, *Geste*, 51–67,
discusses these two motifs in the Chantecler episode in branch II and

in the *Ysengrimus* and other texts, and the changes made by the *Renart* poet. F. Bérier, 'Renart et Tibert, ou comment le goupil "ses moz retorne en autre guise" (branche II, v. 699)', *RTUG*, 55 : 35–53, draws parallels with Lancelot's encounter with Esclados le Roux in Chrétien's *Charrette*: Tibert as guardian of the ford reveals to Renart his essence as a trickster to be tricked. M. Bonafin, 'Fra filologia e antropologia: la genesi del lupo e della vulpe', *Reinardus*, 11 : 25–35, looks at the structure of branch XXIV, its anthropological foundations, possible errors in transmission, and the names of Renart and Isengrin, and finds in the branch a kind of foundation myth of the whole *Roman de Renart*. L. Rossi, 'Renart et Isengrin dans le puits', *Ménard Vol.*, 1123–37, reads the different versions of branch IV as exercises on a theme, for different audiences. C. Zemmour, 'Animalité renardienne et utopie féodale: signifiants et signifiés d'un nouveau monde chevaleresque', *Reinardus*, 11 : 215–30, is a lexicological and hermeneutic study of *bacheler, vassal, vavassor, chevalier*, and *chevalerie*, whose meanings and symbolic values change as they pass from man to beasts.

FABLIAUX. With vol. 10 of the *Nouveau recueil complet des fabliaux (NRCF)*, ed. Willem Noomen, Assen, van Gorcum, xxv + 442 pp., the indispensable new edition of the corpus is complete. In addition to the usual full presentation of the final 14 texts, this volume contains diplomatic and critical editions of a newly discovered MS of *Les Putains et les Lecheors*, and a bibliographical update for the entire collection. *Fabliaux du moyen âge*, ed. and trans. Jean Dufournet, Flammarion, 410 pp., presents 19 texts, selected to be both 'ingénieux' and typical, with a facing modern Fr. prose translation and editorial material including a glossary and O. Jodogne's plot classification. Ziolkowski, *Obscenity*, has a section 'Courting obscenity in Old French'. R. H. Bloch, 'Modest maids and modified nouns: obscenity in the fabliaux' (293–307), analyses the language of the obscene and the erotic, and shows that the courtly and the obscene are not antithetical. C. Muscatine, 'The fabliaux, courtly culture, and the (re)invention of vulgarity' (281–92), tests the hypothesis that obscene language was becoming viewed as increasingly vulgar as a result of the spread of the new courtly codes. P. Nykrog, 'Obscene or not obscene: Lady Reason, Jean de Meun, and the fisherman from Pont-sur-Seine' (319–31), uses *Le Pescheor de Pont sur Seine* to argue that it was possible to write about sexuality openly and affectionately, with a positive and relaxed attitude. K. Busby, 'The diabolic hero in medieval French narrative: *Trubert* and *Wistasse le Moine*', *Papers* (ICLS 8), 415–26, takes a historical and intertextual approach to Trubert and Wistasse, anarchic and diabolic heroes who reflect mid-13th-c. hostility to the nobility and contemporary social instability. F. Calvo and G. B. Chicote, 'Caracterización del espacio urbano en los *fabliaux*', *Medievalia*, 26, 1997:9–16, focuses on the town as a space and a way of life in the fabliaux, which reflect the urbanization of rural society inasmuch as one of their principles is the organization of daily life which town living implies. D. Collins, 'Historia urinalis: re-reading *Les Trois Meschines*', *FS*, 52:397–408, reads the text in legal terms, and shows how it makes sense as a legal conundrum with bilingual puns. J.-L. Leclanche, 'Milon d'Amiens est-il l'auteur du fabliau *Le Fouteur?*', *RLaR*, 102:355–72, bases an affirmative answer on broad similarities of plot and what he takes to be 'analogies remarquables' of detail. M.-T. Lorcin, 'Jeux de mains, jeux de vilains: le geste et la parole dans les fabliaux', Bertrand, *Geste*, 369–82, surveys gestures, their meanings and their relation to speech, with which they are generally associated. A. Ortijo Ocaña, 'A morphological study on the prologues and epilogues of the fabliaux: a rhetorical approach', *RF*, 110:185–201, studies the prologues and epilogues and their preoccupation with the art of composition, in an attempt to contribute to the debate on genre. M. Rousse, '*Estormi* ou l'empreinte du castelet', *Ménard Vol.*, 1139–47, looks for traces of theatrical dialogue in *Estormi*, and wonders if it might be the first Fr. puppet play.

MORAL, DIDACTIC AND ALLEGORICAL WORKS. Ron Baxter, *Bestiaries and their Users in the Middle Ages*, Stroud, Sutton, 256 pp. J.-M. Boivin, 'Prologues et épilogues des isopets', *Reinardus*, 11:3–23, examines the importance of didactic and allegorical, or literary emphasis in Latin isopets and the *Fables* of Marie de France. L. Evdokimova, 'Deux traductions du *Physiologus*: le sens allégorique de la nature et le sens allégorique de la Bible', *ib.*, 11:53–66, studies the interdependence of verse and prose form through a comparison of the bestiaries of Pierre de Beauvais and Guillaume le Clerc. M. Gueret-Laferté, 'La construction allégorique dans le *Château d'amour* de Robert Grosseteste', *Actes* (Rambures), 283–95, places the *Château* in the context of allegorical tradition and underscores the connection between this and vernacular literature. Marie de France, *Les Fables*, ed. Charles Brucker, Paris–Louvain, Peeters, x + 402 pp. E. Schulze-Busacker, 'Le *Romulus* vers 1180: Walter l'Anglais, Alexandre Nequam et Marie de France', *Ménard Vol.*, 1213–33, examines the inheritance of the fable tradition and the rapport between narrative and morality in the work of three contemporary fabulists, concluding that Marie was the first medieval poet to conceive of the fable as an independent literary genre.

LATE MEDIEVAL LITERATURE

By ROSALIND BROWN-GRANT, *University of Leeds*

1. NARRATIVE GENRES

EPIC. C. Raynaud, 'Ganelon dans les enluminures du XIIe au début du XVIe siècle. Première approche', *CRISIMA 3*, 69–89, charts the changing iconographical representation of this character and concludes that his treachery is increasingly interpreted in the later Middle Ages as *lèse-majesté* rather than simply as betrayal. W. L. Hendrickson, 'Geste de Guillaume or de Garin de Monglane?', *Ménard Vol.*, 667–78, contends that the term 'geste' evolves from meaning 'historic exploits' in the Guillaume cycle to meaning more generally 'a group of texts relating to a particular dynasty' in that of Garin de Monglane; whilst S. I. James, ' "Pseudo"-courtly elements in a canonical epic', *Papers* (ICLS 8), 367–74, takes issue with Gautier's exclusive definitions of the *chanson de geste* and offers a more positive assessment of the 'courtly' *Geste de Monglane* with its amorous intrigues, fantastic episodes, and detailed treatment of individual behaviour. V. Naudet, 'Quand le roi frappe la reine: à partir d'une scène de la geste des *Lorrains*', Bertrand, *Geste*, 445–59, compares the treatment of this episode in *Garin le Loherenc* and *Gerbert de Metz* in which the queen, Blanchefleur, is represented as a sacrificial victim struggling to remain loyal to her lineage whilst protesting against the corruption of her husband Pépin's court. D. Collomp, 'Le doigt sur la dent (geste symbolique du serment sarrasin)', *ib.*, 607–24, traces the development of this gesture as a standard topos of supposedly muslim mores in a range of epics from the 13th to the 16th centuries. F. Sinclair, 'Reproductive frameworks: maternal significance in *Berte as grans piés*', *Fest. Emden*, 269–95, argues against the traditional view of the epic as exclusively concerned with patrilineal succession and sees texts such as *Berte* allocating an important role to the mother whose influence affects the positive or negative qualities of her offspring. J. A. Nelson, 'The function of prose in *Godefroi de Buillon*', *ib.*, 327–37, notes how the author of this prose reworking strips his rhymed source down to its essential, factual elements. H.-E. Keller, 'Le clan de Girard de Vienne dans *Galien le Restoré*', *Ménard Vol.*, 713–22, regards this work as a precursor of Renaissance epic in its emphasis on family as a clan of individuals rather than as a traditional hierarchized feudal dynasty. Claude Roussel, *Conter de geste au XIVe siècle. Inspiration folklorique et écriture épique dans La Belle Hélène de Constantinople* (PRF, 222), 452 pp., situates this *chanson de geste* in the context of later medieval reworkings of the folktale *La fille aux mains coupées* and examines how, in transforming it into an epic, the author personalizes and develops his main protagonists whilst at the same time highlighting the didactic and moral import of his text by introducing elements from hagiography. H. Akkari, ' "Mère, tu souffriras et tu erreras": la souffrance et l'errance de la mère dans *La Belle Hélène de Constantinople* et dans *Florent et Octavien*', BDBA, 16:7–18, likens the suffering undergone by mothers sent unjustly into exile to the exploits of knights and deems their struggle to safeguard the family unit to anticipate the *roman familial*; whilst R. Bellon, 'Le renforcement affectif de la négation par l'expression d'une valeur minimale dans *La Belle Hélène de Constantinople*', Demarolle Vol., 105–18, examines F. Möhren's linguistic category of reinforcement in the light of this text. M.-J. Pindivic, 'La déclaration amoureuse dans la chanson de *Doon de Maience* et ses adaptations en prose', BDBA, 15, 1997:19–29, analyses how reworkings of the 14th to 16th c. vary in their treatment of this theme compared to the original version. I. Weill, 'Le château d'Oridon dans la chanson d'*Auberi le Bourgoin*', *Actes* (Rambures), 209–19, reads this work featuring a cruel and despotic lord presiding over a magnificent castle as a transposed representation of the political conflicts between feudal barons and the monarch which typified the reigns of Louis VI and Louis VII.

ROMANCE. *Two Medieval Outlaws: The Romances of Eustace the Monk and Fouke Fitz Waryn*, trans. Glyn Burgess, Cambridge, Brewer, 1997, x + 210 pp., is a modern English version of *Li Romans de Witasse le Moine* and *Fouke le Fitz Waryn*, with information on historical figures and MS tradition, as well as a useful index of proper and place names. I. Iñarrea Las Heras, '*Le Livre du Voir-Dit* de Guillaume de Machaut: una nueva formulación del amor cortés', RLMed, 10:117–40, argues that M. places greater stress on personal experience than on ideal forms of amorous behaviour, thus putting forward a more naturalistic conception of love. F. Bouchet, 'Les "signes" de l'amour: stratégies sémiotiques de la déclaration amoureuse dans le *Méliador* de Froissart', BDBA, 15, 1997:167–78, examines how the various knights use their words and chivalric deeds as signs by which to declare their love for their ladies, despite being obliged to remain incognito; whilst in 'Rhétorique de l'héraldique dans le roman arthurien tardif. Le *Méliador* de Froissart et le *Livre du Cuer d'Amours espris* de René d'Anjou', *Romania*, 116:239–55, Bouchet contrasts F.'s use of heraldry as a metonymic device which simultaneously hides and reveals the knight's identity with R.'s more static representation of arms as heraldic emblems of his illustrious knights. C. Rollier-Paulian, 'Le dénouement du *Roman du Conte d'Anjou*: une réussite ou un échec?', PRIS-MA, 14:175–91, re-evaluates the romance's lengthy ending, stressing the religious and social significance of its didactic message of restitution and reparation; whereas in 'L'image de la mère dans le *Roman du Conte d'Anjou*', *BDBA*, 16:247–60, she argues that, due to his position at the court of Philippe le Bel, Jehan Maillart's preoccupation with upholding the social order leads him to suggest that a mother's role is simply to ensure the legitimacy of succession and thus the transfer of male power from one generation to the next. C. Ferlampin-Acher, 'Le charme d'*Artus de Bretagne*', *Ménard Vol.*, 513–28, highlights its evocation of an ideal courtly world, reduced use of the fantastic and pathos, and valorization of verbal ruse and trickery; whilst in 'Les "deceptions" dans *Perceforest*: du "fantosme" au "fantasme"', *CRISIMA 3*, 413–30, she examines the significance of different types of illusion and apparition as formative moments of betrayal in the protagonists' moral itinerary. M. Szkilnik, 'Passelion, Marc l'Essilié et l'idéal courtois', *Papers* (ICLS 8), 131–38, demonstrates that these two characters from *Perceforest* and *Ysaïe le Triste* respectively point to epic influence on later medieval romance as they reveal how violence, cruelty, and infidelity are the other side of the chivalric and courtly ideal of justice, generosity, and devotion. P. Victorin, 'La Reine Yseut et la Fée Morgue ou l'impossible maternité dans *Ysaïe le Triste*', *BDBA*, 16:261–76, argues that the author here transforms the figure of Yseut into a mother as a pretext for his continuation of the prose *Tristan* which, paradoxically, takes on a more burlesque and parodic tone as the dwarf Tronc largely usurps Yseut's nurturing role. S. Sturm-Maddox, 'Alterity and subjectivity in the *Roman de Mélusine*', *Papers* (ICLS 8), 121–29, contends that the impossibility of attributing a fixed identity to the character of Mélusine, whose fairy 'otherness' makes her thoughts and feelings inaccessible to mortals, is symbolically linked to the inevitable decline of the dynasty that she has founded. A. Caillaud, 'The search for power: a female quest in Antoine de la Sale's *Petit Jehan de Saintré*', *FCS*, 24, 1997[1998]:74–83, maintains that the negative portrayal of Belle Cousine warns the reader against renegotiating the gender roles involved in courtly love within an established male hierarchy. R. Dubuis, 'La notion de *Joie* et son expression dans *Saintré*', *RTUG*, 55:113–23, analyses the ironic contrast between the text's extensive use of the term 'joie' and the author's disillusionment with an impossible ideal of love; whilst in 'Du bon usage de la "nouvelle" dans *Saintré*', *Demarolle Vol.*, 325–38, Dubuis puts the work's enduring appeal down to its blurring of generic distinctions. J. Dufournet and A. Poujet, 'La loi de la duplicité dans les *Cent Nouvelles Nouvelles*', *ib.*, 339–52, stress how the narrator highlights the theme of trickery, and verbal ruse in particular, in order to teach the reader not to confuse appearance with reality. C. Brucker, 'Si/ainsi en moyen français: autour de *Bérinus*', *ib.*, 133–48, compares and contrasts the relative occurrence and function of these two adverbs in this 14th-c. romance with Villehardouin's chronicle and Denis Foulechat's *Policratique*. M. Thiry-Stassin, 'Larmes de femmes dans le *Roman de Troie* en prose (version Bodmer 147)', *Ménard Vol.*, 1377–89, notes the greater role given to women's laments in this version which she links to the shift of interest from women as mothers to women as lovers of the male hero. J. H. M. Taylor, 'The significance of the insignificant: reading reception in the Burgundian *Erec* and *Cligès*', *FCS*, 24, 1997[1998]:183–97, argues that, by acculturation, the later *prosateur* assimilates a puzzling and disturbing model of Arthur's Britain to a more familiar and ordered Burgundian model of government; N. J. Lacy, 'Adaptation as reception: the Burgundian *Cligès*', *ib.*, 198–207, shows how, in the reworked text, irony is excised, style homogenized, and dialogue reduced to a minimum, probably in accordance with the literary taste of the later period; whilst M. Colombo-Timelli, 'Syntaxe et technique narrative: titres et attaques de chapitre dans l'*Erec* bourguignon', *ib.*, 208–30, is a stylistic analysis of how Erec's actions are highlighted at the expense of Enide. *L'istoire de tres vaillans princez monseigneur Jehan d'Avennes*, ed. Danielle Quéruel (Bibliothèque des Seigneurs du Nord), Villeneuve-d'Ascq, Presses Universitaires du Septentrion, 1997, 219 pp., is a new critical edition of this anonymous 15th-c. Burgundian prose romance which forms the first part of a trilogy of texts that also includes *La Fille du Comte de Ponthieu* and the *Roman de Saladin*. Based on Paris BNF ms. fr. 12572, with Paris Arsenal 5208 as a control, this edition contains a substantial glossary and several small reproductions of ink and watercolour miniatures from the text. J. Cerquiglini-Toulet, 'Une parole muette: le rire amoureux au Moyen Age', *Ménard Vol.*, 325–36, surveys the variations on the theme of smiles and laughter as symptoms of an amorous disposition in a range of mostly 14th-c. romances and lyrics.

2. POETRY

David. A. Fein, *François Villon Revisited* (TWAS, 864), 1997, xiii + 187 pp., surveys V.'s life and *œuvre*, devoting chapters to the *Lais, Testament,* and other poems, and examining his use of elements from the Bible and the *Danse Macabre.* Robert R. Daniel, *The Poetry of Villon and Baudelaire: Two Worlds, One Human Condition* (Currents in Comparative Romance Languages and Literatures, 52), NY, Lang, 1997, vi + 196 pp., adopts a more innovative approach in comparing the two poets' works in terms of their emphasis on the physical rather than the spiritual world and of their exploration of the themes of decay, mortality, and transience. J. Ribard, 'Le *Lais* de François Villon et sa thématique symbolique', *Demarolle Vol.*, 353–62, sees V.'s winter symbolism as positive, with its evocation of Christmas as a time heralding salvation and its image of being frozen suggesting a spiritual withdrawal from worldly disappointments. J.-C. Delclos, '*L'Entroubli* de Villon ou la page que l'on ne peut tourner', *ib.*, 363–74, reinterprets the famous stanzas XXXVI–XXXIX of the *Lais* as expressing V.'s state of emotional and intellectual stagnation in failing to leave Paris for Angers and in finding his poetic inspiration run dry. A. Slerca, 'Un motif mythique de la *Ballade des pendus* de François Villon', *RLaR*, 102 : 179–90, traces the folkloric and mythical sources behind V.'s image of the human body being reduced to dust and ashes by the hostile elements of the natural world. B. N. Sargent-Baur, 'Odd man out: Villon at court', *Papers* (ICLS 8), 57–65, assesses V.'s court poetry as the impersonal and somewhat lacklustre productions of a figure who received little patronage from the aristocratic milieux of his day. C. Martineau-Génieys, 'L'espace dans le "Lais" et le "Testament" de Villon', *Ménard Vol.*, 957–68, discusses the representation of Paris as an enclosed and claustrophobic space which echoes V.'s own emotional isolation from his surroundings. C. Deschepper, ' "La Métamorphose Villon": pièce en trois actes', *LR*, 52 : 3–20, reads V.'s last two poems and a *sermon joyeux*, the *Sermon de saint Belin*, as a triptych providing an ironic commentary on the Parliament of Paris which freed the author from the Châtelet in 1463. P. Sélamme, 'Villon, une mésaventure ignorée. "La pierre et la porte" [*Le grès et l'huis*]. Un essai d'approche des huitains XCV et XCVI du *Testament* (v. 990–1005)', *MA*, 104 : 91–105, reads these lines as a satirical and parodic attack on two of V.'s contemporaries — Jehan Cornu and Pierre Bobignon — for their role in a bloody confrontation between students and soldiery in 1452. M.-P. Suárez, 'La mère et la femme fatale chez Villon', *BDBA*, 16 : 237–46, compares the figure of V.'s mother praying to the Virgin to the *planctus* of Mary in Passion plays of the period and sees this pious representation as a counterbalance to his usual image of women as faithless lovers. M. Laccassagne, 'Poétique et politique du corps dans l'oeuvre d'Eustache Deschamps', Bertrand, *Geste*, 321–37, reveals how D. makes satirical use of the image of the body in a number of his 'ballades morales' in order to deliver political and moral lessons against irrational inaction and insatiable greed which he regards as undermining good government in the French state. *Le Purgatoire d'Amours*, ed. Sandrine Thonon (Travaux de la Faculté de Philosophie et Lettres de l'Université Catholique de Louvain, 41, Section de Philologie Romane, 15), Louvain-la-Neuve, Louvain U.P., 175 pp., is the first modern critical edition of this *prosimetrum*, a late 15th-c. contribution to the debate on courtly love, which is based on Paris Arsenal 5113. M. Santucci, 'Adam de la Halle, auteur des *Ver d'amours* et des *Ver de le mort*?', *Ménard*

Vol., 1183–92, compares these two works with that of Hélinand de Froidmont on which they are heavily reliant and concludes that Adam was indeed the author of the former but not the latter text, which she deems to be inferior to his usual standard. R. Crespo, 'Due congetture fuorvianti: R.1541 (Richard de Fournival), v.15 e v.26', *CN*, 58:91–100, corrects Lepage's edition by reading 'je' for 'ne' in 'qe je vausise avoir moie' (v. 15) and by substituting 'nului' for 'ne la' and restoring the 'mais' in 'c'ains mais nului vi or en ai' (v. 26); whereas in 'R.1278 (Richard de Fournival)', *Romania*, 116:394–414, Crespo follows Zarifopol and Lepage in taking the *a* MS as the basis of a new critical edition of this poem, to which he appends a full set of explanatory notes. M. Amri, 'Symbolisme animal et souvenir amoureux dans le *Bestiaire d'Amours* de Richard de Fournival', *BDBA*, 15, 1997:31–43, discusses how the author deploys memory in order to recall painful experiences of love as part of his plea to his lady to requite his passion. Sylvia Huot, *Allegorical Play in the Old French Motet: The Sacred and the Profane in Thirteenth-Century Polyphony* (Figurae: Reading Medieval Culture), Stanford U.P., 1997, 236 pp., is a ground-breaking study which examines the allegorical and parodic interaction between the multiple voices of the motet as they articulate competing secular and religious discourses of desire. G. Mombello, 'A propos d'une édition préoriginale de la ballade de Clément Marot. Deux Noëls du XVI siècle', *Ménard Vol.*, 993–1006, transcribes two poems from Seville Biblioteca Colombina 15.2.16(8), one of which is an earlier version of a ballad printed in the 1532 edition of the *Adolescence clementine*. G. Gros, 'Écrire et lire au *Livre de Pensée*. Étude sur le manuscrit personnel des poésies de Charles d'Orléans (Paris, B.N.F., fr. 25458)', *TLit*, 11:55–75, examines C.'s progressively deepening introspection as he abandons pure lyricism and becomes more resigned to his fate as a captive; whilst R. C. Cholakian, 'Charles d'Orléans: the challenge of the printed text', *FCS*, 24, 1997[1998]:119–26, sees C.'s writing primarily as an act by which he attempts to secure the volatility of the spoken word. J. H. M. Taylor, 'Inescapable rose: Jean le Seneschal's *Cent Ballades* and the art of cheerful paradox', *MAe*, 67:60–84, assesses the intertextual relations between this work and the *Roman de la Rose*, concluding that the author here offers a sophisticated and deliberately ambiguous analysis of the amatory state. L. C. Brook, 'The optimistic love-poet: Philippe de Beaumanoir', *Papers* (ICLS 8), 197–206, examines how, in the *Salu d'Amours* and the *Conte d'Amours*, P. appeals to the lady to alleviate his suffering in the confident expectation that she will answer his pleas; whilst in 'The *Demandes d'Amour* of the Chantilly and Wolfenbüttel manuscripts', *FCS*, 23, 1996[1997]:222–35, Brook stresses the importance of these two large collections of *demandes*, a genre which was derived from an aristocratic social game. A. Armstrong, 'Two more rebus-poems by Jean Molinet?', *Scriptorium*, 51, 1997:76–80, is an edition of two previously unattributed rebus-poems by M. preserved in Paris BNF ms. fr. 19165, with suggested solutions to the puzzles they contain. David Cowling, *Building the Text: Architecture as Metaphor in Late Medieval and Early Modern France* (Oxford Modern Languages and Literature Monographs), Oxford, Clarendon Press, x + 245 pp., examines how the *rhétoriqueurs*, and Jean Lemaire de Belges in particular, employ metaphors of the human body, the state, memory and the text as buildings in order to deliver a variety of didactic and political messages to their literary patrons and to fashion the self as a voice of authority. R. Trachsler, 'Cent sénateurs, neuf soleils et un songe. Encore sur Machaut, la Sybille et le chaînon manquant', *Romania*, 116:188–214, identifies *Ovide moralisé*, XIV, vv. 1121–88 as the source of the Sibylline episode in the *Fontaine amoureuse* and analyses how M. changes the significance of this passage in his discussion on the nature and function of dreams as part of the lover's experience. Isabelle Bétemps, *L'Imaginaire dans l'oeuvre de Guillaume de Machaut* (Bibliothèque du XVe siècle, 59), Champion, 472 pp., examines M.'s debt to and dialectic with the key sciences of his day (astronomy, arithmetic, geometry, medecine, and geography, etc.) in his construction of a poetic universe which privileges instability and ambiguity over certainty and fixity. M. Boulton, 'The lady speaks: the transformation of French courtly poetry in the fourteenth and fifteenth centuries', *Papers* (ICLS 8), 207–17, compares and contrasts the nostalgia for a lost ideal expressed by the male voice in Alain Chartier's *Belle dame sans merci* with the critique of courtly ideology voiced by the female figures in Machaut's *Voir-Dit* and Christine de Pizan's *Livre du Duc des Vrais Amans*. Catherine Attwood, *Dynamic Dichotomy: The Poetic 'I' in Fourteenth- and Fifteenth-Century French Lyric Poetry* (Faux Titre, 149), Amsterdam, Rodopi, 228 pp., is an innovative study that discusses the different ways in which Machaut, Froissart, Deschamps, and Christine distinguish between their authorial voice and the first-person speaker of their texts. Attwood concludes that the key relationship each explores is that between, respectively, for M., the 'I' and the 'Other'; for F., the 'I' of the present and that of the past; for D., the 'I' and a range of externalized personae; and for C., the 'I' and various external actants such as Fortune, which brings about the subsequent transformation of this first-person voice. Two timely additions to the study of C.'s lyric poetry are *The Love Debate Poems of Christine de Pizan: Le Livre du Debat de deux amans, Le Livre des Trois jugemens, Le Livre du Dit de Poissy*, ed. Barbara K. Altmann, Gainesville, Florida U.P., 294 pp., which is a new critical edition of these three texts based on Harley 4431, featuring an extensive introduction offering interpretive analysis of the poems and a discussion of the MS tradition, as well as a useful glossary. *Christine de Pizan and Medieval French Lyric*, ed. Earl Jeffrey Richards, Gainesville, Florida U.P., ix + 241 pp. is an important collection of mostly new essays, whose principal aim, according to the editor (1–24) is to stress the innovative nature of C.'s lyric output: W. D. Paden argues that she radicalizes the carefully defined generic forms of late medieval lyrical genres by introducing a more subjective tone than that of her literary predecessors (27–49); J. C. Laidlaw compares C.'s *Cent balades* to both Machaut's works in this genre and the *Livre des cent balades* in order to show how she combines formal innovation with a more personal and polemical content (53–82); B. K. Altmann examines the thematic relationship between the 'lay mortel' and the *Cent ballades d'Amant et de Dame* to which it is appended and concludes that the former acts as an *envoi* to the latter by summing up the perils for women of passionate love (83–102); J. Laird and E. J. Richards read the *Duc des vrais amans* not as a romance but as a dramatized collection of lyric and prose in which C. stages a dialogue between various male and female voices that exposes the faults and limits of courtly love and values (103–31); N. Margolis analyses how C. deploys both clerkliness and courtliness in her *complainte* poems in order to expound her vision of woman's real place in the process of *fin'amor* (135–54); L. J. Walters reveals how C.'s use of the *translatio studii* topos in her lyric poems and the *Mutacion de Fortune* enables her to represent herself as an authoritative commentator on the political and social ills then affecting the French state (155–67); C. McWebb discusses how, in the *Cent ballades d'Amant et de Dame*, C. revises the empty formalism of courtly lyric in order to create a new kind of female subjectivity (168–83); B. M. Semple traces the development of C.'s phenomenology of beauty from her emphasis on its immediate impact on the audience's passions in the lyric to her portrayal of a more intellectual and internalized meditation on aesthetics in the dream-vision (187–205); and E. J. Richards contends that C. renews the medieval lyric by reintroducing history and experience into her poems in line with her politically committed prose *œuvre* (206–29).

3. DRAMA

Jean Molinet, *Les Pronostications joyeuses*, ed. Jelle Koopmans and Paul Verhuyck, Geneva, Droz, 255 pp., is an important new critical edition of M.'s parodic predictions — complete with suggestions on how to decode his cryptic messages — which includes readings from Cambridge, Gonville, and Caius College, MS 187/220, a version not consulted by Dupire, the previous editor. A. Hindley, 'Les VII Pechie

Morteil: dramatizing sin in the Old French *Moralité*', *RoS*, 32:21–32, re-evaluates various morality plays for their narrative, dramatic, and visual representation of the individual's struggle with the forces of evil. M.-O. Bodenheimer, 'L'expression dramatique de la déclaration amoureuse dans *Le Jeu de Robin et Marion* d'Adam de la Halle', *BDBA*, 15, 1997:145–55, stresses the importance of the knight's declaration to the shepherdess as the motor of the action in this form of dramatized *pastourelle*. J. Enders, 'Medieval snuff drama', *Exemplaria*, 10:171–206, assesses the difficulties of determining true levels of violence in medieval plays, citing the alleged execution of a convicted murderer in 1549 during a performance of the Judith and Holofernes story in Tournai. Graham A. Runnalls, *Etudes sur les mystères. Un recueil de 22 études sur les mystères français, suivi d'un répertoire du théâtre religieux français du Moyen Age et d'une bibliographie* (Champion-Varia, 14), Champion, 503 pp., is a major collection of reprinted articles from 1973–96 which cover key issues such as generic convention, performance, MS tradition, dating and technical vocabulary. E. Pinto-Mathieu, 'Château et mondanité dans la Passion de Jean Michel (XVe siècle)', *Actes* (Rambures), 229–39, analyses the representation of the palaces of Herod and Mary Magdalene in this play both as a valuable source of information on 15th-c. manorial life and as negative symbols used to warn the audience against the dangers of worldliness and vanity. J. D. Wilkins, 'Corps et biens: the body as currency in fifteenth-century Mystères de la Passion', *FCS*, 24, 1997 [1998]:254–72, maintains that the prevalence of metaphors of the body to express the ransom and redemption exchange between God and Satan is determined by contemporary preoccupations with drama and commerce. J.-C. Bibolet, 'Les gestes d'adoration, de prière, d'offrande et de violence dans *Le Mystère de la Passion de Troyes*', Bertrand, *Geste*, 93–107, points out the greater number of stage directions given in the Troyes version compared with those in Gréban; whilst V. Dominguez-Vignaud, 'Les gestes de Marie dans les Mystères de la Passion: les *Planctus* dans la *Passion du Palatinus*, la *Passion Nostre Seigneur* et la *Passion* de Gréban', *ib.*, 201–17, shows how the representation of Mary's sorrow at the foot of the Cross evolves from being purely lyrical to increasingly dramatic. M.-O. Bodenheimer, 'Le rôle da la Mère dans les *Miracles de Nostre Dame par personnages*', *BDBA*, 16:49–57, assesses the literal and spiritual aspects of motherhood in this play; whereas H. Charpentier, 'Figures de la mère dans le *Mistere du Viel Testament*', *ib.*, 59–70, sees Sara, Rebecca, and Rachel as more developed individuals here than in the Vulgate, which thus emphasizes their maternal role in establishing the lineage of Abraham. R. Deschaux, 'Structure et sens du *Mystère du roy Advenir*', *RTUG*, 55:97–102, gives a synopsis of this reworking in dramatic form of the legend of Barlaam and Josaphat and analyses its literary qualities, particularly its varied used of verse forms, as well as its didactic and religious message; P. Walter, 'Noms de diable dans deux Mystères du XVe siècle: *La Pacience de Job* et *Le Mystère du roy Advenir*', *ib.*, 103–12, traces the folkloric origins of the names of various demons which they mention; whilst Y. Le Hir, 'Sur les citations latines dans la Moralité *L'Omme pecheur*', *ib.*, 125–31, inventories the different types of Latin quotations cited and assesses their function in delivering the text's message of repentance. B. Roy, 'Getting to the bottom of St. Caquette's cult', Ziolkowski, *Obscenity*, 308–18, offers a radically new interpretation of *Le Grant Voiage et pelerinage de sainte Caquette* as a witty and scatological farce about how a woman cures her sexual frustration by kissing an obscene relic. **Recueil de farces (1450–1550). Vol. XII*, ed. André Tissier, Geneva, Droz, 404 pp., is the latest volume in the series and contains editions of the *Deux Savetiers*, *Brus*, *Le Savetier Audin*, *Martin de Cambrai*, and *La Pipée*.

4. HISTORICAL AND POLITICAL LITERATURE

Froissart, *Chroniques. Livre I Le Manuscrit d'Amiens*. Vol. V: *Lexique*, ed. George T. Diller, Geneva, Droz, 359 pp., is an invaluable analytical glossary to the whole of the four previous volumes of this important critical edition. Diller is also the author of ' "Pour la cause de ce que j'estoie françois". Langue(s) et loyauté(s) dans les *Chroniques* de Froissart', *MA*, 104:461–71, which argues that F. uses his text as a 'défense et illustration' of the superiority of the French language. M. Zink, 'La fin des *Chroniques* de Froissart et le tragique de la cour', *Papers* (ICLS 8), 79–95, reads the ending as F.'s attempt to impose a tragic symmetry on historical events by equating the fates of Edward II and Richard II of England, thus stressing the instability of the fortunes of kings. C. Blons-Pierre, 'L'expression de la rapidité dans les *Grandes Chroniques de France*', *Ménard Vol.*, 161–72, is a stylistic analysis which compares the distribution of verbs and adverbs expressing speed and movement across the first four volumes of this chronicle. Brigitte Roux, *Les Dialogues de Salmon et Charles VI: Images du pouvoir et enjeux politiques* (Cahiers d'Humanisme et Renaissance, 52), Geneva, Droz, 174 pp., is a handsomely produced study of the two MSS. containing different versions of Pierre Salmon's early 15th-c. political treatise on kingship and government. It examines the intricate relationship between text and illumination in these versions for the way in which S. encodes his pro-Burgundian message and subtly undermines the authority of the ailing king, Charles VI. F. Duval, 'Sébastien Mamerot', *Romania*, 116:461–91, offers a new perspective on the life and works of this little-known mid-15th-c.

compiler and translator, with a useful appendix of extracts from historical documents which mention the author as well as short passages from his four major texts. N. Nabert, 'La mère dans la littérature politique à la fin du Moyen Age (XIVe-XVe siècles)', *BDBA*, 16:191–202, argues that such texts are informed by both the idealized maternal images of didactic literature and the contemporary polemic surrounding the legitimacy of succession. A. Strubel, 'Gaston Phébus et l'intelligence des bêtes', *Ménard Vol.*, 1281–95, relates his anthropomorphic typology of animals according to their capacity for reasoning or ruse to literary and mythological tradition as well as to G.'s own personal experience of hunting; whilst J.-C. Faucon, 'La représentation de l'animal par Marco Polo', *Médiévales*, 32, 1997:97–117, argues that M.'s descriptions of animals emphasize realism over exoticism and symbolism. J. Dufournet, ' "Environ ce temps je vins au service du roi" (Philippe de Commynes, livre III, ch. xi', *CRISIMA 3*, 469–80, shows how C. justifies his shift of allegiance from Charles le Téméraire to Louis XI in August 1472 by claiming disloyalty to be endemic in contemporary society; whilst J. Blanchard, 'Commynes le diplomate: "archéologie" d'une formation intel-lectuelle', *Ménard Vol.*, 147–59, argues that the *Mémoires* break with the traditional symbolic and hieratic representation of monarchy, and privilege instead the viewpoint on affairs of state of professional diplomats like C. himself. M. Slattery, 'King Louis XI — chivalry's villain or anti-hero: the contrasting historiography of Chastellain and Commynes', *FCS*, 23, 1996[1997]:49–73, shows how the former attacks the king for undermining chivalric values by retreating from battle whereas the latter praises Louis's successful use of diplomacy in order to avoid combat. G. Small, 'Qui a lu la chronique de George Chastelain?', *Burgundica*, 1:115–26, analyses the reception of this text amongst its contemporary audience and accounts for its appeal amongst both the Burgundian nobility interested in their ancestral heritage and the incoming Hapsburg rulers curious about the past history of their newly acquired territories. E. Gaucher, 'Joinville conteur: les anecdotes dans la *Vie de saint Louis*', *IL*, 49, 1997:10–16, argues that J.'s use of seemingly digressive anecdotes serves both to underline the prestige of his saintly protagonist as well as himself as authentic, eye-witness narrator, and to lighten an otherwise dry didactic work with more entertaining passages evoking the exoticism of the Holy Land; whereas in 'Du bon usage de la trahison, dans l'historiographie des XIVe et XVe siècles', *CRISIMA 3*, 499–507, Gaucher reveals how the authors of the *Chanson de Bertrand du Guesclin* and the *Livre des faits du maréchal Boucicaut* replace the feudal notion of honour and loyalty with a more pragmatic and ambivalent concep-tion of betrayal. D. Lalande, 'Nicolas de Gonesse est-il l'auteur du

"Livre des fais du Mareschal Bouciquaut"?', *Ménard Vol.*, 827–38, rejects this attribution on the grounds that the style of this work differs substantially from that of G.'s translations of Plutarch and Valerius Maximus; whilst A. J. Kennedy, 'Christine de Pizan's *Livre du corps de policie*: some problems in the identification and analysis of her sources', *ib.*, 733–44, laments the lack of good critical editions of Middle French sources such as this translation of Valerius Maximus which was used by C. and others in their political and historical works. Kennedy is also responsible for an excellent new critical edition of C.'s *Livre du Corps de policie*, Champion, xlii + 231 pp. Based on Chantilly 294, an autograph manuscript, accompanied by a full scholarly apparatus including a particularly useful glossary, it replaces Lucas's rather unsatisfactory edition of 1967 which was transcribed from a version of the text produced long after C.'s own lifetime. R. Brown-Grant, ' "Hee! Quel honneur au femenin sexe!"': female heroism in Christine de Pizan's *Ditié de Jehanne d'Arc*', *JIRS*, 5, 1997 : 123–33, argues that, far from proposing Joan as a feminist *exemplum*, C. presents her as a salvific heroine atypical of ordinary womanhood in order to increase her propagandistic value as a force behind whom the French nation should unite against the English; whilst J.-F. Kosta-Théfaine, 'Entre poésie et prophétie: les sources du *Ditié de Jehanne d'Arc* de Christine de Pizan', *RZLG*, 22 : 41–56, surveys the biblical and medieval elements which enhance this text's status as a prophetic discourse.

5. RELIGIOUS, MORAL AND DIDACTIC LITERATURE

Fauvel Studies: Allegory, Chronicle, Music, and Image in Paris, Bibliothèque Nationale de France, MS français 146, ed. Margaret Bent and Andrew Wathey, Oxford, Clarendon Press, 1997, xix + 666 pp., is a monumental interdisciplinary collection of 27 essays on this multi-faceted but little-studied satire and comes complete with an index of MSS and musical compositions. J. E. Merceron, 'Obscenity and hagiography in three anonymous *Sermons Joyeux* and in Jean Molinet's *Saint Billouart*', Ziolkowski, *Obscenity*, 332–44, argues that, whilst the anonymous works conform to the bawdy tradition in simply coupling the language of sex and religion in order to mock the Church's sexual and moral values, M.'s text experiments with the semiotic and semantic elements of the Christian, bawdy and courtly traditions in its obscene allegory of a 'vit' and a 'cul' pursuing a 'con'. A.-M. Legaré, 'Allégorie et gestualité dans un manuscrit du *Pèlerinage de vie humaine* en prose', Bertrand, *Geste*, 341–67, examines the illumination cycle accompanying this text preserved in Bibliothèque publique et universitaire de Genève, MS fr. 182, for the influence of Quintilian's

Institutio oratoria on its representation of both hand gestures and body language in general. W. Pfeffer, 'The *Dit des monstiers*', *Speculum*, 73:80–114, offers a critical edition and English translation of this 14th-c. work, with a commentary on its linguistic, textual, and historical significance, and a useful glossary of the churches which it mentions. M. Léonard, '*Le Dit de la Honnine*', *Ménard Vol.*, 879–95, is an edition of this previously unpublished tale which compares the destruction wreaked by a caterpillar on a garden with the corruption brought about by a low-born woman of her noble husband and his court. Léonard is also the author of *Le 'dit' et sa technique littéraire des origines à 1340* (Nouvelle Bibliothèque du Moyen Age, 38), Champion, 1996, 455 pp., an important reassessment of this polymorphous genre — accompanied by an appendix listing all 684 works making up the 'dit' corpus — which examines its key internal characteristics and relationships to other genres, and concludes that it represents a major step in the move towards the more personalized poetry of the later middle ages. F. Clier-Colombani, 'Le coup de foudre dans *L'Ovide moralisé* ou la faillite de l'amour', *BDBA*, 15, 1997:179–211, shows how the interaction between text and image in the Rouen MS provides a moral lesson against the perils of love by representing the amorous encounters between gods and mortals as brutal and non-consensual; whereas in 'La mère dans l'*Ovide moralisé*', *ib.*, 16:71–108, she argues that the text's moralizations reduce the different models of maternity illustrated by pagan queens and goddesses to a single type of motherhood, one which is exemplified by the Virgin Mary as submission to God's creative power. Renate Blumenfeld-Kosinski, *Reading Myth: Classical Mythology and Its Interpretation in Medieval French Literature* (Figurae: Reading Medieval Culture), Stanford U.P., 1997, 314 pp. discusses how various texts from the mid–12th c. to 1430 rework classical myths according to their particular political, poetic, and didactic agendas, with chapters devoted to Anglo-Norman romances of antiquity, the *Roman de la Rose*, the *Ovide moralisé*, Machaut and Froissart, and Christine de Pizan. G. Souillac, 'Charisme et prophétisme féminins: Marguerite Porete et le *Miroir des simples âmes*', *AJFS*, 35:261–78, examines how M. presents herself as a female prophet in order to legitimate her claim to attain divine knowledge unmediated by the hierarchy of the Church; whilst M. G. Sargent, 'The annihilation of Marguerite Porete', *Viator*, 28, 1997:253–79, sees the heterodoxy implicit in M.'s attempt to reformulate ideas about male and female subjectivity as the main factor which led to her persecution. G. Ouy, 'Trois prières inédites de Gerson', *Demarolle Vol.*, 27–38, is a transcription of Paris BNF MS fr. 25552, fols 75–80, which contain both a particular and a general prayer to St John the Evangelist (Jean Gerson's patron saint) as well as one addressed to St

Agnes. L. J. Walters, 'The Tournai *Rose* as a secular and a sacred epithalamium', *Papers* (ICLS 8), 251–66, argues that by incorporating references to the Song of Songs and elements of Franciscan spirituality into its illumination cycle, this MS of Gui de Mori's reworking of the *Rose* functions as both a commemoration of the wedding of a real-life couple and a celebration of the soul's pursuit of divine love. E. Martin, 'Away from self-authorship: multiplying the "author" in Jean de Meun's *Roman de la Rose*', *MP*, 96: 1–15, reveals how, in the midpoint and apologia passages, J. layers multiple subjectivities in order to disavow any authorial responsibility; whilst A. Planche, ' "Ne valoir une pomme, une bille, une cive . . ." L'expression concrète de la valeur nulle dans *Le Roman de la Rose*. (Partie Jean de Meun)', *Demarolle Vol.*, 118–32, examines the place of the *Rose* in the development of negative comparisons due to its extensive use of disparaging images taken from the domains of food, amusements, and dress. T. Van Hemelryck, 'Où sont les "Neuf Preux"? Variations sur un thème médiéval', *SFr*, 42: 1–8, argues for the influence of the *Ubi sunt?* topos on the tradition of the *Neuf Preux*, with particular reference to George Chastellain's use of these two themes in his *Miroir de Mort*. C. Segre, 'Due nuove attestazioni di "Les Douze moys figurez" ', *Ménard Vol.*, 1235–46, transcribes a version of this text contained in Tommaso III di Saluzzo's *Chevalier errant* (Paris BNF MS fr. 12559) using Torino Biblioteca Nazionale L.V.6 for variants. M. Colombo-Timelli, 'Le *Purgatoire des mauvais maris*. Introduction et édition', *Romania*, 116:492–523, is a critical edition of a late 15th-c. Burgundian work based on the Colard Mansion incunable (Paris BNF Rés.p.Y2.244), with a discussion of the text's place in the Querelle des Femmes. R. Deschaux, 'Sourires et joies dans le *Champion des Dames* de Martin le Franc', *Ménard Vol.*, 407–16, comments on M.'s use of comic anecdotes and puns as part of his pro-women contribution to the Querelle and his substitution of a conception of love based on Faith, Hope, and Charity for that governed by Venus and physical passion. D. Ruhe, ' "Pour raconte ou pour dottrine". *L'exemplum* et ses limites', pp. 331–51 of *Les Exempla médiévaux: nouvelles perspectives*, ed. Jacques Berlioz and Marie-Anne Polo de Beaulieu, Champion, 464 pp., compares the use made of *exempla* by the Chevalier de La Tour Landry and the Menagier de Paris in their respective courtesy books for women and concludes that the latter emphasizes more the aesthetic and entertaining aspects of his examples than their strict didactic import; whilst A.-M. De Gendt, ' "Plusieurs manières d'amour": le débat dans *Le Livre du Chevalier de la Tour Landry* et ses échos dans l'œuvre de Christine de Pizan', *FCS*, 23 1996[1997]:121–37, examines the attack on *fin'amor* voiced by the

Chevalier's wife and suggests its possible influence on the representation of Sibylle Monthault de la Tour in C.'s works. Alcuin Blamires, *The Case for Women in Medieval Culture*, Oxford, Clarendon Press, 1997, 279 pp., is a pioneering study of the philosophical and theological tradition of pro-feminine arguments which established writers such as C. were able to draw upon in their defence of women against misogynist opinion. L. C. Reis, 'Le prologue au *Livre des Trois Vertus* de C.', *RoN*, 39:47–52, analyses how the opening passages of this work link back thematically to her earlier *Cité des dames*. Christine de Pizan, *The Book of the City of Ladies*, trans. Earl Jeffrey Richards, NY, Persea Books, rev. edn., lxv + 281 pp., is an updated version of this important translation of the *Cité des dames* which first appeared in 1982, and features a new foreword by Nathalie Zemon Davies as well as a new introduction on recent developments in C. scholarship. M. Jeay, 'C.: chroniques de la trahison', *CRISIMA 3*, 453–65, examines how she explores the issue of women's betrayal in love and fatal loss of reputation in society across a range of lyrical, didactic, and political texts. J. A. Wisman, 'C. and Arachne's Metamorphoses', *FCS*, 23, 1996[1997]:138–51, shows how her representation of Arachne as a highly skilled artist challenges Arachne's image as vain and untalented in the male exegetical tradition. A. Suranyi, 'A fifteenth-century woman's pathway to fame: the *Querelle de la Rose* and the literary career of C.', *ib.*, 204–21, is a survey of her defence of women texts up to, during, and after the *Querelle* which is heavily reliant on previous scholarship. J.-P. Beaulieu, '*L'Avision Christine* ou la tentation autobiographique', *Littératures*, 18:15–30, sees this text as proto-modern in its exploration of self-representation within the impersonal framework of the allegorical dream-vision and its breaking down of the distinction between the public and private spheres. L. Dulac, 'A propos des représentations du corps souffrant chez C.', *Demarolle Vol.*, 313–24, demonstrates how, across a variety of works, she uses the image of the suffering human body as part of her political and moral analyses of the ills of her contemporary society; whilst in 'Littérature et dévotion: A propos des *Heures de contemplacion sur la Passion de Nostre Seigneur* de C.', *Ménard Vol.*, 475–84, Dulac offers a preliminary study of literary techniques in one of C.'s most neglected religious works. J.-L. Picherit, 'La fournaise dans la littérature du Moyen Age', *RLaR*, 102:167–77, discusses how C., Gerson, and Deschamps use the image of the oven from the Book of Daniel as a symbol of moral purification or as a metaphor for hell. Two important general collections of essays have also appeared in this bumper year for *études christiniennes*, the first of which is *Christine de Pizan and the Categories of Difference*, ed. Marilynn Desmond, Minneapolis–London, Minnesota U.P., xix + 287 pp. In this volume, which groups papers based on a conference held at Binghampton University in October 1995 and reflects some of the main strands in current American scholarship, C. Cannon Willard offers an overview of C.'s political treatises (3–15); R. Krueger examines C.'s critique of the process of teaching and her anxiety about the failure of moral instruction to reform the social order (16–40); D. Wolfthal analyses how she reinterprets the traditional rape scenario of women as victims of sexual violence by representing them as forceful avengers against their assailants in the *Epistre Othea* and the *Cité des dames* (41–70); M. A. C. Case compares C. with modern critical race theorists in order to show how she legitimates her experiences to give authority to her otherwise marginalized voice in the Querelle des Femmes (71–87); T. Fenster re-assesses the importance of C.'s choice of French over Latin for the development and prestige of the vernacular as a didactic medium in the later Middle Ages (91–107); B. M. Semple argues that, in the *Avision Christine*, she condemns the pursuit of knowledge which leads to intellectual arrogance and instead advocates pursuit of the spiritual life undertaken in humility and acknowledgement of one's ignorance (108–27); M. Weitzel Gibbons shows that the miniature of the *Bath of the Muses* episode in the version of the *Chemin de long estude* contained in Harley 4431, fol. 183, functions as a multi-layered image of female intellectual authority (128–45); M. H. Green contends that C. probably excluded the figure of the Salernitan doctor Trotula from her *Cité des dames* because of the latter's association with the misogynist medical tradition of revealing the 'secrets of women' (146–78); J. L. Kellogg examines how, in the *Epistre Othea* and the *Mutacion de Fortune*, C. takes issue with the misogynist aspects of Ovid by reinterpreting his myth of Ceyx and Alcyone in order to produce a more authoritative discursive voice for herself and other women in society (181–94); D. McGrady maintains that by reconceptualizing the poet-patron relationship in the Harley 4431 MS of her collected works, C. transforms the patron's traditional power over literary creation into a valorization of the writer's position as author and no longer simply as court entertainer (195–214); C. J. Brown demonstrates the varied reception of C.'s works in the late 15th and early 16th c. in France and England whereby French printers of her texts highlight her gender in order to attract a largely female readership whereas English printers play down or even efface her identity as woman author in their attempts to please a more male audience (215–35); and M.-A. Bossy argues that the copy of her *Fais d'armes et de chevalerie* contained in British Library MS Royal 15.E.VI which was presented to Margaret of Anjou by John Talbot, Earl of Shrewsbury, on the occasion of her marriage to Henry VI of England was designed to enhance the prestige of the giver as a soldier and connoisseur of French culture at the expense of both C.'s status as author and Margaret's importance as receiver of the gift (236–56). The second of these volumes, also based on conference proceedings but representing more the European dimension of C. scholarship, is *Sur le chemin de longue étude . . . Actes du colloque d'Orléans Juillet 1995*, ed. Bernard Ribémont, Champion, 204 pp. In this collection, S. G. Bell analyses the reception of the *City of Ladies* in a series of lost 16th-c. tapestries produced for various Renaissance queens and princesses (7–12); A. Birrell compares the love relationship between husband and wife in C.'s *Trois Vertus* with medieval Chinese love poetry (13–24); R. Brown-Grant reads the *Epistre Othea* as a mirror for princes which, like John Gower's *Confessio Amantis*, links personal morality with social ethics in all spheres of human activity (25–44); C. Brucker examines the significance of the terms 'hauteur', 'gloire', and 'renommee' for C.'s moral and didactic project of encouraging the reader to pursue virtue and attain salvation (45–64); M. Closson offers a rather descriptive overview of the educational possibilities open to women in the French Middle Ages (65–76); L. Dulac accounts for the somewhat disparate structure of the *Avision Christine* by relating it to key themes explored by C. in earlier texts such as the substitution of Opinion for Fortune and the linking of personal and collective misfortune (77–86); M. Guarinos discusses how, in the *Trois Vertus*, C. exhorts her female readers to balance their responsibility as moral individuals against solidarity with other members of their sex (87–100); A. J. Kennedy reveals how the *Ditié de Jehanne d'Arc* was read by the literary critic Gustave Cohen during the Occupation as a lesson in moral fortitude and a defence of French cultural values (101–10); J. Laidlaw reassesses C.'s *virelais* in the light of her 14th-c. poetic predecessors and her own lyric output with its emphasis on women as victims of passionate love (111–26); G. Ouy and C. M. Reno outline the form that their forthcoming catalogue of C.'s autograph MSS will take (127–35); A. Slerca situates the *Chemin de long estude* in the tradition of myth narratives on the creation of the universe and notes C.'s original use of both irony and the polemical dialogue (135–48); A. Tarnowski reads C.'s representation of Pallas Athena as a symbol of the author's intellectual aspirations both as a purveyor of wisdom and an instructor in chivalric prowess (149–58); L. J. Walters examines how C. models her transformation into a man in the *Mutacion de Fortune* on the gender change involved in the story of St Perpetua whilst transposing the religious inspiration behind the saint's life into a more secular and humanist set of ideals (159–82); and M. Zimmermann discusses the early 20th-c. German reception of C. which tends to gloss over her provocative status as proto-feminist in favour of a less threatening view of her as wife, mother and patriot (183–204).

6. MISCELLANEOUS

J. E. Merceron, 'Cooks, social status, and stereotypes of violence in medieval French literature and society', *Romania*, 116:170–87, analyses a range of mainly 13th-c. texts, such as the *Bataille de Caresme et Charnage* and the *Merveilles de Rigomer*, for their pejorative portrayal of cooks as characters who direct their violence against the religious estate and the military elite, often as the instruments of a third party. M. A. Rouse and R. H. Rouse, 'The goldsmith and the peacocks: Jean de le Mote in the household of Simon de Lille, 1340', *Viator*, 28, 1997:281–303, examines the relationships between illumination, *orfèvrerie* and poetic composition in the commissioning of the *Li parfait du paon* and the allegorical *Voie d'enfer et de paradis*. A. Smets and B. Van den Abele, 'Manuscrits et traités de chasse français du Moyen Age. Recensement et perspectives de recherche', *Romania*, 116:316–67, is a detailed inventory of MSS containing hunting treatises with a brief but useful introduction to the authors and works cited.

THE SIXTEENTH CENTURY

By CATHERINE REUBEN, *Kingston University*

1. GENERAL

1998 was, among many other things, a year of league tables. Following this trend, Table 1 ranks 16th-c. literary figures by the number of mentions in titles of articles or reviews (source: ISI, 1 January 1998–April 1999), and books, counted manually. Though this method has serious limitations, it gives some idea of the balance of research.

Table 1:   16th-century French authors in titles of 1998 publications

	Articles/Reviews	Books
Montaigne	100	10
Rabelais	45	5
Ronsard	17	3
Du Bellay	15	
Marot	14	2
Marguerite de Navarre	11	
Labé	10	
Palissy	9	
d'Aubigné	7	1
Lemaire de Belges	6	1
Budé	5	
Scève	5	
Baïf	4	
Papillon	3	
Thenaud	2	
La Boétie	2	
Sala	2	
Lefèvre d'Etaples	2	
de la Taille	1	2
Du Bartas	1	1

Montaigne wrote, 'Il se faut réserver une arriere boutique toute nostre, toute franche, en laquelle nous establissons nostre vraye liberté et principale retraicte et solitude.' (*Essais*, Bk 1, Ch. 39 'De la solitude'). Given the scale of Montaigne studies, there can be few corners of his *arrière boutique* not yet explored.

HUMANISM, SCIENCE, AND IDEAS

Michel Jeanneret, *Perpetuum mobile: Métamorphoses des corps et des œuvres de Vinci à Montaigne*, Macula, 1997, 331 pp., starts with Leonardo da Vinci's remark that 'the principle of all life is movement'. J.'s theme embraces art, science, geography, poetry, religion and, of course, literature to remind readers that the 16th-c. Reformation was a time of upheaval and such terrible wars that people thought the very cosmos was affected, or even vice versa. The humanists felt that they had progressed beyond the static view of life held in the Middle Ages. J.'s seminal book plots the continuation of movement, starting with Du Bartas' *La Semaine*, which extends the first chapter of Genesis to more than 6000 lines (see p. 112). He discusses, amongst other topics, Clément Marot's translation of Ovid's *Metamorphoses*, 'transmuer celluy qui les autres transmue', Montaigne's 'grotesques et corps monstreux' and even the idea of self-made man. J. provides a novel view of the Renaissance as a time of change and unrest as opposed to harmony and order. An English translation is to be published early in 2000 by Johns Hopkins U.P., Baltimore.

T. Conley, 'A chaos of science', *RQ*, 51:934–41, follows up some of Jeanneret's themes and indicates the explosion of scientific curiosity in the 16th c. that matched the explosion in art, literature, and philosophy. Though ordered by a supreme creator, the world was also seen to be composed of a dizzying variety of flora and fauna. Much of the science in the 16th c. was merely of observation and classification rather than explanation, and this diverts C. in mid-essay from his fascinating theme, but he finally returns to it.

A massive book of similar scope to Jeanneret's is Francis M. Higman, *Lire et découvrir: La circulation des idées au temps de la Réforme*, Geneva, Droz, 768 pp. It is a compendium of H.'s articles going back to 1970 and will be invaluable to those interested in the interaction of theology and literature in the Reformation. It includes Luther and Calvin, for example translations into French of Luther and 'Calvin polémiste', and also 'Farel, Calvin, Olivétan, sources de la spiritualité gallicane' and wide-ranging articles on 'The Reformation and the French Language' and 'Religious pamphlets from the Counter-Reformation'. The book provides an enjoyable overview of the period together with detailed backing for the specialist.

Arnaud Tripet, *Entre Humanisme et rêverie*, Champion, 330 pp., like Higman's book, is a collection of papers over the years, except that T.'s work extends from Renaissance to Romanticism, under the main headings of *Questions de poétique et de rhétorique*, *La France et l'Italie*, *Figures genevoises*, and *Romantisme de l'aube au crépuscule*. As in much of the year's work, the theme of laughter recurs in several of the chosen pieces such as *Le Rire et la littérature* (1995) and *Le Badin de la farce* (1994). T. covers an intriguing mix of Italian and French writers including André Della Santa, Boccacio, Petrarch, Leopardi, Rabelais, Ronsard, Du Bellay, Montaigne, Rousseau, Mme de Staël, and Baudelaire.

F. Higman, *BHR*, 60:551–55, enthusiastically discusses G. Gadoffre's **La Révolution culturelle dans la France des humanistes: Guillaume Budé et François Ier*, Geneva, Droz, 1997. He traces Gadoffre's view of the French in the early 1500s as 'un peuple inculte et philistin' to the revolution, which Gadoffre sees as based on the value of culture and which brought about the view of France as 'la mère des arts' (Du Bellay) and laid the foundations for *l'Europe des Lumières*.

One of the more interesting series of papers to be published during the year was based on a colloquium organized in 1994 by the Committee for Renaissance Studies at Princeton University with the support of the Center for French Excellence. F. Rigolot's introduction, 'The Renaissance crisis of exemplarity', *JHI*, 59:557–63, is followed by M. Jeanneret, 'The vagaries of exemplarity: distortion or dismissal', *ib.*, 565–79; K. Stierle, 'Three moments in the crisis of exemplarity: Boccaccio-Petrarch, Montaigne and Cervantes', *ib.*, 581–95; T. Hampton, 'Examples, stories, and subjects in Don Quixote and the Heptameron', *ib.*, 597–611; F. Cornilliat, 'Exemplarities: a response to Timothy Hampton and Karlheinz Stierle', *ib.*, 613–24; and D. Engster, 'The Montaignian moment', *ib.*, 625–50. Exemplarity in its most extreme form was the appeal to a classical or religious source as the fount of truth, but in a wider interpretation it could be the use of literary exempla or parables as rhetorical devices. Even Don Quixote could be a source of such exempla, and the Heptaméron contrasts the exempla of male romance heroism and female chastity. 'The classical texts were cut up into flexible and recyclable units [. . .] and fragments put together in anthologies [. . .] with commentaries designed to make them user friendly'(see A. Moss, p. 95). Exemplarity is in either case central to the Renaissance battle between authority and the recourse to experience or experiment. Cornilliat describes Montaigne as 'our most sacred example of non-exemplarity' but E. MacPhail, 'In the wake of Solon: memory and modernity in the *Essays* of Montaigne', *MLN*, 113:881–96, quotes him as claiming that the recent discoveries in geography, astronomy, and medicine 'only accentuate the precariousness and instability of scientific doctrines, which are always subject to supersession'. At the opposite pole was Francis Bacon's paradox that the moderns are the true ancients because they benefit from a greater store of experience than their predecessors. Although Bacon was wrong about geocentrism, he was right on the issue of the corrigibility of science. M. got it wrong in this case and, in his other writings, appears to modify this view. It would perhaps have been better to state this categorically rather than to enter various lukewarm defences that make the eminent philosopher seem more like a 16th-c. ' "disgusted" of Tunbridge Wells'. This excellent debate deserves to run and run.

PROSE, POETRY, AND CULTURE

C. Jomphe, 'Comment disposer le long poème? Quelques réflexions de la Renaissance française sur l'historien, l'orateur et le poète', *BHR* 60:395–403, writes of the opposition between nature and art in Renaissance poetic theory — a question of changing the order of events: 'Créée à partir de pièces détachées, l'œuvre doit atteindre à l'unité parfaite'. Nathalie Dauvois, *De la 'Satura' à la bergerie: Le prosimètre pastoral en France à la Renaissance*, Champion, 320 pp. deals with 16th-c. prose and verse deriving from classical sources.

H. Campagne, 'Disputes et "crimes verbaux": la querelle littéraire au XVIe siècle en France', *RHLF*, 98:3–15, draws a parallel between duels and literary quarrels in 16th-c. France. As writers were exempt from the former, the quarrels took on an almost legal form, defining the image and background of the writers and sometimes even their role in the State. For instance, an unknown writer could attack a well-known author and thus get a name for himself. Who would have heard of Sagon were it not for his famous quarrel with Clément Marot? That the academic quarrel remains alive and well was illustrated by an exchange of letters between M. Simonin, *RHLF*, 98:688–89, and C. Blum, *ib.*, 689–90. The question was whether S.'s article on M.'s *Exemplaire de Bordeaux* had appeared before B.'s comments and that B. had ignored it. B. claimed he was quoting L. Desgraves from 1980 and that S.'s article, like his, was part of conference proceedings and published later.

H. David Brumble, *Classical Myths and Legends in the Middle Ages and Renaissance: a Dictionary of Allegorical Meanings*, London, Fitzroy Dearborn, xiv + 421 pp. is a comprehensive reference work to aid the understanding of literature based on classical or biblical sources. The term 'allegory' is interpreted widely to include moral, physical, natural, and cosmic allegories, together with astrology, emblems, and typology. B. provides full explanations of such diverse topics as the Muses, Hecate, Hector, Potiphar's wife, Mohammed, and Godfrey of Bouillon, but also includes love, reason, gluttony, and friendship. Quotations are all in English but sources, cross references, and bibliographies are profuse. On a related topic is P. Cifarelli, 'Fables et nouvelles à la Renaissance. A propos des fables dans quelques recueils français de nouvelles au seizième siècle', *Reinardus*, 11:37–51.

She compares fables and short stories published between 1531 and 1585 and notes changes in the narrative syntax and didactic role of the fable outside the works of the humanists. Much has been written on the problems of defining the genres at the time, but it seems that the fables appeared most frequently in *nouvelles* or *emblèmes*. The fables have often lost their moral force and have become part and parcel of the narrative text, with the authors using the well-known fables to enliven their stories. A feature of many legends is the prodigious birth and this topic is discussed in B. Dunn-Lardeau, *‘Prodigious births and death in childbirth in *Le Palais des nobles dames* (Lyons 1534)’, *RAR*, 21.3, 1997:43–62.

There have been recent translations of two seminal books: Terence Cave, *Cornucopia. Figures de l'abondance au XVIe siècle: Erasme, Rabelais, Ronsard, Montaigne*, Macula, 1997, 367 pp., and Frances A. Yates, *Les Académies en France au XVIe siècle*, PUF, 1996, vii + 511 pp. These are still important, although Y. wrote hers 50 years ago. In an essay on them, F. Lestringant, ‘La Renaissance entre tragédie et comédie’, *Critique*, 54:420–34, draws comparisons between Europe at the end of World War II and the 16th c. after the Wars of Religion and comments on Y.'s positive message that, even in the midst of so much barbarism and horror, it was right that these academies of intellectuals should have been debating ‘les fondements de la tradition euro-péenne’. L. sees the translation of C.'s *Cornucopia* of 1979 as a reply to Yates, in that it is through the wide diversity of language — the cornucopia — that freedom of ideas is upheld. L. quotes from the preface which, like the rest of the book, has been revised by C. for the translation: ‘Le dispositif esthétique et même philosophique de cette époque (la Renaissance) favorise la composition d’ouvrages ou le sens foisonne, d’ouvrages dont les significations virtuelles dépassent les contraintes d’une pensée univoque.’

M. M. Fragonard, *BHR*, 60:567–70, compares C.'s translation to that of J. Lecointe (*L'idéal et la différence* (1993)), ‘qui en réalise à bien des égards l’approfondissement théorique grâce à une enquête plus suivie sur les formes d’enseignement de l’écriture, le rôle de l’idée dans les processus de création, les formulations théoriques de plusieurs siècles et la longue genèse qui finit par mettre en équivalence différence = valeur nouveauté = différence valorisée, originalité = valeur absolue du texte, démonstration rigoureuse d’une lente évolution collective, conflictuelle, faite de déplacements notionnels lents et parfois équivoques’.

In discussing the vexed and complex question of what exactly is the ‘poétique de la silve’, P. Galand-Hallyn, *BHR*, 60:609–39, concludes that, together with Horace’s *Epître aux Pisons*, the *silve* ‘en imposant brièveté relative, sans désordre impromptu, ainsi qu’une certaine humilité thématique, [. . .] dispensait les poètes de l'aventure épique et semblait praticable même par des auteurs non chevronnés, ce qui pouvait rassurer les poètes français assez peu confiants encore en leur génie latin [. . .]'. She feels that *la silve* influenced poets, both Italian and French, such as Macrin, Marot, Bourbon, Scève, and Ronsard, and maybe even Montaigne.

Olivia Rosenthal, *Donner à voir: écritures de l'image dans l'art de poésie au XVIe siècle*, Champion, 504 pp., takes the idea that 'Un texte se regarde comme une image' to imply 'placer la poésie au cœur d'une interrogation sur les relations entre les arts.' In considering how authors themselves and, in particular poets, talk about poetry, R. includes texts that are not themselves poetic — 'Nous avons voulu tirer de certaines associations surprenantes, de certains rapprochements inattendus, des modes nouveaux d'appréhension du texte littéraire.' The poetry is restricted to love poetry 1575–1620, but the volume includes *Montaigne et la peinture de soi, le spectacle de poésie, sonnet et inscription, la fable*, and *une poésie en temps de guerre*.

Jacques dit Sylvius Dubois, *Introduction à la langue française suivie d'une grammaire (1531)*, ed. Colette Demaizière, Champion, 448 pp. is a fascinating book, a French translation adding to the title [. . .] *une grammaire latino-française inspirée des auteurs hébreux, grecs et latins*. It was printed in 1531 by Robert Estienne, who printed many of the Reformation Bibles, a year after François Ier opened the *Collège des lecteurs royaux*. Thus the problems of Reformation scholars translating biblical texts into vulgar tongues were echoed in the lay world where many medical practitioners, especially barber-surgeons, knew no Latin and needed works in the vernacular.

Claude Faisant, *Mort et résurrection de la Pléiade*, ed. Josiane Rieu et al., Champion, 816 pp. has an exceptionally thorough reference section. It traces the reputations of the Pléiade poets, and in particular Ronsard, over the centuries. R. has been accused of being a *pédant* but also a *barbare*. His style is 'sprinkled with Greek and Latin' but also 'full of triviality', and critical opinion has varied over the years. Another book about the Pléiade, G. Castor, **La poétique de la Pléiade: Etude sur la pensée et la terminologie du XVIe siècle*, Champion, 320 pp., has been translated into French by Yvonne Bellenger.

Pilgrimage is essentially a medieval concept yet paradoxically the Renaissance was concerned with discovery, invention and innovation in which travel was a key part. Thus pilgrimage for the lay person became easier just as it became outmoded. The first travel guides were written by Loys Balourdet (1601) and Henri de Castela (1604). Wes Williams, *Pilgrimage and Narrative in the French Renaissance*, Oxford, Clarendon, 326 pp. advances this paradox and takes the view that pilgrimage was of much greater importance in French Renaissance culture than previously supposed.

Molière's M. Jourdain's remark, 'Pourquoi toujours des bergers?' signals the end of the pastoral novel in Europe, which flowered briefly from the middle of the 16th c. Françoise Avocat, *Arcadies malheureuses: Aux origines du roman moderne*, Champion, 530 pp. considers why the decline of the genre was so rapid. Instead of shepherds, novels had heroes. Thus heroic values were questioned in the light of the loss of the Arcadian idyll. Arcadia itself was compared with Utopia, when the pastoral novel re-emerged briefly in the second half of the 18th c. Utopias are also reviewed in *Utopia 1: 16th and 17th Centuries*, ed. David Lee Rubin and Alice Stroup, Charlottesville VA, Rookwood, 224 pp.

CONFERENCES, COLLECTIONS, AND BIBLIOGRAPHIES

Two volumes have been published in a new series concerned with interdisciplinary research. They are based on study days organized by the Ecole Nationale des Chartes and the Centre de recherches sur l'Espagne des XVIe and XVIIe siècles and both have a Franco-Spanish bias. The first is entitled *Le Pouvoir des livres à la Renaissance*, Geneva, Droz, 160 pp., and has contributions from F. Barbier, F. Delpech, B. Pinchard, I. Diu, J. Balsamo, C. Val Julián, P. Büttchen, and D. de Courcelles. The second is *Traduire et adapter à la Renaissance*, Geneva, Droz, 144 pp., and has contributions from F. Mariani Zini, 'Langue et traduction de la poésie chez Politien: *Doctaque me triplici recinet facundia lingua*' (11–34); F. Géal, 'Enjeux idéologiques de la traduction au XVIe siècle: l'exemple d'une des premières versions en castillan des *Colloques* d'Erasme' (35–64); C. Val Julián, 'Traduire au Nouveau Monde: pratiques de la traduction en Nouvelle-Espagne au XVIe siècle', (65–88); J. Balsamo, 'Traduire de l'italien: ambitions sociales et contraintes éditoriales à la fin du XVIe siècle' (89–98); D. de Courcelles, 'La Silva de varia lección de Pedro Mexiá (Seville, 1540; Paris, 1552): traduction et adaptation en Espagne et en France à la Renaissance' (99–124); and M. H. Smith, 'Points de vue et images du monde: anamorphoses de textes géographiques, de Strabon à Giovanni Botero' (125–40).

A haute voix: diction et prononciation au XVIe et XVIIe siècles. Actes du colloque de Rennes des 17–18 Juin 1996, ed. Olivia Rosenthal, Klincksieck, 260 pp., indicates that in the Renaissance no distinction was made between written and spoken discourse, and poetry was read aloud before being printed. For instance, 'Ronsard insiste [. . .] sur l'existence conjointe de deux sources de poétique: l'oral et l'écrit et il semble refuser que l'un (l'écrit) anéantisse l'autre (l'oral).' Contributors are G. Mathieu-Castellani, J.-C. Monferran, P. Lartigue, J. Vignes, I. His, F. Mouret, O. Millet, E. Buron, H. Merlin, L. Norman, G. Clerico, M.-L. Demonet, and H. Meschonnic.

A Festschrift for Yvonne Bellenger was *La Naissance du monde et l'invention du poème. Mélanges de poétique et d'histoire littéraire du XVIe siècle, offerts à Yvonne Bellenger*, ed. J.-C.Ternaux, Champion, 497 pp. 26 papers are included under the headings of *Les formes de la création poétique, Le monde du poète, Le miracle du poème, Du Bellay-Ronsard*, and *Du Bartas*. Perhaps because of the importance of B.'s work on Du Bartas, there is emphasis on creation, poetic creation and the creation of the world. D. Ménager's article 'Le "Fiat lux" dans la littérature de la Renaissance' (105–20), examines how Genesis (1 : 3) was understood in the Hexamera at the end of the 16th and beginning of the 17th centuries. Other examples include J. C. Nash, 'Invention et plaisir créateur: Ronsard, Du Bellay, Scève' (317–34), and F. Lestringant, 'De la "Première" à la "Dernière semaine" ou de la réversibilité du monde selon Du Bartas, d'Aubigné, Augier Gaillard et Michel Quillian' (435–54).

*Sources et fontaines du moyen âge à l'âge baroque, ed. François Roudaut, Champion, 496 pp., is the proceedings of a conference at the Université Paul-Valéry, 28–30 November 1996. The proceedings of a conference held in Nice, 5–6 December 1997, have been published as **Aspects du lyrisme du XVIe et XVIIe siècles: Ronsard, Rousseau, Nerval*, ed. M.-H. Cotoni, J. Rieu, and J.-M. Seillan, Nice U.P., 266 pp. Revised versions of papers presented at the 25th annual French Literature Conference, Columbia, SC, 1997 have been published as **Religion and French Literature*, ed. Buford Norman, Amsterdam, Rodopi, xi + 219 pp. See also *Rabelais pour le XXIe siècle*, p. 100.

Recent bibliographies include the annual **Bibliographie internationale de l'humanisme et de la Renaissance*, vol. XXVIII, Geneva, Droz, 1997. A cumulative edition for 1969–98 on CD-ROM will appear shortly. Jean Paul Barbier, **Ma Bibliothèque poétique*, IV: *Contemporains et disciples de Ronsard*, Geneva, Droz, 558 pp. is the fourth part of a monumental catalogue covering all the poets in the second half of the 16th century. Yvonne Bellenger, *Du Bartas* (Bibliographie des écrivains français, 12), Memini, 171 pp., deals with Du Bartas.

C. Mazouer, 'Vingt ans de recherches sur le théâtre du XVIe siècle', *NRSS*, 16:310–25, takes as its starting point Madeleine Lazard's *Le Théâtre en France au XVIe siècle* (1980), and updates it with a bibliography of plays, playwrights, theatre, theatrical life and criticism. See also D. R. Carlson, 'The writings of Bernard André', p. 111.

2. MONTAIGNE

EDITIONS

Pride of place goes to *Corpus et oeuvres de Montaigne*, CD-ROM, ed. Claude Blum, Geneva, Slatkine — Paris, Champion, 1997. J. Céard, 'Nouveautés sur Montaigne', *Critique*, 54:456–63, complains that it is expensive and requires a sophisticated computer, which he does not have. However, it contains the editions of all the stages of Montaigne's work from the 16th and 17th c., and will be of use to both specialists and lay readers who can have translations into English, German, Spanish and Italian and with modern script. Despite a few quibbles, C. welcomes the CD and is pleased that literary studies can benefit from advances in IT.

A massive and scholarly new edition has also appeared, Michel de Montaigne, *Essais I*, ed. André Tournon, 3 vols, Imprimerie nationale, 667, 880, 685 pp. J. Céard, *Critique*, 54:456–63, welcomes an attempt to replace P. Villey's edition of the *Essais* by a more up to date critical edition. He points to the difficulties inherent in organizing the five stages of the *Essais* and mentions that the *Essais I* edited by A. Tournon have been punctuated in such a way as to emphasize the 'nouveau langage requis, selon lui [Montaigne], par une philosophie de l'incertitude et de l'aventure intellectuelle.' But Tournon discredits the 1595 edition of the *Essais* and, according to Céard, thus reopens the debate as to what is the authentic text.

The 'Manuscrit de Bordeaux' is an example of the 1588 edition of M.'s *Essais* published by Abel L'Angelier, the first to include the *troisième livre* and the last to be revised by the author himself. M. Simonin, 'Montaigne, son éditeur et le correcteur devant l'exemplaire de Bordeaux de Essais', *Adirel*, 11:75–93, asks what M. intended to do with this edition, which seems first of all to have been intended for the printer and then written over with his own notes and corrections. It was finally printed in the *Editions Municipales*, 1906–23, and S. gives a fascinating insight into the history of printing.

Pierre Leschemelle, *Montaigne tout entier et tout nu: Anthologie des Essais*, Imago–PUF, 256 pp., is a collection of 1694 quotations from the *Essais* classified under such headings as *miracles et fantasies, erreur et vérité, modération et mesure, paternité, imaginations de la mort* and *les cannibales*. This seems to be a direct descendant of the commonplace books that were such a feature of the 16th-c. literary scene (see exemplarity, p. 89) They were similarly collections of authoritative quotations organized by traditional subjects, but usually in Latin and in manuscript rather than printed form. Erasmus' *Adages* and M.'s *Essais* derived in part from commonplace books. They are discussed by Ann Moss, *Printed Commonplace-Books and the Structuring of Renaissance*

Thought, Oxford, Clarendon, 1996, 345 pp., reviewed by R. W. Clement, *SCJ*, 29:589–91.

LUCRETIUS

During the year, Michael Andrew Screech published not only *Laughter at the Foot of the Cross* (see p. 99) but also *Montaigne's Annotated Copy of Lucretius*, Geneva, Droz, xxi + 515 pp., which must surely be the year's major event in Montaigne research. Anyone who has been privileged to work with 16th-c. books will greet with pleasure this minutely annotated description of M.'s copy of Lucretius. The copy was found by chance at Sotheby's — M.'s signature was overwritten by the subsequent owner, Despagnet, also from Bordeaux. That and the slow verification of its authenticity — S. refers constantly to the débâcle of Hitler's diaries — provide a gripping detective story for lovers of Montaigne. The Lucretius is the Lambinius edition of *De Rerum Natura* 1563–64, but S. has provided a concordance so that 'with some guidance' (which is duly provided) lines of Lucretius can be traced and, in the Loeb, read in English translation, or in Guillaume Budé in French. Some of the *bons mots* of the *Essais* originate with the notes written on this copy. M.'s notes are in Latin and French, and his most frequent French comment is 'contre la religion', which is ironic considering the inter-Christian conflicts of M.'s time.

THEMES FROM THE *ESSAIS*

David Quint, *Montaigne and the Quality of Mercy: Ethical and Political Themes in the Essais*, Princeton U.P., xviii + 172 pp., feels that the ethical and political themes in the *Essais* should be read as a response to the horrors of the French civil wars. Q. quotes M.'s letter to Henry IV (1590) trying to persuade the King to be merciful to the Parisians if he wants them to recognize his claims. Q. considers the critical responses to *Des Cannibales* and deals with some of M.'s other *essais* in a readable way.

What does it mean to be a sceptic and is it really possible to be one? Hubert Vincent, *Vérité du scepticisme chez Montaigne*, L'Harmattan, 140 pp., writes about M.'s scepticism and why M. wanted to be a sceptic, with an analysis of the main issues of his scepticism. Jan Miernowsi, *L'Ontologie de la contradiction sceptique: Pour l'étude de la métaphysique des Essais*, Champion, 164 pp., explores the abstract principles underlying the discourse of M.'s *Essais* and the contradiction inherent in his scepticism. Whereas this appears to be negative, Miernowski feels that it is positive in the sense that M. is constantly urging the reader to pursue the ' "point" infiniment fuyant de la raison'. D. L. Sedley, *'Sublimity and skepticism in Montaigne', *PMLA*, 113:1079–92, continues with the scepticism theme. G. Defaux, 'Montaigne among the sceptics: an assessment', *FrF*, 23:147–66, reappraises M.'s scepticism and concludes 'De toutes les vanitez la plus vaine c'est l'homme.' D. puts forward three propositions, first that M. never had a 'crise sceptique', second that Christian scepticism had existed in France since the 1520s, for example the group at Meaux under the protection of Marguerite de Navarre, and third that M. was not a pure pyrrhonian but more an academic, used to giving opposing arguments. M.'s aim is not himself to doubt but to make others doubt. D. asks whether this is a new way of considering M. and whether the group at Meaux had widespread influence on theology during the century.

Montaigne and La Boétie are always described as friends, although the word can have a variety of meanings from casual acquaintances to much loved and constant companions. T. Conley, 'Friendship in a local vein: Montaigne's servitude to La Boétie', *SAQ*, 97:65–90, in a highly technical article lavishly illustrated with 16th-c. maps of the Dordogne, shows the extent to which the two friends' concepts of friendship differed. La B. saw it as an association of equals, characterized by faith, constancy and good ways of living. In *L'Amitié*, M. invokes La B.'s writings in order to efface them; 'He puts "friendship" in the thematic place that La B. had assigned to "servitude" '. The topic is developed further in *Freedom over Servitude: Montaigne, La Boétie, and On Voluntary Servitude*, ed. David Lewis Schaefer, Westport CT, Greenwood, viii + 252 pp., an interdisciplinary collection of papers on the relation between M.'s *Essais* and the writings attributed by M. to La Boétie. Articles are D. L. Schaefer, 'Montaigne and La Boétie' (1–30); R. P. Runyon, 'The vanishing center' (87–114); M. Platt, 'Montaigne, of friendship, and on tyranny' (31–86); R. Reynolds-Cornell, 'Smoke and mirrors: covert dissent in Montaigne's *Essays* and overt dissent in the discourse *On Voluntary Servitude*' (115–26); and D. Martin, 'Montaigne, author of *On Voluntary Servitude*' (127–88). The first two of these have added translations into English of *On Voluntary Servitude* and the *Twenty-Nine Sonnets* attributed to La B. and constituting the 29th chapter of M.'s Book 1. These appeared in all editions published during M.'s lifetime and are an integral part of the *Essais* despite the oblivion into which they have fallen. Schaefer, Martin, and Reynolds-Cornell all take Arthur Armaingaud's view that M. himself was the author both of *On Voluntary Servitude* and of the other works that he published in La B.'s name.

J. Brody, 'Philosophy, philology, literature', *PLit*, 22:258–60, expounds his theory that 'language drives thought, and not the other way around'. For instance, in *Of Repentance*, B. feels it rewarding to read the essay as a 'philologically structured narrative organized around the implicit sub-textual statement: "to re-form is to de-form".' He works similarly on the use of eating and drinking in *Of Experience*. This analysis is persuasive, well expressed and easily comprehensible to the lay reader, as with the image of an autonomous semantic network: 'Like a spider in the middle of its web, it pulls into its orbit whole families of satellite words.' B. feels that the philological approach to the essays helps to reveal the meaning through an analysis of its brilliant and unique style.

MONTAIGNE AND OTHERS

The intellectual links between England and France appear to have been surprisingly strong, considering the difficulties of travel in the 16th c. (see *Imagining Rabelais in Renaissance England*, p. 101). D. Farley-Hills, in 'Another *Hamlet* crux', *NQ*, 45:334–36, discusses Chapman, Marston, and Jonson's Blackfriars play, *Eastward Ho*, as a mockery of *Hamlet*. He suggests that the authors were influenced by Montaigne and that in particular they knew of M.'s essay *Of the Lame or Crippel* when they fashioned the scenes of Ophelia's madness.

Philippe de Commynes was a royal servant ('the French Machiavelli') and historian whose *Mémoires*, published in 1524, cover the years 1464–98. M. mentions him only three times, and M. Tetel, 'Montaigne's glances at Philippe de Commynes', *BHR*, 60:25–39, has provided a rather Leavis-like analysis of what M. might have learned from C. and why he did not mention the latter's chapters on Savonarola. M. and C. were both concerned with the aggrandisement and preservation of a unified monarchical state, but C. had the ear of kings, dealt only with a single superior and operated in the Italian diplomatic mode, whereas Montaigne was 'free-lance' and had continually to look over his shoulder. T. considers the silence of M. about Savonarola to be 'deafening' and ascribes it to something more than mere prudence about a controversial figure.

Thierry Gontier, *De l'Homme à l'animal: Paradoxes sur la nature des animaux, Montaigne et Descartes*, J. Vrin, 316 pp., quotes from Pierre Bayle's article 'Péreira' in his dictionary, saying 'De tous les objets physiques, il n'y en a point de plus abstrus, ni de plus embarrassant que l'âme des bêtes. Les opinions extrêmes sur ce sujet sont ou absurdes, ou très-dangereuses; le milieu que l'on veut y garder est insoutenable.' G. observes that M. opts for the 'very dangerous' angle, while Descartes opts for the 'absurd', while the middle way, rejected by Bayle, is that of Aristotle, which allows animals life and feelings but denies they have the noetic faculties of man.

In spite of the salary of Bernard André (p. 111) and the complaints of Du Bellay (p. 104), scarcely anyone in the Renaissance made a living out of writing. George Hoffmann, *Montaigne's Career*, Oxford, Clarendon, 188 pp., reveals the time and effort M. had to put into managing his family's property and that he had to perform professional tasks such as financing, proof-reading and revising for his editor. None the less, M.'s books did make a profit and H. calculates that the French public at that time were spending more than half a million *livres* per year on books compared with the annual budget for Henri II's army in 1559 of 1.9 million *livres*. Parisians alone were buying three to four hundred thousand volumes per year in mid-century.

Two papers dated 1997 did not appear until 1998. They were M. Debaisieux, *'Marie de Gournay contr(e) la tradition: du Proumenoir de Monsieur de Montaigne aux versions de l'Enéide', *RAR*, 21.2, 1997:45–58; and S. Charles, *'Le Procès de Montaigne par Malebranche: la véracité à l'aune de la vérité moderne', *ib.*, 21.3, 1997:25–42.

3. RABELAIS

Edwin M. Duval, *Design of Rabelais' Quart livre de Pantagruel*, Geneva, Droz, 158 pp., is the third and final volume about the design of the Pantagrueline epics. Its purpose is to discover a coherence of form and meaning in a work that is apparently fragmentary, disjointed, and ambiguous.

Michael Andrew Screech, *Laughter at the Foot of the Cross*, London, Allen Lane, 1997, 352 pp., is a book allying literature and religion in a readable way and was reviewed in the British broadsheets. The laughter, in so far as Jesus is concerned, is often mocking. S. distinguishes between the Latin Vulgate 'illudo' in Matthew and Luke meaning cruel laughter, and the Greek 'empaizō' in Matthew and Mark, meaning to mock or scoff as a child, pitilessly. S. goes back to the Psalms (xxii 7–8) 'Laugh me to scorn' to show that the account of the Crucifixion was foreshadowed in the OT, a conclusion fully in accord with the 16th-c. Christian hebraists. But having looked amongst others at Lucian, Socrates, Plato, Erasmus, Luther, and Rabelais, S. suggests that Christian laughter can be charitable. In his thoughts on Dante, he remarks that it is 'laughing at the world, certainly, but less than you might expect; laughing rarely at oneself; very, very often, laughing at other Christians in their error. It was better than burning them.'

Barbara Bowen, *Enter Rabelais Laughing*, Nashville, TN, Vanderbilt U.P., xv + 230 pp., is a compulsive read for lovers of Rabelais. Bowen points out that, although we laugh at the books, the main characters themselves are not often laughing. The key word, rather than 'rire', is 'joyeux'. Bowen echoes Screech when she asserts that 'joie' most often comes close to the Christian ideal of joyful confidence in God and his Gospel. Laughter may well accompany this joy, but it need not do so. B. argues that R. was a 'humanist for whom comedy and serious purpose were inseparable, and whose love of theatre coloured his views on humanism, rhetoric, and even medicine and law.' In subsequent work, 'Janotus de Bragmardo in the Limelight', *FR*, 72:229–37, B. feels that R's books are 'profoundly theatrical' and has written an enjoyable and instructive analysis of J. de B.'s speech requesting the return of the bells of Notre Dame, which Pantagruel has hung about his horse's neck. B. recapitulates the traditional features of Ciceronian rhetoric — invention, disposition, elocution, memory and pronunciation — and applies them to J. de B.'s ridiculous speech, pointing out the puns and humour in the Latin quotations, which would not easily be understood by the modern student. More seriously, her epilogue considers 'whether, in 1533–1534, R. did not still cherish a hope which he would later lose [. . .] that laughter was powerful enough to destroy the obscurantist enemies of enlightened Christian humanism'.

R. A. Hallett and P. Derks, 'Humor theory and Rabelais', *Humor*, 11:135–60, present 'a psychological model [. . .] for the analysis of comic literature. Two dimensions and their interactions are defined; the aggressive/affiliative and the nonsense/incongruity-resolution'. Affiliative devices, aggression, and nonsense also play a role. As the authors conclude that R.'s humour is involved in all these combinations, the theories are probably of more help to scholars of humour rather than those of Rabelais. There is little about humour emphasizing the important humanist message of R.'s works and, according to the bibliography, the authors have consulted nothing more up-to-date on R. than 1923.

One is entitled to a moment of millennial mockery at the title of the conference proceedings, *Rabelais pour la XXIe siècle*, ed. M. Simonin, Geneva, Droz, 450 pp., but the table of contents is studded with the famous names of Renaissance scholarship. J. C. Margolin, 'Rire avec Erasme, à l'ombre de Rabelais' (9–30) brings up such questions as 'Jésus, a-t-il ri?''and the subject is considered further in D. Ménager, 'Rabelais et le "propre de l'homme"' (31–40). Three articles examine the Abbé de Thélème and its architecture, physically, and metaphorically: M. Huchon, 'Thélème et l'art sténographique' (149–60), D. Desrosiers-Bonin, 'L'Abbé de Thélème et le temple des rhétoriqueurs' (241–48), and J. Guillaume, 'Le "Manoir des Thélèmites": rêve et réalités' (249–64). Other contributors are F. Rigolot, M. L. Kuntz, B. Pinchard, T. Dagron, P. J. Smith, P. Desan, G. Demerson, M. Majorano, G. Mathieu-Castellani, P. Maréchaux, F. Goyet, B. Braunrot, G. M. Masters, G. Defaux, E. M. Duval, J. Balsamo, J.-C. Sournia, R. Cooper, B. Roy, M. Jeanneret, L. D. Kritzman, R. C. La Charité, M. De Grève, H. Baudry, N. Dauvois, and M. Tetel.

Thierry Pech, *Rabelais, fais ce que tu voudras*, Michalon, 119 pp., is part of a collection which considers the role of law in classical and contemporary writing. P. reminds us that R. was, for his contemporaries, a 'civiliste distingué', that R. took issue with the legal problems of the time and that *Pantagruel* was composed mainly for a public from the liberal professions. The frontispiece of the first edition shows a book of law.

M. Harp discusses 'Panurge's thirst as metaphor in the works of François Rabelais', *RoN* 38:179–89. She thinks that we identify with Panurge because he is an ordinary man searching for certainty in an uncertain world, and that his search is exemplified by thirst, which must be quenched not only by wine but by wisdom. Reading is therefore seen as a drink which, if swallowed, will lead to a better life. By reading Panurge's story, the reader will end as did Panurge, sated and wise. A. P. Durand, in 'Le-rire-est-le-propre-de-l'homme: the text of Rabelais' works viewed as Menippean satire', *ib.*, 303–10, discusses the history of satire and decides that R's intellectual satire indeed fits in with Relihan's definition of *satire ménippée*. The authority of D.'s work is perhaps diminished by his failure to mention the basic book dealing with this problem, Dorothy Coleman, *Rabelais: A Critical Study in Prose Fiction* (1971).

J. Berchtold, in 'Le Songe d'Epistemon — L'enfer comique des héros humiliés dans le Pantagruel', *Fest. Geith*, 191–205, compares R's enfer with that of Erasmus and Lucien de Samostrate and discusses the characters confined therein. For instance, Ulysses, Achilles, Agamemnon and Helen were already featured in Homer; and Hector, Paris, Dido and Aeneas were in Virgil.

Anne Lake Prescott, *Imagining Rabelais in Renaissance England*, Yale U.P., xviii + 257 pp., considers 'how early modern English writers read, cited, judged, enjoyed, reviled, imagined, and appropriated François Rabelais — or, often, the name "Rabelais"' before Thomas Urquhart's 1653 translation. This fascinating account shows R.'s reputation across the channel in many guises, including John Eliot's *Ortho-epia Gallica* (1593) somewhat altered as in the descriptions of Thélème applied to Philip II's Escorial and Webster's *The White Devil* (1612). R. seems to have been viewed as an authorial 'pick-and-mix' and used and abused as a source of humour and even madness, often with little reference to the writer and his works.

In 'The ethic of timing and the origin of the novel', *Symposium*, 52: 155–64, E. MacPhail analyses the change of tenses and moods (e.g. from subjunctive to indicative) in Rabelais and Cervantes as fantasy slowly becomes fact in the mind of the fantasist. Psychologists see the tendency to imagine that a wished-for event has already occurred as a characteristic of childishness. M. is perhaps illustrating the way in which this naiveté is conveyed by the authors.

4. RONSARD

Ronsard's popularity in the 20th c. rests principally on his love poems and one must welcome a pocket-sized reprint from 1970 of *Pierre de Ronsard, Sonnets pour Hélène*, ed. Malcolm Smith, Geneva, Droz, 240 pp. In a new postface, Daniel Ménager highlights some of the points of contention in the interpretation of and background to the sonnets. He feels that S.'s edition is still one of the most complete and precise.

The diminutive in R.'s French is not familiar but can be used for tragedy. Y. Loskoutoff's article '"Lycidas en Pierrot et Philis en Toinon": the use of the diminutive in the "Amours" of Ronsard', *RHLF*, 98: 195–213, examines the diminutive as a device that can be used in various ways, not at all rustic. 'Si le diminutif connut son apogée littéraire à l'époque de la Pléiade, l'engouement excessif auquel il donna lieu, on le sait, causa sa chute.' V. Denizot, 'Les Devises en miroir: de la "folie" de l'âme au style éperdu dans *Les Amours* de 1552', *NRSS*, 16: 267–82, has examined the inscriptions under the portraits of Ronsard and Cassandra in the 1552 edition of *Amours* and claims that, whereas R.'s would encourage a poetic style 'fou et éperdu', the sub-text for Cassandra's is envy. She concludes that R.'s 'projet poétique' can be interpreted under these preliminary headings. D. moves on to comment on the portrayal of Petrarch's Laura, Scève's Délie, and Du Bellay's Olive. So the creation of woman takes on different forms: 'Démonstration de la puissance des dieux chez Pétrarche, effet de leur imagination chez Scève, concession libérale de leur part chez du Bellay, [. . .] chez Ronsard [. . .] elle est réellement un cadeux des dieux [. . .]'.

M. Bull, 'Ronsard's Hymne de l'automne and Nonno's Dionysi-aca', *FSB*, 67: 13–14, claims that the meeting of Bacchus and Autumn in R.'s poem is modelled on Bacchus' encounter with the deserted Ariadne. He can find no classical source for the whole of the poem but notes that R. in 1552 is the first French poet to name a volume of poems in French 'Amours'. He surmises that this is because the name recalls Ovid's 'Amores' with their erotic connotations, permissible in Latin, but which did not fit in with the Petrarchan inspiration in that there are parallels with episodes in Nonnon's 5th-c. Greek epic, *Dionysica*.

Y. Bellenger, 'Les Amours de Ronsard, 1552', *BHR*, 60:719–23, suggests three reasons for using the title, to do with linking Petrarch and Ovid, and points out how few 16th-c. poets use 'Amours' alone as a title, preferring rather to link it to a name. Yvonne Bellenger, *Lisez la Cassandre de Ronsard: Etude sur Les Amours (1553)*, Champion, 1997, 184 pp., is a reading of the *Poems for Cassandra* in the light of modern critical opinion, which looks at the extraordinary variety, force and musicality of these sonnets and emphasizes the originality of the young Ronsard vis-à-vis Petrarch and the French and Italian imitators of the *Canzoniere*. B. quotes Etienne Pasquier's advice from *Recherches de la France*: 'Lisez la Cassandre de Ronsard, vous y trouverez cent sonnets qui prennent leur vol jusques au ciel, vous laissant à part les [. . .] Amours de Marie et d'Hélène. Car en ses premières, il voulut contenter son esprit, et aux secondes et troisièmes vacquer seulement au contentement des sieurs de la cour.'

Ygaunin, *Pindare*, III, is third of a series on the influence of Pindar. Following Marot's 'badinage' as the Pléiade poets chose to see it, Ronsard presented the King, the Queen, the nobles and the poets with solemn praises. He had confidence in the immortality of his erudite poetry which, like that of Pindar, associated myth and reality in rich and harmonious language and metre. Y. wonders whether one can refer to 'Pindarism' in the same way as 'Petrarquism', that is to refer to poets who have common themes, images, and metrical forms, and share a concept of love. Thus their poetry becomes an intellectual and technical exercise as much as an expression of real feeling. F. Rouget, 'Ronsard palimpseste', *RoN*, 39:25–33, reads a political sub-text in R.'s odes to the royal family (1550–55). He suggests that, through the poet's irony, these apparent praises can be read as a subversive picture of relationships at the royal court. For instance, from 1555, when Diane de Poitiers becomes an influential figure at court, R. flatters her but, after her disgrace in 1566, he removes from his works the poems that he dedicated to her.

E. Ahmed, '"Quel genre de querelle?"', Pierre de Ronsard et Janne', *ib.*, 38:255–61, argues that, in 'A Janne impitoiable', R. tries to redefine the tradition of love for the second half of the century. A. concludes, unsurprisingly, that R. was a man of his time and was more homophobic and misogynistic than would be considered correct today.

Roberto E. Camo, *Ronsard's Contentious Sisters — the Paragone between Poetry and Painting in the Works of Pierre de Ronsard*, Chapel Hill, North

Carolina U.P., 277 pp., describes how R.'s poems on paintings 'have
provided insights into his own poetic genius and the principles of the
Pléiade school of poetry [. . .]. Throughout these extraordinary
verses, R. directly engages prevailing conceptions of human knowledge and metaphysical ontology, beauty and artistic affectivity.' C.'s
theme is that R.'s pronouncements on the paragone between poetry
and painting are more complex and significant than previous
scholarship has revealed.

5. Du Bellay

The cash problems afflicting academics in our own time are reflected
by V. A. Brown, 'Language as power in the exchange of commodities;
the poet as merchant in "La Deffence et illustration de la langue
francoyse"', *SFr*, 124:9–25. Du Bellay's attempts to validate his new
poetic activity are closely aligned to attempts to get patronage. He
uses praise, hyperbole, and promise of immortality as commodities in
exchange for financial support. While he bemoans the wretched state
of the French language, he also grumbles about the conditions under
which the poet has to operate. Du B. advanced a new concept of
poetry to try to establish the poet as a source of authorized truth and
at the same time sought sponsorship. A poet should not have to
appeal to the king; the king should implore the poet to immortalize
him (see also *Montaigne's Career*, p. 99).

E. Buron, 'Praise and consolation — enunciative fiction in the
"Regrets" of Joachim Du Bellay', *BHR*, 60:323–348, seeks to view
Du B.'s *Regrets* as an artificial journey, whilst keeping the fiction that
the author wished the work to be seen as sincerely meant nostalgia.
C. Skenazi, 'Le Poète et le roi dans "Les Antiquitez de Rome" et "Le
Songe" de Du Bellay', *ib.*, 41–55, suggests that the *Antiquitez* is linked
with military events and negotiations which preceded the treaty of
Cateau-Cambrésis of 1559, a year before Du B.'s book was published.
She seeks a historical perspective on the structure as well as on the
'genre' of *Antiquitez de Rome* and *Le Songe*. R. G. Czapla, *'The subject
and form of post-classical poems to Rome (Hildebert von Lavardin,
Joachim du Bellay, Andreas Gryphius) [. . .]', *Daphne*, 27:141–83,
shows the influence of Du B.'s work on the 17th-c. poet and dramatist,
Andreas Gryphius (1616–64).

6. Marot

From the base of a wide variety of translations of M.'s poem 'A une
Damoyselle malade', D. R. Hofstadter, *Le Ton beau de Marot*, NY,
Basic, xxiv + 632, has evolved a book on translation and many other

things such as computers and love of language, loosely based around Clément Marot's poem. This is a subjective book — H. is a self-confessed grown-up Holden Caulfield — and academics are not accustomed either to the bouncy tone or the breadth of vision and subject. However, lovers of poetry, language and culture will revel in this work, whose index includes both 'Anglo-Saxon' and 'rubber baby-buggy bumpers'. Unsurprisingly, H.'s book attracts detailed criticism from professional poetry critics. S. Burt, 'Blimey, M'sieur, c'est-un-peu-dodgy', *PRev*, 87, 1997 : 16–18, in an article that gets the award for Title of the Year, comments: 'Hofstadter on computers and word games should charm most non-specialist readers (and charmed me) [. . .] But when the Ton Beau turned to the arts I missed not only some sign that Hofstadter enjoys any difficult poetry in English, but some indication that he cared what the writers of the past have to say about translating poetry or about reading it.'

Benôit de Cornulier, 'Petite métrique de chambre. Sur une lettre de Clément Marot à une demoiselle', *SFr*, 125 : 288–94, has taken the poem which figures so largely in Hofstadter and argues for an 'enchaînement rétrograde' in its reading as: 'Ma mignonne// Je vous donne/ Le bon jour// Le sejour/ C'est prison : // Guerison/ Recouvrez// Puis ouvrez/ Vostre porte,// Et qu'on sorte/ Vistement// Car Clement/ Le vous mande.'

D. J. Shaw, 'Clément Marot's Humanist contacts in Ferrara', *FS*, 52 : 279–90, provides further evidence for the intellectual rehabilitation of M. by showing 'the extent to which a vernacular poet who was not himself a university man [. . .] could be accepted into the circles of those at or close to the centre of contemporary humanist culture.' S. quotes letters by Auerbach, Gois, Sinapius, Calvin and others mentioning Marot and praising his intellectual as well as his poetic qualities. This is of special relevance to studies of his Psalm translations. M.'s religious poetry and his poetic translation of the Psalms — describing it as a paraphrase is pandering to Du Bellay's hostile comments in the *Deffence* — is examined by L. K. Donaldson-Evans, 'Marot and the religious poetry of the late sixteenth century in France', *AJFS*, 35 : 129–40. In the light of his influence on Ronsard and the religious poetry of the late 16th c., the later poets' general condemnation of M. must be ascribed to jealousy. The rehabilitation of Marot's religious poetry is continued with D. Hüe's consideration of MS. BNF, f. fr. 2205 containing a rondeau and a chant royale, both signed 'Marot'. In attributing these to Jean or Clément, H. makes the point that Clément's poetry owes much to that of his father and that his religious poetry, in particular, was encouraged by participation with Jean in the Puy de Rouen, thus continuing the medieval tradition and showing how blurred was the line between medieval and early Renaissance poetry. Other interpretations are nonetheless possible. Marot might have been following archaic styles out of piety or because of the wishes of his patron.

F. Lestringant, *Clément Marot de l'adolescence à l'enfer*, Padua, Unipress, 123 pp., wants the reader to share his pleasure at reading M. and tries at the same time to situate the poet in the history of French culture. He covers M.'s lyric poetry but also his Psalm translation and tries to link the attitudes of Calvin and M. concerning this work. Of more interest is the remainder of this chapter dealing with the influence of the Psalms in the New World and on the explorers such as Léry. It seems to fit with the changes described by Jeanneret in *Perpetuum Mobile* (p. 88).

7. MARGUERITE DE NAVARRE

The long-awaited second volume of the new critical edition of Marguerite de Navarre, **Heptaméron*, ed. Renja Salminen, Helsinki, Suomalainen Tiedeakatemia, 1997, 317 pp., has appeared with commentary. It is based on the text of BNF. fr. 2155. S. explains the generation and variants of the work and describes the three successive versions of the *Heptaméron*.

C. Thysell, 'Gendered virtue, vernacular theology, and the nature of authority in the *Heptaméron*', *SCJ*, 29:39–53, considers Marguerite de Navarre's *Heptaméron* as a possible reply to Calvin's letter to the Queen referring to the 'spiritual libertines' in her employ. T. argues that the story's 'attention not only to the discernment of virtue but also to a new locus of authority, which relies upon neither conscience nor gender suggests that [. . .] M. de N. was concerned with presenting or working out her position on themes similar to those in Calvin's treatise.' T. sees parallels with Marguerite de Porete and the late medieval Beguine movement.

The question of vengeance is ever present in the Heptameron, and I. Morrison, 'La Vengeance dans l'*Heptaméron*', *BHR*, 60:57–68, points out that, at the time, private vengeance could be seen as a form of justice. For the *nobles d'épée*, vengeance is linked with war and with protecting their honour, but could also be linked with rebuttal in love. However, women can also avenge themselves, for 'Souvent les femmes de grant cueur sont plustost vaincues de l'ire de la vengeance que de la douleur de l'amour'. In the Bible, the question arises as to whether God can make use of man's vengeance even if it is criminal while, on the other hand, the vengeance is criminal even if its purpose is divine. M. concludes that M. de N.'s discretion on the subject comes more from tact than prudence, in an attempt to link Christianity and realism.

W. Kemp and D. Desrosiers-Bonin write about 'Marie d'Ennet-
ières et la petite grammaire hébraïque de sa fille d'après la dédicace
de l'epistre à Marguerite de Navarre 1539', *BHR*, 60:117–34. This
article is instructive on two counts: firstly because it shows women's
desire for learning in the first half of the 16th c., even to the extent of
their knowing Hebrew and teaching it to their children, and second
that the Hebrew language had attained a certain popularity if gentile
children were using simplified Hebrew grammars. It is also further
proof of the close links between these women; their circle even
included M. de N.

8. Agrippa d'Aubigné

How many readers of Agrippa d'Aubigné, 'qui souffre d'une réputa-
tion douteuse d'auteur calviniste, sectaire et fanatique, persécuté,
condamné à mort et qui fut contraint à l'exil', realise that he was the
grandfather of Françoise d'Aubigné, Madame de Maintenon, the
mistress of Louis XIV? Madeleine Lazard, *Agrippa d'Aubigné*, Fayard,
567 pp., feels that d'A. has come back into fashion and that his life is
so intimately involved with his work that the one illuminates the
other. In the *Tragiques*, the remorse of the soldier who inflicts pain and
death in the cause of religion is mingled with the anguish of the
Calvinist, one of God's elect, but nonetheless a sinner facing
damnation and having to confess his sins. L. presents d'A. at the court
of Henri III and Henri IV but persecuted by Louis XIII against the
background of the wars of religion. 'En apportant sur les guerres
civiles le triple témoignage d'un technicien, d'un témoin et d'un
partisan passionné, son ouvrage s'avère particulièrement précieux.'

At the end of his life, d'A. was afraid that much of his work which
remained in MS form might be lost or destroyed by his enemies. He
therefore entrusted the collection to a friend, Pastor Théodore
Tronchin, whose library, enriched by MSS of Rousseau and Voltaire,
is now in Geneva University and has been reviewed by J.-R. Fanlo,
'Sur quelques volumes manuscrits d'Agrippa d'Aubigné', *Adirel*,
11:107–20. Some were ready for publication, some were circulated
in MS form, and others were so extreme that, at the time, they never
saw the light of day. For example, there is a startling letter from d'A.
to the Doge of Venice proposing an alliance with the Protestants. d'A.
did not keep the MSS of the various stages of his printed work, and
the MSS in which he scribbled his poetry are difficult to follow. Paper
was expensive and he would write in the blank spaces of previous
MSS or old letters. One item — T160, a family book — is bound and
so has kept its original structure. It contains not only d'A.'s writings
but also those of his children. F. points out the contrast between the

printed works, intended for public consumption, and this volume, intended for private and family use.

The Société des amis d'Agrippa d'Aubigné has produced *Actes du colloque: Le livre entre Loire et Garonne (1560–1630); Un outil de guerre, de paix et d'oubli* (Albineana, 9), Champion, 204 pp.

9. MINOR WRITERS

HUMANISTS

The Estienne family were famous as printers and humanists. Charles Estienne, *Paradoxes*, ed. Trevor Peach, Geneva, Droz, 335 pp., provides tongue-in-cheek paradoxes such as 'Pour l'estroitement logé', 'Pour l'infirmité du corps', and 'Il vaut mieux souvent pleurer que rire'. These are free paraphrases, published in 1553, of Ortensio Lando's *Paradossi* (1543) and were extremely popular at the time. In his introduction, P. attempts a self-confessed rudimentary typology of the paradoxes into those with a profound moral or existential content, such as exile, and others that are merely superficial. The book is dedicated to C. A. Mayer, pioneer of Marot studies and expert on Lucian, who died in May 1998.

An exhibition of 'Cartes et Figures de la Terre' in 1980 led to the book Chantal Liaroutzos, *Le Pays et la memoire: pratique et représentations de l'espace français chez Gilles Corrozet et Charles Estienne*, Champion, 360 pp. L. writes of a 'poétique de l'espace', which is made up of the 16th-c. maps, plans, and portolans (books of sailing directions) as well as the texts that explain the scientific facts. She continues, 'Une représentation didactique de l'espace suppose une vision du monde, partagée ou du moins partageable par l'auteur et le lecteur. Dans la mesure où cette vision est prise en charge par le texte en tant qu'objet de plaisir, il me semble que l'on est autorisé à parler d'une poétique.' Amongst the texts are the first French road guide, first historical guide to Paris and first agricultural manual. L. feels that these works of 'vulgarisation du savoir' are intended to instruct and please, and that together they invent an original relationship between what is given to see, to read or to do. L. provides an original insight into the scientific background, which is so important to the philosophy and literature of the 16th century.

Following her critical edition of Sponde's *Méditations sur les Pseaumes* (Champion, 1996), Sabine Lardon, *L'Ecriture de la méditation chez Jean de Sponde*, Champion, 314 pp., has analysed the *Méditations* in two parts. The first examines S.'s use of words under such headings as the legitimacy of the word, palimpsest on the Bible, and polyphony with one voice. The second concentrates on poetry and rhetoric, with the argumentative strategy and a meditation in poetic prose.

As part of the wider interest in religious writing in the 16th c.,
I. Backus, 'Renaissance attitudes to New Testament apocryphal
writings: Jacques Lefèvre d'Etaples and his epigones', *RQ,*
51:1169–98, explains the influence of L. d'E. and his translations of
the Bible on the generation of Clément Marot. She tells us more
about L. d'E.'s methods of work through his attitude to the New
Testament apocryphal writings. She concludes that 'to Lefèvre and
his contemporaries, the term *apocryphon* covered a multitude of
meanings, only one of which was "a Christian text of dubious origin,
not to be made generally available"'. Collections of such texts only
became possible in the 16th c. once the writing had acquired a fully
dubious status. The texts had to be definitively marginalized, if that is
not an oxymoron, before they could be collected and published.

POETS

Much research in recent years has been concerned with the
reassessment of minor writers and the discovery of early examples of
the trends that characterized Renaissance literature. With the
comparison of two MSS in the BN, R. Trachsler, 'Pierre Sala et le
"récit-cadre"', *Reinardus*, 11:185–203, is starting to rehabilitate
Pierre Sala from his position as an 'attardé' without originality to one
of the first exponents in French of the 'récit-cadre' of Boccacio, and
in any case earlier than Marguerite de Navarre's *Heptaméron*. The
'Prouesses et Hardiesses de plusieurs roys et empereurs' was dedicated
to François Ier with the intention of proving that the King, with his
exploits at the Battle of Marignon, was in the direct line of hero-kings
stretching from King David and Charlemagne. C. Lachet, 'Le
Chevalier au lion au XVIe siècle', *MA*, 104:545–49, has reviewed in
detail *Le Chevalier au lion de Pierre Sala*, ed. Pierre Servet, Champion,
1996, 272 pp., which he dates as 1522. Servet explains how Sala
rewrote the novel by Chrétien de Troyes, simplifying the narrative by
cutting the story of the two daughters of the Lord of the Noire Epine,
the fantastic adventure at the castle of Pesme Aventure and the
combat between Yvain and Gauvain. Sala adds to the role of the
narrator, centres the story on the love between Yvain and the lady of
Landuc and adds some bawdy episodes. The novel gains in gallantry
but loses in knightly and symbolic adventures. Lachet lists corrections
to Servet's text, which he otherwise admires, and comments on Sala's
poetic technique.

In the person of Pierre d'Anché, not even mentioned in the new
edition of the *Dictionnaire des lettres françaises 1992*, there is another poet
ripe for rehabilitation. J. C. Mühlethaler, 'Pierre d'Anché', *Reinardus*,
11:131–48, shows how his *rondeaux* illustrate the problems of moving

from the aesthetics of the Middle Ages to those of the Renaissance. The poem can be read on several levels, including the erotic, as is shown by a comparison with poets such as Charles d'Orléans and Jean II de Bourbon.

Louise Labé has become a popular subject for research in recent years possibly as part of a feminist agenda, but her prominence at the time, along with that of Marguerite de Navarre, implies that the barriers to women could be overcome. F. Rigolot, 'Louise Labé and the "Climat Lyonnois"', *FR*, 71:405–13, asks how the daughter and wife of ropemakers could reach prominence in literary circles and be authorized to publish a 'feminist manifesto' and a collection of love poems. R. explains her surmounting the sex barrier in terms of the cultural freedom among Lyons intellectuals distant from the Sorbonne. The Lyons poets were different and perceived themselves as separate from the Pléiade. Meanwhile, her surmounting of the class barrier is less convincingly explained.

Almangue Papillon was a *valet de chambre* to François Ier and a friend of Marot; his work is discussed in C. Hampton, *'François Ier as the chaste lover: Almangue Papillon's "nouvel amour"'*, *MLR*, 93:642–58.

C. Alduy, 'Les "erreurs" de la versification dans *Délie* de Maurice Scève', *NRSS*, 16:249–66, has taken line 6 of *Délie*, with its assurance that his beloved can read in the poem 'mainte erreur, mesme en si durs epygrammes' as an invitation to a metatextual reading, which examines a number of disturbing phenomena within the text. A. considers these under various headings, notably *les dizains atypiques, la fragmentation du vers, le dizain retaillé* and *concurrence des structures formelles* with, as an appendix, *le découpage strophique des dizains*. In a complex argument, A. challenges some of F. Rigolot's views (1982).

There is currently growing interest in Renaissance triumphs and magnificences and a series edited by Margaret McGowan describes many of them. Maurice Scève, *The Entry of Henri II into Lyon, September 1548*, ed. Richard Cooper, Arizona, Tempe, 1997, 326 pp., is the fifth volume in the series, and a facsimile of the 1549 Guillaume Rouillé publication with woodcuts by Bernard Salomon. It includes other eyewitness accounts and background information, hitherto unpublished, on the problems of the City Fathers in organizing such an event, when they were uncertain of the date of arrival or length of stay of the King and his entourage. C. comments that Scève's account is coloured by what he would have liked to have happened rather than what actually happened and that, for example, a gladiatorial combat did not in fact take place. On a related theme is G. Poirier, *'Le Retour de Pologne d'Henri III: images alexandrines du roi au Bucentaure'*, *RAR*, 21.1, 1997:41–56.

R. D. Cottrell focuses on the topical subject of peace-making in 'Allegories of desire in Jean Lemaire's "Concorde des deux langages"', *FrF*, 23:261–300. This is superficially an attempt to achieve a 'cease-fire' in the linguistic and cultural hostilities between France and Italy. Because of L.'s prior assumption of the superiority of French — he was the last of the *rhétoriqueurs* — the text cannot reduce hostility. Indeed, it sheds doubt on the whole idea of concord by casting it in the role of 'apparence' 'vifves ymages' and the imaginary. It allegorizes not concord but the impossibility of concord. L. himself was fascinated by architecture and was involved in the erection of the church of Brou. David Cowling, *Building the Text: Architecture as Metaphor in Late Medieval and Early Modern France*, Oxford, Clarendon, 245 pp., explores the vogue for allegorical buildings at that time and claims it to have been a tool of persuasion as well as a fashion. L. was able to combine panegyric of his patrons with advertisement of his own talents and provided an ideology for Ronsard and the Pléiade when the fashion for architectural allegory changed.

André Berry, *L'oeuvre de Pey de Garros: Poète Gascon du XVIe siècle*, ed. Philippe Gardy and Guy Latry, Bordeaux U.P., 1997, 264 pp., describes the Gascon poet, 1525/30–1583, who rose to be *avocat général* and knew Marguerite de Navarre. He wrote 58 *Psaumes gascons*, some modelled on the translations by Marot and de Bèze, but also *Poesias gasconas — Eglogues, vers héroïques and epîtres*. This important Renaissance Gascon figure was much involved in the battles of his century and wrote the first piece of what was to be called modern Occitan literature.

Flaminio de Birague, *Les Premières œuvres poétiques*, ed. Roland Guillot and Michel Clément, Geneva, Droz, clxxxix + 434 pp., is a critical edition of the works of a minor French Renaissance poet, who both suffered and benefited from being the second cousin of the frightening Chancellor of Charles IX and Henry III. Between the end of 1581 and the beginning of 1585, there were three editions of these poems. The editors believe that the changes shed light not only on the author but also on aesthetic and sociological aspects of poetry under the Valois kings. Petrarchan love had an influence as well as 'la sémiotique sociale de la poésie valoisienne à la recherche d'un équilibre entre ordre et variété que l'édition de 1585 semble sinon atteindre, du moins approcher.'

The English King Henry VII employed a salaried poet, Bernard André, as his *praeco virtutis*. D. R. Carlson, 'The writings of Bernard André', *RenS*, 12:229–50, has assembled A.'s works and 18 pages of the article are devoted to this list. His works are mainly in Latin, with some in French and none in English. That the King should employ a poet who wrote only in 'foreign' languages indicates the low status of English at the start of the 16th century.

G. Banderier, 'Observations sur le texte de la Sepmaine', *BHR*, 60:725–37, has rediscovered an edition of Du Bartas' *La Sepmaine* (a description of the first week of Creation). Printed in Nîmes in 1581, it figured in M. Louis Desgrave's *Répertoire bibliographique des livres imprimés en France au seizième siècle. Bibliotheca Bibliographica Aureliana*, (1976), but was unknown to Du Bartas specialists and discovered independently. After careful examination, B. finds small differences between the editions of B. Jaquy in Nîmes (Bibliothèque Municipal, 32633) and in Besançon (Bibliothèque Municipal, 203.780) which he cannot explain. He lists the five editions that Y. Bellenger used for collating the text of her edition: G78 Michel Gadoulleau, Paris, 1578; F78 Jean Fevrier, Paris, 1578; C81 Jacques Chouet, Geneva, 1581 (texte de base); A84 L'Angelier, Paris, 1584; and Cot 84 D. Cotinet, Paris, 1581. B. suggests that in future J81 Bastien Jaquy, Nîmes, 1581, should also be used and gives a table of variants between C81 and J81.

Philibert Bugnyon, *Les Erotasmes de Phidie et Gelasine (1557)*, ed. Gabriel-A. Pérouse and M.-Odile Sauvajon, Geneva, Droz, xlii + 270 pp., is a critical edition of the work of a Mâconnais lawyer working in Lyons, who wanted to be a poet. In his youth, B. was influenced by Marot and later Ronsard, but he eventually became a devotee of Scève, and these poems carry echoes of *La Délie*.

NOVELISTS AND PLAYWRIGHTS

Jean de La Taille was an early author of tragedies. Four essays on his best-known work, *Saül le Furieux* and its sequel *La Famine, ou les Gabaonites* appear in *Saül le Furieux, Jean de La Taille*, Ellipses, 108 pp., contributed by M. H. Garelli-François, J.-F. Chevalier, J.-Y. Boriaud and C. Ferradou. In *Par ta colère, nous sommes consumés: Jean de la Taille, auteur tragique*, Orléans, Paradigme, 238 pp., M. Fragonard has gathered essays by herself, F. Charpentier, C. Z. de Nolva, O. Millet, A. Michel, R. Lebègue, M. Soulié, P.-L. Vaillancourt, P. Ricoeur, and F. Lestringant, to shed light on the rebirth of tragedy among the passions and politics of the wars of religion.

Maurice Daumas, *Le Système amoureux de Brantôme*, l'Harmattan, 211 pp., deals with the work of Pierre de Bourdeille, Seigneur de Brantôme. D. considers *Les Dames galantes* both as a literary work and a historic document illuminating military and court life, and the manners of the end of the 16th century.

Théodose Valentinian, *L'amant resuscité de la mort d'amour (1558)*, ed. Véronique Duché, Geneva, Droz, 424 pp., is a critical edition.

D. claims V. to be the pen name of Nicolas Denisot, who also took the nom de plume of Conte d'Alsinois, apparently because he was involved on the wrong side of the famous Marot/Sagon quarrel and had his Latin verse roundly condemned. The novel failed at the time of its original publication because the text is unreadable and the plot difficult to follow, but perhaps its lack of success was also due to its moral message of spirituality rather than sensuality.

Nothing is known about the author of *La Mariane du Filomène (1596)*, ed. Nicole Cazauran and Isabelle Pantin, Klincksieck, 194 pp., which perhaps explains its neglect heretofore. It has many of the elements expected from the 16th c. — a varied style with the charm of the pastoral added to a tragic story and involving fantastic visions. It is written in the first person.

THE SEVENTEENTH CENTURY

By Elfrieda Dubois, *sometime Reader in French,
University of Newcastle upon Tyne,* and J. P. Short, *formerly Senior Lecturer in French
at the University of Sheffield*

1. General

Critique, 615–16, 'Les classiques décoiffés', contains reprints and translations. 'La Renaissance entre tragédie et comédie': F. Yates, 'Les académies en France au XVIe siècle' (420–34); T. Cave, 'Cornucopia (1979/1997)'; C. Jouhaud, 'Les rencontres du Nouveau Monde' (1996/97)' (435–46); 'Une Renaissance en mouvement': M. Jeanneret, 'Perpetuum mobile. Métamorphoses des corps et des œuvres de Vinci à Montaigne' (447–62), attempts to see the late Renaissance in terms of a new critical sensibility; J. Céard, 'Nouveautés sur Montaigne' (456–63), discusses C. Blum's *Corpus des œuvres de Montaigne*, CD-ROM, multilingual edition, and Montaigne, *Essais I*, ed. A. Tournon; 'Manger Dieu': F. Lestringant, 'Une sainte horreur ou le voyage en Eucharistie XVI–XVIIe siecle (1996)' (464–77), analyses the controversial religious issues concerning the Eucharist; 'De l'homme accompli à l'homme inachevé': C. Ossola, 'Du courtisan à l'homme de la rue' (478–87), discussed as a study of *courtoisie*; 'La Forme humaine et ses ombres' (488–500) reviewing Agnès Minazzoli, *'L'Homme sans image. Une anthropoligie négative*, 2 vols, Darmon, 1996, emphasizes the importance of scepticism; 'Le théâtre classique ou les Règles du plaisir': J. Lichtenstein, 'Dix leçons sur le théâtre classique français (1996)' (501–10), is reviewed as a renewal in classical doctrine studies; 'Un imaginaire classique': Thomas Pavel, 'L'Art de l'éloignement. Essai sur l'imagination classique (1996)' (511–16), discusses the various forms of imagination; 'Figures de l'épicurisme à l'âge classique': Jean-Claude Darmon, 'Philosophie épicurienne et littérature au dix-septième siècle (1996)' (517–25), stresses the central role of Gassendi; 'Un Discours à pratique' (526–47) reviews Louis Marin, *Pascal et Port-Royal* (1997), a collection of articles published 1976–93; 'Le Papillon et le Lion' (543–57), a review of Marc Fumaroli, *Le Poète et le Roi* (1997), discusses La Fontaine's political role; 'Des Mémoires succincts au *Mémoires* tout court' (558–73), reviewing Saint-Simon, *Traités politiques et autres écrits*, ed. Yves Coirault (1996) points to 'une vie d'écriture' and suggestions of reform; 'Les Ruines de Port-Royal ou la Résistance transfigurée': 'Le jansénisme au XVIIIe siècle' (574–90), on Catherine Maire, *De la cause de Dieu à la cause de la Nation* (1998), shows the political transformation of Jansenism.

LitC, 34, is dedicated to 'La périodisation de l'âge classique': J. Rohou, 'Plaidoyer pour une périodisation critique' (5–12), suggests including the 'coupure' 1650–60 in 1610–1715; A. Croix, 'L'historien et son nombril. Essai sur la périodisation au XVIIe siècle' (15–25), looks at aspects of mentalities, economics, and population, with a view to reconstructing time at 10-year intervals; D. Souiller, 'Périodes du XVIIe siècle français et périodes du XVIIe siècle européen' (27–46), compares political and cultural developments in various parts of Europe with French ones; H. Marlin and D. Ribod, 'Enfin vinrent Malherbe, Galilée, Descartes. Périodisation littéraire, périodisation culturelle: problèmes théoriques, problèmes histo-riques' (47–71), discusses the 'querelle des lettres', Balzac and Galileo, the position for and against Descartes; J.-P. Cavaillé, 'De la construc-tion des apparences au culte de la transparence. Simulation et dissimulation entre le XVIe et le XVIIIe siècle' (73–102), presents an historical approach to the metaphysical problem at different social levels, and contrasts *civilité* and *sincerité*; B. Chédozeau, 'Pour une périodisation des rapports entre littérature et religion au XVIIe siècle' (103–17), investigates the links between the two, close in the baroque age, the Augustinian distinction betwen the two cities, Bossuet's providentialism and the eventual laicization of religion; A. Viala, 'Institution littéraire, champ littéraire et périodisation: l'institution du siècle' (119–29), pleads for periods according to categories, e.g. *doctes, libertins, grotesques, galants* etc.; G. Molinié, 'Peut-on périodiser un XVIIe siècle stylistique et esthétique?' (131–38), considers the problem from the point of view of language; P. Pasquier, 'Les âges de Protée: la périodisation de la vie théâtrale' (139–60), considers the 'moments tournants', 1620, 1640–50 as transition, and 1660; A.-E. Spica, 'Emblématique et périodisation au XVIIe siècle' (191–201), analyses the use of various emblems and distinguishes periods accordingly with a high point at 1639–60; under 'Frontières', M.-M. Fragonard, 'Changements, ruptures et sentiment de rupture du XVIe au XVIIe siècle' (205–16), comments on the gradual changes between 1590 and 1620, arguing that the 16th c. came to an end with the death of Marguerite de Valois (1615); E. Bury, 'Frontières du classicisme' (217–35), suggests various criteria, lin-guistic and aesthetic, as well as significant dates, *Le Cid*, *L'Ecole des Femmes*, mundane literature of the mid-century, later the *Querelle*; J. Grimm, 'Quand s'arrête le siècle de Louis XIV?' (237–48), rejects the category 'siècle' in favour of a deconstruction of historical discourse; under 'Perspectives': A. Becq, 'Le XVIIe siècle au miroir du XVIIIe' (351–66), examines the divergent viewpoints; P. Force, 'L'ère libérale commence-t-elle au XVIIe siècle?' (267–78) points to the emergence of economic viewpoints in Locke and Mandeville;

D. Riou, 'Le XVIIe siècle et la question du sujet' (279–92), comments on the emerging subjectivity, in its modernity, pointing to La Rochefoucauld. D. Course, 'Parure et dévotion: les pierres précieuses du Père Le Moyne', *DSS*, 201:579–94, discusses the metaphorical rhetoric in sermons for female audiences, used by Jesuit preachers, stressing a 'dévotion honnête'; E. Méchoulan, D. Vaillancourt and M.-F. Wagner, 'L'Entrée dans Toulouse ou la ville théâtralisée', *ib.*, 613–37, outlines royal visits and describes Louis XIII's in 1621 in its elaborate details; M.-O. Bonard, 'Essai d'Iconographie au XVIIe siècle: le Pélican et le Coeur', *ib.*, 639–48, based on emblem books, explores the imagery in a religious post-tridentine context; G.-M. Leproux, 'La corporation des peintres et sculpteurs à Paris dans les premières années du XVIIe siècle', *ib.*, 649–68, deals with the first two decades and comments on the uneasy rivalry between the corporations; S. Uomini, 'Clio chez Calliope: eléments doctrinaux et critiques de l'historiographie romanesque française du premier dix-septième siècle', *ib.*, 669–79, examines pre-classical historiography in its relation to fiction with its aesthetic considerations; V. Grégoire, ' "Pensez-vous venir à bout de renverser le pays?": la pratique d'évangélisation en Nouvelle France d'après les *Relations* des jésuites', *ib.*, 681–707, examines religious and political aims, and the misunder-standings arising from the different mentalities of the French and the Amerindians; S. Ben Messaoud, 'Lettre de Boileau à Antoine Arnauld', *ib.*, 709–14, is a critical study of an unpublished copy; G. Dubouchet et al., 'Le Chapelle Bessé et Port-Royal d'après des documents inédits', *ib.*, 715–31, study from documents at the *Minutier*.

J.-P. Cavaillé, 'Galanterie et histoire de "l'antiquité moderne": Jean Chapelain, *De la lecture des vieux romans*, 1647', *DSS*, 200:387–415, starting from a reference to Lancelot, analyses Chapelain's generally neglected text; S. Houdard, 'Des fausses saints aux spirituelles à la mode: les signes suspects de la mystique', *ib.*, 417–32, follows the ambiguous history of largely ostentatious, false mysticism among women in the 16th and 17th c.; P. Zoberman, 'Epistolarité et intertextualité: Madame de Sévigné et l'écriture de la lettre', *ib.*, 433–52, reassesses the style of the letters in a context of quotations from conversations and readings; J.-P. Cléro, 'Pascal et la figure d'Archimède', *ib.*, 491–504, examines the status of Archimedes in the second half of the century, when Pascal's complex geometrical arguments and Leibniz's algebraic approach, have undermined it; R.-G. Guérin, 'Les horoscopes au XVIIe siècle', *ib.*, 505–13, examines the place of astrology within scientific developments.

CDs, 7.1, 1997, contains: K. A. Hoffmann, 'Palimpsests of know-ledge: feasts of words: Antoine Furetière's *Dictionnaire universel*' (47–59), comments on the convoluted origins of the texts quoted, and hybrid definitions, including chocolate and its varieties; J. F. Boltano, 'Le "Point fixe" judéo-chrétien dans les *Pensées de Pascal*' (61–70), looks at Pascal's perspective of Judaism in relation to Christianity, including chronology; A. Vizier, 'Pascal et l'herméneutique' (71–103), based on *Pensées* 274, 452, 502 (L), questions the usual apologetic purpose, and suggests a hermeneutic consideration involved, also pointing to Pascal's non-inimical attitude to Jews; R. Morel, 'Un défi à la sémiotique picturale moraliste et temporalité dans une gravure du XVIIe siècle' (105–20), discusses the Candale story, as pictured in a 17th-c. Dutch painting, together with its original account, a story transformed into a spatial unity in the Van de Venne picture; P.-J. Salazar, 'Temps prioritaire et champ historique chez Roger de Piles' (121–31), discusses his *Cours de peinture par principles*, allowing for both allegorical and historical paintings, as related to his time; F. Dumora-Mabille, 'Quand dire c'est voir: *Moyse sauvé* de Saint-Amant ou la scène de l'écriture' (133–48), comments on the poetic and visual writing, on the principle of 'ut pictura poesis'; P. Dostie, 'Du faste au dépouillement: deux manières de peindre Mme de Sévigne' (149–60), based on two descriptions in letters to Bussy, of the funeral of the Grand Condé and the marriage of the comte de Guiche to Marie-Christine de Noailles which took place at night, as a *cérémonie discrète*; A. Suozzo, '*Le Parasite Mormon* or the "heretical" novel' (161–68), attributes it to La Mothe le Vayer, but argues that several authors are involved, and that it is written in an unorthodox style, a literary heresy; J. Serroy, 'Des Histoires comiques au roman comique' (169–77), looks at Sorel's *Bibliothèque française*, chap. 9 on 'narration fabuleuse' the relation between fiction and reality, and links it to the *Roman comique*; M. Debaisieux, '*Première journée* de Théophile ou l'exorcisme de la tradition' (179–92), first published in *Fragments d'une histoire comique* (1632) interprets it as partly autobiographical and, together with other episodes, leads to an ambiguous conclusion; A. Wallis, 'Le *Roman comique*: récit spec(tac)ulaire' (193–203), points to the theatricality of the novel, both as 'theatrum mundi' and theatre within the theatre; A. M. Menke, 'The widow who would be Queen: the subversion of patriarchal monarchy in *Rodogune* and *Andromaque*' (205–14), discusses the two widows, in their freedom and their royal positions, from a feminist angle; C. Biet, 'La Veuve et l'ideal du mari absolu' (215–26), examines Célimène and Alceste in their contrasting positions; D. Kuizenga, ' "Fine veuve" ou "veuve d'une haute vertu"? Portraits de la veuve chez Mme de Villedieu' (227–39), comments on the variety of descriptions, the independent well-to-do widow, the virtuous, the coquette, including the *Mémoires de la vie de Henrietta Sylvie de Molière*, a widow; A. Wolfgang, 'La duplicité d'un roman par lettres: *Le Porte-feuille* de

Mme de Villedieu' (241–53), discusses the narrator in the letters and concludes that it is an intrigue in letter form, not a *roman à clefs*.

B. E. Schwarzbach, 'Remarques sur la date, la bibliographie et la réception des *Opinions des Anciens sur les Juifs*', *La Lettre Clandestine*, 6, 1997[1998]: 51–63, based on Basnage, *Histoire des Juifs* (1706–16), traces its further history. *EMF*, 3, 'Signs of the Early Modern 2: 17th century and Beyond' contains: C. Randall, 'Possessed personae in Early Modern France' (1–16), bridges the 16th and 17th c., and includes Du Bellay's *Les Regrets*, D'Aubigné's *Les Confessions du Sieur de Sancy*, and Malherbe as seeking to find his way as a poet; L. Daston, 'The cold light of facts and the facts of cold light: luminiscence and the transformation of the scientific fact' (17–44), comments on the centrality of scientific experiment, referring to Galileo, Descartes, Kepler, Boyle, and Bernoulli, and concludes on the change in the conception of factuality, in view of singular and regular phenomena; H. Melchy, 'Descartes's method: the writing of the subject' (45–68), discusses Heidegger's interpretation of Descartes and reaffirms the *Discours* as a founding document for modern philosophy; J.-P. Beaulieu and H. Fournier, 'Le Discours politique de Marie de Gournay sur la modernité d'une prise de parole' (69–79), discuss *Les Advis ou présens de la demoiselle de Gournay*, seeing in them a feminine approach; B. El-Beshti, 'Signifying texts and displaced contexts: orientalism and the ideological foundation of the Early Modern European state' (80–93), discusses Koran translations, in English, 1649, from the French of Sieur du Royer resident in Alexandria, which provided knowledge of the culture in the then still powerful Turkish Empire; J. O. Newman, 'Almost white, but not quite: "race", gender, and the disarticulation of the imperial subject in Lohenstein's *Cleopatra* (1680)' (94–120), discusses this German play and compares it to Benserade's *Cléopâtre*; S. Bryson, 'Rules and transgressions: *Imitatio naturale* and the Quarrel of the Ancients and Moderns' (121–48), analyses the viewpoint of both sides and their respective representatives; J. Dejean, 'The invention of a public for literature' (149–68), investigates the public's reaction to the literature of its time, on the basis of *Le Mercure galant* (1672–1710) with readers' letters, and also looks at the *Querelle*, when the French, at the beginning, thought like Bossuet and ended up thinking like Voltaire; *EMF*, 4, 'Utopia 16th and 17th centuries', includes: A. Stroup, 'French Utopian thought: the culture of criticism. A problematic legacy' (1–30), states that England invented Utopia and France outpublished it after 1650, accounting for utopian writings, based on the *Journal des savants*, in their subversive tendencies; T. J. Reiss, 'Utopia versus état du pouvoir; ou prétexte du discours politique de la modernité: Hobbes, lecteur de la Boétie? Preliminaires' (31–83), admits that there is no evidence of Hobbes having read La Boétie, and attempts a parallel study, with an emphasis on political issues; T. Meling, 'Diana's domain: the displaced center of feminine Utopia in Honoré d'Urfé's *L'Astrée*' (84–124), comments on place and time and recounts the different forms of the myth, including its form in the novel; for V. Kelly, 'The play of Utopia and Dystopia: mindscape and landscape in Descartes and Poussin' (125–64), Descartes wishing to reform ways of thinking, breaks with the usual world, and thus presents a utopia, while Poussin's Phocion landscape, related to France, working in Rome, looks at the centre from the margin, a speculative parallel; A. Stroup, 'Foigny's joke' (165–93), discusses utopian paradoxes, around Gabriel de Foigny's *La Terre* (1676), an imaginary journey — the joke concerns hermaphroditism, the story has a social–moral implication, of a subversive character; C. F. Martin, 'L'Utopie, le souverain et l'individu: le cas des Sévarambes' (194–214), claims that the *Histoire des Sévarambes*, by Denis Veiras, published in England in 1677–79, presenting an imaginary travelogue into different countries, is a disguised political novel, critical of Louis XIV's regime. *From the Royal to the Republican Body Incorporating the Political. Seventeenth- and Eighteenth-Century France*, ed. S. E. Melzer et al., University of California Press, 267 pp., contains: Introduction (1–10); J. Merrick, 'The body politic of French absolutism' (11–31), discusses rituals of the monarchy and rhetoric in resistance; A. Zanger, ' "Betwixt and between": Louis XIV's martial and marital bodies' (32–63), reprint of a 1997 article; M. Franks, 'The King, cross-dressed, power and force in royal ballets' (64–84), reprint from *DR*, 18.4, 1994; S. M. Clary, 'Unruly passions and courtly dances: technologies of the body in baroque music' (85–112), discusses baroque music and art in relation to the monarchy, referring to Lully and Marais; J. Roach, 'The Sun King and the Code Noir' (113–30), discusses the exploitation of slave labour in late 17th-c. France and the legal position of slaves. Roméo Arbour, *Les Femmes et les métiers du livre en France de 1600 à 1650*, Chicago, Garamond Press — Paris, Didier Érudition, 1997, viii + 314 pp., examines the professional, legal, and personal position of women 'éditeurs-imprimeurs', throughout France, with a *Répertoire des femmes éditrices*, as 'imprimeurs and marchandes'. Madeleine Bertaud, *Le XVIIe siècle Littérature Française* (Collection Phares), rev. edn, Nancy U.P., 203 pp., divides this 'manuel pour etudiants' into two parts, from Malherbe to Scudéry, and *le siècle de Louis XIV*, succinctly refers to the main fugures, and adds useful synoptic tables and dates, a most useful student guide. André Charrak, *Musique et Philosophie à l'âge classique*, PUF, 130 pp., covers the 17th and 18th c. and looks at Descartes's *Compendium musicae* and Rameau's writings, discusses the relation between mathematics and music, points to the physical basis of harmonies, and pursues the study into the 18th century, and the nature of musical pleasure. Kathryn A. Hoffmann, *Society of Pleasures: Interdisciplinary Readings in Pleasure and Power during the Reign of Louis XIV*, McMillan, 1997, xv + 240 pp., takes readings from a wide range, the known and the marginal; begins with the spectacles of power, centred on *Bajazet*, follows on with 'Pathways of Pleasure', centred on *Dom Juan* as Christian folklore, assesses the social place of the bourgeoisie, discusses social habits of feasting and fasting, including the rise of the fashionable chocolate, and ends on the decay of the body as 'disrobing the Court'. Claudine Poulouin, *Le Temps des Origines, L'Eden et le Déluge et 'les temps reculés' de Pascal à l'Encyclopédie*, Champion, 667 pp., I: *La Crise de l'universalisme et la Nouvelle représentation de l'Histoire Universelle*, looks at a new conception of history, secular and sacred, dating from the later 16th c., which spread both by publication and among the 'communauté savante'; II: *Retrouver l'unité de l'histoire*, looks at the 'temps reculés', critically, with references to Huet, Fontenelle, the relation between myth and history; III: *L'Histoire universelle et l'abîme des temps*, mainly covers the 18th c., dealing with chronology, different from that of the church, assesses some historians, Boulainvilliers, Mabillon and Montfaucon, and concludes on the changes between 1680 and 1725. Jean Rousset, *Dernier Regard sur le Baroque*, Les Essais, Corti, 187 pp., qualifies it as a minor autobiography of a past adventure, recalls the arts of the visual and of the word in dialogue, a 'dialogue romanesque', pursues the destruction of dialogue in *Le Rouge et le Noir* to Balzac, with his insistence on gesture, and ends on the voice of Charlus.

TL, 11, *Le Manuscrit littéraire: Son statut, son histoire du Moyen-Age à nos jours*, ed. Luc Fraisse, includes: G. Schrenck, 'Pierre de L'Estoile devant ses manuscrits: la fadaise et la sagesse' (95–105), comments on the important manuscripts, basis for the Journal, and which present an important document for many aspects of the time; J. Mesnard, 'L'Original des *Pensées* de Pascal avant et après Victor Cousin' (121–49), discusses and reprints Cousin's report on the manuscript in 1842–43, reviews the discovery of further manuscripts, after the 'Original des Pensées', and discusses Sainte-Beuve's lectures, indifferent to more recent discoveries; M. continues on the findings and publications from Brunschvicg to the most recent, and concludes on the importance of the manuscript as such and its composition; D. Van Der Cruysse, 'Le miroir brisé: le sort des correspondances de Madame Palatine' (151–63), looks at Madame's enormous correspondence of 60,000 letters in two languages, and discusses their partial publications, a large number of manuscripts being no longer extant; the 850 French letters available are a document of the period and reveal her personality; H. Carrier, 'De la "Vie du cardinal de

Rais" aux *Mémoires*, ou les singulières tribulations d'un grand texte' (165–82), attempts to trace the history of the *Mémoires*, composed 1675–77, to its first publication in 1717, discusses the gaps and mutilation of the manuscript, and its various interpretations, the itinerary of the original through a monastic library and then into public property, its inadequate handling by those who copied from the original, and concludes on the hazardous history of manuscripts in the 17th and 18th centuries; R. Duchêne, 'Quelques manuscrits de lettres du XVIIe siècle: les avatars de textes immuables' (183–93), comments on 17th-c. letter writing, the first draft, a copy and the letter itself to be read and circulated, the fate of letters at the hand of the recipients; D. discusses Bussy-Rabutin's use of letters in his writing, including his cousin's letters, which he handled freely: letters were copied and often falsified, unless an autograph copy became available. F. Briot, 'L'Empire des cygnes (poétique de travestissement sexuel au XVIIe siècle)', *RSH*, 252–54:37–48, discusses the subject in Furetière, in *L'Astrée*, as a 'suspense équivoque', leading, in Choisy and others, to a 'poétique de l'oubli'.

P. Yarrow, 'Henriette d'Angleterre', *SCFS*, 20:95–107, outlines Henriette's life from a variety of contemporary sources, and comments on her talents and her royal standing. A. E. Zanger, 'Perspectives on 1660s monumentalities, print-culture and the marriage of Louis XIV', *ib.*, 109–23, from pamphlets of the period, follows contemporary events, in detail, and notes that the King's image was then under construction. Delphine Denis, *"De l'air galant" et autres Conversations (1653–1684): Pour une étude de l'archive galante*, Champion, 380 pp., places the text in Madeleine de Scudéry's interests, the *samedis* with their literary conversation, and looks at style and language, and the text of *L'air galant* from *Artamène*, 1653 (1684). Individual chapters are devoted to: *De la Conversation* (from *Histoire de Sapho*), with its setting in antiquity, on the modern idea of *honnêteté*; *De parler trop ou trop peu, Et comment il faut parler* (from *Clélie*, 1658), the need for discernment and following usage; *De la Raillerie* from *Artamène*; *De la Politesse*, from *Conversations nouvelles sur divers sujets* (1684), and passages from *Artamène*, on the subject of 'politesse' in relation to 'galanterie'; *De la manière d'écrire les lettres*, from *Clélie* (1655), on modern usage, practised by 'honnêtes gens', Pugot de la Serre, *Le Secrétaire à la mode* (1640), models for 'billets doux'; *De la manière d'inventer une fable* from *Clélie* (1658/80), defending fiction and the novel as a form of myth; *Le Songe d'Hésiode*, from *Clélie* (1658), interprets it as literary history for a mundane public; *De la poésie française jusqu'à Henri [IV]*, from *Conversations nouvelles* (1684), concerns 'les Modernes'.

Joan Dejean, *Ancients against Moderns. Culture Wars and the Making of a Fin de Siècle*, Chicago U.P., 1997, xvii + 216 pp., using the American notion of culture wars, comments on the 'fin de siècle' from 1690 as an 'affair' of modernity. D. looks at the position of the public and the transformation of mentalities, with a section on the human heart; she investigates the expression of emotions, in novels and in piety, and analyses culture and civilisation as binary elements. *Nature et culture à l'âge classique (Actes du congrès: Idées, thèmes et formes 1580–1789)*, ed. Christian Delmas and Françoise Gevrey, Toulouse–Le Mirail U.P., 1997, 128 pp., has articles relevant to the 17th c.: B. Périgot, 'Mien et tien: l'adage de la communauté des biens de Platon à Rousseau' (29–45), refers to Bossuet, *Discours de l'Histoire universelle*; F. Berlan, 'Langues naturelles et naturelle des langues chez les théoriciens français d'Henri Estienne à Riverol' (47–60), discusses Malherbe, Vaugelas and particularly Bouhours and the notions of natural and authentic in expression; A. Viala, 'Le naturel galant' (61–76), investigates the literary expressions of 'galanterie' in relation to human nature; C. Delmas, 'Le mythe dans le théâtre classique entre nature et culture' (77–85), looks at the treatment of myths in *Bérénice*, *Dom Juan*, and their theatrical transformation; D. Lopez, 'Entre nature et culture la poésie en question au XVIIe siècle' (87–101), looks at the nature of inspiration, natural genius and a more rationalized poetry than that of the 16th c.; J.-Ph. Grosperrin, 'Barbarie et voix de la nature dans les tragédies de Crébillon (1700–1720)' (103–28), discusses the rhetoric of barbarity and its language. Alain Niderst, *Les Français vus par eux-mêmes: Le Siècle de Louis XIV. Anthologie des mémorialistes du siècle de Louis XIV*, Laffont, xvii + 910 pp., covers the years of the reign, private life, 'la vie au jour le jour', events, intellectual and cultural history; 'le Monde' is concerned with social classes and institutions, 'Les Grandes Figures' include members of the royal family, royal mistresses, ministers and clergy; a final chapter 'Les Grands Evénements', deals with the Fronde, the Spanish marriage, Foucquet, military achievements, Versailles, and James II in exile, and ends with the disastrous year of 1709. Pierre Zoberman, *Les Cérémonies de la parole: L'éloquence d'apparat en France dans le dernier quart du XVIIe siècle*, Champion, 713 pp., deals with official speech-making and its rhetoric in learned circles, in the *parlements* (Paris and provincial) and in local administration; Z. takes much source material from the *Mercure*, and analyses formal speeches and eulogies, including those of the king. Provincial *académies*, mainly dating from the 18th c., have largely followed Parisian practice in a lower key; Z. covers legal bodies, 'éloquence de la robe', in Paris and the provinces, and special occasions ('rentrée du parlement') and 'remonstrances'; at the municipal level, there were occasions for 'harangues' and 'compliments' of a set pattern, a useful source of information on formal rhetoric in specific settings.

2. POETRY

LA FONTAINE. *Le Fablier*, 10 (*Actes du Colloque de Reims, 5–6 juin*), is devoted to 'La Fontaine et le Moyen Age' introduced by J. Adnet (11–13). M. Fumaroli, 'Allocution inaugurale' (17–19), discusses 17th-c. interest in the Middle Ages and explains the importance of the group of young men known as *La Table Ronde* to which La Fontaine was attached from 1642–56. This group considered that the heritage of the Middle Ages and the 16th c. ought to be appreciated with as much sympathy as the poets of antiquity. J. Boivin, 'Des prologues des *Isopets* à ceux des *Fables* de La Fontaine. L'élaboration d'une poétique' (21–27), discusses two medieval adaptations of the collection of *isopets* known as *Anonymus Neveleti* and a possible influence of the prologues and epilogues in these adaptations on the *Fables*. D. Bouchet, 'Les figures animalières de la cour et du pouvoir du *Roman de Renart* aux *Fables* de La Fontaine' (29–37), analyses, not the influence of the *Roman de Renart* on the *Fables*, but the way in which both exploit the same material and reflect similar preoccupations; L. Harf-Lancner, 'L'Isopet médiéval et la fable de La Fontaine "Les Membres et l'estomac"' (39–45), discuss the relevance of this fable in the 17th c. and demonstrates that it must be interpreted very differently in a period of centralized monarchy; M. O. Sweetser, 'La Fontaine conteur: vieilles histoires, nouvelle manière' (47–54), puts forward the view that the *Contes*, especially those involving clever scoundrels and gullible women, represent an original treatment by La Fontaine which goes far beyond his sources; D. Quéruel, '*Les Rémois*: du fabliau au conte de La Fontaine' (57–65), examines the various possible sources of this *Conte* and concludes that there is no single source but that La Fontaine chooses and rejects as it suits him; F. P. Sweetser, '*Les Cent Nouvelles Nouvelles* et La Fontaine' (67–70), recounts the elements of the *Nouvelles* which La Fontaine used as sources for some of his erotic *Contes*; M. Santicci, 'La Fontaine et Martial d'Auvergne: incidences de *L'Imitation des arrêts* sur la langue et la poétique de l'auteur' (73–81), analyses with great skill some of the legal language used in the *Fables* and finds affinities with the language used in *L'Imitation* of Martial d'Auvergne (1460–66) which is a parody of the style of the *Parlement*; P. Dandrey, 'La Fontaine et l'imaginaire médiéval' (83–88), sees four ways in which La Fontaine can be linked to the Middle Ages: imitation, derivation, allusion and references and, finally, in a further contribution, 'Du nouveau sur *La Cigale et la Fourmi*' (127–32), P. Dandrey provides a stimulating and original analysis of a well-known fable showing that if it is to yield up all its meaning it is necessary to take many things into account which might not, at first sight, seem relevant. A. Soare, ' "Le corbeau et le renard" ou la fugue en /ra/ et /ar/', *DFS*, 42:59–76, analyses the art of La Fontaine in this fable by examining with originality the delicate play of sounds in the elaboration of the vocabulary used and shows how this creates a pattern throughout the poem.

MALHERBE. Raymond Baustert, **L'Univers moral de Malherbe. Etude de la pensée dans l'œuvre poétique*, 2 vols, Berlin–NY–Paris, Lang, 1997, 957 pp., is a reworking of a thesis originally written in 1981. The aim is to integrate Malherbe into the currents of thought of his period and it shows clearly the links between Malherbe's thought and the period in which he lived but does not throw a great deal of light on his poetry. It has the merit of bringing proof to what has always been thought about Malherbe's attitude to politics and religion but does not stimulate any great new interest in his poetry.

THEOPHILE DE VIAU. J. Patterson, 'Théophile de Viau: in turbo clamor, in fora silentium', *DFS*, 42:17–19, examines the facts of the trial of Théophile and looks at the motives of Garasse and Molé in attacking him. It goes on to discuss the social and ideological context of his poetry.

TRISTAN L'HERMITE. C. Rizza, 'La mythologie dans *Les Amours*', *CTH*, 20:5–16, shows that by using the mythological code the poet can give to the discourse of love the polished and learned tone which society required. L. Grove, 'Glasgow University Library SMAdd.392: treize poèmes inédits de Tristan?', *ib.*, 29–51, is a description of 13 poems ascribed to Tristan in a MS addition found in a copy of Otto van Veen, *Amorum Emblemata* (Antwerp, 1608) in Glasgow University Library. The arguments for the attribution are recited and the poems are reproduced and discussed. S. Berregard, 'Tristan poète de l'amour est-il un précurseur des Romantiques?' *ib.*, 52–61, goes over the arguments that have been put forward to support this thesis and then expresses reservations showing that in order to sustain the thesis totally irrelevant criteria have to be brought to bear. G. argues that the view is itself a Romantic one.

3. DRAMA

Jean Dubu, *Les Églises chrétiennes et le théâtre (1550–1850)*, Grenoble, PUG, 1997, 204 pp., deals mainly with the 17th c. in spite of its title. It throws a more exact light on precisely what the relationships were between the church and the theatre in this period. D. shows that the traditional view of the Church as being implacably opposed to the theatre must be modified and that it was rather those churches that issued from the Reformation which were responsible for much anti-theatre polemic. He also shows however that there was a gradual movement towards disapproval from the middle of the 17th c.

introduced surreptitiously into dioceses by rigorist bishops. Michel Gilot and Jean Serroy, *La Comédie à l'âge classique*, Belin, 1997, 384 pp., is a very useful account which covers a longish span but with four chapters devoted to the 17th century. There is a great deal of helpful information with extracts illustrating points made in the text. As a means of acquiring much basic knowledge concerning the development of comedy in the 17th-c. it would be difficult to find fault with this manual as much that would be hard to find is here to hand. Its merit is as a work of reference rather than a work of criticism. Laurent Thirouin, *L'Aveuglement salutaire: le réquisitoire contre le théâtre dans la France classique*, Paris, Champion — Geneva, Slatkine, 1997, 292 pp., discusses the attack made on the theatre in the later part of the 17th c. but points out that it is not necessarily easy to identify the parties involved. This opposition did not have much influence on the theatre-going public but it was because the theatre was successful that the attacks were made. While making many useful observations T. tends to overlook previous contributions to the debate on the morality of the theatre. *Dictionnaire des œuvres théâtrales françaises du XVIIe siècle*, ed. Marc Vuillermoz, Paris, Champion — Geneva, Slatkine, 864 pp., is a detailed listing of 17th-c. plays with a very full account of each with discussions of performance, publication etc. but its usefulness is somewhat restricted by choosing only to deal with plays having a modern edition available in 1992. The works of 35 authors are examined, and this is profitable, but the restriction imposed makes for many regrettable omissions. A. Bontéa, 'Tragédie et histoire universelle', *SCFS*, 20:57–70, looks at the function of tragedy and its links with history or mythology seen as history and pays particular attention to the role of the king as a creature of history. F. Epars-Heussi, 'L'exposition dans le théâtre classique: approche pragmatique et textuelle', *DSS*, 198:95–112, reviews the different methods used to convey information in expositions and explores the variety from a textual point of view so that the difference between the relationship author/personage and author/reader-spectator is brought out. R. Fajon, 'Le crime d'amour ou la passion coupable à l'opéra: de la mort de Lully à l'Europe galante', *ib.*, 9–13, shows that the concept of love and passion changes from the time of the operas of Lully and Quinault in the 1670s and 1680s where love is portrayed as an heroic passion to a sombre passion in the 1690s where it is a source of unhappiness and rarely reaches fulfilment. J. della Gorce, 'De l'opéra-ballet aux fragments', *ib.*, 27–50, shows that from full operas the genre became a series of extracts which did not demand much concentration but allowed immediate appreciation by the use of surprise and curiosity. The *fragments*, although not created by Lully, benefited by the kind of spectacles he had created. A. Stefanovic,

'*Médée* de Charpentier: l'interprétation du passé comme pas vers le futur', *ib.*, 63–89, looks at the role of Charpentier in moving on the opera towards the 18th c. by examining the treatment of *Médée* and comparing his technique with that of Lully in the opera of the 1670s. A. Kablitz, ' "Wiedererkennung". Zur Funktion der Anagnorisis in der klassischen französischen Tragödie (Corneille: *Oedipe* — Racine: *Iphigénie en Aulide*)', Peil, *Erkennen*, 455–86, comments on Aristotle's definition of anagnorisis in the *Poetics* as against Plato's anamnesis. He deals with Corneille's and Racine's transformation of their Greek sources in *Oedipe* and *Iphigénie en Aulide* according to their own concept of tragedy. *A haute voix: diction et prononciation aux XVIe et XVIIe siècles*, ed. Olivia Rosenthal, Klincksieck, 260 pp., has two articles relevant for the 17th c.; H. Merlin, 'Effets de voix, effets de scènes; Mondory entre *Le Cid* et la *Marianne*' (155–76), discusses Mondory's acting career, his use of voice and manner of recitation; L. Norman, 'Entendre les vers comiques: l'intervention du poème écrit dans *Mélite*, *Les Visionnaires* et *La Comédie des Académistes*' (177–89), discusses the diction of alexandrines, the voice of the author and that of the characters.

BOYER. *Tyridate* suivie de *Le Fils supposé*, ed. L. Sergent, Geneva, Droz, 272 pp., is the first modern edition of these two texts of 1649 and 1672 respectively.

CLAVERET. *L'Esprit fort*, ed. C. Scherer, Geneva, Droz, 1997, 176 pp., is the first modern edition of this 1637 text. The introduction tells what is known about the life of Claveret and gives a full analysis of the play and useful additional information.

CORNEILLE. Georges Forestier, *Corneille. Le sens d'une dramaturgie*, Sedes, 136 pp., is the second *volet* of the author's *Essai de génétique théâtrale. Corneille à l'œuvre* (1996) (see *YWMLS*, 58 : 132) and is equally rewarding and stimulating. It continues the theme of this book in placing the emphasis on the dramaturgical aspects of Corneille's plays rather than on their political meaning. He discusses the reception of Corneille's tragedies in the 17th c. and puts forward the view that, although the plays are not political in the accepted sense of the term, they have the power to make contemporaries think of what is really political. Judd D. Hubert, *Corneille's Performative Metaphors*, Charlottesville, Rookwood Press, 1997, 254 pp., also concentrates on the theatrical and poetical sides of Corneille's plays rather than on moral, social, or political dimensions. H. demonstrates the very large diversity of dramatic structures used by Corneille although not all the plays are discussed nor are the absentees noted. This is, however, a contribution to the understanding of Corneille which has much that is original, not least the suggestion that Corneille's characters have too much perspicacity to fit into the role of tragic victims. André Le

Gall, *Pierre Corneille en son temps et en son œuvre. Enquête sur un poète de théâtre au XVIIe siècle*, Flammarion, 1997, 605 pp., is a very full biography based on sound research but which relies for its effect on its narrative quality rather than on any new light it sheds on the life of Corneille. Every piece of evidence is followed meticulously so that a very full picture of the life of the dramatist emerges and being written in a vivid and striking style it is easy to follow this well-told story of the lawyer's son from Rouen making his way in the world of 17th-c. drama. On the way a very full account is given of the theatrical and literary background of 17th-c. France, so that the career of Corneille is seen in this context. *LitC*, 32, is a special issue devoted to *Cinna, Rodogune* and *Nicomède*, introd. P. Ronzeaud, 'Corneille dans tous ses états critiques. Pour une lecture plurielle de *Rodogune*' (7–40). This is a survey of recent Cornelian criticism, especially the work of G. Forestier and M. Fumaroli. H. Merlin, 'Corneille et la politique dans *Cinna, Rodogune* et *Nicomède*' (41–61), examines the question of power in these three plays and how they interact with each other; G. Forestier, 'Politique et tragédie chez Corneille, ou de la "broderie"' (63–74), defends his interpretation of the tragedies as not being specifically 'politiques' and explains what he means by 'broderie' in describing what politics contribute to tragedy; P. Pasquier, 'Le héros tragique cornélien dans le *Discours* de 1660 ou comment s'accommoder avec Aristote' (77–89), discusses Corneille's interpretation of Aristotle and attempts to reconcile his presentation of the 'héros vertueux' with Aristotle's view of what constitutes a tragic hero; L. Picciola, 'Janus, héros cornélien' (91–104), sees heroism as having two faces like Janus and examines Cinna, Séleucus and Attale specifically from this point of view; J. Emelina, 'Corneille et la catharsis' (105–20), discuss the meaning of catharsis and shows that pity becomes enfeebled in Corneille, being overtaken by stoicism; C. Biet, 'Plaisirs et dangers de l'admiration' (121–34), looks at admiration and shows that 'to admire' needs to be redefined. The effect on the spectator is what is most important; H. Baby, 'De la nature du sensible dans l'œuvre de Pierre Corneille: les exemples de *Cinna, Rodogune* et *Nicomède*' (135–58), examines the family links which add to the tragedy of the relationships in these plays. Strong blood links are necessary to make the tragedy work; E. Minel, 'Dénouement dynamique et dénouement problématique. Un aspect du travail de l'histoire dans la tragédie cornélienne' (158–69), examines aspects of denouements and shows that they tend to change from being complete and firm to ones that open perspectives on the future leaving a number of questions unanswered, and D. Moncondh'huy, 'De la catastrophe comme tableau. A propos de *Cinna, Rodogune* et *Nicomède*' (177–87), explores the use of the 'catastrophe' as a 'tableau' in these tragedies, especially *Rodogune*, and shows that this helps to explain the direction taken by the action and the characters. *PFSCL*, 25, is devoted to the comedies of Corneille with an introduction by A. Niderst which underlines the variety of the comedies and the danger of neglecting them, underestimating them and ignoring what they bring to the study of Corneille (109–11); Y. Bellenger, 'La dérobade devant l'amour: Ronsard et Montaigne précurseurs d'Alidor' (113–27), discusses ideas expressed in Ronsard and Montaigne which foreshadow the stance adopted by Alidor towards love; M. F. Wagner, 'L'éblouissement de Paris: promenades urbaines et urbanité dans les comédies de Pierre Corneille' (129–44), discusses what is meant by 'la scène est à Paris' and the relationship between urbanity and the setting of the comedies in Paris; C. Mazouer, 'L'épreuve dans les comédies de Pierre Corneille' (145–56), shows that the main kind of 'épreuve' treated is where will is involved but sometimes where love is involved; 'épreuves' help to make young people stable and bring them to maturity; M. Margitic, 'Humour et parodie dans les comédies de Corneille' (157–65), argues that although the word 'humour' did not exist in the 17th c., what the word means nowadays did, and M. defines this and examines its role in the comedies. S. Dosmond, 'Les confident(e)s dans le théâtre comique de Corneille' (167–75), tries to define 'confident' and claims that, except for Lyse (*L'Illusion comique*) there are no real 'confident(e)s' in the comedies. The so-called 'confident(e)s' fulfil other functions. J. C. Vuillemin, 'Hypocondrie, illusion et dramaturgie: Cloridan, Eraste et autres Orphées baroques' (177–91), brings together Rotrou's *Hypocondriaque* and Corneille's *Mélite* and argues that madness in the theatre of the 1630s was a method of creating an illusion/delusion and the treatment of it was to fall in love with the illusion/delusion of the madman and create a world in tune with his madness. A. Soare, 'Sur un mensonge du *Menteur*: "poudre de sympathie" et "résurrections" tragi-comiques' (193–202), defines the tragi-comedy not by its happy ending but as a nightmare from which one wakes up. Corneille uses this idea in *Le Menteur* à propos of the invention by Dorante of the 'death' and 'resurrection' of Alcippe. F. Lasserre, 'La raison d'être des *a parte* dans *Le Menteur*' (203–11), suggests that Corneille's use of *a parte* in his portrait of Dorante can be seen as an indication that he intended to present a portrait of an author of plays. E. Minel, 'Du *Menteur* à sa *Suite*: de la valeur comme vaine sociabilité à la valeur en liberté surveillée ou d'une théâtralité problématique à une théâtralité autonome' (213–24), discusses the change of values in the two plays. In *Le Menteur* Dorante is seeking justification for himself whereas *La Suite* provides justification for him. J. D. Hubert, 'Corneille et le mélange des genres' (225–31), points out that many of the heroic stances assumed by Cornelian heroes and heroines have comic echoes; J. Dubu, '*Les Plaideurs* et Corneille' (233–39), shows that Racine uses some of Corneille's verses and parodies them in *Les Plaideurs*; J. Gaines, 'The comic hero from Corneille to Molière' (247–54), discusses relationships between fathers and sons in Corneille and Molière and makes the point that the clash of the generations becomes important when questions of inheritance are examined; and R. Goodkin, '*Nicomède* 1 and 2: the fraternal heritage of Pierre and Thomas Corneille' (255–65), shows that *Nicomède* and *La Mort d'Annibal* seem to question the notion of primogeniture and this reflects some unease in society with this practice. A. Howe, 'La Troupe du Marais et la première de *Mélite* (1629–1631): trois documents inédits', *AJFS*, 31:279–94, shows that the date of the first performace of *Mélite* is almost certainly 1629 or possibly early 1630 according to three newly discovered documents concerning the leasing of possible theatres in 1629–31. Id., 'La publication des œuvres de Pierre Corneille (1637–49), sept documents inédits', *RHLF*, 98:17–41, is a survey of documents in the *Minutier central des notaires de Paris* which details the dates of the publication of the plays of Corneille by tracing the agreements made between certain publishers for the right to publish, thus throwing light on the evolution of the text of *Le Cid*. C. Gossip, 'The unity of *Horace*', *MLR*, 93:345–55, examines concepts of unity in *Cinna* and *Le Cid* and argues that there is not such a substantial break in the unity of *Horace* as has often been alleged but shows that the nature of the conflict in the tragedy is not as simple as is sometimes thought. A. Zuerner, 'Disguise and the gendering of royal authority in Corneille's *Clitandre*', *FR*, 71:757–74, suggests that the way transvestite characters are portrayed seems to show that in 17th-c. France one's masculinity or femininity was determined less by anatomy than by one's relationship to the king. B. Rubridge, 'Catharsis through admiration. Corneille, Le Moyne and social uses of emotion', *MP*, 95:316–33, examines the meaning of catharsis as applied to admiration and sees Corneille's use of it as being, to some degree, based on Le Moyne's *Traité du poéme héroique*. Id., 'The code of reciprocation in Corneille's heroic drama', *RR*, 89:55–75, examines the idea that Corneille's heroes base their behaviour on a pattern of exchange that reflects the realities of relationships especially between the powerful and those over whom they exercise their power. B. Louvat and M. Escola, '*Oedipe* de Corneille ou le complexe de Dircé', *DSS*, 200:453–70, asks what is the subject of *Oedipe* and argues that it is a competition between a *comédie héroique* and a tragedy, a conflict of legitimacy between the daughter of Laius and the king of Thebes who do not know they are brother and sister. A. Georges, 'Le sens des stances de *Polyeucte*', *ib.*,

471–82, dismisses previous interpretations of the *stances* and by analysing them from a theological point of view demonstrates that they are vital for a full understanding of the role of Polyeucte. C. Carlin, 'Corneille's confessional discourse in the 1660s', *SCFS*, 20:71–82, argues that the plays of this period display a new preoccupation with the question of human frailty so that the nature of the moral conflict is different from that in earlier plays. R. Goulbourne, 'Visual effects and the theatrical illusion in Pierre Corneille's early plays', *PFSCL*, 49:531–44, attempts, by looking at the theatricality and the visual dimension of Corneille's early play (up to *Rodogune*), to show the importance, hitherto underestimated, of visual devices in the treatment of his themes.

MOLIÈRE. Marco Baschera, *Théâtricalité dans l'œuvre de Molière* (*PFSCL*, Biblio 17, 108), 271 pp., sets about closing the gap between a purely literary reading of a play and a purely theatrical one. B. provides a dense and probing exploration of the means whereby a written text becomes a performance by actors. The space between these two states of an author's creation as the written text is transformed into an action performed by actors is seen to be critical and difficult to define. For this reason the comedies of Molière lend themselves particularly well to analysis of this kind and the chapters dealing with the influence of the commedia dell'arte and the mask yield interesting results. The discussion of *La Critique de l'Ecole des Femmes* and *L'Impromptu de Versailles* is also very productive and the final chapter on *Le Misanthrope* is both original and stimulating. C. E. J. Caldicott, **La Carrière de Molière. Entre protecteurs et éditeurs*, Amsterdam, Rodopi, 242 pp., urges us to re-evaluate Molière as a great courtier and man of letters and not as the traditional playwright of the people. Patrick Dandrey, *La Médecine et la maladie dans le théâtre de Molière*, 2 vols, Klincksieck, 716, 845 pp., is a vast survey of everything to do with illness and medicine as a theme in literature leading up to a detailed examination of all those comedies of Molière dealing with the subject. The first volume concentrates on the Sganarelle plays with special attention paid to *Dom Juan*. There is also a very long analysis of *L'Amour médecin* with a discussion of love as an illness and the various theories which support this idea. The originality of Molière in his treatment of this theme is underlined and also its relevance to the understanding of *Tartuffe*. The second volume deals firstly with melancholy with special reference to *Monsieur de Pourceaugnac* with an examination of possible sources and, secondly, with a very detailed analysis of *Le Malade imaginaire*. Every aspect of hypochondria is looked at and its history as a literary theme traced over a large array of works. A very interesting conclusion which D. arrives at is that 'la maladie imaginaire d'Argan procède d'un modèle de pensée et de culture libertines'. This is by far the most complete treatment of this subject yet undertaken and it is difficult to see how it can be superseded. Roger Duchêne, *Molière*, Fayard, 789 pp., recounts the life of Molière based on every known fact, rigorously excluding legends which are shown to be legends. As the method used is chronological the plays appear in their appropriate place and are fitted very clearly into context. In doing this the background of theatrical life in 17th-c. France is very well described and the author's thorough knowledge of the period allows him to paint a very full picture. Thus not only is this an accurate and readable life of Molière it is also as complete an account as it is possible to have of the circumstances in which Molière's plays were written and performed. There are also a series of *annexes* detailing the family history of Molière and a listing of all the plays performed by his troupe in Paris between Easter 1659 and February 1673 which includes not only his own plays but those by other playwrights. A. Erskine, 'Good and bad scepticism in *Amphitryon* and *Le Mariage Forcé*', *SCFS*, 20:17–27, discusses the Christian sceptical ideas in Montaigne and Charron and shows that in Molière's two plays scepticism is a virtue which must be controlled. J. Clarke, 'Molière's double bills', *ib.*, 29–44, examines the choice of plays available to the public in Molière's programming and discusses the pairing of plays in his repertory. C. Spencer, 'O Grès suspends ton vol! *L'Ecole des Femmes* ou l'Esprit de la lettre', *DSS*, 200:483–89, analyses the text of Agnès's letter as a model of modern literary theory substituting *lettre* for *grès* or *grès* for *lettre*. The problem lies in the discrepancy between Agnès's lack of experience and her first, astonishingly successful, attempt to express her feelings in a letter. A. Calder, 'Humour in the 1660s: La Rochefoucauld, Molière and La Fontaine', *SCFS*, 20:125–38, claims that the cynical humour of these three authors is closely connected with the realities of court life. The court is seen as a microcosm of everything that is wrong with the world and irony is used to show the ultimate emptiness of court life. J. Le Boulay, 'La naissance de Don Juan', *RLMC*, 20:25–36, sets out to prove that in *Dom Juan* there is a complete change in the rules. Don Juan is clear about the things of this world but is blind to the forces that make him what he is while Sganarelle is the reverse; he is blind to what is obvious but knowledgeable about his subconscious. J. Carson, 'On Molière's debt to Scarron for *Sganarelle, ou le Cocu Imaginaire*', *PFSCL*, 49:545–54, traces the influence of Scarron's *Le Jodelet duelliste* (1652) on Molière's play. By a comparison of situations in the two plays C. concludes that Molière owes Scarron 'a not inconsiderable debt for character traits, discourse structure, textual elements, stage situations and individual scene structure'.

RACINE. Racine, *Théâtre complet*, ed. J. Rohou and P. Fièvre, Livre de Poche, 1148 pp., has an interesting introduction discussing the development of tragedy and Racine's interpretation of it. The text used is that of the 1697 edition but all the variants are given at the bottom of the page and each tragedy has a substantial notice making this a very useful edition providing much necessary information in a convenient form. *EsC*, 38.1, is a Tercentennial Issue devoted to Racine, introd. H. Stone. T. Murray, ' "Animé d'un regard": the crisis of televisual speed in Racine' (11–22), discusses *Andromaque* with special reference to the visual impact of the past as translated into the present. There is a movement of the visual from one plane to another. K. Horowitz, 'The second time round: the concept of *antériorité* as it structures and controls Racinian theatre' (23–33), attempts to show that the present in Racine is a duplication of the past and that the tragedies replay the actions of the past. S. Gearhart, 'Racine's politics: the subject/subversion of power in *Britannicus*' (38–48), examines the theme of power and its implications for undertanding the relationship between Néron, Narcisse and Burrhus. M. Langin, '*Bajazet* à la lettre' (49–59), discusses the historicity of *Bajazet* particularly with regard to the credulity of the protagonists who are all seen as being credulous in different ways. R. Goodkin, 'Thomas Corneille's *Ariane* and Racine's *Phèdre*: the older sister strikes back' (60–71), claims that Ariane is blinded by a sense of superiority and is not really Thésée's first choice and is abandoned for Phèdre but *Phèdre* sees the revenge of Ariane; Aricie is the means whereby this is done. S. Melzer, 'Myths of mixture in *Phèdre* and the Sun King's assimilation policy in the new world' (72–81), attempts to show that the myths in *Phèdre* are part of a political rhetoric designed to camouflage the reality of French assimilationist policy in the new world. D. Thomas, 'Racine redux, the operatic afterlife of *Phèdre*' (82–94), discusses Rameau's opera *Hippolyte et Aricie* and its use of *Phèdre*. H. Stone, 'Marking time: memorialising history in *Athalie*' (95–104), sets out to show that the temple is the *lieu de mémoire* linking the Jews of the present to their past. S. examines *Athalie* from the point of view of the role of memory in constructing the Jews' attitude towards her and the role played by memory as opposed to history. M. Greenberg, 'Racine's Oedipus: virtual bodies, originary fantasies' (105–17), is a densely argued and elaborately developed thesis based on the role of the body, or rather absence of the body, in Racinian tragedy using much psychoanalytical material to pin down what is really tragic in Racine. A more developed version of this article entitled 'Racine, Oedipus, and absolute fantasies' appears in *Diacritics*, 28.3:40–61. G. Forestier, 'Ecrire *Andromaque*; quelques hypothèses génétiques', *RHLF*, 98:43–62, explores the different sources of *Andromaque* showing that

Racine's use of ancient sources was not simply a copying of stereotypes figures but that he took concepts of characters (especially women in love) and created a new kind of character based on the subtle mingling of hints from antiquity and modern i.e. 17th-c. understanding of passion. V. Schröder, 'Racine et l'éloge de la guerre de Hollande: de la campagne de Louis XIV au "dessein de Mithridate"', *DSS*, 198:113–34, demonstrates persuasively the case for a reading of *Mithridate* which takes into account a possible link between Mithridate's plan to march on Rome and Louis XIV's invasion of Holland at the beginning of the Dutch War in 1672 at the time Racine was composing his tragedy. R. Barnett, 'Infinite regress: expansion of naught in Racine's *Phèdre*', *EsC*, 38, 1:35–45, analyses the role of language in *Phèdre* showing that Phèdre's unceasing search to explain herself in language is destructive and finally destroys her. Language is self-indulgent and is ultimately doomed to fail; the more frenzied the attempt, the more certain the defeat. R. Calder, ' "La seule pensée du crime": *Phèdre*, contrition and casuistry', *SCFS*, 20:45–56, examines the question of moral rigour in *Phèdre* arguing that, as early as 1676, Racine was thinking of 'conversion' and seeking approaches to Port-Royal. R. Barnett, 'Poétique et marginalité: les interstices du tragique racinien', *ib*., 153–62, probes the role of speech and silence in Racine's tragedies and grapples with the language codes involved. R. Lack, ' "Les replis tortueux de l'intertextuel", Racine and Lautréamont, prosody and prose', *FrF*, 23:167–78, traces signs of Racine, specifically the *récit de Théramène* in the work of Lautréamont. F. Lagarde, 'Effets de Racine', *DSS*, 200:521–28, discusses a wide range of reactions to Racine including those of Rimbaud, Proust, and Gide who wonder how evil and tragedy can produce music and beauty.

TRISTAN L'HERMITE. N. Mallet, 'Les plaintes de la mal aimée: passion et scénographie dans la tragédie d'*Osman*', *CTH*, 20:17–27, argues that Tristan's depiction of La Fille du Mouphti in this tragedy reveals an independent stance on his part towards contemporary ethical attitudes; she is a striking figure who foreshadows some heroines of Racine.

4. PROSE

INDIVIDUAL AUTHORS

BALZAC. *LitC*, 33, *Fortunes de Guez Balzac*, ed. Bernard Beugnot, contains: B. Beugnot, 'Reviviscences balzaciennes, 1597–1997' (5–8) and 'Lettres posthumes' (9–16); M. Fumaroli, 'Le premier redécouvreur de Guez de Balzac, Joseph Joubert' (21–26), quotes from Joubert's *Carnets* 1897–98; J. Mesnard, 'Balzac et les écrivains de

Port-Royal' (29–43), refers to Balzac's *Lettres* of 1624, some Messieurs and the Arnauld family had personal contacts, as stylists followed on Balzac; A. Génetiot, 'Les Romains de Balzac aux origines de la conversation classique' (45–66), argues a 'rhétorique de la conversation' and a 'classicisme à la romaine' could be derived from the *Cycle des Romains*, since Balzac wanted to be 'Le Tite-Live de l'hôtel de Rambouillet'; N. Doiron, 'Orasius, Phyllarque et Narcisse, La sophistique à l'époque classique' (67–77), discusses La Mothe le Vayer's criticism of Balzac in *Hexamérion rustique* (1671) and links it to sophistry in Balzac and, generally in the 17th c.; E. Bury, 'Balzac et Boileau' (79–91), considering Balzac as 'ouvrier du clacissime' and Boileau, with a certain dependence on him, as the 'régent du Parnasse', points to quotations and similarities. G. Declercq, 'Bouhours lecteur de Balzac ou du naturel' (93–113), discusses Bouhours's criticism of Balzac's style as grandiloquent, reflecting his use of hyperbole, since Bouhours prefers 'le natural'; the different periods in the century account for the unfavourable criticism. R. Zuber, 'Guez de Balzac et Pierre Bayle' (115–25), quotes from Bayle's writings and appreciations of Balzac's work, but also corrects him from his own erudition; B. Bray, 'Balzac XVIIIe–XXe siecle', investigates manuals from 1624 to 1936; J.-M. Goulemot, 'L'épistolier au siècle des lumières'; M. Bury, 'Balzac face à la critique du XIX siècle'; B. Veck, 'Guez de Balzac chez Francis Ponge, De la distance au "mariage" ou l'indispensable satellite'; E. van der Schueren, 'Guez de Balzac et Constant Huygens, aux frontières des modèles éloquents'; V. Kapp, 'Guez de Balzac en Allemagne'; G. Malquari Fondi, 'La traduction italienne des lettres de Guez de Balzac, Venise 1688'; P.-J. Salazar, ' "The author writes like a Briton": la réception de Balzac en Angleterre'.

BAUDOUIN. Jean Baudouin, *L'Histoire négropontique*, ed. Laurence Plazenet, Champion–Slatkine, 403 pp., based on the second edition of 1731, presents the author, *académicien* and prolific writer; the novel, a love story, said to be extracted from a manuscript by the author, is set in Algiers, Tunis and Morocco, with travels and shipwrecks, ghostly appearances, and also some religious background of Christians versus Turks. The novel belongs to the Baroque period, and in some ways, to the Counter Reformation.

BOSSUET. Michel Crépin, *Le Tombeau de Bossuet*, Grasset, 1997, 229 pp., introduces his account of Bossuet's activities and writings with 'Bossuet notre antipode', and places him in his time, underlining the contrast with the present and his relationship with the King, his family and the Court. C. analyses his role as tutor to the Dauphin, comments on the controversy with Fénelon under the heading 'ironie et mysticisme' which put an end to mystical tradition, and looks at Bossuet's writings and sermons.

FÉNÉLON. *Œuvres II*, ed. Jacques Le Brun, Gallimard, 1997, 1,830 pp., contains *Télémaque*, copiously annotated and commented, reinstating a once widely read text; other texts include *Réfutation du Système de Malebranche sur la nature de la grâce*, some *Opuscules théologiques*, *Instructions sur les sacrements*, few letters in view of the Orcibal edition of the *Correspondance*. Fénélon's political stance in *Plans de gouvernement, dits Tables de Chaulnes*, written in 1711, shows his radicalism.

FRÉNICLE, NICOLAS. *L'Entretien des Illustres Bergers*, ed. Stéphane Macé, Champion, 281 pp. This collection of eclogues of 1634, in the Virgilian manner, is linked by prose passages, critically reflecting on the contents and stylistic form of the eclogues, generally in dialogue form. It illustrates the then fashionable pastoral genre: poets, disguised as shepherds, set in a *locus amoenus*, along the Seine, near Saint-Germain-en-Laye, recite their poems, on love but also on the nature of poetic creation, and their love of the countryside. This first modern edition relies on M. Cauchie's identification of the real poets behind the disguised names.

GOURNAY, MARIE DE. *Textes relatifs à la calomnie*, ed. Constant Venesoen (*PFSCL*, Biblio 17, 113), 193 pp., contains 'Adieu de l'Ame du Roy de France et de Navarre Henry le Grand à la Royne', 'Défense des Pères Jésuites' (1610), 'Le Remerciment des Beurrières de Paris, au Sieur de Courbouzon Mongommery ou L'Anti-Gournay' (1610), 'De la Mesdisance et qu'elle est principale Cause des Duels' (1634), 'Considération sur quelques Contes de Cour' (1634). V. presents the text in the political and religious setting of the period: the defense of the Jesuits receives its first modern edition, together with its critical reply; the texts on *Médisance* and *Contes de Cour* show her moralizing approach. Marie Le Jars de Gournay, *Les Advis, Ou, Les Presens de La Demoiselle de Gournay*, ed. Jean-Philippe Beaulieu and Hannah Fournier, vol. 1, Rodopi, Amsterdam, 1997, 262 pp., is based on the editions of 1626 and 1634, together with a biographical account and commentaries; a second volume is projected to cover the whole work.

LA BRUYÈRE. *Les Caractères*, ed. Louis Van Delft, Imprimerie nationale, 544 pp., presents La B. as a spectator, looking at life and other people; D. refers to Montaigne, to humanistic and mundane elements, and comments on the position of the first readers.

LAMY. Bernard Lamy, *La Rhétorique ou L'Art de parler*, ed. Christine Noëlle-Clauzade, Champion, 495 pp., is based on the 1715 edition, and refers to the earlier versions from 1675 onwards, examining the theory of rhetoric and its relation to logic, ethics, and all means of persuasion, and including a historical perspective on classical sources and an examination of language and style.

LA ROCHEFOUCAULT.   Jean Lafond, *La Rochefoucauld, l'homme et son image*, Champion, 184 pp., contains 11 articles (seven reprinted from the 1996 edition); new items are 'Les Maximes en leur temps', which discusses the 'discours discontinu'; 'L'intention et l'utilité du mal', looking at Augustinian mortality, 'amour-propre' and 'amour de Dieu'; 'Esthétique, éthique et morale' examines their relationship; 'De la maxime 282 au couple fait et droit' distinguishes empirical reality (*fait*) from the idea (*droit*). Charlotte Schapira, *La Maxime et le Discours d'Autorité*, Sedes, 1997, 176 pp., investigates the *maxime* in relation to proverbs and clichés in their linguistic structure; S. distinguishes various categories of *maximes* and discusses the quotability of the genre, referring to modern forms of the genre.

NINON DE L'ENCLOS.   Françoise Hamel, *Notre dame des amours*, Grasset, 394 pp., a novelistic biography (1623–1705), accounts for her libertine upbringing and contacts and her establishment at the Marais; lists her lovers and places her enforced stay at the 'Madelonnettes' and her friendships within a historical setting.

PASCAL.   *Œuvres Complètes*, 1, ed. Michel Le Guern, Pléiade, xlviii + 1378 pp., contains *Actes officiels*, P.'s life by Mme Périer, his arithmetic and scientific writings, the *Polémiques* with P. Noël, the *Provinciales* and the controversies around them.

PERRAULT.   Yvette Saupé, *Les 'Contes' de Perrault et la mythologie. Rapprochements et influences* (*PFSCL*, 104), 1997, 241 pp., gives a full account of the various origins of the *Contes*, with a 'vieux fonds gaulois'. S. discusses titles, themes and myths, including a 'bestiaire mythique', examines the significance of the myths within the 17th-c. setting, and ends on their development in a burlesque vein. F. Ringham, 'Riquet à la Houppe: conteur, conteuse', *FS*, 52:291–304, compares the versions by Perrault and Catherine Bernard, accounting for the different emphasis in one and the other on grounds of gender. Perrault stresses 'esprit', associated with power, while Bernard has Riquet falling in love with Mama, a beautiful but stupid princess. R. analyses the structure of the Bernard version in detail, and finds tensions in both versions. Lorraine Piroux, *Le Livre en trompe l'oeil ou Le jeu de la dédicace Montaigne, Scarron, Diderot*, Kimé, 192 pp., gives a critical review on definitions of a *dédicace*. Chap. 2 deals with 'Les scandales de Scarron' (87–125), the farcical character of Part I of the *Roman comique*, dedicated to Retz, with Scarron then in search of an income, a *risqué* present. P. considers the *Roman comique* as a 'débauche verbale' and the reader as accomplice. Richard Parish, *Le Roman comique* (GCCGFT), 115 pp., deals with the literary context and the role of the travelling players: two chapters examine the structure of the novel and reflect on the author, the persona and the narrator, and with it on the human condition as it emerges from the book; P. concludes on the novel as entirely *sui generis*, a strange mixture. Fausta Garavini, *La Maison des Jeux. Science du roman et roman de la science au XVIIe siècle*, Champion, 318 pp., translated from the Italian by Arlette Estève, is mainly concerned with Sorel's *Francion*, as it represents libertinage and Sorel's *Science universelle* (1641, 1644, and reprints); G. examines the different aspects of science in the then modern and controversial context, has a chapter on a comparative study of the *Roman comique* and the *Roman Bourgeois*, as showing novelists reflecting on the novel within the novel; a brief chapter is added on *Tartuffe*, *Dom Juan* and *Le Misanthrope*.

5. Thought

Jean-Charles Darmon, *Philosophie épicurienne et littérature au XVIIe siècle: Études sur Gassendi, Cyrano de Bergerac, La Fontaine, Saint-Evremond*, PUF, 387 pp., begins with the classical antecendents and Montaigne. The first part explores the ideas in Gassendi's writings, his imagination and images, looks in particular at the *Exercitationes* and moves on to the debate between Gassendi and Descartes, with a discussion of 'De la Pneumatologie Gassendienne au "Double Trésor" de La Fontaine', including the *Discours à Madame de la Sablière*; a futher chapter explores the notion of 'idée', image, and fantasy, with reference to the *Dispositio*. The second part explores Gassendi's influence on Cyrano, La Fontaine and Saint-Evremond, the epicurean ideas in *L'Autre Monde*, in various images, and looks at some fables presenting a 'figuration du plaisir', including *Le Renard et la Panthère*, *Le Loup et le Chasseur*, emphasizing the importance of 'jouir', seen in Saint-Evremond, 'le gassendisme mondain', as a 'libertin honnête, a search for 'tranquillitas' in old age. The conclusion acknowledges the main line of his study as an 'anthropologie de l'imaginaire'. P.-J. Salazar, ' "L'Eclat et la catastrophe" or sceptic independence', *SCFS*, 20:1–16, begins with François de Maucroix and his way of living away from troubles, and moves on to La Mothe le Vayer on the subject of human diversity, and how to live well. S. finds in Saint-Evremond a distinction between the practice and the theory of living, comments on the notion of fantasy, as related to a manner of living, and links it to Le Vayer's insistence on diversity, concluding with the comment that scepticism as rhetoric as opposed to philosophical scepticism, may have secured the tranquillity of an independent life. Marianne Alphant, *Pascal: Tombeau pour un ordre*. Hachette, 222 pp., begins with 'Dans la chambre d'un mort', the postmortem on the body, and moves from there to the fate of the manuscripts and editions, and the order of the fragments, under 'Pascal absconditus'. A. discusses Gilberte's hagiography and Pascal's own use of pseudonyms, indicates theatrical features and ends on later comments on Pascal, as if there could never be an end to the *Pensées*. R.-L. Barnett, 'Pascal's prescripts: the semiotics of suspension', *ZFSL*, 108:241–57, based on criteria from L. Marin and Derrida, suggests an ontological–oratorical structuration, and from the corpus of Pascal scholarship, a dialectic of inside–outside in the structure of the apologetics. C. Meurillon, 'Oubli de soi, oubli de Dieu: écriture et oubli chez Pascal', *RSH*, 252–54:23–36, investigates 'oubli' and 'écriture' (man's weakness as seen in 'oubli'; forgetting oneself and the world would lead to conversion into the presence of God) and links it to the experience of time transformed in writing. A. Vizier, 'Pascal et l'herméneutique', *ib.*, 71–103, argues his hermeneutic interpretation from *Pensées* 274, 452, 502 (L), emphasizing Pascal's attitude to Jews where he breaks with the then traditional views. P. Sellier, 'Vers un nouveau "Port Royal". Bilan 1969–94', *French Studies in Southern Africa*, 23, 1997:10–28, is a bibliography. Henry Phillips, *Church and Culture in Seventeenth-century France*, CUP, 1997, 334 pp., organizes the study under the leitmotiv of space, of belief among clergy and laity, and finds negative and positive sides of the Tridentine reform. Under the heading of 'space of representation', P. considers church buildings, art, theatre, books, and literature; on education describes the main teaching orders, Jesuits, Oratorians, Lazarists, as well as Protestant schools and establishments for girls. P.'s discussion of ideas covers religious controversies, approaches to Scripture, theological positions, Augustinian influence, scientific trends (mostly around Descartes), and the *Académie des Sciences*, unbelief, libertinage and scepticism. John Kilcullen, *Sincerity and Truth. Essays on Arnauld, Bayle, and Toleration*, OUP, xii + 228 pp., sketches out the origins of Jansenism in his chapter on Arnauld, and discusses the teaching on sin. P. Bayle becomes the centre of enquiry into the rights of conscience, and toleration, with a historical perspective. K. comments on the ethics of belief and enquiry in scientific matters, and sums up Bayle's lines of argument. *Humanisme et Politique. Lettres Romaines de Christopher Dupuy à ses frères, 1646–1649*, vol. II, ed. Kathryn Willis Wolfe, and Philip Wolfe (*PFSCL*, Supplements, 103), 1997, 258 pp. In 84 letters, following a first volume of 1988, the eldest Dupuy brother, a Carthusian of Bourg-Fontaine, sent to Rome as procurator, reports on Roman intrigues and on book purchases, and comments on letters received from Paris, at the time of the Fronde. Much of the correspondence is concerned with book buying for libraries, transport, and dealing with book sellers. B. Neveu, 'L'Esprit de Réforme à Rome sous Innocent XI, 1676–89', *DSS*, 199:203–18, discusses the controversial situation in Rome over the Jansenist question, Jansenists in Rome, and the role of the Maurists. N. comments on the pontiff's reforming measures as to simplicity and order, in Rome and in the church, Innocent XI being known for his Jansenist sympathies. E. Caron, 'Défense de la chrétienté ou gallicanisme dans la politique de la France à l'égard de l'Empire ottoman à la fin du XVIIe siècle', *ib.*, 359–72, comments on the enmity between Christian powers in Europe and the Turkish Empire, as Louis XIV pursued a policy of alliance with La Porte, before making his peace with the other powers in Europe and abandoning La Porte. The central part of the volume is on 'La Reconquête catholique en Europe centrale'. Yves Krumenacker, *L'Ecole française de spiritualité: Des mystiques, des fondateurs, des courants et leurs interprètes*, Postface by Jean Dujardin, Cerf, 660 pp., follows, in nine chapters, the history of Bérulle's spirituality and influence over the centuries to the present, considering Bérulle as dominating the so-called French school of spirituality. K. places Bérulle within his period, a low ebb in the church; a complete renewal was undertaken in which Bérulle played an important role. K. gives an account of Bérulle's career (1575–1629): he brought the reformed Carmelites from Spain, helped to reform the clergy by setting up the Oratory and a college, gave spiritual guidance, always Christ-centred, and also came under the influence of Augustinian pessimism; he had considerable influence in the 17th c., on Saint-Sulpice and its seminary through Olier, when the Oratorian colleges practically shared the education of boys with the Jesuits, and took on various charitable works and missions. The subsequent development of the 'École Française', and how much it was Berullian, is perhaps slightly obscured by other influences in later years; a transformation occurred in the 18th century, in post-Revolutionary France, when Saint-Sulpice, through Emery, contributed to a religious renewal (ultramontane, with Marian devotions), alongside several other renewals, some of which may have been influenced by Bérulle's spirit, such as the Lazarists, or Grignion de Montfort. A return to Bérulle in our century owes much to the writings of Bremond. This is a useful reference work covering several centuries, but with no bibliography, other than notes. *La Philosophie clandestine à l'Age classique*, ed. Antony McKenna and Alain Mothu, Oxford, Voltaire Foundation, 1997, 539 pp., contains: M. Sankey, 'Lire le manuscrit clandestin: *L'Autre Monde* de Cyrano de Bergerac' (279–89), compares three clandestine manuscripts (Munich, B.N., Sydney), and concludes on the different 'dénouements'; A. Del Prete, 'Entre Descartes et Malebranche: le *Traité de l'infini créé*' (307–19), discusses the *Traité* in the light of nine manuscripts with a view towards the 18th century. *PFSCL*, 49, 'Littérature et Philosphie au XVIIe siècle', ed. E. Bury and J.-C.

Darmon, 367–623, contains: J.-C. Darmon, 'Littérature et philosophie au XVIIe siècle: relations, passages, partages (remarques liminaires sur quelques questions en suspens)' (371–79), refers to an enigmatic relation between the two, and suggests investigating writers' personal libraries; A. Minazzoli, 'Formes de penser, manières d'écrire: existe-t-il un style sceptique?' (381–96), suggests a style of seekers, with elements of doubt and suspense, largely based on Montaigne; P. Cahné, 'Note sur la comédie du *Menteur* — charge ironique de la parole du philosophe' (397–99), is a brief note on the 'philosophe ironique'; J.-C. Darmon, 'Gassendi et la rhétorique de Descartes' (401–29), examines their respective positions with regard to rhetoric; P. Force, 'Pascal et la philosophie: problèmes de réception' (431–39), discusses the reactions to Pascal through the 18th, 19th and 20th cs; R. Damien, 'Gabriel Naudé et la critique des romans' (441–49), comments on the adverse attitudes to novels, as 'bavardage' for feeble minds, no more than 'songs' and 'mensonge'; O. Bloch, 'Littérature, théâtre et philosophie à propos de Molière' (451–60), states that Molière's philosphical views can only indirectly be deduced from his plays; I. Delpla, 'Bayle, pratiques de la diversité' (461–68), discusses the diversity of readers' taste; F. Rouget, 'De la sage femme à la femme sage: reflexions et reflexivité dans les *Observations* de Louise Boursier' (483–96), gives an account of Boursier's published personal experiences as a midwife (1563–1636); M.-C. Pioffet, 'Relations de missions et intertextualité: les voies de Paul Lejeune et de Chrestian Leclerq' (497–509), looks at the accounts of Jesuit missionaries; F. Lasserre, 'Un ouvrage sous-estimé: *La Comédie des comédiens* de Gougenot, 1631/2' (511–22), attempts to rehabilitate a neglected play (there is a modern edition of 1974); K. Willis Wolfe, 'The baroque paradox of Cyrano de Bergerac's *Pédant joué*: exploiting a conventionalised form to express an anti-authoritarian content' (523–30), mentions its only 19th-c. performance at the time of Rostand's *Cyrano*; R. J. Goulbourne, 'Visual effects and the theatrical illusion in Pierre Corneille's early plays' (531–44), emphasizes the visual quality of the plays and the playing with conventions: J. Carson, 'On Molière's debt to Scarron for Sganarelle in *Le Cocu imaginaire*' (545–54), refers to Scarron's *Le Jodelet soufflet é*, 1652; C. B. Kerr, 'Sous le signe de l'Europe: *Le Menteur* de Jean-Marie Villigier' (555–70), a play produced at Strasbourg in the 1990s; T. Meding, 'Adamas, Alexis, and the fashioning of the Androgyne in *L'Astrée*' (571–80), outlines the fluid gender boundaries and the aesthetic principles underlying them; P. Trzebiatowski, 'The hunt is on: the duc de Nemours, aggression and rejection' (581–93), comments on Nemours as a gamesman, since love is a war, and the eventual failure of his spying; G. Banderier, 'Du *Saint Louis* à la *Louisiade*: note sur la réception du P. Le Moyne au XVIIIe siècle' (595–97), refers to a publication of 1774, *Les Quatre Premiers Chants de la Louisiade. Chroniques de Port-Royal, Port-Royal et l'Histoire*, Bibliothèque Mazarine, 372 pp., contains: B. Chédozeau, 'Situation de l'Histoire en France au XVIIe siècle' (7–14), assesses the conceptions of historians, the Jesuits neutral in their historical works, while Augustinian-inspired writings look at history from a religious angle; H. Savon, 'Godfroi Hermant, Biographie des Pères de l'Eglise' (15–42), examines the writings, as a critical study to avoid hagiography; J.-M. Delabre, 'Robert Arnauld d'Andilly et l'Histoire des Juifs' (43–51), discusses his translations of Flavius Josephus, elegant, but erroneous, yet a 'succès de librairie'; J. Mesnard, 'Port-Royal et saint Louis; (53–73), compares versions of Le Nain de Tillemont, Filleau de la Chaise, and stresses Port-Royal's devotion to Saint Louis; J. Lesaulnier, 'Aux sources de l'Historiographie Port-Royaliste, tradition orale et récits symboliques' (75–105), comments on the 'mise en mémoires' made in historical writing practised at Port-Royal, with a tendency to dramatization.

THE EIGHTEENTH CENTURY*

By D. A. DESSERUD, *Associate Professor of Politics,*
University of New Brunswick at Saint John

MONTESQUIEU

CORRESPONDENCE, WORKS, BIOGRAPHY. *Correspondance, I, 1700–1731, lettres 1–364,* ed. Louis Desgraves and Edgar Mass, with C. P. Courtney, J. Ehrard and A. Postigliola (*Oeuvres complètes de Montesquieu,* 18), Oxford, Voltaire Foundation, lxxxxviii + 476 pp. The first of a projected four volumes covering M.'s correspondence. It covers the period of M.'s life from before his time at the collège de Juilly, up to his return from his travels in Europe. Of the 277 letters printed here, 30 are new. Contains extensive notes, including biographical details of the correspondents, and manuscript varia. This will certainly be the definitive edition of M.'s correspondence, and is also the first volume available of the much anticipated new series of M.'s complete works. Louis Desgraves, *Inventaire des documents manuscrits des fonds Montesquieu de la Bibliothèque municipale de Bordeaux,* Geneva, Droz, 368 pp., is an important contribution to Montesquieu studies, containing as well the newly catalogued material which has only recently (1993) emerged; Id., *Chronologie critique de la vie et des oeuvres de Montesquieu,* Champion, 611 pp. **De l'Esprit des lois (édition partielle): Livres I et XIII (imprimé et manuscrit),* ed. Alberto Postigliola et al., Oxford, The Voltaire Foundation, xxxv + 105 pp.

THOUGHT AND INTELLECTUAL RELATIONSHIPS. D. W. Carrithers, 'Montesquieu's philosophy of punishment', *HPT,* 19:213–40. M. is the first significant author of the enlightenment to discuss the relationship between punishment, crime, and legislation, yet little has been written on M.'s philosophy of punishment. C. argues that M. promoted a moderate, utilitarian, and retributivist philosophy, and refused to make sharp distinctions between public and private morality. An important study on a neglected aspect of M.'s work. Jean Lechat, *La Politique dans l'"Esprit des lois",* Nathan, 126 pp. Jean Ehrard, *L'Esprit des mots: Montesquieu en lui-même et parmi les siens,* Geneva: Droz, 336 pp., is a collection of critical essays which looks at M. on sovereignty, happiness, superstition, and the Inquisition; Id., 'Diderot lecteur de Montesquieu', pp. 175–90 of *Amicitia Scriptor: littérature, histoire des idées, philosophie. Mélanges offerts à Robert Mauzi,* ed. Annie Becq, Charles Porset, and Alain Mothu, Champion,

---

* This section appears in a reduced form while new contributors are being sought.

358 pp. Jean-François Chiappe, with Éric Vatré, *Montesquieu, l'homme et l'héritage*, Monaco, Rocher, 471 pp. C. Betts, 'Constructing utilitarianism: Montesquieu on Suttee in *Lettres persanes*', *FS*, 51, 1997 : 19–29. Is M.'s letter cxxv on suttee in India meant to be an attack on that practice? Or should it be read as a metaphorical attack on Christianity? B. argues that neither approach works. Letter cxxv is an explication of the utilitarian pleasure-pain principle. P. Kra, 'The name Rica and the Veil in Montesquieu's *Lettres persanes*', *SFr*, 42 : 78–79. L. J. Marso, 'The stories of citizens: Rousseau, Montesquieu, and de Staël challenge Enlightenment reason', *Polity*, 30 : 435–63, discusses how all three writers cautioned against the model of masculine, excessively individualistic autonomy that was emerging from Enlightenment thought. This model excludes women, a problem addressed by all three. G. W. Jones, 'The Spirit of the Nakaz: Catherine II's literary debt to Montesquieu', *SEER*, 76 : 658–71.

RMon is a new journal devoted to Montesquieu studies, and will publish once a year. The first volume (1997) contains: J.-P. Courtois, 'Des voix dans le traité' (7–24); E. Pii, 'La Rome antique chez Montesquieu' (25–38), which looks at M.'s soujourn in Rome (1728) that marked the transformation of M. from having a literary attitude to having a scientific attitude. M.'s experience taught him much about modern politics, but it also brought him into contact with works by Italian authors such as Machiavelli, Doria, and Gravina. This experience was profoundly influential to his composition, not just of *EL*, but the *Considérations* as well. This was, after all, the first book he completed upon returning to France. D. W. Carrithers, 'La philosophie pénale de Montesquieu' (39–64). M. Porret, 'Les "lois doivent tendre à la rigueur plutôt qu'à l'indulgence". Muyart de Vouglans *versus* Montesquieu' (65–96), demonstrates that by arguing that moderate punishments were characteristic of democracies, and severe punishments better suited to tyrannies, M. undermined arguments in favour of severe punishment. Muyart de Vouglans countered this position in an essay (1785) on punishment, 'addressed' to Montesquieu, 'Lettre sur le système de l'auteur de *L'Esprit des lois* touchant la Modération des Peines'. Porret includes the full text of V.'s essay. G. Mairet, '"L'esprit général" et la constitution de la *res publica* européenne' (97–112). E. Mass, 'Le Montesquieu de Victor Klemperer (1914–1915)' (113–32). In J.-P. Courtois, 'Montesquieu au présent. La jurisprudence du réel. Entretien avec Michel Chaillou' (133–48), Chaillou discusses why he finds M. still so important today; he prefers M.'s *Voyages* and the *Pensées* to 18th-c. fiction, works which reflect too well the rhetoric of their time. L. Desgraves, 'Montesquieu académicien honoraire de l'Académie des sciences, des belles-lettres et des arts d'Amiens (1750) (173); Id., 'Un projet d'édition des *Œuvres de Montesquieu en 1949*' (174); C. Volphilhac-Auger, 'Montesquieu et Barbey. L'enfant, le moineau et la *Vieille Maîtresse*' (175–76).

The second volume (1998) contains: G. Barrera, 'Montesquieu et la mer' (7–44), which explores the theme of the sea throughout M.'s writings, from navigation, commerce and exploration to 'l'esprit de la mer'; H. Drei, 'Le mot et le concept de vertu chez Machiavel et Montesquieu' (45–54); C. Volpilhac-Auger, 'Les rois de Prusse sous le regard de Montesquieu' (55–66), which looks at M.'s voyage in Germany, part of his travels which have not received the attention that his voyage in Italy and England have; N. Plavinskaia, 'Catherine II ébauche le *Nakaz*: premières notes de lecture de *L'Esprit des lois*' (67–88); M. Troper, 'Montesquieu en l'an III' (89–106), which argues that while it is true that the constitution of year III borrowed M.'s theory of the balance of powers, M. did not recommend such an impossible balance as contained there; F. Lotterie, 'L'oracle désavoué. Montesquieu selon Sainte-Beuve, ou les lumières sans la politique'(107–18); A. Amiel, 'Hannah Arendt lectrice de Montesquieu' (119–38); C. Spector, '*L'Esprit des lois* de Montesquieu: entre libéralisme et humanisme civique' (139–64), which discusses M.'s 'civic humanism' as presenting a counterpoise to the extreme liberty M. found in England. M.'s 'liberalism' is resolutely plural. C. Larrère, 'Vers un nouveau Montesquieu? Entretien avec Claude Nicolet' (165–75).

THE ROMANTIC ERA

POSTPONED

THE NINETEENTH CENTURY (POST-ROMANTIC)

POSTPONED

THE TWENTIETH CENTURY, 1900–1945

By ANGELA M. KIMYONGÜR, *Lecturer in French at the University of Hull*

1. ESSAYS AND STUDIES

The surrealist movement continues to be the focus of critical attention with a number of important studies on the subject. Elza Adamowicz, *Surrealist Collage in Text and Image. Dissecting the Exquisite Corpse* (Cambridge Studies in French, 56), CUP, 264 pp., presents a subtle and rigorous analysis of *collage*, both as a process and as individual works, aiming to reposition *collage* at the centre of surrealist activity. The study situates itself in the context of recent reassessments of surrealism which focus less on the spontaneous nature of surrealism than on the conscious complexity of its production. *Collage* takes its place in this framework as a deliberately subversive process of 'détournement'. Jack J. Spector, *Surrealist Art and Writing 1919–1939: The Gold of Time* (Contemporary Artists and their Critics), CUP, 1997, ix + 322 pp., in a stimulating and thoughtful analysis, proposes a new approach to surrealism which identifies the role played by the largely middle-class education of surrealist writers and artists under the Third Republic in the development of their critique of bourgeois values. Critical of approaches to surrealism which attempt to separate the movement from its historical and political context, S. demonstrates how surrealist (male) writers and artists, referred to as 'suburban adolescents in revolt', were caught between their desire to reject the values of their class of origin and the way in which their education had so permeated their intellectual horizons that they unconsciously reproduced bourgeois values in their art. This is seen in a particularly acute way through their ambivalent attitudes towards the Other, whether female, non-Western or working-class. Questions of gender, in particular the role of women within the surrealist movement are considered in two volumes. *Surrealist Women. An International Anthology*, ed. Penelope Rosemont, London, Athlone Press, xxvii + 516 pp., is a very rich volume which has as its aim 'the recovery of surrealism's lost voices', the work of those female surrealists who are normally left out of anthologies of surrealist writing. R., herself a surrealist, presents women surrealists as being at the very centre of the international surrealist movement from its inception, and, while recognizing some of the contradictions inherent in early surrealist attitudes to women, nonetheless insists on the intrinsically counter-patriarchal nature of the movement. The texts are arranged chronologically, and each author is presented through an informative introduction. This is a valuable source work for both the general reader and for the specialist, who may discover a number of previously lost voices. Marie-Claire Barnet, *La Femme cent sexes ou les genres communicants. Deharme, Mansour, Prassinos*, Berne, Lang, 323 pp., has similar aims to those of the preceding volume in her attempt to bring out of critical oblivion the 'trois illustres méconnues' who form the subjects of this study. B. inscribes her study within a recent tradition of re-reading and re-evaluating surrealism. Her chosen authors are presented as doubly subversive — operating both as women writers and as surrealists: 'la subversion de la subversion surréaliste'. The study focuses on questions of the ambiguity of sexual identity, and the plurality of surrealism which these writers explore. While upholding the importance of the female contribution to surrealism, B. emphatically refuses a ghettoization of female surrealists. Her insistence on their integration within the movement is reflected in the chapter which focuses on the classic themes of surrealism: hysteria, *l'amour fou* and beauty. Heike Laube, *Les Surréalistes sans le savoir oder die Gothic Novel aus surrealistischer Sicht* (EH, 13, Französische Sprache und Literatur), 288 pp. Peter D. Tame, *The Ideological Hero in the Novels of Robert Brasillach, Roger Vailland and André Malraux* (Ars Interpretandi, 6), NY, Lang, xxvi + 518 pp. is an ambitious study which aims to show that despite the obvious ideological differences between the three authors studied, there is a significant amount of common ground between their concepts of the ideological hero and the ways in which these heroes are represented in their novels. Providing detailed analyses of Brasillach's Fascist Man, Vailland's Bolchevik and Malraux's New Man, T. convincingly demonstrates that each writer operates a similar hierarchy of heroes, from the pioneer hero, usually a historical figure, to the model hero, an ideal figure acting as an example to the follower hero who is often more problematical and at the centre of a learning process in the novel. Despite their status as committed writers, the three are seen as ideologically unorthodox, giving less importance in their representations of hero figures to ideology than to individual qualities. Parallels are also seen in the use of heroic and ideological discourse. T. argues that the continued significance of these writers has more to do with the qualities of their heroic characters than with their ideological credentials *per se*. This is a very clearly written and methodical study, with many insights for those interested in these three novelists, or more generally in the discourse and practice of political fiction. Michel Aucouturier, *Le Réalisme socialiste* (Que sais-je?), PUF, 128 pp., focuses primarily on the development of socialist realism within the former Soviet Union, but also looks briefly at the impact of this doctrine on other socialist countries and on France in the 1930s. *Les Ecrivains face à l'histoire: France 1920–1996: Actes du colloque*, ed. Antoine de Baecque (BPI en Actes), Bibliothèque publique d'information, 244 pp., contains the results of a 'journée d'études' on the question of *engagement* itself stemming from an exhibition at the Centre Pompidou. The volume does an admirable job in casting interesting new light on a subject often deemed 'dépassé'. It includes S. Added, 'Jacques Copeau et le "théâtre populaire" dans les années Vichy' (21–44), on the involvement of Copeau in the Vichy régime; A. Simonin, 'La lettre aux directeurs de la résistance de Jean Paulhan' (45–74), on Paulhan's critique of the *épuration*; E. Loyer, 'Engagement/désengagement dans la France de l'après-guerre' (77–111), on the reaction against *engagement* in the 1950s, with particular reference to the *Hussards*; C. Ibos, 'L'intellectuel comme intellectuel défiguré' (113–38), on the figure of the commmunist intellectual in the wake of 1956; F. Vergès, '"Il y a deux France ...".': Ecrivains noirs et colonialisme (1920–1960)' (139–73), on the conflict between black writers and colonialism; and C. Bourseiller, 'Les causes des peuples: les écrivains et le gauchisme' (175–224), on the involvement of writers in the extreme left in the late 1960s. Géraldi Leroy, *Les Ecrivains et l'histoire 1919–1956* (128, 189), Nathan, 128 pp., provides a lucid and readable synthesis of relations between writers, intellectuals and history, in particular politics. Conscious of the sacrifice, both artistic and personal, that this choice represented for many writers, L. aims to correct what he sees as the undervaluing of political literature. He does not, as many critics on the subject have done, limit his analysis to the Left, but seeks to place the activities of the right-wing intellectual in the frame. Topics covered include the reactions to World War I, the rise of fascism and the Right in the 1930s, relations with the French Communist Party, the Occupation and *engagement*. L. Stern, 'The creation of French-Soviet cultural relations. VOKS in the 1920s and the French intelligentsia', *AUMLA*, 89:43–66, makes use of unpublished archive material to explore the role of French intellectuals in establishing cultural links between France and the USSR at a time when visits to the Soviet Union by French intellectuals were particularly frequent. Claire Gorrara, *Women's Representations of the Occupation in Post-'68 France*, London, Macmillan, vii + 168 pp., is another welcome contribution to ongoing attempts to give due recognition to women's contributions to French culture. This volume concentrates on women's narratives of the Occupation. Acknowledging the importance of recent re-evaluations of *les années noires*, notably Rousso's *Le Syndrome de Vichy*, G. takes issue with the marginalization in such works of women's perspectives on the experience of occupation and resistance. The study focuses on two different generations of writers: those who were active in the Resistance and wrote about it after the event, and those who were children at the time or who were born after the war and reflect on the Resistance experience through the experience of their parents. This is a wide-ranging and interesting study which casts new light on its complex subject. Micheline Kessler-Claudet, *La Guerre de quatorze dans le roman occidental* (128, 188), Nathan, 128 pp., provides a useful introduction to the literature of World War I, focusing on France, Germany and the USA. The study is divided into four sections which explore in turn the narrative structures of war fiction, the imagery of war, the experience of the soldier, and different literary and intellectual responses to war. The author puts forward a convincing argument for seeing the literature of the First World War as a major turning point in the development of the modern novel. *Gender and Fascism in Modern France*, ed. Melanie Hawthorne and Richard Golsan, Dartmouth, New England U.P., 1997, ix + 229 pp., is a fascinating volume of essays which set out to explore the complex relations between gender and fascism as elaborated in works from the *fin-de-siècle* to the present day. The usual association between fascism and masculinity is found to be simplistic, and several essays focus on the relationship between fascist ideology and the feminine. Relevant to this section are: M. Hawthorne, on the cultural uses made of Rachilde's writing (27–48); M. J. Green, on Trilby's construction of a heroine who is the embodiment of fascist ideals (49–68); M. Guyot-Bender, on Corinne Luchaire's supplement to the collaborationist daily *Les Temps nouveaux*, and its contribution to the construction of gender during the Occupation (69–82); and A. Loselle, on Morand's 'representation of a masculinist ideology under threat of erasure by the feminine' (101–18). Romana N. Lowe, *The Fictional Female. Sacrificial Rituals and Spectacles of Writing in Baudelaire, Zola and Cocteau* (Currents in Comparative Romance Languages and Literatures, 54), NY, Lang, 1997, xii + 239 pp., is a closely-argued investigation into patterns of sacrificial violence against women in 19th-c. and 20th-c. French literature. L. focuses on well-known works (eg. Cocteau's *La Machine infernale*) to show how the ritual elimination of a female figure is associated with the restoration of a patriarchal order which had been thrown into disorder by a transgressive female character. The re-establishment of order through ritual violence is not merely observed, but also seen as profoundly misogynistic. The literary patterns identified are read against the theories of René Girard, who is seen to be complicit in a tendency which, far from being a literary aberration, has profound and widespread implications for the perception of women within the patriarchal order. A. Kershaw, 'Homosexuality and transgression in three political novels of the 1930s', Duffy, *Transgression*, 219–34, is included in a volume of conference papers on the theme of transgression in French literature, and contains an analysis of novels by Louise Weiss, Edith Thomas, and Drieu la Rochelle, focusing on the presentation of homosexuality as a trangressive force and the way in which this presentation relates to and clarifies the very different political messages of the three texts. D. Holmes, ' "Quel fleuve noir nous emportait . . .": Sex and the woman reader at the *fin-de siècle*,' *NFS*, 37.1:51–67, in a special number on 'French Erotic Fiction', examines the presentation of eroticism and desire in novels by Tinayre. Her novels are seen as distinct from novels by Rachilde, Vivien, and Colette which offer much more of a challenge to patriarchal perceptions of sex. While the latter authors wrote for a limited, self-selecting audience sympathetic to notions of sexual transgression, T.'s audience was primarily composed of middle-class women. Hence her representations of desire, while affirming the reality of female desire, had to operate within the constraints of such women's experience. D. E. Hamilton, 'Gender, genre and politics in French detective fiction of the 1930s: Camille Hedwige's *L'Appel de la morte*', *FMLS*, 34:56–68, is an interesting appraisal of H.'s attempt to rework the genre conventions of detective fiction in order to challenge the traditional gendered ordering of society. Hamilton also looks at the way H. moves away from the classic focus of the whodunnit and concentrates instead upon the study of psychological motivation, the 'why?' of murder rather than the 'who?'. Teresa Bridgeman, *Negotiating the New in the French Novel. Building Contexts for Fictional Worlds*, London, Routledge, xi + 274 pp., is one of a number of new studies of the novel. This volume draws on insights from stylistics and narratology in order to provide an ambitious and detailed re-reading of a number of canonic texts. The texts are chosen as instances of innovative novels which have in different ways challenged readers' expectations of the novel, and in which authors have invited readers to a renegotiation of the conventions of the novel and of reading. B. focuses particularly on the question of genre shift and the ways in which such shifts affect the relationship between text and reader. Of particular interest for this period is a chapter on Céline's *Voyage au bout de la nuit*. Henri Mitterand, *Le Roman à l'oeuvre: genèse, motifs et valeurs* (Ecriture), PUF, 310 pp., takes a critical stand against what he calls 'la dérive postmoderne', the tendency of methodologies to focus exclusively on form at the expense of the specificity of individual authors and their time. In its place he calls for 'une critique d'analyse, de complicité et de plaisir', a fusion of established methodologies alongside the new. Such an inclusive approach underpins this study in which M. applies the insights afforded by genetic criticism, as well as by the relationship between history and politics and by questions of style, to the themes of time and space in Zola, Céline, Aragon, and others. Denis Pernot,

Le Roman de socialisation en France 1889–1914 (Ecriture), PUF, 239 pp., is a wide-ranging and lucid analysis of this particular form of didactic novel which emerged in the latter part of the 19th-c.. P. places this development firmly in its ideological and social context, in an attempt to understand society's need to guide its youth into respectable adulthood, to determine why the novel form was used to accomplish this task and to show how the novelist took on the role of pedagogue. Admitting that to read such novels is often to 'travailler dans la banalité', P. establishes a corpus of some 100 novels which illustrate a certain ideological conformism emanating from the 'romancier-pédagogue' and a level of banality from which few, with the exception of Barrès, were able to escape. Michel Jarrety, *La Critique littéraire française au XXème siècle* (Que sais-je?), PUF, 128 pp., contains a succinct presentation of the evolution of French literary criticism from the influence of Lanson to the importance of 'critique génétique'. John Sturrock, *The Word from Paris. Essays on Modern French Thinkers and Writers*, London, Verso, xv + 206 pp., is a collection of essays, originally written for the *Times Literary Supplement* and the *London Review of Books*, revised and brought together for this volume. While they were originally intended for a general, though informed, readership rather than for a more specialized audience, this in no way detracts from the quality of the writing and insights which the essays provide. This is a lively collection which, taken together, provides an entertaining and perceptive introduction to the world of modern French thought and literature. Of particular interest for this period are essays on Proust, Barbusse and Céline. *Making Connections. Essays in French Culture and Society in Honour of Philip Thody*, ed. James Dolamore, NY, Lang, 283 pp., is a collection of essays which judiciously reflects Professor Thody's own wide-ranging interests in the field of French Studies. There is a predominance of articles with a comparative slant, a tribute to his own enthusiasm for 'making connections' across cultures. Jean Lescure, **Poésie: histoire de Messages 1939–1946*, IMEC, 480 pp.

2. THEATRE

Michel Lioure, *Lire le théâtre moderne. De Claudel à Ionesco*, Montrouge, Dunod, 190 pp., seizes from the beginning upon the contradictory implications of a title such as 'Lire le théâtre' and reflects on the ambiguous position of theatre, poised as it is between spectacle and literature. While acknowledging the importance of spectacle, L. argues that theatre is just as much 'miroir d'un siècle' as is literature. The first section is given over to questions of dramatic art. This is followed by an analysis of the major trends and playwrights of the first two-thirds of the century. The final section contains a short anthology of writing on theatre by a number of its practitioners and commentators, including Claudel, Camus and Sartre.

3. POETRY

Ygaunin, *Pindare*, VII, and Ygaunin, *Pindare*, VIII, form the final two volumes of a series which attempts to trace the influence of Pindar, seen as a 'phare', down through the generations up to the 20th-c.. In volume VII, Y. sees the influence of Pindar at work in Valéry's poetry through his search for poetic perfection. In the subsequent volume, he considers the poetry of Claudel and Montherlant, focusing upon the cosmic resonances of Claudel's language, and seeing in Montherlant the continuation of P.'s celebration of athleticism in his 'mystique du sport'. *Le Lis et la langue. Actes de la journée d'étude du centre de recherche Poésie, poétique et spiritualité*, ed. Dominique Millet-Gérard, Paris-Sorbonne U.P., 170 pp., contains a series of papers all focusing on the relationship between spirituality and poetry, including: H. Levillain, 'Le Saint et l'écrivain' (9–20); C.-P. Perez, 'Art, science et religion au temps du symbolisme' (21–32); C. Bayle, 'La Dimension sotériologique de l'écriture dans les oeuvres en prose de Pierre Reverdy' (33–43); S. Guermès, 'La Poésie d'Yves Bonnefoy: une nouvelle alliance' (45–58); B. Bercoff, 'Contemplation et détachement dans la poésie de Francis Ponge' (59–69); A. P. de Beaufort, '*Bientôt vous devenez une île heureuse*: quelques aspects de la poésie de Marie-Claire Bancquart' (71–81); R. Vaissermann, 'La Création du Verbe et la création verbale chez Péguy' (83–98); P. Delaveau, 'De l'exil vers le centre: la poésie en quête du secret' (99–112); O-T. Venard, 'Note de poétique théologique, saint Thomas d'Aquin et la métaphore' (113–47); D. Millet-Gérard, '*Poetica restituta. La Revue thomiste* et les poètes' (149–61).

4. INDIVIDUAL AUTHORS

ALBERT-BIROT. Debra Kelly, **Pierre Albert-Birot. A Poetics in Movement. A Poetics of Movement*, Farleigh Dickinson U.P., 1997, 440 pp.

APOLLINAIRE. Jean Burgos, Claude Debon, and Michel Décaudin, *Apollinaire en somme* (Littératures de notre siècle, 7), Champion, 279 pp., comprises, as the title suggests, an attempt to provide 'une approche globale' to A.'s work and to assess recent research. This attempt at a synthesis is made difficult by internal contradictions in A.'s work and the lack of a coherent corpus. Undeterred, the authors embark on a study which emphasises the unity of A.'s work. Debon's section 'Fils de personne' concentrates on the question of the

construction of A.'s identity, both personal and poetic. Décaudin in
'L'Ecrivain et son temps', focuses on A.'s relationship with the
contemporary literary scene, while Burgos attempts to provide in
'Sur les sentiers de la création' an insight into A.'s poetics, emphasizing his preoccupation not with an aesthetic ideal, but rather with
poetic truth. E.-A. Hubert, 'Autres scolies sur *Alcools* d'Apollinaire',
RHLF, 98 : 113–22, locates the source of 'Les Colchiques' not in A.'s
stay in Rhénanie as has been previously assumed, but in his reading
of *De la vie d'Apollonius Hyanéen*. H. attributes a note in A.'s 'Agenda
russe' to his reading of this text and uses this to identify parallels
between 'Les Colchiques' and the source text. Faik Konitza and
Guillaume Apollinaire, *Une amitié européenne*, Esprit des Péninsules,
240 pp.

ARAGON. In the wake of the centenary celebrations of his birth,
Aragon continues to attract substantial critical attention. John
Bennett, *Aragon, Londres et la France libre. Réception de l'oeuvre en Grande-
Bretagne, 1940–1946*, L'Harmattan, 271 pp., contains a very detailed
and meticulously researched analysis of the reception accorded A.'s
resistance poetry in Great Britain, demonstrating that alongside very
favourable views of his work, there were those, notably Arthur
Koestler and the surrealists Mesens and Brunius, who attacked his
return to traditional verse forms and maintained that his patriotism
was false and self-serving. B. succeeds in bringing alive the spirit of
the time from an original perspective, and at the same time makes a
staunch defence of A. from the accusations laid against him. Maryse
Vassevière, *Aragon romancier intertextuel ou les pas de l'étranger*, L'Harmattan, 381 pp., is an illuminating and scholarly study of intertextuality
in A.'s final novels, where its use is seen as a means of understanding
the writer and his relation to history and writing. The choice of the
final novels as a corpus is justified by the significant use of the intertext
in these novels, which in its turn is seen as being A.'s strategy for
dealing with the crises of 1956 and of re-evaluating his past, its
silences and its 'oublis'. The intertext is seen as a 'discours de
contrebande d'un genre nouveau', which also helps the reader to
orientate himself in these difficult and complex works. *Les Engagements
d'Aragon*, ed. Jacques Girault and Bernard Lecherbonnier (*Itinéraires et
contacts de cultures*, 23–24), L'Harmattan, 1997, 165 pp., contains the
papers from a centenary conference on A.'s work. Divided into four
sections, the papers trace a chronological view of A.'s career which
emphasizes the complementarity of his political and literary activities.
The first section, 'L'heure de la révolte' explores Aragon's surrealist
years and his movement towards the Communist Party. Section two,
'L'Engagement' reflects on the period from his membership of the
PCF to World War II. The third section 'La Militance' explores A's

political and literary activities in the 1950s and 1960s, while the final section 'Le Fou' looks at his latter years. Nedim Gürsel, *Le Mouvement perpétuel d'Aragon. De la révolte dadaïste au monde réel*, L'Harmattan, 1997, 195 pp., sees the notion of 'mouvement perpétuel' as the only constant of A.'s work, but within this constant change he sees an inner unity. From this standpoint, G. embarks upon an analysis of A.'s poetry where 'mouvement perpétuel' is seen as a dialectical movement between modernity and tradition, between 'rupture' and 'continuité'. While A.'s poetry is known to find its source in the Dadaist and Surrealist *avant-garde*, G. contends that long before the return to traditional verse forms during the Resistance, there is a strong thread of tradition in A's early poetry. These two poles are explored with sensitivity in the two main sections 'poésie de rupture' and 'poésie de continuité'. *Aragon, le mouvement perpétuel*, ed. Nicolas Alain and Henriette Zoughebi, Stock, 1997, 203 pp., is a collection of essays written not by academics but by creative artists. Each essay focuses on an individual work of Aragon's, from *Le Paysan de Paris* to *Henri Matisse, roman*. Jean Albertini, *Non, Aragon n'est pas un écrivain engagé! Textes inconnus ou méconnus*, Grigny, Paroles d'Aube, 152 pp., comprises a slim, though useful, anthology of lesser known texts by A., brought together under this deliberately provocative title in order to demonstrate to the reader the inadequacy of popular preconceptions about the writer. In his introduction to the texts, Albertini shows himelf to be a passionate defender of Aragon's frequently battered reputation, and invites the reader to use the volume as a starting point to better knowledge of 'une des grandes voix [. . .] de ce siècle'. *Recherches croisées Aragon/Elsa Triolet, 6*, ed. Equipe de Recherche Interdisciplinaire sur Elsa Triolet et Aragon, Besançon, Annales Littéraires de l'Université de Franche-Comté, 280 pp. Louis Janover, *Cent ans de servitude: Aragon et les siens*, Arles, Sullivers, 103 pp. W. Bohn, 'Louis Aragon and the critical muse', *RR*, 89:367–79, explores the influence of Apollinaire on A.'s 'critique synthétique', a form of criticism which attempted to comment on works of art while retaining its own creative identity.

ARTAUD. L. A. Boldt-Irons, 'In search of a forgotten culture: Artaud, Mexico and the balance of matter and spirit', *RR*, 89:123–38, discusses A.'s writings on Mexican culture which for him, in the predominance it accorded the body, was a truer culture than Western culture with its insistence on the superiority of intellect and spirit over body. During his visit to Mexico, A. discovered that the culture he sought was actually tainted by European culture but nonetheless his discovery of Mexican culture enabled him to attain a balance between body and culture. E. Grossman, 'Poétique de l'aliénation chez Antonin Artaud', *EsC*, 38.4:136–42, examines the influence of A. on philosophical thought, particularly in the area of the relationship between alienation and truth, madness and writing.

BARRÈS. Marie-Agnès Kirscher, *Relire Barrès*, Villeneuve d'Ascq, Presses Universitaires du Septentrion, 351 pp., is a committed and scholarly attempt to rehabilitate B., to encourage a critical reading, or re-reading, which is long overdue. Disparaging of the reasons behind B.'s fall into relative obscurity, K. makes an impassioned plea for a serious re-evaluation of his work, which has fallen victim, firstly to ideologically motivated neglect, and secondly to the assumption that such neglect of his works implies a lack of artistic substance. K. maintains that if we are ready to read such authors as Céline and Blanchot in full knowledge of their political views, then it is high time for an objective reassessment of Barrès Ida-Marie Frandon, *Barrès tel qu'en lui-même: modernité et déracinement*, Fontainebleau, La Pirole, 273 pp. C. Perry, 'Reconfiguring Wagner's *Tristan*: political aesthetics in the works of Maurice Barrès', *FrF*, 23:317–35, analyses the influence of Wagnerian music and drama upon B.'s political thought.

BERNANOS. Claire Daudin, *Georges Bernanos. Une parole libre*, Desclée de Brouwer, 91 pp., describes itself very accurately as 'une oeuvre de sympathie et de passion'. Part biography and part critical introduction to the thought and writing of B., this is a very readable and accessible work which provides some sensitive insights into B. the man and the writer. *Bernanos: création et modernité*, ed. Max Milner (Actes et Colloques, 55), Klincksieck — Lublin, Presses de l'Université Marie-Curie-Sklodowska, 290 pp., contains a collection of conference papers which aim to go beyond the traditional religious and ideological interpretations of B. and to look at what is modern in his use of literary forms. The papers are divided into four sections. The first section considers the notion of B.'s modernity; the second focuses on aspects of his literary creativity; the third proposes new readings of the major literary texts, while the fourth section takes a comparative approach, looking at parallels between B. and other writers in their treatment of similar themes. Jean-Christian Pleau, *Bernanos. La part obscure* (Currents in Comparative Romance Languages and Literatures, 56), NY, Lang, 129 pp., also seizes on B.'s modernity. P. reflects that while B. now seems very distant from us in terms of his political and religious affiliations, nonetheless this distance is invaluable in assessing the 'littérarité' of his work, and in allowing us to see beyond the confines of doctrine, of a Catholicism which is after all not so transparent, to the 'part obscure' in B.'s writing. P. focuses on themes of obscurity and ambiguity, which he sees as integral to B.'s modernity. François de Saint-Cheron, *Georges Bernanos*, Publications ADPF, 47 pp., published under the aegis of the Ministère des Affaires Etrangères, is a useful introduction to B., arranged thematically around a number of his key preoccupations and places which influenced his thought. Robert Colonna D'Istria, *Georges Bernanos: le poète et le prophète*, France-Empire, 195 pp. *Etudes Bernanosiennes, 21: Bernanos et la modernité*, ed. Michel Estève (*RLMod*, Georges Bernanos), Lettres Modernes 223 pp.. Sébastien Lapaque, *Georges Bernanos encore une fois*, Lausanne, Age d'Homme, 126 pp.

BOUSQUET. Nicole Bhattacharya, *Joë Bousquet: une expérience spiri-tuelle*, HICL, 364, 482 pp., is a substantial and scholarly volume which aims, through detailed textual analysis, to reinstate at the heart of B.'s work the metaphysical and mystical elements which for Bhattacharya constitute 'son originalité et sa grandeur'.

BRETON. *André Breton*, ed. Michel Murat (Cahiers de l'Herne, 72), Herne, 480 pp. Alain and Odette Virmaux, *Breton*, Vilo, 160 pp. André Veilwahr, *S'affranchir des contradictions: André Breton de 1925 à 1930*, L'Harmattan, 414 pp.

CAILLOIS. P. F. De Domenico, 'Revenge of the novel: Roger Caillois's literary criticism in the wake of the 1930s', *RR*, 89: 381–410, explores C.'s critique of the novel in the 1940s in which he questions its value as political expression, arguing that as a product of the imagination, the novel becomes a substitute for rather than an encouragement to revolutionary activity. In this way C. is seen to subvert contemporary notions of the novel at a time when it was synonymous with politically responsible artistic activity.

CÉLINE. Nicholas Hewitt, *The Life of Céline. A Critical Biography*, Oxford, Blackwell, xvi + 360 pp., is a substantial new work, one in which the author admits from the outset the difficulties involved in writing about C., difficulties stemming from the contradictions inherent in his dual identity as great Modernist writer and as rabid anti-Semite; and difficulties in establishing biographical accuracy when confronted with C.'s construction of a persona often at variance with the reality of his life. H. manages to cut through these problems and offers a rigorously documented yet very readable biography. Partly as a corrective to C.'s own unreliable accounts of his life, C. is placed firmly within his social and geographical context: the social context of his upbringing in *Belle Epoque* Paris, the cultural and intellectual context of inter-war Montmartre, his experiences as a doctor in the working-class suburbs of Paris and later during the Occupation of France. This is an authoritative study which will be of interest not only to C. scholars, but also to students of the cultural and social history of France at this time. R. Scullion, 'Writing and resistance in Louis-Ferdinand Céline's *Féerie pour une autre fois* I', *EsC*, 38.3: 28–29, presents this novel as C.'s written resistance to the charges laid against him after World War II, and as an attempt to disprove the allegations on which these charges were based. S. shows

how C. defended his political pamphlets which, having been republished during the Occupation, were subject to particular scrutiny
during the *épuration*. M. Prévost, 'Acte de parole, acte d'écriture.
Céline, le mot écrit et l'imputabilité dans la trilogie allemande', *SFr*,
41, 1997:283–92, also presents a Céline rather belatedly aware of
the implications of committing his contentious views to paper,
realising that society takes the written word more seriously than it
does the spoken. P. demonstrates how, in recognition of this
realization, C.'s later literary production undergoes a transformation.
In his German trilogy he presents himelf as 'un chroniqueur',
recounting what happened, but paradoxically also as a poet detached
from the world, this as a form of self-protection.

CENDRARS.   Amanda Leaman, *Shades of Sexuality: Colour and Sexual
Identity in the Novels of Blaise Cendrars* (Faux Titre, 137), Amsterdam,
Rodopi, 1997, 162 pp., contains a scholarly and perceptive analysis
of the use of colour in C.'s fiction. Colours have symbolic and sexual
implications which are teased out in detailed analyses of C.'s novels.
The use of colour is used to subtle effect in delineating the fragmented
male self, which is compared to a chameleon assuming different
colours, a process which renders the attribution of sexual identity
problematic. Ultimately the male subject is seen to prefer the safety
of sexual neutrality, symbolized by whiteness, to the demands of
sexuality and colour. *Cendrars au pays de Jean Galmot. Roman et reportage*,
ed. Michèle Touret, Rennes U.P., 269 pp., contains a number of
scholarly papers on the topic of the figure of Jean Galmot in C.'s final
novel *Rhum* and the other journalistic texts in which he appears. The
volume is divided into three sections: 'Autour de *Rhum*, le journal et le
livre', on the formal aspects of the work; 'Galmont, l'homme, le héros
selon Cendrars et le romancier' on the figure who inspired the novel,
and finally 'Cendrars reporter' on the writer's career as a journalist.
Michèle Touret, **Blaise Cendrars: le désir du roman 1920–1930* (Cahiers
Blaise Cendrars, 6), Champion, 408 pp. **Brésil: l'utopialand de Blaise
Cendrars: actes du colloque 4–7 août, 1997, São Paulo*, ed. Maria Teresa de
Freitas and Claude Leroy, L'Harmattan, 390 pp.

CHAR.   Serge Velay, *René Char: l'éblouissement et la fureur*, Olbia, 142
pp., is a poetic and evocative assessment of C., rather than an
analytical volume, an approach which is justified in the preface by a
quotation from C. in which he expressed his reservations about the
kind of criticism which reduced 'à une signification et à un projet un
phénomène qui n'a d'autre raison que d'*être*'.

CLAUDEL.   **Claudel et l'Apocalypse, 2* (*RLMod*, Paul Claudel, 17), Les
Lettres Modernes, 208 pp. François Angelier, **Claudel ou la conversion
sauvage*, Salvator, 176 pp. Claude-Pierre Perez, **Le Visible et l'invisible:*

pour une archéologie de la poétique claudélienne, Besançon, Annales Littéraires de l'Université de Franche-Comté, 258 pp.

COCTEAU. Henry Gidel, **Jean Cocteau ou la difficulté d'être* (Les Grandes Biographies), Flammarion, 270 pp. Jean Touzot, **Jean Cocteau, 2. Autour du Requiem: faisant la planche sur les fleuves des morts* (*RLMod*, Jean Cocteau, 2,) Les Lettres modernes, 176 pp. N. Saleh, 'La Correspondance de Jean Cocteau/Maurice Sachs: ligne de la vie; ligne de l'oeuvre', *DFS*, 44:97–114, uses a reading of the unpublished correspondence between C. and Sachs, in particular from 1925, to cast light on a period of crisis in the life of the former, a time when he was undergoing a 'cure de désintoxication' and was forbidden visitors and thus was completely isolated.

COLETTE. Zeina Tamer Schlenoff, *Le Bonheur chez la femme colettienne* (Currents in Comparative Romance Languages and Literatures, 41), NY, Lang, 1997, x + 129 pp., focuses on *La Vagabonde, L'Entrave, Chéri* and *La Fin de Chéri* in order to explore the nature of happiness and the search for happiness in the female characters of these novels. Using insights from feminist literary criticism, S. shows how C. does not present a traditional portrait of feminine happiness, but concentrates instead on strong characters who manage to overcome difficulties in their lives, to triumph over their situation in the search for identity and happiness, and who therefore offer positive role models for the woman reader. Marie-Christine Clément, *Colette au jardin*, Albin Michel, 192 pp., explores C.'s interest in gardens and in nature generally. It is amply and stunningly illustrated with photographs, but also contains a substantial amount of text which aims to evoke 'l'âme jardinière de Colette', both through reference to C.'s own life and through quotations from her work. H. Christiansen, 'Finding a room of her own in Colette's *La Vagabonde*', *DFS*, 44:81–96, presents a reading of *La Vagabonde* as a forerunner of Woolf's *A Room of One's Own*, exploring as it does the tensions between the central character's desire for personal space in which to write and to work, and the desire for love, which threatens the former and on which she ultimately turns her back in order to retain her autonomy. M. Hawthorne, '"C'est si simple ... C'est si difficile": the ideological ambiguity of Colette's *La Chatte*', *AJFS*, 35:360–68, against the background of recent theories about C.'s right-wing sympathies during the Occupation, proposes a new reading of *La Chatte* which, while ambiguous, reflects a 'disturbingly conservative trend' in some of her pre-World War II fiction. M. Rosello, '"L'heure du reflet pourpre": Erotisme-phénix dans le *Duo* de Colette', *NFS*, 37.1:71–87, considers the role of the erotic text in *Duo*, a series of love letters which while central to the novel and its dénouement, form an absence at its centre, since they remain hidden from the reader. Jean Chalon,

*Colette: éternelle apprentie (Les Grandes Biographies), Flammarion, 420 pp. **La grande Colette*, ed. Société des amis de Colette (Cahiers Colette, 20), Rennes U.P., 244 pp.

CREVEL. A. Marangoni, 'Au carrefour de Crevel et d'Eluard', *SFr*, 42:59–65, is an interesting analysis of an unpublished poem in the Fonds Tzara, ostensibly written by C., whose papers were kept by Tristan Tzara after C.'s suicide. While the origins of the poem suggest that it is C.'s, Marangoni suggests that it reads like a poem by Eluard. A detailed reading of the poem and consideration of extratextual factors seem to suggest that it is 'du Crevel écrit à la manière d'Eluard'. M. dismisses the hypothesis that it could have been written by C. unaware of the influence of Eluard; accepts the possiblity that Eluard could have left his own poem among C.'s poems, but comes down on the most likely explanation: that C. wrote it in honour of Eluard.

DELTEIL. Denitza Bantcjeva, **Joseph Delteil*, Lausanne, Age d'Homme, 374 pp.

DUHAMEL. Arlette La Fay, **Duhamel revisité*, Les Lettres Modernes, 231 pp.

FONDANE. *Faux traité d'esthétique*, ed. Anne Van Sevenant, Paris-Méditérannée, 128 pp. *Europe*, 827, is a special number which contains a range of papers on F.

GIDE. Daniel Moutote, *André Gide et Paul Valéry. Nouvelles recherches* (Littérature de notre siècle, 9), Champion, 357 pp., is a collection of M.'s articles on G., some previously published, others not, gathered together from a period of some 30 years. They are wide-ranging in their coverage and do not focus exclusively, as the title might suggest, on G. and V. Instead the volume contains articles on various influences on G.'s writing (Nietzsche, Valéry, Dostoyevsky, and Hesse), as well as articles on G. and *engagement*, on the *Journal* and *Corydon*. Naomi Segal, *André Gide: Pederasty and Pedagogy*, Oxford, Clarendon Press, xxii + 387 pp., is an ambitious and complex contribution to G. studies in relation to issues of gender and homosexuality. Taking as her starting point theories of hydraulics presented as a process of draining, filling and depositing both bodily fluids and knowledge, S. draws together the strands of pedagogy and pederasty in G.'s fictional and non-fictional writings. His sexuality is seen through this framework as a complex interplay of masculinity and femininity, desire, and undesire. *Retour aux Nourritures Terrestres. Actes du colloque de Sheffield 20–22 mars 1997*, ed. David H. Walker and Catharine S. Brosman (Faux Titre, 141), Amsterdam, Rodopi, 1997, xx + 263 pp., contains proceedings of a conference held to celebrate the centenary of the publication of *Les Nourritures terrestres*. The volume is divided into four sections, arranged thematically. Section I on sources and literary influences includes: C. Debard, 'Les sources antiques dans *Les Nourritures terrestres*' (3–26); P. Pollard, 'L'arrière-plan des *Nourritures terrestres*: sources et parentés orientales' (27–45); J. Gillespie, '*Les Nourritures terrestres* comme manuel de délivrance: le rôle des résonances bibliques' (47–64). Section II on earlier critical reactions to *Les Nourritures terrestres* includes: M. Drouin, 'Quelques aperçus relatifs au dialogue André Gide–Marcel Drouin, à propos des *Nourritures terrestres*, avec un inédit' (67–74); P. Fawcett, 'Sur Gide, Pierre Louÿs et la "Ronde de Grenade"' (75–85); C. Brosman, 'Roger Martin du Gard, *Les Thibault* et *Les Nourritures terrestres*' (87–105); J. Sarocchi, '*Les Nourritures terrestres*, par Albert Camus' (107–21). Section III contains detailed textual analyses, including: P. Lachasse, 'La diversité des écritures dans *Les Nourritures terrestres*' (125–139); D. Steel, 'Ponctuation, typographie et mise en page dans *Les Nourritures terrestres*' (141–54); M. Tilby, 'Ecriture et émancipation dans *Les Nourritures terrestres*' (155–69). Section IV on 'Lecteurs et lectures d'aujourd'hui' contains E. Méron, ' *Les Nourritures terrestres*: livre de chevet pour accéder à l'autonomie morale' (173–97); D. Setterfield, 'Mise en abyme, rétroaction et autobiographie dans *Les Nourritures terrestres*' (199–209); D. H. Walker, 'La nature et l'imaginaire dans *Les Nourritures terrestres*' (211–36); A. Goulet, *Les Nouvelles Nourritures*: une autre symphonie pastorale?' (237–63). Eric Marty, André Gide, *Entretiens Gide-Amrouche*, Tournai, La Renaissance du Livre, 316 pp., is a new and updated edition of the series of radio interviews between G. and Amrouche in 1949. The interviews are preceded by a long introduction to G. and his writing career. There is a broadly chronological organization with each interview focusing on a specific work or works, or on literary and intellectual figures associated with a particular period in G.'s life., but the lack of a table of contents or index makes this book difficult to use as a reference work. Alan Sheridon, *André Gide: a Life in the Present*, London, Hamish Hamilton, xix + 709 pp. Mic Chambles-Ploton and Jean-Baptiste Leroux, *Les jardins d'André Gide*, Chêne, 168 pp. *L'Ecriture d'André Gide 1. Genèse et spécificités. Centre Culturel International de Cérisy-la-Salle. Colloque 1996* (*RLMod*, André Gide, 10), Les Lettres Modernes, 271 pp. Claude Martin, *André Gide ou la vocation du bonheur, vol. 1: 1869–1911*, Fayard, 699 pp. Anton Alblas, 'Dear Diary: Gide and his Journal', *AJFS*, 35:348–59, explores the concept of the 'intimate addressee' in an attempt to examine the complex relationship G. developed with his *Journal*. A. demonstrates that G. saw his diary writing as a conversation with a friend, a relationship which had to be sustained, and this in turn explains G.'s preoccupation with the quality and format of paper he used, since for him the notebook and the addressee were one and the same. Anne Greenfeld, ' "Chemin bordé d'aristoloches": dandyism, projection and self-satire in *Paludes*', *AJFS*, 35:189–98, discusses *Paludes* as a satire which G. directed at his own symbolist views as elaborated in *Le Traité de Narcisse*. D. Setterfield, '*Mise en abyme*, retroaction and autobiography in André Gide's *Tentative Amoureuse*', FS, 52:58–70, through an examination of the triangular relationship in *La Tentative amoureuse* between author, narrator, and Luc, elaborates on the difference between traditional autobiography and G.'s autobiographical fiction, particularly focusing on the question of retroaction. D. Steel, 'Fiction, relativity theory, quantum chaology and big bang: the case of *Les Caves du Vatican*', *FrCS*, 8:1–17, explores some of the echoes found in *Les Caves du Vatican* of early 20th-c. developments in theoretical physics, placing these in the context of literary modernism.

GIONO. Ibrahim H. Badr, *Jean Giono. L'esthétique de la violence* (Currents in Comparative Romance Languages and Literatures, 60), NY, Lang, 240 pp., is a detailed and sensitive study of the inner contradictions found in G.'s novels whereby his pacifist ideology is replaced by 'une esthétique de la cruauté et de la violence', seen particularly in G.'s representation of war. Given the profound effect of war upon G. this preoccupation with violence is seen as unsurprising, even in a pacifist writer. The relationship between 'idéologie', which condemns violence, and 'imaginaire', which promotes the aesthetic of violence, is examined and found to be not contradictory but complementary. Hubert Laizé, *Leçon littéraire sur Les Grands Chemins de Jean Giono* (Major), PUF, 147 pp., is one of two guides to G.'s novel, which is identified from the outset as 'déroutant'. More extended and less schematic than is typical of the genre, this study is an accessible and well ordered analysis of the novel, though more specialized readers may be disappointed by the lack of a bibliography. Maryse Adam-Maillet et al., **Jean Giono. Les Grands Chemins*, Ellipses-Marketing, 128 pp.

GIRAUDOUX. Natacha Michel, **Giraudoux: le roman essentiel* (Coup double), Hachette, 224 pp. A. Job, **Giraudoux-Narcisse: genèse d'une écriture romanesque*, Toulouse, Mirail U.P., 270 pp. Bernard Howells, **'Feminist writing by men: the feminine voice and the feminine heroic in the plays of Jean Giraudoux'*, *JIRS*, 5, 1997:191–202.

GREEN. *Julien Green*, ed. Jean Touzot (Littératures contemporaines, 4), Klincksieck, 269 pp., is an attempt to remedy what is seen by the author as the relative critical neglect of G. The volume contains a wide range of articles on various aspects of G.'s writing. Wolfgang Matz, **Julien Green: le siècle et son ombre* (traduit de l'allemand) (Arcades, 58), Gallimard, 189 pp.

GUILLOUX. Yves Loisel, **Louis Guilloux (1899–1980)*, Spezet, Coop Breizh, 288 pp.

JOUVE.   *RSH*, 250, is a special number on 'Pierre Jean Jouve' and includes a range of articles on various aspects of his work.

LOTI.   Alain Quella-Villéger, **Pierre Loti: pèlerin de la planète*, Bordeaux, Aubéron, 560 pp.

MALRAUX.   Jean-François Lyotard, **Chambre sourde: l'antiesthétique de Malraux*, Galilée, 112 pp.

MARITAIN.   James V. Schall, **Jacques Maritain: the philosopher in society*, Rowman and Littlefield, 224 pp.

MARTIN DU GARD.   W. Donald Wilson, *La Structure de dédoublement. Objectivité et mythe dans Les Thibault de Roger Martin du Gard*, Birmingham, Alabama, Summa, 1997, vii + 238 pp., is a substantial study of *Les Thibault* which sees the whole work as structured by a 'bipolarité fondamentale'. W. analyses the ways in which a series of oppositions, of 'dédoublements' between the two brothers Jacques and Antoine, between maternal and paternal orders, between myth and objectivity, relate to the overarching oedipal theme of the work. The oppositions are attributed to a fundamental ambivalence in M. du G. himself as regards his role as writer, aspiring to a realistic representation of events, yet at the same time subverting the realist ethos by the introduction of the mythic element into the novel.

MAURIAC.   Susan Wansink, *Female Victims and Oppressors in Novels by Theodor Fontane and François Mauriac* (Currents in Comparative Romance Languages and Literatures, 53), NY, Lang, 139 pp., is a clearly argued analysis, though rather limited in scope, focusing as it does on only four novels in total. It divides women into two groups — the victims and oppressors of the title — and traces the presentation of their respective plights. The victims are free spirits punished for their transgression of social conventions, while the oppressors struggle against the confines of the female role by seeking to dominate the weak. Both groups accept rather than challenge the social order which condemns them as women to such limited horizons. The study presents the usual difficulty of comparative works which use original quotations, since it is only partially accessible to those not competent in three languages. The bibliography focuses almost exclusively on critical works before 1984. E. J. Gallagher, 'The Eucharist in Flaubert's *Madame Bovary* and Mauriac's *Thérèse Desqueyroux*', *DFS*, 44: 115–22, considers the very different ways in which the sacraments of the Catholic Church, in particular the Eucharist, are used by F. and M. to underpin their very different views on faith. For F. the Eucharist provides only an illusory comfort for Emma and none at all for Charles; while M. holds out hope for Thérèse's eventual salvation, hinted at during her attendance at the Eucharist, despite her failure to undergo conversion at the end of the novel. M.-C. Huet-Brichard, 'L'Homme qui avait peur de son ombre ou les perversions du jeu autobiographique dans les *Mémoires Intérieures* de Mauriac', *Littératures*, 3 : 101–13, explores the contradictions and paradoxes of a complex text which is 'ni autobiographique, ni essai, ni journal' in an attempt to untangle the puzzle which the *Mémoires* present, that of a writer who fears self-revelation and yet seems unable to prevent himself from writing his memoirs. Not least of the paradoxes examined is that this somewhat old-fashioned writer has renewed the genre of autobiography.

MICHAUX. *Henri Michaux. Corps et savoir*, ed. Pierre Grouix and Jean-Michel Maulpoix, Fontenay-aux-Roses, ENS Editions, 381 pp., contains a number of seminar papers on different aspects of M.'s writing of the body and consciousness, including: C. Mayaux, '*Dessins commentés* ou le fantôme du poète' (17–31) a discussion of the tension between two types of writing, the *compte-rendu* and *écriture poétique;* Françoise Bianchi, 'Henri Michaux et le corps en morceaux' (31–56), which considers the image of the body and its transformation into 'une poétique de l'écriture'; C. Dangles on 'Etats du corps: du physique à la métaphysique' (57–65); B. Ouvry-Vial, *A propos de la main et de la mer dans un passage de *Connaissance par les gouffres'* (67–79), which focuses on representations of the subject in the hallucinogenic writings; D. Séris, 'Les Meidosems: l'entreprise para-doxale du portrait' (81–101), on the face as the centre of questions of identity; C. Gjorven and P. Grouix on 'Nul/ et ras . . ./ et risible . . . Lecture de *Clown*' (103–34); M. Sandras, 'La prose à découvert d'Henri Michaux: sur quatre textes de *Passages*' (137–48), which investigates 'les maladies de la prose'; C. Coste, on 'Michaux moraliste dans *Poteaux d'angle*' (149–72); C. Fintz, 'Sagesse de Michaux: entre posture et imposture' (173–90), which presents a reading of the first chapter of M.'s aphorisms; J.-M. Maulpoix, 'Une morale par des traits' (191–96), on *Poteaux d'angle* as a preparation for mental combat; P. Sauvanet on 'Michaux musicien' (197–212); J. Roger, 'Le savoir du ventriloque: les "ravagés"' (213–230), which discusses M.'s writings on paintings of mental illness; A.-E. Halpern, 'Michaux, Artaud: visages, ravages ou les mirages de l'autoportrait' (233–51), which examines the representation of the human face by the two poets in their paintings; M. Fondo-Valette, 'L'énigme du visage: Michaux et Lévinas' (253–75), which proposes a 'rapproche-ment fécond' between the writer and the philosopher; M. Hubert, 'Cioran et Michaux, "une intimité à distance"' (275–96), which explores Cioran's reading of M.; S. Thiry, 'Michaux et Dubuffet: rencontre de deux hommes du commun' (297–324), which discusses their common opposition to the cultural alienation of man; M. Kober, 'La part du sable: Henri Michaux et Georges Henein' (325–43), which examines the impact of M. on H. in the context of their encounter with Egypt.

PAGNOL. Jean-Jacques Jelot-Blanc, *Pagnol inconnu, M. Lafon, 476 pp.

PAULHAN. Michael Syrotinski, *Defying Gravity: Jean Paulhan's Interventions in Twentieth-Century French Intellectual History, NY State U.P., ix + 207 pp.

PÉGUY. Michel Leplay, *Charles Péguy*, Desclée de Brouwer, 200 pp., is a sensitive and readable account of the intellectual and spiritual itinerary of 'un maître en socialisme et spiritualité', an attempt to remedy the caricatural versions of the writer which have been promoted by those claiming him as their own. L. sees him as neither philosopher, theologian nor poet, but simply as a writer for whom writing was not an easy vocation. Annette Aronowicz, *Jews and Christians on Time and Eternity. Charles Péguy's portrait of Bernard-Lazare*, Stanford U.P., xvi + 185 pp., revisits the notion of P. as misunderstood, only to reflect ironically that he is not well-known enough in the United States to have been misunderstood in the first place. The author therefore sees herself as introducing P. to her audience as a new figure. This is, however, no general introduction to P., but a scholarly and subtle analysis of one his lesser-known pieces of writing. Despite the rather obscure nature of the text in question, A. demonstrates clearly its actuality by relating the portrait of the Jewish writer Bernard-Lazare to wider questions of the relationship between Jews and Christians, and to representations of the Other, particularly as regards tensions between the representation of the particular and the universal. This leads into a reflection on the relevance of P. today in the context of debates on otherness and multi-culturalism. *L'Egalité au tournant du siècle. Péguy et ses contemporains*, ed. Françoise Gerbod and Françoise Mélonio (Varia, 13) Champion, 199 pp., also complains of 'insuffisances' in analyses of P. and describes itself as a re-evaluation of a partially understood P. It is a volume of conference papers which place P. in the context of 19th- and early 20th-c. reflections on 'égalité'. Divided into three sections, the collection begins with a series of papers on 'L'héritage du XIXème siècle', looking at the revolutionary origins of the concept of 'égalité'. Section II, 'Les années 1900' contains articles on Brunetière, Maurras, Sorel and Christian democracy, while Section III, 'L'égalité selon Péguy' places P. in this overall context. Critical of materialist notions of 'l'égalité comptable' and dismissive of equality in law, P. is shown to propose a view of equality as a means to attaining 'la cité harmonieuse'.

SAINT-JOHN PERSE. Colette Camelin, *Eclat des contraires: la poétique de Saint-John Perse*, CNRS Editions, 315 pp., is a scholarly and clearly structured analysis of S.-J. P.'s 'poétique', insisting particularly that despite perceptions of his work being at a remove from the mainstream of 20th-c. poetry, and despite his own 'refus de toute historicité', his work is actually very much a part of the major currents of modern poetry. C. considers his relationship with such representatives of modernity as Claudel, Breton and, in the domain of painting, Braque.

PONGE. M.-L. Bardèche, 'Ponge ou le parti pris des gloses', *Poétique*, 115:369–83, reflects on the paradoxical nature of P.'s use of common places and fixed expressions to say something new, and analyses what he calls 'les modalités du défigement'. S. Meitinger, 'Naissance du poème, naissance au poème. *La Fabrique du pré* de Francis Ponge', *ib.*, 116:495–509, is a close analysis of the development of this poem from notes and sketches to the finished product, a process which invites 'une approche phénoménologique de l'expérience créatrice'.

PROUST. Marion Schmid, *Processes of Literary Creation: Flaubert and Proust*, Oxford, Legenda, xvi + 218 pp., aims to study 'the genetic processes which shaped two of the great masterpieces of modernity', namely *L'Education sentimentale* and *A la recherche du temps perdu*. Divided into three sections, the study begins with a useful overview of genetic criticism before analysing the elaboration of the *avant-textes* of each work in order to identify how two very different practices of writing provided the framework for the published texts. In so doing, S. questions the critical assumptions resulting from F.'s characterization as a programmatic writer, and that of P. as an immanent, spontaneous writer. She demonstrates that the *avant-textes* actually show F. to be more spontaneous a writer than has been assumed, while P.'s manuscripts reveal a more systematic approach than one might expect. The study ends with a plea for a bridging of the gap between author and text which is the inheritance of structuralist approaches to literature, and for dialogue between genetic scholars and critics of the published text, between *avant-texte* and published text. This is an excellent, scholarly analysis with insights both for the specialist and the non-genetic scholar. Ian McCall, *'Je', 'il', and 'vous'. Narrator, Protagonist and Narratee from Jean Santeuil to A la recherche* (Currents in Comparative Romance Languages and Literatures, 55), NY, Lang, xix + 261 pp., is an example of such a dialogue between 'critique génétique' and 'critique littéraire'. Making use of published drafts of *A la recherche*, M. examines the development of narrative voice from *Jean Santeuil* to *A la recherche*, the former novel being seen as the first version of the latter, rather than *Contre Sainte-Beuve*. The study begins with an analysis of the relationship between narrators and protagonist and the use of the first-person narrator in *Jean Santeuil*, as a prelude to a full investigation of the transition from third- to first-person narrator in *A la recherche*. Detailed comparisons are made between Jean and Marcel in order to assess the impact of the change of narrative voice between the novels. The final chapter addresses the question of the relationship between the narrator and narratee/reader and the way in which this evolves between the two novels. The conclusion suggests the reasons for these changes. Raymonde Coudert, *Proust au féminin*, Grasset–Le Monde de l'Education, 311 pp., proposes a detailed re-reading of P. through a focus on his 'écriture au féminin'. The study ranges widely across P.'s female characters, concentrating particularly on Albertine, Oriane, and Odette, and discusses in particular the centrality of the figure of the mother in *A la recherche*. Malcolm Bowie, *Proust Among the Stars: How to Read Him; Why to Read Him*, London, Harper Collins, xix + 348 pp., is not, as the author points out, aimed at the Proust scholar, but at a more general readership. It provides an authoritative introduction to *A la recherche* which affirms and revels in the primacy of the Proustian text over and above the biography of the writer. Arranged in chapters, each of which takes a major theme of the novel ('Death', 'Art', 'Time' etc.), it is very much a personal appreciation of the text, but one which is full of insights to be shared. It is very well written and readable, without ever being superficial. Isabelle Zuber, *Tableaux littéraires: les marines dans l'oeuvre de Marcel Proust* (PUE), viii + 279 pp., presents a detailed analysis of the way in which P. makes use of seascapes within his fiction and inscribes them into the text. By making comparisons with other literary evocations of the sea, Z. also seeks to identify the very specific status of the seascape in P.'s works. While other writers describe the sea in order to reflect a certain mood or as a 'décor symbolique', P.'s seascapes are presented not simply as verbal reconstructions of the sea, but as verbal pictures in their own right which are fully integrated into the narrative and thematic structure of the work. The study provides a useful overview of art criticism and of literary texts about the sea which provides a context within which P.'s work can be placed in order to provide new insights into his evocation of the passage of time. Mieke Bal, *The Mottled Screen: Reading Proust Visually*, Stanford U.P., xi + 284 pp., is, like Zuber's work, preoccupied by visual images in P., but the analysis operates on a rather different plane. This is a much more original and theoretical exploration of the complexities of the relation between text and image, between the verbal and the visual in *A la recherche*. Bal places at the centre of her analysis the notion of flatness as an image of writing which is explored in relation to painting and photography. Colleen Lamos, *Deviant Modernism. Sexual and Textual Errancy in T. S. Eliot, James Joyce and Marcel Proust*, CUP, x + 269 pp., is a subtle and rigorous comparative analysis which offers a re-evaluation of these three canonic male modernist writers. L. disputes the notion of modernism as a masculine, politically conservative genre, presenting it instead as a complex site of confusions and anxieties surrounding gender and sexuality which reflect a wider contemporary crisis of gender and sexual identification. Concentrating upon discrepancies between the authors' avowed intentions and their textual practice, L. examines these errant elements in the texts, asserting a connection between them and the gender anxieties and homosexual desires which suffuse the works and yet which are disavowed by the authors. The section on P. challenges the notion of *A la recherche* as a search for truth, focusing instead on the importance of errors and departures from P.'s stated aims. This textual errancy is associated with sexual errancy in the novel, and particular attention is paid to the figure of Albertine. It is a pity that in such a wide-ranging and scholarly work, the notes are not complemented by a bibliography. Thierry Laget, *L'ABCdaire de Proust*, Flammarion, 120 pp., is an attractively illustrated introduction to P. for the general reader or student. Concise and accessible entries are given, in alphabetical order, on a range of topics, including the major characters, themes and places associated with *A la recherche*. Julia Kristeva, *Proust: questions d'identité* (Special Lecture Series), Oxford, Legenda, 29 pp., is an incisive examination of the complex nature of identity, whether it be national, religious or sexual, as explored in *A la recherche*, with particular reference to the Dreyfus Affair. Luc Fraisse, **La Correspondance de Proust: son statut dans l'oeuvre: l'histoire de son édition*, Besançon, Annales littéraires de l'Université de France-Comté, 212 pp. Christian Gury, **Lyautey-Charlus*, Kimé, 296 pp. Robert Kahn, **Images, passages: Marcel Proust et Walter Benjamin*, Kimé, 240 pp. N. Aubert, 'Marcel Proust: de la pratique traduisante à la métaphore', *FrF*, 23:217–33, examines P.'s experience of translation and the effect this had on his own use of language and metaphor in translating lived experience into words. R. Debray-Genette, 'Oriane aux cercles', *Poétique*, 114:221–31, analyses the evolution from *avant-texte* to published text of a particular portrait of Oriane in *Le Côté de Guermantes I*. L. Fraisse, 'Lanson et Proust: parallèle entre deux esthétiques', *FrF*, 23:197–216, is an interesting examination of the parallels between the views of Lanson and of P., who appear not to have met or known each other, on questions of literary aesthetics. P. Piret, **'L'essence infuse. Expérience affective et programme d'étude dans Combray'*, *Poétique*, 114:209–19. Jean-Claude Polet, 'Vérité ou mensonge. Le statut de l'art dans *Combray* de Marcel Proust et *La Femme pauvre* de Léon Bloy', *LR*, 52:75–93, examines the two authors as representative of opposed tendencies in the philosophy of art. Polet traces the aesthetic itinerary outlined by

P. in *Combray* and compares this with the aesthetic views espoused by Bloy in *La Femme pauvre*, concluding that P. is a Platonist, while B.'s essentially theological aesthetics is Augustinian. L. S. Lerner, 'The genesis of Jewish Swann', *RR*, 89:345–65, is an interesting investigation into the reasons why Swann's Jewish identity was down-played in the published version of *Du côté de chez Swann* as compared to its elaboration in the *avant-texte*. L. maintains that existing explanations of this change of emphasis fail to explain why the theme of his Jewishness re-emerges at the time of Swann's illness and the Dreyfus Affair. L. argues that the suppression of Swann's Jewish identity in the early part of the novel paves the way for its dramatic revelation during the Dreyfus Affair, and for the way in which the theme emerges again in *Le côté des Guermantes II* and *Sodome et Gomorrhe* when Swann is 'revealed as essentially — and not simply "originally" — a Jew'. M. Schmid, 'Repression and return: the masturbation scene in Proust's *Du côté de chez Swann*', *RoS*, 31:69–82, traces in detail the genetic elaboration of this scene which, as the *avant-texte* demonstrates, caused P. some difficulty in composition. S. examines the various constraints operating during the drafting of this scene and the way in which the author overcame them, and in doing so examines the conflict between authorial repression and expression.

QUENEAU. Claude Debon, *Doukiplédonktan?: études sur Raymond Queneau*, Presses de la Sorbonne Nouvelle, x + 231 pp., gathers articles written by the author over a period of 16 years, together with two previously unpublished pieces. The articles are organized in four sections. The first section concentrates largely on Q.'s surrealist period; the second section on his prose works; the third on his poetry and the final section collects together a number of general studies. J. Meizoz, 'Queneau, les linguïstes et les écrivains. "Fautes"; de français et littérature', *Poétique*, 115:351–67, sees Q.'s writing, both his novels and his linguistic research, and his interest in 'le français parlé écrit' as part of a wider examination of French language variation, and identifies his writing as 'une critique en acte de la pétrification de la langue française'. M.'s analysis of Q.'s challenges to standard French places him in the context of contemporary linguistic analysis which questions the conventions of French spelling and syntax.

RIVIÈRE. E. Ford, 'Jacques Rivière and the adventure novel', *RoQ*, 45:213–17, identifies the main features defined by R. in his manifesto 'Le Roman d'aventure' in which he promoted a new kind of novel, and shows how those rebelling against Symbolism such as Gide and Alain-Fournier were making use of these features in their work. While making it clear that Proust's *A la recherche* is not a psychological adventure novel in the sense intended by R., F. shows some similarities between P.'s novel and the form envisaged by R.

ROMAINS. Dominique Memmi, **Jules Romains ou la passion de parvenir*, Dispute, 96 pp.

SEGALEN. Y. Schlick, 'On the persistence of a concept: *Segalen's René Leys* and the death(s) of exoticism', *AJFS*, 35 : 199–214, presents *René Leys* as a problematic text in that it undermines S.'s celebration of the exotic and his belief in its aesthetic, ahistorical purity. This historical novel demonstrates throughout the failure of the quest for the exotic, and affirms that the exotic object cannot, despite S.'s wish that it was so, be isolated from history. For Schlick, this novel demonstrates the reactionary nature of S.'s exoticism. **Victor Segalen*, ed. Christian Doumet and Marie Dollé (Cahiers de l'Herne, 71), Herne, 450 pp. Kenneth White, *Les finisterres de l'esprit. L'itinéraire de Victor Segalen: la voix du désert*, Cléguer, Editions du Scorff, 96 pp. C. Forsdick, **'Edward Said, Victor Segalen and the implications of post-colonialism'*, *JIRS*, 5, 1997 : 323–39.

SIMENON. Bernard Alavoine, *Georges Simenon: parcours d'une oeuvre*, Amiens, Encrage, 183 pp., is, as the title suggests, an introductory work, one with a clear intention to place S.'s work, described by the author as 'une oeuvre hors du commun', on a serious critical footing. The study is divided into three sections: a biography, followed by a thematic reading of the novels (excluding the Maigret novels and those written under a pseudonym, which are to be dealt with in a subsequent volume), and concluding with an evaluation of S.'s mixed critical reception.

SUARÈS. Robert Parienté, *Bonjour [. . .] André Suarès*, Marseille, Editions Autres Temps, 32 pp., provides a brief but useful and sensitive introduction to the life and work of this little-known writer. **André Suarès*, ed. Claudine Irles and Robert Parienté, Arles, Actes Sud, 197 pp.

TRIOLET. L. M. Birden, 'Elsa Triolet's *Le Cheval blanc* as a French *bylina*', *CLS*, 35 : 255–77, explores the influence of the traditional Russian oral epic, the *bylina*, on Triolet, detailing the ways in which she makes use of traditional narrative techniques and epic heroes in her novel *Le Cheval blanc*.

VALÉRY. *Reading Paul Valéry. Universe in Mind*, ed. Paul Gifford and Brian Stimpson (Cambridge Studies in French, 58), CUP, xi + 317 pp., is an important volume of essays by a number of international V. scholars. It is intended as a long overdue attempt to view as a unified whole the work of a writer which is seen as fragmented by the critical establishment. A second aim is to re-examine V. in order to remedy the discrepancy between the ways in which he is perceived by specialists on the one hand, and by 'the wider constituency of French Studies' on the other. A third aim is to ensure that V.'s work is opened up to a broader audience, and that he is judged on the whole of his *oeuvre*. Pierre Girardet, *Paul Valéry: de l'enfant et du rêve*, Berne, Lang, 130 pp., is written not by a literary or philosophical specialist of V., but by a paediatrician. Consequently the approach is an unusual one. The study is organized in two discrete sections: the first one on the presence of the child in V.'s work, based primarily on the *Carnets*. The second part, previously published as a separate work, analyses V.'s concept of dream and his opposition to Freud. Valéry, *Le partage de midi. "Midi le juste". Actes du colloque international tenu au collège de France le 18 novembre 1995*, ed. Jean Hainaut (Varia, 10), Champion, 271 pp., contains a wide range of papers on various aspects of V.'s thought and writings. William Kluback, *Paul Valéry. The Realms of the Analecta* (AUS), 163 pp., continues K.'s very personal and idiosyncratic reflections on V. His approach is fluid, dispensing with a fixed structure, and proposing instead what he describes as a 'wandering through the Analecta'. The subsequent exploration and search for insights finishes with a modest 'I refuse to conclude' in lieu of a formal conclusion, accepting that with V. there is no possible point of conclusion, but only a temporary halt in his reflections. J. Duchesne-Guillemin, *'Le Secret de Paul Valéry', LR*, 52:93–105.

VERCORS. W. Kidd, 'Vercors's republican march: iconography, ideology and a war-time récit', *FrCS*, 9:114–20, contains an analysis of V.'s short story *La Marche à l'étoile*, written in 1943, and published in the collection *Le Silence de la mer*, in memory of his Jewish father. The story traces the multiple links between his father's search for freedom which brought him to France, the republican and ideological iconography of the star, and French resistance to collaboration. P. Schulman, 'Vercors et Duras: l'Occupation des silences', *NZJFS*, 19:14–25, examines the themes of silence and of alienation in V.'s *Le Silence de la mer* and D.'s *Hiroshima, mon amour*.

WEIL. Athanasios Moulakis, **Simone Weil and the Politics of Self-denial*, Missouri U.P., 266 pp.

THE TWENTIETH CENTURY SINCE 1945

By H. G. McINTYRE, *Lecturer in French, University of Strathclyde*

1. GENERAL

C. W. Nettelbeck, 'Novelists and their engagement with history: some contemporary French cases', *AJFS*, 35:243–57, looks at how four chosen novelists — Modiano (*Dora Bruder*), Le Clézio (*Poisson d'or*), Echenoz (*Un an*), and Darrieussecq (*Truismes*) — deal with socio-political realities and contribute to the larger process of reshaping France's sense of its own past. Noting the obvious differences between them, N. illustrates how these writers treat various experiences or examples of social exclusion — wartime deportation of the Jews, unemployment, immigration — and use their art to facilitate the integration of these experiences into the French, longer-term collective memory. J. Kaempfer, 'Le latin des Nouveaux Romanciers', *Poétique*, 113:45–59, cautions against the easy assumption that 'déprédations burlesques' of Latin and classical learning in Simon, Pinget, and Butor indicate the *nouveau roman*'s contempt for tradition. On the contrary, a more circumspect consideration of allusion and intertextuality in general reveals the 'relations complexes et ambigues' which these texts maintain with the classical and Christian Latin tradition and, ironically, the amount of traditional background classical culture needed for a proper appreciation of the new genre. C. Britton, 'The representation of popular culture in the *nouveau roman*', *AJFS*, 35:75–86, looks in some detail at Butor, Sarraute, and Robbe-Grillet to assess how the *nouveau roman* uses popular culture to define its position vis-à-vis traditional or classical literature and in relation to postwar modernity. A wide-ranging, clear and well-illustrated discussion encompasses *L'emploi du temps*, *Degrès*, *Vous les entendez*, *Les Gommes*, and other texts and brings out the differences of attitude among individual practitioners. A. Maazaoui, 'Poétique des marges et marges de la poétique', *EsC*, 38.1:79–89, is chiefly concerned to develop a critique of criticism of marginal writing and to suggest an analytical model for analysis which takes into account the characteristic constituents of the *texte mineur*. However, since he draws on a range of contempororary *beur* writing as his source material, the article will have appeal to the non-theorist also. G. Brajot, 'Le rôle de l'état: cinquante ans de politique théâtrale; 1945–1997', *RHT*, 4:365–88, provides a long and informative background reference source. While there is no discussion of individual authors or works, it describes the development and fluctuations of French cultural politics as they have affected postwar theatrical activity in France, emphasizing the remarkable consistency and continuity of these policies over forty years and the substantial increase in public subsidy during that time. M.-F. Christout, 'Petites scènes parisiennes, un prodigieux foyer de création: 1945–1960', *ib.*, 311–18, chronicles the postwar explosion of theatrical activity in Paris, providing a reference treasure-house of names of theatres, plays, and producers. J. Cramesnil, 'Une aventure théâtrale en marge de l'institution: La Cartoucherie de Vincennes', *ib.*, 327–48, describes the circumstances of the reconstruction and conversion of the former Cartoucherie but, in so doing, provides some interesting information, both in the body of the article and in a number of appendices, on the various companies (Théâtre du Soleil, Théâtre de l'Aquarium etc.) who have occupied the premises over the intervening years as well as some general comment on the post–1968 theatrical climate in Paris. M. Bishop, 'Profanes marginalités: D'Adonis, Stéphan et Bancquart à Chedid, Rognet et Stétié', *EsC*, 38.1:91–102, is not a synthetic study but a series of paragraph-length offerings or reflections on the poets of the title, plus for good measure Jaccottet, Dohollau, Bonnefoy, Baude, Vegliante, Albiach, du Bouchet, and Tellermann. They may be linked by the notion of marginality but the comment is concise not to say terse in places and the whole fragmentary. M. Whorton, 'Looking for kicks: promiscuity and violence in contemporary French fiction', *NFS*, 37:89–105, tackles the relationship between the erotic and the pornographic and the use of pornography in serious literature. A lot of the essay is broad in scope and general in content, drawing on a range of theoreticians — Bataille, Lacan, Deleuze, Sontag — but there is also some reference to specific examples of contemporary French erotic fiction: Joel Hespey, *S.M.: roman*, Clothilde Escalle, *Pulsion*, Edouard Malvande, *Déballage* and Marie L., *Confessée*. C. Robinson, 'Sexuality and textuality in contemporary French gay fiction', *FS*, 52:176–85, ponders on the recurrence of the same thematic strategies in contemporary gay writers such as Yves Navarre, Eric Jourdan, Guy Hocquenghem, and Renaud Camus as in the canonical triumvirate of Proust, Gide, and Genet, emphasizing in particular the preponderance of intertextual allusions and suggesting that the reasons for this are more complex than merely preventing the reader from adopting a single position. He indicates both the common and distinguishing factors in how these references are used across a range of novels to depict gay sexuality, arguing that the reader's complicity with the various narrative codes or devices employed depends on how he/she responds to combinations of variables in the text which constrain interpretation. J. E. Flower, *Short French Fiction: Essays on the Short Story in France in the Twentieth Century*, Exeter U.P., 182 pp., provides a varied and interesting collection of essays by different experts on a selection of short stories by Aymé, Sartre, Camus, Yourcenar, Duras, de Beauvoir, and Tournier. All of the contributions are informed and thought-provoking and, as the editor points out in his introduction, open up broader issues than the individual stories they analyse. The volume is very well rounded off by an interesting chapter by J. Gratton, 'From the *Nouvelle* to the *Nouvellistique*', which berates the apparent academic bias against short fiction in contemporary France and the consequent lack of critical attention, as well as tackling some of the areas deliberately avoided in the introduction, such as generic definitions.

2. INDIVIDUAL AUTHORS

ARTAUD. L. A. Boldt-Irons, 'In search of a forgotten culture: Artaud, Mexico and the balance of matter and spirit', *RR*, 89: 123–38, retraces A.'s journey to Mexico to escape an old-world European civilization characterized by the primacy of intellect and mind over 'organs, nerves and blood'. The article examines how A. prioritizes images of the body and its organs in *Le Rite du Peyotl chez les Tarahumoras*, but does none the less touch on the question of the authenticity or veracity of A.'s account and acknowledges those — like Le Clézio — who doubt that A. could ever have found what he was looking for among the Tarahumoras or anywhere in the real Mexico.

AYMÉ. See GENERAL.

BECKETT. S. Critchley, 'Who speaks in the work of Samuel Beckett?', *YFS*, 93: 114–30, focuses on the trilogy, exploring the dramatic tension deriving from the disjunction between narrative time and the non-narratable time of the narrative voice ('the time of dying'). This tension is described from the symmetries and dissymmetries of the two parts of *Molloy* to its most radical expression in *L'Innommable* where disjunction takes place within the unit of the sentence itself. Blanchot is called on to help provide an answer to the question posed in the title. Who speaks? Not the 'I' of a controlling authorial consciousness but the 'Not I' of the insomniac narrative voice. M. Engelberts, 'Théâtre et oppression dans *Catastrophe* de Samuel Beckett: réflexivité moderniste et référence politique', *RHT*, 2: 169–90, seeks to reconcile two opposing views of this work, written for Vaclav Havel in 1982, as either self-evidently realist and political or as B.'s most obviously metatheatrical play. The detailed and thoughtful analysis argues that political oppression and theatre are intimately linked in *Catastrophe* in which B. demonstrates by means of theatre-in-the-theatre that drama, being a peculiarly social art form, is open to the same 'rapports de domination' (e.g. between producer, director, actor, stage crew etc.) as exist in society at large.

BLANCHOT. D. Wilkerson, 'Transgression, masochism and subjectivity: the sacrifice of self to the (feminized) space of literature in Maurice Blanchot', *AJFS*, 35 : 228–42, draws on Foucaultian notions, as well as B.'s own conceptualization of transgression, along with a dash of masochism à la Deleuze, in order to demonstrate in two texts — *Thomas l'obscur* and *L'Arrêt de mort* — that the writing subject in B. 'in its transgressive propulsion outside itself and into a simulacral feminine mode simultaneously brings into focus the limits of Western logocentrism based on an active/passive paradigm and displaces them through the codification of a passive *jouissance* for the whole subject'. Put more succinctly, 'B. in his representation of the feminine as that which enables the male subject to free himself from himself in the space of the work and thereby guarantee its authenticity, therefore transgresses the phallo(hetero)centric matrix of representation even while affirming its limits.' *YFS*, 93, is a special issue devoted to B. Two articles might be of interest to the literary critic: H. de Vries, ' "Lapsus Absolu": notes on Maurice Blanchot's *The Instant of My Death'* (30–59), approaches this most puzzling and generically unclassifiable of *récits* — fiction, literary criticism, philosophy, autobiography? — via Derrida's *Parages* and wonders if the title does not run counter to the central characteristics of B.'s preoccupation with death in earlier works. A lengthy and detailed discussion, drawing on Levinas, Heidegger, and Adorno, argues that this is not a natural death or suicide but 'a failed, delayed and finally a delegated execution'. D. Rabaté, 'The critical turn: Blanchot reads des Forêts' (69–80), looks at B.'s friendship with des Forêts and the various commentaries devoted to des Forêts by B. over the years, emphasizing their political empathy in the fifties — their common opposition to de Gaulle — and defending B.'s reading of des Forêts against that of Bonnefoy.

BONNEFOY. A. Pearre, 'En attendant Eros: Yves Bonnefoy et l'érotisme', *FrF*, 23 : 85–100, goes in search of the 'fonction poétique' of B.'s eroticism. The discussion flits over a few writings before settling on *De vent et de fumée* which is prefaced by remarks on the ambiguous nature and the positive and negative function of eroticism in general and its spiritualization in B. and concluding that B.'s eroticism is 'fertilement ambigu, hésitant entre le sensuel et le spirituel.'

BUTOR. See GENERAL.

CAILLOIS. P. F. De Domenico, 'Revenge of the novel: Roger Caillois' literary criticism in the wake of the 1930s', *RR*, 89 : 381–410, is a long and informative study, clearly argued throughout, of C.'s reactions to the political and intellectual debates of the thirties and how they led to his prolonged questioning of the value of literature as a means of political expression. The article argues that the title *Puissances du roman* is misleading since it masks the novel's fundamental impotence and inability to galvanize the masses into revolutionary action, which makes the *roman engagé* of the time an inherently futile activity. C.'s identification of the primary functions of myth in human evolution in *Le Mythe et l'homme* are also considered since it is due to its loss of mythic quality that the novel in C.'s view is an ineffective tool for political transformation.

CAMUS. V. Howells, 'Clamence as a Lucifer figure in Camus' *La Chute*', *RoS*, 31 : 45–56, takes as its starting point a parallel between *La Chute* and Dante's *Inferno*, in particular Clamence's similarities to Dante's Lucifer but complicates things by suggesting a number of other possible identities for Clamence. It develops into an interesting and wide-ranging survey of the style, structure and background of *La Chute* while always returning to the central Lucifer figure of Clamence. Id., 'Crossing the cultural divide: Camus and the problem of race in *La Pierre qui pousse*', *FMLS*, 34 : 353–65, argues that *Le Premier Homme* suggests the need to reconsider the traditional Eurocentric view of C.'s writing. She undertakes this revision by setting aside previous psychoanalytical and sociological approaches to *La Pierre qui pousse* and offers instead a detailed textual analysis to illustrate how racial difference remains an obstacle to the elusive *royaume*. Touching on aspects such as geographical location, paralinguistic modes of expression, and the macumba ceremony, she concludes that C.'s positive closure is a contrived ending which fails to reconcile or resolve contradictions in his relationship to the ethnic Other. (See also GENERAL.)

CIXOUS. M. Manners, 'The vagaries of flight in Hélène Cixous' *Le Troisième Corps*', *FF*, 23 : 101–14, considers the Gradiva figure as a trope of gender-transgressive verticality and Freudian mediation. Discussion develops into a three-way comparison with Jensen's 1903 novel of the same name and Freud's analysis of it in *Delusion and Dream*.

DARRIEUSSECQ. See GENERAL.

DE BEAUVOIR. See GENERAL.

DE DUVE. R. Chambers, ' "Sida Mon Amour." Aids eroticism in Pascal de Duve's *Cargo Vie*', *NFS*, 37 : 123–36, starts from the basic premise that the eroticism of Aids and the HIV virus in *Cargo Vie* mirrors the relationship of the text to its desired readership, making the reading/writing relationship inherently erotic by nature. Both Eros and Thanatos figure prominently in the subsequent discussion since this 'exercise in transformative erotics' is seen as a reproach to those, symbolized by the writer's lover, who turn away from Aids and its consequences. De Duve repudiates and transcends the mere eroticism of sexuality of those who are only *sidérables* in order to attain the superior, 'flamboyant' eroticism of disease and dying of those who are actually already *sidérés*.

DES FORÊTS. *RSH*, 249, is a special issue devoted to D. J. Roudaut, 'Des propriétés sonores d'une étendue insoupçonnée' (19–33), begins with a close look at language and its effects — sonority, musicality, alliteration etc. — in *Les Mégères de la mer* before moving on to broader issues in *Poèmes de Samuel Wood* which he distinguishes from those of *Les Mégères de la mer* by their 'vigilance'. J.-M. Gleize, 'Altitude zéro' (35–40), looks back with the benefit of hindsight at D.'s response in *Tel Quel* 10 (1962) to their survey 'La littérature d'aujourd'hui' to which Barthes, Sarraute, Butor, Cayrol, and Robbe-Grillet also contributed. F. Delay, 'Qui y a-t-il dans *Le Bavard*?' (41–50), elicits the help of Jean-Benoît Puech, D.'s Boswell, in identifying intertextual material in *Le Bavard*, finding *inter alios* Kleist, Kafka, Dostoievsky, Constant, Hemingway, and Faulkner. From his French sources, D. draws turns of phrase rather than ideas or substance while foreign influences, e.g. Kafka, *Rapport pour une académie* or Kleist, *De l'élaboration progressive des pensées dans le discours*, operate more on the level of thought than language. D. Viard, 'La parole par défaut' (51–64), concentrates on *Ostinato*, acknowledging her debt to predecessors such as Roudaut and Rabaté in exploring D.'s central preoccupation with expressing self or the absence of self in a 'langue en peine de parole' and emphasizing what is for her the central paradox of *Ostinato*, that D. is not writing for his 'improbable lecteur' but for himself. N. Barberger, 'L'hypothèse de l'enfant' (65–74), discuses the sense of loss, of 'ce qui fait défaut', which haunts D.'s writing and attempts to recover or reconstitute the child he might have been in *Une mémoire démentielle*. Beckett is drawn into the discussion for the sake of comparison. J.-M. Maulpoix, 'Qui a peur de Samuel Wood?' (75–80), no sooner asks the question: who is speaking in *Poèmes de Samuel Wood*? than he declares it a futile enquiry. None the less undaunted, and despite the confusion of two voices in the work, he asserts fairly confidently that *Samuel Wood* is definitively the 'voix même' of D.'s poetry. G. Macé, 'Une identité défaillante' (81–86), despite its brevity, squeezes in references to a number of texts from *La Chambre des enfants*. It is a series of reflections and reactions with no particular point to labour. D. Rabaté, '*Ostinato* et la question de l'achèvement' (87–103), cites D.'s own warning that *Ostinato* is only an 'état provisoire' of a work in progress as a preliminary to exploring the notion of *achèvement* which constitutes the 'moteur, inquiétude [and the] insécurité' of *Ostinato*. This long and thoughtful intervention, always clearly argued, concludes that *Ostinato* is not some kind of Proustian *récapitulation de soi* but in fact invents a whole new way of envisaging the role of memory which emancipates literature from Proustian dominance.

DURAS. J. Game, 'The writing of the in-between: a study of Marguerite Duras' *La Vie matérielle*', *FF*, 23:337–52, is offered as a first attempt to read *La Vie matérielle* as a primary source for the study of D.'s work. With theoretical input from Deleuze, it concentrates principally on temporal and spatial aspects of 'in-betweenness' with a view to clarifying D.'s thinking on the relationship between self, being, and writing. M. Hanrahan, 'Je est une autre: of Rimbaud and Duras', *MLN*, 113:915–36, seeks to remedy what she perceives as a lack of historical perspective in D. criticism. The study falls into two parts. The first explores the relationship between self and other and the poetics of alterity in *Le Ravissement de Lol V. Stein* in the light of Rimbaud's famous dictum, Rimbaud being one of the few authors whom D. has explicitly acknowledged as an influence. The second part flips the coin to look at Rimbaud and draw parallels in the light of the analysis of *Lol V. Stein*. (See also GENERAL.)

ECHENOZ. M.-S. Armstrong, 'Le Parcours zolien de Jean Echenoz', *RR*, 89:429–44, detects amidst the multifarious influences which make up E.'s 'intertextualité foisonnante' the primal but neglected presence of Zola. After pinpointing 'vignettes zoliennes' from the Rougon-Macquart in E.'s early novels, the discussion proceeds to a detailed consideration of *Lac* to illustrate E.'s veritable obsession with Zola. The discussion is not only detailed but ingenious also in finding references to Zola in the names Zog 1er d'Albanie and Jean Echenoz, as well as a partial anagram of Echenoz himself in Mouezy-Eon. (See also GENERAL.)

ERNAUX. S. McIlvanney, 'Annie Ernaux: un écrivain dans la tradition du réalisme', *RHLF*, 2:247–66, sees E., who uses the classic techniques of realism, as an unusual synthesis of modernism and tradition. She examines various general aspects of E.'s realism — the choice of working class milieus, the notion of *bienséance*, linguistic registers, the recurrence of themes and characters — before concentrating on two specific aspects, *représentativité* and *objectivité*, in *La place* and *Une femme*. The conclusion underlines the way in which E.'s realism aims to swing the literary balance in favour of her preferred working-class settings in a literary tradition which is still 90 per cent bourgeois.

GENET. M. Paganini, 'Écriture carcérale: l'échappée belle', *EsC*, 38.3:40–50, is largely devoted to G. and his 'langage d'institutions', illustrating how G.'s predilection for word-play and his tendency to juxtapose ideas result in a proliferation of meaning and a rich texture of allusions which culminate in a 'rhétorique de l'imprécision'.

Discussion is based on G.'s prose only, principally *Miracle de la Rose*. Claude Puzin, *Jean Genet: Les Bonnes, Le Balcon*, Nathan, Collection Balises, 128 pp. Ian H. Magedera, *Jean Genet: Les Bonnes*, GIGFL, 76 pp. (See also GENERAL.)

GRACQ. P. Auraix-Jonchière, 'De Barbey à Julien Gracq. *Le Roi Cophetua*, complexe Aurevillien?', *RR*, 89:243–58, cites Barbey d'Aurevilly as one of the more complex of several literary influences on G. Despite some general discussion of influence and similarities, the premise of the article is that evidence for an 'authentique textualité' can only come from a detailed reading, in this instance of one of G.'s most enigmatic texts, *Le Roi Cophetua*, which takes its sustenance from two d'Aurevilly texts in *Diaboliques, Le Rideau cramoisi*, and *Le Bonheur dans le crime*. It would appear, however, that G., by modifying his sources, in particular by changing the portrayal of female figures, has altered their meaning.

LE CLÉZIO. A. Trouvé, 'Une lecture de *La Ronde* de Le Clézio', *RHLF*, 1:123–130, examines this short text in search of an answer to the question of how to read L., more specifically how to reconcile that 'volonté d'ouverture et de renouvellement' which is the basis of his inspiration and vision with the idea of a constant reprise of the same themes and motifs. Any neorealist reading is misleading since the text only appears to be a *récit objectif*. Beneath the surface lurks a 'riche matériau fantasmatique' which works on the reader's subconscious and encourages us to an 'exploration active', which counteracts in advance the sclerosis of any fixed system of values. (See also GENERAL.)

MALET. T. Bridgeman, 'Paris-Polar in the fog: power of place and generic space in Léo Malet's *Brouillard au Pont de Tolbiac*', *AJFS*, 35:58–74, looks at the relationship between M.'s detective Nestor Burma, hero of the *Nouveaux Mystères de Paris* series and Burma's past and surroundings. This well-organized and clearly signposted paper highlights aspects of *Brouillard* which set it apart from other volumes in the series. The central and cohesive role M. accords to Paris creates allusive links to the city's 19th c. and its literature in particular. These, in conjunction with the importance of place and memory as the dominant forces in the narrative undermine the detective-novel model. In the end, the tensions between Burma, Paris and his own past redefine not only Burma's role in the novel but also the novel's status within the *roman policier* genre.

MODIANO. See GENERAL.

PEREC. S. Levy, 'Le temps mode d'emploi', *Littérature*, 109:98–115, looks at the somewhat particular configuration of time in *La Vie mode d'emploi*. Beginning from the apparent contradiction between the movement implicit in the title and the 'immobility' of the content and descriptions, it tries to reconcile these by joining up the pieces of a typical Perec puzzle. Whether or not the attempt is successful, even with the help of Borges, any elucidation of P. must be welcome.

PINGET. See GENERAL.

PONGE. J.-C. Rebejkow, 'La Fin de l'automne dans Le Parti pris des choses de Francis Ponge', *IL*, 2, sets out to demonstrate how autumn is used as a metaphor for P.'s work, but in fact his ambitions are much wider. The analysis leads to comparisons with *Le cycle des saisons* and to a rereading of *Pluie* and a reappraisal of *La Fin de l'automne* as a manifesto or a 'poétique nouvelle de l'écriture.' M.-L. Bardèche, 'Ponge ou le parti pris des gloses', *Poétique*, 115:369–83, surveys the various linguistic or stylistic strategies adopted by P. to combat the 'caractère impropre des paroles' — i.e. the *saleté* or inevitable degradation of language in use — which the writer is constrained none the less to put up with. These strategies include manipulating the semantic associations and connotations of a phrase, various kinds of syntactic modifications, homophonic *défigement*, and paradigmatic derivation.

QUENEAU. J. Meizoz, 'Queneau, les linguistes et les écrivains', *Poétique*, 115:351–67, reviews Q.'s long-standing and central interest in matters linguistic, with particular reference to his rejection of 'le français filandreux' of some of his contemporaries and his own tripartite project to renew literary French (lexis, syntax, and spelling) by redefining a style based on the contemporary spoken language. The result is a clear and informative background study detailing various formative influences on Q.'s thinking; the example of Ramuz, Frei's ideas on correctness and incorrectness, the work of Vendryès and Marouzeau between 1900 and 1914.

SARRAUTE. J. Rothenberg, 'Nathalie Sarraute's changing genres: from "*disent les imbéciles*" to *Elle est là*', *AJFS*, 35:215–27, assesses how well the subtlety and ambiguity of S.'s tropisms translate from her novels to her plays. A comparison between the complex fiction '*disent les imbeciles*' (1976) and *Elle est là* puts to the test a suggestion made to S. by Arnaud Rykner that each of her plays derives from a preceding novel. Rothenberg finds an important shift of emphasis between novel and play, due to the different demands of the dramatic genre, particularly in the treatment of characters which are presented with more marked sexual stereotyping and in more clearly defined social relationships than in the novel. S.'s innate and strong sense of form ensures a successful transition to the more anthropomorphic theatrical genre.

SARTRE. *CAIEF*, 50, reprints a number of papers on S. given at its 49th conference in July 1997. Among those of most interest to the non-philosopher are: R. Goldthorpe, '*Les Mots*: "Soi-même comme un autre" ' (231–45), which situates *Les Mots* vis-à-vis the evolution of S.'s thinking on the self, particularly *l'altérité du soi*. Although the discussion is theoretical in nature for the most part, it will provide useful background material, along with some reference to the *Carnets de la drôle de guerre*, for the literary critic. J.-F. Durand, 'Le jeu de vivre: une lecture des *Carnets de la drôle de guerre*' (247–62), sees in their form and preoccupations a response to a time of uncertainty when we hear the 'craquements' of S.'s thinking. He also finds in the *Carnets* the first traces of the developing notions of exteriority and historical authenticity which will constitute the *jeu de vivre*. G. Rubino, 'De Roquentin au dernier touriste: poétique(s) et anti-poétique(s) de la ville' (263–78), looks at S.'s portrayal of townscapes from *La Nausée* to the fragments of the unfinished *La Reine Albemarle ou le dernier touriste*. *La Nausée* stands apart from other portrayals which are seen through the eyes of visitors and tourists. Bouville, moreover, represents inauthenticity, whereas elsewhere S. attributes sense and essence to towns. S. Teroni, 'L'Arc de Philoctète; Sartre et l'attirance pour le don' (279–95), takes as its starting point S.'s identification with the unlikely figure of Philoctète and broadens in scope to encompass wider issues, notably 'la problématique du don', which the writer considers one of the basic elements of the thematic and structural unity of S.'s writing. Despite the largely theoretical orientation, there is some reference to *Les Mouches*, *Le Diable et le bon dieu* and *Saint Genet*. J.-F. Louette, '*Huis clos* et ses cibles (Claudel, Vichy)' (311–30), looks at the origins and targets of S.'s anti-religious theatre as exemplified by *Huis clos*. Making an initial detour via *Les Mots* to sketch in S.'s anti-religious family background, L. analyses *Huis clos* as an attack on the prevailing Catholic ethos of Vichy theatre. He is mostly concerned to argue that *Huis clos* is a 'réécriture critique' of Claudel's *Le Soulier de satin*. (See also GENERAL.)

SIMON. A. Clément-Perrier, 'Regard sur un motif du *Jardin des Plantes*', *Poétique* 115:273–85, moves from a synopsis of a planned cinematic montage at the end of *Le Jardin des Plantes* to a consideration of S.'s sensitivity to the visual in general and the importance of the visual and descriptive in his writing before finally settling on the many and various symbolic meanings of the *paon* in his work. In the process, the discussion moves well beyond *Le Jardin des Plantes* and into other areas, e.g. *Orion aveugle* and *La Route des Flandres*. N. Piégay-Gros, 'La Voix dans les romans de Claude Simon', *Poétique*, 116:487–94, feels on the other hand that too much emphasis on the visual and descriptive in S.'s novels has tended to obscure an essential aspect of his work, its *vocalité*. She argues that, far from being opposed, *parole* and *regard* are closely interdependent and that the voice in S. is not merely a 'surcroît de signification' but meaning itself since, despite the absence of any 'discours psychologique', the voice suggests those invisible characters which the narration does not represent.

TOURNIER.   See GENERAL.

YOURCENAR.   See GENERAL.

FRENCH CANADIAN LITERATURE
POSTPONED

CARIBBEAN LITERATURE

By MARY GALLAGHER, *University College Dublin*

1. GENERAL

Rayonnants écrivains de la Caraïbe, Guadeloupe, Martinique, Guyane, Haïti: Anthologie et analyses, ed. Régis Antoine, Maisonneuve et Larose, 292 pp., is a critical anthology which contextualizes 100 excerpts from 20th-c. Caribbean writing in French and Creole. It is organized into six rubrics: treatment of place (from realism to surrealism and magical realism); the subject (in relation to questions of community, childhood, and gender); love and romance; resistance and the struggle for liberation; issues of colour and race; and, finally, the politics of Caribbean writing (especially with respect to issues of readership, language choice, and cultural assimilation). Jack Corzani, Léon-François Hoffmann, and Marie-Lyne Piccione, *Littératures francophones, II. Les Amériques: Haïti, Antilles-Guyane, Québec*, Belin, 320 pp., is a detailed, incisive, and pedagogically excellent overview of the field. Richard D. E. Burton, *Le Roman marron: études sur la littérature martiniquaise contemporaine*, L'Harmattan, 1997, 282 pp., presents a slightly pugnacious and highly stimulating analysis of the novels of Glissant, Chamoiseau, and Confiant. The starting point is a study of the cultural and literary centrality in these works of the 'mythe du marron et du marronage', a mythology of resistance which is then compared with the actual history of the maroon, or runaway slave. The reductive binarist logic underlying the literary use of the maroon myth is sharply criticized. Having situated the function of the latter in relation to Glissant's prose fiction and to the shift in dominance from Negritude through 'Antillanité' to 'Créolisation' and/or 'Créolité', Burton analyses three major novels by Chamoiseau and the carnivalesque prose style of Confiant. Lise Gauvin, *L'Écrivain francophone à la croisée des langues*, Karthala, 1997, 183 pp., presents interviews with Patrick Chamoiseau, René Dépestre, and Simone Schwarz-Bart on their linguistic vision and practice. Belinda Jack, *Negritude and Literary Criticism: The History and Theory of 'Negro-African' Literature in French*, London, Greenwood Press, 1996, 208 pp., concentrates on the secondary discourse, showing both the seminal force and the instability of Negritude as a critical concept. The study traces the movement's history and pre-history in and through, for example, Haitian literary programmes and the Caribbean diaspora in 1930s Paris, illustrating the 'critical tautology' incestuously linking the cultural/literary area defined by the critical discourse of Negritude and the criteria used to evaluate the area in question. Of interest because of a chapter on writers of the Haitian diaspora is Pierre Nepveu, *Intérieurs du Nouveau-Monde: essais sur les littératures du Québec et des Amériques*, Montreal, Boréal, 382 pp. B. Ormerod, 'Magical realism in contemporary French Caribbean literature: ideology or literary diversion?', *AJFS 34*, 1997:216–26, studies parody, irony, and other forms of distance which might lead one to question the function and value of the use of magic realism in texts by Confiant, Pineau, Chamoiseau, and Condé, asking whether sometimes it does not promote a 'picturesque fantasy of Caribbean life'. M.-D. Le Rumeur, 'Histoire sainte: les inter-textes dans l'expression franco-caribéenne', *ASCALFY*, 3:52–62, is a detailed exploration of the Biblical intertext in Francophone Caribbean writing, while B. Jones, 'Telling the story of King Béhanzin', *ib.*, 13–22, studies the French Caribbean response (oral, written, and filmic) to the resonant figure of the last king of Dahomey, Béhanzin, exiled to Martinique in the late 19th c. In the case of Micheline Rice-Maximin, *Karukéra, présence littéraire de la Guadeloupe*, Lang, 197 pp., the specificity and also the limitations of the book are implicit in its explicit thesis, namely that the principal inspiration of Guadeloupean literature is the continuity of the latter with the 'histoire marronne de l'île'. This thesis also perhaps explains the fact that the Guadeloupean-born Saint-John Perse is not mentioned at all. More surprising is the lack of any comparative angle and, in particular, the absence of any discussion of the 'Créolité' movement so predominant in the sister island. Roger Toumson, *Mythologie du métissage*, PUF, 267 pp., adopts a philosophical approach to the history of the concept identified as 'une mythologie propre à l'Amérique'. Only in the final two chapters, following an exhaustive historical consideration of cultural relativism, is the inter-face between literature and 'métissage' addressed. The writing of the 'romanciers créolistes' is studied in this light (from a linguistic and semiological point of view) and is deemed metalinguistic in nature and, largely, inauthentic and stereotypical. In Myriam Chancy, *Framing Silence. Revolutionary Novels by Haitian Women*, New Brunswick–London, Rutgers U.P., 1997, 224 pp., the enunciative frame of the study itself is foregrounded, while, on a related topic, G. Romain, 'Before black was beautiful. The representation of women in the Haitian national novel', *FR*, 71, 1997:55–65, seems to suggest that it is sufficient for certain (male) writers to write of the nation and of the representation of women and of women's concerns in order to qualify as Haiti's first 'nationalist and feminist novelists'. J. Dayan, 'Erzulie: a woman's history of Haiti?', Gould, *Post-Colonial Subjects*, 42–60, shows how the trajectories of several female characters in Haitian literature (notably in the writing of Chauvet and of Dépestre) are interwoven with historical realities and with (voodoo) myths.

2. INDIVIDUAL AUTHORS

CÉSAIRE. Gregson Davies, *Aimé C.*, CUP, 1997, 208 pp., like
J. Michael Dash's *Édouard Glissant*, appears in the series 'Cambridge
Studies in African and Caribbean Literature'. Concise biographical
contextualization leads to careful and condensed, rich, and lively
analyses of the poetry (over four chapters) with the drama being
studied in one long chapter. The study never loses sight of the dual
orientation of C. as politician and as poet, as man of words and of
ideas. Insightful and respectful attention is paid to C.'s texts (cited,
happily, both in French and in English).

CHAMOISEAU. M.-C. Rochmann, 'Une autofiction: *Solibo Magnifique* de C.', Mathieu, *Francophonie*, 83–91, provides a challenging
reading of the circulation at work in *Solibo Magnifique* between the text
and the 'hors-texte', and between the fiction of the poet/author and
the memory of a people, while D. Delteil, 'Le récit de l'enfance
antillaise à l'ère du soupçon', *ib.*, 71–82, presents a close narratological and textual study of C.'s *Antan d'enfance*, offering in particular an
illuminating comparison with Raphaël Confiant's *Ravines du devant-
jour*. M. McCusker, 'Telling stories/creating history: C.'s *Texaco*',
ASCALFY, 3:23–33, comments lucidly on C.'s approach to history
and writing and to memory and story.

CHAUVET. R. Scharfman, 'Theorizing terror: the discourse of
violence in C's *Amour Colère Folie*', Gould, *Post-Colonial Subjects*, 229–45,
argues that C.'s discourse enacts the return of all that was repressed
in Haiti (racially, socially, and sexually), deconstructing and resisting
oppressive power by exceeding it through the violence of the text.

CONDÉ. C. L. Miller, 'After negation: Africa in two novels by C.',
Gould, *Post-Colonial Subjects*, 173–85, uses subtle narratological ana-
lysis in order to account for the persistence of a preoccupation with
Africa in C.'s work, even after the continent's supposed 'negation' in
Heremakhonon.

CONFIANT. V. Loichot, 'La créolité à l'oeuvre dans *Ravines du
devant-jour* de Raphaël C.', *FR*, 71:621–31, is both textually and
intertextually attentive.

DÉPESTRE. E. Pessini, '*Hadriana de tous mes rêves* de René Dépestre
ou comment on guérit un zombi', *Francofonia*, 34:93–112, analyses
the structure and resonances of D.'s text, showing how the revitalized
zombi myth provides meta-literary comment on writing about a place
from which one is exiled.

GLISSANT. C. Bongie, 'Resisting memories. The creole identities
of Lafcadio Hearn and Edouard G.', *Sub-Stance*, 26, 1997:153–78,
subtly compares Hearn's colonial and G.'s postcolonial valorizations
of the creolization process, showing how both visions remain attached

to the value or to the 'memory' of the settled, rooted identity which the process of creolization challenges. Unlike his heirs, G. is shown to highlight the ambivalence or nostalgia which lies at the heart of his own postcolonial poetics.

MAXIMIN. K. Gyssels, 'Le jazz dans le roman afro-antillais. Consonances de la diaspora noire dans l'oeuvre de M.', *Europe*, 75, 820–21: 124–33, studies how M.'s writing increasingly integrates the principles of jazz (improvization, variations on repeated themes, dialogical structure), using them to structure both the form and the content of his novels.

OLLIVIER. N. Aas-Rouxparis, '*Passages* d'Ollivier: dérive et diversité', *Neue Romania* 18, 1997: 117–26, is a densely argued article on a rich text.

SAINT-JOHN PERSE. Mary Gallagher, *La Créolité de Saint-John Perse*, NRF, Gallimard, 470 pp., concentrates on the Caribbean connection, and in particular on the central, unique and creative character of the poet's Creole identity.

SCHWARZ-BART. K. McKinney, 'Memory, voice and metaphor in the works of Simone S.-B.', Gould, *Post-Colonial Subjects*, 22–41, explores the value of language, imagination, and storytelling, suggesting an interesting reading of the Wybavor tale in *Pluie et vent sur Télumée Miracle*: namely as a political allegory of a dependent Guadeloupe surrendering its will and its voice to France. D. Deblaine, 'S.S.-B.: au delà du mythe du moi', Mathieu, *Francophonie*, 157–68, most notably clarifies the chronology of composition of S.-B.'s two sole-authored novels.

WARNER-VIEYRA. E. Mudimbe-Boyi, 'Narrative "je(ux)" in *Kamouraska* by Anne Hébert and *Juletane* by W.-V.', Gould, *Post-Colonial Subjects*, 124–39, shows how a madness-muffled discourse becomes, through literary creation, a public discourse of resistance.

AFRICAN AND MAGHREB LITERATURE

POSTPONED

III. OCCITAN STUDIES

LANGUAGE

By KATHRYN KLINGEBIEL, *Associate Professor of French,*
University of Hawaii at Mānoa

1. BIBLIOGRAPHICAL AND GENERAL

C. Bonnet continues his faithful service to Occitan bibliography with
'Occitan Language', *MLAIntBibl,* 1996[1997], III, 198. K. Klingebiel
provides 1996 listings in 'Current Studies in Occitan Linguistics
1996', *CRLN,* 46, 1997:29–42, and 'Occitan Linguistic Bibliography
for 1996', *Tenso,* 13, 1997:66–113. Similarly for 1997, 'Current
Studies in Occitan Linguistics 1997', *CRLN,* 47:29–40. G. Gouiran
has edited another valuable *Bibliographie des adhérents, BAIEO,* 13,
1997, 163 pp., listing work done by AIEO members from 1980 to
1997.

Four sets of proceedings of particular interest to Occitanists
appeared in 1998. Individual articles from *Atti* (Palermo); *AIEO 5;*
and *BAIEO,* 14, have been listed in relevant sections below. *Leng(M),*
42, 'La Contribution des Méridionaux aux premières études de
linguistique romane', 226 pp., includes papers from the 1996 colloquium 'De François Raynouard à Auguste Brun' with a thoughtful
avant-propos by D. Baggioni and P. Martel (7–23). B. Schlieben-Lange,
'Préhistoire de la romanistique: la contribution des Méridionaux
avant Raynouard', *ib.,* 27–43: history, philological study of the
troubadours, and lexicography (from the 16th c. onward) all contributed to the growth of pre-Raynouard comparative *romanistique* in the
Midi, integrating synchrony and diachrony. The search for origins
yielded various hypotheses: Provençal as the mother of Romance
(C.-F. Achard) or as the meeting point of Romance, Celtic, Germanic,
Greek, and Latin (C.-F. Bouche); Vulgar Latin as the mother of
Romance (J.-P. Papon) (see also *YWMLS,* 59:258). J.-B. Marcellesi,
'Le romanisme de Raynouard', *ib.,* 45–53, finds in Raynouard a
precursor of sociolinguistics in his focus on oral language as a key
factor in the split between northern and southern Gallo-Romance.
For historian R. Merle, the eventual rejection of Raynouard's
etymologizing graphy stems from failure to recognize that Provençal
had both an autonomous past and a future (as a language):
'Raynouard et la graphie du provençal: une rupture culturelle', *ib.,*
55–58. D. Baggioni, 'Raynouard et sa postérité: les rendez-vous

manqués de la linguistique romane française avant sa professionnalisation "parisienne"', *ib.*, 59–81: during the 1860s, Paris effectively pre-empted Raynouard's work, 'le premier romanisme français'.

J. Bourquin, 'La Question des dialectes et des patois dans la philologie romane du XIXe siècle (1840–1872) d'après les ouvrages qui ont concouru pour le Prix Volnay', *ib.*, 83–101; from the viewpoint of a unitary France, the patois were seen as corruptions of a 'central' language or as witnesses of an earlier language state. P. Martel, 'Les Félibres, leur langue, et les linguistes, ou le grand malentendu', *ib.*, 105–22, describes the lack of common ground between literary Félibres and Paris-based philologists studying Gallo-Romance. P. Boutan, 'La *Revue des Langues Romanes*, le Félibrige, et Michel Bréal', *ib.*, 123–33: Bréal's encouragement to study *les langues d'oc* slowed but could not prevent the inevitable prohibition against use of regional languages in schools. G. Bergougnioux, 'L'Université et les patois (1850–1914)', *ib.*, 135–52: by the end of the 19th c., support from Paris for field work had dwindled or disappeared. G. Brun-Trigaud, 'Un aspect de la dualité Paris/Montpellier: l'enquête Tourtoulon et Bringuier', *ib.*, 153–62: the power struggle between Paris and Montpellier soon negated any possible benefits of the first field work undertaken in France, Tourtoulon and Bringuier's search for the boundary between oïl and oc (1873–75). J.-C. Chevalier, 'Le baron de Tourtoulon et la constitution d'une géographie linguistique', *ib.*, 163–70, looks at Tourtoulon's theoretical approach and methodology, which focused on spoken language, on the individual speaker, and on a careful distinction between language structure and language function. M. Décimo, 'De quelques correspondants méridionaux de Gaston Paris et Paul Meyer', *ib.*, 171–86: correspondents in the Midi had concerns about career issues and teaching positions, surveys and scientific missions, academic honours, publications, and questions about language.

P. Knecht, 'O. Bloch, A. Brun et l'étude de la diffusion du français dans l'espace patoisant', *ib.*, 189–97, subtitled 'de la rencontre souhaitable, mais non advenue, entre histoire de la langue et dialectologie'. Bloch, dialectologist and author of the linguistic atlas of the Vosges, addressed the spread of spoken French, just as Brun studied diffusion of written French in the Midi. J.-C. Bouvier, 'Auguste Brun et Walter von Wartburg. Essai de mise au point sur une polémique', *Leng(M)*, 42, 1997:199–211, maps 212–13. While Wartburg applied superstratum theory to the dialect fragmentation of Romania, Brun's insistence on substrata went beyond linguistics into anthropology. A. Valli, 'Quelques réflexions à propos de l'ouvrage de A. Brun, *Le Français de Marseille. Étude de parler régional*', *ib.*, 215–26, looks respectfully at Brun's work on linguistic variation and interference. That work is further examined by G. Saunders, 'Language contact in the south of France from 1550 to 1789: a tribute to Auguste Brun', pp. 297–303 of *Recent Studies in Contact Linguistics*, ed. W. Wölck and A. de Houwer (Plurilingua, 18), Bonn, Dümmler, 1997, xv + 484 pp.

2. MEDIEVAL PERIOD (TO 1500)

GENERAL

GENERAL. W. D. Paden's important *An Introduction to Old Occitan*, NY, MLA, xxvi + 610 pp., is packaged with a CD of troubadour poetry read by the author and sung by E. Aubrey. Chapters cover descriptive morphology, historical phonology, historical morphology, syntax, and lexicon; among the valuable appendices is a 140-page glossary.

GRAPHOLOGY AND SCRIPTOLOGY. W. Meliga, '*Ca/cha* nella scripta trobadorica', *Atti* (Palermo), VI, 339–49, analyses a corpus of some 2800 initial and medial examples of these two spellings, corroborating Appel's view that choice of velar or palatal graphy is determined by individual lexeme: 'cha' predominates in reflexes of CANTARE, CANTIONEM.

MORPHOSYNTAX. P. Skårup, *Morphologie élémentaire de l'ancien occitan* (Études romanes, 37), Copenhagen, Copenhagen Museum Tusculanum Press, 1997, 146 pp., is reported to cover morphology and morphophonology of O Occ; its primary intended audience is linguists and philologists. Id., *'En oldfransk og en oldoccitansk morfolgi', *Her(A)*, 19, 1997:69–74. R. Teulat, 'Les types syntaxiques *mon paire* et *lo meu paire* dans les plus anciens textes', *AIEO 5*, 7–16, concludes that the choice between the two types is a matter of stylistics: the first is more frequent in the *Évangile de St-Jean*, but much less frequent in religious texts in verse (1 in 7 examples) or in rhymed troubadour poetry (1 in 10). N. Quint, *EOc*, 21, 1997:2–13, finds 42 instances of the second conditional in the latter part of the *Canso de la crozada*; this rare form (Lim. *aurias plan volgut que t'embracera*) was used most often in hypotheticals, occasionally in potentials, less frequently as a conditional.

LEXIS AND LEXICOLOGY. F. J. M. Raynouard's *Lexique roman, ou Dictionnaire de la langue des troubadours comparée avec les autres langues de l'Europe latine*, 1st edn, Sylvestre, 1844, has been reprinted in 6 vols, Nîmes, Lacour, 1996, 3,598 pp. X. Ravier, 'Sur le lexique du peuplement en Gascogne et en Languedoc: les mots fondamentaux', *NRO*, 31–32:37–60. J. de Cantalausa, 'Du gallo-roman parlé à l'église au VIIIe siècle au gallo-roman écrit du Xe siècle', *AIEO 5*, 3–6, presents C.'s *Le Gallo-roman parlé du VIIIe siècle, le gallo-roman écrit* *du Xe siècle. Glossaire historique et étymologique*, 2nd edn (see *YWMLS*, 59:260). M. Brea and F. Campo, 'El vocabolario provenzal-italiano de Angelo Colocci', *Atti* (Palermo), IV, 339–50, examine the first eight folios of Vat. lat. 4796 for vocabulary of Folquet de Marseille and Arnaut Daniel as transcribed by 'il più romanista degli umanisti'. M. Pfister, 'L'avenir de la recherche lexicographique de l'ancien occitan', *Rothwell Vol.*, 161–71, reports great progress since the time of Raynouard, but much work yet to be done by the current generation of O Occ dictionaries: DOM, DAG, DAO and its supplements, as well as in future editions of texts. J.-P. Chambon provides *'Notes lexicologiques d'ancien occitan', *Lorenzo Vol.*, 797–806 (*anninou, dobla, lasge, salle, trap, via forc, voybres*).

PARTICULAR SEMANTIC FIELDS. E. W. Poe, 'O Occ/OF *tifeignon*: its meaning and its etymology', *RPh*, 51:287–301, identifies this medieval mystery cosmetic as antimony, *tifeignon* resulting from conflation of Lat. (S)TIBI(UM), TIPINUM 'antimony' with OF *tifer*, of Germanic origin. J.-P. Chambon, 'Un catalanisme passé inaperçu: Aocc *cavet* "sorte de houe"', *RLR*, 101, 1997:207–09; apparently a hapax, this term is traced here to Cat. *càvec* 'hoe'. M. Perugi, 'Autoren- und Überlieferungsvarianten bei Marcabru 293,4 "Al prim comens de l'ivernaill". Zu v.58 *garaigno(n), garanno(n)* "Hengst"', *ZrP*, 114:258–68, examines variations on the lexeme 'stallion' in various MSS; cf. mod. Occ *garagnoun, grignoun, gragnou*. A. Callewaert, '*Entreb(r)escar los motz*: à propos d'un terme poétologique chez les troubadours', *AIEO 5*, 115–22, starts from the Celtic **brisca* 'honey-comb', in an attempt to trace the *historique* of honey-making and its literary ramifications in medieval Europe, including (allegedly) the troubadours' *entreb(r)escar* as a hermetic term for saying the unsayable. J. Rüdiger, '*Tolosa e paratge*: Aristocratie urbaine et grammaire d'une mentalité', *BAIEO*, 14:72–78, outlines the grammar of *cortesia*, that foundation of 12th-c. Occitan society.

ONOMASTICS. In a seminal work, P.-H. Billy, *La 'condamine'. Institution agro-seigneuriale. Étude onomastique* (Beihefte zur ZrP, 286), Tübingen, Niemeyer, xvii + 412 pp., traces (i) *condamines* in the arrondissement of Issoire (Auvergne); (ii) the etymology of *condamine* < Lat. CONDAMINA, CONDOMINA < CONDOMA 'ensemble des habitants d'une ferme; exploitation menée par des personnes' (value first attested in southern Italy beginning in the 4th c., and widespread in France 7th–14th c.); (iii) its semantic extension: medieval name > place name > modern name; (iv) the onomastic extension of the term. Id., *'Pour un atlas toponymique et historique: les noms des institutions agro-seigneuriales. 1. Les Terres indominicales', pp. 41–65 of *Actes du VIIIe Colloque de la Société Française d'Onomastique (Aix, octobre 1994)*, ed. P.-H. Billy and J. Chaurand, Aix-en-Provence,

Université de Provence, 386 pp. J.-P. Chambon, *'Sur une technique de la linguistique historique: l'identification des noms de lieux, en particulier dans les textes du passé (avec des exemples concernant l'Auvergne et ses marges)', *LALIES*, 17, 1997:55–100. Id. and M. R. Bastardas i Rufat trace several Occ. and Cat. personal names. '*Jatbertus* = *Teudbertus*. Note sur quelques noms de personne occitans et catalans en *Jat-* d'origine germanique', *NRO*, 27–28, 1997:67–73. R. Lafont provides a *'Note d'onomastique textuelle: les noms en *ma-* et en *cor-* dans les chansons de geste', *Fabre Vol.*, 133–47. X. Ravier, *'Géolinguistique et toponymie: un exemple gallo-roman méridional', *NRO*, 27–28, 1996:19–45.

HISTORICAL SOCIOLINGUISTICS. J. Herman, 'La Situation linguistique dans la Gallia Narbonensis et les origines de la séparation du domaine français et du domaine provençal', *Atti* (Palermo), IV, 455–66, analyses Latin texts from Provincia Narbonensis to find a need for further study of autonomous linguistic evolution in this region. S. Sarrazin, *'Le Catalan face à l'occitan (XIIe–XVe siècles): pour une rédéfinition de la bipartition *ibéro-* vs *gallo-roman*', Camps, *Languedoc*, 339–50.

TEXTS. Gérard Gouiran and Michel Hébert, *Le Livre "Potentia" des États de Provence (1391–1523)*, CTHS, 1997, xcii + 537 pp. Vital for an understanding of Provençal social, political, legal, and economic history, these 48 texts of the *Livre des états de Provence* (named for the gallows pictured on its binding) are mostly transcriptions of assembly sessions, in which business was transacted and the Provençaux could dialogue with their sovereign. F. J. Oroz, 'A raíz de dos recientes publicaciones', *AIEO* 5, 91–101, reviews favourably and in detail: M. de Riquer, **Vidas y retratos de trovadores*, Barcelona, Galaxia, 1995, xxxiii + 335 pp.; and R. Cierbide, **Guilhem Anelier de Tolosa, La Guerra de Navarra (1276)*, Pamplona, Presidencia del Gobierno de Navarra, 1995, 816 pp. M.-R. Bonnet, 'Le Style direct dans les textes médiévaux non littéraires en langue d'oc', *AIEO* 5, 45–61, studies the relationship between direct style and oral speech as found in medieval non-literary Occitan texts, concluding that direct discourse is chosen in order to lend credence to what is being written, to enhance its validity, and to give an appearance of spontaneity. M. Brea, 'Traducir *de verbo ad verbo* (El códice Vat. Lat. 4796)', *AIEO* 5, 103–07, examines problems of word-by-word translation in the 16th-c. MS Chariteo, containing texts of Folquet de Marselha and Arnaut Daniel and their translations into Italian by Bartolomeo Casassagia. F. Pic, 'Note bibliographique sur les traductions occitanes de l'*Opusculum tripartitum* ou *Instruction des curés* de Jean Gerson: *L'Instruction dels Rictors* (Toulouse, 1555–Rodez, 1556)', *Leng(M)*, 41, 1997:129–43 (plates 144–45), documents the seven

extant Occitan versions of this *manuel de conduite du bon chrétien* by
J. Gerson, theologian and *predicateur* (1363–1429). C. van der Horst,
'Documents linguistiques, examen dialectologique', *AIEO 5*, 17–29,
presents his personal data base of ten documents of the Basses-Alpes/
Alpes-Maritimes (from P. Meyer's *Documents linguistiques*), plus *Le Jeu
de Sainte-Agnès*, with vocabulary, commentaries, and linguistic observations. M. S. Corradini Bozzi has published a first volume of *Ricettari
medico-farmaceutici medievali nella Francia meridionale* (Accademia Toscana
di Scienze e Lettere 'La Colombaria', Studi, 159), Florence, Olschki,
505 pp. Edited are relevant texts from three manuscripts: *Princeton,
Garrett 80*; *Auch, Archives du Dép. du Gers I 4066*; and *Chantilly, Musée
Condé 330*. Vol. 2 will contain texts found in MSS *Cambridge, Trinity
College 903* and *Basel, Bibl. de l'Univ. DII 11*; vol. 3 will provide a
complete lexicon. R. Cierbide offers background history and linguistic
notes to 'La Règle et les établissements de l'Ordre de Saint-Jean-de-
Jérusalem', *AIEO 5*, 75–90, from the Navarese MS in the Archivo
Histórico Nacional. Id. and E. Ramos Remedios have edited
**Documentación medieval del monasterio de Santa Engracia de Pamplona-Olite
(ss. XIII–XVI)*, San Sebastián, Eusko Ikaskuntza, 1997, xx + 204 pp.
J. Lafitte edits and comments on 'Ua carta d'afranquiment de
Biscarròssa (1398)', as transcribed by D. Pinzuti, *LDGM*, 9,
1997:5–13. A. Gouron, 'Sur les plus anciennes rédactions coutum-
ières du Midi: les "chartes" consulaires d'Arles et d'Avignon', *AMid*,
109, 1997:189–200, studies charts from Arles (*c.*1156) and Avignon
(*c.*1158) and traces their authors to a single group of Provençal jurists.
R. A. Lodge, 'The consular records of Montferrand (Puy-de-Dome)',
Rothwell Vol., 105–25, gives a description of the municipal account-
books of Montferrand (1258–1390); close statistical analysis of variant
spellings procures a certain level of insight into the process of
language change in this region. *TLP*, 35–36, 'Mélanges dédiés à la
mémoire de Manfred Höfler', ed. M. Bierbach et al., 482 pp.,
contains O. Philippe and J.-C. Rivière, 'Le Livre de dépenses de la
seigneurie de Lavaurs (Jaleyrac, Cantal) (1509) (suite)', 317–29, a
diplomatic transcription, with notes, glossary and commentary, of a
short text dated 1509 from northwest Cantal.

DIALECTS

LIMOUSIN. A. Higounet-Nadal, 'Toponymes et vocables: Sainte-
Marie en Périgord au Moyen Age', *BSHAP*, 125:419–33. Churches
and places originally named for Sainte Marie were renamed in
honour of Notre-Dame, perhaps due to the influence of courtly
literature. This same author studies 'Le Périgord dans le grand
Cartulaire de La Sauve Majeure [bénédictine]', *ib.*, 57–66: the

cartulary conveys a wealth of local economic, juridical, topographic, and demographic detail (see *YWMLS*, 59:261).

AUVERGNAT. J.-P. Chambon, 'L'Identité langagière des élites cultivées d'Arvernie autour de l'an Mil et la *scripta latina rustica*: réflexions à propos du *Breve de libros* du chapitre cathédral de Clermont (984–1010)', *RLiR*, 62:381–408. This list of some 40 works in the Clermont cathedral chapter library yields new insight into awareness of the difference between Latin and the vernacular among medieval Auvergnat clerics, whose deliberate use of a semi-vernacular scripta appears to contradict Brunel's view that a lack of learning caused a switch to the use of Occitan in writing. Id., 'Sur la date, la localisation et le lexique d'un document partiellement rédigé en ancien occitan d'Auvergne: le censier des vignes à part de fruits du cartulaire de Sauxillanges', *Leng(M)*, 43:37–50, dates this text at mid-12th-c., places it in Sauxillanges itself, and details: *en amont, claus* 'vineyard', *coireir* 'leather worker', *custodia* 'surveillance', *esser a terz/quart* 'to pay a percentage tax on produce', *rasa* 'irrigation ditch', *trella* 'vineyard with trellis'. Id. and C. Hérilier, 'Sur un des plus anciens textes en occitan d'Auvergne: un bref de cens, passé inaperçu, du monastère de Sauxillanges', *ib.*, 7–36. The cartulary of Sauxillanges (B.N. lat. 5454), with more than 1000 items, is the single most valuable source of information about 9th-c. to 12th-c. Auvergne. Piece no. 11, a *bref de cens*, is edited (25–26, with notes, glossary, and index, 26–28).

3. POST-MEDIEVAL PERIOD

GENERAL

GENERAL. *Occitans!*, suppl. to vol. 81 (Oct.-Dec. 1997) contains the programme of the 1997 General Assembly of the IEO (Carcassonne, 8–9 Nov. 1997) and related materials, among which: J.-F. Blanc, 'Quin occitanisme per deman?' (28–29), calling for an end to irresponsible attitudes towards the IEO and the language and culture it champions; and J. Sibille, 'Lei tres foncions de l'IEO: orientacions per l'amassada generala de 1997' (29–33). P. Javaneau, *Un coup d'oeil synoptique sur l'espace-temps occitan*, *Lemouzi*, 137, 1996:70–78. P. Cichon, *Konstanten und Entwicklungen in der Stellung des Okzitanischen in Gesellschaft und Schule*, *Fest. Kremnitz*, 75–90. R. Lafont, *1964–1994: La question occitana sus trenta annadas*, *ib.*, 57–74. J.-P. Dalbera, 'La Base de données THESOC. État des travaux', *AIEO* 5, 403–17, reviews the *historique* and objectives of the relational data base of the Thesaurus Occitan (THESOC), with sample records, discussion of procedures, planned components (texts, dictionary, bibliography, maps, digitized sound recordings, etc.), and future directions of development. J.-L. Fossat, 'Vers un "Hesphonic" occitan: mouvement de naturalisation et exploration de la problématique de l'asymétrie de l'écrit et de l'oral', *ib.*, 419–45, presents problems associated with entering ethnotexts into a data base, particularly those transliterated into phonetic spelling or 'graphies patoisantes'. Not all texts could be converted automatically, even if a device were available, since spelling occasionally carries some 'fonction informative'. L. Fornés, 'La Llenga valenciana entre l'occità, el català i l'aragonés (estudi en el diasistema occitano-romànic)', *ib.*, 669–76, proposes the inclusion of Aragonese in a globalizing *sistema d'Oc* (Bec's *occitano-roman*). A. Fontelles, 'El conjunt occitano-romànic: implicacions socials, politics i culturals', *ib.*, 725–37, compares and contrasts three theories to account for Valencian as a language: *valencianista* (direct evolution from Latin), *catalanista* (taking a global view of Catalan), and the *occitanista* (taking a global view of *occitano-roman*). J. Fischer, **'Sprachkontakte in Okzitanien- und Romanisch-Bunden', pp. 17–25 of *Grenzüberschreitungen: Beitrage zum 9. Nachwuchskolloquium der Romanistik*, ed. T. Stauder and P. Tischer, Bonn, Romanistischer, 1995, 216 pp.

ORTHOGRAPHY. M. Audoièr, 'Lo sector lingüstic', *L'Occitan*, 126, 1997:6–7, expresses surprise at attacks on the IEO-Sector Linguistic and on the Alibertian norm for Occitan spelling, particularly as developed in the work of J. Taupiac, who, together with R. Teulat, has worked for more than 30 years to correct lacunae in Alibert's proposals. C. Laux, in his series 'La Vida de la lenga', looks at the final consonant of 'Lo *tomatat*' [tomato juice], *ib.*, 11; and the various possibilities for handling 'Lo cas de -*m* final', *ib.*, 127, 1997:7. In learned words that have entered Occitan since the time of Alibert, one admissible solution is to add a final -*e*, e.g. *sinonime*; otherwise, to pronounce final [m], or yet again, final [n], as in popular words. J. Cerdà Subirachs, 'Projet d'unification orthographique catalano-occitane: l'utopie étymologiste', *BAIEO*, 14:97–102, outlines the veritable *utopie étymologiste* of Miquel Ventura Balañà (1879–1939), who called in vain for an etymology-based unification of all the varieties of Oc, including Catalan.

MORPHOSYNTAX. R. Chatbèrt, *Oc(N)*, 322, 1997:40–42, examines stylistic dislocations, both right (*Los ausirem cridar, lo fats*) and left (*Lo regiment, las femnas i anatz pas*). P. Gauthier, 'Formes verbales occitanes dans les textes poitevins-saintongeais du XIIIe au XVIIIe siècle', *Atti* (Palermo), VI, 177–89, documents the progressive loss of Occitan forms (personal endings, moods and tenses, imperfect subjective, simple past) in dialect texts from this region on the west-northwest boundary of Occitania. J. Taupiac, 'Lo morfèma de la primièira persona del singular en occitan', *AIEO* 5, 387–92, reviews

Language 193

opinions of various codifiers of the Occitan verb: Salvat, Alibert, Taupiac, Sauzet-Ubaud's *Vèrb occitan* (1995; see *YWMLS*, 57:270), as regards first- and third-person endings for indicative imperfect, subjunctive present/imperfect, and present conditional. T. questions certain forms apparently eliminated by Sauzet-Ubaud and proposes to offer both choices in such cases, thereby noting 'l'usatge socializat'. P. Sauzet, 'Futur e clitics', *AIEO 5*, 393–402, analyses clitics not only in terms of phonological stress, but also of syntactic *taxicitat* (autonomy), thus arguing for interpretation of *a, va, fa,* and *aver* as clitics.

LEXIS AND LEXICOLOGY. C. Bonnet, 'Le terreau des lettres: vitalité de la lexicographie occitane', *RFHL*, 90–91, 1996:163–72, provides an eloquent and meticulous overview of recent work in all areas of modern Occitan lexicography, particularly rural *langues du terroir*. L. Piat, *Dictionnaire Français-occitanien, donnant l'équivalent des mots français dans tous les dialectes de la langue d'oc moderne*, 2 vols (Rediviva), Nîmes, Lacour, 1997, xx + 491, 496 pp., repr. from Montpellier, Imprimerie Centrale du Midi, 1893–94. Desgrouais, *Les Gasconismes corrigés, ouvrage utile à toutes les personnes qui veulent parler et écrire correctement* (Rediviva), Nîmes, Lacour, 1997, xxiii + 442 + 9 pp. (fac. of the second edn, Toulouse, Veuve Douladoure, 1802). P. Blanchet, **Corpus littéraire ou enquête orale: Problème de méthode dans l'élaboration d'un dictionnaire d'une langue non normée', *LexL*, 12–13, 1995:41–52.

PARTICULAR SEMANTIC FIELDS. K. Klingebiel, 'Occ. *can* "quand": étude diachronique', *Atti* (Palermo), III, 373–85, studies extension of Lat. *quando* as a function of regular semantic evolution in conjunctions. Without ever losing its original temporal and causal values, Occ. *can* is found as an adversative, concessive, conditional, hypothetical, completive, and consecutive conjunction, eventually as simple equivalent of *que*. Clear parallels between the extension of *can* and *cora* 'when', 'at what time?', are described in another study based on recent work in semantic universals: K. Klingebiel, '*Cora, quora* "quand": étude sémantique', *AIEO 5*, 31–43. 'Per un "vocabulari representatiu" verbal de l'occitan normal: Vocabulari verbal, 2 (*espofar-voutejar*)', *CEPONB*, 7, 1997:107–16. J.-P. Chambon, **Vergere* est roman', *Ménard Vol.*, 337–48. J.-P. Dalbera, **La Morille est-elle bien une "brunette"? Étymologie, géolinguistique et sémasiologie', pp. 423–37 of *Mots chiffrés et déchiffrés*, Champion, 738 pp. Id., **L'Ours, le hérisson et la châtaigne ... et autres fables. Vers une modélisation du changement lexical', pp. 141–58 of *Les Zoonymes*, Nice, Publications de la Faculté des Lettres, 1997.

ONOMASTICS. C. Camps, **A propos des noms de famille Greffeuille et Pégourier', *Fabre Vol.*, 149–58. J.-P. Chambon, **Sur les noms de lieux du type de *Cistrières* (France) et *Sestriere* (Italie)', *RIOn*,

3, 1997:419–32. Id., *'A propos du 'troisième point de vue' en anthroponymie. Les noms de personne-supports (esp. *Diente*, it. *Bocca*, fr. *Visage*)', *Fest. Pfister*, III, 149–68.

SOCIOLINGUISTICS. T. Meisenburg, 'Les Occitans et la langue d'Oc: unité et diversité. Perception interne et externe à travers le temps et l'espace', *AIEO 5*, 657–67, studies different situations of diglossia pertaining to Occitan, as compared to monoglossia, or internal variation within a single language. R. Formanek, 'Le Voyage d'une allemande dans le Midi de la France en 1804: les considérations de Johanna Schopenhauer', *ib.*, 677–85, focuses on the writer's underlying assumptions and choice of descriptive topoi (natural beauty, corruption, and dirt in the cities, smell of garlic) rather than on the rich detailing of post-Revolutionary Bordeaux, Toulouse, Montpellier, and Marseilles. C. Coulon, '*La codina dau païs*: cuisine et recompositions identitaires dans le Sud-Ouest occitan', *ib.*, 749–60, reads cookbooks of Third Republic vintage as ethnotexts to find that popular culinary tradition in the southwest (as in most other regions) of France is transmuted into an expression of regional (non-Paris-centred) 'otherness'. H. P. Kunert, 'Les Occitans en Italie et en France: un problème de conscience linguistique', *ib.*, 717–24, examines applications of the term *occitan* in France and Italy; the term is defined by opposition to a dominant language, rather than to surrounding dialects. H. Jeanjean, 'L'Axe Toulouse-Barcelone de la Croisade à l'époque moderne: changements et permanence', *ib.*, 587–94, examines long-term consequences of the relationship between *les pays occitans* and Catalonia, and of their (artificial) separation 800 years ago, concluding that renewed cooperation cannot solve all the problems faced today. C. Lagarde, 'Les Espagnes à Toulouse au XXe siècle', *ib.*, 595–605, examines Toulouse as crossroads and capital of Spanish exile during and after the Spanish Civil War.

RevO, 5, 1997: 21–25, provides a 'Virat d'uèlh sus l'ensenhament de l'occitan: desfís? sotlèu?'. Despite some success at the pre-school level of the *calandreta*, the situation remains uneven. I. Quentin, P. Baccou, and P. Albert, 'Calandretas: practica de regents', *ib.*, 63–70, provide an optimistic review of 15 years' worth of *calendreta* pre-schooling, which must now make a place for itself in the next millennium. N. Rouland, 'Las politicas juridicas de França dins lo domeni lingüistic', *ib.*, 89–134, presents a very complete account of France's reticence toward its own regional languages: the French constitution is the only one in Europe to make reference to a single, exclusive 'langue officielle'. A French-language version of this paper appeared in *Revue Française de Droit Constitutionnel*.

G. Kremnitz, 'Perspectives pour l'occitan et les autres langues minoritaires en France, ou possibilité et limites des politiques linguistiques', *AIEO 5*, 687–94, outlines a vast research agenda to document the evolution of linguistic minorities within France as well as beyond: changes in numbers of speakers, in spoken and written forms of each language, in linguistic awareness, and in normativization/normalization (where applicable). Id. *'Möglichkeiten und Grenzen von Sprachpolitik für Minderheiten. Annäherung an eine Typologie', *QVR*, 10, 1997[1998]:7–23, deals mainly with Occitan materials. Id., *'Français-occitan', Goebl, *Kontaktlinguistik*, 1188–95. N. Sano, 'L'Occitan: comment "la langue minoritaire" pourrait exister', *BAIEO*, 14:122–26, points out the ease with which minority languages can fit into a multicultural society. *'L'occitan dins lo mond/ Occitan in the World/L'Occitan dans le monde', Toulouse, Conservatoire Occitan, 1995, 16 pp. R. Lafont, *Quarante ans de sociolinguistique à la périphérie*, L'Harmattan, 1997, 236 pp. Id., *'Langues en contact/ langues en conflit: trente ans de sociolinguistique périphérique, cinq concepts revisités', *BrL*, 12:27–38. H. Boyer, 'Configurations et traitement des conflits de langues intra- et inter-communautaires: un cadre de référence sociolinguistique', *Leng(M)*, 41, 1997:95–102, offers a preliminary sketch of a highly theoretical 'protocole d'observation des situations linguistiques complexes'.

J. Fourié examines 'La premsa d'òc pendent la derrièra guerra: l'exemple de "La Tèrra d'Oc"', *GS*, 32, 1997:363–71. M. Koszul, 'De l'Ukraine à l'Occitanie: Mykhajlo Drahomanov et le régionalisme français', *Leng(M)*, 44:21–40; Drahomanov's call (1872–75) for Ukrainian nationalism was based on the 'Felibrige rouge', the Languedoc-Montpellier model which aimed to transform France into a federated state, as against the Provençal 'Félibrige blanc', both conservative and royalist. G. Kremnitz, *'Pigüé: le mythe de la langue. Occitan, français et espagnol dans une petite ville argentine', *QVR*, 10, 1997[1998]:66–76. J.-C. Bouvier briefly outlines the 'État actuel des travaux sur les ethnotextes', *FM*, 65.1, 1997:35–43, with some attention to two directions of study: linguistic awareness and regional varieties of French. A. Kisters, 'Nouvelle musique occitanophone: Un exemple de régionalisme dans la culture musicale populaire', *BAIEO*, 14:115–21, links the role of music to the rebirth and reaffirmation of regional identity. Id., *Un païs que vòl cantar. Okzitanische Musik der Gegenwart als Beispiel für Regionalismus in der populären Musikkultur* (Beihefte zu *QVR*, 2), Vienna, Praesens, 1997.

TEXTS. Y. Gourgaud, 'Occitan normat e literatura', *CEPONB*, 7, 1997:117–21, discusses the translation of *Joan-l'an-pres* into standard Occitan. M.-C. Coste-Rixte, 'De l'identité à la traduction', *Leng(M)*,

44:85–98, reflects on the process of translating 1995 Nobel-prize-winning poet Seamus Heaney (*Selected Poems*, 1965–1975) into what the author terms her own hybrid *provençal rhodanien*. P. Cabanel, *'Patois* marial, *patois de Canaan*: Le Dieu bilingue du Midi occitan au XIXe siecle', Lagrée, *Parlers*, 117–31.

4. GASCON AND BÉARNAIS

ORTHOGRAPHY. In accordance with reforms for Gascon spelling formulated in early issues of *LDGM*, F. Beigbeder calls for re-establishing final consonants in 'Mots gascons dont l'étymon latin s'achève par "-nt", "-nn" ou "-nd"', *LDGM*, 9, 1997:38–42. Likewise, J. Lafitte, 'Escriver "-n[s]" en gascon', *ib.*, 43–48, advocates unequivocal spellings. Id., *'De la reduccion de "-nn-" etimologic', *ib.*, 10:9–10. Id., *'La graphie du béarnais chez Lespy', *ib.*, 21–41 (see LEXIS below). Id., *'Punts de grafia', *ib.*, 42–44, treats 'œ'/'oè' in Alibert's work, and prepositional *sens*/*sents*/*xents*/*xetz* 'without' vs *senns* 'meaning'.

MORPHOSYNTAX. J. Allières, 'Note sur le "futur du passé" en gascon moderne', *EOc*, 21, 1997:19–20. The second conditional, generally a *conditionnel de concordance* in Gascon, is found in indirect interrogatives after a main verb in the past tense: gasc. *sabè pas se vengora* 'il ne savait pas s'il viendrait'; in some areas it coexists with the first conditional, but in the valley of Barèges-Gavarnie this is the sole conditional available.

LEXIS AND LEXICOLOGY. V. Lespy and P. Raymond, *Dictionnaire béarnais ancien et moderne. Gascon classique de Béarn et de Bayonne d'après les Fors de Béarn et de Navarre, le Livre d'or de Bayonne, la Coutume de la Soule et les Archives des Pyrénées-Atlantiques; et Gascon parlé à la fin du XIXe s. en Béarn et pays voisins, Bas-Adour, Chalosse, Bigorre, et Armagnac proche*, Belin-Beliet, Lo Princi Negre, 36 + xiii + 613 pp. This important diction-ary of Béarnais, originally published in Montpellier, Impr. Centrale du Midi, 1887, has been revised and reissued by J. Lafitte, with preface by J.-L. Fossat, introduction by R. Darrigrand, biographical sketches by J. Staes, and approximately 1000 comments and correc-tions taken by Lafitte from Rohlfs, Coromines, Bec, and others. The map figuring in this new edition of Lespy is presented by J. Lafitte, *'Ua carta de l'espaci occitanò-romanic', *LDGM* 10:19–20. Id. studies Gascon vocabulary in *ib.*, 10–14 ('*reguèrc*, en gascon et en occitan'; 'les mois de l'année d'après le *Registre* de B. de Luntz, notaire de Fébus' (XIVe s.); and *ib.*, 10:25–27 (*gallicisme*, not *francisme*; *la gentor*, not *lo gento*). B. Manciet looks at *'Idiotismes gascons. Los S', *Oc(N)*, 39, 1996:44; and 'Idiotismes (Grande-Lande)', *ib.*, 41, 1996:44.

ONOMASTICS. J.-B. Orpustan asks: 'Le Nom de *Biarritz* est-il définitivement expliqué?', *NRO*, 31–32:282–85.

SUBDIALECTS. P. Poujade, 'Situacion lingüistica de la Val d'Aran al sègle XVIIe: produccion en occitan', *TOc*, 2, 1997:55–70, uses some 500 documents (1600–1710) from the Archiu Generau d'Aran (Vielha) to present the linguistic reality of modern Aranese, which remains the only dialect of Occitan to enjoy official language status on the soil of France. G. Hammermüller, *'Sprachnormierung als Mittel im Überlebenskampf einer okzitanisch-gaskognischen Varietät: "era lengua aranesa"', Müller, *Sprachnormen*, 95–107.

SOCIOLINGUISTICS. M.-A. Chateaureynaud, 'Lecture de l'enquèsta "Praticas e representacions de l'occitan dens los Pirenèus Atlantics"', *Leng(M)*, 43:117–42. 1000 interviewees were generally agreeable to the teaching of Occitan; those who speak the language on a daily basis saw no need for official recognition or protection. Continuing her description of the situation, 'L'Occitan aujourd'hui dans les Pyrénées-Atlantiques', *BAIEO*, 14:103–5, C. sees an even split between Occitan and Basque in the coastal area from Biarritz to Bayonne, while rural areas further inland continue to use Béarnais on a daily basis and, in fact, take pride in their *béarnitude*, which is neither Gascon nor Occitan. 'Signalisation bilingue', *PGA*, 53, 1997:6–9, examines historical evidence for bilingual road signs in the communes of Bas-Adour, e.g., *Angles* (mod. Anglet), attested 1188.

TEXTS. J. Eygun, 'Ensai d'inventari deus catechismes imprimits en occitan (sègles XVI-XIX)', *AIEO 5*, 629–47, is an inventory of printed catechisms. The earliest are Protestant (1564), although Occitan was rarely used in Protestant versions; the first Catholic catechisms appeared in 1640–50. Id., 'Essai de comparaison des graphies des fors de Béarn (1552) et de Soule (1553), premiers livres imprimés en occitan gascon', *Leng(M)*, 43:51–68, with 'Errata', *ib.*, 44:169–70, finds need for further study of the relationship between graphic traditions in Gascon and Occitan as a whole. H. Thun, *'Normprobleme bei der Übersetzung der Bibel in eine romanische Kleinsprache. R. Canton, "Lous Ebanyèlis en lengue biarnese (1994)"', Müller, *Sprachnormen*, 227–44.

5. SOUTHERN OCCITAN
LANGUEDOCIEN (INCLUDING S. PERIG.)

ORTHOGRAPHY. J. Taupiac continues his series 'L'Occitan blos' (see *YWMLS*, 59:270). '*Nud, nuda. Polit, polida*', *L'Occitan*, 126, 1997:12, sees the principle of a strictly phonological spelling as unrealistic when it conflicts with tradition; the IEO approach, in accordance with the Alibertian norm, thus calls for *polit* (not *polid)/*polida*, and the disambiguation of homophonic *conte, compte, comte*.

MORPHOSYNTAX. In his long-running series 'Questions de lenga', R. Chatbèrt looks at *o . . . tot* (*o mangèt tot*), particular uses of *anar*, verbal periphrases, and use of *poder, voler*, etc., as auxiliary (*eretz pas poguts venir*), in 'De l'un e de l'autre', *Oc(N)*, 324, 1997:37–39; see *YWMLS*, 57:270 and 59:270.

LEXIS AND LEXICOLOGY. C. Laux has written an admirable new *Dictionnaire français-occitan. Languedocien central*, Puylaurens, Section du Tarn de l'IEO, 1997, 584 pp., preface by C. Rapin. Introductory sections cover language, orthography, alphabet, pronunciation, and grammar; a list of Occitan proper names concludes the volume. A. Moulis, *Dictionnaire français-languedocien*, 2 vols (Collection Colporteur), Nîmes, Lacour, 1997, 711 pp., has been reprinted; originally self-published in 1978, it details vocabulary of the Comté de Foix. C. Rapin continues his series 'Nostra lenga'. 'Lo superlatiu', *Lo Lugarn*, 59, 1997:23, outlines grammatical and lexical strategies for both absolute and relative superlative: *plan, reire* and other intensifiers; learned *-isme*; expressions such as *que jamai pus, es bèla que non sai*; doubling; and syntactic structures, e.g., *qual es lo païa mai ric?*. Id., 'Illusions', *ib.*, 60, 1997:23, examines uses of this semi-learned word, e.g., *per diabolical illusion* 'folie', from fol. 77, *Elucidari de las proprietats de totas res naturals*. Of interest to Occitanists will be R. Botet, **Vocabulaire spécifiquement roussillonnais: Avec traduction en français et en catalan normalisé*, Canet, Trabucaire, 1997, 351 pp.

ONOMASTICS. B. and J.-J. Fénié give a overview of *Toponymie occitane* (Sud-Ouest Université, 8), Bordeaux, Sud-Ouest, 126 pp. This slender volume with its valuable maps includes concise chapters on pre-Latin, Latin, and Germanic formations, the bulk of the presentation being devoted to Languedocien Occitan (39–98). E. Nègre, *'Quelques toponymes toulousains. 1. rue Joutx Aigues; 2. Le Férétra; 3. Le Bazacle; 4. Place Saintes Scarbes; 5. Cuisines; 6. Basse Cambe', appeared in two parts: *L'Auta*, Toulouse, 1996:308–10, and *ib.*, 1997:18–22, 46–51. Id., **Cantayrac serait-il Uxellodunum?*', *Chronique, Supplément au Bulletin de Littérature Ecclésiastique*, Toulouse, 3, 1996:69–75. A. Soutou, *Soulage, nom de lieu languedocien lié à la transhumance depuis le VIIIe s.', *NRO*, 27–28, 1996:75–85. F. Vidaillet, N. Pousthoomis-Dalle, and P.-H. Billy, *'Archéologie et toponymie: essai sur un terroir de moyenne montagne, Durfort dans le Tarn', *ib.*, 27–28, 1996:169–97. M. Péronnet, *'Le Territoire du praxème "Cévennes / Cévenol" : définir une identité', Camps, *Languedoc*, 365–80.

SOCIOLINGUISTICS. G. Behling, 'La Transmission de la langue et de la culture occitanes. Deux études sur les motivations et les contradictions de la transmission culturelle dans la région Languedoc-Roussillon', *Leng(M)*, 41, 1997 : 7–93. Among parents of pre-schoolers, quality of schooling is stressed above other factors in the choice of Occitan, while many 11– to 15–year-olds are attracted by the orality of Occitan culture or wish to communicate with their grandparents. Id. returns to this discussion in 'La Transmission culturala occitana e las relacions inter-generacionalas' (sub-titled 'Enquèsta sus las motivacions dels collegians dins la region lengadòc-Rosselhon, 1994–95'), *RevO*, 5, 1997 : 27–61. E. Hamel, **Aide-Mémoire Langues et cultures régionales Languedoc-Roussillon, 1985–1996*, Canet, Trabucaire, 1997, is a comparative study of Occitan and Catalan, with discussion of regional politics and blueprints for needed changes.

TEXTS. C. Laux, 'L'Occitan, langue du droit et des affaires dans les registres notariaux de l'Albigeois au XVIe siècle', *AIEO* 5, 649–55, continues his study of Occitan as the language of law and business in Albi during the period 1534–40, adding two *notaires* to the five previously studied (cf. *YWMLS*, 59 : 273). Before 1534, Latin was the standard; by 1540, Occitan was eliminated in favour of French. Id., *'L'Occitan langue du Droit dans le milieu des notaires de l'Albigeois au XVIe siècle', pp. 181–92 of *Pouvoir et société en Pays Albigeois (Actes du colloque 'Pouvoir et sociéte en Pays Albigeois')*, Toulouse, Presses de l'Université des Sciences Sociales. Id. also provides a series of short articles devoted to 'Les Registres d'Antoine Vinel, notaire de Rabastens': 'Lo passalís de Rabastens', *EcR*, 196, 1997 : 9–11; 'Le Transport fluvial du pastel', *ib.*, 197, 1997 : 9–11; and 'Décoration de la chapelle du château de Rabastens', *ib.*, 199, 1997 : 11–13. J.-P. Chambon, 'L'*Instruction dels rictors, vicaris et autres ayant charge d'armas aus diocesis de Rodes et de Vabres per mestre Joan Jarson*: un cas de trans-dialectalité languedocienne au milieu du XVIe siècle', *ib.*, 103–27, with maps 124–27. Examining the so-called Rouergat translation of this work, printed in Rodez in 1556, C. proposes an origin in the area of Foix (languedocien ariégeois) and concludes: 'en plein 16e s., le repli d'horizon langagier qu'implique la patoisisation en cours de l'occitan n'est pas encore complet' (118). M. C. Alen Garabato, 'Aperçu des résultats d'une analyse lexico-sémantique et socio-pragmatique du texte toulousain de la période révolutionnaire', *BAIEO*, 14 : 79–90, bases this study on 59 extant revolutionary texts from Toulouse that provided a rallying point for the people, rather than a source of objective information.

PROVENÇAL

GENERAL. **Archives, propriété publique: bicentenaire des Archives départementales, 1796–1996, Catalogue de l'exposition (Avignon, juillet–octobre, 1996)*,

Avignon, Archives départementales du Vaucluse, 1996, 72 pp. J.-P. Chambon and A. Fryba-Reber, *'Sus la draio que condus d'Auro en auro en païs brodo (Sur la voie qui conduit de Vienne à Genève). Lettres et fragments inédits de Jules Ronjat adressés à Charles Bailly (1910–1918)', *CFS*, 49, 1995–96 [1997]: 9–63. R. Bertrand, *'Usages religieux du provençal aux XVIIIe et XIXe siècles', Lagrée, *Parlers*, 107–16.

LEXIS AND LEXICOLOGY. K. Mok, 'Alphonse Daudet, traducteur de provençal', *AIEO 5*, 617–22, discusses two types of calques on Provençal found in Daudet's translations : words attested in French dictionaries but used by Daudet with a different meaning (*lampade* 'rayon de lumiere', *espérer* 'attendre'); and words not found in standard dictionaries, e.g. *vesprée, mistralade*. Y. Rebufat and C. Rostaing, *Le Vocabulaire populaire des proses d'almanach au début du Félibrige, 1855–1892*, Grasse, Viéure! Canta! Parla!, 1997, 114 pp. J.-P. Dalbera, *'L'Élevage en Provence: notes lexicologiques, étymologiques et géolinguistiques', pp. 269–94 of *L'Élevage en Provence*, Mouans-Sartoux, CRDP. J. Castaño Ruiz studies *'La langue du *Pouèmo dóu Rose*: étude du lexique chromatique', Gardy, *Mistral*, 65–82.

PARTICULAR SEMANTIC FIELDS. P. Blanchet, 'Calice, calisson, cal-zone, chausson . . . e tutti quanti: point sur une étymologie difficile entre métaphore et symbolique', *ZrP*, 114:447–61, is an exploratory paper, arguing for derivation from both Gr. *kalàthion* and Gr.-Lat. *calice*, but content to leave the final analysis to specialists.

ONOMASTICS. S. Seror, *'Les noms des juifs du Comtat du XVIe au XVIIIe siècle', *REJui*, 156, 1997:305–32. A.-M. de Cockborne, *En parcourant les actes de baptême, mariage, sépulture: Beaumes-de-Venise*, Avignon, Cercle Généalogique de Vaucluse, 1995, 30 pp. R. Breton and S. Bonamy, *'Les Lieux-dits de Saze: étude systématique', *Rhodanie*, Vaison-la-Romaine, 1995:3–15.

SUBDIALECTS. G. Castellana, *Dictionnaire Français-Niçois*, Nice, Serre, 1997, v + 421 pp. (1st edn Nice, Éd. Ludographiques Françaises, 1949). Id., *Dictionnaire Niçois-Français*, Nice, Serre, ii + 267 pp. (1st edn, Nice, Serre, 1952).

SOCIOLINGUISTICS. P. Bérengier, 'Li capoulié dóu Felibrige, la lengo e l'identita dins li discours de Santo-Estello de 1876 à 1982', *AIEO 5*, 695–99, reviews more than 100 years' worth of a search for identity in the key words: *raço, èime* 'soul', *lengo, freirejacioun, unita dins la diversita*. N. Nivelle presents an overview of 'Marselha, sa cultura e son image', *ib.*, 739–48. J.-C. Bouvier and C. Martel, 'Pratiques et représentations de la langue d'oc en Provence: le "vrai provençal" et les autres', *ib.*, 701–15, report that informants of the *Atlas linguistique et ethnographique de Provence* frequently claimed they did not speak 'true Provençal', a term that appears to conflate notions of language purity, geographical identification, and the whole of *la langue d'oc* in its historical context.

TEXTS. R. Teulat, **'Teodòr Aubanèl: Lo Libre de l'Amor (1–6)',* *Lo Convise*, 19, 1997:2–7; and **'Lo Libre de l'Amor (7–10)', ib.,* 20, 1997:2–8.

6. NORTHERN OCCITAN

LIMOUSIN (INCLUDING N. PERIG.)

ORTHOGRAPHY. M. Puyrigaud, 'Estudi o ben tot estudi! La grafia dau lemosin: lo peiregòrd', *BP*, 1992, 2:24–29, deals with 's', 'ei', and 'es' and agrees that standard Occitan spelling is also necessary.

PARTICULAR SEMANTIC FIELDS. Y. Lavalade, **Bestiaire occitan: bestiari lemosin*, Neuvic-Entier, Ed. de la Veytizou, 172 pp. M. Chapduèlh, **'La Ringueta*: festa deus juecs tradicionals a Sarlat', *PN*, 71–72, 1996:1–40.

ONOMASTICS. P. Gauthier, **Noms de lieux du Poitou. Vienne. Deux-Sèvres. Vendée*, Paris, Bonneton, 1996, 232 pp. J. Roux, **'Les noms de lieux et la carte linguistique de la vallée de la Crempse'*, pp. 47–60 of *La Vallée de la Crempse en Périgord*, Église-Neuve-d'Issac, Fédérop, 1996, 192 pp. J.-P. Bitard, 'De Peyragude en Peyrevive: microtoponymes périgourdins évoquant des mégalithes (1)', *BSHAP*, 125:25–44, surveys 315 place names from the arrondissement of Bergerac, based on various properties of stones: colour, shape, position, etc. Part 2, *ib.*, 239–58, surveys the arrondissements of Nontron, Périgueux, and Sarlat. Id., 'Entau s'apelen nòstras comunas', *BP*, 1997, no. 1:28, surveys Neuvic-sur-l'Isle/Nuòuvic; Périgueux/Peireguers; Riberac/Rebairac; Saint-Astier/Sench Astier; Saint-Aulaye/Sebta Aulàia.

SUBDIALECTS. P. Monteil, *Le Parler de Saint-Augustin: description linguistique d'un micro-dialecte occitan de Corrèze*, 2 vols, Limoges U.P., 451 pp.. Vol. 1 covers phonetics and phonology, morphology, syntax; vol. 2 is devoted to lexicon, presented in the author's phonetic spelling and accompanied by etymological notes. N. Quint provides an 'Aperçu d'un parler occitan de frontière: le marchois', *BAIEO*, 14:126bis–34, characterizing this Limousin subdialect as an 'ensemble de parlers très marqués phonétiquement et lexicalement par le français, avec un noyau lexical de base et une morphologie globalement occitans'. L. Jagueneau, **'La Langue occitane en Poitou-Charente'*, pp. 25–26 of *La Langue poitevine-saintongeaise: Identité et ouverture*, ed. M. Gautier, Mougon, Geste, 1996.

SOCIOLINGUISTICS. J. Marty-Bazalgues, 'Compliments et mono-logues pour mariage en situation de diglossie. 2. Un corpus d'homme de la région de Gramat (Lot)', *Leng(M)*, 40, 1996:89–121, discusses two Quercy rituals that had disappeared by mid-century: compliments to the newlyweds (best wishes from the families combined with good advice from the community at large) followed by a humorous monologue. A third segment in this series, *ib.*, 41, 1997:167–77, presents unpublished Occitan texts by P. Verlhac and J. Cubaynes, who illustrate tolerance for use of both languages in diglossic occasions where French would have been considered more socially correct (see *YWMLS*, 59:265). T. Jones, 'L'Engagement occitan de trois écrivains limousins', *AIEO 5*, 623–28, compares and contrasts the writing careers of three writers from Corrèze: Claude Duneton (known for *Parler croquant*, 1973), Yvon Bourdet (*L'Éloge du patois*, 1977), and Marcelle Delpastre (two volumes of *Mémoires*, 1993).

TEXTS. G. Bazalgues, 'Pierre Verlhac (1868–1955): De l'École laïque au Félibrige et à la Résistance', *Leng(M)*, 44:139–57, discusses the voluminous output of P. Verlhac, composer of popular songs, conteur, and félibre, with an eye to tracking the fate of a quasi-oral 'sous-littérature'. An anthology is planned.

AUVERGNAT

ONOMASTICS. P.-H. Billy, *'L'anthroponymie historique. Essai sur la Basse-Auvergne', *NRO*, 29–30, 1997:19–62.

SUBDIALECTS. J.-B. Martin, *Le Parler occitan d'Yssingeaux (Haute-Loire)*, Yssingeaux, Histoire et Patrimoine-Ville d'Yssingeaux, 1997, 264 pp.

PROVENÇAL ALPIN

MORPHOSYNTAX. J. Sibille traces the second conditional in the Occitan-speaking valleys of Italy, where the lack of a preterite tense may explain its survival: 'Nòta sus la subrevivéncia de la segonda forma de conditional de l'occitan vièlh dins l'Auta Val Doira e la Val Cluson (Itàlia)', *EOc*, 21, 1997:13–18. H. P. Kunert, 'L'Infinitif dans l'occitan de Guardia Piemontese', *RLR*, 101, 1997:167–75, describes a reduced form of the infinitive, e.g., *vèlhou chantë*, used after auxiliaries, modals, and *far* and found only in Calabria and in the Balkans.

PARTICULAR SEMANTIC FIELDS. H. Bessat and C. Germi, '*Balme* dans les dialectes et les toponymes de l'arc alpin occidental et à sa périphérie', *Atti* (Palermo), v, 69–77, maps 78–81, underline the correlation of toponymy and dialectology.

SUBDIALECTS. M. Camps i Prat, 'Éloi Abert et le choix de la langue de création littéraire', *AIEO 5*, 607–16. Abert (1848–1914) chose explicitly to write in his *drômois* dialect, in order to educate people and preserve the dialect's riches. His work (see also *YWMLS*, 57:297) includes 100 poems, ten prose texts, and three plays, briefly reviewed here within the confines of L. Aracil's *rationalisme oligarchique*, as revised by X. Lamuela. H. Schook, *Petit guide de conversation français-occitan drômois*. Ponet, Lo Pitron, 1996. C. Fréchet, *Dictionnaire du parler de la Drôme: De Abader à Zou, Valence, E & R, 1997, 192 pp. N. Quint, *Le Parler occitan alpin du pays de Seyne: Alpes-de-Haute-Provence, L'Harmattan, 131 pp. A. Genre, *Atlante Toponomastico del Piemonte Montano, Fasc. 6, Roccasparvera: area occitana, Torino, Università degli studi, Dipartimento di scienze del linguaggio — Alessandria, Edizioni dell'Orso, 1995, 84 pp. T. Pons and A. Genre, *Dizionario del dialetto occitano della Val Germanasca, con un glossario italiano-dialetto*, Alessandria, Edizioni dell'Orso, 1997, 478 pp., a revision and updating of Pons's 1973 edn. J. Fischer, 'L'occitanico nel Piemonte', *Atti* (Palermo), v, 309–18, studies Piemontese Occitan in relation to Italian.

LITERATURE

By Catherine Léglu, *Lecturer in French, University of Bristol*

1. Medieval Period

William E. Burgwinkle, *Love for Sale: A Materialist Reading of the Troubadour Razo Corpus* (The New Middle Ages, 5), NY, Garland, 1997, 346 pp. B. reads the *razo* corpus as a construction of a cultural fantasy, ascribing this to Uc de Saint-Circ. He explores the effects on cultural production of the nascent capitalist economy of Northern Italy, and suggests that the troubadour corpus functioned as a promotion of this. B.'s book works well with Saverio Guida, *Primi approcci a Uc de Saint Circ*, Soveria Manelli, Rubbettino, 1996, 254 pp., which collects articles published in 1990–95, plus two new studies, proposing Uc's authorship of most of the *vidas* and *razos* (75–144) and of a song collection in MS *H* (171–213). New editions: *La Chanson de Sainte Foi: texte occitan du XIe siècle*, ed. Robert Lafont (TLF), 185 pp. *Le Breviari d'Amor de Matfre Ermengaud*, vol. III (8880T–16783), ed. Peter T. Ricketts, with the assistance of Cyril P. Hershon (Publications de l'AIEO, 5), London, AIEO, xiii + 479 pp., brings the *Breviari* edition to its third volume. Michael Routledge, 'La *Vie de Sainte Marie Madeleine* du manuscrit de Bertran Boysset (*q*): Texte et traduction', *FL*, 125, 1997:9–89. *Garin Lo Brun, L'ensegnamen alla dama'*, ed. Laura Regina Bruno, Rome, Archivio Guido Izzi, 1996, 235 pp. Frede Jensen, *The Troubadours: A Bilingual Anthology* (StH, 39), NY, Lang, xiii + 593 pp., provides a good selection of poems with clear translations. See also the excellent *Songs of the Troubadours and Trouvères: An Anthology of Poems and Melodies*, ed. Samuel N. Rosenberg, Margaret Switten, and Gérard Le Vot (GRLH, 1740), xi + 378 pp., with CD. William D. Paden, *An Introduction to Old Occitan*, NY, MLA, xxvi + 610 pp., with CD featuring readings and sung performances. Gérard Lomenec'h, **Aliénor d'Aquitaine et les troubadours*, Bordeaux, Sud-Ouest, 189 pp. Nadine Henrard, *Le Théâtre religieux médiéval en langue d'Oc* (BFPLUL, 243), Geneva, Droz, 639 pp., examines the extant corpus of plays and staged works from the 11th to the 16th c., through MSS, stage directions and versification. Robert Lafont, *Histoire et anthologie de la littérature occitane, volume 1: L'Age classique, 1000–1520*, Montpellier, Les Presses du Languedoc, 1997, 274 pp., is an introduction to the poetry of the troubadours, the Jeux Floraux and the Rhétoriqueurs, which emphasizes the continuity of Occitan literature beyond 1300. Alvaro Galmés de Fuentes, *El amor cortés en la lírica árabe y en la lírica provenzal*, Madrid, Cátedra, 1996, 158 pp., continues the heated debate on the intertextual relationships between

Iberian and Occitan literature. Articles: G. Sigal, 'Courted in the country: women's precarious place in the troubadours' lyric land-scape', Tomasch and Gilles, *Text and Territory*, 185–206, analyses the treatment of gender, class, and hybridity in the *pastorela*, focusing on Marcabru, and suggests this genre may reinforce the inhuman representation of the *canso domna*; a companion piece to S.'s mono-graph, *Erotic Dawn-Songs of the Middle Ages: Voicing the Lyric Lady*, Gainsville, Florida U.P., 1996, xii + 241 pp. S. discusses the *alba* as a challenge to feminist readings of the courtly *domna*. The study is comparative, and places the *alba* alongside the *Tageliet* and *aube*. S. Kay, 'Text(s) and meaning(s) in the *alba* of Giraut de Bornelh', *Coleman Vol.*, 1–10, reads the text as a play on religious and erotic discourse. A. Deyermond, 'Lust in Babel: bilingual man-woman dialogues in the medieval lyric', *Dutton Vol.*, 199–221, locates ana-logues for Raimbaut de Vaqueiras's bilingual *tenso* in Iberian and British (Welsh/English) multilingual poetry. C. Léglu, 'Identifying the *Toza* in Medieval Occitan *Pastorela* and Old French *Pastourelle*', *FS*, 52 : 129–41, analyses how the texts identify their object in social and familial terms. Also by L., 'Images of exile and the Albigensian Crusade', *NRe*, 4 : 7–22, examines the political agendas in the *vidas*, and their relation to representations of modern Occitania. N. Klassen, 'Self-reflexiveness and the category of the will in early troubadour poetry of fin'amors', *FMLS*, 34 : 29–42, examines Guilhem IX and Bernart de Ventadorn in terms of theories of subjectivity. S. Gaunt, 'Discourse desired: desire, subjectivity and *mouvance* in "Can vei la lauzeta mover"', Paxton, *Desiring Discourse*, 89–110, proposes a new reading of the song, based on the stanza-order in MSS rather than on Appel's critical edition. *Atti* (Palermo), VI, contains: L. Borghi Cedrini, 'Osservazioni sulla tradizione manoscritta di Peire Milo' (37–45), which attempts to establish the status of this 'minor' poet; M. S. Corradini Bozzi, 'Per l'edizione della versione occitanica del *Thesaurus Pauperum*' (87–93); I. Hardy, '*Mayres de Dieu*: contrafactum occitan d'une chanson de Raoul de Soissons' (225–34), which identifies the song by Arnaut Vidal de Castelnaudary (1324) as a *contrafactum* from OF and suggests this contributed to its success; C. Lee, 'Le canzoni di Riccardo Cuor di Leone' (243–50), places the *rotrouenge* (PC 420, 2) in OF tradition, and the exchange with Dalfin d'Auvergne (PC 420, 1/ 119, 8) in the Occ. repertoire; P. T. Ricketts, 'Le problème du ms. *H* du *Breviari d'Amor*' (439–44), examines an instance of *mouvance*; D. Billy, 'Une *canso* en quête d'auteur: *ja non agr'obs qe mei oill trichador* (PC 217, 4b)' (543–56), studies *contrafacta* of a *chanson* by the Châtelain de Coucy and relates this song to an *unicum* in MS *a* attributed to Guilhem Figueira; C. Phan, 'Les *trobairitz* et la technique du contrafactum' (693–702), reconsiders the definition of *contrafactum* in terms of melodies; M. Spampinato Beretta, 'Le citazioni trobadoriche nel *Roman de la Rose* di Jean Renart' (753–64). *Jung Vol.*, 1, has a section on Occitan literature (31–182): G. Hilty looks at the Prologue of the *Chanson de Sainte Foi* (33–45); L. Rossi analyses Cercamon (67–84); P. G. Beltrami discusses Bertran de Born's *domna soisebuda* (101–17); G. Tavani reconsiders attribution and edition problems for Raimon Vidal's 'Entre.l Taur e.l doble signe (PC 411, 3)' (131–49). In *Fest. Mölk:* E. Schulze-Busacker, 'Une réécriture chrétienne des *Disticha Catonis: Lo Libret de bos ensenhamens* de Raimon de Cornet' (61–80) gives a list of cross-references; N. Pasero studies intertextuality in terms of Guilhem IX and Jaufre Rudel's treatment of bad counsel (133–42); P. Cherchi traces the 'lost glove' story in Giraut de Bornelh's corpus and its possible influence on Petrarch (143–53); E. Poe offers a lively reading of an obscene *cobla esparsa* by Montan, 'Vostr'alens es tant putnais' (PC 306, 4) and traces an 'old whores' subgenre (155–74); V. Pollina studies 'madrigal' style in troubadour melodies (175–84); H.-E. Keller looks at Raimon Vidal's use of citations (185–92). M. Zink, 'Résumé du cours "La Mémoire des troubadours" et du séminaire "Guiraut Riquier et Matfre Ermengaud: à l'école des troubadours" donnés au Collège de France, 1997', in *Annuaire du Collège de France*, 1996–97:859–79. K. Klingebiel, 'Lost literature of the Troubadours: a proposed catalogue', *Tenso*, 12, 1997:1–23; V. Fraser, 'Two contrasting views of love in the songs of the Troubadours and the Trobairitz', *ib.*, 24–51, contrasts the *gap* with the songs of Castelloza. *Tenso*, 13.2, is a special issue on cross-cultural exchange, edited by W. D. Paden, with articles by S. N. Rosenberg on the 27 Oïl songs in Occ. MSS (18–32), C. Kleinhenz on the 3 Occ. sonnets extant (33–49), and W. D. Paden on Bonifaci Calvo's use of Occ. and Gal.-Ptg. (50–71). D. Billy, 'Anamorphoses: De la forme à son interprétation dans la poésie des troubadours: Le cas de "Mout m'es bon e bel" (PC 364, 29)', *RLaR*, 102:117–46, examines the patterning of Peire Vidal's song. J.-P. Chambon and C. Vialle, 'Sur la structure chronologique de *Guillaume de la Barre*', *ib.*, 373–86, look at the treatment of time in a narrative text, as does M.-G. Grossel, 'Conclure le roman en terre d'Oc: L'exemple de *Jaufré*', *PRIS-MA*, 14:117–34. A. Espadaler, 'El Rei d'Aragó i la data del *Jaufré*', *CN*, 57, 1997:199–207, dates the text *c.*1271–74. P. Lorenzo Gradín, '*Jaufre* o el orden ambiguo', *Mandach Vol.*, 201–19; R. Lafont, '*Girart de Roussillon*, un texte occitan', *ib.*, 29–50; L. also proposes that the Occ. text of *Fierabras* is the model in 'Les Origines occitanes de la chanson de geste: Le cas de *F(i)erabras*', *CCMe*, 41:365–73. E. Aubrey, 'The dialectic between Occitania and France in the thirteenth century', *EMH*, 16, 1997:1–53, emphasizes the influence of Occ. courtly material over the OF corpus, noting pastiche and parody of Occ. in the motet and *pastorela*. G. Hasenohr, 'La Prédication aux fidèles dans la première moitié du XIIe siècle: L'enseignement des sermons "limousins"', *Romania*, 116:34–67, analyses the language and content of Saint-Martial sermons. R. Harvey, 'Marcabru, *Aujatz de chan* (PC 293, 9): nouvelles questions', *ZRP*, 114:106–35, explores issues arising from a new edition of the *vers*. L. Paterson, 'Marcabru et le lignage de Caïn: "Bel m'es cant son li frug madur" (PC 293.13)', *CCMe*, 41:241–55, re-edits the song, exploring the lineage of Cain image. P. Bec, 'La tenson médiévale et ses avatars: genre ou forme fixe?', *Atalaya*, 8, 1997:135–50, offers a typology up to the 15th-c. C. Jewers, 'Reading and righting: issues of value and gender in early women poets', *Exemplaria*, 10:97–122, reads the Comtessa de Dia in terms of the reception of women's poetry from Sulpicia onwards. A. Brusoni, 'Problemi attributivi nel canzoniere di Gui de Cavaillon', *MedRom*, 22:209–31, identifies Esperdut (PC 142) and Guionet (PC 238) as the same author as Gui de Cavaillon (PC 192). S. Guida, 'Il Limosino di Briva', *CN*, 57, 1997:167–97, identifies Arnaut de Tintinhac as the target of Peire d'Alvernha's poets' gallery, vv. 25–30. *AIEO* 5, 1, includes: Focusing on Toulouse poets, W. Pfeffer (109–14) and R. Manetti (193–204) re-examine Peire Raimon de Tolosa; I. Szabics analyses Peire Vidal (185–92); P. Hutchinson reads Guillem Figueira's 'D'un sirventes far' (237–48); J. Rüdiger looks at Toulouse as a symbolic concept (253–60); F. Zemplenyi re-addresses the Cathar links (249–52); D. Hoekstra looks at the MSS of the *Canso de la Crotzada* (205–10). Intertextual links with other lyric corpuses are explored by A. Touber for the Minnesang (153–66), A. Schippers for Hebrew poetry (275–82), C. Pulsoni for Petrarch (69–74). Music is examined by E. Aubrey on the generic value of melodies (297–306); G. Le Vot on the use of modern research tools (307–36); R. Lug proposes a horse-riding rhythm for performance (337–50). More generally, S. Joseph analyses the intertextual field of Peire d'Alvernha's *Al dessebrar del païs* (PC 323, 3) (179–84); M. Winter-Housman examines the *descriptio puellae* topos (123–32); M. Cabré looks at the professional identity of Cerverí de Girona (211–24); A. Fassò studies Marcabru (PC 298, 15) (225–36); C. Léglu examines defamation in Occ. poetry (269–74). *BAIEO*, 14, 'Actes du Colloque "Jeunes Chercheurs en Domaine Occitan" (Montpellier, 28 février–1 mars 1997)': V. Barberis, 'Illustration et défense du mot-refrain' (7–23); A. Brusoni, 'Problèmes d'attribution dans le chansonnier de Gui de Cavaillon' (25–29); M. Coderch, 'Bernart de Ventadorn: La voix d'un idéal. L'incompréhension des sexes à travers l'oralité' (41–46); P. Olivella Madrid, 'A propos de l'oeuvre de Raimon de Cornet copiée en Catalogne' (51–63); C. Pulsoni, 'Les problèmes d'attribution de la lyrique des troubadours' (51–63); G. Caïti-Russo, 'Projet de recherche: pour une poétique de la politique dans l'Italie du XIIIe siècle' (31–34); A. Callewaert, 'La conscience littéraire des troubadours' (35–39); L. Ernvall, 'De Bernart de Ventadour à Peire Cardenal: réminiscences d'une société féodale dans les poésies des troubadours' (47–49).

2. 1500 AND BEYOND

Joëlle Ginestet, *Jean Boudou: La force d'aimer*, Vienne, Praesens — Pau, SFAIEO – Société des Amis de Jean Boudou, 1997, x + 169 pp. is a critical appreciation of the works of Boudou. Philippe Gardy's volume of the *Histoire et anthologie* (see previous section), *L'Age du Baroque, 1520–1789*, 249 pp., traces the carnivalization of the language, which allows Occ. to become a tool for the expression of political or religious dissent. *Le Siècle d'or de la poésie gasconne (1550–1650), anthologie bilingue*, ed. Pierre Bec, Les Belles Lettres, 1997, 430 pp., gives 64 poems, by 12 authors. Marcelle D'herde-Heiliger, *Frédéric Mistral et les écrivains occitans dans Lou Tresor dóu Felibrige*, Pau, SFAIEO, 413 pp., traces most of the citations found in the dictionary. *RLaR*, 102.2, is a special issue on Pierre Godolin, with six articles on this 17th-c. Toulousain writer. *AIEO 5*, ii: Studies of Jean Boudou: B. Vernhieras interprets *l'Aucel blu* (471–76); W. Calin explores the satire of Occitanism in *la Santa Estela del centenari* (477–80); J. Ginestet looks at Boudou's thematic use of black and white (481–93); U. Hahn examines the role of dual and fragmented identities (493–98); H.-E. Keller analyses *La montanha negra* (499–504). On the *moundi* writers, C. Torreilles presents the early 19th-c. treatment of Godolin as a symbol of a lost past (571–86); M.-C. Alen discusses the anonymous *Miral moundi* (1781) (537–48). C. Bonnet presents links between the circle of Adrien de Montluc and Toulouse (549–52); P. Gardy traces a style in *moundi* 17th-c. writing (553–70); X. Ravier interprets a poem by Antonin Perbosc and its translations (505–12); D. Julien looks at Robert Lafont's treatment of language (527–36). E. Gauzit interprets a 'cathar' song (351–85). Modern reception of the Albigensian crusade is examined by M. Albisson in the Félibres Gras and Laforêt (439–46), by A. Krispin in the German poet Nikolaus Lenau's epic poem of 1838–42 (447–54) and A. Rieger in Peter Berling's popular novel *Les Enfants du Graal* (1991) (455–70), which she interprets as specific to German culture. *BAIEO*, 14, presents the research of D. Cambiès on the 'prehistory' of the Occ. novel, 1800–1906 (91–96), U. Hahn on the poetry of René Nelli (107–13), and A. Kisters on regionalism in new Occ. language music (115–21).

IV. SPANISH STUDIES

LANGUAGE

POSTPONED

MEDIEVAL LITERATURE

By JANE E. CONNOLLY, *University of Miami*, MARÍA MORRÁS, *Universitat Pompeu Fabra, Barcelona*, and M. DOLORES PELÁEZ BENÍTEZ, *Simmons College*

1. GENERAL

James F. Burke, *Desire Against the Law: The Juxtaposition of Contraries in Early Medieval Spanish Literature*, Stanford U.P., xv + 315 pp., proposes that the medieval aesthetic is one of balancing codes of restraint with the realm of desire. The study begins with general theoretical considerations and reflections on the opposition of the law and the carnivalesque in music and manuscripts, and then focuses on specific literary texts: *Auto de los reyes magos, Poema de mio Cid, Milagros de Nuestra Señora, Razón de amor, Libro de buen amor, Conde Lucanor*. José Luis González Molero, *La 'librería rica' de Felipe II. Estudio histórico y catalogación*, M, Biblioteca Nacional, 879 pp., gives notice of the provenance and characteristics of a great number of medieval MSS preserved today in the library of El Escorial; the book is difficult to use because it lacks an index. Manuel Ariza and Ninfa Criado, *Antología de la prosa medieval*, M, Alhambra, 371 pp., is a reissue of an anthology of modernized texts (1985) with a second editor added. Carmen Bobes et al., *Historia de la teoría literaria. II: Transmisores. Edad media. Poéticas clasicistas*, M, Gredos, 471 pp., gives a clear and well-organized overview of medieval rhetoric based on standard secondary sources (Murphy, Kelly, Faulhaber, Minnis, etc.). Jesús Montoya and Isabel de Riquer, *El prólogo literario en la edad media*, M, UNED, 336 pp., following a general introduction on the concept and function of prologues in medieval literary theory, consider a number of well-known Castilian and Romance texts from Berceo to the Marquis of Santillana. Fernando Gómez Redondo, *Historia de la prosa medieval castellana. 1. La creación del discurso prosístico: el entramado cortesano*, M, Cátedra, 1220 pp., is a major reference work giving an exhaustive overview of the making of Castilian prose from its origins to Don Juan Manuel, with special attention to the creation of new genres and their social context. It includes an extensive series of works (translations, short narratives, non-literary texts) normally excluded in other literary histories. D. Hook, 'Some codicological observations on

British Library MS Egerton 289', *BHS(G)*, 75:437–51, examines script, *mise en page*, MS foliation and illumination in order to refine Brian Powell's account of MS development. A. J. Cárdenas, 'Ethical editing at the end of a millennium, or "How one should [edit] with a view to greater happiness in this world and the next"', *La corónica*, 26.2:135–42, discusses reading and editing medieval MSS vis à vis Dagenais's reader/manuscript model, suggesting that the author/text paradigm not be entirely supplanted. J. Acebrón Ruiz, '*No entendedes que es sueño, mas vissyón çierta:* de las visiones medievales a la revitalización de los sueños en las historias fingidas', Beltrán, *Caballerías*, 249–57, attempts to discover the distinction between *sueño* and *visión* by examining their use in texts ranging from Alfonso X to the 15th c.

2. THE EARLY RECONQUEST AND HISPANO-LATIN LITERATURE

R. Wright, 'The dating of the earliest *fuero* translations', *BHS(G)*, 75:9–16, argues that chancery politics, cultural developments, and an assessment of the *carta-puebla* of Zorita de los Canes all point to dating the earliest translations of local *fueros* after 1230, and possibly even 1240.

3. EARLY LYRIC POETRY, EPIC, BALLADS
KHARJAS, LYRIC POETRY

R. Hitchcock, 'La hispanicidad y la arabicidad: dos contracorrientes en la cultura de la España medieval', *Actas* (Birmingham), 1, 222–29, in a reappraisal of the topic, states that any attempt to divide the Iberian peninsula in different and isolated areas, some Christian and others Muslim, leads to a distortion of historical reality. F. López Estrada, 'Evocación de Emilio García Gómez; sus estudios sobre lírica medieval', *García Gómez Vol.*, 13–25, stresses the influence of García Gómez's editions and studies. Á. Galmés de Fuentes, 'Las jarchas mozárabes y la tradición lírica románica', *ib.*, 27–53, maintains that the *jarchas* are to be considered a homogeneous *corpus* within romance lyric. R. de Zayas, 'La jarcha y su melodía', *ib.*, 55–72, considers the only *jarcha* melody that has come down to us: it was still sung in the 16th-c. and was preserved by the famous musician Francisco Salinas through reference to the refrain 'Qalbi bi-qalbi'. C. Alvar, 'Poesía culta y lírica tradicional', *ib.*, 99–111, points out that traditional lyric has not survived in a 'pure' state, but appears in all Romance literatures intertwined with cultured elements that make of this kind of poetry a hybrid. V. Beltrán, 'Poesía tradicional:

ecdótica e historia literaria', *ib.*, 113–35, casts light on the manipulation of traditional poems by editors, who normally take the refrains from their context and modify the text to conform to the canonical forms of what is considered to be traditional lyric; the author advocates a return to the study of the original texts as they stand in the *cancioneros*. M. Frenk, 'Símbolos naturales en las viejas canciones populares hispánicas', *ib.*, 159–82, concentrates on the air, the dark woman, the moon, and the tree. J. M. Pedrosa, 'Reliquias de cantigas paralelísticas y de villancicos glosados en la tradición oral moderna', *ib.*, 183–215, illustrates his theme with abundant examples. Id., '*Las tres llaves* y *Los huevos sin sal*: versiones hispanocristianas y sefardís de dos ensalmos mágicos tradicionales', *Sefarad*, 58:153–66, traces common formulae in traditional Christian religious *ensalmos* and their Sephardic counterparts. S. Armistead and J. H. Silverman, 'Nueve adivinanzas de Estambul (Colección Milwitzky)', *ib.*, 31–60, edit and study them: four have Peninsular analogues, two originate in the Balkans, while the origin of the rest remains uncertain, all of which confirms the tradition's culturally eclectic character.

EPIC

M. Vaquero, 'Señas de oralidad en algunos motivos épicos compartidos: *Siete Infantes de Lara, Romanz del infant García, y Cantar de Sancho II*', *Actas* (Birmingham), 1, 320–27, looks at some notable motifs related to treason shared by the three texts and considers their presence a sign of orality.

POEMA DE MIO CID

A. D'Agostino, 'Angustia y esperanza: *Cantar del Mio Cid*, v. 14*b*', *RLMed*, 10:49–65, is a sharp analysis of vv. 11–14b of the poem that leads to the verification of an omission in the manuscript after v. 14, the defense of Pidal's conjecture in v. 14b, and the convincing proposition of an alternative hypothetical v. 14b that would include the poem's key word *ganança*. N. J. Dyer, 'Gender and manuscript culture in Alfonsine historiography', *La corónica*, 26.2:161–71, in a consideration of *Poema de mio Cid* and *Crónica de veinte reyes*, sketchily examines 'gendered characters' (Jimena, Elvira, Sol, *niña de nuef años*, Félix Muñoz) and argues that reception theory must consider gender questions, noting that physical MS evidence suggests particular interest in 'gender-based material'. J. L. Girón Alconchel, 'La cohesión en el *PMC* y el problema de su comienzo', *Actas* (Birmingham), 1, 183–92, argues on the basis of lexical coherence that there are no missing lines in the opening of the poem. I. Zaderenko, 'El procedimiento judicial del riepto entre nobles y la

fecha de composición de la *Histoira Roderici* y el *Poema de mio Cid*',
RFE, 78:183–94, points out that the judicial procedure in the *PMC*
follows closely the regulations as established in the *Ordenamiento de
Nájera* of 1185, and thus that date must be taken as the year *a quo* for
the poem's composition.

BALLADS

Luis Díaz Viana, **Una voz continuada. Estudios históricos y antropológicos
sobre la literatura oral*, M, Visor, 205 pp. Mariano de la Campa
Gutiérrez, *Antología de la épica y el romancero*, prol. S. Armistead and
A. Valenciano, B, Hermes, 235 pp., gives a rich repertoire from the
modern oral tradition. Diego Catalán, *Arte y poética del romancero oral.
Parte segunda. Memoria, invención artificio.* M, Siglo XXI, 339 pp., is the
second volume of what represents one of the most exhaustive and
groundbreaking studies concerning the stylistic devices of the *romancero*. Víctor Millet, *Épica germáncia y tradiciones épicas hispánicas: Waltarius
y Gaiferos. La leyenda de Walter de Aquitania y su relación con el romance de
Gaiferos*, M, Gredos, 366 pp., argues that the Spanish tradition is not
related to the Germanic legend but to the French versions of it; the
book includes an edition of the known Spanish texts. V. Castro Lingl,
'*La dama y el pastor* and the ballads of the *Cancionero general*: the portrayal
of the experienced woman', *Macpherson Vol.*, 133–46, focuses on the
female protagonist and how she flaunts her desire instead of trying to
conceal it. H. Pomeroy, 'From Greece to Spain and back: a Sephardic
ballad's journey', *ib.*, 147–57, compares the known versions of a
ballad tracing its origins to a Greek source. S. G. Armistead,
'Melisenda and the *chansons de geste*', *La corónica*, 27.1:55–68, examines
the formulaic theme of the forthputting princess in *Sleepless Melisenda*
and its Old French congeners, hypothesizing that the ballad drew on
a now lost Hispanic form of *Amis et Amile*. L. A. Bernard, ' "Sobre las
ocho cabezas": nuevas aportaciones textuales al Romancero de los
Infantes de Lara', *ib.*, 69–80, edits four Infante de Lara ballads held
in BNM 22.028. O. Anahory-Librowicz, 'Romances judeoespañoles
en Gibraltar', *Sefarad*, 58:5–30, with a bibliographical appendix by
S. Armistead (21–30), edits them and concludes that they are related
to the Moroccan and Andalusian traditions, and that they tend to be
brief. I. Katz, 'The traditional tunes of the Gibraltar romances', *ib.*,
58:117–26, refers to the Oro collection. (See also BERCEO.)

4. THIRTEENTH AND FOURTEENTH CENTURIES

POETRY

CUADERNA VÍA VERSE. **Proverbios morales de Sem Tob de Carrión*, ed.
Paloma Díaz-Mas and Carlos Mota, M, Biblioteca Nueva, 306 pp.

M. Garcia, 'La *copla cuaderna* du métier de clergie', Garcia, *Formes fixes*, 51–58, comments on the originality of the *cuaderna vía,* attained by imposing intense metrical and rhythmic constraints on a French model. P. Caraffi, 'La malinconia del re nel *Libro de Apolonio*', *Melli Vol.*, 195–203, believes melancholy is viewed as a characteristic not proper to royalty.

BERCEO. A. Deyermond, 'Narrativas abiertas y cerradas en la poesía castellana', Paredes, *Formas breves*, 21–53, focuses on the *Milagros de Nuestra Señora* and on several *romances* (*El prisionero, El Conde Arnaldo, Los Siete Infantes de Lara, La serrana de la Vera, Moraima, Blancaniña)*, observing that in most there is a mixture of closed and open endings.

LIBRO DE BUEN AMOR. P. Cherchi, ' "Coita non ha ley": *Libro de Buen Amor*, 928A', *MedRom*, 22 : 113–15, provides a new argument in favour of the transcription of the abbreviation *drho* in v. 928a of *LBA* as *derecho* rather than *dicho* by revealing the Latin source of the sententia 'cota non ha ley' in the *Decretum*. E. Francomano, ' "Saber bien e mal": the fall and the fruits of reading the *Libro de buen amor*', *La corónica*, 26.2 : 211–26, sees in the *LBA* the linguistic consequences of the Fall, arguing that fallen language produces much of the text's ambiguous readings. W. Casillas, 'El significado arquetípico de las serranas en el *Libro de buen amor*', *ib.*, 27.1 : 81–98, relies exclusively on Northrop Frye's theory of archetype, identifying in the *serranas* the *mythos* of satire and irony. M. J. Lacarra, 'El *Lba*, ejemplario de fábulas profanas', Paredes, *Formas breves*, 237–52, highlights the overwhelming majority of tales in prose before turning to the scarce examples in verse, among them the fables included in Juan Ruiz's book, which are related to the vernacular collections derived from the Oriental tradition.

OTHER POETRY. A. Dorón, 'La imagen de Alfonso X el Sabio en la creación literaria hebrea', *Actas* (Birmingham), I, 129–39, in fact is limited to the poetry by Todros Ha-Levi Abulafia, one of the most outstanding Hebrew poets of this period. L. M. Haywood. 'Al "mal pecado" de los troyanos: lírica y modos narrativos en la *Historia Troyana Polimética*', *ib.*, 216–21, studies the relationship between the narrative and the lyrics.

PROSE

ALFONSO X EL SABIO. H. Salvador Martínez, 'From script to print: beyond textual criticism in medieval Spanish manuscript culture', *La corónica*, 26.2 : 173–88, considers several Alfonsine examples from *General estoria* and *Estoria de España* to show that MS culture (i.e., the cultural environment in which the MSS were produced) may only be fully understood through the incorporation of significant MS variant readings, 'all contemporary references, variations of the story and possible influences', a difficult task that will be facilitated by a 'digitalized culture'. R. González-Casanovas, 'Fernando III como rey cruzado en la *Estoria de España* de Alfonso X: la historiografía como mitografía en torno a la reconquista castellana', *Actas* (Birmingham), I, 193–204, says everything in its title. (See also POEMA DE MIO CID.)

DIDACTIC LITERATURE. Marta Haro Cortés, *Libro de los cien capítulos (dichos de los sabios en palabras complidas)*, M, Iberoamericana — Frankfurt am Main, Verveuert, 216 pp., is an important contribution to the study of wisdom prose: the author traces the relation of the work to *Flores de filosofía* and the second *Partida*, dating its composition to 1280. Eloísa Palafox, *Las éticas del exemplum. Los Castigos del rey don Sancho IV, El Conde Lucanor y el Libro de buen amor*, Mexico, UNAM, 181 pp., studies the relationship between the three texts as exemplary discourses with different aims: in the first text the objective is to raise Don Sancho's image to a messianic range; the second is part of Don Juan Manuel's strategy to fight against his marginalization from power; and the *LBA* shows how knowledge is manipulated, and in that sense becomes an 'anti-exemplary' work. G. Cándano Fierro, 'Tradición misógina en los marcos narrativos de *Sendebar* y *Calila e Dimna*', *Actas* (Birmingham), I, 99–105, reviews matter related to women in these wisdom works. J. Paredes and P. Gracia, 'Hacia una tipología de las formas breves medievales', Paredes, *Formas breves*, 7–12, review a number of the most representative *exempla* (from *Disciplina clericalis, Sendebar, Calila e Dimna, Barlaam e Josafat*), miracles (Alfonso X and Berceo) and some other verse forms related to the *fabliaux* and *lais* to conclude that in order to establish a typology the structural is the only valid criterion. B. Darbord, 'Formas españolas del cuento maravilloso', *ib.*, 103–21, observes certain constants (the happy ending, a connection with folklore, the aristocratic class of the characters) in the most representative samples (tale 9 from *El Conde Lucanor, Libro de los gatos, Los siete sabios de Roma*).

DON JUAN MANUEL. *Laberinto de Fortuna*, ed. Maxim Kerkhoff, M, Castalia, 277 pp., uses the critical edition published in Colección Castalia Maior (1997), to which the author adds numerous explanatory notes and a solid introduction. R. Wilhelm, 'Geschichtenerzählen und Lebenspraxis Funktionen des Erzählen im *Conde Lucanor* und im *Decameron*', *RF*, 110:37–67, focuses his discussion primarily on *Decameron*, but comments briefly on the use of *exempla* in *Conde Lucanor*. G. B. Kaplan, 'Innovation and humour in three of *El Conde Lucanor*'s most amusing *exemplos*: a Freudian approach', *Hispanófila*, 123:1–15, concludes that Don Juan Manuel employed humour in *exempla* 20, 31, and 32, an element lacking in their sources, in order for them to conform to the text's didactic structure. M. L. Lobato, 'El arte de "façer cartas" de Juan Manuel', *Actas* (Birmingham), I, 230–39, takes a look at the extant 591 letters related to Don Juan Manuel. (See also DIDACTIC LITERATURE.)

OTHER PROSE WRITERS.   M. Faccon, 'Due traduzzioni iberiche della *Vida de Santa María Egipciaca*. Fonti possibili', *RLMed*, 10:83–99, studies the 14th-c. Castilian translation in prose of *VSME* contained in two codices (780 of Biblioteca Nacional de Madrid, and h-III–22 of Biblioteca de El Escorial) and two versions of a 14th-c. Portuguese translation in prose contained in MSS 266 and 771 of the Mosteiro de Alcobaça preserved in the Torre do Tombo in Lisbon. C. L. Scarborough, 'Santa María Egipcíaca: la vitalidad de la leyenda en castellano', *Actas* (Birmingham), I, 302–10, classifies all the known versions and focuses on the one derived from a French source. H. Ó. Bizarri, 'Etapas de transmisión y recepción de los *Castigos y documentos del rey Sancho IV*', *ib.*, 84–91, summarizes the conclusions reached in the course of a critical edition in progress. M. L. Cuesta Torre, 'Ética de la guerra en el *Libro del caballero Zifar*', Beltrán, *Caballerías*, 95–114, focuses on the justification of war and the means to make peace. J. M. Cacho Blecua, 'Del exemplum a la historia ficticia: la primera lección del *Zifar*', Paredes, *Formas breves*, 209–36, examines the making of the first chapters, which are a kind of *speculum principis* that later evolves into a narrative pattern. A close look is given to the materials on which the king's councils are built: *Flores de filosofía*, *De preconiis Hispaniae* by Juan Gil de Zamora, the *Moralia Dogma philosophorum* attributed to William of Conches, and several vernacular collections (*Barlaam y Josafat*, *Ysopete historiado*, *General Estoria*, etc.)

LÓPEZ DE AYALA.   Germán Orduna, *El arte narrativo y poético del canciller Ayala*, M, CSIC, 228 pp., gives fine analyses of the narrative technique of the *Crónicas*, based on the prosody of oral narration, and of the uses of the 'I' in the *Rimado de Palacio* as the thread that structures the poem. J. López-Arias, 'López de Ayala: rasgos sobresalientes de su narrativa', *Hispanófila*, 122:1–16, summarizes the chronicler's narrative techniques.

5.   FIFTEENTH CENTURY

GENERAL, BIBLIOGRAPHY, EARLY PRINTING

Two nice and well-documented books increase our knowledge of early printed books in Spain: J. Canto Bellod and A. Huarte Salves, introd. M. Sánchez Mariana, *Catálogo de incunables de la Universidad Complutense*, M, Univ. Complutense, 266 pp.; R. Rodríguez Álvarez and M. Llorden Miñambres, *El libro antiguo en las bibliotecas españolas*,

Oviedo U.P., 322 pp. M. Pérez González, *Actas del congreso Internacional sobre Humanismo y renacimiento*, León, 686 pp.

POETRY

CANCIONEROS. I. Macpherson and A. Mackay, *Love, Religion, and Politics in 15th-c. Spain*, Leiden, Brill, xvi + 286 pp., is a series of fascinating previously published studies, with updated bibliography and some additions to build them into a coherent volume. J. Jurado, *El cancionero de Baena. Problemas paleográficos*, M, CSIC, 322 pp., studies in full detail the volume now in Paris, but does not add anything of significance beyond A. Blecua's well known article on the subject. J. Whetnall, 'Adiciones y enmiendas al *Cancionero del siglo XV*', *Macpherson Vol.*, 195–218, gives a list of 49 new poems or fragments of poems. L. M. Haywood, 'Romance and sentimental romance as *Cancionero*', *ib.*, 175–94, makes a full inventory of *cancionero* poetry in sentimental and chivalresque romances which Brian Dutton did not take into account. M. Masera, 'Tradición oral y escrita en el *Cancionero musical de Palacio*: el símbolo del cabello como atributo erótico de la belleza femenina', *ib.*, 159–74, examines thoroughly her material, but overlooks studies on traditional poetry from previous centuries. J. N. H. Lawrance, 'La muerte y el morir en las letras ibéricas al fin de la Edad Media', *Actas* (Birmingham), 1, 1–26, contrasts Garcilaso's *decorum* in treating death in the *Elegía en la muerte de don Bernardino de Toledo* with the morbid and macabre lachrymosity found in the 15th-c. elegiac poems by the Marqués de Santillana, Pero Díaz de Toledo, Fernán Pérez de Guzmán, the *Danza de la muerte* and others. V. A. Burrus, 'Role playing in the amatory poetry of the *Cancionero*', Gerli, *Poetry*, 111–33, insists on the necessity of taking into account the social milieu in which this type of poetry was produced, a perspective which is actively pursued by I. Macpherson, 'The game of courtly love: *Letras, divisas* and *invenciones* at the court of the Catholic Monarchs', *ib.*, 95–110 (repr. in Macpherson and Mackay). M. Johnston, 'Cultural studies on the *Gaya ciencia*', *ib.*, 235–53, examines the most important approaches current in cultural studies and applies them to *cancionero* poetry, taken as a discourse of social, political, and economic power. R. Rohland de Langbehn, 'Power and justice in *Cancionero* verse', *ib.*, 199–219, uses as a starting point for discussion various poems by Fernán Pérez de Guzmán, Juan de Mena and Gómez Manrique. J. Rodríguez Puértolas, 'Jews and *conversos* in 15th-c. Castilian Cancioneros: texts and contexts', *ib.*, 187–97, concentrates on Valera's poems included in the *Gallardo*. A. Deyermond, 'Bilingualism in the *Cancionero* and its implications', *ib.*, 137–70, has two objectives: placing bilingual and multilingual Castilian *cancioneros* in a European context and tracing the reasons for the use of another language rather than the poet's own; the study includes a final section on open research subjects. M. Garcia, 'In praise of the *Cancionero:* Considerations on the social meaning of the Castilian *Cancioneros*', *ib.*, 47–56, views poetic anthologies as physical entities, i.e., as volumes, exemplifying his approach with the *Cancionero de Oñate-Castañeda.* J. Weiss, 'Medieval vernacular poetics and the social meaning of form', Garcia, *Formes fixes*, 171–86, looks at what the theoretical treatises have to say on fixed forms and finds that they seem to foster such forms as canonical. V. Beltrán, 'Tipología y génesis de los cancioneros. Los cancioneros de autor', *RFE*, 78:49–101, is an interesting analysis of how personal *cancioneros* where composed; as a point of departure the author examines in detail the cases of Auzias March, Álvarez Gato, Gómez Manrique, and Juan del Enzina. Id., 'The typology and genesis of the *Cancioneros*: compiling the materials', *Actes* (Caen), 19–46, offers an even broader approach to the same subject, establishing the structural tendencies observed in several anthologies and concluding that these can give some information on the compiler's intentions. Id., 'De la cantiga de amor a la canción cuatrocentista. Protohistoria de una forma fija', Garcia, *Formes fixes*, 59–72, considers the latter a derivation of the former, from which it keeps several characteristics (the semantic structure, the use of parallelism, the importance of lexical repetition and the abstract vocabulary) and to which the influence of the metrical structure of the *zéjel* (already present in the famous *cantiga* by Alfonso XI) has been added. M. Morrás, 'Fortuna de las formas zejelescas en la poesía castellana', *ib.*, 113–34, follows the evolution of this type of strophe in several *cancioneros*, examining how this form starts as a loose metrical pattern and ends as a fixed form. E. Beaumatin, 'Travailler sur corpus: observations sur les compositions monostrophiques dans le *Cancionero de Baena*', *ib.*, 21–28, takes on a metrical analysis of the shortest *Baena* poems with statistical considerations on the authors and verse length. C. Tato, 'Poetas cancioneriles de apellido *Montoro*', *RLMed*, 10: 169–81, reduces to two people the four Montoro surnames in the *Cancionero de Palacio (SA7)*: Alfonso de Montoro, identified with Sancho Alfonso de Montoro, author of most of the poems in the *Cancionero*, and Juan de Montoro, from whom we have only one extant composition. N. F. Marino, 'A life of their own: reading the rubrics of the *Cancionero de Baena*', *RoN*, 38: 311–19, argues that the rubrics in *Baena* lead to courtly consciousness, studies the discrepancy between them and the compositions they precede in some cases, and concludes that Baena's manipulation of his readers through rubrics controls the reception of the texts. J. Gornall, 'How reliable is a *razo*? Attribution and genre in Baena 40/556 and 557', *La corónica*, 26.2:227–41, proposes Villasandino as the author of *Baena* 40/536, noting similarities to another poem by him (552).

SANTILLANA.   Ll. Cabré, 'Notas sobre la memoria de Santillana y los poetas de la Corona de Aragón', *Macpherson Vol.*, 39–52, considers Santillana's familiarity with the Catalan poets he quotes.

JORGE MANRIQUE.   A. Hermida, 'Silent subtexts and *cancionero* codes: On Garcilaso de la Vega's revolutionary love', Gerli, *Poetry*, 79–92, tries to figure out if the linguistic and stylistic change in Garcilaso is the consequence of a social change and takes as a point of departure a detailed analysis of Manrique's use of the concept of 'secreto amor'.

JUAN DE MENA.   L. Vasvari, '*Las trescientas preñadas* de J. de M.: la política de la traducción y pedantería latinizantes', *Actes* (Caen), 27–40, indirectly refutes Lázaro Carreter's famous article on the *arte mayor* when she states that Mena's language is the normal product of an era in which Latin held the utmost prestige. E. Beaumatin, 'Pour l'analyse métrique du *Laberinto de Fortuna*: un réexamen des propositions de Jacques Robaud sur l'art mayor', *LNL*, 92 : 65–94, is a rather opaque proposal to solve the problem of the different distribution of rhythmic ictus in Mena's poem. B. Weissberger, 'Male anxieties in *Carajicomedia*: a response to female sovereignty', Gerli, *Poetry*, 221–34, dicusses the literary image of queen Isabel by comparing the *Laberinto the Fortuna* with this parody. M. Duffell, 'Juan de Mena's "La flaca barquilla"', *Macpherson Vol.*, 53–67, confirms the poem's authorship based on stylistic, linguistic, thematic, and metrical analysis.

OTHER POETS.   J. C. López Nieto, 'Algunas precisiones sobre la fecha de la muerte de Gómez Manrique', *RLMed*, 10 : 141–46, brings forward the already probable date of 11 November 1490 to *c.* 3–6 or 7 November of the same year as possible dates for Manrique's death. A. Beresford, 'Poverty and (in)justice: temporal and spiritual conflict in a *Pregunta* by Ferrán Sánchez de Talavera (ID 1657)', *Macpherson Vol.*, 25–38, points out the inadequacy of God's answer, which constitutes the mechanical repetition of the standard religious message, to the poet's plea. M. Brownlee, 'Francisco Imperial and the issue of poetic genealogy', Gerli, *Poetry*, 59–78, tries to demonstrate that the poet from Seville strategically used several episodes from the *Divina Commedia* and a French *dit* in order to represent himself as the only *poeta dezidor* (who masters both philosophy and rhetoric). D. McGrady, 'Macaronic Latin and religious parody in Soria's "Transeat a me calix iste"', *BHS(L)*, 75 : 265–72, proposes a witty explanation of the poem based on the reading of its first line as macaronic Latin, which then allows the conversion of most lexical items into sexual euphemisms. M. Campos Souto, 'La poesía de García de Padilla: edición y estudio', *Macpherson Vol.*, 89–103, identifies the poet as a *freile* from the order of Calatrava who was related to the Aragonese party, and critically edits the two extant poems by him. R. Boase, 'The identity of two poets: the Marquis of Astorga (*c*.1462–1505) and Puertocarrero', *ib.*, 106–32, identifies the former as Pedro Álvarez Osorio, poet at the service of the Duque de Alba, García Álvarez de Toledo, and of Fadrique Enríquez, admiral of Castile; Puertocarrero is Luis Fernández de Puertocarrero. C. Alvar, 'La poesía de mosén Diego de Valera', *Melli Vol.*, 1–13, divides the poetry in three groups belonging to distinct textual traditions. M. Gerli, 'Reading Cartagena: blindness, insight and modernity in a *Cancionero* poet', Gerli, *Poetry*, 171–83, is a successful attempt to disclose the attractive side of this kind of poetry in a brilliant interpretation of Cartagena's poems which considers its intellectual complexity along with its artistic, linguistic, and ideological significance. A. Deyermond, 'Women and Gómez Manrique', *Macpherson Vol.*, 69–87, studies the relation between the poet and his wife, Juana de Mendoza; it is through her that he establishes a close relationship with the monastery of Calabanzos (Palencia), which must be considered in the light of the female literary circles of this age.

PROSE

CHIVALRESQUE AND SENTIMENTAL FICTION. N. Porro, *La investidura de armas en Castilla del Rey Sabio a los Católicos*, Valladolid, Junta de Castilla y León, 368 pp., compares legal and historical documents with the ceremonies depicted in literary texts, showing that the latter were configured according to real procedures. J. M. Lucía, 'Libros de caballerías impresos, libros de caballerías manuscritos (observaciones sobre la recepción del género editorial caballeresco', Beltrán, C*aballerías*, 311–41, stresses the peculiarities of this type of fiction underlining the role of the press in shaping uniformity for chivalresque narration, helping thus to create the genre as such. J. Guijarro, 'Notas sobre las comparaciones animalísticas en la descripción del combate de los libros de caballerías. La ira del caballero cristiano', *ib.*, 115–35, concludes that such comparisons have an ethical value. C. Domínguez, ' "De aquel pecado que le acusaban a falsedat": Reinas injustamente acusadas en los libros de caballerías (Ysonberta, Florençia, la santa Emperatrís y Sevilla)', *ib.*, 159–80, breaks the texts into sequences and motifs and maps the similarities between them. C. Alvar, 'El *Tristán en prosa* del ms. 527 de la Bibliothèque Municipale de Dijon', *ib.*, 19–61, studies the correspondences with the French *Queste* and places this text within the Spanish and the Romance traditions. A series of texts have been published by the Instituto de

Estudios Cervantinos at Alcalá de Henares. These include an edition of Francisco de Barahona's *Flor de caballerías*, ed. J. M. Lucía, 321 pp., as well as a number of reading guides: P. Gracia provides the material for *Baladro del sabio Merlín (Burgos, Juan de Burgos, 1498)*, 74 pp.; J. M. Lucía for *Oliveros de Castilla (Burgos, Fadrique Biel de Basilea, 1499)*, 56 pp.; M. L. Cuesta, *Tristán de Leonís*, 78 pp.; and M. del R. Aguilar for *Felixmarte de Hircania de Melchor Ortega (Valladolid, Francisco Fernández de Córdoba, 1556)*, 68 pp. I. A. Corfis, 'Empire and romance: *Historia de la Linda Melosina*', *Neophilologus*, 82:559–75, studies the parallels between Isabeline politics and the chivalric romance *Historia de la Linda Melosina* (1489), a translation of Jean d'Arras's *Mélusine*. D. Gagliardi, 'La *Historia de la linda Melosina*: una o due versioni castigliane del romanzo di Jean D'Arras?', *MedRom*, 22:116–41, studies the two preserved Castilian editions, the first one published in Tolosa by Parix in 1489 (T1489) and the second in Seville by Cromberger in 1526 (S1526), and argues that the lost edition published in Valencia in 1512 (V1512) was an elaboration of the text in T1489, while S1526 could be a corrected reprint of V1512. E. J. Sales Dasí, 'California, las amazonas y la tradición troyana', *RLMed*, 10:147–67, suggests that the medieval tradition of the Trojan legend is the literary source that inspired and provided for Montalvo the necessary details to elaborate the Amazon's episode in his *Sergas de Esplandián*. C. J. Donahue, 'Written versus visual text: a study of two illuminations in ms. P of the *Libro del Cauallero Çifar*', *RoN*, 38:233–39, analyses the artist's manipulation of the figure of the mother in an illuminated *exemplum*, concluding that she is portrayed as a noble Virgin-like intermediary rather than a sinner as it appears in the written text, and relates this softening to the fact that MS P pertains to the mid or late 15th-c., when the concept of *imitatio Christi* became important for many medieval women. V. Blay Manzanera, 'El Más Allá de *Triste deleytaçión* y el mito de Verbino', *BHS(L)*, 75:137–52, considers the allegory contained under the rubric 'La ventura que alló el E° [yendo] a ver a su Senyora' (fols 154ᵛ–93ᵛ).

DIEGO DE SAN PEDRO.   R. Folger, 'Memorias en *Siervo libre de amor*: el papel de la psicología medieval en la ficción sentimental', *La corónica*, 26.2:197–210, examines *Siervo* from the perspective of medieval theories of memory. M. L. Indini, 'Uno sconosciuto testimonio del *Carcer d'amore*', *Melli Vol.*, 387–402, gives notice of an unknown copy of the Italian translation in the Biblioteca Passerini-Landi de Piacenza (Fondo Comunale KK.XI.10).

ALONSO DE CARTAGENA.   N. G. Round, ' "Pérdóneme Séneca": the translation practices of Alfonso de Cartagena', *BHS(G)*, 75:17–29, considers Cartagena's attitude toward the original Senecan and pseudo-Senecan texts he translated and his definition of translation itself, giving particular attention to the case of *De remediis fortuitum*.

OTHER PROSE WRITERS. V. Campo, 'La traducción castellana del *Contra Hipócritas* de Leonardo Bruni', *RLMed*, 10:9–46, is a critical edition of *Contra los Ipócritas*, a medieval Castilian translation of the *Oratio in hypocritas* by the Italian humanist Leonardo Bruni. J. Herrero Prado, 'Pero Díaz de Toledo, señor de Olmedilla', *ib.*, 101–15, presents Pero Díaz de Toledo as a member of an illustrious *converso* family who had an important social influence in the service of Santillana and Juan II of Castile with both his juridical and literary works. C. Wilkins, 'El devocionario de sor Constanza: otra voz femenina medieval', *Actas* (Birmingham), 1, 340–49, examines an unpublished religious work by a nun, granddaughter of King Pedro I of Castile, focusing on the passages dealing with Jesus's Incarnation and Passion. The author concludes that the work must have been written for the nuns of the convent. Id. edits the text as *Book of Devotions. Libro de devociones y oficios* (EHT, 52), 123 pp. A. Ward, 'Las fuentes de la *Genealogía de los reyes de Navarra* de García de Eugui', *Actas* (Birmingham), 1, 328–39, stresses the work as the first history to consider Navarre as a kingdom worthy of its own chronicle, and studies its sources, which date to the 13th-c. L. Funes, 'El lugar de la *Crónica particular de San Fernando* en el sistema de las formas cronísticas castellanas de principios del siglo xv', *ib.*, 176–82, remarks that this chronicle, by abandoning the universalist view of historiography typical since Alfonso X, prepares the way to the particular chronicles of the 15th c. **Texto y Concordancias de El tratado de menescalcia. Biobliothèque Nationale de Paris, Ms. Esp. 214*, ed. María Isabel Montoya Ramírez, HSMS, 4 pp. + 2 microfiches. **Text and Concordance of Generaciones y semblanzas. Fundación Lázaro Galdiano, MS. 435*, ed. Roger Folger, HSMS, 6 pp. + 2 microfiches.

THEATRE

P. Lorenzo Gradín, 'El arte del actor en los siglos xii y xiii', *MedRom*, 22:161–89, analyses the Latin liturgical and school dramas produced between the 12th and 13th cs; she insists particularly on their *didascalias*, with directions for the actors that depart from the mere ritual experience, and examines the first theatrical romance text, *Jeu d'Adam*, where the initial *didascalia* gives specific instructions for the gesticulation and the diction required from the actors.

ALJAMIADO LITERATURE
POSTPONED

LITERATURE, 1490–1700 (PROSE AND POETRY)
POSTPONED

LITERATURE, 1490–1700 (DRAMA)
POSTPONED

LITERATURE, 1700–1823

By GABRIEL SÁNCHEZ ESPINOSA, *Lecturer in Hispanic Studies,*
The Queen's University of Belfast

1. BIBLIOGRAPHY AND PRINTING

BIBLIOGRAPHY. M.-D. García Gómez, *La biblioteca regalista de un súbdito fiel: Melchor de Macanaz*, Alicante, Instituto Juan Gil-Albert, 218 pp., is the inventory of the library — 538 works — which, in 1716 on his departure for exile, was requisitioned from this statesman, undoubtedly one of the most radical intellectuals of the reign of Philip V.
BOOKS AND PRINTING. J. Blas Benito, 'Pascual Carsi y Vidal, encuadernador de Carlos IV y de su Real Imprenta', *Encuadernación de arte*, 11:33–46, situates the figure of this bookbinder at the climax of the Neo-classical aesthetic in the art of book design during the reign of Charles IV. Carsi learned his trade in England between 1789 and 1797.

2. THOUGHT AND THE ENLIGHTENMENT

M. Bolufer, *Mujeres e Ilustración: la construcción de la feminidad en la España del siglo XVIII*, V, Institución Alfonso el Magnánimo, 427 pp., deals, from a perspective of cultural history, with the diverse representations of femininity at work in the debate which developed around the theme of women in 18th-c. Spain, on issues that were intellectual (renewed by B.-J. Feijoo with his essay 'Defensa de las mujeres'), social (education, luxury, medicine, family, participation in the Economic Societies), and literary (women as readers and writers). J. Gómez de Enterría, *Voces de la economía y el comercio en el español del siglo XVIII*, Alcalá U.P., 1996, 260 pp., brings together a useful glossary of neologisms within 18th-c. economics — words to be found everywhere in the works of reformist and enlightened writers — stating the first appearance of each term. By the same scholar is 'Consideraciones sobre la terminología científico-técnica de carácter patrimonial en el español del siglo XVIII', *BRAE*, 78:275–301. R. Haidt, *Embodying Enlightenment: Knowing the Body in Eighteenth-Century Spanish Literature and Culture*, NY, St Martin's Press, 279 pp., examines, through the lens of theories of gender and the body, the cultural construction of masculine bodies during the Spanish Enlightenment. While chapters 1 and 2 are devoted to the experience of the body as conveyed in medical and anatomical treatises (M. Martínez and B.-J. Feijoo) and 18th-c. erotic poetry (J. Meléndez Valdés), chapters 3 and 4 analyse the antithetical figures of the *petimetre* and the *hombre de bien* (J. Cadalso). J. H. R. Polt, 'Anton Raphael Mengs in Spanish Literature', pp. 351–74 of *Homenaje a don Luis Monguió*, ed. J. Aladro-Font, Newark, Juan de la Cuesta, 1997, summarizes the reception given to the person and work of the Saxon painter — in Spain in the years 1761–69 and 1774–77 — by the Spanish poetry of the Enlightenment (T. de Iriarte, J. Meléndez Valdés and M.-J. Quintana). I. Pulido Bueno, *José Patiño: el inicio del gobierno político-económico ilustrado en España*, pr. publ., Huelva, 368 pp., falls short of the study that this reformist minister under Philip V deserves since it omits all relevant information regarding his intervention in shaping cultural life during the period of his government (for example, his distrust of G. Mayans).

3. LITERARY HISTORY

GENERAL

F. Baasner, 'Una *época clásica* controvertida. La polémica sobre el Siglo de Oro en la historiografía literaria española de los siglos XVIII y XIX', *RLit*, 60 : 57–78, analyses the formation of the concept of 'Siglo de Oro' in Spanish literature from the 16th to the 19th c., the authors of the 16th and 17th cs themselves being the first to use it as a way of establishing their own canon. J. Checa Beltrán, *Razones del buen gusto (poética española del neoclasicismo)*, M, CSIC, 358 pp., is a study of Spanish poetics published between 1737 (I. Luzán) and 1827 (F. Martínez de la Rosa). The structure follows the principal categories and genres of Neoclassicism. As far as the turn of the century period is concerned, the author finds in the poetics a confrontation, not between Neoclassicism and Romanticism, but between old and modern Neoclassicism. F. Sánchez Blanco, *El ensayo español 2: el siglo XVIII*, B, Crítica, 1997, 373 pp., outlines in the introduction the characteristics of this essentially polymorphous genre of 18th-c. Spanish literature. The anthology brings together *ensayos* written by 22 authors — some of them little known — and pays more attention to the reigns of Philip V and Ferdinand VI, than to the better known reigns of Charles III and Charles IV.

DRAMA

El teatro europeo en la España del siglo XVIII, ed. F. Lafarga, Lérida, Lleida U.P., 1997, 442 pp., is divided into three sections. The first, under I. Urzainqui, studies the presence of foreign theatre theoreticians in Spain in the 18th c. The second, which deals with the translations of the different dramatic genres, has been entrusted to known specialists: French tragedy (J.-A. Ríos Carratalá), French comedy (F. Lafarga), French drama (M.-J. García Garrosa), Metastasio and the Italian melodrama (P. Garelli), Goldoni (A. Calderone and V. Pagán) and English and German theatre (J. Álvarez Barrientos). The third section of the book consists of a bibliographical catalogue of the manuscript and printed translations of plays produced in 18th-c. Spain. J.-M. Leza, 'Metastasio on the Spanish stage: operatic adaptations in the public theatres of Madrid in the 1730s', *EMus*, 26:623–30, centres on the operas *Dar el ser el hijo al padre* and *Por amor y por lealtad, recobrar la majestad: Demetrio en Siria*, both staged on 31 January 1736, and based on the *Artaserse* and *Demetrio*, respectively. Five of the 19 operas performed in Madrid between 1730 and 1750 were adaptations of P. Metastasio. Unfortunately, music scores have not survived. The most important modifications are the two-act structure, following the *zarzuela* model, and the incorporation of comic figures, who change the balance of the works. E. Palacios Fernández, *El teatro popular español del siglo XVIII*, Lérida, Milenio, 343 pp., brings together articles previously published in journals, conference proceedings and literary histories, some with additions, grouped under the polemical and certainly anachronistic title of 'teatro popular', which in this book means any 18th-c. theatrical manifestation which is not rigidly neoclassical, including sentimental comedies. Nevertheless, the book is of great value to those who are interested in a wide variety of theatrical subgenres and topics which range from the *teatro de bandoleros* to the *zarzuela*. One outstanding section is his commentary on *El rapto de Ganimedes* by J. de Cañizares. J. E. Varey, *Cartelera de los títeres y otras diversiones populares de Madrid: 1758–1840. Estudio y documentos* (Fuentes para la Historia del Teatro en España, 8), London, Támesis, 1995, 495 pp., provides a complete collection of announcements and advertisements relating to the heterogeneous variety of popular entertainments — cribs, puppets, magic lanterns, shadow plays, automatons, *totilimundis*, scientific, and pseudo-scientific experiments, circus performances and dioramas — which appeared in the *Diario de Madrid* from its commencement in 1758. Altogether some 485 documents are collected, from which the relevant information pertaining to the identity of the impresario, the venue of the show, the date, time and price has been extracted. 11 posters corresponding to the different types of performances are included in the appendix. The insertion of a very useful and detailed map of Madrid in 1800 will undoubtedly allow the reader to locate the urban layout of these paratheatrical shows.

PERIODICAL LITERATURE

J.-P. Clément, *El Mercurio Peruano, 1790–1795*, 2 vols, Frankfurt, Vervuert — M, Iberoamericana, 1997, 307, 329 pp., devotes the first volume to a rigorous study (authors, material and economic aspects, reception, themes and ideology) of this periodical of enlightened orientation produced by the Sociedad Académica de Amantes del País de Lima, which succeeded in publishing 416 numbers. The second volume is an anthology of 34 articles.

4. INDIVIDUAL AUTHORS

ANDRÉS. J. Checa Beltrán, 'Poesía y filosofía: Juan Andrés y el "estilo espiritoso"', *RLit*, 59, 1997:423–35, reflects upon the denunciation by the neoclassical writer J. Andrés of the new literary style arising from the fashionable combination of philosophy and poetry brought about by the Enlightenment, characterized by the prioritizing of *ingenio* and *imaginación* at the expense of *juicio* and *buen gusto*. The term 'espiritoso' — 'spiritoso' in the original Italian — has its origin in the French 'esprit'.

AZARA, FÉLIX DE. Á. Mones and M.-A. Klappenbach, *Un ilustrado aragonés en el Virreinato de La Plata: Félix de Azara (1742–1821): estudios sobre su vida, su obra y su pensamiento*, Montevideo, Museo Nacional de Historia Natural, 1997, 231 pp., is basically a critical bio-bibliography (with commentary), which includes 22 unpublished letters by the enlightened explorer and naturalist.

CADALSO. R. P. Sebold, 'El subtexto costumbrista de las *Noches lúgubres*, de Cadalso', *Dieciocho*, 21:7–19, looks in depth at the connection between Cadalso's *costumbrismo* and that of R. Mesonero, M.-J. de Larra and S. Estébanez Calderón.

CAÑIZARES. J. de Cañizares, *Don Juan de Espina en su patria. Don Juan de Espina en Milán* ed. S. Paun de García, M, Comunidad de Madrid–Castalia, 1997, 281 pp., edits these two *comedias de magia* from the Madrid edition of 1745. The eponymous legendary magician is derived from a mysterious Spanish musician and collector of the reign of Philip IV.

FERNÁNDEZ DE MORATÍN, LEANDRO. R. Andioc, 'Sobre Moratín y Goya', pp. 9–36 of *Goya y Moratín en Burdeos, 1824–1828*, Bilbao, Museo de Bellas Artes de Bilbao, 142 pp., is a masterly comparison of the personalities and works of the playwright and the painter. L. Fernández de Moratín, *Il vecchio e la giovane*, ed. B. Tejerina, Nápoles, Liguori 1996, 507 pp., compares and contrasts the Spanish play and the Italian prose translation by P. Napoli Signorelli, published in Venice in 1805.

FORNER. *Juan Pablo Forner y su época (1756–1797)*, éd. J. Cañas Murillo and M.-Á. Lama, Mérida, Editora Regional de Extremadura, 623 pp., is the proceedings of a conference which took place in Cáceres on 17–20 November 1997. The following articles stand out amongst those included: P. Álvarez de Miranda, 'Forner, escritor de encargo. Nuevos datos para su bibliografía' (35–55); M.-Á. Lama, 'Sobre papeles manuscritos de Juan Pablo Forner' (123–98); F. Lopez, 'Las ideas políticas de Forner' (199–215); P. Deacon, 'Señas de identidad de Juan Pablo Forner: una aproximación a las *Demostraciones palmarias*' (379–99); D. T. Gies, 'Forner, la amistad y la patria: *La escuela de la amistad o el filósofo enamorado* (1796)' (449–60); J. Pérez Magallón, 'De concursos, vicios y sátiras: Forner y Moratín en 1782' (509–23); and J. Álvarez Barrientos, 'Forner traduce a Mencke: las *Declamaciones contra la charlatanería de los eruditos* (1787)' (567–83).

GARCÍA DE LA HUERTA. V. García de la Huerta, *Poesías*, ed. M.-Á. Lama, Mérida, Editora Regional de Extremadura, 1997, 602 pp., collects the poetic output of this writer, normally thought of as only the author of tragedies. For the editor, Huerta's exile in 1768–77 prevented his development of a more neoclassical style of poetry, more in tune with the central decade of the Spanish literary Enlightenment.

GUTIÉRREZ. R. P. Sebold, 'Sadismo y sensibilidad *en Cornelia Bororquia o la víctima de la Inquisición*', pp. 65–78 of *I Congreso internacional sobre novela del siglo XVIII*, ed. F. García Lara, Almería U.P., 311 pp., relates this anticlerical novel published in Paris in 1800 by the extrinitarian monk L. Gutiérrez to the Gothic novel *The Monk* (1796) by M.-G. Lewis and the erotic novels *Justine* (1791) and *Juliette* (1796) by the Marquis de Sade. *Cornelia Bororquia* is a fierce attack on the authoritarianism of the Spanish Catholic Church of the time and its thought police the *Inquisición*. Other influences are the sentimental comedy and novel.

JOVELLANOS. *Jovellanos, ministro de Gracia y Justicia*, ed. G. Anes, B, Fundación la Caixa, 234 pp., is the catalogue of the exhibition which took place in Gijón in the former *Instituto de náutica y mineralogía* between May and June 1998, to commemorate the short but significant period of Jovellanos at the head of the Justice ministry, from November 1797 to August 1798. Outstanding among the studies included is N. Glendinning 'Los amigos de Jovellanos' (41–56), an overview of the diverse circles of acquaintances and friends of the Asturian writer that takes into account the particular understanding of friendship held by the Spanish *ilustrados*.

MONTENGÓN. Pedro Montengón, *Eusebio*, ed. F. García Lara, M, Cátedra, 993 pp., makes available again a much needed university edition of this novel, based on the first edition (1786–88), which was significantly altered in 1807 with a view to evading the prohibition by the Inquisition. The editor re-uses the text that he established in his previous edition of 1984.

NOROÑA. Conde de Noroña, *Antología poética*, ed. S. Fortuño, M, Cátedra, 1997, 273 pp., is basically devoted to his original poetry published in 1799–1800, tending to give less attention to his translations, which appeared in 1833 under the title *Poesías asiáticas*, and his epic poem *La Ommíada* (1816), centred on the caliphate of Cordoba.

SAMANIEGO. E. Palacios Fernández, 'Las *Fábulas* de Félix María de Samaniego: fabulario, bestiario, fisiognomía y lección moral', *RLit*, 60:79–100, addresses the question of the reception of fables within the contemporary debate on educational reform.

SEMPERE Y GUARINOS. J. Sempere y Guarinos, *Ensayo de una biblioteca española de los mejores escritores del reinado de Carlos III*, Valladolid, Junta de Castilla y León–Consejería de Educación y Cultura, 1997, 3 vols, is a new facsimile edition of this important dictionary of authors originally published during the final years of the reign of Charles III, between 1785 and 1789. Bearing in mind the availability on the Spanish market of an identical facsimile edited by a private publishing house (Gredos), it is remarkable that a public cultural institution should spend its restricted funds on a new and costly facsimile that adds nothing to the one available, above all when we consider the need for similar facsimiles in genres such as the press. This publication has a superfluous introduction by J.-J. Lucas Jiménez, the president of the *Junta* of Castilla and León, in accordance with recent Spanish custom.

TRIGUEROS. C.-M. Trigueros, *Los menestrales*, ed. F. Aguilar Piñal, Seville U.P., 1997, 200 pp., is an edition of the *comedia* awarded a prize together with *Las bodas de Camacho* by J. Meléndez Valdés, in the competition organised by the Ayuntamiento of Madrid in 1784, on the occasion of the birth of the twin princes, sons of the then Prince of Asturias. This neoclassical *comedia*, which seeks to dignify manual work, has never been republished since its publication in 1784 in the presses of A. de Sancha. Aguilar Piñal recounts the polemic that followed this prize. Trigueros's text is accompanied by R. de la Cruz's *Loa*, written for the opening of the comedia. The appendix identifies the theatre books belonging to Trigueros, according to the recently discovered inventory of his private library.

VARGAS PONCE. F. Durán López, *José Vargas Ponce (1760–1821). Ensayo de una bibliografía y crítica de sus obras*, Cadiz U.P., 1997, 216 pp., is a bibliography (with commentary) of the widely dispersed work of this enlightened naval officer who served twice as director of the Academia de la Historia. Durán López bases his work on the thorough investigation of the papers remaining in the Academia de la Historia — the 58 volumes of the Colección Vargas Ponce — and in the library of the Museo Naval in Madrid. Despite the positive contribution made by this work, the cataloguing lacks consistency.

VIERA Y CLAVIJO. J. Cebrián, 'El héroe en la poesía didáctica de Viera y Clavijo', *NRFH*, 45, 1997:391–408, studies the new poetic role given to some contemporary scientists within the didactic poetry of the Spanish Enlightenment — especially the chemists J. Priestley and J.-A. Sigaud de Lafond and the doctor J. Ingenhousz in *Los aires fijos* (1780), and the experimental physicist B. Franklin in *Las Cometas* (1811).

LITERATURE, 1823–1898

By DEREK FLITTER, *Senior Lecturer in Modern Spanish Language and Literature,*
University of Birmingham
(This survey covers the years 1997–98)

1. GENERAL

The latest two volumes in the *Historia de la literatura española* project
directed by Víctor García de la Concha supply up-to-date critical
coverage of the period in general: Vol. 8, *Siglo XIX (I)*, ed. Guillermo
Carnero, M, 1996, 870 pp., is the work of some 30 specialists gathered
under the general headings 'Introducción a la primera mitad del siglo
XIX español' (essential socio-cultural contextualization as well as
anticipation of themes to come), 'Coordenadas y cauces de la vida
literaria' (on literature in the institutions: University, libraries,
publishing houses, etc.) and 'El Romanticismo decimonónico: teoría
y polémica' (on questions of terminology, chronology, and contemporary critical debate), as well as genre-based chapters on *costumbrismo*,
theatre, poetry, and narrative. The volume sets very high standards
indeed. One of its many virtues is its inclusive and clearly ordered
coverage; another is its impressive set of bibliographical references,
although here, with each chapter carrying its own bibliography, there
is inevitably a great deal of repetition. Despite the undoubted
excellence of so much of the writing, there are, as this reviewer sees it
at least, two significant problems with the volume: firstly, the
exclusion from the book of the work of the Romantic historians,
whose perspectives on the past and whose construction of a *casticista*
national identity are at the core of Spanish Romanticism and are
effectively interrelated to so much of what we find in literary criticism
and creative literature of the period; secondly, it seems at best
inadvisable in a volume of this sort to lend any real credence to
narrowly constructed theories of a 'romanticismo dieciochesco' of
1770–1800, given that such ideas are demonstrably misleading and
have been discarded in favour of a much more thoroughgoing and
judicious view of cultural history in so much recent criticism. Vol. 9,
Siglo XIX (II) ed. Leonardo Romero Tobar, 1023 pp., is equally
impressive in the quantity and quality of its coverage. It likewise
contains two chapters given to thorough contextualization — 'Introducción a la segunda mitad del siglo XIX en España' and 'Del
Realismo al fin de siglo. Sociedad y arte literario' — which are then
followed by a chapter on theatre, an excellent discussion of poetry of
the period under the subtitle 'Tradiciones poéticas y líricas de la
modernidad', another first-rate discussion of narrative under the

heading 'Entre literatura fantástica y relato realista' (Valera and Pereda figure here), two chapters on 'La plenitud del relato realista', one of which is dedicated in its entirety to Galdós, and a discussion of patterns in late-century narrative taking the reader from Naturalism to the *fin de siglo*. The volume closes with a substantial chapter on literary criticism, with due attention given to Menéndez Pelayo, Valera, Pardo Bazán, and Clarín. In this volume as in the preceding one, however, one does lament the absence of any material binding Spanish historiography into the over-arching framework. E. Inman Fox, 'La invención de España: literatura y nacionalismo', *Actas* (Birmingham), IV, 1–16, in fact reveals so much of the possibilities for an effective synthesis, by mapping out the construction of a national identity in the form of an institutional liberal historiography, from Modesto Lafuente to the Centro de Estudios Históricos. This piece was originally a prelude to the same author's study *La invención de España. Nacionalismo liberal e identidad nacional*, M, Cátedra, 1997, 224 pp., which carries much further F.'s investigation of such mouth-watering themes as 'la institucionalización de la cultura nacional' and 'la comunidad imaginada', moving from Modesto Lafuente's famous general history to the period of the II Republic. A vast amount of work remains to be done on what F. calls 'el discurso de la identidad nacional', particularly the intellectual cross-references: between, for example, *casticismo* and *intrahistoria*. His book makes an important start in this regard, although it might have proved more advanta-geous, as far as the overall vision of the work is concerned, to have initiated the historical discussion some ten years earlier; that is, with the several general histories of Spain appearing in the decade of the 1840s that went such a long way towards determining the nature and outlook of the discourse F. describes.

Culture and Gender in Nineteenth-Century Spain, ed. Lou Charnon-Deutsch and Jo Labanyi, Oxford, Clarendon Press, 1995, 296 pp., is a collective volume that forcefully reveals the instability of sexual categories, portraying a process of fluctuation and upheaval at work in areas of female definition and setting out a larger pattern in which prescriptive differentiation yields, in the course of a protracted period of renegotiation, to an eventual collapse of predetermined gender boundaries. The volume contains the following essays: J. Labanyi, 'Liberal individualism and the fear of the feminine in Spanish Romantic drama'; N. Valis, 'Autobiography as insult', on the representation of Romantic *poetisas*; J. Mandrell, ' "Poesía . . . eres tú" or the construction of Bécquer and the sign of woman'; S. Kirkpatrick, 'Fantasy, seduction and the woman reader: Rosalía de Castro's novels'; M. Bieder, 'Gender and language: the womanly woman and manly writing'; A. Blanco, 'Gender and national identity:

the novel in nineteenth-century Spanish literary history'; D. Urey, 'Woman as language in the first series of Galdós's *Episodios nacionales*'; S. Hart, 'The gendered Gothic in Pardo Bazán's *Los pazos de Ulloa*'; A. Sinclair, 'The force of parental presence in *La Regenta*'; C. Jagoe, 'Monstrous inversions: decadence and degeneration in Galdós's *Ángel Guerra*'; G. Scanlon, 'Gender and journalism: Pardo Bazán's *Nuevo Teatro Crítico*'; A. Lee Six, 'Mothers' voices and Medusas' eyes: Clarín's construction of gender in *Su único hijo*'; L. Charnon-Deutsch, using illustrations from 19th-c. periodicals, analyses the 'politics of difference' in late-century exoticism. **El ensayo español de Jovellanos a Larra (1781–1837)*, ed. José Pallarés Moreno, Málaga, Ágora, 1995, 225 pp. Jesús Torrecilla, *El tiempo y los márgenes*, Chapel Hill, NCSRLL, 1996, 206 pp., analyses the progressive European and traditional Spanish elements in the thought and work of Larra, Galdós, and Unamuno. T. views Larra as overwhelmed by Spain's backwardness, aware that to achieve integration into the modern world it must either learn from translated materials and become foreign to itself or else remain an irrelevance. In Galdós's *Gloria* he detects the need and possibility of Spanish adaptation to Europe and the recognition that *casticista* traditionalism could not be expected abruptly to turn its back upon centuries of national history, while in the eponymous protagonist of *Ángel Guerra* T. sees a man torn between rebellion against and conformity to tradition. Wadda C. Ríos-Font, *Rewriting Melodrama. The Hidden Paradigm in Modern Spanish Literature*, Lewisburg, Bucknell UP, 1997, 233 pp., makes a systematic re-reading of Spanish melodrama, beginning with its incipient formulaic projection early in the 19th c. and following its evolution into the first decades of the 20th. R.-F. detects specifiable formal and ideological structures in melodrama's early period, elucidates the combination by Echegaray of such patterns with other forms of drama, notably tragedy, and moves on to consider 'writing against' or 'subverting' melodrama by, amongst others, Galdós, Benavente, and Valle-Inclán. C. de Zulueta, ' "El nuevo renacer de España". La Institución Libre de Enseñanza', *RHM*, 51 : 161–77, merges evocative personal memoir with a general history of the *Institución*. M. del C. Simón Palmer, 'Memorias familiares', *Actas* (Birmingham), IV, 254–60, deals with three different memoirs written by women connected with important historical figures of the Peninsular War: the popular heroine 'Agustina de Aragón' and the generals Torrijos and Espoz y Mina. E. Rubio Cremades, 'El *Semanario Pintoresco Español*: el artículo de costumbres y géneros afines', *ib.*, 248–53, looks at the diversity of representative *costumbrista* production appearing in the journal. M. P. Espín Templado, 'El costumbrismo del teatro breve durante el último tercio del siglo XIX y sus raíces románticas', *ib.*, 130–39, argues that the *Género*

Chico, particularly in terms of theme, characterization, and plot, derived much of its realistic observation from much earlier *costumbrista* collections and Romantic periodicals. M. Versteeg, 'El mundo ficticio de los sainetes madrileños finiseculares: entre populismo y tradición popular', *ib.*, 284–92, looks at carnivalesque elements of the *Género Chico* from a Bakhtinian perspective. P. Fernández, 'El monopolio del mercado internacional de impresos en castellano en el siglo XIX: Francia, España y "la ruta" de Hispanoamérica', *BH*, 100:165–90, reveals how French publishers attempted to steal a march on their Spanish counterparts in a rapidly expanding market by flouting the laws of copyright, and how Spanish publishers reacted to this in the late century by increasing the production of books in Castilian. A. Viñao, 'Liberalismo, alfabetización y primeras letras (siglo XIX)', *ib.*, 531–60, argues against the prevailing view that the legislation of *desamortización* was harmful to primary education, claiming that the policy of liberal governments between 1838 and 1860 was beneficial after the much more detrimental consequences of the Peninsular War and the rule of Ferdinand VII, and considerably more helpful than the practices of conservative and neo-Catholic administrations of the later *Restauración*. L. Romero Tobar, 'Lectores y lecturas en la primera mitad del siglo XIX: balance y y perspectivas de investigación', *ib.*, 561–76, surveys current knowledge of types of reader and text in the transformation of the literary world of the *Ancien Régime* into that of the popular illustrated press, the *folletín* and the *novela por entregas*. J.-F. Botrel, 'Teoría y práctica de la lectura en el siglo XIX: el arte de leer', *ib.*, 577–90, speculates on the effects of listening and reading aloud on the reception and interpretation of literature.

2. ROMANTICISM

Philip W. Silver, *Ruin and Restitution. Reinterpreting Romanticism in Spain*, Liverpool U.P. — Nashville, Vanderbilt U.P., 1997, 175 pp., is a provocative study that seeks nothing less than to depose the paradigmatic reading advanced by exiled Republican scholars and other partisans of liberal Romanticism that had, until recently, provided something of a critical consensus. S. underlines instead the preeminence of a substantial and politically interested Spanish Romanticism, one that communicated a broad *moderado* community of thought and effectively defined the historical bourgeois struggle for political and ideological hegemony. S. underlines that this essentially conservative majority Romanticism dovetails with the post–1844 hegemony of *moderantismo* and with the imaginative invention, by Romantic historians, of modern Spain. Bécquer appears as a late conservative Catholic and mediævalizing Romantic. Within S.'s wider chronology,

Spain had no high Romantic movement of its own but saw the dissemination, in discrete historical instances, of the detritus of the broader European phenomenon. He dismisses more or less wholesale the 'romantic posturings' of Espronceda and designates Larra an exceptional — and marginal — figure at odds with the greater whole. While this 'reinterpretation' in fact coincides with a substantial body of other recent criticism, it is invaluable in its postulation of intimate connections between a conservative literary Romanticism, Spanish Romantic historiography, and the virulently *casticista* element in the construction of the modern idea of Spain. A Spanish version of the same has appeared as *Ruina y restitución: reinterpretación del romanticismo en España*, M, Cátedra, 1996, 177 pp. María Rosa Saurín de la Iglesia, *Cancionero liberal contra Fernando VII*, Fasano, Schena, 232 pp., is a fascinating anthology of political (and enormously satirical) verse, much of it gathered from the pages of the publication *El Español Constitucional*, prefaced by an illuminating and cogent introduction, making the volume an invaluable one for the study of Spanish Romanticism. S. Kirkpatrick, 'Eighty-one years of scholarship on the Romantic period', *His(US)*, 81:803–10, in a relatively balanced historical overview, reminds us of the seismic shifts in critical opinion regarding Romanticism in Spain. L. Izquierdo Izquierdo and T. Gil Poy, 'Las representaciones dramáticas en Valencia, 1832–1850', *RLit*, 59, 1997:19–66, is enormously informative, and enables us to measure with considerable clarity the fortunes both of French Romantic drama and of an original Spanish Romantic theatre during a controversial period. M. Palenque, 'La recepción del drama romántico francés en Sevilla (1835–1845)', *ib.*, 60:131–52, is essentially concerned with Hugo and Dumas *père*; P. reminds us, amongst other things, that Seville had seen a performance of *Lucrèce Borgia* before the play's controversial première in Madrid.

3. REALISM AND NATURALISM

M. Yáñez, *Siguiendo los hilos. Estudio de la configuración discursiva en algunas novelas españolas del siglo XIX*, Berne, 1996, 200 pp. P. Bly, 'Eighty-one years of articles on nineteenth-century Spanish realist/ naturalist novelists in *Hispania* (1917–98): an overview and listing', *His(US)*, 81:811–17, is very helpful in its documentation. Y. Lissorgues, 'La expresión del erotismo en la novela "naturalista" española del siglo XIX: eufemismo y tremendismo', *RHM*, 50, 1997:37–47, comments on the limitations placed upon imaginative expression of the erotic and of the connections between physiology and spirit, outlining a 'naturalismo radical' fiercely resisted by moralists on account of the perceived threat contained in its 'sexo escrito'; socio-cultural prohibition, L. contends, produced a necessarily euphemistic treatment of the erotic in novels such as *Lo prohibido*. T. Dorca, 'Reformulando la poética de la novela española del siglo XIX: el caso del relato de tesis', *ib.*, 266–79, contends that Galdós, Alarcón and Pereda, in their respective 'novelas tendenciosas', wrote in the service of a transcendent over-arching pattern of religion, sociology or science.

4. INDIVIDUAL AUTHORS

ALARCÓN. M. Yáñez, 'Una lectura carnavalesca de *El sombrero de tres picos*', *Actas* (Birmingham), IV, 293–301, provides an intelligent scrutiny of the symbolical, sociological, and metaliterary implications of the carnivalesque in A.'s novel.

ALAS. *Cuentos*, ed. Ángeles Ezama with preliminary study by Gonzalo Sobejano, B, Crítica, 1997, 424 pp., maintains the largely excellent record of this series, with thoughtful and perceptive commentary on a wide range of tales. Paula Preneron Vinche, **Madam Bovary — La Regenta. Parodia y contraste*, Murcia U.P., 1997, 330 pp. R. Vila-Belda, 'La estrategia del injerto en *La Regenta*', *RHM*, 51:13–21, uses the metaphor of the article's title to show the novel as depicting the failed organic union or physical grafting between various of its characters. E. Delgado, '*La Regenta* llevada al cine: apuntes para una re-interpretación en imágenes', *RoQ*, 45:109–13, briefly reflects on the 1974 film scripted by Juan Antonio Porto and directed by Gonzalo Suárez. S. Wegschal, '¿"Incertidumbre moderno" o "moralismo medieval"?: la interpretación de la ambigüe-dad textual en *Su único hijo* de Clarín', *RHM*, 51:257–72, scrutinizes the textual ambiguities surrounding Antonio Reyes's parentage. As W. sees it, the narrative is deliberately ambiguous, signposting the deceptions of a society driven by rumour and gossip, while A., in typically mediæval terms, allows each reader to opt for a moral solution through the exercise of *libre albedrío*. S. Miller, 'De la cuentística de Alas y Pardo Bazán en los años noventa, con referencia a Galdós', *RoQ*, 45:35–44, uses A.'s 'Benedictino' and Pardo Bazán's 'Sara y Agar' to differentiate between their respective authors' techniques and thematic material, arguing that A. was more 'oppor-tune' in addressing the intimate ongoing conflicts of middle-class urban society. P. Ríos Sánchez, '"Diálogo edificante", alegoría de Clarín sobre la intolerancia religiosa española a fines del siglo XIX', *RLit*, 60:463–89, examines an 1893 'palique' in which A. responded to episcopal intransigence, and indeed to that of Madrid society, concerning the dedication of a Protestant church in the capital.

C. Richmond, 'Los demonios de Leopoldo Alas, "Clarín": una indagación musical', *His(US)*, 81:853–63, deals with A.'s development of the diabolic in terms of plot and theme, affirming the influence of the operas of Gounod, Boïto, and Meyerbeer as well as referring to the human experience of the author himself.

BÉCQUER. **Rimas y leyendas*, ed. T. Sánchez Santiago, M, 297 pp. Mario A. Blanc, **Las 'Rimas' de Bécquer: su modernidad*, M, Pliegos, 1997, 185 pp. T. Lewis, 'Gender, discourse, and modernity in Bécquer's *Rimas*', *REH*, 31, 1997:419–47, reads B.'s poems as conditioned by a divided society, one of an imploding political régime and a waning cultural aesthetic that wrenches artists out of Romanticism and casts them into modernity. Elegant in its explication of B.'s enforcement of discursive power over women, L.'s piece is, for this reader at least, disingenuous in its depiction of a Madrid emblematized by street barricades and brutal repression (curiously implied to be the essential background to Rima xxxiv, 'Cruza callada'). L. Caparrós Esperante, 'Bécquer. Estética del borrador', *BH*, 99, 1997:437–55, contends that the reconstruction of a 'plano antetextual' reinforces some of the conclusions of B.'s own poetic theory, particularly concerning the role of memory, but denies the existence of the 'abismo' between idea and form that dominated it; much of C.E.'s piece is then given over to the enduring problems of the corrections to the *Libro de los gorriones* manuscript and of the ordering of the *Rimas*. A. Esteban, 'Bécquer y Ricardo Palma: el sustrato hispano-alemán', *Hispanófila*, 119, 1997:9–22, elucidates the presence of *Rimas* and *Leyendas* within the poetry of Palma on two levels, designated respectively 'sentimental-formativo' and 'germánico-ideológico'.

CABALLERO. *Fernán Caballero, hoy. Homenaje en el bicentenario del nacimiento de Cecilia Böhl de Faber*, ed. Milagros Fernández Poza and Mercedes García Pazos, El Puerto de Santa María, Ayuntamiento, 287 pp., contains the proceedings of the 1996 colloquium: M. Fernández Poza, 'Introducción: "Fernán Caballero" en el bicentenario de su nacimiento' (7–15); J. del Moral, 'Liberales y románticos en la España isabelina: la consolidación del Estado Español Contemporáneo' (19–43), outlines Romantic elements present in the territorial reorganization of Spain after 1833; A. Langa Laorga, 'La obra de Fernán Caballero como fuente histórica: pinceladas de vida cotidiana' (45–65), stresses (in authentically Romantic fashion) the value of imaginative literature in the reconstruction of social history; A. Gómez Yebra, 'Actualidad de los elementos folclóricos recopilados por Fernán Caballero' (67–88), underlines both the inherent significance of F.C.'s collections of popular material and their contribution as a source of inspiration for later Andalusian poets such as Jiménez,

Lorca and Alberti; D. Flitter, 'La historia que nos llega: Fernán Caballero y la poética de la tradición' (89–105), locates F.C.'s imaginative vision of history within the parameters of a traditionalist historiography dominant within the Romantic period in Spain; M. Cantos Casenave, 'Los cuentos de Fernán Caballero: una visión poética de la realidad' (107–26), considers the idealized reality of F.C.'s stories in the service of her moralizing mission; M. Mayoral, 'Doña Cecilia o el arte de disimular la superioridad' (129–39), argues that F.C.'s projection of her persona was conditioned by contemporary association between womanly intellect and 'deficiencia moral'; M. Fernández Poza, 'El Epistolario de Fernán Caballero: correspondencia y corresponsales' (141–72), presents a broad historical contextualization of the life and work of F.C. within Romantic aesthetics and views the author's letters as a privileged insight into her personality; L. Suárez Ávila, 'Fernán Caballero pionera en la recolección del romancero oral' (173–87), is a well documented contribution to study of F.C.'s ballad-collecting; M. Ravina Martín, 'Nuevas cartas inéditas de Fernán Caballero' (189–246), is a progress report on the ongoing classification of F.C.'s letters housed at the Archivo Histórico Provincial de Cádiz which reproduces 30 letters to Fermín de Iribarren Ortuño and six to Ángela Böhl de Faber; R. Montes Doncel, 'Fernán Caballero: algunos procedimientos lingüísticos para la consecución de la ironía' (247–59), is an illuminating close analysis of F.C.'s style; M. P. Moliner and J. Prado, 'La representación del sujeto femenino en la narrativa de Böhl de Faber' (261–74), address the paradoxical question of F.C.'s status and relevance as writer's combining with her reinforcing of masculine authority and patriarchal tradition; A. Carmona González, 'Fernán Caballero en la prensa sevillana' (275–87), takes an informative look at F.C.'s contributions to the Seville press. R. Quirk, ' "La mère", "La madre", Fernán Caballero, her mother and a tale of Trafalgar', *RHM*, 51:5–12, takes Cecilia Böhl's earliest published work to elucidate the literary and personal relationships between the author and her mother Francisca Larrea. E. Paz-Soldán, 'Lo extranjero y la esencia de España en *La Gaviota*', *RoN*, 37, 1997:281–88, probes the intellectual construction of 'esencia' as driven by conservative ideology and eventually as a form of *costumbrista* poetics; for P.-S., Spain is imaginatively constructed out of its opposition to 'lo extranjero' and tradition out of its opposition to modernity, ironical, he avers, when the material for self-definition is seen to be largely imported.

CASTRO. See LARRA below.

DONOSO CORTÉS. R. A. Herrera, **Donoso Cortés: Cassandra of the Age*, Grand Rapids, Eerdmans, 1996, 166 pp.

ESPRONCEDA.   L. Caparrós Esperante, 'El discurso metapoético en *El diablo mundo*', *RLit*, 59, 1997:437–63, contends that E.'s poem narrates the story of poetry and of the Romantic hero as poet, that it systematically opposes truth and lie, literature and life, and that it contains an appeal for a renovated poetic language that could only stem from a fresh dynamic vision of life and reality that itself constituted the 'mission' of the poet.

GÓMEZ DE AVELLANEDA.   The 'Diálogo Crítico' section of *REH*, 32, is dedicated to readings of *Sab*: S. Stein, 'Gertrudis Gómez de Avellaneda's bourgeois liberal *Sab* story' (153–69), contends that the novel protects the status quo instead of promoting the possibility of real social transformation, its rhetoric and plot operating in such a way as to perpetuate inequalities of race and gender; D. Sommer, 'A program of reading, not a reading for program' (171–74), argues, on the contrary, that the text both foresees change and legitimates it; W. Luis, 'How to read *Sab*' (175–86), thoroughly contextualizes the novel within the parameters of Spanish and Cuban political and intellectual history. M. de los A. Ayala, '*Dos mujeres*, novela reivindicativa de Gertrudis Gómez de Avellaneda', *Actas* (Birmingham), IV, 76–83, considers this novel's anticipation of several of the salient themes and emphases of the later Realist novel. R. Pagés-Rangel, 'Para una sociología del escándalo: la edición y publicación de las cartas privadas de Gertrudis Gómez de Avellaneda', *RHM*, 50, 1997:22–36, concerns the publication, originally in 1907, of Tula's love letters to Ignacio Cepeda; their editor, it is argued, repressively reconstructed their female subject according to a form of narratological teleology, an authoritarian manipulation of a writer who had ironically assumed her own authority by editing her own *Obras completas* many years earlier.

HARTZENBUSCH.   L. Materna, 'Lo femenino peligroso y el orientalismo en *Los amantes de Teruel*, de Juan Eugenio Hartzenbusch', *Actas* (Birmingham), IV, 192–201, reads H.'s play — in its significantly altered 1858 version rather than the Romantic text of 1837, which is surely unwise given M.'s argument — as articulating the threat posed by a subversive feminine 'Other', contending that the posited conflict represents an *Ancien Régime* menaced and eventually supplanted by a new and unnerving bourgeois liberal social order.

HÚMARA Y SALAMANCA.   *Ramiro, Conde de Lucena*, ed. Donald L. Shaw, Málaga, Ágora, 169 pp., supplies the modern reader with long-overdue access to an historically significant text, one previously, as S. notes, 'casi totalmente inasequible'; this, together with its status as 'primera novela romántica española', would alone justify such an edition. The shrewd and perceptive critical introduction makes it, however, an indispensable text for both specialist and general reader seeking a full understanding of the complex gestation of Romanticism in Spanish imaginative literature.

LARRA. *Artículos*, ed. J. Álvarez Barrientos, B, 249 pp. W. Ríos-Font, 'From Romantic irony to Romantic grotesque: Mariano José de Larra's and Rosalía de Castro's self-conscious novels', *HR*, 65, 1997:177–98, drawing on material from Walter Scott to Wolfgang Iser and Linda Hutcheon, examines L.'s *El doncel* and Rosalía's *El caballero de las botas azules* as anticipations of modern-day metafiction, as narratives that self-consciously seek a solution to the representational problems of Romantic irony.

MARTÍNEZ DE LA ROSA. Pedro Ojeda Escudero, *El justo medio. Neoclasicismo y romanticismo en la obra dramática de Martínez de la Rosa*, Burgos U.P., 1997, 347 pp. D. Schurlknight, '*La conjuración de Venecia* as/in context', *REH*, 32:537–55, forges persuasive connections between *La conjuración* and the contemporary political scene, according to which the playwright's conservatism leaves a powerful imprint on his text and the drama itself becomes a vehicle for the manipulation of public thought, part of the *con-text* in which the Estatuto Real appeared.

MESONERO ROMANOS. L. M. Fernández, 'Mesonero Romanos agente de negocios. Correspondencia inédita con Remigio García de Caamaño', *HR*, 65, 1997:317–28, sheds light on the writer's management of the family business inherited from his father in 1820.

PALACIO VALDÉS. R. Krauel, 'La función ideológica de los clérigos en *La fe*, de Armando Palacio Valdés', *RCEH*, 21, 1997:313–28, appeals for a reconsideration of appraisals of *La fe* as an anti-clerical novel on three grounds: the moral qualities of Gil Lastra; the emphasis on literary humour rather than ideological antagonism; and the novel's revelation of a code of moral conformity to Catholic orthodoxy.

PARDO BAZÁN. *La cuestión palpitante*, ed. R. de Diego, M, Biblioteca Nueva, 382 pp. *Los Pazos de Ulloa*, ed. María de los Ángeles Ayala, M, Cátedra, 1997, 405 pp., uses the 1886 *princeps* text, A. providing a balanced and thoroughgoing introduction under headings such as the composition, publication, and reception of the work, its Naturalist features, narrative structures and political commentary. M. Bieder, 'Sexo y lenguaje en Emilia Pardo Bazán: la deconstrucción de diferencia', *Actas* (Birmingham), IV, 92–99, examines P. B.'s self-differentiation from contemporary *literatas* via her exemplification of a postulated 'lenguaje sin sexo'. C. Karageorgou-Bastea, 'La figura del narrador en *Insolación*: apertura e incertidumbre', *Neophilologus*, 82:235–45, focuses on the means by which the novel's narrative voice transcends ideological affiliation by proposing an 'open field' of ethical principles of freedom, love, and social convention; irony, it is argued, serves to reveal the flux between thesis and antithesis that is a feature of P. B.'s narrative fiction. R. Medina, 'Dulce esclava, dulce histérica: la representación de la mujer en *Dulce dueño* de Emilia Pardo Bazán', *RHM*, 51:291–303, describes the novel as an 'alegato moralista' that depicts 19th-c. woman's enforced seclusion in the world of the spirit, at a remove from the pleasures of the body and, although empowered to write from her inner space, socially silenced by the madhouse and thus 'cuerda para lo divino, pero histérica para lo humano'. A. Hills, 'Dos arquetipos femeninos en los cuentos de Emilia Pardo Bazán', *RoQ*, 44, 1997:171–80, via Julia Kristeva and Maria Aurèlia Capmany, examines P.B.'s depiction of the 'mujer culpable' and 'mujer fuerte'. M. Vidal Tibbits, '*Sic transit amicitia*: la correspondencia entre Emilia Pardo Bazán y Narcís Oller', *CH*, 20:107–15, examines a correspondence primarily concerned with literary matters, initiated in 1883 and ending abruptly after P.B.'s visit to the Barcelona Exposición Universal of 1888, and more specifically reconstructing the two writers' face-to-face encounters as detailed in Oller's *Memòries literàries*. Y. Latorre Ceresuela, 'Emilia Pardo Bazán desde la poesía: nuevas claves de una escritora en plena revisión', *Ínsula*, 607, 1997:8–9, is a reflection upon the publication of the late Maurice Hemingway's edition of P.B.'s *Poesías inéditas u olvidadas* (EHT, 51), Exeter U.P., 1996, 179 pp. (See also ALAS above.)

PEREDA. M. Iarocci, 'On the ideology of metaphor in Pereda's *Peñas arriba*', *RHM*, 51:236–56, examines rhetorical figuration and some of its functions in the late 19th-c. novel, emphasizing the relationship between metaphorical discourse and authorial ideology. P.'s idealization, it is argued, necessarily drew upon Romantic epistemology, translating a Romantic metaphorical order into the idiom of the Realist novel and at the same time resisting an opposing metaphorical construct generated by bourgeois liberalism. P. Bly, 'Escenas marítimas en *Lo prohibido* y *Sotileza*', *Actas* (Birmingham), IV, 100–06, examines connections between Chapter XXVIII of *Sotileza* and José María Bueno de Guzmán's holiday trip to San Sebastián from Galdós's novel, while differentiating between the two in terms of their narratology and psychological insight. S. García Castañeda, 'Catorce cartas de Pereda a Enrique Menéndez Pelayo (1895–1905)', *RoQ*, 44, 1997:107–18, introduces and annotates letters found among the recipient's personal papers housed at the Biblioteca Menéndez Pelayo, Santander.

PÉREZ GALDÓS. The published *Actas del Quinto Congreso Internacional de Estudios Galdosianos (1992)*, 2 vols, Las Palmas, Ediciones del Cabildo Insular de Gran Canaria, 515, 565 pp., contains some 90 new contributions to Galdós scholarship. Vol. 1, headed by P. Ortiz

Armengol's opening address, 'Aproximación de Galdós al Nobel' (7–16), is dedicated to 'Poética, narrativa y crítica textual' and contains the following studies: A. Acosta Peña, 'Aspectos significativos de las novelas *Nazarín* y *Halma*' (19–29); E. Avilés Arroyo, 'Univocidad de dos personajes galdosianos: Nazarín y Benina' (31–37); L. Behiels, 'La búsqueda del amor, de la verdad y de la historia: *Los duendes de la camarilla* (1903)' (39–49); C. Cervelló, 'Algunas consideraciones sobre la relación entre tema y estructura en *La de Bringas*' (51–58); V. Chamberlin, 'Verosimilitud y humorismo de los apodos en *Fortunata y Jacinta*' (59–65); M. del P. Escobar Bonilla, '*Nazarín* y *Halma*: novelas complementarias' (67–76); P. Esterán Abad, '*La fontana de oro*: tres desenlaces para una novela' (77–87); A. Ezama Gil, 'El manuscrito de *Celín*: análisis crítico de un cuento maravilloso galdosiano' (89–97); J. Gallego, 'Los manuscritos de *Voluntad*' (99–107); D. Gallego and C. Alonso, 'El orador y el discurso en *El amigo Manso*' (109–24); M. J. García Domínguez, 'La descripción de don Lope: un proceso de creación lingüística en *Tristana* de Galdós' (125–35); R. González Santana, 'Narcisismo, "ofelismo" y cosificación de la mujer en *Fortunata y Jacinta* y *Nana*' (137–54); H. Gold, 'El principio ornamental en la narrativa galdosiana' (155–63); F. González Povedano, 'Reflexiones sobre el exclusivismo, la intransigencia y el fanatismo religiosos en las novelas de primera época de Galdós' (165–74); T. Guerra Bosch, 'El usurero Torquemada: de tipo a personaje' (175–86); M. T. Hernández, 'De *La fontana de oro* a *El caballero encantado*. Evolución de un estilo' (187–94); O. Izquierdo Dorta, 'Estudio del proceso de creación en el manuscrito del cuento "¿Dónde está mi cabeza?"' (195–208); J. Konieczna-Twardzikowa, 'Los polacos de *Miau*. Problema de la traducción del estereotipo' (209–13); M. Moreno Martínez, 'Psicología y narrativa. A propósito de *Tristana*' (215–23); M. O'Byrne Curtis, ' "La razón de la sinrazón": configuraciones de la locura en *La sombra*' (225–34); A. Padilla Mangas, 'La tertulia como elemento estructural, en dos novelas de Galdós: *La incógnita* y *Realidad*' (235–43); J. Peñate Rivero, 'Niveles intertextuales de *La novela en el tranvía*' (245–53); A. Polizzi, '*La novela en el tranvía* o la transgresión del realismo' (255–61); F. Quevedo García, 'El espacio narrativo, medio caracterizador en *Tormento*' (263–70); R. Rodríguez Marín, 'El galicismo en las *Novelas españolas contemporáneas* de Galdós' (271–82); J. Sinnigen, 'Historias nacionales y pasionales: *La incógnita* y *Realidad*' (283–90); G. Smith, '*Ángel Guerra* y el acto de contar: hacia una clasificación narratológica de las novelas de Galdós' (291–96); H. Turner, 'Tropologías del arte realista de Galdós' (297–304); J. Whiston, 'Las galeradas (perdidas) de *Lo prohibido*' (305–15); M. Yáñez, 'Saloma la Baturra, hilo romántico de la tercera serie de *Episodios nacionales*' (317–28); G. Gullón, 'Influencias

socio-culturales en la narrativa de Galdós' (329–39); M. Aguinaga
Alfonso, 'Novela urbana y novela regional: Galdós y Pereda del
costumbrismo a la novela' (341–50); V. Bagno, 'Las inquietudes
religiosas de los héroes de las novelas rusas y su huella en la obra
galdosiana finisecular' (351–57); R. Dash, 'El Pitusín de Galdós y
Perucho de Pardo Bazán: primos hermanos del naturalismo'
(359–66); J. Egea, 'Maneras de soñar: Cervantes y *Misericordia*'
(367–73); A. Fernández Sein, 'Torquemada, seducido y abandonado'
(375–82); J. M. González Herrán, 'La revolución de julio de 1854 en
la novela: José María de Pereda, *Pedro Sánchez* (1883), Benito Pérez
Galdós, *La revolución de julio* (1903)' (383–92); M. Krow-Lucal,
'Fornarina/Fortunata: Rafael, Fernández y González, y la creación
galdosiana' (393–401); M. D. Madrenas and J. Ribera, 'B. P. Galdós
y N. Oller: la superación de la novela realista' (403–18); C. Merchán
Cantos, 'La erótica de la narración en el *Banquete* y *Misericordia*'
(419–35); S. Miller, 'La metáfora del espejo y la óptica de Galdós y
Echegaray' (437–44); M. del C. Rodríguez Acosta, '¿Galdós es lector
de Unamuno?' (445–53); M. de los A. Rodríguez Sánchez, 'Un
cuento desconocido de C. Ruth Morell: "¡Plafz! Cuento azul"'
(455–69); L. Romero Tobar, 'Del "nazarenito" a *Nazarín*' (471–85);
J. Sánchez-Gey Venegas, 'Acerca de la mujer (Tristana): el Galdós de
María Zambrano' (487–93); C. Servén, 'El becerro que estercola: de
Palacio Valdés a Galdós' (495–501); 'Sesión plenaria. Proyecto de
investigación Galdós: del texto a la realidad construida' (503–09).

Vol. II contains the sections 'La obra de Galdós en relación con
otras disciplinas', 'Galdós y el teatro' and 'Galdós y la historia', and
comprises: J.-F. Botrel, 'La cornucopia del texto y de la obra' (9–21);
A. Delgado Cabrera, 'Galdós y Buñuel' (23–33); M. del P. García
Pinacho, 'El periodismo como tema en los artículos de *La Nación*'
(35–40); M. López-Baralt, '*Fortunata y Jacinta* según televisión española: la lectura cinematográfica del clásico galdosiano por Mario
Camus' (41–59); R. Navarrete-Galiano, '*Viridiana*: una recreación
cinematográfica de "Leré"' (61–68); P. Martínez, 'Pérez Galdós y el
mundo editorial de su época' (69–89); S. Piskunova, 'La obra de
Galdós y tipología de la cultura del siglo XIX' (91–96); A. Ramírez
Jáimez, 'La recepción de la obra de Galdós en Alemania a la luz de
las traducciones' (97–107); F. Ríos, '*Nazarín*. De Galdós a Buñuel.
Fidelidades, adaptaciones y equívocos' (109–20); E. Roca Roca, 'De
la primera república a la Constitución de 1876, en los *Episodios
nacionales* de Pérez Galdós' (121–39); S. de la Nuez, 'Estructura
significativa en una tragicomedia del último teatro galdosiano'
(141–56); C. Alonso García, 'Aportaciones a la biografía galdosiana
a través de las cartas de López Pinillos a Pérez Galdós: primera
época' (157–64); J. Avila Arellano, 'El desastre del 98 en la obra de

Benito Pérez Galdós (1895–1905)' (165–75); C. Enrique, '*Fortunata y
Jacinta* ante la crítica de su tiempo: el silencio a una gran novela'
(177–83); P. Faus Sevilla, 'La España finisecular vista por Benito
Pérez Galdós y Emilia Pardo Bazán' (185–203); E. Fierro Sánchez,
'Galdós, el 98 y hoy' (205–10); V. Fuentes, 'Las novelas galdosianas
de los 90 y la crisis finisecular de la modernidad' (211–20); M. I.
García Bolta, 'El africanismo de Galdós en *Aita Tettauen*' (221–30);
C. Menéndez Onrubia, 'El melancólico declinar de la tradición
española en Cuba y el particular simbolismo modernista galdosiano
en *Alma y vida*' (231–41); J. L. Mora, 'La imagen de España en el
último Galdós' (243–55); J. Oleza Simó, 'El debate en torno a la
fundación del realismo. Galdós y la poética de la novela en los años
70' (257–77); P. Bly, 'El encanto de las artes visuales: relaciones
interdisciplinarias en la novela galdosiana' (279–92); A. Cao, 'Inter-
textualidad mítico-religiosa en *Electra* de Galdós' (297–301); C. Díaz
Castañón, 'Galdós en la escena de hoy' (303–13); I.-A. Fuentes
Herbón, '*Doña Perfecta* y *La casa de Bernarda Alba*. La encarnación de la
ideología reaccionaria en el personaje literario femenino' (315–23);
M. del M. López Cabrera, 'El teatro de Galdós representado en Las
Palmas de Gran Canaria, durante los últimos años del siglo XIX'
(325–32); L. López Jiménez, 'Vicisitudes de la adaptación escénica
en francés de *El abuelo*' (333–43); B. Madariaga de la Campa, '*Una
gloria nacional*, episodio dramático inspirado en la vida de Galdós'
(345–49); J. Navarro de Zubillaga, 'Espacio, arquitectura y esceno-
grafía en el teatro de Galdós' (351–73); J. J. Páez Martín, 'Galdós en
Las máscaras' (375–90); J. Kronik, ' "¿Qué es un Galdós?" Los estudios
galdosianos en la edad posmoderna' (391–401); M. L. Acosta
González, 'Estanislao de Kostka Bayo, una base histórica en la obra
galdosiana' (405–18); A. Armas Ayala, 'El lector de Galdós' (419–26);
C. Bastons i Vivanco, 'A vueltas con la relación Benito Pérez
Galdós—Cataluña' (427–36); J. Fernández Sanz, 'Las epidemias de
cólera del siglo XIX vistas por Pérez Galdós' (437–51); C.-N. Kérek
de Robin, 'Cultura y poder en *Torquemada en la Cruz* o la estrategia de
la araña' (453–61); Y. Latorre Ceresuela, 'El arte en *Lo prohibido*'
(463–69); J. Marrero Cabrera, 'Una vacante en la Real Academia de
la Lengua en el otoño de 1904' (471–501); G. Ribbans, 'Galdós frente
a la historia en los *Episodios nacionales* y las novelas contemporáneas'
(503–10); J. Rodríguez Puértolas, '*Casandra* y la modernidad'
(511–22); I. Calvo Gil et al., 'Aproximación histórica a la quinta serie
de los *Episodios Nacionales*' (523–32); D. Urey, 'Representando la
historia en *La batalla de los Arapiles*' (533–42); R. Cardona, 'Galdós
desde nuestro fin de siglo' (543–56); M. del P. Escobar Bonilla,
'Conclusiones' (557–58).

Tristana, ed. and introd. Gordon Minter, Bristol, Bristol Classical Press, 1996, 164 pp., contains a cogent and well-structured thematic introduction and helpful textual annotation. *La loca de la casa (1893)*, ed. and introd. Lisa P. Condé, Lewiston, Mellen, 1996, 150 pp. J. Kronik, 'The present state of Galdós studies', *HR*, 65, 1997:431–44, is a schematic overview primarily concerned with the critical output of 1992 and 1993. *Benito Pérez Galdós. Aportaciones en ocasión de su 150 aniversario*, ed. Eberhard Gesler and E. Povedano, Frankfurt/M., Iberoamericana, 1995, 220 pp. John H. Sinnigen, *Sexo y política: lecturas galdosianas*, M, 1996, 283 pp. Teresa M. Vilarós, *Galdós: invención de la mujer y poética de la sexualidad. Lectura parcial de 'Fortunata y Jacinta'*, M, Siglo XXI, 1995, 174 pp. S. López, 'The Gothic tradition in Galdós's *La sombra*', *His(US)*, 81:509–18, demonstrates that, while G.'s short novel appropriates devices and elements from British Gothic fiction, its emphasis on the theme of honour and on 'el qué dirán' make it profoundly entrenched in Hispanic culture. H. Gold, 'Painting and representation in two nineteenth-century novels: Galdós's and Alas's skeptical appraisal of Realism', *ib.*, 830–41, regards the references to the visual arts contained in *La sombra* and *Doña Berta* as reflections of a commonly felt scepticism for the putative validity and efficacy of mimetic representation. M. Santana, 'The conflict of narratives in Galdós' *Doña Perfecta*', *MLN*, 113:283–304, argues that G. was responding to the canonized forms of fiction of his age and presenting his own alternative aesthetics of the novel. S. affirms that G.'s critical reading of 'costumbristic writing' (Fernán Caballero and Pereda) and of idealist poetics saw him react against the 'discursive pieties' of a *costumbrismo bonachón* centred on tradition, faith and national identity that was unable to contain the transformations of the modern world. M. Schnepf, 'A note on Galdós, Ortega Munilla, and *La desheredada*', *RoN*, 39:3–8, comments on Ortega's announcement of G.'s forthcoming (but as yet untitled) novel and the accompanying declaration of its desire to censure the abuse of alcohol. A. Tsuchiya, 'On the margins of subjectivity: sex, gender, and the body in Galdós's *Lo prohibido*', *RHM*, 50, 1997:280–89, persuasively argues that the novel challenges culturally generated categories of gender and sexuality, and, ultimately, any notion of coherent subjectivity, as the ironic discourse of Bueno de Guzmán deconstructs the dominant phallocentric discourses of the period, thus anticipating postmodern interrogation of the subject. O. Calvelo, 'Fortunata y Mme Bovary', *Actas* (Birmingham), IV, 115–21, examines the introduction of these characters by their respective authors before considering the structures of social ascent and descent, and ultimately of centripetal and centrifugal movement, that the two novels articulate. S. Lakhdari, 'El ratón y la custodia: el problema de la unidad temática en *Fortunata y Jacinta*', *ib.*, 186–91, supplies a psychoanalytical explanation of the chapter *Las Micaelas por dentro*, arguing that an apparently unstructured narrative functions much more coherently upon a 'nivel inconsciente'. G. Ribbans, 'La visión de "Dios" por Luisito Cadalso en *Miau*', *ib.*, 227–33, applies to a very specific excerpt a cogent and probing narratological and linguistic analysis of its content, stressing the verisimilitude and psychological accuracy of G.'s text. T. Fuentes Peris, 'Drink and degeneration: the "deserving" and the "undeserving" poor in Galdós's *Ángel Guerra*', *RoS*, 29:7–20, suggests that G. questioned the system of categorization and labelling implemented by the late-century bourgeoisie, perceiving a refusal on the novelist's part to comply with contemporary views on alcoholism conditioned by class structures. J. González Alonso, 'El Don Juan en zapatillas de *Tristana*', *REH*, 31, 1997:295–308, reflects on the character of Don Lope as an outmoded Don Juan subjected to the merciless gaze of 19th-c. Realism, as a literary figure whose attributes are perilously transferred to Tristana, who in turn awakens from her false dream at the cost of mutilation; unlike Lope, who successfully adapts his donjuanism to the prescriptions of contemporary society, Tristana, in a novel of literary deceptions, is inexorably marginalized by it. A. Smith, '*Nazarín*, masculino, femenino: aspectos de la imaginación mitológica galdosiana', *RHM*, 50, 1997:290–98, specifies a shift from patriarchal to matriarchal discourse: *Nazarín*, S. feels, marks a crisis of form and style in which the mythological imagination offers a fresh basis for the art of the novel, while the triumph of an 'hembra varonil' or 'amazona' figure exemplifies a feminine mythological impulse later culminating in *Halma* and *Misericordia*. G. Minter, 'The Seven Deadly Sins in Galdós's *El abuelo*', *RoS*, 32:33–44, elucidates ways in which exchanges between characters within the text are calculated to instruct after the fashion of a catechism, with each of the seven sins subtly embodied in an individual.

L. Behiels, 'Diosas y madres en la obra tardía de Benito Pérez Galdós', *Actas* (Birmingham), IV, 84–91, deals with the mythical figure of 'la madre' found under various names and in different guises in *El caballero encantado* and the final four *Episodios Nacionales*. D. Urey, 'Mythological resonances in Galdós's early *Episodios Nacionales*', *His(US)*, 81:842–52, affirms the significance of Classical mythology as a component part of G.'s intertextual design, highlighting the prominent role played by Homer and Ovid in the mythological parameters of the ten novels contained in the First Series. A. Andreu, 'Historia y literatura en un texto de Benito Pérez Galdós', *Actas* (Birmingham), IV, 50–56, looks at G.'s literary recreation of the

'Combate del 2 de mayo' of 1866 as found in La *vuelta al mundo en la 'Numancia'*.

L. Conde, 'Adultery in Galdós' *Realidad*', *RomSt*, 31: 19–32, focuses upon the psychological characterization of Augusta within the play's underlying problems and tensions, arguing that a mixed response from audience and reading public stresses the difficulty of ethical judgement of Augusta's predicament, one aggravated by the society of the period and detrimental to that society's future. J. Gabriele, 'Historia y feminismo en *Santa Juana de Castilla* de Galdós', *Actas* (Birmingham), IV, 140–48, deals with G.'s dramatization of Juana's desire for autonomy and for liberation from an oppressive social order, elements that exemplify the play's revisionist perspective on history and on the myths of the past. L. Condé, 'Galdós and his leading ladies', *BHS(L)*, 75, 1997:79–91, considers the performances involved in the creation, presentation and reception of *Realidad*, *Voluntad* and *Santa Juana de Castilla*, with reference to the actresses Concha-Ruth Morell, María Guerrero and Margarita Xirgu.

There is a cluster of articles dedicated to G. in *Studies in Honor of Gilberto Paolini*, ed. Mercedes Tibbits, Newark, Juan de la Cuesta, 1996, 496 pp.: F. Pérez, 'El texto de la intransigencia: proceso y dinámica en *Gloria*'; M. O'Byrne Curtis, 'La representación de la ciudad en la narrativa galdosiana'; G. Smith, 'Augusta Orozco and other angels: questions of gender and power in Galdós' *Torquemada*'; F. Barroso, 'El ideal y la realidad en *Tristana*'; H. Turner, 'The poetics of suffering in Galdós and Tolstoy'. (See also PEREDA above.)

PULIDO Y FERNÁNDEZ. K. Larsen, 'Dr. Pulido y Fernández's "brave new" pharmacy', *RoQ*, 45:45–54, takes a look at an 1883 short story by a prolific author and medical man, a tale dealing with material that had recently revolutionized medical thought and practices and which was to foreshadow events and ideas of our own century.

RIVAS. R. Sebold, 'Destino y locura: la novela del duque de Rivas', *RLit*, 60:101–30, argues that 'El moro expósito' is in essence a revelation of the modern novel in its process of gestation; S. feels that, while it partakes of the old epic genre, it is peculiarly modern in its depiction of Mudarra as hero, in its complicated plot that functions as a simulacrum of the chaos of existence, and in its representation of a paranoid Kerima dominated by specifiable *idées fixes*.

ROS DE OLANO. J. Acebrón Ruiz, '*Sic pani corvus additur*. Elementos paródicos en "Maese Cornelio Tácito", de A. Ros de Olano', *Actas* (Birmingham), IV, 17–25, examines the ironic configuration of the heraldry and lineage of the Palomino de Pan-Corvo family in this tale of 1868.

VALERA. Robert G. Trimble, *Don Juan Valera en sus novelas*, M, Pliegos, 215 pp., is a rather slight study of the authorial presence of V. in his eight full-length novels, one in which a potentially fertile line of inquiry is subjected to excessive categorization, with consequently superficial coverage: each chapter, dealing with a single novel, has sections sometimes no more than half a page long with headings such as 'Comentario no-ficticio — Filosofía' or 'Comentario no-ficticio — Moralización', so that the end result is principally one of opportunities missed. T. Langford Taylor, **The Representation of Women in the Novels of Juan Valera*, NY, Wor(l)ds of Change, 1997, 130 pp. F. M. Acero Yus, 'Un poco más sobre *Nescit labi virtus* de Valera', *RLit*, 59, 1997: 145–47, cites a letter to Gumersindo Laverde in which V. spoke of the Latin motto as providing a title for his forthcoming novel. C. Moreno Hernández, 'Valera, Flaubert y las ilusiones', *BHS(L)*, 75, 1997: 65–77, identifies Juan Fresco as the best representative of V.'s aesthetics, and views *Las ilusiones* as an apologist work designed to reveal the presence of Romanticism in Realism and, as such, as a novel closely related to *L'éducation sentimentale*. S. Miranda García, '*Morsamor*, una lectura *ibérica*', *CHA*, 570, 1997: 125–33, deals with the novel's projection of an Iberian historical ideal of 'despliegue lusoespañol'. M. C. Piñero Valverde, 'Un pionero de los brasilianistas: don Juan Valera', *Actas* (Birmingham), IV, 202–07, looks briefly at V.'s contribution to the study of Brazilian literature. The same writer's 'Don Juan Valera y el indianismo romántico brasileño', *CHA*, 570, 1997: 107–23, surveys V.'s articles for the *Revista Española de Ambos Mundos* that provided the material for his *De la poesía de Brasil*.

ZORRILLA. *Cada cual, con su razón*, ed. and ann. Jorge Manrique, Valladolid, Ayuntamiento, 1997, 293 pp., is an excellent addition to studies of Z.'s lesser-known work. Consisting of a thoroughgoing introduction, a facsimile of the autograph manuscript plus 'traslado' into this first modern printed edition, and a plethora of well-focused notes to the text, it will prove invaluable to the understanding of Z.'s developing powers as a dramatist. W. de Ràfols, 'Writing to seduce and seducing to write about it: graphocentrism in *Don Juan Tenorio*', *RHM*, 50, 1997: 253–65, stresses Don Juan's reliance upon visual signs and the written word and specifies the polysemous but indeterminate letter whose meaning shifts for both character and spectator. I. Bergquist, 'El pastelero y el rey: Gabriel de Espinosa visto por Zorrilla y sus contemporáneos', *ib.*, 5–21, looks at the historical figure of Espinosa and his depiction in literature by Z., Escosura, and Fernández y González, arguing that for the imaginative writer it was indispensable to allow at least the possibility of Espinosa and King Sebastian's being one and the same, and concluding that Z.'s representation is the most fascinating and convincing despite (or because of) its being furthest from history. T. Lewis, 'Zorrilla and 1848: contradictions of historico-nationalist Romanticism in *Traidor, inconfeso y mártir*', *His(US)*, 81:818–29, challenges the revisionist picture of a triumphant historico-nationalist Romanticism, regarding it as just one element in a broader cultural revolution: the emergence of a bourgeois society in Spain. The moment is characterized, L. feels, by *Traidor*'s neutralization of the threat of 'legal revolution' contained in the Spanish experience of 1848, in which Z. acknowledges the 'felt legitimacy' of Romantic rebellion but preserves the social status quo by transposing that rebellion into the realm of inner spirituality. While questionable in some of its connections (few would entirely share, for example, the emphases of this ideological depiction of the Spain of the 1840s), L.'s piece is a significant contribution to the current debate and offers considerable potential for further research.

LITERATURE, 1898–1936

By K. M. SIBBALD, *McGill University*

1. GENERAL

BIBLIOGRAPHY. A useful summation covering 1993–96 is contained in C. Byrne, 'Review of miscellanies', *BHS(G)*, 75:293–305; while F. Maguire, 'Review of miscellanies. Part I: A-L', *BHS(L)*, 75:499–515, lists collections from 1995–96, containing specific criticism on Gerardo Diego, José Bergamín, and Ramón J. Sender not covered here.

PERIODICAL HISTORY. D. Guemárez-Cruz, 'Juan Ramón Jiménez editor de la revista *Índice*', *BHS(G)*, 75:355–70, not only examines closely the genesis of the review that soon followed *España* and *La Pluma* as the preferred organ for the new literature advocated by Jiménez, maestro and mentor of the 1927 Generation, but also, more surprisingly, pinpoints the considerable role of Enrique Díez-Canedo in making the whole enterprise a success. Overlapping with our period's contributors, *La codorniz. Antología. 1941–1978*, ed. Melquíades Prieto and Julián Moreiro, M, Edaf, 253 pp., with a prologue and an epilogue by veteran humorists Antonio Mingote and Chumy Chúmez, respectively, is a useful reminder of how humour provided often the only vehicle to circumvent Francoist literary censorship.

LITERARY AND CULTURAL HISTORY. Much of the year has been devoted to celebrating the centenary of (the Generation of) 1898, while the *año enlorquecido* has certainly dominated the media with all sorts of celebrations of García Lorca. In somewhat more subdued tones, the centenaries of the birth of Vicente Aleixandre, Dámaso Alonso, and Rosa Chacel, and the death of Ángel Ganivet have also been duly feted. Impossible, therefore, to cover every literary junket, although what follows here and under individual authors sums up some of the more representative acts of homage in special editions, special issues, proceedings and specially commissioned works. Quite typical of the 1898 Generation as special topics are: Javier Leralta, **Viajes y viajeros. Andanzas literarias por España de la Generación del 98*, M, Viajes Ilustrados, 198 pp., and Eduardo Martínez de Piston, *Imagen del paisaje. La Generación del 98 y Ortega y Gasset*, M, Caja de Ahorros y Monte Piedad de Madrid, 22 pp., making hay out of the familiar theme of the Generation as armchair travellers; José Miguel Fernández Urbina, *Los vascos del 98*, San Sebastián, Bermingham Edit., 335 pp., zeroing in on Unamuno, Baroja, and Maeztu and modernity; José Luis Calvo Carrillo, *La cara oculta del 98*, M, Cátedra, 442 pp., on

mystics and intellectuals at the turn of the century; and *En el 98*, ed.
José Carlos Mainer and Jordi García, M, Visor, 178 pp., on the 'new'
writers. Among the special issues are the following with special
reference to our period. *'El 98. Lecciones de un fin de siglo', *Boletín
de la Institución Libre de Enseñanza*, 28–29, M, Fundación Francisco
Giner de los Ríos, 1997, 160 pp. *CA*, 72, is dedicated to '1898:
¿desastre o reconciliación?' and contains of interest here: C. Chaparro
Gómez, 'Extremadura: del 98 al 98' (103–10), contrasting the vision
of Unamuno and Baroja in the 1890s of the province as 'atraso y
desdicha, de abandono y pobreza, de enfermedades y carencias' with
present progress; I. Reguera, 'La Generación del 98 y la idea de
España' (133–39), tracing how an abstract concept became an
aesthetic problem and, finally, a literary motif from Ganivet to
Unamuno, Maeztu, Antonio Machado, and Azorín, on to Ortega
and down through the Francoist years; and I. Román Román,
'Regeneracionismo y utopía en la literatura del 98' (160–74), a light-
hearted look at the *madre patria* in Galdós, Pereda, Azorín and Felipe
Trigo. Concentrating on the American point of view: *CAm*, 211,
devotes most of the issue to 'En el 98', with relevant essays here being:
J. C. Mainer, '1898 en la literatura: las huellas españolas del *desastre*'
(46–55), which illustrates by way of Clarín, Valle-Inclán, Azorín and
Unamuno, as well as testimony from Eduardo López Bago, Manuel
Ciges Aparicio, and Felipe Trigo, that many considered blood shed
in the colonies the result of mismanagement by the state and the
sacrifice of the poor, and were opposed to the government's policy of
toros y guerra symbolized in the misguided *corrida patriótica* of 12 May
1898; M. D. Albiac Blanco, 'Regeneracionismo y estética en la
literatura española de la preguerra europea' (56–64), that reads
Baroja y Pérez de Ayala to find the prologue to the war in the Treaty
of Versailles of 1783; M. L. Laviana Cuetos, 'Memoria del 98 en
España' (65–71), celebrating the happy end of colonialism by setting
1898 in opposition to 1492; M. Rojas Mix, 'Reflexiones sobre
América en la España de los 98' (84–88), which traces the use of
'Hispanoamérica' *versus* 'Latinoamérica' and the predilection for
'hispanidad'; while L. Toledo Sande, '95 vs 98' (89–99), revisiting the
date 24 February 1895 and the initiation of hostilities finds some far-
fetched parallel with the date of the death of Lady Diana. Still from
the opposite shore: *CHA*, 577–78, is a monographic issue dedicated
to 'El 98 visto desde América', of which the part designated
'Repercusiones literarias' is of most interest here: T. Alfieri, 'La
Generación del 98 en el ensayismo argentino' (201–13), discovers the
presence of Unamuno, Azorín, and Maeztu in Martínez Estrada,
Manuel Gálvez, and Eduardo Mallea; D. Cvitanovic, 'Concepto y
paradoja: los flujos barrocos del 98 en la Argentina' (213–37), also

finds, in a very loose definition of the Baroque, evidence of Unamuno in Martínez Estrada, Gálvez, Mallea, and, even, Borges; E. de Zuleta, 'El 98 desde la Argentina: una aproximación bibliográfica' (239–41), most usefully indicates, first, the reaction of the Spanish community in Argentina to the war and the intervention of the United States, and the part played later in the reception in the Argentine press of five representative figures (Unamuno, Azorín, Baroja, Maeztu and Antonio Machado) by Guillermo de Torre, Francisco Ayala, and Ricardo Baeza; P. González Rodas, 'Unamuno y Colombia' (243–92), zeroes in on Unamuno's correspondence with and about Tomás Carrasquillo, Max Grillo, Samuel López, Francisco de L. Rendón, Gabriel la Torre, Luis Tablanca, José Eustasio Rivera, Baldomero Sansón Cano, Santiago Pérez Triana, Julio Vives Guerra, José Asunción Silva, Rafael Uribe Uribe, and Enrique Pérez; M. Caballero, '¡Llegaron los americanos! El 98 en la narrativa puertorriqueña' (293–98), briefly discusses influence in René Marqués, Manuel Zeno Gandía, Rosario Ferré, and Edgardo Rodríguez Juliá; while C. Arroyo Reyes, 'Entre el regeneracionismo y el *Volksgeist*' (299–315), gives an account of Peruvian writer Víctor Andrés Belaúnde's readings not only of Ganivet, Unamuno, and Azorín, but Joaquín Costa and Ricardo Macías Picavea as well. Nearer home, *ALEC*, 23, concentrates on 1898, *fin de siècle*, and modernity, in a major collection that deserves serious attention and contains: J. Blasco, 'Hospital de furiosos y melancólicos, cárcel de degenerados, gabinete de estetas . . .' (19–49); R. A. Cardwell, 'Antonio Machado and the search for the soul of Spain: a genealogy' (51–79); M. P. Celma Valero, 'Mario Raso de Luna y el pensamiento teosófico en España' (81–98); L. Fernández Cifuentes, 'Cartografía del 98: fin de siglo, identidad nacional y diálogo con América' (117–45); S. M. Hart, 'Some notes on literary print culture in Spanish America: 1880–1920' (165–80); C. L. Jrade, 'Modernism on both sides of the Atlantic' (181–96); F. La Rubia-Prado, 'La cuestión del género literario: el "Ortega vanguardista" y los formalistas rusos' (187–216); J. Macklin, 'Religion and modernity in Spain: *Camino de perfección* and *La voluntad*' (217–47); G. Navajas, 'La modernidad como crisis. El modelo español del declive' (277–94); G. Nouzeillas, 'La ciudad de los tísicos: tuberculosis y autonomía' (295–313); N. R. Orringer, 'Redefining the Spanish Silver Age and 98 within it' (315–26); W. C. Ríos-Font, 'To hold and behold: eroticism and canonicity at the Spanish *fin de siglo*' (355–78); M. P. Rodríguez, 'Modernidad y feminismo: tres relatos de Carmen de Burgos' (379–403); M. Santos Zas, 'Valle-Inclán, de puño y letra: notas a una exposición de Romero de Torres' (405–50); D. L. Shaw, 'More about *abulia*' (451–64); C. C. Soufas, Jr., 'Tradition as an ideological weapon: the critical redefinition of modernity and modernism in early 20th-century Spanish literature' (465–77); R. C. Spires, 'El Donjuanismo y las construcciones sociales de las *Sonatas*' (479–94); J. Torrecilla, 'Valle-Inclán y la apropiación nacionalista de las vanguardias' (495–515); M. Ugarte, 'Azorín and the politics of modernist identity' (517–30); A. Zamora, 'Construcciones y derribos. Arquitecturas ideológicas de la novela de tesis española en la coyuntura entre dos siglos' (531–57); and S. J. Schumm, '*Tristana* and the encrypted enigma of *El secreto del acueducto*' (655–69). Testimony of a life's work, †Victor Ouimette, *Los intelectuales y el naufragio del liberalismo (1923–1936)*, 2 vols, V, Pre-Textos, 535, 596 pp., examines two generations of intellectuals in the context of their socio-political activities in a period of constant crisis between the abdication of Isabel II in 1868, through war, dictatorship and the Second Republic until the Civil War in 1936. Chapters on Unamuno and 'el eterno liberalismo español' (71–274), Azorín and 'el liberalismo instintivo' (275–460) and 'Antonio Machado and 'el liberalismo cordial' (461–526), form the first volume, while in the second figure Pío Baroja and 'el liberalismo iluso' (15–102), Ortega y Gasset and 'el liberalismo imperativo' (103–287), Gregorio Marañón and 'el liberalismo inquieto' (290–444), and Pérez de Ayala and 'el liberalismo de la racionalidad' (445–589). There is much useful quotation from the periodical writings, intelligent contextualization with other European men of stature and a committed sense of dialogue between these various modern 'clercs' that makes this a work for leisured reading and obligatory consultation. Perhaps to be read as a postscript, Pedro Laín Entralgo, *Hacia la recta final. Revisión de una vida intelectual*, B, Galaxia Gutenberg, 415 pp., continues the debate. C. Zulueta, '"El nuevo renacer de España". El Instituto Libre de Enseñanza', *RHM*, 51:161–77, does some personal reminiscing about the 'Insti', María de Maeztu's classes, the medieval nature of the Spanish education system and the extraordinarily high illiteracy rates, with some warm words for Unamuno, Azorín, Antonio Machado, and Ramiro de Maeztu at the *Residencia*. M. Gallego Roca and J. E. Serrano Asenjo, 'Un hombre enamorado del pasado. Las crónicas de Antonio Marichalar en la revista *The Criterion*', *NRFH*, 46:67–96, documents well Marichalar's contributions between 1923–38, showing the affinity of taste for actuality and tradition that made Ortega, Eliot and Pound his true contemporaries, and highlighting the considerable achievement of this 'double agent' in introducing modern Spain to English readers. *Monteagudo* (Murcia), 3, is devoted to 'Epistolarios and literatura del siglo XX' but of relevance here: F. J. Díaz de Castro, 'La autobiografía del 27: los epistolarios' (13–35) reviews some 30 collections of letters, mainly by and between Salinas, Guillén,

Diego, Juan Larrea, Aleixandre, and García Lorca; E. Bou, 'Defensa de la voz epistolar' (37–60), examines the range and register of Salinas's epistolary voice and reproduces four unpublished letters dated 13 October 1937, 2 January 1948, 31 January 1950 and 2 September 1950 to Catherine Centeno, Guillermo de Torre, Solita Salinas and Juan Marichal, and José Ferrater Mora, respectively; B. Ciplijauskaité, 'La construcción del yo y la historia en los epistolarios' (61–72), compares Guillén's correspondance with wife Germaine to that of Salinas and Margarita, to find in both cases that the boomerang effect of writing and reception is (auto)biography in the making; G. Morelli, 'Historia y exégesis de una antología poética a través del epistolario inédito Aleixandre-Macrì' (73–84), illustrates the perfect *chiasmo* made by Aleixandre's letters full of important annotations to two anthologies, the first compiled by Macrì, *Poesia spagnola del Novecento* (1952), and Dario Puccini's collection *Poesie* (1961); and, the jewel in the crown, C. Fernández Hernández, 'Correspondencia del Archivo "Carmen Conde-Antonio Oliver"', (85–115), is a fascinating selection of 15 letters written between 1925–34 by Juan Ramón, Ernestina de Champourcín, Juana de Ibarbouru, Dulce María Loynaz, Raimundo de los Reyes, Concha Méndez, María Zambrano, Jorge Luis Borges and sister, Norah, and Jorge Guillén. Relations between art and literature are explored. M. S. Fernández Utrera, 'Los héroes de la vía media: representación de la nueva humanidad en el discurso artístico y literario de la vanguardia española', *BHS(G)*, 75:491–516, uses portraits by Diego Rivera and Victorio Macho; Javier Pérez Bazo, **La vanguardia en España. Arte y literatura*, Toulouse, CRIC, 546 pp.; and Margaret H. Persin, *Getting the Picture: The Ekphrastic Principle in Twentieth-Century Spanish Poetry*, Lewisberg, Bucknell U.P., 1997, 257 pp., defines a strategy to analyse how individual writers inscribe certain objects of visual art, whether canonized or not, into particular 'visions' of language, ideology and art that affect how their readers interpret issues of intertextuality, genre, gender, and liminality in discourse; of relevance here, the first chapter on Manuel Machado was previously published (see *YWMLS*, 51:352), while chapter 2 deals with how Alberti and Picasso interface in 'the writerly / painterly text', and Persin concentrates on *Los 8 nombres* to differentiate between the Renaissance fixed-point perspective and the multiperspectival preference of Modernism. *La Torre*, 9, dedicates a special number to 'Literatura y ciencia', of which of interest here: J. Hoeg, 'Heidegger, Ortega y el problema de la abulia en *Camino de perfección* de Pío Baroja' (597–614), binds technology and culture together in Fernando Osorio; and N. R. Orringer, 'Antonio Machado y la ciencia de los sentimientos provisionales' (637–53), points out parallels between

Alexander Pfänder's phenomenology and Machado's poetry. The seventh art form is well served: Luis Gasca, *Un siglo de cine español. Un catálogo completo de toda la producción cinematográfica de nuestro país*, B, Planeta, 572 pp.; José Luis Borau, *Diccionario del cine español*, M, Alianza, 1106 pp.; and Jenaro Talens and Santos Zunzunegui, *Historia general del cine*, M, Cátedra, 348 pp. Particular perspectives are represented: Iris M. Zavala coordinates *Breve historia feminista de la literatura española (en lengua castellana)*, Vol. 5, *La literatura escrita por mujeres. Desde el siglo XIX hasta la actualidad*, B, Anthropos, 301 pp., is of interest here; while Lidia Falcón and Elvira Siurana, *Catálogo de escritoras españolas en lengua castellana (1860–1992)*, M, Comunidad de Madrid, 296 pp., is a handy *vademecum*. From an anthology of brief excerpts from the work of the 11 Hispanic Nobel Prize winners, together with introductory critical studies of varying length and worth, come: F. La Rubia-Prado, 'Jacinto Benavente', Mujica, *Premio Nóbel*, 26–36, explicating Benavente's theatrical success and reading closely *Los intereses creados* from a postmodern stance; S. Daydí-Tolson, 'Vicente Aleixandre', *ib.*, 185–90, commenting in general terms upon Rubén Darío's early influence in a lifetime dedicated to experimentation in poetry; and G. Palau de Nemes, 'Juan Ramón Jiménez', *ib.*, 83–93, the best documented and most serious essay, situating Jiménez in both European and American modernism and touching upon the mystical aspect of his work to point out the *via unitativa* in *Animal de fondo*. J. Doce, 'Carta desde Inglaterra. Españoles en Oxford', *CHA*, 575:103–08, is a highly speculative view of both Jorge Guillén and Luis Cernuda in Oxford among fellows and dons that owes more to Javier Marías's *Todas las almas* than the reality of a *lector* in Spanish or an academic visitor in that venerable institution.

2. POETRY

Poetas de 98, ed. Miguel García Posada, M, Alfaguara, 344 pp., is a timely anthology; reaching further into this century, José María Balcells, *De Jorge Guillén a Antonio Gamoneda*, León U.P., 242 pp.; while, augmenting the 1972 edition with representative work from over 30 authors classified as 'forgotten' or 'unknown', *Poetas españoles del siglo veinte desde 1925 hasta hoy*, ed. Albert Bensoussan and Claude Le Bigot, Rennes U.P., 1996, 203 pp., shows that José Moreno Villa, Ernestina Champourcin, Juan José Domenchina and others have, apparently, yet to be discovered. *En torno al 27*, ed. Antonio A. Gómez Yebra, Málaga, Diputación de Málaga, 229 pp., collects essays on José Moreno Villa, Emilio Prados, Manuel Altolaguirre, José María Hinojosa and Jorge Guillén. Antonina Rodrigo, *Aleluyas de Mariana Pineda, Angel Ganivet, Federico García Lorca*, Granada, Fundación Caja de Granada, 95 pp., also reproduces drawings from *gallo* (1927–28). *Imágenes para una generación poética (1918–1927–1936). Sala de exposiciones de Plaza de España*, M, Comunidad de Madrid, 227 pp., is a pleasant piece of memorabilia from the exhibition which ran from 25 September to 22 November 1998. **Traducir poesía. Luis Cernuda, traductor*, ed. Emilio Barón, Almería U.P., 160 pp. J. Calvetti, 'Homenaje a Manuel Machado', *BAAL*, 62, 1997:85–90, is a spirited revindication of a poet ignored for political reasons, which adds less familiar devotees like Carlos Mastronardi and Conrado Nalé Roxlo to the usual list, and re-reads 'Un hidalgo' and 'Felipe IV' but finds little new to say. Manuel Salinas edits with critical apparatus, Emilio Prados, *Diario íntimo, Málaga, Diputación de Málaga, 45 pp.

INDIVIDUAL POETS

ALBERTI. (Auto)biography fleshes out literary criticism: D. Gagen, ' "Más progreso que Federico": Alberti in the Salinas-Guillén correspondence', *BHS(L)*, 75:191–200, pinpoints a certain disappointment in the relationship that characterizes Salinas as a rather dyspeptic father figure and Guillén as the absent older brother to A. (and García Lorca) as *enfant terrible*; R. Havard, 'Rafael Alberti, Maruja Mallo, and Giménez Caballero: materialist imagery in *Sermones y moradas* and the issue of surrealism', *MLR*, 93:1020–67, takes some interesting quotations from A.'s conversations with Geoffrey Connell recorded in November 1979 to elucidate A.'s method of exploiting evangelical Christianity in the Freudian beginning of the journey *via* surrealism and materialist metaphysics to communism, according both A.'s painter-companion Mallo and the Jesuits their due as influences; while Id., 'The sons of the fathers: Jesuit echoes in Rafael Alberti's *Sobre los ángeles* and *Sermones y moradas*', *RoS*, 31:33–44, pursues further the connection with the Society of Jesus. H. Laurenson, ' "Cortas las faldas, cortas las melenas": the reinvented feminine in Rafael Alberti's *Cal y canto*', *MLR*, 93:71–82, analyses the mutilation, violation, victimization, and violence done to the sublime and sublimated feminine forms of A.'s earlier poetry, in what is seen as the true predecessor of *Sobre los ángeles* wherein A. would express the need to purify a self-destructive dynamic his pysche could no longer sustain. (See also LITERARY AND CULTURAL HISTORY above).

ALEIXANDRE. Interest quickens during this the centenary year. Alejandro Duque Amusco edits and introduces *Prosa*, M, Espasa Calpe, 417 pp., which contains *Los encuentros, Evocaciones y pareceres* and *Otros apuntes para una poética*; A.'s contributions to a distinguished poetry review are republished in facsimile form as **Vicente Aleixandre. 'Litoral' en el centenario de su nacimiento*, Málaga, Revista Litoral, 251 pp.

José Olivio Jiménez, **Vicente Aleixandre. Un aventura hacia el conocimiento*, Seville, Renacimiento, 135 pp. *BFFGL*, 23, is largely devoted to a useful *homenaje* comprising: 'Un poema inédito de Vicente Aleixandre' (11–14), entitled 'La amada niña', which comes from a letter dated 12 August 1941 sent to José Luis Cano, and is reprinted with an earlier letter from Cano dated 16 October 1938; L. de Luis, 'Vicente Aleixandre: algunas contradicciones, algunos recuerdos' (19–26), is some very personal reminiscing; G. Morelli, 'Vicente Aleixandre prosista' (27–45), looks at *Los encuentros* to find Azorín as the probable model, although the company includes Rubén Darío, Gómez de la Serna, Juan Ramón, Rafael Alberti and Pablo Neruda, with echoes of Picasso and Dalì, Gabriel Miró and Pérez Galdós; F.J. Díez de Revenga, 'Vicente Aleixandre en su paraíso. "Hablo de mí, pero hablo del Mundo . . ."' (47–66) offers an explanation that complements previous commentaries by José Luis Cano, Carlos Bousoño and Leopoldo de Luis; while A. Duque Amusco, 'Revisión de las fuentes literarias de *Pasión de la tierra* de Vicente Aleixandre' (67–80), uses A.'s interview with Giancarlo Depretis in 1974 and a letter dated 1 April 1929 to Juan Guerrero Ruiz to decipher echoes of Lautréamont, Rimbaud, Roger Vitrac, Robert Desnos, René Crevel, Max Jacob, Paul Éluard, Louis Aragon, José Moreno Villa, and José María Hinojosa, that might well be read together with Rosa Fernández Urtasun, *La búsqueda del hombre a través de la belleza*, Kassel, Reichenberger, 1997, 163 pp., a comparative study of A. and French surrealism. A. Poust, 'Vicente Aleixandre in the crossfire: classicism vs romanticism', *His(US)*, 81:287–98, deftly dodges the bullets to come to the judicious conclusion that the mix of opposing political and cultural positions, first, in the 1920s and, then again, in the 1940s, provided different scenarios for different readers that had little to do with A.'s own aesthetic. (See also LITERARY AND CULTURAL HISTORY above.)

ALONSO. Another centenary also produces a critical flurry: *Poesía y otros textos literarios*, ed. Valentín García Yebra, M, Gredos, 747 pp., has a prologue by Víctor García de la Concha; while **Hijos de la ira. Diario íntimo*, B, Galaxia Gutenberg, 220 pp., has sketches by Pla-Narbona; and Fernando Huarte Morton and Juan Antonio Ramírez Ovelar, **Bibliografía de Dámaso Alonso*, M, Gredos, 132 pp., is a useful adjunct to further criticism.

BERGAMÍN. Nigel Dennis edits with critical apparatus *Las ideas liebres. Aforística y epigramática 1935–1981*, B, Destino, 125 pp. R. Fernández Romero, 'El vacío en la poesía de José Bergamín', *ECon*, 11.1:27–40, relies heavily upon previous criticism to elucidate B.'s *catolicismo agónico* in poetry about death and the after life in which a

Pascalian fear of emptiness translates a vision of Hell. (See also BIBLIOGRAPHY above.)

CHAMPOURCÍN. Milagros Arizmendi selectively edits, with an epilogue by Clara Janés, *Cántico inútil. Cartas cerradas. Primer exilio. Huyeron todas las islas*, Málaga, Diputación Provincial–Centro Cultural de la Generación de 27, 1997, 365 pp., which follows the standard 1991 anthology by José Angel Ascunce (see *YWMLS*, 54:333), but fails to give either criteria for her selection or notes to the text. C.'s (auto)biographical memoir of Juan Ramón Jiménez is augmented in an important second edition, *La ardilla y la rosa*, Huelva, Fundación Juan Ramón Jiménez, 193 pp.

GARCÍA LORCA. First, the centenary re-editing of the collected works begins as a series: *Poema del cante jondo*, Granada, Comares, 117 pp., *Canciones*, Granada, Comares, 159 pp., *Romancero gitano*, Granada, Comares, 149 pp., *Doña Rosita la soltera o el lenguaje de las flores. Poema granadino del novecientos, divido en varios jardines. Con escenas de canto y baile*, Granada, Comares, 89 pp., and *La casa de Bernarda Alba. Drama de mujeres en los pueblos en España*, Granada, Comares, 95 pp.; for the *Clásicos Universales Losada* series, Luis Martínez Cuitiño prologues and annotates not only *Romancero gitano (1924–1927)*, B, Océano, 129 pp., but *Bodas de sangre*, B, Océano, 156 pp., and *La casa de Bernarda Alba. Drama de mujeres en los pueblos en España*, B, Océano, 137 pp.; Daniel Zarza illustrates **Canciones y poemas para niños*, Cooper City, Span Press, 1997, 90 pp.; the theatre is well served, Annabella Cardinali provides an introductory study for *Títeres de cachiporra. Tragicomedia de don Cristóbal y la señá Rosita*, M, Cátedra, 245 pp., which follows the annotated text established by Christian de Paepe, Pedro Provencio edits with critical apparatus *Bodas de sangre. La casa de Bernarda Alba*, B, Edaf, 205 pp., and Mario Hernández prologues *La casa de Bernarda Alba*, M, Alianza, 101 pp., with illustrations by Juan Cobos Wilkins; Andrew A. Anderson edits *Diálogos*, Granada, Comares, 85 pp.; and Eutimio Martín selects and annotates *Antología comentada*, 2 vols, M, Ediciones de la Torre, with reproductions of sketches by the author. Biography looms large: **Federico García Lorca. Vida*, ed. Gonzalo Armero, Granada, Huerta de San Vicente, 28 pp.; Ian Gibson, *García Lorca. Biografía esencial*, B, Península, 100 pp.; Jacinto S. Martín, **García Lorca, bachiller*, M, Alhulia, 284 pp.; Mario Hernández prologues the reprinting of José Mora Guarnido, *Federico García Lorca y su mundo*, Granada, Fundación Caja de Granada, lxiii + 239 pp.; A. A. Anderson, 'Federico García Lorca y Sebastià Gasch: escenas de una amistad epistolar', *BFFGL*, 23:83–105, documents G.L.'s passage through the *Ateneíllo de Hospitalet* and the friendship surrounding *gallo* that ended with Gasch's disillusionment with the public figure who returned to Barcelona in 1935; and, as a

curious twist, M. de Paco, 'García Lorca, personaje dramático',
Monteagudo, 3:117–27, records fact making fiction in the appearance
of G.L. as a main character in theatre plays by José María Camps
(1961), José Antonio Rial (1969), Fina de Calderón (1977), José
Gerardo Manrique de Lara (1985), Fernando H. Guzmán (1982),
Lorenzo Píriz-Carbonell (1982, 1990), and Alberto Miralles (1995).
A. A. Anderson, 'Bibliografía lorquiana reciente XXIII (1984–1998)',
BFFGL, 23:129–50, is particularly useful both for the record kept of
doctoral theses not noted here and, more importantly, for the first
instalment of the as yet incomplete bibliography of special issues,
anthologies, collections and editions celebrating the centenary.
Symbols and imagery fascinate the critics: Pedro Guerrero Ruiz and
Veronica Dean Thacker, *Federico García Lorca. El color de la poesía*,
Murcia U.P., 211 pp.; Javier Salazar Rincón, '*Por un anfibio sendero . . .*'
Los espacios simbólicos de Federico García Lorca, B, PPU, 374 pp.; and
Federico García Lorca en el espejo del tiempo, ed. Pedro Guerrero Ruiz,
Alicante, Aguaclara, 324 pp. R. Lozano Miralles, '*Impresiones y paisajes*
en el contexto de la obra juvenil: proyectos y géneros', *BFFGL*,
23:107–25, argues the strong link between G.L.'s juvenilia and the
rest of his work and G.L.'s clear ideas from an early stage on
authorship and the organic unity of his work. D. E. C. Nordlund,
' "Cementerio judío": Lorca's cryptic dream of the wandering Jew',
RHM, 51:46–63, explicates the poem showing G.L.'s sympathetic
rendition of the suffering of Jews in the diaspora following his visit to
the New York Sephardic synagogue Shearith Israel and its cemetery
on 18 January 1930. Paul Julian Smith, *The Theatre of García Lorca:
Text, Performance, Pyschoanalysis*, CUP, 185 pp., formulates some controversial interpretations of four major plays: in the first chapter
Yerma is seen as the 'intersexual type' within the anxiety of bisexuality
of Gregorio Marañón and contemporary medical practice; Chapter
2 takes note of the 'translation of introjection' by the luminary of the
Harlem Renaissance, Langston Hughes; in Chapter 3 *Así que pasen
cinco años* is read within the paradigm of *Corydon*, homosexuality and
Freud's analytical two-step; while Chapter 4 looks at subsidized
cinema and Lluis Pasqual's performances of the unplayable, all
argued from a return to Freud's own words questioning the basis of
confession and societal restraint. In comparative vein: E. L. Santos-
Phillips, 'Discourses of power in the film versions of *The House of
Bernarda Alba* and *Like Water for Chocolate*', *HisJ*, 18:9–22, uses
Foucault to explain the techniques and tactics of domination in both
works.

GUILLÉN.   *Cántico: Selected Poems*, ed. Donald McCrory, Bristol,
Bristol Classical Press, xliii + 94 pp., aims primarily at students with
its basic introduction, not very useful notes, bibliography and

vocabulary; the 'Introduction" (vii-xl) covers G.'s biography and draws some interesting parallels between the poet and Ortega y Gasset that deserve consideration, but Guillén's pseudonym for the articles in *El Norte de Castilla* was Félix de la Barca not de la Carpa as stated. E. Mathews, 'Heroic vocation: Cervantes, Guillén and "Noche del Caballero" ', *MLR*, 93 : 102–33, proposes Cervantes as the literary source of the example of enduring human fulfilment and cites a number of G.'s poems without explaining the connection very carefully. (See also LITERARY AND CULTURAL HISTORY above.)

HERNÁNDEZ. José María Balcells prologues **El rayo que no cesa*, B, Océano, 170 pp.; while, in the same series, Elvio Romero edits with an introductory study **Cancionero y romancero de ausencias*, B, Océano, 108 pp. At either end of the literary scale: Antonio Gracia, *Miguel Hernández. Del 'amor cortés' la mística del erotismo*, Alicante, Instituto Juan-Gil Albert, 82 pp., complements an earlier collection of essays in the same series **Miguel Hernández. Tradiciones y vanguardias*, ed. Serge Salaün and Javier Pérez Bazo, Alicante, Instituto Juan-Gil Albert, 1996, 268 pp.

JIMÉNEZ. E. Ralston, 'Juan Ramón Jiménez, en familia. Cartas inéditas a su hermana Ygnacia y a su sobrino Enrique, hijo de Ygnacia', *His(US)*, 81 : 475–89, collects and reproduces four undated letters and cards from the 1940s that show J.'s genuine family feelings despite the recognition he was 'un poco raro y tímido', and record his reiterated desire to destroy all his uncorrected work published in the period 1899–1914. (See also PERIODICAL HISTORY above, and MACHADO, A. below.)

MACHADO, A. F. de Giovanni, 'Legitimación intelectual y proyecto creador: Antonio Machado ante Gregorio Martínez Sierra, Rubén Darío y Juan Ramón Jiménez', *RHM*, 51 : 22–29, takes up A.M.'s alusions to intellectual mentors and weaves an intricate web of socio-political exchanges in which Juan Ramón was the most likely cultural mediator. J. Malpartida, 'Poética y filosofía: el pensamiento literario de Antonio Machado', *CHA*, 571 : 109–20, is a very personalized apology in favour of A.M.'s combination of poetry and philosophy that adduces little that is new. E. Scarlett, 'Antonio Machado's fountains: archeology of an image', *MLN*, 113 : 305–23, gushes about the metapoetic dialogue between the feminine discourse of water and the poet's masculine discourse of solitude in writing that brings solace. (See also LITERARY AND CULTURAL HISTORY above.)

SALINAS. **Narraciones completas*, B, Península, 262 pp. R. K[atz] Crispin, 'How to re-invent the self despite the world: a reading of Pedro Salinas' *Todo más claro*', *Inti*, 46–47 : 27–40, first uses Heidegger and Lacan to read closely the following poems, 'Camino al poema', 'Hombre en la villa', 'Pasajero en museo', 'Nocturno de los avisos',

'Contra esa primavera' and 'Cero', and then she goes on to 'The poems of the *Largo lamento* era: the memorialization of love as art', *Hispanófila*, 124 : 1–14, in which she discovers the intimate connection of love and loss with poetry in an internalization that is neither pyschic escape nor mere digression but rather poetic integration. (See also LITERARY AND CULTURAL HISTORY above.)

3. PROSE

Some useful anthologies appear: for the general reading public, *Cien años de cuentos. Antología del cuento español en castellano*, ed. José María Merino, M, Alfaguara, 575 pp.; and for the specialist, María Teresa García-Abad García, *La novela cómica*, M, CSIC, 1997, 294 pp., follows the line of research taken by Alberto Sánchez Alvarez-Insúa (1996) and José Antonio Pérez Bowie (1996) (see *YWMLS*, 59 : 340), highlighting the social context, 1916–19, and comparing this series with *La novela teatral*, and giving also a useful description of each work, whether by writers of repute like Antonio Paso, Arniches, and Muñoz Seca or now forgotten figures like Manuel Moncayo, Francisco Torres, and Manuel Linares Becerra; and *Proceder a sabiendas (Antología de la narrativa de vanguardia española, 1923–1936)*, ed. Domingo Rodenas de Mayo, B, Alba, 1997, 556 pp., whose introductory essay gives details of the 'other' Generation of 1927, prose writers like Botín Polanco, Díaz Fernández, Corpus Barga, Verdaguer and Ximénez de Sandoval who, together with better known exponents of new narrative techniques, García Lorca, Dámaso Alonso, Diego, and Salinas, had Ortega y Gasset as publicist for this new 'dehumanized' art, to be read with Id., *Los espejos del novelista. Modernismo y autoreferencia en la novela vanguardista española*, B, Península, 287 pp. Carmen de Urioste Azcorra, **Narrativa andaluza (1900–1936): erotismo, feminismo y regionalismo*, Seville U.P., 1997; 140 pp. Manuel Aznar Soler edits with full critical apparatus, to which Miguel Angel González-Sanchís adds a bio-bibliographic epilogue, Max Aub, *San Juan*, V, Pre-Textos, 265 pp. J. Whiston, ' "La virtud de la palabra": Manuel Azaña's diaries of the Spanish Civil War', *Neophilologus*, 82 : 411–24, enquires into why what should have been the democratic consolidation of a brilliant parliamentary career turned, instead, into a nightmare as hopes for peace in the Republic were dashed in wartime defeat, and, by quoting well and at length, illustrates the dreadful irony of a resolute, clear-minded politician powerless to act because of his principled commitment to the Republican Constitution. Rafael Cansinos Asséns, *Obra crítica, ed. Alberto González Troyano, Seville, Diputación de Sevilla, 745 pp. Juan Chabás, **Puerto de sombra. Agor sin fin*, ed. Javier Pérez Bazo, M, Espasa Calpe, 337 pp. In time for the centenary of her birth, Rosa Chacel, *Alcancía. Estación Termini*, ed. Carlos Pérez Chacel and Antonio Piedra, Salamanca, Junta de Castilla y León, 409 pp. José Esteban prologues José Díaz Fernández, *El blocao. Novela de la guerra marroquí*, M, Viamonte, 122 pp. O. Ayala, 'Antonio Espina. Los años oscuros (1936–45)', *ECon*, 11.1:41–59, documents the period before exile in Mexico in 1947 from letters to wife Mercedes Abreu and an unpublished letter from Ortega and Santos Martínez, ex-secretary of Manuel Azaña, dated 25 June 1946. Elizabeth Rojas Auda, *Visión y ceguera de Concha Espina. Su obra comprometida*, M, Pliegos, 152 pp., tries to equate feminism in *La esfinge maragata* (1914) and Christian Socialism in *El metal de los muertos* (1920) without signal success. F. Lough, '*El profesor inútil* and the ethical aesthetics of Benjamín Jarnés', *BHS(G)*, 75:469–90, adduces a parallel with Herbert Marcuse to teach the lesson that supposedly 'elitist' art may have as its mission social change. Juan Carlos Ara Torralba, *Del modernismo castizo. Fama y alcance de Ricardo León*, Saragossa U.P., 1996, 562 pp., does a little literary resuscitation, outlining how this conservative opportunist constituted an enviable literary reputation by turning at the right time from young militant into Catholic propagandist for *casticismo*. K. S. Larsen, 'Lust, madness and a bowl of cherries: Gabriel Miró's *La cerezas del cementerio*', *Inti*, 46–47:95–108, mixes together Freud and Krafft-Ebbing with some Cervantine characters, Huysmans, Oscar Wilde, Bosch, and Juan Valera in the 'soup of sexuality' that is this watershed novel. Eduardo Jiménez Urdiales, *La narrativa de José Moreno Villa. 'Evoluciones' y 'Patrañas'*, Málaga, Diputación de Málaga, 212 pp. Florencio Friera Suárez, *Ramón Pérez de Ayala, testigo de su tiempo*, Gijón, Fundación Alvargonzález, 1997, 570 pp. Francisco Carrasquer Launed selects with an introductory study, Ramón J. Sender, *Rimas compulsivas*, Corunna, Sociedad de Cultura Valle-Inclán, 148 pp.

INDIVIDUAL WRITERS

AZORÍN. New editions become available: *Doña Inés (Historia de amor)*, ed. Jorge Urrutia, M, Biblioteca Nueva, 157 pp.; Miguel García Posada prologues *Valencia. Madrid*, M, Alfaguara, 426 pp., while Santiago Riopérez y Milá provides an introduction, notes, and bibliography to the same text: *Valencia*, M, Biblioteca Nueva, 208 pp.; Miguel Angel Lozano Marco coordinates the mammoth *Obras escogidas*, 3 vols, I. *Novela completa*, II. *Ensayos*, and III. *Teatro. Cuentos. Memorias. Epistolario*, M, Espasa Calpe, 1574, 1634, 1675 pp., while Mario Vargas Llosa provides a prologue to the much slimmer volume *Obras selectas*, M, Espasa Calpe, 186 pp. The proceedings of various international congresses spill into print: *Azorín en el primer milenio de la lengua castellana*, ed. Estanislao Ramón Trives and Herminia Provencio Garrigós, Murcia U.P., 344 pp.; and **Azorín. Fin de siglos (1898–1998)*, ed. Antonio Díez de Mediavilla, Alicante, Aguaclara, 230 pp. Two for the price of one, José Luis Castillo Puche, *Azorín y Baroja. Dos maestros del 98*, M, Biblioteca Nueva, 90 pp. (See also LITERARY AND CULTURAL HISTORY above).

BAROJA. Inevitably some new editions for the centenary: *Aquí París, M, Caro Raggio, 243 pp.; **El Mayorazgo de Labraz*, M, Alfaguara, 263 pp.; while Luis Mateo Díez prologues *Silvestre Paradox. Paradox, rey*, M, Comunidad de Madrid, 585 pp. L. Rubio García, 'Dos cartas de Don Pío Baroja al duque de Dosfuentes', *RLit*, 60: 199–203, reproduces two letters dated 3 April 1914 and 22 August 1944, respectively, in which B. complains of his countrymen's lack of manners, declares himself a 'nihilista', and muses on possible Jewish blood in the veins of Lope, Cervantes, Calderón and Velázquez. Beatriz de Ancos Morales, *Pío Baroja. Literatura y periodismo en su obra*, M, Fundación Universitaria Española, 503 pp., is well-documented. Ramón Emilio Mandado Gutiérrez, **Pío Baroja (1872–1956)*, M, Ediciones del Orto, 94 pp. R.G. McArthur, 'Pío Baroja's *El árbol de la ciencia*: objectification as a means of survival', *RCEH*, 22: 531–40, uses Freud to argue melancholia as the root cause of Andrés Hurtado's repeated exercises in objectification which lead, inevitably, to his suicide. (See also LITERARY AND CULTURAL HISTORY and AZORÍN above).

BLASCO IBÁÑEZ. The 70th anniversary of B.I.'s death causes renewed critical interest. Some readily accessible editions all published in Madrid by Cátedra: *La bodega*, ed. Francisco Caudet, 475 pp.; *La maja desnuda*, ed. Facundo Tomás, 475 pp.; *Mare nostrum*, ed. María José Navarro, 511 pp.; and *El préstamo de la difunta y otros relatos*, ed. José Más and María Teresa Mateo, 303 pp. Jeremy T. Medina, *From Sermon to Art. The Thesis Novels of Vicente Blasco Ibáñez*, V, Albatros, 98 pp., is scholarly. Various proceedings from events organized by the Diputació de Valencia and the Centre Cultural La Beneficiencia get quickly into print: from sessions held 12 March–30 April, 14 May–30 June and 17 July–31 August 1998, respectively, come three publications under the rubric *Vicente Blasco Ibáñez*, V, Diputación de Valencia, 1. *Y el periodismo se hizo combativo*, 103 pp., 2. *Vicente Blasco Ibáñez y el novelista universal*, 117 pp., and 3. *Blasco Ibáñez, viajero*, 99 pp.

GANIVET. Just in time to mark the centenary come: first, two new editions of G.'s record of his stay in Helsinki, *Cartas finlandesas. Hombres del norte*, ed. Fernando García Lara, Granada, Diputación Provincial–Fundación Caja de Granada, 375 pp., with a long and useful 'Estudio preliminar' and notes to the texts by Nil Santiáñez-Tió (13–76), and the editor's short 'Historia del texto' (77–80) giving details of previous editions, while the same *Cartas finlandesas. Hombres del norte*, ed. Antonio Gallego Morell, M, Espasa Calpe, 276 pp., has fewer details. Continuing the *obras completas* project (see *YWMLS*, 58:362), *El porvenir de España*, ed. Fernando García Lara, Granada, Diputación Provincial–Fundación Caja de Granada, 191 pp., with a magistral 'Estudio preliminar' by Pedro Cerezo Galán; *Los trabajos del infatigable creador Pío Cid*, ed. José Montero Padilla, M, Castalia, 521 pp. Two studies on G.'s thought to be read together: Miguel Olmero Moreno, *El pensamiento de Ganivet y actualidad de Ganivet*, Granada, Diputación–Fundación Caja de Granada, 331 pp., and Nelson R. Orringer, *Ángel Ganivet (1865–1898). La inteligencia escindida*, M, Ediciones del Orto, 94 pp. M. Aronna, 'Ángel Ganivet's *Idearum español*: virginity, figleafs and the medicalization of history', *JHispP*, 19, 1994–95[1998]:17–42, press-gangs Alfred Fouillée, Foucault, and Krafft-Ebing into service, alongside psychologists and neurologists like Henry Maudsley, Jean-Étienne Esquirol, Théodule Ribot, and Pierre Janet, to interpret Spanish sexual-national transgressions in what he describes as a spiritual (auto)biography of 19th-c. Spain. In a meaty review article, C. A. Longhurst, 'New perspectives on the novels of Ángel Ganivet', *BHS(G)*, 75:371–78, takes a hard look at recent critical work by Nil Santiáñez-Tió and Raúl Fernández Sánchez-Alarcos (see also *YWMLS*, 58:362), to find in this melancholy and maladjusted individual one of the most powerfully original and creative minds of the *fin-de-siècle* in Spain. (See also LITERARY AND CULTURAL HISTORY above.)

GÓMEZ DE LA SERNA. The *obras completas* proceed apace with **La ciudad. Madrid-Buenos Aires (1919–1956)*, ed. Ioana Zlotescu, B, Galaxia Gutenberg, 1119 pp., with Juan Pedro Gabino revising the texts and a prologue by Luis Candell. Alan Hoyle, *El humor ramoniano de vanguardia*, MUP, 1996, 34 pp., nicely explicates the work. G. Roof Nunley, '*La mujer de ámbar* and the tradition of the Italian chronicle', *RoQ*, 45:219–30, corrects the short-sighted vision of Ramón as 'madrileño por los cuatro costados' and insightfully situates his 1927 Neapolitan novel within the specific literary travelogue tradition so that Naples appears not merely as a picturesque backdrop but rather constitutes the text itself.

D'ORS. *Eugenio d'Ors, del arte a la letra*, ed. Laura Mercader et al., M, Museo Nacional Centro de Arte Reina Sofía, 131 pp., illus., comes complete with the diskette 'Literatura artística de Eugenio d'Ors. Catálogo razonado'. Vicente Cacho Viu, *Revisión de Eugenio d'Ors. 1902–1930*, B, Publicaciones de la Residencia de Estudiantes–Quaderns Crema, 1997, 382 pp., puts O. in a Spanish perspective to challenge the usual pigeon-holing, and publishes for the first time over a hundred letters grouped meaningfully according to historical progression and/or contents, which, written in both Catalan and Spanish over the period 1904–30, document O.'s travels and residence in France and Italy, fortunes and misfortunes in Barcelona, and a life spent between Madrid and Paris, and include correspondence with cousin Antoni Rubió i Lluch, wife María Pérez-Peix, Joan Maragall, Enric Pont de la Riba, Francisco Giner de los Ríos, Ortega, and Unamuno.

ORTEGA. *Boletín Ortegiano*, VI, ed. José Luis Molinuevo and Domingo Hernández Sánchez, M, Fundación José Ortega y Gasset, 128 pp., continues with a 'Bibliografía sobre Ortega y Gasset 1989–1997', with details on unedited texts, translations and re-editions, as well as monographs and doctoral theses on O. not noted here; the particular unit 'Bibliografía cubana' (45–50) is a useful compendium of items not readily accessible. Heilette Van Ree, *Ortega y el humanismo moderno. (La conformación de los modelos de análisis cultural)*, Saragossa, 1997, 166 pp., has its genesis in work by Miguel Enguídanos (1983), José María Pozuelo, and E. Inman Fox (1997), but uses Hayden White as guide, and Johan Huizinga and Jacob Burckhardt as mentors, in reordering O. within the new fashion for cultural studies. (See also D'ORS above.)

UNAMUNO. New editions make one of the Generation of 1898's major players more accessible for the centenary: Gonzalo Torrente prologues *Niebla*, M, Alianza, 101 pp.; Demetrio Estébañez Calderón introduces *Tres novelas ejemplares y un prólogo*, M, Alianza, 312 pp.; Laureano Robles provides full critical apparatus for *Alrededor del estilo*, Salamanca U.P., 192 pp.; and José María Valverde selects and introduces, *Antología poética*, M, Alianza, 143 pp. F. La Rubia-Prado, '*Amor y pedagogía*: ceguera y lucidez de Miguel de Unamuno', *Symposium*, 52 : 2–20, bucks the usual critical trend by re-reading U.'s 'prólogo-epílogo' of 1934 to trace a line on imagination and characterization through Coleridge, Schelling, and Schlegel, right to Paul de Man to establish *organicismo* and irony as the twin poles of U.'s poetics. (See also LITERARY AND CULTURAL HISTORY and D'ORS above.)

VALLE-INCLÁN. As with others of the 1898 Generation, new editions abound: *Sonata de otoño. Memorial del Marqués de Bradomín*, Badajoz, Universitas, 148 pp., comes with an introduction by José M. Bustos Gisbert and illustrations by José Luis Rufes Zazo; *Luces de Bohemia. Esperpento*, ed. Gregorio Torres Nebrera, Badajoz, Carisma, 1997, 241 pp.; *Tirando Banderas. Novela de tierra caliente*, B, Galaxia Gutenberg, 257 pp., is replete with illustrations by Alberto Gironella; while Julián Marías prologues **Obras selectas*, M, Espasa Calpe, 849 pp. D. Dougherty, 'Valle-Inclán y la dirección de escena: una carta olvidada de 1916', *Estreno*, 24.1 : 26–29, publishes a text from *La*

Tribuna dated 28 January 1916 directed at Ramón Pérez de Ayala, in order to use Pierre Bourdieu to explicate the plea for the modernity of the Spanish scene under the direction of Gregorio Martínez Sierra, Cipriano Rivas, and Rafael Cansinos Asséns, rather than yet another personal attack on Fernando Díaz de Mendoza and his stranglehold on the Teatro de la Princesa; and Id., 'El hilo de Ariadna: nueva bibliografía de Valle-Inclán', *ECon*, 10.2, 1997:91–94, picks up the latest criticism, 1993–95, as well as ordering items differentiating between *edición* and *emisión* in V.-I.'s very fragmented editorial and publication activity. C. Feal, 'Entre la guerra y el amor: el Marqués de Bradomín en la *Sonata de invierno*', *ib.*, 11.1:61–80, explores the two ways to enter a real man's world; J. Torrecilla, 'Exotismo y nacionalismo en la *Sonata de estío*', *HR*, 66:35–66, finds in the portrait of Niña Chole and Tierra Caliente the exotic dimension of America that extends a narrow concept of nationalism. In comparative vein: J. Montero, 'El subtexto esproncediano de *La pipa de Kif*', *ECon*, 11.1:81–90, cites *El diablo mundo*; Luis Lorenzo Rivero, *Goya en el esperpento de Valle-Inclán*, Sada, Ediciós do Castro, 221 pp.; Dolors Sabate Planes, *Ramón María del Valle-Inclán en Alemania. Recepción y traducción del esperpento, Kassel, Reichenberger, 239 pp.; while D. Johnston, 'Valle-Inclán: the mirroring of the *esperpento*', *MoD*, 41:30–48, discusses the difficulties of rendering V.-I.'s 'idiolects' for English audiences and reviews translations by Anthony Zahareas, Gerald Gillespie, John Lyon, and María Delgado in which not only the words but also their cultural specificity in the text do not always come through clearly.

4. THEATRE

Critical work on the drama of the period is also noted above under GARCÍA LORCA, UNAMUNO, and VALLE-INCLÁN. Items not recorded here on Azorín, García Lorca, Unamuno, and Valle-Inclán may be found in L. M. Pottie, R. Cameron, and C. Costello, 'Modern drama studies: an annual bibliography', *MoD*, 41:181–302, see particularly section E: Hispanic (242–51); while information on reviews and doctoral theses, as well as certain items on Cernuda and García Lorca, is made available in P. L. Podol, 'El drama español del siglo XX: bibliografía selecta del año 1996', *Estreno*, 24.1:58–64. Reviewing the century in theatre, *Teatro y pensamiento en la generación del 98, M, Fundación RESAD, 247 pp.; R. Domenech, '1898 . . . 1998', *Estreno*, 24.1:24–25, 44, contrasts in general terms the popular theatre of the 1890s of Enrique Gaspar, Pérez Galdós, Benavente, and Dicenta with the minority theatre of the 1990s that, nevertheless, keeps some 30 plus theatres open for business between October and June, and concludes, unsurprisingly, that the leading lights of this century have been Valle-Inclán, García Lorca, and Buero Vallejo; while M. F. Vilches de Frutos, 'Nuevos enfoques críticos para la historia del teatro español del siglo xx: las páginas teatrales en la prensa periódica', *ib.*, 50–57, points to recent scholarly interest in contemporary press reviews as a way of both writing and interpreting a history of the stage in the early part of this century, citing the work of such critics as Manuel Machado and Ramon J. Sender in *La Libertad*, Enrique Díez-Canedo and Ricardo Baeza in *El Sol*, Luis Araujo-Costa in *La Época*, Juan Chabás in *Luz*, and Antonio Espina in *España*, as the source material for information upon productions, ideology of the period, the making of the canon and the growth of a national theatre. Eduardo Pérez Rasilla selects with a long introduction *Antología de teatro breve español (1898–1940)*, M, Biblioteca Nueva, 1997, 379 pp., giving an overview of the Spanish theatre from Echegaray to the innovations of Valle-Inclán and García Lorca, followed by a 'typology' of the one-act play, and a useful and representative collection of 12 texts including Enrique García Álvarez, *El palco del Real*, Arniches's *Los milagros del jornal*, Muñoz Seca's *Adán y Evans*, *Chiquita y bonita* by the Quintero brothers, Bergamín's *El criado de Don Juan*, Unamuno's *La princesa doña Lambra*, Azorín's *La arañita en el espejo*, Gómez de la Serna's *Beatriz*, *¿Qué has hecho hoy para ganar la guerra?* by Max Aub, Valle-Inclán's *Ligazón*, García Lorca's *Quimera*, and *Los sentados* by Miguel Hernández. J. E. Checa Puerta, 'La actividad empresable de Gregorio Martínez Sierra: una apuesta renovadora en la órbita del teatro comercial de preguerra', *ALEC*, 23:821–48, documents the forming of Martínez Sierra's company in 1915, the intrigues between his leading actor Enrique Borrás and his lover Catalina Bárcena, a repertory that included plays by Bjornson, Renard, Dumas, Musset, Marivaux, and Turgenev in translations by Cansinos-Asséns, Eduardo Marquina, and Enrique de Mesa, and his talent for making money in the cause of improving and modernizing the Spanish theatre. J. Dowling, 'En un mesón de la Mancha, en un salón de París: Cervantes y Manuel de Falla', *HisJ*, 18, 1997:23–36, recounts the illustrious history of Falla's interpretation of a scene from *Don Quixote* from the first presentation of the music in Seville in March 1923 and the official *estreno* at the home of the Princesse de Polignac, Winnaretta Singer, more vulgarly known as Madame Machine à Coudre, with Wanda Landowska at the piano and Wladimir Golschmann conducting, through subsequent concerts in Paris, Madrid, Zurich, Berlin and Venice, all of which helped make Falla a world renowned composer. From a contemporary perspective, M. F. Vilches de Frutos, 'La temporada teatral española", *ALEC*, 23:849–96, see particularly 'El teatro del primer tercio del siglo xx'

(853–55), has news of Mario Gas's production of *Martes de Carnival* at the María Guerrero, Francisco Vidal's staging of *El embrujado* at the Lara, Lluis Pasqual's review *Haciendo Lorca* with veteran actors Nuria Espert and Alfredo Alcón, and *La zapatera prodigiosa* at La Latina, Unamuno's *El otro* at the Sala Olimpia, and *Me siento pulga*, a collage of texts by Gómez de la Serna, Jardiel Poncela, and Miguel Mihura. Francisco J. Díaz de Castro and Almudena del Olmo Iturriarte edit with a solid introduction Jacinto Benavente, *Los intereses creados*, M, Espasa Calpe, 209 pp. In a facsimile version, María Zambrano prologues the modern one act mystery play by Concha Méndez, *El solitario*, M, Caballo Griego para la Poesía, 48 pp. Carlos Serrano, *Carnival en noviembre. Parodias teatrales de 'Don Juan Tenorio'*, Alicante, Instituto de Cultura Juan Gil-Albert, 1996, 483 pp., with a useful catalogue of nearly 200 texts written between 1844 and 1944 inspired by Zorrilla's work and an anthology of ten parodies, which could do with some explanation of the criteria governing such a diverse selection that includes: Mariano Pino Bohiga's *Juan el perdío* (1848) in heavy Andalusian dialect; the Catalan version *L'agüello pollastre* (1859) by Chusep B. Baldor; the anonymous, pornographic skit *Don Juan Notorio* (1874); a 'feminized' *Doña Juana Tenorio* (1876) by Rafael María Liem; a Robin Hood look-alike, *Las mocedades de don Juan* (1977) by Juan de Alba; the metatheatre of *El novio de doña Inés* (1884) by Javier de Burgos; a fin-de-siècle *Tenorio modernista* (1906) by Pablo Parellada; José María Dotre's *Román Osorio* (1907) in which Doña Inés plays *cigarera* to Don Juan as a drunk; Lluis Millà i Gaciò's short monologue *El Xuti del Tenorio* (1907); and *Tenorio el del siglo XX* (1917) by J. Huete Ordóñez, a musical set in Madrid. In more exotic vein: V. D. Almazán Tomás, 'La actriz Sada Yacco: el descubrimiento del teatro japonés en España', *ALEC*, 23:717–31, gives a full account of the triumphal European tour in 1902 of the actress who broke a strict sex barrier to bring authentic Meiji theatre to the West in such (Spanish) productions as *Kesa*, *El Shogun* and *La geisha y el caballero*, while, at the same time, bridging different continents and cultures in her versions of *The Merchant of Venice* and *La Dame aux camélias*; M. Martín Rodríguez, 'El *Teatro del Grottesco* en España: los estrenos de Luigi Chiarelli hasta 1936', *ib.*, 751–73, documents the presentations first in Italian then in Spanish of *La maschera e il volto* in December 1923 and January 1924, and *Fuochi d'artificio* in April 1926 and 1930, respectively; while, a little nearer home, *Teatro de la emigración asturiana en Cuba*, ed. Alfredo I. Álvarez and Virginia Gilamate, Oviedo U.P., 1997, 325 pp.

LITERATURE, 1936 TO THE PRESENT DAY

By Omar García-Obregón, *Queen Mary and Westfield College, University of London*, and Irene Mizrahi, *Boston College*

1. General

Margaret C. González, *Literature of Protest. The Franco Years*, U.P. of America, 125 pp., explores the relationship between Spanish literature and political opposition under the Franco Regime. Ch. 1 introduces the two related theories (political discourse and literary generation) which, in G.'s view, 'establish a foundation for the transition to democracy in Spain'. Ch. 2 deals with the mythic foundations of Spanish culture, literature, and politics. Ch. 3 studies literary, physical, and temporal alienation, as well as alienation through perspective, characterization, and lack of communication. Ch. 4 discusses the regime's coercive force vs the opposition's disruptive force, concluding that the manner in which these forces are linked in the censored literature 'suggests the omnipotence of the regime and the futility of disruptive protest'. Ch. 5 examines various groups within Francoist society and how their interaction with the regime and with one another maintains the oppressive society of the former. Ch. 6 concludes by explaining how all the aforementioned aspects facilitated the preparation for a political transition. Catherine Davies, *Spanish Women's Writing 1849–1996*, London, The Athlone Press, 334 pp., is a study that, following Kirkpatrick's findings, departs from 1846, the moment by which women's place in literature had been established, and aims to foreground a feminine literary tradition (with its distinctive cultural and political agenda) subsequent to that period through an examination of 150 years of women's writing from a feminist perspective. Of particular importance to this section are part II (1912–44), which analyses works by C. de Burgos, Montseny, Chacel, and Laforet, and part III (1944–96), which focuses on texts by Rodoreda, Martín Gaite, Tusquets, Falcón, Conde, and Diosdado. *Spanish Women Writers and the Essay. Gender, Politics, and the Self*, ed. Kathleen M. Glenn and Mercedes Mazquiarán de Rodríguez, Missouri U.P., 294 pp., is an excellent book that explains why the essay, traditionally considered as a 'masculine' form, is an attractive genre for Spanish women writers and how they have reshaped it with the incorporation of a variety of strategies that aim to capture and influence the reader. It contains 13 sections (including the introduction) written by different scholars on essays by Arenal, Bazán, C. de Burgos, Martínez Sierra, Nelken, Chacel, Zambrano, Martín Gaite, Falcón, Roig, Puértolas, and Montero. M. A. Soler,

'Literatura y crítica en la revista *Nuestra España* (1939–1941)', *Ojáncano*, 14:29–42, calls attention to the first exile magazine, *Nuestra España*, published monthly in Cuba, 1939–41. J. Escalona Ruiz, 'El exilio literario desde *Ibérica*', *ib.*, 65–76, is of a documentary nature, mainly highlighting the importance of the journal *Ibérica por la libertad*, founded in New York by Spanish exiles. E.R. concentrates on the literary coverage from 1953–64; the latter being the year when it focused on politics until its demise in 1974.

2. PROSE

(This section includes 1997 materials postponed from vol. 59)

GENERAL

Daniel Gier, *La Castilla rural en la narrativa de posguerra*, Junta de Castilla y León, Consejería de Educación y Cultura, 1997, 144 pp., analyses the correspondence between novels, travelling books, essays, and articles written from 1898 to 1974 that deal with the Castilian landscape and its 'reality' during those years. G.'s study includes texts by Unamuno, Azorín, Ortega y Gasset, Pérez de Ayala, Arconada, Cela, Fernández Santos, Ferres, Caballero Bonald, Nieto, López Pacheco, Delibes, J. Goytisolo, Sánchez Ferlosio, and Aldecoa, and argues that a recurrent duality interweaves in these texts: while in some descriptions the Castilian field is represented as a place in which the farmers' work is sentimentally combined with a tergiversated vision of the landscape, in other descriptions, the same texts present a less subjective approach to the concrete experiences of the farmer and his particular difficulties, and even include suggestions for solutions. The fourth edition of Martínez Cachero's wide-ranging book, *La novela española entre 1936 y el fin de siglo. Historia de una aventura*, M, Castalia, 1997, 877 pp., adds a useful commented bibliography of criticism about the Spanish novel published between 1936 and 1995 to the six chapters of previous editions. Juan Ángel Juristo, *Ni Mirto ni Laurel. Tres años de narrativa española*, M, Huerga & Fierro, 1997, 274 pp., is a collection of 56 commented reviews of novels by authors such as Matute, Landero, García Morales, Llamazares, Aparicio, Grandes, Marías, Chirbes, Martín Gaite, and Merino, as well as other postwar writers. According to J.'s preface, this compilation of reviews, previously published in *El Mundo* (1994–96), has a double purpose: to attest to the occupation of today's literary critic and to justify it in view of factors such as the politics of the post-Franco era, the academic institutions, the competition between publishing houses, the market, and the mass media. J. Gracia, 'Crónica de la narrativa española', *CHA*, 565–66, 1997:257–61, is mostly devoted to reviews of memoirs and novels centred on the reconstruction of private experiences, including Pardo's *Autorretrato sin retoques*, Castilla del Pino's *Pretérito imperfecto*, Martínez Sarrión's *Una juventud*, Cercas's *El vientre de la ballena*, Martínez de Pisón's *Carreteras secundarias*, Casavella's *Un enano español se suicida en Las Vegas*, Casares's *Dios sentado en un sillón azul*, Fonollosa's *Poetas en la noche*, and Vila-Matas's *Extraña forma de vida*. T. R. Franz, 'Mist and mountain in three sagas of Cela, Montero, and García Márquez', *Ojáncano*, 12, 1997 : 69–80, discusses mountain and mist as well as their closest and clearest determiners as common symbols in Cela's *Mazurca para dos muertos*, Rosa Montero's *Temblor*, and García Márquez's *Cien años de soledad* in order to show 'the process by which these symbols create meaning absent from or unfocused in the purely narrative dimension of the works'. C. Murcia, 'Écriture romanesque et mémoire historique dans le roman espagnol postfranquiste', *RLC*, 1997, no.2 : 191–97, argues that the presence of the Civil War's collective memory as a literary theme in novels such as Llamazares's *Luna de lobos*, *La lluvia amarilla* and *El río del olvido*, Vázquez Montalbán's *Galíndez*, Azúa's *Cambio de bandera*, Atxaga's *Obabakoak* and *El hombre solo*, Molina Foix's *La quincena soviética*, and Guelbenzu's *La tierra prometida* operates as a 'counter-example' in the narrative of the 80s and 90s, which tends to treat subjects of actuality, leaving behind '*la España negra*' and its political history. E. Bouju, 'Transition démocratique et déplacement des repères romanesque en Espagne (1976–86)', *ib.*, 199–210, claims that from the late 70s the Spanish novel is engaged in a reconstruction of an aesthetic modernity based on a 'universal intertextuality', in which foreign genres and sub-genres (e.g. journalistic chronicle, science fiction, detective novel, and *roman noir*) function as references mostly for ironic and demystifying ends. Umbral, Montero, Grosso, Maldonado, Pinilla, C. García, Buiza, Bermúdez Castillo, Saiz Cidoncha, Rato, Calle, Ferrero, Muñoz Molina, Guelbenzu, Vázquez Montalbán, Mendoza, Ortiz, Mayoral, Millás, Guerra Garrido, Savater, Sastre, Torrente Ballester, Benet, and Marsé are among the authors covered. T. Dorca, 'Joven narrativa en la España de los noventa: la generación X', *REH*, 31, 1997 : 309–24, successfully defends the literary quality of the novel of the 90s through a 'recontextualization' focused on aspects such as techniques of composition, themes, and cosmic vision. D.'s study includes Juan Bonilla's *Nadie conoce a nadie*, Gabriela Bustelo's *Veo Veo*, Martín Casariego's *Qué te voy a contar* and *Mi precio es ninguno*, Ismael Grasa's *De Madrid al cielo*, Ray Loriga's *Lo peor de todo* and *Caídos del cielo*, Pedro Maestre's *Matando dinosaurios con tirachinas*, José Ángel Mañas's *Mensaka* and *Historias del Kronen*, Daniel Múgica's *La ciudad de abajo*, and Benjamín Prado's *Nunca le des la mano a un pistolero zurdo*. J. Marí, 'Embrujos visuales: cine y narración en Marsé y Muñoz Molina', *ib.*, 449–74, analyses Muñoz Molina's *Beltenebros* and Marsé's

El embrujo as examples of a type of postmodern novel that incorporates references, themes, conventions and narrative tools taken from films, and argues that a fascination with the experience of narration is one of the consequences that this incorporation has on the reading processes of both novels, in which a different approach to the 'reality' of the narration is presented. G. Navajas, 'De Unamuno a Antonio Muñoz Molina. El proyecto moderno y el siglo XXI', *Siglo XX*, 15, 1997: 131–46, proposes that, from a cultural perspective, *la modernidad* is not a finished entity, as thinkers such as Lyotard suggest, but a non-limited model of understanding which is receptive to changes and to enlargements of the options' repertory. N. establishes a parallelism between Unamuno and Muñoz Molina, and argues that these authors can be considered as different paradigms of modernism despite the century that separates them in time.

C. X. Ardavín, 'La novela española del desencanto político', *Ojáncano*, 15:47–59, sees the novel as a good yardstick to measure the political disenchantment during the transition to democracy in Spain, but emphasizes 'la inexistencia de una interpretación unívoca del desencanto por parte de la novelística postfranquista'. At the same time, it highlights the focal point given to memory in the novels of this period. J. Ferrer Solá, 'La estética del fracaso en la actual narrativa española', *CHA*, 579:17–25, reviews the 'aesthetics of failure' which F.S. claims have as a first referent Laforet's *Nada*. He includes the work of Delibes, Juan Antonio Zunzunegui, Francisco Candel, Antonio Rabinad, and Ignacio Aldecoa from the Franco period, and swiftly moves on to cover up to the end of the century, with works by José Ángel Mañas, Francisco Casavella, José A. Garriga Vela, Pedro Maestre, and Ramón de España. F. Valls, 'El bulevar de los sueños rotos', *ib.*, 27–37, includes works that show disenchantment and the moving away from utopias, from Lourdes Ortiz's *Luz de la memoria* (1976) to Belén Gopegui's *La conquista del aire* (1998). V. alludes to the apathy that rules the day in terms of political engagement, but also warns about the dangerous simplistic conclusions that could lead to compare this attitude with that of those in power before. Some authors covered are: Juan José Millás, José María Merino, Juan José Armas Marcelo, Esther Tusquets, José María Guelbenzu, Mariano Antolín Rato, José Antonio Gabriel y Galán, and Manuel Vicent. J. Gracia, 'Una resaca demasiado larga: literatura y política en la novela de la democracia', *ib.*, 39–47, highlights the lack of political engagement in what has been called 'literatura light'. G. claims the political is still rooted in the post-war period under Franco. He calls attention to the elements that escape today's novels, which pay little attention to analytic minutiae. J. Rodríguez, 'Memoria y voz narrativa', *ib.*, 49–58, claims the emphasis of the narrative of the last quarter of the century is on individuality, portrayed through the abundance of autobiographical and first person narration and the importance given to memory in today's narrative. J. Gracia, 'Entrevista con José-Carlos Mainer', *ib.*, 59–70, is an illuminating interview on the subject of the novel post–1975, with particular reference to some authors and their works, such as Luis Mateo Díez, Javier Marías, Muñoz Molina, Vázquez Montalbán, and Miguel Sánchez-Ostiz, among others. M. L. Abellán, 'Conquista y rechazo de la literatura del exilio: Sender, Ayala y Aub', *Ojáncano*, 14: 19–28, is on the role of censorship during the Franco years and how it affected the publication and distribution of works by writers included in the title.

R. C. Spires, 'Discursive constructs and Spanish fiction of the 1980s', *JNT*, 27.1 : 128–46, focuses on Luis Goytisolo's *Teoría del conocimiento* (1981), Cristina Fernández Cubas's *El año de Gracia*, and Javier Marías's *Todas las almas* (1989), studying their relationship with contemporary theoretical debates and socio-historical facts.

INDIVIDUAL AUTHORS

ALDECOA. José Manuel Marrero Henríquez, *Documentación y lirismo en la narrativa de Ignacio Aldecoa*, Las Palmas de Gran Canaria U.P., 1997, 252 pp., studies A.'s narrative in the context of manifestos and debates of the 50s and 60s about available literary options, arguing that, although A. puts his style in service of social themes, he does not subscribe to pre-established paradigms (e.g. the Marxist postulates of social realism, the existential metaphysics of the transcendental novel, or the abstract forms of objectivism), but rather to a poetic narrative (comparable to Baudelaire's poetic prose) which is informed by the 'difference in repetition' of multiple literary models.

ATXAGA. J. A. Ascunce Arrieta, 'Planos autobiográficos en *Memorias de una vaca* de Bernardo Atxaga', *Versantes*, 31, 1997 : 107–26, analyses the novel as composed of two narrative nuclei, a biographical one associated with the fact of existence (the first eight chapters) and a creative one associated with the fact of writing (the last chapter), arguing that the latter is subordinated by the former, even if, from the point of view of the story's materiality, the opposite appears to be the truth.

AUB. V. Geninazza, 'L'apprendistato di un "falsario": *Luis Álvarez Petreña* di Max Aub', *Acme*, 50.3, 1997: 251–66, studies the three editions of this first work of A. (published in 1934, 1965, and 1971) and its connection with other works — e.g. *Jusep Torres Campalans* (1958) and *Antología traducida* (1963) — demonstrating that the taste for the creation of phoney biography and other fabrications is a constant characteristic of A.'s literary career.

CABALLERO BONALD. M. J. Ramos Ortega, 'El escenario del mito en la narrativa de Caballero Bonald', *ECon*, 11.2:27–42, points to the world of C.B.'s childhood as the source for his creativity in the cycle from *Ágata ojo de gato* (1974) up to *Campo de Agramante* (1992), works marked by memory and anticipation. R.O. claims that C.B. brings myth to bear on the existential issues relevant to us today.

CASTILLA DEL PINO. J. M. Pozuelo Yvancos, 'Función narrativa, perspectivismo y construcción del otro en *Una alacena tapiada* de Carlos Castilla del Pino', *RO*, 197, 1997:61–73, is a compelling study of the unidentified narrator of the novel, indicating that his function is to objectivate and thus neutralize the perspectivism inherent in the information and deductive processes of the other characters, thereby reconstructing the circumstances of his protagonist's suicide with a 'superior' knowledge.

CELA. K. G. Eller, 'Cela's *Oficio de tinieblas 5*: nihilism, demolition and reconstruction of the novel', *Neophilologus*, 81, 1997:223–29, claims that C.'s text creates a 'ritual of darkness' which represents the absolute rejection of commonly accepted beliefs, facts, and traditions. E.'s argument about the reader, who, in the critic's words, is 'left with a rather original reading experience which is strange, humorous and entertaining as well as frustrating, depressing, shocking and offensive', seems more convincing than his argument about C.'s attempt to change literature, rather than politics or society, through his demolition and recreation of the knowledge found in history books, encyclopedias, ancient and modern texts, and the Bible. E.'s article also includes a brief but interesting discussion about the work's value as literature.

CHACEL. M. Mori, 'Rosa Chacel en su diario', *RO*, 209:101–18, calls attention to the diary of Rosa Chacel, particularly the third and last volume, *Estación termini*, which puts an end to *Alcancía*, which covers over 40 years of C.'s life. C. Janés, 'Rosa Chacel: la pasión por la libertad y una página borrada', *ib.*, 119–34, is an overview of the topic of freedom as presented in C.'s works, starting with her first novel, *Estación. Ida y vuelta*, which J. affirms 'Era nada menos que la invención del *Nouveau Roman* treinta años antes de que apareciera en Francia'.

DELIBES. T. Boucher, 'Delibes and "the question concerning technology"', *Ojáncano*, 15:33–46, is on the connection between D.'s two rural novels *El tesoro* and *El disputado voto del señor Cayo*. B. focuses 'specifically on Heidegger's concept of the essence of technology' in the essay mentioned in the title. B. claims that D.'s novels respond 'to a post-romantic questioning of the relationship between man and nature in much the same mode as Heidegger'.

ESPINA. O. Ayala, 'Antonio Espina. Los años oscuros', *ECon*, 11.1:41–59, rescues the Republican E., concerning the years from his imprisonment and admission to a mental hospital until he went into exile. A. focuses on E.'s life; of importance are some letters that had not been published before.

ESPINOSA. J. I. Moraza, 'Miguel Espinosa: estudio introductorio (I)', *Ojáncano*, 12, 1997:81–103, is a sophisticated study in three sections: the first deals with the life and general stature of E. (1929–82), the second focuses on his essays, and the third on his fiction. In M.'s view, E.'s entire work has not yet received the critical attention it deserves. Id., 'Miguel Espinosa: estudio introductorio (II)', *ib.*, 15:3–31, examines the characteristics of E.'s work as he attempts to bring academic rigour to his fiction in a somewhat Borgesian way; particular attention is given to *Escuela de mandarines*, *La fea burguesía* and *Tríbada*.

GOYTISOLO, JUAN. P. J. Smith, 'Juan Goytisolo and Jean Baudrillard: the mirror of production and the death of symbolic exchange', *Antípodas*, 8–9, 1997:111–29, a reprint of the text that appeared originally in *Representing the Other* (OUP, 1992), shows how neither G. nor B. can avoid the trap of idealizing the marginal or deviant subject when they set it up as the paradigm of rebellion, despite these authors' shared commitment to the cause of cultural pluralism and their mutual awareness of the problems involved in attempting to 'represent' the Other. For the cultural critic, concludes S., 'their failures in this area may be as important as their successes'. T. Jermyn, 'The accursed share: sacrifice in Juan Goytisolo's *Makbara*', *Neophilologus*, 81, 1997:231–51, is a reading of G.'s novel in the light of G. Bataille's theory of the desire to lose as the basis of human nature. J.'s study, which includes the treatment of sexuality in *Makbara*, shows both 'the fundamental difference that exists between the two writers vis-à-vis significance of eroticism in the social sphere, and how this difference reveals a basic contradiction' in G.'s work.

GOYTISOLO, LUIS. M. Pillado-Miller, 'Una lectura rizomática de *La paradoja del ave migratoria*, de Luis Goytisolo', *REH*, 31, 1997:113–27, applies the concept of *rizoma* developed by Deleuze and Guattari in *Mille plateaux* to G.'s novel, suggesting that this concept can illuminate the novel's underlying process of transformation and repetition which frustrates any critical attempt to systematize the material of the text. A. M. Sobiesuo, 'History and artifice in Luis Goytisolo's *Recuento*', *CH*, 20.1–2:99–106, examines the manipulation of Spanish history in G.'s first novel of the tetralogy *Antagonía*; structure and content are the focal points of this analysis.

LAFORET. A. G. Andreu, 'Huellas textuales en el *bildungsroman* de Andrea', *RLit*, 59, 1997:595–605, compares Andrea's *bildungsroman* with other examples of the genre, and claims that it has particular characteristics due to the plurality of textual layers which deny the apparent effect of continuity and coherence of Andrea's narration, and, consequently, the aspect of evolution and development of the protagonist. The absence of B. Jordan's work on *Nada* in the context of A.'s study is a serious oversight.

MARÍAS. R. Christie, '*Corazón tan blanco:* the evolution of a success story', *MLR*, 93:83–93, is a reading of M.'s novel in the light of the neo-Darwinian ideas of Richard Dawkins and Daniel Dennett applied to cultural issues, extrapolated here to offer a new reading of M.'s text.

MARINA. F. J. Higuero, 'Doble deconstrucción en *Elogio y refutación del ingenio*, de José Antonio Marina', *Ojáncano*, 14:3–17, concentrates on the role of the signifier as manifested in the essay in the title, which emphasizes the deconstruction of 'reality', where the signifier reigns supreme without any desire to reach ultimate signifieds; H. views M.'s use of language as a game moving away from teleological points.

MARSÉ. K. A. Thorne, 'The revolution that wasn't': sexual and political decay in Marsé's *Últimas tardes con Teresa*', *HR*, 65, 1997:93–105, pays original attention to the play of homosexual desire and its connection to societal boundaries in the novel, arguing that this desire (upon which the entire text hinges) 'is responsible for the anti-hero's fate and will serve to keep in place the stranglehold of class divisions'.

MARTÍN GAITE. M. S. Collins, 'Inscribing the space of female identity in Carmen Martín Gaite's *Entre visillos*', *Symposium*, 51.2, 1997:66–78, argues that space and spatial relations play an essential role in M.G.'s novel, in which they function structurally and symbolically to inscribe the subjectivity of the major, primarily female characters. C. M. Jaffe, 'Patterns of fiction and desire: childhood reading in Carmen Martín Gaite's *Retahílas*', *MLN*, 112, 1997:182–200, analyses the novel in the light of J. Wyatt's account of women's reading (1990) in order to show how the novel's narrative concerns (in particular, the entanglement of life and literature) are illuminated by scenes of the childhood reading of the female protagonist. M.G.'s evocation of childhood reading — so argues J. — also 'calls into question the status and practices of the reader(s) of her own novel'. D. J. McGiboney, '*El cuarto de atrás* de Carmen Martín Gaite: space, text, and inscription', *CRR*, 17:79–85, examines 'the restrictive and patriarchal characteristics' of the mysterious visitor in M.G.'s novel.

MARTÍN-SANTOS. A. Acereda, 'Tiempo de silencio: el lenguaje como subversión', *Ojáncano*, 12, 1997:43–55, analyses the novel's language (particularly its neologisms, word games, paronomasias, antitheses, paradoxes, hyperboles, comparisons, metaphors, etc.) as an instrument of protest against the empty rhetoric of Franco's regime.

MENDOZA. M. Herráez, 'La otra cara de lo histórico', *CHA*, 561, 1997:127–29, discusses M.'s *Una comedia ligera*, highlighting the differences between this novel and the author's previous production, in which, so claims H., historicism was not as consubstantial in the corpus of the text as it is in *Una comedia*, a novel that also rejects irony as a necessary element of postmodern narrative.

MOIX. C. Arkinstall, 'Ana María Moix's *Las virtudes peligrosas* and the theatre of the gaze', *BHS(L)*, 75:201–19, centres on the short story in the title, but without losing sight of other stories that also form the collection of the same title. A. examines the symbolic importance of the Paris opera theatre as a setting, paying particular attention to 'the representation of narcissism and its association with lesbianism in Western patriarchal thought'. R. Cornejo-Parriego, 'Desde el innominado deseo: transgresión y marginalidad de la mirada en "Las virtudes peligrosas" de Ana María Moix', *ALEC*, 23:607–21, explores the reciprocity of the female gaze in this short story, and the diversity of interpretation to which the work has been subjected, usually being included by critics within a lesbian discourse. R. Krauel, 'Funambulismo sobre la frontera de un género: "una novela" de Ana María Moix', *ib.*, 23:641–53, is on the issues of genre concerning the brief text 'Una novela' which has also been classified as poetry.

MONTERO, ISAAC. Eufemia Sánchez de la Calle, *Isaac Montero: Pionero de la novela española de posguerra*, M, Pliegos, 1997, 174 pp., studies M.'s life and narrative work, arguing that the latter evidences a formal evolution (the three periods studied in chapters 3, 4, and 5) without ever abandoning the denunciatory purposes characteristic of social realism.

MONTERO, ROSA. J. Escudero, 'Rosa Montero a la luz de sus fantasmas', *REH*, 31, 1997:333–48, is an account of E.'s interview with M. about the key aspects of her work, her journalistic career, and her ideas about politics and other themes of actuality, followed by the author's response to it ('Vivir en una nube', *ib.*, 348–51). K. Thompson-Casado, 'Elements of the *novela negra* in Rosa Montero's *Te trataré como una reina*', *ECon*, 10.2, 1997:21–34, studies the elements of this traditional masculinist genre in M.'s novel, indicating that they play the double role of exposing the conservatism of the genre and of challenging the reader's social attitudes, therefore pushing him/her to examine his/her own interpretations.

MUÑOZ MOLINA. W. Sherzer. '*El jinete polaco*: the autobiographical fiction of Antonio Muñoz Molina', *ECon* 10.1, 1997:7–22, is a superb study of the structural elements (in particular, narrative voice, temporality, and closure or resolution) and their role in the creation of the meaning of the novel as autobiographical fiction. Theoretical writings on autobiography by W. L. Howard, P. Lejeune, and J. Starobinski, as well as other novels by M.M. are included within the context of the article. L. Fernández Martínez, 'La proximidad de los fantasmas: *Beatus ille* y *El jinete polaco* de Antonio Muñoz Molina', *Versantes*, 31, 1997:77–106, examines the similarities between the two novels, and argues that these connections reveal the creation of a personal imaginary world which at the same time implies the reflection of a collective experience. E. Amann, 'Genres in dialogue: Antonio Muñoz Molina's *El jinete polaco*', *RCEH*, 23:1–21, analyses the 'conflation of diverse literary genres', concentrating on the dominant discourses present: the Byzantine novel, the gothic, and the *Bildungsroman*. The novel is contrasted to *Frankenstein*. The interaction of genres and the socio-political message also receive critical attention.

ORTIZ. C. M. Rivera Villegas, 'Cuerpo, palabra y autodescubrimiento en *Urraca*, de Lourdes Ortiz', *BHS(L)*, 74, 1997:307–14, claims that the novel exemplifies the main characteristics of feminist narrative of self-discovery as they appear in Rita Felski's *Beyond Feminist Aesthetics: Feminist Literature and Social Change* (1989).

POMBO. W. J. Weaver III, 'Literatura y cultura popular en *Telepena de Celia Cecilia Villalobo*', *Ojáncano*, 14:43–63, studies the role of high culture and popular culture in Álvaro Pombo's 1995 novel. W. claims television becomes the focal point of the novel, highlighting the erasure of boundaries between reality and fiction.

PRADA. J. A. Pérez Bowie, 'La historia como ficción en *Las máscaras del héroe*, de Juan Manuel de Prada', *ECon*, 11.2:61–72, centres on metaliterature and the creative process of reinventing the past in P.'s work.

ROJAS. D. Glad, 'The demons of Carlos Rojas', *WLT*, 71.1, 1997:75–80, proposes to introduce the non-Spanish-reading public to Rojas's fiction through the study of three periods: his early work (1957–68), his later work (1978–90), and his last novel to date, *Alfonso de Borbón habla con el demonio* (1995).

SÁNCHEZ FERLOSIO. K. G. McConnell, 'The geographical frame in *El Jarama*: an implied reminder of the Spanish Civil War', *ECon* 10.1, 1997:37–53, looks at the geographical references of the novel from an historical perspective to show how they are not arbitrary points in space but implied reminders of the war. I. D'Ors, 'Nombre, rostro e identidad: Rafael Sánchez Ferlosio, teoría y práctica narrativa', *ALEC*, 23:623–39, is on the importance of face and name in terms of identity, concentrating on the thematic aspect of *El testimonio de Yarfoz*, a travel narrative without a teleological purpose, at the same time that it takes into account other works such as *Las semanas del jardín*.

SAVATER. P. J. Smith. 'Social space and symbolic power: Fernando Savater's intellectual field', *MLR*, 93:54–68, studies Savater's *Contra las patrias* and *Ética como amor propio* in the light of Bourdieu's theories of 'intellectual field' as the articulation of the space between works, producers, and institutions, suggesting that S. 'comes to occupy the finely balanced position of what Bourdieu calls the "consecrated heretic" or "heresiarch", and Savater's political and philosophical analyses are underwritten by unacknowledged movements from the social to the symbolic and back again'.

SENDER. M. J. Schneider, 'Thematic representation and "skiascopic" vision in Ramón Sender's *El rey y la reina*', *MLN*, 112, 1997:166–81, shows how the novel is about 'the interplay between aesthetic and individuation on the one hand, and politics and history on the other' by means of an excellent study of an aspect generally overlooked by scholars: the relational import of 'thematic clusters' within the structure of the novel. H. Ahumada Peña, '*El lugar del hombre* de Ramón J. Sender, la validación social como vía de acceso a la dignidad humana', *RCL*, 52:83–92, is on the social context of S.'s novel *El lugar del hombre* (1939); A.P. highlights the importance of reflecting on human nature and the role of the individual in society in S.'s work.

SERRANO PONCELA. A. Villagrá, 'Voces revividas del exilio en *La viña de Nabot* de Segundo Serrano Poncela', *Ojáncano*, 14:77–88, focuses on S.P.'s novel, published posthumously, which marks the end of his entire career in exile. V. studies the testimonial value of the novel in terms of exile writing.

UMBRAL. P. J. Smith, 'Modern Times: Francisco Umbral's chronicle of distinction', *MLN*, 113:324–38, is food for thought on the role of U.'s writing in Spain, and his 'aestheticization of everyday life'. S. claims 'that Umbral's writing practice, unique in Spain, is exemplary of Bourdieu's concept of "distinction" or "the judgment of taste"'.

VÁZQUEZ. J. Gracia, '*La vida perra de Juanita Narboni* de Ángel Vázquez', *CHA*, 568, 1997:113–15, defines the novel as both a chronicle and a confession, and argues that Juanita's recount of her life in Tangiers, a life of solitude and alienation, represents the antithesis of usual narratives about Tangiers. Memory and irony as thematic and structural devices are other aspects of the novel discussed in G.'s article.

VÁZQUEZ MONTALBÁN. G. Tyras, 'Manuel Vázquez Montalbán ou la réinvention du roman (noir) à la mort de Franco', *RLC*, 1997, no.2:210–24, studies V.M.'s literary trajectory, seeing *Galíndez* (1990) as the culmination of a literary project which is mostly based on referential tension and hermeneutic code. J. F. Colmeiro, 'Dissonant voices: memory and counter-memory in Manuel Vázquez Montalbán's *Autobiografía del general Franco*', *STCL*, 21.2:337–59, shows how V.M.'s novel challenges conventional notions of authorship, referentiality, and self-referentiality, thereby forcing the reader 'to examine the dissonant discourses of historiography and memory and to ascertain the political function of writing as counter-discourse'. W. C. Ríos-Font, 'Literary value, cultural production, and postmodern fragmentation: Manuel Vázquez Montalbán and the Spanish literary institution', *REH*, 32:375–84, develops an interesting discussion about the task of academic literary criticism upon the critical reactions provoked by Montalbán's work, particularly his bestsellers, the detective narratives.

ZAMBRANO. F. La Rubia-Prado, 'Filosofía y poesía: María Zambrano y la retórica de la reconciliación', *HR*, 65, 1997:199–216, analyses Z.'s *Filosofía y poesía*, claiming that Z. examines the dynamics between philosophy and poetry from an analytic stance and, at the same time, from a very concrete practical position of writing which is based on the notion of 'organic form' and the cosmic vision created by it.

3. POETRY

GENERAL

J. J. Lanz, 'La joven poesía española. Notas para una periodización', *HR*, 66:261–87, studies the interaction between the poetic generation of 1968 and younger generations, arguing that all these generations have influenced one another and have maintained a certain continuity in their evolution, despite the plurality of tendencies evidenced in their poetry since the 'novísimos' onwards. L.'s article includes an interesting debate concerning the proliferation of poetic anthologies from the 1970s to the present time. J. M. Parreño, 'Noni Benegas: sobre poesía escrita por mujeres', *RO*, 208:77–91, is an interview with B. about her wide-ranging anthology of contemporary women's poetry. Questions presented include: the anthology as a strategic device to challenge the literary canon, women as subjects rather than objects of the poem, language re-possession as a key element in feminine poetry, special critical tools required for the study of women's poetry, consequences of women's entrance into the literary canon, relevance of the so-called 'poetry of experience' in contemporary women's poetry, and feminist dimensions of the latter.

INDIVIDUAL AUTHORS

ALONSO. D. Villanueva, 'Dámaso Alonso uno y dual', *RO*, 210:27–37, examines A.'s *Vida y Obra*, initially published in 1984 and reproduced in *Antología de nuestro monstruoso mundo. Duda y amor sobre el Ser Supremo* (Cátedra, 1985), emphasizing interior tensions such as faith vs doubt, professional vs creative aspirations, and deep horror vs child-like vitality.

BRINES. C. J. Morales, 'Toda la poesía de Francisco Brines', *CHA*, 573:149–52, is on the collection of B.'s works published by Tusquets in 1997.

CIRLOT. 'Dossier: Cirlot y el no-dónde', *Barcarola*, 53, 1997:51–191, is dedicated to the life and works of Juan-Eduardo Cirlot.

CRESPO. B. Matamoro, 'La realidad entera: visión del mundo y la labor poética de Ángel Crespo', *CHA*, 575:121–28, examines the chronological organization of C.'s latest work, the three volumes of *Poesía* (Ciudad Real, 1926–Barcelona, 1995), arguing that, since C. subscribes to a 'progressive' strategy of publication, comparable to that of Juan Ramón Jiménez or Jorge Guillén, *Poesía* should be considered as the canonical edition of C.'s poetic work.

DOCE. C. J. Morales, 'El aliento y la memoria: diálogos', *CHA*, 575:135–36, is a review of *Diálogos en la sombra*, D.'s third poetry book.

FAGUNDO. Silvia Rolle, *La obra de Ana María Fagundo: una poética femenino-feminista*, M, Fundamentos, 1997, 285 pp., is divided into 3 chapters: 'Tres etapas de una trayectoria poética', 'Cuerpo femenino/cuerpo textual', and 'Vida/arte: dos obras de creación'. R.'s study covers F.'s total poetic output, examining some of the constants in F.'s poetry, such as the presence of the island and the death of her father in her earlier works, the use of poetry as an act of discovery, and F.'s feminine/feminist poetics. The book also includes a useful bibliography for any scholar working on F.'s poetry.

FERNÁNDEZ CALVO. J. Cenizo Jiménez, 'La poesía de Manuel Fernández Calvo', *Alaluz*, 30.2:32–37, is brief and more impressionist than analytic, on metrics and themes, especially on the role of religion in the work of this priest and poet.

FUERTES. M. Payeras Grau, 'Gloria Fuertes posee la poesía', *Alaluz*, 30.2:7–31, is a broad study of the constant elements in terms of thought and style, present in F.'s works, particularly the role of themes and language, and includes a mini-anthology of F.'s poetry (20–31).

GARCÍA MONTERO. C. González-Badía, '*Completamente viernes*: una cala en la vida y en la esperanza', *CHA*, 575:142–44, analyses G.M.'s recent book (1998), seeing it as the continuation of a poetic trajectory initiated in *Las flores del frío* (1991) and *Habitaciones separadas* (1994), in which love, the autobiographical experience and the valorization of the quotidian appear as central postulates of his poetry.

4. DRAMA

GENERAL

C. Leonard, '*Agonía* and *Sueños de Ginebra*: Spanish alternative theatre at the end of the twentieth century', *ALEC*, 23:733–49, sets the background on Spanish alternative theatre and then concentrates on the metadramatic play *Agonía* by Luis Miguel González Cruz, and on the feminist play *Sueños de Ginebra* by Juan Mayorga. Both writers are selected as representative of this generation, and L. claims that 'while theatre in general and Alternative Theatre in particular do not play a large role in Spanish society at the close of the twentieth century, they remain significant'. M. F. Vilches de Frutos, 'La temporada teatral española 1995–1996', *ib.*, 849–96, complies with the documentation role of this project. V.F. acknowledges a positive change in attitude with reference to the topic of 'crisis teatral'. Of special interest for this section are pp. 855–61. F. Martín Iniesta, 'Teatro español en la democracia', *CHA*, 572:95–98, gives an overall picture of theatre during and after Franco, which might be of little interest to specialists. R. Mahieu, 'Teatro en Cádiz', *ib.*, 573:75–78, is on the *Festival Iberoamericano de Teatro* and the cooperation between Latin America and Spain. Ó. Cornago Bernal, 'Bases teóricas para una historia de la escena española contemporánea', *Gestos*, 26:37–56, is an ambitious coverage of the diversity of approaches to theatre.

INDIVIDUAL AUTHORS

ALONSO DE SANTOS. C. Santolaria Solano, 'José Luis Alonso de Santos y el teatro independiente: veinte años de vinculación (1960–1980)', *ALEC*, 23:791–810, is a documentary account of the life and work of A.S., highlighting the formative years of the playwright which led to his success post-Franco. P. Thompson, '*Bajarse al moro*: a socio-political examination of the "family" and contemporary Spain', *ib.*, 811–19, is on the significance of the play in examining the traditional family values imposed by the Franco regime, parodying the fact that they are still in place post–1975, co-existing with progressive idealism.

BUERO VALLEJO. S. Monti, 'Goya en las tablas. *El sueño de la razón* de Buero Vallejo', *ALEC*, 23:775–89, studies this play's intertextuality with Goya's paintings, and compares it with other works by B.V. The paintings are seen as the main referent of the dialogue.

FALCÓN. M. Halsey, 'A history of their own: the long road of women's memory in Lidia Falcón's *Las mujeres caminaron con el fuego del siglo*', *CH*, 20.1–2:57–67, points out that the play represents history rewritten by women. H. studies the autonomy given to women in F.'s work, both in terms of vision and expression. H. covers the importance of gender in this play, and claims F. 'gives us a history of feminism in Catalonia'.

MARTÍN RECUERDA. Ángel Cobo Rivas, *José Martín Recuerda: Vida y obra dramática*, Caja General de Ahorros de Granada, 367 pp., analyses M. R.'s life (the social, political, religious, and familiar environment of his youth, his years at the University of Granada and the Instituto Padre Suárez, his work at the theatre of the University of Granada and Teatro de la Casa de América, his experience in Madrid and his emigration to the US, his return and professional work in the University of Salamanca) and dramatic work (dedicating a section to *El engañao y Caballos desbocaos*, the Lope de Vega prize in 1975).

V. CATALAN STUDIES

LANGUAGE

By Sílvia Llach and Pep Serra, *Universitat de Girona*, and Bernat Joan i Marí, *Universitat de les illes balears*

1. Phonetics and Phonology

J. Jiménez, 'Valencian vowel harmony', *RivL*, 10:137–61, analyses Valencian vowel harmony, a phenomenon by which the two [RTR] mid-vowels /ɛ/, /ɔ/ in stressed position spread the features Front and Round to the vowel /a/. Valencian vowel harmony is explained as a means to make the features of stressed [RTR] mid-vowels more perceptible, following the postulates of Optimal Domains Theory. The uniform behaviour of both vowels is made to follow from the fact that the features Front and Round belong to the same class, Colour features. P. Serra, 'El patró sil·làbic del sard a la fonologia de l'alguerès', Maninchedda, *Sardegna*, 511–21, studies two alternative processes that exist in the Catalan variety spoken in Alghero: the inclusion of a paragogic vowel in the consonantal group and the elimination of a consonant from the group. S. proposes that both processes follow the same purpose, i.e. a tendency to exclude final consonants. The article also suggests that this influence can be seen as a projection of Sardinian syllabic pattern in Algherian phonology. D. Recasens, M. D. Pallarès, and J. Fontdevila, 'An electropalatographic and acoustic study of temporal coarticulation for Catalan dark /l/ and German clear /l/', *Phonetica*, 55:53–79, aims to achieve a thorough understanding of the relative prominence of the consonantal and vocalic effects in lingual co-articulation in VCV sequences with consonants specified for different degrees of tongue dorsum involvement in their articulation. The results show that electropalatographic and F2 frequency data in /VlV/ sequences reveal more prominent C-to-V effects for Catalan dark /l/ than for German clear /l/, which is in agreement with the existence of high lingual requirements on the formation of two constriction places for dark /l/. M. Wheeler, 'Fonètica històrica i teoria fonològica', *Actes* (Palma), 299–337, summarizes some recent elements of General Linguistics to contribute to wider and more explicative historical phonetics. In particular, the author uses three currents of linguistics: the relation

---

* The editor wishes to thank Daniel Grau for his assistance in co-ordinating this section.

between phonetics and phonology (Ohala), prosodic theory (especially Optimality Theory), and the Labovian view on the regularity of phonetic change and lexical diffusion. E. Bonet and M. R. Lloret, *Fonologia Catalana*, B, Ariel, 222 pp., present a description and a systematical analysis of the phonological phenomena in Central Catalan, based on the model of Classical Generative Phonology. *El món dels sons*, ed. M. A. Pradilla (Biblioteca Gregal, 1), Benicarló, Alambor, 212 pp., contains: J. Rafel, 'Teoria fonològica i inventari de fonemes' (17–30), on changing conceptions of the phoneme and other invariable categories; B. Palmada, 'Les preguntes i les respostes de la fonologia' (33–46), on the advantages of new directions in phonology, studying two different processes to demonstrate that the use of arguments from phonetics provide a functional explanation and increase the amount of realism in phonology; M. R. Lloret, 'L'ús de l'Alfabet Fonètic Internacional' (81–96), on some of the uses of the IPA (1993) for translating the sounds of Catalan; D. Recasens, 'Fonètica articulatòria experimental' (99–113), on electropalatography and magnetometry; and M. A. Pradilla, 'Entonació' (117–49), on the different perspectives involved in the study of intonation.

2. Lexis and Morphology

Gran Diccionari de la Llengua Catalana, B, Enciclopèdia Catalana, 1781 pp., is based on the *Diccionari de L'Enclopèdia Catalana* (3rd edn, 1993), including new items — new words admitted by the linguistic norm; a wider range of scientific and technical vocabulary; 6350 new entries; grammatical monographies; lists of vocabulary grouped by subjects; verbal models and dialectal varieties — and distinguishing between those entries accepted by the norm and those not accepted. The content of entries has been extended. I. Creus, R. González, and J. Julià, 'Dialectalismes i diccionaris: entre la tradició i la variació', *Sintagma*, 10:61–80, reflect on the presentation of dialectal features in some Catalan lexicographical texts, paying special attention to those problems which derive from lexical selection and the semantic scope of these units. At the same time, to these are added aspects inherent in the lexical component such as the internal or external variation they undergo. The examples used come in large part from research carried out for the preparation of the *Pronunciation Dictionary of North-western Catalan (Lleida variety)*.

J. Corbera, 'Les denominacions alguereses dels mamífers terrestres no domèstics, dels rèptils i dels petits invertebrats no artròpodes', Maninchedda, *Sardegna*, 567–81, studies the Algherian denomination of animals and underlines the influence of Sardinian and the Algherian intrinsic solutions. C. also comments on the graphical and identification errors which have appeared in the bibliography of this subject. M. Pérez Saldanya, *Del llatí al català: morfosintaxi verbal històrica* (Col·lecció Biblioteca Lingüística Catalana, 22), Valencia U.P., 329 pp., belongs to the tradition of studies on historical grammar, while incorporating a reinterpretation of the changes from the current perspectives and theoretic models. It gives a lot of importance to the factors that are the basis of the linguistic change: organization tendencies of the flexive paradigms, general cognitive principles, grammaticalizations of grammatical implications and syntactic reanalysis. R. Estopà, J. Vivaldi, and M. T. Cabré, *Sistemes d'extracció automàtica de (candidats a) termes: estat de la qüestió* (Papers de l'IULA. Sèrie Informes, 22), B, IULA, 66 pp., describe and compare the main systems of automatic terminology extraction so as to give an overview of the current state of the art, leading to the definition of criteria that could lead to the proposal of a methodology-combined system of terminology extraction. M. R. Lloret, 'Sobre l'estructura morfològica dels noms en català i en castellà', *Atti* (Palermo), II, 557–66, analyses the identification of the lexical basis — based on the proposal of identification between the lexeme and the traditional radical — and the grammatical character of the terminations of the Catalan and Spanish nouns: a distinction between the regular markers of gender and other terminations is suggested. L. Pons, 'Pronoms personals i possessius en català: varietat de formes a la llengua parlada', *ib.*, 679–91, deals with the concept of reference to the three grammatical persons, based on the material of the *Atles Lingüístic del Domini Català* (ALDC). The aspects related to the morphology or the phonetic nature of these elements are studied and a comparison is drawn between the observed results and the content, which follows from both the prescriptive and descriptive grammar. M. Grossman, 'Formazione dei nomi di agente, strumento e luogo in catalano', *ib.*, 383–92, studies the morphological processes which govern the formation of nouns with agentive, instrumental, and locative semantic roles in Catalan, distinguishing early levels of derivation, which always correspond to the formation of agentive nouns, and the later levels of derivation, which lead to instrumental and locative nouns, in this order. F. Esteve et al., 'El diccionari de l'Institut. Una aproximació sistemàtica', *EMarg*, 60 : 5–96, evaluate the *Diccionari de la Llengua Catalana* as a contribution to the Catalan lexicographical tradition, while analysing the explicit and implicit criteria which guided the project and its elaboration in order to determine their intrinsic consistency, their coherence towards the lexicographical tradition and, also, the systematization which has been applied to all this work. M. P. Perea, 'De re lexicogràfica', *ib.*, 96–120, compares dictionaries published from 1995 to 1997. This study mixes, both chronologically and typologically, the works published during this period, and underlines the newest and most important factors. Works establishing the terminology of different specialized fields include: C. Barberà, *Lèxic de les plagues i malalties dels conreus de Catalunya*, B, Institució Catalana d'Estudis Agraris, 117 pp.; M. M. Ramon, *Lèxic bàsic d'Internet català-anglès*, Palma de Mallorca, Universitat de les Illes Balears, 46 pp.; J. Úbeda, *Lèxic musical: els noms de la música*, Vilassar de Mar, Oikos-tau, 240 pp.; *Vocabulari de filosofia: català-castellà-anglès-alemany*, B, Servei de Llengua Catalana, Univ. de Barcelona, 84 pp.; *Vocabulari de ciències dels aliments: català-castellà-anglès-francès*, B, Servei de Llengua Catalana, Univ. de Barcelona, 58 pp.; *Vocabulari d'anatomia patològica: castellà, català, anglès*, B, Servei de Llengua Catalana, Univ. de Barcelona, 24 pp.; *Lèxic de les industries manufactureres: instruments musicals, jocs i joguines, joieria i bijuteria, fotografia, material esportiu*, B, Enciclopèdia Catalana, 63 pp.; *Lèxic de productes farmacèutics*, B, Enciclopèdia Catalana, 86 pp.; *Lèxic de béns d'equipament*, B, Enciclopèdia Catalana, 59 pp.; *Lèxic d'indústria bàsica i productes metàl·lics*, B, Enciclopèdia Catalana, 38 pp.; M. T. Cabré i Castellví, J. Freixa, and E. Solé, *Descripció quantitativa dels neologismes documentats durant l'any 1995 a la premsa en català* (Papers de l'IULA. Sèrie Informes, 23), B, IULA, 31 pp.

3. Syntax, Semantics, and Pragmatics

A. Fernández and G. Vázquez, 'Verbs d'actitud', *Sintagma*, 10:45–60, proposes a new semantic class of attitude predicates, defined intentionally, using syntactic as well as semantic criteria, and extensionally. The hypothesis upon which this work is based is that of Levin — verbs that have the same meaning also present an identical syntactic behaviour — even though there are several differences between this approach and hers. J. Roca Pons, 'Alguns aspectes de gramàtica catalana', *Actes* (Bloomington), 45–68, studies the behaviour of clitics and verbal aspect and mode, suggesting a new categorization, which arises from the use of clitics and aspect within the sentence. D. Adger and J. Quer, 'Clausal polar determiners in Catalan embedded questions', Fullana, *Central Romance*, 65–81, argue for the existence of Clausal Polarity Items (determiner-like polar elements that head unselected embedded questions), and account for the distribution and interpretation of embedded yes/no questions that are not selected by an interrogative matrix predicate. J. Solà, 'Clitics are inflection. Evidence from Catalan', *ib.*, 213–25, argues that Romance pronominal clitics are to be treated as inflectional affixes, and that this view, once implemented in Minimalist terms (i.e. making inflection trigger movement), allows for an interesting account of the proclisis/enclisis alternations in Catalan. L. Casanova, 'Un estudi tipològic del català col·loquial', *Sintagma*, 10:5–25, describes the word order of the basic constituents of the Catalan sentence. The study considers the preferred sentence within the different word orders, i.e. the sentence that is statistically more frequent. It compares the preferred sentence with the sentence with canonical word order: subject-verb-object. X. Villalba, 'Right dislocation is not right dislocation', *ib.*, 226–55, offers a comprehension analysis of dislocation processes in Catalan. It shows that CLRD (Clitic Right Dislocation) and CLLD (Clitic Left Dislocation) have a set of distinguishing properties which cannot be explained neither by an analysis taking CLRD to be the mirror image of CLLD nor by one taking CLRD to be the covert counterpart of CLLD. M. J. Cuenca, 'Processi di gramaticalizzazione: il caso dei connettivi in catalano e in spagnolo', *Atti* (Palermo), 195–204, studies the process of grammaticalization as a process through which an element acquires a grammatical function. This study is applied in particular to the Catalan and Spanish connectors, and emphasizes the aspects associated to this process, i.e., the modification of the meaning, the reinforcement of the pragmatic meaning and the change of category.

4. Sociolinguistics

J. Gifreu, 'L'espai comunicacional català', *Nació secreta*, 19–35, is on the construction of a communication area around the Catalan countries, sustained by several mass media. Antoni Artigues and Rosa Calafat, *Ecologia lingüística*, B, La Busca, 76 pp., show the relations between the general schema of Ecology for natural inter-action and the interaction between language communities. In some sense, the same kinds measures which are used to protect nature can be applied to language policy, in order to mantain some less used languages, in Europe and all around the world. J. Carbonell, 'Una plana del llibre d'Europa', *Nació secreta*, 111–15, is about the history of Catalan language and its present in European context. Bernat Joan, *Un espai per a una llengua*, V, Tres i Quatre, 122 pp., writes upon methodology in Sociolinguistics and the support that the sociolinguist can take from Social Psychology, especially in fields like the investigation of language attitudes.

MEDIEVAL LITERATURE

By LOLA BADIA, *Professor of Catalan Literature at the Universitat de Girona*

1. GENERAL

BIBLIOGRAPHY AND COMPUTERIZED MATERIALS. *BBAHLM*, 11:
1–79, includes information on Catalan for the year 1997. *Repertori de
catalanòfils*, IV-V, ed. J. Brumme (*ELLC*, 36–37), 376, 241 pp., updates
information on Catalan scholars. E. Duran et al. publish the first issue
of: *Repertori de manuscrits catalans (1474–1620)* 1: Barcelona: Arxiu Històric
i Biblioteca de Catalunya, B, IEC, 391 pp. Studies on the works of
M. Batllori: *Jornades sobre l'obra de Miquel Batllori*, B, IEC, 77 pp.;
*Miquel Batllori, historiador humanista. Cicle sobre la seva obra (17 de febrer–17
de març de 1998)*, ed. J. Solervicens, B, RABLB– Fundació Caixa de
Sabadell, 82 pp.; M. Cabré, 'Miquel Batllori, medievalista', *BRABLB*,
46:357–73, and A. L. Moll Benejam, 'Miquel Batllori: del Renaixe-
ment a la Il·lustració', *ib.*, 397–414. Three new issues of AITCC
contain 'Els cançoners catalans. Concordances': J. Perramon, *Cançoner Vega-Aguiló. B, Biblioteca de Catalunya, Ms. 8* (AITCC, 1–B);
S. Gascon, *Jardinet d'orats. B, Biblioteca Universitària, MS 151* (AITCC,
6); and J. Torruella, *Cançoner dels Masdovelles, B, Biblioteca de Catalunya,
MS 11* (AITCC, 7).

COLLECTED ESSAYS AND HISTORICAL CONTEXT. R. Aramon Serra,
Estudis de Llengua i Literatura, ed. J. A. Argente and J. Carbonell, B,
IEC, 1997, 773 pp., with 16 works on medieval literature, and two on
history of the Catalan language; J. Bastardas, '*Els camins del mar' i altres
estudis de llengua i literatura catalanes*, B, PAM, 212 pp., gathers
contributions on the linguistic and literary analysis of ancient texts;
for M.-C. Zimmermann see AUSIÀS MARCH below. Archive research
on the cultural background: J. Hernando Delgado, 'L'ensenyament a
Barcelona, segle XIV. Documents dels protocols notarials. Segona
part: Instruments notarials de l'Arxiu de la Catedral de Barcelona i
de l'Arxiu històric de la Ciutat de Barcelona (1294–1400)', *ATCA*, 16,
1997:131–298, contributes to the history of literacy; J. Aurell, 'La
imagen del mercader medieval', *BRABLB*, 46:23–44, describes the
cultural outline of medieval merchants; J. A. Rabella, *Un matrimoni
desavingut i un gat metzinat. Procés criminal barceloní del segle XIV* (TEEC
63), B, Curial-PAM, 416 pp., is a linguistic study of a criminal trial
held between 1374 and 1377.

M. de Riquer, *Catorze generacions d'una família catalana*, B, Quaderns
Crema, 489 pp., studies his ancestors since the 14th c. from his
private archive in a book of success. A contribution on literary
reception: A. Cortijo Ocaña, 'Women's role in the creation of

literature in Catalonia at the end of the fourteenth and beginning of the fifteenth century', *La corónica*, 27.1:7–20.

2. LYRIC AND NARRATIVE VERSE

AUSIÀS MARCH

Printed matter related to the sixth centenary in 1997 (but now J.J. Chiner has suggested that March was born in 1400, see below). Two anthologies: *Pagine del canzoniere*, ed. C. di Girolamo, Milan, Luni, 400 pp., translates into Italian with useful comments poems 1, 2, 3, 8, 10, 15, 23, 25, 28, 29, 42, 45, 46, 64, 68, 76, 77, 79, 80, 81, 82, 83, 86, 89, 95, 101, 105, 111, 118, 122a, and 122b; A. March, *Tria de poemes*, ed. J. Pujol and F. Gómez, B, Biblioteca Hermes, 220 pp., is an introduction to poems 1, 4, 11, 13, 18, 19, 23, 29, 39, 46, 76, 79, 81, 87, 89, 97, and 105. Two readings of poem 105: M. Prats, *Sobre el 'Cant espiritual' d'Ausiàs March*, B, Fundació Joan Maragall–Editorial Claret, 28 pp., and P. Bruno, 'Ausias March in the light of Dante', *Actes* (Bloomington), 101–08. J. J. Chiner Gimeno, *Ausiàs March i la València del segle XV (1400–1459)*, V, Generalitat Valenciana, 1997, 607 pp., is a new biography of March, with 400 new documents, from his birth onwards. *L'Ausiàs March llatí de l'humanista Vicent Mariner*, ed. M. A. Coronel Ramos, V, Edicions Alfons el Magnànim, 1997, 909 pp., edits a valuable 17th-c. Latin translation of March. V. Fàbrega, *Veles e vents. El conflicte eròtic a la poesia d'Ausiàs March*, Lleida, Pagès, 188 pp., explores the impossibility of being happily in love from a severe Christian point of view about lust and sin. F. Garcia-Oliver, *En la vida d'Ausiàs March*, B, Edicions 62, 281 pp., uncovers many links between biography and lyrics. M.-C. Zimmermann, *Ausiàs March o l'emergència del jo* (Biblioteca Sanchis Guarner, 40), B, PAM — V, Valencia U.P, 316 pp., gathers her readings on March from the point of view of the poetical 'I'. The volume *Lectures d'Ausiàs March. 15 de gener–10 de desembre de 1997*, ed. A. Hauf, V, Fundació Bancaixa, 264 pp., contains the following readings of single poems: G. Walters (17–40) on 1; A. Espadaler (43–58), 3; C. di Girolamo (63–82), 25; A. Hauf (85–127), 27; L. Cabré (129–53), 45; X. Dilla (155–79), 47; L. Badia (181–203), 64; M.-C. Zimmermann (205–37), 97; and R. Archer (239–64), 105. On the posterity of March: E. Duran, 'La valoració renaixentista d'Ausiàs March', *ELLC*, 35, 1997:93–108.

OTHER POETS

Two contributions on the Catalan troubadour Cerverí: M. R. Bastardas, 'Sobre el vers 19 de l'alba de Cerverí de Girona', *BRABLB*,

46:375–87, and M. Cabré, 'Ne suy juglars ne·n fay capteniments: l'ofici de trobador segons Cerverí de Girona', *AIEO 5*, 1, 211–20. Two studies by P. Olivella on the Catalan reception of R. de Cornet, a neglected Occitan poet of the 14th c.: 'À propos de l'oeuvre de Raimon de Cornet copiée en Catalogne', *BAIEO*, 14:51–63, and 'Raimon de Cornet, una mostra de poesia tolosana a Catalunya', *AIEO 5*, 1, 167–78. An analysis of an anthological poetry manuscript: S. Martí, 'El cançoner del Marquès de Barberà (S1/BM1). Descripció codicològica', *BBAHLM*, 11, 1997:461–502. *Contra las mujeres: poemas medievales de rechazo y vituperio. Estudio y edición*, ed. R. Archer and I. de Riquer, B, Quaderns Crema, 313 pp., is an edition and study of a *corpus* of the troubadouresque genres *mala canso*, *comiat*, and *maldit*. D. Billy, 'Contrafactures de modèles troubadouresques dans la poésie catalane (XIVe siècle)', *Actes* (Amsterdam), 51–74, finds eleven 14th-c. Catalan poems metrically dependent on troubadouresque schemata. J. de Sant Jordi, *L'amoroso cerchio. Poesie dell'ultimo trovatore*, ed. D. Siviero, Milan, Luni, 1997, 150 pp., translates the whole *corpus* of the poet into Italian, with new commentaries. M. Garcia Sampere, 'The religious poetry of Bernat Fenollar, Joan Escrivà, and Roís de Corella in its literary context', *CatR*, 11.1–2, 1997:73–82, explores the sources and devices of devotional contemplation.

NARRATIVE VERSE

Two contributions on the Occitan-Catalan roman *Jaufré*: J. Alturo, 'Restes codicològiques del més antic manuscrit de Jaufré amb algunes consideracions sobre aquesta novel·la provençal', *BRABLB*, 46:9–22, from the evidence of a new fragmentary manuscript of the beginning of the 13th c., asserts that the poem was written for king Alfons II of Aragon in the 12th c.; A. Espadaler, 'El Rei d'Aragó i la data del *Jaufré*', *CN*, 57, 1997:199–207, uses literary arguments to date the poem between 1268 and 1276, at the times of king Jaume I. A. Batallé Català, 'Representació social i tòpic de la igualtat davant de la mort a través de la figuració del joc dels escacs (de Jaume de Cèssulis i Innocent III/Joan de Gal·les a Francesc Eiximenis i Ausiàs March)', *LlLi*, 9:7–47, investigates the allegorical meaning of the chess game, and M. J. Rubiera Mata, 'Un relat àrab de viatge al més enllà (Buluqiya), possible font de la *Faula* de Torroella', *Veny Vol.*, 71–80, suggests a new source. On Jaume Roig, A. Carré, 'Fou la poma, un préssec o un gotim de raïm', *ELLC*, 35, 1997:65–70, and G. Colon, ' "Vellós" en un passatge de l'*Espill* de Jaume Roig', *ib.*, 51–64.

3. DOCTRINAL AND RELIGIOUS PROSE

RAMON LLULL AND LULLISM

Two volumes of the Latin *opera omnia*: *Raimundi Lulli Opera Latina 130–133 in Monte Pessulano et Pisis anno MCCCIII composita* , ed. A. Madre (*Raimundi Lulli Opera Latina*, 22 = Corpus Christianorum. Continuatio Medievalis, 114), Turnhout, Brepols, 364 pp., and *Ramundi Lulli Opera Latina 106–113 in Monte Pessulano et Ianuae anno MCCCIII composita*, ed. W. Euler (*Raimundi Lulli Opera Latina* 23 = Corpus Christianorum. Continuatio Medievalis, 115), Turnhout, Brepols, 290 pp. Two translations into French and German: R. Lulle, *Anthologie poétique*, ed. A. Llinarès, Paris, Éditions du Cerf, 204 pp., and R. Lull, *Das Buch vom Heiden und den drei Weisen*, ed. T. Pindl, Stuttgart, Philipp Reclam jun., 306 pp. Two monographs: R. González Casanovas, *La novela ejemplar de Ramón Llull: interpretaciones literarias de la misión*, M–Gijón, Ediciones Júcar, 204 pp., is a superficial introduction to Llull's narrative; J. N. Hillgarth, *Ramon Llull i el naixement del lul·lisme*, ed. A. Soler (TECC 61), 436 pp., is the updated Catalan version of the unavailable *Ramon Lull and Lullism in Fourteenth Century France* (1971). *SLu*, 36, 1996[1997], contains: F. Domínguez, 'El *Dictat de Ramon* y el *Coment del dictat*. Texto y contexto' (47–67); M. Idel, 'Dignitates and Kavod: two theological concepts in Catalan mysticism' (69–78); M. Pereira, 'Un innesto sull'*Arbor scientiae*. L'alchimia nella tradizione lul·liana' (79–97); C. Lohr and A. Madre, 'Pseudo-Raimundus Lullus *Liber ad memoriam confirmandam*: Zeuge der lullistische Tradition an der Wende des 15./16. Jarhunderts' (99–121); E. Pistolesi, ' "Paraula és imatge de semblança de pensa". Origine, natura e sviluppo dell'*affatus* lulliano' (3–45). *Ib.*, 37, 1997, contains: W. Artus, 'Acuerdo y desacuerdo sobre la creación entre Tomás de Aquino y Raimundo Lulio' (105–14); P. Beattie, 'Eschatology and Llull's *Llibre contra Anticrist*' (3–24); J. Gayà, 'Ramon Llull en Oriente (1301–1302): circunstancias de un viaje' (25–78); J. E. Rubio, 'Alguns antecedents de la figura T de l'Art quaternària al *Llibre de contemplació en Déu*' (79–104). From *Actes* (Palma): A. Bonner, 'Ramon Llull: autor, autoritat, il·luminat' (35–60); J. N. Hillgarth, 'Els començaments del lul·lisme a Mallorca' (21–34); H. Hina, 'La construcció d'una tradició cultural: Ramon Llull i la Renaixença' (143–55); E. Pistolesi, 'El rerefons de l'*affatus* lul·lià' (73–92); J. E. Rubio, 'Una incursió lul·liana en l'*ars memoriae* clàssica al *Llibre de contemplació en Déu*' (61–72). Other contributions include: J. Butinyà, 'Reflexiones sobre la fuente arábiga del *Libre del gentil* luliano', *RFR*, 14.2, 1997:45–61, and G. Colon, 'La forma "malenconi" de Llull i els fets occitans', *Veny Vol.*, 27–37; L. Martín Pascual, 'Algunes consideracions sobre la relació entre les faules del *Llibre de les bèsties* de Ramon Llull i l'original oriental', *CatR*,

11.1–2, 1997:83–112. Two lullian issues of specialized journals: *Ars brevis*, 3 (Número extraordinari. *Jornades Universitàries Ramon Llull al llindar del segle XXI*), B, Ramon Llull U.P., 175 pp., contains contributions by A. Badia Margarit (9–31), J. M. Vidal (33–53), J. M. Ruiz Simon (55–65), C. Llinàs (67–100), E. Colomer (101–12), and A. Nieto (113–26), and *Revista Española de Filosofía Medieval*, 5 (Monográfico Ramón Llull), 312 pp., gathers studies by C. Llinàs (11–20), K. Reinhardt (21–32), D. Urvoy (33–40), V. Serverat (41–60), S. Trías Mercant (61–74, 109–20); J. M. Soto Rábanos (75–88), and W. Künzel and C. Heiko (89–109). Two contributions on Llull in *ZK*, 11: E. Jaulent, 'Arbor scientiae: Immanenz und Transzendenz im Denkens Llulls' (8–32), and R. Krüger, 'Kosmologisches Wissen, das Konzept des Universums und die Kugelgestaldt der Erde bei Ramon Llull (1232–1316)' (33–78). On lullism: J.-A. Ysern Lagarda, 'Els *Principis de medicina* lul·lians del MS Mil.II.384 (Biblioteka Uniwersytecka, Wroclaw)', *BBAHLM*, 11, 1997:447–59, describes an Italian translation of Llull's work. J. Perarnau, 'De Ramon Llull a Nicolau Eimeric. Els fragments de l'*Ars amativa* de Llull, en còpia autògrafa de l'inquisidor Eimeric integrats en les cent tesis antilul·listes del seu *Directorium Inquisitorum*', *ATCA*, 16, 1997:7–129, shows new Inquisition documents against Llull; P. Rosselló Bover, 'L'aportació de Rafael Ginard i Bauçà al lul·lisme', *Actes* (Palma), 158–81, studies a 20th-c. Maiorcan lullist.

RELIGIOUS AND MEDICAL WRITERS

J. M. Ribera Llopis, 'Anotacions a una imatge vicentina: illa punició i/o glòria', *RFR*, 14.2, 1997:357–64, deals with an allegory of the other world; D. J. Viera, 'Vicent Ferrer's Catalan Sermon on Margaret of Antioch', *Actes* (Bloomington), 293–304, analyses a sermon by Vicent Ferrer. D. M. Rogers, 'La llengua oral al *Regiment de la cosa pública* de Francesc Eiximenis', *Actes* (Palma), 431–38, is a stylistic study. A new issue of critical edition of the medical works of A. de Vilanova: *Regimen Almarie (Regimen castra sequentium)*, ed. M. McVaugh and L. Cifuentes (*Arnaldi de Vilanova Opera Medica Omnia*, X.2), B, Univ. de Barcelona, 228 pp. J. Veny, J. Arrizabalaga, and L. García Ballester present a renewed edition of the first Catalan treatise on the Plague of the 14th c.: J. d'Agramont, *Regiment de preservació de pestilència*, B, Edicions Proa–Enciclopèdia Catalana, 125 pp.

4. HISTORICAL AND ARTISTIC PROSE, NOVEL

HISTORIOGRAPHY

M. M. Batlle, 'La Fi del comte d'Urgell: un text escrit en dues etapes', *EMarg*, 58, 1997:93–100, explains the double redaction of this 15th-c. chronicle. C. Domínguez, 'Repertorio de materiales hispano-medievales para el estudio de las cruzadas. 1. El manuscrito 152 de la Biblioteca de Catalunya', *BBAHLM*, 11, 1997:503–18, finds in that manuscript a fragment of a lost Catalan chronicle on the Crusades. A. Espadaler, 'El retrat del rei en Jaume a la Crònica de Bernat Desclot', *Veny Vol.*, 63–69, shows Occitan and Latin patterns in Desclot's portrait of the king; J. Moran Ocenrinjauregui, *Cronicó de Perpinyà (segle XIII)*, B, PAM, 67 pp., is the first edition of that old text, with a study of its linguistic features.

TIRANT LO BLANC

An abbreviated edition, J. Martorell, *Tirant lo Blanc*, ed. I. Grifoll, B, Biblioteca Hermes, 371 pp., and a French translation, J. Martorell, *Tyrant le Blanc*, by the Comte de Caylus (1737), ed. J. M. Barbera, Paris, Gallimard, 1997, 641 pp. Some articles: R. Alemany, 'A propósito de la reutilización de dos fuentes en el *Tirant lo Blanc*', *RFR*, 14.2, 1997:15–25, and J. Pujol, 'Micer Johan Bocaci i Mossèn Joanot Martorell: presències del *Decameron* i de la *Fiammeta* al Tirant lo Blanc', *LlLi*, 9:59–100, deal with the sources of the novel, a subject that has been studied systematically by J. Pujol; R. Alemany and J. L. Martos, 'Llull en el *Tirant lo Blanch*: entre la reescriptura i la subversió', *Actes* (Palma), 129–42, and M. Piera, 'Llull i el concepte de la croada evangelitzadora al Tirant lo Blanch de Martorell', *ib.*, 113–25, are two approaches to the same problem; R. Beltran, 'El conjur d'Eliseu al Tirant lo Blanch: poesia i oralitat en la literatura culta', *ib.*, 461–78, analyses chapter 262 of the novel; R. Mérida Jiménez, 'La desaparición de Morgana: de Tirant lo Blanch (1490) y Amadís de Gaula (1508) a Tyran le Blanch (1737)', *BRABLB*, 46:135–56, belongs to comparative literature; M. Piera, '"Com Tirant vencé la batalla e per força d'armes entrà en lo castell": rape and conquest in *Tirant lo Blanc*', *Actes* (Bloomington): 259–80, and her '"Lletres de batalla" de mujeres en *Tirant lo Blanc* y *Curial e Güelfa*: la verbalización del discurso femenino dentro del código caballeresco', *La corónica*, 27.1:35–53, develop topics of gender studies.

JOAN ROÍS DE CORELLA AND NARRATIVE TEXTS

S. M. Cingolani, *Joan Roís de Corella. La importància de dir-se honest*, V, Edicions Tres i Quatre, 318 pp., studies the chronology and the literary sources of Corella's works aiming for a comprehensive interpretation of them. On *Curial e Güelfa*: C. Merril, 'They came to Carthage burning: Curial, Güelfa, Aeneas, and St. Augustine of Hippo', *Actes* (Bloomington), 189–98, reads *Curial i Güelfa* together with Chaucer and St. Augustine; F. Pieras Guasp, 'Amor bilingüe: estudi comparatiu del lèxic sentimental a Curial e Güelfa i algunes obres literàries castellanes del segle XV', *Actes* (Palma), 479–93, compares Catalan and Castilian sentimental texts; A. M. Saludes Amat, 'Ricerca paradigmatica o trionfo della letterarietà nelle strategie narrative del *Curial e Güelfa*', *Chiarini Vol.*, 197–211, discusses the relationship between the novel and a poem of the troubadour Rigaut de Berbezilh. On other texts: J. M. Ribera Llopis, 'Una altra lectura del Ramon de Perellós prèvia al seu viatge (primera part)', *RevAl*, 8, 1997:233–51, finds in Giraldus Cambrensis a source for the description of Ireland in Perellós's *Viatge al Purgatori*.

5. TRANSLATIONS AND OTHER GENRES AND TEXTS

T. Martínez Romero, *Un clàssic entre els clàssics. Sobre traduccions i recepcions de Sèneca a l'època medieval* (Biblioteca Sanchis Guarner, 42), Valencia U.P. — B, PAM, 268 pp., combines already published articles and new contributions on the medieval Catalan translation of Seneca's works. J. M. Perujo Melgar, 'Les veus de Troia: oralitat en l'obra de Jaume Conesa', *Actes* (Palma), 445–59, analyses the style of the Catalan version of Guido delle Colonne's *Historia troiana*. C. Wittlin, 'La Vida de Santa Caterina de Sena de Miquel Peres: ampliació literària d'extrets escollits en el Chronicon d'Antonino de Florència', *Actes* (Bloomington), 305–32, studies the circumstances and the style of an hagiographic text. Three contributions to medieval Catalan epistolography: *De València a Roma. Cartes triades dels Borja*, ed. M. Batllori, B, Quaderns Crema, 218 pp., offers 64 familiar letters written between 1473 and 1504; A. Rubio Vela, *Epistolari de la València medieval, ii* (Biblioteca Sanchis Guarner 43), Valencia U.P. — B, PAM, 458 pp., edits 166 letters, and D. Bratsch-Prince, 'A queen's task: Violant de Bar and the experience of royal motherhood in fourteenth-century Aragón', *La corónica*, 27.1:21–34, develops a gender study using some letters of the queen.

6. DRAMA

P. Coccozzella, 'A Sibyl for the Catalan "Passion" of the late Middle Ages', *Actes* (Bloomington), 109–32, analyses the character Sybil in B, Biblioteca Universitària, MS 1029. M. Gómez Muntané, 'A propósito de *Déu vos salve, Verge imperial*, un canto monódico del misterio de

Elche', *BRABLB*, 46:199–212, studies musical aspects of that piece. J. Castaño and G. Sansano, *Història i crítica de la 'Festa d'Elx'*, Alicante U.P., 395 pp., gather fundamental contributions to Catalan medieval liturgical drama already published by J. Massot, J. Romeu, F. Massip, etc. A. A. MacDonald, 'The Catalan-Occitan Easter play', *Romania*, 115, 1997:495–518, studies the BNP manuscript n.a.f. 4232. R. Miró Baldrich, *La processó de Corpus i els entremesos. Cervera, segles XIV-XIX* (TECC 60), 258 pp., documents some late medieval performances of liturgical drama.

LITERATURE (NINETEENTH AND TWENTIETH CENTURIES)

By Margarida Casacuberta, *Lecturer in Catalan Literature at the Universitat de Girona,* and
Marina Gustà, *Lecturer in Catalan Literature at the Universitat de Barcelona*

1. General

N. Garolera, *L'escriptura itinerant. Verdaguer, Pla i la literatura de viatges*, Lleida, Pagès, 174 pp., collects some articles previously published by the author, now with an introduction on general subjects about travel literature. *Veny Vol.,* II, has of course a miscellaneous character; among other contributions, some on Balearic literature of the two last centuries must be considered (those of M. Salord, F. Salord, G. Sampol, J. A. Mesquida, J. Massot, J. M. Ribera, R. Cabré, and P. Arnau). 'El jardí teatral' is the title of the monographic issue which constitutes *Faig Arts*, 38, with several erudite, critical, and theoretical articles (by J. Paré, J. Noguero, P. Ley, F. Massip, J. Casas, T. Casares, and F. Foguet) on the past and present of theatre in Catalonia, in both sides of dramatic performance and literary text. A complete and documented report on the new erudite and critical contributions to the study of Catalan literature in the 19th and 20th c. is given in J. Aulet, 'Estudis recents de literatura catalana contemporània', *SdO*: 71–75, 149–51, 662–66, 928–32.

2. Renaixença

M. Cahner, *Literatura de la Revolució i la Contrarevolució (1789–1849). Notes d'història de la llengua i de la literatura catalanes*, B, Curial, 447 pp., is of capital importance for the study of the not very well known relationship between literature and society in the early 19th c., as well as providing a lot of material which will be of great interest in the sight of historical sociolinguistics. P. Farrés, 'Una lectura de les tragèdies de Víctor Balaguer', *EMarg*, 59, 1997: 5–22, is a suggestive work devoted to a very important personality, in spite of the small volume of studies dedicated to him up till now. Two polemical articles on one of the institutional sides of literature in the Renaixença are: M. Almirall, 'Els republicans i els Jocs Florals (1859–1883): el mite de la unitat', *RCat*, 117, 1997: 33–38, answered in X. Vall, 'Almirall i els Jocs Florals', *ib.*, 125: 29–54. Very useful, indeed, and not only from the point of view of literary history, is the work of C. Duran i Tort, *Índexs de 'La Renaixença' (Barcelona, 1871–1880)* B, Barcino,

470pp. Both sides of research, collecting and reading, are at the basis of J. Requesens i Piqué, *Estudis verdaguerians de Jaume Collell*, B, Barcino, 526 pp., in fact the only contribution of the year on the figure of the capital poet in the Catalan 19th c. Another major writer, Narcís Oller, has deserved a volume by A. Yates, *Narcís Oller. Tradició i talent individual*, B, Curial, 347 pp., in which the author collects, and enriches, the fine quantity amount of work that for years he has devoted to the novelist. M. Corretger, 'Pere Nanot Renart, referent històric i moral de *La bogeria* de Narcís Oller', *SdO*:630–33, and V. Martínez-Gil, 'L'evolució textual de *L'Escanyapobres*', *EMarg*, 61:81–89, are both noteworthy contributions, although not about the prime subject of Oller's work.

3. MODERNISME

The critical edition of Joan Maragall, *Poesia*, ed. G. Casals, B, La Magrana, 834 pp., is indeed the year's most important work on the literature of that movement: to establish the text with care means here also to read it in many senses, as no further information about the writing of every poem has ever been offered. Poetry is as well the matter of X. Vall, 'Algunes fonts d' "El pi de Formentor" ', *RCat*, 133:108–30, a study on one of the most famous poems ever written in Catalan. P. Arenas i Sampera, *Una aventura poètica moderna (el poema en prosa en la literatura catalana)*, B, Curial–PAM, 296 pp., fails in the pursuit of that poetic form during the *Modernisme*, as description was not the only way to proceed. 1998 has commemorated the decline which means a point of no return in Spanish politics, as well as a very productive reaction among intellectuals. The specific reflection of all that in Catalonia has been, during 1998, a point of interest. However, the proceedings of several meetings are still not available. In the meantime: I. Cònsul, 'El 98 en la literatura catalana', *SdO*:101–04. About the same period, but on the Majorcan cultural milieu, D. Pons i Pons has published a lot of interesting material: 'El grup de *L'Almudaina* en la Mallorca d'entre els dos segles (1897–1905)', *EMarg*, 61:5–17; *El diari 'L'Almudaina' en l'època de Miquel S. Oliver*, Binissalem, Di7, 165 pp.; *Ideologia i cultura a la Mallorca d'entre els dos segles (1886–1905). El grup regeneracionista de 'L'Almudaina'*, Palma de Mallorca, Lleonard Muntaner, 366 pp. The intellectual life of Barcelona, and the amount of effort that leading it required, can be tasted with the reading of *Els epistolaris de Carles Rahola. Antologia de cartes de cent corresponsals (1901–1939)*, ed. N.-J. Aragó and J. Clara, B, PAM, 618 pp. J. Castellanos, *Intel·lectuals, cultura i poder*, B, La Magrana, 280 pp., focuses, through some wise approaches, on personalities of different weight in the written history of contemporary Catalonia, but with a common wish (the building of the nation), which they approach from different ideological positions: A. Gaudí, J. Massó i Torrents, R. D. Perés, C. de Montoliu, E. D'Ors, J. Pijoan, and N. M. Rubió i Tudurí.

4. NOUCENTISME

With regard to the last years, interest in Noucentisme seems to decrease, though maybe temporarily. R. Campi, 'Sobre "La generació anàrquica": Dues cartes entre Pere Coromines i Joan Estelrich', *EMarg*, 62:73–88, provides some interesting documents in order to understand Noucentisme's complex final crisis. V. Alsina i Keith, 'Lluís Nicolau d'Olwer i les traduccions de la Fundació Bernat Metge', *ib.*, 89–105, is a contribution on a matter that was an obsession in the movement's goals. A biographical aspect of the poet is the centre of J. Medina, *Les dames de Josep Carner*, B, PAM, 100 pp., with almost no new information. A critical edition of Carner's greatest poem, *Nabí*, ed. J. Coll, B, Edicions 62, has also appeared.

5. THE TWENTIETH CENTURY

Knowledge of the literary scene from the crisis of Noucentisme to the Civil War grows still quite slowly. On cultural, and literary, sociability: N. Real, 'Espais de literatura popular i de consum en català: M. del Carme Nicolau', *SdO*: 204–07, and Id., *El Club Femení i d'Esports de Barcelona, plataforma d'acció cultural*, B, PAM, 129 pp.; F. Foguet i Boreu, 'Lyceum Club de Barcelona. Una aposta per un "teatre intel·ligent" (1934–1937)', *SdO*:654–57. Two poets have been honoured: Marià Manent and Bartomeu Rosselló-Pòrcel. 'Marià Manent en el seu centenari', *ib.*, 691–700, counts on works by R. Pla i Arxé, J. Palau i Fabre, and S. Abrams. An academic ambition guides M. Roser i Puig, *El llegat anglès de Marià Manent*, B, Curial — PAM, 248 pp., an investigation of English and North American influences in M.'s poetry and criticism. On Rosselló: J. Palau i Fabre, Bartomeu Rosselló-Pòrcel, profeta dels temps moderns', *SdO*:387–89, and S. Alzamora, ' "Imitació del foc", o la necessitat de ser absolutament modern', *ib.*, 390–92. Still on poetry: V. Panyella, 'Simona Gay, poeta rossellonesa', *ib.*, 208–11. A single work on J. V. Foix has appeared: A. Martí, *J. V. Foix o la solitud de l'escriptura*, B, Edicions 62, 210 pp. With regard to another centenary: J. Triadú, 'Ferran Canyameres. El centenari d'un escriptor entre l'arrelament i l'aventura', *SdO*: 131–32. Beyond biography, though following the long life of a personality of great interest, M. Llanas, *Gaziel: vida, periodisme i literatura*, B, PAM, 481 pp., proposes a suggestive global view on the

figure of an intellectual at several modern crossroads. On a particular
literary aspect, Id., 'Gaziel, lector de Shakespeare', *LlLi*, 9:365–87.
Actes del I Simposi Internacional de Narrativa Breu (Valencia, abril), B,
PAM, 488 pp., is half devoted to Mercè Rodoreda's short stories,
from the early works in the 1930s up to her last output, with
contributions from J. M. Balaguer, C. Arnau, M. Aritzeta, M. Cam-
pillo, C. Gregori, A. Bernal, V. Simbor, M. Gustà, M. Casacuberta,
C. Cortès, M. J. Cuenca, Ll. Meseguer, J. Aulet, and J. Martínez
Blanch. The young R. is also focused in R. Porta, 'Mercè Rodoreda i
el periodisme satíric', *SdO*: 548–50. C. Arnau, finally, has exhumed a
few pages of an unfinished work of R.'s, probably written in 1961: '*El
pont de les tres roses*, de Mercè Rodoreda. Un projecte', *ib.*, 538–41.
Three worthy contributions to the knowledge of all the faces of
Llorenç Villalonga's life and works are: Ll. Villalonga, *Cartes i articles.
Temps de preguerra (1924–1936)*, ed. and introd. J. Pomar, Palma de
Mallorca, Moll, 275 pp., which contains documentary materials of
great interest; V. Simbor i Roig, 'La utopia segons Llorenç
Villalonga', *LlLi*, 9:173–205, concentrates on a characteristic point
of reference in the writer's novels of the late period; and X. Vall,
'Llorenç Villalonga i l'existencialisme', *EMarg*, 62:105–16, is a well-
documented and suggestive study of the reflection in V.'s work of a
philosophy at which the novelist used to look ambiguously.

   Literature in time of war continues to be explored, especially with
regard to cultural sociability. J. Massot, *Tres escriptors davant la guerra
civil*, B, PAM, 284 pp., is the enriched, last, and in fact new, version of
an acute and each time more documented view of those three men in
time of war, and at professional and moral crossroads. Other
contributions are all on theatre and come from the same author:
F. Foguet i Borau, 'Erwin Piscator a Catalunya (1936)', *SdO*:312–15,
is the result of scrupulous research around an almost mythical event;
'L'Associació d'Autors de Teatre Català. Seixanta anys enrera', *ib.*,
479–81, and 'El teatre amateur català en temps de guerra
(1936–1939)', *EMarg*, 62:7–40, are both of documentary value.

   The postwar landscape is of course very wide. First of all, the end
of the war and exile must be looked at: D. Serrano i Balaguer, 'Edició
i recepció de *K. L. Reich*, de J. Amat-Piniella', *EMarg*, 61:89–99;
J. Arévalo (ed.), 'Set cartes de Just Cabot a Lluís Capdevila', *ib.*, 59,
1997:57–80; J. Mengual Català, 'Una aproximació al teatre català a
Mèxic', *ib.*, 101–10; two writers with an important role in Mexican
exile have been studied: J.-V. Garcia Raffi, *Lluís Ferran de Pol i Mèxic:
literatura i periodisme*, B, PAM, 487 pp., is a long monograph about the
writer and the activist; 'Sobre Anna Murià', *SdO*:793–804, contains
articles by J. Aulet, S. Abrams, N. Real, and I. Pelegrí. With respect
to poetry: A. Mohino i Balet, 'La poesia de Rosa Leveroni a la llum

de "Confessions i quaderns íntims"', *ib.*, 451–55; *Epistolari Rosa Leveroni — Josep Palau i Fabre (1940–1975)*, ed. N. Barenys, B, PAM, 172 pp., is of great help in reading the poetic works of both writers; P. Rosselló Bover, 'Miquel Gayà o la fidelitat a la llengua i a la poesia', *SdO*: 634–37; and the very valuable survey by M. Pons, *Poesia insular de postguerra: quatre veus dels anys cinquanta*, B, PAM, 528 pp., on the poetry of Llorenç Moyà, Jaume Vidal Alcover, Josep M. Llompart, and Blai Bonet. The last-named, recently deceased, was also the object of more than an interview: S. Alzamora, 'Blai Bonet, delicada agressió', *SdO*: 48–53. J. Perucho has been honoured in *Joan Perucho o la mirada darrera el mirall*, ed. R. Cabré, B, Universitat — Vic, Eumo, 171 pp., with, among others, articles by A. Trapiello, F. Valls, A. Vilanova, R. Cabré, and J. Guillamon. J. Malé, 'Algunes consideracions sobre el llenguatge d' *Or i sal*, de Joan Brossa', *EMarg*, 59, 1997: 111–18, analyses linguistic performances in a dramatic play by Brossa. Gabriel Ferrater's life and poetry is a little clearer thanks to R. Gomis, *El Gabriel Ferrater de Reus*, B, Proa, 183 pp., a biographical approach to the poet's youth, and S. Oliva, 'La mètrica d' "In memoriam", de Gabriel Ferrater', *LlLi*, 9: 405–21. Related, in some way, to the memory of those days and those places, A. Nomen, 'Xavier Amorós, testimoniatge i memòria', *SdO*: 461–63. In spite of being a review, J. Aulet, 'La màscara de Baltasar Porcel', *ib.*, 409–10, is as good as any brief approach to P.'s theatre. *Memòria Any Pla 1997*, B, Generalitat de Catalunya, 175 pp., should perhaps, with regard to its content, be qualified as a kind of 'institutional survey' about last year celebration of P.'s centenary; however, the main purpose is to inventory all the material, academic or not, the year has seen with the writer as a pretext. A single contribution to the study of P., A. Camps, 'El *Zibaldone* de Josep Pla', *SdO*: 201–03, confirms that P.'s year has really come to an end.

Today's role and value of literature and of literary research in Catalonia have been looked at, according to different faces and senses of writing. First of all, a homage and an award have made the work of two historicians the focus of interest: *Jornades sobre l'obra de Miquel Batllori*, B, IEC, 77 pp., with contributions by J. Massot, J. Molas, A. Hauf, E. Duran, A. Mestre Sanchis, and H. Raguer, and *Miquel Batllori, historiador i humanista*, ed. J. Solervicens, Sabadell, Caixa de Sabadell — B, RABLB, 82 pp., with contributions by M. de Riquer, J. Romeu, M. Carbonell, J. Bada, and J. Massot, collects articles on all the aspects of B.'s bibliography. J. Castellanos, 'El Premi d'Honor. De Jordi Rubió a Joaquim Molas', *SdO*: 610–11, and A. Pons, 'Joaquim Molas, Premi d'Honor de les Lletres Catalanes', *ib.*, 612–13, consider the different reasons for the award to one of the most important critical, historiographical and didactic works of the last 40 years. 'Jaume Fuster, un comiat', *ib.*, 348–60, with articles by G. J. Graells, M. Aritzeta, V. Llorca, and A. Munné-Jordà, is a homage to the early deceased novelist. The same sad event causes 'En la mort de Maria Mercè Marçal', *ib.*, 764–82, with contributions by J. Sabadell, M. Ll. Julià, V. Panyella, and P. Gimferrer, which aim at the central role of M. in last year's poetry, with special regard to the feminist activism of the writer. Quim Monzó goes on confirming his supremacy among not so young writers, in the field of short story: 'Quim Monzó', *RECat*, 1, 220 pp., with articles by M.-C. Zimmermann, J. Vallcorba, J. Gàlvez, S. Pàmies, M. Ollé, and A. Charlon, among others. We must finally single out three reviews of today's literature. The most important is the one contained in *Caplletra*, 22, 1997, with the following contributions worthy of mention: I. Cònsul, '25 anys de novel·la: 1970–1995' (11–25); F. Calafat, 'Entre el llenguatge i la realitat. 25 anys de poesia catalana' (27–48); V. Simbor, 'Sobre la novel·la històrica actual' (105–28); J. Aulet, 'La poesia catalana i el boom de l'any 1972' (139–52); C. Batlle, 'La nova dramatúrgia catalana: de la perplexitat a la diversitat' (49–68); and others by C. Gregori, V. Alonso, E. Balaguer, M. Aparicio, and F. Carbó. The two other surveys are: 'L'estat actual de la literatura catalana', *SdO*: 258–63, with opinions by D. Castillo, J. Vallcorba, M. Pessarrodona, J. Triadú, J. Murgades, S. Pàmies, C. J. Guardiola, and J. Molas, among other critics and creative writers; and 'La literatura al País Valencià, avui', *ib.*, 17–42, with contributions by A. Bernal, C. Gregori, V. Simbor, V. Alonso, F. Carbó, R. J. Rosselló, and F. Pérez Moragon, who speak about the last 20 years' production.

VI.   PORTUGUESE STUDIES

LANGUAGE

By STEPHEN PARKINSON, *Lecturer in Portuguese Language and Linguistics,*
University of Oxford

1.   GENERAL

Holtus, *Lexikon*, VII, has sections on contacts with other Romance
varieties (V. Noll, 109–21), African and Asian languages (W. Bal,
395–410; G. Cardona, 410–19) and S. American languages
(W. Dietrich, 489–99), and a brief account of contrastive studies (J.
Schmidt-Radefeld, 864–73). S. Parkinson, Price, *Encyclopedia*,
364–70, covers the development of EPtg. A. Castilho, 'A gramaticalização', *ELL*, 19, 1997:25–64, distinguishes lexical, syntactic and
discourse levels of grammaticalization. Id., 'Língua falada e gramaticalização', *FLP*, 1, 1997:107–20, contrasts the discourse functions
of *mas* (preserving the inclusivity of Lat. MAGIS) and its grammaticalized syntactic function of con(tra)junction. *Para a história do
Português Brasileiro*, 1, *Primeiras Ideias*, ed. Ataliba Teixeira de Castilho,
SPo, Humanitas–FFLCH–FAPESP, 254 pp., contains orientation
articles by R. V. M. Silva (21–52) on BPtg in general, and A. T. de
Castilho (61–76) on São Paulo; sketches of syntactic research
programs (79–140), J. A. Ramos, 'História social do português
brasileiro: perspectivas' (153–67) and various surveys of diachronic
corpora (171–254). *Pesquisas linguísticas em Portugal e no Brasil*, ed.
Eberhard Gärtner (Linguistica iberoamericana, 4), Frankfurt am
Main, Vervuert — Madrid, Iberoamericana, 1997, 137 pp., has
mainly bio-bibliographical essays on Ptg and BPtg linguistic traditions; see also E. Gärtner on BPtg grammars, *Fest Woll*, 271–83.
Telmo Verdelho, *As origens da grammatografia e da lexicografia latino-
portuguesas*, Aveiro, INIC, 1995, 594 pp., is a broad and amply
documented study and inventory of writers and sources up to the end
of the 16th c. M. F. Gonçalves, 'As ideias linguísticas em Portugal no
século XVIII', *Confluência*, 13.1, 1997:37–59, develops a framework of
problemáticas to distinguish different authors and their works. L. L.
Fávero, 'História das idéias lingüísticas: gramáticos e ortógrafos
portugueses dos séculos XVI e XVII', *FLP*, 1, 1997:95–105, is yet
another general presentation. M. C. Rosa, 'Línguas bárbaras e
peregrinas do Novo Mundo segundo os gramáticos jesuitas: uma
concepção de universalidade no estudo das línguas estrangeiras',
RevEL, 6.2, 1997:97–149, describes the cultural context to the writing
of vernacular grammars by Jesuits in Brazil: *reduzir à arte* — grammar

on the Latin model — needed considerable supplementation. T. Meisenburg, 'Portugiesisch: ganz schön schwer? Zum *Diálogo em defensão da lingua portuguesa* von Pêro de Magalhães de Gândavo', *Fest. Woll*, 97–106.

E. Bechara, 'Epifânio Dias e Eça de Queirós', *FLP*, 1, 1997:51–59, recalls D.'s non-prescriptive approach to syntactic innovation. J. G. Herculano de Carvalho, 'Ortografia e as ortografias do Português', *Confluência*, 13.1, 1997:39–46, returns to the fray in favour of the 1986 proposals for wholesale abolition of accents and silent letters. Fernando Pessoa, *A língua portuguesa*, ed. Luísa Medeiros, L, Assírio & Alvim, 1997, 198 pp., collects the poet's scattered thoughts on topics including orthography and international languages. D. Santos, *APL 13*, II, 259–74, collects examples of translationese in childrens' literature, as an object lesson to lexicographers and language students. *Letras de Hoje*, 32.4, 1997, has studies on the acquisition of Ptg phonology and syntax.

2. HISTORICAL

GENERAL. José Pedro Machado, *Ensaios Arábico-Portugueses*, L. Notícias, 1997, 319 pp., reprints lexical and historical articles. I. Roberts, 'Creoles, markedness and the Language Bioprogram hypothesis', *ELL*, 19, 1997:11–24, suggests weak parameter setting as a GB characterization of creole syntactic features. A. Baxter and D. Lucchesi. 'A relevância dos processos de pidginização e crioulização na formação da língua portuguesa no Brasil', *ib.*, 65–84, restate the argument for early creolization ('irregular linguistic transmission') with reference to Helvécia BPtg, but with no concessions to the opposing (Tarallo) point of view. D. A. Costa Martins, *Atti* (Palermo), IV, 175–83, confirms the similarity of baby talk, foreigner talk, and pidgins.

On non-literary texts, A. H. A. de Emiliano, 'Modelos representacionais vs modelos operacionais na escrituralidade notarial médio-latina', *RFCSH*, 10, 1997:415–30, and 'Significado lingüístico de errores de copista en la lengua notarial del siglo xi', pp. 407–20 of *Actas del II Congreso Hispanico del Latin Medieval (León, 11–14 de noviembre de 1997)*, I, ed. Maurilio Pérez González, León U.P., develops the idea of an 'equivalência representacional entre grafias latinas e romances que coexistiam em variação sincrónica': apparent errors can be significant alternations. A. M. Martins and C. Albino, 'Sobre a primitiva produção documental em português. Noticia de um noticia de aver', *Lorenzo Vol.*, 105–21, insist on the documentary significance of *notícias* as private memoranda, and study an example of an early (probably 12th-c.) inventory.

M. T. Brocardo, 'As variantes como objecto de estudos lingüísticos diacrónicos', *Atti* (Palermo), VI, 47–57, gives a valuable classification of variants in a 15th-c. chronicle. **A Carta da Caminha: testemunho lingüístico de 1500*, ed. Rosa Virgínia Mattos e Silva, Salvador, EDUFBA, 1996.

M. de B. Pessoa, 'Proposta de periodização para a história do português brasileiro', *AIL 5*, 229–45, gives priority to the consciousness of the 'língua comum' in identifying three periods, with 1750 and 1922 as key dates. M. A. Cohen, S. Prado, and C. T. Seabra, 'BTLH, Banco de textos para pesquisa em lingüística histórica — dados de Barra Longa MG', *FLP*, 2:119–42, give samples of 18th- and 19th-c. non-literary documents.

PHONOLOGY. L. C. Cagliari, 'A escrita do português arcaico e a falsa noção de ortografia fonética', *AIL 5*, 57–69, and G. Massini-Cagliari, 'Escrita do Cancioneiro da Biblioteca Nacional de Lisboa. Fonética ou ortográfica', *FLP*, 2:159–78, make much of the orthographic variability and indeterminacy of OPtg, making few allowances for graphemics or complexities of transmission. G. Massini-Cagliari and L. C. Cagliari, 'De sons de poetas ou estudando fonologia através da poesia', *RANPOLL*, 5:77–105, see poetry as a source of phonological information; this is put into practice by G. Massini-Cagliari, 'Atribuição de acento em português arcaico', *AIL 5*, 183–206, applying metrical phonology to OPtg (which is basically trochaic despite courtly poets' preference for *agudo* rhymes), and 'O percurso histórico da acentuação português através da análise do ritmo das cantigas de amigo', *RevEL*, 5.2, 1996:5–33.

R. Marquilhas, 'Importância das fontes judiciais no conhecimento do português seiscentista', *ELL*, 19, 1997:163–78, and 'Mãos inábeis nos arquivos da Inquisição. Fontes para o estudo fonológico do português do século XVII', *Lorenzo Vol.*, 761–67, identifies and lists usable sources. E. Bechara, 'Testemunho de *Os Lusíadas* em factos de fonética sintática', *Fest. Woll*, 251–60, follows Rodrigues in accepting original readings as an index of vowel contractions. J. G. H. de Carvalho, 'Contribuições para a história da língua galaico-portuguesa', *ib.*, 41–47, gives a brief review of past tense morphology.

SYNTAX. *ELL*, 19, 1997, has S. B. B. Costa, 'Adverbiais na Crónica de D. Pedro' (239–52), an inventory. R. V. Mattos e Silva, 'Observações sobre a variação no uso dos verbos *ser, estar, haver, ter*, no galego-português ducista' (253–86), finds very low frequencies of *estar* and *ter*. C. Galves, 'Do português clássico ao português europeu moderno. Uma análise minimalista' (105–28), links the increasing preference for enclisis with the loss of Verb-second word order. A. M. Martins, 'Mudança sintática: clíticos, negação e um pouquinho de scrambling' (129–61), traces the loss of freedom of positioning of clitics, in relation to the structure of AgrS; and three studies using João de Barros's pedagogical texts: S. Cyrino (189–96) showing B.'s system of accents to be syntactic not phonetic; M. A. Moraes (197–216) on word order in main clauses; and I. Ribeiro (217–38) on embedded sentences.

LEXICON. C. Rocha, '*Saber* e *conhecer* em documentos portugueses da idade Média', *Atti* (Palermo), I, 329–37, gives a semantic analysis of near synonyms. C. A. A. Murakawa, 'A unidade lexical heresia nos documentos da Inquisição portuguesa', *ib.*, III, 607–12, finds a wide range of *crimes* categorized as heresy. T. Verdelho appreciates '*O Vocabulário da lingoa da Iapam* (1603), uma fonte inexplorada da lexicografia portuguesa', *ib.*, 951–55.

3. PHONETICS AND PHONOLOGY

Graça Maria Rio-Torto, *Fonética, fonologia e morfologia do português. Conteúdos e metodologia*, Coimbra U.P. — Colibri, 115 pp., is a very basic manual with bibliography. J. Moraes et al., *Português falado*, V, 33–53, give formant data from a range of urban dialects. J.-P. Zerling and L. Castro, *'Les diphthongues orales en portugais de Portugal. Étude acoustique préliminaire', *TIPS*, 27, 1997:91–116. M. B. M. Abaurre and E. G. Pagotto, *Português falado*, VI, 495–526, find strong phonemic and allophonic nasalization in tonic syllables and preceding /ɲ/. E. Bechara reflects on 'Pronúncia de nomes próprios: o problema Gandavo ou Gândavo', *AIL 5*, 53–56.

M. H. M. Mateus, 'Ainda a subespecificação na fonologia do Português', *APL 13*, II, 63–73, sticks to her earlier conclusions (*YWMLS*, 59:384), while admitting that underspecified /i/ and coronals need to be specified early in derivations to act as triggers for assimilation rules. H. H. do Couto 'As sequências qu- e gu- mais vogal', *RevEL*, 5.2, 1996:35–43, is a simplistic attempt to derive labiovelars from underlying velar + /u/ sequences. W. L. Wetzels, 'The lexical representation of nasality in Brazilian Portuguese', *Probus*, 9, 1997:203–32, adduces familiar evidence in favour of a biphonemic (bimoraic) analysis, insisting that nasal monophthongs are VN but diphthongs are VV: an interesting corollary is the analysis of /R/ and /ɲ/ as geminates. S.-H. Lee, 'O acento primário do português do Brasil', *RevEL*, 6.2, 1997:5–30, has separate rules of noun and verb stress (neither of them quantity-sensitive) working at different levels of a prosodic Lexical Phonology. D. Callou, Y. Leite, and J. Moraes, 'O sistema pretônico do português do Brasil e a regra de harmonia vocálica', *Atti* (Palermo) IV, 95–100, find low levels of vowel raising. M. A. de Oliveira, 'Reanalisando o processo de cancelamento do (r) em final de sílaba', *RevEL*, 6.2, 1997:31–58, finds complex individual and group variation in Belo Horizonte data, as do D. Callou, J. Moraes, and Y. Leite, *Português falado*, VI, 465–93, for São Paulo.

PROSODY. L. C. Cagliari, *Português falado*, II, 39–64, shows syntactic units marked intonationally. J. Moraes and Y. Leite, *ib.*, 65–77, try to establish syllable-timing with studies of variable speed of speech. L. Bisol, *ib.*, II, 21–38, V, 55–96, gives prosodic accounts of external vowel sandhi. M. Vigário, *APL 13*, II, 359–76, analyses the deletion of final mute e in similar terms. L. C. Cagliari and G. Massini-Cagliari, 'Quantidade e duração silábicas em Português do Brasil', *DELTA*, 14:47–59, find a range of length effects dependent on stress and prosody rather than moraic structure. P. A. Barbosa, *CEL*, 31, 1996:33–53, attempts to model duration computationally. L. R. Couto, *'Le rhythme en espagnol et en portugais. Syllabique ou accentuel?', *TIPS*, 27, 1997:63–90.

4. SYNTAX AND MORPHOLOGY

M. A. Kato et al., *Português falado*, VI, 303–68, give a full account of BPtg. interrogatives (*construções-Q*). In two meaty articles based on NURC data, M. A. Kato et al., *Português falado*, V, 201–74, return to the analysis of BPtg as a variably pro-drop language, while M. Dillinger et al., *ib.*, 275–324, claim a basic VO sentence pattern for BPtg. J. A. Peres, 'Convenções e desvios na língua portuguesa', *RILP*, 16, 1996:9–16, distinguishes three degrees of linguistic (im)propriety. M. M. P. Scherre, 'Variação linguística, mídia e preconceito linguístico', *ib.*, 17–38, looks at non-standard plurals. R. G. Camacho, *Português falado*, VI, 253–74, and E. Pezatti, *ib.*, 275–99, study functional word order (oddly labelled as *estrutura argumental*). *Alfa*, 41, 1997, is devoted to 'Estudos de gramática funcional': S. Votre, 'Um paradigma para a lingüística funcional' (25–40), accepts the partial autonomy of syntax and semantics, giving useful examples of grammaticalization and degrammaticalization; M. L. Braga and G. M. Silva, 'Discurso e abordagens quantitativas' (41–55), find variation explained by information content; on word order, R. A. Berlinck (57–78) shows that VS order can be used to background information, while E. G. Pezatti and R. G. Camacho (99–126) see BPtg as a VSO language only now moving to SVO; M. C. Mollica, 'Anáforas em relativas no Português do Brasil' (171–79), uncovers factors favouring the still infrequent use of 'pronome sombra' in relative clauses. M. M. P. Scherre, 'Concordância nominal e funcionalismo' (181–206), argues that agreement inside NPs reflects functional principles, with only unpredictable information needing to be marked. M. M. Cavalcante, 'A omissão de complementos verbais', *LingLit*, 23, 1997:171–215, ranks semantic factors governing null objects in a BPtg spoken corpus. S. G. C. Pereira, *APL 13*, II, 185–97, considers predicative and restrictive readings of *beber o chá quente*. H. T. Valentim, ' "Ele há várias coisas . . ." - uma abordagem enunciativa', *ib.*, 353–58, somehow attributes meaning to the dummy subject *ele*.

GB SYNTAX. E. Raposo, 'Definite/zero alternations in Portuguese', *LSRL 27*, 197–212, neatly explains a range of null objects and zero determiners by the same feature, a null determiner. M. Lobo, 'Fenómenos relacionados com o Parâmetro do Sujeito Nulo em português', *Atti* (Palermo), II, 567–76, claims that pro-drop in EPtg is not simply optional. C. Novaes, 'Representação mental do sujeito nulo no português do Brasil', *RevEL*, 6.2, 1997:59–80, proposes that the null subject is pronominal in 1st person forms and variable elsewhere. E. Mourão, 'Restrições à ocorrência da CV e do pronome lexical sujeitos no português', *ib.*, 189–212, looks at pronouns in complement and coordinated structures. M. H. C. Lopes, 'Sintaxe dos nomes deverbais eventivos', *APL 13*, II, 15–30, analyses action nominals in terms of aspectual functional heads, with thematic roles interpreted only in Logical Form.

TENSE AND ASPECT. D. Santos, *Atti* (Palermo), III, 777–87, uses a corpus of translations to describe the imperfect. O. Campos and A. C. S. Rodrigues, 'Tempos verbais: uma nova abordagem', *ib.*, II, 123–29, describe preterite-perfect contrasts in terms of 'transitivity'; O. Campos et al., *Português falado*, VI, 415–62, on discourse function of the preterite-imperfect contrast.

MODALITY. Maria Helena Araújo Carreira, *Modalisation linguistique en situation d'interlocution. Proxémique verbale et modalités en Portugais*, Louvain-Paris, Peeters, 1997, 347 pp., focuses on distancing values of tenses, deixis and address, applying the approach to the imperfect in *Atti* (Palermo), IV, 33–39. M. H. M. Neves, *Português falado*, VI, 163–99, gives a functionalist overview of modality, with NURC examples. E. Gärtner, 'Modo verbal e classificação semântica dos verbos', *AIL 5*, 119–30, distinguishes ten classes of mental verbs by their modal properties and selection of mood in complement clauses. P. T. Galembeck, 'O subjuntivo em elocuções formais (Projetos NURC/SP e RJ)', *Atti* (Palermo), II, 359–69, finds modal values confirmed by speakers' preference for the infinitive in final clauses. M. H. C. Campos, 'Approche énonciative de quelques faits de modalité', *ib.*, III, 169–77, distinguishes epistemic (grammatical) and deontic (lexical) values of *dever*. B. Lohse, 'Modalidade epistémica e quantificação nominal', *AIL 5*, 131–41, insists on the modal nature of the contrast between present and future subjunctives, which represent two types of epistemic modality. H. Martins and V. Medeiros, *ib.*, 169–75, cite examples of 'flutuação' in subjunctive use in spontaneous speech.

ADVERBS. *Português falado*, II, has a subsection on adverbial syntax: R. Ilari on aspectual values (151–92) and on focus (193–212); A. T. de Castilho on *adverbios modalizados* (213–60); M. H. M. Neves on time and manner (261–96); and studies on adverb position by M. A. Oliveira (297–303) and S. Possenti (305–13). *APL 13*, II, has obvious comments on *sempre* by A. C. M. Lopes (3–14), on *mesmo* by B. Moreira (75–83), and on *então* by O. C. Silva (317–27).

PRONOUNS. M. Groppi, 'Um caminho para o estudo dos pronomes', *FLP*, 1, 1997:121–49, tries to apply a classification of pronouns into strong, weak and clitic. J. M. Barbosa, 'Sobre os chamados verbos reflexos e pronominais', *Fest. Woll*, 245–50, usefully distinguishes pronouns with complement functions (*lavar-se*) from all other cases of extended person-number marking.

NOUN PHRASES. A. L. Müller, 'A estrutura do sintagma nominal con argumentos genitivos', *CEL*, 31, 1996:71–89, uses X-bar syntax to distinguish three types of genitives. C. N. Correia, 'O valor dos determinantes em português europeu', *Atti* (Palermo), III, 157–67, gives a Culiolian account of zero determiners; A. Moreno, *APL 13*, II, 85–91, similarly covers negative values of *qualquer*. A.-M. Spanoghe, 'L'expression de l'áppartenance inaliénable en portugais, un probléme discursif?', *Atti* (Palermo), II, 783–94, links article use to 'définitude'. M. T. F. Oliveira, *APL 13*, II, 175–84, finds some relative clauses of the type *um N que* which are ambiguous between restrictive and non-restrictive readings.

VERBS. M. A. C. Mota, 'Les traits *nombre* et *personne/nombre* en portugais — l'óral dans ses variétés', *Blanche-Benveniste Vol.*, 339–45, draws together a wide range of cases of non-standard number-marking and (non-) agreement. M. H. M. Neves, 'Estudo das construções com verbo-suporte em português', *Atti* (Palermo), III, 577–88, highlights the stylistic versatility of V + N constructions (also *Português falado*, VI, 201–29). M. L. Braga describes gerundial constructions, *Português falado*, VI, 231–50. B. F. Head and L. Semenova, *AIL* 5, 267–72, list 'semi-predicative' uses of *a* + infinitive in EPtg.

DISCOURSE. *Atti* (Palermo), IV, has a cluster of discourse studies of conversation: B. Brait, 'Estratégias interacionais e configuração do texto falado' (51–63) on self-conscious elements in NURC dialogues; H. Gryner, 'Variação modal como estratégia argumentativa' (131–37) on the modal contrasts as an index of speaker attitude; L. L. Fávero, M. L. Andrade, and Z. G. O. Aquino (183–91) on self-correction; D. L. P. Barros (213–21) on *aceleração/deceleração*. With some overlap, *Português falado*, V, has NURC-based discourse studies of *decelaração* by M. Silva and I. Koch (327–38), asides by C. Jubran (339–54) and self-correction (355–66) by L. Fávero et al.; *ib.*, vi, has M. Risso et al. (821–94) on the definition of discourse markers, J. G. Hilgert (131–47) on paraphrase, and M. Souza and M. Crescitelli (149–59) on interruption. M. Basilio, *ib.*, ii, 81–97, is on discourse functions of adjectives. Repetition is a popular topic for functionalist studies: I. G. Villaça Koch. 'Peculiaridades da repetição no português falado no Brasil', *Atti* (Palermo), iv, 295–300, is a ragbag of lexical, syntactic, and discourse data; M. L. Andrade, 'A repetição como elemento condutor do tópico discursivo', *FLP*, 2 : 179–204; A. T de Castilho, 'Para uma sintaxe da repetição — Lingua falada e gramaticalização', *LingLit*, 23, 1997 : 293–330; L. A. Marcuschi, *Português falado*, vi, 95–129. On discourse structures, C. Jubran et al., *ib.*, ii, 357–97, try to identify topics as discourse units; S. C. Gavazzi, 'Fechamento de subtópicos em diálogos assimétricos', *RevEL*, 6.2, 1997 : 81–96. J. S. B. Neves, *APL 13*, ii, 135–42, describes causal constructions using *porque* and *portanto*.

STYLISTICS. R. C. P. da Silveira, 'Discursos científicos: argumentação científica em língua portuguesa e a situação de comunicação expositiva', *Atti* (Palermo), iii, 821–27, has obvious comments on discourse structure. *Fest. Woll* has the inevitable section on stylistics: U. L. Figge, 'Tempora un innere kalender in einer portugiesischen Erzählung' (139–52) on past tenses in literary use; M. Hummel (153–76) on adverbial adjectives in Eça; C. Hundt (177–94) on the re-use of set phrases in journalistic language; and C. Ossenkop (195–209) on diminutives in a folk tale.

MORPHOLOGY. Graça Maria Rio-Torto, *Morfologia Derivacional. Teoria e aplicação ao Português* (Colecção Linguística, 12) O, Porto Editora, 249 pp., essential reference for morphological studies, contains revised versions of earlier work, and new items including 'Operações e paradigmas genolexicais do português' (83–107, also *FLP*, 2 : 39–60) and 'Regras de formação de palavras em português: achegas para um quadro general' (109–32), giving an extensive classification of word-formation processes; 'Morfologia dos adjectivos étnicos' (223–30); 'Sincronia, diacronia, e análise genolexical' (133–48), arguing for complementary approaches to neologisms. A. Villalva, 'Identidade das estruturas morfológicas', *ib.*, ii, 861–66, identifies three types of nominal base for affixation. V. Kehdi, 'A derivação regressiva em português', *FLP*, 2 : 205–13, is a survey of problems, noting that for many V-N pairs the direction of derivation cannot be established. *Português falado*, ii, has I. M. Alves (99–109) on negative prefixes, O. Campos and A. Rodrigues (111–34) on noun concord, I. B. Costa on *-zinho* (135–47); *ib.*, v, contains L. Gamarski on past participles (99–117), M. H. M. Neves on argument structure in derived nouns (119–54), and R. Camacho and E. Pezatti on countable nouns (155–83); *ib.*, VI, has M. Basilio and H. Martins on denominal verbs (371–91), and L. Gamarski on -*nte* (393–413). W. M. Cano, 'O elemento *tele-* no português atual do Brasil', *Atti* (Palermo), III, 535–46, compares compounds with *tele-*, *disque-* (= 'dial') and *ligue-*. M. J. Marçalo, *ib.*, 471–83, is on *guarda-* compounds. L. A. Pagani, 'Descrição da flexão regular em Português: aplicação de uma ferramenta computacional', *CEL*, 31, 1996: 55–69, uses PC-KIMMO to model regular verb inflection.

5. LEXICON

M. Vilela, 'O léxico do Português: perspectivação geral', *FLP*, 1, 1997: 31–50, gives a fine overview of how to treat new words; on an area of heavy importation, M. G. Kriger, 'A terminologia da informática no Português brasileiro: da adaptação à transgressão', *RILP*, 16, 1996: 131–35. José Pedro Machado, *Estrangeirismos na Língua Portuguesa*, L, Notícias, 1994, 253 pp., casts his net very wide

LEXICOGRAPHY. D. Messner, **Dictionnaire des dictionnaires portugais*, Salzburg, 5 vols, 1994–1996, has got to AJU (see *Atti* (Palermo), III, 499–502). D. Kremer, 'Zu einem Historischen Wörterbuch des Portugiesischen', *Lorenzo Vol.*, 1077–1138, offers ample documentation of names of professions and personal names. Equally rich is N. Nunes, 'A terminologia do açúcar nos documentos dos séculos XV e XVI na ilha da Madeira', *APL 13*, II, 155–73. C. A. A. Murakawa, *ib.*, 105–13, compares Nascentes with later BPtg and Ptg dictionaries. L. T. Martins, 'O dicionarista brasileiro Francisco Fernandes', *AIL 5*, 177–81, gives a brief biography of a respected 20th-c. lexicographer. I. M. Alves presents the 'Dicionário de Neologismos do Português contemporâneo do Brasil', *Atti* (Palermo), III, 7–12. M. F. B. Nascimento et al., *APL 13*, II, 115–34, introduce the Ptg implementation of LE-PAROLE.

ETYMOLOGY. On imported words, A. G. da Cunha, 'Três exotismos quinhentistas (O Bétel, a Coca e a Cola)', *Confluência*, 11.1, 1996: 33–38; A. Blank goes bananas in *Fest. Woll*, 1–18; A. G. da Cunha, 'Origem e difusão dos vocábulos *azoto, hidrogênio, nitrogênio* e *oxigênio*. Estudo histórico etimológico', *Lorenzo Vol.*, 1033–36, shows French forms predominating in first attestations. More traditionally, Id., 'O latim gratus e seus derivados e compostos no vocabulário português', *FLP*, 1, 1997: 61–77, charts the extensive family of *agradar*. M. Freeman, *Rothwell Vol.*, 17–36, traces 14th-c. English *pots of osey* to Azoia. A. A. Fernandes, 'A toponímia da Beira Alta no *Dicionário Onomástico Etimológico* de José Pedro Machado', *Beira Alta*, 67, 1997: 253–92, has sensible critical comments.

SEMANTICS. A. S. Silva, *APL 13*, II, 281–93, has more data on the polysemy of *deixar* in protoype semantics (*YWMLS*, 59:389) and cognitive semantics. E. M. F. S. Nascimento, *Atti* (Palermo), III, 613–20, is superficial on portmanteau words in Guimarães Rosa. M. C. Augusto, 'Maleitas e outros achaques: tabu e eufemismo na nomenclatura das doenças', *AIL 5*, 25–40, compares Ptg euphemisms with other languages. A. M. de Oliveira 'Tabu lingüístico: um estudo do vocábulo do diabo em Grande Sertão: veredas', *Atti* (Palermo), IV, 547–53, is mainly lists. M. G. Funk, 'A genericidade dos provérbios portugueses na teoria e na prática', *AIL 5*, 103–18, sees generic reference as a result of, but not a criterion for, proverbial status for set phrases. B. Poll, 'Les collocations portugaises. Un approche métalexicographique', *Atti* (Palermo), III, 695–702, has a weak definition of collocation.

REGISTER. C. Maciel, *FLP*, 2:19–38, studies word frequencies in successive Brazilian constitutions. R. M. F. Queirós dos Santos Fréjaville, *AIL 5*, 81–101, gives an inventory of the terminology of pollution in Fr. and Ptg. M. A. Barbosa, *Atti* (Palermo), III, 25–34, finds 'conjuntos noêmicos' in ecological terminology, as C. T. Pais, *ib.*, 661–72, does for political vocabulary. Other register studies include M. E. Barcellos da Silva, *ib.*, 35–42, on fishermen's lexicon, and M. L. S. de Pretto, *ib.*, IV, 231–35, on employment law.

6. DIALECTOLOGY AND SOCIOLINGUISTICS

BRAZIL. M. Cohen et al., 'Filologia bandeirante', *FLP*, 1, 1997:79–94, describe a dialectological project to study the influence of the 17th- and 18th-c. expeditions known as *bandeiras* in the preservation of archaic features of Ptg in rural BPtg varieties. S. F. Brandão, 'O Atlas Etnolingüístico dos Pescadores do Estado do Rio de Janeiro (Região Norte)', *Atti* (Palermo), IV, 299–307, describes an atlas with quantitative data. L. A. da Silva, 'Projeto NURC: Histórico', *LdA*, 10, 1996: 83–90, traces its origins and dispersion into local research projects. Among individual dialectological studies, H. Pisciotta, 'Geografia lingüística e diacronia', *Atti* (Palermo), IV, 555–61, relates terms for the uterus to phases of colonization; S. A. M. Cardoso, 'Inovação e conservadorismo no léxico rural brasileiro', *ib.*, 109–19, lists innovations and (phonetic) archaisms from Bahia and Sergipe; J. Mota. 'Variantes palatais do português do Brasil', *ib.*, 475–83, compares non-standard *muito* [mutsu] and normal palatalization of /t d/; S. A. M. Cardoso, 'Outros caminhos de Santiago. Designações de inspiração cristã no léxico rural brasileiro', *Lorenzo Vol.*, 1037–47, maps *caminho de Santiago* (Milky Way), *verônica* (medallion), *matinas*, and *São João/Santana* (June/July). M.-M. P. Scherre and A. J. Naro, 'Sobre a concordância de número no português falado do Brasil', *Atti* (Palermo), IV, 509–23, re-run the data on concord, with education and saliency still the main factors.

PORTUGAL. M. C. F. Gouveia, *Atti* (Palermo), II, 339–49, sees a link between S. Ptg. archaisms (*párvoa, soa*) and extensions of fem -*a*. J. N. Corrêa Cardoso, *AIL 5*, 71–80, traces the replacement of *de que* by plain *que* in complement clauses. M. V. Navas Sánchez-Élez, *Atti* (Palermo), II, 645–51, finds no solution for 1pl. -*emos* in Barranquenho 1st conjugation verbs.

AFRICA. A. M. M. Martinho, 'Lusofonia em Angola e Moçambique: implicações educativas', *Confluência* 11.1, 1996:25–32.

7. CREOLES

Two long-overdue republications are Sebastião Rodolfo Dalgado, *Dialecto indo-português de Ceilão*, introd. Ian Smith., L, CNCDP, 301 pp, and Id., *Estudos sobre os crioulos indo-portugueses*, introd. Maria Isabel Tomás, L, CNCDP, 187 pp. T. Stolz gives an overview of Ptg creoles in Holtus, *Lexikon*, VII, 618–37, with a separate section on Papiamentu by M. P. A. M. Kerkhof (644–61). M. Ploae-Hanganu, 'A dinâmica lexical do crioulo português da África', *AIL 5*, 255–65, gives samples of classic types of lexical and semantic change in creoles, urging a full study. Nicolas Quint-Abril, *Dicionário Caboverdiano (variante de Santiago)-Português*, L, Verbalis, 111 pp., is also available on CD-ROM. C. P. Costa Martins, 'Presença da língua inglesa no léxico crioulo de Cabo Verde', *AIL 5*, 153–68, lists borrowings from English and American, with notes on phonetic and morphological adaptation. H. H. do Couto, 'Os provérbios crioulos de Guiné-Bissau', *RILP*, 16, 1996:100–14.

MEDIEVAL LITERATURE
POSTPONED

LITERATURE, 1500 TO THE PRESENT DAY
POSTPONED

VII. GALICIAN STUDIES

LANGUAGE

POSTPONED

LITERATURE

By Dolores Vilavedra, *Department of Galician Philology, University of Santiago* and Derek Flitter, *Senior Lecturer in Modern Spanish Language and Literature, University of Birmingham*

1. General

The final three volumes (III-V) of the collective *Historia da literatura galega*, Vigo, ASPG–A nosa terra, 643–90, 961–1280, 1281–1600 pp., complement earlier instalments published in 1996 and 1997 (*YWMLS*, 59:421); while evidencing those same problems detected in their predecessors, these volumes provide a useful new — if markedly ideological — focus dominated by an emphasis on socio-historical context. A. Requeixo, *Escritores mindonienses*, Ferrol, Sociedad de Cultura Valle-Inclán, 162 pp., meticulously documents the contribution to Galician literature of a long list of Mondoñedo writers and of the area's periodical press. X. R. Pena, 'Algunhas reflexións arredor da conformación dunha literatura periférica', *AELG*, 1997:145–60, reflects upon the allegedly peripheral nature of Galician literature with reference to opinions on the question expressed by the region's most noted specialists. M. Valcárcel, 'Prensa literaria en Galicia: desalienación cultural e afirmación dunha identidade', *Actas* (Lisbon), 269–312, is a comprehensive survey of the contribution made by the periodical press to the development of an autochtonous literature. A. Requeixo, 'Literatura galega e medios de comunicación: o estado da cuestión ás portas do século XXI', *ib.*, 313–32, approaches the same issue from a strictly contemporary perspective. E. Río, 'Textos metaliterarios nas letras galegas no período 1920–55', *AELG*, 1997:161–72, is a summary of a much larger doctoral thesis dealing with these issues. J. Ribera and O. Rodríguez, 'Aproximación ás relacións literarias galego-catalanas. Noticias históricas e bibliográficas', *Madrigal*, 1:97–100, provides a brief historical survey of relationships between the respective literatures. X. Frías, 'Nos confíns da literatura galega: escritores asturianos en galego', *RLLCGV*, 5:223–40, surveys the production of Asturian authors writing in Galician. K. B. Valentine and G. Valentine, 'Galician folklore:

starting a dialogue', *GalR*, 2:80–84, is intended to stimulate intellectual exchange. The weighty *Lorenzo Vol.* has given a belated public airing to numerous literary studies, such as A. Tarrío's 'Tempo e novela: da melancolía á vertixe (ensaio)' (377–90), which, with reference to Pérez Galdós and Blanco-Amor, analyses the capacity of prose fiction to generate specific reactions in the reader. M. T. Caneda, 'Literatura, traducción e reconfiguración da identidade nacional: a "apropiación" galega do *Ulises*', *Grial*, 137:87–97, evidences the ideological loading of translation, using as an example the Galician version of Joyce's novel.

2. NARRATIVE

X. C. Domínguez, 'A diversificación do xénero narrativo dende 1975', *Actas* (Lisbon), 87–111, synthesizes the development of the genre since the death of Franco and the multiplicity of critical interpretations deriving from it. S. Gaspar, 'La narrativa (1975–97)', *RLLCGV*, 5:249–62, supplies a panoramic survey of the given period. D. Vilavedra, 'A narrativa galega, na procura de novos camiños', *AELG*, 1997:195–201, is a critical examination of the year's production.

3. THEATRE

Do novo teatro á nova dramaturxia (1965–95), ed. M. Vieites, Vigo, Xerais, 257 pp., provides a first systematic examination of theatrical writing and scenography of the period, one which saw a progressive reception and definition of Galician theatre. From the same author come: 'De la brevedad como elección a la brevedad como maldición. Apuntes sobre la dramática breve gallega', *Art teatral*, 10:65–71, seeking to account for the historical fortunes of this genre in Galician; an 'Estudio preliminar' (pp. 17–180) to *La nueva dramaturgia gallega*, Madrid, Asociación de Directores de Escena de España, 491 pp., examining theatrical production since 1965 in its literary, scenographic and socio-historical context and prefacing an anthology of the work of some 20 playwrights; and 'Sen présa . . . sen pausa . . . camiño de ningures', *AELG*, 1997:211–16, evaluating the year's dramatic production. D. Vilavedra, 'El teatro gallego después de 1975: una incipiente madurez', *RLLCGV*, 5:297–311, takes Vieites's proposals as a point of departure while seeking to modify certain of their conclusions. A. Abuín, 'De *poioumenos* e outros usos postmodernos: unha tendencia no teatro galego actual', *BGL*, 19:83–90, is concerned with the prevalence, in contemporary Galician drama, of elements of metatheatre as conceived by theories of postmodernism.

4. POETRY

Grial, 140, is a monographic issue dedicated to 'Poesía última 1985-98', which includes a selection of poems by writers emerging during this period and a cluster of articles; among these are: H. González, 'Repensar, fatigándose, desde a desorde actual' (651–65), seeking to make a fresh classification of work appearing since 1985; A. Casas, 'Lírica difusa, ou xéneros en tempo indecoroso' (667–89), scrutinizes the various new generic models explored by Galician poets; M. Romero, 'Poetizar o mundo como muller. Movemento poético da *Festa da palabra silenciada*: trece anos de poesía galega de mulleres' (691–716), evaluates a flourishing Galician women's poetry with special reference to the group of writers emerging out of the influential journal named in the title; I. Cochón, 'Dicción, contradicción e nación: a incorporación do mundo no discurso poético último' (717–30), aims to document how Galician poetry of the period sought to revise and extend those stereotypical images of Galician identity found in official discourse; T. Seara, 'A diversificación da poética intimista no período 1985-97' (731–44), surveys the diverse poetic projections of the lyrical self found in this verse. H. González, 'De poesía e de poetas no cincuenta aniversario de *Cómaros verdes*', *AELG*, 1997 : 203–10, provides a critical evaluation of the year's production. H. González, 'Poesía gallega desde 1975 hasta hoy: entre la palabra y la realidad', *RLLCGV*, 5 : 263–76, supplies a panoramic reassessment of the period. The same writer's 'La destrucció dels tòpics a la recent poesia de dones', in *Bellesa, dona i literatura. Actes del Congrés Internacional 12–14 de març 1997*, ed. A. Carabí and M. Sagarra, Barcelona, Centre Dona i Literatura–Universidad de Barcelona, CD-ROM, proposes several lines of thought concerning women's poetry of the 1990s converging in its subversion of canons of beauty. M. María, 'Do Rexurdimento á renovación dos anos oitenta', *Actas* (Lisbon), 195–228, is an historical survey, defined by period, from the pen of one of modern Galician literature's most eminent poets.

5. MEDIAEVAL LITERATURE

The dedication of the *Día das Letras Galegas 1998* to three mediaeval troubadours produced a tidal wave of published material, much of it in a form intended simply to commemorate or popularize their verse. Several volumes are, however, notable for the intellectual rigour of their content. Henrique Monteagudo, Luz Pozo Garza, and Xesús Alonso Montero, *Tres poetas medievais da ría de Vigo. Martín Codax, Mendiño e Xohán de Cangas*, Vigo, Galaxia, 350 pp., is a collaborative venture: M.'s 'O marco histórico-literario. A lírica trobadoresca galego-portuguesa' (13–162) establishes specifiable generic character-istics for the closely related *cantigas de romaría* and *cantigas de santuario*; P.G.'s 'Os poetas do mar de Vigo' (163–246) proposes an audacious new reading that challenges the cyclical pattern customarily attrib-uted to the seven poems by Martín Códax; A.M., for his own part, produces a critical survey of the editions, translations, literary tributes and forms of poetic recycling generated by the three troubadours under the heading 'Fortuna literaria dos tres poetas da ría de Vigo' (247–334).

Martín Codax. Mendiño. Xohán de Cangas. Día das Letras Galegas 1998, ed. X. L. Couceiro and L. Fontoira, Santiago de Compostela U.P., 188 pp., contains a wide range of articles, among which: R. Álvarez and H. Monteagudo, '¿Sedía-m' eu? A propósito do *incipit* da cantiga de Meendiño' (45–64), offer a fresh interpretation of the notoriously polemical opening of Mendiño's poem; M. Brea, '*E verrá i, mia madre, o meu amigo*' (65–76), takes on some of the problems surrounding Martín Codax's 'Mia irmana fremosa, treides comigo'; X. L. Couceiro, 'A edición da cantiga de Mendiño' (77–95), makes an effective review of the various editions and interpretations of the text; E. Fidalgo, '*Corpo velido, corpo delgado*: a descrición física da amiga' (97–112), examines the self-portrait of the female protagonist of *Eno sagrado, en Vigo*; P. Lorenzo, 'Tres xograres, tres ermidas e un só mar' (133–42), evaluates those elements linking the work of these trouba-dours to the *cantiga de romaría*; L. Martínez, '¿Fonosimbolismo en Mendinho?' (151–59), scrutinizes phonic elements in Mendiño's text.

Flitter, *Ondas,* contains the proceedings of the Birmingham sympo-sium held in May of 1998. F.'s preface, 'Limiar: As ondas no tempo' (v-vii), is followed by some wide-ranging papers: X. L. Méndez Ferrín, 'Meendinho connosco' (1–11), argues for the origins of much of Meendiño's phrasing and imagery in the Psalms and makes an engaging historico-literary depiction of the island of San Simón; H. Monteagudo, 'Cantores de santuario, cantares de romaría' (12–37), is a thoroughly documented and densely argued appraisal of pilgrim elements in the *cantigas*; M. C. Rodríguez Castaño and M. C. Vázquez Pacho, 'O proxecto Lírica Galego-Portuguesa (LGP), primeira fase do Arquivo Galicia Medieval (AGM)' (38–48), detail the mammoth research project currently being undertaken under the auspices of the *Instituto Ramón Piñeiro* in Santiago; J. Paredes Núñez, 'As cantigas satíricas de Afonso X, o Sábio: problemas de inter-pretação' (49–57), reveals some of the lexical subtleties and sexual innuendoes of this verse, highlighting the pressing need for an annotated critical edition; M. P. Ferreira, 'A música das cantigas galego-portuguesas: balanço de duas décadas de investigação

(1977–1997)' (58–71), underlines recent discoveries in this area and maps out some of those rich veins yet to be worked; S. Parkinson, 'Two for the price of one: on the Castroxeriz *Cantigas de Santa María*' (72–88), argues convincingly and in considerable detail that *cantigas* 242 and 249 are elaborations of the same collected miracle story, two separate compositions resulting from what was originally a single piece; T. López, 'Meendinho e familia' (89–107), considers the presence of motifs deriving from the *cantigas* — elements of 'neotrobadorismo' — in the work of modern poets, including Álvaro Cunqueiro and Luz Pozo Garza; S. Gutiérrez García, 'A corte poética de Afonso III o Bolonhês e a materia de Bretaña' (108–23), argues against the allegedly peripheral cultural positioning of the Iberian Peninsula within mediaeval western Europe, stressing the role of Afonso III of Portugal in a broadening of literary and artistic horizons; R. Zenith, 'Translating the *Cantigas*: how to lose gracefully' (124–31), provides an insight into the translator's art with special reference to his own English version of Pero Meogo's 'Levou-s'a louçana, levou-s'a velida'; G. Lanciani, '*Nojo tom'e quer prazer* é de Fernão Velho?' (132–38), argues that the said piece is not a composition by Fernan Velho but, instead, a much later anonymous addition to the original manuscript; G. Videira Lopes, 'Os ciclos satíricos nos Cancioneiros peninsulares' (139–46), surveys the historical context and often elusive meaning of those examples, commonly found in the mediaeval lyric, of variations upon a single theme; X. R. Pena, '*En Vigo, eno sagrado*: ciclos e secuencias líricas no cancioneiro de amigo' (147–57), examines the arguments for and against specific structural patterning of poem cycles in the *cantigas*, preferring to view individual poems as fragmentary imaginative insights rather than as exactly ordered components of a precisely organized whole; G. Tavani, 'Ainda sobre Martin Codax e Mendinho' (158–73), returns to the enduring textual questions surrounding the single surviving *cantiga* of Mendiño and the equally persistent interpretative problems posed by those of Martín Codax. M. P. Ferreira has also provided 'The layout of the *cantigas*: a musicological overview', *GalR*, 2:47–61, eliciting the contribution of musical structures to the meaning of the *cantigas*, even in the absence, within surviving manuscripts, of the planned musical notation.

Among the contributions to *Lorenzo Vol.* are numbered a cluster of articles dealing with mediaeval verse: X. B. Arias, 'O motivo do "casamento da senhor" nas cantigas d'amor' (123–34), posits an effective chronological pattern for this motif, according to which significant evidence of poetic influence is perceptible; I. Castro, 'O fragmento galego do *Livro de Tristán*' (135–50), provides up-to-date coverage of work on the manuscript; X. M. Gómez, 'A manifestación do marabilloso de orixe cristiá no texto historiográfico' (151–76), analyses supernatural visitations found in the Galician translation of the *Crónica general*; X. Filgueira, 'A remuneración do axente lírico na poesía galego-portuguesa medieval' (185–86), studies the various methods of payment given to mediaeval *cantores*.

6. Individual Authors

AMOR MEILÁN. M. T. Araújo Torres, 'Introducción' (11–47) to *Baixo do alpendre e outros relatos*, Santiago, Xunta–CILLRP, 172 pp.

BLANCO AMOR. C. Blanco, 'Parodia e destrucción xenérica en *A esmorga* de Blanco Amor', *Lorenzo Vol.*, 333–46, underlines the novel's subversive content. The collective volume *Homenaxe a Blanco Amor 1998*, Corunna, Espiral Maior, 138 pp., is primarily an ensemble of imaginative literature and biographical recollections dedicated to B.A., the highlight of which is C. Rodríguez's 'Sobre os anxos de E. Blanco Amor' (69–79), dealing with an unpublished collection of B.A.'s poems in Castilian and, more specifically, with the motif that was to emerge as central to a poetic canon of homosexual love in Spanish poetry.

BLANCO TORRES. An early avalanche of publications concerning the life and work of the honorand of the *Día das Letras Galegas* for 1999 includes: J. Blanco Valdés, *Hipertensión cívica. Aproximación á vida e a obra de R. Blanco Torres*, Sada, O Castro, 398 pp., possibly the most comprehensive and well documented biographical study, with a selection of his work and bibliographical information; M. Villar, 'Introducción' (pp. 10–82) to *Orballo de media noite*, Vigo, Xerais, 148 pp., B.T.'s only published imaginative work in Galician.

CASTRO E ANDRADE. X. L. Couceiro, 'Atribución indebida', *Lorenzo Vol.*, 283–98, casts fresh light on the life of Isabel de Castro e Andrade and on the contested authorship of the famous sonnet usually attributed to her.

CASTRO. C. Blanco, 'A subversión múltiple. "Estranxeira na súa patria" de R. de Castro', *Unión Libre*, 3:37–48, analyses the various strategies employed by the author to communicate a sense of alienation from the surrounding world. J. Gómez Montero, 'O vaso quebrado. Imaxes da identidade na poesía de R. de Castro', *AELG*, 1997:11–46, proposes a hermeneutic reading of the poetry centred on the construction of the subject and its aesthetic configuration. A. López, ' "Soya cos meus pensamentos". A adxectivación das mulleres nos *Cantares gallegos* de Rosalía', *Lorenzo Vol.*, 255–82, reaches some suggestive conclusions regarding a 'hermeneutics of suspicion' in the adjectivization of the female figure in Rosalía's collection.

CUNQUEIRO. X. Alonso and G. Avenoza, 'Dous poemas en catalán de A. Cunqueiro', *Madrigal*, 1:27–38, is a facsimile edition, with Galician translation and literary and linguistic commentary, of two poems written in Catalan. M. Carracedo, 'O teatro descoñecido de Cunqueiro', *ATO*, 34:69–84, reproduces an unpublished theatrical text written by C. in Catalan and premiered in 1938, with a well documented appraisal of its reception by public and theatre critics. J. Kabatek, 'F. Hölderlin en galego (con especial referencia ás traduccións de A. Cunqueiro)', *BGL*, 20:5–22, is an historical survey of H.'s fortunes in Galician, in which C.'s translations are subjected to close scrutiny. C. Paz, '*Xan, o bo conspirador*, un texto revolucionario', *Art teatral*, 10:74–78, stresses the play's originality in its historical moment.

CURROS ENRÍQUEZ. E. López Varela, *A poesía galega de M. Curros Enríquez*, 2 vols, Corunna, Deputación, 1–1034, 1037–1969 pp., is a weighty study: the first volume contains an extensive preliminary study (85–305) and an annotated edition of C.E.'s published poetry in Galician; the second includes C.E.'s journalism, his unpublished poetry and his verse written in Castilian Spanish, together with a documentary appendix. R. Gutiérrez, ' "A Rosalía", Curros Enríquez e o canon', *BGL*, 19:103–09, analyses the poem's symbolism with reference to contemporary paradigms and evaluates its contribution to the critical reception of C.E. The facsimile edition of *A virxe do cristal*, Santiago, Xunta, 64 pp., includes J. M. Paz's, 'Comentario preliminar' (ix–xxxiii), which pays particular attention to metrical patterns. P. Vázquez Cuesta, 'Curros Enríquez, traductor de Guerra Junqueiro', *Lorenzo Vol.*, 299–308, examines C.E.'s Castilian translations of the Portuguese poet.

DIESTE. R. Varela, 'O diálogo en *A fiestra valdeira* de R. Dieste', *BGL*, 19:65–82, analyses the characteristics of dramatic dialogue as evidenced by the text in question.

FERREIRO. A. Acuña, 'Os Juegos Florais da A. C. Ac. "Santa Cecilia" (Marín): poemario premiado de C. E. Ferreiro e variantes voluntarias posteriores', *Madrigal*, 1:13–26, salvages an unpublished collection of poems and considers its relationship to F.'s subsequent work.

GARCÍA LORCA. The centenary of Lorca's birth has inspired an abundance of work on his cluster of Galician poems: X. Alonso Montero, 'Presencia dos *Seis poemas galegos* de García Lorca na poesía galega', *Actas* (Lisbon), 115–29, is a closely documented overview of intertextual connections with these poems found in subsequent Galician literature. L. Alonso, 'García Lorca: "Poeta da alta herba" no seu itinerario galego', *ib.*, 229–40, summarizes the enduring debate concerning G.L.'s relationship with Galicia and his poems in the Galician language. X. A. García, 'García Lorca e Lorenzo Varela: dous cabodanos e un poema esquecido', *ATO*, 34:77–81, finds traces of G.L.'s poetic practice in a poem in Castilian dedicated to G.L. by Varela in a homage volume. L. Pérez, 'E. Blanco Amor e F. García Lorca', *Homenaxe a Blanco Amor 1998*, 45–59, debates the thorny question of the literary and linguistic authorship of the Galician poems in the context of G.L.'s friendship with Blanco Amor. A. Pociña, 'F. García Lorca, tema dos poetas galegos', *Lorenzo Vol.*, 347–64, examines the Lorquian motifs deriving from G.L.'s Galician poems.

GONZÁLEZ GARCÉS. A new edition of G.G.'s *Poesía galega*, Corunna, Espiral Maior, 118 pp., contains an extensive and rigorously analytical introduction in the form of a 'Limiar' (9–39) by X. L. Valcárcel.

GONZÁLEZ REIGOSA. See MÉNDEZ FERRÍN.

IGLESIA ALVARIÑO. L. Rodríguez, 'No cincuentenario de *Cómaros verdes*', *AELG*, 1997:85–108, examines the reception of this work within the Galician literary context of its period and assesses its significance within I.A.'s overall output.

LAMAS CARVAJAL. M. P. García Negro, 'Introducción' (pp. 13–45) to a new edition of L.C.'s complete poetical work in Galician, 530 pp.

LEIRAS PULPEIRO. R. Reimunde, *Ben pode Mondoñedo desde agora. A esencia popular na obra e na lingua de M. Leiras Pulpeiro*, Fundación Caixa Galicia, 220 pp., approaches L.P.'s life and work from the standpoint of that work's popular inspiration, in a text that reproduces a great deal of previously unpublished material.

LOIS VÁZQUEZ. M. T. Monteagudo's 'Biobibliografía' (pp. 11–56) figures as an introduction to *Alira de Elfe. A Reina Loba e outros relatos*, Santiago, Xunta–CILLRP, 160 pp.

LÓPEZ-CASANOVA. C. Mejía, 'Una aproximación a *Asedio de sombra* de A. López-Casanova', *Madrigal*, 1:79–82, outlines the thematic and symbolic motifs of this collection.

MANUEL ANTONIO. *De catro a catro*, Vigo, Galaxia, 112 pp., contains an excellent textual analysis in the form of an 'Introducción' (9–59) by H. González.

MÉNDEZ FERRÍN. C. Mejía and M. M. López, 'Recreación medieval en *Percival e outras historias* (1958) de X. L. Méndez Ferrín y en *Irmán Rei Artur* (1987) de C. González Reigosa', *RLLCGV*, 5:277–96, looks at the convergent uses made by the two writers of the Materia de Bretaña. J. Rutherford, 'The artisan-translator and the artist-translator: Méndez Ferrín into English', *GalR*, 2:73–79, illustrates practical questions of translation in writing of the gestation of *Them and Other Stories*.

MURGUÍA. On the 75th anniversary of the author's death, there was an abundance of published studies. Deserving of especial mention is H. Rabunhal, *Manuel Murguía*, Santiago, Laiovento, 146 pp., an intellectual biography that pays particular attention to historical context and that reproduces some of M.'s most important texts. *A nosa terra. Cadernos A nosa cultura*, 19, 79 pp., is a monographic issue under the title 'Volver a Murguía' that contains a range of material on this multi-faceted writer.

NEIRA VILAS. C. De Oliveira, 'Os narradores artífices: X. Neira Vilas e Rachel de Queiroz', *ATO*, 34:29–37, examines, from a comparativist perspective and in the vein of Walter Benjamin, the relationships between the respective authors' work.

OTERO PEDRAYO. *A lagarada. O desengano do prioiro*, ed. H. Monteagudo, Vigo, Galaxia, 202 pp., contains an exploratory piece by M. Vieites, 'A obra dramática de Otero Pedrayo. Entre a tradición e a (pos)modernidade' (7–39), that formulates the essential premises for a re-evaluation of O.P.'s dramatic output. X. Alonso Montero has edited, with a preliminary 'Estudio' (pp. 9–28), O.P.'s unpublished poem 'A Estadea ou pranto polo Seminario de Estudos Galegos', together with a facsimile of the autograph manuscript, 47 pp. C. Patterson, 'Landscape, philosophy and identity: a Galician response to the legacy of 1898', *GalR*, 2:62–72, examines *Arredor de si* in the light of O.P.'s Spanish predecessors; A. Risco, 'Unha lectura de *O purgatorio de Don Ramiro* de Otero Pedrayo', *Lorenzo Vol.*, 309–19, interprets from a mythological and anthropological perspective the presence of a supernatural realm in O.P.'s text. X. R. Barreiro, 'Ficción e realidade histórica na novela *O señorito da Reboraina*', *ib.*, 321–32, is an evaluation of those features that mark out the novel as an historical work. X. M. Salgado, 'Otero Pedrayo y el teatro', *Art teatral*, 10:79–86, sees a leading specialist in O.P.'s work outline a general picture of his writing for the stage.

OUTEIRIÑO. M. C. Rábade, 'E o silencio na lira de Outeiriño', *Dorna*, 24:115–28, provides an analysis of polyphony, especially in the form of intertextual references, in the collection *Depósito de espantos*.

PÉREZ PLACER. I. Soto, 'Os relatos galegos de H. Pérez Placer', *BGL*, 19:21–63, examines P.P.'s short fiction, outlining its thematic content and formulating some essential interpretative strategies.

PONDAL. M. X. Queizán, *Misoxinia e racismo na poesía de Pondal*, Santiago, Laiovento, 81 pp., is an attempt, on the part of a well-known feminist activist, to define the sexist and racist ideology informing P.'s literary production.

POZO GARZA. V. Sanjurjo, *Entre la llum i l'ombra. L'obra poética de Luz Pozo Garza*, Barcelona, Parsifal, is a stylistic analysis of P.G.'s Galician poems that pays particular attention to intertextuality and musicality.

RODRÍGUEZ FER.   O. Novo, 'A luz da rosa negra. Eróticas de C. Rodríguez Fer', *AELG*, 1997:131–43, surveys the principal thematic motifs of R.F.'s erotic verse.

ROMPENTE.   H. González, 'Rompente, poderosa pomada', *AELG*, 1997:47–84, provides an important study of the artistic output of the Rompente co-operative, a grouping that played a salient role in the renovation of Galician verse in the years immediately before and after 1975.

VARELA.   See GARCÍA LORCA above.

VILLAR PONTE.   *Entre dous abismos. Nouturnio de mesao e morte*, 151 pp., ed. E. X. Ínsua with an extensive introduction (9–109), provides a thoroughgoing analysis both of these texts and of the hitherto neglected contribution of their author to Galician drama of the period.

VIII. LATIN AMERICAN STUDIES

SPANISH AMERICAN LITERATURE
THE COLONIAL PERIOD

POSTPONED

THE NINETEENTH CENTURY

By Annella McDermott, *Department of Hispanic, Portuguese and Latin American Studies, University of Bristol*

1. General

G. Aching, *The Politics of Spanish American Modernismo*, CUP, 1997, 183 pp., offers a close reading of selected texts with a view to understanding the links between aesthetics and notions of Spanish American cultural autonomy. The principal texts explored are by Darío, Julián del Casal, and José Enrique Rodó: there is also a chapter dealing with a number of *modernista* literary journals. Timothy G. Compton, *Mexican Picaresque Narratives*, Lewisburg, Bucknell U.P. — London, Associated U.P., 1997, 147 pp., examines at length eight narratives from the 16th to the 20th c., among them Lizardi's *El Periquillo Sarniento* and *Don Catrín de la Fachenda*. Rita Gnutzmann, **La novela naturalista en Argentina (1800–1900)*, Rodopi, Amsterdam, 239 pp. R. Gnutzmann, 'La batalla del naturalismo en Buenos Aires', *RIAB*, 48:53–68, chronicles the debate on this literary movment in the Buenos Aires press, and in critical writing, from 1879. Martha I. Gonzales Ascorra, **La evolución de la conciencia femenina a través de las novelas de Gertrudis Gómez de Avellaneda, Soledad Acosta de Samper y Mercedes Cabello de Carbonera*, NY, 1997. N. Jitrik, 'La estética del romanticismo', *Hispamérica*, 76–77, 1997:35–47, examines the role played by Romanticism in the formation of the Latin American nations. G. Marún, 'Darwin y la literatura argentina', *La Torre*, 3:551–77, is concerned with the influence of Darwin on such novels as Eduardo Holmberg's *Dos partidos en lucha* (1875) and *Olimpio Pitango de Monalia* (published posthumously in 1915), on Sarmiento and Alberdi, and on articles in *La Revista Literaria* (June–October 1879). Klaus Meyer-Minnemann, **La novela hispanoamericana de fin de siglo*, Mexico, F.C.E., 1997, 382 pp. Cristóbal Pera, **Modernistas in París: el mito de París en la prosa modernista hispanomericana*, Berne, Lang, 1997, 207 pp. Dolores Phillips-López, **La novela hispanomaericana del modernismo*, Geneva, 1997, 314 pp. *Narrativa fantástica del siglo XIX (España e Hispanoamérica)*, ed. Jaume Pont, Lleida, Milenio, 1997, 433 pp., has articles on Tomás Carrasquilla, Rubén Darío, Gertrudis Gómez de Avellaneda, Juana Manuela Gorriti, Amado Nervo, and Ricardo Palma. I. A. Schulman, 'Modernismo/Modernidad y el proyecto de alzar la nación', *JILAS*, 4:121–31, concentrates on aspects of *modernista* writing linked to nation-building. Sara V. Rosell, *La novela antiesclavista en Cuba y Brasil, Siglo XIX*, M, Pliegos, 1997, 192 pp., deals with Gertrudis Gómez de Avellaneda, *Sab*, Cirilo Villaverde, *Cecilia Valdés*, Maria Firmina dos Reis, *Ursula* and Bernardo Guimarães, *A Escrava Isaura*.

2. INDIVIDUAL AUTHORS

BELLO, ANDRÉS.   M. Gomes, 'Las silvas americanas de Andrés Bello: una relectura generológica', *HR*, 66:181–96, explores B.'s use of open imitation of existing works.

DARÍO, RUBÉN.   J. M. Martínez, 'Sobre la recepción y el contexto de *El fardo*', *Atenea*, 478:215–31, amongst other considerations, traces similarities between this story by D. and *Un naufragio* by the Chilean Pedro Balmaceda Toro. Uncertainty about the dates of composition of both stories make it difficult to be sure who influenced whom, though the writer opts for D. as the author of the original text. J. Martínez Domingo, 'Un carta inédita de Rubén Darío a Algernon Charles Swinburne', *BHS(G)*, 74, 1997:279–92, enlarges upon D.'s knowledge of English, in particular his ability to write in that language. J. M. Martos, 'Góngora, Velásquez y Rubén Darío: el diálogo imposible de *Trébol* (*Cantos de vida y esperanza, Otros poemas, VII*)', *HR*, 66:171–80, examines the poem in the light of Riffaterre's theories.

ECHEVERRÍA, ESTEBAN.   M. A. Cabañas, 'Géneros al matadero: Esteban Echeverría y la cuestión de los tipos literarios', *RCLL*, 48:133–47, examines the reasons for E.'s failure, or refusal, to publish this text in his lifetime, and the difficulties of assigning it to a particular genre.

GÓMEZ DE AVELLANEDA, GERTRUDIS.   B. Pastor, 'A romance life in novel fiction: the early career and works of Gertrudis Gómez de Avellaneda', *BHS(G)*, 75:169–81, points out that while G. de A.'s life may be seen as an example of romance, the novel was her preferred genre for the expression of her feminist views.

MARGARIÑOS CERVANTES, ALEJANDRO.   M. C. Burgueño, '*O Caramuru* y *Caramurú*: sus relaciones en la formación de un protoimaginario nacional uruguayo', *RevIb*, 64:117–28, looks at intertextual relations between M.C.'s novel and the epic poem by the Portuguese José de Santa Rita Durão.

MANSILLA, LUCIO V. S. Rotker, 'De dandys y cautivas: ocultamientos en la frontera', *CAm*, 212:82–89, centres on silences in M.'s *Una excursión a los indios ranqueles*, in particular the absence of detailed description of captive white women; attention is also drawn to contradictions between certain attitudes expressed in the book and M.'s public actions, or later writings.

MÁRMOL, JOSÉ. C. Lindsay, 'The two *Amalias:* irony and influence in José Mármol's novel and Rosario Ferré's short story', *JILAS*, 4:5–19, focuses on the different approach to nation-building expressed in the two works.

MARTÍ, JOSÉ. Carmen Alemany, *José Martí: historia y literatura ante el fin del siglo XIX*, Alicante U.P. — Havana, Casa de las Américas, 1997, 266 pp., publishes papers delivered at the international colloquium held in Alicante in 1995. Besides some papers on historical questions, it contains: C. Vitier, 'España en Martí' (15–30); R. Fernández Retamar, 'Forma y pensamiento en José Martí' (31–41); T. Fernández, 'José Martí y la invención de la identidad hispanoamericana' (43–50); I. A. Schulman, 'Narrando la nación moderna' (51–73); A. Sorel, 'José Martí: un creador del siglo XIX para el siglo XXI' (75–86); F. García Marruz, 'Los *Versos sencillos*' (89–108); B. Varela Jácome, 'Análisis estilístico de *Versos sencillos*' (109–26); C. Alemany Bay, 'Intuiciones sobre el proceso de creación de los *Versos libres* de José Martí' (127–34); E. Marini-Palmieri, 'Los *Versos libres* de José Martí: notas para una poética de lo hirsuto' (135–46); C. Ruiz Barrionuevo, '"En un domingo de mucha luz": poesía y literatura en los años previos a *Ismaelillo*' (147–58); R. Mataix, 'José Martí, protagonista del mito: la utopía americana de Lezama Lima' (159–67); M. A. Auladell, 'Literatura y educación en el inicio del modernismo: la aportación de José Martí' (169–78); J. Gomáriz, 'Las metamorfosis del poeta e intelectual ante la modernidad en *Lucía Jerez*' (179–99). A. Azougarth, 'Martí orientalista', *CAm*, 210:12–20, points to the difference between the attitude to the Orient of the majority of *modernista* writers, for whom it was largely an imaginary or literary construct, and the attitude of M., who had a genuine interest in the historical reality of the Arab and Muslim world. **José Martí y su periódico 'Patria'*, ed. Salvador Bueno, Barcelona, Puvill, 1997.

VARGAS VILA, JOSÉ MARÍA. A. Correa Ramón, 'José María Vargas Vila: un caso de recepción literaria manipulada', *JILAS*, 4:133–41, makes the point that negative images of the lifestyle of this writer, and of the *modernistas* in general, have obscured discussion of the literary merits of their work.

VILLAVERDE, CIRILO. S. Fischer, 'Sketches of a colony: Cuba in the 1800s', *JLACS*, 7:131–49, looks at Cirilo Villaverde's *Excursión a*

Vuelta Abajo, arguing that the narrative's concern with beginnings 'reflects a generalized desire among the Cuban elites at the time to eradicate a pictorial tradition that had been the domain of coloured artisans'.

THE TWENTIETH CENTURY

By D. L. SHAW, *Brown-Forman Professor of Spanish American Literature in the University of Virginia*

I. GENERAL

GENERAL WORKS. *Latin American Postmodernisms*, ed. R. A. Young, Amsterdam, Rodopi, 1997, 282 pp., a collection of essays chiefly on individual countries and authors; *Twentieth Century Spanish American Literature since 1960*, ed. D. W. Foster, NY, Garland, apparently collects 32 previously published articles, many by leading critics. See too his *Sexual Textualities. Essays on Queer/ing Latin American Writing*, Austin, Texas U.P., 1997, 180 pp. J. Bracho, *El discurso de la inconformidad. Expectativas y experiencias en la modernidad hispanoamericana*, Caracas, Fundación CELARG, 1997. I. Corona, '¿Vecinos distantes? Las agendas posmodernas en Hispanoamérica y el Brasil', *RevIb*, 182–83:17–38. S. Mattalía, *Modernidad y fin de siglo en Hispanoamerica*, Alicante, Gil Albert, 1996, essays on literature. N. Linstrom, *The Social Conscience of Latin American Writing*, Austin, Texas U.P., 200 pp. See too her 'Escritoras judías brasileñas e hispanoamericanas', *RevIb*, 182–83:287–97, a quick survey. G. Siebenmann, *Poesía y poéticas del siglo XX en la América Hispana y el Brasil*, M, Gredos, 1997, 475 pp., is very thorough. C. Alemany Bay, *Poética coloquial hispanoamericana*, Alicante, Alicante U.P., 1997, 221 pp. R. L. Williams, *The Modern Latin American Novel*, NY, Twayne, 177 pp., a brief survey from the 1940s to now. D. L. Shaw, *The Post-Boom in Spanish American Fiction*, Albany, SUNY U.P., 224 pp., discusses its emergence and major representative writers. L. P. Zamora, *The Usable Past. The Imagination of History in Recent Fiction of the Americas*, CUP, 1997, 272 pp. *La invención del pasado*, ed. K. Kohut, Frankfurt, Vervuert, 1997, 256 pp., on historical novels by García Márquez, Carpentier, Poniatowska, etc. in the context of postmodernism. J. Rodríguez-Luis, *El enfoque documental en la narrativa hispanoamericana*, Mexico D. F., FCE, 1997, 137 pp. A. Llerena, *Realismo mágico y lo real maravilloso*, Gaithersburg, Hispamérica, 1997, 333 pp. E. Camaid-Freixas, *Realismo mágico y primitivismo. Relecturas de Carpentier, Asturias, Rulfo y García Márquez*, Lanham, U.P. of America, 349 pp., takes too restricted a view of the movement. S. Menton, *Historia verdadera del realismo mágico*, Mexico D. F., FCE, 256 pp., casts his net very wide. A. Ubidia, 'Cinco tesis acerca del realismo mágico', *Hispamérica*, 78, 1997:101–07, attempts to establish distinctions. S. Henigen, 'The trapped bachelor', *BHS(G)*, 75:221–35, surveys ambivalence about the homeland in novels from

Asturias to Allende. P. Collard, *El relato breve en las letras hispánicas actuales*, Amsterdam, Rodopi, 1997. *RIAB*, 46, 1996, is devoted to the *microrelato* with 12 articles and an anthology. *La dramaturgia en Iberoamerica*, ed. O. Pellettieri and E. Rovner, BA, Galerna, 198 pp., a general survey by countries. Fernando de Toro and Alfonso de Toro, *Acercamientos al teatro actual (1970–1995)*, Frankfurt, Vervuert, 253 pp., essays. N. Martínez, 'Dramaturgia femenina y fin de siglo en América Latina', *LATR*, 31.2:5–16, is a general survey of outlooks rather than figures. E. Suárez-Galbán, '*Orígenes* y *Asomante*', *La Torre*, 3, 1997:497–521, studies these two famous reviews.

GENDERED WRITING. S. Reisz, *Voces sexuadas: género y poesía en Hispanamérica*, Lérida U.P., 1996. *Caribbean Women Fiction Writers*, ed. H. Bloom, Broomhall, Chelsea House, 1997, 192 pp. *The Transforming Voices of Women Caribbean Writers and Scholars*, ed. A. Newson and L. Strong-Leek, NY, Lang, 237 pp. R. Scott. *'Novia que te vea* y *Sagrada memoria*: dos infancias judías en Hispanoamérica', *RIAB*, 45.4, 1995.

ON MORE THAN ONE AUTHOR. R. Hernández, 'La calavera en el espejo', *REH*, 51:30–45, is unanalytic on López Velarde and Vallejo. E. Sklodowska, *Todo ojos, todo oídos. Control e insubordinación en la novela hispanoamericana 1895–1935*, Amsterdam, Rodopi, 1997, 216 pp., includes studies of M. Azuela's *Los de abajo*, J. E. Rivera's *La vorágine*, and D. M. Loynaz's *Jardín*. S. Fernández, *Visión periodística de la literatura*, BA, HomoSapiens, 1997, 188 pp., carries essays on Arlt, Cortázar, Borges, Neruda, and others. M. Gomes, 'Quiroga, Rivera y la formación del canon mundonovista', *Atenea*, 477:135–62, relates them to *modernismo, expresionismo*, and the avant-garde. W. Luis, 'El desplazamiento de los orígenes en la narrativa caribeña de Reinaldo Arenas, Luis R. Sánchez y Julia Alvarez', *La Torre*, 3, 1997:39–71, is on exile and identity. A. Rivero-Potter. 'La mujer cibernética en "Salvad vuestros ojos" de Huidobro y Arp, "Anuncio" de Arreola y "El eterno femenino" de Castellanos', *ib.*, 579–96, is on robotization. M. Scarano, *La reinvencion de la memoria*, Rosario, B. Viterbo, 1997, 192 pp., is on historical novels by Carpentier, Posse, and Roa Bastos. O. R. López, *La crítica latinoamericana*, Medellín, Autores Antioqueños, 1996, 149 pp., is in fact an analysis of six short stories including ones by García Márquez, Rulfo, and Bryce Echenique, plus Bombal's *La última niebla* and Menchú's *Me llamo Rigoberta Menchú*. G. Geirola, 'Protocolos de obediencia, dinámica perversa y fantasías masculinas en Oscar Villegas y Eduardo Pavlovski', *LATR* 32.1:81–98, analyses Villegas's *Santa Catarina* (1969) and Pavlovski's *El Señor Galíndez* (1973).

2. INDIVIDUAL COUNTRIES

ARGENTINA

GENERAL. *Oralidad y argentinidad. Estudios sobre la función del lenguaje hablado en la literatura argentina*, ed. W. B. Berg and M. K. Schaffaner, Tübingen, Narr, 1997, 250 pp. J. J. Sebreli, *Escritos sobre escritos*, BA, Sudamericana, 1997, 572 pp., essays on H. A. Murena, A. Girri, O. Massotta, V. Ocampo, Borges, etc. *La caja de la escritura*, ed. M. Martínez Richter, Frankfurt, Vervuert, 1997, 136 pp., contains remarks by six Argentine prose writers. *Aspects du récit fantastique rioplatense*, ed. M. Esquerro, Paris, L'Harmattan, 1997, 149 pp., includes essays on S. Ocampo and Cortázar. P. L. O'Connell, 'Individual and collective identity through memory in three novels of Argentina's *El Proceso*', *His(US)*, 81:31–41, examines Giardinelli's *Santo Oficio de la memoria*, T. Mercader's *En estado de memoria* and A. M. Shua's *El libro de los recuerdos*. C. M. Topuzian, *'Teoría literaria e intelectuales en Buenos Aires en los últimos años 80: "Babel"'*, *Chasqui*, 26.2, 1997:44–55. N. Fernández de la Barca, *'Notas sobre los viajes en Mansilla, Saer y Aira'*, *RIAB*, 45.4, 1995. J. Martínez Tolentino, *La crítica literaria sobre Alfonsina Storni*, Kassel, Reichenberger, 1997, 92 pp. J. Prieto, 'Cimbelina en 1900 y pico', *LALR*, 32.1:25–49, is on Storni's feminist re-write of Shakespeare. A. Laera, 'Genealogía de un mito imposible: la 'cautiva' de Leopoldo Lugones', *RIAB*, 47, 1997:1161–72, reprints and analyses 'Lokomá'. V. Unruh, 'Las ágiles musas de la modernidad. Patricia Galvão y Norah Lange', *RevIb*, 182–83:271–86, sees more similarities than differences. M. Gomes, 'Juan Gelman en la historia de la poesía hispanoamericana reciente', *ib.*, 181, 1997:649–64, contrasts him with Neruda. M. Nicholson, 'Davantara Sarolamor, the rhetoric of charm in the poetry of Olga Orozco', *LF*, 24:57–67, is on her exploration of the occult.

PROSE. D. Kandiyoti, 'Comparative diasporas', *MFS*, 44:77–122, includes consideration of A. Gerchunoff's *Los gauchos judíos* (1910). S. Serafín, 'Il concetto di solitudine nella narrativa di Eduardo Mallea', *RI*, 61, 1997:27–38, goes over old ground. U. Kröpfl, 'Der Nachlass Leopoldo Marechals', *Cahiers d'Histoire des Littératures Romanes*, 21, 1997:393–415, is on *La cacique* (1978).

BORGES. A. Louis, *Jorge Luis Borges, œuvres et manœuvres*, Paris, L'Harmattan, 1997. N. E. Alvarez, *Discurso e historia en la obra narrativa de Jorge Luis Borges. Examen de Ficciones y El Aleph*, Boulder, SSSAS, 255 pp., is technical but not very illuminating. J. Woscoboinik, *The Secret of Borges. A Psychoanalytic Inquiry into his Work*, Lanham, U.P. of America, 256 pp. R. Lefère, *Borges y los poderes de la literatura*, Berne, Lang, 278 pp. F. I. Yudin, *Nightglow: Borges's Poetics of Blindness*,

Salamanca U.P. 1997, 127 pp., is innovative and original. E. Fishburn, *Borges and Europe Revisited*, London, Institute for Latin American Studies, 128 pp. B. E. Strong, *Poetic Avant-garde: The Groups of Borges, Auden and Breton*, Evanston, Northwestern U.P., 1997, 384 pp. *Variaciones Borges*, 5, has ten essays on 'Conjecture' in Borges and six other miscellaneous items; no. 6 has six essays on *Seis problemas* and seven other items. J. J. Sebreli, 'Borges, nihilismo y literatura', *CHA*, 565–66, 1997:91–125, is a sharp critique by a fellow writer. N. Palenzuela, 'Unamuno y Borges', *ib.*, 79–89, is inadequately researched. J. M. Barrera López, *La Revista Grecia*, Seville, Alfar, 1997, 142 pp., is relevant to Borges and *Ultraismo*. R. A. Green, *'Borges en La Revista Multicolor de los Sábados'*, *RIAB*, 45.4, 1995. C. Meneses, 'Una carta de juventud de Jorge Luis Borges', *CHA*, 575:89–92, reproduces another to Sureda of 1921. G. García, *'Contracrítica, un texto desconocido de Borges'*, *Letras de Buenos Aires*, 16, 1996. A. Huici, *Los mitos clásicos en la obra de Jorge Luis Borges*, Seville, Alfar, 300 pp. H. Morris, 'What Emma knew', *IJHL*, 10–11, 1997:165–202, suggests father/daughter incest as a theme in 'Emma Zunz'. A. Rivero-Potter, 'Complementaridad e incertidumbre en "El jardín de senderos que se bifurcan" de Borges', *La Torre*, 3, 1997:459–74, analyses the tale from the standpoint of sub-atomic theory. S. G. Dapía, *'An approach to Borges's "Tlön, Uqbar, Orbis Tertius"'*, *Chasqui*, 26.2, 1997:94–107. R. I. Díaz, 'Borges en Guayaquil', *RHM*, 50, 1997:315–25, is vague on Borges and history. A. Rodríguez Persico, 'Borges 1970', *Hispamérica*, 78, 1997:109–16, is on *El libro de arena*. S. Heaney and R. Kearney, 'Jorge Luis Borges: el mundo de la ficción', *CHA*, 564, 1997:55–68, a fascinating interview by the Nobel Laureate.

OTHER NARRATIVE. M. L. Snook, *In Search of Self. Gender and Identity in Bioy Casares' Fantastic Fiction*, NY, Lang, 134 pp. J. M. Sardiñas, 'El juego de perspectivas en *La invención de Morel*', *CAm*, 209, 1997:93–99, is on the novel's narrative strategy. N. Balutet, '¿Qué se esconde dentro de una muñeca rusa?', *STLi*, 31 : 1127–32, praises the structure of Bioy's 'Una muñeca rusa'. P. N. Klingenburg, *Fantasies of the Feminine. The Short Stories of Silvina Ocampo*, Lewisburg, Bucknell U.P. E. C. Santos Phillips, 'Bibliografía sobre Silvina Ocampo', *RIAB*, 47, 1997:149–57, a handy check-list. M. L. Bueno, *'La escritura de E. Sábato', ib.*, 45.4, 1995. C. Alonso, *Julio Cortázar: New Readings*, CUP, 224 pp. H. Zampaglione, *El París de Rayuela. Homenaje a Cortázar*, B, Lunweg, 1997, 122 pp. H. M. Cavallari and G. P. García, 'La crítica de *Rayuela*', *IJHL*, 10–11, 1997:203–22, an interesting critical analysis. M. Martínez-Góngora, 'Gregorovius y la decadencia', *RHM*, 51:341–53, contrasts Gregorovius and Traveler in *Rayuela*. A. M. Rodríguez, *'Oliverio Girondo y Julio Cortázar',*

Letras de Buenos Aires, 16, 1996. P. J. McNab, 'Shifting symbols in Cortázar's *Bestiario*', *RHM*, 50, 1997:335–46, is on the multiple symbolism of the tiger. G. Fabry, 'Las aporías de la visión en la novelística de Manuel Puig', *RCL*, 51, 1997:29–38, is on his paradoxical view of the act of seeing. L. Davies, 'Psychoanalysis, gender and angelic truth in Manuel Puig's *Pubis Angelical*', *MLR*, 93:400–10, is on parodic elements in the novel. R. Roffé, 'Entrevista a Manuel Puig', *CHA*, 573:61–70, is as usual chiefly biographical and on sexual repression. E. Sisson Guerrero, **Juanamanuela, mucha mujer* y *Para ser una mujer* de Marta Mercader', *Chasqui* 26.2, 1997:3–14. A. Solomianski, 'El cuento de la patria. Una forma de su configuración en la cuentística de Ricardo Piglia', *RevIb*, 181, 1997:675–88, is chiefly on 'Las actas del juicio' and 'El gaucho invisible'. H. R. Morell, 'Después del día de la fiesta', *ib.*, 665–74, is on Griselda Gambaro's 1994 novel questioning modernity. L. J. Beard, 'La sujetividad femenina en la metaficción feminista latinoamericana', *ib.*, 182–83:290–311, discusses Luisa Futoranski alongside Helena Parente Cunha of Brazil. A. Fitts, 'Alejandra Pizarnik's *La condesa sangrienta* and the lure of the absolute', *LF*, 24:23–35, sees the collection as figuring forth the author's poetic obsessions. B. Boling, 'The gaze of the body and the text in Silvia Molloy's *En breve cárcel*', *Hispanófila*, 123:73–89, is on the lost presence of the lesbian body. J. Logan, 'A study on exile and subjectivity', *REH*, 50, 1997:391–402, is on Tununa Mercado's autobiography *En estado de memoria* (1990). G. L. García, *Oscar Massotta, BA, Atuel, 1996, 83 pp. C. Manzoni, 'Migración y frontera en la escritura de Héctor Tizón', *Hispamérica*, 78, 1997:29–37, is on his picture of provincial life. *Quimera*, 167, 'Nuevos aires porteños' introduces three new writers: Rodrigo Fresán, Alan Pauls, and Juan Forn. *Teatro, postmodernidad y política en Eduardo Pavlovski*, ed. J. D. Ubatti, Concepción (Uruguay), Búsqueda, 1997, with five essays. *El teatro y su crítica*, ed. O. Pellettieri, BA, Galerna, 296 pp., essays on the theory and practice of Argentine theatre. R. Patiño, 'Los suplementos culturales en la transición argentina', *Hispamérica*, 78, 1997:3–16, discusses cultural journalism.

BOLIVIA

E. Paz-Soldán, 'Sexualidades cuestionadas y el "trauma histórico" en *Pisagua* de A. Arguedas', *REH*, 32:249–69, asserts that it 'alegoriza la caída de la mujer'.

CHILE

G. Lillo and J. G. Renart, **Re-leer hoy a Gabriela Mistral*, Ottawa U.P., 1997, 188 pp. S. Tamura, **Los sonetos de la muerte de Gabriela Mistral*, M,

Gredos, 1997, 318 pp. M. Ryan-Kobler, 'Beyond the Mother Icon', *RHM*, 50, 1997:327–34, is on Mistral's conflictive self-view. B. D. Willis, 'Vicente Huidobro's "Non Serviam" and M. de Andrade's "Parabola d'A escrava que não é Isaura"', *Chasqui*, 26.2, 1997:56–71, is excellent on avant-garde poetics. H. Méndez Rodríguez, *Neruda's Ekphrastic Experience, Mural Art and Canto General*, Lewiston, Bucknell U.P., an original comparison of the poetry with Mexican muralism. M. Persin, 'Writing and women's work in the later poetry of Pablo Neruda', *REH*, 32:229–47, reviews Neruda's later evolving views. L. E. Zamudio, **Una interpretación mítica de 'La rosa separada' de Pablo Neruda*, Mexico D. F., UNAM. G. Kirkpatrick, 'Dos poemas narrativos de los años cincuenta', *RevIb*, 182–83:159–69, discusses Neruda's *Canto general* alongside J. Cabral de Melo Neto's *Morte e vida severina*. D. Ulloa Cárdenas, 'Neruda: humilde traductor', *Atenea*, 476, 1997:83–99, is on his translation of *Romeo and Juliet*. H. Lavín Cerda, 'El ritual de Gonzalo Rojas', *Gaceta del Fondo de Cultura Económica*, 332:48–52, comments by a friend on his life and work. I. Dölz-Blackburn, 'Nicanor Parra: reputación, biografía y crítica, 1969–96', *RIAB*, 47, 1997:175–226, a survey of journalistic comments. N. Binns, 'Los medios de comunicación masiva en la poesía de Nicanor Parra', *RCL*, 51, 1997:81–97, is on antipoetry and postmodernity. A. Skármeta, 'Lobos y ovejas', *ib.*, 117–19, is on this 1976 collection of poems by Manuel Silva Acevedo. M. Ostria González, 'Tomás Harris y Juan Pablo Riveros', *Atenea*, 476, 1997:109–17, briefly introduces these two new poets. E. Echevarría, **La novela social de Chile. Trayectoria y bibliografía 1903–1973'*, *RIAB*, 45.4, 1995. D. Oelker, '*Juana Lucero* [1902] de Augusto d'Halmar', *Atenea*, 476, 1997:47–61, is on the reception of Naturalism in Chile. L. A. Chesak, **José Donoso. Escritura y subversión del significado*, M, Verbum, 1997, 125 pp. C. A. Trujillo, 'José Donoso', *RCL*, 51, 1997:131–37, is anecdotal on Donoso's arrest in 1985. L. García-Moreno, 'Margins and medallions: rival narrative modes in José Donoso's *El obsceno pájaro de la noche*', *REH*, 32:29–55, sees it as ambiguous about the oligarchy. L. Torres, 'La "conseja maulina" y la indeterminación en *El obsceno pájaro de la noche*', *RCEH*, 22:473–96, is on its ambiguities. L. García-Moreno, **'Art, gender and power in José Donoso's *El lugar sin límites*', *Chasqui*, 26.2, 1997:26–43. J. Gilkison, 'Literal and metaphorical truth in José Donoso's *La desesperanza*', *BHS(G)*, 75:17–37, is on its meaning in context.

C. Alfieri, 'Jorge Edwards, la ficción de la memoria', *CHA*, 571:123–38, a long and meaty interview. B. Schultz-Cruz, 'Narrativa y sociedad en cuatro novelas de Jorge Edwards', *La Torre*, 3, 1997:101–13, is on their theme of the insufficiency of the bourgeois vision. C. Correa Zapata, **Isabel Allende*, B, Plaza y Janés, 224 pp.

C. Pinet, 'Choosing Barrabás', *Hispamérica*, 123:55–65, explores the symbolism of the dog in *La casa de los Espíritus*. J. Koene, 'Entre la realidad y la ficción. La parodia como arma de subversión en "Tosca" de Isabel Allende', *RoN*, 38:263–70, is on the tale's parody of the traditional role of woman. C. Perricone, 'Genre and metarealism in Allende's *Paula*', *His(US)*, 81:42–48, sees it as exemplifying a new kind of realism. J. D. Cid Hidalgo, 'El acto de "leer" en "Un viejo que leía novelas de amor"', *Atenea*, 477:241–47, on the relation of reading to living in Luis Sepúlveda's novel. L. Morales, 'Narracíon y referentes en Diamela Eltit', *RCL*, 51, 1997:121–29, an important interview. B. Schultz-Cruz, '*Vaca sagrada*', *Hispamérica*, 123:67–72, is on sexuality and power in Eltit's novel. G. García Corrales interviews Darío Oses in *Hispamérica*, 78, 1997:45–55, on new Chilean fiction. M. L. Hurtado, 'La experimentación de formas dramáticas en la escrituras femeninas/escrituras de la mujer en Chile', *LATR*, 31.2:33–43, a quick survey of I. Aguirre, I. Stranger, and others. See too her *Teatro chileno de la modernidad, identidad y crisis social*, Irvine, Gestos, 1997, 215 pp.

COLOMBIA

H. Luque Muñoz, 'Tendencias de la nueva poesía colombiana', *Universitas Humanística* (Bogotá), 43.4, 1996:51–60, very helpful. L. M. Giraldo, 'De las utopías a las escrituras del vacío en la narrativa colombiana', *ib.*, 71–82, postulates a downward spiral. L. Ortiz, *La novela colombiana hacia finales del siglo XX*, NY, Lang, 1997, 173 pp. J. G. Cobo Borda, *Silva, Arciniegas, Mutis, García Márquez y otros, escritores colombianos*, Bogotá, Imprenta Nacional, 1997, 551 pp. M. Comfield, 'Parodia, paradoja, cliché y fabulación en la obra de García Márquez', *CMar*, 135:36–48, tries to cover too much ground. R. Mautner, '¿E a mágica? A representação da realidade social em Jorge Amado e Gabriel García Márquez', *RevIb*, 182–83:171–92, examines magical realist elements. B. S. Castañeda, 'Aproximaciones críticas al monólogo en *La hojarasca*', *RIAB*, 47, 1997:103–17, analyses his use of the technique. J. Corwin, *La transposición de fuentes indígenas en Cien años de soledad*, Mississippi U.P. 1977, 93 pp. M. Parra, 'La crítica de la razón instrumental en *Cien años de soledad*', *La Torre*, 3, 1997:73–85, is on its unmasking of ideological constructs. R. Campos, 'Un relato sospechoso: *Crónica de una muerte anunciada*', *Atenea*, 477:221–38, is on its radical ambiguity. F. López, '*Crónica de una muerte anunciada* de Gabriel García Márquez, ou le crime était presque parfait', *BH*, 96, 1994:545–61, sees Angela as the prime mover. A. M. Penuel, 'The contingency of reality in García Márquez's "Un señor muy viejo con unas alas enormes"', *RoN*, 38:191–97, is on the tale's Cervantine perspectivism. F. Fajardo-Acosta, 'A vision of redemption in Gabriel García Márquez's "La prodigiosa tarde de Baltasar"', *HisJ*, 17.1:31–45, is on arts and the 'higher truth'. H. Araujo, 'Un mimetismo lucrativo', *Quimera*, 171:54–58, examines García Márquez's influence on seven women writers. D. L. Shaw, 'Darío Jaramillo's *Cartas cruzadas* as a post-boom novel', *NNR*, 5:19–35, sees it as a test-case example. J. M. Pardo, 'Desarrollo del teatro colombiano 1960–95', *Universitas Humanística* (Bogotá), 43.4, 1996:63–69, a useful survey.

COSTA RICA

Protestas, interrogantes y agonías en la obra de Rima de Valbona, ed. J. A. Arancibia and L. Jiménez, San José, Perro Azul, 1997, 434 pp., has 23 essays on most aspects of her work. P. Fumero, *Teatro, público y estado en San José 1880–1914*, San José, Costa Rica U.P., 1996, 245 pp., is the first attempt at a social history of the theatre in Costa Rica.

CUBA

E. J. Mullen, **Afro-Cuban Literature*, Westport, Greenwood, 240 pp. I Alvarez Borland, *Cuban American Literature of Exile*, Charlottesville, Virginia U.P., 208 pp., includes essays on Cabrera Infante, Arenas etc. C. A. Salgado, 'Lezama y Joyce', *La Torre*, 3, 1997:475–96, examines Joyce's influence on *Paradiso*. N. Catelli, 'Lezama Lima sobre la tarea de la cultura en América', *CHA*, 565–66, 1997:189–200, is on *mestizaje* chiefly in *La expresión americana*. L. A. Ulloa and J. C. Ulloa, 'Lezama Lima: configuración mítica de América', *MLN*, 113:364–79, is on the search for an American essence in *La expresión americana*. A. González Pérez, **'Raza e ideología en la poesía afrocubana de Nancy Morejón', *RIAB*, 45.4, 1995. S. Chaple, *Estudios de narrativa cubana*, Havana, Unión, 1996, 313 pp., has 11 essays, six on Carpentier. R. Chao, **Conversaciones con Alejo Carpentier*, M, Alianza, 315 pp. S. Millares, 'La constante del viaje en las ficciones de Alejo Carpentier', *Atenea*, 477:201–20, is too descriptive. V. Unruh, 'The performing spectator in A. Carpentier's fictional world', *HR*, 66:57–77, sees performance as a kind of enquiry. C. Ramos de Nadal, **'La reivindicación del negro en *El Camino de Santiago*', *Letras de Buenos Aires*, 16, 1996. G. T. Castillo-Feliú, '*Viaje a la semilla*', *Secolas*, 29:5–12, is on its reversal of time order. G. Maturo, 'De los pasos perdidos de Alvar Núñez a los *Pasos* de Alejo Carpentier', *Atenea*, 477:181–200, in part sees *Los pasos perdidos* as a search for self. F. Valerio-Holguín, 'Las estrategias de Virgilio Piñera durante la Revolución Cubana', *RoQ*, 45:89–97, is on his adaptation after 1959. A. Cusato, 'Tres tristes tigres', *StLI*, 30, 1997:73–83, is on its structure. A. Rivero-Potter, **Essays in Honor of Severo Sarduy*, Boulder, SSSAS, 136 pp. J. García Méndez, '*De donde son los cantantes*', *LNL*, 33–34:56–61, is a critique of the French and the Cátedra editions. M. Poümer, 'Severo Sarduy, néo-baroque sévère ou sérieusement néo-romantique', *ib.*, 43–51, tries to situate *De donde son los cantantes*. J. M. Saint-Lu, 'Les sens, l'essence, le sens. Remarques sur *De donde son los cantantes* de Severo Sarduy', *LNL*, 33–34:9–16, is too discursive. A. E. Vadillo, 'La metamorfosis del signo lingüistico', *Symposium*, 52:95–103, is on the food-sex metaphor in *Maitreya*. L. A. Ulloa and J. C. Ulloa, '*Pajaros de la playa* de Severo Sarduy: final de juego', *Hispamérica*, 78, 1997:17–27, is on its treatment of Aids. J. Abreu, *A la sombra del mar*, B, Casiopea, 224 pp., a memoir of Reinaldo Arenas's eight months on the run in Cuba before his capture and imprisonment, by a close friend. E. M. Santí, 'Fresa y chocolate: the rhetoric of Cuban reconciliation', *MLN*, 113:407–25, is about guilt and repentance in the film version. S. Regazzoni, 'Escritoras cubanas: Mirta Yañez', *StLI*, 30, 1997:95–103, is introductory. J. Febles, '*Requiem por Yarini* de Carlos Felipe', *ETL*, 25.1:15–29, relates it to Zorrilla's *Don Juan Tenorio*. See too his 'Recontextualización poemática en *La dolorosa historia de amor secreto de don José Jacinto Milanés*', *LATR*, 31.2:79–95, examining the technique of this 1974 play by Abelardo Estorino. J. B. Alvarez, **(Re) escritura de la violencia en la cuentística novísima cubana', *Chasqui*, 26.2, 1997:84–93. J. Febles and A. González Pérez, **Matías Montes Huidobro*, Lewisburg, Mellen, 1997, 258 pp. M. Viñalet, 'Freddy Artiles: un autor polifacético', *LATR*, 32.1:99–106, a brief introduction. C. Manzoni, 'Vanguardia y nacionalismo: itinerario de *La Revista de Avance*', *CAm*, 208, 1997:127–33, is chiefly on its questionnaire in no. 26 (1928).

DOMINICAN REPUBLIC

C. Tirado Bramen, 'Translating exile: the metamorphosis of the ordinary in Dominican short fiction', *LALR*, 51:65–78, is on 'Lulú' by J. Alcántara and 'La Marimanta' by Viriato Sención.

GUATEMALA

G. Bellini, 'Vuelta a *El Señor Presidente*', *StLI*, 31:95–125, rather too discursive. C. Camplani, '*El santo de fuego* de Mario Monteforte Toledo', *ib.*, 30, 1997:61–72, is on the pessimism of this 1986 play. E. J. Westlake, 'Performing the Nation in Mario Galich's *El tren amarillo*', *LATR*, 31.2:107–17, examines this anti-imperialist play of the 50s.

MEXICO

A. Salinas, *Dios y los escritores mexicanos*, Mexico D.F.; Nueva Imagen, 1997, 309 pp., includes references to J. Agustín, R. Garibay, V. Leñero, C. Monsiváis, E. Poniatowska, and others. M. E. de Valdés, **The Shattered Mirror. Representations of Women in Mexican Literature*, Austin, Texas U.P., 284 pp. A. G. Choncíño, 'Poesía del lenguaje en México', *HR*, 66:245–60, is useful on this new trend of the 70s and 80s. J. J. Arreola, **Ramón López Velarde*, Mexico D.F., Alfaguara, 1997, 145 pp. B. Rodríguez, **El imaginario poético de Ramón López Velarde*, Mexico D. F., UNAM, 1996, 247 pp. G. Gordon, **Carlos Pellicer. Breve Bibliografía*, Mexico D.F., Consejo Nacional, 1997, 106 pp. J. Quiroga, **Understanding Octavio Paz*, Columbia, S. Carolina U.P., 192 pp. E. Poniatowska, **Octavio Paz*, Barcelona, Lumen, 220 pp. F. R. Alvarez, 'Octavio Paz: hacia una metapoética de la modernidad', *His(US)*, 81:20–30, is lucid. J. A. Pastén, 'Elaboración de una poética en los ensayos tempranos de Octavio Paz', *RHM*, 51:72–86, is on Paz's antagonism towards his cultural milieu. J. A. de Ory, 'Octavio Paz y la India', *CHA*, 581:33–38, is superficial and descriptive. B. L. Lewis, **'Paz y la novela latinoamericana', *RIAB*, 45.4, 1995. A. Brickhouse, 'Hawthorne in the Americas', *PMLA*, 113:227–42, includes a commentary on Paz's *La hija de Rappaccini*. I. L. Camargos Walty, 'O diálogo Brasil/América hispánica na crítica de Silvano Santiago e Octavio Paz', *RevIb*, 182–83:229–39, is banal on their Latinamericanness. M. E. Maciel, 'América Latina reinventada: Octavio Paz e Haroldo de Campos', *ib.*, 219–28, compares their outlook. C. Pulgar Machado, 'Entrevista a Adolfo Castañón sobre Octavio Paz', *La Gaceta del Fondo de Cultura Económica*, 335:46–51, contains comments by a friend and collaborator. M. J. Bas Albertos, *La poesía de Jaime García Terrés*, Alicante U.P., 1996, 158 pp., is merely introductory. A. Ruiz Abreu, 'Novela de la crisis y crisis de la novela', *Nexos* (Mexico), 241:183–92, a handy review of fiction in Mexico today. *Ínsula*, 618–19, is on modern Mexican prose with articles on M. L. Guzmán, Paz, Arreola, Fuentes, Rulfo, E. Garro, Ibargüengoitía, Elizondo, Pitol, J. E. Pacheco, Monsiváis, Monterroso, Mastretta, and A. García Bergua. E. Perassi, 'Breve homenaje a la narrativa de Los Contemporáneos', *StLI*, 30, 1997:85–94, is on their prefiguration of the future of fiction. J. P. Duffey, 'A war of words: orality and literacy in Mario Azuela's *Los de abajo*', *RoN*, 38:173–78, is on the contrast of Demetrio and Luis. R. M. Ochoa, *Escritoras mexicanas vistas por escritoras mexicanas*, Mexico

D.F., 1997, 203 pp., rather scrappy and anecdotal. P. Méndez, 'Genealogía y escritura en *Balún-Canán* de Rosario Castellanos', *MLN*, 113:339–63, interprets the narrator's family as an allegory. C. Merithew, 'La búsqueda eterna de "otro modo de ser humano y libre" de Rosario Castellanos', *LF*, 24:95–110, is aggressively old-style feminist. M. L. Gil, '*Oficio de tinieblas*', *StLI*, 31:133–50, is on the notion of an 'estética matriarcal'. G. Fares, *Ensayos sobre la obra de *Juan Rulfo*, NY, Lang, 152 pp. A. Vital, *Juan Rulfo*, Mexico D.F., Consejo Nacional. *RCEH*, 22, is a special no. on Rulfo with ten good articles. D. Cohn, 'Catherine Ann Porter's Miranda stories and Juan Rulfo's *Pedro Páramo*', *Hispanófila*, 124:65–86, contrasts their visions. M. A. Arango, 'Aspectos religiosos en tres cuentos de *El llano en llamas*', *Iris*:9–22, is under-researched.

M. Van Delden, *Carlos Fuentes, Mexico and Modernity, Nashville, Vanderbilt U.P., 262 pp. C. Helmuth, *The Postmodern Fuentes, Canbury, Bucknell U.P., 1997, 150 pp. L. Valenzuela, 'Una duda vital y activa', *CMar*, 140:65–67, a brief appreciation by a fellow-writer. *JILS*, 8.1, is a special number on literary reactions to the 1985 earthquake in Mexico, with references to Poniatowska, C. Pacheco, C. Monsiváis, and J. E. Pacheco. J. T. Espinosa, 'Palinuro, escultura del artista adolescente', *BH*, 99, 1997:457–70, is on Del Paso's parody of 'La Onda' and his influence on Allende. S. Lucas Dobrian, '*Querido Diego*', *RCEH*, 22, 1997:33–44, compares Angelina in Poniatowska's novel with Frida Kahlo, Rivera's other mistress. K. S. López, 'Internal colonialism in the testimonial process. Elena Poniatowska's *Hasta no verte, Jesús mío*', *Symposium*, 52:21–39, is again on author/informant. N. Martínez, 'Silencios que matan: el cuerpo político en *Hasta no verte, Jesús mío* de Elena Poniatowska', *LF*, 24:9–21, is on dissidence and oral authority. I. T. Agheana, '*Muchacho en llamas* de Gustavo Sainz, una novela por hacer', *IJHL*, 10–11, 1997:237–48, is on the protagonist's self-discovery. H. Subirats, 'Acoso y fuga de Sergio Pitol', *CHA*, 567, 1997:73–80, a brief interview. S. Pitol, 'The narrator', *Review*, 56:51–59, is autobiographical. S. Serafín, 'Il sorriso inquietante di Juan José Arreola', *StLI*, 30, 1997:105–35, is on the ludic quality of his work. J. Pellicer, '*La viuda*: una femineidad utópica', *RevIb*, 181, 1997:689–96, analyses the message of this 1994 novel by M. L. Puga. C. M. Rivera, 'Las mujeres y la Revolución Mexicana en *Mal de amores* de Angeles Mastretta', *LF*, 24:37–48, is on Emilia's self-discovery. J. Ortega, 'Carmen Boullosa', *La Torre*, 38, 1996:167–81, a handy introduction to this difficult writer. J. A. Payne, 'A World of her Own. Exilic metafiction in Angelina Muñoz-Haberman's *Morada interior* and *Dulcinea encantada*', *RCEH*, 22, 1997:45–63, is on the theme of exile. L. I. Underwood, '*Ascensión Tun* de Silvia Molina', *ETL*, 25.1:80–90, introduces this

1993 novel. J. E. Bixler, *Convention and Transgression. The Theatre of Emilio Carballido*, Lewisburg, Bucknell U.P. 1997, 256 pp., reviews his experimentalism. P. Méndez, '*Orinoco*, Carballido y su 'diario de navegación', por el teatro', *REH*, 32:491–510, sees the play as allegorical. J. Rea, 'El conflicto de conciencias en los dramas de Vicente Leñero', *LATR*, 31.2:97–105, is on threats to spirituality. L. H. Quackenbush, 'El espacio y tiempo negativos en *Los fantoches* y *Jesucristo Gómez*', *ib.*, 17–31, brings new concepts to bear on these plays by Leñero and Carlos Solórzano. P. Rosas Lopátegui and J. C. Reid, 'La ironía metafórica en *Benito Fernández* de Elena Garro', *ib.*, 51–67, analyses her critique of racialism and classism. S. Wehling, 'Typewriters, guns and roses: shifting the balance of power in Sabina Berman's "Entre Villa y una mujer desnuda"', *LF*, 24:69–79, is on history seen as a fictional construct. F. Reyes Palacios, 'Ideología y grotesco en dos obras recientes de Adam Guevara', *LATR*, 32.1:69–79, is on the limitations of his social criticism.

NICARAGUA

W. Detjens, '*La mujer habitada* de Gioconda Belli', *ETL*, 25.1:60–71, is thin and descriptive on sexual roles in the novel. J. Febles, 'Juego, represión y represión del juego en "El centerfielder" de Sergio Ramírez', *La Torre*, 3, 1997:427–39.

PANAMA

H. López Cruz, 'Factores discursivos en la narrativa de Rosa María Britten. Feminismo y negritud', *Secolas*, 29:55–60, is on her view of these two issues. See too his 'La negritud como historia no oficial en las dos primeras novelas de R. M. Britten', *RoN*, 39:53–59, similarly thematic.

PARAGUAY

R. Ferrer, 'Narrativa paraguaya actual', *CMar*, 137:53–57, 138:51–54, a quick survey. H. C. Welt-Basson, 'Augusto Roa Bastos's trilogy as postmodern practice', *STCL*, 22:335–55, is on the unity of the trilogy. A. Albonico, 'Augusto Roa Bastos en sus últimas novelas', *StLI*, 30, 1997:21–25, a slight survey. G. Minardi, 'Josefina Pla: una voz a recuperar', *LF*, 24:157–72, is on female characters in her stories. G. da Cunha-Giabbai, **La cuentística de René Ferrer. Continuidad y cambio en nuestra expresión*, Asunción, Anandura, 1997, 171 pp.

PERU

Literatura peruana hoy, ed. K. Kohut et al., Frankfurt, Vervuert, 1997, 330 pp., appears to be chiefly on younger authors. *The Poetry and Poetics of César Vallejo*, ed. A. Sharman, Lewiston, Mellen, 1997, 200 pp., has good essays by major critics. S. Hart, 'Was César Vallejo guilty as charged?', *LALR*, 51:79–87, analyses the cause of his imprisonment. C. Tisnado, 'El personaje lesbiano en la narrativa peruana contemporánea', *RoN*, 38:343–49, surveys examples from 1919 to 1996. J. Marcone, 'De retorno a lo natural: *La serpiente de oro*', *His(US)*, 81:299–308, is on the originality of Ciro Alegría's novel as a *novela de la selva*. M. Aleza Izquierdo, **Aspectos lingüísticos de la narrativa de J. M. Arguedas*, Valencia, Tirant Lo Blanc, 1996, 114 pp. **José María Arguedas: recuerdos de una amistad*, ed. A. Ortiz, Lima, Univ. Pontificia, 1996, 309 pp. C. A. Sandoval, '*El sexto* de José María Arguedas', *RevIb*, 181, 1997:697–709, is on its questioning of Peruvian identity. E. Kristal, **The Novels of Mario Vargas Llosa*, Nashville, Vanderbilt U.P., 256 pp. H. Establier, **Mario Vargas Llosa y el nuevo arte de hacer novelas*, Alicante U.P. 182 pp. *Conversación de otoño. Homenaje a Vargas Llosa*, ed. V. Polo García et al., Murcia, CAM, 1997, 499 pp., has numerous articles on most aspects of his work. *Ínsula*, 624, is a Vargas Llosa number with interesting essays. *CHA*, 574, has a section on Vargas Llosa, with two interviews and four useful essays. A. I. Ballesteros, '*Pantaleón y las visitadoras*', *StLI*, 30, 1997:137–48, is on the stage version. P. Allatson, '*Historia de Mayta*: a tale of queer cleansing', *REH*, 32:511–35, considers it homophobic. J. L. de la Fuente, 'Los "Cuadernos de navegación" de Bryce Echenique', *BH*, 96, 1994:203–15, sees the two novels as picaresque. G. Díaz, 'Treinta años de dramaturgia en el Perú (1950–1980)', *LATR*, 31.2:173–88, is a handy survey.

PUERTO RICO

C. D. Hernández, **Puerto Rican Voices in English: Interviews with Writers*, Westport, Praeger, 1997, 251 pp. C. L. Montañez, **El personaje femenino en la cuentística de varias escritoras puertorriqueñas*, NY, Lang, 117 pp. B. Torres Caballero, 'La función de la comida en la obra de E. Rodríguez Juliá', *La Torre*, 3, 1997:523–31, is on the symbolic value of food. C. M. Concepción, 'Una lectura de *Solar Montoya* de Enrique Laguerre', *ib.*, 1–13, is on this conservationist novel of 1941. E. Irrizarry, '*La proa libre* caribeña de Enrique Laguerre', *ib.*, 441–57, studies this 1996 *novela* as Ganivetian. L. R. Sánchez, 'Why do you write?', *Review*, 56:5–13, gives an interesting answer. G. Tineo, 'En torno a lo popular en la narrativa de L. R. Sánchez', *BH*, 96,

1994:235–43, is on its connection with *antillanía*. I. M. López, '*The House on the Lagoon*', *IJHL*, 12:135–44, is too descriptive on Ferré's novel. R. Perales, *Cincuenta años de teatro puertorriqueño: El arte de Victoria Espinosa*, Mexico D.F., Escenología.1996, 258 pp. R. E. Soto-Crespo, 'Infiernos imaginarios', *MFS*, 44:215–39, includes discussion of A. Marat's play *Dios en el Playgirl de noviembre* (1966).

URUGUAY

G. San Román, **Amor y nación. Ensayos sobre literatura uruguaya*, Montevideo, Fundación Banco de Boston, 1997, 156 pp. P. O'Connell, 'Delmira Agustini, Rubén Darío y la "Tabula Rasa"', *ETL*, 25.1:72–9, is as usual on Delmira's subversiveness. O. Prego, '"El hijo"', *CMar*, 136:47–50, checks this tale with H. Quiroga's famous *Decálogo*. R. Varela, 'Comentario de un cuento fantástico: "Las moscas"', *RCEH*, 22:511–29, uses several interpretative approaches. A. Atorresi, **Un amor a la deriva, Horacio Quiroga y Alfonsina Storni*, BA, Solaris, 1997, 294 pp. P. Lange, 'De la ocularidad hacia lo imaginario', *Quimera*, 172:58–64, is on Felisberto Hernández's odd vision of reality. M. A. Petit, 'Etica y estética, compromiso y ficción en J. C. Onetti', *CMar*, 136:51–57 is superficial on his political stance. E. Gurski, 'Revisiting Onetti's "Un sueño realizado"', *IJHL*, 10–11, 1997:223–35, sees it as manipulating our vision of reality. J. Cordones-Cook interviews Teresa Porzecanski, in *Hispamérica*, 78, 1997:39–44, with interesting remarks. P. Dejbord, 'Nuevas configuraciones del exilio en *La nave de los locos*, *Solitario de amor* y *Babel bárbara* de Cristina Peri Rossi', *RHM*, 50, 1997:347–62, is on her re-working of the theme of exile. R. Roffé, 'Entrevista a Cristina Peri Rossi', *CHA*, 581:93–106, is useful on her exile feelings and on her work.

VENEZUELA

W. Martínez, **Lo más reciente de la poesía venezolana en los años 80*', *Revista de Literatura y Artes Venezolanas*, 2.1, 1996. Y. M. Rodríguez, **La narrativa de Salvador Garmendia*, Lewisburg, Mellen, 1997, 108 pp. A. López Ortega, 'Razón y sinrazón del relato venezolano 1970–1995', *Quimera*, 170:26–29, is a brief survey.

BRAZILIAN LITERATURE

By MARK DINNEEN, *Spanish, Portuguese and Latin American Studies, University of Southampton*

1. GENERAL

P. Maligo, *Land of Metaphorical Desires: The Representation of Amazonia in Brazilian Literature*, NY, Lang, 208 pp., seeks to show how the writers' own ideals and aspirations are embodied in their depiction of Amazonia. The principal figures referred to are Inglés de Sousa, Euclides da Cunha, and Dalcidio Juranir. *A história contada: capítulos de história social da literatura no Brasil*, ed. S. Chalhoub and L. A. de M. Pereira, R, Nova Fronteira, 362 pp., is a collection of 12 essays which discuss the relationship between literature and history. Writers covered include Alencar, Amado, Mário de Andrade and especially Machado de Assis. R. Ingel, *Imigrantes judeus/escritores brasileiros: o componente judaico na literatura brasileira*, SPo, Perspectiva, 1997, 260 pp., is a thoroughly researched survey of Brazilian Jewish writers since the colonial period to the present. It is a valuable source of information for a growing area of interest, though short on analysis. D. B. Lockhart, *Jewish Writers of Latin America: a Dictionary*, NY, Garland, 1997, 612 pp., highlights Jewish themes in brief entries on ten Brazilian writers, including Lispector, Scliar, and Rawett. G. Bilharinho, *Romance brasileiro: uma leitura direcionada*, Uberaba, Instituto Triangulino de Cultura, 208 pp., gathers together over 40 brief, and in some cases superficial, essays on novelists writing between 1870 and 1970. M. D. Ledgerwood, *Images of the 'Indian' in Four New World Literatures*, Lampeter, Mellen, 232 pp., includes 19th- and 20th-c. Brazilian literature in a discussion of the construction of myths about indian culture. J. A. Miranda, 'Origens do conceito de literatura brasileira: o papel de Joaquim Norberto de Sousa Silva e seu *Bosquejo da história da poesía brasileira*', *Caravelle*, 70:135–50, examines S.'s contribution to the study of the origins of Brazilian literature. *RevIb*, 182–83, is dedicated to the comparative study of Brazilian, Spanish American and Caribbean literatures and culture. I. Corona, '¿Vecinos distantes? Las agendas críticas posmodernas en Hispanoamérica y el Brasil' (17–38), compares contemporary criticism in Spanish America and Brazil with particular reference to different responses to postmodernism. L. H. Costigan, 'Exclusões (e inclusões) na literatura latino-americana: índios, negros e judeus' (55–80), is a broad survey of changing perceptions of national culture which emphasizes the presentation of different races in Brazilian literature since the 19th century. R. Antelo, 'Uma literatura centaúrica' (81–94), discusses the debate on Latin American modernity in the light of Nietzchean thought. A. L. Andrade, 'Da casa do romance ao xadrez de casas: formas industriais/texturas culturais' (195–207), considers the relationship between Brazilian literature and the country's cultural heterogeneity. M. E. Maciel, 'América Latina reinventada: Octávio Paz e Haroldo de Campos' (219–28), compares the two poets' theories on literature. I. L. Camargos Walty, 'O diálogo Brasil/América hispânica na crítica de Silviano Santiago e Octavio Paz' (229–39), identifies similarities in the way the two writers confront the cultural legacy of colonialism. L. Franco Moreira, 'Plenitude e privação: Antônio Cândido na virada do século', *RCLL*, 47:17–27, discusses C.'s *O discurso e a cidade*. F. Sussekind, 'Relógios e ritmos: em torno de um comentário de Antônio Cândido', *ib.*, 29–52, points out that the frequent presentation of Brazilian literary development as a series of homogeneous phases has impeded understanding, and that different literary systems have coexisted at every moment. A. Anoni Prado, '*Raízes do Brasil* e o modernismo', *NovE*, 50:211–18, reviews the development of Sérgio Buarque de Holanda's ideas on Brazilian literature and culture. J. H. Hernesto, *A nação e o paraíso: a construção da nacionalidade na historiografia literária brasileira*, Florianopolis, UFSC, 1997, 215 pp. *Autores brasileiros: biobibliografias*, Part 1, R, Ministério da Cultura, 197 pp., contains a series of biographical sketches on Brazilian writers, but is brief and far from comprehensive. D. de Almeida Prado, *Seres, coisas, lugares: do teatro ao futebol*, SPo, Letras, 1997, 229 pp., is a collection of essays on diverse aspects of Brazilian culture which includes sections on Rubem Braga and Artur Azevedo. C. A. Baumgarten, *A crítica literaria no Rio Grande do Sul: do romantismo ao modernismo*, Porto Alegre, EDIPUCRS, 1997, 248 pp.

2. COLONIAL

E. Lopes, *Metamorphoses: a poesia de Cláudio Manuel da Costa*, SPo, UNESPL, 1997, 209 pp., extols the pioneering role of C. and the *Inconfidência Mineira*. The close analysis of rhyme, metre, and language is for the specialist, but the discussion in the early chapters of the historical and cultural context will be of more general interest. J. Pereira Furtado, *Uma República de leitores: história e memória na recepção das cartas chilenas*, SPo, HUCITEC, 1997, 230 pp., examines how interpretation of the poem attributed to Gonzaga has changed in accordance with the prevailing theoretical currents of each period. L. M. Bernucci, 'Os pecados do lado debaixo do Equador: notas sobre a épica sacra na América Latina', *RevIb*, 182–83:107–15, briefly refers to Itaparica, Durão, and Basílio da Gama in a comparison of Brazilian and Spanish American religious poetry.

M. C. Burgueño, '*O Caramuru y Caramurú*: sus relaciones en la formación de un protoimaginário nacional uruguayo', *ib.*, 117–28, is a comparative study of Durão's epic poem and the 19th-c. novel by the Uruguayan Alejandro Magariños Cervantes. P. Peres, 'Domingos Caldas Barbosa e o conceito de *crioulização do Caribe*', *ib.*, 209–18, emphasizes B.'s originality as an Afro-Brazilian poet.

3. NINETEENTH CENTURY

R. Schwarz, *Duas meninas*, SPo, Companhia das Letras, 1997, 152 pp., is a thought-provoking study of Machado's *Dom Casmurro*, which focuses particularly on questions of literary form. E. H. Douglass, 'Machado de Assis's *A cartomante*: modern parody and the making of a Brazilian text', *MLN*, 113:1036–55, reads the short story in the light of Hutcheon's definition of parody, to show how the work assimilates the debate on national identity versus cosmopolitanism. On the same short story, A. Villaça, 'Machado de Assis: traductor de si mesmo', *NovE*, 51:3–14, examines its incorporation of elements from other cultural traditions. E. E. Fitz, 'Machado, Borges e Clarice: a evolução da nova narrativa latinoamericana', *RevIb*, 182–83:129–44, refers to M.'s *Memórias póstumas de Brás Cubas* in a comparative study of the way the three authors reject the tenets of realism. M. Meyer, *As mil faces de um herói-canalha e outros ensaios*, R, Editora UFRJ, 348 pp., deals with Machado de Assis. See also G. Ramos under TWENTIETH CENTURY: POETRY for a discussion of Machado's poetry. P. Beattie, 'Conflicting penile codes: modern maculinity and sodomy in the Brazilian military, 1860–1916', pp. 65–85 of *Sex and Sexuality in Latin America*, ed. D. Balderston and D. J. Guy, New York U.P., 1997, 288 pp., discusses Caminha's treatment of homosexuality in *Bom crioulo*. E. Fraga, 'Teatro brasileiro no fim do século XIX', *LBR*, 35.2:3–17, is a historical survey of the theatre in the last decades of the century, which concludes that, though a period of intense activity, efforts centred on producing works of popular entertainment and that intellectual and aesthetic dimensions were of secondary concern. J. R. Faria, 'Notas sobre o naturalismo teatral no Brasil', *ib.*, 19–35, argues that the significance of naturalist plays of the late 19th c., like those written by Aluísio Azevedo, has not been adequately recognized by critics. A. M. Tenório Vieira, 'A crítica teatral de Machado de Assis', *ib.*, 37–51, examines M.'s critical evaluations of the attempts made to develop a theatre of national expression and how, from the process, he drew lessons for the writing of his own fiction. L. M. Martins, 'Efeitos de ilusão; o teatro de Qorop-Santo', *ib.*, 53–68, studies the way Q. (José Joaquim de Campos Leão) broke with the conventions of realist theatre and emphasized instead the role of illusion.

4. TWENTIETH CENTURY

POETRY

M. M. do Carmo, *Paulicéia scugliambada, Paulicéia desvairada: Juó Bananére e a imagem do italiano na literatura brasileira*, Niterói, EDUFF, 233 pp., offers an interesting discussion on the interaction between the popular and the erudite in Brazilian modernism. It focuses on the writing of B., a popular São Paulo journalist, arguing that his use of satire, parody, and linguistic experimentation captures much of the spirit of early modernist poetry. J. P. Paes, *Os perigos da poesia e outros ensaios*, R, Topbooks, 1997, 207 pp., contains 25 short essays which discuss such poets as Jorge de Lima, Murilo Mendes, and Flávio Luis Ferrarini, as well as broader questions of poetry. B. D. Willis, 'Necessary losses: purity and solidarity in Mário de Andrade's dock side poetics', *His(US)*, 81:261–68, considers A.'s theories on poetic creation, particularly the role of the conscious and the unconscious. M. D. dos Santos, **Ao sol carta é farol: a correspondência de Mário de Andrade e outros missivistas*, SPo, Annablume, 305 pp. G. Ramos, *Ironia à brasileira: o enunciado irônico em Machado de Assis, Oswald de Andrade e Mario Quintano*, SPo, Pauliceia, 1997, 204 pp., opens with an extended discussion on the concept of irony and then contrasts its use in the poetry of the three writers. L. Franco Moreira, 'A lua e o domador: símbolos literários e divisões sociais na poesia nacionalista de Cassiano Ricardo e Leopoldo Marechal', *RevIb*, 182–83:145–58, compares the use the two poets make in their work of symbols of national identity. G. Kirkpatrick, 'Dos poemas narrativos de los años cincuenta: *Morte e vida severina* y *Canto general*', *ib.*, 159–69, identifies elements of the epic in the poems by Melo Neto and Neruda. M. Ayres, 'Reflejos de la mística del siglo de oro español en el Brasil: una lectura de la poesía de la madre María José de Jesús', *ib.*, 255–70, is an introduction to the religious verse of a poet largely ignored by the critics. J. Schwartz, 'Um Brasil em tom menor: Pau-Brasil e Antropofagía', *RCLL*, 47:53–65, returns to the question of Oswald de Andrade's search for national cultural identity. H. Osakabe, 'Porque a rosa é mística: uma leitura da poesia de Adélia Prado', *ib.*, 67–75, is a brief summary of the main components of P.'s poetry. M. L. dos Santos Sisterolli, **Da lira ao ludas: travessia. Leitura poética de Gilberto Mendonça Teles*, SPo, Annablume, 230 pp.

DRAMA

LBR, 35.2, is a special issue on the Brazilian theatre. V. H. Adler Pereira, 'Endemias e vanguardias: teatro brasileiro no fim do milênio' (69–86), presents a pessimistic view of a theatre badly affected in the

1990s by state indifference and public apathy. F. M. Clark, 'Theater, actress, woman: Isis Baião's *As da vida também voltam* and *Essas mulheres*' (87–97), discusses B.'s search for new forms and devices in her plays, in order to challenge patriarchal values. D. S. George, 'Gerald Thomas's postmodernist theatre: a Wagnerian *Antropofagia*?' (99–106), extols the originality of T.'s work and presents a picture of a dynamic Brazilian dramaturgy in the 1990s that contrasts with Adler Pereira's view previously mentioned. S. J. Albuquerque, 'Entrevista com Alberto Guzik' (113–17), is an interview with a major drama critic who gives an overview of the strengths and weaknesses of the Brazilian theatre today. N. Afolabi, 'A visão mítico-trágica na dramaturgia abdiasiana', *His(US)*, 81 : 530–49, deals with Abelias do Nascimento's 1973 play *Sortilégio II*. Focusing on the role of the Afro-Brazilian hero, the article examines the play's treatment of race relations in Brazil. A. Pereira, 'A poética do oprimido e o papel do espectador no jogo e debate teatrais', *Caravelle*, 70 : 151–64, studies the adaptation of Boal's *teatro do oprimido* in Europe and the US and assesses the consequences that has for the original political objectives.

PROSE

R. J. Oakley, *The Case of Lima Barreto and Realism in the Brazilian 'Belle Epoque'*, Lampeter, Mellen, 216 pp., examines how L.B.'s views on artistic creation manifest themselves in his writing, especially in the relation between form and content. O. argues that previous critics have paid insufficient attention to L.B.'s reading of European writers, and especially the influence of Tolstoy's conception of art. V. Soares de Oliveira, *Literatura, esse cinema com cheiro*, SPo, Arte e Ciência, 111 pp., is a brief but highly readable study of the prose of Alcântara Machado, which has tended to be eclipsed by the major modernist poets. The book attempts to reaffirm A.'s position within Brazilian modernism, focusing particularly on his innovative use of colloquial language. R. A. Franconi, *Erotismo e poder na ficção brasileira con-temporânea*, SPo, Annablume, 1997, 187 pp., is a valuable study of fiction of the 1980s which seeks to show how eroticism in the work of such writers as Fonseca, Trevisan, Haroldo Maranhão, and Radua Nassar challenges political oppression. V. M. P. Milanesi, *Cyro dos Anjos: memória e historia*, SPo, Arte e ciência, 1997, 108 pp., is a good introduction to A.'s three novels, which are studied in the light of Goldmann's genetic structuralist approach. W. Nogueira Galvão, *Desconversa*, R, UFRJ, 264 pp., includes discussion on da Cunha, Guimarães Rosa, Mário de Andrade, and Lispector in a wide-ranging collection of essays on literary topics. *Entre resistir e identificar-se: para uma teoria de prática da narrativa braliseira de autoria feminina*, ed. P. Sharpe,

Florianópolis, Editora Mulheres, 1997, 200 pp., consists of 12 essays offering different perspectives on contemporary women's writing, and in particular the quest for female identity through literature. The main writers considered are L. Fagundes Telles, H. Parente Cunha, L. Luft, M. Colasanti, and N. Piñon, all of whom contribute essays themselves. H. Owen, 'The anxiety of confluence: James Joyce's *The Dead* and Clarice Lispector's *A partida do trem*', pp. 99–109 of *Hers Ancient and Modern: Women's Writing in Spain and Brazil*, ed. C. Davies and J. Whetnall, MUP, 1997, 147 pp., uses Cixous's analyses of J. and L. in a comparative study of the two works. M. M. Lisboa, 'Whatever happened to baby boys? Motherhood and death in Lygia Fagundes Telles', *ib.*, 111–29, examines the treatment of the theme of maternity in two of F.T.'s stories of the 1980s. M. Gomes Mendes, *Edição crítica em uma perspectiva genética de 'As tres Marias' de Rachel de Queiroz*, Niteroi, EDUFF, 324 pp., uses Q.'s original drafts to provide a detailed study of the novel's evolution through the various stages of its writing. L. A. Ferreira, *Roteira de leitura: O cortiço de Aluísio Azevedo, SPo, Ática, 1997, 128 pp. K. S. López, '*Modernismo* and the ambivalence of the postcolonial experience: cannibalism, primitivism, and exoticism in Mário de Andrade's *Macunaíma*', *LBR*, 35.1:25–38, seeks to show how the paradox of Brazilian Modernism, searching for the cosmopolitan whilst seeking to affirm the national, is embodied in A.'s novel. W. Nogueira Galvão, 'Clarice Lispector: uma leitura', *RCLL*, 47:67–75, briefly considers aspects of L.'s writing that explain its originality. B. Waldman, 'O estrangeiro em Clarice Lispector', *ib.*, 95–104, focuses on Jewish cultural elements in L.'s fiction. H. D. Fernández L'Hoeste, *Narrativas de representación urbana: un estudio de expresiones culturales de la modernidad latinoamericana*, NY, Lang, 208 pp., includes brief reference to Lispector in an examination of the effects of accelerated urbanization on Latin American writing. See also E. E. Fitz under NINETEENTH CENTURY for a comparative study of Lispector, Machado de Assis, and Borges. D. E. Marting, 'Clarice Lispector (post)modernity and the adolescence of the girl-colt', *MLN*, 113:433–44, uses post-structuralist philosophical ideas to shed light on L.'s *Seco estudo de cavalos*. L. Helena, *Nem musa, nem medusa: itinerários da escrita em Clarice Lispector, Niteroí, EDUFF, 1997, 124 pp. C. Williams, 'More than meets the eye, or a tree house of her own: a new look at a short story by Clarice Lispector', *PortSt*, 14:170–80, analyses the confrontation of self and other in L.'s *A menor mulher do mundo*, by highlighting the story's concern with inequalities between men and women and the relationship between the colonizer and the colonized. F. Arenas, 'Being here with Vergílio Ferreira and Clarice Lispector: at the limits of language and subjectivity', *ib.*, 181–94, is a comparative study of the writing of F. and L. which emphasizes the shared concern they show for the limitations of subjectivity and of language. L. Sá, 'An epic of the Brazilian revolution: Callado's *Quarup*', *ib.*, 195–204, considers C.'s novel in the light of Lukács's *Theory of the Novel*, linking the two works through the Marxist view of social change which they share. S. Dennison, 'Ever decreasing circles: Chico Buarque's hidden agenda in *Estorvo*', *ib.*, 255–66, focuses on the role of the novel's narrator, and draws out parallels with Machado's *Memórias póstumas de Brás Cubas*. D. Treece, ' "It could all be different": an introduction to the fiction of João Gilberto Noll', *ib.*, 267–76, emphasizes the originality of N.'s writing in a discussion of its objectives and achievements. E. Piza, *O caminho das aguas: estereótipos de personagens negras por escritoras brancas*, SPo, EDUSP, 213 pp., deals with children's literature written by four women authors in the 1970s and 80s. It examines how the black characters in their work replicate stereotypes but also convey the intimate concerns of the authors. J. R. Whitaker Penteado, *Os filhos de Lobato: o imaginário infantil na ideología do adulto*, R, Dunya, 1997, 394 pp., is a very thorough study of L.'s writing for children, interesting in its observations on the ideology conveyed, but unconvincing in its attempt, through questionnaires and interviews, to assess its impact on its readers. L. Costa Lima, *Terra ignota: a construção de 'Os sertões'*, R, Civilização Brasileira, 1997, 298 pp., is a valuable new study of the work, which investigates thoroughly its scientific and literary bases, and then takes up again the debate on its significance in the construction of Brazilian cultural identity. T. Franco Carvalhal, 'Limiares culturais: as complexas relações do sul/sur', *RevIb*, 182–83:97–106, makes brief reference to João Simões Lopes Neto and Sergio Faraco in a comparison of concepts of the 'south' in Argentine and Brazilian literature. R. R. Mautner Wasserman, 'E a Mágia? A presentação da realidade em Jorge Amado e Gabriel García Márquez', *ib.*, 171–192, examines the relationship between the 'real' and the 'magical' in G.M.'s *Cien años de soledad* and A.'s *Gabriela, cravo e canela*. V. Unruh, 'Las ágiles musas de la modernidad: Patrícia Galvão y Norah Lange', *ib.*, 271–86, argues that both G. and the Argentine L. demonstrate the paradoxical relationship of women writers with the Latin American avant-garde. N. Lindstrom, 'Escritoras judías brasileiras e hispanoamericanas', *ib.*, 287–97, is a broad survey of the role of Jewish cultural elements in the work of such writers as Lispector and Célia Igel Teitelbaum. L. J. Beard, 'La sujetividad feminina en la metaficción feminista lati-noamericana', *ib.*, 299–311, seeks to show how Parente Cunha's work challenges traditional notions of female identity. **Navegar e preciso, viver: escritos para Silviano Santiago*, ed. E. M. Souza and W. Melo Miranda, Belo Horizonte, UFMG, 1997, 365 pp. I. Avelar, 'The angel of history's forged signature: the ruins of memory and the task of mourning in a Brazilian post dictatorial novel', *MFS*, 44: 183–214, uses aspects of Nietzchean philosophy to examine how Silviano Santiago's 1981 novel *Em liberdade* confronts Brazil's recent political past. D. A. de Castro, *Roteiro de leitura: Vidas Secas de Graciliano Ramos*, SPo, Ática, 1997, 136 pp.

IX. ITALIAN STUDIES

LANGUAGE

By ADAM LEDGEWAY, *University Assistant Lecturer in Romance Philology, University of Cambridge*, and ALESSANDRA LOMBARDI, *Part-time Lecturer in Italian, University of Cambridge*

1. GENERAL

Ramat Vol. pays a well-deserved tribute to a key Italian figure in the field of linguistics with a collection of 29 articles spanning R.'s wide-ranging interests, many relating to Italo-Romance topics. *Lepschy Vol.* brings together in honour of a much respected scholar a collection of essays within the fields of literature, visual arts, history, and language (three articles). The buoyant state of Italian linguistics is confirmed by the following volumes of conference proceedings: *SLI 30*, with a strong bias towards articles devoted to historical topics of Italo-Romance interest; *SLI 29*, containing 25 articles falling within the three areas of 'La "lingua d'Italia" in Italia', 'La lingua "degli italiani"' and 'La "lingua d'Italia" fuori d'Italia'; *Qasis, 2: atti della 3ª giornata italo-americana di dialettologia. La negazione nelle lingue romanze*, ed. Paola Benincà and Cecilia Poletto, Istituto di Fonetica e Dialettologia CNR, iii + 112 pp., henceforth *QASIS*, 2, heralding the second volume in a series intended to report on the research from field inquiries conducted for the Syntactic Atlas of Northern Italy. The present volume focuses on aspects of the syntax of negation, bringing together three articles dealing with northern Italian dialects and one article devoted to Italian; Benincà, *Romance Syntax*, further highlights the central role played by Italian linguists and Italo-Romance data in recent developments in generative syntax with a collection of seven previously published articles dealing almost entirely with topics of Italo-Romance interest; **Lessico e grammatica. Teorie linguistiche e applicazioni lessicografiche. Atti del Convegno interannuale della Società di Linguistica Italiana, Madrid 21–25 febbraio 1995*, ed. Tullio De Mauro and Vincenzo Lo Cascio, Ro, Bulzoni, 1997, x + 462 pp.; **Italica matritensia: Atti del 4. Convegno SILFI: Società Internazionale di Linguistica e Filologia Italiana, Madrid 27–29 giugno 1996*, ed. Maria Teresa Navarro Salazar, F, Cesati, 538 pp.; **Storia della lingua italiana e storia letteraria. Atti del I. Convegno ASLI, Associazione per la Storia della Lingua Italiana, Firenze 29–30 maggio 1997*, ed. Nicoletta Maraschio and Teresa Poggi Salani, F, Cesati, 153 pp. Also of general interest are the following two volumes of already published essays by two eminent scholars in the field: *Scritti scelti di R. Lazzeroni*, ed. T. Bolelli and S. Sani, Pisa, Pacini, 1997, xxi + 344 pp., and Tullio De Mauro, *Prima persona singolare passato prossimo indicativo*, Ro, Bulzoni, 168 pp. The external history of Italian and the socio-linguistic situation in modern-day Italy receive a thorough, albeit concise, treatment in M. Parry, 'Italian', Price, *Encyclopedia*, 254–59.

2. HISTORY OF THE LANGUAGE, EARLY TEXTS, AND DIACHRONIC STUDIES

Gianni Viola, *La lingua italiana fra tradizione letteraria e società civile: un sommario di storia della lingua italiana*, Ro, Bulzoni, 225 pp., provides a comprehensive overview of the external history of the language particularly useful for undergraduate courses, including chapters on: 'L'italiano nel sistema delle lingue', 'Formazione e ragione dei canoni letterari', 'L'italiano che fece l'Unità', 'L'italiano di fine millennio', 'La diffusione dell'italiano nel mondo. La teoria della traduzione e della ricezione'. M. Metzeltin, 'Proposta di una storia dell'italiano attraverso le sue grammatiche: storia concezionale e storia della lingua', *SLI 29*, 129–51, explores the evolution of gràmmars in relation to the history of the language, highlighting their significance as a linguistic tool in evaluating changes in linguistic attitudes. *La questione linguistico-musicale*, a somewhat neglected area in studies on the history of the language, forms the topic of Ilaria Bonomi, *Il docile idioma. L'italiano lingua per musica*, Ro, Bulzoni, 320 pp., with chapters on: 'L'uso dell'italiano nell'opera fuori d'Italia nel Seicento e nel Settecento', 'La questione linguistico-musicale in Francia, Inghilterra e Germania', 'La coscienza del primato dell'italiano lingua per musica nei teorici italiani del Settecento', 'La fine di un dominio', 'Conclusione ottocentesca'. B. examines the privileged role of Italian during the centuries in which Italian opera predominated in Europe, tracing how in this most Italian of art forms the Italian language acquired the prestigious status of 'the language of music'. Of interest to students of the history of the language is the new edition of Luca Serianni's *Lezioni di grammatica storica italiana*, Ro, Bulzoni, 161 pp., which benefits from a considerable reworking of the original text, an extended introductory section, and the inclusion of a number of exercises. The publication of Martin Maiden, *Storia linguistica dell'italiano*, Bo, Il Mulino, 307 pp., underlines the success enjoyed by the original English edition of M.'s authoritative internal history of the language. This new Italian edition contains a number of corrections and additions to the original text, as well as an introduction by A. Stussi. C. Giovanardi, **La teoria cortigiana e il dibattito linguistico nel primo Cinquecento*, Ro, Bulzoni, 275 pp. M. Pastore Passaro, 'From theory to history and poetry: Dante's hunt in the forest of dialects',

Language

RStI, 16:104–15, analyses the value of Dante's *De vulgari eloquentia* as a linguistic work, championing it as a pioneering study in the field of historical linguistics. F. M. Devoto, 'Produzione e ricezione del linguaggio negli studi italiani della seconda metà del Settecento', *LS*, 33:231–66, establishes that, alongside the well-documented traditional debates on language, research on language production and speech pathologies were flourishing in the latter half of the 18th c., providing the stimulus for a different and innovative perspective on language.

G. Gorni, 'Restituzione formale dei testi volgari', *SFI*, 56:5–30. S. Bertelli, 'Il copista del *Novellino*', *ib.*, 31–45. S. Orlando, 'Una pagina preziosa di fine Trecento', *ib.*, 47–55. M. Malinverni, '*Lectiones faciliores* e varianti redazionali nella tradizione delle rime di Panfilo Sasso', *ib.*, 203–28. R. Baldini, 'Zucchero Bencivenni, *La santà del corpo*', *SLeI*, 15:21–300. Mario Piotti, '*Un puoco grossetto di loquella*'. *La lingua di Niccolò Tartaglia. La 'Nuova Scientia' e i 'Quesiti et inventioni diverse'*, Mi, LED, examines the historical importance of the use of the northern vernacular in the scientific texts of Niccolò Tartaglia, a 16th-c. mathematician who was the first in his field to use the vernacular at a time when Latin was still the language of science. P.'s work offers a clear and detailed study of Tartaglia's language, with individual sections dedicated to phonetics, morphology, syntax, and lexis. The role played by alternations in grammatical person in Montale's *Mottetti* (*Le Occasioni*) is studied in L. Tomasin, 'Sulle persone grammaticali nei *Mottetti* di Montale', *LS*, 33:301–26.

R. L. Bruni, 'Il Lucidoro (1634) o chiave della Toscana Pronunzia (1674) di Bernardino Ambrogi', *Lepschy Vol.*, 494–508, examines Ambrogi's 17th-c. little known treatise on Tuscan pronunciation, highlighting A.'s interest in the spoken language and his relaxed linguistic attitudes to non-Tuscan norms. L. Ramello, **Il Salterio italiano nella tradizione manoscritta: individuazione e costituzione dello stemma delle versioni toscane: edizione critica della versione veneta*, Alessandria, Orso, 1997, 491 pp. A. Zangrandi, 'Il lessico del *Marco Visconti* di Tommaso Grossi nella prima edizione milanese. La componente dialettale e popolare', *LS*, 33:267–300, evaluates the popular features of Marco Visconti's vocabulary, particularly in the light of Grossi's Manzonian ideas on language and their fulfilment in the novel. D. Zancani, 'Appunti per una storia del piacentino antico. La testimonianza di scolari del Trecento', *Lepschy Vol.*, 479–93, unearths several unpublished 14th-c. Piacentino texts to shed some light on the general linguistic features of the early dialect, which is shown to belong to the Lombard, rather than Emilian, dialect group.

Nunzio La Fauci, **Per una teoria grammaticale del mutamento morfosintattico: dal latino verso il romanzo*, Pisa, ETS, 1997, 86 pp. F. Sabatini and

V. Coletti, *La lingua italiana: come funziona, come si usa, come cambia*, F, Giunti, 1997, 48 pp. S. Luraghi, 'On the directionality of grammaticalisation', *STUF*, 51 : 355–65, challenges traditional claims about the unidirectional nature of grammaticalization processes with an examination of the fate of the present participle from Latin to modern Italian. Despite the loss of its original verbal usage, L. contends that the *-ante/-ente* suffix is still nonetheless highly productive, having acquired the status of a derivational suffix in modern Italian. This shift from an inflectional to a derivational suffix is championed by L. as a prime example of degrammaticalization. L. Renzi, 'Pronomi e casi. La discendenza italiana del lat. QUI', *SGI*, 17 : 5–36, traces the development of early Italian case distinctions in the pronominal paradigm, providing persuasive evidence in favour of recognizing a residual binary case system parallel to early Gallo-Romance varieties. S. Luraghi, 'Omissione dell'oggetto in frasi coordinate: dal latino all'italiano', *SLI 30*, 183–96, investigates the emergence of the obligatory use of a resumptive pronoun in early Italian coordinated structures, where Latin allowed a gapping strategy. L. links the rise of such resumptive pronouns to the loss of object drop in Italian. N. Vincent, 'Tra grammatica e grammaticalizzazione: articoli e clitici nelle lingue (italo)-romanze', *ib.*, 411–40, explores the interaction of ILLE and IPSE in the formation of the D(eterminer)-system, with particular reference to Italo-Romance data, highlighting the merits of an analysis which brings together the insights of both generative and grammaticalization theories of language change. M. Palermo, *L'espressione del pronome personale soggetto nella storia dell'italiano*, Ro, Bulzoni, 1997, 374 pp. G. Fiorentino, 'La clausola relativa debole e il pronome relativo in italiano', *SLI 30*, 215–33. Two studies that deal specifically with the development of the conjunction *perché* are M. Samardzic, 'I valori della congiunzione *perché* nell'italiano antico', *ib.*, 235–46, which reveals through an examination of 14th-c. Tuscan texts that the development of the conjunction in modern Italian is characterized by a gradual weakening of its original semantico-syntactic properties, while M. Bertuccelli Papi, 'Dalla sintassi del discorso alla sintassi frasale: *che* (*ché?*) e *perché* nella prosa toscana del '2–300', *ib.*, 247–66, analyses the distribution of *che* and *perché* in early Tuscan prose, demonstrating how at first the causal connector *che* assumes a discoursal rather than syntactic function, whose role as a dependent marker is signalled solely by inference and pragmatics. B. adduces evidence to demonstrate that its subsequent development into a subordinating clause connector is marked by the introduction of a preposition. K. Hölker, 'Un caso di delocutività: l'assenza dell'articolo davanti al possessivo con nome di parentela in italiano (e in altre lingue romanze)', *ib.*, 567–76, offers an original account of the absence of the article in conjunction with possessives modifying singular, unqualified kinship terms in modern Italian. Noting that such bare possessive forms mirror the syntactic distribution of the old Tuscan enclitic possessives, H. maintains that the 'free' possessive forms assimilated the syntax of the enclitic forms at an early date when their own syntactic properties were still in a state of flux and subject to considerable instability. G. de Boer, 'Appunti sulla storia recente delle costruzioni comparative in italiano', *ib.*, 671–86, surveys the history of the comparative construction and the changes in its syntax from 16th-c. to present-day Italian. D. Cerbasi, 'Le costruzioni causative in italiano, spagnolo e portoghese', *ib.*, 457–68, views the process of syntactic re-analysis and auxiliation in the development of the Romance analytic causative as characterized by a greater degree of grammaticalization in Italian than in Spanish or Portuguese, a fact which explains the differing behaviour of the causative construction in Italo- and Hispano-Romance.

3. PHONOLOGY

Certamen Phonologicum. Papers from the Third Cortona Phonology Meeting April 1996, ed. Pier Marco Bertinetto et al., T, Rosenberg and Sellier, 1997, 291 pp. P. M. Bertinetto, 'La sillabazione dei nessi /sC/ in italiano: un'eccezione alla tendenza "universale"?', *QLLP*, 11 : 12–27, reconsiders from a phonological perspective the problems posed by the syllabification of the sequence /sC/ in Italian, a grey area where experimental phonetic evidence highlights a high degree of oscillation between hetero- and tautosyllabic outputs. B. concludes that the question remains unsettled, although acknowledging that the evidence of modern Italian strongly suggests a shift from an original heterosyllabic output to a tautosyllabic realization. L. Turchi, 'Sui gradi di apertura delle vocali medie dell'italiano davanti ai nessi /sC/', *ib.*, 139–54, contends (pace Marotta) that the preponderance of /ɛ/ and /ɔ/ over /e/ and /o/ before the sequence /sC/ cannot be taken as evidence in favour of the heterosyllabic realization of this sequence, the predominant presence of open vowels in such contexts being explained by recourse to other factors. P. M. Bertinetto, 'Against prosodic phonology: boundary strength and linguistic ecology (concerning intervocalic /S/-voicing in Italian)', *ib.*, 37–47, presents evidence for a fine-grained scale of boundary strength in order to capture the different behaviour of a number of Romance varieties with respect to the rule of intervocalic /S/-voicing, deriving the varying distribution of [s] vs [z] in French, standard Italian and northern Italian from a modulation of the level of strength of the morpheme boundary and by its position relative to the fricative segment. B. Gili Fivela and P. M. Bertinetto, 'Incontri vocalici tra prefisso e radice (iato o dittongo?)', *ib.*, 102–22, examines the behaviour of vowel-final prefixes attached to vowel-initial roots, arguing that in addition to vowel deletion, one of the two adjacent vowels be may phonetically weakened to a glide in spontaneous speech, giving rise to a diphthong.

4. MORPHOLOGY

A. Blank, 'Kognitive Italienische Wortbildungslehre', *ItStudien*, 19:5–27. G. Crocco Galèas, 'La base dei processi morfologici in italiano', *SGI*, 17:245–72, postulates, contrary to word-based approaches, that the morpheme should be viewed as the prototypical base of Italian morphological rules. S. Scalise, 'Aspetti problematici della semantica in morfologia derivazionale', *Ramat Vol.*, 467–80, investigates some aspects of the derivational semantics of the two polysemous suffixes *-aio* and *-ata*. The results of the analysis, which S. argues hold more generally of all affixation processes, reveal that word formation rules are characterized both by a 'core' of semantic regularity, where meaning constitutes a predictable extension of the semantic values of the base, and a degree of semantic irregularity where the interpretation of the derived word is not predictable on the basis of the interaction between base and suffix. R. Veland, 'Les adverbes en *-mente* dans trois langues romanes (espagnol, français, italien)', *RF*, 11:427–44, concludes following an examination of a small survey of various sources that Italian adverbs in *-mente*, on a par with their French congeners, prove increasingly less frequent and productive in the modern language than their Spanish counterparts. M. Maiden, 'Metafonesi, "parola", "morfema": alcune riflessioni metodologiche', *ItStudien*, 19:44–63, presents an overview of M.'s previously argued reconstruction of the history of metaphony, highlighting in particular the central importance accorded to the word in his account. Id., 'Towards an explanation of some morphological changes which "should never have happened"', pp. 241–54 of *Historical Linguistics 1997*, ed. Monika S. Schmid et al., Amsterdam–Philadelphia, Benjamins, ix + 409 pp., draws on some apparent 'unnatural' morphological developments from the history of Romanian feminine plurals and Italian gerunds to challenge the view that 'naturalness' in morphology be equated with notions of transparent mapping between form and meaning.

5. SYNTAX

The central role played by Italian in recent developments in generative syntactic theory is highlighted by the appearance of

Haegeman, *Comparative Syntax*, which applies the insights of recent generative research to a number of traditional and current issues in comparative syntax, with five out of the 11 contributors drawing heavily, if not predominantly, on Italo-Romance data. Contributions of particular interest to Italianists include: A. Cardinaletti, 'Subjects and clause structure' (33–63), accounting for the patterns of cross-linguistic variation in the distribution of preverbal subjects in Italian varieties (Italian, northern and central Italian dialects), English and French by postulating the existence of two preverbal subject positions within IP, a higher AgrP which hosts overt subjects (e.g. *lui*) and a lower one hosting weak subjects (pro or subject clitics); G. Giusti, 'The categorial status of determiners' (95–123), examining the distribution of items traditionally labelled determiners, including articles, demonstratives and quantifiers, and arguing that such items do not form a homogeneous syntactic category: only articles should be considered of the category D(eterminer); M. T. Guasti, 'Romance causatives' (124–44), which despite the deceptive title, focuses entirely on the syntax of Italian causatives, capitalizing on the observation that the Italian construction, though clearly analytic in nature, mimics the behaviour of morphological causatives in many respects. This ambivalent behaviour of the Italian causative is interpreted as the reflex of an incorporation process of the infinitive into the causative verb, on a par with morphological causatives, followed by the excorporation of the causative raising to IP. This would account for the superficial presence of two morphologically independent verbs. Research into the pro-drop parameter continues to make frequent use of Italian data: L. Rizzi, 'A parametric approach to comparative syntax: properties of the pronominal system', *ib.*, 268–85; R. Manzini and L. Savoia, 'Null subjects without pro', *UCLWPL*, 9, 1997: 303–13, attempts to reformulate the parameter within a minimalist framework without recourse to pronominal empty categories and DP movement. Instead, the content of the Null Subject Parameter is derived from a theory of feature movement, with languages varying in terms of whether such features are realized overtly (northern Italian dialects) or covertly (Italian). E. Torrego, 'Nominative subjects and pro-drop INFL', *Syntax*, 1 : 206–19, explores within a comparative perspective the syntax of nominative subjects in Italian, Spanish, and Catalan infinitival clauses, concluding that such subjects are licensed by a D-feature with weak agreement features in Tense. J.-Y. Pollock, 'On the syntax of subnominal clitics: cliticisation and ellipsis', *ib.*, 300–30, attempts to deduce the different behaviour of Italian *ne* and French *en* in such minimal pairs as **il primo capitolo ne è interessante (di questo libro)* vs *le premier chapitre en est interéssant (de ce livre)*

from principles of Universal Grammar and the proper characterization of the Null Subject Parameter. Other significant research into
the syntax of subjects includes: C. Dobrovie-Sorin, 'Impersonal *se*
constructions in Romance and the passivization of unergatives', *LI*,
29:399–437, offers a reinterpretation of Cinque's [± arg] *si* distinction, arguing for two kinds of impersonal *si* in Italian and Romance
unergative clauses: a nominative *si* limited to finite clauses (*si canta*),
where nominative is licensed by the finite specification of the verb,
and an accusative middle-passive *si* restricted to infinitival clauses
(*sembra essersi lavorato a sufficienza*), where the non-finite specification of
the verb precludes the possibility of the clitic bearing nominative
case. Manuela Pinto, *Licensing and interpretation of inverted subjects in
Italian*, Utrecht, Led, 1997, ix + 261 pp., offers an extensive description of subject inversion and the interpretative effects related to the
structural position of the subject, persuasively deriving inversion from
the interaction of the EPP and conditions on economy through the
verb's ability to license a loco/temporal argument (LOC). If the latter
is raised to check the EPP, the subject remains *in situ* yielding VS,
thereby capturing in a highly natural way the interpretative differences between *Dante ha telefonato* 'Dante has rung' vs *Ha telefonato Dante*
'Dante has rung (here/us)'.

Romance in HPSG, ed. Sergio Balari and Luca Dini, Stanford,
CSLI, xxxi + 402 pp., brings together a collection of articles investigating a number of Romance topics not previously studied in detail
from the perspective of HPSG theory. Six of the eight contributors
deal with issues relating directly to Italian, confirming the impact of
Italian on the theory: V. Allegranza, 'Determiners and functors: NP
structure in Italian' (55–107), is a fascinating account of the syntax
and semantics of Italian NPs that incorporates much of the DP
analysis — without giving up the assumption that the head of the NP
is the noun — by collapsing all nominal specifier structures into a
single head-functor structure; L. Dini, 'Null complements in Italian'
(219–65), advances an interpretation of the behaviour of certain
phonetically unrealized complements and unrealized subjects in *si*-
constructions and infinitival sentences in purely semantic terms
without appealing to empty categories; C. Grover, 'English missing
objects and Italian restructuring' (267–304), develops and extends a
raising analysis of English missing object constructions to Italian
restructuring phenomena (tough-constructions, clitic climbing and
object promotion in *si*-constructions) treated as local dependencies;
P. Monachesi, 'Decomposing Italian clitics' (305–57), proposes a
lexical account of cliticization which draws a crucial distinction
between affix-like clitics (e.g. *lo*) and word-like clitics (e.g. *loro*) to
explain certain idiosyncracies that each category shows with respect

to clitic climbing; A. Sanfilippo, 'Thematically bound adjuncts' (359–95), pursues a richer typology of grammatical dependencies with the incorporation of the categories 'quasi-argument' and 'thematically bound adjunct' into the traditional argument/adjunct distinction. Under these assumptions, S. advances an analysis of clitic dislocation constructions as involving a thematically bound adjunct, a type of strong dependency where extraction lexical rules are responsible for both gap creation and cliticization.

C. Marello, 'What qualifies as an elliptical Noun Phrase in Italian? Opinions of grammarians, lexicographers and native speakers', Korzen, *Clause Combining*, 107–23, reports the results of a small survey investigating native speakers' intuitions in relation to such NPs as *un bicchiere di (acqua) minerale gassata* and *la (autostrada) Torino-Savona*, traditionally labelled elliptical by grammarians and lexicographers alike. M.'s results reveal that native speakers do not generally perceive grammatical ellipsis at all in such NPs. Rather, the syntactic role of such heads is redistributed over the remainder of the NP and their exact semantic interpretation is determined by the remainder of the utterance and/or pragmatic knowledge. The syntax of adjectival positions is investigated in: G. Berruto, 'Sulla posizione prenominale dell'aggettivo in italiano', *Ramat Vol.*, 95–108, which provides a useful sketch of the well-known problems of adjectival position in Italian, concluding with some remarks on the increasing use of prenominal adjectives in modern Italian; G. Cinque, 'On the evidence for partial N-movement in the Romance DP', Benincà, *Romance Syntax*, 159–76, an ambitious attempt to explain Italian adjectival positions within a system that exploits a number of functional projections between D and NP. G. Longobardi, 'Reference and proper names: a theory of N-movement in syntax and logical form', *ib.*, 177–214, draws heavily on Italian data, including such minimal pairs as *Il mio Gianni ha finalmente telefonato* vs *Gianni mio ha finalmente telefonato*, in support of overt N-to-D movement in Italian and ultimately the DP hypothesis. G. Cinque, 'L'ordine relativo degli avverbi di frase in italiano (e in altre lingue)', *Ramat Vol.*, 141–49, examines the distribution of various classes of sentential adverb in Italian, highlighting the constraints operating on their respective ordering; Id., 'On the relative order of certain "lower" adverbs in Italian and French', Benincà, *Romance Syntax*, 99–111, compares ordering restrictions on a class of Italian and French adverbial phrases belonging to the lower portion of clause following the active past participle (e.g. *già/déjà*, *mica/pas*), highlighting the identical behaviour of the two languages in this respect. V. Bianchi, 'On the structural position of time clauses', *QLLP*, 11:66–90. P. Acquaviva, 'Negation and operator dependencies', *QASIS*, 2:61–84, compares the distributional properties of Italian negative indefinites with those of English negative quantifiers and polarity items, demonstrating the more restricted nature of the former. P. Blumenthal, 'Für eine Lehre von der Konnexion: Komplementsatz und direktes Objekt im Italienischen', *ZRP*, 114:1–52. C. Schwarze, 'A lexical-functional analysis of Romance auxiliaries', *TL*, 24:83–105, pursues an LFG account of the syntax of Romance perfective and passive auxiliaries. The choice of perfective auxiliary in Italian is related to the conceptual/argument structure by way of a rule of 'agentless role configurations', e.g. *Il temporale era/*aveva cominciato a notte fonda* (subject ≠ Agent) vs *Il panettiere aveva/*era cominciato a lavorare a notte fonda* (subject = Agent), whereas the choice of passive auxiliary is determined by the interplay of constituency, semantics, and discourse pragmatics. A. Belletti, 'Generalized verb-movement', Benincà, *Romance Syntax*, 28–80. F. Beghelli, 'Mood and the interpretation of indefinites', *LRev*, 15:277–300, illustrates through an examination of subjunctive contexts in Italian and modern Greek that mood choice is generally able to restrict the availability of referential readings of indefinites, e.g. *Gino sosteneva che una donna ricevette il premio. Il suo nome era Ines* (indicative/specific interpretation) vs *Gino propose che una donna ricevesse il premio. *Il suo nome era Ines* (subjunctive/non-specific interpretation). Data from Italian and the dialects figure heavily in Alessandra Giorgi and Fabio Pianesi, *Tense and Aspect. From Semantics to Morphosyntax*, OUP, xv + 319 pp., 1997, which explores the interaction between morphosyntax and semantics within a minimalist framework through an examination of the variety of tense and aspectual forms in Romance and Germanic, their distribution and interpretation. The high degree of cross-linguistic variation observed within this area is accounted for in terms of a theory of features which can be variously realized as a syncretic category within a single structural head or scattered across several projections. The proposed analysis offers, in addition, a particularly convincing account of extraction from subjunctive contexts and complementizer deletion in Italian. L. Rizzi, 'The fine structure of the left periphery', Benincà, *Romance Syntax*, 112–58, undertakes a detailed examination of Italian topic and focus structures, providing evidence for a more articulated structure of the CP domain.

6. SEMANTICS

A. Vecchiato, 'Verbi e significati. La semantica lessicale di C. J. Fillmore', *LS*, 33:79–109. M. Moneglia, 'Determinazione empirica del senso e partizione semantica del lessico', *SGI*, 17:363–98. P. M.

Bertinetto, 'Sui connotati azionali ed aspettuali della perifrasi con-
tinua (*andare/venire* + gerundio)', *Ramat Vol.*, 109–28, examines aspect
and actionality in relation to the properties of the continuative
periphrasis and their interaction in determining the type of predicate
which can occur in this periphrasis. P. Ribotta, '*Ormai* ed espressioni
di tempo affini: considerazioni sintattiche e semantiche', *SGI*,
17:273–328, undertakes an examination of the semantic and syntactic properties of the adverb *ormai*, comparing its behaviour with
that of associated temporal expressions. In contrast to its traditional
classification as a temporal adverb, R.'s findings reveal that *ormai*
appears, rather, to behave like a sentential adverb, alluding to either
a prolonged process in time, e.g. *tagliuzzate gli spinaci ormai scongelati*,
or a missed opportunity, e.g. *ormai l'ha scoperto Giulio*. P. Ramat,
'Perché *veruno* significa "nessuno"?', *SLI 30*, 397–409, traces the
semantic development of *veruno* from positive to negative quantifier in
Italian and various northern Italian dialects.

7. PRAGMATICS AND DISCOURSE

G. Tamburini, 'L'ordine dei costituenti e l'articolazione dell'informa-
zione in italiano: un'analisi distribuzionale', *SGI*, 17:398–443, analyses word order variations in terms of topic and comment.
E. Lombardi Vallauri, 'Focus esteso, ristretto e contrastivo', *LS*,
33:197–216, compares broad, narrow, and contrastive focus in
English and Italian, suggesting that a focus cannot have a contrastive
meaning unless precise syntactic and discourse features first make it a
narrow focus. M. Dardano, G. Frenguelli, and A. Pelo, 'Struttura
della frase e testualità: il caso delle proposizioni consecutive nell'italiano antico', *SLI 30*, 293–310, establishes a typology of consecutive
clauses on the basis of some samples of 12th-, 14th-, and 17th-c. prose
and verse. I. Korzen, 'On the grammaticalisation of rhetorical
satellites. A comparative study on Italian and Danish', Korzen *Clause
Combining*, 64–86, presents and discusses the results of a corpus
derived from an empirical survey conducted on Danish and Italian
university students asked to reproduce two Mr Bean episodes. K.'s
findings highlight some fundamental differences between Italian and
Danish text structure and clause combining as they appear in the
grammaticalization of various rhetorical units.

8. LEXIS

Tullio De Mauro, **DAIC. Dizionario avanzato dell'italiano corrente*, T,
Paravia, 1997, 1385 pp. M. Drago and A. Boroli, **Dizionario fondamentale della lingua italiana*, Novara, De Agostini, xiii + 1522 pp. **Dizionario italiano: le 50,000 parole della lingua di oggi: significati, usi, fraseologia,*

pronuncia, ortografia, grammatica, sintassi, etimologia, ed. F. Melotti and I. Sordi, Mi, Rizzoli, 1997, xxiii + 1191 pp.

M. G. de Boer, 'Riflessioni intorno a un saluto: la storia di *ciao*', *RLFRU*, 17:10–24, retraces the origins of *ciao* to 18th-c. Venetan, chartering its gradual adoption throughout the Peninsula in three phases between 1800–1950, spreading first to Lombardy and Piedmont, then Sicily and Rome, and finally to the remainder of the Peninsula. M. Sartor Ceciliot, 'Cucuc, cucuriel, cucurissa. Saggio linguistico e folcloristico', Mioni, *Dialetti*, 127–34. O. Lurati, 'Per la storia etimologica dei nomi delle testualità orali: il caso di filastrocca', *QS*, 19:113–21, re-examines the origins of *filastrocca* retracing the term to the fusion of two imperatives *fila e st(r)occa*. S. Orlando, 'Aggiunte "bolognesi" al corpus delle CLPIO', *SLeI*, 15:5–20. F. Gambino, 'Gli *Evangelii* di Jacopo Gradenigo', *ib.*, 15:301–18. S. Telve, 'Il lessico della librettistica verdiana', *ib.*, 319–437. F. Rainer, 'Les premières traces de l'italianisme *agio*', *RLiR*, 62:377–80. S. C. Sgroi, 'Chi ha paura del dialetto? Ancora un caso di enantiosemia', *QS*, 19:127–29, examines the meaning of *malfidata* in such expressions as *una persona malfidata*, for which most modern dictionaries offer the definition 'diffidente'. S. challenges this definition, observing that in modern usage *malfidata* generally has the opposite meaning of 'infido', a semantic change which S. retraces to the simple confusion of two opposite, if not complementary, points of view whose origins are to be sought in the influence of northern dialects on Italian. G. Alfieri, 'La "lingua d'Italia": ambiti e usi di una definizione', *SLI 29*, 28–57, scans the centuries leading up to Italian Unification for the way in which the historical experiences of the Peninsula contributed to the various definitions applied to the Italian language.

9. SOCIOLINGUISTICS

Lorenzo Coveri, Antonella Benucci, and Pierangela Diadori, *Le varietà dell'italiano. Manuale di sociolinguistica italiana*, Ro, Bonacci, 322 pp., presents a clear and well-illustrated overview of sociolinguistic variation in modern Italy, ideal for a student text, with chapters on the following topics: 'Il modello della variazione e la situazione sociolinguistica italiana', 'Le varietà diatopiche', 'Le varietà diastratiche', 'Le varietà diafasiche', 'Le varietà diamesiche', each containing a wide selection of authentic illustrative texts and exercises. D. Spadea, 'Aspetti linguistici della lingua pubblicitaria su Internet', *QS*, 19:87–101, compares the use of Italian in general advertisements with those appearing on the Internet, with particularly interesting results for the areas of grammar and lexis. It emerges that while in the language of canonical advertisements there is a widespread use of 1st and 2nd person imperatives, advertisements on the Internet exhibit a tendency towards a more impersonal style, characterized by the use of complex nominalizations and simple verbal constructions limited to the present tense. E. Burr, 'Questione della lingua, lingua media und Zeitungssprache', *ZRP*, 114:269–89, examines the features of journalistic styles of Italian. C. Marazzini, 'La lingua degli stati italiani. L'uso pubblico e burocratico prima dell'unità', *SLI 29*, 1–27, studies the significance of the official, public, and bureaucratic uses of the vernacular and their relationship to Latin in the Peninsula prior to Unification. R. Sardo, 'Continuità formulare e integrazione morfosintattica nella lingua burocratica della Sicilia vicereale e borbonica', *ib.*, 68–94, explores the influence of two distinct administrative regimes on the linguistic features of 17th-c. Sicilian legal documents. S.'s study reveals that the gradual abandonment of Latin was accompanied by the concomitant integration of Tuscan morphosyntax in the bureaucratic language of the time. P. Bellucci et al., 'Studi di sociolinguistica giudiziaria', *ib.*, 226–68, pursues a fascinating inquiry into the language used by the Italian underworld, paying particular attention to the linguistic behaviour of women in the courtroom and the language recorded in extracts of speech taken from tapped telephone conversations. C. Grassi and R. Weilguny, 'Per lo studio dell'italiano del diritto e dell'amministrazione in uso sotto la Monarchia austroungarica', *ib.*, 357–63. J. Visconti, 'L'elaborazione di un glossario comparativo dei condizionali nel linguaggio giuridico: un progetto europeo', *Lepschy Vol.*, pp. 509–26, highlights the frequent use of complex conditional connectives in legal language with examples drawn from a comparative Italian, English, French, and German corpus. L. Briganti, 'L'italiano politico-amministrativo della Repubblica Cisalpina. Bandi e proclami del Dipartimento del Rubicone', *SLI 29*, 95–112, considers the lexis and pragmatic-communicative aspects of public notices published during the short-lived two-year existence of the Cisalpine Republic. A. Nesi, 'Usi dell'italiano in Corsica durante l'Ottocento', *ib.*, 113–28, provides a synthesis of the status of Italian in 19th-c. Corsica, a significant period in the linguistic history of the island during which the cultural and institutional role of Italian was clearly declining. G. Iannàccaro, 'La "lingua della volontà". Intorno a testamenti milanesi di fine Ottocento', *ib.*, 152–73, critically examines the language of 19th-c. Milanese holographic wills, a form of linguistic production which hitherto has received scant attention from specialists. E. Martínez Garrido and M. Rodríguez Fierro, 'Il discorso fascista italiano e il suo debito all'oratoria romantica', *ib.*, 174–94, assesses through a comparative textual analysis of writings by Foscolo and D'Annunzio the extent to which the lexicon used in the Romantic period can be considered a fundamental part of Fascist discourse. V. Deon, 'Una lingua democratica: la lingua della Costituzione', *ib.*, 195–211, on the basis of a study of the *Atti dell'Assemblea Costituente* demonstrates how linguistic considerations, in particular lexis, syntax, and pragmatics, were of prime importance in the final drafting of the Italian Constitution. P. Desideri, 'Metalinguaggio e retorica dell'attenuazione nel discorso politico di Aldo Moro', *ib.*, 212–25. M. E. Piemontese, 'Il linguaggio della pubblica amministrazione nell'Italia di oggi. Aspetti problematici della semplificazione linguistica', *ib.*, 269–92, raises a number of problems inherent in past and present attempts to simplify the language of public administration which, despite increasing but frequently disjointed efforts, have met with little success. F. Liverani Bertinelli and C. Carnevali, 'Usi istituzionali dell'italiano in atti legislativi ed amministrativi della Repubblica di San Marino', *ib.*, 449–70. J. Nystedt, 'Ricchezza (o povertà) lessicale nei documenti italiani della CEE', *ib.*, 471–91. P. Diadosi, 'L'italiano degli stranieri nei programmi delle radio di Roma e Milano', *ib.*, 293–314, takes a first look at the linguistic characteristics of the Italian used by an increasing number of non-native speakers working in public broadcasting. D. Höhmann, 'Interlingue e strategie comunicative di un gruppo di ragazzi tamil in Italia', *RID*, 21 : 177–90, explores the linguistic production of a group of immigrant Tamil children, analysing their communicative strategies, their types of utterance, and the linguistic features of their interlanguages.

10. PSYCHOLINGUISTICS AND LANGUAGE ACQUISITION

D. Antelmi, *La prima grammatica dell'italiano: indagine longitudinale sull'acquisizione della morfosintassi italiana*, Bo, Il Mulino, 1997, 237 pp. C. Nelli, 'L'acquisizione della morfologia libera italiana. Fasi di un percorso evolutivo', *SGI*, 17 : 329–62, examines the acquisition of free morphemes of all morphological classes: articles, clitics, auxiliaries, prepositions. The results of the study establish that the acquisition of free morphemes follows a precise and gradual path articulated into three successive developmental phases. U. Bortolinu, L. B. Leonard, and M. C. Caselli, 'Specific language impairment in Italian and English: evaluating alternative accounts of grammatical deficits', *LCP*, 13 : 1–20, reports the results of a comparative study of the use of grammatical morphology in Italian and English children with a specific language impairment. While articles are found to be used to a similar degree in both groups of children, Italian-speaking children are reported to make greater use of noun and verb inflections and copular forms than their English-speaking counterparts, a pattern of findings consistent with processing accounts based on morphological richness and the durational properties of grammatical morphology. *L'apprendimento linguistico all'università: le lingue speciali*, ed. Maria Pavesi and Giuliano Bernini, Ro, Bulzoni, 323 pp.

11. DIALECTOLOGY

Extensive discussion of both northern and southern Italian dialects figures in Michele Loporcaro, *Sintassi comparata dell'accordo participiale romanzo*, T, Rosenberg and Sellier, xiv + 272 pp., which offers a clear and comprehensive account of Romance participle agreement in both perfective and passive periphrases. Unprecedented in both empirical coverage and level of detail, the present volume establishes within a Relational Grammar framework a systematic inventory of agreement patterns throughout Romance, taking into account more than 60 different agreement systems. Also considered are rival theoretical analyses developed within the Principles and Parameters framework, as well as issues relating to the acquisition of participle agreement. G. Carpaneto, **L'Italia dei dialetti*, Ro, Rendina, 1997, 237 pp. An important reference work for all Italian dialectologists is the new revised and enlarged edition of Manlio Cortelazzo and Carla Marcato, *I dialetti italiani: dizionario etimologico*, T, UTET, xli + 723 pp. *Dialetti, cultura e società. Quarta raccolta di saggi dialettologici*, ed. Alberto M. Mioni, Maria Teresa Vigolo, and Enzo Croatto, Padua, CSDI-CNR, vii + 345 pp., henceforth Mioni, *Dialetti*. M. Alinei, 'La teoria della continuità ed alcuni esempi di lunga durata nel lessico dialettale neolatino', *RID*, 21:73–96, defends a stronger version of the 'Continuity Theory' drawing on dialect data to demonstrate that the presence of Latin and its different territorial forms in Italy may be dated back to the second millennium B.C. This hypothesis is sharply criticized in L. Renzi, 'Alinei, ovvero il latino prima di Roma', *ib.*, 191–202, who rejects A.'s theory which fails to take account of firmly established concepts of Romance Philology and dialectology.

NORTHERN DIALECTS. Concise overviews of northern Italian dialects appear in Price, *Encyclopedia*: M. M. Parry, 'Piedmontese' (260–61); P. Benincà, 'Lombardy' (261–62); P. Benincà, 'Venetan' (263–65); M. Parry, 'Ligurian (Genoese)' (266–68); L. Vanelli, 'Emilian-Romagnol' (268–69). Laura Vanelli, *I dialetti italiani settentrionali nel panorama romanzo*, Ro, Bulzoni, 280 pp., contains a collection of ten essays, one of them previously unpublished, bringing together some of this eminent linguist's most significant work. Notwithstanding the more general title, these articles concentrate on two main topics:

subject and object clitic pronouns and the definite article. The previously unpublished 'Da "li" a "i" storia dell'articolo definito maschile plurale in italiano e nei dialetti settentrionali' (215–44) suitably complements V.'s previous work on the masculine singular definite article embodied in her 1992 article. Through a detailed analysis of the distribution of *li* in early texts, its modern outcome *i* is argued to be the result of a process of palatalisation *li* > *gli* > *i*, documented quite clearly in Friulan. The article concludes with an appendix tracing the distribution of *gli* in Dante to the present day. C. Poletto, 'L'inversione interrogativa come "verbo secondo residuo": l'analisi sincronica proiettata nella diacronia', *SLI 30*, 311–27, proposes a single structural analysis for generalized inversion (verb second) and interrogative inversion, two phenomena previously treated separately. N. Munaro, '*Wh-in situ* in the northern Italian dialects', Fullana, *Central Romance*, 189–212, provides a formal account of the distributional properties of *Wh*-phrases in a number of northern Italian dialects. The absence of overt *Wh*-movement in dialects of the northern Veneto and eastern Lombardy follows from a requirement of structural and categorial matching between the *in situ* *Wh*-phrase and a *Wh-scope* marker (covert in Venetan but overt in eastern Lombard) in the domain of CP, licensed by the raising of the inflected verb to the relevant functional head. In dialects spoken in the Canton Ticino, by contrast, the absence of interrogative inversion precludes the licensing of a *Wh-scope* marker in the CP domain, with the consequence that *Wh*-phrases *in situ* are not subject to any restrictions. Theoretical aspects of negative structures raised by data drawn from northern dialects are investigated in R. Zanuttini, 'Re-examining negative clauses', Benincà, *Romance Syntax*, 81–98, which provides a unified account of the contrasts in the syntactic expression of sentential negation in a wide range of Romance varieties, especially Italian and northern Italian dialects. Z. relates them to a common LF structure by the raising of the negative marker to a PolP projection. By the same author, 'Negation and verb movement', Haegeman, *Comparative Syntax*, 214–45, examines the expression of sentential negation in a number of Romance languages, demonstrating, in particular, that the behaviour of negation in northern Italian dialects provides strong evidence for postulating a more articulated IP structure containing two NegP projections. P. Portner and R. Zanuttini, 'The force of negation in *Wh*-interrogatives and exclamatives', *QASIS*, 2: 1–37, explores the relationship between negation and clausal type with an examination of so-called expletive negation in Paduan interrogative and exclamative sentences, paying special attention to the different semantic and syntactic properties of expletive and 'real' negative markers. R. Manzini and L. Savoia,

'The position of clitic and adverbial negation in Italian varieties', *ib.*, 39–60, discusses three significant parameters in negation in northern Italian dialects: the pre- or postverbal position of the negator, the position of preverbal negators with respect to clitics and the effects of preverbal negators on V-to-C movement in main clause interrogatives. M. M. Parry, 'On negation in the Ligurian hinterland', *ib.*, 85–112, examines the behaviour of negation strategies in northwestern varieties of Piedmont and Liguria in relation to Jespersen's cycle, exploring the factors which have contributed to the change from preverbal to postverbal negation in some varieties but not in others. P.'s analysis highlights the variation in positions occupied by the negator with respect to various types of object clitic and the special status of reflexive clitics among the latter.

PIEDMONT.   C. Brero, *Dizionario piemontese: italiano-piemontese, piemontese-italiano*, Mi, Vallardi, 1997, xxxiii + 237 pp. G. Pasquali, *Nuovo dizionario piemontese-italiano*, Sala Bolognese, Forni, 1997, xxxi + 621 pp., a reprint of the 1870 edition. C. Bocca and M. Centini, *Proverbi e modi di dire piemontesi: l'amore e l'amicizia, il lavoro e la famiglia, il denaro e la fortuna nelle espressioni più colorite e argute della saggezza popolare subalpina*, Ro, Newton Compton, 302 pp. A. Sella, *Modi di dire e proverbi popolari biellesi: nuova raccolta (con presentazione di Corrado Grassi)*, Alessandria, Orso, xxvii + 550 pp. B. Buono, 'Note sulla lingua cancelleresca sabauda nel Cinquecento da documenti dell'Archivio di Stato di Simancas (1536–1561)', *StP*, 27:301–564. G. Gasca Quierazza, 'Devozione alla Santa Sindone: una cantica in Piemontese della metà dell'Ottocento', *ib.*, 3–18. A. Rossebastiano, 'Sindone', *ib.*, 19–20. K. Gebhardt, 'Contribution à l'étude des mots *Piémont* et *piémontais*', *ib.*, 63–78. C. Goria, 'Subject clitics in Piedmontese: a minimalist analysis', Fullana, *Central Romance*, 101–21, reconsiders the status of subject clitics proper and the auxiliary clitic *l'* in Turinese in the light of recent theoretical developments. The results of G.'s analysis single out a number of advantages of a minimalist approach within an Agr-less system over rival analyses such as Poletto's typology of subject clitics and analyses based on Kayne's 1994 antisymmetry approach to syntax. Piedmontese clitics are explored from a diachronic perspective in two contributions. M. M. Parry, 'The reinterpretation of the reflexive in Piedmontese: "impersonal" *se* constructions', *TPS*, 96:63–116, traces the development of passive and impersonal *se* in Piedmontese from its first vernacular attestations to the present day, revealing the existence of both types of *se* in early texts, a fact which makes it impossible to determine conclusively whether the impersonal use of *se* developed out of its passive use. Equally problematic is the task of evaluating the influence of Italian on innovations in the use of *se*, which P. prefers to view as a natural continuation of the reanalysis of the originally reflexive SE. M. M. Parry, 'La sintassi dei pronomi soggetto in piemontese', *SLI 30*, 329–44, traces the emergence of subject clitics and their syntactic development from the earliest medieval texts of the Piedmont area. D. Ricca, 'Una perifrasi continua-iterativa nei testi piemontesi dal Cinquecento all'Ottocento: tenere + participio passato', *ib.*, 345–68, identifies in Piedmontese texts dating from the 15th–17th c. the existence of an aspectual periphrasis consisting of *tenere* + participle which, unlike the superficially similar resultative periphrasis of other Romance varieties, is demonstrated to mark continuative-iterative aspect.

LIGURIA. F. Toso, **Dizionario genovese: italiano-genovese, genovese-italiano*, Mi, Vallardi, 509 pp. M. Cuneo, 'Il lessico degli animali marini in Liguria: distribuzione areale', Mioni, *Dialetti*, 55–89. Id., 'L'uso dell'infinito nei dialetti liguri: infinito con soggetto espresso e infinito flesso nel dialetto di Cicagna (GE)', *RID*, 21 : 99–132, presents extensive evidence from the dialect of Cicagna to show that the distribution of infinitives with explicit subjects is sensitive to the control properties of the governing predicate: only infinitival complements to predicates which allow non-obligatory control may license an explicit subject. A very restricted case of agreement marking on the infinitive of 'to be' in conjunction with modal verbs is also discussed, which C. interprets as a form of inflected infinitive comparable to similar Tuscan and Apulian constructions.

LOMBARDY. E. Berni, **Vocabolarietto mantovano-italiano per le scuole e pel popolo*, Mantova, Tre Lune, viii + 158 pp., is a facsimile reprint of the 1882 edition. E. Albonico, **Vestiss & svestiss: vestirsi una volta nei canti della tradizione lombardo-ticinese*, Muzzano, San Giorgio, 1997, 78 pp. + 1 compact disc. M. Cantella, **Antichi proverbi comaschi*, Vimercate, Meravigli, 1997, 121 pp. C. Beretta, **Toponomastica in valcamonica e lombardia: etimologia, relazioni con il mondo antico*, Capo di Ponte, Ed. Del Centro, 1997, xvi + 240 pp. M. Merlo, **Proverbi pavesi*, Pavia, EMI, 1997, 402 pp., reprint of 1982 edition.

VENETO. **El cao del zhucàro: dal veneto all'italiano*, ed. Graziano Zanin et al., Stangella, Linea AGS, 1997, 283 pp. D. Soranzo, 'I cognomi tratti dagli etnici delle città del Veneto. Problematiche, analisi e diffusione', Mioni, *Dialetti*, 165–80. G. Tardivo, 'Excursus dialettale veneto sulle carni', *ib.*, 181–90. E. Croatto, 'Appunti di avifauna dialettale zoldana (Belluno)', *ib.*, 207–20. S. Mazzaro, 'Il liventino ed il veneto settentrionale: cenni su testi antichi e moderni', *ib.*, 293–326. C. M. Sanfilippo, 'Per il testo della tenzone tridialettale veneta: un caso di paraipotassi', *ib.*, 341–45. L. Corrà, 'La lingua degli atti di un processo svoltosi a Feltre nel 1545', *SLI 29*, 58–67, examines the language of the proceedings of a 16th-c. trial held in the province of Feltre which, though written in a Venetian-based vernacular, reveals considerable oscillation between Venetian and Tuscan linguistic forms. E. Banfi 'Tà taliánika di un poliziotto eptanesio in una commedia neogreca del 1836', *ib.*, 398–413. N. Munaro, 'L'evoluzione diacronica del sintagma interrogativo *che cosa* nei dialetti veneti settentrionali', *SLI 30*, 267–92, traces the development of the interrogative *che cosa* in texts from the Bellunese area dating from the 16th c. to the present day. From an original nominal use, *cossa* is demonstrated to undergo a process of grammaticalization resulting in its eventual use as an interrogative operator in conjunction with *che*, subject to overt *Wh*-movement in earliest texts but appearing *in situ* in the modern dialects. These data are interpreted within a minimalist framework as an example of economy in overt movement, whereby the historically documented loss of overt *Wh*-movement is viewed as a consequence of the principle of Procrastinate.

EMILIA-ROMAGNA. L. Paraboschi, *Posti e luoghi dell'Emilia Romagna: l'origine dei nomi, dei comuni e delle località: nomi antichi per antichi nomi*, Modena, SIGEM, 1997, 201 pp., J. Hajek, 'Analisi acustica delle quantità segmentali in area bolognese', *RID*, 21:133–48, presents the results of a study carried out in the province of Bologna confirming the presence of long consonants in Bolognese using experimental phonetic data. M. Loporcaro, 'Syllable structure and sonority sequencing', LSRL 27, 155–70, Amsterdam–Philadelphia, Benjamins, viii + 349 pp., explores the problems of syllabification of word-initial consonant clusters in Emilian dialects which are demonstrated to pattern like onsets, a result which precludes interpreting the Sonority Sequencing Generalization as an absolute constraint on phonological representations.

TRENTINO. F. Bonenti, *Glossario dialettale di Bondo e Breguzo*, Bondo (Trento), Gruppo culturale Bondo Breguzo, 1997, 328 pp. A. Bertoluzza, *Dizionario dell'antico dialetto trentino: 4000 mila voci dialettali, proverbi, sciolingua, indovinelli, filastrocche, cantilene. In appendice: testi dialettali a confronto*, Trento, L'Adige, 1997, 334 pp. S. Schmid and M. T. Vigolo, 'I tedeschismi nei dialetti nònesi e solandri', Mioni, *Dialetti*, 135–63.

CENTRAL AND SOUTHERN DIALECTS. Concise overviews, though perhaps too general in their coverage, appear in Price, *Encyclopedia*: M.-J. Dalbera-Stefanaggi and G. Moracchini, 'Corsican' (103–05) and L. Vanelli, 'Central and southern Italy' (269–73), the latter contrasting with the individual entries provided in the same volume for northern Italian dialects. Traditional questions relating to the availability of infinitival complementation in dialects of the extreme south are addressed in two articles: S. Cristofaro, 'Aspetti diacronici e sincronici della subordinazione infinitiva in alcuni dialetti calabresi e pugliesi e nelle lingue balcaniche: una prospettiva tipologico-funzionalista', *SLI 30*, 495–518, compares the widespread reduction in infinitival usage and concomitant increase in finite clauses in southern Calabrian and Salentino dialects with similar phenomena in the Balkan languages, concluding that infinitival usage is more resistant in contexts characterized by a high degree of semantic integration between matrix and subordinate clauses. A. Ledgeway, 'Variation in the Romance infinitive: the case of the southern Calabrian inflected infinitive', *TPS*, 96: 1–61, proposes a gradient notion of finiteness in terms of the features [± Agr, ± Tense] to explain the variation in form and function exhibited by the various species of Romance infinitive, with interesting consequences for the so-called finite *mu*-clauses of the *dialetti grecanici* of southern Calabria, which are innovatively analysed as inflected infinitival clauses. M. Cennamo, 'Transitività e inaccusatività in testi antichi abruzzesi e napoletani', *SLI 30*, 196–213, illustrates some aspects of unaccusativity in early Abruzzese and Neapolitan texts with evidence from auxiliary selection and past part. agreement with subjects of unaccusatives. Her analysis provides evidence for the existence of different stages in the weakening process of a preceding active system, manifested in the gradual substitution of *avere* as perfective auxiliary with intransitives and the elimination of past participle agreement in conjunction with original unaccusatives. G. Cocchi, 'Ergativity in Romance Languages', Fullana, *Central Romance*, 83–99, adopts an analysis based on split ergativity in an attempt to explain the distribution of the perfective auxilaries in central-southern Italian dialects where auxiliary alternation is sensitive to both person and tense. M. Loporcaro, 'Fattori interni ed esterni nella spiegazione del mutamento sintattico: la riduzione dell'accordo participiale nelle varietà (italo-)romanze', *SLI 30*, 91–110, draws on a wide range of dialect data to defend the superiority of internal factors in explaining the demise of past part. agreement in Romance, concluding that syntactic change operates independently of phonetic and morphological factors. Id., 'Ancora sull'etimo della particella pronominale *ne* di I plurale: la testimonianza dei dialetti del Meridione', *Atti* (Palermo), 1, 161–72, presents persuasive historical evidence from a number of southern Italian dialects which favours deriving the first person plural clitic *ne* from NOS, rather than the traditional etymon INDE. Id., 'L'assimilazione fonosintattica di -T finale nei dialetti della zona Lausberg', *Morschini Vol.*, 237–44.

TUSCANY. S. Giannini, 'Forma e funzioni del clitico *ni* in lucchese', *Ramat Vol.*, 215–45, traces the diachronic development of the 3rd person indirect object pronoun *ni* in dialects of western Tuscany, highlighting its change from a clitic pronoun to an affixal person marker in the modern dialects.

THE MARCHES. *I dialetti della Marca Ascolana*, ed. Maria Gabriella Mazzocchi, Senigallia, Sapere Nuovo, 1997, 145 pp. H. J. Nibirt, 'Processes of vowel harmony in the Servigliano dialect of Italian: a comparison of two non-linear proposals for the representation of vowel height', *Probus*, 10:67–101, investigates within the framework of Prosodic phonology three phonological harmonization processes (post-tonic vowel copying, metaphony, and pre-tonic vowel raising) and tonic vowel reduction.

UMBRIA. S. Giulietti and A. Batinti, *La variabilità linguistica nell'area orvietana: la comunità di Parrano*, Ellera Umbra, Era Nuova, 171 pp.

LAZIO. L. Cimarra, *Mazzabbubbù: repertorio del folclore infantile civitonico*, Civita Castellana, Biblioteca Comunale Enrico Minio, 1997, 235 pp. P. D'Achille and C. Giovanardi, 'Conservazione e innovazione nella sintassi verbale dal romanesco del Belli al romanaccio contemporaneo', *SLI 30*, 469–93, analyses the syntax of the two infinitival constructions *stare a* and *dovere da* in a corpus of texts from Belli to the present day. The results highlight a number of innovative trends in modern Romanesco, including the growing use of *stare* + gerund over its rival *stare a* + infinitive and the expansion of the *dovere da* + infinitive construction unknown in the writings of Belli and Trilussa.

CAMPANIA. S. Tambascia, *Grammatica e lessico del dialetto castelvetrese*, Ro, Il Calamo, 203 pp. N. Vincent, 'On the grammar of inflected non-finite forms (with special reference to Old Neapolitan)', Korzen, *Clause Combining*, 135–58, returns to the topic of finiteness and inflected non-finite verb forms in old Neapolitan, focusing on the syntax of the inflected gerund. Although the grammar of the inflected gerund is identical to that of the inflected infinitive, V. maintains that the distribution of the inflected gerund appears to be driven more by considerations of discourse than does that of the inflected infinitive. This point is reinforced by a comparison with the use of the gerund in the writings of Dante, both with and without a lexical subject, demonstrating that the availability of a system of person inflections does not alter the grammatical distribution of the construction. A. Ledgeway, '*Avé(re)* and *esse(re)* alternation in Neapolitan', Fullana, *Central Romance*, 123–47, examines the rich array of auxiliary alternations according to verb class, person, and tense exhibited by Neapolitan and other Campanian varieties. Drawing on Kayne's 1993 modular approach of Romance auxiliary selection, the observed range of alternations is derived from the interaction of finiteness and Case, two general conditions on clausal licensing in Neapolitan.

APULIA.   *Salento: monografia regionale della Carta dei dialetti italiani*, ed. Giovan Battista Mancharella, Lecce, Grifo, 412 pp. G. B. Mancarella, 'Regionalismi lessicali in una carta brindisina del 1382', Mioni, *Dialetti*, 289–92.

CALABRIA.   R. M. Lucente, *Lu vancielliu secunnu Mattio. Versione di Raffaele Maria Lucente in calabrese-cosentino*, introd. Raffaele Ortale and Anna Scola, Bo, CLUEB, 1997, xxvii + 125 pp. J. Trumper and E. Straface, 'Varia etymologica I', Mioni, *Dialetti*, 225–54. L. Di Vasto and J. Trumper, 'Varia etymologica (et geolinguistica) II. Elementi latini arcaici, bizantini periferici, punici e brettici nell'area Lausberg e nella Calabria settentrionale', *ib.*, 255–86. J. Trumper, 'Aspetti storici del lessico marino in genere e di quello calabrese in particolare', *RID*, 21:149–74, outlines the difficulties inherent in studying the direction of lexical borrowing in seafaring and marine vocabulary. In particular, T. focuses on the nature and formation of Calabrian marine lexicon and, after investigating its sources, concludes that it seems to be largely borrowed. N. Misiti, 'Aspetti particolari del lessico marinaresco calabrese', Mioni, *Dialetti*, 105–25. M. Loporcaro and A. Mancuso, 'Interdentale ma anche laterale: /l/ prevocalica in alcuni dialetti della (Pre)Sila', Bertinetto, *Unità*, 77–90, reports the existence of an interdental lateral in three dialects from the province of Cosenza, a sound considered to represent an intermediate stage in the diachronic development from an original lateral approximant to interdental fricative. M. Loporcaro et al., 'La neutralizzazione delle vocali finali in crotonese: un esperimento percettivo', *ib.*, 91–100. In addition to the articles by Cristofaro and Ledgeway mentioned above, another significant contribution to the debate on infinitival usage, as well as auxiliary selection, is A. Lombardi, 'Calabria greca e Calabria latina da Rohlfs ai giorni nostri: la sintassi dei verbi modali-aspettuali', *SLI 30*, 613–26, which considers the differing syntactic behaviour of modal and aspectual verbs in two very distinct groups of Calabrian dialects, demonstrating that the distribution of infinitival and *mu*-clauses to such verbs in Southern Calabria hinges on the selection of the category Tense in the embedded clause. The effects of auxiliary choice on modals and aspectuals in northern Calabrian dialects, investigated from a RG perspective, highlight a sensitivity to the epistemic/deontic distinction, the former calling for *essa* (e.g. *nun c'è pututu escia* 'he couldn't have gone out') and the latter *avire* (e.g. *nun ha pututu escia* 'he wasn't able to go out'). Similar questions are followed up by L. in 'Linguistic fragmentariness in the Calabrian dialects: the distribution of the perfective auxiliaries in Latin Calabria and Greek Calabria', Fullana, *Central Romance*, 149–69, which evaluates the validity of traditional dialect divisions on the basis of syntactic evidence, comparing and contrasting participle agreement and the distribution of perfective auxiliaries in conjunction with reflexives throughout the region.

SICILY. G. Vicari, *Il canto del signum. Prefazione di Rosario Antonio Rizzo*, Caltanissetta, Lussografica, 1997, 95 pp. *Aspetti della variabilità: ricerche linguistiche siciliane*, ed. Mari D'Agostino, Palermo, CSFLS, 1997, 213 pp. Historical investigations into the synthetic and analytic expressions of modality are explored in D. Bentley, 'Modalità e tempo in siciliano: un'analisi diacronica dell'espressione del futuro', *VR*, 57:117–37, which challenges the traditional account of Sicilian *aviri a* + infinitive, arguing that the periphrasis denotes not only modality but also prototypical futurity, with the virtual disappearance of the synthetic future in modern Sicilian ascribed to diastratic variation in old Sicilian; and in Id., 'Modalità perifrastica e sintetica in siciliano. Un caso di grammaticalizzazione?', *SLI 30*, 369–83, presenting the findings of a diachronic analysis of Sicilian periphrastic and synthetic modal structures, which challenge the idea that semantic change involving deontic and epistemic structures ultimately depends on the cognitive basicness/abstractness of such notions. M. Mazzoleni, 'Convergenze e divergenze nella morfosintassi dei costrutti condizionali lombardo-siculi', *ib.*, 627–45, identifies in Lombard Gallo-Sicilian dialects some typologically rare asymmetrical combinations of the subjunctive in the apodosis and imperfect indicative/conditional forms in the protasis, ascribing such combinations to widely-attested phenomena of Lombard-Sicilian symbiosis and hybridism.

12. SARDINIAN

S. Colomo, *Vocabularieddu sardu-italianu, italianu-sardu: liberamente tratto dal Vocabulariu sardu-italianu, italianu-sardu del canonico e studioso Giovanni Spano edito a Cagliari nel 1851–52*, Nuoro, Archivio Fotografico Sardo, 1997, 562 pp. M. Pittau, *I nomi di paesi, citta, regioni, monti, fiumi della Sardegna: significato e origine*, Cagliari, Gasperini, 1997, 254 pp. G. Spano, *Proverbi sardi: trasportati in lingua italiana e confrontati con quelli degli antichi popoli*, Nuoro, Ilisso, 1997, 365 pp. M. M. Parry, 'Sardinian', Price, *Encyclopedia*, 273–75. F. Mameli, *Il logudorese e il gallurese*, Villanova Monteleone (Sassari), Soter, 258 pp. P. Iorio, *L'italiano parlato dai sardi*, Oristano, S'Alvure, 1997, 172 pp. H. J. Wolf, 'Sarde *pettora, liporra*, le mèrinos et le suffixe *-inu*', *RLiR*, 62:331–46.

13. ITALIAN ABROAD

A. Petralli, 'L'italiano e la revisione dell'articolo sulle lingue della Costituzione federale svizzera', *SLI 29*, 430–48. J. Cremona, 'La "lingua d'Italia" nell'Africa settentrionale: usi cancellareschi francesi nel tardo cinquecento e nel seicento', *ib.*, 340–56, discusses the use of Italian in 16th-c. Tunis with three new texts. A. Cassola, 'L'italiano dei francesi a Malta (1798–1800)', *ib.*, 364–76, is a first attempt to describe the Italian used during the French period in Malta, highlighting the salient characteristics of the language used by the French administration through the analysis of a few passages from the bilingual French-Italian *Journal de Malte*. G. Brincat, 'L'italiano della Corona Britannica', *ib.*, 377–97, examines the elements which characterize the type of Italian that was used in the administration of Malta during the period of British rule, with a brief exploratory examination of a few documents representative of four different stages in the evolution of the Italian spoken on Malta. R. Fontanot, 'La lingua italiana in Istria dopo la fine della Jugoslavia', *ib.*, 414–29. F. Ursini, 'La "lingua d'Italia" sulle coste orientali dell'Adriatico fra Trecento e Quattrocento', *ib.*, 324–47. M. Cortelazzo, 'Usi linguistici fuori d'Italia nel Medioevo: le repubbliche marinare in Levante', *ib.*, 315–23.

DUECENTO AND TRECENTO I
DANTE

By CATHERINE KEEN, *St John's College, Cambridge*
(This survey covers the years 1996, 1997 and 1998)

I. GENERAL

Considerations of D.'s literary achievements tend to invite reflection on the context of D.'s poetic activity, and his relations with past and contemporary writers: and in the past two years, this has provided material for several studies. Enrico Malato, *Dante e Guido Cavalcanti: il dissidio per la Vita Nuova e il 'disdegno' di Guido*, Ro, Salerno, 1997, 117 pp., in two studies also published elsewhere, on the relationship between D. and C., offers interpretation of the rupture in their poetic and personal relations: M. suggests an early, radical divergence based on opposite understandings of the nature and effects of love, in a new chronology of poetic exchanges, with the *VN* preceding *I' vegno il giorno* and *Donna me prega*; and making connections with D.'s retrospective analysis of their connection, and divergence over the compatability of love with reason (Virgil) in *Inf.* x's pessimistic prognosis of C.'s possible mortal or eternal illumination. M. Cursietti, 'Dante, Guido e l'"annoiosa gente" (a proposito della "paternale" di un presunto sonetto di Guido Cavalcanti e di un libro recente)', *L'Alighieri*, 39:106–12, offers interesting readings of D.'s and Cavalcanti's texts to reveal their literary divergence over poetic elitism. Antonio Gagliardi, **Guido Cavalcanti e Dante: una questione d'amore*, Catanzaro, Pullano, 1997, 147 pp. P. V. Mengaldo, 'Dante come critico', *Parola del Testo*, 1, 1997:36–54, an impressive survey of D.'s activity as critic of Italian poetry, (esp. *DVE*, *Purg.* XXIV-XXVI), showing the durability of his categories and hierarchies, and the motivations for his assessments of predecessors and contemporaries.

On questions relating more broadly to language and poetics: Paolo Baldan, *Nuovi ritorni su Dante*, Alessandria, Orso, 106 pp., a collection of B.'s recent studies into one volume, focuses on themes from the *Inf.*: especially noteworthy is his interpretation of the Veltro prophecy as a reference to the *DC* itself, with its programme of moral and political conversion, based on links between the prophecy's language and the terminology of medieval paper production. Ignazio Baldelli, *Dante e la lingua italiana*, F, Accademia della Crusca, 1996, 31 pp., plays on his title to suggest that 'Dante è la lingua italiana', and offers a brief, engaging survey of D.'s linguistic achievements and importance, both in revising his own linguistic agenda (from the *VN* to the

DVE to the *DC*), and creating the idea of a politico-linguistically unified 'Italy', to which the language and politics of the present nation-state are still indebted. Domenico De Robertis, **Per una cittadinanza dantesca: considerazioni sulla lingua della Commedia*, F, Le Lettere, 1997, 19 pp. William Franke, *Dante's Interpretive Journey*, Chicago U.P., 1996, xi + 250 pp., brings the hermeneutical thinking of philosophers like Heidegger and Gadamer to bear on the *DC*, investigating its mimesis of truth and insistence on temporality, and its divulgatory intent, reflected in the choice of vernacular and historicized narration. Heideggerian analysis of the *DC* also informs John Took's *Ethics and Existence in Dante: a new theological perspective*, UCL Centre for Italian Studies, Occasional Papers, 1, 65 pp., which presents readings of D.'s ontological concerns in three essays originally delivered as a lecture series and still retaining an engaging informality of tone in his invitation to understand D. as '*the* Christian-existentialist poet in our tradition' (1). G. Gorni, 'Anniversari: Dante e il tempo ciclico', *LC*, 26, 1996: 111–23, for the 675th anniversary of D.'s death, underlines the importance of cyclicity both in D.'s stylistics (rhyme, figure, etc.), and in his structuring of themes — love, nature, religion — springing from a Christian understanding of remembrance and repetition. Milivoje Pejovic, **Dante Alighieri: la conscience poétique et l'œuvre*, Paris, Éditions du Titre, 1996, 207 pp. B. Porcelli, 'La nominazione dei protagonisti nel *Fiore*, nella *Vita nuova*, nella *Commedia*', *Italianistica*, 27: 221–34, investigates name symbolism in the canonical texts (Beatrice, Virgilio) and in the *Fiore*, focusing on the negative connotations of D[ur]ante's endurance/obstinacy in *Purg.* in contrast to positive overtones in *Fiore* (ascribed definitely to D.).

On the portrayal of Beatrice: Bruno Pinchard, *Le bûcher de Béatrice: essai sur Dante*, Paris, Aubier, 1996, 300 pp., gives an impressionistic personal study of almost the whole of D.'s output, focusing on the significance of the experience of love, symbolized in the relationships with B., and also, patriotically, with Florence, and exploring D.'s relationship to broad strands of cultural discourse (courtliness, *romanitas*, political philosophy, mysticism, etc.). D. De Vita, ' "Fu chiamata da molti Beatrice" ', *Belfagor*, 53 : 1–26, revives the question of B.'s identity, making the novel suggestion that the actual 'Beatrice' of the *VN* was Piccarda Donati, Bice Portinari being instead only one of the *donne-schermo*, and proposing that Piccarda's notable piety would also account for a devotion to a form of marked Christian ascetic humility that De V. attributes to the D. of the *VN* and which, after disruption by the philosophical pursuits of *Cvo*, is extended later, as shown in the *DC*, into a more direct devotion to the Church and to Christ. M. Pazzaglia, 'Beatrice nella *Vita nuova* e nella *Commedia*', *LC*, 25, 1996: 21–38.

On D.'s place with regard to medieval intellectual culture: Zygmunt G. Barański, *'Sole nuovo, luce nuova': saggi sul rinnovamento culturale in Dante*, T, Scriptorium, 1996, 319 pp., is a welcome collection of B.'s work on aspects of D.'s poetics from the past 15 years, in which he has cogently explored D.'s linguistic experimentalism and his contextualization of reference and innovation especially in relation to definitions of the 'comic'; the diverse collection ranges from passages of close reading to discussions of attribution (on the *Ep. to Cangrande* and the *Fiore*). *Bibliologia e critica dantesca: saggi dedicati a Enzo Esposito*, II: *Saggi danteschi*, ed. Vincenzo De Gregorio, Ravenna, Longo, 1997, 438 pp. Reudi Imbach, *Dante, la philosophie et les laïcs*, Fribourg, Éditions Universitaires — Paris, Éditions du Cerf, 1996, x + 265 pp. Romano Pasi, *Dante, i medici e la medicina*, Ravenna, Essegi, 1996, 89 pp., suggests, not always convincingly, that D.'s medical knowledge was more formal and extensive than often appreciated, was cultivated during youthful studies at Bologna, and was consolidated in maturity by study and contact with distinguished medical contemporaries. Interest in his scientific knowledge is pursued also by Gotthard Strohmaier, in four essays on D. and Arabic culture, in *Von Demokrit bis Dante: die Bewahrung antiken Erbes in der arabischen Kultur*, Hildesheim, Olms, 1996, x + 558 pp., a collection of S.'s articles from the 1960s to the present. D. Sperduto, 'Tra ragione e fede: l'immortalità dell'anima in Dante', *EL*, 21.4, 1996: 35–48, relates divergences in the discussion of immortality in *Cvo* (soul) and *DC* (soul and body), to Scholastic discussions of divergence between faith and reason, suggesting D.'s revision moves him (perhaps unconsciously) from Thomism towards Duns Scotus and William of Ockham.

D.'s politics are discussed in: *Dante and Governance*, ed. John Woodhouse, Oxford, Clarendon, 1997, xi + 179 pp., a stimulating collection of ten essays on a very broad range of political themes: alongside a series of excellent *letture* of particular cantos, more global surveys are provided by P. Armour, 'Dante and popular sovereignty' (27–45); G. Holmes, '*Monarchia* and Dante's attitude to the Popes' (46–57), with its provocative dating of the treatise; R. Cooper's engaging 'The French dimension in Dante's politics' (58–84). Further political and cross-cultural themes are approached by A. Carile, 'Dante e Bisanzio', *L'Alighieri*, 38, 1997: 23–42, assessing D.'s attitudes to Byzantine political claims, especially in relation to the *Mon.* and the *translatio imperii* issue, and to hellenistic studies, especially Aristotle and Pseudo-Dionysius.

Further general studies include: *Dante: Contemporary Perspectives*, ed. Amilcare A. Iannucci, Toronto U.P., 1997, xxii + 299 pp., a collection of 14 very diverse essays showing the impact of contemporary critical trends on discussion of D.'s poetics, literary culture, politics, and reception, by a distinguished group of scholars, mostly based in North America, and covering both minor works and the *DC*. Alessandro Cosi, **Poesia come musica nella Commedia di Dante*, Lecce, Grifo, 1996, 165 pp. F. P. Kirsch, 'Dante im Prozeß der Zivilisation', *Fest. Birkhan*, 61–79, places D. in the context of the changing political and intellectual culture of his time, and assesses his 'Renaissance' versus 'medieval' outlook. Franco Masciandro, *La conoscenza viva: letture fenomenologiche da Dante a Machiavelli*, Ravenna, Longo, 129 pp., includes four essays on diverse aspects of the *DC*, covering the symbolism of the 'punto' as sign of concrete temporality versus numinous atemporality, in spiritual and in linguistic questions; connections between the serpentine attributes of Geryon and of Virgilian dialectical ratiocination; considerations of the literal and metaphorical 'return to Eden' and reflections on the Words of God and of poetry; and the meanings of the term 'bellezza' in *Par.*'s oscillations between earthly imperfections and paradisal fulfilments. W. Ross, 'Dante an der Schwelle der Jahrhunderte', *DDJ*, 73:195–206, a short, personal essay on D.'s outlook and achievement. Giorgio Santangelo, **Dante e la Sicilia, e altre letture dantesche*, Palermo, Palumbo, 1996, 261 pp. **Seminario dantesco internazionale. Atti del convegno internazionale*, *Princeton*, ed. Zygmunt G. Barański, F, Le Lettere, 1997, 389 pp. *Villari Vol.*, has three essays on D.: Z. G. Barański, ' "Orpheus id est pulchra vox": philological notes on Dante, Orpheus, Horace, and other writers' (1–18); L. Pertile, 'Il silenzio di Geri (*Inferno* XXIX. 1–36)' (19–28); C. Keen, 'Signs of *fiorentinità*: the Baptistery and its meanings in Dante's Florence' (29–42). *Studi offerti a Luigi Blasucci dai colleghi e dagli allievi pisani*, ed. Lucio Lugnani, Marco Santagata, and Alfredo Stussi, Lucca, Pacini Fazzi, 1996, xix + 596 pp., offers four disparate but very stimulating essays on D.: L. Battaglia Ricci, 'Testo e immagini in alcuni manoscritti illustrati della *Commedia*: le pagine d'apertura' (23–50); F. Ceragioli, 'Le rime petrose di Dante' (169–92); B. Porcelli, 'Tempi nel Purgatorio' (427–40); M. Tavoni, 'Il nome di *poeta* in Dante' (545–78). W. A. Therivel, 'Praised be Italy for the birth of the visitor personality and Western civilization; praised be Italy for Gregory VII at Canossa, Alexander III at Legnano, Innocent III at Runnymede; for Dante, Petrarch, Boccaccio', *RStI*, 15.1, 1997:25–40, offers an extravagant account of the importance of Italian power-structures and -struggles to the development of the 'visitor personality' typical of Western civilization, and its creative capacities, exemplified in D. and the other *corone*.

2. FORTUNE

Reception of D. by early readers is much discussed: Robert Hollander, *Boccaccio's Dante and the Shaping Force of Satire*, Ann Arbor, Michigan U.P., 1997, 225 pp., provides a useful presentation of essays on B.'s knowledge of D. published over the past 15 years (chapter 6, 'Day Ten of the *Decameron*: the myth of order', 109–68, with Courtney Cahill), in which H. argues that the *Decameron* shows a detailed knowledge of D. and reveals constant awareness of its own relation to its recent vernacular predecessor; the Appendix, on '*Hapax legomenon* in Boccaccio's *Decameron* and its relation to Dante's *Commedia*' (169–220), suggesting that there is still fruitful philological and interpretative work to be done in this area. M. Lenzen, ' "La discoverta del vero Dante": Giambattista Vico und Dante', *DDJ*, 72, 1997:97–114, analyses Vico's paralleling of D. and Homer, as historicizing poets of a 'heroic age', and shows how this prepares the way for later Romantic readings of Dante. C. Pulomi, 'Per la fortuna della *De vulgari eloquentia* nel primo Cinquecento: Bembo e Barbieri', *Aevum*, 71, 1997:631–50, discusses Trissino's 're-launch' of the *DVE*, through MS circulation and through translation, and notes use of and comments on the text by Bembo and Barbieri for their discussions of vernacular literature, especially the poetry of Provence. M. Simonetta, 'La lingua esiliata: buoni proposti e cattivi "supposti" in un testo machiavelliano', *RStI*, 15.1, 1997:41–54, analyses M.'s abuse of D. and his politics in the *Discorso intorno alla nostra lingua*, arguing that M.'s ironic spirit and habit of dissimulation allow the critique to read as inverted praise for D.'s patriotism.

Later reception is discussed in: Giovanni Capecchi, *Gli scritti danteschi di Giovanni Pascoli, con appendice di inediti, Ravenna, Longo, 1997, 198 pp. Giorgio Cavallini, *Montale lettore di Dante (e altri studi montaliani)*, Ro, Bulzoni, 1996, 123 pp., in which the first of three essays investigates reception of D. in M.'s activities as critic and poet, and his dialogue with D.'s linguistic, formal, and thematic procedures. *Dante's Modern Afterlife: Reception and Response from Blake to Heaney*, ed. Nicholas Havely, Basingstoke, Macmillan, 288 pp., a stimulating collection of essays on Anglo-Saxon reaction to D. over the past two centuries, considering religion, literature, criticism, visual art, and concluding with Heaney's translation of *Inf.* II; Eduardo Dall'Alba, *Drummond, leitor de Dante, Caxias do Sul, Rs. Educs., 1996, 109 pp. In Alison Milbank, *Dante and the Victorians*, MUP, x + 277 pp., a detailed and stimulating analysis of the reception of D. by 19th-c. British writers, artists and scholars, three sections entitled 'History', 'Nationalism', and 'Aesthetics' trace a kind of Dante mania, first introduced by the Romantics, and later prominent throughout the century in cultural discourse, and in developing ideologies of British and Italian nationhood. The final section on 'Unreal cities' looks at reception of D.'s eschatology and at the influence of Victorian perceptions of D. over his new appropriations in Pound and T. S. Eliot. M. Bryden, 'No stars without stripes: Beckett and Dante', *RR*, 87, 1996:541–56, discusses B.'s enduring interest in D., especially in adaptations of the waiting theme of Ante-Purgatory, using B.'s notes and texts of the *DC* held at Reading University. A. Ciccarelli, 'Dante and Italian Futurism', *LDan*, 18–19, 1996:30–40, looks at Futurism's rejection of the *DC*. H. Heintze, 'Der Fremde Dante Victor Klemperers', *DDJ*, 73:181–95. G. P. Raffa, 'Eco and Calvino reading Dante', *Italica*, 73, 1996:388–409, discusses the two writers' appreciations of the encyclopedic and syncretic aspect of D.'s cosmic vision, discussing possible analogues/*querelles* in their critical and creative writing. J. Tambling, 'Terragni, fascism and allegory: reading the Danteum', *The Italianist*, 17, 1997:123–44, surveys the ideological reading of D. underlying the unbuilt monument and its textual and architectural shortcomings and anxieties. E. Travi, 'Federico Ozanam lettore di Dante', *Testo*, 35:123–30. A. Vallone, 'La "lectura dantis" di Antonio Pagliaro', *DDJ*, 73:119–26. M. Verdicchio, 'Overreading and underreading Dante in North America', *ItQ*, 127–28, 1996:77–86, discusses recent critical trends, including a survey of some 20 book-length studies from 1986–1990. On cinema and D.: A. A. Iannucci, 'From Dante's *Inferno* to *Dante's Peak*: the influence of Dante on film', *FoI*, 32:5–35, classifies the *Inf.* as a 'producerly' text, and offers a survey of cinematic versions, allusions, and adaptations from silent film to the 1990s. H. Teschke, 'Pasolini und Dante: *Divina Mimesis*', *ItStudien*, 19:202–27, on the modifications and the success of the project of 'rifare Dante' in *Divina Mimesis*.

COMPARATIVE STUDIES. G. Angeli, 'Figure della povertà da Boezio a Christine de Pisan', *RLMC*, 49, 1996:143–62, notes the theme of virtuous poverty, often connected to discussions of *Fortuna*, in medieval literature, including the *Cvo* and *DC*. G. M. Anselmi, 'Dante, Boccaccio e "il buon Lizio"', *SPCT*, 56:91–95, outlines structural parallels, besides the reappearance of L. as a character, between the contrasts of past chivalric glory and present decadence in *Purg.* XIV and the *Decameron*'s Days 5 and 4. *Dante e Pound*, ed. Maria Luisa Ardizzone, Ravenna, Longo, 245 pp. G. Bárberi Squarotti, 'La candida cerva (*RVF* 90): dal mito a Beatrice', *REI*, 44:79–95, traces Petrarchan allusions to the B. of *Purg.* and *Par.* S. N. Brody, 'The fiend and the Summoner, Statius and Dante: a possible source for the *Friar's Tale*, Ds 1379–1520', *ChRev*, 32, 1997:175–82, suggests a possible Dantean inspiration in parallels between Statius's and the fiend's elucidations to their mortal interlocutor of the connection between 'the soul of an immortal being and the form it assumes' (180). K. Brownlee, 'The practice of cultural authority: Italian responses to French cultural dominance in *Il Tesoretto, Il Fiore* and the *Commedia*', *FMLS*, 33, 1997:258–69, examines receptions of a paradigmatic French cultural product, the *Roman de la Rose*, challenged in all three texts by a developing vision of Italian cultural autonomy, climaxing in the *DC*'s aggressive assertions of past (Roman) and present Italian supremacy. Mario Luzi, *Mitografia dell'esule: da Dante al Novecento*, Na, ESI, 1996, 108 pp. C. Di Donna Prencipe, 'L'*exul immeritus* nell'opera di Foscolo', *LC*, 27:57–68, underlines F.'s engagement with D. as poet of patriotic and moral revival, commenting especially on *Ortis* and *A Dante*. A. Dunker, 'Dantes Odysseus in Auschwitz: Primo Levis "Der Gesang des Ulyss"', *DDJ*, 71, 1996:77–98. L. Fiedler, 'Dante: verdi pensieri in verde ombra', *Belfagor*, 52, 1997:2–21, translates into Italian F.'s essay on his own, and D. G. Rossetti's, translations of *Al poco giorno* (texts given), with interesting commentary on technical questions regarding D.'s poetic and philosophical goals, and on translation problems; the following article, M. Marazzi, 'Amore e morte nella sestina petrosa', *ib.*, 22–26, notes F.'s enthusiasm for D., in his creative as well as critical work, and the reciprocal respect for his own work in Italy. S. Hirakawa, 'The *Divine Comedy* and the Nô Plays of Japan: an attempt at a reciprocal elucidation', *CLS*, 33, 1996:35–58, finds unexpected structural and cultural parallels between the *DC* and the Japanese 'mugen nô' tradition of plays where earth and afterworld intersect. Stefano Jacomuzzi, *Le insegne della poesia: studi su Dante e sul Manzoni*, T, SEI, 1996, xxx + 106 pp. G. Magrini, 'Luzi e il Veglio di Creta', *ParL*, 47, 1996:51–58. B. Marx, 'Petrarkismus im Zeichen von Dante: Pietro Bembo und die Asolani', *DDJ*, 73:9–50. R. A. Mechanic, 'In pursuit of earthly justice: the Albarosa episode of Boiardo's *Orlando Innamorato* as a "positivization" of *Inferno* v', *CJIS*, 20, 1997:157–70, suggests an intertextual relationship where B. echoes language and themes (sibling and amorous relationships; the moral teleology of textual interpretation) from D., but gives a positive moral outcome. B. Porcelli, 'Echi purgatoriali nei *Pastori* di *Alcyone*', *Italianistica*, 27:437–40. C. C. Soufas, 'Dante and the geography of Lorca's *Bodas de sangre*', *RoN*, 37, 1997:175–82, on the symbolic geography of misdirected love in L. and *Inf.* xv-xvi in particular. Andrew Thompson, *George Eliot and Italy: Literary, Cultural and Political Influences from Dante to the Risorgimento*, Basingstoke, Macmillan, x + 243 pp., investigates aspects of E.'s reception of D. and the deployment of ideas derived from the *VN* and *DC* about moral choice, spiritual development, and the allegorical journey in several of her novels, as well as tracing her enthusiasm for Risorgimento conceptions of Italy, with their prominent use of D.'s life and writings. W. Tommasino, 'Beatrice e Clizia nel cammino salvifico di due poeti', *LC*, 27:19–41, compares the biographic and poetic roles of D.'s B. and Montale's C., both writers finding metaphysical illumination in myths of a muse. S. Vazzana, 'Dante in Frezzi', *L'Alighieri*, 39:83–98.

3. TEXTUAL TRADITION

I leave aside the large number of recent editions of the *DC* and minor works in or with translation (English, French, German), although noting that their number, and the often distinguished writers engaged with D.'s texts, suggests an encouraging revival of general interest in Dante. A number of new critical editions reveal the extent to which Dante still poses philological and interpretative challenges at a more scholarly level. Dante Alighieri, *La Commedìa: testo critico secondo i più antichi manoscritti fiorentini*, ed. Antonio Lanza, Anzio, De Rubeis, 1996, cxxvi + 818 pp., offers numerous revisions to the Petrocchi *vulgata* (1966–67), beginning with the title accentuation, to produce a distinctively 'early Florentine' text, following the reading of the single MS Trivulziano 1080 wherever possible, against the more 'Italian' and comparative Petrocchian standard; the substantial methodological and critical issues a new edition raises are thoughtfully discussed in the introduction. A detailed review appears in R. Stefanini, 'Fra Commèdia e Com(m)edìa: risalendo il testo del poema', *LDan*, 20–21, 1997:3–32. L. Cassata, 'Contributi al testo critico del *Paradiso*', *La Parola del Testo*, 2:185–94, makes a variety of suggestions on passages from the *Par.* Dante Alighieri, *Vita Nova*, ed. Guglielmo Gorni, T, Einaudi, 1996, xlviii + 392 pp., also offers substantial revisions to the standard critical edition (Barbi 1932), again beginning with the title (adopting D.'s Latin *'incipit'* form), and immediately visible within the text in the new division into 31 rather than 42 'paragrafi', and in the more archaicizing forms preferred overall; the introduction and commentary elucidate G.'s preferences and approach, opening fruitful lines for discussion. He returns to these issues in 'Appunti sulla nuova *Vita Nova*', *LC*, 26, 1996:7–20. Dante Alighieri, *Commedia: Paradiso*, ed. and comm. Anna Maria Chiavacci Leonardi, Mi, Mondadori, 1997, lvi + 1309 pp., completes her edition of the *DC* (1991–97), with a clear and elegant presentation of the *Par.*, amply glossed and noted. The commentary tradition is also receiving attention, with a critical edition of Guglielmo Maramauro's *Expositione sopra l'Inferno di Dante Alligieri*, ed. Pier Giacomo Pisoni and Saviero Bellomo (Medioevo e Umanesimo, 100), Padua, Antenore, xiii + 546 pp. Luigi Pirandello, *Chiose al Paradiso di Dante*, ed. Giuseppe Bolognese, T, San Paolo, 1996, 220 pp., offers a critical edition of Pirandello's various notes and comments on the *Par.* (the very brief *Inf.* and *Purg.* references appear in an appendix, pp. 205–14), discussing his engagement with D., and especially the stylistically and thematically challenging poetics of the *Par.* I also note a few of the recent editions of the Latin works with accompanying translations and commentary: Dante, *De vulgari eloquentia*, ed. and trans. Steven Botterill, CUP, xxix + 105 pp.; Dante Alighieri, *L'eloquenza in volgare*, ed. and trans. Giorgio Inglese, Mi, Rizzoli, 199 pp. *Dante's Monarchia*, trans. and comm. Richard Kay, Toronto, Pontifical Inst. Medieval Studies, xliii + 449 pp., with a detailed and accessible apparatus. Further, on the latter work, P. Shaw's 'The *stemma codicum* of Dante's *Monarchia*', *ISt*, 51, 1996:5–26, traces a 'three-branch tree' (p. 24) of readings, contributing importantly to the understanding of the textual tradition; the same scholar investigates 'Le correzioni di copista nei manoscritti della *Monarchia*', *StD*, 63, 1991[1997]:281–312, a detailed discussion of textual and philological points, investigating the 8 out of 19 principal MSS of the *Mon.* that show considerable uncertainty about the form and meaning of the text transcribed, and the extent to which these corrections are caused by contamination.

New insights on 14th-c. reception appear in M. Seriacopi, 'La storia nella storia: Paolo, Francesca e Lancillotto in un commento inedito del XIV secolo al v canto dell'*Inferno*', *L'Alighieri*, 39:45–53, on a commentary where the Lancelot story appears *in extenso* as a context for the *Inf.* v narrative. M. Petoletti, 'Un chiosatore lucchese a Dante della fine del Trecento', *Aevum*, 71, 1997:371–87, discusses the authorship and sources of MS Ambrosiano D 539 inf. L. C. Rossi, 'Per il commento di Martino Paolo Nibia alla *Commedia*', *MedH*, 96, 1997:1677–1716, discusses N.'s contribution to vernacular discussion of the *DC* in the humanist age, and provides the texts of his Latin dedicatory letter to Guglielmo di Monferrato and his elegy addressed to the reader.

4. Minor Works

Giovanni Cappello, *La dimensione macrotestuale: Dante, Boccaccio, Petrarca*, Ravenna, Longo, 247 pp., urging a rigorous application of Corti's original notion (1976) of the 'macrotext' against loose usage in subsequent criticism, applies it to D. in two essays on the *VN* and the *Rime*, and the problem of authorial versus editorial-critical 'macrotext' constructions, analysing their implications for evaluation of D.'s poetics and especially his intertextuality and his experimentalism.

On the *VN*, G. Brugnoli, 'Un libro della memoria asemplato per rubriche', *La Parola del Testo*, 1, 1997:55–64, addresses the narrative function of D.'s 'asemplare' in the *VN*. M. Farnetti, 'Dante e il libro della memoria', *CLett*, 25, 1997:419–34, discusses the narratological and metatextual resonances of the *incipit* to the *VN*. C. A. Mangieri, ' "Messer Brunetto" e "Messer Giano" in un sonetto di Dante Alighieri', *ib.*, 627–36, advances an intriguing but not fully convincing proposal for a new 1314 dating for the *VN*, contemporary with *Purg.* publication, and a polemical meaning for the 'pulzelletta' sonnet's dedicatees in relation to the *VN* text. R. Martinez, 'Mourning Beatrice: the rhetoric of threnody in the *Vita Nuova*', *MLN*, 113:1–29, discusses D.'s rhetorical and allegorical allusions to *Lamentations* in the structuring of images of loss and mourning in the *VN*, highlighting the importance of commentaries on the Christological exegesis of *Lamentations*, and their implications for the understanding of B. in the *VN* and the *Purg.* M. Picone, 'Eros e poesia da Dante a Petrarca', *Italianistica*, 27:9–18, proposes that the *VN* forms D.'s *ars amatoria*, reconciling the conflicting medieval visions of *fol'amor* and *fin'amor* in a conscious summation of traditions, via the passage from the opening dream to the closing vision, and briefly commenting on the parallel, but negative, summation of love tradition in Petrarch. Id., 'Theories of love and the lyric tradition from Dante's *Vita nuova* to Petrarch's *Canzoniere*', *RoN*, 39:83–94, covers very similar ground. S. Sarteschi, 'Lode e dolcezza nel xxvii della *Vita Nuova*', *CLett*, 26: 3–21, highlights the significance of the concept of *dolcezza* in the text of the *VN* and its anticipations of the *DC*.

On the *Rime*, debates over the authenticity of the *tenzone* with Forese Donati continue, and tend increasingly towards rejection: R. Stefanini, '*Tenzone* sì e *tenzone* no', *LDan*, 18–19, 1996:111–28, offers a pertinent review of the problem of the *appendice dantesca* in general, before turning to the *tenzone*, concurring with Cursietti's 1995 study via a discussion of stylistic univocity (forged exchange), dissimilarity in tone from Duecento comic-realism (forged chronology), and opacity of linguistic *gergo* or code, adding philological observations. E. Esposito, '*Tenzone* no', *La Parola del Testo*, 1, 1997:268–71. A. Lanza, 'A norma di filologia: ancora a proposito della cosidetta "Tenzone tra Dante e Forese" ', *L'Alighieri*, 38, 1997:43–54, also views the exchange as a forgery. G. Gorni, ' "Nevicate alpi" tra Iacopo e Dante', *La Parola del Testo*, 1, 1997:255–67, discusses another question of attribution, and E. Pasquini, 'Appunti sulle *rime dubbie* di Dante', *LC*, 26, 1996:37–54, reviews the whole corpus of *rime dubbie*, rejecting the majority as apocryphal, and maintaining just six serious candidates; while S. De Laude, 'Per la lettura di un sonetto di Dante: qualche nota su *Ne le man vostre* (*Rime* LXVI)', *ASNP*, 1, 1996:173–85, turns to a work now normally considered canonical, and discusses the history of its various attributions. A. Battistini, 'Lo stile della Medusa: processi di pietrificazione in *Io son venuto al punto della rota*', *LC*, 26, 1996:93–110, finds in the poem a poetics of stylistic "petrification" around repetition. M. Chiamenti, 'The representation of the psyche in Cavalcanti, Dante and Petrarch: the *spiriti*', *Neophilologus*, 82:71–81, discusses the adoption of the Aristotelian natural science of *spiriti* in the early lyric, and the diminution of *prosopopeia* from Cavalcanti and D. to the later Petrarch. E. Fenzi, ' "Sollazzo" e "leggiadria": un'interpretazione della canzone dantesca *Poscia ch'amor*', *StD*, 63, 1991[1997]:191–280, offers a lengthy analysis of these two terms, and of their public and moral implications, tracing connections between D.'s usage and that of Brunetto, Guittone, and the Occitan poets (*solatz*). E. Graziosi, 'Dante e Cino: sul cuore di un giurista', *LC*, 26, 1996:55–91, reassesses the exchanges over inconstancy to suggest that D.'s relation of love to Aristotelian natural science actually justifies passages between passions, and she relates this to D.'s and C.'s shared juridical and poetic status as exiles. M. Pazzaglia, 'Due canzoni dantesche: *Amor che movi tua vertù da cielo* e *Io sento sì d'Amor la gran possanza*', *LC*, 26, 1996:21–35, highlights the *canzoni*'s thematic continuity with the *VN* and *stilnovismo*, in D.'s engagement with questions regarding love, and stylistic diversity reflecting experimentalism after the homogeneity pursued in *VN*. L. Peirone, 'Frequenza dei nomi nelle *Rime* dantesche: retorica e semantica', *EL*, 21.1, 1996:37–41, notes divergences between the *DVE*'s theoretical limitations of lexis, and the less restrictive practice of the *rime*. G. Sansone, 'Il nome disseminato: Brunetto, Bondie, Dante', *La Parola del Testo*, 2:9–20, suggests an acrostic of 'Beatrice', unveiling the *donna-schermo* device, may be hidden in the sonnet *Voi che per la via d'Amor*.

On the *DVE*, R. J. Lokaj, 'Il volgare illustre quale *trames* dantesco nel ritorno a Dio', *L'Alighieri*, 39:55–82, on the ethical/anagogical implications of linguistic thought in *Cvo* and *DVE*. M. Pastore Passaro, 'From theory to history and poetry: Dante's hunt in the forest of dialects', *RStI*, 16.1:104–15, offers a survey of linguistic ideas from the *VN* to the *DC*, focusing on the imagery of the hunt in *DVE* and revealing its tendency to 'prove' D.'s own supremacy in linguistics and poetry.

On the *Cvo*, Peter Dronke, *Dante's Second Love: The Originality and the Contexts of the Convivio*, Society for Italian Studies Occasional Papers, 2, 1997, vi + 76 pp., offers a reading of Dante's attitude(s) to philosophy in the *Cvo*, especially urging the coherence of Books III and IV and drawing attention to Neoplatonic influences on D's thought in the text.

On the *Mon*, M. Palma di Cesnola, '*Isti qui nunc*, la *Monarchia* e l'elezione imperiale del 1314', *SPCT*, 57:107–30, returns to the dating debate, suggesting that *Mon*. III.xv offers a chronologically-specific reference to imperial electors, *isti qui nunc*, to mark a publication date between April and October 1314, and a corresponding interruption of composition between *Par*. v and vi.

On the *Eclogues*: G. P. Raffa, 'Dante's mocking pastoral muse', *DaSt*, 114, 1996:271–92, discusses the Latin poetics of the *Eclogues*, suggesting a subtle mockery by D. of Giovanni del Virgilio's Latin predilections.

On the *Ep. to Cangrande*, S. Giovannuzzi, '*Sive anagogicus*: a proposito dell'*Epistola a Cangrande*', *ParL*, 47, 1996:29–39, while offering cautious support for D.'s authorship, rejects the 'anagogicus' reference (§7) as both uncharacteristic and philologically unsubstantiated. G. Padoan, 'Il Vicariato Cesareo dello Scaligero: per la datazione dell'*Epistola a Cangrande*', *LItal*, 50:161–75, analyses the historical sequence surrounding the conferral, confirmation, and revocation of titles of Vicariate on Cangrande, to suggest that the form of the *Ep.*'s salutation makes it fall in the window July 1319 to July or August 1320.

The question of the *Fiore* has also received considerable attention over recent years, with new proposals on its authorship, intention, and status: *The Fiore in Context: Dante, France, Tuscany*, ed. Zygmunt G. Barański and Patrick Boyde (William and Katherine Devers Series in Dante Studies, 2), Notre Dame U.P., 1997, xxii + 409 pp., records the proceedings of an international conference at which substantial contributions on the *Fiore*, and on the question of its authorship, were made by 13 speakers, and a survey on the *status questionae* of authorship conducted involving 24 more: this publication of papers and discussion confronts 'questions of attribution', 'the MS and the text', 'France and Italy', 'literary context', and 'the *Fiore* and the *DC*', and the volume offers a valuable cross-section of the range of current opinions and critical approaches to the *Fiore*. Elsewhere, M. Cursietti, 'Ancora per il *Fiore*: indizi cavalcantiani', *La Parola del Testo*, 1, 1997:197–218, boldly proposes a possible Cavalcantian paternity for the *Fiore*. R. Fasani, 'Il *Fiore* e Brunetto Latini', *SPCT*, 57:5–36, offers equally definite arguments for Brunetto, with his rhetorical training and familiarity with French language and culture, as the poet. A. Mazzucchi, 'A proposito della "consecuzione *R[ose]-F[iore]*-Angiolieri": un supplemento d'indagine sulla "danteità" del *Fiore*', *StD*, 63, 1991[1997]:313–34, suggests that A.'s sonnet *Dante Allaghier, Cecco, tu' serv'amico* is citing the *Fiore* in its allusion to Amore as 'tu' signor antico', and thus attests D.'s recognized Trecento paternity of the *Fiore*. D. Senior, 'The authority and autonomy of the *Fiore*', *FoI*, 32:305–31, avoids questions of authorship to investigate narrative technique, and Durante's critical self-definition in relation to the textual traditions established by the *Rose*, around the key terms *tradigione* and *fedeltate*; she returns to these themes in 'Love, sex and gender in Durante's *Fiore*', *The Italianist*, 17, 1997:29–43, pointing to divergences from the *Rose*, especially in the *fiore*-beloved's personal autonomy, and a different vision of the nature and acquisition of knowledge as an individual and not public endeavour.

5. COMEDY

Longer general studies of the *DC* include Giuliana Angiolillo, *La nuova frontiera della tanatologia: le biografe della Commedia*, 3 vols, F, Olschki, 1996, 182, 308, 268 pp., a somewhat unwieldy set of volumes, which combines biographical material with evidence from *letture* of selected cantos, alongside a study of D.'s understanding of death, from the *VN* to the *Par.*, both in relation to the individual and as humanity's collective destiny, in D.'s highly personal eschatological vision based on a new vernacular (hence collective) intellectual culture. Carmelo Ciccia, *Dante e Gioacchino da Fiore*, Cosenza, Pellegrini, 157 pp., discusses D's attitude to Joachimite thought in two main areas: regarding J.'s vision of Italy's special place in the Trinitarian scheme of Ages of world history; and regarding the imagery, visual and mystical, of the *Liber figurarum* and its possible connections with the *DC*, especially the *Par.* Ugo Dotti, *La Divina Commedia e la città dell'uomo: introduzione alla lettura di Dante*, Ro, Donzelli, 1996, 146 pp., proposes a political reading of the *DC* based around the theme of justice, presenting D. as a reforming poet with 'humanist' concerns for the renewal of the secular order and a revival of the intellectual and political virtues of Rome. Raffaele Giglio, *Il volo di Ulisse e di Dante: altri studi sulla Commedia*, Na, Loffredo, 1997, 198 pp. Edward G. Miller, *Sense Perception in Dante's Commedia*, Lewiston, Mellen, 1996, vi + 365 pp., assesses especially the importance of Platonic influence, and its Augustinian mediation, on D.'s thinking with regard to sense experience and its role in the development of intellectual and spiritual faculties. There are also some reflections on D.'s influence on Ariosto, Tasso, and Milton. Riccardo Scrivano, *Dante, Commedia: le forme dell'oltretomba*, Ro, Nuova Cultura, 1997, 192 pp., a survey of symbolic and rhetorical aspects of the *DC*, focuses on D.'s topographical imagination, with an interesting study of the symbolic topography of light in the *Par.*, and on the status attributed to poets, especially Statius's role in *Purg.* as a *figura Dantis*. Marianne Shapiro, *Dante and the Knot of Body and Soul*, Basingstoke, Macmillan, xiv + 226 pp.

Language, poetics, and eloquence are much discussed: S. Botterill, 'Dante's poetics of the sacred word', *PLit*, 20, 1996:154–62, surveys representations of eloquence in the *DC*, from Virgilian 'parola ornata' to St Bernard's 'parola santa', and discusses their implications for D.'s authorial rhetoric, in particular for his 'questing' approach to extensions/limitations of linguistic capacity. G. Casagrande, 'Parole di Dante: *aborrare*', *StD*, 63, 1991[1997]:177–90, uses Uguccione's etymologies to suggest a new reading of *aborrare* as indicating *stupor*. F. Coassin, 'L'ideale della "armonia": musica e musicalità nella *Commedia*', *MedRom*, 20, 1996:412–36, studies sound patterns, contrasting the aural and symbolic dissonances of *Inf.* with the harmonies of *Par.* C. Delcorno, 'Dante e il linguaggio dei predicatori', *LC*, 25, 1996:51–74, outlines the importance of rhetorical and thematic connections between the *DC* and medieval sermon literature, both absorbing and transmitting influences. W. Hirdt, 'Phantasie und Konstruktion: Anmerkungen zu Dantes *Göttlicher Komödie*', *DDJ*, 72, 1997:7–43, on eschatological literature and D.'s hermeneutics in the making of the 'ghost story' of the *DC* and its significance, both for D. and for later centuries. G. Ledda, 'Tópoi dell'indicibilità e metaforismi nella *Commedia*', *StCrit*, 12, 1997:117–40, urges further exploration of Curtius's 'inexpressibility topos', here pursued in an investigation of the importance of figural language in the *DC*, with brief comment on the impact of points where the topos is reversed into directness. V. Lucchesi, 'Giustizia divina e linguaggio umano: metafore e polisemie del linguaggio umano', *StD*, 63, 1991[1997]: 53–126, re-examines five cases of *contrapasso* in *Inf.* and *Purg.*, arguing against over-mechanical allegorism and proposing a study of D.'s language as indicating a 'contrapasso semantico' (63), combining homonymous terms, etymologies, and theological exegesis to offer the reader multiple interpretative possibilities. E. A. Millar, 'Dante, "miglior fabbro"', *EL*, 23.4:1–17, takes the Valley of the Princes episode (*Purg.* VII) as an interconnecting point between theologically, poetically, and politically significant moments in the three *cantiche* (Limbo's castle, the Earthly Paradise, the rose of Empyrean). N. Mineo, 'Gli Spirituali francescani e l'"Apocalisse" di Dante', *RLI*, 102:26–46, surveys prophetic passages — the Veltro, the Earthly Paradise pageant, the *cinquecento dieci e cinque* — in relation to Spiritual thought on the last things, emphasizing syncretic combination of radical spirituality with traditional exegesis, and with Ghibelline political aspirations for a reformatory imperial mission. C. Moevs, 'Is Dante telling the truth?', *LDan*, 18–19, 1996:3–11, discusses the problem of the *DC*'s truthfulness, stressing the importance of a developing distinction between historical and literary truth, for medieval understanding and exegesis of the poem and for its relation with theological orthodoxy. S. Pearce, 'Dante and the art of memory', *The Italianist*, 16, 1996: 20–61, surveys D.'s use of classical and medieval memorial techniques and his structuring of the *DC.* as a recollection. W. Ross, 'Der Canto als Form', *DDJ*, 71, 1996:9–22, surveys the structure of the *DC* and discusses the musical/epic implications of D.'s terminology of 'canto', 'cantica', and 'commedia'.

A debate on 'D. and the arts' in *DaSt*, 114, 1996, brings together several articles on the visual qualities of the *DC*: P. Barolsky, 'The visionary art of Michelangelo in the light of Dante' (1–14); J.-P. Barricelli, 'Dante: *Inferno* I and the Arts' (15–40); B. J. Watts, 'Sandro Botticelli's response to *visibile parlare*' (41–78). More considerations of D. and the visual arts appear in V. Borsò, 'Dalí begegnet Dante: Transposition des Blickes und Abenteuer der Augen', *DDJ*, 73:153–80. D. Dombrowski, 'Beobachtungen zu Botticellis Dante-Illustrationen', *DDJ*, 71, 1996:45–74, notes the architectural and synthesizing visions of Botticelli and of D. Visual splendours are provided in Charles H. Taylor and Patricia Finley's *Images of the Journey in Dante's Divine Comedy*, London, Yale U.P., 1997, xvi + 295 pp.: beautiful images from 14th- to 20th-c. artists are accompanied by minimal text presenting idiosyncratic criticism based on Jung and focused as much on the illustrators as on the poet. The exhibition catalogue *Francesco Scaramuzza e Dante*, ed. Corrado Gizzi, Mi, Electa, 1996, 319 pp., reproduces a large number of S.'s illustrations to the *DC*, with a series of short essays on his appreciation of D. and on Dantean iconography. Art and theology intersect also in J. Mazzaro, 'Dante and the image of the "Madonna Allattante"', *DaSt*, 114, 1996:95–112, drawing out the theology of motherhood in Marian cults and the figures of Beatrice, Virgil, and others in the *DC.* E. Pasquini, 'Le icone parentali nella *Commedia*', *LC*, 25, 1996:51–74, also analyses metaphors of family relationship and makes interesting reflections on the parental figuring of Virgil and his works in the *DC.*

Sources and questions of intertextuality provide the focus for: N. Borsellino, 'Metamorfosi in *Commedia*: da Ovidio a Dante', *FC*, 22, 1997:3–19, on D.'s renewals of metamorphosis myths from classical to Christian contexts; T. Brückner, '*Führen* und *geführt werden* in Vergils *Aeneis* und Dantes *Commedia*', *DDJ*, 72, 1997:115–38; G. Brugnoli, 'Le arpie di Dante', *Aevum*, 71, 1997:359–70, with detailed source-lists for scriptural and literary Harpy lore, suggesting both that the Harpies fit the wild Maremman landscape of wood and hunt and that, figurally, their connections with prophecy ('tristo annunzio di futuro danno' *Inf.* XIII, 12) fit the sequence's allusions to exile and establish intratextual links with the Cacciaguida *canti* of *Par.*; Enzo Esposito et al., **Memoria biblica nell'opera di Dante*, Ro, Bulzoni, 1996, 119 pp.; F. Ferrucci, 'Tre note dantesche', *LItal*, 49, 1997:89–92, which reviews *Inf.* III, 136, underlining an *imitatio Christi* in D.-character's faint, and *Inf.* V, 100 and 103, a semi-parodic revision of *stilnovista* Amore as a maleficent deity, and *Purg.* XIV, 17, for its echoes of Lucan. V. Jewiss, 'Monstrous movements and metaphors in Dante's *Divine Comedy*', *FoI*, 32:332–46, surveys D.'s use of monsters from classical literature (Virgil, Ovid) as guardians and symbols in *Inf.* and *Purg.* (the Griffin), noting their 'marginal' position in MSS illumination and in the circles of D.'s afterworld topography, but also their accommodation within the schemes of Divine Grace. J. Leeker, 'Geschichtsmythos als moralisches Exempel: Dante und Theben', *DDJ*, 73:127–51, surveys D.'s borrowings from Theban myth with reference to his use of individual protagonists as moral allegories and his interpretation of Statius's version of the myth as a *dehortatio a civili bello*, especially in *Inf.* R. Wilson, 'Prophecy by the dead in Dante and Lucan', *ISt*, 52, 1997: 16–37, outlines a strong presence of classical, besides Biblical, notions of prophecy in D., especially in *Inf.* M. Shapiro, 'Dante's two-fold representation of the soul', *LDan*, 18–19, 1996:49–90, discusses sources for D.'s representations of the souls in the three *cantiche*, emphasizing debts to Lucan as well as Virgil. M. Veglia, '*Lucerna ardens*: appunti su Cavalcanti, Virgilio e il problema del *disdegno*', *Italianistica*, 26, 1997:9–21, finds parallels between the situations of C. and V., figures whose example benefits others but is self-destructive through intellectual pride, but significant divergences between C.'s 'disdegno' towards Beatrice and V.'s constructive acceptance of her commission/meaning.

On D.'s scientific knowledge, S. Gilson, 'Dante's meteorological optics: refraction, reflection and the rainbow', *ISt*, 52, 1997:51–62, underlines D.'s reference to Aristotelian ideas, rather than contemporary technical treatises, when creating optical images, which then synthesize scientific with scriptural and mythological allusion. R. Podgurski, 'Where optics and visionary metaphysics coincide in Dante's *novella vista*', *ItQ*, 135–36:29–38, highlights mystical elements in D's uses of light theory and *perspectiva* in the Empyrean.

Studies of history and geography in the *DC* include: A. Cottignoli, 'Cronaca e poesia nella *Commedia* dantesca', *LC*, 25, 1996:75–86, and G. Di Pino, 'Le valenze del fiume nella *Divina Commedia*', *StD*, 63, 1991[1997]:127–39, which explores D.'s 'hydrographic' imagery of rivers: more specific and more complex than that of the sea, ranging as it does from markers of afterworld symbolic topography to metonymic 'sources' of origin for person or place (esp. for the Arno) and to symbols of temporality and, in the Empyrean, of eternity.

6. INFERNO

I monstra nell'Inferno dantesco: tradizione e simbologie. Atti del XXXIII Convegno storico internazionale, Spoleto, Centro di Studi sull'Alto

Medioevo, 1997, x + 288 pp., collects 11 studies on *monstra* in D.'s sources and in *Inf.*: five *letture* of specific examples provide detailed illustration of D.'s techniques of allusion and reinvention; D.'s range of different sources is surveyed in: U. Pizzani, 'I *monstra* nella cultura classica' (1–26); G. Cremascoli, 'L'immaginario dei *monstra* biblici' (27–42); M. Donnini, '*Monstra* in testi mediolatini' (43–72); A. Orchard, 'The sources and meaning of the *Liber monstrorum*' (73–106); B. Spaggiari, 'Antecedenti e modelli tipologici nella letteratura in lingua d'oïl' (107–40); P. Armour, 'I *monstra* e *mirabilia* del mondo ai tempi di Dante' (141–60), which stresses the closeness of the categories of the monstrous and the marvellous in D.'s culture, investigating the *mirabilia* of *VN*, *Purg.*, and *Par.*, as well as infernal *monstra*. Monstrous figures and their meanings are discussed also in: S. M. Barillari, 'L'animalità come segno del demoniaco nell'*Inferno* dantesco', *GSLI*, 174, 1997:98–119, on the diabolic meaning of bestial images — of animals, but especially of mixed *monstra* — whose morphology enriches the allegorical representation of sin and duplicity through the underworld. B. Basile, 'Mostri delle *Storie d'Ercule* nell'*Inferno*', *LC*, 25, 1996:7–20, discusses intertextual sources, predominantly classical, for D.'s depictions of Cerberus, Cacus, and Geryon. V. Di Benedetto, ' "Fatti non foste a viver come bruti" ', *GSLI*, 173, 1996:1–25, outlines the correspondences between *Cvo* and *DC* over images of bestiality and the renunciation of commitment to truth, showing sources also in Boethius and Cicero. J. C. Nohrnberg, 'The descent of Geryon: the moral system of *Inferno* XVI–XXXI', *DaSt*, 114, 1996:129–88, relates G.'s anatomy to the topography of Hell and traces structural alternations of verbal and pecuniary sin in Malebolge matching the enchained structure of *terza rima*. S. Tomasch, 'Judecca, Dante's Satan and the *Dis*-placed Jew', Tomasch and Giles, *Text and Territory*, 247–67, suggests that Christianist readings have neglected the tensions surrounding explicit and unconscious repressions of Judaism in the *Inf.*, especially in Giudecca's symbolic name (mimicking historic ghetto terminology), and in the parodies of circumcision and the eucharist evoked, implicitly, by D.'s Satan. S. Vazzana, 'Dov'è la "matta bestialitade"? (Ancora sulla struttura aristotelica dell'*Inferno*)', *L'Alighieri*, 38, 1997:95–108, on the Aristotelian origins of defining a super-sin, *matta bestialitade*, seen as corresponding to the treachery of Cocito. A survey of the *cantica* as a whole appears in V. Moleta, 'Virgil in Cocytus', *LDan* 20–21, 1997:33–47, a deceptively plain title for what is an engaging vision of the choreographies of the role of V. in Hell, instructorly prominence alternating with a focus on D.-character's autonomous judgements, exercized on the civic monuments of Dis, as part of a Florentine *metanoia* of which he is both protagonist and prophet.

On particular *canti*, *Inf.* I is represented by: P. Armour, 'The twelve Ambassadors and Ugolino's Jubilee inscription: Dante's Florence and the Tartars in 1300', *ISt*, 52, 1997:1–15, shedding possible new light on the Veltro prophecy; G. Casagrande, 'Parole di Dante: il "lungo silenzio" di *Inferno* I, 63', *GSLI*, 1997, 174:243–54, proposing a visual/spatial reading of *silenzio*, to give 'uno che nella grande selva appariva indistinto', and tracing the etymology *silva/silen/silentium;* V. R. Giustiniani, ' "Bene ascolta chi la nota" ', *ZRP*, 114:301–03, offering philological discussion of various passages and suggests that *Inf.* I finds D. running out of the wood, as ''l piè fermo sempre era 'l più basso' (1, 30). On *Inf.* II: R. Mercuri, 'Il canto II dell'*Inferno*', *L'Alighieri*, 39:7–22, and M. Roddewig, 'Lectura Dantis: *Inferno* III', *DDJ*, 72, 1997:139–60. On *Inf.* IV: P. A. Cantor, 'The uncanonical Dante: the Divine Comedy and Islamic philosophy', *PLit*, 20, 1996:138–53, argues that D.'s prominence in the 'Western Canon' obscures his familiarity with aspects of Islamic culture and his dependence on the Orient for much knowledge of, for example, the 'Western' Aristotle, suggesting especially sympathies for Averroes and reading Limbo as a representation of the Possible Intellect in its inhabitants' eternal philosophic activity. F. Salsano, 'Il canto IV dell'*Inferno*', *L'Alighieri*, 39:23–36, is a perceptive account of the 'supernatural register' of mysteriousness on entry to the realm of the dead and of the insufficiencies of Limbo's heroes. On *Inf.* V: T. Barolini, 'Minos's tail: the labor of devising hell (*Inferno* 5.1–24)', *RR*, 87, 1996:437–54, highlights the importance of physical and ideological aspects of M. in relation both to Virgil (poet and character), and the predominantly classical world of Limbo, and to the classical and contemporary sinners who confess to and are judged by Minos; L. Derla, 'Francesca, una Beatrice incompiuta (*Inf.* V 73–143)', *ItQ*, 133–34, 1997:5–20; G. Gorni, 'Francesca e Paolo: la voce di lui', *Intersezioni*, 16, 1996:383–89, argues that P., not F., utters the line (107) of 'vendetta' on Gianciotto's predestined place in Caina; D. Maddox, 'The Arthurian intertexts of *Inferno* V', *DaSt*, 114, 1997:113–28; L. Palladino, 'Paolo und Francesca in der Kunst des 19. Jahrhunderts', *DDJ*, 73:75–98; B. Telleschi, 'L'ingenuità di Francesca', *Belfagor*, 52, 1997:348–49, underlines F.'s romantic 'Bovarism'. On *Inf.* VI: G. Arnaldi, 'Il canto di Ciacco' (Lettura di *Inf.* VI)', *L'Alighieri*, 38, 1997:7–20, on the political detail of Ciacco's 'prophecy' about the events of May 1300. On *Inf.* VII: M. Roddewig, 'Lectura Dantis: *Inferno* VII — Der Fortuna-Gesang', *DDJ*, 71, 1996:99–124; and M. Saccenti, 'Dalla soglia della quarta lacca alla palude di fango (*Inf.* VII)', *L'Alighieri*, 38, 1997:21–33, on the canto's two poles, demonic Pluto and angelic *Fortuna*. On *Inf.* VIII: M. Picone, '*Inferno* VIII: il viaggio contrastato', *L'Alighieri*, 38, 1997:35–50, provides a convincing elucidation of the theme of the journey — physical and narratological — as exemplified in a canto that is 'intermediary' between the river and the city of Dis, and between the classical shortfalls of Phlegyas/Virgil and the Christian authority of the Messo/Dante. On *Inf.* x: J. T. Chiampi, 'Farinata's exile from the city of the resurrection', *RStI*, 15.1, 1997:1–24, discusses the 'analytical typology' whereby F.'s apparent epic grandeur is undercut and becomes the antitype of the true ancestor, patriot, and believer, Cacciaguida, in *Par.* xv-xvii; C. López Cortezo, 'Las tres "orribili infermitadi" del canto x del *Inferno*', *LDan*, 18–19, 1996:41–48. On *Inf.* xi: T. Santelli, '*Inferno*, canto xi', *L'Alighieri*, 38, 1997:51–72. On *Inf.* xii: U. Carpi, 'I tiranni (a proposito di *Inf.* xii)', *ib.*, 39:7–31, provides a detailed reading of the contemporary implications of D.'s comments on the decline of feudal leadership and the malignancy of papal politics. On *Inf.* xiii: S. Vazzana, 'Il "disdegnoso gusto" di Pier delle Vigne', *ib.*, 91–94; L. Scorrano, '*Inferno* xiii: un orizzonte di negazione', *DDJ*, 73:99–118. On *Inf.* xvi: M. Chiamenti, 'Due *schedulae* ferine: Dante, *Rime* ciii 71 e *Inf.* xvi 45', *LN*, 59:7–10, suggests a mutual illumination between the bestial implications of the terms 'scherzare' in the *petrose* and 'fiera moglie' in the *Inf.* M. Dell'Aquila, 'Il canto XVI dell'*Inferno*', *L'Alighieri*, 39:37–46. On *Inf.* xix: L. Sebastio, 'La contenta labbia di Virgilio: dinamiche culturali in *Inferno* xix', *RLettI*, 15, 1997:9–34, examines the canto's indications about literary authority, using intertextual references, to *Mon.* and *Ep.* xi in particular, to emphasize D.'s affirmation of poets' philosophic and political stature. On *Inf.* xxi: A. Battistini, 'L'arte d'inabissarsi o la retorica della "tenace pece" (*Inf.* xxi)', *L'Alighieri*, 38, 1997:73–92, explores the range of registers and civic allusions from high to low. On *Inf.* xxii: G. Costa, 'Il canto xxii dell'*Inferno*', *ib.*, 39:47–89, offers a detailed account of the commentators' opinions on this canto, revealing anxieties over the comic crudity surrounding the devils and the damned. On *Inf.* xxiv: I. Baldelli, 'Le *fiche* di Vanni Fucci', *GSLI*, 174, 1997:1–38, displays the medical and sexual implications of the canto's language, especially the 'fiche'. On *Inf.* xxvi: Id., 'Dante e Ulisse', *LItal*, 50:358–73, besides a close analysis of U.'s rhetoric, suggests some historical analogues for his ill-fated voyage 'off the map' beyond the Mediterranean; C. Chierichini, 'La terza Satira di Persio "fra le righe" di *Inferno* xxvi', *L'Alighieri*, 39:95–103, suggests a possible source for Ulisse's speech in Persius, possibly via Augustine; M. Dell'Aquila, 'Le Sirene di Ulisse (*Inf.* xxvi: qualche chiosa dopo tante letture)', *EL*, 21.2, 1996:3–25, returns to the question of Ulysses's sin, stressing the ambiguity of admiration for intellectual adventure, with condemnation of disobedience, in D.'s portrayal of the questing hero/sinner; A. Del Biondo, 'La sirena latente: Ulisse nella *Divina Commedia* (*Inferno* xxvi)', *Versants*, 29, 1996:91–104; K. Münchberg, 'In Gespräch mit Odysseus: zum Verhältnis von Allegorie und Dialog in Dantes *Commedia, Inferno* xxvi', *DDJ*, 72, 1997:83–96, explores D.'s deployment of theological and poetic modes of allegory in the Ulysses encounter, through the devices of intertextuality (with Virgil, Ovid and others) and iconicity (the *contrapasso*); W. Stull and R. Hollander, 'The Lucanian source of Dante's Ulysses', *StD*, 63, 1991[1997]:1–52, cites Lucan as a source for D.'s depiction of Ulysses, a figure of the Latin poet's militarily and rhetorically untrustworthy Julius Caesar (and in turn, Caesar as anti-type of Virgil's Aeneas), also engaging critically with Bloom's (1994) and Barolini's (1992) interpretations of Ulysses as a counterpart to a 'dark Dante'. On *Inf.* xxviii: S. Grazzini, 'Per l'origine e la storia del dantesco *trullare* (*Inf.* xxviii 24)', *LN*, 58, 1997:79–84, gives a detailed survey of Latin sources for *trullare*, which proves to have a more literary genealogy, and more extended senses, than commentary often indicates; M. T. Lanza, 'Nota su Dante (*Inferno* xxviii, 22–42): lo strazio di Maometto', *MC* 26:75–76, suggests Mohammed's wound may expose testicles, rather than bowels, and thus suggest literal and symbolic profanation of human (and divine) creative force; G. Tardiola, 'Bertran cefaloforo: percorsi iconico-tematici di una configurazione dantesca', *La Parola del Testo*, 1, 1997:66–77, surveys a range of hagiographic, folkloric, and chivalric sources for the motifs of the 'cefaloforo' and the 'testa parlante' combined in Bertran. On *Inf.* xxx and xxxi: L. Derla, 'Infernali tragicommedie (su *Inferno* xxx e xxxi)', *Italianistica*, 26, 1997:225–36, re-examines the medieval significance of 'comic' and 'tragic', and the Christian ideology that eluded or elided classical meanings, illustrating D.'s combination of both modalities in these canti to create mixed 'tragicomic' effects. D. Modesto, 'Son sans lumière: an investigation into Dante's Nembrot of *Inferno* xxxi', *Altro Polo*, 18, 1996:38–52, investigates the intertextual resonances between Nimrod and Roland to suggest that the horn-sounding is neither hunting-call nor warning but part of the *contrapasso* of the treacherous, perpetually recalling Roland's (the *figura Christi*'s) betrayal at the hands of proud Ganelon (Lucifer), and a presage of the Last Judgement, when suffering will be redoubled. On *Inf.* xxxiii: E. Raimondi, 'Le figure interne di Ugolino', *LC*, 25, 1996:87–100, draws out the effective deployment of intertextual links with the Bible, both in U.'s narrative, and in the invective against Pisa, and underlines the indications of cannibalism. On *Inf.* xxxiv: G. Farris, 'L'anti-trinitarismo di Lucifero nei *Sermones* di Jacopo delle Varazze e nel canto xxxiv dell'*Inferno*', *CLett*, 25 1997:211–24, reveals trinitarian and anti-trinitarian structures in

D.'s theology of damnation (and redemption), linked to contemporary demonological lore.

7. PURGATORIO

The *cantica* has received a detailed study in John A. Scott's *Dante's Political Purgatory*, University Park, Pennsylvania U.P., xi + 295 pp., an original reading of the *Purg.* from a purely political viewpoint, focusing on D.'s reaction to the activities of Henry VII and on the context and forms of his reformatory political vision. Arguing that the *cantica*'s theoretical and historical references converge on the imperial issue, S. leads up to a political interpretation of the myth of Eden in the Earthly Paradise pageant, with its confirmation of D. in his vatic role, as pilgrim and as poet, and to the active life of political engagement. Other general studies include: M. Baine Campbell, ' "Nel mezzo del cammin di nostra vita": the palpability of *Purgatorio*', Tomasch and Gilles, *Text and Territory*, 15–28, underlining the corporeality of D.'s narrative in the *Purg.* and classing it as 'travel writing' in its focus on transition rather than arrival; J. T. Chiampi, 'Dante's education in debt and shame', *Italica*, 74, 1997:1–20, stressing the importance of shame to develop *pietas* — Aeneas and Augustine provide pagan and Christian examples — and a sense of purpose such as awareness of human humility and indebtedness for redemptive grace arouse in *Purg.*, especially the Earthly Paradise pageant sequence; N. R. Havely, 'Poverty in Purgatory: from *Commercium* to *Commedia*', *DaSt*, 114, 1996: 229–44, finding intertextual resonances for *Purg.* with a favourite Spiritual Franciscan text elaborating an allegory of mountain-purification and a rejection of cupidity; P. Williams, '*Accidia* as the personal sin of the character Dante in the *Comedy*', *RoS*, 32:57–68, drawing her arguments from the discourse on love and choice in *Purg.* XVII and making connections with the *Cvo*'s pursuit of the *donna gentile* to suggest that the shortcoming confessed in *Purg.* XXX and XXXI reflects a moral *accidia* in diversion from celestial to philosophical goods.

Single-canto studies include, on *Purg.* V: P. De Stefano, '*Purgatorio*: canto V', *LC*, 27:91–100. On *Purg.* X–XII: J. T. Chiampi, 'Visible speech, living stone and the names of the word', *RStI*, 14.1, 1996:1–12, focuses on the divine sculptures, and stone-weighted sinners, as illustrations of the redemptive *renovatio* of Christian humility before the 'rejected cornerstone' of Christ. M. Collareta, 'Visibile parlare', *Prospettiva*, 86, 1997:102–04, shows D.'s debt to Augustinian notions of sign and gesture as 'verbum visibile' (103), and to iconographic convention in the sculptures of *Purg.* X. József Pál, 'Il simbolismo della parola nel *Purgatorio* (Dante, *Commedia*,

Purgatorio, canto N° XII)', *Neohelicon*, 23, 1996:129–40, addresses linguistic play in the canto with regard to name, poetic artifice, and acrostic symbolism. A. Vettori, 'La breccia silenziaria in *Purgatorio* X', *LDan*, 20–21, 1997:78–100, underlines the importance of prayer and liturgy in the structure of *Purg.* in general, and in canto X's sculptures as an articulate, but silent, 'visibile parlare' by and with God. On *Purg.* XIV: B. Guthmüller, ' "Che par che Circe li avesse in pastura" (*Purgatorio* XIV, 42): Circes-Mythos und Metamorphose in Dantes *Commedia*', *DDJ*, 73:51–74, offers stimulating insights into D.'s use of the theme of metamorphosis, drawing on Ovid and Boethius. Observant points about D.'s Ulisse and Glauco are also raised. On *Purg.* XVI: J. Tambling, 'Dante and the modern subject: overcoming anger in the *Purgatorio*', *NLH*, 28, 1997:401–20, investigates the rejection of 'moderno uso' in *Purg.* XVI, suggesting that this apparent assertion of univocal relations between text and referent actually draws attention to elusivity and doubleness in the poetics and theme of the sequence. On *Purg.* XIX: G. Muresu, 'Il richiamo dell'antica strega (*Purgatorio* XIX)', *RLI*, 100.1, 1996:5–38, examines the quality and chronology of the dream of the siren, stressing its revelatory nature, its allegorical value regarding Virgil-Reason and Divine Grace, and the connections between avarice and pride outlined in the subsequent encounter with Hadrian. On *Purg.* XX: A. I. Iannucci, 'The mountainquake of *Purgatorio* and Virgil's story', *LDan*, 20–21:48–59, urges an extended intratextual reading of *Purg.* XX, 128 (the liberating earthquake), to make connections with the Limbo sequence and provide a symbolic summary of the question of the virtuous pagans. On *Purg.* XXIV: S. Giovannuzzi, 'Brunetto e Francesca in *Purgatorio* (sul canto XXIV)', *FC*, 22, 1997:161–85, investigates the recapitulations of *Inf.* and of the lyric tradition in the encounters with Forese and Bonagiunta, suggesting that D. sums up the poetic past in order to liberate the narration of the return/renewal of Beatrice in *Purg.* XXX. On *Purg.* XXVI: R. Stefanelli, 'Il canto XXVI del *Purgatorio*', *LC*, 27: 69–89, revisits the questions of poetic precedence and category in the meetings with Guinizelli and Arnaut. On *Purg.* XXVII: S. Bargetto, 'Il "battesimo di fuoco": memorie liturgiche nel XXVII canto del *Purgatorio*', *LItal*, 49, 1997:185–247, is a detailed and illuminating study of the canto's echoes of baptismal theology (by water, by fire, by blood), in D.-character's poetic, moral, and spiritual *renovatio* from the limitations binding the journey through terrestrial structures with Virgil, renounced in adhesion to Beatrice/Christ. M. Dell'Aquila, 'Il canto XXVII del *Purgatorio*', *LC*, 27:43–55. On *Purg.* XXX–XXXIII: J. Levenstein, 'The pilgrim, the poet, and the cowgirl: Dante's alter-*Io* in *Purgatorio* XXX-XXXI', *DaSt*, 114, 1996:189–208, is a dense and stimulating reading of D.'s allusions to the myths of Argus and Io, and the metier of literature, in the canti surrounding the meeting with Beatrice. G. Oliva, 'Il ritorno dell'antico amore: techniche di rappresentazione e codici culturali nell'Eden dantesco', *LC*, 27:7–17. R. Psaki, 'Dante's redeemed eroticism', *LDan*, 18–19, 1996:12–19, on the shift from erotic to disembodied love for Beatrice occurring at the end of *Purg.* M. Shapiro, 'The widowed crown: "men che di rose e più che di viole" (*Purg.* XXXII, 58)', *ib.*, 20–21, 1997:59–77, supports politicizing interpretations of the pageant (notably Armour 1989), glossing the traditional symbolism of violets as signs of Christian martyrdom, but also of widowhood, a state with secular allegorical significance in the *DC* as a condition of political injustice. J. Stark, 'Once again, Dante's five hundred, ten and five', *RoQ*, 44, 1997:99–106, suggests that the reference is to line numbers in the *Aeneid* (ll. 500, 10, 5), forming an allegorical prophecy about the qualities of the ideal ruler (a lower-case *dux*) to revive Aenean leadership in Italy.

8. PARADISO

R. Beal, 'Bonaventure, Dante and the Apocalyptic Woman clothed with the Sun', *DaSt*, 114, 1996:209–28, suggests that D.-io as well as Beatrice may parallel the Apocalyptic Woman, following the Bonaventuran exegesis as an allegory of the contemplative soul. A. M. Chiavacci Leonardi, 'Il *Paradiso* di Dante: l'ardore del desiderio', *LC*, 27:101–12, provides a stimulating overview of D.'s Christian and exilic poetics in the *Par.*, noting D.'s lifelong commitment to intellectual exploration reflected in *Par.*'s triply innovative approach to genre (a first-person epic), language (definitive expressive equality of the vernacular with Latin), and conception of the cosmos's structures, incorporating corporeal history within the apparent intangibilities of eternity. A. Cornish, 'Beatrice and the astronomical heavens', *LDan*, 18–19, 1996:20–29, links themes of salvific and educational love between *VN* and *Par*, around desire for Beatrice and for knowledge of the divine. N. Havely, 'The blood of the Apostles: Dante, the Franciscans and Pope John XXII', *ISt*, 52:1997:38–50, links D.'s critical portrayal of the Papacy in *Par.* XVIII and XXVII to Church repression of Spiritual Franciscanism from 1316. E. Pasquini, 'Il *Paradiso* e una nuova idea di figuralismo', *Intersezioni*, 16, 1996:417–27, urges *Par.*'s perfection of the technical and conceptual experimentation of the whole *DC*, especially in D.'s deployment of figural parallels between sequences within and outside the poem, and traces interconnections progressing towards the Empyrean. Close readings of particular cantos include, on *Par.* XIII: C. Cahill, 'The limitations of difference in *Paradiso* XIII's two arts: reason and poetry',

DaSt, 114, 1996:245–70, which presents a vivid reading of D.'s representation of Thomist thinking on the 'unity within difference' of divine creation, as contrasted with the Daedalan shortcomings of God's *artisti*, whether Nature, poet, or craftsman. On *Par.* XVII: M. Papio, 'Dante's re-education of conscience (*Paradiso* XVII)', *LDan*, 18–19, 1996:91–109, on the theological and epistemological revelations achieved at the meeting with Cacciaguida. On *Par.* XXII: C. Di Fonzo, ' "La dolce donna dietro a lor mi pinse / con un sol cenno su per quella scala" (*Par.* XXII, 100–101)', *StD*, 63, 1991[1997]:141–75, explores sources for ladder imagery of spiritual ascent (and descent), in scripture and mystical writing, employed in the *DC* in both the 'macroscala' of the whole journey of *Par.* and the 'microscala' of cantos XXII and XXIII, where it also anticipates the final ascent into the Empyrean, as Di F. argues in an analysis of linguistic connections between these cantos and XXXIII. W. Hübner, 'Antike Kosmologie bei Dante', *DDJ*, 72, 1997:45–81, discusses sources for D.'s paradisal cosmology, focusing especially on *Par.* XXII. On *Par.* XXVII: A. Vallone, '*Paradiso* XXVII', *ib.*, 71, 1996:23–44.

DUECENTO AND TRECENTO II
(EXCLUDING DANTE)

POSTPONED

HUMANISM AND THE RENAISSANCE

By PAOLO. L. ROSSI, *Senior Lecturer in Italian Studies, Lancaster University* and GERALDINE MUIRHEAD, *Lecturer in Italian, Manchester Metropolitan University*

1. GENERAL

Il canone della letteratura. Antologia degli autori da Dante a Marino, ed. Giorgio Bárberi Squarotti and Riccardo Verzini, T, Tirrenia, 621 pp., is a useful collection which attempts to give an overall appreciation of literary production, though it is not at all clear what selection criteria have been applied. It covers both poetry and prose and provides biographies, a chronology of works, critical assessments, and annotated extracts. Antonio Piromalli, *La letteratura calabrese,* 2 vols, Cosenza, Pellegrini, 1996, 464, 399 pp., has good chapters on Greek humanism, the present state of studies on 15th-c. prose, and the evolution of devotional literature dedicated to specific saints. The chapter on the 16th c. is an excellent fusion of social, political, cultural, and literary history, showing how texts were inspired by banditry, local political conditions, heretical movements, and piracy. The approach taken in this volume has much to commend it. The introduction of CD-ROM technology has made a significant contribution to our ability to read, compare, and analyse texts. *Art Theorists of the Italian Renaissance,* ed. Deborah Howard and Amanda Lillie, Cambridge, Chadwyck-Healey, 1997, CD, contains 90 first or early editions of treatises on art and architecture. The series *Archivio Italiano,* Ro, Lexis, has made available: Torquato Tasso, *Tutte le opere,* ed. Amedeo Quondam, 1997; *Archivio della tradizione lirica da Petrarca a Marino,* ed. by the same, 1997; Giordano Bruno, *Opere complete,* ed. Nuccio Ordine. *Letteratura Italiana Zanichelli CD-ROM dei testi della letteratura italiana,* ed. Pasquale Stoppelli and Eugenio Picchi, Bo, Zanichelli, is a CD containing 780 texts which can be explored using the powerful search engine. This is an excellent research tool as all the texts are taken from good, and many from critical, editions. It comes with a useful reference volume: Nadia Cannata, *Dizionario biografico compatto degli autori della letteratura italiana,* 1997, 431 pp. A series of texts by Ariosto, Machiavelli, Cellini, Michelangelo, Tasso, Vasari, Galileo, Prosatori del Cinquecento, Prosatori del Seicento, F, D'Anna, 1996–97, is available on diskette, in hypertext format.

Beer, *Saggi,* includes a discussion of the innovations and complexities of dialogue structure as well as the literary and philosophical background to Guazzo's *Civil Conversazione. Sondaggi sulla riscrittura del Cinquecento,* ed. Paolo Cherchi, Ravenna, Longo, 157 pp., offers new insights into the creative process. An essay by A. Quondam on imitation and plagiarism in classicism is followed by studies of plagiarism in Franco, Doni, Dolce, Fioravanti, L. P. Rosello, Garzoni, E. Tasso, and A. Farra. Claudio Giovanardi, *La teoria cortegiana e il dibattito linguistico nel primo Cinquecento*, Ro, Bulzoni, 275 pp., identifies the features of a proposed Roman courtly language 'basata su una varietà toscaneggiante e tuttavia non del tutto toscanizzata, quale dovette apparire il cosidetto "romanesco di seconda fase" '. Annick Paternoster, *Aptum. Retorica ed ermeneutica nel dialogo rinascimentale del primo Cinquecento*, Ro, Bulzoni, 276 pp., sets out to examine the methodological links between *rhetorica docens* and *rhetorica utens* and the tradition of humanist dialogue with a detailed study of Bembo and Aretino. *Posthomerica I. Traduzioni omeriche dall'antichità al Rinascimento*, ed. F. Montanari and S. Pittalunga, Genoa U.P., 1997, 157 pp., has an article by R. Fabbri on the development of Greek studies in the 15th c. that traces the theoretical stances taken with regard to Homer and the stylistic experimentation in the translations of the Iliad. *Traduire et adapter à la Renaissance,* ed. Dominique de Courcelles, Paris, École des Chartes, 142 pp., contains six essays which explore the ways in which texts were translated, copied, transferred, and adapted across national language boundaries. The topics covered include the internal difficulties in Poliziano's creative process inherent in his use of Latin, Greek, and the vernacular, and the way translations from the Italian had much to do with commercial concerns. *Regards sur la Renaissance italienne. Mélanges de litterature offerts à Paul Larivaille*, ed. Marie-Françoise Piéjus, Nanterre, Paris X U.P., 474 pp., has 35 essays that sustain a high level of scholarship. There are sections on politics and philosophy, Aretino, Machiavelli, chivalric literature, theatre, Tasso, and aesthetics. Katia Marano, *Apoll und Marsyas*, Bern, Lang, 222 pp., points to concern with hubris in literary interpretations of the myth, whereas in the visual arts it was treated in a fundamentally different manner. Bernadine Barnes, *Michelangelo's Last Judgement. The Renaissance Response*, Berkeley, California U.P., 171 pp., examines the works of Aretino, Lomazzo, Vasari, Dolce, Varchi, Gilio, and Paleotti, to identify what visual images meant to a contemporary audience and the artist's awareness of this audience. Giancarlo Mazzacurati, *Rinascimento in transito 1528–1532*, Ro, Bulzoni, 1996, 231 pp., includes an essay on Alemanni which examines the social and cultural changes in Florence after the Medici restoration and how Alemanni had to refashion his activities to be employable as *poeta di corte*. *The Search for a Patron in the Middle Ages and the Renaissance*, ed. David G. and Rebecca L. Wilkins, Lampeter, Mellen, 1996, 264 pp., has 13 essays including a study of the relationship between L. de' Medici, Botticelli, and Landino's commentary on Dante, and an analysis of the way in which Salviati communicated the propaganda of Cosimo I and how this was related to the histories of Florence written after 1540. *With and without the Medici. Studies in Tuscan Art and Patronage 1434–1530*, ed. Eckart Marchand and Alison Wright, Aldershot, Ashgate, 187 pp., comprises seven studies, which include the editors' thorough historical essay on the difficulty of separating cultural or artistic patronage from political patronage, a discussion of the links between the Medici and the Lanfredini families, and an assessment of the possible influence of antique Bacchic saracophagi on poets, musicians, and artists associated with L. de' Medici. *Concepts of Beauty in Renaissance Art*, ed. Francis Ames-Lewis and Mary Rogers, Aldershot, Ashgate, 258 pp., comprises 16 essays on topics which include: the theorists' view of the relationship between *bellezza, gratia,* and the beauty of craftsmanship; the impact of Ficino's writings on the evolution of different theories of aesthetics; and the instance of the artist as beauty in Vasari's *Vite*; the treatment of movement in Vasari, Dolce, Lomazzo, Bembo, and Castiglione, and the different connotations of the terms *grazia* and *leggiadria*. D. S. Chambers, *Individuals and Institutions in Renaissance Italy*, Aldershot, Ashgate, 389 pp., is a collection of 16 articles, most already published, covering educational institutions, Mantua, Venice, spas, English connections with Italy, and papal elections. The two new studies are on protonotary Francesco Gonzaga and Marin Sanudo.

FEMINISM AND WOMEN'S STUDIES. *The Feminist Encyclopedia of Italian Literature*, ed. Rinaldina Russell, Westport CT, Greenwood, 1997, x + 402 pp., gives a different slant on the major literary figures, movements, and genres as it focuses on aspects which are usually ignored. *Gender and Society in Renaissance Italy*, ed. Judith C. Brown and Robert C. Davis, London, Longman, xi + 255 pp., is a collection of 10 essays that explore the advantages and limitations of gender as an analytical tool. The high standard of scholarship and analysis gives a new and authoritative perspective on themes such as medical practice, sexuality, religious reform, and art history. The entry of women into male-dominated professions is explored in Orietta Pinessi, *Sofonisba Anguissola, un 'pittore' alla corte di Filippo II*, Mi, Selene, 111 pp. *Picturing Women in Renaissance and Baroque Italy*, ed. Geraldine A. Johnson and Sara F. Matthews Grieco, CUP, 1997, xiv + 321 pp., comprises nine essays which examine women as subjects, producers, patrons, and viewers of art. Of particular note are J. M. Musacchio on image magic and mediating devices to encourage the conception of heirs, and S. F. Matthews Grieco's study of moralizing broadsheets and wayward women in Counter-Reformation Italy. Catherine E. King, *Renaissance Women Patrons*, MUP, 272 pp., examines a number of treatises to extrapolate the advice given about the education of women and about what a woman should and could concern herself with in terms of patronage. Cristelle L. Baskins, *Cassone Painting,*

Humanism and Gender in Early Modern Italy, CUP, 264 pp., limits itself to panels (primarily based on texts by Virgil, Livy, and vernacular sources) showing female protagonists from the ancient world and seeks to understand the motives of the readers and spectators. It claims that 'the expanded narrative treatment characteristic of painted wedding chests allow viewers to test well-worn tropes and to cross clearly delineated iconographic boundaries'.

BIBLIOGRAPHY, PRINTING, AND PUBLISHING. *Bibliografia generale italiana dal secolo 15 al 1997*, Munich, Saur, CD-ROM, contains over 600,000 records which cover classical and modern literature, scholarly publications, conference proceedings, reference books and periodicals. Alfredo Serrai, *Storia della Bibliografia*, VIII: *Sistemi e tassonomie*, ed. Marco Menato, Ro, Bulzoni, 1997, 836 pp., marks the end of this valuable project and deals with the problems of how material was classified and organized for public consultation. Anna Bosco and Luca Seravalle, *I manoscritti della Biblioteca Chelliana di Grosseto. Catalogo*, 1, Grosseto, Biblioteca Chelliana, 197 pp., has a useful introduction followed by a full description of 188 MSS with appropriate indexes. The collection includes works by Acciaiuoli, L. Benucci, and Petrarch. *I manoscritti del fondo Certosa di Calci nella Biblioteca Medicea Laurenziana di Firenze*, ed. Giovanna Murano, F, Regione Toscana, 1996, 109 pp. + 21 pls, is a description of the MSS moved from the island of Gorgona to Florence in 1972. The introduction looks at the contents of the collection and the activities of the scriptorium.

A number of studies have full critical apparatus. *Gli incunaboli della Biblioteca Fardelliana*, ed. Margherita Giacalone and Maria Rosaria Mercadante, Trapani, Biblioteca Fardelliana, 82 pp., is a beautifully produced volume with a catalogue of 125 books and essays on the cultural and intellectual climate in Trapani that led to the development of private and religious libraries; on the humanist G. F. Pugnatore; and on the incunable collection and the illuminations. Cristina Moro, *Gli incunaboli delle biblioteche ecclesiastiche di Udine*, Udine, Forum, xviii + 268 pp., traces the evolution of the Seminario, Arcivescovile, Bartoliniana, and Capitolare libraries with details of 190 books. Marina Bonomelli and Ivanoe Riboli, *Le cinquecentine della Raccolta Molli, conservate alla Fondazione 'Achille Marazza' di Borgomanero*, II: *Edizioni di Venezia*, Borgomanero, Fond. Achille Marazza, 1997, 248 pp., is the final volume of the series and lists 352 works. Marco Ferri, *Edizioni del XVI secolo nel Fondo Mabellini, Biblioteca Federiciana di Fano*, Fano, Regione Marche, 108 pp., lists 226 volumes accompanied by an essay by F. Battistelli which traces the origins of printing in Fano and the development of the Biblioteca Comunale. Rosario Carrara, Lina Loglio, and Giovanni Spinelli, *Le cinquecentine della*

Biblioteca S. Giacomo di Pontida, Pontida, San Giorgio Maggiore, 1997, 381 pp., gives a description of 487 books followed by full indexes. In an appendix R. Zilioli Faden deals with incunables and G. Mazzucco with bindings. *Private Libraries in Renaissance England. A Collection and Catalogue of Tudor and Early Stuart Book-Lists*, v, PLRE *113–37*, ed. R. J. Fehrenbach and E. S. Leedham-Green, MRTS, xxxii + 376 pp., continues an excellent project. The lists, taken mainly from probate inventories, give a valuable insight into intellectual interests, purchasing patterns, and availability of texts. Italian authors include: D. Acciaiuoli, Cardano, Della Casa, Castiglione, Machiavelli, Manuzio, Della Porta, and Valla.

   Catalogo delle Biblioteche d'Italia. Toscana, 3 vols, Ro, Istituto Centrale per il Catalogo Unico — Mi, Bibliografica, 1997, 364, 365–745, 746–983 pp., is an indispensable guide for planning research, listing collections, opening hours, and periods of closure. *Aldus Manutius and Renaissance Culture. Essays in Memory of Franklin D. Murphy*, ed. David S. Zeidberg, F, Olschki, 336 pp., comprises 15 studies in four sections. 'Aldus and the Renaissance' has essays on the links between Venetian culture, printing enterprises, and Florence, on the reaction to changing conditions with new strategies for marketing and publicity, and on Bembo's life and links with Manutius. 'Aldus and the classics' looks at the publishing history of the *Epistolae diversorum philosophorum*, the development and acceptance of the Aldine italic, the contribution of the self-enumerated index to religious and intellectual debate, and Aldus and classical scholarship in terms of the number and form of his texts. 'Aldus and the art of the book' covers the links between Aldus, illuminations, and woodcuts, and the possible existence of an Aldine bindery. 'The influence of Aldus' investigates the fortunes and composition of Latin grammars, Paolo Manutius's Tridentine publishing house in Rome, the reception of Aldine books in the New World and Spain, and the changing face of Aldine collecting in France.

   La Bibliofilia, 100, includes O. Ferrari, 'Nuovi documenti per la storia della tipografia padovana del '400' (1–25); A. Tura, 'Sull'anno di stampa di due edizioni di Ripoli' (43–46); and P. Bellettini, 'Sugli *Annali della tipografia cesenate* di Franco Fioravanti' (47–82). Angela Nuovo, *Il commercio librario a Ferrara tra XV e XVI secolo. La bottega di Domenico Sivieri*, F, Olschki, xxix + 303 pp. + 8 pls, is a well-researched study of one of the most important humanist centres which, though it had the right conditions for the setting up of a vigorous printing industry, was faced with great difficulties due to the activities of Venetian booksellers who imported Venetian texts rather than selling local imprints. The second part of the study comprises an inventory and a critical description of 426 items. Angela Nuovo, *Il commercio librario dell'Italia del Rinascimento*, Mi, Angeli, 287 pp., continues the high quality of scholarship of the previous study and is particularly illuminating on the subject of book fairs, the evolution of the book trade, and book catalogues. Ugo Rozzo, *Lo studiolo nella silografia italiana (1479–1558)*, Udine, Forum, 145 pp., is a fascinating study of *'il luogo dei libri'* which shows how an iconographical analysis can make a significant contribution to the study of books, printing, and the rise of libraries. *Le Pouvoir des livres à la Renaissance*, ed. Dominique de Courcelles, Paris, École des Chartes, 156 pp., contains eight essays examining libraries, prefaces, dedications, and the works of the early translators. *Piante e vedute di Napoli dal 1486 al 1599*, ed. Ermanno Bellucci, Na, Electa, 95 pp., is an important contribution to our understanding of the printing and publishing process, and the methodology behind creating an image of the city, with descriptions of 26 maps.

A number of studies deal with bindings. Francesco Malaguzzi, *De libris compactis. Legature di pregio in Piemonte: il Vercellese*, T, Centro Studi Piemontesi, 148 pp. + 134 pls, has a scholarly introduction that reviews binderies, bindings, bibliophiles, and libraries. Id., *De libris compactis. Legature di pregio in Piemonte: il Biellese*, T, Centro Studi Piemontesi, 1996, 174 pp. + 127 pls. (*Il Canavese* was published in 1995.) P. F. Gehl, 'Describing (and selling) bindings in sixteenth-century Florence', *ISt*, 53 : 38–51. *Legature bolognesi del Rinascimento*, ed. Anthony R. A. Hobson and Leonardo Quaquarelli, Bo, CLUEB, 122 pp. + 60 pls, deals with early 15th- and 16th-c. binders, bindings, and clients, followed by a full description and illustrations of the bindings.

2. HUMANISM.

Poggio Bracciolini, *De infelicitate principum*, ed. Davide Canfora, Ro, Storia e Letteratura, cl + 79 pp., is a critical edition with a scholarly introduction that traces the development of Bracciolini's ideas, the influences that helped to shape the dialogue, and how it related to events at the court of Pope Eugenius IV. Jacopo Ammannati Piccolomini, *Lettere (1444–1479)*, ed. Paolo Cherubini, 3 vols, Ro, Ministero per i Beni Culturali e Ambientali, 1997, 494, 495–1401, 1402–2408 pp., is a monumental critical edition, with a scholarly introduction, of one of the richest collections of letters left by a humanist which range far beyond the strictly biographical. Platina, *On Right Pleasure and Good Health*, ed. Mary Ella Milham, MRTS, 511 pp., is a critical edition and translation of the *De honesta voluptate et valetudine*. The introduction shows how Platina did not slavishly follow any previous ancient genre and used 'dialectal Italian as well as borrowings and adaptations from other languages'. Luisa Pesavento, *L'umanista e il principe. La 'vita ducum' di Pietro Lazzaroni*, Pisa, ETS, 1997, 268 pp., gives the Latin text, with detailed commentary and notes preceded by a scholarly introduction, of an encomiastic work by a Lombard humanist dealing with the aspirations, functions, and cultural activities of learned men. Leon Battista Alberti, *De statua*, ed. Marco Collareta, Livorno, Sillabe, 54 pp., gives the Latin with translation, followed by an essay that examines Alberti's idea of 'image-making' and his emphasis on the intellectual as opposed to the manual aspect of artistic production, and on the rational nature of art. Marc van der Poel, *Cornelius Agrippa the Humanist Theologian and his Declamations*, Leiden, Brill, xiv + 303 pp., is a well-documented and argued study stressing the importance of understanding A.'s Neoplatonism in order to make sense of the seemingly disparate topics he addressed, and maintaining that, despite his fierce polemical nature and anti-scholastic stance, he stood for tolerance. *Pietro Andrea Mattioli, Siena 1501 – Trento 1578. La vita, le opere*, ed. Sara Ferri, Perugia, Quattroemme, 1997, 405 pp., comprises 21 studies which cover M.'s multifarious career as humanist, poet, doctor, cartographer, writer on secrets and alchemy, student of natural history, and translator of Dioscorides. Giovanni Iorio, *Dal Trecento al Cinquecento*, Cassino, Garigliano, 1996, 167 pp., gathers seven essays dealing with Alberti, humanism, antiquity, and the development of new modes of expression, and reassessing Filetico on education, culture, and poetry. *Storia dell'architettura italiana. Il Quattrocento*, ed. Francesco Paolo Fiore, Mi, Electa, 562 pp., includes an excellent essay by H. Burns which examines the way in which Alberti's philological method was applied to the grammar, language, and theology of Valla, the influence of Flavio Biondo, and Alberti's archeological methodology for reconstructing the past. A new journal dedicated to Alberti, *Albertiana*, 1, comprises ten studies on topics which include: A.'s constant innovative dialogue with antiquity and new way of investigating sources; the *Zuffa tra mostri marini*, epigraphy, and humanist classical studies; A.'s winged eye and Cosimo Bartoli; classical and medieval elements in the *Ludi matematici*; the concept of man in the *Momus*; editions, MSS, and copyists of A.'s Italian works. D. Pietragalla, 'La fortuna dei *Rerum gestarum Alfonsi regis libri* di Bartolommeo Facio. Stampe, lettori, volgarizzamenti', *ASI*, 156:257–91. A. Maranini, ' "L'ordo historicus" di Bargeo', *SUm*, 1:39–65, shows that Pietro Angeli da Barga had a mnemonic end in mind when compiling his list of Greek and Roman writers. B. Mitrovic, 'Paduan Aristotelianism and Daniele Barbaro's commentary on Vitruvius' *De Architectura*', *SCJ*, 29:667–88. D. J. Murphy, 'Greek epigrams and manuscripts of Damiano Guidotto of Venice', *RenS*, 12:476–94.

E. M. Duso, 'Un nuovo manoscritto esemplato da Felice Feliciano', *LItal*, 50:566–86. G. Ianziti, 'Bruni on writing history', *RQ*, 51:367–91. R. Righi, '*Otium* e *negotium*: i due poli dell'inconscio bembiano', *SPCT*, 56:95–117. Anne Reynolds, *Renaissance Humanism at the court of Clement VII. Francesco Berni's 'Dialogue against Poets' in Context*, NY, Garland, 1997, 400 pp., assesses the influence and activities of Giberti, Sanga, Calvo, and Aretino as well as the cultural, social, and political undercurrents at the papal court. W. H. Woodward, *Vittorino da Feltre and other Humanist Educators*, Toronto U.P., 1997, xxviii + 261 pp., is a welcome reprint with a new foreword. Patrick Gilli, *Au miroir de l'humanisme. Les représéntations de la France dans la culture savante italienne à la fin du moyen âge*, École Française de Rome, 1997, 638 pp., explores: the language and images used by Pius II in his attempts to foster interest in the crusade against the Turks; the distinction drawn by Italians between Gauls and Latin peoples; the invention, popularity, and political ramifications of the legend of Charlemagne; the historiographical activity of the humanists and the French dimension in their histories; the consequences of the failure by French rulers to cultivate humanist historiography in their favour. Virginio Longoni, *Umanesimo e Rinascimento in Brianza*, Mi, Electa, 73 pp., consists of well-documented archival studies divided into three parts: *La cultura*, *I cantieri*, and *Gli artisti*. Of particular interest is the first section, which examines the development of grammar schools, the curriculum, and the humanist teachers. Vittore Branca, *La sapienza civile. Studi sull'umanesimo a Venezia*, F, Olschki, xix + 316 pp., is a rich feast of 18 studies on humanism centring on the figure of Ermolao Barbaro, 14 of them already published. The topics covered include the political and cultural interests of Barbaro's circle; *l'umanesimo volgare* in Bembo; Lauro Quirini, commerce, and humanist books; G. Gardi and Castiglione; and Galileo and Venetian humanism. L. Pertile, 'Plurilinguismo. di Trifon Gabriele — o di Giason Denores', *Lepschy Vol.*, 177–96. Kenneth Gouwens, *Remembering the Renaissance. Humanist Narratives and the Sack of Rome*, Leiden, Brill, xvi + 232 pp., is an important scholarly contribution to understanding the effects of the Sack of Rome on curial humanism and Roman humanist discourse. The writings of Alcionio, Corsi, and Valeriano show how they were forced to reassess the role of papal Rome as cultural arbiter as well as their own identities. C. G. Nauert, 'Humanism as a method: roots of conflict with the scholastics', *SCJ*, 29:427–38. Peter Godman, *From Poliziano to Machiavelli. Florentine Humanism in the High Renaissance*, Princeton U.P., 366 pp., examines the careers, writings, and personalities of Poliziano, M. Adriani, and Machiavelli to reveal an ever-changing social, political, and cultural climate. The study stresses the shared values and uncovers the human dimension, replete with envy and animosity unavoidable in the search for patronage and survival. Antonio Natali, *Andrea del Sarto*, Mi, Leonardo, 218 pp., points to the humanist learning and taste that lay at the heart of Sarto's methodology and emphasizes the links to the aesthetic theories and Ciceronian ethics that developed in 15th-c. Florence. It analyses the notions behind terms such as *gravitas, elegantia*, and *suavitas*, and sees Sarto's lifestyle as being linked to Ciceronian precepts set out in the *De Officiis*. The year's most significant contribution to the Renaissance retrieval and refashioning of antiquity is Giulio Bodon, *Enea Vico fra memoria e miraggio della classicità*, Ro, L'Erma di Bretschneider, 1997, 302 pp. + 303 pls, which sets out with laudable clarity and conciseness Vico's interest in humanist erudition, collecting, and the representation of antiquity. The book is divided into three sections respectively covering his life, his representations via drawings and etchings, and his antiquarian studies. The kind of humanist interest in antiquity that led to a real desire to catalogue, interpret, and reconstruct the past is the subject of Federico Rausa, *Pirro Ligorio: tombe e mausolei dei Romani*, Ro, Quasar, 1997, 155 pp., which investigates L.'s methodology and his links to contemporary antiquarian proccupations, including the tendency to fabricate and to reconstruct, albeit using all available source material. The enigmatic nature of Ligorio's real projects are examined in Enzo Pinci, *Pirro Ligorio opzione per il magico-simbolico*, T, Testo e Immagine, 93 pp., which assesses his methodology in combining classical elements, often derived from coins and medals, with innovations. Ligorio lamented the destruction of the classical heritage while at the same time contributing to it. The preoccupation with archeological studies and collecting can be seen in *Forschungen zur Villa Albani. Katalog der antiken Bildwerke*, v, ed. Peter C. Bol, Berlin, Mann, 678 pp. + 352 pls, which continues a monumental catalogue of antique figure sculpture, masks, reliefs, and inscriptions found at Villa Albani in the gardens and the building itself. How the dialogue with the past that engaged the humanists was also a preoccupation of architects is explored in a number of important studies. E. H. Gombrich et al., *Giulio Romano*, CUP, 338 pp, comprises five essays, including M. Tafuri on how *sprezzatura* and precepts of dissonance and irony in Castiglione may link Giulio's work in Mantua to Rome, and how the 'surpassing of the ancients was the product of representation to the extent of being a fiction'. It proposes that Giulio's art, 'thanks to its eccentricity, can be read as fully humanist: his linguistic games, the dynamic of his contrasts, his own excesses, relativize the myths to which Cinquecento culture entrusted itself'. C. L. Frommel sees Giulio's work as the most coherent manifestation of the classical, though his antiquity is filtered and interpreted: there is borrowing of exquisite detail but no slavish imitation. H. Burns shows how Giulio assimilated the antique from childhood and adapted ancient models in his work, an antique-modern synthesis. The importance of his collection of antique coins and medals is underlined. Christof Thoenes, *Sostegno e adornamento. Saggi sull'architettura del Rinascimento: disegni, ordini, magnificenza*, Mi, Electa, 258 pp., comprises 15 essays, including a perceptive study of Bramante which stresses his appreciation of the impossibility of reproducing classical antiquity and his concern with only imitating '*la bella maniera*'. Another essay questions the whole notion of a rediscovered classical canon regarding the orders, and postulates that 'the classical language' was invented by Alberti, Filarete, Francesco di Giorgio, and Raphael in the 15th c. and by Serlio, Vignola, Palladio, and Scamozzi in the 16th c. *L'architettura civile in Toscana: il Rinascimento*, ed. Amerigo Restucci, Siena, Monte dei Paschi, 1997, 574 pp., is a beautifully produced volume with five essays which examine: the meaning of the term 'civic humanism' and the way in which humanist writing was related to a new concept of the city and its relationship to the citizen; the way new styles and tastes reflected the advice given by humanists; the humanist view of the classical concept of *otium*, and the countryside as seen in Alberti and G. Rucellai. C. Van Eck, 'Giannozzo Manetti on architecture: the *Oratio de secularibus et pontificalibus pompis in consecratione basilicae Florentiae* of 1436', *RenS*, 12 : 449–75. All these studies add a new dimension to our understanding of the nature of 'revived antiquity'. Stephen J. Campbell, *Cosmè Tura of Ferrara: style, politics, and the Renaissance city, 1450–1495*, New Haven, Yale U.P., 207 pp., investigates local humanist cultural values and the writings of L. Carbone, Alberti, and Guarino of Verona to show how Tura's work was aimed at satisfying and embodying these values, particularly in negotiating the relationship between poetry and painting. The calligraphic nature of his style can also be seen as a self-conscious invention linked to manual dexterity and to the audience's expectations. *La biblioteca di un medico del Quattrocento. I codici di Giovanni di Mario da Rimini nella Biblioteca Malatestiana*, ed. Anna Manfron, T, Allemandi, 257 pp., examines the *scrittoio* in Cesena where Giovanni worked. There are four scholarly essays which look at the wide cultural interests of the doctor, his links to humanist circles, the way he built up his collection, and his annotations. Maurizio Bonora, *I tarocchi del Boiardo*, Mantua, Casa del Mantegna, 1997, 35 pp., uses the evidence in the MS of Pier Antonio Vita and humanist court culture to reconstruct the place of the tarot and the allusions and significance of Boiardo's project. V. N. Zabughin, 'Storici bizantini e umanisti italiani (nota critica)', *Intersezioni*, 18 : 341–59. Y. Haskell, 'Renaissance Latin didactic poetry on the stars: wonder, myth and science', *RenS*, 12:495–522, compares the literary devices, classical reflections, and choice of subject matter in Pontano's *Urania*, L. Buonicontri's *De rebus coelestibus*, and G. Buchanan's *Sphaera*. *Rinascimento*, 37, 1997, includes: G. Ianziti, 'Writing from Procopius: Leonardo Bruni's *De bello italico'* (3–27); L. Canfora, 'Tucidide e Machiavelli' (29–44); M. Campanelli, 'Pietro Bembo, Roma e la filologia del tardo Quattrocento: per una lettura del dialogo *De Virgilii culice et Terentii fabulis'* (283–319). Andrea Alciato, *Emblemata, Lyons 1550*, trans. and ann. Betty I. Knott, Aldershot, Scolar Press, 1996, xxx + 226 pp., has a useful introduction by J. Manning followed by a facsimile of the 1550 edition interleaved with English translations of, and notes on, the Latin verse.

PHILOSOPHY AND HISTORY OF IDEAS. Paolo Casini, *L'antica sapienza italiana. Cronistoria di un mito*, Bo, Il Mulino, 373 pp., is an original and enjoyable evaluation of the changing interpretations of the myth of Pythagoras, particularly in the 15th and 16th c., and of its relationship to the idea of a *philosophia perennis*. *L'ermetismo nell'antichità e nel Rinascimento*, ed. Luisa Rotondi Secchi Tarugi, Mi, Nuovi Orizzonti, 240 pp., is a disparate collection which would have benefitted from a clear editorial definition of 'hermeticism'. Mino Gabriele, *Alchimia e iconologia*, Forum, Udine, 1997, 175 pp. + 151 pls, contains 10 studies including the significance of the marble intarsia of Hermes Trismegistus in Siena Cathedral. H. Vredeveld, ' "Hippocrates coitum comitiali morbo similem judicavit": a note on Marsilio Ficino, *De Vita*, I, 7', *BHR*, 60:741. Giovanni Pico della Mirandola, *On the Dignity of Man, On Being and the One, Heptaplus*, trans. Charles Glenn Wallis, Paul J. W. Miller, and Douglas Carmichael, Indianapolis, Hackett, 174 pp., is a reprint of the 1965 translation in an inexpensive edition with a new, if totally inadequate, bibliography. *Giovanni Pico della Mirandola*, ed. Gian Carlo Garfagnini, 2 vols, F, Olschki, 1997, lv + 349 pp., 350–721 pp., assembles 43 essays that cover humanist anthropology, Christian doctrine and the Heptaplus, Pico and late 15th-c. Aristotelianism, and the double inquest on the *Conclusiones*, Cabbalistic magic, Giovanni and Gianfrancesco Pico and Savonarola, P.'s early poetry and his works in the *volgare*, and his Hebrew books. *Giovanni e Gianfrancesco Pico. L'opera e la fortuna di due studenti ferraresi*, ed. Patrizia Castelli, F, Olschki, 368 pp., comprises 18 essays on such diverse topics as: the mythologizing of the figure of Giovanni by the humanists; his *filosofia della poesia* in the *Commento*; the extent of his use of cabbalistic sources in the *Conclusiones*; the Greek, Latin, patristic, biblical, and Hebrew sources of the *Disputationes*; his interpretation of Plato's *Parmenides* and the influence of the *Commento*; and his fortunes and reception. Vico Allegretti, *Esegesi medievale e umanesimo. L'Heptaplus di Giovanni Pico della Mirandola*, Ravenna,

Girasole, 1997, 94 pp., is a well-researched study of both sources and methodology which points to the medieval respect for *traditio* and *auctoritas* and offers a new perspective on Renaissance exegesis. Giovan Battista Della Porta, *Le zifare o della scrittura segreta*, ed. Raffaele Lucariello, Na, Filema, 1996, 92 pp., reproduces Book 16 of the *Della Magia Naturale*, taking into account the textual variations of the 1611 and 1677 editions. The introduction gives an assessment of Della Porta's methodology. Nicola Cusano, *La caccia della sapienza*, ed. Graziella Federici Vescovini, Casale Monferrato, Piemme, 162 pp., is a translation of the *De venatione sapientiae*, written in 1432, which deals with the distinction between knowledge and wisdom. Lorraine Daston and Katherine Park, *Wonders and the Order of Nature 1150–1750*, NY, Zone Books, 511 pp., looks at the social, political, and religious interpretations of Nature, and the use made of unusual and imagined natural phenomena. Nancy G. Siriasi, *The Clock and the Mirror. Girolamo Cardano and Renaissance Medicine*, Princeton U.P., 1997, xiv + 361 pp., investigates C.'s belief in astral powers and the attention he paid to the regularities of the heavenly clock. It also gives a clear analysis of the theme of medical self-examination in his *Vita* and how this fits into the work's structure. Gianluigi Magoni, *Le cose non dette sui Decani di Schifanoia. Una lettura astronomica*, Ferrara, Corbo, 1997, 110 pp., casts some new light on the significance of the Decani, which are seen as reproducing forms of constellations or star clusters. The most important publication this year on magic is Richard Kieckhefer, *Forbidden Rites. A Necromancer's Manual of the Fifteenth Century*, University Park, Pennsylvania State U.P., 384 pp., which has an excellent introduction discussing the MS, the purpose (for entertainment, power, and knowledge), the sources, and the techniques necessary for magic, followed by the Latin text. Claire Fanger, *Conjuring Spirits: Texts and Traditions of Medieval Ritual Magic*, University Park, Pennsylvania State U.P., xviii + 284 pp., makes a compelling case for a reassessment of the extent and nature of this tradition, which underlies later developments in the early modern period. Stuart Clark, *Thinking with Demons. The Idea of Witchcraft in Early Modern Europe*, OUP, xvii + 827 pp., is a fundamental study that mines the writings of the demonologists to reveal how their ideas were part of current developments and stances in other areas of intellectual and cultural debate. The study stresses the historical longevity of, and the linguistic options available for, demonological theory, and argues that 'by taking up the intellectual positions they did, witchcraft authors were [. . .] declining to take up others'. Renzo Beltrame, *La prospettiva rinascimentale. Nascita di un fatto cognitivo*, Ro, Società Stampa Sportiva, 1996, 119 pp., seeks to clarify the mathematical basis of Brunelleschi's and Alberti's theories and speculates on why three-dimensional perspective appeared in 15th-c. Florence.

BRUNO. Anna Foa, *Giordano Bruno*, Bo, Il Mulino, 107 pp., traces the way in which Bruno came to symbolize freedom of thought. *Rinascimento*, 37, 1997, includes: E. Scapone, 'Giordano Bruno e la composizione del *De Vinculis*' (155–231); and N. Tirinnanzi, 'Giordano Bruno e i tipografi londinesi' (437–58). G. Candela, 'An overview of the cosmology, religion and philosophical universe of Giordano Bruno', *Italica*, 75:348–64. G. Aquilecchia, 'Giordano Bruno', pp. 325–68 of *Storia della letteratura italiana*, ed. Enrico Malato, Ro, Salerno, 1997, is a major contribution from the foremost present-day Bruno scholar. Id., 'Sonetti bruniani e sonetti elisabettiani (per una comparazione metrico-tematica)', *FAM*, 11, 1996:27–34. Id., 'Bruno at Oxford. Between Aristotle and Copernicus', pp. 117–24 of *Giordano Bruno 1583 - 1585: The English Experience / L'esperienza inglese. Atti del Convegno (Londra, 3–4 giugno 1994)*, ed. Michele Ciliberto and Nicholas Mann, F, Olschki, 1997. Id., 'L'ecdotica ottocentesca delle opere italiane di Bruno', pp. 1–17 of *Brunus redivivus. Momenti della fortuna di Giordano Bruno nel XIX secolo*, ed. Eugenio Canone, Pisa–Ro, Istituti Editoriali e Poligrafici Internazionali, 1997. Giordano Bruno, *De la causa, principio et uno*, introd., trans., and ann. Morimichi Kato, Tokyo, Toshindo, is a Japanese edition based on the critical text established by G. Aquilecchia in his recent Belles Lettres edition.

RELIGIOUS THOUGHT AND THE CHURCH. *Carlo Borromeo e l'opera della 'Grande Riforma'. Cultura, religione e arti del governo nella Milano del primo Cinquecento*, ed. Franco Buzzi and Danilo Zardin, Cinisello Balsamo, Silvana, 1997, 383 pp., investigates how a new religious and social message was transmitted. It gives an analysis of the propagandistic use of the popular press, the contribution of music, and the place of celebrations and festivities to promote particular religious agenda. It also examines the contents of Borromeo's library, investigates the linguistic elements in his prose, and his influence on the fine arts. Massimo Firpo and Dario Marcatto, *I processi inquisitoriali di Pietro Carnesecchi (1557–1567). Edizione critica*, I: *I processi sotto Paolo IV e Pio V (1557–1561)*, Ro, Archivio Segreto Vaticano, cxix + 577 pp., in its scholarly introduction draws on material in the Archivio del Sant'Ufficio for an account of the charges brought against Carnesecchi and the various stages of the trial. A. Prosperi, 'Una esperienza di ricerca nell'Archivio del Sant'Uffizio', *Belfagor*, 53:309–45, discusses the problems raised by the newly accessible material. *Suspended License. Censorship and the Visual Arts*, ed. Elizabeth C. Childs, Seattle, Washington U.P., 1997, 422 pp., is a collection of 12 essays including studies of Aretino and the censorship of Michelangelo's *Last Judgement*, and of the Inquisitors' suspicions that Veronese's work might be crypto-Protestant and an attack on the doctrines of the Church. B. Peria, 'Tintoretto e l'"ultima cena"', *Venezia Cinquecento*, 13:79–139, reveals an iconography that dealt with fundamental theological issues.

SAVONAROLA.   The quincentenary of S.'s death has been marked by a number of studies. Eugenio Garin et al., 'Frate Girolamo Savonarola e il suo Movimento', *Memorie Dominicane*, 29, 715 pp., is a rich, well-balanced collection of 24 essays that include studies of prophecy and of S. and Lorenzo de' Medici; analyses of the *Apologeticus de ratione poeticae artis;* essays on S.'s influence in Lucca, on anti-Savonarolan texts, on S. and Dominican reform in the South of Italy, on Savonarolan iconography, and on De Sanctis and Savonarola. 'Libri di vita, libri di studio, libri di governo: Savonarola e Giorgio Antonio Vespucci', *Memorie Domenicane*, 28, 1997, contains 10 essays including an in-depth study of the MS tradition of the *Tratado de Milagros* attributed to S., a catalogue of the Greek and Latin books in the *scrittoio* and library of the humanist scholar and teacher G. A. Vespucci, an investigation into the diffusion of G. F. Pico's *Vita Savonarolae*, and a biography of Vespucci. *Savonarola e la politica*, ed. Gian Carlo Garfagnini, F, Sismel, 197, 269 pp., comprises 14 studies divided into four sections 'Il pensiero politico' (devoted to analyses of the prophetic/political sermons to show S.'s insistence on the necessity of the political act); 'L'assetto istituzionale: influenze e mutamenti' (on the changes in the administration of the state during his period of influence); 'La (ri)organizzazione della società' (on the impact of charitable institutions and S.'s struggles with, and manipulation of, the pre-existing political and social structures). The last section deals with the rediscovered autograph of the *Sermones in primam divi Joannis Epistolam. Savonarola: democrazia, tirannide, profezia*, ed. Gian Carlo Garfagnini, F, Sismel, 312 pp., is an excellent collection of 14 essays covering the problems of interpreting S.'s political and social messages, the role of prophecy and the problem of tyranny, war in S.'s preaching, S. and the Florentine republican tradition, Machiavelli on S.'s political activity, S. and the public dimension of tyrannicide, S. as ideologue and prophet, contemporary views of the political reasons behind the trials of S. and his followers, and interpretations of S. in the age of Cosimo I. *Savonarole: enjeux, débats, questions*, ed. Anna Fontes, Jean-Louis Fournel, and Michel Plaisance, Paris, Sorbonne Nouvelle, 1997, 322 pp., comprises essays on S.'s preference for coalitions in reaching consensus for political action, and on the burning of the vanities and a new concept of carnival; a philological study of D. Benivieni's *Dialogo della verità della dottrina* which highlights the prophetic themes and the relationship between the clergy and the faithful; discussion of the contrasting theories concerning the soul in S. and Ficino; analysis of the documentation of S.'s trial; and studies of the attacks on, and defence of, S. after the Medici restoration, of the translation and editing of G. F. Pico's *Vita Savonarolae*, and of S. and G. F. Pico and the use of scepticism in a reassessment of Ficino's philosophical positions. Girolamo Savonarola, *Apologetico. Indole e natura dell'arte poetica*, ed. Antonino Stagnitta, Ro, Armando, 111 pp., is a translation of the *Apologeticus de ratione poeticae artis* with a thorough introduction that explores the link between content and language and emphasizes the importance of the text for understanding the psychology of Savonarola. Id., *Fede e speranza di un profeta*, ed. Adriana Valerio, Mi, Paoline, 213 pp., gives a good outline of S.'s religious and social ideas followed by a selection of writings. Id., '*Sermones in primam divi Joannis epistolam*', *secondo l'autografo. Testo latino con traduzione italiana fronte*, ed. Armando F. Verde and Elettra Giaconi, F, Sismel, xxxii + 312 pp., is a critical edition including a useful index of sources with an introduction that traces the history of the MS, analyses the themes, and takes issue with recent critical opinion on the question of S.'s belief in his power to 'trasformare il cuore degli uomini'. *Catalogo delle edizioni di Girolamo Savonarola (secc. XV-XVI) possedute dalla Biblioteca Nazionale Centrale di Firenze*, ed. Piero Scapecchi, F, Sismel, xxxix + 72 pp., has an introduction discussing the early printers of the texts in Florence and other centres and sets out the genesis of the Nazionale's collection with two appendices. It lists the books sold in 1855, details the contents of the Carteggio Capponi, and provides a list of works with full critical apparatus. Giovanfrancesco Pico della Mirandola, *Vita di Hieronimo Savonarola (volgarizzamento anonimo)*, ed. Raffaella Castagnola, F, Sismel, xxxiii + 98 pp., reproduces the text with linguistic and historical notes. A preface by G. C. Garfagnini offers possible reasons for the paucity of G. Pico studies and examines the compositional history of the text and its theme of prophecy. The introduction compares the Italian version to the Latin original and discusses the picture painted of Savonarola. Armando Verde and Donald Weinstein, *Savonarola: la vita, le opere*, Venice, Marsilio, 89 pp., gives a useful chronology and extracts from S.'s writings. It includes essays examining S.'s call for a life of Christian virtue which would renew the Church and make Florence prosperous and free, and the heated debate over S. that started during his lifetime and which still rages. A. F. Verde and E. Giaconi, 'Convento S. Marci florentiae', *Rinascimento*, 37, 1997:67–154. Angelo da Valombrosa, *Lettere*, ed. Loredana Lunetta, F, Olschki, 1997, xxx + 123 pp., presents correspondence which contributes much to an understanding of the Savonarola controversy by documenting the shift from positive to negative attitudes. Andrea Drigani and Raimondo Sorgia, *Savonarola eretico o 'santo contestatore'*, Mi, Paoline, 233 pp., stresses the positive religious aspects of the Savonarolan moment and the lasting value of his teaching. Ivan Cloulas, *Savonarola o la rivoluzione di Dio*, Casale Monferrato, Piemme, 437 pp., is a well-written biography. Paolo Luotto, *Il vero Savonarola e il Savonarola di L. Pastor*, F, Sismel, xvi + 622 pp., is the second edition, with a new preface, of a study first published in 1900 which disagreed with Pastor's conclusions. It pointed out that S.'s ideas were very close to Thomism and that, accordingly, his actions were orthodox and justified. Felice Tocco, *Savonarola profeta e ribelle*, ed. Fulvio De Giorgi, Genoa, Marietti, 146 pp., examines the positions taken on S. in the 19th and 20th c. (centred on the figure of Tocco himself) and also includes two essays on S. and Contarini.

3. POETRY.

D. Looney, *Compromising the Classics: Romance Epic Narrative in the Italian Renaissance*, Wayne State U.P., Detroit, 1996, 244 pp. attempts to understand the evolution of the romance epic in the three acknowledged masters (Ariosto, Boiardo, and Tasso) by examining the combined influence of classical sources, Renaissance humanism, and the demands of contemporary culture. S. Jossa, *Rappresentazione e scrittura. La crisi delle forme poetiche rinascimentali (1540–1560)*, Na, Istituto Italiano per gli Studi Filosofici – Vivarium, 1996, 373 pp., with direct reference to contemporary texts and criticism, especially G. B. Giraldi and S. Speroni, illuminates the 'profondo conflitto ideologico', which for him governed the debate on poetics and poetic form (1540–50). *Le varie fila. Studi di letteratura italiana in onore di Emilio Bigi*, ed. Fabio Danelon, Hermann Grosser, and Cristina Zampese, Mi, Principato, 1997, 352 pp., commemorates Bigi's 80th birthday with contributions ranging from the 13th to the 20th c. The section on the 16th c. is particularly rich, including: C. Zampese, 'Considerazioni sul primo libro degli *Amori* di Bernardo Tasso' (74–95), which looks at the Petrarchan influences on the sonnets first published at Venice in 1531; A. D. Piovano, 'Le edizioni cinquecentesche degli scritti di Olimpia Fulvia Morata' (96–111), concerning a Ferrarese writer who before her premature death in 1555 completed dialogues, Latin translations, and Greek epigrams; A. G. S. Galbiati, 'Un poeta satirico del Cinquecento: Giovanni Agostino Caccia' (112–34); H. Grosser, ' "Semplice gravità" o stile della tragedia nei *Discorsi* del Tasso' (135–49), where the author, pre-empting a work already begun on the *Torrismondo*, focuses on Tasso's style in order to 'chiarire meglio gli orientamenti teorici del Tasso in materia di stile tragico nel lasso di tempo che intercorre tra la stesura dei *Discorsi sull'arte poetica* e quella dei *Discorsi sul poema eroico*'. **Per Cesare Bozzetti. Studi di letteratura e filologia italiana*, ed. Simon Albanico et al., Mi, Fond. Mondadori, 1996, xvi + 746 pp., has a section on 15th–16th-c. poetry which contains a number of notable articles which include: A. T. Benvenuti, 'Ruggiero e la fabbrica dell'*Innamorato de Orlando*', considering Ruggiero the epicentre of Boiardo's poem and linking it to contemporary works like *Aspromonte, Spagna,* and *Borsias,* while C. Mazzoleni examines the *Rime* of G. G. Trissino particularly through the last MS which predates the first edition of 1529; and S. Longhi and G. Rabani proposing two readings of *Baldus*: the first, 'Le muse del *Baldus*', reviewing *topoi* connecting the work to models stretching from Dante to Ariosto and the second, 'Tra Rinaldo e Orlando: sul *Baldus* di Folengo', tracing the marked affinities between the *Baldus* and the *Furioso*. In the 16th-c. section O. Grande, 'Curzio Gonzaga e le sue opere', provides a thorough yet succinct account of G.'s life and verse, especially his epic poem *Fidamante*, while several articles focus upon the two Tassos. R. Cremante, 'Appunti sulle rime di Bernardo Tasso', looks at the *Amori* of 1531; C. Saletti, 'Un sodalizio poetico: Bernardo Tasso e Antonio Brocardo', examines the two authors' experiments with the pastoral in the 1520s; L. Poma, 'Un lungo equivoco storico: la stampa Osanna della *Liberata*', heralds the much-awaited critical edition of the text and also proves by detailed textual analysis that S. Gonzaga organized the Mantuan publication of T.'s poem in 1584; and finally C. Dionisotti reviews the considerable Basile-Marchand edition of the *Rime* of Tebaldeo which seeks to overturn Croce's dismissal of him as 'poeta nullo' by restoring his reputation as critic, philologist, and Latin poet. Dionisotti's one criticism, however, is that greater significance was not accorded the contemporary local influences upon Tebaldeo and his work. A range of scholarly articles in Bodo Guthmüller, *Mito, poesia, arte. Saggi sulla tradizione ovidiana nel Rinascimento*, Ro, Bulzoni, 1997, lxxii + 355 pp., demonstrates how Ovid's *Metamorphoses* were an unparalleled source-book in both the Middle Ages and Renaissance, including: 'Concezioni del mito antico intorno al 1500' (37–64); and 'Le *Metamorfosi* di Ovidio in forma di romanzo' (97–123). N. Gardini, **Le umane parole. L'imitazione nella lirica europea del Rinascimento da Bembo a Ben Johnson*, Mi, Bruno Mondadori, 248 pp., a comparative study of *imitatio* in lyric poetry from 16th-c. Italy to 18th-c. Europe, is based primarily upon three sets of comparisons, Tasso – Ovid, Tasso – Petrarch, and Petrarch – Ovid, which are intended to illustrate in the remaining chapters the gradual overturning of the Petrarchan model. **Gendered Contexts: New Perspectives in Italian Cultural Studies*, ed. L. Benedetti, J. L. Haviston, and S. Ross, NY, Lang, 1996, 221 pp., the result of two conferences held at Johns Hopkins University between 1990 and

1992, looks at questions of gender in Italian literature from Boccaccio's *novelle* to 17th-c. theatre. The 16th-c. lyric is well served by two essays: R. J. Rodini maintains that works by Gaspara Stampa, Vittoria Colonna, Chiara Mattaini, and Michelangelo subvert the Petrarchan model either by cloaking expressions of female sexuality or by having a male addressee as the love object. R.'s argument is complemented by O. Sears, 'Choosing battles? Women's war poetry in Renaissance Italy', which shows how women poets functioned within two contrapuntal traditions being both poet and object of verse. Exploring *commedia dell'arte*, R. Kerr analyses the device of transvestism in three plays (*Li finti servi*, *L'innocente persiana*, and *Il Marito*) showing the complexity of depicting the sexes but particularly using it as a yardstick against which to discuss the parameters of bourgeois capitalism.

ARIOSTO. *Cinque Canti. Five Cantos*, trans. A. Sheers and D. Quint, Berkeley, California U.P., 1996, 349 pp., unlike previous prose translations comes as a parallel text edition. Quint's introduction charts the fortunes of the text while maintaining controversially that, intended as a sequel to the *Furioso*, it is incomplete but not unfinished. The fundamental collaboration between W. Binni and a pupil in Walter Binni, *Metodo e poesia di Lodovico Ariosto e altri studi ariosteschi*, ed. Rosanna Alhaique Pettinelli, F, La Nuova Italia, 1996, 471 pp., produces an invaluable overview of A. criticism. Binni's analysis of its stages is complemented by his pupil's appendix, whose title, 'Linee della critica ariostesca dal 1950 ad oggi' (423–61), indicates its important range. Demarcating the principal stages of research over some 45 years, she isolates the contemporary focus as being 'il versante umanistico della cultura ariostesca'. Stefano Jossa, *La fantasia e la memoria. Intertestualità ariostesche*, Na, Liguori, 1996, 194 pp., gives a highly readable synthesis of all his writings on the *Furioso*, in particular those on the issue of A.'s absorption and transformation of sources: 'Dittologia e aggettivazione: la "forma" della riscrittura' (15–70), 'La "mediazione" dei moderni' (71–124), and 'Stratigrafie ariostesche' (125–74), which identifies Poliziano as a source, thus preparing for the comparative study that concludes the book. The predominant argument of Clare Carroll, *The Orlando Furioso: A Stoic Comedy. The Limits of Theory*, MRTS, 1997, vii + 299 pp., is revealed in the title chosen for the introductory chapter, 'The limits of theory'. She seeks to demonstrate her 'stoic' contention through detailed textual analysis (she provides skilful translations) and by reference to contemporaries (Leonardo and Machiavelli) and to modern criticism (M. Foucault and H. Kenner). E. Saccone, 'Wood, garden, *locus amoenus* in Ariosto's *Orlando Furioso*', *MLN*, 112, 1997:1–20.

BATTIFERRA. In an attempt to break the silence surrounding the career of the most eminent 16th-c. Florentine woman of letters, V. Kirkham, 'Laura Battiferra degli Ammanati's first book of poetry. A Renaissance holograph comes out of hiding', *Rinascimento*, 36:351–92, publishes a collection of 187 poems (including 41 by her famous male correspondents) which shows her not only at the centre of Florentine cultural life but also as Medici propagandist.

BOIARDO. The ten eclogues (composed in 1463–64) that arguably established B.'s reputation as a Latin poet are turned into excellent Italian in Matteo Maria Boiardo, *Pastoralia. Testo critico*, comm. and trans. S. Carrai, Padua, Antenore, 1996, 143 pp. M. Praloran, 'La più tremenda cosa al mondo. L'avventura arturiana nell'*Innamoramento de Orlando*', *La Parola del Testo*, 1, 1997 : 141–57, attempts to trace the Arthurian sources in B.'s poem, especially in the figures of Lancelot, Tristan, Guiran, and Courtois. M. Villoresi, 'Le donne e gli amori nel romanzo cavalleresco del Quattrocento', *FC*, 23:3–43, after a chronological comparison with romances in *ottava rima* such as *L'Ancroia, Il Danese, I Cantari di Rinaldo,* and *L'Altobello,* concludes that the *Innamorato* is an essential point of reference for study not only of female characters, but also the rituals of falling in love, in 15th-c. chivalric literature.

COLONNA. With the discovery of a new manuscript of the *Rime* from the Biblioteca Nazionale Vittorio Emanuele di Napoli, T. B. Toscano, 'La formazione napoletana di Vittoria Colonna e un nuovo manoscritto delle sue *Rime*', *SPCT*, 57:70–106, provides new insights into Colonna the poet, especially in her Ischian years, and opens up the debate regarding her *Rime amorose* in particular.

DELLA CASA. *Per Giovanni Della Casa. Ricerche e contributi. Gargnano del Garda (3–5 ottobre 1996),* ed. Gennaro Barbarisi and Claudia Berra, Mi, Cisalpino, 503 pp., is an important contribution to Della Casa studies. The conference looked at a range of his works beyond the *Galateo*. In a first section devoted to the poetic works, the discussion opens with A. L. Serianni, 'Lingua e stile delle poesie di Giovanni Della Casa' (11–60); G. Tanturli, 'Dai "Fragmenta" al Libro: il testo di inizio nelle rime del Casa e nella tradizione petrarchesca' (61–91), which conducts a close linguistic comparison between Della Casa's *Rime* and Petrarch verse; and G. Dilemmi, 'Giovanni Della Casa e il *nobil cigno:* "a gara" col Bembo' (93–122). His comic and erotic verse is considered in A. Corsaro, 'Giovanni Della Casa poeta comico. Intorno al testo e all'interpretazione dei *Capitoli*' (123–78), and A. Masini, 'La lingua dei *Capitoli*' (179–206). The 16 Latin texts composed between 1551 and 1555 are examined in G. Parenti, 'I carmi latini' (207–40).

MICHELANGELO. Michelangelo, *The Poems*, ed. and trans. Christopher Ryan, London, Dent, 1996, xxxviii + 354 pp., is a highly readable prose translation of M.'s poems. Comprehensive endnotes to each poem complement the facing prose translations in pursuit of the stated aim of 'facilitating direct appreciation of the original'. Christopher Ryan, *The Poetry of Michelangelo. An Introduction*, Madison, Fairleigh Dickinson U.P., xiii + 345 pp., studies the poems in chronological perspective within three main periods.

NANNINI. Remigio Nannini, *Rime*, ed. Domenico Chiodo, pref. G. Bárberi Squarotti, T, RES, 131 pp., reproduces the first edition (1547) of a verse collection ranging well beyond sonnets and madrigals and here given meticulous attention by the editor.

NOGAROLA. R. Rabbani, 'Due sestine di Giovanni Nogarola (ante 1413)', *FC*, 21, 1996:77–95, looks at sestinas by a Veronese scholar born *c.* 1385.

PICO DELLA MIRANDOLA. The analysis offered in Giovanni Pico della Mirandola, **I Sonetti*, ed. G. De Sica, Mi, La Vita Felice, 1996, 96 pp., is concerned with exploring and unravelling the density of meaning in P.'s text. Given that this is the stated objective, additional notes on archaisms and mythological references would have usefully supplemented the prose translation of the original.

PULCI. Luigi Pulci, **Morgante. The Epic Adventures of Orlando and His Great Friend Morgante*, trans. Joseph Tusiani, introd. and ann. Edoardo A. Labano, Bloomington, Indiana U.P., 1104 pp., is a commendable translation of the first Italian Renaissance epic which retains something of the music of the Italian verse while maintaining the pulse of the narrative. It will widen Pulci's appeal to non-Italianists. Mark Davie, *Half-Serious Rhymes: The Narrative Poetry of Luigi Pulci*, Dublin, Irish Academic Press, 323 pp., presents two main arguments: the discrepancy between P.'s penchant for digression and stated desire to push the narrative forward in the *Morgante*, and his successful reworking of material not only in the *Morgante* but also in his lesser works. Id., 'The connotations of *riso, ridere* in Pulci's *Morgante*', *Lepschy Vol.*, 165–76.

TAEGIO. R. Rabbani, 'Apollonio fatto meneghino: da Antonio Pucci a Paolo da Taegio', *LItal*, 50:62–83, traces the fortunes of a chivalric work by Pucci (already existent in an anonymous chivalric tradition), *Cantari di Apollonio di Tiro*, which was recast by the noted 15th-c. Milanese advocate P. da Taegio as *L'Historia de Apollonio de Tiro*, published in Milan in October 1492.

TASSO. A thought-provoking contribution to the creation of T. Tasso's female characters and to the representation of women generally in the Renaissance Epic is provided by M. Migiel, **Gender and Genealogy in Tasso's Gerusalemme Liberata*, Lewiston, Mellen, 223 pp.

Focusing upon the complex lineage of the poem's heroines (Clorinda, Erminia, Sofronia, and Armida), the work is seen no longer in terms of male genealogy but as a poem about 'daughters without fathers or mothers'. This theme is further linked to T.'s problematic relationship with his own father Bernardo, professionally as well as personally. Torquato Tasso, *Discorso della virtù feminile e donnesca*, ed. Maria Luisa Doglio, Palermo, Sellerio, 80 pp., is a new edition of T.'s 1580 essay. Looking at the *Aminta, Rime,* and *Gerusalemme Liberata,* Doglio argues for the modernity of his female figures: 'Il Tasso modifica e sovverte il canone dei trattati del Cinquecento sulla donna sostituendo alle eroine antiche le moderne principesse e facendo di donne vive, note in tutte le corti, i nuovi modelli'. S. Zatti, *L'ombra del Tasso: epica e romanzo nel Cinquecento,* Mi, Bruno Mondadori, 1996, ix + 315 pp., presents a detailed analysis of the influences on Tasso's epic, especially Ariosto and Trissino. L. Benedetti, *La Sconfitta di Diana. Un percorso per la Gerusalemme Liberata,* Ravenna, Longo, 148 pp., presents a rereading of T.'s female characters, both pagan and Christian. Using the goddess Diana as a symbol of female power and autonomy, B. examines the figures of Clorinda, Armida, and Erminia (as well as two Christian couples, Sofronia–Olindo, Gildippe–Odoardo) to demonstrate the negative consequences of the subjection of the pagan women. G. Picco, *'Or s'indora or verdeggia'. Il ritratto femminile dalla 'Liberata' alla 'Conquistata',* F, Le Lettere, 1996, 163 pp., applies a philological analysis to the alteration, editing, or development of Clorinda, Armida, and Erminia between the two works to decipher the difficult stages in T.'s elaboration and re-elaboration of the two texts. *Formazione e fortuna del Tasso nella cultura della Serenissima. Atti del convegno di studi nel IV centenario della morte di Torquato Tasso (1595–1995), Padova–Venezia 10–11 novembre 1995,* ed. Luciana Borsetto and Bianca Maria da Rif, Venice, IV, 1997, 322 pp., explores three main areas: T.'s youth in Venice and Padua, the crucial influence of this on his writings, and the success of his poetry in the Veneto from the 17th to the 19th c. To be particularly noted is G. Resta, 'Formazione e noviziato del Tassino' (17–34), where a new date is proposed for the composition of the *Discorsi dell'arte poetica* (Spring 1565), and G. Da Pozzo, 'La memoria tassiana dell'esperienza veneta' (189–210). *Dal Rinaldo alla Gerusalemme: il testo, la favola. Atti del Convegno internazionale di studi Torquato Tasso quattro secoli dopo, Sorrento, 17–19 novembre 1994,* ed. Dante Della Terza, Sorrento, Città del Sorrento, 1997, 341 pp., is the first of two volumes celebrating the birth of the poet with a range of articles focusing on the *Liberata,* the *Conquistata,* and T.'s dramatic works and correspondence. Here I note in particular G. Da Pozzo, 'Dall'*Aminta* al *Torrismondo:* manierismo costruttivo e coerenza della tragedia'; P. Larivaille, 'Dalla prassi alla teoria, l'allegoria nella

Gerusalemme Liberata'; M. Rossi, 'Fortuna figurativa dell'epica tassiana a Firenze e Venezia fra Cinque e Seicento'. Secondly, *Torquato Tasso quattrocento anni dopo. Atti del convegno di Rende, 24–25 maggio 1996,* ed. A. Daniele and F. W. Lupi, Soveria Mannelli, Rubbettino, 1997, 155 pp., proposes *inter alia*: D. Della Terza, 'Armida dalla *Liberata* alla *Conquistata*: genesi ed evoluzione di un personaggio' (47–60); and A. Oldcorn, ' "ogni altezza s'inchina". Lettura del *Re Torrismondo*' (79–92). I also note G. Da Pozzo, 'Ultimi assalti e vittoria differita nei canti finali della *Gerusalemme liberata*', *ItStudien*, 19:83–108.

4. DRAMA

J. I. Cope, *Secret Sharers in Italian Comedy from Machiavelli to Goldoni*, Durham, NC, Duke U.P., 1996, x + 221 pp., argues unconvincingly for a new genre of Italian Renaissance comedy characterized by the sharing of secrets, mistaken identities, and unresolved endings. The extensive synopses of plots, complemented by lengthy quotes in both Italian and English, do not persuade that the works of Machiavelli and Cecchi exemplify this new genre, or that it reached its apogee with Ruzante and Goldoni. Among the problems presented by this work, the dates of plays are not given, chronological order is not maintained, and the 17th c. is glossed over. A. G. Gramigna, 'La leggenda di Didone: amore e tragedia', *Ariel, 12.1,* 1997:63–77, for the Italian Renaissance theatre concerns Giraldi and Dolce. M. A. Katritzky, 'A German description of the Florentine *intermedi* of 1565', *ISt,* 52, 1997:63–93.

DE' SOMMI.   C. dal Molin, 'Un "ipotesi" sulla datazione della *Fortunata* di Leone de' Sommi: rappresentazione mantovana e torinese', *SPCT,* 55:95–106, points out the inaccuracy of the received dating of the composition and first performance of De' Sommi's text by means of the manuscript recently discovered at the Biblioteca Nazionale, Turin.

DOLCE.   A. Neuschäfer, ' "Io già di Colco gran Regina fui . . .". Medea als Magierin oder Möderin? Deutungen im italienischen *Cinquecento*', *ItStudien,* 19:140–55, analyses D.'s adaptation of Euripides with reference to his earlier *Didone* and to Seneca's *Thyestes*.

MACHIAVELLI.   Niccolò Machiavelli, *Opere,* ed. Corrado Vivanti, 1, T, Einaudi — Paris, Gallimard, cxliii + 1243 pp., is a large volume divided into six sections which looks at M.'s major works, political and historical, but also includes the *Mandragola*. Rejecting a purely allegorical interpretation, V. has a new approach to M.'s 'badalucco', based upon the author's own assertions as to the comic nature of his work.

RUZANTE. P. Vescovo, *Da Ruzante a Calmo tra 'Signore Comedie' e 'Onorandissime Stampe'*, Padua, Antenore, 1996, 241 pp., by focusing upon two authors, Ruzante and Calmo, over a period of 20 years from 1530 to 1550, aims to provide 'un'immagine della cultura rinascimentale veneta vista attraverso il teatro e la letteratura teatrale'.

TASSO. See TASSO under POETRY, above.

5. PROSE

La novella del grasso legnaiuolo, introd. Paolo Procaccioli, pref. Giorgio Manganelli, Mi, Garzanti, xliv + 97 pp., has an excellent introduction that traces the MS and printed tradition. It gives the version, with notes, of A. Manetti. Angelo Ugoleto, *Il libro di tuti li chostumi*, pref. Carlo Antinori, Parma, Maccari, is a facsimile of the 1498 Parma edition which was printed in three parts, the novelty residing in the fact that each part is self-contained and could have been sold separately. This genre which deals with advice to merchants was popular in the second half of the 15th c. Ugolino da Pisa, *Dei bagni della Porretta*, ed. Mahmoud Salem Elsheikh, Bo, CTL, xxv + 123 pp., is a critical edition of Biblioteca Riccardiana MS 1192, the vernacular version, by Francesco de Andrea Ciati, of Ugolino's lost Latin treatise on hydrology. The appendices contain critical editions of Tura da Castello, *Proprietà e virtù del bagno della Porretta*, in the Biblioteca Nazionale, Florence, and his *Recetta de l'aqua del Bagno de la Porretta*, in the Biblioteca Universitaria, Bologna. Piero Toffano, *La scrittura autobiografica fino all'epoca di Rousseau*, Fasano, Schena, 271 pp., comprises 10 essays, including an excellent study by G. Rabitti, 'Isotopie dell'io. Percorsi autobiografici da Boccaccio a Lorenzo de' Medici', which yields many new insights and sees Boccaccio's methodology as making a decisive break with the past. The analysis also covers A. S. Piccolomini, Ghiberti, Alberti, A. Traversari, the letters of A. Macinghi Strozzi, and V. da Bisticci. A. Valori, 'Da lei viene ogni utile e ogni onore. Le lettere di Alessandra Macinghi Strozzi ai figli e la tutela del patrimonio morale della famiglia', *ASI*, 156 : 25–72. Cesare Nappi, *Memoriale Mei. Ricordi de mi. Con l'appendice del memoriale secondo*, ed. Leonardo Quaquarelli, Bo, EdG, 1997, l + 237 pp., gives the full text of the *memoriale* written by a well-read humanist notary. The excellent introduction sets out the nature and the structure of such texts and analyses the particular themes of learning, scholarship, and antiquarianism, paying particular attention to the theme of friendship. S. Lo Re, 'Fresca e rugiadosa in quella penitenza', *Intersezioni*, 18 : 33–45, looks at the unpublished autobiographical writings of Baccio de Filippo di Niccolò Valori. S. Agostini, 'La memoria bifronte. Le scritture del bolognese Antonio Lamberti', *SUm*, 1:87–124, indicates that, in contrast to Florence, in Bologna the *libro di famiglia* as a genre seem to have become more popular at the end of the 16th c. Id., 'Biografie e biografi di Benedetto Varchi: Giambattista Busini e Baccio Valori', *ASI*, 156:671–736. M. E. Bratchel, 'Chronicles of fifteenth-century Lucca: contributions to an understanding of a restored republic', *BHR*, 60:7–23, points to a rich chronicle tradition, explores literary topoi and evaluates the links between prose and verse chronicles. *Vita del Principe Giovanni Andrea Doria scritta da lui medesimo incompleta*, ed. Vilma Borghesi, Genoa, Compagnia dei Librai, 1997, lii + 194 pp. + 9 pls, has a scholarly introduction that reviews the MS tradition followed by an edition of the text in the Biblioteca Civica Berio in which Doria describes his early life on board ship and his career as Admiral of the Spanish fleet. A. Gentile, 'Boccaccio a Venezia', *Venezia Cinquecento*, 14:5–45, examines the changes introduced when the *Decameron* was illustrated. C. Elam, ' "Che ultima mano!" Tiberio Calcagni's marginal annotations to Condivi's *Life of Michelangelo*', *RQ*, 51:475–97, reveals Michelangelo's reaction to errors and confirms other anecdotes. G. W. McClure, 'The *Artes* and the *Ars moriendi* in late Renaissance Venice. The professions in Fabio Glissenti's *Discorsi morali contra il dispiacer del morire detto Athanatophilia* (1596)', *RQ*, 51:92–127. Marco Fabrizio Caroso, *Nobiltà di dame*, Bo, Forni, 1997, is a facsimile of the second edition (1600) and centres on a dialogue between teacher and pupil on the art of dancing, its origins and the etymology of terms. Originally titled *Il ballerino* the text has much of interest for literary, social, and cultural historians.

ANDREA DA BARBERINO. Gloria Allaire, *Andrea da Barberino and the Language of Chivalry*, Gainesville, Florida U.P., 1997, xiv + 183 pp., seeks to establish a corpus of genuine texts, to set out the main elements of his style, and to correct critical misunderstandings, often based on corrupt texts, which have led to his works being labelled as 'popular' and 'unlearned'.

ARETINO. Paul Larivaille, *Pietro Aretino*, Ro, Salerno, 1997, 555 pp., is a major biographical contribution. G. Aquilecchia, 'Pietro Aretino e la "Riforma cattolica" ', *NRLett*, 1996, no. 2:9–23. L'Arétin, *Ragionamenti*, 1, ed. Giovanni Aquilecchia, introd., trans., and ann. Paul Larivaille, Paris, Les Belles Lettres, xcviii + 212 pp., is another milestone in Aquilecchia's collaboration with Les Belles Lettres in the production of bilingual editions of Italian Renaissance texts.

CASTIGLIONE. Baldesar Castiglione, *Il libro del Cortegiano*, ed. Walter Barberis, T, Einaudi, xci + 460 pp., is based on MS Laurenziano-Ashburnhamiano 409, while the dedicatory letter is taken from the 1528 *editio princeps*. The excellent introduction traces Castiglione's preoccupations with the printing and revision of the text, and his correspondence with V. Colonna. It also gives an assessment of court literature, seeing Castiglione as 'l'ultimo esempio di una grande stagione della retorica'. S. D. Kolsky, 'Old men in a new world: Morello da Orona in the *Cortegiano*', *Italica*, 75 : 330–47. Id., 'Graceful performances: the social and political context of music and dance in the *Cortegiano*', *ISt*, 53 : 1–19.

CELLINI. P. L. Rossi, 'Sprezzatura, patronage, and fate: Benvenuto Cellini and the world of words', pp. 55–69 of *Vasari's Florence. Artists and Literati at the Medicean Court*, ed. Philip Jacks, CUP, xvi + 320 pp., dispels the myth of the *Vita* as a product of spontaneous dictation by pointing out the carefully planned structure of the work and the possibility that the MS is a *bella copia*. It also shows how Cellini's writing was a strategy, employed also by other artists, for professional and social advancement at court.

COLONNA. Francesco Colonna, *Hypnerotomachia Poliphili*, ed. Marco Ariani and Mino Gabriele, 2 vols, Mi, Adelphi, 467, cxvii + 1207 pp., is an excellent piece of scholarship. The first volume gives a facsimile of the Aldine edition of 1499, while the second has a thorough introduction that takes us through Polifilo's journey, followed by a standardized Italian version. The real and lasting value of this edition lies in the scholarly commentary that sets out the classical sources and the references to works in Latin and the *volgare*. There are also valuable notes on the historical aspects of the work and useful indexes.

DELLA CASA. *Per Giovanni Della Casa* (see POETRY, above), also includes several contributions on his prose writings. For the *Galateo*: G. Barbarisi, 'Ancora sul testo del *Galateo*' (253–70); C. Berra, 'Il *Galateo* "fatto per scherzo" ' (271–35); and S. Morgana, 'Le "lingue" del *Galateo*' (337–69). M. Mari, 'Le lettere di Giovanni Della Casa ad Annibale Rucellai' (371–419), presents and transcribes 19 letters. The volume also contains items by S. Albonico on Della Casa's orations (437–56) and by S. Carrai on his Latin biography of Bembo (419–35); it concludes with contributions by C. Vecce (457–67) and P. Passavino (469–79) on the *An uxor sit ducenda*.

FRANCO. Veronica Franco, *Lettere*, ed. Stefano Bianchi, Ro, Salerno, 145 pp., reproduces, with corrections, the text of the *editio princeps* (1580) comprising 50 letters put together by Franco herself. The introduction points out the echoes of Seneca and Alberti and the deliberate literary purpose of the collection. All but two lack any dedication and were intended as *exempla*.

GHIBERTI. Lorenzo Ghiberti, *I commentarii*, ed. Lorenzo Bartoli, F, Giunti, 316 pp., finally clarifies this difficult text. What emerges is a *zibaldone* where Ghiberti amended, and commented on, specific texts on topics such as optics, perspective, and anatomy. The excellent introduction sets out Ghiberti's methodology and the complex nature of the work, as well as giving a sensitive analysis of the structure and themes.

LOMAZZO.   *Le tavole del Lomazzo*, ed. Barbara and Giovanni Agosti, Brescia, L'Obliquo, 1997, 96 pp., is a thorough study of Lomazzo's methodology and research sources which illuminates how writers of the period put together material for their biographical portraits.

MACHIAVELLI.   *Machiavelli*, ed. John Dunn and Ian Harris, 2 vols., Cheltenham, Elgar, 1997, xiii + 600, ix + 631 pp., is a collection which, taken as a whole, is a monument to M. studies. It allows a historical assessment of changing interests in and critical approaches to him, and of the different ideological positions taken. It contains 53 essays ranging from Macaulay's (1827), Lord Acton's (1907), and Croce's (1930) to the new approaches of Gilbert, Hans Baron, and J. H. Whitfield, and contemporary studies by J. N. Stephens, H. C. Butters, J. G. Pocock, V. Kuhn, M. L. Colish, and P. J. Osmond. Robert A. Kocis, *Machiavelli Redeemed. Retrieving his Humanist Perspectives on Equality, Power and Glory*, Bethelem, Pa., Lehigh U.P., 264 pp., argues that to understand M. as a man and thinker all his writings should be investigated and that, if this is done, it will render his philosophy plausible, coherent, and modern. The study offers new insights into M.'s contribution and place in the history of political thought. Emanuele Cutinelli-Rèndina, *Chiesa e religione in Machiavelli*, Pisa–Ro, Istituti Editoriali e Poligrafici Internazionali, 334 pp., presents a scholarly analysis that sees M. not only opposed to the Church but 'fondamentalmente e consapevolmente "anticristiano"'. Religion is seen as a basic aspect in his comparisons of the contemporary world with that of antiquity and inextricably linked to major themes in all his writings. Jader Jacobelli, *Machiavelli e/o Guicciardini alle radici del realismo politico*, Mi, Mursia, 262 pp., adopts a novel approach in comparing and contrasting their careers, opinions, and writings with regard to the vicissitudes of Florentine, Italian, and European politics. H. Jaeckel, 'I "Tordi" e il "Principe Nuovo". Note sulle dediche del *Principe* di Machiavelli a Giuliano e a Lorenzo de' Medici', *ASI*, 156:73–92. Mario Martelli et al., **Cultura e scrittura di Machiavelli*, Ro, Salerno, xx + 692 pp. F. Fedi, ' "Personaggi" e "paradossi" nei *Discorsi* machiavelliani: il caso di Virginia e Appio Claudio', *LItal*, 50:485–505. M. L. Colish, 'Machiavelli's *Art of War*. A reconsideration', *RQ*, 51:1151–68.

MASUCCIO SALERNITANO.   Donato Pirovano, *Modi narrativi e stile del 'Novellino' di Masuccio Salernitano*, F, La Nuova Italia, 1996, 281 pp., concentrates on Masuccio's emphasis on the abnormal, unusual traits in human nature and life, and the overwhelming forces that lead to tragic ends, his fascination with horror and morbidity, and the biting acerbic nature of his humour.

MEDICI. Lorenzo de' Medici, *Lettere*, VII, *(1482–1484)*, ed. Michael Mallett, F, Giunti, 578 pp., continues the meticulous scholarship of the project, covering the period of the Ferrarese war which began in May 1482 and ended with the Peace of Bagnolo. The correspondence reflects the intense, yet ineffective, diplomatic activity of Florence during this period, and the letters of 'raccomandazione' indicate Lorenzo's increasingly influential position as a patron and his close relationship with the new popular government in Siena after the *coup d'état* of June 1482.

NICCOLÒ DA CORREGGIO. Domizia Trolli, *La lingua delle lettere di Niccolò da Correggio*, Na, Loffredo, 1997, 278 pp., is a detailed linguistic analysis of 280 letters written between 1462 and 1507, which covers phonetics and morphology and includes an exhaustive glossary. The letters reveal preoccupations with family, politics, and court.

PICCOLOMINI. Norbert Seeber, *Enea Vergilianus. Vergilsches in den 'Kommentaren' des Enea Silvio Piccolomini (Pius II)*, Innsbruck, Wagner, 1997, 172 pp., is a detailed study of classical themes, language, and structures in the *Commentari*. It traces echoes of Virgil's Camilla, specific Virgilian word groupings and a statistical analysis of Virgilian elements. This is an important study that sheds much light on humanist learning and borrowing. Pius II (Enea Silvio Piccolomini), *I commentari*, ed. Mino Marchetti, 2 vols, Siena, Cantagalli, 1997, xxviii + 432, 435–923 pp., is based on the text published in 1584 (Rome, Domenico Basa) which followed the Codex Corsiniano 157 written by Giovanni Gobellino. The expurgated parts of the Basa edition have been restored, and it is a pity that notes have not been included. There is a good introduction by D. Balestracci.

SANUDO. Marin Sanudo, *I diarii 1496–1533. Pagine scelte*, ed. Paolo Margaroli, Vicenza, Neri Pozza, 1997, 699 pp., has a scholarly introduction that examines the structure of the work and places it within the historiographical tradition. There are also good notes and useful indexes.

TASSO. Alessandra Coppo, *All'ombra di malinconia. Il Tasso lungo la sua fama*, F, Le Lettere, 266 pp., is a scholarly study that charts the changing face of Tasso first by setting out autobiographical information found in his writings, particularly in the letters, and then by showing how the theme of *la malinconia* was later manipulated in Italy, France, and England. Torquato Tasso, *Dell'arte del dialogo*, ed. Guido Baldassarri, makes use of the critical edition of 1971 (*RLI*, 75) with an excellent introduction that analyses the themes and Tasso's theoretical position.

VASARI. *Vasari's Florence. Artists and Literati at the Medicean Court*, ed. Philip Jacks, CUP, xvi + 320 pp., comprises 14 essays including: J. Shearman on Vasari and the paragons of art, which assesses his professional agenda and his criteria for praise or blame; P. Barolsky on the *Vite* as a poetic work of ' "fantasy", "invention", and "ingenuity" in its own right; D. Cast on how the social status of art could be raised by regarding the practical side as a product of *phronesis* as well as *techne*; sections on 'Vasari as artist and connoisseur', and '*Istorie* and the representation of history'.

ZUCCARI. *Federico Zuccari. Le idee, gli scritti,* Mi, Electa, 1997, 193 pp., assembles 12 essays that investigate: the annotations to Vasari's *Vite*, which reveal disagreements and dislikes; the correspondence with Francesco Maria II of Urbino displaying esteem and affection between artist and Duke; the *terzine* for the life of his brother Taddeo; the way *virtù* and *fortuna* are at the heart of his writings, the latter relating to mental and intellectual effort seen as an important element in enhancing the artist's status; Z.'s contribution to the evolution of the artists' academy; the coming together of art and faith in the theory of angels in the *Idea dei pittori* and the links to Dante and G. M. Tarsia.

SEICENTO

By MAURICE SLAWINSKI, *Lecturer in Italian Studies, University of Lancaster*

I. GENERAL

An important event, well beyond the book's status as a 'student primer', is the publication of Domenico Sella, *Italy in the Seventeenth Century*, London, Longman, 1997, xii + 246 pp., which is effectively the first summary, in any language, of the revisionist view of the *Seicento* which has emerged over the last 30 years. Particularly welcome is its critique of the dubious concept of *rifeudalizzazione*. The chapter on social class and social relations is also worthwhile (despite not sufficiently emphasizing the differences between the elites of the *dominante*, of the larger subject cities, and of the smaller towns), as is that on Church-State relations. Would that the chapter on 'Culture' were as stimulating (and up-to-date): given that most of its sources (Getto, Spini, Asor Rosa) have been amply superseded, it had been better not written at all; and the crucial issue of the relationship between elites and *intellettuali* (in both Gramscian and Weberian senses) is scarcely touched upon.

LITERARY HISTORY, POETICS, GENERAL CRITICISM. Eraldo Bellini, *Umanisti e Lincei. Letteratura e scienza a Roma nell'età di Galilei*, Padua, Antenore, 1997, 320 pp., is a broad-ranging tableau of literary culture in Rome in the early years of Urban VIII's papacy, from the enthusiasms surrounding his election, through the encouragement of classicism in literature and experimentalism in natural philosophy, to literary debates like the one provoked by Agazio Di Somma's claim that *L'Adone* had surpassed the *Liberata*, and attempts by intellectuals of the Barberini circle to produce a new code of conduct for the courtier–cleric–*letterato*. The study stops short of considering the sudden end of this 'mirabil congiuntura', no doubt because so much has been said about it in connection with Galileo (here present only in the background), yet the links between Ciampoli, Cesarini, Mascardi et al. and the New Science are hardly sufficient to explain a change of course which may have been maturing for some time before (nothing is said, for example, of Urban's progressive captivation under the very different spell of Campanella, from 1626).

P. Frare, 'La "nuova critica" della meravigliosa acutezza', pp. 223–77 of *Storia della critica letteraria in Italia*, ed. G. Baroni, T, UTET, 1997, 624 pp., traces a summary history of *Seicento* literary criticism from Beni ('moderno ma non barocco') to the precursors of Arcadia (neither baroque nor modern?) viewed largely from the perspective of the *concettisti*, while relegating classicism to a marginal role contradicted by its place at the Roman heart of Counter-Reformation culture and investing it with a purity and separateness difficult to substantiate: *Seicento* classicism is always a *baroque* classicism, far from opposed to conspicuous artifice and *meraviglia*, and in theory as much as practice *Seicento* poetics are far less polarized, far more of a continuum, than the traditional picture originating in Stigliani's demonization of Marino suggests. Frare only partially breaks from this (though his essay does have the merit of suggesting that modernity and progress lie more on the side of those who engage with the problematic of *concettismo* than those who seek to re-establish the link with the classicism of the *Cinquecento*.

LITERATURE AND THE VISUAL ARTS. M. Rossi, 'Raffigurazione e riscritture della *Liberata* da Firenze a Venezia: un intervento di Bernardo Castello recuperato', *SV*, 34, 1997:165–86, discusses the influence of the *Liberata* in Florence (where for reasons the article does not make wholly clear the story of the First Crusade became linked with Medici propaganda) from P. A. Bargeo's *Syrias* to *Seicento* pictorial cycles in various Medici residences to Giulio Strozzi's 'rewriting' of the *Liberata* in his *Venezia edificata*, published 1621–24 with engravings by Tasso's most famous illustrator. I also note W. Hirdt, 'Fonti e motivi letterari della "Buona Ventura" del Caravaggio', *StIt*, 17, 1997:49–75; R. Villa, '"Vecchio lattante e pargoletto antico": rinvii letterari in una scena del Caravaggio con due tavole fuori testo', *Belfagor*, 52, 1997:655–76.

BIBLIOGRAPHY, PRINTING AND PUBLISHING. Maria Maira Niri, *La tipografia a Genova e in Liguria nel XVII secolo*, introd. G. Pistarino, F, Olschki, xxxii + 688 pp. + xlv plates, catalogues 1574 editions, though how complete the inventory is may be doubted, given that only 461 editions by Giuseppe Pavoni are recorded, as against the 533 listed by Ruffini (*YWMLS*, 58:547). The somewhat bitty introduction contains useful data concerning, inter alia, book censorship and distribution of titles by subject-matter, but hardly amounts to a clear overview of printing in Liguria and its dependence on aristocratic patronage: as the overwhelming prevalence of Italian titles over Latin, large formats (folio, 4°) over small (12° or less), and the magnificent engraved title pages and *anteporte* reproduced in the plates imply, this is not commercial printing like that of contemporary Venice, Milan, or Naples, but a mixture of official publication and a kind of vanity publishing (works written by or dedicated to the city's leading patricians). Entries are presented chronologically and divided by publisher (with a brief introduction outlining the activities of each). As well as a chronological summary giving the total number of editions per year (a graph would have provided the information more effectively), indexes of authors and titles of anonymous works, of dedicatees, and of owners of exemplars checked, there is also a valuable appendix of documents (contracts, *suppliche* to the authorities, and printers' wills).

Franco Fioravanti, *Annali della topografia cesenate*, Manziana, Vecchiarelli, 1997, 265 pp., includes details of some 200 *Seicento* imprints, covering a wide range of disciplines, including a number of entries of interest for the study of provincial literary culture; P. Bellettini, 'Sugli *Annali della tipografia cesenate* di Franco Fioravanti', *La Bibliofilia*, 100: 47–80, offers several corrections and some additions.

Giulio Busi, *Libri ebraici a Mantova. Le edizioni del XVII, XVIII e XIX secolo nella biblioteca della Comunità ebraica*, Fiesole, Cadmo, 1997, 570 pp., catalogues a significant number of 17th-c. editions.

A. Capaccioni, 'Alcuni aspetti dell'attività editoriale di un comune del ducato di Urbino: Gubbio nel XVII secolo', pp. 289–305 of *Storici, filosofi e cultura umanistica a Gubbio tra Cinque e Seicento*, ed. P. Castelli and G. Pellegrini, Spoleto, CSAM, xii + 688 pp., gathers the surviving information concerning the (extremely modest) publishing activities of that period (just ten brief pamphlets — though oddly the bibliographical details provided for them amount to nothing more than short title and date, when a full description would have been appropriate). G. Lombardi, 'Tipografia e commercio cartolibrario a Napoli nel Seicento', *StS*, 39: 137–59, presents a rapid overview of the Neapolitan book-trade (probably second only to Venice's), and lists the 'operatori del libro' (some 500 booksellers, printers, paper sellers, publishers, with the dates during which they are known to have been active).

Libri, tipografi, biblioteche. Ricerche storiche dedicate a Luigi Balsamo, F, Olschki, 1997, 2 vols., xviii + 700 pp., contains one essay of *Seicento* interest: Mario Infelise, ' "Ex ignotus notus"? Note sul tipografo Sarzina e l'Accademia degli Incogniti' (207–33), piecing together the little that is known concerning one of the printers most closely connected with Loredano's Academy.

CENSORSHIP. Pierre-Noël Mayaud, *La Condemnation des livres coperniciens et sa révocation à la lumière de documents inédits des Congrégations de l'Index et de l'Inquisition*, Ro, PUG, 1997, 352 pp., the first major publication resulting from the opening of the Archivio Storico of the Holy Office, is of both particular and general interest; the reconstruction of the events of 1613–16 is prefaced by chapters outlining the functioning of the Congregation of the Index and followed by chapters on their impact, with the related condemnation of works by Campanella and Galileo. The second half of the work deals with the partial revocation of the decrees of 1616 and 1633, starting in the 18th c.

CHURCH HISTORY, RELIGIOUS ORDERS. Roberto Bellarmino, *Consigli per un vescovo*, ed. and trans. P. Giustiniani and L. Longobardo, Brescia, Morcelliana, 110 pp., is the Italian translation of *Admonitio ad episcopum Theanensem* (1616), really a series of *quaestiones* (from whether it is permissible to solicit an episcopal see to the nature of the incumbent's title to diocesan revenues) which Bellarmino answers by drawing on the Church Fathers, the Tridentine decrees, and contemporary controversists.

Andrea Pozzo, ed. V. De Feo and V. Martinelli, Mi, Electa, 1996, 256 pp., is strictly speaking a work of architectural and art history, but the Jesuit Pozzo (1642–1709), best remembered perhaps for the painted dome of S. Ignazio in Rome, was arguably the most influential exponent and theorist of the grandly prospective, illusionistic style promoted by the Order throughout Europe in the second part of the *Seicento*, closely related to Jesuit oratory of the period and the main source of the 'international Baroque' which dominated the visual and 'plastic' arts for almost a century. Of specifically literary and dramatic interest is the chapter by V. Martinelli, ' "Teatri sacri e profani" di Andrea Pozzo nella cultura prospettico-scenografica barocca' (94–113), and M. Carta and A. Menichella, 'Il successo editoriale del Trattato' (230–33), concerning his *Prospettiva de' pittori e architetti* (1693–1700); but no less interest and relevance is the discussion of the 'rhetoric' and programmatic content of pictorial cycles and church buildings.

G. Raffo, 'I Gesuiti a Genova nei secoli XVII e XVIII. Storia della Casa Professa di Genova della Compagnia di Gesù dall'anno 1603 al 1773', *ASLSP*, 36, 1996:151–403, consists of an introduction to and translation of the original MS Latin chronicle by the Jesuit Raffo.

Stefano Villani, 'I Quaccheri contro il Papa. Alcuni pamphlet inglesi del '600 tra menzogne e verità', *StSec*, 39:165–202, is more directly concerned with the history of the movement than that of the Church of Rome. It is interesting to note, however, that (thanks largely to the importance of Livorno for England's Levantine trade) even geographically and numerically marginal religious movements like early Quakerism reached to the centre of the Catholic world, though its actual impact would appear to have been insignificant.

COURT SOCIETY. Irene Fossi, *All'ombra dei Barberini. Fedeltà e servizio nella Roma barocca*, Ro, Bulzoni, 318 pp., reconstructs the career of Cardinal Giulio Sacchetti, from the advancement strategies of his Florentine banker father (who settled in Rome in mid-*Cinquecento*) which determined his entry into the Curia, through assiduous service of Urban VIII and the Barberini, to his failure to secure for himself the ultimate prize of the papacy in the 1644 and 1655 conclaves. It is an interesting story, though the account is over-long, repetitious, and too prone to summarize events with a series of stock phrases about service, tact, and family *utile* rather than let them speak for themselves through a clear narrative constructed out of the vast quantity of archival material consulted. The result is that though the portrait rings true, we have largely to take it on trust, since the protagonists are seldom allowed to speak for themselves.

EPISTOLARY RELATIONS. Alessandro Antelminelli, *In forma di republica o stati. La corrispondenza del residente fiorentino a Londra (1645–1649)*, ed. O. Santini, F, CET, 1997, 288 pp., is the political correspondence of "Amerigo Salvetti" (Antelminelli had assumed this alias for fear of assassination by agents of the Republic of Lucca) to Cosimo II's secretary of state, Giovan Battista Gondi. A. Mirto, 'Lettere di Antonio Magliabechi a Bernardo Benvenuti', *StSec*, 39:205–42, publishes 19 letters of some interest for the mechanisms of cultural exchange and book circulation in the final quarter of the *Seicento*.

GENDER. Elisabetta Graziosi, *Avventuriere a Bologna. Due storie esemplari*, Modena, Mucchi, 250 pp., pieces together the surviving fragments of the literary biographies of Christina di Northumberland Paleotti (1649–1719), granddaughter of 'Ruberto Dudleio Conte di Warwick', and Teresa Zani (1664–1732): exemplary precisely because what survives of both their lives and their poetry consists of mere fragments, which Graziosi argues is the inevitable condition of women's writing in this period. The story, suspended between literary history and *cronaca mondana* (with more than a hint of scandal in Christina's case, since the sexual mores of her circle would have been better suited to the Paris of the *philosophes* than Papal Bologna), is indeed an interesting one, and the lively, polemical tone in which it is presented not inappropriate, though it might have been told in briefer, more linear fashion. The verse comprises a handful of sonnets published in anthologies edited by various *arcadi* — though in Christina's case it predates the establishment of the Academy and its various *colonie*, belonging rather to mid-*Seicento* Petrarchan classicism.

Quaderni franzoniani, 8, 1995[1996], is entirely devoted to 'Congregazioni laicali femminili e promozione della donna in Italia nei secoli XVI e XVII', including S. S. Macchietti, 'Per una pedagogia dell'educazione femminile in Italia nei secoli XVI e XVII' (21–57), which focuses on what theorists said of the moral and socializing functions of female education, but unfortunately tells us little of its practical contents.

LITERARY BIOGRAPHY. Uberto Motta, *Antonio Querenghi (1546–1633). Un letterato padovano nella Roma del tardo Rinascimento*, Mi, Vita e Pensiero, 1997, viii + 364 pp., is somewhat misleadingly titled, since the most important period of Roman residence of this

remarkable *eminence grise* of Italian letters began in 1605, and his long
intellectual itinerary constitutes a *trait-d'union* between the literary
culture of the mid-to-late *Cinquecento* (Della Casa, Speroni, Tasso,
Patrizi all figure prominently in his education) and the 'classical
restoration' promoted by Urban VIII: a dense volume packed with
new detail, though not perhaps used to best advantage, since at the
end no very clear picture emerges either of the man or his cultural
role.

Giorgio Cosmacini, *Il medico ciarlatano. Vita inimitabile di un europeo del
Seicento*, Ro–Bari, Laterza, vi + 172 pp., reconstructs the career of
Giuseppe Francesco Borri, splendidly known as 'il coglionatore', a
notable (but by the standards of the mid *Seicento* far from unique)
adventurer, author of *Istruzioni politiche date al Re di Danimarca* (pub.
1660) as well as medical and alchemical treatises.

T. Biganti and V. I. Comparato, 'Vincenzo Armanni da segretario
ad "archivista"', pp. 72–110 of *Storici, filosofi*, cit., traces the main
events of Armanni's two careers, as papal diplomat in England and
Germany and as student of genealogy, history, and epigraphy in his
native Gubbio (where he spent the second part of his long life after
the onset of blindness, after which, *secretario* that he had been, he in
turn had to make systematic use of *amanuenses*): an appetiser rather
than a definitive study of an extraordinary figure who, paradoxically,
only became really important and cosmopolitan in his enforced
retreat. His papers — particularly the letters addressed to him by
letterati from all over Italy and beyond — still await thorough
investigation. M. Slawinski, 'Tra periferia e centro: la carriera
esemplare di Guidubaldo Benamati eugubino', *ib.*, 539–98, reconstructs the literary career of this friend and supporter of Marino as
(again) typical of the relationship between major and minor cultural
centres and of the *Seicento* trend for the production of literature to
move towards the latter. G. de Miranda, 'I volti molteplici della
cortigiana virtú. Per un "portrait masqué" di Giambattista Basile
nella sua prima maturità (1606–1612)", *Quaderni dell'Aprosiana*, 5,
1997:7–19, pieces together autobiographical reflections and documentary evidence from the works of this period, relating to Basile's
self-refashioning from *uom d'armi* to *uomo di lettere*.

LANGUAGE. P. B. Diffley, 'Paolo Beni e la lingua italiana: la
prospettiva di un umanista di Gubbio', pp. 331–73 of *Storici, filosofi*
cit., gives an invaluably clear account of Beni's views, making a
persuasive case for their possessing much greater coherence than is
generally assumed. I am less convinced, however, by the assertion of
their modernity and wonder whether they would not benefit from
greater contextualization in the cultural politics of the period. M. A.
Mastronardi, 'Innovazione e modelli. La "questione della lingua" in

Puglia fra Sei e Settecento', *ArSP*, 50, 1997:89–166, considers the views of Giovanni Cicinelli, Giuseppe Silos, Tommaso Luigi Francavilla, and Giacinto Gimma. S. Bozzola, 'Glossario frugoniano', *SLeI*, 14, 1997:153–282, glosses some 800 neologisms and rare forms drawn from his study of the *Tribunale della critica* (for which see section 4 below).

PATRONAGE, ACADEMIES, ORGANIZATION OF CULTURE. M. Miato, *L'Accademia degli Incogniti di Giovan Francesco Loredan, Venezia (1630–1661)*, F, Olschki, 296 pp., is a disappointing contribution to a subject on which more information would be very welcome. The study (really three distinct essays: on Loredano himself; on the activities of the Academy; on the printer Francesco Valvasense, closely connected with Loredano, and his trial for printing and selling unlicenced and forbidden books) is exceedingly naive in the use of its sources, riddled with factual inaccuracies, poorly written, and worse proof-read (starting with the odd-looking title). Some useful data does emerge here and there, and the appendix, containing details of some 144 editions published by Valvasense between 1644 and 1680 is also of some value (though given the rest of the work its accuracy and comprehensiveness cannot be taken for granted). But the real nature of the Accademia (which I for one suspect existed chiefly in Loredano's mind and in the pages of the books whose publication he promoted) remains unclear. Symptomatic of Miato's unwillingness to tackle the fundamental questions are the indexes (appendices IV–VI) of its presumed members: it is noted that a number died before the Accademia's official 1630 foundation (some of them, not spotted by the author, were dead before Loredano was even born!), but no attempt is made to explain this strange fact.

D. Capaldi, '*Logos, ludus, eros* nell'incontro accademico di veglia tra cinquecento e seicento', *ItStudien*, 19:64–82, sees a transition from ritualized (socialized) erotic play to narcissistically theatrical self-display in the evolution of academic activities; but quite apart from the question of what this would prove, the evidence is scant, to say the least, since the argument stands on a comparison between the *veglie* of the *Accademici Intronati* (entertainments specifically staged for the ladies such as we know the academies continued to promote long into the *Seicento*) and the virtuoso displays of the Accademia degli Incogniti, whose existence was largely, if not exclusively, cartaceous.

THE COUNTER-REFORMATION CHURCH. *Cheiron*, 27–28, 1997, is entirely dedicated to 'Chiesa Romana e cultura europea in antico regime', ed. C. Mozzarelli, and includes F. Rurale, ' "Modo suggerito al Signor Cardinale Barberino per aver uomini dotti da valersene per rispondere alle scritture et alle stampe che ogni giorno si divulgano contro i dogmi della fede e contro l'autorità del Pontefice". Note a margine' (235–54), consisting of the text of an anonymous memorandum written, it would appear, at the Cardinal's request in 1641/42. It is interesting for the lack of confidence it shows, at the end of a long pontificate which had particularly wanted to be distinguished by the attention it paid to intellectuals, in the ability of Church institutions to provide competent theologians and polemicists. It is prefaced by general remarks concerning the doctrinal and political debates of the period.

MISCELLANEOUS CONTRIBUTIONS.   P. Castelli, 'Il *Baculus Daemonium* di Carlo Olivieri. Demoni ed esorcismo a Gubbio e la discussione sulla possessione nella riforma cattolica', pp. 375–437 of *Storici, filosofi*, cit., discusses a 1618 treatise in the context of the Church's affirmation, against the claims of physicians, of the supernatural causes of 'possession' and 'melancholy', the primary role of exorcism in treatment of such conditions, and its relationship to the cult of St Ubaldo. On the latter subject we also have E. Paoli, 'La ricezione post-tridentina delle *vitae* medievali di S. Ubaldo: metamorfosi agiografiche fra Cinque e Seicento', *ib.*, 439–79.

M. S. Rollardi, 'A. Groppoli di Lunigiana. Potere e ricchezza di un feudatario genovese (secc. XVI-XVIII)', *ASLSP*, 36.1, 1996, 148 pp., is of some indirect literary interest since one of the proprietors of the fief was Anton Giulio Brignole Sale.

2.   POETRY

L. Giachino, ' "Atomi fecondi". Rassegna di edizioni e studi sulla poesia barocca (1989–1996)', *LItal*, 50:264–306, is very far from being comprehensive. G. Jori, ' "Sentenze maravigliose e dolci affetti". Jacopone tra Cinque e Seicento', *ib.*, 506–27, documents an aspect of the revival of interest in pre-Petrarchan poetry. M. L. Doglio, 'Il "Teatro Poetico" del Principe. Rime inedite di Carlo Emanuele I di Savoia', *StSec*, 39:3–31, publishes 37 *canzoni*, sonnets, and madrigals on amorous and religious subjects, taken from manuscripts in the Biblioteca Reale, Turin, and attributes them to the Duke of Savoy, though the evidence as given in the brief introduction (essentially the presence on the texts of the royal cipher) is by no means conclusive. In fact, the very first of the 'inediti' in question is actually Marino's *Canzone dei baci*, evidently transcribed from the 1602 *princeps* of the *Seconda parte delle Rime* or a later re-edition, which on the information supplied makes one wonder whether all (or any) of the others are by the Duke or whether we are dealing with fragments of a poetic 'scrap book' prepared for him. The same reservations must apply to the same scholar's, 'Il teatro del principe e il teatro del mondo: inediti di Carlo Emanuele I di Savoia e Valeriano Castiglione', *Croce Vol.*, 203–11, which publishes five further poems (a sonnet and four madrigals) attributed to Carlo Emanuele and a madrigal to the Duke for New Year 1627, accompanied by a brief letter, both by Castiglione. Rather oddly, no indication is given as to where they were found.

T. Montanari, 'Sulla fortuna poetica di Bernini. Frammenti del tempo di Alessandro VII e di Sforza Pallavicino', *StSec*, 39:127–64, surveys verse celebrations of Bernini and his work in the classically inclined literary circles of the Rome of Fabio Chigi and Queen Christina.

On Genoese dialect poetry we have *Gian Giacomo Cavalli, *In servixio dra patria e dra coronna*, ed. F. Toso, introd. F. Croce, Recco-Genova, Le Mani, 1997, 70 pp., being the text of two odes for the election of doges Giorgio Centurione (1621) and Leonardo della Torre (1632) and one on the occasion of the 1625 war against the Duke of Savoy. Also by F. Toso, *'Una poesia in genovese di Anton Giulio Brignole Sale', *A Compagna*, 29, 1997:4–5.

WORDS AND MUSIC. *La musica, la poesia, la spada. Diego Personè 'virtuoso gentil'huomo' del XVII secolo*, ed. L. Costi, introd. M. Marti, Lecce, Conte, 1997, 272 pp., contains four contributions relating to the music of this late polyphonist (and swordsman) and his 'paroliere' Girolamo Cicala: E. Bandiera, 'I Personè a Carpignano Salentino tra Cinque e Seicento' (11–27), sketching the history of this family of the minor nobility; G. Rizzo, 'Un secentesco sodalizio salentino, tra letteratura, musica e scherma (A. Grandi, G. Cicala, D. Personè)' (29–39), reconstructing aspects of Lecce's lively literary culture; L. Cosi, '*Il III libro di Madrigali a cinque voci* di Diego Personè. *Otia e negotia* di un "virtuoso gentil'homo"', considering his surviving musical output (41–57) and following it with an edition of the texts and music (59–229). The volume concludes with a bibliographical study: M. G. Brindisino, 'Polifonisti di Terra d'Otranto nel repertorio a stampa tra Cinque e Seicento' (231–71). I also note F. Chiarelli, 'Tradition and "gusto del secolo" in Monteverdi's *Il Sesto Libro de' Madrigali*', *ISt*, 53:52–66.

CAMPANELLA. *Poesie*, ed. F. Giancotti, T, Einaudi, clx + 694 pp., is the fruit of half a century's work on C.'s poetry and without doubt a considerable improvement on what has been available to date, including the 'poesie sparse', translations from Greek and Latin, and the late Latin verse (with Italian parallel text), as well as the *Scelta di poesie filosofiche* (based on a collation of the autograph corrections in the exemplar of the *editio princeps* in the Biblioteca dei Gerolamini, Naples, made before some of these were 'restored' into illegibility). The introduction strikes a good balance between asserting the importance and absolute originality of C.'s poetry, and not over-estimating its actual literary achievement. The presentation of the texts, however, seems to me to be flawed. In the first place, the fact that each composition is prefaced by an often lengthy note by the editor (discussing chronology, relation to other poems, variants, etc.), and followed by equally lengthy textual notes (some explicatory, some a good deal more discursive), as well as C.'s own glosses, means that the texts are buried deep in a mass of commentary, not all of it immediately helpful (169 poems, mostly sonnets and madrigals, stretch to nearly 700 pages). It may be the fashion to give this kind of prominence to the *apparato*, but valuable though it generally is in this case, its presence is very obtrusive, and the overall effect unwieldy, an obstacle rather than an aid to reading. Better to have kept the notes accompanying the text to the essential minimum, and given the rest of the information as end notes. A more fundamental criticism is that while it is clear that orthography and punctuation have been very significantly modernized, absolutely no information is given either as to the nature of the original or the criteria adopted. Given the extreme rarity of the *princeps* and the substantial autograph evidence, this seems a serious omission, tending implicitly to confirm the idea that what counts is more the philosopher than the poet. I would gladly have swapped the 40–page bio-bibliographical summary (which adds little to Firpo's *Dizionario Biografico degli Italiani* entry) for some idea of how the text we are given actually relates to what C. wrote. Concerning this edition see also F. Giancotti, 'Postille a una nuova edizione delle poesie di Campanella', *BrC*, 4:423–26, which includes some corrections.

CHIABRERA. *Maniere, scherzi e canzonette morali*, ed. G. Raboni, Parma, Fond. Bembo–Guanda, xliv + 578 pp., is a significant addition to the growing body of late-*Cinquecento*/early-*Seicento* poetry now available in modern critical editions. Generally accurate (though the occasional editorial choice leaves me doubtful) and usefully annotated, what impact it will have on the study of the period remains to be seen, but for my part, I cannot help but sympathize with De Sanctis's criticism of Chiabrera: 'sgraziato nell'intreccio delle rime [. . .] talora dà in dissonanze e stonature'. Furthermore, his verse seems as vacuous to me in this annotated edition as it did before (and Raboni makes no claims as to content): however skilful his handling of a variety of metres and rhyme schemes (carefully recorded here), his success seems to have been due more to the fact that he was safe, and safely *musicabile*, taking none of the risks with himself or his subject matter that Tasso or Marino took. Raboni's introduction and the note prefacing each composition have the considerable merit of brevity, making realistic claims concerning C.'s importance and not

engaging in the debatable lengthy disquisitions which have characterized some recent Fondazione Bembo editions. The 'Note al testo'
and *apparati* are precise and to the point, the latter including a
thorough account of the printed and manuscript tradition, with
significant variants. Even more useful, given the (very sensible)
decision *not* to attempt an edition of all Chiabrera's lyrics, but only
these, persuasively presented here as the best and most influential
collections put together by the author himself (about a fifth of his total
lyric output), is an appendix providing an overview of that production:
an inventory of all manuscript and printed sources, and an index of
first lines of all the known texts.

F. Bianchi, 'Per una definizione critica del Chiabrera: riflessioni su
una questione ancora aperta', *Croce Vol.*, 213–29, removes some of
the literary commonplaces surrounding Chiabrera the master-versi-
fier, but only to make room for some of his own ('uomo che si
interessa ai grandi problemi del suo tempo') which are almost wholly
unsubstantiated.

CIRO DI PERS. Lorenzo Carpané, *La tradizione manoscritta e a stampa
delle poesie di Ciro di Pers*, Mi, Guerini, 1997, 228 pp., is a painstaking
reconstruction of the textual tradition of one of the major mid-*Seicento*
poets, whose unwillingness to publish, leading to numerous partial
posthumous editions, makes the establishment of a critical text
difficult. It has to be said, however, that the conclusion, outlining the
criteria to be followed in preparing such a critical edition, makes one
wonder whether the job is worth the effort, since what is proposed
does not vary greatly from the edition by M. Rak (T, Einaudi, 1978)
while Carpané has now provided comprehensive details of the
variants.

MARINO. F. Gambonini, 'Bibliografia delle opere a stampa di
G. B. Marino: 1700–1940 (IV)', *StSec*, 39:243–322, concludes an
exhaustive survey (the term hardly does justice to its minute precision)
and includes a series of invaluable indexes. Whoever said bibliography was dull? The evidence of Marino's ongoing 'capillary'
presence over a 250-year period when, it was assumed, he had been
largely ignored will warrant extensive re-writing of the history of his
reception.

M. Slawinski, 'Marino tra Umbria e Inghilterra', *RELI*, 10,
1997[1998]:53–80, discusses aspects of Marino's career: his membership of the Accademia degli Insensati of Perugia and his authorship
of an aborted panegyric to Ann of Denmark, 'reina d'Inghilterra', in
relation to Aldobrandini patronage, and the subsequent literary
geography of *concettismo*. S. Carrai, 'Minturno, Marino e un modulo
oraziano', *Italique*, 1:93–101, suggests that, formally at least, the
famous rejection of heroic poetry of *Rime* I, 'Altri canti di Marte'

derives from Horace, via a sonnet of Minturno — but the evidence seems thin. P. Paolini, 'Su alcuni madrigali del Tasso (e due del Marino)', *EL*, 23.1:53–76, uses Marino's 'mechanistic' approach to composition largely as a foil to exalt Tasso; but since the latter's virtues as identified here are no less mechanical, all that really shows through is the futility of this kind of phoneme-crunching. A. Fabrizi, 'Due postille mariniane', *StSec*, 39:323–27, identifies verses attributed to Ennius in Cicero's *Tusculanorum disputationum* as a likely source for the *sdrucciole* of the dithyramb of *Adone* XII, and records a number of *Settecento* references to Marino (in Muratori, Rousseau, Bettinelli, Alfieri, Gori Gandellini), suggesting once again that his influence was more pervasive, and judgements of him less thoroughly negative, than has generally been assumed.

I also note V. de Maldé, *'Percorsi intertestuali negli scritti polemici di Giovan Battista Marino', pp. 81–118 of *Bufere e molli aurette. Polemiche letterarie dallo Stilnovo alla 'Voce'*, ed. M. G. Pansa, Mi, Guerini, 1996, 326 pp., which deals with the literary fall-out of the feud with Murtola; R. Simon, *'Le symbolisme hermétique dans l'*Adone* de G. B. Marino', *CER*, 8:117–39.

TASSONI. S. Longhi, 'Il vestito sconveniente. Abiti e armature nella *Secchia rapita*', *Italique*, 1:103–26, considers the comic inversions produced by 'vesti e armature bizzarre, mal combinate [...] sconvenienti', suggesting that the game goes beyond humour, engaging in a critique of the heroic code through a series of allusions and cross-references to more orthodox epics.

3. DRAMA

DRAMATIC TEXTS. Giovan Battista Andreini, *Amor nello specchio*, ed. S. Maira and A. M. Borracci, Ro, Bulzoni, 1997, 144 pp., presents the text of a 1622 play in a format which I find heavy going: no-one could quarrel with the stated aim to preserve clues as to performance, but this seems to entail some very odd punctuation, which far from reflecting the speaking voice simply conceals (and occasionally obliterates) the sense, and highly arbitrary decisions as to which spellings to preserve and which to standardize or modernize. The notes are not particularly helpful, and the introduction's claim that the play's real subject is lesbian love seems to me to lack any serious evidence.

Francesco Maria Marini, *Il fazzoletto. Tragicommedia inedita del secolo XVII*, ed. F. Toso and R. Trovato, CTLin, 1997, lxxi + 306 pp., is the first edition of this text, from a manuscript which tells us it was 'recitata in Genova l'anno 1642 nel Palazzo Reale' (in honour of the author's father, Doge Agostino Marini) in a mixture of Italian and

Genoese. The editor's arguments for the play's cultural and linguistic significance (as constituting an intervention in the debate over the excesses of *concettismo*, supposedly instigated by Matteo Pellegrini, and a critique of 'hypercorrect' Tuscan forms) are interesting, but far from proven.

M. Sarnelli, 'Il neosenechismo di Francesco Bracciolini', *StSec*, 39:33–78, discusses Senecan themes in B.'s tragedies *L'Evandro* (1612), *L'Arpalice* (1613), and *La Pentesilea* (1614); Id., 'Per un'ipotesi drammaturgica "regolare" nel primo seicento', *RLI*, 102:425–51, reads Prospero Bonarelli's *Solimano* (1619) and *Medoro incoronato* (first performed 1623, pub. 1645) as 'revisionist' interpretations of the Aristotelian theory of tragedy. V. Guercio, 'Tirannide e machiavellismo in scena pastorale: sulla *Galatea* di Pomponio Torelli', *GSLI*, 175:161–209, returns to the political reading of this 1603 pastoral first suggested by Croce but rejected by subsequent critics. The argument (equating Poliphemus to a tyrant) is only partially convincing: though I am certain that this supposedly escapist genre is indeed much more political than generally supposed, Guercio's interpretation seems a little forced.

OPERA AND ORATORIO. I. Mamczarz, *'Il melodramma del Seicento e l'"Industria teatrale": il ruolo delle macchine teatrali e della scenotecnica nella trasformazione del melodramma', *Atti* (AISLLI 15), 117–37. F. Bussi, ' "Ancien Régime" dei teatri musicali piacentini tra Seicento e Settecento', *ASPP*, 47, 1995[1996]:161–67, records a small number of 17th-c. performances.

SPECTACLE. M. Slawinski, 'Consuming the Revels: eating as spectacle at the Medicean Court', *NCo*, 24, 1997[1998]:32–55, discusses public banqueting and the distribution of food and wine to the 'plebs' on the occasion of the great dynastic celebrations of 1539–1608, as actualized metaphors, when the material and symbolic orders of society are intended momentarily to coincide, and through them traces the progressive dissolution of Renaissance representations of an idealized community where 'court' and 'plebs' coexist in symbiotic harmony. Changes in the ways court spectacle is produced and consumed are related to the political and economic transformations of Early Modern Italy and presented as the basis for a cultural-materialist redefinition of the Baroque as a historiographical category. The definition of the Baroque is also the subject of T. Koswan, 'Jeu de miroirs, phénomène baroque', *RHT*, 199:197–206, which exhumes the old *canard* concerning Bernini's 1637 *Commedia dei due teatri* as one of the 'jeux de miroirs [. . .] représentatifs de ce qu'on appelle le baroque', but leaves us none the wiser as to why they are representative.

E. Gavazza, 'Le vittorie di Minerva. Il Gran Balletto di Madama la Duchessa di Valentinese danzato in Monaco l'anno 1655', *Croce Vol.*, 231–47, reconstructs the spectacle designed by Orazio de Ferrari to a programme by Francesco Fulvio Frugoni.

4. PROSE

Sergio Bozzola, *La retorica dell'Eccesso. 'Il Tribunale della Critica' di Francesco Fulvio Frugoni*, Padua, Antenore, 1996, 330 pp., is a rhetorical-stylistic analysis of the fifth *latrato* of the *Cane di Diogene* (a work which one struggles to place within the sub-categories of *Seicento* prose), as measured against the classic *schemata* and *figurae*, the sub-types of metaphor proposed by Tesauro and those of modern linguistics-inspired revisions of rhetoric (which interestingly prove less capable of accounting for Frugoni's ingeniousness than Tesauro's). How far it advances understanding of this *caso limite* of baroque prose remains to be seen however — perhaps until such time as the study of style and content converge in Bozzola's own planned edition of the *Tribunale* (pencilled in for a future Fondazione Bembo volume).

HISTORIOGRAPHY.   Camillo Tutini and Marino Verde, *Racconto della sollevatione di Napoli accaduta nell'anno MDCXLVII*, ed. P. Messina, Ro, ISIEMC, 1997, lxxii + 664 pp., publishes the text of a chronicle originally written as a day-to-day account of Masaniello's Revolution by Verde, then revised and added to by Tutini (both of them supporters of the defeated, 'popular' side). An extensive introduction deals with the authors, their milieu, and their political views, as well as the text's complex history, testified to by a number of surviving drafts and copies. It is questionable whether the decision to adopt hyper-conservative 'criteri di trascrizione' is the right one for a lengthy historical document of this kind, since it hardly facilitates reading, while its significance in relation to the history of the language is marginal. However, this remains a substantial work of scholarship.

G. Galasso, 'Motivi e forme della storiografia italiana tra Cinque e Seicento', pp. 31–55 of *Storici, filosofi*, cit., traces the evolution (and involution) of historical writing, to its decline in the later *Seicento*, the end of a tradition which is seen as the necessary premise of its *Settecento* renewal.

NARRATIVE.   Lucrezia Marinella, *Arcadia felice*, ed. F. Lavocat, F, Olschki, lxviii, 220 pp., is altogether a strange package. The work's principal claims to fame are the sex of its author (though unlike some contemporary pastoral dramas it does not seem much touched by gender politics) and the fact that it is virtually the only Italian pastoral *romanzo* of the period (though that ignores both the presence of strong pastoral elements in other prose narratives and the question whether this strangely dated book, a throwback to Sannazaro, with linguistic echoes of Francesco Colonna, is a *romanzo* at all). The text provided is characterized by inexplicable oscillations between slavish adherence to the sole extant edition and unnecessary corrections and interpolations, accompanied by exceedingly long and sometimes quite superfluous footnotes. The equally lengthy introduction casts around for reasons to exhume the work, considers several in a half-hearted fashion, and comes to no conclusions.

Fulvio Pevere, *L'ordine della retorica. La riscrittura del mondo nelle novelle di Maiolino Bisaccioni*, T, Tirrenia, 174 pp., has some interesting things to say concerning Bisaccioni's extensive output of *novelle* (four collections between 1637 and 1664), though it is by no means certain on the evidence of this study (a doctoral thesis) whether they deserved a full-length monograph; and while the final chapter (following three dealing with internal structure, narratology, and rhetoric) attempts to place them in socio-political context (interestingly, the titles of three of the collections explicitly raise the question of the relationship between literary 'fiction' and historical 'truth'), the conclusion that faced with the irresolvable contradictions of politics Bisaccioni can only retreat into the Utopia of literature seems a little superficial. Utopias are not merely escapes: both in content and form they posit alternatives which cannot but reflect back on the real world. If narratological and linguistic Utopias (and dystopias) are a constant of the *Seicento*, from Marino to Frugoni, that is a response to very material circumstances (as Bisaccioni's fellow *Accademico insensato* Ferrante Pallavicino discovered, it was dangerous to tackle political issues head-on), not necessarily a sign of disengagement.

A. Coppola, 'L'*Albergo* di Maiolino Bisaccioni', *NLe*, 1996, no. 4–7 : 147–54, is altogether too brief and naive an account to do more than skim the surface of the text, yet its observation that 'potrebbe altrimenti intitolarsi *Pensieri sui principi e l'arte del governare*' may come closer to its partially concealed concerns than some of Pevere's subtler lucubrations.

L. Spera, 'Permanenze secentesche. La narrativa barocca italiana nel XVIII secolo: un episodio francese', *StSec*, 39 : 79–95, describes the treatment of *romanzi* (and *novelle* collections) in the *Bibliothèque Universelle des Romans* (1775–1789). Another aspect of the reception of the genre outside Italy is discussed in J. Miszalska, '*Il Cretideo* di G. B. Manzini tradotto in polacco', *ib.*, 97–124.

SACRED ORATORY. A. Maggi, 'Memoria ed immagini emblematiche nel *Funerale fatto nel Duomo di Torino*, di Luigi Giuglaris', *ib.*, 111–24, discusses a complex description of the *apparato funebre* for the 1637 funeral of Vittorio Amedeo di Savoia in terms of the 'mnemonic' relation between words and images; but despite appealing to a variety of currently fashionable topics, from Camillo's *Teatro* to sacred oratory (the Jesuit Giuglaris was a leading exponent, singled out by Croce to exemplify its supposed vices), the drift and purpose of the argument escape me.

5. THOUGHT

BIOLOGY, MEDICINE, AND THE NATURAL WORLD. G. Weber, *L'anatomia patologica di Lorenzo Bellini (1643–1704)*, F, Olschki, 170 pp., discusses the Florentine physician's anatomical studies, which are said to point to developments in late 18th-c. physiology. *Marcello Malpighi, anatomist and physician*, ed. D. Bertoloni Meli, xii + 174 pp., contains a large number of contributions which space prevents me from detailing. I also note A. Ottaviani, 'La natura senza inventario: aspetti della ricerca naturalistica del Linceo Fabio Colonna', *Physis*, 36, 1997:91–113.

ETHICS AND POLITICS. Torquato Accetto, *Della dissimulazione onesta*, ed. S. S. Nigro, T, Einaudi, 1997, xl + 76 pp., derives from Nigro's earlier edition (Genoa, Costa & Nolan, 1986) itself based on the text of the first (and only) 17th-c. edition, possibly supervised by Accetto himself. In line with the present more 'conservative' fashions, the new version sticks closer to the *princeps*. It is prefaced by an elegant though not particularly substantial introduction and accompanied by notes of varying interest: excellent those on sources, parallels, and intertextual echoes; sometimes superfluous the glosses and observations on style.

Virgilio Malvezzi, *Davide perseguitato*, ed. Denise Aricò, Ro, Salerno, 1997, 145 pp., republishes another of Malvezzi's exemplary, aphoristic biographies, with an introduction which essentially summarizes the arguments of a previous article (*YWMLS* 59:550). But while the conservative, rigidly Catholic views of this well-connected aristocratic historian and political moralist are certainly interesting, claims as to his importance in contemporary culture and the development of historiography seem to me yet to be substantiated.

Linda Bisello, *Medicina della memoria. Aforistica ed esemplarità nella scrittura barocca*, F, Olschki, xx + 300 pp., is to my knowledge the first monograph dedicated to a genre, the collection of aphorisms, maxims, brief exemplary stories, and the like, clearly of great significance in the *Seicento*. Its scope is principally, though not exclusively, Italian, and the sources on which it draws extensive (though far from exhaustive). The result is disappointing however: a dutiful trawl through the literature which touches on all the commonplaces (*stupor* and wonder, encyclopaedism, the debate over the 'stile laconico', prudence, *dissimulazione*, etc.) yet fails to come up with any answers as to why the earlier traditions of *florilegia, avvertimenti,* and exemplary lives should have led to what was effectively a new, autonomous form, or how this related to a wider crisis of humanist values. (The tradition originates in the anti-scholastic, practical objectives of the discursive, rhetoricized 'new logic' of the Quattrocento, yet aphorisms also claim axiomatic status within the Aristotelian revival of the Counter-Reformation: a contradiction which constantly surfaces in the way their functionality as axioms, foundations of a binding, objective philosophical discourse, is undermined by the aphorists' love of antithesis, oxymoron, paradox.) On a closely related theme, R. Bragantini, 'Discorsi della prudenza: esempi italiani tra secondo Cinque e primo Seicento', *AFLLS,* 37 : 9–28, points to the breakdown and rejection of the Renaissance tradition of didactic *exempla,* fables and apologues (as typified by two very different texts: Giovan Pietro Giussani's *Brancaleone* and Virgilio Malvezzi's *Ritratto del privato politico cristiano*).

B. Anatra, 'La leggenda nera in Italia: Boccalini e Tassoni', *AFLFUC,* 15, 1996–97 : 159–66, returns to these authors' anti-Spanish polemics without, however, adding anything of substance to what Croce had noted early this century.

THEOLOGY. Roberto Bellarmino, *Scritti Spirituali (1615–1620),* ed. G. Galeota et al., 3 vols., Brescia, Morcelliana, 924, 842, 648 pp., consists of Italian translations of works from the last years of the Cardinal's life, learned meditations with a strongly theological flavour, each prefaced by a brief introduction: *Elevarsi interiormente a Dio* and *La felicità eterna dei Santi in Paradiso* (Vol. I), *Il Gemito della Colomba, cioè l'utilità spirituale del pianto* and *Le sette parole di Cristo sulla Croce* (Vol. II), *Il dovere del principe cristiano* and *L'arte di ben morire* (Vol. III).

François Laplanche, *Bible, sciences et pouvoirs au XVIIe siècle,* Na, Bibliopolis, 1997, 146 pp., is concerned with both the epistemological and natural-philosophical problems of biblical exegesis and the political context of the debate. Its scope is European — Protestant as well as Catholic — rather than simply Italian, but is all the more useful for that (for the debate as it related to Galileo's discoveries, see below).

L. Conti, 'Galilei e Paolo Beni: astrologia, determinismo e Inquisizione', pp. 307–29 of *Storici, filosofi,* cit., despite the prominence given to Galileo's name, is almost exclusively concerned with Beni's 1603 attempt to resolve the controversy then raging between Dominicans and Jesuits over the exact relationship between Divine Grace and human free will, an effort which came close to the position of the Jesuit Molina and resulted in the prohibition of his work by the Dominicans (who controlled the Holy Office).

CAMPANELLA. Luigi Firpo, *I processi di Tommaso Campanella*, ed.
E. Canone, Ro, Salerno editrice, 350 pp., reconstructs Campanella's
first trials and publishes the relevant documents from Roman and
Neapolitan archives.

G. Ernst, 'Il cielo in una stanza: l'*Apologeticus* di Campanella in
difesa dell'opuscolo *De siderali fato vitando*', BrC, 3, 1997:303–34,
publishes a new version of C.'s defence of his astrological beliefs and
of the rituals to ward off harmful influences as compatible with the
doctrine of free will and within the bounds of nature (hence not
constituting a demonic pact) from a Vatican manuscript mistakenly
ascribed to one Giulio Cesare Lagalla, prefaced by a lucid introduction to the text's history and significance in the development of C.'s
thought. V. Frajese, 'L'*Atheismus triumphatus* come romanzo filosofico
di formazione', *ib.*, 4:313–42, reads this key text as an implicit denial
of the accusations laid against C. in his 1599 heresy trial, arguing that
the ideas attributed to him then are the same as those he refutes
here — plausible enough, but from this to arguing that it makes it a
forerunner of the *Bildungsroman* seems to me a considerable leap. M.-
P. Lerner, 'L' "incertaine et changeante fortune" posthume de
Campanella entre Dominicains et Jésuites', *ib.*, 369–99, is of considerable interest, though not so much for the fact that C. would prove
more popular with the Jesuits than with his own order (*nemo propheta
in patria*) as for its reconstruction of some of the arguments relating to
the debate on Grace and salvation, showing just how intricate the
question was and how fine some of the distinctions between Catholic
and Protestant positions were. M. Fintoni, ' "Folle l'occhio mortal del
basso mondo". Menzogne e annichilazione in Tommaso Campanella', *ib.*, 301–12, contrasts C.s views on deception with those of
his classical sources. W. Neuber, 'La redenzione immaginata. Andreae, Campanella e la crisi dell'utopia all'inizio del Seicento', *ib.*,
93–106, relates Johan Valentinus Andreae's departures from his
source, the *Città del Sole*, to the very different climate of introspection
characterizing contemporary German protestantism.

F. Arato, ' "Genoa, del mondo donna". Intorno a un sonetto di
Tommaso Campanella', *Croce Vol.*, 149–62, considers C.'s ambivalent
view of the Genoese Republic, connecting it with his shift from
hostility to Spain, to the millenarian expectations of the *Monarchia di
Spagna*, to the resumption of hostility as he enters the sphere of French
royal patronage, while also emphasizing the underlying coherence of
his political thought (the objectives remain constant, even though he
may frequently change his mind as to which institutions may best
promote them). T. Tornatore, 'Tre manoscritti inesplorati della *Città
del Sole*', *ib.*, 149–201, re-examines the question of the genealogy of
the veritable 'selva' of manuscript versions on the basis of three which

had hitherto received little attention, the two British Library versions and one now at the University of Kansas, but concludes rather despairingly that 'più ci si immerge [. . .] più ci si rende conto di quanto sia utopico costringerla a svelare tutti i suoi misteri'.

C. Longo, 'Fra' Tommaso Campanella e la Congregazione di Propaganda Fide', *AFP*, 68 : 347–67, traces Campanella's interest in missionary work and provides a brief appendix reproducing relevant documents.

I also note: R. Hagengruber, 'La fondazione del punto matematico nella filosofia di Tomaso Campanella', *BrC*, 3, 1997 : 77–92; C. Leijenhorst, 'Motion, monks and golden mountains: Campanella and Hobbes on perception and cognition', *ib.*, 93–121; O. Faracovi, 'Sull'oroscopo di Campanella', *ib.*, 245–63; M.-D. Couzinet, 'Notes sur les *Medicinalia* de Tommaso Campanella', *Nuncius*, 13 : 39–67; P. Ponzio, 'Tommaso Campanella e la *Questio singularis* di Jean-Baptiste Poysson', *Physis*, 34, 1997 : 71–97.

GALILEO AND THE NEW SCIENCE. Paolo Ponzio, *Copernicanesimo e teologia. Scrittura e natura in Campanella, Galilei e Foscarini*, Bari, Levante, 196 pp., rehearses the well-known controversy sparked off by Foscarini's defence of G., but though it does fill in some of the theological background and detail, it does not appear to me to break new ground concerning the underlying epistemological questions. I. A. Kelter, 'A Catholic theologian responds to Copernicanism: the theological *Judicium* of Paolo Foscarini's *Lettera*', *RenR*, 21 : 2, 1997 : 59–70, considers a brief anonymous judgement, adducing it as proof that the real argument was not between heliocentrism and geocentrism, but 'the celestial-terrestrial distinction', which may be partly true (though Bellarmine among others had not insisted upon it when lecturing at Louvain) but really leaves us none the wiser concerning its claim to elucidate 'the theological climate' in Rome around 1616 (particularly since we know nothing of the date or authorship of the document). Much the same can be said of A. Poppi, 'La lettera del cardinale Carlo Conti a Galileo su cosmologia aristotelica e Bibbia (7 luglio 1612): l'approdo galileiano alla nuova ermeneutica biblica', *AMAP*, 199, 1996–97 : 131–58: though it does serve to remind one that the issue had been brewing for some time prior to 1616 and that Galileo, as his Copernican resolve stiffened, had been conscious of the need to confront the theological issues, the claims that he would produce 'una soluzione lucida e definitiva del problema ermeneutico della Bibbia nei confronti della scienza naturale', and that the exchange with Conti was the route towards this, seem excessively simplistic in the light of what we now know of the intricacies and contradictions of the subsequent debate.

The question is discussed much more thoroughly by E. McMullin, 'Galileo on science and Scripture', pp. 271–347 of *The Cambridge Companion to Galileo*, ed. P. Machamer, CUP, xii + 462 pp., who concludes that Galileo painted himself into a corner: he could not refrain from endorsing the argument (derived from Augustine) that an alternative, non-literal interpretation of Scripture should only be sought when the letter contradicted *demonstrable* philosophical truths, but an irrefutable demonstration of heliocentrism was precisely what he was unable to produce, either in 1616 or in 1633. M. Pera, 'The god of theologians and the god of astronomers. An apology of Bellarmine', *ib.*, 367–87, takes the same issues in a different direction, suggesting that Bellarmine may have been more alert to the potential damage to faith of a conciliation with science on Galileo's terms, than those popes, from Leo XIII to John Paul II, who have sought to accommodate modern science by distinguishing its concerns from those of theology, while emphasizing the underlying truths common to both; P. Redondi, 'From Galileo to Augustine', *ib.*, 175–210, takes a broader view of Galileo's attempt to reconcile science and faith, pointing to dependence on and parallels to Augustine. Other, more technical contributions on Galileo's science in this collection include: W. A. Wallace, 'Galileo's Pisan studies in science and philosophy' (27–52); P. Machamer, 'Galileo's machines, his mathematics, and his experiments' (53–79); R. Feldhay, 'The use and abuse of mathematical entities: Galileo and the Jesuits revisited' (80–145); W. Hooper, 'Inertial problems in Galileo's preinertial framework' (146–74); W. Shea, 'Galileo's Copernicanism: the science and the rhetoric' (211–43). All are highly accomplished but the purpose of the volume as a whole seems questionable: many aspects of Galileo's work and career are not touched on; the rather anodyne introduction by Machamer suggests a student reader, but many of the contributions, though not covering wholly new ground, are clearly pitched at a higher level of specialization, while the final two essays, by M. Segre, 'The never-ending Galileo story' (388–416), and P. Galluzzi, 'The sepulchres of Galileo: the "living" remains of a hero of science' (417–47), would not be out of place in a book for the general public. A perfunctory bibliography and even more perfunctory index compound the sense of confusion.

Mario Biagioli's *Galileo Courtier* (*YWMLS*, 55:579) continues to arouse debate, with M. Clavelin, 'Galilée homme de cour. Sur un ouvrage de Mario Biagioli', *RHSc*, 51:115–26, and J. C. Pitti, 'Will the real Galileo please stand up?', *Physis*, 34, 1997:313–20, both concerned to stress the limits of his patronage-driven model of scientific research (though one suspects that the real target is sociological relativism in its more extreme forms, not Biagioli, who despite the occasional rhetorical gesture is generally rather more cautious in his claims).

L. Degryse, 'Acteurs et mise en scène dans le *Dialogue sur les deux grands systèmes* de Galilée', *ChrI*, 55–56:31–48, attempts to read the *Dialogo* 'dans une perspective théâtrale', though it is difficult to see what new insights are afforded by this (not particularly novel) idea. H. Gatti, 'Giordano Bruno's *Ash Wednesday supper* and Galileo's *Dialogue of the two major world systems*', *BrC*, 3, 1997:283–300, considers parallels already noted by Giovanni Aquilecchia (see *YWMLS* 57:541), whose work passes unacknowledged here. F. Favino, 'A proposito dell'atomismo di Galileo: da una lettera di Tommaso Campanella ad uno scritto di Giovanni Ciampoli', *ib.*, 265–82, is perhaps most interesting for the evidence it presents of Ciampoli's commitment to atomism (as evinced in a 1639 anonymous manuscript dialogue which Favino attributes to him), possible indirect corroboration for the view that this played some part in Galileo's downfall. I also note: M. Fehér, 'Patterns of argumentation in Galileo's *Discorsi*', *ISPS*, 12:17–24; W. A. Wallace, 'Galileo's regressive methodology, its prelude and its sequel', pp. 229–52 of *Method and Order in Renaissance Philosophy of Nature: the Aristotle Commentary Tradition*, ed. D. A. Di Liscia et al., Aldershot, Ashgate, 1997, xii + 416 pp., which also contains M. Camerota, 'Flaminio Papazzoni: un aristotelico bolognese maestro di Federico Borromeo e corrispondente di Galileo' (271–300).

D. Bertoloni Meli, 'Shadows and deception: from Borelli's *Theoricae* to the *Saggi* of the Cimento', *BJHS*, 31:383–402, draws an interesting sketch of the talented but far from original 'Galilean' attempting to negotiate the conflicting demands of the new science, his patron Leopoldo de' Medici, and the Jesuit scientific establishment (particularly the highly influential Cardinal Sforza Pallavicino and Honoré Fabri, with whose astronomical studies he competed for priority). Three letters from Borelli to Leopoldo concerning his rivalry with 'quel cervellaccio' (i.e. Fabri) are appended to the article. I also note D. Aricò, 'Giovanni Antonio Roffeni: un astrologo bolognese amico di Galileo', *Il Carrobbio*, 24:67–96.

SETTECENTO

By G. W. SLOWEY, *Lecturer in Italian, University of Birmingham*

1. GENERAL

Raffaele Gianesini, *I proclami napoleonici (1797) della Biblioteca V. Joppi di Udine*, F, Olschki, 1997, 234 pp., has a mass of information on the printing, iconography, signatories, and so on, of these important documents. V. Trombetta, 'Intellettuali e collezionismo librario nella Napoli austriaca', *ASPN*, 114, 1996[1997]:61–93, examines the Domenico Greco collection in the Biblioteca Nazionale di Napoli, which the author describes as put together from the point of view of branches of knowledge rather than merely interest in individual books, beginning with a discussion of the collections of private libraries in 18th-c. Naples, and continuing with an account of printing against the background of the Church's *Index librorum prohibitorum.* Zefirino Campanini, *Istruzioni pratiche ad un novello capo-stampa, o sia regolamento per la direzione di una tipografica officina (1789)*, ed. Conor Fahy, F, Olschki—London, MHRA, 398 pp., presents the only manual which has survived from the days of hand printing, written by a man who worked all his active life as a compositor for Bodoni in Parma. C. Fahy, 'La descrizione del torchio tipografico nel *Dizionario delle arti e de' mestieri* (1768–1778) di Francesco Griselini', pp. 277–91 of *Libri, tipografi, biblioteche: ricerche storiche dedicate a Luigi Balsamo*, F, Olschki, 1997, discusses the work of this Venetian writer, whose dictionary, as its author proudly says, 'non è più una servile traduzione, ma una compilazione del migliore', though, as Fahy points out, it still remains, basically, a translation from French.

LITERARY HISTORY AND BACKGROUND. *L'illuminismo: dizionario storico*, ed. Vincenzo Ferrone and Daniel Roche, Ro–Bari, Laterza, 1997, 673 pp., contains a wide series of articles, divided into four main categories: *Valori, idee, linguaggio*; *Immagini, simboli, rappresentazioni*; *Pratiche*; *Spazi*, and which looks at Enlightenment influences in such countries as the USA. There is also an extensive and extremely valuable bibliography by Antonio Trampus, and an afterword on the impact of the Enlightenment in the 19th and 20th centuries. G. Dioguardi, 'Enciclopedismo nel XVIII secolo', *Belfagor*, 53:208–15, surveys the vast theme with reference to *StSet*, 16, 1996. E. Brambilla, 'Università, scuole e professioni in Italia dal primo '700 alla Restaurazione', *AISIGT*, 23, 1997[1998]:153–208, deals with periods of reform in areas such as Piedmont in the 1760s and 1770s, examining the evidence of French influence and the development of Enlightenment thought, particularly in the sciences, while pointing out that studies in philosophy tended to remain in the hands of conservative thinkers. The article explains how, while the *laurea* in law was awarded largely as a result of money or influence, from the 1770s onwards there is a noticeable acceleration in reform in universities and schools, leading to extensive changes to legal qualifications and practice during the period of French domination. V. Ferrone, 'The Accademia Reale delle Scienze: cultural sociability and men of letters in Turin of the Enlightenment under Vittorio Amedeo III', *JModH*, 70:519–60, discusses the importance of the founding of the Academy, and the recognition of the widespread political dissent based on Enlightenment culture, and shows the development of the *letterato* in Turin and the role of freemasonry in the cultural and political life of Piedmont. A. Mattone and P. Sanna, 'La "rivoluzione delle idee": la riforma delle due università sarde e la circolazione della cultura europea (1764–1790)', *RSI*, 110:834–942, beginning with a description of the appalling state of the universities of Cagliari and Sassari, outlines the reform of studies in law and philosophy and the introduction of courses in physics, mathematics and the natural sciences, pointing in particular to Francesco Cotti's *Storia naturale di Sardegna* (1774–78) and the work of Plazza. The article further discusses the development and promotion of Sardinians in the university world, and the problems associated with the transfer from 'outsiders' to local teachers, which led to further lively debates on Sardinian culture and in particular on the status of Sardinian as a language, with the work of Matteo Madao in the area of philology, which also became part of the argument about the honour of Sardinia. There is also an examination of literary, particularly poetic, presentations of scientific matters, an example being *Il tesoro della Sardegna* (1779) by Antonio Porqueddu, and the article concludes by showing how the crisis of absolutism in the 1790s found its most fervent interpreters amongst those who had studied at the reformed universities. Maria Teresa Silvestrini, *La politica della religione. Il governo ecclesiastico sabaudo del XVIII secolo*, F, Olschki, 1997, 428 pp., deals with the Concordats of 1727 and 1741 between the court of Turin and the papacy, and highlights different aspects of the Church's relationship with, and impact on, not only Vittorio Amedeo II and Carlo Emanuele III, but all levels of society. Jacopo Riccati and Giovanni Poleni, *Carteggio (1715–1742)*, ed. Marco Soppelsa, F, Olschki, 1997, 350 pp., contains a series of seventy letters, giving a great deal of interesting information on new thinking in Venice, especially in the field of scientific development. Serviliano Latuada, *Descrizione di Milano ornata con molti disegni in rame, tomo quinto, Milano, Giuseppe Cairoli, 1737*, Mi, La Vita Felice, 381 pp., one volume in what was originally a series of five, demonstrates different ways of approaching the presentation of the city. D. Tongiorgi, 'Una "filosofia della storia" nell'università del Settecento. Note su Aurelio Bertola (con inediti di Ippolito Pindemonte)', *GSLI*, 174:481–521, discussing the setting up of a chair of universal history in the University of Pavia, entrusted to Aurelio de' Giorgi Bertola, shows how Bertola, in his *Filosofia della storia* (1787), asserted the supremacy of modern institutions over the old. The work was praised in three poems by Pindemonte which are reproduced at the end. *Imperiale e real corte*, ed. Concetta Giamblanco and Piero Marchi, Ro, Pubblicazioni degli Archivi di Stato, 1997, vii + 530 pp., is an extensive inventory, covering all aspects of the organization of the granducal court in Tuscany after the arrival of Peter Leopold in 1765, with interesting sections on libraries and museums. C. Triarico, 'La corrispondenza di Leonardo Ximenes. Inventario delle filze del carteggio conservate nel Fondo Nazionale della Biblioteca Nazionale Centrale di Firenze', *Nuncius*, 18:209–46, examines some forty years of Ximenes' correspondence, covering controversial issues such as Newtonian physics and natural sciences as well as his reviews for the *Storia letteraria d'Italia* and his *Catechismo storico del Concilio di Trento*. G. Fiori, 'Vita intellettuale, religiosa, artistica e sociale a Piacenza tra Sette e Ottocento: il Consorzio di S. Cecilia, l'Accademia degli Agitati, la Conversazione dei Cavalieri e il Circolo di Lettura', *BSPia*, 93:43–79, chooses a number of institutions whose existence has long been forgotten and reconstructs their role in the spread of ideas in Piacenza. R. Unfer Lukoschik, 'Elisabetta Caminer Turra (1751–1796). Una letterata veneta per l'Europa', *AARA*, 247, 1997:215–51, presents a Venetian intellectual who worked to promote Enlightenment ideas in different cultural arenas, including the theatre, where she ran foul of Carlo Gozzi who condemned her translations, though she was later responsible for the production of plays by Beaumarchais and Diderot. She was also extremely active in publication of such material as the *Giornale enciclopedico*. When this ran into censorship problems, she set up her own printing press and produced controversial works such as her translation of Méhégan's *Tableau de l'histoire moderne* and Berquin's *L'ami des enfans* and other works on women's education. A. Montanari, 'Giovanni Bianchi (Iano Planco), studente di medicina a Bologna (1717–19) in un epistolario inedito', *StRmgn*, 46, 1995[1998]:379–94, draws on Bianchi's correspondence to demonstrate his acquaintance with the world of letters and academies, where he became secretary to the Accademia de' Letterati at Rimini. A. R. Capoccia, 'La casa di esercizi spirituali di Foligno (1729–1773)', *AHSJ*, 67:161–206, draws on extensive archival material to present a picture of Jesuit activity in Foligno, where the retreat house had a number of distinguished intellectual directors, and concludes with a selection of the documents used. Giuseppe Bonaccorso and Tommaso Manfredi, *I Virtuosi al Pantheon 1700–1758*, introd. Vitaliano Tiberia, Ro, Nuova Argos, xxvi + 148 pp., provides much information on the members of the cultural elite who belonged to this Academy, launched in 1542 and still in existence. *RMC*, 5, 1997[1998] has a number of articles on the importance of Holy Years for the cultural life of the city in the 18th c.: D. Rocciolo, 'Preparare il giubileo: il ruolo del vicariato nell'anno santo 1725' (521–52); S. Nanni, ' "Anno di rinnovazione e di penitenza. Anno di reconciliazione e di grazia". Il giubileo del 1750' (553–87); B. Dompnier, 'Le pardon sans pèlerinage. La France, le jubilé de 1751 et Rome' (589–617). G. Addeo, '*Il Vero Repubblicano*', *CLett*, 26:51–61, discusses a periodical published for the first time on the arrival of André-Joseph Abrial as French political commissar in Naples in 1799; although it ran for only four issues, it was seen by many later republicans and democrats as having contributed substantially to the cause of liberty. By the same author is 'La libertà di stampa nella Repubblica napoletana del 1799', *ASPN*, 114, 1996[1997]:243–93, which asserts the comparative lack of collaboration of Neapolitan *letterati* in the literary and scientific fields for most of the 18th c., discussing censorship, both religious and political, as well as the origins of the city's *stampa periodica*, before moving on to an analysis of the press freedom introduced by the French in 1799. The author points out that while there still remained some form of press control, this period saw the publication of important periodicals such as Eleonora De Fonseca Pimentel's *Monitore*. A. Borelli, 'Istituzioni e attrezzature scientifiche a Napoli nell'età dei lumi', *ib.*, 131–83, considers Bernardo Tanucci's limited response to calls for the development and reform of the economy, agriculture, and scientific structures by such important figures as Genovesi, while pointing out that developments in medicine and printing showed that works in Italian and foreign translations in the field of sciences were in demand. The article also deals with the founding in 1778, after the fall of Tanucci, of the Reale Accademia delle Scienze e Belle Lettere and the Reale Accademia Militare which, towards the end of the century, was the most active centre for research in chemistry. R. Librandi, 'Sul lessico dell'economia negli scritti di Antonio Genovesi e Ferdinando Galiani', *Atti* (AISLLI, 15), 239–52. P. Matarazzo, 'La formazione civile del suddito nel Regno di Napoli alla fine del XVIII secolo: i catechismi degli stati di vita', *AAPN*, 46, 1997[1998]:173–94, examines Marcello Eusebio Scotti's *Catechismo nautico*, which devoted the last of its five chapters to the education of women, and looks at other works, such the *Catechismo di agricoltura pratica e pastorizia* by Teodoro Monticelli, which emphasize the need for socio-economic development and deal with religion from the point of view of social utility. P. Amodio, 'La diffusione del pensiero di John Locke a Napoli nell'età di Vico', *AASN*, 108, 1997 [1998], is a bibliographical study of references in writings relating to debates on Locke in Naples, together with lists of principal editions of Locke to be found in Neapolitan libraries and of places where Locke is mentioned by Vico. John Ingamells, *A Dictionary of British and Irish Travellers in Italy 1701–1800*, New Haven, Yale U.P., 1997, lii + 1070 pp., is an immensely useful publication of the archive which Sir Brinsley Ford gave to the Paul Mellon Centre in 1988, covering some six hundred travellers. L. Polezzi, 'Thomas Jones. Autobiografia e viaggio nelle memorie di un paesaggista gallese in Italia', *Intersezioni*, 18:67–84, describes the painter's journeys in Italy and his links with Rome and Naples in the period 1776–80. On travellers in the other direction is J. Lindon, 'L'Inghilterra della rivoluzione industriale nelle descrizioni di viaggio italiane tardo-settecentesche', *Atti* (AISLLI, 15), 177–88, which discusses principally the *Giornale del viaggio d'Inghilterra* of Carlo Castone della Torre di Rezzonico. P. Sárközy, ' "Ognor l'util cercando". Poesia e scienza nella cultura arcadica', *ib.*, 189–97, on Arcadia as more than a mere poetic manifestation: a vast cultural movement embracing the natural sciences and exerting its influence as far afield as Hungary.

2. PROSE, POETRY, DRAMA

Il Caffè, 1764–1766, ed. Gianni Francioni and Sergio Romagnoli, T, Bollati Boringhieri, 2 vols, clxxviii + 404 pp., ix + 848 pp., is a revised edition of the 1993 original. R. Giglio, 'Bibliografia delle opere e delle edizioni di S. Alfonso M. de Liguori', *CLett*, 26, 100:503–23. F. M. Dovetto, 'Produzione e ricezione del linguaggio negli studi italiani della seconda metà del Settecento', *LS*, 33:231–66, distinguishes different approaches in 18th-c. discussion of language, including important work on the physiology of speech and hearing which went largely unnoticed, scholars preferring to concentrate on the goal of a people who could communicate in a national language. The writings of Domenico Cotugno and Francesco Soave, and Cesarotti's differences of opinion with Vico, are given particular attention. N. Jonard, 'Images du paysan au XVIIIe siècle. Mythes et réalités', *REI*, 44:7–22, looks at the depiction of the countryside in Parini and Goldoni, also examining Passeroni's *Cicerone* and descriptions which were essentially 16th-c. Arcadian by writers such as Zaccaria Betti. R. Schwaderer, 'Die Aufklärung in Italien — eine Epoche ohne Roman?', *ItStudien*, 19:184–201, questions the impression given by major histories of Italian literature that the *romanzo*, in prose or in verse, disappeared during the Settecento, and points out that it remained extremely popular as mass literature, though not used by the *letterati* to express new ideas. The article also claims that the place of the *romanzo* in the literary system was taken by autobiography, the two forms coming together at the end of the century in Foscolo's *Ultime lettere di Jacopo Ortis*. Franco Fido, *La serietà del gioco. Svaghi letterari e teatrali nel Settecento*, Lucca, Pacini Fazzi, 235 pp., collects essays published over the last ten years on subjects including Goldoni, Chiari, Tommaso Crudeli, and Carlo Gozzi. C. Alberti, ' "Natura sì, ma bella dee mostrarsi". Sentimenti, artifici e interpretazioni sceniche', Beniscelli, *Naturale*, 155–80, examines the evolving role of the theatre and actors, beginning with Riccoboni's *Dell'arte rappresentativa* of 1728, discussing the importance of Giustina Renier Michel's translations of Shakespeare, and concluding with Antonio Fortunato Stella's great collection, *Teatro moderno applaudito* (1796–1801). C. Tacchini, 'Francesco Saverio Salfi, un teorico "d'avanguardia" nel panorama teatrale italiano sette-ottocentesco', *Ariel*, 12.3, 1997:41–61, looks at S.'s activity in Milan during the revolutionary *triennio*. Reinhard Strohm, *Dramma per musica. Italian Opera Seria of the Eighteenth Century*, New Haven, Yale U.P., 1997, x + 326 pp., contains a large number of articles, many on librettists such as Zeno, Metastasio, and Antonio Salvi, and on theatres such as the Teatro Capranica in Rome. Pietro Spezzani, *Dalla commedia dell'arte a Goldoni*, Padua, Esedra, 1997, 477 pp., a collection of essays most of which have previously appeared, has a first part devoted to the language of the Commedia dell'Arte, including a chapter on 'Il linguaggio di Pantalone pregoldoniano' (55–120) to set the context for the second part of the book, 'Studi sulla lingua del Goldoni', which ranges over the language of Pantalone, Goldoni's translations from his own dialect plays, an analysis of comic language in *La bancarotta*, *Le femmine puntigliose*, and *Il ventaglio*, the 18th-c. editions of Goldoni and linguistic variants. C. Bertoni, 'La prosa in versi: dal *Cicerone* al *Poeta di teatro*', *LCrit*, 25–27, 1993–95[1997]:203–24, on Passeroni's lengthy autobiographical *Cicerone*, reopens discussion of the link with Sterne's *Tristram Shandy* and looks at possible similarities with *Il poeta di teatro* by Filippo Pananti. Dionisotti, *Ricordi*, contains a number of Settecento items: 'Appunti sul Quadrio' (11–32), on Francesco Saverio Quadrio's *Storia e ragione di ogni poesia* and other writings; 'Biografie e dizionari storici' (43–53), which looks at Italian versions of encyclopaedic works, particularly French, and shows how Italian *letterati* were reluctant to admit the value of French writing; 'Ricordo di Cimante Micenio' (55–79), on the Arcadian poet Luigi Godard; 'Un sonetto di Iacopo Durandi' (81–103); 'Un sonetto del Minzoni' (105–13), on Onofrio Minzoni's *Sulla morte di Cristo*; 'Un sonetto su Shakespeare' (115–41), on 'Ecco l'Anglo Shak'speare: in queste carte' of Giovanni De Coureil. A. Beniscelli, 'Wertherismo in scena: tra Sografi e Foscolo', *LItal*, 50:220–36, examines Antonio Simone Sografi's *Verter* (1794), discussing the introduction of a new character, Giorgio, not in Goethe's original, in a play which distances the element of passion in order to 'farsi portavoce delle ragioni "istruttive" del dovere', and also pointing out how Foscolo, in his *Jacopo Ortis*, 'censura drasticamente la posizione di Goethe'. O. Rouvière, 'De Zeno à Goldoni: trois versions de *Griselda*', *ISV*, 19:75–97, is mainly concerned with Goldoni's adaptation of Zeno's libretto for Vivaldi in 1735, and, while welcoming the reduction in size, laments the weakening of the characterization. By the same author is '*Siroe* de Vivaldi, ou Metastasio à Venise', *ib.*, 18, 1997:45–59, which looks first of all at Vivaldi's changes to Metastasio's text in 1727, and then examines the 'Venetian' character of the libretto. L. Pancino, 'Le opere di Vivaldi fra libretti e partiture. *La verità in cimento; La virtù trionfante dell'amore e dell'odio, overo il Tigrane; Giustino*', *ib.*, 19:5–30, concerns the single libretto (1720) for all three operas, examining variants and borrowings. B. Anglani, 'Tra "nobile natura" e "riso vile". Goldoni e Pietro Verri', *LCrit*, 25–27, 1993–95[1997]: 171–201, questions the traditional division of Goldoni's contemporaries into friend or foe and examines Verri's standpoint in relation to the political function of culture, his ambiguous response to G.'s veiled comments in the foreword to *Il festino* (1754). E. Sala Di Felice, '*Ut drama pictura:* la muta eloquenza di Tiepolo e la facondia pittorica di Metastasio', *Intersezioni*, 18:47–66, sees Metastasio and Tiepolo as 'i due artisti forse più compiutamente rappresentativi del Settecento italiano sullo sfondo europeo', interpreting theatre and painting as parallel and interactive semiotic codes, and asserting that both aspired to the whole range of rhetorical device — *docere, movere*, and *dilectare*. C. Timms, 'Music and musicians in the letters of Giuseppe Riva to Agosto Steffani (1720–27)', *MusL*, 79:27–49, explores the period of Riva's time as diplomatic representative of Modena in London and his involvement in its flourishing cultural scene. N. Treadwell, 'Female operatic cross-dressing: Bernardo Saddumene's libretto for Leonardo Vinci's *Le zite 'n galera* (1722)', *COJ*, 10, 2:131–56, claims that the character of the cross-dressed Belluccia goes beyond the usual confines of her sex, allowing her, in common with other 'real-life' cross-dressers, 'a taste of the linguistic and social privileges of men': although order is restored there is the potential for a more subversive discourse. Maria Augusta Morelli Timpanaro, *A Livorno nel Settecento. Medici, mercanti, abati, stampatori: Giovanni Gentili (1704–1784) ed il suo ambiente*, Livorno, Belforte, 1997, 148 pp., discusses G.'s cultural links with printers and publishers, including his collaboration on the *Magazzino toscano d'istruzione e di piacere* and his translations of articles from the *Spectator*, *Tatler*, and *Guardian*.

3. Individual Authors

ALFIERI. Vittorio Alfieri, *Vita scritta da esso. Testo e concordanze*, ed. Stefania De Stefanis Ciccone and Pär Larson, Viareggio, Baroni, 1997, 785 pp., makes no claims to be a critical edition, pointing out that its real purpose is to act as the basis for this extremely useful concordance. G. P. Marchi, ' "Sentiva il nulla di tutte queste cose . . ." Due nuove lettere di Vittorio Alfieri', *GSLI*, 175: 236–41, gives the text of two letters contained in a Vatican Library manuscript. E. Rossi, 'Teatro, persuasione e potere: l'*Agamennone* di Alfieri', *Italianistica*, 26, 1997: 19–33, emphasizes the protagonist's sense of fate as belonging to a family predestined to do wrong, and where the autonomy of individuals is limited, and contrasts it with the ambition for power. The article also points out that the figure of Egisto has a much more prominent role than in Greek or Latin sources. T. Coppola, "L'*Eneide* tradotta da Vittorio Alfieri: *imitatio* ed *aemulatio* stilistica', *RLI*, 102: 467–83, shows how Alfieri brings to his version of the *Aeneid* 'una radicalizzazione espressiva degli stilemi virgiliani' with no intention of hiding his tendency to amplify the Latin original: if *imitatio* is not always rigid, *aemulatio* in rhetorical and metrical analogy is always evident. A. Di Benedetto, 'La "repubblica" di Vittorio Alfieri', *StIt*, 19: 53–78, discusses especially *Della tirannide* and *Del principe e delle lettere*, pointing out that A. was one of the first figures in Italy to see the crisis of absolutism and therefore to reject the idea of the ruler as protector of letters. Gaetano Polidori, **La Magion del Terrore con note che contengono le memorie di quattro anni nei quali l'autore fu segretario del Conte Alfieri*, ed. Roberto Fedi, Palermo, Sellerio, 1997, 164 pp.

BARETTI. Cristina Bracchi, *Prospettiva di una nazione di nazioni*, Alessandria, Orso, 189 pp., is a searching and sensitive reinterpretation of that key essay in 18th-c. mediation between Italy and England, B.'s *Account of the Manner and Customs of Italy*. Bracchi explores not only its 'intertextual' relation with contemporary English travel literature, but even the variants between B.'s English original and 18th-/19th-c. Italian translations and between the two editions produced by B. himself.

CASTI. Giambattista Casti, *Melodrammi giocosi*, ed. Ettore Bonora, Modena, Mucchi, xxxix + 257 pp., contains the texts of *Teodoro in Corsica*, *Il re Teodoro in Venezia*, *Prima la musica e poi le parole*, *Cublai gran Can de' Tartari* and *Catalina*, which show Casti's satirical and parodistic approach to *opera seria*. G. Cartago, '*Gli Animali parlanti* di Giovan

Battista Casti e la traduzione di William Stewart Rose', *Acme*, 51, 2:97–110, points out the use of political language in Casti as central not only to his writing but to his life. This is not reflected to the same extent in Rose's version, essentially a new work born of a different culture.

CESAROTTI. Melchiorre Cesarotti, *Drammaturgia universale antica e moderna*, ed. Paola Ranzini, Ro, Bulzoni, 305 pp., reproduces C.'s universal catalogue of drama productions (excepting modern comedy) down to the year 1800.

DA PONTE. Lorenzo Da Ponte, *Memorie*, ed. Armando Torno and Max Bruschi, Mi, Gallone, 1997[1998], 2 vols, xxxv + 205 pp. and 271 pp., is a straightforward presentation of the text with brief notes.

DE ROGATI. L. Tufano, 'Francesco Saverio De Rogati (1745–1827): poeta per musica', *AISS*, 14, 1997:345–93, assesses the cultural contribution of a figure previously known only for his libretto for Niccolò Jomelli's opera *Armida abbandonata*. A discussion of his chamber cantatas and his translation of Rousseau's *Pygmalion* is followed by an appendix containing De Rogati's *Riflessioni sul dramma intitolato Armida abbandonata* of 1784.

FEDERICI. G. Henry, 'Alle prese con "naturale e artificiale": Camillo Federici', Beniscelli, *Naturale*, 181–200, identifies different concepts of *natura* — from that of the learned whose *natura* appears very artificial to that of those who would follows Goldoni's notion of the 'gran libro del mondo' — and deals with the figure of Federici, who worked for Francesco Barisan's theatre in Castelfranco after having been resident writer at the S. Angelo theatre in Venice.

GOLDONI. In the Edizione Nazionale, we have two items: Carlo Goldoni, *Un curioso accidente*, ed. Ricciarda Ricorda, Venice, Marsilio, 206 pp.; Id., *Teatro di società*, ed. Enrico Mattioda, Venice, Marsilio, 657 pp., containing *L'avaro*, *Il cavaliere di spirito*, *L'apatista*, *La donna bizzarra*, and *L'osteria della posta*, that is, the plays written between 1756 and 1762 for the private theatre of Francesco Albergati Capacelli. Id., *La locandiera*, Mi, La Spiga, 77 pp. Id., *Il campiello*, ed. Roberto Verti, Bo, Compositori, 117 pp., contains Maria Ghisalberti's libretto, based on G.'s play, for Ermanno Wolf-Ferrari's opera. Angela Paladini Volterra, *"Oh quante favole di me si scriveranno"*. *Goldoni personaggio in commedia*, Ro, La Goliardica, 1997, 393 pp., deals with stage representations of G. under three main headings: theatrical discussion and controversy; the stage and G.'s autobiography; texts that pay homage to G. The book covers plays about G. from 1754 to 1920 (but deliberately omits plays such as Gozzi's *L'amore delle tre melarance* where G. appears under a pseudonym) and concludes with an anthology of nine of the texts. F. Vazzoler, 'Per una rilettura della *Pamela fanciulla*', *Croce Vol.*, 357–90, observes how G. creatively modifies Richardson's novel, substituting theatre dialogue for the monologues originally told through letters, in a fashion which shows G. developing a new way of presenting tragedy. N. Pirotta, 'Divagazioni su Goldoni e il dramma giocoso', *RIM*, 32:99–108, looks at the use of *dramma giocoso* as a subtitle along with *dramma comico*, concentrating on G.'s *Il Conte Caramella* of 1751. R. Candiani, 'Sulla fortuna di Carlo Goldoni e del suo teatro musicale a Milano: *L'Arcadia in Brenta* del 1750', *GSLI*, 175:84–106, examines this libretto as one of the first to treat the theme of *villeggiatura* showing G.'s great capacity to renew material in the context of what suited actors and audiences. *Tra commediografi e letterati. Rinascimento e Settecento veneziano*, ed. Tiziana Agostini and Emilio Lippi, Ravenna, Longo, 1997, x + 274 pp., has three articles on the Settecento: M. Donaggio, 'La raccolta Pasquali delle commedie goldoniane: prospettive e strategie di un'edizione di pregio, ma incompiuta' (171–83), which examines the Pasquali edition from its beginnings in 1761, as an attempt to produce a high-quality work, against the reality of the incomplete project, abandoned in 1778; A. Zaniol, 'Filosofi, mercanti e servitori: le "spie" inglesi del teatro goldoniano tra stilizzazione esotica e modello culturale' (185–207), which places *Il filosofo inglese* (1754), as 'una vera e propria *summa* delle idee goldoniane', in the context of G.'s interest in English themes, manifested at different times in such works as *Ritornata di Londra*, but also reflected in changing master-servant relations; M. Bordin, 'Sul lieto fine goldoniano come "imperfetta" conclusione. Preliminari e due analisi (*La famiglia dell'antiquario* e *Il geloso avaro*)' (209–37), which points out the problematic endings of the two plays, claiming that even in plays where a happy resolution seems to be achieved (e.g. in *I rusteghi*) it is no more than a precarious moment of pause in a world where it is not easy to resolve disorders within bourgeois families. G. Tocchini, 'Libretti napoletani, libretti toscoromani: nascita della commedia per musica goldoniana', *StMus*, 26, 1997[1998]:377–415, discusses G.'s apparent reluctance to value his libretto production, and examines possible links with the libretti of Gennarantonio Federico and the Neapolitan tradition. *Carlo Goldoni and Eighteenth-Century Theatre*, ed. Joseph Farrell, Lewiston, Mellon, 1997, 262 pp., contains: A. Beniscelli, 'La presenza di Goldoni nel teatro di Carlo Gozzi' (13–33), which shows how Gozzi was not an outright enemy of G., but followed him to a certain extent in his use of Pantalone and *zanni* characters, and occasionally even in his views on theatre development; G. Callan, 'Marivaux's *La fausse suivante* and Goldoni's *La bottega del caffè* as physical theatre' (37–54), which contrasts G.'s concentration on the functioning of society with Marivaux's view of a self-destructive society; E. Cervato, 'Goldoni and women: female characters and their social background' (75–89), analysing the female characters in four of G.'s dialect plays, but concluding that their role is largely confined within the bounds of the status quo; M. Günsberg, 'The Angel-in-the-House, or Virtue Punished' (91–115), which describes the overtly moralizing tone of G.'s plays as it affects gender portrayal, with the angel-in-the-house figure (to be found in *La putta onorata* and *La buona moglie*) as the most extreme example of female virtue; D. O'Grady, 'Goldoni's women: widows and wiles' (117–31), which shows how G. develops the role of the comic soubrette, juxtaposing the figures of servant and mistress; A. Tosi, 'Linguistic etiquette in eighteenth-century Venice and rules of address in Carlo Goldoni' (133–57), which sets out to show how a linguistic study examining social structures, modes of address, and linguistic etiquette, as well as G.'s use of irony in plays such as *La locandiera* and *Gl'innamorati*, can clarify some of the comic effects of G.'s plays; A. Wilkin, 'Goldoni and Modena' (159–72), which uses the *Mémoires* to explore G.'s family connections with Modena; R. Andrews, 'Goldoni's Venetian twins: whose side is the audience on?' (175–92), which looks at G.'s attempts to convey a moral message in *I due gemelli veneziani*, where he manipulates our sympathy in favour of Tonino, though not always successfully for a modern audience; J. Farrell, 'Citizen Goldoni? Reform, rebellion and the enigma of *Il feudatario*' (193–218), where the supposed committed nature of the play is seen against the background of the tension between peasant and aristocrat, in which there is no sense of Goldoni having any view of faults of government; C. Maeder, 'Goldoni's libretti for *opera seria*' (219–32), in which the author claims that G. occasionally caricatures the story and style of *opera seria*, and exaggerates rhetorical devices in libretti which reflect the socio-cultural problems of classical tragedy; P. Puppa, 'Goldoni antiquario' (233–51), which deals with some of the plays involving dislocation of time or space and discusses G.'s interest in antiquarianism. Unavailable for comment at the time were the proceedings of the bicentenary conference held in Venice in April 1994 entitled *Carlo Goldoni, 1793–1993*, ed. Carmelo Alberti and Gilberto Pizzamiglio, Venice, Regione del Veneto, 1995, 438 pp., whose contents we note here: G. Padoan, 'L'erede di Molière' (23–54); S. Romagnoli, 'Goldoni e gli illuministi' (55–78); F. Fido, 'Patrizi, popolani, borghesi in maschera: rileggendo *Il festino*' (79–88); N. Mangini, 'La fortuna del teatro goldoniano in Europa nel Settecento. Quadro di riferimento dei principali percorsi' (89–98); G. Henry, 'Per un Goldoni nuovo' (99–120); F. Angelini, 'Autobiografia *cum figuris*'. Note sui frontespizi istoriati dell'edizione Pasquali' (123–30); F. Decroisette, 'Gli intertesti goldoniani: bilancio e prospettive' (131–36); P. Vescovo, 'La Riforma nella tradizione' (137–56); F. Vazzoler, 'Qualche (modesta) proposta sul "libro del teatro"' (157–60); C. Alberti, 'Alla sorgente dei "caratteri"' (161–76); A. Fabiano, 'Goldoni a Parigi: una diversa prospettiva di indagine' (177–94); R. Chlodowski, 'Goldoni, Diderot e Puskin' (195–204); G. Gronda, 'Goldoni, Marivaux e i teatri parigini' (205–20); J. Hösle, 'Goldoni sui palcoscenici di lingua tedesca: bilancio del bicentenario' (221–26); L. Nyerges, 'Goldoni librettista e commediografo sulle scene ungheresi' (227–32); M. Vieira de Carvalho, 'Goldoni et le chemin vers le "naturel" dans le théâtre et l'opéra au XVIIIᵉᵐᵉ siècle' (233–46); D. Goldin Folena, 'Teatro e melodramma nei libretti goldoniani' (249–60); T. Emery, 'La riforma goldoniana tra commedie e libretti e la riscrittura de *La gastalda*' (261–70); I. Crotti, 'Il carattere e il "baule": il viaggio di Giocondo' (271–96); L. Comparini, 'Le vicende della "parvenue" tra libretto e romanzo' (297–306); F. Licciardi, 'Di alcune compagnie di attori-cantanti e cantanti-attori nella critica fra Sette e Ottocento' (307–24); B. Anglani, 'I *Mémoires*: bilanci e prospettive' (325–40); K. Hecker, 'Le donne in Goldoni ovvero: trappole da evitare. Considerazioni sul personaggio femminile nelle commedie goldoniane. Appunti per una ricerca' (341–56); S. Ferrone, '*La locandiera* di Goldoni secondo Visconti' (357–68); G. Pullini, 'Goldoni sulla scena italiana degli anni Novanta' (369–76); A. Tenenti, 'Il mondo settecentesco nelle *Memorie* goldoniane' (377–88); Tavola Rotonda with G. Pizzamiglio, G. Bosetti, M. Scaparro, L. Squarzina, P. Trevisi, G. Vacis, A. Momo (389–420); C. Alberti, 'Le illustrazioni dell'edizione Grimaldo (1856–1865)' (421–26).

GORANI.   A. Volpi, 'Da avventuriere a scrittore: Giuseppe Gorani nella storiografia', *BSP*, 67:185–95, describes the rehabilitation of G.'s memory from early dismissal of him as an adventurer and opportunist to the recognition of his interest in Enlightenment ideas and of his qualities as a writer and traveller. R. P. Coppini, 'Una voce fuori dal coro. Giuseppe Gorani critico di Pietro Leopoldo', *ib.*, 179–84, deals with G.'s *Il vero dispotismo*, and the *Mémoires secrets et critiques des cours, des gouvernements et des moeurs des principaux états d'Italie* which were highly critical of Peter Leopold's government, which he described as economically and politically restrictive.

GOZZI.   Carlo Gozzi, *Fiabe teatrali*, ed. Stefano Giovanuzzi, Mi, Mursia, 257 pp. *Carlo Gozzi. Letteratura e musica. Atti del convegno internazionale, Centro tedesco di studi veneziani, Venezia, 11–12 ottobre 1995*, ed. Bodo Guthmüller and Wolfgang Osthoff, Ro, Bulzoni, 1997, 328 pp., contains the following items: A. Beniscelli, 'Carlo Gozzi tra romanzi "antichi" e "moderni"' (13–34), on G.'s satirical attacks against the theatre of Goldoni and Chiari, and his ability, in *La Marfisa bizzarra*, to imporre direction on 'academic' elements in the theatre as well as on the taste for the contemporary; B. Guthmüller,

' "Xele romanzi, o no xele romanzi ste vicende?" *I due fratelli nemici* di Carlo Gozzi' (35–51), which discusses the changes made by G. in basing his play on Agustín Morelo's *Hasta el fin nadie es dichoso*, and his intention to create between comic and serious elements a relationship very different from the Spanish original by using Brighella and Tartaglia to express the 'riflessione metateatrale'; G. Pizzamiglio, 'Modelli autobiografici e tentazioni romanzesche nelle *Memorie inutili* di Carlo Gozzi' (53–76), which looks at the influence of Cellini's *Vita* on G. and passes to a discussion of the moral dimension, harking back to Arcadia and Zeno, whereby he remains 'tenacemente ancorato alle radici conservatrici'; N. Mangini, 'Le *Memorie inutili* di Carlo Gozzi. Il problema della cronologia' (77–90), which examines some of the problems arising from G. starting his autobiography as a response to Pier Antonio Gratarol's *Narrazione apologetica* and then later changing the basis on which he writes, a process which explains some of the changes of structure and style in the three volumes of the Palese edition; C. Alberti, ' "Il grano e la zinzania". Carlo Gozzi giudica la scena europea di fine Settecento' (91–118), which begins with G.'s dispute with Sacchi's company in the 1780s in order to demonstrate how G. remained faithful to his view of the theatre and to illustrate the reasons for his attacks on French plays and on Albergato Capacelli, Baretti, and Napoli Signorelli; P. Vescovo, ' "La più lunga lettera di risposta che sia stata scritta . . ." Riflessioni sull'ultimo Gozzi' (119–41), which the author sees as introductory to G.'s comments on the *frammenti* which follow the letter, where G. attempts to redefine his position in theatre history; R. Unfer Lukoschik, ' "La bella infedele". La *Turandot* nella versione di F. A. Cl. Werthes' (143–67), which looks at the publishing success of G.'s works in German, drawing mainly on Werthes' translation of *Turandot* to show how he modifies in particular the figure of Calaf and Turandot, whose driving force is no longer divine providence but love; R. Schwaderer, ' "Gozzi romantisch". L'immagine di Carlo Gozzi nel romanticismo tedesco' (169–85), which examines the part played in the creation of a kind of Gozzi myth by Goethe, who had been one of the earliest to introduce G. to Germany, describing him as 'Gozzi König der Genien und wahrer Freund', and goes on to look at G.'s influence on people such as Ludwig Tieck and the two Schlegel brothers. The second part of the volume is concerned with musical representations of G.'s work and contains: M. Russo, 'Il balletto *La figlia dell'aria* di Salvatore Viganò da Gozzi' (193–228); U. Skouenborg, 'E. T. A. Hoffmans Idee der romantischen Oper und J. P. E. Hartmanns dänische Oper *Ravnen* (H. C. Andersen nach Gozzis *Corvo*' (229–42); T. Siedhoff, 'Auf der Suche nach der romantischen Oper. Carlo Gozzi und Richard Wagners oper *Die*

Feen' (243–54); W. Osthoff, 'Turandots Auftritt. Gozzi, Schiller, Maffei und Giacomo Puccini' (255–81); P. Weber-Bockholdt, 'Einige Beobachtungen zu Prokofjews Oper *Die Liebe zu den drei Orangen* nach Carlo Gozzi' (283–99); G. Oestelli, '*La donna serpente* di Alfredo Casella' (301–18). A. Momo, 'Carlo Gozzi: teatro filosofico e meta-teatro', Beniscelli, *Naturale*, 143–54, asks what 'mondo' in the Goldoni sense could G. find as a model for his theatre, concluding that, although G. draws on our emotions, he does not require us to believe in the reality of what he writes.

LONGANO. R. Giordano, 'L'*Autobiografia* di Francesco Longano', *CLett*, 26:139–56, sets Longano in context as 'colui che meglio di tanti altri incarna l'insegnamento genovesiano', examining his auto-biography in conjunction with the much better-known autobiograph-ies of Vico, Giannone, and Genovesi.

MELI. A. Di Benedetto, 'Aspetti e carattere della *Bucolica* di Giovanni Meli', *ib*., 241–55, discusses the genre of writings on the seasons and the particularly Sicilian nature of Meli's poem, while pointing out that his shepherds and shepherdesses are basically the same as in the main stream, and also noting the essentially conservat-ive nature of the poem.

METASTASIO. *EMus*, 26.4, is entirely devoted to Metastasio on the occasion of the tercentenary of his birth, and contains: R. Strohm, 'Dramatic dualities: Metastasio and the tradition of the opera pair' (551–61), in which he examines the phenomenon of paired dramas, tracing their history in late 17th- and 18th-c. opera and looking at various pairs which Metastasio wrote for Vienna between 1730 and 1752; W. Hiller, 'Reforming Achilles: gender, *opera seria* and the rhetoric of the enlightened hero' (562–81), which examines M.'s *Achille in Sciro* (1736) against the background of other theatrical treatments of the same subject, emphasizing M.'s 'elegant' comprom-ise between love and honour; R. Savage, 'Staging an opera: letters from the Caesarian poet' (583–95), pointing out that M. wrote for singers and actors, as his libretti are essentially concerned with 'the manifestation of character in action or response to action', and showing the detailed nature of M.'s stage directions; D. Neville, 'Opera or oratorio? Metastasio's sacred *opere serie*' (596–607), which examines the importance of the moral content in M.'s moral dramas, whether they were meant for theatre or chapel; M. Burden, ' "Twittering and trilling": Swedish reaction to Metastasio' (609–21), dealing with the reception of M.'s works in Sweden from the 1750s, many of them set to music by Francesco Uttini, and also looking at the later influence on Swedish opera of Domenico Michelessi and Francesco Algarotti; J.-M. Leza, 'Metastasio on the Spanish stage' (623–31), which looks at adaptations of M. in Madrid between 1731 and 1747. S. Olcese, 'Poesia e musica in Metastasio', *RLI*, 102:452–66, argues that the fact that Metastasio is more famous than most of his composers demonstrates his success in adding dignity to the poetic text of the libretto, which he saw as poetry for music, in perhaps the last period in which elements of production and characterization were still the prerogative of the poet, not the musician. Andrea Chegai, *L'esilio di Metastasio. Forme e riforme dello spettacolo d'opera fra Sette e Ottocento*, F, Le Lettere, 317 pp.

MONTI. Vincenzo Monti, *Poesie (1797–1803)*, ed. Luca Frassineti, Ravenna, Longo, 626 pp., covers all of what the editor refers to as the poetic production of 'Monti cittadino', that is, during what might be called his republican period, from the sonnet, 'Costei che nata fra il giumento e il bue' through to the versions of Persius's Satires, and *Caio Gracco, La Musogonia, Il Prometeo* and the *Canti in morte di Lorenzo Mascheroni*. A. Bruni, 'Lettere montiane inedite', *StCrit*, 13:109–21, publishes six letters, one of which contains a verse of a *canzone* for Adelaide Calderara. F. Finotti, 'Il "sublime patetico" del Monti', *LItal*, 50:523–53, draws on the *Prosopopea di Pericle* (1779), which described the heroic sense of vitality of the past and the animating power of art, and also looks at *La bellezza dell'universo* of 1781, which claims that beauty has not merely an aesthetic value, but is the animating power of creation, set alongside the 'orrido fascino della rovina'.

MURATORI. Ludovico Antonio Muratori, *Carteggio con AA - Amadio Maria di Venezia*, ed. G. Fabbri and D. Gianaroli, F, Olschki, 1997, 492 pp., is the latest volume in the national edition of M.'s correspondence.

PARINI. *Interpretazioni e letture del 'Giorno'*, ed. Gennaro Barbarisi and Edoardo Esposito, Bo, Cisalpino, 701 pp., are the proceedings of a conference held at Gargnano del Garda in 1997 and contain: G. Bárberi Squarotti, 'Il vero Ettore; l'eroe del *Giorno*' (11–60); A. M. Mutterle, 'Osservazioni sullo stile satirico nel *Giorno*' (61–74); R. Leporatti, 'Sull'incompiutezza del *Giorno*' (75–116); W. Spaggiari, 'L'edizione Reina' (117–60); G. Biancardi, 'Alcune osservazioni sulla dedica e sul proemio del primo *Mattino*' (161–76); C. Donati, 'La nobiltà milanese nelle fonti documentarie e nella satira pariniana' (177–204); G. Barbarisi, 'I Verri e l'idea del *Giorno*' (205–50); G. Mazzocchi, 'I trattenimenti del Padre Guilloré e di Carlo Maria Maggi' (251–74); G. Carnazzi, 'L'altro ceto: "ignobili" e Terzo Stato nel *Giorno*' (275–92); G. Santato, 'I Lumi nel *Giorno*. Voltaire e i "nuovi Sofi": dal *Mattino* e dal *Mezzogiorno* al *Giorno*' (293–350); M. Mari, 'La ricchezza linguistica del *Giorno*' (351–80); C. Berra, 'Le figure di permutazione nel *Mattino* e nel *Mezzogiorno*' (381–422);

F. Spera, 'La voce dei personaggi' (423–42); E. Esposito, 'L'endecasillabo del *Giorno*: prospezioni' (443–66); F. Tancini, 'Gusto e buon gusto nel primo *Giorno*' (467–92); P. Gibellini, 'La mitologia classica nel *Giorno* (e dintorni)' (493–510); C. Vecce, 'Gioco e società nel *Giorno*' (511–28); M. A. Terzoli, 'Le gloriose "opre" di un Don Giovanni milanese' (529–52); G. Benvenuti, 'La *Sera* di Parini e l'occasione mancata del Giovin Signore' (553–78); I. Magnani Campanacci, 'Suggestioni iconografiche nel *Giorno*' (579–620); L. Clerici, 'Bibliografia della critica e delle opere di Giuseppe Parini' (1947–1997). G. Biancardi, 'Per il testo della prima redazione del *Mattino*: appunti sulle stampe milanesi del 1763', *SPCT*, 55, 1997:51–76, examines various MS and print variants in the context of Dante Isella's 1996 edition of *Il giorno* (Mi, Fond. Pietro Bembo—Parma, Guanda), drawing on Parini's own well-documented dissatisfaction with the first edition of his poem, where some of the problems were due to fascicules from different printings being bound together. R. Martinoni, 'Bricciche pariniane. Intorno alla cronologia del *Mattino* e alla stampa del *Mezzogiorno*', *StCrit*, 13:143–52, suggests a dating for the completion of *Il mattino* 18 months before the first edition (Milan 1763) and deals with Parini's concerns about printings of *Il mezzogiorno* outside Milan in 1765.

PINDEMONTE. G. Pizzamiglio, 'Ippolito Pindemonte e il teatro nel carteggio con Isabella Teotochi Albrizzi', Beniscelli, *Naturale*, 201–21, looks briefly at the nearly 500 letters, written between 1784 and 1828, to examine some of Pindemonte's thoughts on the theatre, with some particularly interesting comments on Alfieri, and on his own play, *Arminio*.

SILVA. *QA*, 5, is devoted to a conference held at Cinisello Balsamo in 1997, entitled *Ercole Silva (1756–1840) e la cultura del suo tempo*, and contains: C. Nenci, 'Ercole Silva: erudizione e bibliomania' (13–25); G. Guerci, 'Galeotto fu il libro: la serie di dame e la Robinia pseudoacacia' (26–30), which mentions links between S. and Manzoni; A. Sartori, 'Ercole Silva, le sue epigrafi in biblioteca' (41–49), on S.'s books on epigraphs; M. David, 'Ercole Silva e le colonne di San Lorenzo' (50–58), which looks at S.'s writings on gardens; V. De Michele, 'Aspetti della cultura naturalistica di Ercole Silva' (59–63), which discusses S.'s library collections on mineralogy, palaeontology, and zoology; G. Gaspari, 'La biblioteca ritrovata. Aspetti del collezionismo librario di Donato ed Ercole Silva' (67–72); M. Ferrari, 'In margine al volume *Catalogo della Biblioteca Silva in Cinisello*' (73–78), for which see the following item. *Catalogo de' libri della Biblioteca in Cinisello*, ed. Roberto Cassanelli et al., Cinisello Balsamo, Centro di Documentazione Storica, 1996, is the photographic reprint of the catalogue of Ercole Silva's large collection.

SPALLETTI.   R. Caira Lumetti, 'In margine al *Saggio sopra la bellezza* di Giuseppe Spalletti', *CLett*, 26:41–49, discusses S.'s polemic with Monti, seeing his *Saggio* (1765) as central to arguments on the notion of beauty.

VERRI.   G. Santato, ' "Industria" e pubblica felicità in Pietro Verri', *Atti* (AISLLI, 15), 199–237, is concerned with V.'s ideas on poverty and the *industrioso cittadino*, particularly as expressed in the *Discorso sulla felicità* and the *Discorso sull'indole del piacere e del dolore*.

VICO.   Giambattista Vico, *De antiquissima Italorum sapientia*, ed. Giovanni Adamo, F, Olschki, xxxiv + 476 pp., presents the 1710 Naples text in photographic reproduction, and the critical apparatus compares that text with the Bari 1914 edition by Giovanni Gentile and Fausto Niccolini. Id., *Principj di scienza nuova d'intorno alla comune natura delle nazioni. Concordanze e indici di frequenza dell'edizione Napoli 1744*, ed. Marco Veneziani, F, Olschki, 1997, xl + 1046 pp., offers an extremely useful tool in analysing Vico's conceptual structures, and also in comparing this text with the 1725 *Scienza nuova*. M. S. Stella, 'G. B. Vico. Considerazioni attuali sulla storia', *AASN*, 108, 1997[1998]:245–89, discusses V.'s approach to history, including his idea of a 'storia ideale eterna', and the link between civilization and religion, as well as looking at V.'s notions on social communication and language. *BCSV*, 26–27, 1996–97, contains: J. Trabant, 'Tristi segni. Per una semiologia vichiana' (11–27); M. Lollini, 'Il mito come precomprensione storica aperta nella *Scienza nuova* di Giambattista Vico' (29–53); M. G. Pia, 'Gravina e Vico: la poesia "sub specie temporis et imaginationis" secondo la "Metaphysica mentis" spinoziana' (55–74); G. Cacciatore, 'Vico e la filosofia pratica' (77–84); R. Mazzola, 'Il "Sanchuniaton" di Vico tra mito dell'antichissima sapienza e origine della scrittura' (85–99); Id., 'Religione e Provvidenza in Vico' (101–26); V. Gess-Kurotschka, 'Il desiderio e il bene. Christian Wolff e le origini della moderna filosofia pratica in Germania' (127–57); R. Vitti Cavaliere, 'Annotazioni su Hanna Arendt e Vico' (159–83); G. Acocella, 'Ugo Spirito e lo storicismo "vichiano" di W. Sombart' (185–203); G. Cacciatore and S. Caianiello, 'Vico anti-moderno?' (205–18); G. Cacciatore and F. Tessitore, 'Alcuni "storicisti" tra "devoti" e "iconoclasti" vichiani' (219–25); G. Lissa, 'Massoneria e illuminismo di Giuseppe Giarrizzo' (227–40); B. Pinchard, 'Nuovi pensieri sulla dualità' (241–46); S. Caianiello and M. Sanna, 'Una lettera inedita vichiana' (325–31); P. Amodio, 'A proposito del capov. 304 della *Scienza nuova* del 1744' (333–38); S. Caianiello, 'Per il progetto di un catalogo internazionale delle prime edizioni vichiane' (339–52); M. Riccio, 'Nota sul termine "Ragion di Stato" nella *Scienza nuova* 1744' (353–56); R. Mazzola,

'Noterelle vichiane' (357–60); A. Traversa, 'Una fonte petroniana in un'opera giovanile di Vico' (361–65).

OTTOCENTO
POSTPONED

NOVECENTO

By ROBERTO BERTONI, *Lecturer in Italian, Trinity College, Dublin* and
CATHERINE O'BRIEN, *Professor of Italian, University College, Galway*
(This survey covers the years 1997 and 1998)

1. GENERAL

Gianfranco Contini, *Postremi esercizi ed elzeviri*, T, Einaudi, 281 pp.,
comprises texts written by C. from 1971 to 1989, including items on
Bilenchi, Montale, Gadda, Palazzeschi, and Pizzuto; a 'Postfazione'
by C. Segre (255–58); and a 'Nota ai testi' by G. Breschi (259–62).
Dionisotti, *Ricordi*, among its three dozen essays gathers many on
20th-c. intellectuals, scholars and writers, including Santorre Debenedetti, Fortunato Pintor, Carlo Calcaterra, Sapegno, Gobetti, Pavese,
Lalla Romano, Augusto Campana, Delio Cantimori, and Arnaldo
Momigliano. *Atti* (AISLLI 15) gathers contributions on miscellaneous
aspects of the theme 'Letteratura e Industria' as well as over a score
of essays on individual writers. The latter are registered below.
Among the former we note: L. Ballerini, 'La legge dell'ingratitudine:
letteratura e industria tra le due guerre' (581–618); C. De Michelis, 'I
romanzi della fabbrica' (835–52); G. P. Brunetta, 'Cinema come
mondo' (853–60); G. L. Beccaria, 'L'automobile, un'officina di
parole' (1147–87); G. Lepschy, 'La lingua dell'industria' (1189–96).
The concluding section 'Macchine e poesia' comprises contributions
by M. Petrucciani, L. Davì, E. Solonovic, P. Barbaro, and G. Giudici.
Piero Cudini, **Breve storia della letteratura italiana del Novecento*, Mi,
Bompiani, 240 pp. **Dizionario critico della letteratura italiana del Novecento*,
ed. Enrico Ghidetti e Giorgio Luti, Ro, Editori Riuniti, 1997.
Carmine Di Biase, **Novecento letterario italiano. Ricognizioni*, Na, Liguori,
1997, 363 pp. Giorgio Luti, *La letteratura italiana del Novecento*, Ro,
Editori Riuniti, 120 pp., an 'opera di carattere prevalentemente
divulgativo' which sees the Novecento as 'epoca di crisi e d'instabilità',
includes a section on poetry (13–38), one on narrative (39–84), one
on criticism (85–118), and a floppy disk. **L'identità del Novecento. Atti
del seminario di studi di Forte dei Marmi*, ed. Valeria Nicodemi, Palermo,
Palumbo, 1997. Giuseppe Petronio, *Il piacere di leggere. La letteratura
italiana in 101 libri*, Mi, Mondadori, 1997, 364 pp., contains commentaries on the 101 books chosen — the Novecento section begins with
Pascoli and ends with Tabucchi. Cesare Segre, *Letteratura italiana del
Novecento*, Ro–Bari, Laterza, xii + 118 pp., underlines the relevance
of social commitment and textual analysis for literary criticism,
discusses the position of 20th-c. Italian writers in relation to foreign
authors, identifies a 'linea lombarda', examines Jewish Italian

literature and antifascism, surveys authors and movements, identifies Saba, Croce, Svevo, Montale, Gadda, Calvino, and Zanzotto as essential authors, and sees contemporary poetics as fragmented and based less on movements than on individual voices. Sergio Solmi, *La letteratura italiana contemporanea*, II, Mi, Adelphi. Giacinto Spagnoletti, *I nostri contemporanei*, Mi, Spirali, 1997, 274 pp. *La nuova critica letteraria nell'Italia contemporanea*, ed. Arnaldo Colasanti, Rimini, Guaraldi, 1996, 350 pp. Michele Dell'Aquila, *Le sirene di Ulisse e altra letteratura*, Fasano, Schena, 1997, 270 pp., gathers articles (some previously published) which for the Novecento concern Croce, Gentile, Russo, Donadoni, C. Levi, and poetry in Apulia in the last twenty years. *Sequenze novecentesche per Antonio De Lorenzi*, Modena, Mucchi, 1996, 262 pp., hereafter *De Lorenzi Vol.*, is a posthumous tribute from colleagues and friends, the main contents of which are noted below.

INTELLECTUAL MOVEMENTS, LITERARY THEORY, CRITICISM, PERIOD-ICALS, PUBLISHING. For the first half of the Novecento, from Futurism to Fascism, we note: Cinzia Sartini Blum, *The Other Modernism: F. T. Marinetti's Futurist Fiction of Power*, Berkeley, California U.P., 1996, xii + 212 pp.; F. Perfetti, 'Il futurismo e il suo tempo', *Il Veltro*, 42:31–43, which argues that the attitudes of Futurism to politics were a result of its rejection of 'passatismo'; A. Iacobelli, 'La modernità come tradizione: l'esperienza della *Ronda*', LCrit, 25–27, 1993–95[1997]:71–103; S. Albertini, 'Dante in camicia nera: uso e abuso del divino poeta', *The Italianist*, 16, 1996[1997]:117–42. The Resistance movement and the concept of political commitment are the topics of several essays. *Letteratura e Resistenza: cerchi concentrici. Atti del Convegno di Fano, 26–27 maggio 1995*, Bo, CLUEB, 1997, 311 pp., ed. Andrea Bianchini and Francesca Lolli, includes the following contributions: A. Battistini, 'Introduction' (7–24) and 'Un anomalo scrittore comunista: Antonio Meluschi' (193–222); G. Falaschi, 'La memorialistica dalle guerre garibaldine alla guerra di liberazione' (25–42); B. Falcetto, 'Neorealismo e scrittura documentaria' (25–42); A. Asor Rosa, 'L'influenza della Resistenza nella letteratura con-temporanea' (95–106); S. Pivato, 'Letteratura e guerra a Rimini' (265–74); F. Lolli, 'La Resistenza di un editore: Einaudi' (59–94); G. Ghiandoni, 'Letteratura di Resistenza: i giornali clandestini delle Marche 1943–1944' (275–88); R. Galaverni, 'Prima che il gallo canti: la guerra di liberazione di Cesare Pavese' (107–56); A. Andreini, 'Vittorini e il romanzo della Resistenza' (157–72); C. Milanini, 'Calvino e la Resistenza: l'identità in gioco (173–92); M. Zancan, 'L'esperienza, la memoria, la scrittura di donne' (223–38); G. C. Ferretti, 'Il mito della Resistenza in Pasolini' (259–64); C. Donati, '*Fisarmonica rossa* di Franco Matacotta: le ragioni biografiche e i temi poetici' (289–304). *Italian Resistance Writing: An Anthology*, ed. Philip

Cooke, MUP, 1997. *RivF*, 88.1, 1997, an issue entitled *Filosofia e politica*, contains contributions by Beřti, Bobbio, Ciliberto, De Giovanni, Losurdo, Tardi, Vattimo, Veca, Viano, and Zolo on the attitudes of contemporary intellectuals to political commitment. Nello Ajello, *Intellettuali e PCI dal 1958 al 1991*, Ro–Bari, Laterza, 1997. Alfonso Berardinelli, *L'eroe che pensa. Disavventure dell'impegno*, T, Einaudi, 1997, 206 pp., discusses political commitment in a postmodern society. A. L. De Castris, 'La cultura del Novecento', *Allegoria*, 26, 1997: 107–11, argues that the majority of politically committed 20th-c. Italian intellectuals have been more concerned with the 'primacy of culture' than with practical life.

Turning to the second half of the century, a number of essays deal with Italian modernism and postmodernism. Remo Ceserani, *Raccontare il postmoderno*, T, Bollati Boringhieri, 1997, 242 pp., places Italian postmodernism against the historical background of the development of 'neocapitalism' since the 1950s, and discusses Italian and foreign postmodernist theory and creative works. G. Guglielmi, 'L'autore come consumatore', *Il Verri*, 42.4–5, 1997: 64–77, interprets postmodernism as a legacy left by early 20th-c. modernism, and concludes that the difference between the avant-garde and postmodernism consists in the fact that the former was self-reflective and non-conformist while the latter is commercial and hedonistic. M. Jansen, 'Tradizione del nuovo o novità della tradizione? Avanguardia e postmoderno messi a confronto in occasione della morte del Gruppo 63', pp. 5–26 of *Scrittori degli anni Novanta* (Narrativa, 12), ed. Marie-Hélène Caspar, Centre de Recherches Italiennes, Université Paris X-Nanterre, Publidix, 1997, examines Italian critical debate on the 'neoavanguardia' in 1963, 1984, and 1993, and traces a development from the poetics of novelty in the 1960s to a critical variety of postmodernism in the 1980s and finally to a recovery of tradition in new guises in the 1990s. E. Sanguineti, 'Elogio dell'antitesi. Il significato dell'avanguardia oggi', *Allegoria*, 29–30:219–29, the text of an interview given to G. Mazzoni, confirms his anarchist conception of the avant-garde and its role to destroy middle-class capitalist morality.

The fantastic is the topic of a number of books. Giacinto Spagnoletti, *Letteratura e utopia. Alle origini della fantascienza*, Ro, Empiria, 137 pp., briefly examines the *genre* of Utopia in Italy from Casanova's *Jcosameron* to Fileno Carabba's *La foresta finale*. Stefano Calabrese, *Fiaba*, F, La Nuova Italia, 1997. Monica Farnetti, *L'irruzione del vedere nel pensare. Saggi sul fantastico*, Pasian di Prato, Campanotto, 1997, 187 pp. Paola Rodari, *Enciclopedia della favola. Volpi e lupi*, Ro, Editori Riuniti, 1997.

Miscellaneous topics are as follows. *AnI*, 15, 1997, a thematic issue on Italian literature and anthropology, includes O. Pelosi, 'Anthropology and literature' (which examines a number of relevant general themes such as myth, psychoanalysis, play, sacrifice, food, and the body), and other essays by N. Pioleddu on D'Annunzio, G. P. Raffa and M. Friguletti on Carlo Levi, M. Pine and S. Parussa on Pasolini, and M. Lollini on Calvino. *AnI*, 16, devoted to Italian cultural studies, includes the following 20th-c. contributions: M. Brose, 'Dido's turn: cultural syntax in Ungaretti's *La terra promessa*' (121–43), which relates *La terra promessa* to the *Aeneid* and sees U. as identified with both the exiled Aeneas and the abandoned Dido; K. Pinkus, ' "Black" and "Jew": race and the resistance to psychoanalysis in Italy' (145–62), examining the reasons for Fascist aversion to psychoanalysis; E. Neremberg, 'Love for Sale, or That's *Amore:* representing prostitution during and after Italian Fascism' (213–35), which includes an analysis of Pratolini's *Cronache di poveri amanti;* and A. Perry, 'Fallen partisans: hagiographic imprints in Italian Resistance biography' (237–59), where a 'sacrificial model of death' is found in biographies of fallen partisans. *Aut aut*, 282, 1997, a special issue on humour and paradox, includes essays by M. Mizzau, A. Polidori, and A. Rovatti. *Stato e frontiera: dalla Mitteleuropa all'Europa unita? Atti del XII congresso A.I.P.I.*, *Ratisbona, 29–31 Agosto 1996*, ed. Michel Bastiaensen, Corinna Salvadori Lonergan, and Luisa Quartermaine, assisted by Bart Van den Bossche and Giovanna Domenichini (*Civiltà Italiana*, 20), F, Cesati, 271 pp., exploring the literary and linguistic concept of 'frontiera', comprises an introduction by B. Dorner, M. Sachau, and A. Schmidt; contributions by F. Tomizza and G. Morandini on their own position as 'scrittori di frontiera'; literary criticism: N. Dupré (on G. Morandini), L. Pavan (on 'miti and soggetti erranti', or 'zingari'), G. Giacomazzi (on Jewish culture), S. Nemmert (on the concept of *Mitteleuropa*), D. Aristodemo (on G. B. Angioletti), M. Spunta (on A. Tabucchi), G. Pintorno (on F. Vegliani), A. Luzi (on V. Sereni), D. Mangano (on C. Sgorlon), B. Van den Bossche (on P. V. Tondelli), R. Gennaro (on G. Ungaretti), H. Salaets (on S. Slataper); a section entitled 'Italiano fuori d'Italia' (essays by J. Eynaud on Italian culture in Malta, A. Moc on Italian and Polish Futurists, G. Řabac-Condrić on Italian language and culture in Dalmatia, L. Šimunković on Italo-Dalmatian correspondence, and A. Kalling on translation from Italian into Estonian); and a section on linguistics (essays by B. Villata, A. Scarsella, and S. Widlak). *Autoritratto italiano. Un dossier letterario 1945–1998*, ed. Alfonso Berardinelli, Ro, Donzelli, 176 pp., contains a selection of passages by Italian writers on the theme of national identity. *I segni incrociati. Letteratura italiana del Novecento e arte figurativa*, ed. Marcello Ciccuto and Alexandra Zingone, Viareggio, Baroni,

884 pp., gathers essays on the relationship between literature and the visual arts in the works of writers such as Caproni, Fortini, Savinio, Tabucchi, and Ungaretti. *Sicilia. Mito e tradizione letteraria. Giornate di studio in ricordo di Saro Contarino (Arcavacata, 8–9 febbraio 1996)*, ed. Franca Ela Consolino and Nicola Merola, Soveria Mannelli, Rubbettino, 140 pp. L. E. Ruberto, 'Immigrants speak: Italian literature from the border', *FoI*, 31, 1997: 127–44. Martino Marazzi, *Little America. Gli Stati Uniti e gli scrittori italiani del Novecento*, Mi, Marcos y Marcos, 1997, 206 pp. Giancarlo Quiriconi, *Luoghi dell'immaginario contemporaneo. L'io, l'altro, le cose*, Ro, Bulzoni.

Literary theory is represented by various essays. Luciano Anceschi, *Cos'è la poesia*, Bologna, CLUEB, 185 pp., the text of the last university course held by A. in 1980–81, illustrates his concepts of poetics and phenomenological interpretation of texts through constant questioning on the nature and meaning of poetry. R. Nisticò, 'Luciano Anceschi', *Belfagor*, 52, 1997: 287–301, reviews Anceschi's work and analyses his conception of 'autonomia e eteronomia dell'arte', of the phenomenology of 'open' works, of literary 'institutions' (i.e. style, analogy, and symbol), of 'implicit and explicit poetics', and of the Baroque, Hermeticism, and the Neo-Avantgarde. Alberto Cadioli, *Il critico navigante. Saggio sull'ipertesto e la critica letteraria*, Genoa, Marietti, 155 pp., adopts the concept of hypertext as an essential tool for literary analysis. Maria Corti, *Per una enciclopedia della comunicazione letteraria*, Mi, Bompiani, 1997, 114 pp., discusses intertextuality, the concept of 'places of the mind', oral vs written literature, the fantastic and realism. She analyses samples from early as well as 20th-c. works. F. Curi, 'Canone e anticanone', *Intersezioni*, 17, 1997: 495–511, questions Bloom's approach to the classical canon, and sees the Novecento as a century in which the canon has been exposed both to 'legislation' and freedom from strict rules. According to C., 20th-c. avant-garde experiments have created an 'anticanon'. Id., *Canone e anticanone. Studi di letteratura*, Bo, Pendragon, 1997, 127 pp., develops the above-mentioned article, and analyses texts by authors such as D'Annunzio and Montale. *Allegoria*, 29–30, includes a section entitled 'Sul canone' (5–102) which comprises: R. Luperini, 'Introduzione. Due nozioni di canone' (5–7), distinguishing between canon as determined by historical and intrinsic value and canon as formulated by readers' reactions; C. Rivoletti, 'Introduzione al saggio di Jauss. La categoria dell'orizzonte di attesa e la sua revisione' (8–22); H. R. Jauss, 'Il lettore come istanza di una nuova storia letteraria' (23–41); A. Battistini, 'Il canone in Italia e fuori d'Italia' (42–57), contrasting the social criteria on which the concept of canon is based in the English-speaking world with the mainly academic criteria on which it rests in Italy, and discussing the views of Aristotle, Bloom, and

Luperini on the canon; R. Ceserani, 'Appunti sul problema dei canoni' (58–74), examining the word's etymology, sees the concept of canon as pluralistic and reviews recent debate stemming from Bloom's theory; G. Guglielmi, 'Letteratura, storia, canoni' (83–90), advocating a return to historical awareness in contrast to recent lack of historicity in formulating the notion of canon; N. Pasero, 'Canone, norma, sanzione: breve nota' (91–94); C. Segre, 'Il canone e la culturologia' (95–102), offering a 'modello tipologico' to enable future historians of literature to move easily between one canon and another, interpreting changes in the canon as cultural changes. Franco D'Intino, *L'autobiografia moderna. Storia forme problemi*, Ro, Bulzoni, 370 pp., is a study of the origins of autobiography and its development to the present time. Umberto Eco, *Kant e l'ornitorinco*, Mi, Bompiani, 1997, xvi + 454 pp., examines the relation of signs to reality, and the concepts of cognitive types and cognitive strategies. Isabella Pezzini, *Le passioni del lettore. Saggi di semiotica del testo*, Mi, Bompiani. Marina Polacco, *L'intertestualità*, Ro–Bari, Laterza, 82 pp., examines some aspects of the theory of intertextuality (including a discussion of the concepts of 'imitation' and 're-writing', and of the difference between 'hypotext' and 'hypertext'), and gives some examples of textual analysis (including Calvino's *Se una notte d'inverno un viaggiatore*).

A number of essays are about theory of or debate on women's writing. *Lapis. Sezione aurea di una rivista*, Ro, Manifesto Libri, 319 pp., includes a chapter entitled 'Nascita di sé, nascita della scrittura' discussing various aspects of women's writing. The introductions to the various sections of *Critiche femministe e teorie letterarie*, ed. Raffaella Baccolini et al., Bo, CLUEB, 1997, 354 pp., assess the present status of criticism on women's writing and the position of women intellectuals in Italian literary and academic institutions. C. Mazzoni, 'Parturition, parting and paradox in turn-of-the-century Italian literature (D'Annunzio, Aleramo, Neera)', *FoI*, 31, 1997: 343–66. *The Feminist Encyclopedia of Italian Literature*, ed. Rinaldina Russell, Westport, Greenwood, 1997, 402 pp. Marina Zancan, *Il doppio itinerario della scrittura. La donna nella tradizione letteraria italiana*, T, Einaudi, 234 pp., laments the scant presence of women in the Italian literary tradition, underlining the importance of the few women writers who have emerged over the centuries. Their contribution is examined especially in terms of subjectivity and creative imagination. One chapter is devoted to a detailed analysis of Sibilla Aleramo. There are also essays on individual pre-20th-c. authors.

An overview of the history of criticism is *Storia della critica letteraria in Italia*, ed. Giorgio Baroni, T, UTET, 1997, 598 pp. A. Di Benedetto, 'Benedetto Croce: un critico ben temperato', *Belfagor*, 52,

1997: 125–37; D. Della Terza, 'Benedetto Croce critico: la presenza dell'antico', *FAM*, 13, 1997: 71–86, analyses Croce's essays on Homer, Terence, and Virgil. Pier Vincenzo Mengaldo, *Profili di critici del Novecento*, T, Bollati Boringhieri, 150 pp., advocates a philological, philosophical, and militant variety of literary criticism in short but dense studies of Croce, Borgese, Montale, Solmi, Debenedetti, Contini, Fortini, Cases, Zanzotto, Pasolini, Calvino, Segre, Garboli, Baldacci, Raboni, and Magris. Aldo Trione, **Estetica e Novecento*, Ro–Bari, Laterza, 1996.

The following essays focus on periodicals. 'Per il centenario di una rivista', *RLI*, 101.1, 1997: 5–63, includes G. Amoretti, 'La *Rassegna* dal 1893 al 1915' (5–16); G. Ponte, 'La *Rassegna* diretta da Achille Pellizzari' (17–30); S. Verdino, 'La *Rassegna* di Binni nel periodo genovese e fiorentino' (31–41); Q. Marini, 'Quattro numeri monografici della *Rassegna*' (42–61); A. Bemporad, 'Ricordo della *Rassegna della letteratura italiana*' (62–63). E. Esposito, 'L'intatto aroma. Novecento letterario in *Belfagor*', *Belfagor*, 53: 417–54, contains a critical-historical introduction and a list of articles published in *Belfagor*. A. Longoni, '*Alfabeta*. I discorsi itineranti di una rivista di cultura', *Autografo*, 35, 1997: 15–34, reconstructs the debate on 'impegno' held in *Alfabeta* and assesses its relevance in the social and cultural context of the 1980s.

On publishing: Gabriele Turi, **Storia dell'editoria nell'Italia contemporanea*, F, Giunti, 1997.

2. POETRY

Le notti chiare erano tutte un'alba, ed. Andrea Cortellessa, Mi, Bruno Mondadori, anthologizes D'Annunzio, Commisso, Rebora, Ungaretti, Saba, Jahier, Marinetti, Moscardelli, and others who wrote of the First World War. Joseph Tusiani and Giovanni Cecchetti, *Voci di poesia. Saggi di struttura poetica da Dante a Campana con uno studio sulla traduzione*, Salerno, Laveglia, 1997, 202 pp., bring together ten articles already published elsewhere. *Dialect Poetry of Southern Italy. Texts and Criticism. A Trilingual Anthology*, Brooklyn, Ontario, Legas, 1997, 511 pp., presents contemporary dialect poetry from Abruzzo, Lazio, and further south, and from Sicily and Sardinia, with Sicilian, Italian, and English versions of these poems. Ronald De Rasy, *Il narrativo della poesia moderna*, F, Casati, 1997, 260 pp. Anna Dolfi, *Terza generazione. Ermetismo e oltre*, Ro, Bulzoni, 1997, 457 pp., hereafter *Terza generazione*, is a useful study of major figures such as Luzi, Bigongiari, Caproni, Gatto, Bodini, Jacobbi, Tentori, Landolfi, Bilenchi, Dessì, and Macrì. Silvio Ramat, *La poesia italiana 1903–1943*, Venice, Marsilio, 1997, 505 pp., is a valuable collection of 41 critical essays on major poets of that time. Claudia Salaris, *Luciano Folgore e le avanguardie. Con lettere e inediti futuristi*, F, La Nuova Italia, 1997, 387 pp., looks at the role of Florence in the context of futurism and the forms of cultural renewal in literature up to the post-war period. *Come leggere la poesia del Novecento. Saba, Ungaretti, Montale, Sereni, Caproni, Zanzotto*, ed. Stefano Carrai and Franco Zambon, Vicenza, Neri Pozza, 1997, 138 pp. Vittorio Esposito, 'Poeti italiani (o padani?) del secondo Novecento (1945–1995)', *RStI*, 15.2, 1997:208–15, criticizes Cucchi and Giovanardi in their anthology *Poeti italiani del secondo novecento (1945–1995)* for ignoring the progress made by poets outside the north of Italy since 1945. Giovanni Bonalumi, Renato Martinoni, and Pier Vincenzo Mengaldo, *Cento anni di poesia nella Svizzera italiana*, Locarno, Dadò, 1997, 423 pp. L. Fontanella, 'Poeti emigrati ed emigranti poeti negli Stati Uniti', *Italica*, 75:210–25, deals with Italian poets who went to the USA almost 100 years ago, Italo-American poets, and Italian poets who emigrated following the Second World War. M. Marrucci, 'I poeti sperimentali negli anni dell'antisperimentalismo', *Allegoria*, 29–30:156–84, evaluates the work of Leonetti, Volponi, Porta, and Sanguineti. P. Giovannetti, 'Al ritmo dell'ossimoro. Note sulla poesia in prosa italiana', *ib.*, 28:19–40, is an overview of poetic prose from the 18th century to today. A. I. Villa, 'Incontri crepuscolari. L'asse Roma–Firenze', *ON*, 22.1–2:133–84, details the poetic and cultural links between the crepuscular poets in Rome (in particular Corazzini) and Florence (Palazzeschi and Moretti) with Papini's Florence and journals such as *Leonardo*, *Hermes*, and *Regno*. G. Salvadori, 'L'officina di *Lacerba* tra anarchia e futurismo', *CLett*, 26:357–68, analyses the contribution of Soffici, Papini, Palazzeschi, and Tavolato towards the development of *Lacerba*. L. Farina, 'A new dictionary of twentieth-century Italian poetry', *Italica*, 74, 1997:576–88. R. Deidier, 'Looking at the 1980s: some notes linking poetics and poetry', *WLT*, 71, 1997:255–59. E. Ghidetti, 'Un modello francese per la prima antologia della poesia italiana del '900', *REI*, 43, 1997:285–96. G. Consonni, 'I luoghi dei viandanti: città e periferia nella poesia del Novecento', *Belfagor*, 52, 1997:649–53. M. Bettarini, 'Donne e poesia - prima parte: dal 1963 al 1979', *Poesia*, 119:57–73, looks at the impact made by women in those years. Ib., 'Donne e poesia - seconda parte: dal 1980 al 1989', *ib.*, 121:61–76, looks at further progress in these years. Enrico Elli, *Cultura e poesia tra Ottocento e Novecento*, Modena, Mucchi, 1997, 300 pp., includes for the Novecento pieces on poetic language from Pascoli to Montale and on Sbarbaro, Ungaretti, Pirandello, Santucci, Loy, Tamaro, Mazzantini, Facetti. R. Feldman, 'On translating Italian poetry', *FMLS*, 33, 1997:3–16.

3. NARRATIVE, THEATRE

Essays on narrative are as follows. Carla Benedetti, *Pasolini contro Calvino. Per una letteratura impura*, T, Bollati Boringhieri, 203 pp., analyses Pasolini's and Calvino's poetics, and favours Pasolini's opposition to institutional politics, his thematic literary nuclei, and his conception of literature as action, in contrast with Calvino's playing with literary conventions. Cristina Benussi, *Scrittori di terra, di mare, di città. Romanzi italiani tra storia e mito, Mi, Pratiche. Gian Paolo Biasin, *Le periferie della letteratura. Da Verga a Tabucchi*, Ravenna, Longo, 1997, 151 pp., defines the concept of 'literary periphery' as a terrain of apparently minor details which constitute lateral but relevant starting points for an understanding of texts. B. sees literary criticism as a combination of stylistic and sociological analysis, and examines works by Verga, Tozzi, Svevo, Paola Drigo, Primo Levi, Calvino, and Tabucchi. G. Borri, 'Una contrapposizione "ideologica" d'inizio secolo: *Gli Ammonitori* di Giovanni Cena (1904) e *La nuova arma (la macchina)* di Mario Morasso', *Atti* (AISLLI 15), 559–67. Lidia De Federicis, *Letteratura e storia*, Ro–Bari, Laterza, 80 pp., is a brief introduction to the structures and themes of historical novels written after Manzoni's *I promessi sposi*. Pier Giorgio Conti, 'Dietro alcune figure dello straniero nella letteratura svizzero-italiana', *Cenobio*, 47, 1998:23–34. Gigliola De Donato, *Gli archivi del silenzio. La tradizione del romanzo storico italiano*, Fasano, Schena, 1997, 324 pp., combines Lukács's theory with semiotics to examine the 20th-c. Italian historical novel. *Scrittori a confronto. Incontri con Busi, Corti, Magris, Morandini, Pazzi, Sanguineti, Sanvitale, Tabucchi, ed. Anna Dolfi e M. C. Papini, Ro, Bulzoni. Elio Elli, *Cultura e poesia* (see POETRY, above), includes an essay on Pirandello's novels seen at the intersection between archaic society and modernity (225–37), and an essay on collective memory in Rosetta Loy's and Susanna Tamaro's novels (pp. 267–98). M. Ganeri, 'Il ritorno postmoderno del romanzo storico: implicazioni teoriche e culturali', *Allegoria*, 26, 1997:112–20, defines Italian 'neo-historical novels' (published in recent decades by authors such as Consolo, Maraini, and Morante) as a postmodern literary genre which portrays a degraded past and anticipates an apocalyptic future against the background of a contemporary society where the ideology of the end of history seems to prevail. Margherita Ganeri, *Postmodernismo*, Mi, Bibliografica, 94 pp., summarizes some postmodern theory and draws attention to Calvino's intertextuality, Consolo's historical novel, Eco's hyper-novel, Malerba's political allegory, Volponi's sense of tradition, and Tabucchi's portrayal of the multiple self. Guido Guglielmi, *La prosa italiana del Novecento*, II: *Tra romanzo e racconto*, T, Einaudi, 209 pp., focuses on the 'antinaturalismo' visible to a greater or lesser degree in the works of a number of 20th-c. Italian writers. In particular, G. analyses the modernist poetics of Gadda, Pirandello, and Svevo; myth in Pavese, Sanguineti, and Vittorini; the theme of play in Calvino; alienation and ideology in Moravia; he also includes essays on Bilenchi, Delfini, Fenoglio, and Landolfi. Paolo Mauri, *L'opera imminente*, T, Einaudi, 187 pp., contains book reviews and essays on authors such as Alvaro, Malerba, and Biamonti. F. Merlanti, 'Genova nel romanzo italiano fra Ottocento e Novecento: trasfigurazione, realtà, mistero', *Resine*, 76:3–27, examines how Genoa is portrayed by Arpino, Baratono, Ceccardi, Tabucchi, and others. P. Orvieto, 'Il romanzo erotico-trasgressivo tra le due guerre: il primo decennio (1919–1929). Guido da Verona, Luciano Zuccoli, Pittigrilli e altri', *StIt*, 16, 1996[1997]:43–83. Giorgio Patrizi, *Prose contro il romanzo. Antiromanzi e metanarrativa nel Novecento italiano*, Na, Liguori, 1996, viii + 215 pp. Roberto Paoli, *Borges e gli scrittori italiani*, Na, Liguori, 1997, 152 pp., contains a section on Borges' influence on Calvino, Eco, Sciascia, Tabucchi, and other authors, and a section on the influence of Italian writers on Borges. Franco Petroni, *Le parole di traverso. Ideologia e linguaggio nella narrativa d'avanguardia del primo Novecento*, Mi, Jaca Book, 133 pp., analyses some aspects of Slataper's, Tozzi's, and Pea's work. Eugenia Roccella, *La letteratura rosa*, Ro, Editori Riuniti, 148 pp., outlines the development of the 'romanzo rosa' from the last century to its most recent manifestations reflecting commercial strategies dictated by the growth of mass society. Gino Tellini, **Il romanzo italiano dell'Ottocento e del Novecento*, Mi, Bruno Mondadori, 560 pp. Enrico Testa, *Lo stile semplice*, T, Einaudi, 1997, 264 pp., focuses on contemporary novels written in a 'lingua semplice', or average standard Italian, in contrast with the 'espressionismo' of some other novels. David S. Watson and B. Mortara Garavelli, 'Temi giudiziari, *inventio*, e invenzione letteraria negli ultimi decenni', *StIt*, 17, 1997:107–19. Paola Zanotti, *Il modo romanzesco*, Ro–Bari, Laterza, 82 pp., differentiates *romance* from *novel*; discusses some of the features of *romance* (passive reader, rewriting of folklore, fantasy, lack of depth, happy ending, function of protagonists, tension between realistic and non-realistic procedures), and concludes that *romance* survives in 20th-c. science fiction and popular literature, and also in some sophisticated novels such as Calvino's *Il barone rampante* and Benni's *La compagnia dei Celestini*.

Some essays focus specifically on fiction written by women. Adriana Cavarero, **Tu che mi guardi, tu che mi racconti. Filosofia della narrazione*, Mi, Feltrinelli, 1997. S. Wright, 'La guerra al femminile, tra esperienza e comunicazione letteraria: *L'Agnese va a morire, Lessico familiare, Prima e dopo*', *FoI*, 32:63–85. **Novelle d'autrice tra Otto e Novecento*, ed. Paola Bulzon, Ro, Bulzoni, 304 pp.

The following essays are about Italian narrative in the 1990s. *La Bestia*, 1997, no. 1, a thematic issue on the so-called 'cannibali' writers, includes essays by D. Brolli and A. Guglielmi, and an interview with E. Sanguineti. Giuseppe Amoroso, **Il cenacolo degli specchi. Narrativa italiana 1993–1995*, Caltanissetta–Ro, Sciascia, 1997, 565 pp. T. Arvigo, 'La narrativa italiana degli anni Novanta', *NC*, 120, 1997:377–414, identifies the following four different ways of using language in several Italian novels published in the 1990s: (i) Tamaro's 'linea normativa', or standard Italian; (ii) Del Giudice's, Biamonti's, and Tabucchi's 'linea espressiva'; (iii) Consolo's and Ortese's 'espressionismo classico'; and (iv) Ballestra's and Brizzi's 'neoespressionismo' characterized by slang, neologisms and idiolects. A. prefers Brizzi and Ballestra to the 'cannibali'. She dismisses Tamaro as a writer of 'ovvietà', but values Tabucchi, Malerba, Del Giudice, Ortese, Cavazzoni, Loy, and Benni. Raffaele Cardone, Franco Galato, e Fulvio Panzeri, *Altre storie. Inventario della nuova narrativa italiana fra gli anni '80 e '90*, Mi, Marcos y Marcos, 1997, 216 pp., is a useful annotated inventory of authors, novels, and tendencies. A. Cortelessa, 'Gaddismo mediato. La "funzione Gadda" negli ultimi dieci anni di narrativa italiana', *Allegoria*, 28:41–78, identifies and examines Gadda's influence on Ballestra, Mari, Ottieri, and other recent writers. C. Covito, 'In search of the Italian language: integrated Italian', which can also be read in the original Italian on the author's private www pages (carmencovito.com), *WLT*, 71, 1997:309–12, ascribes the diffusion of standard Italian to the development of the mass media and observes that some writers (such as Capriolo and Tamaro) resist the adoption of 'italiano parlato' and instead use high registers. In fiction-writing, C. is in favour of what she calls 'italiano integrato', a variety of written Italian combining 'parlato' with the language of the literary tradition. C.'s examples of 'italiano integrato' are Arbasino's, Busi's, and Ballestra's novels. Lidia De Federicis, *Prove a carico. Due anni di percorsi della narrativa italiana*, T, L'Indice, 1997, 92 pp. (supplement to *L'Indice*, 14.5, 1997) collects articles published from 1995 to 1997 on novels reviewed according to their tendencies. R. Donnarumma, 'Esecuzione sommaria', *Allegoria*, 25, 1997:163–64, accuses Ammanniti, Ballestra, Brizzi, Caliceti, Culicchia, Nove, Santacroce, and Scarpa of being commercial and trivial; he defines the Italian they use in their stories as 'inglese da discoteca'. R. Luperini, 'Giovani e cannibali solo *basic instinct*', *L'Indice*, 14.3, 1997:10, provides a brief but dense sketch of some linguistic and thematic inconsistencies of the 'cannibali'. F. Petroni, 'La neoavanguardia battezza i cannibali', *Allegoria*, 27, 1997:129–31. Marino Sinibaldi, *Pulp. La letteratura nell'era della simultaneità*, Ro, Donzelli, 1997, 95 pp., identifies an Italian 'pulp' genre. S. values

Benni but expresses reservations about the 'cannibali'. V. Spinazzola, 'La letteratura del Novecento. Industria editoriale, sistema formativo, canone', *Allegoria*, 27, 1997: 95–104, invites academic critics to be less stern about the recent democratization of literature and the use of everyday language in fiction. *Tirature '98*, ed. Vittorio Spinazzola, Mi, Il Saggiatore, 1997, 250 pp., includes a section entitled 'Una modernità tutta da raccontare' on the Italian novel in the 1990s.

Contributions on the theatre range from B. Nuciforo Tosolini 'Futurismo: teoria e pratica teatrale' *De Lorenzi Vol.*, 53–80, to Luca Ronconi, **Lezioni per l'attore di teatro*, T, Fornovelli, 1997, and particularly Richard Andrews, *A Theatre of Community Memory: Tuscan Sharecropping and the Teatro Povero di Monticchiello* (Society for Italian Studies, Occasional Papers, 4), Leeds, Maney, 128 pp., which examines the economic and cultural collective history of the people of the village of Monticchiello near Siena, and explores the themes, forms, language, and social functions of its community theatre in the last 30 years.

4. Individual Authors

ALVARO. G. Savarese, 'L'autobiografia tra "alto" e "basso" mnemonico. (In margine a Alvaro autobiografo mancato)', *EL*, 22.4, 1997: 35–44, discusses some aspects of autobiography as a genre, and detects hidden autobiographical aspects in A.'s work. G. Rimanelli, 'Letteratura come racconto. Alvaro e Tozzi, compagni di viaggio', *StIt*, 16, 1996[1997]: 121–40.

ARBASINO. M. Lunetta, '*Fratelli d'Italia 3*: un enorme metaromanzo, la conversazione ininterrotta', *Il Ponte*, 53.5, 1997:92–102, shows how A. portrays existential emptiness and social catastrophe in a language made up of multiple registers.

ARDIZZI. T. Manduca, 'L'industria edile nei romanzi di Maria Ardizzi', *Atti* (AISLLI 15), 1113–22.

BALESTRINI. T. Pagano, 'Le avanguardie entrano in fabbrica: scrittura e rivoluzione in *Vogliamo tutto* di Nanni Balestrini', *Atti* (AISLLI 15), 1025–37.

BANTI. *L'opera di Anna Banti. Atti del Convegno di studi, Firenze, 8–9 maggio 1992*, ed. Enza Biagini, F, Olschki, 1997, xxvi + 206 pp., includes biographical information and essays on B.'s historical novels, on her interest in the visual arts, and on her identity as a woman writer (contributions by E. Biagini, L. M. Savoia, B. Magnolfi, A. Paolucci, G. Barblan, P. Bigongiari, C. Garboli, M. Gregori, G. Leonelli, G. Fink, M. Ghilardi, R. Guerricchio, J.-M. Gardair, E. Biagini, R. Loy, E. G. Belotti, M. C. Papini, G. Livi, L. Fortini, M. L. Strocchi, G. Nava, G. Luti, A. Nozzoli, and M. Volpi).

BASSANI. R. Cotroneo, 'La ferita indicibile' and 'Cronologia', pp. ix–xciv of Giorgio Bassani, *Opere*, Mi, Mondadori, examines Ferrara as an imaginary place in B.'s work, sees his fiction as independent of rigid ideological and psychological definitions, detects intertextual reference to the visual arts, and underlines the importance of B.'s exploration of the inner self. C. Della Coletta, 'La cultura del giardino. Miti e appropriazioni letterarie nel *Giardino dei Finzi-Contini*', *MLN*, 113:138–63, discusses some of B.'s literary models. B. Moloney, 'James Joyce and the *Storie ferraresi*', *JAIS*, 5, 1997: 231–43, analyses B.'s work in relation to Joyce's *Dubliners* and *A Portrait of the Artist*, and to Croce's concepts of 'paralisi storica' and 'storia mitizzata'.

BELLONCI. Maria Bellonci, *Opere, ed. Emilio Ferrero, Mi, Mondadori, 1997, cviii + 1556 pp., contains introductions by M. Onofri and V. Della Valle.

BERNARI. N. Cacciaglia, 'Considerazioni su *L'ombra del suicidio (Lo strano Conserti)* di Carlo Bernari', *Atti* (AISLLI 15), 749–61. R. Capozzi, 'Tecniche pittoriche e cinematografiche nelle prime opere di Carlo Bernari', *FoI*, 31, 1997:389–407, highlights some of the symbolic elements interwoven with the realism of B.'s early works.

BERTOLUCCI. G. Palli Baroni, ' "Il gatto selvatico". Attilio Bertolucci dirige il mensile aziendale dell'ENI', *Atti* (AISLLI 15), 929–34. T. Peterson, 'Pascolian intertexts in the lyric poetry of Attilio Bertolucci', *RStI*, 14.1, 1996:153–64. G. Pontiggia, 'Attilio Bertolucci. *Opere*', *Poesia*, 112, 1997:38–40, is an overview of B.'s *œuvre* as collected in Mondadori's 'I Meridiani' edition.

BIAMONTI. R. Cavalluzzi, 'Allegoria del viaggio e dell'attesa in un romanzo di Biamonti', *Italianistica*, 26, 1997:503–06, analyses the novel *Attesa sul mare*. V. Coletti, 'Umanità in fuga nel dilagare del paesaggio. Francesco Biamonti fra i grandi sperimentatori della prosa novecentesca', *L'Indice*, 15.3:6, defines B. as an experimental writer who interweaves poetry and prose, description and storytelling.

BIANCHINI. A. M. Jeannet, *'Exiles and returns in Angela Bianchini's fiction', *Italica*, 75:93–111.

BIGONGIARI. *Per Piero Bigongiari. Atti della giornata di studio, Firenze, 25 novembre 1994*, ed. Enza Biagini, Ro, Bulzoni, 1997, 191 pp., contains a number of wide-ranging studies on B. by S. Agosti, G. Isella, T. O'Neill, A. Fongaro, J.-M. Gardair, S. Crespi, I. Lavergne, A. Brettoni, L. Tassoni, M. Ajazzi Mancini, E. Biagini. G. Chiappini, 'Per ricordare Piero Bigongiari', *CV*, 52, 1997:425–28. A. Dolfi, 'Su Bigongiari, le lettere e la *land art*', *Terza generazione*', 27–42. *Poesia*, 111, 1997, offers tributes to B. from R. Carifi, 'Omaggio a Piero Bigongiari' (16–18); M. De Angelis, 'Un maestro nobile e generoso' (19); and S. Ramat, 'Saluto lieve a Piero Bigongiari' (19).

BO. V. Greglio, 'Carlo Bo: Leopardi come vita', *CLett*, 25, 1997:551–61, establishes parallels between B.'s and Leopardi's pitiless questioning of life and living.

BONAVIRI. S. Zappulla Muscarà, 'Postfazione', pp. 179–87 of Giuseppe Bonaviri, *Il fiume di pietra*, Mi, Mondadori, 1997, argues that in B.'s fiction realism dissolves into myth, dreams, surrealism, and multilingualism. Franco Zangrilli, **Il fior del ficodindia. Saggio su Bonaviri*, Acireale, La Cantinella, 1997, 141 pp. Franco Zangrilli, *Sicilia isola-cosmo. Conversazione con Giuseppe Bonaviri*, Ravenna, Longo, 128 pp., sketches a biographical and critical profile of B. followed by a long interview. R. Bertoni, 'Bonaviri ermetico: il motivo del *rito di passaggio*', *The Italianist*, 16, 1996[1997]:161–75.

BONTEMPELLI. F. Airoldi Namer, 'Massimo Bontempelli: una vita intensamente inoperosa', *Atti* (AISLLI 15), 681–706. M. Mascia Galateria, 'Il viaggio di una Fiat 522 in un racconto novecentista di Massimo Bontempelli', *ib.*, 707–19.

BORGESE. P. Gerbi, 'Giuseppe Antonio Borgese politico', *Belfagor*, 52, 1997:43–69, studies the complex attitudes to Fascism of the early Borgese. G. Bevilacqua, 'La questione tedesca nella riflessione di G. A. Borgese', *RLMC*, 49, 1996[1997]:349–56.

BRANCATI. Gian Carlo Ferretti, *L'infelicità della ragione nella vita e nell'opera di Vitaliano Brancati*, Mi, Guerini, 138 pp., discusses ambivalence in B.'s work — between reason and senselessness, angelic and non-angelic women characters, and comedy and tragedy. Domenica Perrone, *Vitaliano Brancati. Le avventure morali e i 'piaceri' della scrittura*, Mi, Bompiani, 1997, 232 pp., defines B.'s realism as complex, based on the relationship between reality and dreams, autobiographical allusions, and an intertextual dialogue with Pirandello and Leopardi.

BRIZZI. Anna Comodi, **Tratti lessicali e morfosintattici del parlar giovane in Jack Frusciante è uscito dal gruppo*, Perugia, Guerra.

BUFALINO. F. Caputo, 'Il fotografo delle parole. In ricordo di Gesualdo Bufalino', *Autografo*, 34, 1997:49–56, analyses the interrelated motives of photography, circular patterns, and death in *Tommaso e il fotografo cieco* (B.'s last book) and in some of B.'s other works. E. Papa, 'Gesualdo Bufalino', *Belfagor*, 52, 1997:561–77, finds cross-fertilization between poetry and prose in B.'s language, highlights the thematic antitheses of life vs death and disease vs health, and concludes that B. was politically moderate but deeply concerned with 'sicilianità' and 'storia minore'. **Simile a un colombo viaggiatore. Per Bufalino*, ed. Nunzio Zago, Comiso, Salarchi.

BUFFONI. P. Valesio, 'Franco Buffoni or oblique illuminations', *YIP*, 1, 1997:12–15.

BULGHERONI. A. Giorgio, 'Parola e passione materna: 'Gli Orti della Regina' di Marisa Bulgheroni', *Lepschy Vol.*, 315–26.

BUZZATI. A. Brambilla, 'Appunti sulle *Cronache terrestri* di Dino Buzzati', *Cenobio*, 47:3–11. C. Cochi, 'La macchina nei racconti di Dino Buzzati', *Atti* (AISLLI 15), 935–40. G. Hofmann, 'Von Eros zu Heros: Dino Buzzatis militarischer Zauberberg *Il deserto dei tartari*', *RF*, 108, 1996:146–56. Elena Lardo, *L'universo tangente. Una lettura della narrativa di Dino Buzzati*, Ro, Nuova Cultura, 1996, 65 pp. E. Nerenberg, 'Tartar control: masculinity and *impegno* in Buzzati's *Il deserto dei tartari*', *Italica*, 74, 1997:217–34. Angelo Colombo, *'Un linguaggio universalmente comprensibile'. Correzioni e varianti nei primi racconti di Buzzati*, Seren del Grappa, DBS, 1996, 110 pp. We also note G. Carnazzi's *Introduction to B. at pp. i-xlviii of *Opere scelte*, Mi, Mondadori; Giorgio Cavallini, *Buzzati. Il limite dell'ombra*, Ro, Studium, 1997; and S. Lazzarin, *'Preliminari a uno studio dell'inter-testualità buzzatiana', *Italianistica*, 26, 1997:303–11.

CALVINO. *Autografo*, 36, devoted to C., includes: M. McLaughlin, 'Il carteggio Calvino–De Giorgi: problemi di datazione' (13–32); C. Martignani, 'Viaggio nelle città di Italo Calvino' (33–48); N. Leone, 'Le copertine di Calvino: altri mondi possibili' (49–66); E. Borsa, 'Calvino e il saggio: *Lezioni americane* e altro' (67–86); N. Trotta, 'Due inediti sulla *Panchina* di Italo Calvino' (117–32). *Alì Babà. Progetto di una rivista 1968–1972 (Riga*, 14), Mi, Marcos y Marcos, 321 pp., includes and discusses letters exchanged between Calvino, Celati, and others on a plan for a never-published literary journal. R. Andrews, 'Calvino's (fictional) women', *Villari Vol.*, 171–83, analyses 'Calvino's tendency to show his fictional females as *l'altro*, seen from outside, filtered through the consciousness of an observing male', a tendency partly contradicted and partly confirmed by those works (such as *Il cavaliere inesistente*) where female characters are 'in charge of the text offered by the male author'. P. Antonello, 'Paesaggi della mente. Su Italo Calvino', *FoI*, 32:108–13, investigates the relationship between nature, culture, and mental maps in 'Dall'o-paco' and other works by Calvino.

A. Botta, 'Calvino and the Oulipo: an Italian ghost in the combinatory machine', *MLN*, 112, 1997:81–89. I. Cartasso, 'Il percorso circolare di Pin come un'"iniziazione mancata"', *FoI*, 31, 1997:63–73, discusses Pin's failed initiation into the world of adults in *Il sentiero dei nidi di ragno*. Simona Chessa Wright, *La poetica neobarocca in Calvino*, Ravenna, Longo, 176 pp., adopts Omar Calabrese's concepts of 'neobarocco' — especially instability and multiple dimensions of reality, mutability, and complexity — to analyse C.'s work, where she finds a search for order against the background of a chaotic universe. Stephen Chubb, *I, Writer, I, Reader: The Concept of*

Self in the Fiction of Italo Calvino, Market Harborough, Troubador, 1997, 146 pp., investigates the theme of the self as textual strategy. One chapter is about death, a theme which was ignored or understated by C.'s critics before recent years. M. Ciccuto, 'L'industria dell'acciaio committente di visite in fabbrica: Ungaretti, Calvino e altri scrittori d'arte', *Atti* (AISLLI 15), 949–62. C. Della Colletta, 'L'Oriente tra ripetizione e diffidenza nelle *Città invisibili* di Italo Calvino', *StN*, 24, 1997: 411–31, finds both a Western orientalist approach and an unbiased intertextual interest in C.'s use of Eastern models.

Europe, 817, 1997, largely given over to C., includes: M.-A. Rubat du Mérac, 'Au commencement était *Le Sentier des nids d'araignées*' (19–29); M. Fusco, 'Un arbre généalogique' (35–34); P. Daros, 'Petite typologie du regard' (35–47); J. Jouet, 'L'homme de Calvino' (48–52); A. Asor Rosa, 'La nature morale de l'inspiration' (53–58); J. Updike, 'Les métropoles de l'esprit' (59–64); P. Citati, 'Le roman du lecteur' (65–69); M. Lavagetto, 'Un écrivain d'apocryphes?' (70–79); D. Del Giudice, 'L'œil qui écrit' (80–83); G. Manganelli, 'Profond en surface' (84–86); M. Belpoliti, 'Le clair miroir de l'esprit' (87–100); J.-P. Manganaro, 'Le regard du comte' (101–07); P. Braffort, 'L'ordre dans le crime' (128–39); Id., 'Une expérience cybernétique avec Italo Calvino' (140–50); C. Milanini, 'Calvino et l'édition de ses œuvres' (151–60); M. Barenghi, 'Calvino et le spectacle. Le théâtre des éventails' (161–60). Id., 'Gli oggetti e gli dèi. Appunti su una metafora calviniana', *De Lorenzi Vol.*, 197–218. B. Ferraro, 'I segni del mondo industriale in alcune opere di Italo Calvino negli anni Cinquanta e Sessanta', *Atti* (AISLLI 15), 941–47. Gian Carlo Ferretti, *Le avventure del lettore. Calvino, Ludmilla e gli altri*, Bari, Manni, 1997, 59 pp., traces C.'s itinerary as a professional reader for Einaudi, and shows how he makes use of reading in his fiction from earlier work such as *Il barone rampante* to Ludmilla, reader-par-excellence, of *Se una notte d'inverno un viaggiatore. Italo Calvino le défi au labyrinthe. Actes de la Journée d'études de Caen, 8–3–1997*, ed. Paolo Grossi and Silvia Fabrizio-Costa, Caen U.P., 146 pp., contains the following contributions: pref. and introd. by S. Vento, P. Grossi, and S. Fabrizio-Costa; M. Barenghi on oblique autobiographical references in C.'s fiction; G. Bonsaver on C.'s development from political commitment to an interest in the ideologies of crisis; P. Laroche on the theme of the city in C.'s fiction; M. Belpoliti on the anthropological concept of sacrifice in C.'s work; M. Fusco on C.'s interpretation of Landolfi; S. Blazina on the concept of Utopia; P. Grossi on C. and Ariosto.

Martin McLaughlin, *Italo Calvino*, Edinburgh U.P., 190 pp., studies C.'s works in chronological order, using a philological approach based on text genetics, intertextuality, and thematic and structural analysis, and distinguishes an initial realist phase from a successive postmodern phase beginning in 1963–64. C. Martignoni, 'Alcuni percorsi nelle *Città invisibili* di Italo Calvino', *Autografo*, 34, 1997: 15–27, analyses C.'s use of first person narrative and other aspects of his fiction. M. J. Calvo Montoro, 'Joseph Conrad and Italo Calvino, o della stesura di una tesi come riflessione sulla scrittura', *FoI*, 31, 1997:74–115, summarizes and discusses C.'s university dissertation on Conrad, and examines the latter's influence on his work. By the same writer, *'Italo Calvino e Ignazio di Loyola: due superatori di prove alla ricerca di una poetica', *ConLet*, 26:805–14. G. Nava, 'La teoria della letteratura in Calvino', *Allegoria*, 25, 1997:169–85, sees a dichotomy between intellectual rationality and existential pessimism in C.'s last works. Eugenia Paulicelli, *Parola e immagine. Sentieri della scrittura in Leonardo, Marino, Foscolo, Calvino*, Fiesole, Cadmo, 1996, 156 pp., includes (115–43) the final chapter *'Le città invisibili* di Italo Calvino: fra microstoria e immagini della memoria'. Also by her, 'Dalla città invisibile alla città futura. Italo Calvino: storia, impegno, linguaggio', *The Italianist*, 16, 1996[1997]:143–60. Francesca G. Pedriali, '"Più per paura che per gioco?"'. Three textual explorations of Calvino's *Il sentiero dei nidi di ragno*', *MLR*, 93: 59–70, shows, among other things, that C.'s 'double poetics of advertisement and conceal-ment' is already present in the 'nocturnal' *Sentiero dei nidi di ragno*, thus anticipating some of his successive stories. F. Pellizzi, 'Metafore della distanza in Borges e Calvino', *StCrit*, 12, 1997:291–307, defines the two writers as practitioners of the 'racconto romanzizzato' or 'pro-romanzo', a genre combining procedures of the novel and the short-story and characterized by its use of 'metaphors of distance'. F. Pierangeli, *Italo Calvino*, Soveria Mannelli, Rubbettino, 1997. A. Pierpaolo, 'Paesaggi della mente. Su Italo Calvino', *FoI*, 32:108–31. K. Pilz, 'Complexity: a paradigm for "One Culture"?', *FoI*, 31, 1997:423–37, relates C.'s vision of the world to post-Newtonian scientific paradigms, and in particular to Prigogine's and Stengers' theories. L. Re, 'Calvino and the value of literature', *MLN*, 113:121–37, discusses C.'s historically variable literary and moral values, from the compact ideology of 'Il midollo del leone' to the sense of social and existential precariousness in *Lezioni americane*. R. Rushing, 'Il cristallo e il mare: l'*enumeración caótica* e l'epistemologia in Calvino e Gadda', *FoI*, 31, 1997:407–22, applies Leo Spitzer's concept of 'enumeración caótica' to both writers and especially to C.'s essays on Gadda. Ulrich Schulz-Buschhaus, *Zwischen 'resa' und 'ostinazione'. Zu Kanon und Poetik Italo Calvinos*, Tübingen, Narr, 50 pp.

CAMILLERI. B. Perelli, '*Un filo di fumo*, romanzo siciliano di Andrea Camilleri', *Italianistica*, 27:99–103, studies C.'s novel in relation to Tasso, Ariosto, and Sicilian fiction.

CAMPANA. P. Brunel, 'Campana, Rimbaud et le mythe de Paris', *REI*, 43, 1997:241–46. C. D'Alessio, '*Toscanità* di Dino Campana: teoria e prassi dell'avanguardia', *FC*, 21, 1996[1997]:487–94. E. Speciale, 'Dino Campana: la notte barbara', pp. 231–48 of *Poétiques barbares/Poetiche barbare*, Ravenna, Longo, reviews C.'s poetry in terms of 'barbarian' poetics. M. A. Grignani, 'Momenti della ricezione di Campana', *Allegoria*, 27, 1997:5–16. P. L. Ladron de Guevara Mellado, 'I *Canti Orfici* del 1928', *RLI*, 102:537–45, discusses 1928 variants from the 1914 edition.

CAMPANILE. U. Eco, 'Achille Campanile: il comico come straniamento', pp. 53–97 of his *Tra menzogna e ironia*, Mi, Bompiani, uses theories of comedy and pragmatic linguistics to analyse C.'s fiction and appreciate it anew.

CAMPO. M. Farnetti, 'Osservazioni sul metodo-correttorio di Cristina Campo', *StN*, 25:331–49, attempts to match the pseudonym of Vittoria Guerrini with C.'s bibliography and poetry. *CV*, 51, 1996[1997]:467–628, publishes papers (ed. M. Farnetti and G. Fozzer) presented at a 1997 conference on Campo by M. G. Rosito, G. Fozzer, M. Farnetti, M. Pieracci Harwell, M. Luzi, P. Simeoni, P. Citati, P. Gibellini, and A. Spina.

CAPRIOLO. G. Palmieri, 'Il grande albero nietzschiano nel giardino narrativo di Paola Capriolo', *Autografo*, 34, 1997: 56–81, shows how Stiller's love for Zeta in C.'s novel *Un uomo di carattere* is modelled on Nietzsche's love for Lou Salomé, and concludes that C.'s novel is postmodern because the author playfully challenges the reader to detect the underlying text based on Nietzsche.

CAPRONI. A. Dolfi, '*Enfasi a parte* e il silenzio della parola', *Terza generazione*, 43–62. R. Orlando, 'Un sonetto di Caproni: note sul linguaggio', *StN*, 25:291–303, offers a linguistic analysis of the poem 'Notte'. G. Caproni, *L'opera in versi*, ed. P. V. Mengaldo, A. Dei, and L. Zuliani, Mi, Mondadori, lxxxi + 1886 pp., is the first critical edition of C.'s poetry with an introduction, bibliography, and notes on his work. S. Ramat, 'Giorgio Caproni, poeta del fil di voce', *Poesia*, 120:20–27, examines C.'s poetry as presented in the Mondadori volume. L. Zuliani, '*Il passaggio d'Enea* di Giorgio Caproni: varianti ed inediti contemporanei', *StN*, 24, 1997:433–55, considers textual variants and unpublished poems in C.'s working papers between 1943 and 1958. M. Lenti, 'Roma nella poesia di Giorgio Caproni', *StRo*, 45, 1997:76–87. E. Rovegno, 'Leggendo *Res amissa* di Caproni: il *Gelo* e l'ultima caccia', *Croce Vol.*, 615–39.

CAPUANA. Franco Manai, *Capuana e la letteratura campagnola*, Pisa, Tip. Ed. Pisana, 1997, 190 pp., focuses on C.'s two collections of short stories *Le paesane* (1894) and *Le ultime paesane* (publ. posthumously in 1923). It seeks to show, by means of a narratological analysis, how, though both collections deal with the representation of life in the countryside, the first is written with narrative techniques that correspond to a positivist vision of the world, while the second adopts procedures that are connected to a relativistic conception of reality. In a detailed discussion, the book also places Capuana's collections in the broader context of the rustic genre in Italian literature.

CARDARELLI. A. Bussolari, 'Cardarelli, la favola e la prosa d'arte', *LS*, 32, 1997:313–33, studies the 'prosa d'arte' of *Favole della genesi*, ascribing its origins to C.'s reading of the classics and to the general context of his poetics. A. Benevento, 'Cardarelli prosatore', *CLett*, 25, 1997:277–305.

CARPI. G. Gronda, 'Analisi in versi', *De Lorenzi Vol.*, 219–28.

CARRERA. E. Livorni, 'Alessandro Carrera ovvero del diuturno discontinuo', *YIP*, 1, 1997:26–28.

CASSOLA. E. Siciliano, 'Per Carlo Cassola', *NArg*, 1997, no. 11:5–7, reappraises C. ten years after his death; in particular he values positively the 'rilievo plastico' of his characters and his vivid spoken Italian.

CELATI. M. Hanne, 'Narrative wisdom in Celati's *Narratori delle pianure*', *RStI*, 14.1, 1996:133–52. P. Kuon, ' "La vita naturale, cosa sarebbe". Modernität und Identität in Gianni Celatis *Narratori delle pianure*', *Italienisch*, 37, 1997:24–36. R. Piazza, 'The narrative imperfect in Celati', *Villari Vol.*, 208–21.

CHIARA. Giancarlo Sala, *Piero Chiara e la sua sentenziosa affabulazione allegorico-pittoresca. Intendimenti artistici, didascalici e iniziatrici*, Poschiavo, Menghini, 1996, 318 pp.

CLAUDIO. E. Giachery, 'Per Dino Claudio', *CLett*, 25, 1997: 121–27. A. Luzi, 'Natura e società nella poesia di Dino Claudio', *CJIS*, 20, 1997:281–93.

CONTINI. See GADDA and MONTALE, below.

CONSOLO. G. Alvino, 'La lingua di Vincenzo Consolo', *Italianistica*, 26, 1997:321–33, sees C.'s experimental fiction as characterized by his 'turbinosità espressiva' rather than by his 'lucido razionalismo nutrito di passione sociologica'. E. Esposito, ' "Nulla è sicuro, ma scrivi". Un romanzo civile (o forse un poema)', *L'Indice*, 15.11:11, reviews *Lo spasimo di Palermo*, pointing to Vittorini as the main source of its experimental nature. P. Farinelli, 'Strategie compositive, motivi e istanze nelle opere di Vincenzo Consolo', *Italienisch*, 37, 1997:38–54.

CORAZZINI. M. Gaetani, 'Tra lamento e rifacimento: Corazzini poeta manierista', *RStI*, 14.1, 1996:87–119. S. Morotti, 'La poesia dialettale di Corazzini', *CLett*, 26:285–312, offers a stimulating analysis of the thematic and metrical nature of C.'s dialect poetry. A. I. Villa, 'Sergio Corazzini schedatore del *Leonardo*: un testo corazziniano disperso', *ON*, 22:3:211–13, assesses the way journalism impacted on C.'s work.

DEBENEDETTI. V. Pietrantonio, 'La quarta dimensione di Giacomo Debenedetti', *RLI*, 100.2–3, 1996[1997]:117–28.

DE CARLO. R. Carnero, 'Dal romanzo "superficiale" al romanzo "generazionale": Andrea De Carlo negli anni ottanta', *Il Ponte*, 53.11, 1997:67–90, traces the Milanese writer's development from *Treno di panna* to *Due di due*.

DE CÉSPEDES. T. De Matteis, '*Quaderno proibito* di Alba de Céspedes: un diario in scena', *Ariel*, 12.1, 1997:93–100, concerns her stage adaptation of the novel.

DE CHIRICO. G. Sanguinetti Katz, 'Il mondo della macchina nell'opera di De Chirico', *Atti* (AISLLI 15), 651–55.

DEL GIUDICE. R. Tordi, '*Manovre di volo* di Daniele Del Giudice', *ib.*, 1133–43.

DESCALZO. F. De Nicola, 'Giovanni Descalzo e il mondo operaio', *Atti* (AISLLI), 741–47.

DESSÌ. M. Dell'Aquila, 'Giuseppe Dessì: i racconti', *Italianistica*, 27:393–400, surveys their main themes and sees them as preparatory materials for his novels.

DI GIACOMO. A. Benvenuto, 'Il punto su Salvatore Di Giacomo (1985–1996)', *EL*, 22.2, 1997:83–102, surveys a decade of Di G. criticism.

DURANTI. J. M. Kozma, 'Bio-fictive conversations and the uncentred woman in Francesca Duranti's novels', *The Italianist*, 16, 1996[1997]:176–90.

ECO. *Reading Eco. An Anthology*, ed. Rocco Capozzi, Bloomington, Indiana U.P., 1997, 476 pp. Id., 'Metaphors and intertextuality in Eco's neo-baroque narrative machine: *The Island of the Day Before*', *RStI*, 14.1, 1996:165–89. G. P. Raffa, 'Walking and swimming with Umberto Eco', *MLN*, 113:164–85, analyses *L'isola del giorno prima* and interprets it by reference to *Sei passeggiate nei boschi narrativi.Staunen über das Sein. Internazionale Beiträge su Umberto Ecos 'Insel des vorigen Tages'*, ed. Thomas Stauder, Darmstadt, WBG, 1997, viii + 367 pp.

ERBA. P. M. Forni, 'L'aquilone, lo svagato e gli ireos gialli (tra Pascoli e Erba)', *FC*, 33:459–72, considers the use of Pascolian themes in two Erba poems. *The Metaphysical Streetcar Conductor (Sixty poems of Luciano Erba)*, ed. Alfredo de Palchi and Michael Palma, NY, Gradiva, 151 pp., contains an introduction to E.'s poetry and valuable parallel-text translations in English.

FALLACI. John Gatt-Rutter, *Oriana Fallaci. The Rhetoric of Freedom*, Oxford, Berg, 1996, 212 pp.

FENOGLIO. W. Boggione, '*La malora* di Fenoglio. Condanna alla privazione e potere salvifico della rinuncia', *Lingua e letteratura*, 27–28,

1997:123–38, suggests that Agostino's hardship in *La malora* may be seen as a way to obtain existential salvation and concludes that F.'s non-religious sense of the sacred may be found in the myth of a symbolic mother earth. L. Bufano, 'Alba come Rouen. Maupassant in Fenoglio', *Il Ponte*, 54.1:67–79, draws an intertextual, stylistic, and thematic comparison between Maupassant's *Contes de guerre* and *I ventitré giorni della città di Alba. Beppe Fenoglio 1922–1997. Atti del convegno di Alba, 15 marzo 1997*, ed. Pino Menzio, Mi, Electa, 63 pp., includes contributions by G. L. Beccaria (9–17), who argues in favour of F.'s symbolic, rather than naturalist, realism, and by M. A. Grignani (19–26), who conducts a textual analysis of *Appunti partigiani*. L. Pavan, ' "E ho una strana potenza di parola": la traduzione in Fenoglio', *LetP*, 103:3–26. M. Pregliasco, 'In forma di fuga. Lettura di *Una questione privata* di Beppe Fenoglio', *StCrit*, 13:79–103.

FILIPPINI.   'Enrico Filippini tra illuminismo e coscienza infelice. Atti dell'incontro di studio di Lugano, 7 febbraio 1997', *Cenobio*, 46.4, 1997.

FLAIANO.   Lucilla Sergiacomo, *Invito alla lettura di Flaiano*, Mi, Mursia, 1996, 264 pp.

FO.   Dario Fo, *Morte accidentale di un anarchico*, ed. Jennifer Lorch, MUP, 1997, 177 pp., contains explanatory notes (122–41), some statements by F. (142–53), a vocabulary (158–77), and an introd. (1–35) on recent Italian history and F.'s political theatre. D. Maceri, 'Dario Fo: jester of the working class', *WLT*, 72:9–14, examines *Mistero buffo*. Chiara Valentini, *La storia di Dario Fo*, Mi, Feltrinelli, 1997, 207 pp., is a biographical and cultural reconstruction of F.'s career.

FONTANELLA.   'A proposito di *Ceres* di Luigi Fontanella: tre interventi di Roberto Deidier, Giulio Ferroni e Valerio Magrelli', *RStI*, 15:2, 1997:240–51, outlines the transatlantic lyricism of these poems. F. Doplicher, 'Punto di contatto: sulla poesia di Luigi Fontanella', *FoI*, 31, 1997:487–96. P. Valesio, 'Luigi Fontanella or writing with green ink', *YIP*, 1, 1997:54–57.

FORTINI.   Thomas E. Peterson, *The Ethical Muse of Franco Fortini*, Gainesville, Florida U.P., 1997, 200 pp., examines the religious, literary, and political substrata of Fortini's work. S. Palumbo, 'Franco Fortini esordiente. Poesie e prose sconosciute', *Poesia*, 118:24–30. T. E. Peterson, 'Commenti sciolti su *Composita solvantur*', *ItC*, 16:99–110. See also PASOLINI, below.

GADDA.   A. Andreini and M. Guglielminetti, *La coscienza infelice. Carlo Emilio Gadda*, Mi, Guerini, 1996, 197 pp. D. Carmosino, 'Tra estetica ed etica: Carlo Emilio Gadda critico militante', *Italianistica*, 26, 1997:279–302. A. Cortelessa, 'Il punto su Gadda. Tentativo di ordinare la bibliografia gaddiana: 1993–1994', *StN*, 24, 1997:

177–223, is the continuation of a survey of criticism on G. published in *StN*, 23. C. D'Alessio, 'L'ingegner Gadda e la macchina. Dall'industria moderna all'officina faustiana', *Atti* (AISLLI 15), 861–76. G. Galli De Ortega, *'Pasticciaccio argentino*, o Carlo Emilio Gadda in Argentina', *EL*, 23.1:41–52, analyses *Indi'* (Italian trans. *Pasticciaccio argentino*), a novel by the Argentinian writer Enrique Maria Butti, and finds reference to G.'s stay in Argentina from 1922 to 1924. Paola Italia, *Glossario di Carlo Emilio Gadda 'milanese'. Da 'La meccanica' a L'Adalgisa'*, Alessandria, Orso, cxxxvii + 377 pp., provides a glossary subdivided into sections on various aspects of G.'s language, and shows how literary language, colloquial registers, dialect, and innovation are interwoven in his work during the Milanese, or early, period. M. Kleinhans, ' "Un caleidoscopico novecento" — Zur Funktion der bildenden Kunst in Carlo Emilio Gaddas Satire *San Giorgio in casa Brocchi*', *RF*, 109, 1997:214–46. M. Marchesini, 'L'etica e il sistema: *I miti del somaro* di Carlo Emilio Gadda', *Italica*, 74, 1997:235–48. L. Minervini, 'La cognizione nella "Meditazione Milanese" di C. E. Gadda', *LCrit*, 25–27, 1993–95[1998]:33–53. Aldo Pecoraro, **Gadda*, Ro–Bari, Laterza, 244 pp. Walter Pedullà, **Carlo Emilio Gadda. Il narratore come delinquente*, Mi, Rizzoli, 1997, 301 pp. Leone Piccioni, **Identikit per Carlo Emilio*, F, Pananti, 1997, 229 pp. Gian Carlo Roscioni, *Il duca di Sant'Aquila. Infanzia e giovinezza di Gadda*, Mi, Mondadori, 1997, 349 pp., is a biographical study of G. up to 1928. Rosalma Salina Borello and Cristiana Lardo, *'L'impossibilità di dire: io'. A proposito della voce narrante in Gadda*, Ro, Nuova Cultura, 1997, 131 pp. A. Scarsella, 'Contini comparatista: dalla traduzione "espressionista" agli universali letterari', Mildonian, *Parodia*, 291–96. M. Versace, ' "Cecità e visione" in una lettura recente del *Pasticciaccio*. Allegoria e ironia in Gadda', *NRLI*, no. 1:277–329, questioning Amigoni's Freudian interpretation, concludes that philosophy and history prevail over psychoanalysis in G.'s outlook on reality. Antonio Zolino, *Il vate e l'ingegnere. D'Annunzio in Gadda*, Pisa, ETS, 1997, 140 pp., compares texts by G. and D'A. and concludes that the latter's influence on G. is particularly evident in *La cognizione del dolore*.

GATTO. A. Dolfi, *'Una notte a Firenze:* ragione delle forme e metamorfosi del paesaggio', *Terza generazione*, 63–87; also, 'Approssimazioni a una lettura di *Desinenze*', *ib.*, 89–114. M. Maggiari, 'Alfonso Gatto: morte e simbolismo materno', *SIAA*, 10:1, 1997:25–33. S. Prandi, 'Esordi di Alfonso Gatto: "Isola"', *ON*, 22.3:151–92, analyses this poem and measures its impact on Hermeticism in 1932.

GINZBURG. Maria Pflug, **Arditamente timida. Natalia Ginzburg*, Mi, La Tartaruga, 1997, is the Italian trans. (by Barbara Griffini) of a biography published in 1995 in German. P. Puppa, 'Natalia Ginzburg: una lingua per il teatro', *ISt*, 52, 1997:151–64, highlights G.'s insecurity in a 'scrittura che ha paura di se stessa'. J. Wienstein, 'Il telefono come espediente drammatico nelle opere teatrali di Natalia Ginzburg', *Atti* (AISLLI 15), 1123–32.

GIUDICI. E. Livorni, 'Giovanni Giudici ovvero del quotidiano sperimentare', *YIP*, 1, 1997 : 66, shows how G.'s passion for the 'rigore sperimentale del quotidiano' is implied in what is mundane and ordinary.

GOVONI. A. M. Brogi, 'Govoni e De Pisis: verso un'idea metafisica', *CLett*, 94, 1997 : 91–111, discusses G.'s momentary dalliance with metaphysics and De Pisis's encounter with the literary experience of metaphysics.

GOZZANO. P. Fasano, 'Il bello stile negli esili versi. Colloqui con Dante di Guido Gozzano', Mildonian, *Parodia*, 241–65. I. Pupo, 'Silenzi gozziani', *RLI*, 101 : 2–3, 1997 : 112–29, outlines the subdued tone in G.'s poetry.

GUERRA. A. Malaguti, 'Il passato che persiste: tempo e tempi verbali ne *I bu* di Tonino Guerra', *ISt*, 52, 1997 : 165–79.

JACOBBI. A. Dolfi, *Terza generazione*, contains the following: ' "Lo specchio cavo" della poesia', 173–210; 'Una passione surrealista', 211–34; 'Ancora sul carteggio Jacobbi–Macrì', 235–68.

LA CAPRIA. L. Manthey, 'Raffaele La Capria auf der Suche nach der verlorenen Harmonie', *Italienisch*, 39 : 42–56, concerns the 1986 collection of essays *L'armonia perduta*.

LANDOLFI. F. Amigoni, 'La bestia folgorosa. Il fantasma e il nome in Tommaso Landolfi', *StCrit*, 12, 1997 : 1–31. Marcello Carlino, *Landolfi e il fantastico*, Ro, Lithos, 150 pp., in a first part examines the fantastic as a genre, while the second part studies its pervasive presence in L.'s work. A. Dolfi, *Terza generazione*, contains the following articles on L. ' "Ars combinatoria", paradosso e poesia' (315–56); 'La camicia di Nesso della letteratura (nota sul diarismo di Landolfi)' (357–68); and 'Poesia, diari: il "differire" autobiografico di Landolfi' (369–81). R. Ferrando, 'Amore e terrore per le parole', *Italianistica*, 26 : 301–08, detects a clash between 'parola assoluta' and the limitations of language in Landolfi. S. Lazzarin, 'Memoria dantesca e modelli folclorici nella *Pietra lunare* di Tommaso Landolfi', *Il Ponte*, 53.3, 1997 : 121–30, sees witchcraft and lycanthropy in the character of Gurù as derived from folklore, and her dual (human and goat) nature as reminiscent of Dante. R. Rabboni, 'Tommaso Landolfi traduttore di Puškin', *De Lorenzi Vol.*, 81–103. D. Tomasello, 'La "luminaria" e la "caligine": il ritorno di T. Landolfi', *CLett*, 25, 1997 : 137–57.

LEVI, C. Giovanni Battista Bronzini, *Il viaggio antropologico di Carlo Levi. Da eroe stendhaliano a guerriero birmano*, Bari, Dedalo, 1997, 397 pp., employs an anthropological approach to illustrate L.'s biography and intellectual concerns, analyses his texts in relation to other writers on the Italian South, and takes into account both his written and his visual work. G. De Donato, *Le parole del reale*. *Ricerche sulla prosa di Carlo Levi*, Bari, Dedalo, 224 pp., compares the written and film versions of *Cristo si è fermato a Eboli*. G. Russo, 'Durata di Carlo Levi', *Il Ponte*, 53.5, 1997:103–12, highlights the importance of L.'s intuition of the destructive potential of modern consumerism and materialism. D. Sperduto, 'La presenza del tempo ne *Il futuro ha un cuore antico* di Carlo Levi', *EL*, 22.4, 1997:93–97, shows how *Il futuro ha un cuore antico* is related to L.'s letters to Linuccia Saba.

LEVI, P. **Primo Levi* (*Riga*, 13), Mi, Marcos y Marcos, 1997, 535 pp., includes contributions by various authors. *Primo Levi. Conversazioni e interviste 1963–1987*, ed. Marco Belpoliti, T, Einaudi, 1997, xxiii + 321 pp. Id., *Primo Levi*, Mi, Bruno Mondadori, 213 pp., is a repertory of L.'s main concepts and works. *Primo Levi. Un'antologia della critica*, ed. Ernesto Ferrero, T, Einaudi, 1997, xxiii + 413 pp. Giovanna Bellini and Giovanni Mazzoni, **Primo Levi e la memoria dell'Olocausto*, Ro–Bari, Laterza. V. Brombert, 'Primo Levi and the Canto of Ulysses', *RLC*, 70, 1996:313–25. G. D'Angelo, '*La chiave a stella* di Primo Levi: una sfida al labirinto', *Atti* (AISLLI 15), 1059–74. I. Dovara, 'Scienza, tecnica e industria nella vita e nell'opera di Primo Levi', *ib.*, 1053–60. A. Dunker, 'Dantes Odysseus in Auschwitz. Primo Levis *Der Gesang der Ulyss*', *DDJ*, 71, 1996:77–98. R. Gordon, ' "Per mia fortuna . . .". Irony and ethics in Primo Levi's writing', *MLR*, 92, 1997:337–47, examines 'cognitive and communal' irony, some intertextual aspects, and an 'ethical passion which excludes cruelty'. Id., 'Primo Levi: on friendship', *Villari Vol.*, 184–94, analyses L.'s poem 'Agli amici' and outlines the philosophical, ethical, and literary aspects of the concept of friendship in Levi. J. Hösle, 'Primo Levi — in memoriam zum zehnten Todestag', *ItStudien*, 19:117–22. W. Kluback, 'Primo Levi, a friend of Empedocles and Rabelais', *Journal of Evolutionary Psychology*, 18:3–4, 1997:164–73, looks at L.'s poetry and possible textual sourcing from Rabelais and Empedocles. G. Santagostino, 'Tecnologia e rappresentazione in Primo Levi', *Atti* (AISLLI 15), 1039–52. P. Sica, ' "Piombo" e "Mercurio" in *Il sistema periodico* di Primo Levi: un microcosmo fantastico in un macrocosmo autobiografico', *ItQ*, 131–32, 1997:33–38, underlines the existential weight of 'Piombo' and 'Mercurio', thus denying that they may be seen as gratuitous fantastic digressions.

LODOLI. E. Trevi, 'Ritratto dell'artista da fuggiasco. Marco Lodoli e la fiaba', *NArg*, 1997, no. 10:88–90, finds L.'s *fiabesco* to lie in the places of the mind which he describes, in 'un'identità tra l'*altro* e il *medesimo* di cui l'altro è rappresentazione', and in L.'s ability to 'manipolare le apparenze'.

LORIA. *La zona dolente. Studi su Arturo Loria*, ed. Marco Marchi, F, Giunti, 1996, 209 pp., are the papers of the conferenze *Omaggio a Arturo Loria* held at Carpi in May 1992 and organized by the Commune and Civic Library of Carpi in collaboration with the Gabinetto G. P. Vieusseux.

LOY. P. Mattei, 'Poesia e libertà', *Poesia*, 103, 1997:6–9, gives the text of an interview with L. on the manner in which liberty and poetry complement each other.

LUZI. G. Cavallini, 'La poesia decide per la vita. Breve nota su Mario Luzi', *Testo*, 36:75–85. A. Dolfi, '*Invocazione*: identità e immagine in *Primizie del deserto*', *Terza generazione*, 13–26. A. Fongaro, 'Valeurs maternelles dans la poésie de Mario Luzi', *REI*, 43, 1997:87–94. M. P. McDonald, 'Il mestiere del critico: una intervista a Mario Luzi', *FoI*, 32:491–509, is also included in *ib.*, 31, 1997:177–95. *Per Mario Luzi. Atti della giornata di studio, Firenze, 20 gennaio 1995*, ed. Giuseppe Nicoletti, Ro, Bulzoni, 1997, 130 pp., includes articles on L. by C. Bo, A. Prete, A. Panicali, G. Gramigna, A. Jacomuzzi, G. Orelli, L. De Nardis, L. Tassoni, S. Vizzardelli. G. Quiriconi, 'Tensioni percettive della recente poesia luziana', *RLI*, 101.1, 1997:143–55. S. Ramat, 'Mario Luzi, la costanza della poesia', *Poesia*, 123:34–36, examines the role of dominant themes in L.'s work. L. Toppa, 'La tendenza occulta della parola diviene azione', *REI*, 44:75–78, records an interview with Luzi. L. Toppan, 'Da *Primizie del deserto*. A *Su fondamenti invisibili*: il dantismo "ideologico" di Luzi', *StN*, 24, 1997:147–74, probes the stylistic links between L. and D. as exemplified in L.'s poetry between 1952 to 1971.

MACRÌ. See JACOBBI, above.

MAFFIA. D. Maraini, 'Le poesie di Dante Maffia', *SIAA*, 11, 47–50.

MAGGIANI. P. Polito, 'Il dono del racconto. Metafore e strategie discorsive ne *Il coraggio del pettirosso* di Maurizio Maggiani', *RevR*, 33:269–88, sees *Il coraggio del pettirosso* as a combination of *Bildungsroman*, metanovel, autobiography, and historical novel and concludes that the epic nature of those passages where the narrator tells the story of his original Apui community is also where the strength of the novel lies.

MAGRELLI. E. Coco, 'Valerio Magrelli', *CHA*, 573:117–19. A. Schneider-Soltanianzadeh, 'Valerio Magrelli oder Das geheime Leben der Dinge', *Italienisch*, 39:92–98.

MAGRIS. Ernestina Pellegrini, **Epica sull'acqua. L'opera letteraria di Claudio Magris*, Bergamo, Moretti & Vitali, 1997, 213 pp. Also by her, 'I *Microcosmi* di Claudio Magris: autoritratto per via obliqua', *Il Ponte*,

53.7, 1997:102–14, finds indirect autobiographical reference, a polycentric self, and allusions to the myth of Orpheus and Euridice. L. Polezzi, 'Magri's *Danubio* and its translations', *MLR*, 93:678–94, places *Danubio* in an eccentric position in the Italian literary canon, where travel literature is relatively unusual. By contrast the English translation was publicized precisely as travel literature for a readership used to canonical books of this type, but intertextual reference to Sterne makes *Danubio*, partly at least, an unusual book in English too. F. Scarpa, 'Translation patterns in *A Different Sea* by Claudio Magris', *The Italianist*, 16, 1996[1997]:191–219.

MAIER. A. Benevento, 'Un romanzo autobiografico. *L'assente* di Bruno Maier', *CLett*, 25, 1997:165–68.

MALAPARTE. Curzio Malaparte, *Opere scelte*, ed. Luigi Martellini, introd. G. Vigorelli, Mi, Mondadori, 1997, cii + 1602 pp. L. Martellini, 'Curzio Malaparte: le "prospettive" dell'industria', *Atti* (AISLLI 15), 803–32. G. Pardini, *Curzio Malaparte. Biografia politica*, Mi–Trento, Luni, 382 pp.

MALERBA. *Conversazione con Luigi Malerba. Elogio della finzione*, ed. Paola Gaglianone, Ro, Nuova Omicron, 91 pp., includes an interview (5–43) in which M. talks about creative writing, commitment, the neo-avantgarde, and literary models, and A. Errico's 'Il racconto infinito' (44–81), an essay on 'realtà multiforme', use of language, and other aspects of M.'s fiction. M. Kern, 'Storia vs. fiction: un appuntamento mancato. *Le maschere* di Luigi Malerba', *RELI*, 10:129–43, points out that real facts and imagined events are partly combined and partly separate at the beginning of the novel but become increasingly united as the story unfolds and turns into a strange historical novel where we find not only what actually happened but also what might have happened. D. Tanteri, 'Una "parodia" italiana di *1984*', Mildonian, *Parodia*, 363–71, concerns the short story *4891* published in *La Repubblica* in 1983.

MANGANELLI. Maurizio De Benedictis, *Manganelli e la finzione*, Ro, Lithos, 175 pp., in a first part surveys general theories about fictional representation and forgery of reality, and discusses the literary concept of 'menzogna' in particular; in the second part he traces the development of M.'s work from a first phase characterized by a less pervasive sense of existential *ennui* to a second nihilist phase. The dark side of M.'s imagination is explored through an analysis of the themes of hell, death, and night. The fragmented self, Jungian psychology, and some aspects of gnostic philosophy are also investigated. Language aspects include 'sconclusione', the Baroque, and 'parola morta e parola fantasma, parola inutile, parola ombra e parola stemma'. S. Lazzarin, '*Centuria*: le sorti del fantastico nel Novecento', *StN*, 24, 1997:99–145, examines *Centuria* against the background of the fantastic genre in the 20th c. V. Levato, 'Giorgio Manganelli: una teoria della letteratura', *FAM*, 13, 1997:115–36, attributes a central role to the concept of nothingness, highlights the importance of language, structure, and digressions over plot and characters, and sums up M.'s poetics as an oxymoron in which 'separazione, odio, afasia, sconclusione' cohabit with their opposites 'unione, amore, linguaggio, sensatezza'. V. Papetti, 'Manganelli e gli inglesi', *NArg*, no. 1–2:356–65, shows how M. developed an interest in a number of authors from English-speaking countries, especially James and Yeats. Graziella Pulce, *Bibliografia degli scritti di Giorgio Manganelli*, F, Titivillus, 1996, 184 pp.

MARAINI. Bruce Merry, **Dacia Maraini and the Written Dream of Women in Italian Literature*, Townsville, Univ. of North Queensland, 1997, 211 pp. M. G. Sumeli Weinberg, 'Ricerca di un futuro tra civiltà industriale e arcaica: *Donna in guerra* di Dacia Maraini', *Atti* (AISLLI 15), 1075–84. S. Wright, 'Dacia Maraini: charting the female experience in the quest-plot: *Marianna Ucria*', *ItQ*, 133–34:59–70, sees the protagonist's dumbness and writing as symbols of women's voicelessness but rediscovery of a collective voice and identity through literature. Marianna's story is related to the myth of Philomela and Procne.

MARINETTI. E. Ivanova, 'Una battaglia a/di colori: *La battaglia di Tripoli* di F. T. Marinetti', *ItC*, 16:143–56.

MENEGHELLO. Luigi Meneghello, **Opere*, ed. Francesca Caputo, 2 vols, Mi, Rizzoli, 1997, xiii + 1988, xxxiv + 904 pp., has introductions by C. Segre and P. V. Mengaldo. See also SVEVO, below.

MERINI. P. Mattei, 'Alda Merini, prigioniera della libertà', *Poesia*, 107, 1997:32–38, records an interview with M. on how she feels incarcerated by life. C. O'Brien, 'Alda Merini: poetry and psychosis', *Villari Vol.*, 195–207, outlines the impact of mental instability on M.'s poetry.

MIANO. B. Maier, 'L'itinerario poetico di Alessandro Miano', *De Lorenzi Vol.*, 187–95.

MICHELSTAEDTER. G. Taviani, 'Contro la "rettorica". Per un'attualizzazione del pensiero di Carlo Michelstaedter', *Allegoria*, 26, 1997:27–40, highlights the contemporary relevance of M.'s stance against rhetoric in a world pervaded by the language of the mass media.

MONTALE. E. Bonora, 'Rassegna montaliana', *GSLI*, 175: 107–29. Eugenio Montale, *Prose e racconti*, ed. Marco Forti, Mi, Mondadori, 1995, cx + 1253 pp. *Montale e il canone poetico del Novecento*, ed. M. A. Grignani and R. Luperini, Ro–Bari, Laterza, 452 pp., under five critical and interpretative aspects of M.'s work, includes: M. Corti, 'Il mio ricordo di Montale' (3–8); L. Blasucci, 'Appunti per un commento montaliano' (11–32); R. Bettarini, 'Sacro e profano' (33–46); F. De Rosa, 'Scansioni dell'ultimo Montale' (47–72); F. Nosenzo, 'Saggio di un commento a *Finisterre* 1945: [I.11] *Lungomare*' (73–94); R. Orlando, ' "O maledette reminiscenze!". Per una tipologia della 'citazione distintiva' nell'ultimo Montale' (95–120); F. Zambon, 'Il problema del commento montaliano' (121–27); W. Krysinski, 'La poesia di Eugenio Montale e il canone del classicismo moderno' (131–51); L. Barile, 'L'eco della "pagina rombante". Montale e Maurice de Guérin' (152–64); M. A. Grignani, 'Montale, Solmi, Praz e la cultura europea: dalla Francia all'Inghilterra' (165–88); T. de Rogatis, 'Alle origini del dantismo di Montale' (189–201); R. West, 'Montale profeta del postmoderno' (202–10); P. V. Mengaldo, 'Montale critico di poesia' (213–39); G. Nava, 'Montale critico di narrativa' (240–60); F. Contorbia, 'Montale critico nello specchio delle lettere: una approssimazione' (261–75); S. Palumbo, 'Montale e la Sicilia, alla scoperta di nuovi talenti' (276–307); M. Forti, 'Montale: introduzione alla "Prosa di fantasia e d'invenzione" ' (311–29); L. Previtera, 'Sulla lingua di Montale narratore in prosa' (330–42); R. Castellana, 'La metamorfosi di Alastor. Note su Montale prosatore (con un racconto raro)' (343–58); R. Luperini, 'Montale e il canone poetico del Novecento italiano' (361–68); G. Guglielmi, 'Montale "Arsenio", e la linea allegorico-dantesca' (369–81); G. Mazzoni, 'Il posto di Montale nella poesia moderna' (382–416); P. Cataldi, 'La questione del canone e la "strana pietà" dei montalisti' (417–23); P. Bigongiari, 'Dal "correlativo oggettivo" al "correlativo soggettivo" (424–28); A. Giuliani, 'Ragionevoli strategie per sorprendere l'invisibile' (429–32); F. Pusterla, 'Dubbi, più che altro' (433–35); E. Testa, 'Un saluto a Montale' (436–40). G. Bárberi Squarotti, 'Lettura dei *Mottetti*', *LItal*, 49, 1997:66–88. G. A. Camerino, 'Spazi d'acqua, specchi e parvenze in Montale (con alcuni echi danteschi)', *Italianistica*, 26, 1997:441–50. M. Capati, 'Montale saggista', *La Cultura*, 36:489–99. Giorgio Cavallini, *Montale lettore di Dante e altri studi montaliani*, Ro, Bulzoni, 1996, 123 pp., outlines M.'s critical appreciation of Dante and evaluates the way his prose writings often impact on his verse. M. Chiamenti, 'Dora 1: Ipotesi', *FoI*, 31, 1997:163–66. E. Citro, 'Eugenio Montale: *In limine*', *Croce Vol.*, 559–86. V. Coletti, 'Montale, la poesia, la morte', *ib.*, 539–57. F. Contorbia, 'Genova — Trieste 1925: Adriano Grande tra Bazlen e Montale', *ib.*, 587–614. F. Croce, *La primavera hitleriana e altri saggi su Montale*, Genoa, Marietti, 1997, 191 pp., looks at varying thematic movements in M.'s poetry and also discusses his relationship with Liguria. P. De Marchi, 'Montale e Kavafis: i "barbari" e altro', pp. 65–86 of *Poétiques barbares/Poetiche barbare*, cit., p. 481, looks at M.'s 'barbarian' affiliation through

Kavafis. V. Di Benedetto, 'Interpretazioni del Montale inedito', *RLettI*, 13, 1995[1997]: 159–88. F. M. Fabrocile, 'Gli anni genovesi di Montale e Messina. Due vite a confronto', *ON*, 22.3: 131–49, examines the 'fondo comune' that existed between M. and Messina in poetry and sculpture. F. Ferrucci, 'Montale e Leopardi', *StCrit*, 12, 1997: 193–97, argues that M.'s development, once he had shed his D'Annunzian and Pascolian scales, consisted of 'un lento avvicinarsi a Leopardi'. C. F. Goffis, '*L'Angelo Nero*, un sogno montaliano in verità', *Italianistica*, 25, 1996[1997]: 233–58. L. Gorgoglione, 'Montale critico', *LCrit*, 25–27, 1993–95[1997]: 9–32. *Eusebio e Trabucco. Carteggio di Eugenio Montale e Gianfranco Contini*, ed. Dante Isella, Mi, Adelphi, 1997, xvii + 334 pp., consists of 150 letters by M. and 42 by C. accompanied by notes explaining the context and purpose of each letter. G. Lonardi, 'Montale, il fantasma dell'opera', *LItal*, 50: 186–219, looks at the way M.'s passion for opera is interwoven in his prose and poetry. R. Luperini, 'A proposito di *Nuove stanze* e di un'edizione commentata delle *Occasioni*', *Belfagor*, 52, 1997: 139–49. B. Moloney, 'Montale e Eliot: affinities and influences', *Ricerca Research Recherche*, 1, 1995[1997]: 9–25. Id., 'Montale on Svevo', pp. 1–14 of *Montale. Words in Time*, ed. G. Talbot and D. Thompson, Market Harborough, Troubadour. M. de las Nieves Muñiz, 'La traduzione come dialogo: il caso Montale-Guillén', *RELI*, 9, 1997: 95–107, examines the links between six Guillén poems translated by M. and six M. poems translated by G. into Spanish. M. Nelson, 'Eugenio Montale's imagery of enduring disenchantment: a close reading of two poems', *ItC*, 15, 1997: 213–27, interprets 'Clivo' and 'Piccolo testamento'. V. Pacca, 'Prime osservazioni sul *Diario postumo*', *Italianistica*, 26, 1997: 461–68. P. Pepe, 'Figurato e infigurabile nell'immaginario. Montale e anche Leopardi', *RStI*, 16.1: 205–26, indicates what is possible and impossible in the poetic discourse of both poets. M. E. Romand, 'Baudelaire occultato o rilevato in Montale, e le armoniche di *Costa San Giorgio*', *RLettI*, 13, 1995[1997]: 467–92. Giuseppe Savoca, *Concordanza del 'Diario postumo' di Eugenio Montale. Facsimile dei manoscritti, testo, concordanza*, F, Olschki, 1997, xxii + 84 + 133 pp. Claudio Scarpati, *Sulla cultura di Montale. Tre conversazioni*, Mi, Vita e Pensiero, 1997, 101 pp., offers some new perspectives on M.'s early poetry collections. J. Schulze, 'Montales *Punta del Mesco*, Mallarmé und eine deutsche Übersetzung', *ItStudien*, 19: 171–83. K. Stierle, 'Im Zwischenreich der Dichtung. Zum poetischen Werk Eugenio Montales', *Italienisch*, 37, 1997: 2–22. *Montale: Words in Time*, ed. G. Talbot and D. Thompson, Market Harborough, Troubador, 208 pp., brings together 15 essays based on papers at conferences in Hull and Melbourne to mark the centenary of M.'s birth. G. Talbot, 'Montale sulla scia di Stravinski: il contesto musicale della "primavera hitleriana"', *StN*, 24, 1997:353–65, illustrates the relationship between Stravinsky's ballet *Le Sacre du Printemps* and the above poem. M. F. William, 'Poetic seacoasts: Montale's "I morti" and Propertius 3.18, 1.11, 3.5', *CML*, 17:2, 1997:149–69, examines M.'s treatment of underworld and seashore in relation to sources in Propertius, Sextus Empiricus, Virgil, and Dante. A. Zollino, 'Poliziano nel *Falsetto* di Montale', *CLett*, 25, 1997:77–90, shows how some verses of Poliziano's *Stanze per la giostra* were used as a subtext in M.'s *Falsetto*. See also UNGARETTI, below.

MORANTE. R. Sodi, 'Whose story? Literary borrowings in Elsa Morante's *La storia*', *LS*, 33:141–53, shows how Debenedetti's *16 ottobre 1943*, Piazza's *Perché gli altri dimenticano*, and Katz's *Black Sabbath* influenced the writing of *La storia*. These three texts are mentioned in the 'Nota conclusiva' to M.'s novel.

MORAVIA. M. J. Stella, 'Indifference as positive reality in *Una cosa è una cosa*', *FoI*, 31, 1997:39–62, compares M.'s concept of indifference with some Buddhist concepts. A. Nari, '*Gli indifferenti* nella riduzione per il teatro di Alberto Moravia e Luigi Squarzina', *RLI*, 100.2–3, 1996[1997]:139–89.

MORSELLI. *Autografo*, 37, a special issue entitled *Ipotesi su Morselli*, includes some M. items and contributions by S. D'Arienzo, D. Vittoz, M. Mari, V. Fortichiari, L. Malerba, M. Morselli, G. Pontiggia, J. Lotman, and E. Borsa. Marina Lessona Fasano, **Guido Morselli. Un inspiegabile caso letterario*, Na, Liguori, 150 pp. E. M. Guidi, 'Spazio del romanzo, spazio della coscienza in *Un dramma borghese* di Guido Morselli', *LetP*, 103:27–36, examines some autobiographical aspects in *Un dramma borghese* and sees this novel as an attempt to 'tracciare una radiografia dell'intellettuale contemporaneo'.

MUSSAPI. E. Gioanola, 'Sulla poesia di Roberto Mussapi', *Testo*, 36:87–102.

NEGRI. C. Mazzoni, 'Difference, repetition, and the mother–daughter bond in Ada Negri', *RStI*, 15.1, 1997:55–74, and '"Di Mamma ce n'è una sola": Fascism, demography and the mother's voice in Ada Negri's *Niobe*', *ItC*, 15, 1997:115–30. L. Picchi, 'Ada Negri: la chiaroveggenza della solitudine', *CV*, 52.1, 1997:21–28.

NOVENTA. E. Urgnani, *Noventa*, Palermo, Palumbo, 225 pp., outlines the link between his poetry and political philosophy.

ORTESE. Monica Farnetti, *Ortese*, Mi, Bruno Mondadori, 213 pp., is an introduction to works and concepts organized in alphabetical order. B. Manetti, 'Ritorno a Toledo', *AnVi*, n.s. 10:112–16. G. Mazzocchi, 'Anna Maria Ortese e l'ispanità', *MLN*, 112, 1997:90–104.

ORTESTA V. Bonito, 'La luce del gelo, lo sguardo e la voce nella poesia di Cosimo Ortesta', *RLMC*, 49, 1996:489–510.

OTTIERI. T. Saverio, *Ottiero Ottieri. Il poeta osceno*, Na, Liguori, 282 pp.

PACI. A. Principe, 'Il ruolo dell'Algoma "Plant" nell'ultimo trittico di Franco Paci', *Atti* (AISLLI 15), 1101–11.

PALAZZESCHI. A. Cortellessa, 'Controdolore e retroguardia. Aldo Palazzeschi tra *Spazzatura* e *Boccanera*', *RLI*, 100.2–3, 1996[1997]: 80–109. M. C. Papini, 'Aldo Palazzeschi, Remy de Gourmont: un gioco di : *riflessi*', *ib.*, 101.1, 1997:116–30, shows how in : *riflessi* P. makes intentional, even explicit, though never openly admitted, reference to G.'s work. N. J. Perella, ' "Servite Domino in laetitia": Palazzeschi and the primacy of laughter', *Italica*, 75:365–76. Anthony J. Tamburri, *A Reconsideration of Aldo Palazzeschi's Poetry (1905–1974): Revisiting the 'Saltimbanco'*, Lewiston, Mellen. S. W. Vinall, 'Parody in Palazzeschi's "La passeggiata": the rewriting of a D'Annunzian *topos*', *Lepschy Vol.*, 273–303.

PAPINI. J. Soldateschi, 'Il giovane "fantastico" Papini', *RLI*, 102.1:131–42, situates P.'s fantastic stories against the background of early-20th-c. hybridism of genres.

PARISE. *Goffredo Parise. Atti del convegno su Parise*, Fondazione Cini, *1995*, ed. Ilaria Crotti, F, Olschki, 1997, 286 pp. P. V. Mengaldo, 'Dentro i *Sillabari* di Parise', *AnVi*, n.s. 10: 81–98, defines *Sillabari* as 'microracconti', showing how one of their aspects, the act of seeing, is characterized by the same fragmentary exactness with which the structure of the text is organized. This orderly precision is in contrast with the recurring motif of chance. P.'s 'puntinismo' may be compared with Walser's and Kafka's work.

PARRONCHI. Alessandro Parronchi, *Lettere a Vasco*, ed. Alessandro Parronchi, introd. Marino Biondi, F, Polistampa, 1996, xxxiii + 428 pp., complements *Lettere a Sandro* (Parronchi's edition of Pratolini's letters to him), published shortly after the novelist's death in 1991, when the 438 missives (May 1941–December 1987) contained in this volume had temporarily disappeared. The correspondence is particularly (though by no means solely) valuable for the light it sheds on Pratolini's fiction.

PASOLINI. Pier Paolo Pasolini, *La meglio gioventù*, ed. Antonia Arveda, Ro, Salerno, 460 pp., is an invaluable commentary and study of the work's genesis with a parallel Italian translation of the Friulan text. M. A. Bazzocchi, *Pasolini*, Mi, Bruno Mondadori, 236 pp., is an alphabetical repertory of P.'s works and concepts. A. Bertoni, 'Pasolini e l'avanguardia', *LItal*, 49, 1997:470–80, runs through P.'s experimental poetics and differentiates it from the experiments of the avant-garde. G. Borghello, 'Una fame di storia e di speranza: Fortini *versus* Pasolini', *De Lorenzi Vol.*, 133–86, outlines the analysis of P.'s work in Fortini's *Attraverso Pasolini* and points to certain parallels with F.'s own work. A. Girardi, 'Pascoli secondo Pasolini', *StN*, 24, 1997:403–10. R. S. C. Gordon, 'Recent work on Pasolini in English', *ISt*, 52, 1997:180–88, reviews essays by P. Rambella and B. Testa, T. E. Peterson, D. Ward, and S. Rohdie. K. Jewell, 'Sexual commerce and culture: Pier Paolo Pasolini's *Caracalla* poems', *Italica*, 75:192–209. Edi Liccioli, *La scena della parola. Teatro e poesia in Pier Paolo Pasolini*, F, Le Lettere, 1997, 339 pp., outlines the strong connection between P.'s poetry and theatre. C. Marazzini, 'Sublime volgar eloquio. Il linguaggio poetico di P. P. Pasolini', *De Lorenzi Vol.*, 105–32, discusses the interplay and tension between the dialect of Friuli and Italian in P.'s verse. S. Mex, 'Die "Verwandlung der Welt" und der (texte-)korporale Rausch: Pier Paolo Pasolinis *Petrolio*', *ItStudien*, 18, 1997:188–98. Andrea Miconi, *Pier Paolo Pasolini. La poesia, il corpo, il linguaggio*, Genoa–Mi, Costa & Nolan, 169 pp., seeks to rescue P. from biographical and ideological interpretations by conducting an analysis of the style and language of his poetry, prose, and films. S. Ramat, 'Pier Paolo Pasolini, Il "Diario" inedito', *Poesia*, 121:2–11, examines the concerns of P. in this work. D. Rondoni, 'Passione per la realtà e senso religioso in Pier Paolo Pasolini', *Testo*, 33, 1997:155–84, traces the development of a dualism constituted by the sacred and the profane in P.'s life and work from his 'sensuosa gioventù' in Friuli to the 'bassa innocenza' he found in subsequent years among the Roman *Lumpenproletariat*. Patrick Rumble, *Allegories of Contamination: Pier Paolo Pasolini's 'Trilogy of Life'*, Toronto U.P., 1996, 207 pp. Giacinto Spagnoletti, *L'impura' giovinezza di Pasolini*, Caltanissetta, Sciascia, 128 pp., provides biographical details of P.'s early years and also analyses his *Diario friulano*. H. Teschke, 'Pasolini und Dante: *Divina Mimesis*', *ItStudien*, 19:202–27.

PASSERINI. D. Duncan, *'Corporeal histories: the autobiographical bodies of Luisa Passerini', *MLR*, 93:370–83.

PASTONCHI. G. Amoretti, '"Tra nette simmetrie": i *Versetti* di Pastonchi', in *Croce Vol.*, 519–38.

PAVESE. G. C. Antoni, 'Il colore del mito. Percezione cromatica e ricuperi culturali nei *Dialoghi con Leucò* di Cesare Pavese', *Intersezioni*, 18:103–27, highlights the function of perception of colour and its symbolic meanings. G. Davico, 'L'uomo solo ascolta la donna dalla voce rauca', *StP*, 26, 1997:11–17, is prompted by the latter's autobiography: Tina Pizzardo, *Senza pensarci due volte*, Bo, Il Mulino, 1996. M. Lanzillotto, 'Materiali pavesiani', *FAM*, 13, 1997, includes two lists of documents from the Archivio Einaudi: the sheets found in P.'s study and the manuscripts found in his home immediately after his suicide in 1950. N. Simborowski, 'From *La famiglia* to the *Taccuino* and *La casa in collina*: Pavese and the need to confess', *MLR*, 92, 1997:70–85. T. Stauder, 'Zur Bedeutung angloamerikanischer

Prätexte für Cesare Paveses frühe Lyriksammlung *Lavorare stanca'*, *ItStudien*, 18, 1997:208–33. Giuseppe Savoca and Antonio Sichera, *Concordanza delle poesie di Cesare Pavese*, F, Olschki, 1997, lvii + 265 pp., comprises concordances, frequency lists, and indexes of P.'s poetry. B. Van den Bossche, ' "La parabola stanca". Le fabbriche del simbolo nei racconti giovanili di Cesare Pavese', *Atti* (AISLLI 15), 791–820. A. Williamson, 'Pavese's late love poems', *American Poetry Review*, 26.5, 1997:40–45.

PAZZI. A. Bernardelli, 'Intervista a Roberto Pazzi. Le contraddizioni di una città di provincia: Ferrara', *RStI*, 15.1, 1997:88–98.

PEA. Marina Fratnik, *Enrico Pea et l'écriture du moi*, F, Olschki, 1997, 401 pp., seeks to bring a new interpretative rigour to bear on P.'s *œuvre* in an impressive combination of textual and Freudian analysis. See also UNGARETTI, below.

PENNA. W. Loddi, 'Per una rilettura di Sandro Penna', *CLett*, 25, 1997:129–36. L. Marcuz, 'Intertestualità nella poesia di Sandro Penna', *StN*, 25:305–29. C. V. Saura, 'La poesia di Sandro Penna: la costruzione e il significato di "Solfeggio" ', *StCrit*, 13:199–216, looks at the form and content of this poem.

PIRANDELLO. *Le fonti di Pirandello*, ed. A. Alessio and G. Sanguineti Katz, Palermo, Palumbo, 1996. *Pirandello zwischen Avantgarde und Postmoderne. Akten der Erlanger und der Münchner Pirandello-Kolloquien*, ed. Michael Rossner, Wilhelmsfeld, Egert, 1997. Roberto Alonge, *Luigi Pirandello*, Ro–Bari, Laterza, 1997. Id., *Madri, baldracche, amanti: la figura femminile nel teatro di Pirandello*, Genoa, Costa & Nolan, 1997, 137 pp. S. Acocella, ' "Effetti speciali" della scrittura pirandelliana. Volti ottusi e specchi deformanti', *FC*, 21, 1996[1997]:391–411. M. Bertone, 'Le burle di John e le prodezze di Max. La fonte milanese della seduta spiritica del *Fu Mattia Pascal*', *Allegoria*, 25, 1997:186–96, indicates G. Negri's *Segni dei tempi* as one of P.'s sources. G. Bolognese, 'I *Giganti* industriali di Pirandello', *Atti* (AISLLI 15), 637–49. A. Bruni, 'Un caso di manzonismo strutturale: *La patente* di Luigi Pirandello', *StIt*, 17, 1997:95–106, points out that Manzoni, frequently mentioned in P.'s essays, is one of the literary models of *La patente*. Francesco Bruno, *Luigi Pirandello. L'arte e il decadentismo*, Na, ESI. Ettore Catalano, *Delitti innocenti. La scena pirandelliana tra veleni e emblemi*, Ro–Bari, Laterza. G. Corsinovi, 'Pirandello e l'industria cinematografica, ovvero, il gioco delle contraddizioni', *Atti* (AISLLI 15), 619–35. Vincenzo Crupi, *L'altra faccia della luna. Assoluto e mistero nell'opera di Luigi Pirandello*, Soveria Mannelli, Rubbettino, 1997. C. Biazzo Curry, 'Il trionfo della teatralità assoluta in *Questa sera si recita a soggetto*', *CJIS*, 20, 1997:207–20, analyses P.'s symbolism with the aid of Lacan's psychoanalysis. M. Ermilli, '*Il viaggio* di Luigi Pirandello. Una lettura antropologica e psicoanalitica', *StCrit*, 12, 1997:157–76. Bianca Baruscotto Fergola, **La teatralità dal senso alla rappresentazione. Sei personaggi in cerca d'autore*, introd. G. Genot, Mi, Angeli, 1997, 170 pp. Roberto Filippetti, **Pirandello narratore e poeta: ragione e mistero*, Castel Bolognese, Itaca Tools, 1997, 148 pp. Anna Gabrielli, **Pirandello*, T, Paravia, 1997. S. Garbarino, 'Osservazioni sulla lingua e sullo stile delle ultime novelle di Luigi Pirandello', *EL*, 22.2, 1997:70–81, in contrast with those critics who see the short stories written between 1931 and 1936 as involutional, interprets them in terms of a development in complexity and refinement of style and lexis, and highlights the semantic field of *noia, niente*, and *vuoto*. Id., 'L'evoluzione di Luigi Pirandello nelle sue ultime novelle', *RLI*, 101.2–3, 1996[1997]:54–79. Elio Gioanola, *Pirandello, la follia. Nuova edizione integrata con saggi su 'Liolà' e i 'Sei personaggi'*, Mi, Jaca Book, 1997, 257 pp. **Pirandello e la sua opera. Atti del XXXIII Convegno di studi pirandelliani, Agrigento*, ed. Enzo Lauretta, Palermo, Palumbo, 1997. W. Leparneo, 'Pirandello e Beckett', *CJIS*, 20, 1997:193–206, compares *Sei personaggi* with *Godot* along the lines of 'assurdità dell'esistenza', 'relatività della verità, molteplicità della personalità, moralità e pessimismo'. A. L. Lepschy, 'Temporal planes in Pirandello's *Questa sera di recita a soggetto*', *Lepschy Vol.*, 264–72. R. Lo Russo, '"In corpore vili": la tragedia della riflessione', *StIt*, 18, 1997[1998]:87–102. M. Maggi, 'Pirandello e il pensiero tragico', *EL*, 22.1, 1997:63–82, points out that human beings, tormented by doubt, experience difficulty in grasping the meaning of the fluctuating and contraditory reality which surrounds them; an awareness of this reality is expressed pessimistically by thinkers such as Leopardi, Dostoevskij, Kirkegaard, Schopenauer, Nietzsche, and Pirandello. His philosophy of relativity demonstrates that he is conscious of the limitations of reason; his poetics of 'umorismo', combining 'riso tragico, sentimento, riflessione, sofferenza e possibilità', aims at destroying 'illusioni' and leads to the verge of nothingness. Marco Manotto, *Pirandello*, Mi, Bruno Mondadori, 306 pp., continues a series of critical essays on writers whose concepts and works are ordered alphabetically as in hypertexts. L. Marseglia, 'Il tramonto della *hybris* e il riso di Pirandello', *CLett*, 25, 1997:513–34. A. Meda, 'D'Annunzio, Pirandello e l'era industriale: due poetiche a confronto', *Atti* (AISLLI 15), 547–57. M. N. Muñiz Muñiz, 'Sulla ricezione di Pirandello in Spagna', *Quaderns d'Italià*, 2, 1997:113–48. T. Pagano, 'Philosophy and toothache: Pirandello meets Montaigne', *RStI*, 15.1, 1997:75–87, presents a 'vertical' reading of *L'avemaria di Bobbio*, arguing that a careful scrutiny of the *novella*'s variants leads into the ideological and technical dimensions of P.'s narrative. C. O'Brien, 'Novità e altro nelle prime raccolte poetiche', pp. 93–103 of *Pirandello* *e la sua opera* (see p. 497), shows how certain themes evident in P.'s theatre can be found in some of his early poetry. *YSPS*, 17, 1997, contains four essays: J. O'Keefe Bazzoni, 'Grotesque innamorata: the transforming object of desire in Pirandello and his contemporaries' (5–33), showing how the character of the *innamorata* in the Commedia dell'Arte survives in more complex female characters in the 20th c., especially in Bontempelli and P.; D. Bini, 'Woman as creator: Pirandello's *L'innesto*' (34–45), highlighting the emotional inclinations of P.'s women characters and their silence, in contrast with the mainly male *raisonneurs*, and seeing the character of Laura in *L'innesto* as depositary of women's values and conjugal love; D. A. Kuprel, 'The hermeneutic paradox: Pirandello's *Così è (se vi pare)*' (46–57), holding that in *Così è (se vi pare)*, rather than a relativistic doctrine, we find a hermeneutic 'process of questioning' or investigation into the plurality of truth linked to an exploration of the 'private core of self-identity', or '*idem*-identity', and to a construction of self-identity in relation to others, or '*ipse*-identity'; F. D'Intino, 'The letter as palimpsest of literature. Pirandello versus Woolf' (58–77), conducting an analysis of the meaning of letter-writing and its status as a literary genre, then drawing a comparison between P. and Woolf: he detects a similarity in their modernist attribution of literariness to ordinary letter-writing, but divergent attitudes to the genre: negative in Pirandello, positive in Woolf. Angelo Pitrone, **Pirandello e i luoghi del caos*, Palermo, Sciascia. E. Providenti, 'Pirandello impolitico', *Belfagor*, 52, 1997:253–73, continued in *Belfagor*, 53:525–52, shows how P.'s political views until 1920 mainly consisted in detachment from politics but also included some restrained sympathy for the left. Filippo Puglisi, *Le nuove correnti di estetica, con al centro Pirandello*, Ro, Bulzoni, 1996, 72 pp. G. Raboni, 'La poesia di Pirandello', pp. 11–16 of *Pirandello e la sua opera* (see p. 497), considers the possibility of Pascoli, Saba, and Gozzano influencing P.'s later poetry collections. G. Rigobello, 'Il motivo del viaggio nella poesia di Pirandello', *ib.*, 105–19. A. Vettori, 'Serafino Gubbio's candid camera', *MLN*, 113:79–107, contrasts P.'s polemic against cinema with the sympathy of the Futurists for technology pointing out that on a sociological level P. sees technology as dehumanizing, whereas on the existential level Serafino's aversion towards cinema is mitigated by the paradoxically positive effect of salvation that his decision to continue working as a film operator has on him. F. Zangrilli, 'La religione nel primo Pirandello, ossia il poeta', *ItC*, 15, 1997:131–45. Id., 'Pirandello e la fede inaridita', *CV*, 52:3, 1997:251–68, examines the treatment of childhood and religion in P.'s poetry and novels.

PIZZUTO. G. Alvino, **'Antonio Pizzuto: referti di un ripudio', *SPCT*, 55, 1997:77–94.

PORTA. P. Valesio, 'Antonio Porta or violence and the door in the wall', *YIP*, 2, 1997:26–33, outlines the firm structures in P.'s work and analyses the poem 'Il tempo della povertà'.

POZZI. E. Borsa, 'Per una lettura antropologica della poesia di Antonia Pozzi', *Cenobio*, 46, 1997:249–62. B. Carle, 'Flower lexicon, metaphor and imagery in Antonia Pozzi's *Parole*', *RomN*, 38, 1997:79–86.

PRATOLINI. R. Rodondi, 'L'ultimo Pratolini', *StCrit*, 12, 1997: 261–90. S. Ross, 'Resistance and the carnivalesque: Florentine festivals in Pratolini's *Cronache di poveri amanti*', *ItC*, 16:183–96. See also PARRONCHI, above.

PRAZ. See MONTALE, above.

PREZZOLINI. See STUPARICH, below.

PROSPERI. *Carola Prosperi: una scrittrice non 'femminista'. Atti della Giornata di studio, 3 aprile 1993*, F, Olschki, 151 pp.

QUASIMODO. C. Del Popolo, 'Quasimodo: "Al padre"', *Italianistica*, 27:251–53, considers the use of the words 'acque viola' and 'acque tempestose' in this poem. A. Traversa, 'Quasimodo e Leonida di Taranto. Un epigramma', *CLett*, 25, 1997:113–20, examines Quasimodo's translation of the poem into Italian.

RABONI. G. Luzzi, 'Giovanni Raboni, *Tutte le poesie (1951–1993)*', *Poesia*, 108, 1997:44–48, outlines change and development in R.'s collected poetry (Garzanti 1997). S. Ramat, 'Mitografo essenziale', *ib.*, 46, examines leading themes in R.'s poetry.

RAGAZZONI. M. Pedroni, 'Osservazioni sulla poesia di Ernesto Ragazzoni', *ON*, 22.3:63–90.

RAMAT. S. Chemotti, 'Il ghiaieto ardente di Silvio Ramat', *CLett*, 25, 1997:535–49. G. Langella, 'L'"Ecce poeta" di Silvio Ramat', *Il Verri*, 43.6:139–43, analyses R.'s view of life and the space allotted in it to poetry.

REBORA. A. Bettinzoli, 'La vita intensa: Rebora, Nietzsche e il frammento "Clemente, non fare così"', *StN*, 24, 1977:283–330, delineates the links between Rebora's moral crisis (1913–15) and his encounter with Nietzsche's writings as expounded in his letters of that period. J. G. Gonzalez-Miguel, 'Spiritualità e poesia mariana di Clemente Rebora (1885–1957)', *CV*, 52, 1997:363–88, examines the treatment of the Virgin Mary in R.'s work. E. Grandesso, '"Umana industria sacra" e tensione civile nei *Frammenti lirici* di Clemente Rebora', *Cenobio*, 47:122–29, and also in *Atti* (AISLLI 15), 569–78.

RICCHI. Renzo Ricchi, *Selected poems*, ed. C. O'Brien, Cork, Lee Abbey Press, 1997, 99 pp., provides an introduction to R.'s poetry together with selected parallel text translations of his poetry.

RODARI. Francesca Califano, *Lo specchio fantastico: realismo e surrealismo nell'opera di Gianni Rodari*, T, Einaudi, 120 pp., attributes an important place to R. in 20th-c. Italian mainstream literature and places him at the crossroads between tradition and innovation: 'il suo contributo innovatore non comporta una rottura con il passato, ma diviene elemento di transizione verso una forma nuova di espressione letteraria'. C. defines his style as characterized (like Calvino's) by a twofold tendency: towards both realism and the fantastic, showing how the former is derived partly from De Amicis and Collodi, but mainly from neo-realism, while the latter, though influenced by surrealist procedures and ideology, is alien to surrealist inclinations towards transgression and exoticism. She also examines comedy, irony, and satire in Rodari in relation to Bergson, Bachtin, and Olbrechts-Tyteca.

ROMANO. V. Consolo, 'Nei mari estremi con Lalla Romano', *Belfagor*, 52, 1997:199–201, sees R.'s fiction as marked by the 'dialectic between nature and culture, instinct and reason, oblivion and memory' and by the existential cycle of birth, love, and death. He defines her linguistic register as 'linear', underlines her interest in the Enlightenment, and argues that *Le parole tra noi leggere* marks the turn towards the formulation of a narrative voice identical to the voice of the biographical author.

ROSSELLI. *Galleria*, 48.1–2, 1997[1998], ed. D. Attanasio and E. Tandello, is a special issue devoted to R. It contains valuable material that covers almost every imaginable aspect of her work with articles by G. Ferroni, N. Lorenzini, G. Spagnoletti, L. Re, E. Tandello, D. Woodard, G. Scartaghiande, R. Deidier, I. Vicentini, A. Cortellessa, L. Pugno, C. O'Brien, M. C. Cardona, D. Di Iorio, A. Giannitrapani, R. Paris, E. Pecora, A. Rosselli, G. Sicari, A. Anedda, D. Attanasio, L. Barile, C. Bordini, M. Caporali, P. Febbraro, M. F. Degli Uberti, V. Lamarque, P. Perilli, D. Pieroni, S. Zanghì, P. Febbraro.

ROSSO DI SAN SECONDO. F. Orsini, 'Espressionismo e "Lebensphilosophie" in *Lazzarina tra i coltelli* di Pier Maria Rosso di San Secondo', *LCrit*, 25–27, 1993–95[1997]:55–70, re-examines the 1923 comedy.

RUFFATO. M. Lenti, 'Cesare Ruffato: la parola e il labirinto', *StN*, 24, 1997:7–38, details the masking of reality in R.'s poetic idiom.

SABA. I. Comar, '*Preludio e fughe* di Saba: la strada verso la significazione', *Italianistica*, 27:199–218, argues that S. recalls Bach's fugues and treats words here like musical notes. E. Guagnini, 'Ancora su Saba: a proposito della "Terza stagione". *ItStudien*, 19:109–16. L. L. Westwater, 'Autobiographical impact: life and art of Umberto Saba and Italo Svevo', *RLA*, 9, 1998:397–405.

SALGARI. *Il caso Salgari*, Na, Vuen, 1997, 268 pp., gathers contributions by various authors.

SANGUINETI.   V. Hand, '*Laborintus II*: a neo-avant-garde celebration of Dante', *ISt*, 53:122–49, conducts a hermeneutic investigation of S.'s libretto, highlighting intertextual reference to Dante, Pound, and Isidore of Seville.

SAVINIO.   Silvana Cirillo, *Alberto Savinio. Le molte facce di un artista di genio*, Mi, Bruno Mondadori, 367 pp., sees S. as a multiform but coherent author concerned with dreams, myth, irony, and death. She analyses *Chants de la mi-mort*, *Hermaphrodito*, *Tragedia dell'infanzia*, *Angelica* and *La nostra anima*, and examines his aesthetics with the support of statements chosen from his *Enciclopedia*, music reviews, and other critical works, highlighting some aspects of his affinity with Apollinaire, Surrealism, and psychoanalysis. M. E. Gutierrez, 'La poetica del "lapsus". Inconscio e linguaggio nell'opera di Alberto Savinio', *FoI*, 31, 1997:439–57, focuses on Freudian aspects such as subconscious use of language, 'arte come shock', and 'spaesamento'. Id., 'Il mito in pantofole. Le Muse domestiche di Alberto Savinio', *ItQ*, 135–36:437–55, highlights S.'s quotidian as well as symbolic rendering of myths and examines some references to Vico and Baudelaire. P. Italia, **Dopo la partenza dell'argonauta. Nuovi testi di Alberto Savinio tra *Hermaphrodito* e *Achille innamorato*', *AnVi*, n.s. 8–9, 1997:51–98. Marco Sabbatini, *L'argonauta, l'anatomico, il funambolo: Alberto Savinio dai Chants de la mi-mort a Hermaphrodito*, Ro, Salerno, 1997, 371 pp., analyses some aspects of S.'s early metaphysical poetics and shows how they anticipate subsequent developments.

SBARBARO.   Vittorio Coletti, *Prove di un io minore. Letture di Sbarbaro: 'Pianissimo' 1914*, Ro, Bulzoni, 1997, 127 pp., looks at the importance assigned by the poet to self, family, and nature in this 1914 collection of poetry. P. Guaragnelli, 'Incamminato verso dove non sa. Allegoria del "congedo" nel primo Sbarbaro', *Allegoria*, 26:41–68. A. Perli, ' "Taci, anima . . .": Sbarbaro e il silenzio della poesia', *EL*, 22.3, 1997:93–103.

SCIASCIA.   M. Chu, 'Sciascia and Sicily: discourse and intertextuality', *Italica*, 75:78–92, applies Said's concept of 'orientalist discourse' to S.'s writing about Sicily and explores the complexities of S.'s position. **Il piacere di vivere. Leonardo Sciascia e il dilettantismo*, ed. Roberto Cincotta and Marco Carapezza, Mi, Vita Felice, 222 pp. *La morte come pena in Leonardo Sciascia*, ed. Italo Mereu, Mi, Vita Felice, 1997, 176 pp., concentrates on the themes of the death penalty and death in general. E. Höfner, 'Theodizeen und mehrlei andere Heilslehren in ihrer Vergleichung zur Lebenspraxis: wie Candide 1943 nach Sizilien kam und was mit ihm geschah. Aufklärungsaufarbeitung in Leonardo Sciascias *Candido ovvero Un sogno fatto in Sicilia*', *ItStudien*, 18, 1997:137–64. M. Onofri, ' "Poi vennero gli americani'': il mondo visto da Racalmuto. Nuovi appunti sul giovane Sciascia', *NArg*, 1997, no 12:59–63, argues that S.'s early literary models were not the American writers he read but their Italian translators and commentators, especially Cecchi and Vittorini; he also examines Pasolini's influence on Sciascia. Id., *Nuovi studi sciasciani*, Mi, Vita Felice, 159 pp., gathers the above essay and others written between 1989 and 1992. A. Pietropaoli, 'Il giallo contestuale di Leonardo Sciascia', *StCrit*, 12, 1997:221–59. Domenico Ribatti, **Leonardo Sciascia: un ritratto a tutto tondo*, Fasano, Schena, 1997. Leonardo Sciascia, *Il giorno della civetta*, ed. Gerry Slowey, MUP, 137 pp., contains explanatory notes, a vocabulary, and an introduction (1–22) dealing with S.'s documentary enquiries, his literary representation of the Mafia and creation of non-conventional detective stories, his enlightened rationality, and with intertextuality. C. Spalanca, 'Leonardo Sciascia e l'infernale mondo dell'industria', *Atti* (AISLLI 15), 1085–99.

SERAO. T. Scappaticci, 'Matilde Serao e il teatro', *Ariel*, 12.2, 1997:91–112, covers both her theatre reviews and the theatre as theme in her narrative.

SERENI, C. C. S. Kolsky, 'Clara Sereni's *Casalinghitudine*: the politics of writing. Structure and intertextuality', *ItQ*, 133–34, 1997:47–58, draws a comparison between S. and Primo Levi, shows how cuisine is used by S. as a way to highlight women's values, and argues that the structure of *Casalinghitudine* reproduces the cycle of life.

SERENI, V. A. Barbuto, 'Letteratura e industria: Vittorio Sereni, "Questo e altro"', *Atti* (AISLLI 15), 963–75. R. Nisticò, 'Ellissi e metamorfosi: una diversa lettura de "La spiaggia" di Vittorio Sereni', *StN*, 24, 1997:379–93.

SERRA. Viola Talentoni, *Vita di Renato Serra*, Ravenna, Girasole, 1996, 204 pp., has an introduction by Marino Biondi.

SERRAO. R. Capek-Habekovic, 'Deconstructed text: Achille Serrao's *Retropalco*', *FoI*, 30, 1997:116–26. G. Rimanelli, 'Un'ombra sussurrata di dolore nella poesia in dialetto di Achille Serrao', *Italica*, 74, 1997:81–91.

SEVERINI. Anne C. Hanson, **Severini futurista: 1912–1917*, Seattle, Washington U.P., 1997.

SILONE. E. Circeo, 'L'umanesimo cristiano e socialista di Ignazio Silone', *Il Veltro*, 41, 1997:191–95. Ignazio Silone, **Romanzi e saggi*, 1: *1927–1944*, ed. Bruno Falcetto, Mi, Mondadori. B. Falcetto, '"Salvarsi dalla letteratura". Il modello di Silone', *NA*, 2207:51–63, argues that by avoiding elitist 'accademismo' and literary evasion S. seeks to 'salvarsi dalla letteratura' and 'dalle sue pratiche dominanti'. Yet he believes in literature: 'La letteratura è per Silone una forma della cultura che possiede una specifica e particolare forza comunicativa e morale'. A biographical study is Ottorino Gurgo and Francesco de Core, *Silone*. *L'avventura di un uomo libero*, Venice, Marsilio, 460 pp. Silvano Scalabrella, **Il paradosso Silone*. *L'utopia e la speranza*, Ro, Studium, 177 pp., has an introduction by M. Castellano.

SINISGALLI. L. Cantatore, 'Arredare la "Stanza cubica": Sinisgalli, *La Botte e il Violino*', *Atti* (AISLLI 15), 921–28. Marino Faggella, *Leonardo Sinisgalli. Un poeta nella civiltà delle macchine*, Potenza, Ermes, 1996, 225 pp., examines the multidimensional aspect of Sinisgalli as poet, critic, painter, and writer. Giuseppe Lupo, *Sinisgalli e la cultura utopica degli anni Trenta*, Mi, Vita e Pensiero, 1996, xii + 280 pp., examines the impact of northern and Milanese culture on the work of this poet from the south of Italy. Id., 'Sinisgalli *industriale*', *Atti* (AISLLI 15), 763–73. F. Vitelli, ' "Pneumatica". Sinisgalli e la rivista *Pirelli*', *ib.*, 877–920.

SOFFICI. Dirk Vanden Berghe, *Ardengo Soffici dal romanzo al 'puro lirismo'*, I: *Modelli narrativi e poetici*; II: *Testi inediti (1908–1910)*, F, Olschki, 1997, 190, 163 pp., analyses intertextuality and the relationship between prose and poetry in the first volume and in the second gathers S.'s previously unpublished texts *La famiglia Turchi*, *Infanzia*, and *Lemmonio Boreo*. S. Bartolini, ' "Parigi o cara": il viaggio di formazione di Ardengo Soffici', *REI*, 43, 1997:203–14. I. Violante, 'Papiers collés: des mots français dans la poésie de Soffici', *ib.*, 215–23.

SOLMI. See MONTALE, above.

STUPARICH, G. and C. G. Manacorda, 'Lettere di Giani e Carlo Stuparich a Giuseppe Prezzolini', *RLI*, 100.2–3, 1996[1997]:117–38.

SVEVO. G. Adamo, 'L'inizio e la fine di *Senilità* di Italo Svevo e di *Libera nos a Malo* di Luigi Meneghello: un esempio di lettura', *Lepschy Vol.*, 253–63. A. Benevento, 'Le *Favole* di Italo Svevo', *EL*, 23.2:91–95, examines *Favole* and draws a comparison with Slataper's *Fiabe*. Sergio Blazina, *Svevo e i luoghi della scrittura*, T, Tirrenia, 101 pp. Giuseppe Antonio Camerino, *Italo Svevo e la crisi della Mitteleuropa*, Mi, IPL, 1997, 304 pp., is a new edition of a 1974 essay with the addition of three chapters and some appendixes. G. Contini, 'Angiolina leggera e sciagurata. Appunti per *Senilità*', *RLI*, 101.1, 1997:103–15, examines the social connotations of Trieste 'sartorelle' in relation to some paratextual autobiographical aspects of *Senilità*. L. D'Ascia, 'Tecnica narrativa e analisi dell'io in *Vino generoso* di Italo Svevo', *RLettI*, 13, 1995[1997]:451–66. M. A. Di Gioia, 'Italo Svevo nella critica anglo-americana (1970–92)', *RStI*, 14.1, 1996:48–86. Brian Moloney, **Italo Svevo narratore. Lezioni triestine*, Gorizia, Goriziana, 200 pp. Id., 'Svevo e Schmitz in Inghilterra', *Metodi e ricerche*, 16.2, 1997:19–29, with the support of documents (especially letters) reconstructs S.'s visits to Great Britain and their influence on his work. Id., 'Montale on Svevo', see MONTALE, above. G. Moretti, 'Le storie di Giacobbe. Strutture bibliche nella *Coscienza di Zeno*', *RLettI*, 13, 1995[1997]:137–58. Giovanni Palmieri, 'Positivismo spiritista. Zeno (Svevo) e i suoi libri', *RLI*, 102:58–66, is a textual analysis of positivistic and spiritualistic aspects in S.'s creative work and biography. Edoardo Saccone, 'Il giorno e la notte. Riflessioni sulla *Novella* di Svevo', *MLN*, 113:108–20, examines S.'s perception of death and his concerns with old age vs youth, health vs disease, and literature vs real life. Giulio Savelli, **L'ambiguità necessaria*, Mi, Angeli, 151 pp. Mario Sechi, *'Etica e verità. Sul pessimismo integrale del primo Svevo', *StCrit*, 13:259–93. Caterina Verbaro, **Italo Svevo*, Soveria Mannelli, Rubbettino, 1997, 153 pp.

TABUCCHI. C. D. KLOPP, 'Antonio Tabucchi: postmodern Catholic writer', *WLT*, 71, 1997:331–34, runs through some of T.'s literary concerns (postmodernist self-consciousness, aversion to conventional endings, use of intertextuality, mixture of low and high literary genres) and some ideological aspects: in particular, he sees T.'s moral indignation at social injustice as linked to Catholicism. Antonio Tabucchi, *Sostiene Pereira*, ed. Bruno Ferraro, T, Loescher, 167 pp. H. Felten, 'Künstlerträume. Zur Superposition von Intertexten und Traumdiskurs in Antonio Tabucchi: *Sogni di sogni*', *ItStudien*, 18, 1997:81–90. J. Heymann, 'Existenzsuche im intertextuellen Niemandsland: Antonio Tabucchi zwischen Fernando Pessoa und Luigi Pirandello', *ib.*, 123–36. B. Ophey, 'Antonio Tabucchi: *La testa perduta di Damasceno Moneiro*', *ib.*, 19:156–60.

TECCHI. P. Tuscano, 'Bonaventura Tecchi a cento anni dalla nascita', *EL*, 23.3:2–47, reappraises T.'s work on the occasion of his centenary (1996).

TESTORI. *Opere 1943–1961*, Mi, Bompiani, 1997, 1 + 1356 pp., the first of three volumes on Testori, has an introduction, a chronology of his life and work, and a critical bibliography. A. Cortellessa, 'Giovanni Testori, poesia e figurazione', *Poesia*, 116:14–17, looks at imagery in T.'s poetry.

TOBINO. M. A. Grignani, 'Piccolo diagramma della scrittura di Tobino', *StIt*, 16, 1996[1997]:85–99.

TOMASI DI LAMPEDUSA. Sandra Cavicchioli, **Le sirene*. *Analisi semiotiche intorno a un racconto di Tomasi di Lampedusa*, Bo, CLUEB, 1997, 268 pp. N. La Fauci, 'Le tre porte del *Gattopardo*', *RELI*, 10:99–113, examines the functions of three doors which figure in *Il Gattopardo*, drawing conclusions on the relationships between 'vero e falso' and 'essere e non essere'. R. Luperini, 'Il "gran signore" e il dominio della temporalità. Saggio su Tomasi di Lampedusa', *Allegoria*, 26, 1997:135–45, analyses T.'s and Montale's sense of failure in the face of the social changes brought about in Italy by the economic miracle. Francesco Orlando, *L'intimità e la storia. Lettura del Gattopardo*, T, Einaudi, 195 pp. G. M. Tosi, 'Le cosmogonie aristocratiche: *Il Gattopardo* di Tomasi di Lampedusa', *Italica*, 74, 1997:67–80, sees the novel as T.'s rediscovery of the moral legacy left by the Sicilian aristocracy and argues that, precisely because *Il Gattopardo* constitutes a sublimation of T.'s aristocratic self, it may be seen rather as a 'cosmogonia delle origini' than a 'testo prettamente realista'.

TONDELLI. Roberto Carnero, *Lo spazio emozionale. Guida alla lettura di Pier Vittorio Tondelli*, Novara, Interlinea, 138 pp. Id., 'Dalla "letteratura emotiva" alla "letteratura interiore": l'itinerario narrativo di Pier Vittorio Tondelli', *CLett*, 25, 1977:739–86. Fulvio Panzeri, *Tondelli: il mestiere di scrittore. Un libro-intervista*, Ro, Theoria, 1997, 187 pp. *Pier Vittorio Tondelli. La lettura, la scrittura*, Mi, Marcos y Marcos, 1997, 128 pp., ed. Fulvio Panzeri and Fulvio Galato, contains some texts by T. and critical contributions by F. Panzeri, A. Spadaro, and S. Novelli.

TOZZI. Giancarlo Bertoncini, *Studi tozziani*, Manziana, Vecchiarelli, 1997, 183 pp. B. Bonfiglioli, 'L'espressionismo tozziano. Note tematiche e stilistiche su *Bestie*', *LS*, 32, 1997:293–311. R. Castellana, 'Inattualità di un classico del Novecento. Rassegna critica di studi su Federigo Tozzi (1987–1996)', *Allegoria*, 27, 1997:17–36. M. Codebò, *La rappresentazione del tempo in *Giovani* di Federigo Tozzi', *RStI*, 16.1:241–54. Id., 'Guy de Maupassant in Federigo Tozzi', *MLN*, 113:213–30, compares some aspects of T. and Maupassant, then some aspects of Maupassant and D'Annunzio, to conclude that similarities between Maupassant and D'Annunzio consist in metonymic contiguity, while Maupassant and T. are linked via a metaphoric relationship based on similes and ideological affinity. M. Fratnik, *Les résidues opaques des descriptions de Federigo Tozzi', *REI*, 44:23–73. L. Melosi, 'Ipotesi su una trilogia: *Bestie, Cose, Persone* di Federigo Tozzi', *RLI*, 100.2–3, 1996[1997]:110–16. N. Mainardi, 'Uomini e rospi. Le nature morte di Tozzi e Viani', *Italianistica*, 26, 1997:413–22. M. Palumbo, ' "Forza lirica" e mondo allegorico: *Tre croci* di Federigo Tozzi', *MLN*, 112, 1997:57–80. B. Liva, 'Tozzi poeta: *Specchi d'acqua*', *FC*, 22, 1997:437–63.

TUROLDO. L. De Luca, 'La morte ispiratrice di David Maria Turoldo', *CV*, 52, 1997:353–62.

UNGARETTI. M. Barenghi, 'Di porto in porto con Ungaretti 1923', *Belfagor*, 53:189–203. L. Caretti, 'Ungaretti e il *Mémoire* su Maurice de Guérin', *FC*, 23, 1997:464–66, produces documentary evidence to show that Maurice de Guérin was the subject of U.'s thesis at the Sorbonne in 1914. P. Epistolari, '*Sentimento del tempo* e la poesia di Valéry', *RLI*, 102:109–20. A. Guastalla, 'Il futuro della tradizione.

Ungaretti e Jacopone', *ON*, 22.3:91–129, offers an overview of the
spiritual and literary bonds that U. felt for Jacopone's *Laudario*.
V. Hand, 'Ambiguous joy: contradictions and tensions in U.'s
L'Allegria (1914–19)', *The Italianist*, 16, 1996[1997]:76–116. B. Itri,
'Perle d'Oriente nell'*Allegria* ungarettiana', *FC*, 22, 1997:294–304,
discusses the impact of Onofri's translations of old Chinese poems on
Ungaretti's *Allegria* and on *Il porto sepolto* in particular. E. Livorni,
Avanguardia e tradizione. Ezra Pound e Giuseppe Ungaretti, F, Le Lettere,
384 pp. E. Lorenzetti, 'Alle origini di Ungaretti: la scoperta di
Kavafis', *Italianistica*, 27:441–51, considers the hidden connection
between the Greek poet Kavafis and the two 'Egyptian' Italian poets
Pea and Ungaretti. M. Marchi, 'In margine agli *Inni* di Ungaretti',
RLI, 102:130–40, documents the first resolute step taken by U. to
return to a Christian faith. L. Melosi, 'Note su *Un Grido e Paesaggi*', *ib.*,
121–29, argues that U. here confronts his past while facing a desert-
like, comfortless future. M. Nota, 'Éléments pour une poétique de la
transition: à propos de *Sentimento del tempo*', *ib.*, 97–108. A. Parronchi,
'L'antagonismo Ungaretti–Montale', *ib.*, 101.1, 1997:130–33. Rosita
Tordi, *Ungaretti e i suoi 'maitres à penser'*, Ro, Bulzoni 1997, 216 pp.,
outlines various influences in Africa and Europe that impacted on
U.'s poetics. A. Zingone, 'Ungaretti *Africano a Parigi*. Due poèmes, la
poesia araba', *RLI*, 102:82–96, shows how three poems and one
letter point to the symbolic axis (East–West) that divides and
complements U.'s work. By the same author, ' "Sentimento della
soverchiante materia". Ungaretti e la civiltà meccanica', *Atti* (AISLLI
15), 775–89. See also CALVINO, above.

VALESIO.   J. Jimenez-Heffernan, 'Sonetos de Paolo Valesio', *CHA*,
565–66, 1997:267–70.

VENTURI.   *Resine*, 71, 1997, a special issue entitled *Omaggio a
Marcello Venturi*, gathers papers from 'Marcello Venturi. La vita
raccontata', a study day held at Genoa in December 1995.

VIANI.   Rolando Bellini, **Lorenzo Viani 1882–1936*, Lugano, Fidia,
1997. See also TOZZI, above.

VIGOLO.   M. Vigilante, 'Giorgio Vigolo 1894–1983', *StN*, 24,
1997:259–80, offers a critical overview of this little-known poet and
writer from Rome.

VILLA.   U. Fracassa, 'Versi fuori stagione: *Vanità verbali* di Emilio
Villa', *Il Verri*, 43.7–8:105–16, evaluates V.'s use of language in some
of his later poetry. M. Graffi, 'Le Galapagos di Emilio Villa', *ib.*,
117–22, asks what language represents for V. in his poetry. G. Spagnoletti, 'Omaggio a Emilio Villa', *Poesia*, 123:2–8, records V.'s
valuable contribution to Italian poetry. A. Tagliaferri, 'Scrittura e

matericità negli ultimi testi villiani', *Il Verri*, 43.7–8: 134–43. A. Zanzotto, 'Come sta Villa?', *ib.*, 7–8: 59–61, is a presentation of what is 'presente e inafferrabile' in V.'s poetry.

VIOLA. Luigi Scorrano, *Il polso del presente. Poesia, narrativa e teatro di Cesare Giulio Viola*, Modena, Mucchi, 1996, 264 pp.

VITTORINI. C. Antonelli, 'Elio Vittorini e il PCI: un andamento erratico', *RStI*, 14.1, 1996: 120–36. G. Bonsaver, 'Vittorini's American translations: parallels, borrowings and betrayals', *ISt*, 53: 67–93, examines V.'s translations from Caldwell, Faulkner, Hemingway, Saroyan, and Steinbeck. He concludes that their influence on V.'s fiction rests less on the originals in English than on the Italian he innovatively adopted as a translator. Id., 'Un Gran Lombardo sbarca a Milano: "Il negozio di stoffe" (con un inedito di Elio Vittorini)', *Lepschy Vol.*, 304–14. M. Pignatelli, 'Editing e maieutica nei "Gettoni" di Vittorini', *EL*, 22.4, 1997: 53–78, examines V.'s activity as an editor and especially the role he played in publishing Rigoni Stern's *Il sergente nella neve*. Felice Rappazzo, *Vittorini*, Palermo, Palumbo, 1996, 286 pp.

VIVIANI. F. Cotticelli, 'Raffaele Viviani: suggestioni e proposte di lettura', *Ariel*, 12.2, 1997: 113–28.

VOLPONI. *StN*, 55, devoted to V., includes the following texts: Paolo Volponi, 'L'acqua e il motore' (5–28), a previously unpublished short story; G. Santato, 'Follia e utopia: poesia e pittura nella narrativa di Volponi' (29–66); A. Guidotti, 'Lettura di *Memoriale*' (67–94); P. Dal Bon, '*Memoriale*: tra lingua e stile' (95–134); E. Zinato, 'Tra lampo lirico e rappresentazione saggistica: le prose minori di Paolo Volponi' (135–56); and G. C. Ferretti, 'Profilo biografico' (157–62). L. Knapp, 'Paolo Volponi: *Le mosche del capitale*', *Allegoria*, 26, 1997: 146–57, examines the protagonist's alienation and his acquisition of consciousness in relation to V.'s biography. Id., 'La città e la storia. *Il sipario ducale* di Paolo Volponi', *ib.*, 27: 159–66, analyses various aspects of the novel, especially the relationship between the character of Dirce and the Renaissance town of Urbino. M. T. Marini, 'Letteratura industriale, simbolo e allegoria: Volponi da *Memoriale* alle *Mosche*', *Atti* (AISLLI 15), 987–98. Maria Carla Papini, *Paolo Volponi. Il potere, la storia, il linguaggio*, F, Le Lettere, 1997, 181 pp., interprets V.'s fiction (ch. 1–5) and poetry (ch. 6–7) in terms of a dialectic 'progetto unitario' characterized by a portrayal of a non-idyllic, difficult relationship between the individual and the outside world, and by a language which explores the 'logiche della società mentre ne dichiara lo scandalo'. In V.'s novels she highlights the combination of a history and politics psychology and characterization, and she investigates the characters' ideologies as well as their Freudian aspects. By the same author, 'Il romanzo del non-romanzo:

Le mosche del capitale di Paolo Volponi', *Atti* (AISLLI 15), 999–1008.
M. X. Wells, '*Memoriale* di Paolo Volponi: l'uomo e la fabbrica, esame delle varianti nel manoscritto', *ib.*, 977–85.

ZANZOTTO. Stefano Dal Bianco, *Tradire per amore. La metrica del primo Zanzotto 1938–1957*, Lucca, Pacini Fazzi, 1997, 202 pp., considers possible semantic implications in the rhythmic, phonic, and metrical aspects of Z.'s early poetry. D. Favaretto, 'Diverse linee d'ascesa al monte', *REI*, 43, 1997:51–65, is the text of an interview with Zanzotto. Maike Albath-Folchetti, *Zanzotto's Triptychon. Eine Studie der Sammlungen 'Il Galateo in Bosco', 'Fosfeni' und 'Idioma'*, Tübingen, Narr, xiii + 298 pp. Uberto Motta, *Ritrovamento di senso nella poesia di Zanzotto*, Mi, Vita e Pensiero, 1996, 180 pp., gives particular consideration to the way autobiography, and psychological and linguistic dimensions, impact on the Paschal theme in Z.'s work.

ZILLE. M. Bordin, 'Il mio "disarmonico fragore". Appunti sulla poesia di Luisa Zille', *StN*, 24, 1997:457–77.

ZOPPI. *Cenobio*, 46.1, 1997, carries 'Giuseppe Zoppi nel primo centenario della nascita. Atti del pomeriggio di studio di Locarno, 26 ottobre 1996', comprising: G. Bonalumi, 'La poesia di Giuseppe Zoppi' (5–13); M. Danzi, 'Zoppi, l'idillio e la "distruzione" dell'idillio' (15–26); M. Noseda, 'L'esordio di Giuseppe Zoppi critico letterario' (28–34); R. Martinoni, 'Ritratto in piedi dell'apostolo. Giuseppe Zoppi e i fratelli Bianconi' (36–42); P. Codiroli, 'Giuseppe Zoppi tra italianità ed elvetismo. I difficili anni Trenta' (44–51); P. R. Frigeri, 'Bibliografia di Giuseppe Zoppi' (53–62).

ZUCCOLI. *Cenobio*, 47.2, carries papers read at a colloquium held at Locarno in September 1997 on 'Luciano Zuccoli e i romanzieri di successo di inizio '900 in Italia': A. Dolfi, 'Su un'edizione de *I lussuriosi* di Zuccoli' (110–14), and V. Coletti, 'Appunti sulla lingua de *I lussuriosi* di Zuccoli' (115–21), preceded by a 'Nota introduttiva' by F. Catenazzi (107–09).

X. ROMANIAN STUDIES*

LANGUAGE

POSTPONED

LITERATURE

By Mircea Anghelescu, *INALCO, Paris/University of Bucharest*

(This survey covers the years 1997 and 1998)

Literary history, criticism, and theory occupy a relatively small area of the Romanian book market. Within that area two trends can currently be discerned: an increase in the number and quality of research tools (besides undergraduate study aids, which are numerous and of unequal value) as opposed to a decrease in the number of monographs and synthetic studies with a high degree of originality and their replacement by collections of studies and articles.

1. Works of reference and of general interest

1997 saw the publication of the fourth and final volume of the first literary history conceived and written after 1989: Dumitru Micu, *Scurtă istorie a literaturii române,* IV, Iriana, 1997, 326 pp. It contains the concluding section of the contemporary period, dealing with playwrights and literary critics. Approximately 200 authors are registered, with short entries based on formal and quantitative criteria. Rather than a history, it is more of a repertory which does not dare to go beyond bibliographical notes or to exclude unimportant authors. Far more interesting (and not from Romania or from a specialist) is Eugène Ionescu, *Littérature roumaine,* Paris, Fata Morgana, 68 pp., a concise synthesis of Romanian literary history from the origins to the post Second World War period published posthumously without any indication as to its date of composition, the origin of the manuscript, or even the name of the editor. Dating probably from the late 1950s, when the author was not yet famous, it contains memorable characterizations, no less memorably phrased, of the most important Romanian writers. It is likely to be most used by Ionescu's own commentators, as revealing preferences and opinions which can be

---

* The place of publication of books is Bucharest unless otherwise stated.

placed under the sign of a capital question: 'comment peut-on être Roumain?'

Among works of reference, the most successful have been the literary dictionaries. The most important one to come out in 1998 was the second volume of *Dicționarul scriitorilor români*, ed. M. Zaciu, M. Papahagi, and A. Sasu, Fundației Culturale Române, 860 pp., comprising names of authors starting with letters D to L. The 406 articles each contain essential information on the writer's biography, *œuvre*, and critical and interpretative fortunes, along with an exhaustive bibliography of his work and a selective critical bibliography at the end of each entry. Important authors such as Delavrancea, Eminescu, Filimon, and so on, are covered, as well as authors who have emerged since 1980, authors in exile whose names could not be mentioned before 1989, and authors from Bessarabia (the Republic of Moldova) or from other areas inhabited by Romanians. The volume also includes a general bibliography, an index, and a list of abbreviations. Another useful dictionary, the first of its kind in Romania, is *Dicționarul analitic de opere literare românești*, ed. Ion Pop, 1, Didactică și Pedagogică, 361 pp., which comprises, from A to D, 176 entries devoted to as many famous titles, both of volumes and of separate pieces: poems like Bolintineanu's *Conrad*, short stories like *Cezara* by Eminescu, plays like *A treia țeapă* by M. Sorescu. Here too the articles are accompanied by a bibliography of editions and a critical bibliography, and the volume has an index. The only problem might be the surprising inclusion of collections of folklore, such as *Doine și strigături din Ardeal* by Jarnik and Bârseanu, which in no case could be considered a Romanian *literary* piece. Doina Ruști, *Dicționar de simboluri din opera lui M. Eliade*, Coresi, 156 pp., takes over, for the word 'symbol', Eliade's meaning of 'revelatory metaphor' and identifies in his works precisely 117 such terms, which are illustrated by means of references to his entire work and explained in relation to Romanian folklore in particular, but with relatively scant reference to universal space: amnesia, androgyne, animal, ark, etc. Each entry ends with a very concise bibliographical note. There have also been two regional dictionaries. Nicolae Busuioc, *Scriitori ieșeni contemporani*, Iași, Junimea, 1997, 416 pp., includes approximately 370 authors born in Iași and its county, or authors active in the area, giving detailed biographical data on their careers. Here one might note some errors in the translated titles and some omissions with regard to texts printed abroad (for example, in the case of G. M. Cantacuzino). Teodor Tanco, *Dicționar literar al județului Bistrița-Năsăud, 1639–1997*, Cluj-Napoca, Virtus Romana Rediviva, 453 pp., includes over 300 names of writers, journals, and literary societies connected with the county concerned. The writers range from the famous (Coșbuc,

Rebreanu) to the obscure, the articles devoted to the latter offering data difficult to find in any other way. However, the author includes too many writers whose relation to the county was of no importance: Blaga who owned some land in the region, the novelist Radu Petrescu who was a school-teacher there at the beginning of his career, etc. This is an obvious case of overzealous research, which nevertheless does not impair the overall importance of the information gathered in the dictionary.

In the field of bibliography, we can signal a few contributions of wider interest. The first is Olimpia Mitric, *Cartea românească manuscrisă din Nodrul Moldovei*, Atos, 367 pp., a catalogue of old Romanian MSS from libraries, or written in scriptories in northern Moldavia, with some conclusions regarding cultural activities in this area in the 16th and 17th c. Produced by a team of researchers coordinated by him, Marin Bucur, *Bibliografia I. L. Caragiale. Text din periodice*, Cultura Naţională – Grai şi Suflet, 1997, 478 pp., comprises 3160 entries for the years 1852–1912, though sometimes different entries refer to the same published text. Mircea Handoca, *Bibliografia Mircea Eliade*, 1, Jurnalul literar, 1997, 320 pp., first published in 1979 and now much enriched since the author's collaboration with E. himself, who gave him access to his personal archives. This first volume comprises only E.'s own works: after a foreword and a chronology of his life, the bibliography proper divides into books and translations of books, articles and interviews, and published and unpublished correspondence, and is rounded off with addenda and an index. A second volume of 339 pp. appeared in 1998, bringing the total number of references to 5992.

Very important documentary material, to a considerable extent already known but now gathered in two compact volumes, is contained in Panait Istrati, *Cum am devenit scriitor*, ed. Al. Talex, 2 vols, Florile Dalbe, 581, 511 pp. The first volume has now appeared for the third time (the first being in 1981, from Scrisul Românesc, Craiova, the second in 1985 from Minerva) but is completed with an 80-page bibliography; the second volume, published for the first time, includes widely known texts such as Istrati's pamphlet against Soviet communism, *Vers l'autre flamme*, but also others which so far have gone practically unnoticed: his open letter to Mauriac, his secret file in the police archives, etc. Another important volume of unknown documents is *Benjamin Fondane et les 'Cahiers du Sud'. Correspondance*, ed. and ann. Monique Jutrin, Gh. Has, and I. Pop, introd. M. Jutrin, Fundaţiei Culturale Române, 333 pp., containing the correspondance between Benjamin Fondane and the Marseilles journal *Cahiers du Sud*: 181 letters between 1932 and 1944, almost half of which are addressed by Fondane to Jean Ballard, the editor of the journal. We might also mention two documentary anthologies: the first dedicated to the leader of the Nationalist Right intellectuals between the Wars: *Nae Ionescu în conştiinţa contemporanilor sai. Memorii, articole, eseuri, interviuri, corespondenţa*, ed. Gabriel Stănescu, Criterion, 463 pp.; the second gathering writing by the most significant supporters of Romania's dissident literary movement of the late 1960s: Leonid Dimov and Dumitru Ţepeneag, *Momentul oniric*, ed. Corin Braga, Cartea românească, 1977, 262 pp. Here most of the texts had never been reprinted in volume. Unfortunately the edition is not accompanied by notes or a bibliography.

Also in the field of works of general interest and use, one should mention editions of the classics or of important writers: the most complete edition of Vasile Voiculescu's *Prose*, ed. Roxana Sorescu, Anastasia, 698 pp., including a number of texts that have never been published in volume before; Mihail Sadoveanu, *Opere*, ed. Cornel Simionescu and Fănuş Băileşteanu, IV, Minerva, 1997, 375 pp., which comprises *Umiliţii mei prieteni* of 1911 and *Bordeenii* of 1912; Mircea Eliade, *Opere*, ed. and ann. Mihai Dascal, II, Minerva, 1997, 395 pp., comprising the novel *Maitreyi;* Petru Maior, *Scripta minora*, ed. Ioan Chindriş, Viitorul românesc, 1997, 398 pp., which includes some rare writings such as his polemics with B. Kopitar, V. Coloşi, etc., but is edited in rather amateurish fashion; Liviu Rebreanu, *Opere*, ed. N. Gheran, vols 16 and 17, Minerva, 672, 695 pp., which include the 1927–44 *Journal* and his travel diary from 1928 to 1943; also Alexandru Busuioceanu, *Istoria literaturii române*, pref. Al. Ciorănescu, Jurnalul Literar, 188 pp., a booklet first printed in Spain in 1942 and now reprinted in both the original Spanish version and the Romanian translation (with a few mistakes in the proper names) and also three more texts, including the important *Literature and Destiny*, 1948, conceived as an introduction to an improved and extended version of the compendium which was never realized; P. Zarifopol, *Pentru arta literara*, ed. Al. Săndulescu, Fundaţiei Culturale Române, 482 pp., and the second and last volume of his collected works.

Diaries and memoirs continue to appeal to the public. Among the large numbers of books published this year which directly concern the history of literature, one must mention Mircea Zaciu, *Jurnal*, IV, Albatros, 465 pp., containing notes from 1982–86; Nicolae Balotă, *Caietul albastru*, Fundaţiei Culturale Române, 824 pp., the diary of a member of the famous 'literary circle' of Sibiu during the Second World War; the second volume of Ion Caraion's *Diary*, ed. Emil Manu, Albatros, 497 pp.; and Marin Preda, *Scrisori către Aurora*, Albatros, 374 pp., where the letters are followed by an interview given by E. Simion.

2. MONOGRAPHS, LITERARY CRITICISM

Monographs and scholarly studies are not very numerous. Emil Turdeanu, *Oameni şi cărţi de altădată*, ed. Ştefan Gorovei and Magdalena Szekely, I, Enciclopedică, 1977, 400 pp. + 16 pl., includes older studies such as *Manuscrise slave din timpul lui Ştefan cel Mare, Miniatura bulgară şi începuturile miniaturii româneşti, Vechea legătură românească de carte*, etc. Originally a PhD thesis, Adriana Babeţi, *Bătălii pierdute. D. Cantemir, strategii de lectură*, Timişoara, Amarcord, 296 pp., combines interest in the mannerist and encoded work of an early 18th-c. author who was an orientalist, geographer, and historian, with a tendency towards an intertextualist modern reading. Ştefan Badea, *Biografia poeziei eminesciene. Constituirea textului poetic*, Viitorul românesc, 1997, 231 pp., pleads for the study of the whole work and of individual variants in order to determine 'the semantic centres of poeticality'. A special kind of monograph is Andrei Corbea, *Paul Celan şi 'meridianul' său. Repere vechi şi noi pe un atlas central-european*, Iaşi, Polirom, 198 pp., where the author examines the poet's personality and work, starting from his origins, back in Cernăuţi, the 'meridian' of his Central-European childhood and teenage life. A solid monograph devoted to one of the pre-eminent figures of Romanian literary and academic life in the interwar period, the aesthetician, essayist, and comparatist Vianu, is George Gană, *Tudor Vianu şi lumea culturii*, Minerva, 290 pp. Vasile Lungu, *Viaţa lui Tudor Vianu*, Minerva, 1997, 198 pp., draws on previously unused documents in state and private archives. *Manuscriptum*, 1997, no. 2–4, is also devoted to this scholar, with unpublished texts and various mementos. Petru Poantă, *'Cercul literar' de la Sibiu*, Cluj-Napoca, Clusium, 1997, 258 pp., researches a literary group, important during the Second World War, which developed around the poet and philosopher Lucian Blaga. It has chapters on formative elements, the group manifesto, the journal influenced by the group, its literary ideas, etc. Younger authors direct their attention towards contemporary writers: a monographic study of a contemporary prose-writer who has lived in Paris for the last 25 years is Nicolae Bârna, *Dumitru Ţepeneag. Introducere într-o lume de hîrtie*, Albatros, 282 pp.; or they tackle forgotten figures of modern literature: Mircea Diaconu, *Mircea Streinu*, n. pl., Bessarabian Institute, 210 pp., is devoted to an expressionist of the end of the 1930s and to his group. A short monograph on the folklore specialist I. Diaconu (1903–1984), famous for six volumes concerned with the region of Vrancea, has been brought out by Paula Diaconu-Bălan, *Ion Diaconu. O viaţă dedicată Vrancei*, Iaşi, Petra-Dia, 133 pp.

A collection of critical studies and essays entirely devoted to Eminescu is George Munteanu, *Eminescu şi antinomiile posterităţii*,

Albatros, 383 pp. A collection of essays with a strong theoretical tendency is Monica Spiridon, *Interpretarea fără frontiere*, Cluj-Napoca, Echinox, 182 pp., whereas Cornel Regman, *Întîlniri cu Clasicii*, Eminescu, 264 pp., comprises traditional-style studies by a critic well versed in his methodology. Ana Selejan, *Literatura în totalitarism, 1955–1956*, Cartea Românească, 398 pp., continues a series of documentary investigations into literary criticism in the 1950s. Mircea Popa, *Reîntoarcerea la Ithaca. Scriitori romȃni din exil*, Oradea, Globus, 1997, 248 pp., assembles studies on Romanian writers in exile, from the famous, such as M. Eliade, E. Cioran, and E. Ionescu, to the less well known, such as Alexandru Busuioceanu, Grigore Cugler, and Lucian Boz. Eugen Simion, *Fragmente critice*, Grai şi Suflet, 366 pp., gathers a fragment of his abundant daily criticism. Florin Manolescu, *Litere în tranziţie*, Cartea Românească, 383 pp., contains studies and notes on current production over the last ten years. Mihai Zamfir, *Retorica anilor '90*, Fundaţiei Culturale Române, 1977, 150 pp., examines the rhetoric of ideological texts after 1989 (the deviant discourse, the European discourse, etc.) in an essayistic but substantial way, while Virgil Nemoianu, *Jocurile Divinităţii*, Fundaţiei Culturale Române, 278 pp., gathers together essays on 'thought, freedom, and religion at the end of the millennium'. One might also mention: Ana Maria Tupan, *Scriitori romȃni în paradigme universale*, Fundaţiei Culturale Române, 212 pp.; George Băjenaru, *Intre sublim şi tragic*, Cerna, 252 pp.; Gh. Crăciun, *In căutarea referinţei*, Piteşti, Paralela 45, 251 pp.; and Traian Ştef, *Ridicolul*, Piteşti, Paralela 45, 148 pp., consisting of essays on the meta-aesthetic concept of ridicule and its relationship with the burlesque, the absurd, the grotesque, etc. A volume in honour of Professor I. Ianosi of Bucharest University on his 70th birthday: *Estetică şi moralitate*, ed. Marin Diaconu, Crater, 636 pp., contains *inter alia* G. Liiceanu, *Repères pour une herméneutique de l'habitation*, and G. Achiţei, *O permanenţă a culturii romȃneşti: opoziţia traditionalism-modernism*, and a bibliography of Ianoşi's work.

Finally, *RITL*, 45, 1997, 1–2, the most recent issue of the journal, carries two article on as yet unpublished texts: M. Mitu, 'O carte de înţelepciune: *Palatul crailor leşeşti*' (43–60), an anonymous late-18th-c. work, and A. Nestorescu, 'O tragedie "indiană": *Regele de Armgabad de Al. Macedonski*' (145–60), the beginning of an unknown oriental tragedy by the Romanian symbolist Macedonski. I would also note, in the latest issue of the Romanian comparative literature journal, Doina Popa-Liseanu, 'Elementos para una poética comun en *Kyra Kyralina* y *Don Segundo Sombra*', *Synthesis*, 24, 1997:69–81, concerning P. Istrati and the Argentinian Ricardo Guiraldes.

XI. RHETO-ROMANCE STUDIES

By INGMAR SÖHRMAN, *Gothenburg University*

1. BIBLIOGRAPHICAL AND GENERAL

Ulrich Hoinkes and Wolf Dietrich, *Kaleidoskop der lexikalischen Semantik*, Tübingen, Narr, 1997, x + 396 pp. Heidi Siller-Runggaldier and Paul Videsott, *Rätoromanische Bibliographie 1985–1997* (Romanica Ænipontana, 17), Innsbruck, 150 pp., is a carefully compiled and comprehensive bibliography of Friulan, Ladin, and Romansh linguistic books.

2. FRIULAN

BIBLIOGRAPHICAL AND GENERAL. L. Peressi, *Indice delle pubblicazioni della SFF. Supplemento 5 (1991–1996)*, Udine, Societât Filologjiche Furlane, 159 pp. L. Vanelli, 'Friulian', Price, *Encyclopedia*, 265–66, gives a good overview of the language's external situation from the beginnings to the present day, including its maintenance among emigrants. The same scholar, 'A proposito di alcune ipotesi sul friulano preletterario', *Ce fastu?*, 74:7–21, replies to G. Cadorini, 'Cualchi ipotesi sul furlan di prin di scrivilu', *ib.*, 73, 1997:183–201. G. Sanga, 'Il frammento zurighese di Giacomino Pugliese: osservazioni linguistiche e filologiche su un testimone di area friulana (1234 circa)', *ib.*, 211–35, follows G. Brunetti and rejects the supposed Sicilian origin of the Zurich MS (C88 ex 292) on the basis of a linguistic and philological analysis which links it firmly to Friuli. G. Frau, 'Peraulis in libertât: i atlanz lenghistics', *ib.*, 203–10, stresses the importance of linguistic atlases for the study of linguistic change in general and of ASLEF for Friulan in particular.

PHONOLOGY AND MORPHOLOGY. M. Bais, 'La lunghezza vocalica nella lettura di parole friulane e di non parole', *ib.*, 7–29, reports and analyses interesting empirical data. M. Bonifacio, 'Concordanze linguistiche tra l'Istria e il Friuli', *Sot la Nape*, 49.4, 1997:43–46, particularly concerns the suffix *-èo*.

MORPHOSYNTAX. L. Anziutti et al., **Ricercjis par furlan*, Udine, Societât Filologjiche Furlane, 1996, is a collection of prize-winning contributions to the study of Friulan entered for a contest organized by the Societât in 1994.

ONOMASTICS AND LEXIS. Cornelio Cesare Desinan, *Le varianti dei nomi di luogo*, Udine, Societât Filologjiche Furlane, 287 pp., is a fairly complex study of problematic place names. Some of the names discussed by Desinan in his *Itinerari friulane* (see *YWMLS*, 59:603) are reconsidered in P. Merku, 'Su alcuni toponimi sloveni in Friuli', *Ce fastu*, 73, 1997:7–29. Other contributions on place names are M. Buligatto, 'I nomi di luogo a Teôr', *Sot la Nape*, 49.1–2, 1997:63–81, and Id., 'I nomi di luogo a Rivarotta di Teôr', *ib.*, 49.4, 1997:47–56. On Friulan family names in surrounding areas: M. Bonifacio, 'Cognomi di origine friulana a Trieste, in Istria e in Slovenia', *ib.*, 50.3:33–37. Giulio Andrea Pirona et al., *Il nuovo Pirona. Vocabulario friulano*, 2nd edn, rev. Giovanni Frau, Udine, Societât Filologjiche Furlane, 1996, xlvii + 1810 pp., is the result of extensive revision of the original 1935 edition.

3. LADIN

GENERAL. P. Benincà, 'Dolomitic Ladin', Price, *Encyclopedia*, 262–63, provides a general view of the language's external situation from the beginning to the present day. The author does not regard Ladin as a Rheto-Romance variety but sees it as a peripheral dialect with similar conservative features.

MORPHOSYNTAX. N. Bacher, 'Versuch einer Deütsch-Ladinischen Sprachlehre', *Ladinia*, 19, 1995[1996]:1–304, is a critical edition of the German grammar of Ladin (1833) by Nikolaus Bacher, alias Micurá de Rü.

LEXIS M. Bundi, 'Note etimologiche sul dialetto di Novate', *Clavenna*, 35, 1996:205–25. Hans Goebl, *Atlant linguistich dl ladin dolomitich y di dialec vejins*, Wiesbaden, Reichert, comprises four volumes of maps (1–216, 217–438, 439–660, 661–884) and, to facilitate their use, three of indexes: *Index alphabeticus omnium vocum, quae reperiuntur in ALD-I*, 823 pp., *Index alphabeticus inversus omnium vocum, quae reperiuntur in ALD-I*, 833 pp., and *Tres indices etymologici omnium mapparum titulorum qui reperiuntur in ALD-I*, 177 pp. The result of highly skilled investigation, this reference work is of extreme interest to any researcher in Ladin or Rheto-Romance etymology, or in north Italian dialectology.

SOCIOLINGUISTICS AND LANGUAGES IN CONTACT. R. Bernardi, 'Das Ladin Dolomitan, das Sprachplanungsprojekt SPELL und die Angst der Mächtigen', *ASR*, 111:79–84, is a concise presentation of the standardization principles of Dolomitic Ladin, the language planning service SPELL, and existing attitudes and strategies to gain a better position for Ladin. D. Kattenbusch, 'Ladinien', pp. 311–33 of *Handbuch der mitteleuropäischen Sprachminderheiten*, ed. Robert Hinderling and Ludwig M. Eichingen, Tübingen, Niemeyer, 1996, is a thorough description of the sociolingistic situation, focusing on the external aspects, by a researcher who knows the theme well.

4. SWISS ROMANSH

GENERAL. *Schweizer Sprachen, Langues suisses, Lingue svizzere, Linguas svizras*, Ed. Dynamicha, 1997, is the first conversation guide in all the four official languages of Switzerland. It could be seen as a consequence of the promotion of Romansh to official status in 1996. Some general facts and basic grammar are given. I. Söhrman, 'Romansh', Price, *Encyclopedia*, 388–93, offers a general view of the language's external situation from the beginnings until the present day. The effects of the standardization process and the use of Rumantsch Grischun are discussed. M. Bundi, 'Lungatg vegl sursilvan en litteratura e documents communals', *ASL*, 111:7–44, is a linguistic and philological study of three early documents in Sursilvan. *100 onns Romania 1896–1996*, Müster, Societad Studentica all'Union Culturala dalla Surselva Catolica e dil Plaun, 1996, consists mainly of a commented bibliography on teaching materials in Sursilvan during the last century. Language standardization and a sociolinguistic overview of Romansh, as well as the linguistic activities of the cultural organization, are presented.

MORPHOSYNTAX. R. Capeder, 'Von Sprache und Wandel', *Terra Grischuna*, 56, 1997:14–16, concerns Germanization in the Albula Valley. Ulrich Wandruszka, *Syntax und Morphosyntax: eine kategorialgrammatische Darstellung anhand romanischer und deutscher Fakten* (TBL 430), 230 pp., is a contrastive German-Romansh study of syntactic problems.

LEXIS. Andreas Blank, *Prinzipien des lexikalischen Bedeutungswandels am Beispiel der romanischen Sprachen* (ZRP Beiheft 285), Tübingen, 1997, xiv + 533 pp. *Dicziunari Rumantsch Grischun*, ed. Felix Giger et al., Chur, Inst. dal Dicziunari Rumantsch Grischun, fasc. 130–31, IR-ISCHAIAR II. P. Masüger, 'Orientierungsmarken im Lebensraum — Flurnamen', *Terra Grischuna*, 56, 1997:34–36. C. Riatsch, 'Ün rebomb? Üna sombriva? — Problems da traducziun da lirica rumantscha', *ASR*, 110, 1997: 87–102. K. Frank-Spörri and R. Cathomas, 'Success e nonsuccess da pleds rumantschs', *ASR*, 111:45–78, presents and analyses the results of an investigation on the recognition both of presumed obsolete words and of neologisms in Surmeir. The analysis also contains a sociolinguistic part. Chatrina Urech-Clavuoat, *Verbs puters*, Samedan, 1997, 109 pp. K. Wanner, 'Die Wörterbücher der Walser-Mundarten', *Wir Walser*, 35, 1997:5–12.

SOCIOLINGUISTICS AND LANGUAGES IN CONTACT. R. Cathomas, 'Survesta dallas cundiziuns da basa per il svilup della cumpetenza linguistica tier minoritads', *ASR*, 110, 1997:7–51, is a lengthy analysis of language competence among the Romansh-speaking population.

E. Diehmann, 'Das Rätoromanische in der Schweiz', pp. 335–84 of *Handbuch der mitteleuropäischen Sprachminderheiten*, ed. Robert Hinderling and Ludwig M. Eichingen, Tübingen, Niemeyer, 1996, is a fairly thorough description of the sociolinguistic situation, focusing on its external aspects. Jean-Jacques Furer, *Le romanche en péril? Évolution et perspective*, Bundesamt für Statistik, Bern, 1996, 335 pp. + 10 maps, the results and an analysis of the 1990 census on Romansh, is a rich and substantial source of information on the use of Romansh in different situations and by different sexes and generations. Hanspeter Kriesi et al., *Le clivage linguistique. Problèmes de compréhension entre les communautés linguistiques en Suisse*, Bern, Bundesamt für Statistik, 1996, 136 pp., is a statistically-based discussion of the problems that arise in a multilinguistic society like Switzerland. Georges Lüdi et al., *Le paysage linguistique de la Suisse*, Bern, Bundesamt für Statistik, Bern, 1997, 720 pp., contains the results and an analysis of the 1990 census. It deals with Switzerland's four national languages and main immigrant languages, also discussing language loss, multilingualism, and language politics in Switerland. Clà Riatsch, *Mehrsprachigkeit und Sprachmischung in der neueren bündnerromanischen Literatur*, Chur, Bündner Monatsblatt, is an analysis of how language contact (German-Romansh) is reflected in modern Romansh literature, contrasting puristic attitudes and mixed, 'impure' texts, and the consequences that may ensue. Gion Pol Simeon, *Igl muvimaint rumantsch an Surmeir*, Union Rumantscha da Surmeir, 1996, is an account of the particularities and external situation of the central Romansh dialect, Surmiran. The question of the standardizing process is also discussed. This is especially interesting from a Surmiran view as many have suggested that this dialect be made Standard Romansh. The society's linguistic activities and language promotion are also described.

3

CELTIC LANGUAGES

I. WELSH STUDIES

LANGUAGE

By DAVID THORNE, *Reader in Welsh Language and Literature,*
University of Wales, Lampeter

1. GENERAL

P. Simms-Williams, 'Celtomania and Celtoscepticism', *CMCS*,
36: 1–15, continues the discussion of the concept of Celticity as it has
developed in different disciplines. P. M. Freeman, 'The earliest Greek
sources on the Celts', *EC*, 2: 11–48, notes all the early Greek literary
and inscriptional sources up to the 4th c. BC mentioning the Celts,
and provides the original text, a translation and commentary.

2. PHONETICS AND PHONOLOGY

T. D. Griffin, 'The law of sibilants in Brythonic', *SC*, 31: 125–33, re-
examines the changes that occurred in Brythonic involving the
sibilant, arguing that dynamic sibilant analysis is the key to unravelling the law. A. R. K. Bosch, 'Prominence at two levels: stress versus
pitch prominence in north Welsh', *JCLin*, 5: 121–65, examines
dialectal evidence which may question the autosegmental hypothesis
that phonotactic licensing and prominence are equivalent. J. F. Eska,
'Resyllabification and epenthesis in Hispano-Celtic', *ib.*, 71–89, re-
examines a series of 'disturbed' forms in Hispano-Celtic and offers
alternative explanations.

3. GRAMMAR

T. A. Watkins, 'Constituent order in the main/simple verbal
declarative clause in *Math uab Mathonwy*', *SC*, 31: 195–217, completes
his important constituent-order analysis of *Pedeir Keinc y Mabinogi.*
B. M. Jones, 'Necessity and obligation: Part 1, adult Welsh', *ib.*,
239–67, examines the root uses of the lexemes *dylai, i fod, gorfod, rhaid*
and argues that the semantic distinctions discerned in his data allow
speakers to adopt certain social attitudes and postures. R. D. Borsley
and M. Tallerman, 'Phrases and soft mutation in Welsh', *JCLin,*

5:1–49, is a contribution to an on going discussion on the character of soft mutation, the nature of the triggers, the nature of the targets and the relationship between trigger and target. S. Rodway, 'A datable development in medieval literary Welsh', *CMCS*, 36:71–94, attempts to date the use of the 3rd person singular endings -*w(y)s* and -*awdd* in medieval poetry and prose. A. Shisha-Halevy, *JCLin*, 6:63–102, continues his study of modern Welsh syntax, discussing the significance of both the verbal noun in narration and the present-future tense.

4. ETYMOLOGY AND LEXICOGRAPHY

Hywel Wyn Owen, *The Place-names of Wales*, Cardiff, Univ. of Wales Press, xxii + 103 pp., is a guide to a selection of place names in Wales; in addition to a dictionary and brief discussion of the names themselves the valuable introduction concisely describes what the study of place names involves and the likely results of such a study. Iwan Arfon Jones, *Enwau Eryri: Place names in Snowdonia*, Talybont, Y Lolfa, 247 pp., is a discussion of the names of mountains, cliffs, valleys, rivers, streams, and lakes of Snowdonia and provides a grid reference number for each location. Melville Richards, *Enwau Tir a Gwlad*, Caenarfon, Gwynedd, 229 pp., is a more comprehensive and authoritative discussion of the place names of Wales, providing in Welsh much of the material available in the author's academic publications in English. Deric John, *Cynon Valley Place-names*, Llanrwst, Carreg Gwalch, 118 pp., has more modest aims, but is a useful introduction to the place names of the Cynon Valley in Glamorgan.

Heini Gruffudd, *The Welsh Learner's Dictionary*, Talybont, Y Lolfa, 256 pp., is a handy first dictionary aimed at schools and adult learners.

Llyfni ac Afan, Garw ac Ogwr, ed. Hywel Teifl Edwards, Llandysul, Gomer, 320 pp., has an interesting essay on two eminent 18th-c. lexicographers from Glamorgan: R. M. Crowe, 'Thomas Richards a John Walters: Athrawon Geiriadurol Iolo Morganwg' (226–51), traces the influence of Thomas Richards and John Walters on the linguistic work of Edward Williams (Iolo Morganwg). *Y Termiadur Ysgol: Termau wedi'u Safoni ar gyfer Ysgolion Cymru*, ed. Delyth Prys, Bangor, Univ. of Wales, 668 pp., is a useful compilation of terms used across the key stages of the National Curriculum. *Mynegair i'r Beibl Cymraeg Newydd*, ed. Owen E. Evans and David Robinson, Cardiff, Univ. of Wales Press, xii + 1135 pp., is a very impressive concordance of the New Welsh Bible. G. R. Isaac, 'Two Continental Celtic verbs', *SC*, 31:161–71, has notes on *ieuru* and *amPiTiśTi* from the Botorrita inscription. E. P. Hamp, *ib.*, 276 discusses Celtic Ὄκελον. V. Orel, *ib.*, 277–79, considers Gaulish *Dona*. B. Maier, *ib.*, 280 has a note on Gaulish **GENA*. R. Coates, 'A new explanation of the name of London', *TPS*, 96: 203–29, tentatively suggests that the name London is derived from a Celticized river name; the proposed etymology also accounts for the Welsh *Llundein*. Part 48 of GPC (ed. G. A. Bevan) covers RHADUS-RHESYMADAWY. *Fest Birkhan* has one significant contribution relevant to this section: D. Ellis Evans, 'Rex Icenorum Prasetagus' (99–106), considers the interpretation of the proper name Prasetagus, ruler of the Iceni in early Roman Britain. G. Morgan, *JCLin*, 6: 137–39, has a note on *mehyr* in the *Gododdin*.

5. SOCIOLINGUISTICS

Dot Jones, *Statistical Evidence Relating to the Welsh Language 1801–1911 / Tystiolaeth Ystadegol yn Ymwneud â'r Iaith Gymraeg 1801–1911*, Cardiff, Univ. of Wales Press, xiv + 519 pp., is a comprehensive presentation of statistical material relating to the Welsh language in the 19th c. arranged under population, language, education, religion, culture; each section is prefaced by a brief but useful introductory comment. *Iaith Carreg fy Aelwyd: Iaith a Chymuned yn y Bedwaredd Ganrif ar Bymtheg*, ed. Geraint H. Jenkins, Cardiff, Univ. of Wales Press, xiv + 427 pp., is the third volume in a series of studies exploring the social history of the Welsh language, each of the 14 chapters contributing useful discussions to the study of the complex process of linguistic change in different communities. W. T. R. Pryce, 'Ardaloedd iaith yng ngogledd ddwyrain Cymru *c.* 1800–1911' (21–60), shows that in north east Wales the westward retreat of bilingual areas hastened the process of Anglicization, especially in centres of commerce and tourism where English achieved prominence to the detriment of Welsh. D. Ll. Jones, 'Yr iaith Gymraeg yn Sir Drefaldwyn *c.* 1800–1914' (61–95), traces the westward shift of the linguistic boundary in Montgomeryshire during last century and examines the economic, educational and population changes which spearheaded the change. R. Davies, 'Iaith a chymuned yn ne orllewin Cymru *c.* 1800–1914', (97–120), is an entertaining description of Welsh as a community language in south-west Wales in the 19th c. I Mathews, 'Yr iaith Gymraeg yn y maes glo carreg *c.* 1870–1914' (121–41), shows how the seeds which led to the erosion of the language in the anthracite coalfield in the present century were sown during the years leading up to the First World War. P. N. Jones, 'Y Gymraeg yng nghymoedd Morgannwg *c.* 1800–1914' (144–76), focuses on industry, immigration and language use in the industrial valleys of Glamorgan in the last century. O. J. Thomas, 'Yr iaith Gymraeg yng Nghaerdydd *c.* 1800–1914' (177–95), describes the fortunes of the language in the

capital city between 1801 and 1914. S. Rh. Williams, 'Y Gymraeg yn
y Sir Fynwy ddiwydiannol *c.* 1800–1901' (197–223), traces the rapid
demise of the Welsh language in the western valleys of Monmouth-
shire in the last century and describes the change in the nature of the
community during these years of industrialization and in migration.
E. Jones, 'Yr iaith Gymraeg yn Lloegr *c.* 1800–1914' (225–53), is a
careful assessment of the distribution of Welsh speakers in 19th-c.
England; he also provides an interesting analysis of the pattern of use
of the language in the institutions recreated by the migrants. W. D.
Jones, 'Y Gymraeg a hunaniaeth Gymreig mewn cymuned ym
Mhennsylvania' (255–80), describes the Welsh communities of the
last century in Pennsylvania. R. O. Jones, 'Yr iaith Gymraeg yn y
Wladfa' (281–305), is an interesting account of the efforts made to
maintain the Welsh language and its institutions in Patagonia. *Llyfni
ac Afan, Garw ac Ogwr*, ed. Hywel Teifi Edwards, Llandysul, Gomer,
320 pp., has two contributions relevant to this section: B. Thomas,
"Tyfu mas o'r mæs": Pont-rhyd-y-fen a'r æ fain' (138–62), studies the
distribution of the half-open front vowel in a dialect of south-east
Wales; P. N. Jones, 'Pa mor Gymraeg oedd fy nghwm? Cymreictod
cymoedd Garw ac Ogwr ar ddiwedd y bedwaredd ganrif ar bymtheg'
(209–26), is an analysis of the decline of the Welsh language in the
Garw and Ogwr Valleys during the latter half of the 19th c.
    Mari C. Jones, *Language Obsolescence and Revitalisation: Linguistic
Change in Two Sociolinguistically Contrasting Welsh Communities*, OUP,
vii + 452 pp., examines the steady revitalisation of Welsh that is
taking place against a backdrop of contraction with special reference
to two communities: the implications are also explored with reference
to Breton and Cornish. P. W. Thomas, 'Cymraeg swnllyd', *Taliesin*
102:39–65, studies the language of private sector bilingual road
signs. Price, *Encyclopaedia* under 'Welsh' (448–95), includes a useful
and concise discussion encompassing various areas such as early
attestations, official status of Welsh, Welsh in religion, education and
the media, geographical distribution of speakers and dialects. E. H. G.
Jones, 'Bilingualism in the Assembly', *Planet* 131:77–81, is an
assessment of the chances of a working bilingualism being adopted in
the Welsh Assembly. G. P. Davies, 'Statws cyfreithiol yr iaith
Gymraeg yn yr ugeinfed ganrif', *Y Traethodydd*, 153:76–95, explores
the legal history of the Welsh language during the present century
and assesses the significance of the 1993 language act. Marion Löffler,
'Eu hiaith a gadwant': the work of the National Union of Welsh
Societies, 1913–1941', *THSC*, 4:124–52, continues her discussion of
the role of voluntary cultural organizations in the history of the Welsh
language.

6. DIALECTOLOGY

Issues and Methods in Dialectology, ed. Alan R. Thomas, Bangor, Univ. of Wales, 312 pp., has one contribution relevant to this section: G. E. Jones and C. H. Williams, 'A mid-Wales dialect transition zone' (294–312), addresses the notion of dialect transition from a geographical and historical perspective. The data from Brecknock which forms the basis of the study reveals it to be a significant interface between the major northern and southern dialects, with marked affinities with the southeastern Gwentian dialect. The article seeks to interpret the dialect data using evidence from settlement patterns, transportation routes, regional economic development, and cultural systems.

EARLY AND MEDIEVAL LITERATURE

By JANE CARTWRIGHT, *Department of Welsh, Trinity College Carmarthen*

O. J. Padel, 'A new study of the *Gododdin*', *CMCS*, 35:45–55, gives a mixed welcome to John T. Koch's *The Gododdin of Aneirin. Text and Context from Dark-Age Britain* (1997). Having summarized Koch's theory of the *Gododdin's* textual history, Padel criticizes many of the hypotheses put forward in the volume, as well as its difficult style, and calls for a new edition of the Book of Aneirin which is as free as possible from preconceptions about the date and early textual history of its contents. G. R. Isaac, '*Gweith Gwen Ystrat* and the northern heroic age of the sixth century', *ib.*, 61–70, refutes Koch's claims that the poem *Gweith Gwen Ystrat* was composed in the 6th c. and depicts the same events as the *Gododdin* but viewed from the side of the Coeling. He provides a new edition and translation of the poem, together with a metrical analysis, and concludes that the poem was composed in the 11th c. or later. A. Breeze, 'Two notes on Early Welsh poetry: the date of the *Gododdin*, and poet and patron in *The Praise of Tenby*', *SC*, 31:269–75, uses Brittonic loanwords in Old English, namely *truma*/*trwm* and *syrce*/*seirch*, to suggest *c*. 600 as the date of composition of the *Gododdin* and places in context a reference in the 9th-c. *awdl*, *Edmyg Dinbych* to the poet as his lord's bedfellow. Stephen S. Evans, *The Lord's of Battle: Image and Reality of the Comitatus in Dark-Age Britain*, Woodbridge, The Boydell Press, viii + 169 pp., focuses primarily on the literary images of the *comitatus* and assumes that there exists 'a credible correlation between the ideals established by the court poets of this period and the actual behaviour that was exhibited by the members of the Dark-Age warbands'. His rather literal interpretation of *Cynfeirdd* poetry leads him to assume that the descriptions of battles in the 'historical' poems attributed to Taliesin are based on eyewitness accounts. D. G. Jones, 'Dedwydd a Diriaid', *Efrydiau Athronyddol*, 61:65–81, examines the meaning and uses of the contrasting terms *dedwydd and diriaid* in early Welsh saga poetry. C. Cessford, 'Pine marten and other animal species in the poem *Dinogad's Smock*', *Environmental Archaeology* 2:71–72, links archaeological and literary evidence to confirm that Dinogad's '*Peis . . . o grwyn balaot*' was indeed made of pine marten pelts. M. Haycock continues her survey of references to alcoholic beverages in medieval Welsh poetry with ' "Canu y Cwrw" o Lyfr Taliesin', *Dwned*, 4:9–32, which provides a valuable edition of 'Canu y Cwrw', an anonymous religious poem found in the Book of Taliesin, along with a translation into modern Welsh and copious notes.

N A. Jones 'Golwg arall ar "Fawl Hywel ap Goronwy"', *LlC*, 21:1–7, provides new insights into an anonymous, conventional praise poem to Hywel ap Goronwy, one of the minor princes of South Wales who came to power at the end of the 11th c. She suggests a slightly earlier date of composition than that suggested by the poem's editor R. Geraint Gruffydd in *Gwaith Meilyr Brydydd a'i Ddisgynyddion*, ed. J. E. C. Williams *et al*. Cardiff, Univ. of Wales Press, 1994. A. P. Owen, 'Canu arwyrain Beirdd y Tywysogion', *YB*, 24:44–59, considers whether 'canu arwyrain', the ceremonial praise poetry to Welsh princes, can be considered as a specific genre in its own right and in 'Cymeriad yn awdlau Beirdd y Tywysogion – rhai sylwadau', *Dwned*, 4:33–58, she reviews the use of *cymeriad* in the *awdlau* of the *Gogynfeirdd*. She categorizes the various types of *cymeriad*, a stylistic device used to join together the beginning of lines of poetry, and provides a useful list of all relevant poets and their approximate dates. Other valuable contributions which look closely at poetic metre include: R. M. Andrews, 'Sain Broest', *LlC*, 21:166–71, which surveys a variation on the *cynghanedd sain* in 12th- and 13th-c. poetry; P. Lynch 'Einion Offeriad a'r gyhydedd fer', *Dwned*, 4:59–74, whose meticulous analysis of *y gyhydedd fer* in the work of the *Gogynfeirdd* and Einion Offeiriad demonstrates that the latter was not only responsible for the first version of the bardic grammar, but that he also helped establish a new variation on *y gyhydedd fer* as illustrated in the grammar; and R. M. Jones, 'Ffurf y cywydd a'r englyn', *YB*, 24:94–122, extends the analysis begun in 'Gogynghanedd y Gogynfeirdd' (*YB*, 21), by applying the same theoretical stance to the *cywydd* and the *englyn*.

Bleddyn Owen Huws, *Y Canu Gofyn a Diolch c. 1350–c. 1630*, Cardiff, Univ. of Wales Press, xv + 272 pp., is a pioneering study of some 650 poems of request and thanks composed by approximately 150 different poets *c*. 1350–*c*. 1630. The volume traces the popularity and decline of this specifically Welsh genre in considerable detail and provides valuable insights into the relationship between poet and patron, the kind of gifts requested and the poetic techniques employed by the *Cywyddwyr* to describe a wide range of contemporary objects, concluding that the golden age of poems of request and thanks was between *c*. 1450 and *c*. 1525 with fewer *cywyddau* composed by poets requesting gifts for themselves after 1500. Useful lists of poets, gifts requested, thanks for gifts, and numbers of relevant poems are provided in appendices. An edition of 30 poems has been published separately in *Detholiad o Gywyddau Gofyn a Diolch*, ed. Bleddyn Owen Hughes, Swansea, Barddas, 157 pp. Two volumes have been published in the UWCASWC series, *Cyfres Beirdd yr Uchelwyr. Gwaith Llywelyn Goch ap Meurig Hen*, ed. Dafydd Johnston, Aberystwyth, UWCASWC, xiv + 117 pp., contains editions of the 12 poems attributed to Llywelyn Goch ap Meurig Hen (*fl.* 1350–1390). *Gwaith Dafydd Bach ap Madog Wladaidd 'Sypyn Cyfeiliog' a Llywelyn ab y Moel*, ed. R. Iestyn Daniel, Aberystwyth, UWCASWC, xvii + 219 pp., edits the work of two poets associated with Powys: Dafydd Bach ap Madog Wladaidd (otherwise known as Sypyn Cyfeiliog) *c.* 1320–*c.* 1390, and Llywelyn ab y Moel *c.* 1395–1440. Id., 'Rhagolwg ar Gasnodyn', *YB*, 24:26–43, discusses the life and work of Casnodyn, a 14th-c. poet from Glamorgan who wrote in the style of the *Gogynfeirdd. Canu Maswedd yr Oesoedd Canol/Medieval Welsh Erotic Poetry*, ed. and trans. Dafydd Johnston, Bridgend, Seren, 136 pp., is a revised edition of the 1991 volume with the addition of 'Merch o Swydd Lincoln', a 16th-c. macaronic poem by Dafydd Llwyd Ysgolhaig. M. P. Bryant-Quinn, 'Tair marwnad i hynafiaid Catrin o Ferain', *Dwned*, 4:107–24, edits two elegies to Ieuan ap Tudur ap Gruffudd Llwyd and an elegy to his son Tudur ab Ieuan demonstrating that one of the elegies to Ieuan ap Tudur is the work of Ieuan Llwyd Brydydd. Sections of these poems had previously been published as a composite text in *Gwaith Tudur Aled*, ed. T. Gwynn Jones, Cardiff, Univ. of Wales Press, 1926. D. J. Bowen, 'Gwladus Gam a'r beirdd', *YB*, 24:60–91, establishes that Gwladus, the daughter of Dafydd Gam, played an important role in the sponsorship of 15th-c. Welsh poetry. Id., 'Siôn Cent a'r ysgwier-iaid', *LlC*, 21:8–37, is a valuable discussion on the work of Siôn Cent which places the poet's criticisms of 14th-c. squires in their social and historical context, and suggests that Siôn was familiar with the work of Petrus Lombardus, Langland and other English poets who openly condemned the exploitation of the poor by wealthy landowners. H. Fulton, 'Trading places: representations of urban culture in medieval Welsh poetry', *SC*, 31:219–30, uses the poetry of the *Cywyddwyr* as an historical source to document the nature and extent of Welsh participation in the economic and social life of the medieval borough, concluding that, although originally the boroughs provided the locus of Welsh oppression and exclusion, as the period proceeded concerns of nationality became subordinated to economic and social interaction. D. Foster Evans, ' "Y carl a'i trawai o'r cudd": ergyd y gwn ar y cywyddwyr', *Dwned*, 4:75–105, surveys references to guns in the work of the *Cywyddwyr*. R. M. Jones, *Ysbryd y Cwlwm: Delwedd y Genedl yn ein Llenyddiaeth*, Cardiff, Univ. of Wales Press, viii + 459 pp., traces literary imagery relating to national consciousness within Wales, focusing in the first four chapters on texts such as *Armes Prydein*, 'Marwnad Llywelyn ap Gruffudd' and the poetry of Dafydd Llwyd of Mathafarn. R. Wallis Evans, 'Nodiadau ar y cywyddau brud', *LlC*, 21:177–82, classifies the prophetic poems, and notes similarities between the Welsh poems and their English counterparts. G. Thomas provides notes on the work of Dafydd ap Gwilym and 'Naw Englyn y

Juvencus' in 'Nodiadau amrywiol', *LlC*, 21:172–77. A. Breeze, 'The Greek grammar of Theodore Gaza (d. 1475/6) in early Tudor Wales', *BLR*, 16:281–84, briefly discusses a reference to Theodore Gaza's grammar in the poetry of Tudur Aled. Id., 'Margaret Paston's "Grene a Lyere"', *NQ*, 243:29–30, notes references to the English phrase 'blac of lyre' in medieval Welsh poetry.

In comparison to the numerous publications relating to medieval poetry relatively few publications have appeared in the field of Middle Welsh prose. One of the most significant contributions is Pryce, *Literacy*, which includes the following relevant articles: P. Sims-Williams, 'The uses of writing in early medieval Wales' (15–38), a wide-ranging article which considers the difficulties involved in interpreting the limited literary evidence that survives from pre-Norman Wales; S. Davies, 'Written text as performance: the implications for Middle Welsh prose narratives' (133–48), utilizes recent research in performance theory to throw new light on the interaction between orality and literacy, demonstrating that the 11 tales in the *Mabinogion* corpus 'are not written versions of oral stories, but rather the result of composition-in-writing'; D. E. Thornton, 'Orality, literacy, genealogy in early medieval Ireland and Wales' (83–98), also focuses on orality and literacy; W. Davies, 'Charter-writing and its uses in early medieval Celtic societies' (99–112), although primarily concerned with charter-writing, is also of interest to those studying hagiography; L. B. Smith, 'Inkhorn and spectacles: the impact of literacy in late medieval Wales' (202–22), references a number of literary sources; and C. Lloyd-Morgan, 'More written about than writing? Welsh women and the written word' (149–65), opens up a much-neglected field by surveying the scant evidence relating to women's literacy, book ownership and patronage in medieval Wales, concluding that women did have an active role in the production and transmission of literature. A. Breeze reaffirms his view that Gwenllian ferch Gruffudd ap Cynan 'wrote' the *Four Branches of the Mabinogi*, in 'Did a woman write the *Four Branches of the Mabinogi*?', *Stvdi Medievali*, 38:679–705. A pivotal aspect of his argument hinges upon the rather naïve assumption that there are certain passages in the Four Branches 'which would be unusual if the work of a man, but which read naturally as the work of a woman.' Id.,' *The Awntyrs off Arthure*, Cywryd of Kent, and Lavery Burn', *NQ*, 243:431–32, identifies Cywryd Gwent, mentioned in the Welsh triads as the father of Gwenhwyfar, as Krudely of Kent in *The Awntyrs off Arthure*. R. M. Jones, *Tair Rhamant Arthuraidd gydag Arolwg o Derfynau Beirniadaeth Gyfansawdd*, Caernarfon, Gwasg Pantycelyn, 84 pp., draws on Saussurean structuralist theory in his analysis of the three Welsh Arthurian romances. J. R. Davis, '*Liber Landavensis*: its date and the identity of its editor', *CMCS*,

35 : 1–11, argues that this important MS, which contains a number of charters and hagiographical texts, was compiled under the direct supervision of Bishop Urban *c.* 1119–1134. K. L. Maund, 'Fact and narrative fiction in the Llandaff Charters', *SC*, 31 : 173–93, demonstrates that the Narrations attached to charters in *Liber Landavensis* can be divided into particular story-types and warns against using this narrative material as an accurate historical record of ecclesiastical problems and powers in 6th-11th-c. south-east Wales.

Marion Eames, *A Private Language? A Dip into Welsh Literature*, Llandysul, Gomer, 202 pp., is what it purports to be: a basic introduction to Welsh literature for a non-Welsh readership by a successful author of modern Welsh fiction who is well-aware of her non-academic background. It contains a summary of previous work on the *Cynfeirdd*, early Welsh saga poetry, the *Gogynfeirdd*, the *Mabinogion*, Dafydd ap Gwilym and the poets of the gentry. Unfortunately it provides no new translations, the bibliographies are somewhat out-dated and a few errors have crept in. An essential source of reference for the non-Welsh reader as well as the specialist is *The New Companion to the Literature of Wales*, ed. Meic Stephens, Cardiff, Univ. of Wales Press, xv + 841 pp. which accompanies the Welsh volume *Cydymaith i Lenyddiaeth Cymru*, ed. Meic Stephens, Cardiff, Univ. of Wales Press, xiii + 831 pp. Both masterly tomes draw on the work of 320 scholars and provide concise, reliable information on a wide range of texts, authors and genres. They supersede their 1986 predecessors since they contain much revised and updated material as well as over 400 new entries, many of which reflect the most recent research on early and medieval literature. Dafydd Johnston's *Pocket Guide* (1994), a concise, reliable introduction to Welsh literature from the 6th c. onwards, is now available in Welsh: *Llyfr Poced Llenyddiaeth Cymru*, Cardiff, Univ. of Wales Press, x + 143 pp.

LITERATURE SINCE 1500

By KATHRYN JENKINS, *Lecturer in Welsh, University of Wales, Lampeter*

R. G. Gruffydd, 'Y Print yn dwyn ffrwyth i'r Cymro: *Yny Lhyvyr Hwnn*, 1546', *Y Llyfr yng Nghymru*, 1: 1–20, examines issues of authorship and context of the first published book in Welsh, noting that it must be seen as a handbook of religious education. M. P. Bryant-Quinn, *Cymaint Serch i Gymru: Gruffydd Robert, Morys Clynnog a'r Athrawiaeth Gristnogawl (1568)*, Aberystwyth, UWCAWCS, 28 pp., reviews the aims of recusant literature and emphasizes that it was their consciousness of the needs of the people of Wales which spurred the efforts of these exiled authors. G. Bowen, 'Siôn Dafydd Rhys a'i *Institvtiones* 1592', *LIC*, 21:38–49, discusses Rhys's life and work, suggesting influences on his *Grammar* and the author's own aim of presenting the splendours of Wales's bardic tradition to the aristocracy of his day. M. Evans, 'Canu Cymru yn yr unfed ganrif ar bymtheg', *Cof Cenedl*, 13:33–68, is a useful survey of how we now believe poetry to have been performed in the 16th c. and concentrates on the Established Church, and strict and free metre poetry. N. Lloyd, *Ffwtman Hoff: Cerddi Richard Hughes, Cefnllanfair*, Swansea, Barddas, liii + 128 pp., provides history and context for a virtually unknown figure of the Elizabethan Court and publishes his varied poetic output together with works sung to him during his lifetime. G. ap Gwilym, 'Y rheithor a'i blwyf', *Barn*, 428:26–27, eulogizes the Herculean scholasticism of John Davies, Mallwyd. B. F. Roberts, 'Cyhoeddiadau Edward Lhwyd', *Y Llyfr yng Nghymru*, 1:21–58, offers a chronological analysis of Edward Llwyd's work and accounts for his international reputation.

Gweledigaethau y Bardd Cwsg: Ellis Wynne, ed. Patrick J. Donovan and Gwyn Thomas, Cardiff, Univ. of Wales Press, xxxii + 163 pp., is a new edition of this work by the 17th-c. devotional writer, Ellis Wynne, with Thomas providing the necessary textual notes and general introduction. C. Charnell-White and F. Rhydderch, 'Ellis Wynne a'i ferched', *Barn*, 425:37–39, offer a feminist view of Wynne's work and note English influences. K. Jenkins, ' "Songs of Praises": the literary and spiritual characteristics of the hymns of William Williams Pantycelyn and Ann Griffiths', *The Hymn Society of Great Britain and Ireland Bulletin*, 214:98–109, analyses the said qualities of both hymnists in the context of the Methodist Revival and the development of the hymn as a literary genre. *Ffrewyll y Methodistiaid*, ed. A. Cynfael Lake, Cardiff, Univ. of Wales Press, xxxii + 76 pp., is the text of an anti-Methodist *anterliwt* by William Roberts and Lake also discusses the work's context in a stimulating and valuable introduction. Id., 'Cipdrem ar anterliwtiau Twm o'r Nant', *LlC*, 21:50–73, offers a view of Thomas Edwards's career and examines his themes and characters, in particular those of the Fool and Miser, emphasizing Nant's ability to treat abstractions in the person of concrete characters. Id., 'Llenyddiaeth boblogaidd y ddeunawfed ganrif', *Cof Cenedl*, 13:69–101, rightly presents the period as the golden age of folk literature and notes reasons for its gradual demise, namely the increasing influence of the eisteddfod and chapel culture. D. E. Davies, 'Iolo Morganwg (1747–1826): bardism and Unitarianism', *Journal of the Welsh Religious History Society*, 6:1–11, looks at Edward Williams's ideals as literary and religious leader and stresses the intellectual overlaps. A. R. Jones, 'Lewis Morris and "Honest Mr. Vaughan" of Nanmor and Corsygedol', *Journal of the Meirioneth Historical and Record Society*, 13:31–42, notes the connection between the 18th-c. poet and squire William Vaughan; Jones also scrutinizes the form and content of Morris's poems to him. M. Ellis, 'Y bardd Alun a'r *Cylchgrawn*', *Y Casglwr*, 62:3–5, traces John Blackwell's activities as author and notes his lack of penchant for marketing. G. T. Roberts, *The Language of the Blue Books*, Cardiff, Univ. of Wales Press, ix + 260 pp., looks at a cataclysmic period of Welsh history, noting the effect of the report's publication on all aspects of Welsh culture together with their still felt aftermath. J. Aaron, *Pur fel y Dur: Y Gymraes yn Llên Menywod y Bedwaredd Ganrif ar Bymtheg*, Cardiff, Univ. of Wales Press, vii + 247 pp., offers a feminist analysis of the positive and negative images of Welsh women in religion, literature, and in a British context. C. Hopkins, 'Merched Islwyn', *Taliesin*, 102:83–99, suggests psychological complexities as the reason for Islwyn's dependence on female figures. E. G. Millward, *Yr Arwrgerdd Gymraeg: ei Thwf a'i Thranc*, Cardiff, Univ. of Wales Press, viii + 369 pp., is a most significant and enlightening study of the epic in Welsh, tracing its roots to pre-Methodist Revival times on through the 19th c. E. W. James, 'Ann Griffiths, Mary Jones a Mecca'r Methodisitiaid', *LlC*, 21:74–87, looks at the connections of two similar Methodist women with Thomas Charles of Bala, their respect for the scriptures and charts the context of the Methodism that underpinned so much of 19th-c. religion. D. Ll. Morgan, 'Ffydd a gwyddoniaeth yng ngweithiau beirdd oes Fictoria', *ib.*, 88–138, is a most comprehensive survey of the place of the Bible in Victorian poetry given the crisis of faith that was beginning to affect Wales. The author discusses scriptural allusion and dwells on the place of the epic at this time as it attempted to grapple with such subjects as Geology. T. Jones, 'Y baledi a damweiniau glofaol', *Canu Gwerin*, 21:3–21, notes the ways in which popular poetry reflected the increasingly tragic results of industrialization in Wales. B. M. Mathews, 'Dylanwad y sinema ar lenyddiaeth Gymraeg', *Y Traethodydd*, 153:6–24, offers some moral criticism of that media through a variety of Welsh authors. D. A. Thorne, 'Steddfod Spandau', *Y Casglwr*, 64:17, vivaciously examines the circumstances surrounding and reactions to an eisteddfod held at Ruhleben Camp, Spandau, in October 1915, involving some 70 Welshmen. H. Walters, 'Dau lythyr gan Tom Hughes Jones', *Taliesin*, 101:93–102, brings to light correspondence of a contemporary of T. H. Parry-Williams and one time editor of *Y Wawr*. G. Erfyl, 'Poenau Gŵr Pen y Bryn', *Efrydiau Athronyddol*, 61:1–12, explores some theological aspects of a novel by E. Tegla Davies first published in *Yr Eurgrawn* in 1915–16. The author highlights the issue of religious conversion and suggests the possible influence of Evelyn Underhill's study of mysticism published at the same time. D. Z. Phillips, 'Ôl y duwiau: Jane Gruffydd a *Traed mewn Cyffion*', *ib.*, 13–28, discusses the theme of fate in the novel by Kate Roberts. E. Evans, 'Wil Ifan', *Barddas*, 249:11, talks of his father and offers some biographical evidence and observations on his poetry. M. George, 'Wil Ifan: bardd "Bro fy mebyd"', pp. 274–300 of *Llynfi ac Afan, Garw ac Ogwr*, ed. Hywel Teifi Edwards, Llandysul, Gomer, 320 pp., offers a view of Wil Ifan's connections with the Eisteddfod and in particular the reaction to his pioneering *pryddest* of 1925. G. P. Hughes, 'Rhwng Cyfyng Gell a'r gwesty gwyn', *YB*, 24: 151–189, looks at the poetry of I. D. Hooson and the influences upon him. Alan Llwyd, *Cerddi R. Williams Parry*, Denbigh, Gee, xxxvii + 318 pp., is a complete edition of Williams Parry's poems with a comprehensive introduction dealing with his life and his growing disillusionment with human nature; his attitudes to the ravages of death are well-analysed. Another volume in the *Bro a Bywyd* series appeared: T. Emyr Pritchard, *R. Williams Parry 1884–1956*, Swansea, Barddas, 124 pp. B. Griffiths, 'Trwy deg neu trwy dwyll? y cyfyng-gyngor moesol yng ngwaith Saunders Lewis', *Efrydiau Athronyddol*, 61:50–64, looks at Lewis's plays from both a moral and political standpoint. W. O. Roberts, 'Nodiadau ar *Excelsior*', *Taliesin*, 104:19–35, sets the play in the context of the beginnings of the Welsh Nationalist Party and grapples with possible influences on Saunders Lewis. J. G. Griffiths, '*Dail Pren:* y cysodiad cyntaf', *ib.*, 42–60, recites with relish some previously unpublished evidence regarding Waldo's life and personal contacts. B. G. Owens, 'Brenhines y lamp', *Barddas*, 245:2–3, offers an appreciation of an unpublished poem by Waldo Williams. H. Walters, 'Beirniadaeth lenyddol Brinley Richards', *ib.*, 249:36–37, is an appreciation of Brinli's work as poet and adjudicator at the National Eisteddfod. Id., 'Brinli - Bardd "Y Dyffryn"', pp. 38–64 of *Llynfi ac Afan, Garw ac Ogwr*, looks at Archdruid Brinli's career, the hyperbolic reaction to his study of Edward Williams, Iolo Morganwg, and his connections with the National Eisteddfod. M. Strange, 'Cerddi Gwilym R.', *Y Traethodydd*, 153 : 25–40, discusses the work of Gwilym R. Jones as a reflection of his Christian faith as a Welsh speaking Welshman and presents him as a restless poet of meditation. G. Williams, 'Dylanwadau detholus?', *ib.*, 109–11, intimates the influence of folk song on Gwilym R.'s poem, 'Yr oeddwn i yno'. Pennar Davies, *Cudd Fy Meiau*, ed. R. Tudur Jones, Swansea, Tŷ John Penry, 221 pp., is a new edition of a revealing diary, the introduction by Jones tracing intellectual characteristics and patterns. D. S. Jones, *Bobi Jones: Y Farddoniaeth Gynnar*, Caernarfon, Pantycelyn, 104 pp., is a further volume in the *Llên y Llenor* series, emphasizing the fullness of the poet's perspective of life based on Calvinist theology, and traces allusions and explores themes. Id., 'Persbectifau: golwg ar *Sonedau Serch Hen Bensiynwr*', YB, 24 : 123–150, appreciates Bobi Jones's poems to his wife that intimate that their love will survive even death and continue in eternity. J. T. Jones in two articles looks at the renaissance in strict metre Welsh poetry over the last decades, 'Adfywiad y canu cynganeddol diweddar', *Barddas*, 247 : 26–39; 248 : 14–18. The author emphasizes the social revolution of the sixties and asks the questions: how contemporary is *cynghanedd*? What future is there for such poetry? C. M. Jones, 'Sir Benfro a'r gerdd dafodiaith', *LlC*, 21 : 139–50, notes that the dialectical poem is a symbol of national identity; amongst its most prominent themes is the romantic mourning of a disappearing society. E. Lewis, 'Ar lafar gwlad', *Barn*, 426–27 : 60–63, offers a critique of standards for contemporary poets in public performance. I. Llwyd, 'Sawl Cymro fu'n trigo mewn tref?', *Llais Llyfrau*, 2 : 5–6, suggests the need for an urban context to some Welsh poetry and the cross-fertilization of ideas between poets. R. M. Jones, 'Ffurf y cywydd a'r englyn', *YB*, 24 : 94–122, scrutinizes both forms psycho-mechanically. *A Guide to Welsh Literature c. 1900–1996*, ed. Dafydd Johnston, Cardiff, Univ. of Wales, x + 308 pp., is an invaluable collection of articles tracing the development of various literary forms in the 20th c.

A Nation and its Books: A History of the Book in Wales, ed. P. H. Jones, and E. Rees, Aberystwyth, National Library of Wales, xvi + 432 pp., is a major chronological study of the production and supply of books in Wales. D. Johnston, *Llyfr Poced: Llenyddiaeth Cymru*, Cardiff, Univ. of Wales Press, x + 143 pp., is a useful overview. R. M. Jones, *Ysbryd y Cwlwm: Delwedd y Genedl yn ein Llenyddiaeth*, Cardiff, Univ. of Wales Press, xii + 459 pp., is a scholarly, pioneering diachronic study of Welsh nationhood as expressed in literature; the author places particular emphasis on the nation's spiritual history. D. Ll. Morgan, *Y Beibl a Llenyddiaeth Gymraeg*, Llandysul, Gomer, 256 pp., contains much work already published elsewhere and concentrates on the 19th c. I. Ff. Ellis, *Naddion*, Denbigh, Gee, 256 pp., is a collection of creative and critical writings on aspects of 20th-c literature, in particular the literature of the eisteddfod.

II. BRETON AND CORNISH STUDIES

By HUMPHREY LLOYD HUMPHREYS, formerly *School of Modern Languages, University of Wales, Lampeter*

1. BRETON

There is a particularly large number of publications dealing with extralinguistic aspects of Breton, of which the most general is H. Ll. Humphreys, 'Breton', in Price, *Encyclopedia*, 35–40. Y. Le Berre and J. Le Dû, '149. Français-breton', Goebl, *Kontaktlinguistik*, 1252–60, is a remarkably full condensation focussing on the contact situation. R. Hincks, 'Y Llydaweg yn y Bedwaredd Ganrif ar Bymtheg', pp. 359–83 of *Iaith Carreg fy Aelwyd: Iaith a Chymuned yn y Bedwaredd Ganrif ar Bymtheg*, ed. Geraint H. Jenkins, Cardiff, Univ. of Wales Press, xiv + 427 pp. although quite fully documented and generally sound, is excessively restricted to the 19th c., possibly reflecting an editorial directive. Some reference to the status of Breton in pre-Revolutionary and Ducal times would however seem essential in explaining the situation to the incompletely informed public the author addresses.

Some work provides more narrowly thematic discussion. V. Lachuer, *L'Etat face à la langue bretonne*, (= *Klask*, 4), Rennes, Presses Universitaires, 136 pp., examines with extensive quotations and documents, the attitudes and actions of the French administrative machine with regard to Breton since the Revolution. F. Broudic, *Combes a-eneb ar brezoneg*, Brest, Brud Nevez, 127 pp., singles out the confrontation between Church and State (1902–05) which he illustrates with some 60 items from the clerical weekly *Kroaz ar Vretoned*. Y. Le Berre and J. Le Dû, 'Ce que nomme «breton»', pp. 99–116 of *Le Nom des langues I — Les Enjeux de la nomination des langues*, ed. A. Tabouret-Keller (Bibliothèque des cahiers de l'Institut de Linguistique de Louvain, 95), Louvain-la-Neuve, Peeters, 1997, pp. 99–116, is a minute examination of the reality and perceptions of the term. M. C. Jones, 'Death of a language, birth of an identity: Brittany and the Bretons', *LPLP*, 22.2 : 129–42, examines the paradoxical, but not unusual, situation touched upon in an earlier study (see *YWMLS*, 57 : 611), in which a heightened awareness of Breton identity accompanies an accelerating erosion of the traditional speech community which provides its organic foundation. R. L'Hourre, 'Le changement de langue en Basse-Bretagne : pour une approche centrée sur le sujet parlant', *BrL*, 11 : 253–71, discusses social and psychological aspects, seeing similarities between the motivations for language change and those for language restoration.

Other work is concerned with the precise appraisal of the linguistic situation on the ground. F. Broudic, 'La recherche sur la pratique du breton: objet, méthodes et perspectives', BrL, 11:51–75, reviews the extremely varied data he and others have used to try and give a general picture of the situation and finishes by listing a number of specific aspects which could be profitably pursued. Id., 'Littérature et sociolinguistique - relire Flaubert', *Bull. de la Soc. Archéologique du Finistère*, 124:304–12, illustrates the exploitation of fragmentary evidence scattered in literary sources. M. C. Jones, *La Langue bretonne aujourd'hui à Plougastel-Daoulas*, Brest, Brud Nevez, 1998, 71 pp., reports questionnaire-based fieldwork planned in association with the aforementioned author. A. Guillou, 'Les femmes et le breton', *BrL*, 11:227–31, explains three cases of 50–60 year-old women untypically attached to Breton, by a particularly close relationship with the father. G. Le Duc, 'Notes sur la frontière linguistique en 1878 par Gabriel Milin', *Bull. de la Soc. Archéologique du Finistère*, 124:289–90, confirms the overall dependability of Sébillot.

Phonological and grammatical aspects of the language are represented by a rather small number of publications. I. Wmffre, *Central Breton*, Lincom Europa (Languages of the World/Materials, 152), München, 63 pp., is a very useful sketch of a dialect rather grossly misdescribed by Timm (see *YWMLS*, 46:614, 49:559). It is generally sound in substance, but the extremely condensed nature of such a presentation obviously does not permit exhaustive investigation of numerous questions. P. Le Besco, 'Le Breton de Saint-Gildas-de-Rhuys', *EC* 32:244–55, is a tentative phonology based on a corpus of some 200 lexical items recorded from a woman born in 1896, reputedly the last link with native vernacular — barely used at all after pre-school childhood. *The Syntax of the Celtic Languages: A Comparative Perspective*, ed. R. D. Borsley and I. Roberts, CUP, 1996, 368 pp. contains two relevant papers: R. D. Borsley, M.-L. Rivero, and J. Stephens, 'Long head movement in Breton' (53–74), is generally sophisticated and correct in its examples, though the crude umbrella assertion that 'Breton is a VSO language' rings more like a political slogan; and R. Hendrick, 'Some syntactic effects of suppletion in the Celtic copulas' (75–96), touches upon the relationship between the different forms of the present of *beza(ñ)*, but with minimal and sometimes uncertain exemplification. J.-Y. Plourin, 'La phrase bretonne comprenant le verbe ÊTRE au présent de l'indicatif. Conflits de topicalisation', *BrL*, 11:281–300, is a more concrete and useful discussion of this very problematical area of Breton syntax. G. Pennaod, 'Notennoù war an niveriñ', *Hor Yezh*, 213:51–55 justifies a decimal counting system in neo-Breton with remote historical backing.

Lexical material is dominated by G. Mercier, et al., *Ar Geriadur a gomz: dictionnaire vocal du breton*, Saint-Brieuc, TES, a CD-ROM based on Favereau's dictionary (see *YWMLS*, 54;595) providing an oral model as well as enabling the user to manipulate the written data. The most ambitious project of the sort to date in the field of Celtic languages, with over 30,000 entries, it claims to be perfectible rather than definitive. It is a response to the problem of ensuring that Breton learners will have access to native-speaker phonology. The organization of the project is outlined in J.-P. Messager 'Research in speech processing for Breton language learning', *Workshop on Speech Technology in Language Learning (STiLL 98): Proceedings*, Stockholm, pp. 29–31. A glossary of words connected with childhood or used by children is begun by H. ar Bihan, 'Geriaoueg yezh ar vugale hag ar vugale vihan', A-B, *Hor Yezh*, 215:5–27; CH-D, *ib.*, 216:5–32. N. Davalan, 'Un nebeud geriennoù pennaouet e Plounevez-Kintin (Kernev-Uhel)', *ib.*, 212:15–29, is a glossary, with phonemic transcriptions, of some 200 words either uncatered for or differently glossed in existing dictionaries. Thematic glossaries include: P. Herbert, 'Anvioù laboused Europa', *ib.*, 213:5–18, (continuation); R. Mogn, 'Anvioù gwez brezhoneg', *ib.*, 29–43. A sociolinguistically revealing aside is B. Tanguy, 'Un témoignage inédit de Gabriel Milin sur Amable-Emmanuel Troude', *Bull. de la Soc. Archéologique du Finistère*, 125:347–52, claiming gross under-acknowledgement of Milin's key role in the production of Troude's dictionary. Milin's claim that Troude — and incidentally Le Gonidec — did not have a perfect mastery of Breton, foreshadows similar not unfounded accusations made against numerous later language activists of a prescriptive bent.

Toponymy continues to inspire numerous articles. Some are concerned with problems of form: A. Deshayes, 'Toponymie: du traitement du *gw-* lénifié au *v-* de composition', *Bull. de la Soc. Archéologique du Finistère*, 124:286–88. Id., 'Valeur de l'«élément» *Coati-* dans la toponymie finistérienne', *ib.*, 125:352–55 (in which the second syllable could be < *ti*, *hi-*, *di-* but where the whole is quite often < *cozty*); Id., 'La valeur du /f/ en toponymie', *ib.*, 125:356–57 (discussing the possible sources). Others are thematic: B. Tanguy, 'Les activités textiles dans la nomenclature toponymique en Basse-Bretagne', pp. 23–37 of J.-C. Cassard, *Bretagnes: art, négoce et sociéte de l'Antiquité à nos jours* — mélanges offerts au professeur Jean Tanguy, Brest, Fac. des Lettres V. Segalen, 1996, 518 pp. (20 terms discussed); Id, 'Marais, étangs et zones humides dans la nomenclature toponymique en Bretagne', pp. 31–50 of *Marais en Bretagne* (= *Kreiz*, 8) ed. G. Milin, Brest, CRBC/UBO, 1998, 212 pp. (53 terms); Id., 'De Budoc à Budogan ou de l'île Lavret à l'île des Ébihens et des origines de l'abbaye de Saint-Jacut', *Bull. de la Soc. Archéologique du Finistère*,

124:281–86, and Id., 'L'itinéraire religieux de saint Paul Aurélien en Léon', pp. 79–91 of *Actes du colloque international de, Saint-Pol-de-Léon*, Brest, CRBC, 1997, 123 pp., straddle the frontiers between toponymy and hagiography. G. Le Duc, 'Anthroponomastique: saint Gonéry et Alvandus', *Bull. de la Soc. Archéologique du Finistère*, 125:339–40, proposes correcting the second name to Alanus.

Middle and Pre-Modern Breton is scantily represented. P.-Y. Lambert, 'La source du poème moyen-breton des *Pemzec leuenez Maria*', *Bull. de la Soc. Archéologique du Finistère*, 124:290–303, gives a Middle French prose text which may have been the model. G. Le Menn, 'Une ancienne devinette bretonne . . . et une expression grossière (1706)', *ib.*, 125:344–47, provides a full analysis of a rediscovered fragment.

Oral literature is focussed on the collectors. *Œuvres de Luzel: Notes de voyage*, ed. F. Morvan, Rennes, Terre de Brume, Presses Universitaires de Rennes, 1997, 222 pp., reports *some* of his collecting missions. *Œuvres de F. Cadic* [1864–1929]: *Contes et légendes populaires de Bretagne*, ed. F. Postic, vol. 1 (1997), vol. 2 (1998), Rennes, Terre de Brume, Presses Universitaires de Rennes, 346, 332 pp., presents the life and work(s) of this neglected collector (pp. 19–120) and 68 tales of varying length. These are all in literary French versions and although the themes are intact, unfortunately no MSS or notes of oral originals seem to have been preserved.

Literature for popular consumption is dealt with in R. Calvez, 'Vie et mort du paysanisme : *Feiz ha Breiz* (1865–75)', *BrL*, 11:77–96, discussing the ideological and social context of the periodical with abundant illustrative extracts; and Id., '«Les Bretons parlent aux Bretons». Radio Quimerc'h: les débuts de la radio en breton', *BrL*, 11:97, describing the setting up of Breton broadcasting in 1946 and analysing its aims and themes. See also Broudic, *Combes . . .*, above.

The critical approach to literary literature is rather better served than usual. P. Rannou, *Inventaire d'un héritage: essai sur l'œuvre littéraire de Pierre-Jakez Hélias*, Ar Releg-Kerhuon, An Here, 1997, 131 pp., focusses essentially on the French writings, but throws light on much of the work in Breton, as many pieces, apart from the novels, were also published in Breton. Well-documented literary criticism praising and condemning different parts of the oeuvre, but highly critical throughout of Hélias' non-militant involvement with his language. A. Simon, *An Emsav lennegel brezhonek hag an danevelloù berr*, 'Barn', Mouladurioù Hor Yezh, 1998, 140 pp., is an excellent critical presentation of the development and themes of the Breton short story in the 20th century.

2. CORNISH

P. Payton, 'Cornish', Price, *Encyclopedia*, 99–103, provides a concise overall picture, covering both 'historical' and 'revived' Cornish. I. Wmffre, *Late Cornish*, München, Lincom Europa (Languages of the World/Materials 135), 73 pp., is a serious attempt at a synchronic sketch drawing attention to the numerous uncertainties and providing frequent references to comparable forms or situations in Breton and Welsh.

III. IRISH STUDIES

EARLY IRISH

POSTPONED

MODERN IRISH

POSTPONED

IV. SCOTTISH GAELIC STUDIES

By RICHARD A. V. COX, *Lecturer in Celtic, University of Aberdeen*

G. C. Ramchand, *Aspect and Predication: The Semantics of Argument Structure*, Oxford, Clarendon Press, 1997, ix + 250 pp., uses an analysis of Scottish Gaelic in developing an integrated theory of the relationship between the syntax and semantics of predication. Apart from some minor, non-critical, errors, *dh'iàrr* [*sic*] *e not* is oddly translated 'he got a pound', using the verb in a sense which is based upon an assumed outcome, and then contrasted with *bha e ag iarraidh not* 'he wanted a pound' to illustrate a proposed 'change of position/possession' in the object as a result of the action, concomitant with the change in aspect (pp. 47–49). A. Bosch, 'The syllable in Scottish Gaelic dialect studies', *SGS*, 18:1–22, in her summary of researchers' (generally incomplete) descriptions, concludes that syllable structure may not be identical in all dialects. K. Hind, 'The structure of epenthesis in Gaelic', *JCLin*, 5:91–119, applies articulatory phonology to the question of the description of epenthesis whereby a form *marbh* is conceived of as a 'heavy syllable' whose long vowel would be hidden had not /r/ and /v/ failed to 'co-ordinate'. E. P. Hamp, 'Easter Ross *iad-sa*', *SGS*, 18:188, explains /e:čəs/ in terms of a phonological correlation.

W. Gillies, 'Scottish Gaelic', Price, *Encyclopedia*, 417–22, provides a summary account of the history of the literary and spoken language to the present. M. Bangor-Jones, ' "Abounding with people of dyvers languages": the church and Gaelic in the presbytery of Caithness in the second half of the 17th c.', *Northern Studies*, 33:55–66, reveals how the presbytery of Caithness was aware of a significant Gaelic-speaking population, especially in Thurso, Halkirk, Reay, Latheron and Watten, although adequate provision of Gaelic-speaking ministers was not always made for them. A. Jennings, 'Iona and the Vikings: survival and continuity', *ib.*, 37–54, provides a lot of useful information in demonstrating the continuance of the Gaelic church during the time of Norse settlement of Scotland and Iceland, although a few of the links made, rest upon assumption rather than close argument. D. Broun, 'Gaelic literacy in eastern Scotland between 1124 and 1249', in Pryce, *Literacy*, 183–201, examines the evidence from manuscript sources for the survival of Gaelic *literati* within the context of a proliferating Anglo-French culture, noting a number of the orthographic clues present. B. T. Hudson, 'The language of the Scottish Chronicle and its European context', *SGS*, 18:57–73, is a detailed discussion of the identity and significance of Gaelic linguistic forms or their influence in this Latin text compiled from the mid 9th to the late 10th c. R. Ó Maolalaigh, 'Place names as a resource for the historical linguist', in Taylor, *Place-names*, 12–53, discusses the evidence for neuter gender, fossilised forms of the article (to which may be added the originally neuter form in *Beinn na Dùine*, Carloway Lewis), instances of archaic mutations (lenition and eclipsis) and the suffixes *-in* (∼ *-ie*) and *-ach*. S. Taylor, 'Generic-element variation, with special reference to eastern Scotland', *Nomina*, 20:5–22, argues that apparent variation in the forms of certain place names (e.g. *Inchfure* 1463 *Petfure* 1479) is due to the erstwhile existence of more than one name sharing a specific element in common; in some instances rarer generics are seen as having been replaced by commoner ones 'frequently helped along by phonological factors', although these factors are inadequately described. R. A. V. Cox, 'Onomastic luggage: variability in the onomastic landscape', *ib.*, 21:15–28, discusses the movement of place names at various levels mainly with Gaelic and Norse-derived examples from the west of Scotland. G. W. S. Barrow, 'The uses of place names and Scottish History: pointers and pitfalls', Taylor, *Place-names*, 54–74, plots a number of Gaelic, Pictish, Scots, and Anglian place name elements highlighting continuity in patterns of settlement and transhumance and a gradualness in the process of population change in the early history of eastern and southern Scotland. D. E. Meek, 'Place names and literature: evidence from the Gaelic ballads', *ib.*, 147–68, examines the various functions of place names in developing and authenticating tales in the ballad tradition. R. A. Rankin, 'Place names in the *Comhachag* and other similar poems', *SGS*, 18:111–30, studies the identity of places, many in Lochaber, and the meaning of their names cited in this long poem. C. Maclean, *The Isle of Mull: Place Names, Meanings and Stories*, Dumfries, Maclean Publications, 1997, 170 pp., gives no pronunciations but provides a useful, though unindexed, lexical corpus for its area. T. J. Gasque, 'Place names of Scottish Origin in South Dakota', *ICOS 19*, II, 127–32, is of limited interest but contains examples of commemorative (mostly personal) names. I. A. Fraser, 'Mountain, hill or moor? An examination of Gaelic *sliabh* in the place names of the Western Isles of Scotland', *ib.*, 119–26, discusses the geographical and semantic distribution of this element. R. A. V. Cox, 'Old Norse *berg* in Hebridean place nomenclature', *ib.*, 59–65, accounts for the various reflexes of this element in Gaelic and discusses the semantic context for its borrowing into Gaelic. P. Gammeltoft, 'Sowing the wind? Reaping the crop of *bólstaðr*', *Northern Studies*, 33:25–35, summarizes his views on the lexical significance of this generic element in 'greater Scandinavia' with passing reference to Scotland. D. P. Dorward, 'Scottish *mac* names', *ICOS 19*, III, 113–16, only scratches the surface of its subject and lacks linguistic precision. D. E. Thornton, 'Hey, Mac! The name *maccus*, tenth to fifteenth centuries', *Nomina*, 20:67–98, contains a number of Scottish references in an exploration of possible derivations of this personal name. A. Breeze, 'Common Gaelic *básaire* "executioner": Middle Scots *basare* "excutioner" ', *SGS*, 18:186–87, ponders the context for this suggested Gaelic loan-word in Scots.

K. Forsyth, *Language in Pictland* (Studia Hameliana, 2), Utrecht, de Keltische Draak, 1997, 48 pp., argues with some justification against there having been a non-Indo-European Pictish language and that the case for one as presented by the late Professor Kenneth Jackson is unfounded. K. Forsyth, 'Literacy in Pictland', Pryce, *Literacy*, 39–61, centres discussion (because of the complete lack of any surviving Pictish manuscripts) upon epigraphic evidence and, due to their numerical superiority, upon the ogam inscriptions; their significance however — the claim that 'some Pictish ogams can be fully interpreted without difficulty, many can be substantially interpreted' is unproven — is inconclusive. R. A. V. Cox, 'Modern Scottish Gaelic reflexes of two Pictish words: **pett* and **lannerc*', *Nomina*, 20:47–58, in exploring the etymologies of these words, underlines their significance in language contact terms and offers linguistic arguments against using *pit*-names as evidence for the Pictish language. T. Vennemann, 'Pre-Indo-European toponyms in central and western Europe: *bid-/bed-* and *pit*-names', *ICOS 19*, II, 359–63, contains unsupported conjecture equating the generic of *pit*-names to Semitic. P. Dunbavin, *Picts and Ancient Britons: An Exploration of Pictish Origins*, Long Eaton, Third Millennium Publishing, viii + 133 pp., claims to show but does not demonstrate that Pictish origins lie with Finno-Ugrian immigrants; its usefulness lies in the series of translated excerpts it contains from sources on the Picts. C. A. Hromnik, 'Nesa or Ness: what lies below the "Celtic" names of Scotland', *ICOS 19*, II, 199–210, is an equally flawed attempt to identify the origins of the Picts, this time linking them with the tinmen of Cornwall and with the Dravidian language. On the other hand, A. Wolf, 'Pictish matriliny reconsidered', *Innes Review*, 49.2:147–67, while acknowledging that the matter cannot be proven unambiguously either way, lays out a strong case against the likelihood that matrilineal succession was practised amongst the Picts.

L. Gowans, 'Sir Uallabh O Còrn: a Hebridean tale of Sir Gawain', *SGS*, 18:23–55, provides an edition of this prose tale from an unattributed 19th-c. MS. A. Loughran, 'Ceann dubh dìleas/ Cuir a chinn dìlis: a group of Irish and Scottish Gaelic songs', *ib.*, 75–88, discusses the relationship between Irish and Scottish versions of this song of possibly 17th-c. origin. C. Ó Baoill, 'Caismeachd Ailean nan

Sop: towards a definitive text', *ib.*, 89–110, provides a close commentary on this text and its metrics. D. Tratnik, 'Three poems from County Cork in praise of Bobbing John', *ib.*, 167–74, details a 'poetic correspondence' on the Jacobite Rising of 1715 under the leadership of John Erskine. †J. L. Campbell, 'Notes on Poems by Mac Mhaighstir Alasdair', *ib.*, 175–85. *Evan MacColl, The Lochfyneside Bard—Bard Loch Fin*, ed. J. Y. Murray, Furnace Argyll, Crùisgean, 33 pp., contains a brief note on the literary quality of 10 of some of the more well-known songs in this selection of the 19th-c. bard's Gaelic work, but a more extensive biographical commentary. *Màiri Mhòr nan Oran: Taghadh de a h-Orain le eachdraidh a beatha is notaichean*, ed. D. E. Meek, is a welcome revised and expanded edition of the 1977 title. *Moch is Anmoch: the Gaelic Poetry of Donald A. MacNeill and Other Colonsay Bards*, ed. A. M. Scouller, Isle of Colonsay, House of Lochar, 64 pp., contains six songs by the late Oronsay-born bard. The few comments in R. Macdonald's 'Some present-day trends in Gaelic writing in Scotland', *Studies in Scottish Literature*, 29, 1996:85–94, on literary trends leaves plenty of scope in this field of interest. Finally, here, *From Gaelic to Romantic: Ossianic Translations*, ed. F. Stafford and H. Gaskill, Studies in Comparative Literature, 15, Amsterdam–Atlanta, Rodopi, xiv + 264 pp., contains a wealth of essays on Macphersonic or Ossianic influences as well as D. S. Thomson, 'James Macpherson: the Gaelic dimension', pp. 17–26. More peripherally, *Scotlands*, 4.1, 1997, EUP, ii + 130 pp., contains 8 articles in particular on Macpherson and his relation to other Scottish writers.

A. Ross, ' "Harps of their owne sorte"? A reassessment of Pictish chordophone depictions', *CMCS*, 36:37–60, suggests that is impossible to assign the development of the *clàrsach* from a triangular-framed instrument model to any one country or culture and that early depictions of chordophones should be seen as Scotland's response to a range of influences similar to those found in other European societies. B. Hillers, 'Music from the otherworld', in *Procs* (Harvard), 14:58–75, looks at the function of music and its use as a communicative device in modem stories of the otherworld. J. MacKillop, *Dictionary of Celtic Mythology*, OUP, xxix + 402 pp., includes many common Gaelic and a number of specifically Scottish references. Concentration for sources is upon written texts (itself a delimiting factor), but arguably notable omissions may include *Donnán* (Columba and Ninian, for example, are present) and *Shony* (after Martin Martin). L. S. Sugg, 'Summary list of items 488 to 576 in the Carmichael–Watson collection', *SGS*, 18:131–65, describes 122 previously uncatalogued items, much on lore and some unpublished, in the papers of James Carmichael Watson, editor of vols 3 and 4 of *Carmina Gadelica*.

4

GERMANIC LANGUAGES

I. GERMAN STUDIES

LANGUAGE

By CHARLES V. J. RUSS, *Reader in the Department of Language and Linguistic Science, University of York*

1. GENERAL

SURVEYS, COLLECTIONS, BIBLIOGRAPHIES. J. West, Price, *Encyclopedia*, supplies a review of the diachronic, synchronic, and literary aspects of German (193–206) with an appendix on the Germanic languages (206–08). Some of the writings of one of the founders of Germanistik are now made available in: *Hermann Paul: Sprachtheorie, Sprachgeschichte, Philologie. Reden, Abhandlungen und Biographie*, ed. H. Henne and J. Kilian (RGL, 200), xix + 342 pp. This volume contains a diverse range of material. There are obituaries, letters, speeches, articles, reviews, and a full bibliography. The letters are presented with a transcribed page opposite a facsimile. Their orthography is interesting in that P. uses conventional capitals for nouns, while his correspondents, Braune and Sievers, use lower case letters. His speeches, 'Die Bedeutung der deutschen Philologie für das Leben der Gegenwart' (85–105) and 'Gedanken über das Universitätsstudium' (107–27), reflect the spirit of the times. More important for Germanists are his classic articles on lexicography, 'Über die Aufgaben der wissenschaftlichen Lexikographie mit besonderer Rücksicht auf das deutsche Wörterbuch' (131–69), on word formation, 'Über die Aufgaben der Wortbildungslehre' (171–92), and also 'Aufgabe und Methode der Geschichtswissenschaften' (193–250), and 'Über Sprachunterricht' (251–77). Two more controversial pieces are his 'Zur orthographischen Frage' (281–318), where he puts forward the view that there has to be agreement on the criteria for a spelling system before any reform can take place, and 'Gutachten Zu: Th. Siebs: "Deutsche Bühnenaussprache"' (319–21) which is severely critical. This is a fascinating volume which gives insight into some of P.'s views and makes accessible some of his important articles. Jacob Grimm's treatment of Swedish features in S. Sonderegger, 'Jacob Grimms Blick auf das Schwedische', *Fest. Härd*, 273–86.

The topic of pluricentricity of German is dealt with in *Sprache, Kultur, Nation / Language, Culture, Nation* (*NGS*, Texts and Monographs, 12), ed. C. V. J. Russ, ix + 117 pp., which contains the following articles: U. Ammon, 'Die Frage der Teutonismen in der deutschen Gegenwartssprache' (1–14); S. Barbour, 'Why is German a single language? Nationalism and language in German-speaking Europe' (15–25); R. Schrodt, 'Österreichisches Deutsch, Deutsch in Österreich' (26–56); V. Martin, 'Dialect, popular culture and national identity in Austria' (57–76); W. Haas, 'Diglossie im historischen Wandel oder: Schweizerdeutsch auf dem Weg zur eigenen Sprache?' (77–101), and C. V. J. Russ, 'Speech enclaves in Switzerland' (102–17). Also noted: U. Ammon, 'Plurinationalität oder Pluriarealität? Begriffliche und terminologische Präzisierungsvorschläge zur Plurizentrität des Deutschen — mit einem Ausblick auf ein Wörterbuchprojekt', *Fest. Wiesinger*, 313–22. The situation in Switzerland is given splendid treatment in F. Rash, *The German Language in Switzerland* (German Linguistic and Cultural Studies, 3), Berne, Lang, 321 pp. Austria features in a number of articles: J. Ebner, *Wie sagt man in Österreich? Wörterbuch des österreichischen Deutsch* (DT, 8), Mannheim, Dudenverlag, 382 pp.; Id., 'Austriazismen im Kontakt mit anderen Varietäten', *Fest. Wiesinger*, 323–34; Id., 'Die lexikografische Darstellung des österreichischen Deutsch — Bestandsaufnahme und Überlegungen zur weiteren Entwicklung', *Fest. Tatzreiter*, 49–64; R. Muhr, 'Sprache und Land. Die soziale und kuturelle Wirklichkeit Österreichs im Spiegel seiner Sprache', *ib.*, 143–55; P. Ernst, 'Friedrich Schlegels Überlegungen zu einem österreichischen Idiotikon', *Fest. Wiesinger*, 335–44. A culinary feast of Austrianisms is cooked up by E. Erbes, '"Essen und Trinken hält Leib und Seele zusammen"', *Fest. Härd*, 57–74. The fascinating subject of pronouns of address features in W. Besch, *Duzen, Siezen, Titulieren. Zur Anrede im Deutschen heute und gestern*, Göttingen, Vandenhoeck and Ruprecht, 2nd edn, 160 pp. B. focuses on recent developments, looking at the state of affairs before 1968, then subsequent changes, especially in academic circles. He also treats the system of pronouns of address in the GDR and then in a large number of everyday situations, ranging from addressing waitresses, members of religious communities, the army, the family, in firms, contact advertisements etc. There are four W's that determine the choice of pronoun: '*Wer* redet *wen* in *welcher* Situation *wie* an?'. After a short excursion into former customs of address in German and those of other countries there is a section on the difficulties that foreigners face. This chapter has contributions from people from India, Hungary and the Ukraine. B. sees *Du* advancing but *Sie* not dying out. In fact, new forms of address such as

Christian name + *Sie* and surname + *Du* are used in certain situations. This is an extremely readable volume with amusing illustrations, and although not conceived for linguists, it is well documented. M. Durrell, 'Zum Problem des sprachlichen Kontinuums im Deutschen', *ZGL*, 26:17–30, tackles the very difficult problem of colloquial varieties in German. German in contact with other languages shows many faces, as evidenced by: E. Skála, 'Versuch einer Definition des mitteleuropäischen Sprachbundes', *Fest. Wiesinger*, 675–84; M. Norberg, 'Sprachwandel vom Sorbischen zum Deutschen in der Niederlausitz: eine Fallstudie', *IJSL*, 120, 1996:9–27; T. S. Wicherkiewics, 'Ethnic revival of the German minority in Poland', *ib.*, 28–38; A. M. Ramer and M. Wolf, 'Yiddish origins: The Austro-Bavarian problem', *ib.*, 193–209; M. Townson, 'Red socks on the turn', *London Ger. St. VI*, 15–31; R. Quirk, 'Language and concepts of identity', *ib.*, 1–13; G. Kaufmann, **Varietätendynamik in Sprachkontaktsituationen: Attitüden und Sprachverhalten rußlanddeutscher Mennoniten in Mexiko und den USA* (VarioLingua, 3), Frankfurt, Lang, 1997, xx + 369 pp.; Z. Masarík, 'Zum tschechisch-deutschen/österreichischen Sprachkontakt (dargestellt am Beispiel Südmähren-Niederösterreich)', *Fest. Tatzreiter*, 133–41; W. Schabus, 'Konfession und Sprache in südamerikanischen Kolonisationsgebieten mit österreichischem Anteil', *ib.*, 249–80. Also noted: U. Ammon, **Ist Deutsch noch internationale Wissenschaftssprache? Englisch auch für die Lehre an den deutschsprachigen Hochschulen*, Berlin, De Gruyter, xvi + 339 pp.; W. Schneider, **Dem Kaiser sein Bart: Deutschstunde mit 33 neuen Fragezeichen*, Zürich, NZZ, 120 pp.; U. Röding-Lange, **Bezeichnungen für 'Deutschland' in der Zeit der 'Wende': dargestellt an ausgewählten westdeutschen Printmedien* (WBDP, 19), 1997, 353 pp.; W. Dieckmann, 'Sprachliche Ausdrucksformen wissenschaftlicher Autorität', *ZGL*, 25:177–94.

INTERDISCIPLINES. Computer applications are: Y. Duttrich, **Computeranwendungen und sprachlicher Kontext: zu den Wechselwirkungen zwischen normaler und formaler Sprache bei Einsatz und Entwicklung von Software* (EH, XLI, 27), 1997, 266 pp., and **Computerunterstütztes Deutschlernen von Ausländern für die Berufs- und Arbeitswelt — eine Materialsammlung*, ed. G. Kühn, Bielefeld, Bertelsmann, 268 pp. Translation in many forms features in the following: H. Risku, **Translatorische Kompetenz: kognitive Grundlagen des Übersetzens als Expertentätigkeit* (Studien zur Translation, 5), Tübingen, Stauffenburg, 294 pp.; **Übersetzung als kutureller Prozeß: Rezeption, Projektion und Konstruktion des Fremden*, ed. B. Hammerschmid and H. Krapoth (Göttinger Beiträge zur internationalen Übersetzungsforschung, 16), Berlin, Erich Schmidt, viii + 324 pp.; **Fremdsprachendidaktik in Übersetzungswissenschaft: Beiträge zum 1. verbal-workshop, Dezember 1994*, ed.

M. Stegu and R. de Cillia (Sprache im Kontext, 1), Frankfurt, Lang, 358 pp.; J. Albrecht, *Literarische Übersetzung: Geschichte — Theorie — kulturelle Wirkung*, Darmstadt, Wissenschaftliche Buchgesellschaft, 363 pp.; and M. Siegel, *Die maschinelle Übersetzung aufgabenorientierter japanischer-deutscher Dialoge: Lösungen für translation mismatches*, Berlin, Logos Vlg, 1997, 194 pp. Items on the media are: B. Wegenstein, *Die Darstellung von Aids in den Medien: semio-linguistische Analyse und Interpretation* (Dissertationen der Universität Wien, 42), Vienna, WUV-Universtitätsverlag, 402 pp.; and C. di Meola, 'Schlagzeilen in Presse und Werbung', DSp, 26:218–39. Politics features in: S. Elspass, *Phraseologie in der politischen Rede: Untersuchungen zur Verwendung von Phraseologismen, phraseologischen Modifikationen und Verstößen gegen die phraseologische Norm in ausgewählten Bundestagsdebatten*, Opladen, Westdeutscher Vlg, 319 pp.; G. Wolf, *Parteipolitische Konflikte: Geschichte, Struktur und Dynamik einer Spielart der politischen Kommunikation* (Beiträge zur Dialogforschung, 18), Tübingen, Niemeyer, vi + 315 pp.; and K. Watzin, *Politiker im 'Spiegel'-Gespräch: ein Beitrag zur Entwicklung der politischen Sprache in der Bundesrepublik Deutschland* (RBDSL, 67), 220 pp. A large number of items deal with the teaching and acquisition of German as a second language: *Kulturkontraste im universitären Fremdsprachenunterricht*, ed. W. Börner and K. Vogel (Fremdsprachen in Lehre und Forschung, 20), Bochum, AKS-Vlg, 1997, xii + 230 pp.; M. Ott, *Deutsch als Zweitsprache: Aspekte des Wortschatzerwerbs. Eine empirische Längsschnittuntersuchung zum Zweitspracherwerb* (TVS, 27), 1997, 388 pp.; R. Weinert, 'Discourse organisation in the spoken language of L2 learners of German', LBer, 176:459–88; *Die Diagnose des frühen Fremdspracherwerbs*, ed. R. Zangl et al. (TBL, 441), viii + 72 pp.; M. Zanovello-Müller, *L'apprendimento del tedesco in emigrazione: attegiamenti linguistici di persone italiene in Svizzera*, Berne, Lang, 334 pp.; *Speech processing: selected topics from the Czech-German workshops*, ed. H. H. Wodarz (Forum Phoneticum, 63), Frankfurt, Hector, 1997, x + 154 pp.; *Eine zweite Sprache lernen: empirische Untersuchungen zum Zweitspracherwerb*, ed. H. Wegener (TBL, A, Language Development, 24), xi + 281 pp.; K.V. Sánchez, 'Diglossische Prozesse (zwischen Deutsch und Spanisch) unter den spanischen Emigranten der 2. Generation in Deutschland: eine soziolinguistische Studie', IRAL, 36:197–212; and T. Parodi, *Der Erwerb funktionaler Kategorien im Deutschen: eine Untersuchung zum bilingualen Erstspracherwerb und zum Zweitspracherwerb* (TBL, A, Language Development, 22), 220 pp. Items noted on different aspects of children's language are: *Dortmunder Korpus der spontanen Kindersprache*, ed. K. R. Wagner and R. Schulz (Kindersprache, 14), Essen, Die Blaue Eule, 1997, xiii + 215 pp.; A. E. Olah, *Neurolinguistische Aspekte der dysgrammatischen Sprachstörung bei Kindern* (TBL, A, Language Development, 23), x + 286 pp.; H. Pishwa, *Kognitive Ökonomie im Zweitspracherwerb* (TBL, 437), 374 pp.; and S. Döpke, 'Competing language structures: the acquisition of verb placement by bilingual German–English children', *Journal of Child Language*, 25 : 555–84. Technical language contributions are: D. Heller, *Wörter und Sachen: Grundlagen einer Historiographie der Fachsprachenforschung* (FF, 43), 229 pp.; A. Gardt, 'Sprachtheoretische Grundlagen und Tendenzen der Fachsprachenforschung', *ZGL*, 26 : 31–66; and N. Janich, *Fachliche Information und inszenierte Wissenschaft: Fachlichkeitskonzepte in der Wirtschaftswerbung* (FF, 48), 336 pp.

Also noted: *Sprachandrogik*, ed. D. Eggers (Forum Angewandte Linguistik, 31), Frankfurt, Lang, 165 pp.; *Beeinträchtigungen des Mediums Sprache: aktuelle Untersuchungen in der Neurolinguistik*, ed. M. Hielscher et al. (StLi), 247 pp.; and E. Terhardt, *Akustische Kommunikation: Grundlage mit Hörbeispielen*, Berlin, Springer, xii + 505 pp.

GENERAL LINGUISTICS, PRAGMATICS, AND TEXTLINGUISTICS. General linguistic works are: *Sprache und Sprachen: Fachsystematik der Allgemeinen Sprachwissenschaft und Sprachsystematik*, ed. C.-P. Herbermann et al., Wiesbaden, Harrassowitz, 1997, xv + 630 pp.; G. Schunk, *Studienbuch zur Einführung in die deutsche Sprachwissenschaft — vom Laut zum Wort*, Würzburg, Königshausen & Neumann, 1997, 178 pp.; P. Ernst, 'Zum Systemcharakter von Sprache', *Fest. Birkhahn*, 81–98; H. Wegener, 'Zurück zur Sprache! Noch ein Beitrag zur Strukturdebatte', *DaF*, 35 : 72–73; H. Löffler, 'Traumfabrik Sprache oder linguistische "Traumdeutereien"', *Fest. Geith*, 317–24; *Intention — Bedeutung — Kommunikation: kognitive und handlungstheoretische Grundlagen der Sprachtheorie*, ed. G. Preyer et al., Opladen, Westdeutscher Vlg, 1997, 407 pp.; F. Liedtke, *Grammatik der Illokution: über Sprechhandlungen und ihre Realisierungsformen im Deutschen* (TBL, 436), 288 pp.; K.-Å. Forsgren, 'Evolution, Revolution oder Re-Evolution? Gedanken zur Entwicklung der Sprachwissenschaft', *Fest. Härd*, 75–83; H. Nikula, 'Das Ästhetische als Begriff der Linguistik', *ib.*, 211–21; W. Abraham, *Linguistik der uneigentlichen Rede: linguistische Analysen an den Rändern der Sprache* (StLi), 360 pp.; B. Lehmann, *Rot ist nicht 'rot' ist nicht (rot): eine Bilanz und Neuinterpretation der linguistischen Relativitätstheorie* (TBL, 341), 377 pp. Sociolinguistic items are: *Unterdrückte Sprachen: Sprachverbote und das Recht auf Gebrauch der Minderheitensprachen*, ed. K. Bott-Bodenhausen, Frankfurt, Lang, 1996, 215 pp.; A. Linke, 'Sprache, Gesellschaft und Geschichte. Überlegungen zur symbolischen Funktion kommunikativer Praktiken der Distanz', *ZGL*, 26 : 135–54; and S. Augenstein, *Funktionen von Jugendsprache: Studien zu verschiedenen Gesprächstypen des Dialogs Jugendlicher mit Erwachsenen* (RGL, 192), xi + 288 pp. Conversational and discourse studies of the spoken language include: *Neuere Entwicklungen in der Gesprächsforschung: Vorträge der 3. Arbeitstagung des Pragmatischen Kolloquiums Freiburg*, ed. A. Brock and M. Hartung (ScO, 108), 288 pp.; M. Selting et al., 'Gesprächsanalytisches Transkriptionssystem (GAT)', *LBer*, 173:91–122; S. Roman and A. Schwarz, 'How to do funny things with words', *Fest. Geith*, 325–43; B. Andersson, 'Ist ein "Muh" ein relevantes Argument? Überlegungen zur Argumentation aus der Werbung', *Fest. Härd*, 17–32; I. Thonhauser-Jursnick, **Tourismus-Diskurse: Locus amoenus und Abenteuer als Textmuster der Werbung, der Trivial- und Hochliteratur* (EH, 1, 1636), 1997, 279 pp.; H. Kotthoff, **Spaß verstehen: zur Frage von konversationellem Humor* (RGL, 196), xiii + 402 pp.; B. Stitz and C. Walther, **Zur formalen Textanalyse von Verbatimprotokollen eßgestörter Patientinnen: eine vergleichende Untersuchung* (Reihe klinische Psycholinguistik), Frankfurt, VAS, 227 pp.; L. Hoffmann, Paranthesen', *LBer*, 175:299–328; R. Forster, **Mündliche Kommunikation in Deutsch als Fremdsprache: Gespräch und Rede* (Sprechen und Verstehen, 12), St. Ingbert, Röhrig, 1997, 426 pp.; and W. Haas, 'Über die Entstehung von Sprachnormen im Gespräch', *Fest. Wiesinger*, 285–96.

Text linguistic studies are numerous and include: T. Schröder, 'Textstrukturen aus integrativer Sicht. Eine kritische Bestandsaufnahme zur Textstrukturendiskussion', *DSp*, 26:121–37; A.-K. Gramberg, 'Diskursanalyse deutscher und nordamerikanischer Automobilwerbeanzeigen', *ib.*, 174–89; B. Ahrenholz, **Modalität und Diskurs: Instruktionen auf deutsch und italienisch: eine Untersuchung zum Zweitspracherwerb und zur Textlinguistik* (StLi), 266 pp.; K.-E. Sommerfeldt, **Textsorten in der Regionalpresse: Bemerkungen zu ihrer Gestaltung und Entwicklung* (SST, 25), 168 pp.; K. Mudersbach, **Die juristische Vorschrift als holistischer Text* (Speyerer Forschungsberichte, 161), 1996, xxiv + 298 pp.; C. Schwender, **Wie benutze ich den Fernsprecher? die Anleitung zum Telefonieren im Berliner Telefonbuch 1881–1996–7* (Technical Writing, 4), Frankfurt, Lang, 1997, xii + 341 pp.; **Textsorten und Textsortentradition*, ed. F. Simmler (BSG, 5), 1997, viii + 343 pp.; P. Sieber, **Parlando in Texten: zur Veränderung kommunikativer Grundmuster in der Schriftlichkeit* (RGL, 191), vii + 284 pp.; G. Klingenberg, **Das Verarbeiten von Texten bei Aphasie: Untersuchungen zur modalitätsspezifischen Verarbeitung narrativer Texte* (Mentale Sprachverarbeitung, 4), Freiburg, Hochschulverlag, 1997, 220 pp.; C. P. Meister, 'Das XIX. Kapitel in Thomas Manns Erzählung *Das Gesetz*. Intertextualität als lexikalisch-phraseologische Analyse von Ironie', *Fest. Härd*, 239–51; A. Sabban, **Okkasionelle Variationen sprachlicher Schematismen: eine Analyse französischer und deutscher Presse- und Werbetexte* (Romanica Monacensia, 53), Tübingen, Narr, 392 pp.; **Die Sprache des Migrationsdiskurses: das Reden über 'Ausländer' in Medien, Politik und Alltag*, ed. M. Jung et al., Opladen, Westdeutscher Vlg, 1997, 405 pp.; K.-E. Sommerfeldt, **Gestern so und heute anders: sprachliche Felder und Textsorten in der Presse*, Munich, Iudicium, 1997, 171 pp.; and T. Zimmermann, **Mehrfachadressierung*,

Handlung und Konflikt: dargestellt am Beispiel der Asylrechtdebatte vom 26. Mai 1993 (EH, 1, 1656), 568 pp.

2. HISTORY OF THE LANGUAGE

Probleme der Textauswahl für einen elektronischen Thesaurus. Beiträge zur historischen deutschen Wortforschung 1. und 2. November 1996, ed. R. Bergmann, Stuttgart, Hirzel, 174 pp., contains detailed reports on various text corpora which can be used for the history of German. The use of electronic corpora makes possible a much more detailed study of individual changes. The range of vocabulary covered is large, from general language to specialist and technical language. The volume contains the following: M. Schlaefer, 'Vorarbeiten zum Göttinger Akademiethesaurus' (17–21); H-J. Solms and K-P. Wegera, 'Das Bonner Frühneuhochdeutsch-Korpus. Rückblick und Perspektiven' (22–39); U. Götz, 'Zum Korpus des Bamberg-Rostocker Gemeinschaftsprojekts "Die Entwicklung der Großschreibung im Deutschen von 1500–1700"' (40–48); M. Wermcke, 'Vorüberlegungen zum Aufbau elektronischer Textkorpora in der Dudenredaktion' (49–56); H. Kemper, 'Das Korpus des Deutschen Fremdwörterbuchs' (57–68); U. Haß-Zumkehr, 'Das Historische Korpus des Instituts für deutsche Sprache' (69–80); W. Bauer, 'Historische Quellen des WBÖ zu den bairisch-österreichischen Sprachvarietäten des 14.–19. Jahrhunderts' (81–103); P. Ott, 'Möglichkeiten eines schweizerischen Corpusteils (aus der Sicht des Schweizerdeutschen Wörterbuchs)' (104–12); R. Ris, 'Der schweizerische Anteil in den deutschen Großwörterbüchern' (113–26); K. Jakob, 'Techniksprachliche Quellen des 17. bis 19. Jahrhunderts' (127–34); G. Wagenitz, 'Fachsprache und Textarten in der Biologie' (135–44); H. Henne, 'Ein deutscher Thesaurus und die deutschen Wörterbücher des 17. und 18. Jahrhunderts' (145–49), and P.O. Müller, 'Wörterbücher als Thesaurusquellen: Möglichkeiten — Probleme — Grenzen' (150–74).

Germanic is represented by L. Hermodsson, 'Fragen der Völkerwanderung', *Fest. Härd*, 99–112; K-H. Mottausch, 'Die reduplizierenden Verben im Nord- und Westgermanischen: Versuch eines Raum-Zeitmodells', *NOWELE*, 33:43–91, and A. Bammesberger, 'Runic Frisian *weladu* and further West Germanic nominal forms', *ib.*, 121–32. Gothic features in K. Shields, Jr., 'The Gothic genitive plural in -*ê* revisited', *AJGLL*, 9, 1997:239–49; H. Schmeja, 'Gotisch *bilaif*', *BGDSL*, 120:355–67; P.W. Brosman, Jr., 'The Gothic *tu*-abstracts', *FLinHist* 18, 1992:25–37, and S. K. Sen, 'Sanskrit cognates of Gothic *fisks*', *NOWELE*, 33:155–56. Some items on Old Frisian include: R. N. Smith, 'Aspects of the graphonomy of Old Frisian',

ABÄG, 49:257–84; R. D. Fulk, 'The chronology of Anglo-Frisian sound changes', *ib.*, 139–54, and D. Boutkan, 'On labial mutation and breaking in Old Frisian', *ib.*, 77–88. Old Low German is represented by L.-E. Ahlsson, 'Altniederdeutsche Präpositionen aus wortgeographischer Sicht', *Fest. Härd*, 11–15. Old High German features R. Grosse, 'Nomination im Althochdeutschen', *Fest. Fleischer*, 15–21; A. and E. Dittmer, **Studien zur Wortstellung — Satzgliedstellung in der althochdeutschen Tatianübersetzung*, ed. M. Flöer and J. Klempt (SA, 34), 264 pp.; H.-W. Eroms, 'Verbale Paarigkeit im Althochdeutschen und das "Tempussystem"im Isidor', *ZDA*, 126, 1997:1–31; R. Bergmann and U. Götz, 'Altbairisch = Altalemannisch? Zur Auswertung der ältesten Glossenüberlieferung', *Fest. Wiesinger*, 445–61. Grosse, *Wörterbücher*, contains articles on the determination of meaning in OHG and the use of computer technology: I. Koppe, 'Das Fortleben des althochdeutschen Wortschatzes im Neuhochdeutschen und die Bedeutungsermittlung im Althochdeutschen Wörterbuch' (557–64); B. Meinecke, 'Über die Verfahren der Bedeutungsermittlung am volksprachigen Wortschatz der Leges' (65–72); K. Landwehr, 'Über den volkssprachigen Wortschatz der Leges' (73–76), and A. Mikeleitis-Winter, 'Die Nutzung der EDV am Althochdeutschen Wörterbuch' (255–58). The *Althochdeutsches Wörterbuch* continues on its way with volume 4, fasc. 15, *himil-hîuuiski*, cols 1077–156, 1997, and fasc. 16, *hîuuisclîh-holz*, cols 1157–220.

Items on Middle High German include: E. Glaser, 'Das Graphemsystem der Clara Hätzlerin im Kontext der Handschrift Heidelberg, Cpg. 677', *Fest. Wiesinger*, 479–94; R. Hildebrandt, 'Die Adjektive auf -*echt* im deutschen Wortschatz der Hildegard von Bingen', *ib.*, 495–501; W. Kleiber and R. Steffens, 'Das älteste bayerische Herzogsurbar von 1231–1234 als Quelle der mittelhochdeutschen Sprachgeschichte', *ib.*, 517–36; T. Klein, 'Vers und Syntax in frühmittelhochdeutscher Dichtung. Wege zur Datengewinnung und -auswertung', *ib.*, 537–68; F. Patocka, 'Zur Linksversetzung im Mittelhochdeutschen', *ib.*, 611–21, and A. Lötscher, 'Syntaktische Irregularitäten beim komplexen Satz im älteren Deutsch', *BGDSL*, 120:1–28. Lexicographical studies of MHG included in Grosse, *Wörterbücher* deal with explanation of meaning, choice of lemmata and use of computers: I. Lemberg, 'Möglichkeiten der Bedeutungserläuterung im Deutschen Rechtswörterbuch' (77–85); U. Schulze, 'Lemmatisierung und Bedeutungsbestimmung von Substantivkomposita im "Wörterbuch der mittelhochdeutschen Urkundensprache"' (87–93); P. Schmitt, 'Bemerkungen zur Bedeutungsbeschreibung im "Wörterbuch der mittelhochdeutschen Urkundensprache"' (95–115); E.-M. Lill, 'Die EDV — das Ende aller Verzettelung? Der

Einsatz der elektronischen Datenverarbeitung am Deutschen Rechtswörterbuch' (237–47), and U. Recker and P. Sappler, 'Aufbau des
maschinenlesbaren Text- und Belegarchivs für das Mittelhochdeutsche Wörterbuch' (249–53). Two items on Middle Low German:
L. Elmevik, 'Schwed. und norw. dial. koks(a) "Schale, Schöpfkelle"
u.ä. Ein mittelniederdeutsches Lehnwort oder ein Wort anderen
Ursprungs?', *Fest Härd*, 51–56, and G. Korlén, 'Eine mittelniederdeutsche Grammatik aus Uppsala', *ib.*, 145–55.

Early New High German features in: R. Möller, **Regionale
Schreibsprachen im überregionalen Schriftverkehr: Empfängerorientierung in den
Briefen des Kölner Rates im 15. Jahrhundert* (Rheinisches Archiv, 139),
Cologne, Böhlau, viii + 361 pp.; P. Jorgensen, 'Probleme in einem
ripuarischen Text des 15. Jahrhunderts mit der Beschreibung einer
Pilgerfahrt', *Fest. Tatzreiter*, 123–31.

C. Grolimund, *Die Briefe der Stadt Basel im 15. Jahrhundert. Ein
textlinguistischer Beitrag zur historischen Stadtsprache Basels* (BSDSL, 69),
1995, xi + 262 pp., is a rather wordy work which concentrates on the
pragmatic aspects of historical texts. After a detailed discussion of
text linguistics and the historical communication within Basel, G.
homes in on the the text type *Missive* produced by the Council. This
is a kind of letter which has a clear five-part structure. He examines
some of the contemporary instructions that exist for writing such
texts. They were mainly written to other towns, landed princes,
nobles and citizens. Their geographical range was mainly restricted,
although some are sent to Mainz and Frankfurt and even to France.
Most of the letters have the functions of appeal for something and
providing information. There are facsimiles of some letters but no
transcriptions. There is very little actual linguistic analysis but some
is provided when dealing with the formulae for the appeal function.
This lack is intentional and argued for but is, in my personal view,
disappointing. Even in these days of analysis of the organization of
texts some of us still want to see actual linguistic forms.

R. P. Ebert, *Verbstellungswandel bei Jugendlichen, Frauen und Männern im
16. Jahrhundert* (RGL, 190), vii + 188 pp., is an interesting work. E.
examines the word-order construction in subordinate clauses of an
infinitive/past participle and auxiliary verb. The development he
sketches is from *wie du hernach wirst sehen* to *sehen wirst*. He uses a large
range of texts from official administrative texts to private letters and
school books, and has a wide range of informants, both male and
female, young and not so young. There are social differences but they
are not easy to ascertain. Using a computer program, VARBRUL, he
is able to input a wide variety of variables such as stress of the word
before the construction, rhythmic structure of the group etc. and also
the usual socio-linguistic variables. The material is presented with a

plethora of tables. E. comes to the conclusion that the modern order, *sehen wirst*, starts in chancery documents, then is a variable in school, opposing a tendency for the older construction to occur in spoken language. At the end of the century, however, *sehen wirst* has virtually spread throughout all linguistic usage. This type of study is modish in the history of English and this volume is a good example of its successful application to a German situation. Also noted: O. Pausch, 'Italienisch-deutsche Aussprachregeln aus dem Quattrocento', *Fest. Birkhahn*, 132–38; G. Kolde, '*Es sol aber ein bischof unstraflichseyn/ nur äines weibes man.* Ansätze zur graphemischen Differenzierung von unbetontem Indefinitheitszeichen *ein* und betontem Numerale ain/ äin im Spätmittel- und Frühneuhochdeutschen?', *Fest. Geith*, 283–306; J. Korhonen, 'Zur lexikographischen Erfassung von Phrasemen und Sprichwörtern in Josua Maalers Wörterbuch (1561)', *ib.*, 569–84; R. L. Lanouette, 'The attributive genitive in Early New High German: A semantic analysis', *AJGLL*, 10:73–90; W. J. Jones, 'Germanic virginity or Teutonic virility? Attitudes to language among early German purists', *London Ger. St. VI*, 33–70; and I. T. Piirainen, 'Paarformeln in einem deutschen Rechtsbuch aus dem Jahre 1628', *Fest Fleischer*, 37–51. Luther's language features in: A. Lobenstein-Reichmann, **Freiheit bei Martin Luther: Lexikographische Textanalyse als Methode historischer Semantik* (SLG, 46), xiii + 598 pp.; H.U. Schmidt, 'Sprachlandschaften und Sprachausgleich in nachreformatorischer Zeit. Martin Luthers Bibelübersetzung in epigraphischen Zitaten des deutschen Sprachraums', *ZDL*, 45:1–41; W. Besch, '. . . *sein Licht (nicht) unter den Scheffel stellen*', *Fest. Wiesinger*, 463–77.

S. Bendel, *Werbeanzeigen von 1622–1798: Entstehung und Entwicklung einer Textsorte* (RGL, 193), x + 447 pp., is a pioneering work which tackles the development of the advertisement. This presupposes a capitalist environment and also newspapers. Because of restrictive practices many of the goods that we normally associate with advertising do not feature. In fact, books and printed matter are the mostly frequently advertised items. B. analyses the advertisements and produces a scheme to which they conform. Most of them come from newspapers in Switzerland, but there are quite a few from Hamburg and north Germany. Their language is analysed briefly, most useful being a list of *Fremdwörter* used. One of the most important things about the volume is the corpus of over 1450 advertisements B. has put together. H. Takada, *Grammatik und Sprachwirklichkeit von 1640–1700. Zur Rolle deutscher Grammatiker im schriftsprachlichen Ausgleichsprozeß* (RGL, 203), ix + 346 pp., is a wide-ranging work, trying to compare and match up the principles that are put forward by grammarians, particularly Schottel with the practice of linguistic revision of 23 different works. Foremost among these is the Lutheran

Bible. T. uses two extra corpora as well. Three areas are investigated, orthography, *Wortforschung*, which includes inflectional and derivational morphology, and *Wortfügung* which covers syntax. In every section the principles enunciated by the theoreticians are discussed followed by a good number of examples, often with tables and bar charts, which show the development over time. A careful study of the different phenomena will be richly repaid. There is a chapter on the changes in the different version of *Simplicissimus* but it seems not to be explict exactly how it fits into the main scheme of things. The main conclusion is that in orthography and syntax theoreticians and practice go mostly hand in hand, whereas in morphology the theoreticians are rather in advance. This book is a mine of information and very stimulating for anyone interested in the history of German.

A. Fleming-Wieczorek, *Die Briefe an Friedrich Justin Bertuch. Eine Studie zu kommunikativen, sprachlichen und sozialen Verhältnissen im klassichen Weimar* (Sprache & Kultur), Aachen, Shaker, 1996, 180 pp., examines the letters written, from a very wide circle of people, to B. between 1789 and 1798. The research is based on original sources in Weimar. It is a pity that no letter is reproduced to give a flavour of the language. F.-W. identifies features of the letters: whether the correspondents are known to each other in general, known to each other by letter, not known to each other but have been put in touch by a third party, or they do not know each other at all. These parameters influence the forms of address and greetings formulae. The big disappointment is that there are hardly any linguistic forms cited. F.-W. focuses on the communicative and social aspects but sadly neglects the linguistic, i.e. philological. The 18th c. is also represented by the following: G. Lerchner, 'Kommunikationsmaximen im Kontext des 18. Jahrhunderts. Zum sprachhistoriographischen Interesse an Knigges "Über den Umgang mit den Menschen"', *Fest. Wiesinger*, 585–92; C. V. J. Russ, 'Die Sprache von Schillers Mutter in ihren Briefen. Ein Beitrag zur Sprachgeschichte im Südwesten Deutschlands im späten 18. Jahrhundert', *ib.*, 643–50; Goethe features in: J. Mattausch, 'Freie Wortbildung(en) bei Goethe', *Fest Fleischer*, 43–51; Id., 'Wörterbuch und Poesiesprache. Dichterische Wortbedeutungen im Goethe-Wörterbuch', Grosse, *Wörterbücher*, 139–44, and R. Welter, 'Zwischen Bedeutung und Benutzer. Zur Mikrostruktur des Goethe-Wörterbuchs', *ib.*, 145–49. P. Roessler, **Die deutschen Grammatiken der zweiten Hälfte des 18. Jahrhunderts in Österreich: ein Beitrag zur Reform der der deutschen Schriftsprache* (Schriften zur deutschen Sprache in Österreich, 21), Frankfurt, Lang, 1997, 357 pp.; Id., 'Text, Satz, Druck. Prolegomena zu Auswahl und Sprachanalyse von Wiener Drucken des 17. und frühen 18. Jahrhunderts', *Fest.*

Wiesinger, 623–42; Id., 'Die Großschreibung in Wiener Drucken des
17. und frühen 18. Jahrhunderts', *Fest. Tatzreiter*, 205–38; C. Becker,
**Sprachkonzeptionen der deutschen Frühaufklärung: Wörterbuch und Untersu-
chung* (EH, 1, 1659), 422 pp.; M. Herrlich, **Organismuskonzept und
Sprachgeschichtsschreibung: die 'Geschichte der deutschen Sprache' von Jacob
Grimm* (Schriftenreihe Werke der Brüder Jacob und Wilhelm Grimm,
1), Hildesheim, Olms-Weidmann, 222 pp.

Items noted on the language of the Nazi period: C. Schmitz-
Berning, **Vokabular des Nationalsozialismus*, Berlin, De Gruyter,
xli + 710 pp.; and C. Sauer, **Der aufdringliche Text: Sprachpolitik und
NS-Ideologie in der 'Deutschen Zeitung in den Niederlanden'*, Wiesbaden,
DUV, 400 pp.

3.   Orthography

The authoritative source for spelling in Austria, *Österreichisches
Wörterbuch*, ed. O. Back et al., 38th edn, Vienna, *ÖBV* Pädagogischer
Vlg, 1997, 800 pp., has seen a mighty expansion in the number of
words covered. F. Kranz, *Eine Schifffahrt mit drei f. Positives zur
Rechtschreibreform*, Göttingen, Vandenhoeck & Ruprecht, 112 pp., is a
positive account of the new spelling reform. K. achieves this by posing
provocative questions and statements and then replying to them.
After an introductory chapter, showing among other things how
other countries have changed their spelling system, he deals with the
history of the spelling reform, authorities, consequences, and the
content of the spelling reform itself with a final chapter pointing to
the future. Many of the problems and concerns raised by people have
arisen from a wrong identification of spelling with language in
general. This is an extremely informative and cogently argued work
which has ample documentation.

The fact that the whole question of spelling reform has come of age
is evidenced by *Dokumente zur neueren Geschichte einer Reform der deutschen
Orthographie. Die Stuttgarter und Wiesbadener Empfehlungen*, ed. H. Strunk,
2 vols (Documenta Orthographica, Abt. B, 19. und 20. Jahrhundert,
10, 1), Hildesheim, Olms, xiv + 361, 391 pp. Here we have detailed
documentation of the two abortive attempts at spelling reform from
the 1950s. The Stuttgarter and Wiesbadener Empfehlungen both
have pre-histories, the former going back to an initiative of Franz
Thierfelder, the latter resulting from the concern of a Bremen
politician, Willy Dehnkamp. Each section consists of the reproduction
of a selection of minutes, letters and comments, most in facsimile
form, with an introduction, setting them in context. After the
documents there is a chronology of spelling reform from 1901 to
1970, and short biographical notices on the main players. The second

volume is devoted to the Wiesbadener Empfehlungen, focusing on Paul Grebe. Now that a new generation has found the courage to reform German spelling it is instructive to look back at these earlier attempts, which are set down in a systematic and helpful way.

An historical study is *Die Entwicklung der Großschreibung im Deutschen,* ed. R. Bergmann et al. (Germanische Bibliothek, 3, Untersuchungen, n.F., 29), 2 vols, Heidelberg, Winter, xvi + 522, xiv + 523–989 pp. This volume is the result of a major research project. 145 texts from all dialect areas except Switzerland are used. They represent theological, entertaining, and non-fiction texts. The parameters of the use of capitals are set up, comprising syntactic ones, e.g. sentence, clause initial etc., and lexical, e.g. noun, names etc. Each text is then examined and detailed statistics given in volume 1. In volume 2 each parameter is taken and the results for them presented. After that the development is compared to the pronouncements of grammarians. The 16th c. is crucial for the extension in the use of capitals. By 1700 they are used in over 90 per cent of cases as in modern German. The western part of Upper German is the slowest to adopt the new usage. The grammarians seem to have had little effect on usage which has been driven by the writers. However, although we can trace the extension in detail, the authors admit that they cannot answer the question why? This is a very detailed account which must be worked into the handbooks and considered in questions of spelling reform.

Another historical study is U. Riecke, *Studien zur Herausbildung der nhd. Orthographie. Die Markierung der Vokalquantitäten in deutschsprachigen Bibeldrucken des 16. - 18. Jahrhunderts* (Studien zur Geschichte der deutschen Sprache, 1), Heidelberg, Winter, 406 pp. R. tackles the subject of designation of vowel length. This is something which the recent spelling reform did not really tackle, much to the regret of the author. R. uses bible editions since this is one of the most widespread books. The editions come from six areas: Wittenberg/Leipzig/Halle, Lüneburg, Cologne, Nuremberg, Augsburg/Ulm, and Strasbourg. Both the use of doubling of vowel signs, use of *e* and *h,* as well as the doubling of consonants are examined in detail with respect to types and tokens. The analysis is presented in detailed tables and pie-charts as percentages of deviation from the modern standard. The results for the two groups of signs are different. The vowel signs are clearly driven by the East Central German localities. By 1700–50 over 90 per cent of long vowels are designated as in NHG. The use of double consonants is slightly different. Here by the same period there is a variation between 48 per cent for Cologne to 97 per cent for Strasbourg. By the end of the century, however, most centres have over 90 per cent. In all these developments the grammarians seem to have played no significant part. The study emphasizes the leading role of ECG centres in the 17th century. This is a careful study and an important one, if it is representative of the language as a whole. The volume is accompanied by a CD-ROM.

Also noted: H. Birkhahn, 'Grundsätzliches und Spezielles zu einer Rechtschreibreform des Deutschen', *Fest. Wiesinger*, 271–83; J. van Megen and A. Nejt, 'Niederländische und deutsche Orthographie im Vergleich', *DSp*, 26:193–217; F. Simmler, 'Zur Geschichte der direkten Rede und ihrer Interpungierungen in Romantraditionen vom 16. bis 20. Jahrhundert', *Fest. Wiesinger*, 651–74.

4. PHONOLOGY

Various items cover both phonetic and phonological studies: *Phonologie und Psychophysiologie*, ed. R. Foltin and W. Dressler (SÖAW, 649; Veröffentlichungen der Kommission für Linguistik und Kommunikationsforschung, 27), Vienna, Österr. Akad. der Wiss., 1997, 64 pp.; J. Fehr, *Redundanzminderung in der phonologischen Beschreibung* (StLi, 8), x + 122 pp.; J. Neppert, *Elemente einer akustischen Phonetik*, Hamburg, Buske, 340 pp.; I. Albrecht, 'Analyse phonetischer Schwierigkeiten und Konsequenzen für die Unterrichtspraxis (am Beispiel japanischer Deutschlerner)', *DaF* 35:31–36; A. Seddiki, 'Phonetik in der DaF-Lehrer-Ausbildung (an den Universitäten Algier und Oran', *ib.*, 158–61; K. Ehlich and G. Schnieders, 'Intonationsmischungen', *LBer*, 174:153–71; K. Classen et al., 'Stimmqualität und Wortbetonung im Deutschen', *ib.*, 202–45; T. A. Hall, 'A note on secondary stress in German prosodic morphology', *ib.*, 175:414–24; J. Geilfuß-Wolfgang, 'Über die optimale Position von *ge-*', *ib.*, 176:581–88; D. Recasens et al., 'An electropalatographic and acoustic study of temporal coarticulation for Catalan dark /l/ and German clear /l/', *Phonetica*, 55:53–79; G. Zimmermann, 'Die "singende" Sprechmelodie im Deutschen. Der metaphorische Gebrauch des Verbums "singen" vor dem Hintergrund sprachwissenschaftlicher Befunde', *ZGL*, 26:1–16, and Id., 'Phonetische Beobachtungen zum gezierten Sprachgebrauch in Deutsch und Englisch. Nach Zeugnissen der fiktionalen und biographischen Literatur', *ZDL*, 65:129–51.

5. MORPHOLOGY

Fest. Fleischer contains a plethora of articles on derivational morphology: I. Barz, 'Die Ökonomie des Lexikons. Zum Kompositumsverhalten von Synonymen' (265–76); P. Braun, 'Benennungsvorgänge

in Bekanntschaftsanzeigen' (407–13); D.O. Dobrovol'skij, 'Proto-
typentheoretische Ansätze bei der Beschreibung der Idiomatik'
(157–65); L. Draye, 'Nomination, Arealität und Etymologie, am
Beispiel von *pflanzen*' (67–69); L.M. Eichinger, 'Inszenierung auf
verschiedenen Ebenen. Die Verwendung komplexer Verben'
(361–74); J. Erben, 'Zum Problem der Nominationsvarianten,
Bemerkungen zu Bennennungsversuchen in Theaterkritiken Alfred
Kerrs' (399–406); U. Fix, 'Wortzuteilung, Wortverknappung, Wort-
verweigerung, Wortverbot. Die Rolle von Benennungen bei der
Steuerung des Diskurses' (345–59); H. Fleischer, 'Zu vereinigungs-
bedingten Referenzproblemen in der Benennungspraxis der Medien'
(117–32); R. Geier, ' "Das Wort ist eine geheimnisvolle, vieldeutige,
ambivalente, verräterische Erscheinung" (Vaclav Havel). Topoi und
Paraphrasen in politischen Texten' (415–24); G. Gréciano, 'Zur
Festigung von Phraseologie. Eine Merkmalsanalyse' (167–75); H-J.
Grimm, 'Konfixe: Beobachtungen in Tageszeitungen und in Wörter-
büchern' (277–84); W. Heinemann, 'Zu Nominationsproblemen im
Bereich der Verwaltungskommunikation' (441–57); G. Helbig,
' "Grenzgänger" und "Einzelgänger" in der Grammatik' (325–34);
M. W. Hellmann, 'Das "kommunistische Kürzel BRD". Zur Ge-
schichte des öffentlichen Umgangs mit den Bezeichnungen für die
beiden deutschen Staaten' (93–107); D. Herberg, 'Beitritt, Anschluß
oder was? Heteronominativität in Texten der Wendezeit' (109–16);
V. Hertel, 'Nomination dörflicher Rechte im Mittelalter und in der
Frühen Neuzeit' (23–36); C. Kessler, '*Länderkugel* und *die Schwelle im
Brot*. Nominationsstrategien bei Schulanfängern' (459–68); C. Knob-
loch, 'Über Possessivkomposita im Deutschen' (249–63); A. Krause,
and J. Sternkopf, 'Wege onymischer Identifikation' (229–47);
G. Lerchner, 'Nomination und Semiose. Zur Explikation ihrer
kulturell-kommunikativen Geprägtheit' (147–55); K-D. Ludwig,
'Neue Bennungen und Wörterbuch am Beispiel wende-typischer
Lexik' (135–44); G. Michel, 'Okkasionalismen und Textstruktur'
(337–44); H. Naumann, 'Ethnische Kennzeichnungen als Familiennamen: deutsch' (85–92); E. Piirainen, ' "Da kann man nur die
Hände in den Schoß legen." Zur Problematik der falschen Freunde
in niederländischen und deutschen Phraseologismen' (201–11);
H. Poethe, 'In Phraseologismen geronne Alltagserfahrungen mit
Sprache und Kommunikation' (177–90); P. Porsch, 'Phraseologismen
im interkulturellen Vergleich' (191–200); B. Schaeder, 'Wortbildung
und Orthographie: Getrennt- und Zusammenschreibung' (285–96);
A. Simecková, 'Das Reflexivpronomen als Wortbildungselement?'
(297–303); M. Schröder, 'Variation und Intention. Zu signifikanten
Wortbildungsphänomenen in Wörterbuchartikeln von Adelung,

Campe und Eberhard' (53–66); W. Seibicke, 'Alliteration in Personennamen. Annäherung an ein namenästhetisches Phänomen' (219–27); H. Wellmann, 'Transformation, Nomination, Kondensation und Projektion durch Wortbildung. Der Wenderoman in der Literaturkritik' (375–86); N.R. Wolf, 'Diminutive im Kontext' (387–97); G. Yos, 'Benennungen für Einstellungen bei der Redewiedergabe' (425–39). *Wortbildung. Theorie und Anwendung*, ed. A. Simecková-Vachková, Karolinum, Prague, 1997, contains the following articles: F. Danes, 'Zur Theorie und Praxis der Wortbildung' (18–23); L.M. Eichinger, 'Weltansicht in Wörtern. Vom Zweck und Nutzen verbaler Wortbildung' (24–41); W. Fleischer, 'Grundsatzfragen der Wortbildung aus germanistischer Sicht' (42–60); H. Wellmann, 'Die Lexikographie (und Analyse) der transparenten Verben im Deutschen' (61–78); I. Barz, 'Das Wörterbuch im Dienst der Wortbildungsforschung' (79–89); S. Höhne, 'Zur Typologie der Fachkeute. Das Begriffssystem in der Sprache des Finanzwesens' (96–107); M. Knapová, 'Einige Bemerkungen zur Anpassung der Wortbildungsstruktur deutscher Familiennamen in Böhmen' (108–10); S. Olsen, 'Über Präfix- und Partikelverbsysteme' (111–37); M. Schröder, 'Nominale Konversionsprodukte in Langenscheidts Großwörterbuch Deutsche als Fremdsprache' (138–46); A.Simecková, 'Zur Modifikationsfunktion des Präverbs im deutschen komplexen Verb (am Material der NACH- und VOR-Verben)' (147–54); F. Stícha, 'Implizitsmengen und -arten bei der Substantivkomposition' (155–62); M. Thurmair, 'Verbwortbildung und Verbklammer im Deutschen' (163–73); E. Uhrová and F. Uher, 'Deutsche und tschechische Verbalpräfixe vom vergleichenden Standpunkt aus' (174–80); M. Vachková, 'Zur Rolle von Wortbildungskenntnissen beim Studium der philosophischen Texte' (181–85).

Other items are: R. Bergmann, 'Autonomie und Isonomie der beiden Wortbildungssysteme im Deutschen', *Sprachwissenschaft* 23:167–83; G. Inghult, ' "Zwölf Goldmedaillen, zwölf silberne und zehn aus Bronze." Konstruktionen mit der Bedeutung "aus etwas bestehend" im heutigen Deutsch', *Fest. Härd*, 121–32; T. Lindner, 'Zur Geschichte und Funktion von Fugenelementen in Nominalkomposita am Beispiel des Deutschen', *Moderne Sprachen*, 42:1–10; A. Paslawske, 'Transparente Morphologie und Semantik eines deutschen Negationsaffixes', *LBer*, 175:353–85;

B. Mazke, 'Wohin mit *Gesinge, besänftigen, verarzten*? Einige grundsätzliche Bemerkungen zu Status und Abgrenzung der kombinatorischen Derivation', *DaF*, 35:24–27; V. Baskevic, 'Kombinierbarkeitsmodelle von Lexemen im Fremdsprachenunterricht', *ib.*, 28–30; A. Topalova, 'Wortbildungsparadigmen der deutschen und bulgarischen Internationalismen. Eine kontrastive Analyse', *ib.*, 154–57;

S. Vandermeeren, 'Semantik deutscher Substantivkomposita mit Verwandschaftsbezeichnungen, *DSp*, 26:240–55; C. Fraas, 'Interpretations- und Gebrauchsmuster abstrakter Nomina. Ein korpusbasierter Beschreibungsansatz', *ib.*, 256–72; F. Braun et al., 'Können Geophysiker Frauen sein? Generische Personenbezeichnungen im Deutschen', *ZGL*, 26:265–83; Inflectional morphology includes the following: L. Cahill and G.Gazdar, 'The inflectional phonology of German adjectives, determiners, and pronouns', *Linguistics*, 35–36, 1997, 211–46; K-M. Köpcke, 'The acquisition of plural marking in English and German revisited: schemata vs rules', *JCL*, 25:293–319.

6. SYNTAX

General works are: **Syntax des gesprochenen Deutsch*, ed. P. Schlobinski, Opladen, Westdeutscher Vlg, 1997, 283 pp.; E. Hentschel, **Negation und Interrogation: Studien zur Universalität ihrer Funktionen* (RGL, 195), vii + 249 pp.; J. D. Bobaljik, 'If the head fits. . . . on the morphological determination of German syntax', *Linguistics* 35–6, 1997:1029–55. J. Russ, *Teach Yourself German Grammar*, London, Hodder & Stoughton, viii + 248 pp., successfully combines a functional with a structural approach. Other items on grammar are: A. Kasjan, 'Deutschunterricht unter erschwerten Bedingungen: Grammatik als Risiko und Chance', *DaF* 35:168–71; P. Suchsland, 'Wege zum Minimalismus in der Grammatiktheorie. Entwicklungen in der generativen Grammatik (I)', *ib.*, 212–19; P. Rusch, 'Schritte zum Ausbau einer Lernergrammatik', *ib.*, 233–38;

Studies dealing with elements of noun phrases are: **Lexikalische und grammatische Eigenschaften präpositionaler Elemente*, ed. D. Haumann and S. Schierholz (LA, 371), 1997, xii + 206 pp.; U. Kohlmann, **Objektreferenzen in Beschreibungen und Instruktionen: eine empirische Untersuchung zum Zusammenhang von Textstruktur, referentieller Bewegung und Formen von Objektreferenzen* (EH, XXI, 187), 220 pp.; L. Molnárfi, **Kasus und Passivierung: ein Beitrag zur Kasustheorie* (EH, XXI, 189), 1997, 312 pp.; R. Vogel and M. Steinbach, 'The dative — an oblique case', *LBer*, 173:65–90; L. Molnárfi, 'Kasusstrukturalität und struktureller Kasus — zur Lage des Dativs im heutigen Deutsch', *ib.*, 176:535–80; D. Bittner, 'Entfaltung grammatischer Relationen im NP-Erwerb: Referenz', *FLin* 31:255–83; U. Brinkmann, **The Locative Alternation in German: Its Structure and Acquisition* (Language Acquisition and Disorders 15), Amsterdam, Benjamins, 1997, x + 289 pp.; G. Hens, 'Constructional semantics in German: The dative of inaction', *AJGLL*, 9, 1997:191–219. Items dealing with verb phrase elements are: S.Olsen, 'Prädikative Argumente syntaktischer und lexikalischer Köpfe — Zum Status der Partikelverben im Deutschen und Englischen', *FLin* 31:31–29; C. Terzan-Kopecky, 'Zu den Verbalkategorien Aspekt und Tempus', *DaF*, 35:17–23; V. Myrkin, 'Zur Konkurrenz zwischen Futur I und Präsens mit Zukunftsbezug. Antworten auf Fragen von Mayumi Itayami', *ib.*, 108–10; W. Feigs, 'Verbalkongruenz — ein universaler Sprachverarbeitungsprozeß', *ib.*, 220–26; M. Hennig, 'Tempus — gesprochene und geschriebene Welt?', *ib.*, 227–32; and E. Tomczyck-Popinska, 'Verbformen im authentischen und simulierten Alltagsgespräch', *KN*, 49, 1997:19–24. Word order features in M. Krifka, 'Scope inversion under the Rise-fall contour in German', *LI*, 29:75–112; G. Müller, *Incomplete Category Fronting: A Derivational Approach to Remnant Movement in German* (Studies in Natural Language Linguistic Theory, 42), Dordrecht, Kluwer, xvi + 339 pp.; W. Frey and K. Pittner, 'Zur Positionierung der Adverbiale im deutschen Mittelfeld', *LBer*, 176:489–534; Y-M. Park, *Zur Theorie der A-Bewegung: eine universalgrammatische Analyse von Topikalisierungsphänomenen* (LA, 380), viii + 193 pp. Also noted: B. Schwarz, 'Reduced conditionals in German: event quantification and definiteness', *Natural Language Semantics*, 6:271–301; G. Helbig, 'Satzarten — formaler oder funktionale Einheiten?', *DaF* 35:141–47; H. Bergerová, 'Zu Problemen der Nebensatzbeschreibung am Beispiel der Vergleichssätze', *ib.*, 148–53; F. Freund and B. Sundqvist, ' "Frohen Herzens und vollen Portemonnaies." Die F/S-Konstruktion', *Fest. Härd*, 85–97, and D. Büring and K. Hartmann, 'Assymetrische Koordination', *LBer*, 174:172–201.

DSp, 26, contains a number of items on syntax: G. Zifonun, 'Zur Grammatik von Subsumtion und Identität *Herr Schulz als erfahrener Lehrer* [. . .]' (1–17); P. Groth, 'Aspekte der Redundanz' (18–37); D. Clément, 'Wie frei sind die Adjunkte? Plädoyer für eine diffenzierte syntaktische Beschreibung der Adjunkte am Beispiel der durch *während* eingeleiteten Adverbialsätze im Deutschen' (38–62); L. Carlsen, 'Redewiedergabe mit redeeinleitendem *wie*-Satz' (63–89); A. Lötscher, 'Die textlinguistische Interpretation von Relativsätzen' (97–120); U. Brausse, 'Was ist Adversivität? *aber* oder *und*?' (138–59); A. Ogawe, 'Zur Syntax und Semantik von Partikelverben' (160–73); M. Ide, 'Die Formen des Infinitivsubjekts in der *lassen*-Konstruktion. Ihre kontextuelle Bedingungen' (273–89).

Historical studies include M. Kotin, *Die Herausbildung der grammatischen Kategorie des Genus verbi im Deutschen: eine historische Studie zu den Vorstufen und zur Entstehung des deutschen Passivs-Paradigmas* (BGS, 14), 190 pp.; G-J. Gang, *Passivsynonyme als Elemente der wissenschaftlichen Fachsprache im Deutschen. Untersucht am prominenten Fachtexten des 19. und*

20. Jahrhunderts aus den Bereichen der Geisteswissemschaften und der Natur-wisssenschaften (EH, XXI, 188), 1997, 169 pp.; K. Willems and J. van Pottelberge, **Geschichte und Systematik des adverbialen Dativs im Deutschen: eine funktional-linguistische Analyse des morphologischen Kasus* (SLG, 49), xii + 671 pp.

Contrastive studies are C. di Meola, **Der Ausdruck der Konzessivität in der deutschen Gegenwartssprache: Theorie und Beschreibung anhand eines Vergleichs mit dem Italienischen* (LA 372), 1997, viii + 339 pp.; H. Mirault, **La Syntaxe des propositions relatives: étude contrastive des différences structurales d'ordre syntaxique entre le français et l'allemand* (EH, XIII, 226), 1997, 268 pp.; O. Krause, 'Progressiv-Konstruktionen im Deutschen im Vergleich mit dem Niederländischen, Englischen und Italienischen', *STUF*, 50:48–82.

7. SEMANTICS

A major publication is *Wortfamilienwörterbuch der deutschen Gegenwarts-sprache*, ed. G. Augst et al., Tübingen: Niemeyer, xl + 1687 pp. This is a pioneering work, based on the *Handwörterbuch der deutschen Gegenwartssprache* (*YWMLS*, 46:644). There is a detailed introduction and instructions for using the dictionary before the main entries. These are alphabetical, but of the basic lexical item in the word family, after which all the other members are treated even though they do not follow alphabetically, thus for *Feind*, we have *Feindin, feindlich, Feindschaft, feindschaftlich*, then *anfeinden, Anfeindung, befeinden, verfeinden*. This is, of course, ideal for foreign learners and let us hope that a *Studienausgabe* could bring it within their reach. There are also entries for productive affixes. One very good thing about this dictionary is that families of foreign words have the same status as native words. This is not simply a mechanical word formation dictionary but gives full weight to semantic developments as well. All in all a volume which is a must for anyone interested in German.

General items include J. Müller, **Die semantische Gliederung zur Repräsentation des Bedeutungsinhalts innerhalb sprachverstehender Systeme* (Mensch — Maschine — Kommunikation), Munich, Utz, 1997, 162 pp.; M. Keil, **Wort für Wort: Repräsentation und Verarbeitung verbaler Phraseologismen (Phraseo-Lex)* (SI, 35), 1997, x + 253 pp.; K. von Heusinger, 'Antinomien. Zur Behandlung von semantischen Para-doxien, ihren Risiken, Nebenwirkungen und Unverträglichkeiten', *LBer*, 173:3–42; C. Di Meola, 'Zur Definition einer logisch-seman-tischen Kategorie: Konzessivität als "versteckte Kausalität"', *ib.*, 175:329–52; **Betrachtungen zum Wort: Lexik im Spannungsfeld von Syntax, Semantik und Pragmatik*, ed. E. Klein and S. J. Schierholz (StLi), xiii + 250 pp. Some specialist vocabularies feature **Petting statt*

Pershing: das Wörterbuch der Achtziger, ed. G. Fricke and F. Schäfer (Reclam Bibliothek, 1630), Leipzig, Reclam, 180 pp.; **Synonym-Wörterbuch: der treffende Ausdruck — das passende Wort*, ed. S. Kroeber and M. Spalier, Gütersloh, Bertlesmann Lexik, 1997, 711 pp.; **Das große Schimpfwörterbuch*, ed. H. Pfeiffer, Frankfurt, Eichborn, 556 pp. Lexicographical studies are: **Perspektiven der pädagogischen Lexikographie des Deutschen: Untersuchungen anhand von 'Langenscheidt Großwörterbuch Deutsch als Fremdsprache'*, ed. H. E. Wiegand (Lexicographica. Series maior, 86), Tübingen, Niemeyer, x + 405 pp. Contrastive items are B. H. Beile, **Gesangsbeschreibung in deutschen und englischen Musikkritiken: fachsprachenlinguistische Untersuchungen zum Wortschatz* (GASK, 34), 1997, xii + 337 pp.; R. Albert, 'Das bilinguale mentale Lexikon', *DaF*, 35:90–97; I. I. Suscinski, 'Zur Entwicklung eines Wörterbuchs der verstärkenden Wortverbindungen in der deutschen und der russischen Gegenwartssprache', *ib.*, 98–103, and A. Sapavalov et al., 'Interferenzen Deutsch-Russisch bei Internationalismen aus dem Bildungswesen', *ib.*, 239–42.

Borrowing features in A. Sons, 'Aneignung des Fremden. Entlehnungen aus dem Chinesischen', *ZGL*, 36:155–76.

Studies of individual words include: H. Birkhahn, 'Segel', *Fest. Tatzreiter*, 27–37; P. Dalcher, 'Der Huchen und seine Etymologien', *ib.*, 39–47; P. Ernst, 'Zur Herkunft der Wiener Redewendung "einen Karl haben" ', *ib.*, 89–98; D. Boutkan and M. Kossmann, 'Etymologische Betrachtungen zur Dialektgeographie von *Raupe*, *rups*', *ABÄG*, 50:5–11, and W. Meid, 'Eichenkundliches', *Fest. Birkhahn*, 107–14.

Also noted: M. Hornung, 'Rund um die Volksetymologie', *Fest. Tatzreiter*, 119–37; C. M. Blanco, 'Historische Entwicklung der deutschen Paarformeln mit somatischen Komponenten', *NMi*, 99:285–95, and F-J. Schaarschuh, 'Von deftiger und delikater, kannibaler und freundlicher Lexik', *DaF*, 35:111–14.

R. Majut. *Die hippologisch gebildeten Pflanzennamen im Deutschen und Englischen. Ein Beitrag zur vergleichenden Metaphorik*, ed. R. Frisch, Stuttgart, Hirzel, 341 pp. is a compendious dictionary of German and English plant names containing many references to horses, edited and published posthumously. The lemmata are ordered alphabetically, ignoring the words for horse. This is a lot more than a simple historical dictionary. Every name leads off into fascinating philological avenues. This a labour of the love of words, real 'philology' which is not often seen nowadays. There are lists of German, English and Latin words mentioned in the text. It will help to supplement information in other dictionaries.

Also on metaphor: B. Naumann, 'Language and earth: the use of metaphor in geology and linguistics', Debatin, *Metaphor*, 101–12.

8. DIALECTS

A general work is A. Huesmann, *Zwischen Dialekt und Standard. Empirische Untersuchung zur Soziolinguistik des Varietätenspektrums im Deutschen* (RGL, 199), vii + 287 pp., which uses a questionnaire to elicit information on the use of standard and dialect and on the nature of the standard in Germany. She uses informants from six small towns and six cities. The questionnaire is provided in an appendix with a statistical interpretation of the data. Over 2,000 informants were used, 62 per cent were women and 38 per cent men. 56 per cent were between 16 and 30, 35 per cent between 31 and 65 and 8 per cent between 66 and 95. Most had *Abitur*. Hypotheses were confirmed that dialect use was more prevalent in South Germany and in the countryside. Overall dialect competence is being lost, more quickly in the north from parents to children. The use of High German is stagnating. This is a very relevant book for the state of varieties of German in Germany. General questions are also treated in H. Löffler, 'Dialekt und regionale Identität. Neue Aufgaben für die Dialektforschung', *Fest. Wiesinger*, 71–85; K. J. Mattheier, 'Dialektsprechen in Deutschland. Überlegungen zu einem deutschen Dialektzensus', *ib.*, 95–104; N. Berend, **Sprachliche Anpassung: eine soziolinguistisch-dialektologische Untersuchung zum Rußlanddeutschen* (Studien zur deutschen Sprache — FIDS, 14), vii + 253 pp.

General lexicographical problems of dialect dictionaries are dealt with in Grosse, *Wörterbücher*, which contains: P. Ott, 'Wie kommt das Schweizerdeutsche Wörterbuch zu seinen Definitionen?' (21–25); W. Bauer, 'Möglichkeiten und Grenzen der Bedeutungsbeschreibung im Dialektwörterbuch' (27–33); A. R. Rowley, Bedeutungserfassung und Bedeutungsgliederung im neuen Bayerischen Wörterbuch' (35–40); A. Burri, 'Möglichkeiten der Wortfelderfassung im Schweizerdeutschen Wörterbuch' (107–27); B.-D. Insam, 'Zur Phraseologie im Bayerischen Wörterbuch' (117–28); W. Lösch, 'Phraseologismen im Thüringischen Wörterbuch' (129–37); J. Wiese, 'Zur Darstellung von Synonymengruppen im Brandenburg-Berlinischen Wörterbuch' (151–55); R. Mulch, 'Probleme der Synonymie in einem großlandschaftlichen Mundartenwörterbuch' (157–65); R. Goltz, 'Lebenswelt und Mündlichkeit' (167–75); S. Bingenheimer, 'Zur Strukturierung von Bedeutungen in den Wortartikeln des Pfälzischen Wörterbuches. Struktur der Bedeutung — Bedeutung der Struktur' (177–84); H. Weber, 'Wortkarte und Wortbedeutung' (183–93); and G. Kettmann, 'Das Mittelelbische Wörterbuch: Stationen seines Weges nach 1992' (199–208). The same volume also treats the use of computers in dialect lexicography: R. Post, 'Möglichkeiten der elektronischen Strukturierung, Vernetzung und Verfügbarmachung von lexikographischen Daten bei der Arbeit am Pfälzischen Wörterbuch' (211–20); E. Kühn, Intensive Nutzung der EDV im Bereich Verwaltung und Bearbeitung des Sprachdatenmaterials beim WBÖ' (221–32); T. Braun, 'Der Einsatz der EDV beim Preußischen Wörterbuch' (233–35); E. Fischer, '(Postscript) Zeichensätze — Möglichkeiten ihres Einsatzes für (Dialekt) Wörterbücher' (259–64), and G. W. Baur and F. Scheer, 'Vorzüge und Schwierigkeiten in der Nutzung des Computers bei der Arbeit am Badischen Wörterbuch' (265–71).

The *Bayerischer Sprachatlas. Sprachatlas von Bayerisch-Schwaben*, Heidelberg, Winter, continues with volume 5, *Lautgeographie* III, ed. W. König and S. Kuffer, xxxviii + 603 pp. This volume deals with the reflexes of MHG long vowels and diphthongs. An especially interesting section is that on the quantity of long vowels and diphthongs. Shortening before fortis obstruents occurs typically east of the Lech. In some instances reference is made to the *Formenband* and it is to be hoped that this will appear in due time. As with the other volumes this is an essential contribution to the study of variation in this region.

Also noted: **Wörterbuch der obersächsischen Mundarten*, 1, *A-F*, Berlin, Akademie, 712 pp.; B. Barden and B. Grosskopf, **Sprachliche Akkomodation und soziale Integration: sächsische Übersiedler und Übersiedlerrinnen im rhein-/moselfränkischen und alemannischen Sprachraum* (Phonai, 43), Tübingen, Niemeyer, xi + 404 pp.; J. Mlieck, **Samatimerisch: Phonetik, Grammatik, Lexikographie: Geschichte der Mundart der deutschen Gemeinde Sanktmartin am nördlichen Rand des rumänischen Banats* (Berkeley Models of Grammars, 3), Frankfurt, Lang, 1997, xii + 373 pp.

Low German items include J. Wirrer, 'Zum Status des Niederdeutschen', *ZGL*, 26:308–40; D. Stellmacher, 'Gelten für die Darstellung der niederdeutschen Sprachgeschichte eigene Prinzipien?', *BGDSL*, 120:368–75; P. Auer, 'Hamburger Phonologie', *ZDL*, 65:179–97; G. Rohdenburg, 'Zur Umfunktionierung von Kasusoppositionen für referentielle Unterscheidungen bei Pronomen und Substantiven im Nordniederdeutschen'. *ZDL*, 65:293–300; D. Stellmacher, 'Voraussetzungen für die soziolinguistische Erforschung des Saterfriesischen', *Fest. Wiesinger*, 161–66, and H. Böning, **Plattdeutsches Wörterbuch für das Oldenburger Land* (Oldenburger Forschungen, n.F., 7), 4th edn, Oldenburg, Isensee, 186 pp.

Central German features: J. Goossens, 'Schärfung und Diphthongierung von î, iu, û. Moselfränkisch-limburgische Parallelen', *Fest. Wiesinger*, 63–70; M. Pützer and W. J. Barry, 'Geographische und generationsspezifische Verbreitung saarländischer Dialekteigenschaften im germanophonen Lothringen (Frankreich)', *ZDL*, 65:152–78; H. Schönfeld, 'Fremde Mundart im Raum einer Großstadt. Pfälzer in Berlin', *Fest. Wiesinger*, 145–60, and G. Bellmann,

'Zur Passivperiphrase im Deutschen. Grammatikalisierung und Kontinuität', *ib.*, 241–69.

The unity of Upper German is the subject of E. Gabriel, 'Gibt es ein gemeinsames Oberdeutsch?', *Fest. Tatzreiter*, 99–118.

Alemannic features in the following: H. Christen, *Dialekt im Alltag. Eine empirische Untersuchung zur lokalen Komponente heutiger schweizerdeutscher Varietäten* (RGL, 201), xv + 365 pp. This is a pioneering work which aims to provide an empirical investigation of whether utterances in Swiss German dialects can be localized. The reference system used is the *Sprachatlas der deutschen Schweiz*. She uses three groups of informants, all students, born between 1963 and 1976, who represent particularly western Swiss dialects and those around Zürich. The data was elicited in interviews. The starting point for variables was R. Hotzenköcherle's list which is reduced to six phonological and five morphological ones. The role of frequency is examined with reference to verbal forms. The results, carefully presented and represented by many tables, were that speakers could for the most part be easily located even if there were some differences between their speech and the SDS data. There seems to be a convergence of forms at the phonological level but not at the morphological. L. Hofer, *Sprachwandel im städtischen Dialektrepertoire. Eine variationslinguistische Untersuchung am Beispiel des Baseldeutschen* (BSDSL, 72), xiii + 306 pp., is a very wide-ranging, well informed study which comprises a theoretical basis followed by an analysis of Basel data. The theoretical emphasis is on a multivariate statistical analysis of variables. The most important factor is age. The data is drawn from 44 informants, ranging in age from 11 to 62. H. uses a wide range of phonological and morphological variables such as derounding, verb endings etc. The phonological variables are changing in some cases towards larger regional forms, the verb endings towards those of Eastern Switzerland. There is also an analysis of connected speech and of attitudes. The archaic and conservative types of dialect are not in favour and adults have a more homogeneous approach to evaluating varieties. This is often not an easy book to read if you are not too familiar with statistical methods but it contains a mine of information. Other items on Alemannic include: P. Dalcher, 'Dialektologische Aspekte in den Arbeiten über Anglizismen in der deutschsprachigen Schweiz', *Fest. Wiesinger*, 47–62; R. Trüb, 'Wortgruppen im *Schweizerdeutschen Wörterbuch* und im *Sprachatlas der deutschen Schweiz*', *ib.*, 187–204, and M. Waibel, **Walser Weisheiten: Sprichwörter und Redensarten*, Frauenfeld, Huber, 160 pp.

Franconian is treated in A. Rowley, 'Das Präfix *ge-* des Partizip Präterit in den Mundarten des Bayreuther Umlandes — sprachgeographische Modelle', *Fest. Tatzreiter*, 239–48; N. R. Wolf, 'Zum verbalen "Präfix" *ge-* in Dialekten Unterfrankens', *ib.*, 337–45, and Id., 'Mundarträume in Unterfranken. Zugleich eine Überlegung zum Problem "Sprachraum"', *Fest. Wiesinger*, 205–21.

Numerous items on Bavarian include W. Bauer, 'Die Mundart des unteren Zillertales und Umgebung mit besonderer Berücksichtigung von Fügen', *Fest. Wiesinger*, 31–45; R. Reutner, 'Dialekt und Sprachspiel bei Nestroys Vorgängern und Zeitgenossen: Am Beispiel von Franz Xaver Gewy (1764–1819) und Friedrich Kaiser (1814–1874)', *ib.*, 105–24; H. Tatzreiter, 'Monophthongierung im binnenbairischen Mitterpinzgau (Land Salzburg)', *ib.*, 179–86; H. Altmann, 'Deiktische Lokal- und Direktionaladverbien in einem mittelbairischen Dialekt', *ZDL*, 65:257–79; F. Patocka, 'Beobachtungen zur Partikel halt im bairischen Dialektraum', *Fest. Tatzreiter*, 157–76; O. Pausch, 'Ein Gruß Max Mells vom Wallersee', *ib.*, 177–78; R. Reutner, 'Ein kleines Dialektwörterbuch, zusammengestellt aus Belegen in den gedruckten Volksstücken Friedrich Kaisers', *ib.*, 179–204; H. Scheuringer, 'Die Dialektgrenze Innviertel — Hauruckviertel. Über den langen Atem der Geschichte', *ib.*, 281–88; P. Wiesinger, 'Franz Tschischka (1786–1855), der vergessene Pionier der Dialektforschung in Niederösterreich', *ib.*, 315–35, and H. Weiss, 'Logik und Sprache: Der Fall der doppelten Negation im Bairischen', *LBer*, 175:386–413.

Speech islands feature in Z. Masarík, 'Bemerkungen zur mittelbairischen Enklave bei Olmütz', *Fest. Wiesinger*, 87–94; W. Schabus, 'Kontaktlinguistische Phänomene in österreichischen Siedlermundarten Südamerikas', *ib.*, 125–44; S. Zepic, 'Das Vokabular des Essekerischen', *ib.*, 223–38; R. Srámek, 'Zur Wortgeographie der deutschen Lehnwörter in den tschechischen Mundarten', *Fest. Tatzreiter*, 295–306; H. Tyroller, 'Die Abbildung der diachronen und dialektalen Sprachstufen des Italienischen in den Entlehnungen der Sprachinselmundarten im Ostalpenraum', *ib.*, 307–14, and A. Szulc, 'Nachträgliches zu Forschungsgeschichte und Lautlehre des Hochpreußischen', *Fest. Wiesinger*, 167–78.

9. ONOMASTICS

Fest. Fleischer contains the following items on names: W. Seibicke, 'Alliteration in Personennamen. Annäherung an ein namenästhetisches Phänomen' (219–27); H. Naumann, 'Ethnische Kennzeichnungen als Familiennamen: deutsch' (85–92); L. Ortner, 'Die

Benennung von Pflanzen: Deutsche Büchernamen zwischen wissenschaftlicher Nomenklatur und Volksnamen' (305–23); V. Hellfrizsch, 'Zu kirchlich motivierten Ortsnamen Sachsens' (71–83); and E. Eichler, 'Zum Eigennamen als Komplex von Subklassen' (213–17). *Fest. Wiesinger* also contains a number of items in this area: F. Debus, 'Name und Mythos. Elias Canetti als Beispiel' (347–61); E. Eichler, 'Österreich in der slavistischen Namenforschung' (363–70); A. Greule, 'Gewässernamenschichten in Nordostbayern' (371–78); W. Haubrichs, 'Romanen an Rhein und Mosel. Onomastische Reflexionen' (379–414); I. Reiffenstein, 'Ortsnamenforschung und Siedlungsgeschichte am Beispiel des oberen Ennstales' (415–34); and W.-A. Freiherr von Reitzenstein, 'Die *Wiesing*-Namen in Bayern' (435–41). Also noted: F. Eiselt, 'Sprachrelikte und Besonderheiten im mikrotopographischen Namengut des Gerichtsbezirks Hartberg', *Fest. Tatzreiter*, 65–88; J. Hanauer, **Die Flurnamen im Bereich der Marktgemeinde Eslarn*, Kallmünz, Lassleben, 1995, 207 pp.; J. Hodemacher, **Braunschweigs Straßen — ihre Namen und ihre Geschichte*, I, *Innenstadt*, Cremlingen, Elm-Vlg, 1995, 348 pp.; II, 1996, 320 pp.; **Eigennamen in der Fachkommunikation*, ed. R. Gläser (Leipziger Fachsprachen-Studien, 12), Frankfurt, Lang, 1996, 250 pp.; **Ortsnamenbuch des Landes Oberösterreich*, III: *Die Ortsnamen des politischen Bezirkes Schärding*, ed. P. Wiesinger and R. Reutner, Vienna, Vlg der Österr. Akad. der Wiss., 1994, xl + 211 pp., and E. Seidelmann, 'Die Namen der Wutach', *Fest. Tatzreiter*, 289–94.

The processes and results of language contact on names and name-giving is reflected in the contributions to *Onomastica Slavogermanica*, 23, ed. E. Eichler and H. Walther (Abhandlungen der sächsischen Akademie der Wissenschaften zu Leipzig. Philologisch-historische Klasse, 75, 2), Leipzig, Hirzel, 300 pp.: E. Eichler, 'Zu neueren Tendenzen und Zielen der Namenforschung im deutsch-slavischen Berührungsgebiet' (9–19); W.P. Schmid, 'Methodische Bemerkungen zur Klassifikation: Alteuropäisch' (21–28); R. Schützeichel, 'Siedlungsnamenbuch der ältesten Überlieferung. Kurzfassung' (29–32); F. Debus, 'Dichter über Namen und ihr Umgang mit ihnen' (33–59); R. Sramek, '*Acker*-, -*acker* in tschechischen Flurnamen in Mähren' (61–66); K. Rymut, 'Zur Erforschung der deutschen Einflüsse auf die Eigennamen in Polen' (67–68); A. Greule, 'Ortsnamenschichten in Nordostbayern' (69–76); J. Udolph, 'Deutsches und Slavisches in der Toponymie des nördlichen Niedersachsen. Die Ortsnamen des Antes Neuhaus, Kr. Lüneburg' (77–109); F. Reinhold, 'Betrachtungen zu Orts- und Flurnamen im "Thüringischen Wörterbuch"' (111–17); I. Bily, 'Slawische Vollnamen in Ortsnamen des ehemaligen Altsorbischen Sprachgebietes. Ein Beitrag zum slawischen onomastischen Atlas' (119–74); H. Walther, 'Die Landesnatur im weiteren Umfeld

Leipzigs zur Zeit des hochmittelalterlichen Landesausbaus im Spiegel der parallelen altsorbischen und mittelhochdeutschen Toponyme' (177–84); P. Zigo, 'Kategória casu v urbanomyii (Die Kategorie der Zeit in der Urbanomyie)' (185–94); K-H. Hengst, 'Zum Gebrauch der slawischen Ortsnamen im Mitteldeutschen bis zum 10. Jahrhundert' (195–200); V. Hellfritsch, 'Zu einigen Ortsnamen im (vor)erzgebirgisch-vogtländischen Raum. 1: Deutsche Ortsnamen auf -*itz*-. 11: Etymologisches' (201–09); S. Wauer, 'Die Problematik der Namenübertragung am Beispiel der Uckermark' (211–18); J. Dieckmann, 'Anmerkungen zu einigen Ortsnamen im Mecklenburgischen Urkundenbuch' (219–28); H. D. Pohl, 'Flurnamen slawischer Herkunft im Osttiroler Kalser Tal' (229–33); F. Freiherr Lochner von Hüttenbach. 'Bemerkungen zu den Ortsnamen *Weiz* und *Pikeroi*' (235–38); B. Czopek and J. Duma, 'Zum Verhältnis von Orts- und Gewässernamen im Gebiet von Stettin' (239–52); J. Duma, 'Polnische sprachwissenschaftliche Arbeiten zu Hinterpommern. Abriß der Problematik' (253–57); W. Wenzel, 'Herkunft, Bildung und Bedeutung der häufigsten polnischen Familiennamen. Ein Beitrag zur deutschen Personennamenforschung' (259–67); A. Greule, 'Zum Verhältnis von Historischem Ortsnamenbuch und Historischem Ortslexikon' (269–77), and M. Harvalík, 'Vyuzití dialektologie pri zkoumáni pomístních jmen (Zu den Beziehungen zwischen Onomastik und Dialektologie am Material der Flurnamen Böhmens)' (287–91). Also noted: K. Kunze, '*Pape* und *Pfeifer*. Zur Lautverschiebung in Familiennamen', *Fest. Geith*, 307–16; H. Christen, 'Die Mutti oder das Mutti, die Rita oder das Rita? Über Besonderheiten der Genuszuweisung bei Personen- und Verwandtschaftsnamen in schweizerdeutschen Dialekten', *ib.*, 267–81.

MEDIEVAL LITERATURE

By DAVID A. WELLS, *Professor of German at Birkbeck College, University of London*

I. GENERAL

Horst Brunner, *Geschichte der deutschen Literatur des Mittelalters im Überblick* (UB, 9485), 1997, 389 pp., attempts a concentrated survey history of the whole period in a single volume. To avoid a mere list of names and works — even though in some areas the effect is not much more — B. focuses on major works and genres, the lion's share falling to the period 1150–1350. Although the work is of obviously limited value for specialists a surprising amount of factual material emerges, accompanied by basic time-charts and bibliographies. The literary history in Italian proceeds with Donatella Bremer Buono, *La mistica*, 1996, and Michael Dallapiazza, *La letteratura intorno al 1400*, 1997 (La letteratura tedesca medievale), 2 vols, Pisa, ETS, 119, 90 pp. Thomas Bein, *Germanistische Mediävistik. Eine Einführung* (Grundlagen der Germanistik, 35), Berlin, Schmidt, 224 pp., is aimed at the student beginner and in reflecting the modern direction of the discipline will certainly succeed in its intention of rousing curiosity in the subject more than the older and more dryly academic handbooks. An introductory chapter on Hartmann's *Der Arme Heinrich* treats this work as a paradigm for explaining many fundamental concepts. There are then brief but informative sections on many aspects of the cultural and linguistic background and matters of medium, form, and interpretation; a short history of the discipline and the various movements and approaches it has reflected; the historical periods, genres, and text types it embraces; practical guides for study, including the major grammars and reference works and hints on how to use them; summary tables of political and literary history; and a select bibliography of 629 titles. W. H. Jackson, Lutzeier, *Challenges*, 75–96, defends and justifies medieval German in the curriculum. There are pedagogical studies by Ina Karg, *. . .und waz si guoter lêre wernt . . . Mittelalterliche Literatur und heutige Literaturdidaktik. Versuch einer Kooperation* (Beiträge zur Geschichte des Deutschunterrichts, 35), Frankfurt, Lang, 411 pp., and in *MDG*, 45, by G. Behütuns (12–28), U. Reichelt (30–42), and P. Jentzsch (44–66), which indicate some revival of our discipline in German schools.

R. Schnell, *WS XV*, 12–73, takes a fundamental look at recent theoretical approaches to questions of text and transmission, pointing out that conceptions such as the 'open text' are used in quite different contexts and that the postmodernist fashion for denying the role of the author is belied by the literary reality of the period. *Gattungen mittelalterlicher Schriftlichkeit*, ed. Barbara Frank, Thomas Haye, and Doris Tophinke (ScriptOralia, 99), Tübingen, Narr, 1997, 321 pp., includes theoretical discussions of aspects of the subject by T. Luckmann, W. Oesterreicher, P. Koch, B. Frank, D. Tophinke, F. Rädle, P. von Moos, and E. van Houts. Erich Kleinschmidt, *Autorschaft. Konzepte einer Theorie*, Tübingen–Basle, Francke, is highly theoretical but of relevance for the current debate in medieval studies. C. Haase, Bräuer, *Kontext*, 149–60, makes general comments on the computer-based analysis of medieval texts, and R. Bräuer, *ib.*, 161–74, supplies a theoretical basis for a view of the European-wide interaction of literary ideas and motifs. J. L. Flood, *Kolloquium* (Meissen), 370–96, studies the concealing of authors' names through acrostics and similar word-games.

A *Dictionary of Medieval Heroes. Characters in Medieval Narrative Traditions and their Afterlife in Literature, Theatre and the Visual Arts*, ed. Willem P. Gerritsen and Anthony G. van Melle, trans. Tanis Guest, Woodbridge, Boydell, vii + 336 pp., was originally published in Dutch in 1993; to the 86 substantial entries by a team of Dutch scholars Richard Barber adds Robin Hood as an evident concession to the taste of English-language readers! The selection goes far beyond the obvious narrowly heroic figures and includes major Classical and Arthurian personalities and those from *Spielmannsepik* and Reynard the Fox. Storytelling is accompanied by detailed and scholarly accounts of different versions and reception, with basic bibliographical leads. A. Classen, *LiLi*, 109:7–37, interprets a range of texts from the *Hildebrandslied* to the 15th c. as anti-war poetry, and R. Krohn, *MDG*, 45:134–58, places the reception of the period in historical perspective.

Max Wehrli, *Gegenwart und Erinnerung. Gesammelte Aufsätze*, ed. Fritz Wagner and Wolfgang Maaz (Spolia Berolinensia, 12), Hildesheim–Zurich, Weidmann, vii + 331 pp., reprints 20 essays and shorter monographs by W. originally published between the years 1965 and 1996. The texts are essentially photographic reprints which include the original paginations for ease of citation. The subject-matter ranges widely over literary theory, myth and the comic, medieval Latin and biblical epic, the high medieval romance, and the history of the discipline. Karl Stackmann, *Philologie und Lexikographie. Kleine Schriften*, 11, ed. Jens Haustein, Göttingen, Vandenhoeck & Ruprecht, vii + 400 pp., admirably complements the first volume of collected essays (see *YWMLS*, 59:664). This volume contains 16 essays originally published between 1950 and 1996 besides lengthy obituaries for Hans Neumann and Jost Trier. The material reflects a very wide range of interests, including theoretical critique of the 'new philology', historical lexicographical topics, and discussion of the linguistic dimension of literary subjects from *Waltharius* and Old High German to Luther. *Franciscus Junius F.F. and his Circle*, ed. Rolf H. Bremmer Jr (Studies in Literature, 21), Amsterdam–Atlanta, GA, Rodopi, xii + 249 pp. + 17 pls, contains 12 essays with much of value for knowledge not merely of Junius but also of the origins of the discipline. Among the items of specifically Germanic (as distinct from art-historical) interest there is work by C. S. M. Rademaker (biography, 1–17), C. L. Heesakkers (pedagogical activity, 93–119), P. H. Breuker (Frisian and other Germanic studies, 129–57), E. G. Stanley (the Oxford Junius manuscripts, 159–76), P. J. Lucas (printers and types, 177–97), and R. H. Bremmer (correspondence, 199–235). H. Rölleke, *MJ*, 32.1, 1997:5–9, publishes a letter of W. Grimm. Of further interest for *Gelehrtengeschichte* is *Johann Andreas Schmeller und die Bayerische Akademie der Wissenschaften. Dokumente und Erläuterungen*, ed. Richard J. Brunner (BAWA, 115), 1997, 650 pp., while M.-V. Leistner, *BGDSL*, 120:266–72, documents correspondence of Wilhelm Müller, and W. Kofler, *ZDA*, 127:249–70, reviews correspondence between A. Holtzmann, F. Pfeiffer, F. Zarncke, and K. Bartsch. *Germanistik als Kulturwissenschaft. Hermann Paul 150. Geburtstag und 100 Jahre Deutsches Wörterbuch. Erinnerungsblätter und Notizen zu Leben und Werk*, ed. Armin Burkhardt and Helmut Henne, Brunswick, Ars & Scientia, 1997, vii + 94 pp., contains brief contributions on P.'s life and scholarship. Konrad Burdach and Erich Schmidt, *Briefwechsel 1884–1912*, ed. Agnes Ziegengeist, Stuttgart–Leipzig, Hirzel, 312 pp., is a first edition of the complete correspondence, with a total of 344 letters, 96 of B., 248 of S. The introduction reviews the major professional and personal themes of the letters, which appear chronologically and accompanied by a wealth of informative footnotes and an index of the many names of persons mentioned. N. Voorwinden, *ABÄG*, 50:209–24, surveys the polemic of R. C. Boer against A. Heusler. A scholar of more recent eminence is the subject of Christine Jacquemard-de Gemeaux, *Ernst Robert Curtius (1886–1956). Origines et cheminements d'un esprit européen* (Contacts, III, 43), Berne, Lang, xvii + 433 pp. *Geschichtskörper. Zur Aktualität von Ernst H. Kantorowicz*, ed. Wolfgang Ernst and Cornelia Vismann, Munich, Fink, 239 pp., contains an introduction and 14 contributions on historical, critical, and biographical aspects of K.'s life and work. There are studies of K.'s Poznań background and later life (A. S. Labuda, P. T. Walther and W. Ernst), his approach to Frederick II (H. D. Kittsteiner), Castel del Monte (W. Seitter), K.'s philosophy of history (J. Mali, W. Ernst) and significance for medieval studies (O. B. Rader), the conception of *patria* (C. Vismann), the *laudes regiae* (S. Klotz), and above all various facets of the impact of *The King's Two*

Bodies (A. Haverkamp, H. Bredekamp, B. Kriegel, P. Haldar, R. Faber). *Das Mittelalter und die Germanisten. Zur neueren Methodengeschichte der Germanischen Philologie. Freiburger Colloquium 1997*, ed. Eckart Conrad Lutz (Scrinium Friburgense, 11), Freiburg (Switzerland) U.P., 165 pp., contains seven essays which contribute both to an understanding of the fundamental methodologies of the discipline and to *Gelehrtengeschichte*. These ends are achieved in a particularly vivid and immediate form since the scholars discussed are of the present or recent past and their activity impacts on the discipline in its current state. K. Stackmann (11–32) focuses on the problems of transmission and textual editing, with much on the 'new philology'; there are discussions of the respective interests of Hugo Kuhn (B. Wachinger, 33–48), Kurt Ruh (V. Mertens, 49–62), F. Ohly (C. Meier, 63–91), and W. Stammler (M. Curschmann, 115–37); J. Heinzle (93–114) considers research with a social-historical orientation; and H. Fromm (139–58) dwells on the tension between oral and written culture besides other approaches.

The *Katalog der deutschsprachigen illustrierten Handschriften des Mittelalters*, vol. III, fascs 1, 2, ed. Norbert H. Ott and Ulrike Bodemann, Munich, Beck, 160 pp. + 88 illus., is substantially concerned with the *Buch der Natur*, naturally dominated by Konrad von Megenberg's version in its manuscript and printed forms and which with the addition of Peter Königschlacher and Thomas von Cantimpré besides a comprehensive introduction occupies 63 printed pages. Other works represented are Konrad's *Büchlein von der geistlichen Gemahelschaft*, *Christus und die sieben Laden*, *Christus und die minnende Seele*, and the opening of what will prove a very substantial section bringing chronicle literature together. Here the introduction with its attempt at a typological classification, followed by instances of local chronicles from Augsburg and Berlin, indicates that this section will be of value far beyond the specifically iconographic concerns of this fine reference work. Franzjosef Pensel, *Verzeichnis der deutschen mittelalterlichen Handschriften in der Universitätsbibliothek Leipzig*, ed. Irene Stahl (DTM, 70/3), xxxi + 521 pp., is prefaced by a survey by K. Gärtner of the long history of this third catalogue in the series, completed in 1986 and subsequently revised and brought into machine-readable form. P.'s introduction reviews the remarkable thematic range of the collection, and S. outlines the editorial principles followed. The information is supplied in exemplary detail, with the expected codicological descriptions but also a detailed breakdown of the contents into the most minor subsections (e.g. individual sermons), with incipits and full references to the scholarly literature. The indexes of persons, places, subjects, and incipits further enhance the value of an indispensable tool. H. Engelhart, *ZWL*, 57:369–75, comments on the recent catalogue of Stuttgart manuscripts. Arnold Schromm, *Die Bibliothek des ehemaligen Zisterzienserinnenklosters Kirchheim am Ries. Buchpflege und geistiges Leben in einem schwäbischen Frauenstift* (Studia Augustana, 9), Tübingen, Niemeyer, xi + 401 pp., offers more than the relatively specialized subject-matter of the title might imply: in effect a complete cultural and intellectual history of a convent whose library, following secularization in 1802–03, became a significant part of the Oettingen-Wallersteinsche Bibliothek now in Augsburg. The catalogue and related archives are described in meticulous detail as the prelude to the more discursive discussion of the holdings which form the basis for the central chronological review of the history. The second part of the study documents the sources, with lists of the nuns, the sources, bibliography, and full descriptions of the manuscripts and printed books in question. The appendices include 22 plates of interest and full indexes. Other recent work on codicology and early printing includes Bernhard Bischoff, *Katalog der festländischen Handschriften des neunten Jahrhunderts (mit Ausnahme der wisigotischen). 1. Aachen-Lambach*, Wiesbaden, Harrassowitz, xxviii + 495 pp.; Betty C. Bushey, *Die deutschen und niederländischen Handschriften der Stadtbibliothek Trier bis 1600*, Wiesbaden, Harrassowitz, 1996, l + 464 pp.; Nigel F. Palmer, *Zisterzienser und ihre Bücher. Die mittelalterliche Bibliotheksgeschichte von Kloster Eberbach im Rheingau unter besonderer Berücksichtigung der in Oxford und London aufbewahrten Handschriften*, Regensburg, Schnell & Steiner, 356 pp.; *Bibliotheken und Bücher im Zeitalter der Renaissance*, ed. Werner Arnold (Wolfenbütteler Abhandlungen für Renaissanceforschung, 16), Wiesbaden, Harrassowitz, 1997, 206 pp.; *Augsburger Buchdruck und Verlagswesen. Von den Anfängen bis zur Gegenwart*, ed. Helmut Gier and Johannes Janota, Wiesbaden, Harrassowitz, 1997, xiii + 1413 pp.; *Humanistische Buchkultur. Deutsch-niederländische Kontakte im Spätmittelalter (1450–1520)*, ed. Jos M. M. Hermans and Robert Peters (Niederlande-Studien, 14), Münster–Hamburg, Lit, 1997, 208 pp.; Pierre L. Van der Haeghen, *Basler Wiegendrucke* (Schriften der Universitätsbibliothek Basel, 1), Basle, Schwabe, xvii + 359 pp.

OTHER WORKS

Schrift und Gedächtnis, ed. Aleida and Jan Assmann and Christof Hardmeier (Beiträge zur Archäologie der literarischen Kommunikation, 1), 3rd edn, Munich, Fink, 284 pp., is the first volume in a series which extends to text and commentary (*YWMLS*, 57:651). While the 18 contributions (the first by Plato!) to the present volume deal with the origins of the communicative approach by way of early Classical, Egyptian, and Hebrew examples, and also include work on oral tradition derived from modern African and Oriental examples, the specific interest for medievalists is found in essays by H.-G. Gadamer (the theoretical basis of the progression to writing, 10–19), W. Raible (hermeneutics and the written word, 20–23), K. Ehlich (text and speech act, 24–43), W. Haug (development of medieval German written culture, 141–57), H. U. Gumbrecht (orality and written culture in the High Middle Ages, 158–74), and A. Assmann (folklore and writing, 175–93). *Die Vielfalt der Dinge. Neue Wege zur Analyse mittelalterlicher Sachkultur. Internationaler Kongreß Krems an der Donau 4. bis 7. Oktober 1994. Gedenkschrift in memoriam Harry Kühnel*, [ed. Helmut Hundsbichler, Gerhard Jaritz, and Thomas Kühtreiber] (Forschungen des Instituts für Realienkunde des Mittelalters und der frühen Neuzeit. Diskussionen und Materialien, 3), VÖAW, 440 pp., reflects the growing influence of the approaches signified by both *memoria* and material culture (*Realienkunde*). While there are some very subject-specific contributions, e.g. F. Kaspar (207–35) on the public and private dimensions of the medieval dwelling-house, P. Jezler (237–61) on the use of private devotional images, the majority of the essays take a wide basis of examples for inferring more general conclusions of a theoretical or broadly social nature. Among several items which take medieval archaeology as a starting-point, H. Hundsbichler, B. Scholkmann, J. Moreland, and D. Austin each in different ways consider the modern and medieval interpretations of the past, while F. Verhaeghe (263–311) studies its contribution to social networks, S. Schütte (359–73) to civic norms, and H. Steuer (399–428) to daily life. C. Dyer (313–24) addresses the inequalities and cohesive forces implied in material culture. K. Bertau, *Fest. Birkhan*, 15–39, explores the communicative implications of credibility as a hermeneutic category, and *Raum und Raumvorstellungen im Mittelalter*, ed. Jan A. Aertsen and Andreas Speer (Miscellanea Mediaevalia, 25), Berlin, de Gruyter, xxi + 847 pp., contains numerous contributions focusing on the philosophical and scientific aspects of the subject.

A. Classen, *LB*, 87:59–78, comments on Curtius's view of the topos of the book. W. Affeldt, *Mediaevistik*, 10, 1997:15–156, supplies a detailed review of research on women and relations between the sexes in the period. Susan Tuchel, *Kastration im Mittelalter* (Studia Humaniora, 30), Düsseldorf, Droste, 357 pp., finds a surprising quantity of historical and literary material to justify a serious treatment of the subject. There are substantial chapters on topics such as the role of the eunuch in Classical antiquity and in the Middle Ages; castration as a legal punishment; Byzantine and Western practice as evidenced by chronicles; ecclesiastical law and the attitude of the Church, and its reflection in visionary literature; Abelard, the response to whose experience is shown to include almost all other attitudes of the period as a whole; literary instances such as Wolfram's Clinschor and his reception, the beast epic, the fabliau, and *Physiologus. Hausväter, Priester, Kastraten. Zur Konstruktion von Männlichkeit in Spätmittelalter und Früher Neuzeit,* ed. Martin Dinges, Göttingen, Vandenhoeck & Ruprecht, 297 pp., includes work on a range of 'masculist' themes by H. Talkenberger (masculine roles in Württemberg funeral sermons, 29–74); R. Dürr (priestly roles, 75–99); B.-U. Hergemöller (homosexuality, 100–22); P. Barbier (*castrati*, 123–52); C. Bischoff (Hercules and Omphale, 153–86); M. Frank (alcoholism, 187–212); H. R. Schmidt (patriarchalism, 213–36); G. Schwerhoff (blasphemy, 237–63); and F. Loetz (body language, 264–93). C. Lecouteux, *CEtGer*, 33, 1997 : 11–18, considers the medieval background to the dream motif, and R. Bräuer, *Fest. Geith,* 21–30, relates the theme of the dream to medieval fictionality. *Alchemie. Lexikon einer hermetischen Wissenschaft,* ed. Claus Priesner and Karin Figala, Munich, Beck, 412 pp., treats the subject in a series of encyclopaedic articles on major concepts and personalities by a team of 25 international specialists, including both natural scientists and those with more obviously literary and philosophical backgrounds. The result is both informative in an introductory sense, with numerous cross-references, and erudite through the bibliographical leads into the latest literature. A list of alchemical symbols is added, and the detailed index facilitates access when a subject does not appear under the expected heading.

The New Cambridge Medieval History. VII. *C. 1415–C.1500,* ed. Christopher Allmand, CUP, xxi + 1048 pp., the final volume in the chronological sequence, like that on the period 700–900 (see *YWMLS,* 58 : 715) differs totally in structure and content from its predecessor of 1936. The preface dwells on the internationalization of scholarship, the fact that the period is no longer seen as one of decline, and that even the section of chapters on individual European states seeks to present them within a common European framework. In this context T. Scott (337–66) surveys the transition from 'German lands' to a 'German nation', and Hus and Bohemia are treated separately by J. Klassen (367–91). The first section deals with government, with chapters on the theory and practice of politics, representation, and the papacy. The second addresses economic and social developments, with accounts of the nobility (P. Contamine, 89–105), rural Europe (C. Dyer, 106–20), urban Europe (B. Dobson, 121–44), commerce and trade (W. Childs, 145–60), war (C. Allmand, 161–74), and exploration (F. Fernández-Armesto, 175–201). All this is excellent background for literary scholars. What gives a wholly new dimension to the conception of history is the third section on spiritual, cultural, and artistic life, with chapters on religious belief and practice (F. Rapp, 205–19), schools and universities (J. Verger, 220–42), humanism, with some reference to the German contribution (R. Black, 243–77), manuscripts and books (M. Vale, 278–86), printing (D. McKitterick, 287–98), architecture and painting (P. Crossley, 299–318), and music (G. Curtis, 319–33). *Römer und Barbaren. Ein Lesebuch zur deutschen Geschichte von der Spätantike bis 800*, ed. Christina Lutter and Helmut Reimitz, pref. Herwig Wolfram (BsR, 1234), 2nd edn, 320 pp., is a clever anthology in the manner of the recent volume on the period 800–1500 (see *YWMLS*, 59:671). Brief excerpts, none of more than ten pages and most considerably shorter, from the works of some 30 distinguished scholars published by Beck, take us through the chief aspects of the relationship of the Empire and the barbarians, the politics of the early Germanic tribes, the Church and its organization, the economy and society, the rise of the Carolingians, and particular features of Charlemagne's reign. Lutz E. von Padberg, *Die Christianisierung Europas im Mittelalter* (UB, 17015), 307 pp., treats a seminal subject with such clarity of organization that one could only wish for greater length and detail. The greater part of the book is occupied by a chronological account of the spread of Christianity from the pre-Constantinian Empire to the missions to the Slavs in the high Middle Ages, with due attention being paid to individual ethnic groups and the frequent assistance of time-charts and maps (sometimes lacking in legibility of detail). A second part supplies discussion of missionary methods and concepts, the role of preaching and Bible, and the practical and social consequences of conversion. Finally, there are 34 translated excerpts from major sources, with full documentation and bibliography. *'Vae victis!' — Über den Umgang mit Besiegten. Referate gehalten auf der Tagung der Joachim Jungius-Gesellschaft der Wissenschaften Hamburg am 31. Oktober und 1. November 1997*, ed. Otto Kraus, Göttingen, Vandenhoeck & Ruprecht, 226 pp., contains 11 essays on the treatment of the defeated in war in many periods from Ancient Near Eastern civilization to the present day. J. Simon (67–82) reviews numerous historical examples from the early Middle Ages to the 11th c., and the development of legal controls is placed in context by K.-H. Ziegler (45–66) who surveys Roman theory and practice and its Christianization by Augustine. *Das Rittertum im Mittelalter*, ed. Arno Borst, 3rd edn, WBG, 501 pp., is a handy paperback edition of one of the most useful collections to have appeared in the 'Wege der Forschung' series. The 18 essays from the period 1921–76 (see *YWMLS*, 38:572) include the most important recent work on the knightly class and its history and values. Werner Goez, *Lebensbilder aus dem Mittelalter. Die Zeit der Ottonen, Salier und Staufer*, 2nd edn, Darmstadt, Primus, 535 pp., is a full-scale revision and expansion of G.'s *Gestalten des Hochmittelalters* (see *YWMLS*, 45:623). The 22 lives of the earlier volume have been wholly reworked and 12 new essays added. Among the latter are treatments of Popes John XII, Hadrian IV, and Innocent III, Emperor Konrad II, Otloh of St Emmeram, Paulina, and King Henry VII. The approach makes for lively reading and informative scholarship together. The sources are documented in detail and the accompanying bibliographies have been updated. Gerd Althoff, Hans-Werner Goetz, and Ernst Schubert, *Menschen im Schatten der Kathedrale. Neuigkeiten aus dem Mittelalter*, Darmstadt, Primus, x + 358 pp., is an attractively designed book accompanying a series of broadcasts seeking to present the fruits of recent research to a wider public. The contributions focus on aspects of power and government, religion, and above all social history, great emphasis being placed on the 'gemeiner Mann'. If the choice of themes seems somewhat arbitrary — they include monasteries, marriage, death, the Devil, public opinion, and crime and punishment — these are reviewed in vivid detail, with relevant illustrations and full source-references. Ferdinand Opll, *Friedrich Barbarossa*, 3rd revd edn, Darmstadt, Primus, xii + 345 pp., is a re-issue of a comprehensive study which first appeared in 1990 (see *YWMLS*, 52:605). The chief revision is a substantial appendix to the bibliography which takes into account the literature appearing in the wake of the 800th anniversary. Anna Sapir Abulafia, *Christians and Jews in the Twelfth-Century Renaissance*, London–NY, Routledge, 1995, x + 196 pp., admirably complements the work of Heinz Schreckenberg in this area (*YWMLS*, 59:668–69). A. has generally harsher judgements than S. on the major examples of 12th-c. disputation literature, associating this unequivocally with the origins of late-medieval militant anti-Semitism on the grounds that the introduction of rational argument into the debate in the wake of Anselm of Canterbury presupposed a universal Christian concept of reason which effectively excluded and marginalized the Jews. Unsurprisingly Peter the Venerable is repeatedly used to document this view, while elsewhere it depends on a reading of works which can sometimes bear other interpretations and whose general impact on society at large is perhaps in any case questionable. This a fascinating study of great importance for the interest in attitudes to tolerance in medieval literature. T. Haye, *JOWG*, 10:167–80, interprets the political and literary function of Justinus von Lippstadt's *Lippiflorium*. Ernst Schubert, *Einführung in die deutsche Geschichte im Spätmittelalter*, 2nd edn, Darmstadt, Primus, vi + 328 pp., is a re-issue of an admirably clear introduction to the major themes and problems of the later Middle Ages (see *YWMLS*, 54:659). The bibliography has been brought wholly up to date. Gerhild Scholz Williams, *Hexen und Herrschaft. Die Diskurse der Magie und Hexerei im frühneuzeitlichen Frankreich und Deutschland*, rev. edn, trans.

Christiane Bohnert (FGÄDL, 22), 240 pp., is a translation of *Defining Dominion. The Discourses of Magic and Witchcraft in Early Modern France and Germany*, Ann Arbor, Michigan U.P., 1995. W. understands magic as an intellectual and cultural form of expression and focuses on major texts of the period 1400–1650: the Melusine legend, the views of Paracelsus, gender-specific magic (*Malleus Maleficarum*, Johannes Weyer, and Jean Bodin), magic and the 'other' as exemplified by Pierre de Lancre, and the fundamental question of religious dissent. The analyses are vivid and informative, although it is perhaps questionable whether an interpretation of these texts in the light of the categories and preoccupations of the currently fashionable critical discourse provides a wholly satisfying explanation of the phenomena in question. Manfred Heim, *Kleines Lexikon der Kirchengeschichte*, Munich, Beck, 486 pp., is an encyclopaedia which seeks to comprehend the essential concepts of the historical dimension of Christianity in almost 3,000 articles, many of them necessarily very brief. The work is useful for basic names and dates, and frequent cross-references enhance its value. Among the supplementary material is a bibliography and lists of popes and councils. Heinrich Krauss, *Kleines Lexikon der Bibelworte* (BsR, 1270), is an interesting alphabetically arranged dictionary of over 1,000 words and expressions in modern German with a biblical origin. Not surprisingly, much of the phraseology itself derives from Luther. There is a wealth of interesting source material with full biblical reference. Augustinus, *Über Schau und Gegenwart des unsichtbaren Gottes. Texte mit Einführungen und Übersetzung*, ed. Erich Naab (MGG, 1, 14), vii + 296 pp., contains an important collection of Augustine's texts on the subject-matter of the title in the standard edition of A. Goldbacher, with translations on facing pages (pp. 117–271): *De videndo Deo* and the related letter to Fortunatianus, *De praesentia Dei*, and two closely related letters. The introductory material is a substantial aid to making the difficult material accessible, with explanations of the background and composition, summaries of the thought, references to its significance for other Augustinian works, and accounts of the medieval reception. Peter Dinzelbacher, *Bernhard von Clairvaux. Leben und Werk des berühmten Zisterzienzers*, Darmstadt, Primus, x + 497 pp., is a timely new biography which takes into account the wealth of textual work and commentary accompanying the 1990 anniversary. D. divides the life into five substantial phases, within which the material is presented in numerous brief chapters with their own title headings. This allows for informative treatment of significant background topics in almost encyclopaedic detail, besides summaries of historical developments. The overall impression is one of immense learning combined with a vividly readable style. D. does not refrain from citing Frau Ava, the

Kaiserchronik, and other vernacular and Latin literature. The indexing and documentation are comprehensive. *Demons: Mediators between This World and the Other. Essays on Demonic Beings from the Middle Ages to the Present*, ed. Ruth Petzoldt and Paul Neubauer (Beiträge zur europäischen Ethnologie und Folklore, B 8), Frankfurt, Lang, 176 pp., contains an introduction and ten essays on various demonic figures, including work by L. Petzoldt (a broad-brush treatment of the demonic in the late Middle Ages, 13–23); W. Frey (Sibyls in medieval literature, 51–73); N. H. Ott (the iconography of Alexander and Henry the Lion, 75–99); D. Ward (some early medieval cynocephalic demons, 101–09); and R. Petzoldt (vampires, 153–74). Jürgen Werinhard Einhorn, *Spiritalis unicornis. Das Einhorn als Bedeutungsträger in Literatur und Kunst des Mittelalters*, 2nd edn, Munich, Fink, 685 pp., is a substantial revision of the monumental study which was completed 25 years ago and appeared in 1976 (see *YWMLS*, 38:573–74). E. emphasizes that new material comes above all from eastern Germany, while some consideration is now given to the period post–1530. The integration of the illustrations into the text is one particular enhancement among several improvements of layout which make the work more accessible than the first edition notwithstanding the paperback format. The copious bibliography aims at complete updating of all relevant literature. M. Sammer, *Euphorion*, 92:143–221, documents the Western exegetical tradition of the basilisk, and, *LiB*, 51:2–23, the allegorical tradition of the hen, while P. Michel, *Daphnis*, 27:203–29, contributes evidence of various dimensions of understanding of the frog. Günther Binding, *Der früh- und hochmittelalterliche Bauherr als 'sapiens architectus'*, 2nd rev. edn, WBG, 480 pp., links the subject of medieval architecture directly to its wider exegetical, symbolic, and cultural significance as propounded above all in the approach of F. Ohly and his school. This is the first comprehensive treatment of the subject to link the literary and theological sources since that of J. Sauer (1924). B. reviews the relevant activities of the major architectural patrons of the 9th–11th cs and the educational background. The approach to the detail of the subject-matter is thematic, with absorbing sections on the architect/master mason; the foundation and corner stones, and the living stones of the spiritual Ecclesia; tabernacle and temple of Solomon; the exemplary and imitative relationships perceived between different buildings, and above all the figurative representation of the Church; Wisdom 11.21; and the role of the *ordinator aedificiorum*. Heinrich Klotz, *Geschichte der deutschen Kunst. 1. Mittelalter 600–1400*, Munich, Beck, 472 pp. with 404 illus., traces the art of the period through a chronological approach which also focuses on major monuments. The whole account is set out with great clarity and there is an ease of reference between text and illustration, most welcome in this kind of study. The obvious contraints of space mean that perhaps less than justice is done to the pre-Carolingian period, but subsequent periods to the concluding 'Ankündigung der Neuzeit' are impressively covered. Due attention is paid to secular art and to the wider aesthetic dimension of the religious background, with mention of literary references to art and music. Ulrike Liebl, *Die illustrierten Flavius-Josephus-Handschriften des Hochmittelalters* (EH, xxviii, 304), 1997, xii + 277 pp. + 150 pls, includes a catalogue with detailed codicological descriptions of the neglected cycle of illustrations of Josephus. These are discussed in detail and convincingly shown to be an important and distinctive component in the tradition of Western Bible illustration. The introductory chapters have much of interest on the life and work of Josephus, and on the Greek and Latin transformation and reception of his works during the Middle Ages. Norbert Wibiral, *Die romanische Klosterkirche in Lambach und ihre Wandmalereien. Zum Stand der Forschung* (Veröffentlichungen der Kommission für Kunstgeschichte, 4), VÖAW, 56 pp., is a well-illustrated survey and analysis of the Lambach frescoes which draws together a range of findings of the past few decades. Substantially a New Testament sequence designed to support the Gregorian party in the Investiture contest, the particular cultural and literary interest lies in the unique Herod scenes which may reflect a tradition of iconographic illustration of Josephus and the Pseudo-Hegesippus.

2. GERMANIC AND OLD HIGH GERMAN

Allan A. Lund, *Die ersten Germanen. Ethnizität und Ethnogenese*, Heidelberg, Winter, 181 pp., takes a critical look at the scholarship on the origins of the Germanic peoples since the mid-19th c. against the background of present-day cultural and social anthropology. The results reveal the extent to which our understanding rests on the consequences of scholarly constructions supported to only a limited extent by concrete evidence. Above all the analysis of the relevant passages in Caesar and Tacitus shows that the concept of Germania as a coherent entity was in fact a learned fiction invented by Caesar which has influenced all the modern scholarly disciplines that have addressed the subject. L. Motz, *ANF*, 113:29–57, includes German folkloric evidence in a study of the Northern great goddess. D. H. Green, *Language and History in the Early Germanic World*, CUP, xv + 438 pp., derives from a famous cycle of lectures and, though claiming only limited originality, achieves a distinctively clear perspective by placing the linguistic material in a proper relationship to history and archaeology. The contact of the early Germanic peoples with both Classical and Christian civilizations is reflected in the basic structure of the book, but the Celts also receive a chapter. The significance of the linguistic evidence is immediately apparent in the first part with studies of Germanic religion, law, kinship, warfare, lordship, and kingship, underpinned by a general warning of the problems posed by the *interpretatio Romana*. Reciprocal loanwords in Germanic and Latin form the heart of the second part, leading to seminal studies of trade and warfare with the Romans, the names of the days of the week, and the vocabulary of writing. In the final part, the known problems associated with the conversion to Christianity are a prelude to discussions of the respective influences of provincial Roman Christianity, the Merovingians, and the Anglo-Saxons, while contrasts in vocabulary are carefully nuanced and the concluding chapter on the vocabulary of ethics and fate sees in Notker the figure representing the final conjunction of Germanic, Classical, and Christian. The value of this impressive book lies in its ability to combine a wealth of philological and semantic detail with a compelling coherence of the wider cultural argument. Early Germanic legal codes are the subject of work in *Fest. Schmidt-Wiegand* by G. Baumann (the *Lex Frisionum*, 17–24), H. Höfinghoff (the *Lex Salica*, 9–15), and C. Schott (the *Lex Burgundionum*, 25–36). Urs Müller, *Der Einfluß der Sarmaten auf die Germanen* (Geist und Werk der Zeiten, 88), Berne, Lang, 216 pp. C. Giliberto, *ABÄG*, 49:155–68, considers the definition of a corpus of Frisian runes, and A. Bammesberger, *ib.*, 50:13–20, interprets the text of the 'Romulus plate' of the Franks Casket, while R. Nedoma, *Fest. Birkhan*, 115–31, studies some early Germanic appellatives, and E. Ewig, *RVB*, 62:1–16, analyses the early evidence of the legend of the Trojan origin of the Franks.

Althochdeutsche Literatur. Eine Textauswahl mit Übertragungen, ed. Horst Dieter Schlosser, Berlin, Schmidt, 148 pp., is an anthology for student use, with translations on facing pages, intended to replace S.'s *Althochdeutsche Literatur* (see *YWMLS*, 51:637), now out of print. This volume contains substantially less, but its layout makes it significantly easier to use. Thematic grouping has been abandoned in favour of a straightforward chronological presentation. The major shorter texts have been retained complete, the number of excerpts from the longer works reduced. For the glossary, the reader is referred to the internet. Stefan Sonderegger, *Althochdeutsch als Anfang deutscher Sprachkultur* (Wolfgang Stammler Gastprofessur für Germanische Philologie. Vorträge, 2), Freiburg (Switzerland) U.P., 1997, 91 pp., is a substantial monograph. Hans Ulrich Schmid, *-lîh-Bildungen. Vergleichende Untersuchungen zu Herkunft, Entwicklung und Funktion eines althochdeutschen Suffixes* (SA, 35), 671 pp., addresses the most fundamental of adjectival suffixes in a monumental dissertation, the implications of which cannot be restricted to OHG either chronologically or geographically. The greater part of the work (135–442) consists of an alphabetical catalogue of all OHG and Early MHG lexical items including the suffix together with corresponding forms from the other early Germanic languages, a total of 1,019 lemmata, following in general the principles of the Leipzig *Althochdeutsches Wörterbuch*. The accompanying information is substantial and amounts to a valuable lexicographical resource in its own right. The following study, which is accompanied by substantial statistical and tabulated information and indexes, seeks to assess the morphological development of the suffix by way of analysis across the whole geographical area for each grammatical category. Conclusions are detailed in a summary. B. Meineke, Desportes, *Semantik*, 54–91, studies syntax and semantics in the OHG Prudentius glosses. Arne Dittmer and Ernst Dittmer, *Studien zur Wortstellung — Satzgliedstellung in der althochdeutschen Tatian-übersetzung* (SA, 34), 264 pp., has the methodical thoroughness now well-established as a characteristic of this series. Identifying the *Tatian* as an extended prose work especially suited to a topological study, the authors proceed on the basis of J. Lippert's thesis that the Latin version G can serve as a satisfactory basis for comparison. With exhaustive statistical detail of examples the analysis falls in turn on main clauses, subordinate clauses, and non-finite constructions, with concise summaries of the findings at the end of each section. There are general conclusions about transposition of word order, clauses with conjunctions, preservation of Latin word order, and the overriding tendency to change in the direction of German word order, never towards Latin. The work gives substance to what more subjective judgements have long regarded as the features marking the quality of the *Tatian* as a translation. A. Masser, Desportes, *Semantik*, 123–40, addresses syntactical problems in the *Tatian*, and K. Düwel, *Fest. Birkhan*, 539–51, records the later reception and interpretation of the Merseburg Charms, while M. V. Molinari, *ABÄG*, 50:21–45, is unusual in finding a coherence and logical pattern in the text of the *Hildebrandslied*, and U. Schwab, *Fest. Birkhan*, 139–56, discusses *gibada* in the *Heliand* and related runic terms. Dhuoda, *Handbook for her Warrior Son. Liber Manualis*, ed. and trans. Marcelle Thiébaux (Cambridge Medieval Classics, 8), CUP, ix + 276 pp., includes the standard text of Pierre Riché with annotations relating to recent scholarship on points of detail. On facing pages appears the first full translation of the work in English, lively and readable. The introduction ranges over the historical background, the author and her family, the work's genre and intention, and its relationship to Carolingian literature generally. The notes are concisely informative on both scriptural reference and other matters.

ABÄG, 49, is devoted entirely to Old Frisian topics, with an introduction on the state of research by R. H. Bremmer (vii-xvi). In addition to the study of linguistic subjects there is a detailed survey of the relationship between Frisia and the Empire throughout the Middle Ages (N. E. Algra, 1–76), and work on the terminology of verbal insult (R. H. Bremmer, 89–112), the efforts of 17th-c. scholars in the field (K. Dekker, 113–38), and Frisia and its inhabitants in medieval German literature (N. Voorwinden, 303–18).

In Desportes, *Semantik*, Y. Desportes (161–85) addresses semantic, and M. Krause (92–106), modal, aspects of Otfrid, and W. Milde, *Fest. Schmidt-Wiegand*, 37–46, makes broad-brush comments on Otfrid's work. Eva Cescutti, *Hrotsvit und die Männer. Konstruktionen von 'Männlichkeit' und 'Weiblichkeit' in der lateinischen Literatur im Umfeld der Ottonen. Eine Fallstudie* (FGÄDL, 23), 314 pp., seeks to interpret what is known of H.'s life and work in terms of the interaction of the three parameters *ordo*, *medium*, and *genus*. The first two are defined against the background of early medieval social theory and literacy as applied to 10th-c. Saxony, while for the latter C. draws on various perspectives from modern gender studies in addition to Pauline and later understanding of sex roles. While a range of other prominent figures besides H. are drawn into the argument, this turns in the last instance on the interplay of the chosen categories rather than the discovery of new knowledge about the subject. M. Jennings, *MJ*, 33.1:37–52, dwells on H.'s use of typology. Notker's sentence structures in his translation of the Psalms are studied by H. Eilers, Desportes, *Semantik*, 23–45, and his syntactical-semantic relations by S. Sonderegger, *ib.*, 141–60, while A. Näf, *Fest. Geith*, 89–109, addresses N.'s reception of Plato's *Kratylos*, and A. A. Grotans, *Scriptorium*, 51, 1997:251–302, records lexical and graphic cues for reading in N. and his St Gall contemporaries.

3. MIDDLE HIGH GERMAN

GENERAL

Hilkert Weddige, *Mittelhochdeutsch. Eine Einführung*, 2nd rev. edn, Munich, Beck, xii + 210 pp., follows hard upon the first edition (see *YWMLS*, 58:724), suggesting that for German students at least the introduction, which is broadly comparable to M. O'C. Walshe's *A Middle High German Reader*, is indeed appropriate in the current educational context. Corrections and additions relate largely to matters of detail. Hermann Paul, *Mittelhochdeutsche Grammatik*, 24th edn, rev. Peter Wiehl and Siegfried Grosse, Tübingen, Niemeyer, xxiv + 648 pp., is the first revision of this standard work for nine years see *YWMLS*, 51:639). The chief addition is an explanatory list

of phonetic symbols and other signs which will be of great assistance
to the regular user. After the radical changes to the format of the
work in the present generation the editors reveal a welcome openness
to further possible innovations. Beate Hennig, Christa Hepfer, and
Wolfgang Bachofer, *Kleines Mittelhochdeutsches Wörterbuch*, 3rd rev. edn,
Tübingen, Niemeyer, xxv + 496 pp., effectively replaces the first
edition, only five years old (see *YWMLS*, 55:710), since the whole
alphabet, no longer merely A-G, is now treated according to the
revised principle of grouping entries of related words. While users
will certainly dream of an enhanced version covering a greater range
of texts, this is the most practical and accessible one-volume
dictionary of the language now available and seems set to serve the
needs of students and professional scholars alike for a generation.
S. Obermaier, *LiLi*, 112:141–52, considers intercultural problems of
translating from MHG.

B. Schirok, *Fest. Geith*, 111–26, reconsiders the structure and
programmatic content of Codex Sangallensis 857. H. A. Burmeister
and J. Wolf, *ZDA*, 127:45–68 + 8 pls, report recently discovered
manuscript fragments of various 13th-c. works, and K. Klein, *ib.*,
69–84, clarifies the whereabouts of various manuscripts reported as
lost. K. O. Seidel, *JOWG*, 10:371–82, studies scribal comments in
the colophons of MLG manuscripts, while in *Kolloquium* (Meissen),
H. Wenzel (1–28) considers authorial function as reflected in a range
of illustrations, A. Suerbaum (29–37) the conception of the author in
commentary texts, and K. Gärtner (38–45) the MHG terminology of
authorship. O. Pfefferkorn, *ZDP*, 117:399–415, discusses the theoretical problems attending the classification of historical text types.

N. H. Ott, pp. 27–50 of *Demons* (see p. 579 above), reviews the
iconography of demons in late-medieval vernacular manuscripts,
with many pleasant illustrations. A. Classen, *ABÄG*, 50:185–207,
comments on the Jewish contribution to literature of the period. *Die
Anfänge des Schrifttums in Oberschlesien bis zum Frühhumanismus*, ed.
Gerhard Kosellek, Frankfurt, Lang, 1997, 364 pp., includes 18
contributions on authors and works from Upper Silesia. H. Freytag,
JOWG, 10:125–37, reviews literature in Lübeck 1200–1600, and
H. Wernicke, Bräuer, *Kontext*, 135–47, considers Lübeck and the
14th-c. Hanse cities as literary centres, but decides the merchants
were uninterested in *belles-lettres*! B. Pfeil, *ZDA*, 127:26–44, studies
the role of the Bavarian counts of Bogen as patrons of the arts.

Manfred Kern, *Edle Tropfen vom Helikon. Zur Anspielungsrezeption der
antiken Mythologie in der deutschen höfischen Lyrik und Epik* (APSL, 135),
viii + 567 pp., is a Vienna dissertation from the school of H. Birkhan
which seeks to cover the allusions to Classical mythology in the

literature of the period 1180–1300 both systematically and comprehensively. After some consideration of the nature of Classical
reception and allusion in the Middle Ages generally, the main body
of the study includes detailed treatments of expected authors such as
Veldeke, Morungen, and Gottfried, but also of a wide range of themes
relevant to many poets such as the treatment of the goddess of love
and attitudes to the Classical gods as a whole, comparisons of beauty,
the reading of Classical myth as a theme within courtly literature, the
Trojan legend and the origins of chivalry, and the role of allegory in
the presentation of myth. The whole body of material yields a
substantial and coherent interpretative corpus; notable among the
conclusions is the exclusion of Gottfried from the tradition-forming
process, thus corroborating the unique status conferred on him by
quite different literary approaches. J. Knape, Goetz, *Geschichtsbewußtsein*, 317–29, writes on the understanding of the past in MHG versions
of Classical literature, and H. Reinitzer, pp. 83–104 of *'Vae victis!'* (see
p. 576 above), reviews examples of the treatment of the defeated in
battle in all the major classical courtly works. *Knowledge, Science, and
Literature in Early Modern Germany*, ed. Gerhild Scholz Williams and
Stephan K. Schindler (UNCSGL, 116), 1996, xi + 310 pp., includes
work by H. Wenzel (93–116) on metaphors of speech and text against
the background of oral and written traditions, and T. Cramer
(151–92) on natural marvels and their medieval background.
A. Classen, *GN*, 29.1:3–17; 29.2:1–11, uses Walther, Gottfried, and
Freidank to exemplify the 'modernity' of the Middle Ages, and
U. Schaefer, *Das Mittelalter*, 3.1:3–12, surveys and introduces work
on the liberal arts. A. Classen, pp. 133–51 of *Demons* (see p. 579
above), includes *Herzog Ernst* and Wolfram's Cundrie in a study of
medieval attitudes to foreigners and the foreign. Other thematic
studies include Dirk Matejovski, *Das Motiv des Wahnsinns in der
mittelalterlichen Dichtung* (STW, 1213), 1996, 399 pp., while D. Buschinger, Bertrand, *Geste*, 125–43, comments on gesture in the *Rolandslied*
and the Tristan romances of Eilhart and Gottfried, T. Ehlert, *Fest.
Ertzdorff*, 145–71, relates body language and gesture to sex in high
medieval courtly literature, and B. Bastl, *Fest. Birkhan*, 361–415,
includes MHG examples in an account of gestures and places of
intimate contact. A. Classen, *Neohelicon*, 25.1:247–74, includes
Hartmann, Walther, and other authors in a study of the affirmation
of human happiness in this world as a desirable value. K. Andermann,
DAEM, 54:97–117, links the names of castles to the vocabulary
denoting the courtly virtues, and C. S. Jaeger, Peil, *Erkennen*, 19–34,
focuses on the educational dimension of the origin of 'courtly love',
while W. Wunderlich, *MJ*, 33.2:1–13, links the biblical Asahel with
the 'slaves of love' topos, and C. Wand-Wittkowski, *ZDP*, 117:38–54,

argues that the inscriptions on the Munich *Minnekästchen* are typical of the period 1300–50. I. Bennewitz, *Fest. Ertzdorff*, 173–91, studies the treatment of intelligent women and women disguised as men, and C. Tuczay, *Fest. Birkhan*, 307–29, looks at MHG Amazons. Günter Schopf, *Fest und Geschenk in mittelhochdeutscher Epik* (Philologica Germanica, 18), Vienna, Fassbaender, 1996, v + 184 pp., analyses and classifies the different forms of festival and gift, and U. Hirhager, *Fest. Birkhan*, 437–53, documents games making use of grass in the mouth or hand, while G. Blaschitz, *ib.*, 416–36, surveys culinary delicacies in cookery books and literary sources. G. Althoff, *Fest. Ertzdorff*, 3–20, comments on the demonstrative significance of the conduct of Pope and Emperor at the Peace of Venice (1177), and W. Röcke, *JOWG*, 10:281–97, surveys the treatment of the Duke of Brunswick in literature of the late Middle Ages and the early modern period.

EARLY MIDDLE HIGH GERMAN

E. Hellgardt, *Kolloquium* (Meissen), 46–72, surveys the practice of anonymity and naming of authors in literature of the 11th and 12th cs. *Das St. Trudperter Hohelied. Eine Lehre der liebenden Gotteserkenntnis*, ed. Friedrich Ohly and Nicola Kleine (Bibliothek des Mittelalters, 2), DKV, 1402 pp., controversially — in view of current editorial fashions — presents the text (pp. 9–313), accompanied in the manner of the series by a lucid line-by-line translation on facing pages, in a normalized MHG which probably postdates the original by a generation. Ohly admirably justifies this procedure in the light of the manuscript tradition and later transmission, H. Menhardt's earlier approach, and above all the need to make a crucially important early mystical work available to more than philological specialists. The commentary focuses on the historical exegetical traditions which lie behind the work and treats these in exhaustive detail, with surveys of longer passages preceding detailed comments on individual lines. The index of names, concepts, and themes is less complete than envisaged but nevertheless an immensely useful aid to the user. Rooted in Ohly's seminal *Hohelied-Studien*, this volume, in which he acknowledges the assistance of pupils and colleagues over several generations, could hardly be a more fitting monument. The imagery of the work is the subject of H. E. Keller, pp. 121–37 of *Symbolik des menschlichen Leibes*, ed. Paul Michel (Schriften zur Symbolforschung, 10), Berne, Lang, 1995, xxiii + 368 pp. A. Ostheimer, *BGDSL*, 120:223–33, interprets the *Benediktbeurer Gebet zum Meßopfer*, viewing the work not as a prayer related to the mass but as a meditation expressing the new piety associated with Anselm of Canterbury.

M. Dobozy, *Fest. Schmidt-Wiegand*, 47–53, comments on the Oriental bride motif, and C. Kiening, *WS XV*, 211–44, studies the narrative strategies at work in *König Rother*, while L. Miklautsch, *Fest. Birkhan*, 284–306, interprets aspects of *Salman und Morolf*, which is also studied by O. Neudeck, Peil, *Erkennen*, 87–114 (narrative structure), and H. Wuth, *ASNS*, 235:328–44 (the relevance of the theme of *ingenium*). M. Schulz, *BGDSL*, 120:395–434, interprets the conception of *triuwe* in *Herzog Ernst B* on a broad cultural and legal basis, while A. Bihrer, *JOWG*, 10:55–66, interprets the Brunswick *Herzog Ernst* tapestry, and V. Bok, *ib.*, 81–91, reviews the Czech reception of the related legend of Henry the Lion. M. Schulz, *ABÄG*, 50:47–72, interprets the trial scene of the *Rolandslied*, the archaic battle formulae of which U. Schwab, *ib.*, 73–93, compares with other works, and the Imperial interest of which is subjected to a discriminating analysis by K. Zatloukal, *Fest. Birkhan*, 714–33.

Änne Bäumer, *Wisse die Wege. Leben und Werk Hildegards von Bingen. Eine Monographie zu ihrem 900. Geburtstag*, Frankfurt, Lang, xii + 388 pp., is a comprehensive introduction to H.'s life, work, thought, and science. Michaela Diers, *Hildegard von Bingen* (dtv, 31008), DTV, 158 pp., is an attractively presented introductory biography covering the essential data on H.'s life and works. The 61 illustrations are accompanied by explanatory captions and there are brief excursuses rather than annotations, and a good basic classified bibliography. Beutin, *Mystik*, includes a substantial essay by A. Sroka (33–65) on H. and the question of her place in the history of mysticism, while A. Kreutziger-Herr (67–94) addresses her music and its significance.

MIDDLE HIGH GERMAN HEROIC LITERATURE

H.-J. Behr, Goetz, *Geschichtsbewußtsein*, 331–40, writes on the understanding of the past in MHG heroic poetry. C. Glassner, *BGDSL*, 120:376–94, and J. Heinzle and K. Klein, *ZDA*, 127:373–80, study the Melk *Nibelungenlied* fragments. *A Companion to the Nibelungenlied*, ed. Winder McConnell, Columbia, SC, Camden House, xiii + 293 pp., contains 12 coherently arranged essays and an introduction in which McC. points to the reasons for the continuing mythical fascination of the *Nl.* and traces the course of its scholarship. O. Ehrismann (18–41) traces the role of the poet in shaping the image and reception of Kriemhilt; J. L. Flood (42–65) studies the literary tradition of Siegfried's fight with the dragon; F. G. Gentry notes the particular use of key epic concepts (66–78); W. Hasty (79–93) examines different forms of conquest, and E. R. Haymes (94–104) the heroic, chivalric, and aristocratic ethos; J. Heinzle (105–26) supplies a very up-to-date account of the manuscript tradition; W. Hoffmann (127–52) deals with 20th-c. reception; J. T. Lionarons (153–71) surveys the otherworld aspects; W. McConnell (172–205) takes a psychological approach, and J. McGlathery (206–28) compares the eroticism of the *Nl.* with that of Wagner's *Ring*; B. Murdoch (229–50) writes on the political dimension; and W. Wunderlich (251–77) treats different aspects of the problem of authorship. Taken together this book touches on most of the current problems of scholarship and justifies its title. Jan-Dirk Müller, *Spielregeln für den Untergang. Die Welt des Nibelungenliedes*, Tübingen, Niemeyer, vi + 494 pp., is easily the most ambitious and challenging study of the *Nl.* for several decades. Taking issue with the continued reading of the work in terms of a 19th-c. realism, M. argues that its numerous contradictions are not 'errors' to be explained away or avoided by a flight into a historical or genetic approach, but rather the keys to a different aesthetic inadequately defined by a simple tension between oral and written tradition. Reasserting Jauss's 'alterity' concept, M. draws on Ursula Schaefer's term *Vokalität*, and identifies a culture of 'secondary orality' in which the literate and illiterate may participate in each other's medium: hence in oral performance epic formulae revert to implications lost in the written tradition. Rather than follow the action of the *Nl.* M. focuses rather on different perspectives, among them book epic and the memory of legend, social structure, anthropology and the understanding of personality (much here on Kriemhilt's change), transparency and its elimination, spatial constellations, ritual inter-action and its disturbance, and the rejection of the courtly alternative. Not surprisingly, M.'s approach is based not merely on the B text. Although he insists that the 'deconstruction' of the concluding chapter, which finds no single guiding idea in the *Nl.* but rather an anthropology that seeks a break with both contemporary society and older tradition, is not used in the currently fashionable sense, the book nevertheless owes much to current critical concerns while exploiting them in a remarkably measured and fruitful manner. J. E. Härd, pp. 137–54 of *Sozusagen. Eine Festschrift für Helmut Müssener*, ed. Edelgard Biedermann (Schriften des Germanistischen Instituts, Universität Stockholm, 23), Stockholm Univ., Germanistisches Institut, 1996, xiv + 273 pp., comments on narrative strategies in the *Nl.*, which A. Classen, *Fest. Birkhan*, 673–92, interprets as essentially anti-heroic, while for W. Seitter, pp. 149–57 of *Übertragung und Gesetz. Gründungsmythen, Kriegstheater und Unterwerfungstechniken von Institutionen*, ed. Armin Adam and Martin Stingelin, Berlin, Akademie, 1995, 275 pp., the work contains clandestine pacifism. U. Störmer-Caysa, *GRM*, 48:1–25, studies Merovingian and Burgundian marriage law, showing that the former would have obliged Kriemhild to support her brothers against Siegfried, the latter to defend her husband against them. I. Campbell, *Fest. Marson*, 121–36, interprets Gunther's role in the murder plot, and P. Göhler, pp. 215–35 of *Hansische Literaturbeziehungen. Das Beispiel der 'Þiþreks saga' und verwandter Literatur*, ed. Susanne Kramarz-Bein (Reallexikon der germanischen Altertumskunde. Ergänzungsbände, 14), Berlin, de Gruyter, 1996, xxiv + 315 pp., interprets the function of the treasure. The *Nl.* is also mentioned by G. F. Jones, *SN*, 70:83–88, in a survey of treatments of bloodshed.

E. Lienert, *WS XV*, 276–98, points to the use of intertextuality in *Nl.* and *Klage*, and W. Schröder, *MJ*, 33.1:171–83, attacks the 'new philology' as allegedly practised by J. Bumke in his edition of the *Klage*, while E. Tobler, Michel, *Symbolik des menschlichen Leibes* (see p. 586 above), pp. 139–56, notes Germanic and Christian attitudes to the body in *Wolfdietrich D*, and S. Coxon, *Kolloquium* (Meissen), 148–62, studies authorial self-portrayal in *Wolfdietrich* and *Dietrichs Flucht*. U. Kindl, *Fest. Birkhan*, 567–79, studies the reception of *Laurin*.

THE COURTLY ROMANCE

Volker Mertens, *Der deutsche Artusroman* (UB, 17609), 384 pp., is a handy introduction to the subject which, though brief, is probably as comprehensive a treatment of the German manifestations of Arthurian subject-matter in their totality as any other. A major benefit is the discussion of the postclassical romances on their own terms, free from the stigma of 'epigonality'. D. H. Green, Peil, *Erkennen*, 35–56, comments on irony, fictionality, and lying, and the way these are signalled in courtly literature, while R. Voss, *Fest. Ertzdorff*, 21–39, points to the ethical basis of help and pity in the romance, and K. Brunner, *Fest. Birkhan*, 245–62, looks at the realities of sexuality in the period and their reflection in courtly literature. T. Tomasek, Bräuer, *Kontext*, 85–100, studies the 'bold water' episode in versions of the Tristan legend and elsewhere, and M. Unzeitig-Herzog, *Fest. Ertzdorff*, 41–61, surveys courtly combats with dragons. Other work on several romances includes Roland Franz Rossbacher, *Artusroman und Herrschaftsnachfolge: Darstellungsform und Aussagekategorien in Ulrichs von Zatzikhoven 'Lanzelet', Strickers 'Daniel von dem blühenden Tal' und Pleiers 'Garel von dem blühenden Tal'* (GAG, 649), vi + 386 pp.; W. Blank, *Fest. Geith*, 1–19, identifying the melancholic hero in the *Prosa-Lancelot*, Hartmann's *Iwein*, and Wolfram's *Parzival*; P. Priskil, *System ubw — Zeitschrift für klassische Psychoanalyse*, 16.1:56–87, adopting a psycho-analytical approach to Iwein's adventure at the spring (Hartmann), the blood drops in the snow (Wolfram), and other Arthurian motifs; U. Ruberg, Peil, *Erkennen*, 181–94, characterizing the memorial function of painting in the Aeneas, Lancelot, and Tristan romances; F. Büttner, *ib.*, 195–213, explaining the understanding of the representation of the emotions in late–13th-c. pictures; A. Bihrer, *Poetica*, 29, 1997:343–77, surveying 14th-c. embroideries illustrating Arthurian scenes; K. M. Schmidt, Bräuer, *Kontext*, 61–83, asking after the absence of Merlin from the German tradition; S. S. Poor, *MDG*, 45:68–82, commenting on filmic reception of the romance; and H.-C. Stillmark, *ib.*, 84–93, on Tankred Dorst's *Merlin*.

Karen Opitz, *Geschichte im höfischen Roman. Historiographisches Erzählen im 'Eneas' Heinrichs von Veldeke* (*GRM*, Beihefte, 14), Heidelberg, Winter, 254 pp., is a richly informative Marburg dissertation from the school of J. Heinzle, its success achieved through a balance between a focus on the dimension of *historia* according to the contemporary understanding of Virgil, and the recognition that V. was primarily a fictional and not a historiographical writer. There is wide-ranging reference to the French source, to contemporary Latin historiographical works, and to the *Kaiserchronik*, while the greater part of the analysis is all the more convincing for its consistent proximity to the text. H. Vögel, Peil, *Erkennen*, 57–85, interprets Veldeke's *Eneas* in terms of the significance of memory, while W. Freytag, *Fest. Ertzdorff*, 341–61, studies the rhetorical background to the topical epithets used by Eilhart, and J. H. Winkelman, *Fest. Birkhan*, 821–38, studies the neglected Vienna *Tristrant* fragments.

HARTMANN VON AUE

P. Hörner, Hörner, *Hartmann*, 167–283, provides a most useful bibliography of 861 numbered titles on H. for the period 1976–97, designed to complement the earlier work of E. Neubuhr which it resembles in layout and structure. M. Gouel, *ib.*, 155–65, comments on Heinrich von dem Türlin's memorial of H., and Joseph von Lassberg, 'Hartmann von Aue, ein Schweizer, und zwar ein Thurgauer?', ed. V. Schupp, *Fest. Geith*, 127–39, is of interest for H. reception. M. Vladovich, *SM*, 38:707–35, sees the theme of lovesickness in the *Klage* as definitive for H.'s later works. C. Young, *ArLit*, 16:1–21, reassesses the significance of the role of the individual and his character in *Erec*, R. Fisher, *Seminar*, 34:221–34, shows the theme of madness to be significant in *Erec* besides *Iwein*, and W. Fritsch-Rössler, *ASNS*, 235:344–49, comments on the linking of motifs in *Erec*, while F. Brandsma, *Neophilologus*, 82:513–25, analyses the interaction of physical and verbal exchange in *Erec* and other romances, B. D. Haage, *Fest. Birkhan*, 40–48, links Enite's marvellous horse with the humanism of the Chartres school, and C. L.

Gottzmann, Hörner, *Hartmann*, 123–54, includes *Erec* in a comparative study of *Erex saga*. B. Plate, *Mediaevistik*, 10, 1997:219–36, analyses references to feudal law in *Gregorius*. In Hörner, *Hartmann*, P. Hörner (11–49) studies the concepts of *gebote*, *guot*, and *êre* in *Gregorius*, and H. Beifuss (51–89) interprets the work against the background of *riuwe* and *buoze*, while K. Harthun, *MJ*, 33.2:85–104, emphasizes that Arnold of Lübeck's conception of the subject-matter is generically different from H.'s. D. Duckworth, *Mediaevistik*, 10, 1997:157–92, interprets the confession to the farmer by the hero of *Der arme Heinrich*, and J. Klinger, *MDG*, 45:95–104, discusses Tankred Dorst's version of the subject-matter. P. Kern, *Fest. Ertzdorff*, 363–73, explains some differences in *Iwein* compared with its source, M. Eikelmann, *Kolloquium* (Meissen), 73–100, studies the use of aphorism in *Iwein*, and K. Speckenbach, Peil, *Erkennen*, 115–46, makes perceptive comments on a range of problems associated with the identity crisis of Iwein and other heroes, while T. Bein, *LiLi*, 109:39–58, analyses the presentation of fighting and slaying in *Iwein* and five other versions of the work, M. Wynn, *Fest. Ertzdorff*, 131–44, casts light on the abduction of the queen in *Iwein* by studying the motif in a comparative and historical context, U. Siewerts, Hörner, *Hartmann*, 91–122, focuses on the themes of seclusion and recognition in a study of *Iwein*, and H. Zutt, *Fest. Ertzdorff*, 103–20, places Lunete outside the courtly norms.

WOLFRAM VON ESCHENBACH

R. Decke-Cornill, *WS XV*, 494–521, supplies a copious W. bibliography for 1995–96. A. Classen, *OL*, 53:277–95, identifies the 'saracen princess' as a cultural and political bridge-builder in W.'s works and elsewhere and her relative idealization in W., while N. Thomas, *ABÄG*, 50:111–29, aligns Wolfram's 'tolerance' with that of Lessing. D. Yeandle, *Euphorion*, 92:223–48, surveys the history and current state of commentaries on *Parzival*. J. Clifton-Everest, *Fest. Birkhan*, 693–713, makes interest comments on the possible influence of the *chanson de geste* tradition on *P.*, and K. Ridder, *WS XV*, 168–94, studies the authorial roles in *P.*: Hartmann, Kyot, Chrétien, and Wolfram, and their implications for narrator and work. U. Ernst, *Fest. Ertzdorff*, 215–43, writes on love and aggression in *P.*, M. Schnyder, *DVLG*, 72:3–17, interprets the discussion of women in the prologue, 2,23–3,24, and C. Luttrell, *ArLit*, 16:131–69, includes *P.* among the cognate works in a comparative study of the hero's upbringing, while A. Gerok-Reiter, Aertsen, *Individuum*, 748–65, places Cundrie at the centre of a discussion of the emergence of individuality in literature, M. Dallapiazza, *Fest. Ertzdorff*, 121–30, comments on Obilot, and

A. Büchler, *ABÄG*, 50:95–109, upon Trevrizent's psalter and the reckoning of time in *P*. Also noted: Anke Wagemann, *Wolframs von Eschenbach 'Parzival' im 20. Jahrhundert: Untersuchungen zu Wandel und Funktion in Literatur, Theater und Film* (GAG, 646), 278 pp.

There is an Italian translation, W. v. E., *Willehalm*, trans. Michael Dallapiazza (Medioevo tedesco, 1), Pisa, ETS, 1997, 165 pp., its introduction claiming an anti-war ideology for the work. In *WS XV*, K. Schneider (411–16), E. Hellgardt (417–25), and C. Bertelsmeier-Kierst and B. Salzmann (426–38), print recently discovered fragments of *Whm*, and H. A. Burmeister (405–10) comments on the transmission. John Greenfield and Lydia Miklautsch, *Der 'Willehalm' Wolframs von Eschenbach. Eine Einführung*, Berlin, de Gruyter, x + 317 pp., is both a comprehensive introduction and a working companion to the text, chiefly valuable for its admirably clear and concise summaries of the now copious critical literature. The relatively brief first chapter on the poet's life, work, and patronage, is geared towards the problem of the dating of *Whm*. There follows a chapter on the Old French material and a lengthy and well focused stage-by-stage analysis and interpretation of the epic action (pp. 61–167) which, concluding with a discussion of the problem of the incomplete ending, has the germs of a much more elaborate commentary. Later chapters are dedicated to the narrator and his technique, characterization, and specific problems such the prologue, *minne*, the heathen, and political themes. The transmission and reception receive relatively scant attention. Maps, genealogies, bibliography, and indexes assist the reader further. W. Freytag, *ZDA*, 127:1–25, interprets *Willehalm* 2,16–22 against the background of handbooks on *grammatica*, identifying W.'s intellectual approach with that of St Bernard and the Cistercians, and J. Heinzle, *ZDP*, 117:75–80, reaffirms his interpretation of *Whm* 307,26–30, while D. Hüpper, *Fest. Schmidt-Wiegand*, 77–96, comments on text and illustration of *Whm*. C. Kiening and S. Köbele, *BGDSL*, 120:234–65, assess the metaphorical dimension of the two *Titurel* fragments.

GOTTFRIED VON STRASSBURG

A. de Mandach, *Tristania*, 18:53–75, links the composition of *Tristan* with Augsburg rather than Strasbourg, and J.-M. Pastré, *ib.*, 17, 1996:71–84, finds Oriental analogues to the motif of the abduction of cattle in the versions of the *T*. legend. H. Zutt, *Fest. Geith*, 175–89, studies G.'s stylistic juxtaposition of words with the same prefix, and D. Rocher, Peil, *Erkennen*, 169–80, points to the memorial function of *Leich* and *maere* in *T*. C. Young, *WS XV*, 195–210, re-interprets the *T*. prologue, arguing that the *edeliu herzen* concept has a dual function, relating both to the confirmation of a preconceived role and to a fictional process, and pointing to the affinity with developments in 12th-c. eucharistic theology. M. C. Robinson, *Tristania*, 18:1–15, argues that T.'s troubled origins create his subsequent lack of identity and mastery of disguise and deception. J. A. Schulz, *ib.*, 17, 1996:111–23, explores the relation of bodies and clothing to sex and class, and W. Hasty, *MDU*, 90:137–47, re-evaluates the love-power relations in *T*. A. Volfing, *MAe*, 67:85–103, interprets the *huote* excursus as a didactic passage encouraging women to resist psychological pressure, and L. Johnson, *Neophilologus*, 82:247–57, examines the conceptions of time and history in G.'s excursus on women. R. S. Sturges, *Exemplaria*, 10:243–69, understands heterosexual desire in *T*. as a 'social construction', and G. Dicke, *ZDA*, 127:121–48, analyses the narrative layers in the Gandin episode, while S. Philipowski, *BGDSL*, 120:29–35, interprets the Petitcreiu episode in terms of remembering and forgetting. The hunting imagery is the subject of Burkhardt Krause, *Die Jagd als Lebensform und höfisches 'spil'. Mit einer Interpretation des 'bast' in Gottfrieds von Straßburg Tristan* (HS, 12), 1996, 204 pp., and E. S. Dick, *Tristania*, 17, 1996:1–25, interprets G.'s use of *bast* in terms of the pursuit of Utopian love. J. Richardson, *Tristania*, 17, 1996:85–109, returns to the links between T., David, and Orpheus, and W. Schild, *Fest. Schmidt-Wiegand*, 55–75, addresses the legal aspects of Isolde's trial by ordeal. In *Tristania*, 18, P. Dinzelbacher (37–41) notes a 12th-c. reference to the *T*. legend in the life of Alpais of Cudot, A. Classen (43–52) records reception of the legend from the late Middle Ages on, and A. Deighton (17–35) interprets the London *T*. illustrations and the German tapestries, while W. Rankin, *GN*, 29.2:31–35, interprets episodes in *T*. in relation to the Grimm Brothers. Gottfried von Strassburg, *Die Geschichte der Liebe von Tristan und Isolde*, trans. and ed. Dieter Kühn (UB, 4474), 187 pp., is a revised and much abbreviated version of K.'s earlier reworking of G. (see *YWMLS*, 53:646). The author explains his intention to bring the translations of passages of the text closer to the original, and to eliminate the more speculative essays at interpretation. As before, the work occupies an interesting but uncomfortable position between scholarship and creative literature.

OTHER ROMANCES

Ulrich von Zatzikhoven, *Lanzelet mittelhochdeutsch/neuhochdeutsch*, ed. Wolfgang Spiewok (Wodan, 71), Greifswald, Reineke, 1997, xxxvii + 378 pp., includes K. A. Hahn's text with minor corrections, a translation on facing pages, and introductory matter. Y. Yokoyama, *ZDP*, 117:55–74, comments on the lexicography of *Wigalois*, of which

H. Denruyter, *LB*, 87 : 119–38, interprets the animals. D. Klein, *ZDA*, 127 : 271–94, studies the critique of courtly love in *Moriz von Craûn*. P. D. Hardin, *ColGer*, 31 : 97–103, interprets the fragmentary *Der Mantel* in the context of other courtly texts. M. Niesner, *LJb*, 39 : 55–74, interprets Rudolf von Ems's *Der guote Gerhart* in relation to the Arthurian romance. D. Klein, *WS XV*, 299–323, shows Stricker's *Karl der Große* returning — in contrast to Wolfram's *Willehalm* — to the ideology of the *Rolandslied*, and W. Lenschen, *Fest. Geith*, 67–71, notes the treatment of the senses in Stricker's *Daniel*. Anja Kristina Radojewski, '*ôwe, wie sol ich leben?' Eine Studie zur Individuation des Menschen im späthöfischen Roman von Rudolf von Ems bis Heinrich von Neustadt*, diss., Cologne, Hundt, vii + 307 pp., comes from the school of J. Bumke and has much of interest on the emergence of the conception of the individual. K. Klein, *WS XV*, 451–93, documents manuscripts of Ulrich von Türheim's *Rennewart* in full, and G. Hayer, *ib.*, 439–50, prints a fragment of the work from Salzburg. G. Zimmermann, *Fest. Birkhan*, 734–53, analyses Der Pleier's understanding of conflict. K. Cieslik, Bräuer, *Kontext*, 121–34, discusses the ethical values of Konrad von Würzburg's *Engelhard*, among which U. von Bloh, *ZGer*, 8 : 317–34, focuses on friendship and love, and A. Jobst, *JVF*, 43 : 11–25, interprets Konrad's *Herzmaere* as a case-study of the theory of courtly love. K. Klein, *WS XV*, 396–404, comments on the transmission of Albrecht's *Jüngerer Titurel*, and D. Huschenbett, *Fest. Ertzdorff*, 375–88, analyses the bridge of virtues episode in the work. W. Röcke, pp. 243–67 of *Weltbildwandel. Selbstdeutung und Fremderfahrung im Epochenübergang vom Spätmittelalter zur Frühen Neuzeit*, ed. Hans-Jürgen Bachorski and Werner Röcke (Literatur, Imagination, Realität, 10), WVT. Wissenschaftlicher Vlg Trier, 1995, 318 pp., considers the theme in the *Crescentia* and *Mai und Beaflor* romances, and A. Classen, *WW*, 48 : 324–44, finds innovative narrative techniques in *Mai und Beaflor*. Klaus Ridder, *Mittelhochdeutsche Minne- und Aventiureromane. Fiktion, Geschichte und literarische Tradition im späthöfischen Roman: 'Reinfried von Braunschweig', 'Wilhelm von Österreich', 'Friedrich von Schwaben'* (QFLK, 12), xi + 462 pp., adopts an intertextual approach, associating the three late romances with an interest in local subject-matter; Id., *Kolloquium* (Meissen), 239–54, interprets the authorial role in *Reinfried von Braunschweig*. K. Lichtblau, *Fest. Birkhan*, 263–83, interprets the fairy in Konrad von Stoffeln's *Gauriel von Muntabel*, the historical and political background to which is the subject of W. Achnitz, *ASNS*, 235 : 241–66. K.-E. Geith, *Fest. Ertzdorff*, 63–82, emphasizes the courtly and chivalric dimension of *Karl und Galie*, and V. Mertens, *ZDA*, 127 : 149–68, addresses the structure of the Dutch *Walewein*.

Robert Schöller, *Seifrits 'Alexander'. Form und Gehalt einer historischen Utopie des Spätmittelalters*, Vienna, Praesens, 1997, 179 pp., takes a new look at a romance popular in the late Middle Ages but neglected by scholarship, and shows it to have a coherent structure and theme transcending the 'epigonality' attributed in older literature. A programmatic prologue is accompanied by a clear view of the hero as a divine instrument and of history as a rationally ordered process within a framework of *Heilsgeschichte* in which the heathen gods are subordinated to Christ and the theme of a universal Emperor presented as an ideal associated with the potential of Charles IV's rule. E. J. Morrall, *ZDP*, 117:381–98, studies stories of illicit love and attitudes to suicide in Niklas von Wyle's translation of the *Historia de duobus amantibus* and related works. *Valentin und Namelos. Mittelniederdeutsch und Neuhochdeutsch*, ed., trans., and comm. Erika Langbroek, Annelies Roeleveld, and Arend Quak (APSL, 127), 1997, viii + 190 pp., is a handy edition of the MLG version of this verse narrative in 2291 lines based on the 15th-c. Stockholm Cod. Holm. Vu 73 with additions and emendations from the Hamburg 'Hartebôk' text. The apparatus and the accompanying commentary, largely but not exclusively confined to linguistic problems, are clearly laid out, and there is an unpretentious and practical translation on facing pages. The work contains a wealth of popular and typical medieval epic and romance narrative motifs. E. Langbroek and A. Roeleveld, *NdJb*, 121:85–131, analyse the rhymes of *Valentin und Namelos*, and in *ABÄG*, 50:149–65, study their significance for the transmission of the work. W. Wunderlich, Bräuer, *Kontext*, 27–50, places the Reinold legend in its wider European context.

LYRIC POETRY

D.-R. Moser, Bräuer, *Kontext*, 9–25, seeks to identify the social characteristics of the poets of the *Carmina Burana*, and F. H. Bäuml, *Das Mittelalter*, 3.1:95–105, comments on the principles underlying the compilation of the Manesse Song Manuscript, while F. J. Worstbrock, *WS XV*, 114–42, considers the significance of the Budapest early Minnesang fragments, and A. Touber, *Fest. Birkhan*, 652–72, systematically studies various aspects of Romance reception in the lyric. *Actes* (AIEO 1995) includes work on the German reception of the Occitan troubadours by V. Mertens (adaptation of melodies, 269–83), A. Touber (retention of 'hidden' Occitan meanings in the Minnesang, 285–96), and N. Unlandt (comparison of words for God, 297–311). Thomas Cramer, *Waz hilfet âne sinne kunst? Lyrik im 13. Jahrhundert. Studien zu ihrer Ästhetik* (PSQ, 148), 210 pp., is a major contribution to the debate about oral and written tradition in the period in genral. C. challenges what since the work of Hugo Kuhn and P. Zumthor has become the received view that the medieval lyric was designed for oral performance. A large number of examples from Romance as well as MHG texts are assembled to illustrate where comprehension is only possible from a consideration of the written word. Analysis of the manuscript transmission shows that the texts generally show much greater stability than is often assumed. While individual versions are intended for performance, the full meaning of many texts only emerges from reading a plurality of written versions which are seen as the expression of an elaborate aesthetic experiment. Thomas Bein, *'Mit fremden Pegasusen pflügen.' Untersuchungen zu Authentizitätsproblemen in mittelhochdeutscher Lyrik und Lyrikphilologie* (PSQ, 150), 496 pp., like Cramer challenges a whole attitude prevalent in lyric scholarship, in this case the even more fundamental approach to questions of authorship. Both theoretical considerations of the categories involved, besides the study of numerous specific cases, show that the conventional distinction of 'spurious' and 'authentic' strophes in the development of scholarship on the lyric rests on the flimsiest ground. While fashionable modern approaches to the conceptions of author and work with an emphasis on their fluidity provide obvious support for the thesis, the likely transience of such views makes them a less convincing argument than the detailed case histories. B. rightly emphasizes that the designation 'spurious' has consigned many interesting texts to the unvisited attic of scholarship, and by re-investigating them in detail argues their alleged inauthenticity is either fallacious or at best unproven. In *Kolloquium* (Meissen), E. Lienert (114–28) discusses the roles of author and singer in the Minnesang, W. Haubrichs (129–47) identifies and interprets 'biographical fragments', M. Meyer (185–99) focuses on the later lyric, V. Mertens (200–10) writes on Ulrich von Liechtenstein and Hadloub, and C. Kiening (211–38) introduces the 'body' into the discussion of the *Frauendienst*.

G. Rings, *GN*, 29.1 : 18–25, writes on service of God and the lady in Hausen, and R. W. Fisher, *ZDA*, 126, 1997 : 375–96, points to the implications of variations in strophic sequence in six songs of Morungen, while A. Stein, Peil, *Erkennen*, 147–68, interprets his 'Mir ist geschehen als eime kindeline', and N. Henkel, *Kolloquium* (Meissen), 101–13, considers the problem of the authorship of Hartmann's song XII.

Walther von der Vogelweide, *Werke. Gesamtausgabe.* II. *Liedlyrik. Mittelhochdeutsch / Neuhochdeutsch*, ed., trans., and comm. Günther Schweikle (UB, 820), 832 pp., is the final volume of this monumental new edition following the principle of adherence to a single MS — again usually MS C — expounded in detail in the first volume (see

YWMLS, 56:752). S. acknowledges the greater difficulties encountered with the love-lyric in terms of translation and wealth of critical literature to be digested: hence a commentary occupying pp. 535–800 including a metrical analysis of each song. No less interesting is the classification of the songs and after a critique of the efforts of his predecessors S. proposes a tentative grouping into ten broad categories, among which 'Nicht nach dem Schema des Hohen Sanges' avoids many terminological problems, and 'Neue Ansätze' is subdivided into '*frouwen*-Kritik', '*frouwen*-Kritik mit Gesellschaftskritik', and 'Problematisierungen der Minne'. This is altogether a magnificent achievement the sheer scale of which probably means that, notwithstanding the Reclam format, the volumes will be restricted to specialized scholarly use rather than become a standard teaching text. Eric Marzo-Wilhelm, *Walther von der Vogelweide. Zwischen Poesie und Propaganda. Untersuchungen zur Autoritätsproblematik und zu Legitimationsstrategien eines mittelalterlichen Sangspruchdichters* (RBDSL, B 70), 275 pp., is a Regensburg dissertation which thoughtfully addresses the fundamental questions of how W. achieves success with his highly polemical political works in the context of his own and others' understanding of his songs, and what the nature of that unquestioned success in fact was. Less interesting perhaps than the analyses of individual texts is the linking of the subject to the overarching problems of the role of patronage and the representational and performative character of didactic verse, the public function of literature, and the use of 'role play', both a help and hindrance in interpreting the biographical leads. In particular M.-W. casts doubt on the supposed role of W. as a political adviser, suggesting that Thomasin von Zerclaere confirms that his influence was poetic rather than political. R. K. Weigand, *LJb*, 39:9–35, interprets the authorial role and biographical significance of W.'s *Preislied*, and T. Nolte, *ib.*, 37–54, considers the evidence for the audience of the later songs.

D. Buschinger, *Fest. Birkhan*, 605–18, reviews the attitudes to art in late-medieval didactic poets. M. Springeth and U. Müller, Bräuer, *Kontext*, 101–20, take a comparative look at Neidhart and the pastourelle, and E. Hages-Weissflog, *ZDP*, 117:346–60, interprets Neidhart's *Sommerlied* 12 and *Winterlied* 37, while M. W. Adamson, *Neophilologus*, 82:577–88, relates Neidhart's themes to modern popular songs. M. Egidi, *GRM*, 48:405–33, fundamentally re-evaluates the criteria for approaching the didactic strophes on *minne* by Reinmar von Zweter, Litschauer, Konrad von Würzburg, and Frauenlob. B. Kellner and P. Strohschneider, *WS XV*, 143–67, study the organization of the *Wartburgkrieg* strophes and their implications. Heinz Kischkel, *Tannhäusers heimliche Trauer. Über die Bedingungen von*

Rationalität und Subjektivität im Mittelalter (Hermaea, n. F., 80), Tübingen, Niemeyer, viii + 332 pp., addresses one of the most problematic of all medieval poets, his already shadowy existence further shrouded in the mystique of the legend which has arguably come to have more significance than the work, even though the formal variation in the *Leich* genre makes him one of the most productive of the period. The easy option, the identification of T. with the transmission of the Manesse MS C and the rejection of all else as legendary, is eschewed in favour of the attempt to build a complete picture of the poet by proceeding from the least probably authentic 'Hofzucht' by way of the 'Bußlied' to the works in MS C. There is no attempt at an easy or complete answer: K. anchors his efforts in a framework which considers the role and conception of the author in the context of a range of recent and current theoretical works. The textual appendix includes the texts of the 'Bußlied' and 'Hofzucht', complete for the first time, with modern translations. Heidrun Alex, *Der Spruchdichter Boppe. Edition — Übersetzung — Kommentar* (Hermaea, n. F., 82), Tübingen, Niemeyer, vii + 242 pp., is an admirably practical edition which could serve as a model for similar treatment of other minor 13th-c. poets. A.'s brief introduction is followed by an account of the transmission which leads to the nowadays surprising but wholly logical conclusion that a normalized MHG text based on C as *Leithandschrift* represents the best method of presentation. The close line-by-line translations on facing pages are themselves an aid to interpretation. The commentary (pp. 121–59) includes a variety of linguistic, metrical, cultural, and historical detail, and is followed by a facsimile print of the transmission in its entirety, bibliography, and index. Dietrich Gerhardt, *Süsskind von Trimberg. Berichtigungen zu einer Erinnerung*, Berne, Lang, 1997, 394 pp. + supp., is a professedly largely reconstructive attempt to address a poet of whom almost nothing is known apart from his Jew's hat in the famous illustration of the Manesse MS. There is a full account of the evidence of the source and other references to S., but of no less interest is the treatment of the poet in older scholarship which is documented in detail, so that a substantial focus of the work is on reception rather than the main subject. Commentaries on the strophes are supplemented by translations. Of additional interest is a text and study of a 15th-c. polemical dialogue. F. V. Spechtler, *Fest. Birkhan*, 586–90, points to Ulrich von Liechtenstein's reception of Walther, and K. Kellermann, *WS XV*, 324–43, analyses forms of communication in Ulrich's *Frauendienst*. A. Schnyder, *JOWG*, 10:327–39, interprets Günther von dem Forste's *Tagelied* as a parody. P. Kern, *Fest. Birkhan*, 619–28, interprets a strophe of Rumelant von Sachsen, and F. Löser, *WS XV*, 245–75, interprets the riddles in the strophes of Singûf and

Rumelant. Also noted: Reinhard Bleck, *Der Rostocker Liederdichter Hermann Damen (c.1255–1307/9)* (GAG, 655), 200 pp. B. Kellner, *Kolloquium* (Meissen), 255–76, and S. Köbele, *ib.*, 277–98, consider aspects of the authorial role in work of Frauenlob, while A. Diehr, *JOWG*, 10:93–110, interprets Frauenlob's *Minneleich*, and S. Fritsch-Staar, *ib.*, 139–51, records its reception on the Lower Rhine. J. Haustein and K. Stackmann, *WS XV*, 74–103, edit late-medieval strophes using melodies of Frauenlob, and K. Stackmann, *ib.*, 104–13, studies the implications of two related songs in the Frauenlob tradition. Elisabeth Hages-Weissflog, *Die Lieder Eberhards von Cersne. Edition und Kommentar* (Hermaea, n. F., 84), ix + 304 pp., is devoted to the 20 songs of a late lyric poet better known for *Der Minne Regel* based on Andreas Capellanus. After an introduction which focuses on the very limited earlier scholarship, biographical data, and the longer work, the main part of the study consists of an edition of the songs accompanied in each case by a translation, bibliography, notes on transmission and metre, and a detailed line-by-line commentary followed by a more discursive interpretation based on the major themes. A concluding chapter takes a wider view of the collection and its transmission as a whole, and seeks to place E. in the context of the lyric of his time and its reception of both German and Romance traditions. This is a most informative study which effectively rehabilitates a seriously neglected author.

DIDACTIC, DEVOTIONAL AND RELIGIOUS LITERATURE

I. Lommatzsch, *JOWG*, 10:255–68, discusses the function of the *Lucidarius* Prologue A, whether authentic or not. J.-M. Pastré, *Reinardus*, 11:149–60, writes on the destruction of the anthill in *Reinhart Fuchs*, and J. Goossens, *Fest. Schmidt-Wiegand*, 217–26, comments on the structure of the beast epic. R. Disanto, *AION(FG)*, 5.3, 1995:9–26, comments on virtues and vices named in Thomasin von Zerclaere's *Der Welsche Gast*, and H. Wenzel, *Das Mittelalter*, 3.1:73–94, assesses his understanding of the liberal arts, while M. Stolz, *WS XV*, 344–72, analyses the distinctive functions of text and illustration in the work.

Goetz, *Geschichtsbewußtsein*, contains important work on the background to medieval historiography. There are contributions by W. Knoch (history as *Heilsgeschichte*, 19–29), H.-W. Goetz (the attitude to history of high medieval historians, 55–72), J. Ehlers (historical thought in 12th-c. Bible exegesis, 75–84), G. Althoff (commemorative documents and a sense of history, 85–100), A. Angenendt (cyclical and linear time in the liturgy, 101–15), B. Englisch (temporal organization of calendars, 117–29), P. Segl (historical thought of heretics, 131–41), H. Röckelein (other-world visions, 143–60), D. Schlochtermeyer (timelessness in hagiography, 161–77), H. Kugler (history in *mappae mundi*, 179–98), B. Schneidmüller (history in West Frankish and French royal documents, 217–35), T. Zotz (history in German royal documents, 237–55), J. Jarnut (Barbarossa's conception of time, 257–67), and V. Epp (the Classical past and the present in medieval Latin poetry, 295–316). M. Krausová, *JOWG*, 10:235–40, notes geographical references in Thietmar von Merseburg's chronicle, while H.-J. Behr, *ib.*, 17–26, notes aspects of power relations in historiographical texts, and W. Beutin, *ib.*, 39–54, characterizes wider aspects of the mentality of early Saxon historiography. C. A. Meier, Goetz, *Geschichtsbewußtsein*, 357–75, comments on the illustrations in high medieval chronicles. *Die Chronik Ottos von St. Blasien und die Marbacher Annalen*, ed. and trans. Franz-Josef Schmale (Ausgewählte Quellen zur deutschen Geschichte des Mittelalters, 18a), WBG, vii + 275 pp., makes more accessible than hitherto two important 13th-c. chronicles closely associated with the tradition of Otto of Freising. For Otto of St. Blasien's chronicle, the chief interest of which is seen to lie in its account of the Third Crusade, S. follows the standard MGH edition of A. Hofmeister, with some improvements from alternative manuscript readings. The text of the *Annales Marbacenses* follows that of H. Bloch for the years 1152–1238 with their original material. S.'s translations on facing pages are readable and accompanied by informative brief notes. There is a full name index. On the *Sächsische Weltchronik* we note *Die sächsische Weltchronik im Spiegel ihrer Handschriften. Überlieferung, Textentwicklung, Rezeption*, ed. Jürgen Wolf (MMS, 75), 1997, x + 490 + lx pp., while F. Scheele, *Fest. Schmidt-Wiegand*, 123–37, studies the punishment scenes. Raymond Graeme Dunphy, *Daz was ein michel wunder. The Presentation of Old Testament Material in Jans Enikel's Weltchronik* (GAG, 650), 351 pp., is a thoroughly admirable study of one of the most popular world chronicles, which succeeds both in delineating its place in relation to earlier tradition and in characterizing its specific and contemporary features. Building on earlier work on the exegetical traditions inherited by the Early MHG biblical epic, D. shows convincingly that the older views of P. Strauch on the indebtedness to specific sources are largely untenable, and if much greater relative space is devoted to the earlier books of the Old Testament than to the historical and prophetic books, that is a reflection of the interest of medieval writers as much as modern scholars. The subject-matter is clearly subdivided according to the textual pericopes, and well indexed, and in pursuing his conclusions to the characterization of E.'s individualistic stance with its particular features of rationalization and sensationalization, D. writes in an attractively lucid style which combines insight, clarity, and wit. S. Hölscher, *JOWG*, 10:181–90, points to the Welf dynastic interest of the *Braunschweigische Reimchronik*, while U. Bartels and J. Wolf, *ZDA*, 127:299–306, discuss the transmission of Nikolaus von Jeroschin's *Kronike von Pruzinlant*, and J. Wenta, *JOWG*, 10:409–18, studies Detmar von Lübeck's chronicle and its Prussian associations. M. Zips, *Fest. Birkhan*, 839–57, reviews Franciscan historiography in the 13th and 14th cs.

M. Egerding, *ABÄG*, 50:131–47, considers the problem of normative values in Stricker, and F.-J. Holznagel, *Kolloquium* (Meissen), 163–84, studies authorship and transmission in Stricker's minor works, while S. L. Wailes, *MDU*, 90:148–60, points to the narrator's ambivalence in *Pfaffe Amis*, comparing the two versions of this work in *JEGP*, 97:168–76.

Gottzmann, *Osteuropa*, includes six items which impress above all by their attempt to bring the literature of the region into the mainstream of work on the later Middle Ages. F. Löser (7–37) takes a critical look at the conception of *Deutschordensliteratur*, showing that there is no proof that the Teutonic Order was as involved with all the texts as it suggests; M. Gouel (39–78) interprets the *Väterbuch* as a missionary work; and P. Hörner (79–104) points to the significance of the Trinity in Tilo von Kulm. H. Beifuss (105–32) characterizes the unedited German translation of Matthew of Cracow's *Dialogus rationis et conscientiae*, and B. Schnell (133–47) lists the textual evidence of late-medieval Silesian Latin-German vocabularies, while J. Meier (149–68) classifies Early NHG texts from Slovakia. R. D. Schiewer, *OGS*, 26, 1997:24–72, documents an independent Low German sermon tradition. J. Macha and M. J. Schubert, *ZDP*, 117:361–80, print a Cracow fragment of texts on the Virgin Mary from the *Passional*, of which K. Klein, *ZDA*, 127:191–95, lists newly identified fragments, while R. Plate, *ib.*, 295–98, studies the Breslau fragment E of the *Väterbuch*, and A. Hagenlocher, *LiLi*, 109:59–73, places the *Erlösung* at the heart of a study of pacific conceptions in literature *c.*1300. Johannes Fournier, *Das St. Pauler Evangelienreimwerk. 1. Text. 11. Untersuchungen*, 2 vols (*VB*, 19, 20), Berne, Lang, xviii + 408, ix + 328 pp., is a major edition and study of a 14th-c. gospel translation. *Speculum humanae salvationis. Codex Cremifanensis 243 des Benediktinerstiftes Kremsmünster*, comm. Willibrord Neumüller (Glanzlichter der Buchkunst, 7), ADEVA, 1997, viii + 124 + 67 pp., is a welcome facsimile edition in a handy, practical format of the most impressive monument of late-medieval typology. The illustrations and the Latin and German text are generally highly legible, and the book can be used in conjunction with recent editions and studies such as the work of M. Niesner (*YWMLS*, 58:751–52). The commentary contains the essence of N.'s research, with introductory matter on the genre and the manuscript, accounts of the layout and the most significant iconographical features, and a review of the individual illustrations, their biblical sources and typological interpretation. K. Gärtner, *ZDA*, 127 : 182–90, prints a fragment of Bruder Philipp's *Marienleben* from Burghausen, and W. Achnitz, *BGDSL*, 120 : 53–102, edits and studies Peter Suchenwirt's *Die zehn Gebote*.

Heike A. Burmeister, *Der 'Judenknabe': Studien und Texte zu einem mittelalterlichen Marienmirakel in deutscher Überlieferung* (GAG, 654), 379 pp. + 61 pls, adopts a chronological approach to a surprisingly diffuse miracle story which originates in the account of the young men in the furnace and extends to the Grimm brothers and 19th-c. Catholic devotional literature. B. supplies a detailed documentation of the Latin sources and places the legend in its Mariological context. The earliest vernacular version, *Das Jüdel*, is dated against much earlier scholarship, but convincingly, into the 13th c., and possibly even later than 1250. The version in the *Passional* provides an important focus of the later transmission, for which H.-G. Richert's edition and studies supply the basis of a fruitful investigation. Both homiletic and relatively unknown compilatory works provide further examples, while the second part of the dissertation helpfully points the way to future work with a collection of edited texts. W. Frey, *Fest. Birkhan*, 165–86, studies the literary consequences of an alleged host desecration by Deggendorf Jews in 1338. Angela Mielke-Vandenhouten, *Grafentochter — Gottesbraut. Konflikte zwischen Familie und Frömmigkeit in Bruder Hermanns 'Leben der Gräfin Yolande von Vianden'* (FGÄDL, 21), 368 pp., is a Cologne dissertation which enhances the social and cultural importance of this neglected text. M.-V. seeks to bring together a large quantity of relevant but disparate and dispersed material, and also to develop interpretative insights. Textual and editorial problems, and questions relating to the source and analogous works, occupy the early chapters, and form the basis for an analysis of the structure, style, and narrative form. The longest and most readable chapter places the figure of Yolande against the background of her family, society, and religion, exploiting the contribution of J. Bumke's work in this area down to practical matters of everyday life. A final chapter adopts a similar approach to her religious vocation, with much of interest on female piety in general and the personalities who shaped it. J. M. Sullivan, *MDU*, 90 : 161–75, illustrates the use of hagiographical tradition in Brother Hermann's work.

Sonja Kerth, *'Der landsfrid ist zerbrochen.' Das Bild des Krieges in den politischen Ereignisdichtungen des 13. bis 16. Jahrhunderts* (Imagines medii aevi, 1) Wiesbaden, Reichert, 1997, ix + 356 pp., is a Würzburg dissertation which inaugurates a new series dedicated to interdisciplinary research. The work covers over 650 shorter texts from the period and, emphasizing their occasional rather than generic function and the different types of conflict represented, K. identifies the four broad categories of violence in association with legal disputes, crusades against Turks, heretics, and political opponents, confessional wars, and international conflicts. For the various wars discussed there is much detail on the representation of the enemy and of the author's party, the arguments used, and the overall attitude to war, which is seen overwhelmingly in unemotional terms as a normal state of affairs and a means to an end. The propagandistic role of the texts increases throughout the period. F. J. Worstbrock, *MJ*, 32.1, 1997:105–25, surveys 14th-c. Latin school texts. R. Damme, *Fest. Schmidt-Wiegand*, 201–08, notes a neglected MLG-Latin vocabulary; Id. *NdW*, 38:141–80, analyses diatopic marks in the *Vocabularius Theutonicus*. N. Henkel, pp. 261–83 of *Gattungen mittelalterlicher Schriftlichkeit* (see p. 569–70 above), characterizes the *Disticha Catonis* and its variants and prints a 14th-c. German version, and G. Roth, *NdJb*, 121:133–48, surveys MLG didactic literature of the 'mirror' type, while T. Tomasek, *JOWG*, 10:397–408, considers LG riddles from *c.*1300 on. J. Bockmann and J. Klinger, *Das Mittelalter*, 3.1:107–26, interpret the Constance *Minnelehre*, a genre represented by *Mittelhochdeutsche Minnereden und Minneallegorien der Prager Handschrift R VI Fc 26. 1. 'Standhaftigkeit in der Liebesqual.' Eine mittelhochdeutsche Minneallegorie. Edition und Übersetzung*, ed. Michael Mareiner (EH, 1, 1650), 311 pp. Ulrich Steckelberg, *Hadamars von Laber 'Jagd'. Untersuchungen zu Überlieferung, Textstruktur und allegorischen Sinnbildungsverfahren* (Hermaea, n. F., 79), Tübingen, Niemeyer, xi + 359 pp., is a comprehensive treatment of this neglected *Minnerede* based on the insight, which emerges with clarity from the survey of earlier research, that in this case textual criticism and interpretation are intimately associated. Fundamental to the manuscript tradition is the highly complicated question of the numbering and order of the strophes, for which S. brings into play the current theory of 'fluid transmission', seeking the reasons for this with regard to the different facets of the text and extending its implications to the polyvalence of the allegory central to the work. The text is accordingly seen as coherent and — in contrast to earlier researchers — as uncorrupt. The substantial appendix of texts documents major variants from H. Stejskal's edition as prolegomena to a projected new edition. D. Hempen, *Neophilologus*, 82:425–33, points to the dominance of male friendship in *exempla* of *Der Große Seelentrost*, the exemplary function of which is also the topic of E. Feistner, *JOWG*, 10:111–24. R.-H. Steinmetz, *ZDA*, 126, 1997:397–446, edits Latin and German versions of the *Libellus* *muliebri nequitia plenus*, another manuscript of which is reported by D. Roth and R.-H. Steinmetz, *ib.*, 127:307–22. F. P. Knapp, *Fest. Birkhan*, 788–97, introduces the life and work of Ulrich von Wien.

Wörterbuch der Mystik, ed. Peter Dinzelbacher, 2nd edn (KTA, 456), xix + 537 pp., is a welcome reissue of an admirably comprehensive short work of reference (see *YWMLS*, 51:661). The chief enhancements are bibliographical, and are found both in the general list of literature and in easily cross-referenced supplements to individual entries. *Von der Suche nach Gott. Helmut Riedlinger zum 75. Geburtstag*, ed. Margot Schmidt and Fernando Domínguez Reboiras (MGG, 1, 15), xiii + 809 pp., contains a wide range of essays on topics associated with mysticism, many with reference to Latin and medieval German sources which feature in varying degree in the items selectively mentioned here. A first section, on mysticism and spirituality, includes work by M. Schmidt (the tradition of Moses's visions of God, 3–38); A. Deissler (41–50) and L. Ruppert (207–22) on the Psalms; A. Mehlmann (Joachim of Fiore, 83–108); W. Böhme (basic tenets of mysticism, including reference to Eckhart, Seuse, and Tauler, 173–85); J. Sudbrack (implications for pluralist theology, 187–205); W. Eckermann (Wolfgang Ostermair, *c.*1469–1531, 233–48); and J. Stöhr (Trinitarian thought, 249–82). A second section is dedicated to the Middle Ages, with work by F. Bertelloni (Aristotelian reception, 367–87); R. Weier (conception of freedom in Aquinas and Luther, 429–45); P. Walter (reception of the allegorical senses in Erasmus, 447–62); E. Schockenhoff (concepts of deception and lying, 489–507); L. Scheffczyk (sacramental symbols, 547–58); and J. Schumacher (the didactic role of the Church, 559–82). Mariological topics are treated by A. Ziegenaus (585–98) and K. Welker (599–608), while of less relevance to our subject is a final section on natural science and theology. There is a complete name index. In Beutin, *Mystik*, P. Dinzelbacher (13–30) supplies a brief but characteristically informative survey of the role of women in Christian mysticism, while H. Beutin (97–118) characterizes the life and piety of Elizabeth of Thuringia, M. Ankermann (119–38) writes on Mechthild von Magdeburg and Gertrud von Helfta, K. Agricola (139–65) documents the reception of mystic themes in the Wienhausen Song Book, W. Beutin (189–219) compares the accounts of the deaths of various female mystics, and U. Müller (237–49) links Dorothea von Montau to both Sor Juana Ines de la Cruz and Günter Grass! Specifically female mysticism is studied by Wolfgang Beutin, *Anima. Untersuchungen zur Frauenmystik des Mittelalters. II. Ideengeschichte, Theologie und Ästhetik* (BBLI, 23), 235 pp., and A. M. Haas, Peil, *Erkennen*, 1–17, indicates the early history of the term *unio mystica*, while H. E. Keller, *ZDP*, 117:17–37, studies the aggressive characteristics of Frou Minne, especially in Lamprecht von Regensburg's *Tochter Syon*, and in Aertsen, *Individuum*, 605–11, S. Möbuss studies the conception of individuality in Mechthild of Magdeburg; the same volume includes work on Eckhart's understanding of individuality by U. Kern (612–21) and M.-A. Vannier (622–41). W. Störmer-Caysa, *Fest. Birkhan*, 197–210, comments on Eckhart's sermon Q 20a. L. Sturlese, pp. 434–46 of *Die Bibliotheca Amploniana. Ihre Bedeutung im Spannungsfeld von Aristotelismus, Nominalismus und Humanismus*, ed. Andreas Speer (Miscellanea Mediaevalia, 23), Berlin, de Gruyter, 1995, xvi + 512 pp., discusses Eckhart's works in the Erfurt library, and K. Flasch, *FZPT*, 46:130–50, studies the theory of the intellect in Eckhart and Dietrich von Freiberg, while A. de Libera, *ib.*, 151–68, comments on philosophical aspects of E.'s theology, and T. Heimerl, *MJ*, 33.2:105–17, demonstrates the difficulties of Eckhart's accusers in translating his figurative terminology. In Aertsen, *Individuum*, M. Enders (642–64) assesses Johannes Tauler's awareness of individuality, D. Thiel (766–83) studies the conception of individuality in Nicholas Cusanus, and E. Meuthen (784–804) writes on Cusanus's life and work.

Andreas Krass, *Stabat mater dolorosa. Lateinische Überlieferung und volkssprachliche Übertragungen im deutschen Mittelalter*, Munich, Fink, 381 pp. + 7 pls, a Munich dissertation from the school of F. J. Worstbrock, begins with a survey of the monumental transmission of the Latin text, noting that the standard edition of the *Analecta hymnica* (1915) is based on the 'romance' transmission and ignores the significantly deviant 'German' versions, for which a critical edition is offered. The study of the poetics of the sequence focuses on the 12th-c. humanization of Mary and the particular form of piety represented (*compassio*) and leads to the tentative suggestion that the work originates in the 12th-c. Cistercian milieu rather than that of St Francis as usually assumed, although there is no very convincing answer to the objection posed by the much later transmission. The second half of the work doubles the number of known vernacular versions and in documenting these concentrates on the process of translation, a section of editions and analyses according to region, and a consideration of aspects of the aesthetics of production. In its range, detail, and depth of analysis this is a most satisfying and informative achievement. R. Hahn, *Daphnis*, 27:231–61, prints a new Upper German text of the Brendan legend, and I. Kasten, *Fest. Birkhan*, 49–60, studies the place of the book in its various versions; an edition of the Upper German redaction is included in *San Brandano. Un antitipo Germanico*, ed. and trans. Marie-Louise Rotsaert (Univ. degli studi di Cagliari: Dipartimento di filologie e letterature moderne, 12), Rome, Bulzoni, 1996, 288 pp. B. Stark, Aertsen, *Individuum*,

704–21, notes individualistic traits in the biography of St Elizabeth of Thuringia, and P. Strohschneider, *IASL*, 23.1:1–29, compares the substance and function of Johannes Rothe's four accounts of her life. *Das Bild der heiligen Hedwig in Mittelalter und Neuzeit*, ed. Eckhard Grunewald and Nikolaus Gussone (Schriften des Bundesinstituts für ostdeutsche Kultur und Geschichte, 7), Munich, Oldenbourg, 1996, 257 pp., includes work on aspects of the transmission and iconography of the legend by J. Gromadzki, M. Karge, W. Mrozowicz, and G. Muschiol. S. Jefferis, *JOWG*, 10:191–209, documents the transmission of Hermann von Fritzlar's *Heiligenleben* and the LG *Alexius*, and A. Poppenborg, *NdW*, 38:77–16, documents the late-medieval legends of St Catherine of Siena in Lübeck, while S. Fritsch-Staar, *ib.*, 117–39, presents the fictional saint Ontcommer in the Devotio Moderna, J. Knape, *JOWG*, 10:225–34, studies the Graz MLG *Veronica* fragment, and W. Williams-Krapp, *Fest. Geith*, 147–73, assesses the transmission of Dominican vernacular hagiography in the 14th and 15th cs.

Rudolf Stephan, *Teutsch Antiphonal. Quellen und Studien zur Geschichte des deutschen Chorals im 15. Jahrhundert unter besonderer Berücksichtigung der Gesänge des Breviers* (SÖAW, 595), 190 pp., is a monograph on the neglected pre-Reformation vernacular chorale written in the 1950s and supplied with an additional new preface. The text focuses on the number of breviaries in German from the 14th and 15th cs and complements these with a *catalogue raisonné* of the contents of the Munich and the Vienna manuscripts on which the study is based. Many of the hymns, antiphons, and other liturgical texts represented are discussed in some detail, so that there is important literary and theological substance here, besides the obvious musicological interest. H. Beifuss, *Chloe*, 25, 1997:983–94, discusses the edition of Matthäus von Krakau's *Dialogus rationis et conscientiae de communione sive de celebratione missae*. G. Roth, *JOWG*, 10:299–308, studies Alexander and Diogenes in the *Spieghel der leyen*. *Die 'Offenbarungen' der Katharina Tucher*, ed. Ulla Williams and Werner Williams-Krapp (UDL, 98), viii + 71 pp., makes accessible a work consisting of 94 entries from Nuremberg dated to 1418–21. The introduction traces what can be inferred about the author and her family, and analyses the form and content of the work, seeing in it a uniquely individual mystical spirituality. Katharina's subsequent entry into the Nuremberg Katharinenkloster yields knowledge of her considerable library with which her own work is fruitfully confronted. The text (pp. 31–70) is near-diplomatic. A. Volfing, *Kolloquium* (Meissen), 346–69, includes transcriptions of texts in a study of the vision of St John the Evangelist in the Meistergesang, and P. Dinzelbacher, *Fest. Birkhan*, 157–64, prints two other-world visions from a Salzburg manuscript of 1441.

U. Bakker, *NdW*, 38:1–35, analyses the sources of the Loccum *Historienbibel*, and A. Sroka, *JOWG*, 10:383–94, identifies the reception of mystical tradition in the *Wienhäuser Liederbuch*. P. Wiesinger, *Fest. Birkhan*, 211–43, cites 15th-c. German and other examples of the dispute between the devil and saints over the soul of a dead person. M. J. Briški, *Acta Neophilologica*, 31:3–33, studies a prayer book for private use in Ljubljana, and V. Honemann, pp. 101–16 of *Gattungen mittelalterlicher Schriftlichkeit* (see pp. 569–70 above), considers the functional context of a Basle library for lay brethren from the 1480s.

DRAMA. E. E. DuBruck, *FCS*, 24:1–16, reviews research on the drama 1995–96. H. Linke, *ZDP*, 117:1–16, uses examples from the history of work on the drama to illustrate how both chance and intention may determine the course of research. Matthias Schulz, *Die Eigenbezeichnungen des mittelalterlichen deutschsprachigen geistlichen Spiels* (GB, 2), 408 pp., based on R. Bergmann's catalogue and its supplement, is concerned, after careful attention to definitions, with the terms found in the historical documents themselves which refer to plays or parts of plays, or their performance. The identification of the remarkable number of 290 lexemes with over 4,000 examples in the total of 246 texts is itself justification of the value of the study. This is further enhanced by the inclusion of substantial quotations when the terminology is classified. Generic terms of the type play, comedy, act, etc., are distinguished from those which tend rather to be titular descriptions of content. The assessment of the material includes informative conclusions about historical processes such as the transition to modern theatre terminology, and the relationship of the medieval terms to scholarly terminology. W. Milde, Bräuer, *Kontext*, 51–60, connects the *Brunswick Easter Play 4* with the Mary Magdalene miniature in the Gospel Book of Henry the Lion, and F.-J. Schweitzer, *JOWG*, 10:363–70, identifies Christian and pagan myth in the hell scenes of the *Redentin Easter Play*, while C. Dauven-van Knippenberg, *Fest. Birkhan*, 778–87, studies the function of the *Wienhausen Easter Play* fragment. Ulrich Mehler, *Marienklagen im spätmittelalterlichen und frühneuzeitlichen Deutschland. Textversikel und Melodietypen. I. Darstellungsteil. II. Materialteil*, 2 vols (APSL, 128–29), 1997, viii + v + 237, ix + 319 pp., takes up the vexed problem of the scope and definition of the *Marienklage* and its relation to the drama. The second volume supplies the documentation on the basis of which the conclusions are developed: concordances of texts both alphabetical and according to various editions and Latin incipits, notation and transcription of all melodies, and two examples of the application of melodic types. The first volume is in effect an attempt to impose some kind of order upon chaos, R. Bergmann's catalogue and E. A. Schuler's 1951 account of the music being the only earlier work of substantial use. Although the comparative method adopted does not, on M.'s own admission, yield the straightforward classification of *Marienklagen* expected, it does identify a greater number than hitherto of the types and melodies characteristic of the dramatic instances of the form as a whole. H. Linke, *ASNS*, 235:110–15, records readers' notes in the MS of the *Munich Last Judgement Play*. J. R. Erb, *Exemplaria*, 10:371–403, focuses on the obscenity of the Nuremberg *Fastnachtspiele*, adding some suitably vivid translations.

SCIENTIFIC AND SPECIALIZED LITERATURE

Der Oldenburger Sachsenspiegel. Codex Picturatus Oldenburgensis CIM I 410 der Landesbibliothek Oldenburg. Vollständige Faksimile-Ausgabe. Kommentarband, ed. Ruth Schmidt-Wiegand (Codices selecti, 101), ADEVA, 1996, 324 pp., is an important new facsimile edition, while C. Bertelsmeier-Kierst, *WS XV*, 373–95, studies the interaction of text and illustration in legal manuscripts, and *Fest. Schmidt-Wiegand* includes work on legal texts by T. Sodmann (a Münsterland formula, 179–89), G. Kocher (the *Gänsezehent* in Eike von Repgow, 113–21), D. Pötschke (*Sachsenspiegel* glosses, 161–78), D. Werkmüller (a precedent from Ober-Roden, 139–47), and D. Munzel-Everling (the *Kleines Kaiserrecht*, 97–111). P. Lamberg, *JOWG*, 10:241–53, characterizes the theme *under konninges banne* in MLG legal texts, of which R. Schmidt-Wiegand, *ib.*, 311–26, studies the verse prefaces. W. Werner, *Fest. Schmidt-Wiegand*, 149–59, discusses a newly-discovered fragment of Bruder Berthold's *Rechtssumme*, while Goetz, *Geschichtsbewußtsein*, includes G. Dilcher on the legal view of time and history (31–54), and G. Theuerkauf on historical reference in legal texts (201–16). Legal texts and formulae also form the subject of work on Old Frisian in *ABÄG*, 49, by T. D. Hill (the *Fia-eth*, 169–78), T. S. B. Johnston (political ideology in texts and manuscripts, 179–214), B. Murdoch (prologues to legal texts, 215–44), D. P. O'Donnell (literary embellishment, 245–56), A. Sterringa (role of widows, 285–301), and O. Vries (hereditary right to purchase, 319–40). Franz Heiler, *Bildung im Hochstift Eichstätt zwischen Spätmittelalter und katholischer Konfessionalisierung. Die Städte Beilngries, Berching und Greding im Oberamt Hirschberg* (WM, 27), xii + 362 pp., is an Eichstätt dissertation which builds on recent work, also published in this series (see *YWMLS*, 56:765–66) directing attention to the importance of regional civic educational initiatives in the later Middle Ages. The main focus falls on the later 15th c. and the Reformation period, though some of the evidence takes us well into the 17th c. and is sufficiently well-documented for a vivid picture of the school provision in the three tiny townships to emerge. H. draws comparative conclusions about their social composition, ecclesiastical, economic, and political situation, and, for the schools themselves, substantial detail about their foundation and development, size, management, and staffing, the negative impact of the Reformation and their subsequent recovery. The subsequent fate of their pupils is well attested by the records of the *Studienstiftungen* and evidence of their university matriculation.

M. W. Adamson, *Fest. Birkhan*, 501–20, studies the preventative medicine of Michael de Leone, and C. Baufeld, *JOWG*, 10:3–16, studies medical terminology in Everhard van Wampen's LG health treatise, while G. Keil, *Fest. Birkhan*, 454–74, writes on a Luneburg health treatise of 1442, and A. Berndzen, *NdW*, 38:37–75, continues her work on the Lübeck plague treatise of 1484 (see *YWMLS*, 59:706). Gerold Hayer, *Konrad von Megenberg 'Das Buch der Natur': Untersuchungen zu seiner Text- und Überlieferungsgeschichte* (MTU, 110), ix + 533 pp. + 19 pls, marks a major advance in knowledge of the transmission and reception of a seminally important encyclopaedic text, the known importance of which more than justifies the aim of contributing to the eventual establishment of a new edition reflecting its historical impact. With 173 manuscripts and prints besides numerous fragments and excerpts the documentary evidence is more than sufficient for a study with this purpose alone. In exhaustive detail H. proceeds from an analysis of the transmission itself by way of an account of the history of the different versions to a history of the transmission external to the text; the latter culminates in comprehensive conclusions about the spatial and temporal dissemination, and its literary and social context and function. H.'s commentaries dwell on the fundamental question of the possible discrepancy between K.'s authorial intentions and the actual effects of his works: the approach, for example, demonstrates with clarity that what began as a popularizing vernacular text might reach no further than the *litterati* already familiar with the Latin sources! C. Baufeld, *Fest. Birkhan*, 521–38, discusses Heinrich Österreicher's 1491 translation of Columella's *De re rustica*. I. ten Venne, *NdJb*, 121:59–84, cites documents from late medieval Danzig in a primarily linguistic survey.

OTHER LATER MEDIEVAL LITERATURE

C. Bertelsmeier-Kierst, *ZDA*, 127:410–26, surveys the 15th-c. German adaptation of Boccaccio, the subject also of Claudia Bolsinger, *Das 'Decameron' in Deutschland. Wege der Literaturrezeption im 15. und 16. Jahrhundert* (EH, 1, 1687), 235 pp. M. Chojnacka, *SGGed*, 3, 1997:39–56, discusses female figures in the *fabliaux*, and H.-J. Bachorski, *ZGer*, 8:263–81, writes on the mocking of male aggression in fabliau literature, while H. Ragotzky, *BGDSL*, 120:36–52, examines the accommodation of courtly love to the fabliau, exemplified by *Der Sperber* and *Das Häslein*, and B. Beine, *JOWG*, 10:27–38, depicts the portrayal of clerics in *Die Frau des Seekaufmanns*. Also noted: Marga Stede, *Schreiben in der Krise. Die Texte des Heinrich Kaufringer* (Literatur — Imagination — Realität, 5), Trier, WVT, Wissenschaftlicher Vlg Trier, 1993, 353 pp., and D. Wolter, *JOWG*, 10:419–31, which characterizes the erotic fabliaux of the *Rostock Song Book*.

Christian Kiening, *Schwierige Modernität. Der 'Ackermann' des Johannes von Tepl und die Ambiguität historischen Wandels* (MTU, 113), ix + 718 pp. + 40 pls, is a monumental Munich *Habilitationsschrift* which is the first major work on the *Ackermann* for some time and takes a radically new look at the reception and transmission of the text in its late medieval and early modern historical contexts, the ambiguities of which it both mirrors and exemplifies. The central account of the impact and perception of the *Ackermann* and its substantial themes in the century from 1450 is strongly orientated towards its changing perception and function, and is highly informative on a range of other works and the shifts in cultural and philosophical sensibilities of the time. K. also develops the conception of 'modernity' against the background of a number of critical studies. The copious appendices include not only new documentation of the transmission in manuscript and printed versions, but also editions of a German translation of Lothar of Segni, *De miseria humanae conditionis*, Guilhelmus Savonensis, *An mortui sint lugendi an non*, and Menrad Molther, *Dialogus Mortis et Coloni*. Id., *OGS*, 26, 1997:1–23, looks at the figure of Death in the *Ackermann*, and N. F. Palmer, *Kolloquium* (Meissen), 299–322, addresses the question of autobiography and literary fiction in the *Ackermann*, while J. Schulz-Grobert, *ib.*, 323–33, focuses on ploughing and other metaphors of writing. The complex verb forms in the work are analysed by M. Shigeto, pp. 67–82 of *Gesellschaft, Kommunikation und Sprache Deutschlands in der frühen Neuzeit. Studien des deutsch-japanischen Arbeitskreises für Frühneuhochdeutschforschung*, ed. Klaus J. Mattheier, Haruo Nitta, and Mitsuyo Ono, Munich, Iudicium, 1997, 316 pp.

A. Robertshaw, *Kolloquium* (Meissen), 335–45, points to the editorial function of Hugo von Montfort and Oswald von Wolkenstein, and W. Pass, *Fest. Birkhan*, 629–51, records the Viennese reception of O. manuscripts, while A. and U. M. Schwob, *Fest. Geith*, 141–46, find a musical note in O.'s account book for 1418. Also of interest for O. is Gottfried Kompatscher, *Volk und Herrscher in der historischen Sage. Zur Mythisierung Friedrichs IV. von Österreich vom 15. Jahrhundert bis zur Gegenwart* (Beiträge zur europäischen Ethnologie und Folklore, A 4), 1995, 266 pp. S. Schmolinsky, *FCS*, 24:63–73, includes Helene Kottanner in a survey of female autobiography. *The Memoirs of Helene*

Kottanner (1439–1440), trans., introd., and comm. Maya Bijvoet Williamson, Cambridge, D. S. Brewer, xi + 79 pp., makes the important text accessible to an English-language readership. The lucid translation follows Karl Mollay's edition. The prefatory material surveys the biographical and historical background. More speculative is the 'interpretative essay' (pp. 53–71) which takes more account of the literary and fictive dimension of the work.

Werner Faulstich, *Medien zwischen Herrschaft und Revolte. Die Medienkultur der frühen Neuzeit (1400–1700)* (Die Geschichte der Medien, 3), Göttingen, Vandenhoeck & Ruprecht, 341 pp., continues this 'media history', effectively one of literary and cultural developments in general which can be related to a broadly defined conception of 'media'. Two volumes have already appeared (see *YWMLS*, 58:710; 59:671). With chapters on the letter, the various media used by different civic groups, the rural dimension (festival, storyteller, pamphlet, calendar), and, for the end of the period onwards, theatre, sermon, and the various minor forms of printing besides the book itself, the approach becomes relatively more convincing as the Middle Ages progresses. Andrea Klein, *Der Literaturbetrieb am Münchner Hof im fünfzehnten Jahrhundert* (GAG, 652), 244 pp. S. Westphal, *Daphnis*, 27:1–29, studies cursing and sorcery in some late-medieval texts, and A. Classen, *Daphnis*, 27:31–58, documents women writers and song collectors at the end of the period and beyond.

Fünf Palästina-Pilgerberichte aus dem 15. Jahrhundert, ed. and introd. Randall Herz, Dietrich Huschenbett, and Frank Sczesny (WM, 33), xxi + 329 pp., extends significantly the number of texts available in this growing area of late-medieval research. For each of the carefully edited critical editions the introductory matter includes essential biographical, textual, stylistic, and linguistic data, with bibliography and summary of content: the anonymous Austrian *Geschrift und Weisung für die Fahrt zum Heiligen Grab* (F. Sczesny, 1–22); the anonymous Bavarian *Von der Gestalt des Heiligen Grabes zu Jerusalem und des Heiligen Landes darum* (F. Sczesny, 23–96); Girnand von Schwalbach, *Reise zum Heiligen Grab* (D. Huschenbett, 97–138); the anonymous Rhenish Franconian *Fahrt zum Heiligen Grab* (R. Herz, 139–74); and Hans Koppler, *Rais in das heilig land* (R. Herz, 175–224). D. Huschenbett draws the material together in a preface and there is a concluding essay by N. Zwijnenburg-Tönnies (225–60) which relates the pilgrimage texts to earlier literature associated with the stations of the Cross. N. Miedema, *ZDA*, 127:381–409, supplies prolegomena to an edition of the *Indulgentiae ecclesiarum urbis Romae*, and R. Herz, *GJ*, 73:101–04, ascribes a Jerusalem itinerary to Nuremberg, *c.* 1489. Detlev Kraack, *Monumentale Zeugnisse der spätmittelalterlichen Adelsreise. Inschriften und Graffiti des 14.–16. Jahrhunderts* (AAWG, 224), 1997, xi + 571 pp., is an interesting complement to the wealth of work on travel literature, and E. Seebold, *BGDSL*, 120:435–49, identifies a long tradition for the alphabets cited by Mandeville.

Michael Giesecke, *Der Buchdruck in der frühen Neuzeit. Eine historische Fallstudie über die Durchsetzung neuer Informations- und Kommunikationstechnologien* (STW, 1357), 957 pp., first appeared in 1991 but the significance of the approach, inseparable from the growth of the electronic media, can hardly be overestimated and has had a wide resonance in the meantime. With countless examples G. shows the practical and the symbolic and intellectual consequences of printing and the parallels to the progress of electronic technology and the attitudes and fears surrounding it. A supplementary essay takes stock of the current position and argues that the metaphorical system implied by the computer will take time to replace the mythology of the information system established in the late 15th c. A. Fromm, *JOWG*, 10:153–65, reviews the Cologne and Lübeck Bibles as evidence of early printing in the LG area. In Tomasch and Gilles, *Text and Territory*, the place of Gog and Magog in the *mappae mundi* tradition is interpreted by S. D. Westrem (54–75) and K. Biddick (268–93). H.-J. Behr, *FCS*, 24:17–25, locates Michael Wyssenherre's poem on the Duke of Brunswick to Gochsheim (Württemberg). N. F. Palmer, pp. 287–302 of *Boethius in the Middle Ages. Latin and Vernacular Traditions of the 'Consolatio Philosophiae'*, ed. Maarten J. F. M. Hoenen and Lodi Nauta (Studien und Texte zur Geistesgeschichte des Mittelalters, 58), Leiden, Brill, 1997, viii + 376 pp. + 3 pls, writes on the 1473 Boethius translation. F. Fürbeth, *Fest. Ertzdorff*, 389–407, interprets the prefaces to the 1478 print of Niklas von Wyle's works as genuine expressions of his didactic purpose. A. E. Wright, *Wolfenbütteler Beiträge*, 11:53–72, reviews the introduction of vernacular fable collections in the late Middle Ages, and *ib.*, 7–15, studies the manuscript initials of the Nuremberg *Äsop*, while a more exhaustive study is supplied by Brigitte Derendorf, *Der Magdeburger Prosa-Äsop. Eine mittelniederdeutsche Bearbeitung von Heinrich Steinhöwels 'Esopus' und Niklas von Wyles 'Guiscard und Sigismunda'. Text und Untersuchungen* (NdS, 35), 1996, ix + 568 pp., and F. Schanze, *GJ*, 73:105–10, discusses the printer of the German *Äsop* and the Basle *Brandan*. I. Bennewitz, *Fest. Birkhan*, 755–77, studies the relationship of text and illustration in *Neithart Fuchs* prints. For F. J. Worstbrock, Peil, *Erkennen*, 215–43, Hartmann Schedel's *Liber antiquitatum cum epitaphiis et epigrammatibus* epitomizes the humanist appreciation of historical memory, and R. Klein, *JFL*, 58:167–85, surveys Schedel's treatment of Greek history in his world chronicle. C. Meier-Staubach, *Fest. Schmidt-Wiegand*, 191–200, discusses text and illustration in the *Hortus sanitatis*, and M. Ostermann, *GJ*, 73:131–38, studies a Strasbourg letter of 1494 announcing a crossbow tournament.

Sebastian Brant, *Kleine Texte*, ed. Thomas Wilhelmi, I/I, I/2, II (Arbeiten und Editionen zur Mittleren Deutschen Literatur, n. F., 3), Stuttgart-Bad Cannstatt, Frommann-Holzboog, 320, 321–625, 224 pp., is an immense aid to scholarship, with 469 shorter texts of which only about a half have previously been edited in part or whole. The editor rightly prefers a chronological sequence — the majority of the works are dated and the rest mostly datable — to a division into Latin and German, so that B.'s impressive range and development are immediately accessible. Text and punctuation follow the originals with minimal intervention. The third volume supplies full codicological and bibliographical information besides, as appropriate, brief references to the historical and literary background and to sources. The quality of production, characteristic of the publisher, makes the volumes a pleasure to use. S. Fuchs, *Neophilologus*, 82:83–95, interprets Brant's use of the metaphor of ship and book, and M. Rupp, *ZDA*, 127:169–81, studies the image of the crab in Brant and elsewhere.

H. Kokott, *Eulenspiegel-Jb.*, 37, 1997:61–83, studies the organization of animal and human characteristics in *Reynke de Vos*, on which there is a linguistic study, R. Steinar Nybøle, *Reynke de Vos. Ein Beitrag zur Grammatik der frühen Lübecker Druckersprache* (Forschungen zum Niederdeutschen, 1), Neumünster, Wachholtz, 1997, 295 pp. A. Schwarz, *JOWG*, 10:349–61, considers the cunning of *Reynke de Vos* and *Eulenspiegel* on an intercultural basis, and H.-J. Behr, *Eulenspiegel-Jb.*, 37, 1997:13–32, considers various medieval fools as the background to *Eulenspiegel*. Finally, C. Kirschner, *JOWG*, 10:211–23, writes on the theme of city and world in Hermen Bote's historiographical works, and M. Nix, *ib.*, 269–79, studies his connection to the Welfs.

THE SIXTEENTH CENTURY

By PETER MACARDLE, *University of Durham*

1. GENERAL

Jürgen Römer, *Geschichte der Kürzungen. Abbreviaturen in deutschsprachigen Texten des Mittelalters und der frühen Neuzeit* (GAG, 645), 1997, 237 pp. This work, based on a detailed examination of over 700 medieval and early modern manuscripts, discusses the development of abbreviations in German-language texts in the context of the overall evolution of forms of writing. Though the study is not primarily designed as a reference work, the copious list of abbreviations (40–153) will be a useful palaeographical aid. Friedrich-Carl Stechow, *Lexikon der Stammbuchsprüche. Stechow's Stammbuchsprüche-Schlüssel*, Neustadt an der Aisch, Degener, 1996, xiv + 286 pp., proposes a variety of solutions to the meaning of the many entries in *Stammbücher* of the 16th–18th cs which are given as initials only. Josef Ijsewijn and Dirk Sacré, *Companion to Neo-Latin Studies. II. Literary, Linguistic, Philological and Editorial Questions* (Supplementa Humanistica Lovaniensia, 14), Leuven U.P., xiv + 562 pp., is a completely rewritten second edition of this essential tool. It covers the entire field of neo-Latin writing, giving an accurate summary of the current state of research in numerous genres and periods, along with helpful pointers to the direction that further study could take. Hans-Jörg Künast, *'Getruckt zu Augspurg.' Buchdruck und Buchhandel in Augsburg zwischen 1468 und 1555*, Tübingen, Niemeyer, ix + 373 pp., is a comprehensive history of all aspects of printing and the book trade in this important centre. A vast amount of original archival research and personal examination of many printed books has produced extremely detailed information not only on the books produced, but also on the financial structures of the trade, personal and economic networks of printers, and the complex practicalities of distributing the books printed in the city. Over 60 pp. of graphs (293–355) display statistics on book production in an accessible and informative manner.

2. HUMANISM AND THE REFORMATION

B. Guthmüller, 'Formen des Mythenverständnisses um 1500', Horn, *Allegorese*, 37–62. W. Schibel, 'Der antike Mythos in der neulateinischen Literatur Deutschlands — Probleme seiner Erschliessung', pp. 177–89 of *Der antike Mythos und Europa. Texte und Bilder von der Antike bis ins 20. Jahrhundert*, ed. Francesca Cappelletti and Gerlinde Huber-Rebenich, Berlin, Mann, 1997, xi + 250 pp. *Hellas in Deutschland.*

Darstellungen der Gräzistik im deutschsprachigen Raum aus dem 16. und 17. Jahrhundert, ed. Walther Ludwig (Berichte aus den Sitzungen der Joachim-Jungius-Gesellschaft der Wissenschaften, Hamburg, 16.1), Göttingen, Vandenhoeck & Ruprecht, 104 pp. F. Rädle, 'Humanistenlatein und das übrige Leben oder von der Nachsicht der Gebildeten mit den Frommen', *Fest. Wimmel*, 261–74. Herfried Munkler, Hans Grünberger and Kathrin Mayer, *Nationenbildung. Die Nationalisierung Europas im Diskurs humanistischer Intellektueller. Italien und Deutschland* (Politische Ideen, 8), Berlin, Akademie, 350 pp., examines Aeneas Sylvius's thinking on the national identity of the Germans, strategies of *Identitätsbildung* used by German humanists, and the functionalization of Arminius as a national symbol in the 16th c. Noted: Manfred Welti, *Die europäische Spätrenaissance*, Basel, Reinhardt, 336 pp., an interdisciplinary *Mentalitätsgeschichte*.

Work concentrating on specific regions includes the following: *Stadt und Literatur im deutschen Sprachraum der Frühen Neuzeit*, ed. Klaus Garber, Stefan Anders, and Thomas Elsmann (FN, 39), 2 vols, xvii + 546, x + 547–1145 pp., a most informative collection of essays on this flourishing area of early modern literary scholarship. Vol. 1 contains theoretical essays and studies on Upper Germany and the areas dominated by Reformed Protestantism; vol. 2 covers Lutheran *Mitteldeutschland*, the Hanseatic cities, Central Europe, and Catholic Germany; though the brief coverage of this last category suggests there is still a good deal to investigate here. The majority of the essays deal with the 17th and 18th cs. Relevant to the 16th c. are those by K. Garber, 'Stadt und Literatur im alten deutschen Sprachraum' (3–89), W. Adam, 'Urbanität und poetische Form' (90–111), M. Schilling, 'Stadt und Publizistik in der Frühen Neuzeit' (112–41), C. Gellinek, on Münster (186–202), T. Elsmann, on Bremen (203–38), A. Schindling, on Frankfurt (538–46), D. Ignasiak, on Jena (572–602), H. Freytag, on Petrus Vincentius in Bremen (637–57), H. Langer, on Pomerania (729–36), I. Zachová, on Bohemia (988–96), D. Schubert, on the library of the Latin school at St Joachimsthal (997–1006), L. Tsybenko, on Lemberg (1007–29), B. Boge, on the literary production of the Ingolstadt Jesuits (1033–62), D. Breuer, on Munich (1063–91), and H. Marti, on Counter-Reformation Lucerne (1092–113). *The Reformation in Eastern and Central Europe*, ed. Karin Maag, Aldershot, Scolar, 1997, xiv + 235 pp. Particularly relevant to the German-speaking world are the contributions by H. R. Schmidt, on the long-term social effect of the morals courts in rural Berne (155–81), J. Małłek, on similarities and differences between the Polish and Prussian Reformations (182–91), M. G. Müller, on Protestant confessionalization in Prussia (192–210), and R. J. Gordon, on the role of the nobility in the recatholicization of Lower Austria (211–27). M. Włodarski, 'Polen und Basel — kulturelle und literarische Verbindungen im 16. Jahrhundert', *Pirckheimer Jb.*, 12, 1997:91–100. J. Pirożyński, 'Die Krakauer Universität in der Renaissancezeit', *ib.*, 13–38; T. Ulewicz, 'Literarische Kreise und "Gesellschaften" in Krakau und Kleinpolen im Zeitalter der Renaissance', *ib.*, 39–72. H. Wiegand, *ib.*, 187–209, investigates the *Sodalitas litteraria Rhenana* in Heidelberg. F. Machilek, 'Der Olmützer Humanistenkreis', *ib.*, 111–35. R. L. Vice, 'Iconoclasm in Rothenburg ob der Tauber in 1525', *AR*, 89:55–78. J. Gény, 'La ville impériale de Sélestat et sa participation aux mouvements sociaux, politiques et religieux des années 1490–1536', *Annuaire des amis de la Bibliothèque Humaniste de Sélestat*, 48:47–56.

G. R. Dimler, pp. 93–109 of *Emblematic Perceptions. Essays in Honour of William S. Heckscher on the Occasion of his Ninetieth Birthday*, ed. Peter M. Daly and Daniel S. Russell (Saecula spiritualia, 36), Baden-Baden, Koerner, 1997, 241 pp., sees Jesuit emblematic practice as rooted in Renaissance humanism. A. Buck, 'Zum Selbstverständnis der Renaissance', *WRM*, 21, 1997:49–57. C. Kiening, *ZGer*, n.s. 8:302–16, studies writing by Erasmus, Hutten, and Pirckheimer on their own bodies and ailments. C. G. Nauert, Jr, 'Humanism as method: roots of conflict with the scholastics', *SCJ*, 29:427–38.

Protestant History and Identity in Sixteenth-Century Europe, ed. Bruce Gordon, 2 vols, Aldershot, Scolar, 1996, x + 194, x + 202 pp. Though largely historical and theological in focus, this collection contains several contributions exploring ways in which Reformation writing attempted to forge narratives and images of the past which bolstered the self-understanding of the Protestant churches. Particularly relevant are M. Wriedt, on 'Luther's concept of history and the formation of an evangelical identity' (I, 31–45); H. U. Bold, on Bullinger's *Anklag und ernstliches ermanen Gottes* (I, 46–59); B. Gordon, on Protestant images of Savonarola (I, 93–107); P. Biel, on Luther's theory of betrothal and marriage (II, 121–41; and B. Nischan, on 'Ritual and Protestant identity in Late Reformation Germany' (II, 142–58). R. J. Bast, 'From two kingdoms to two tables: The Ten Commandments and the Christian magistrate', *AR*, 89:79–95; P. Friess, 'Die Bedeutung der Stadtschreiber für die Reformation der süddeutschen Reichsstädte', *ib.*, 96–124; D. Myers, 'Ritual, confession and religion in sixteenth-century Germany', *ib.*, 125–43; G. Vogler, 'Kurfürst Johann Friedrich und Herzog Moritz von Sachsen: Polemik in Liedern und Flugschriften während des Schmalkaldischen Krieges 1546/47', *ib.*, 178–206. H. Junghans, 'Plädoyer für "Wildwuchs der Reformation" als Metapher', *Lutherjb.*,

65: 101–08. J. Orschler, 'Protestantische Lehr- und Erbauungsgra-phik. Perspektiven der Erforschung konfessioneller Bilderwelten', *JV*, n.s., 20, 1997: 211–44.

3. Genres

DRAMA AND DIALOGUE

Stephen K. Wright, *Theatre Annual*, 51: 1–14, concludes that the policing of early modern dramatic performances in Germany consti-tuted a ritual display of civic authority and cohesion that comple-mented the action of the plays themselves.

PROSE AND VERSE

Geschlechterbeziehungen und Textfunktion. Studien zu Eheschriften der Frühen Neuzeit, ed. Rüdiger Schnell (FN, 40), x + 317 pp., a collection of essays by several hands, examines differences between about 20 *Eheschriften* written in Latin and German between 1470 and 1580. The widespread assumption that these differences were brought about by actual changes in social and religious thought and behaviour is questioned; the authors conclude that communicative and situative aspects of the texts in question are also (indeed predominantly) responsible. Different languages, addressees and kinds of discourse seem to be much more influential on the varying accentuations of the texts than alleged changes in the social or theological evaluation of marriage and gender-roles in the early modern period. Miriam Usher Chrisman, *Conflicting Visions of Reform. German Lay Propaganda Pamphlets, 1519–1530*, Atlantic Highlands, Humanities Press International, 1996, xiii + 288 pp., examines approximately 300 pamphlets written by lay authors. C. identifies six main social groups from which the authors come: the nobility and knights, the urban elite, learned civil servants and professionals, minor civil servants and technicians, common burghers and artisans. The differences, both in content and style, of the products of these various strata show that early Lutheran preaching was received in a wide variety of ways according to the preoccupations and self-perceptions of different classes, and their divergent visions of the Christian community. This led to several simultaneous, but separate, socio-theological revolutions; that of the urban elite, the 'magisterial' reform, based on the vision of the holy city, won out over those of the knights, peasants and artisans. H. Sievert, *JIG*, 29.2, 1997: 124–46, examines the reception of the *chanson de geste* in four prose romances of the 16th c., two by Johann II of Simmern. W. Klose, Peil, *Erkennen*, 311–23, analyses the *Stammbuch* of Abraham and David Ulrich.

The series *Bibliothek der frühen Neuzeit* continues with Abt. 1. *Literatur im Zeitalter des Humanismus und der Reformation*. 5. *Humanistische Lyrik des 16. Jahrhunderts. Lateinisch und deutsch*, trans. and ed. Wilhelm Kühlmann, Robert Seidel, and Hermann Wiegand, DKV, 1997, 1592 pp. This superb volume offers a representative selection from the work of 20 German neo-Latin poets from Celtis to Caspar von Barth. The poems are printed in newly established editions, with facing German prose translations. There are biographical and bibliographical introductions to each poet, and a vast *Stellenkommentar* (920–1527) with all the necessary source and background material. This volume, the fruit of a collaborative research project in Heidelberg, combines scholarly reliability with accessibility even to the non-specialist reader; it fully meets the extremely high standards set by previous volumes in the series. S. Hohmann, 'Türkenkrieg und Friedensbund im Spiegel der politischen Lyrik. Auch ein Beitrag zur Entstehung des Europabegriffs', *LiLi*, 28:128–58. U. Müller and M. Springeth, *Fest. Geith*, 73–88, investigate the rhymed chronicle in a unique 'Flagellum' MS of *c.* 1595 (British Library, Add. MS 16280).

4. OTHER WORK

Edward Muir, *Ritual in Early Modern Europe* (New Approaches to European History, 11), CUP, xii + 291 pp. Many German examples are discussed in this wide-ranging study of the change in the perception of ritual which took place between 1400 and 1700. Originally thought of as action which brought about real presence, ritual was reinterpreted, largely under the influence of the Reformers, to mean words which communicated merely representational meanings. M. deals with the official and unofficial ritual practices of Christianity, with the civic rituals of government, with carnival and festivity, and with the (alleged) anti-Christian rituals of Jews and witchcraft. W. Müller, 'Erinnern an die Gründung: Universitätsjubiläen, Universitätsgeschichte und die Entstehung der Jubiläumskultur in der frühen Neuzeit', *Berichte zur Wissenschaftsgeschichte*, 21:79–102. M. Pelc, 'Zensur und Selbstzensur in der Bibelillustration des 16. Jahrhunderts', *Frühneuzeit-Info*, 9:194–205. W. Ludwig, *Philologus*, 142:123–61, studies the inscriptions on visual depictions of Erasmus, Melanchthon, Luther, P. Melissus, and H. Rantzau. O. Ulbricht, 'Pesterfahrung: "Das Sterben" und der Schmerz in der frühen Neuzeit', *Medizin, Gesellschaft und Geschichte*, 15:9–35, considers numerous 16th-c. accounts of such illnesses. M. Harrington, 'Bad parents, the state, and the early modern civilising process', *German History*, 16:15–28, deals with German examples, particularly from Nuremberg. J.-P. Bodmer, *Daphnis*, 27:59–92, edits the inventory of books belonging to Heinrich Grob (Zurich, 1566–1614). E. Kleinschmidt, 'Formation und Differenz. Funktionale Konstellationen frühneuzeitlicher Etymologik', Peil, *Erkennen*, 245–63.

5. INDIVIDUAL AUTHORS AND WORKS

AGRIPPA VON NETTESHEIM, HEINRICH CORNELIUS. Henricus Cornelius Agrippa, *Declamation on the Nobility and Preeminence of the Female Sex*, trans. and ed. Albert Rabil, Jr, Chicago U.P., 1996, xxxii + 109 pp., presents a good translation of the Latin text (from Antonioli's critical edition, 1990), and introductory material on A.'s place in the feminist tradition and on his possible literary sources.

AMERBACH, VEIT. G. Frank, 'Veit Amerbach (1503–1557). Von Wittenberg nach Ingolstadt', Scheible, *Melanchthon*, 103–28.

BIDEMBACH, CHRISTOPH. W. Ludwig, *ZWL*, 57:21–35, discusses a recently discovered description of Stuttgart written by B. in 1585.

BOTE, HERMANN. H. Blume, *JOWG*, 10:67–79, investigates the early modern reception of the *Schichtbuch*; J. Schulz-Grobert, *ib.*, 341–48, considers the recently rediscovered *Braunschweiger Titelbuch* as a source for some details of *Till Eulenspiegel*. H.-J. Behr, 'Der *Ulenspiegel* im Umkreis der mittelalterlichen Narrenliteratur', *Eulenspiegel-Jb.*, 37, 1997:13–32; A. Kanngiesser, 'Handwerksbezeichnungen im *Eulenspiegelbuch*', *ib.*, 35–58; A. Schwarz, 'Eulenspiegel am Genfersee', *ib.*, 85–97. A. Classen, 'Der vertrackte, widerspenstige Held Till Eulenspiegel. Sexualität, der Körper, Transgression', *Euphorion*, 92:249–70.

BRANT, SEBASTIAN. Sebastian Brant, *Fabeln*, ed. Bernd Schneider (Arbeiten und Editionen zur Mittleren Deutschen Literatur, n.s., 4), Bad Cannstatt, Frommann-Holzboog, 592 pp. S. Fuchs, ' "[...] und netzen das bapyren Schiff." Schiffsmetapher, Buchmetapher und Autordiskurs im *Narrenschiff* Sebastian Brants', *Neophilologus*, 82:83–95.

CANTIUNCULA, CLAUDIUS. Beate Gabriele Lüsse, *Formen der humanistischen Utopie. Vorstellungen vom idealen Staat im englischen und kontinentalen Schrifttum des Humanismus 1516–1669* (Beiträge zur englischen und amerikanischen Literatur, 19), Paderborn, Schöningh, 271 pp., includes the Basel jurist's German translation of More's *Utopia* (1524) in her study of the development and reception of utopian thinking by various humanist writers.

CASELIUS, JOHANNES. M. Scattola, 'Johannes Caselius (1533–1613), ein Helmstedter Gelehrter', *WNB*, 22, 1997:101–21.

CHEMNITZ, MARTIN. T. Kaufmann, 'Martin Chemnitz (1522–1586). Zur Wirkungsgeschichte der theologischen Loci', Scheible, *Melanchthon*, 183–254.

CHYTRAEUS, DAVID. R. Keller, 'David Chytraeus (1530–1600). Melanchthons Geist im Luthertum', Scheible, *Melanchthon*, 361–71.

CORDUS, EURICIUS. E. Schäfer, 'Euricius Cordus: Vergil in Hessen', *Fest. Wimmel*, 283–314.

DEDEKIND, FRIEDRICH. Barbara A. Correll, *The End of Conduct: 'Grobianus' and the Renaissance Text of the Subject*, Ithaca, Cornell U.P., 1997, xv + 225 pp., illuminatingly interprets *Grobianus* against a tradition of Renaissance civility literature which is actually harsh and aversion-based, drawing much of its effect from the anxiety about the (male) body which it instils in its (male) readers. This reading, in the tradition of Bakhtin, Elias, and Foucault, is also informed by original insights into the role of gender in the conduct literature. The study examines D.'s original text and his revisions of it, including *Grobianus et Grobiana* (1554), as well as translations into German (by Kaspar Scheidt, 1551) and English.

DREYFELDER, TIBURTIUS. R. Hilgers, *RPLit*,20, 1997:188–84, discusses D.'s German translation of G. B. Pigna's history of the ducal house of Este (1580).

DÜRER, ALBRECHT. H. Sahm, 'Dürer als Autor', *Kolloquium* (Meissen), 397–408; H. K. Szépe, 'Bordon, Dürer and modes of illuminating Aldines', pp. 185–200 of *Aldus Manutius and Renaissance Culture. Essays in Memory of Franklin D. Murphy*, ed. David S. Zeidberg and Fiorella Gioffredi Superbi, Florence, Olschki, 336 pp. J. Schulz-Grobert, 'Mit Zirckel vñ Richtscheydt. Dürers Bauernsäule als praktisches Vermessungsinstrument für "theoretisches" Neuland', *ZDP*, 117:321–45.

EBER, PAUL. W. Thüringer, 'Paul Eber (1511–1569). Melanchthons Physik und seine Stellung zu Copernicus', Scheible, *Melanchthon*, 285–321.

EBERLIN VON GÜNZBURG, JOHANN. Geoffrey Dipple, *Antifraternalism and Anticlericalism in the German Reformation. Johann Eberlin von Günzburg and the Campaign against the Friars*, Aldershot, Scolar, x + 244 pp., considers E.'s anti-Franciscan writings along with those of several of his contemporaries as part of a concerted Wittenberg antifraternal campaign. D. also reassesses the chronology and progression of E.'s increasing distance from the Observant Franciscans, and points out ways in which his thought and polemic were influenced by the traditions of his erstwhile order.

ECK, JOHANN. *Threni magistri nostri Ioannis Eckii in obitu Margaretae concubinae suae*, ed. and trans. Franz Wachinger (Studien zur klassischen Philologie, 107), Frankfurt–Berne, Lang, 204 pp., is a commented critical edition of this anonymous satire on Eck. W. (28–36) judiciously weighs up the evidence of authorship and rejects the common ascription of the *Threni* to Simon Lemnius; on stylistic and other grounds, Thomas Venatorius in Nuremberg emerges as a more likely author.

EOBANUS HESSUS, HELIUS. J. Hamm, '*De victoria Wirtembergensi*. Die Restitution Herzog Ulrichs von Württemberg (1534) im Spiegel der neulateinischen Dichtung', *LiLi*, 28:74–99, deals with E. and the lesser-known poets J. Pedius and M. Augustus. W. Ludwig, 'Eobanus Hessus in Erfurt. Ein Beitrag zum Verhältnis von Humanismus und Protestantismus', *MJ*, 33:155–70.

FEYERABEND, SIGMUND. Anne Simon, *Sigmund Feyerabend's 'Das Reyssbuch dess heyligen Lands'. A Study in Printing and Literary History* (WM, 32), x + 227 pp., analyses F.'s great compendium of accounts of pilgrimages to the Holy Land (1584). S. deals with the printing history of the *Reyssbuch*, which was reprinted three times until 1659, with its relation to and adaptation of its source-material, and with its reception-history. There are chapters considering F.'s mixed aims in publishing such an essentially old-fashioned kind of book so late in the 16th c., comparative exemplary analyses of sections dealing with Bethlehem, and an examination of the literary and generic aspects of medieval and early modern pilgrimage literature. K. Skow-Obenaus, 'Women in the Book of Love: The contexts of Feyerabendt's *Das Buch der Liebe*', *ColGer*, 31:105–16. A. Ebenbauer, *Fest. Birkhan*, 552–66, writes on Schubert's opera adaptation of *Fierabras*.

FISCHART, JOHANN. Johann Fischart, *Sämtliche Werke*, ed. Hans-Gert Roloff, Ulrich Seelbach, and W. Eckehart Spengler, Bad Cannstatt, Frommann-Holzboog, continues with II. *Eulenspiegel reimenweis*, ed. Ulrich Seelbach and W. Eckehart Spengler, 480 pp. The edition contains facsimiles of the original illustrations by Tobias Stimmer.

FLACIUS ILLYRICUS, MATTHIAS. B. J. Diebner, 'Matthias Flacius Illyricus. Zur Hermeneutik der Melanchthon-Schule', Scheible, *Melanchthon*, 157–82. J. Knape, 'Petrarca protestantisch. Flacius Illyricus rezipiert Petrarca', *Chloe*, 26, 1997:195–210.

FORTUNATUS. The facsimile reprint of the English translation, *The Right Pleasant and Variable Tragical History of Fortunatus (London, 1676)* (Deutsche Volksbücher in Faksimiledrucken, A, 18), Hildesheim, Olms, vi + 148 pp., includes an afterword and bibliography by Renate Noll-Wiemann.

FRISCHLIN, NICODEMUS. **Nicodemus Frischlin (1547–1590). Poetische und prosaische Praxis unter den Bedingungen des konfessionellen Zeitalters. Tübinger Vorträge*, ed. Sabine Holtz and Dieter Mertens (Arbeiten und Editionen zur Mittleren Deutschen Literatur, 1), Bad Cannstatt, Frommann-Holzboog, 530 pp., contains 21 essays by various hands.

GESNER, CONRAD. J.-D. Müller, 'Universalbibliothek und Gedächtnis', Peil, *Erkennen*, 285–309 (on the *Bibliotheca universalis*).

GRESEL, JAKOB. Eberhard Doll, *Jakob Gresel, 1483–1552. Leben und Vermächtnis eines rheinisch-westfälischen Klerikers und Humanisten*, Bramsche, Rasch, 1997, 313 pp., traces the sparsely documented career of this humanist from his studies at Cologne to his pedagogical and ecclesiastical activity in Osnabrück and Rees. Nearly half of this informative study is devoted to the documents recording G.'s life and work; all are printed in full, many in facsimile. They include much legal and administrative material, giving a rounded picture of the diverse ways in which this scholar interacted with the communities where he lived.

HAGEN, PETER. T. Bürger, *WBN*, 24, 1997:259–61, writes on H.'s *Stammbuch*, recently acquired by the Herzog August Bibliothek in Wolfenbüttel.

HERESBACH, KONRAD. *Humanismus als Reform am Niederrhein. Konrad Heresbach 1496–1576*, ed. Jutta Prieur (Schriften der Heresbach-Stiftung Kalkar, 4), Bielefeld, Vlg für Regionalgeschichte, 1997, 241 pp., the catalogue of a major exhibition, contains (14–134) nine substantial essays by various hands on H.'s wide-ranging literary, theological and political activity.

HESHUSEN, TILEMANN. I. Mager, 'Tilemann Heshusen (1527–1588). Geistliches Amt, Glaubensmündigkeit und Gemeindeautonomie', Scheible, *Melanchthon*, 341–59.

HEYDEN, SEBALD. Sebald Heyden, *Nomenclatura rerum domesticarum*, ed. Peter O. Müller and Gaston van der Elst, Hildesheim, Olms, iv + 36 + 184 facsimile pp., is a facsimile reprint of the editions of the *Nomenclatura* printed in Nuremberg in 1530 and Mainz in 1534.

HISTORIA VON D. JOHANN FAUSTEN. D. Walch-Paul, *Fest. Ertzdorff*, 83–99, reads the *Historia* as a series of 'Gegenbilder' to medieval norms of life and behaviour.

KEPLER, JOHANNES. *Bibliographia Kepleriana. Verzeichnis der gedruckten Schriften von und über Johannes Kepler*, ed. Kepler-Kommission der Bayerischen Akademie der Wissenschaften. *Ergänzungsband zur zweiten Auflage*, ed. Jürgen Hamel, Munich, Beck, xliii + 192 pp. Charlotte Methuen, *Kepler's Tübingen. Stimulus to a Theological Mathematics*, Aldershot, Ashgate, xi + 280 pp., is a profound, wide-ranging study of late-16th-c. intellectual life at the University of Tübingen. M. attempts to show how the interaction between theological and philosophical thinking there may have influenced K.'s own scholarly programme of searching for a harmonizing principle for the universe. After a conspectus of the Württemberg educational system and the Tübingen curriculum, there follow detailed analyses of the place of mathematics and astronomy in Melanchthon's theology, and of the contemporary debates about the relationship between theology and natural philosophy and about the role of observation in the physical sciences.

KRELL, PAUL. H.-P. Hasse, 'Paul Krell (1531–1579). Melanchthons "Enarratio Symboli Nicaeni" (1550) und der Sturz des Philippismus in Kursachsen im Jahre 1574', Scheible, *Melanchthon*, 427–63.

LAGUS, KONRAD. H. E. Troje, 'Konrad Lagus (*c.*1500–1546). Zur Rezeption der Loci-Methode in der Jurisprudenz', Scheible, *Melanchthon*, 255–83.

LIPSIUS, JUSTUS. A. Moss, 'The *Politica* of Justus Lipsius and the Commonplace-Book', *JHI*, 59:421–36.

LUTHER, MARTIN. Martin Luther, *Werke. Kritische Gesamtausgabe*, continues with 67. *Lateinisches Sachregister zur Abteilung Schriften Band 1–60, o–r*, ed. Ulrich Köpf, Weimar, Böhlau, 1997, xii + 750 pp. Renate and Gustav Bebermeyer, *Wörterbuch zu Martin Luthers deutschen Schriften*, Lieferung 3. *Härtiglich–Heilig*, Hildesheim, Olms, iv + 205 pp. Anja Lobenstein-Reichmann, *Freiheit bei Martin Luther. Lexikographische Textanalyse als Methode historischer Semantik* (SLG, 46), xiii + 598 pp., is a semantic and syntactic examination of L.'s use of 'frei', 'Freiheit' and lexically and thematically related terms in a corpus of German-language texts from the period 1517–31. Comparison of the use of the same terms in the writing of those (such as the German peasants) who misunderstood L.'s concept of freedom is also made (327–66). Interestingly, this rigorously linguistic study reveals the theological nature of L.'s understanding of human freedom not as worldly autonomy, but as a freedom that humans can enjoy only insofar as they participate in the unconstrained freedom of God. H. U. Schmid, *ZDL*, 65:1–41, uses 16th-c. and 17th-c. inscriptions to reach a nuanced verdict on the influence of L.'s Bible translation on the phonology of modern German. E. Reichert, Beutin, *Mystik*, 223–36, examines L.'s relation to the mystic tradition. E. Andreatta, 'Aristoteles als literarische Quelle Martin Luthers', *Lutherjb.*, 65:45–52; A. Flegel and H. Junghans, *ib.*, 85–100, edit and comment on three previously unknown letters of L. and Melanchthon; H. Junghans, *ib.*, 109–77, assesses the resonance of the 1996 'Lutherjahr' in scholarship.

MAJOR, GEORG. T. J. Wengert, 'Georg Major (1502–1574). Defender of Wittenberg's Faith and Melanchthonian Exegete', Scheible, *Melanchthon*, 129–56.

MELANCHTHON, PHILIPP. Philipp Melanchthon, *Briefwechsel. Kritische und kommentierte Gesamtausgabe*, Bad Cannstatt, Frommann-Holzboog, is brought to completion by the last two volumes: 9. *Addenda und Konkordanzen*, ed. Heinz Scheible and Walter Thüringer, 403 pp.; 10. *Orte A–Z und Itinerar*, ed. Heinz Scheible, 725 pp. The *Itinerar* section of vol. 10 (275–725) gives an almost daily account of M.'s whereabouts from his arrival at Wittenberg in 1518 till his death, with cross-references to the letters and other documents which provide evidence of this. Scheible, *Melanchthon*, contains a brief treatment by S. of 'Melanchthon als akademischer Lehrer' (13–29), and essays by various hands on 16 of the most influential of M.'s numerous pupils, listed separately in this report. Timothy J. Wengert, *Human Freedom, Christian Righteousness. Philip Melanchthon's Exegetical Dispute with Erasmus of Rotterdam*, OUP, xiii + 239 pp., examines M.'s *Scholia* on Colossians (1527) showing the similarities, but above all the differences, between M.'s exegetical method and that of Erasmus. W. re-appraises the relationship between the two humanists, revealing it as a good deal more distanced than it has often been perceived as being. Analysing the *Scholia*, W. uncovers a 'systematic but largely unnoticed opposition' (11) of M. to E. which is obscured by the fact that M. refrained from attacking E. explicitly. M., he argues, crafted the commentary as a specific refutation of E.'s position on the human will. Jürgen Blum, Wolf-Dieter Müller-Jahncke and Stefan Rhein, *Melanchthon auf Medaillen 1525–1997*, Ubstadt-Weiher, Vlg Regionalkultur, 1997, 200 pp., is a complete illustrated catalogue of an exhibition of all known M. medals; it contains several informative essays on the numismatic M. image. M. Greschat, 'Philipp Melanchthon — ein Intellektueller, Pädagoge und Christ', *Pirckheimer Jb.*, 13:11–25; J. Leonhardt, 'M. als Verfasser von Lehrbüchern', *ib.*, 26–47; R. Decot, 'Vermittlungsversuch auf dem Augsburger Reichstag. M. und die Confessio Augustana', *ib.*, 48–72; B. Bauer, *ib.*, 73–122, compares M.'s mode of doctrinal argumentation with those of Erasmus, Luther and Castellio. W. Metzger and V. Probst, *Daphnis*, 27:685–716, examine three previously unknown letters between M. and W. Reiffenstein. A. Burlando, *Studi Umanistici Piceni*, 17, 1997:49–58, writes on M.'s Latin translation of the dramas of Euripides. T. and U. Rütten, 'Melanchthons Rede "De Hippocrate"', *Medizinhistorisches Journal*, 33:19–55, situates this address in the tradition of Hippocratic medicine of the 16th c. A. Moss, 'Allegory in a rhetorical mode', Horn, *Allegorese*, 395–406.

MÜNSTER, SEBASTIAN. B. Kedar, 'Sebastian Münsters lateinische Psalmenübersetzung', *Theologische Zeitschrift der Universität Basel*, 53, 1997:44–52.

MÜNTZER, THOMAS. P. Matheson, 'The cornflower in the wheatfield: freedom and liberation in Thomas Müntzer', *AR*, 89:41–54.

MUSCULUS, WOLFGANG. M. van Wijnkoop Lüthi, '*Orbis habet libros nostri monumenta laboris*. Wolfgang Musculus und der Buchdruck seiner Zeit', *Daphnis*, 27:539–85.

PARACELSUS. Theophrast von Hohenheim, genannt Paracelsus, *Sämtliche Werke. Theologische und religionsphilosophische Schriften. Register (Indices) der Wörter, Begriffe, Namen und Bibelstellen in den Bänden* IV *bis* VII (Auslegungen zum Alten Testament), ed. Kurt Goldammer and others, Stuttgart, Steiner, iv + 242 pp. *Paracelsus. The Man and his Reputation: his Ideas and their Transformation* (SHCT, 85), ed. Ole Peter Grell, ix + 351 pp., contains, in addition to G.'s introductory essay, 14 updated contributions to a 1993 symposium. In the first, historical, section, A. Cunningham and D. Goltz write on the historical image of P., and S. Pumfrey and H. Breger on the history of Paracelsianism. The second section, on the social and religious P., contains essays by H. Trevor-Roper, B. T. Moran, C. Gilly, H. Rudolph, and U. Gause. The third, on the philosophical and medical P., has contributions by A. G. Debus, O. P. Grell, J. R. R. Christie, F. McKee, and H. Schott. This collection of judicious studies is given unity and added usefulness by a consolidated bibliography and copious indexes. M. Hammond, 'The religious roots of P.'s medical theory', *AR*, 89:7–21.

PEUCER, KASPAR. U. Neddermeyer, 'Kaspar Peucer (1525–1602). Melanchthons Universalgeschichtsschreibung', Scheible, *Melanchthon*, 69–101.

PEUTINGER, KONRAD. J.-D. Müller, 'Konrad Peutinger und die Sodalitas Peutingeriana', *Pirckheimer Jb.*, 12, 1997:167–86. C. S. Wood, *JMEMS*, 28:83–118, discusses the preparation and publication of P.'s *sylloge* of classical inscriptions, *Romanae vetustatis fragmenta* (1505).

PEZEL, CHRISTOPH. R. Wetzel, 'Christoph Pezel (1539–1604). Die Vorreden zu seinen Melanchthon-Editionen als Propagandatexte der "Zweiten Reformation"', Scheible, *Melanchthon*, 465–566.

PIRCKHEIMER, WILLIBALD. Willibald Pirckheimer, *Briefwechsel.* 4., ed. Helga Scheible, Munich, Beck, 1997, xxxiii + 560 pp. The 186 letters written by and to P. between 1519 and 1521 which this vol. edits (a good quarter previously unpublished) cover a crucial period in German history, and shed important light on P.'s initial attitudes to Luther and the Reformation. Each letter has a detailed commentary explaining its context; there are exhaustive indexes.

RHENANUS, BEATUS. R. Walter, 'L'épidémie de peste de 1519–1520 vue à travers la correspondance de Beatus Rhenanus', *Annuaire des amis de la Bibliothèque Humaniste de Sélestat*, 48:65–71; F. Schlienger, 'Correspondance de Beatus Rhenanus', *ib.*, 73–81.

RUBIANUS, CROTUS. E. Bernstein, 'Der Erfurter Humanistenkreis am Schnittpunkt von Humanismus und Reformation. Das Rektoratsblatt des Crotus Rubianus', *Pirckheimer Jb.*, 12, 1997:137–65.

RUCKERSFELDE, JOBUS. E. Könsgen, 'Variorum Carminum Liber ad Cancrinam. Marburgensia aus den Jahren 1583 bis 1592', *Fest. Wimmel*, 131–46.

SACHS, HANS. Brigitte Stuplich, *Zur Dramentechnik des Hans Sachs* (Arbeiten und Editionen zur Mittleren Deutschen Literatur, n.s., 5), Bad Cannstatt, Frommann-Holzboog, 363 pp., examines a large corpus of S.'s plays, representing a variety of sub-genres, from his earliest period till his death. Throughout his career, S. is shown to use a wide variety of carefully considered dramatic effects which he steadily develops and refines. These contribute to the impact of the plays — practical considerations of staging are always uppermost in S.'s mind — and thereby to the didactic purposes which the plays serve.

SCHENK, HIERONYMUS. *Die 'Kinderzucht' des Hieronymus Schenk von Siemau (1502)*, trans. and ed. Marc Pinther, Hamburg, Krämer, 1996, xiii + 169 + 32 facsimile pp., presents a transcription and modern German translation of this Franconian knight's educational treatise, preserved in a single copy at Zwickau; an early example of a humane, humanist pedagogy based on the values of classical antiquity. A substantial linguistic and thematic commentary and a complete facsimile of the *Kinderzucht* are included.

SCHÖNBORN, BARTHOLOMÄUS H.-T. Koch, 'Bartholomäus Schönborn (1530–1585). Melanchthons *De anima* als medizinisches Lehrbuch', Scheible, *Melanchthon*, 323–40.

SIMMERN, JOHANN II. VON. Johann II. von Simmern, *Die Haymonskinder*, ed. Werner Wunderlich (FN, 35), 1997, vii + 585 pp., is an excellent edition of this anonymous prose work of 1535, whose author identifies himself in an acrostic at the beginning. The text is that of the original printing, with minimal normalization and editorial interference; footnotes are brief but helpful. There are sections on the form of the legend and its diffusion in western Europe (with the emphasis on the German-speaking countries), on the author and the printer, and on the reception of the legend up until modern times.

STAPHYLUS, FRIEDRICH. U. Mennecke-Haustein, 'Friedrich Staphylus (1512–1564). Von Wittenberg nach Ingolstadt', Scheible, *Melanchthon*, 405–26.

STIGEL, JOHANNES. S. Rhein, 'Johannes Stigel (1515–1562). Dichtung im Umkreis Melanchthons', Scheible, *Melanchthon*, 31–49); B. Schäfer, 'Johann Stigels antirömische Epigramme', *ib.*, 51–68.

STRIGEL, VICTORIN. E. Koch, 'Victorin Strigel (1524–1569). Von Jena nach Heidelberg', Scheible, *Melanchthon*, 391–404.

STURM, JAKOB. Thomas A. Brady, Jr, *The Politics of the Reformation in Germany. Jacob Sturm (1489–1553) of Strasbourg*, Atlantic Highlands, NJ, Humanities Press International, xix + 280 pp., presents the activity of this urban politician as representative of 'the real Reformation', which 'occurred not on a national level but on a local one'. S., who represented Strasbourg in many key events of the age from the Peasants' War to the Council of Trent, worked in a manner typical of the particularist, regional engagement of many similar figures. B. develops an image of the Reformation as a movement that was not the beginning of German national statehood, but a many-layered phenomenon working itself out in the 'dispersed governance' of the pluricentric Holy Roman Empire.

SYLVIUS, CHRISTOPHORUS. K. Lüthje and H. Freytag, *Euphorion*, 91, 1997:423–30, write on a poem in praise of Hamburg written by S. in 1587.

URSINUS, ZACHARIAS. D. Visser, 'Zacharias Ursinus (1534–1583). Melanchthons Geist im Heidelberger Katechismus', Scheible, *Melanchthon*, 373–90.

VINCENTIUS, PETRUS. H. Freytag, Peil, *Erkennen*, 265–84, analyses V.'s Latin oration in praise of Lübeck (1552).

VOITH, VALTEN. G. Ehrstine, 'Seeing is believing: Valten Voith's *Ein schön Lieblich Spiel von dem herlichen vrsprung* (1538), Protestant "Law and Gospel" panels, and German Reformation dramaturgy', *Daphnis*, 27:503–37.

WEYER, JOHANN. *Witches, Devils, and Doctors in the Renaissance. Johann Weyer, De praestigiis daemonum*, trans. John Shea (MRTS, 73), xciii + 790 pp., offers a translation of this seminal treatise on witchcraft, first published in 1583. W. approached the phenomenon from theological, philosophical, legal, and medical angles; he was impatient of the superstitious beliefs of witch-hunters, and was the first author to understand 'witches' primarily in psychological terms; the treatise is now regarded as a pioneering study of hysteria. The voluminous prefatory material includes an introduction to W.'s life and works, an account of early modern witchcraft and the significance of the *De praestigiis*, a discussion of W.'s place in the psychological tradition, and a bibliography of his works. There are helpful glossaries, notes, and indexes.

WICKRAM, JÖRG. Jörg Wickram, *Sämtliche Werke*, ed. Hans-Gert Roloff, Berlin, de Gruyter, continues with 10. *Kleine Spiele* (ADL, 151), 389 pp. This volume contains W.'s four 'serious' *Fastnachtspiele* — *Die zehen Alter der Welt, Der trew Eckhart, Das Narren Giessen*, and *List der Weiber*, as well as the *Dialogus von der Trunckenheit*. This is a careful edition to high standards. In the case of the very popular *Zehen Alter*, Gengenbach's play of the same title, which W. reworked, is also printed, along with copious background material. P. Frei, 'Zur Konstitution von Innenwelt in Jörg Wickrams *Goldtfaden*', *Fest. Geith*, 31–47.

THE SEVENTEENTH CENTURY

By ANNA CARRDUS, *Exeter College, Oxford*

1. GENERAL

Martin Bircher, *Im Garten der Palme. Katalog einer Sammlung von Dokumenten zur Wirksamkeit der Fruchtbringenden Gesellschaft mit Beigabe eines Ausstellungskataloges (1991)* (WAB, 32), 2 vols, xiii + 632, 163 pp., lavishly illustrated, presents complementary perspectives on B.'s own extensive collection (now held by the Rare Book Library of the University of California in Berkeley) of portraits, documents, and publications relating to members of the Fruchtbringende Gesellschaft. The larger volume catalogues the entire collection and is arranged alphabetically, according to members' names, while the smaller volume is the catalogue to an exhibition of items selected from the collection, held at the Herzog August Bibliothek, Wolfenbüttel in 1991, and is arranged thematically. Both volumes contain detailed commentaries. As reference material they provide a wealth of information which enriches the background to, for example, the critical editions of letters and other work by members of the FG currently being edited by B. and Klaus Conermann; but they also form a valuable and fascinating general resource on 17th-c. literary activities and relationships in their own right. *Chloe*, 28, is a *Festschrift* for Martin Bircher in celebration of his 60th birthday, on the appropriate theme of *Ars et Amicitia*. Apart from contributions discussed below under the names of individual authors, it contains: F. van Ingen, 'Freundschaftskonzepte und literarische Wirkungsstrategien im 17. Jahrhundert' (173–222), which explores the 17th-c. humanist concept of friendship in poems by Opitz, Fleming, Dach, and Zesen, arguing that their expressions of personal friendship exploit rhetorical strategies which tend to aim beyond immediate occasions of gratitude or farewell towards upholding the timeless ideals of the *res publica litteraria*; and that contemporary literature thrives on the practical realization of such ideals — as in the case of the friends whose support of Zesen led to the formation of the Teutschgesinnte Genossenschaft. F. Kemp, 'Handleitung zur Freundschaft. Kardinal Bona in Wolfenbüttel' (295–308), which comments on a 1669 edition of Giovanni Bona's *Manuducio ad Coelum* that includes French and German translations. K. draws attention to the standard of translation, the popularity of this Catholic work in Protestant territories and to B.'s brief chapter on friendship, which offers a Christian definition (in contrast to the humanist definition central to most contributions on the 17th c. in this *Festschrift*) and is reprinted in the article in Latin, French, and German. A. Herz, ' "Wältz recht." Fruchtbringerisches Zeremoniell und sein "Hintergrund" in einem Stich Peter Isselburgs' (353–408), which takes Isselburg's engraving (*c.*1622) of a genial gathering of twelve members of the Fruchtbringende Gesellschaft as the starting-point for a study of the society's ceremonial admission of new members. H. maintains that early initiations follow the general festive custom of including rowdy (yet patriotic) moments of music and dance; these are absent from the rituals of a 1658 initiation in Weimar. He links this change to the rise of absolutism: the widespread passing of decrees designed to suppress unruliness in festive celebrations of all kinds coincides with the stricter norms of courtly self-control adopted by the society in the latter half of the 17th c. W. W. Schnabel, 'Über das Dedizieren von Emblemen. Binnenzueignungen in Emblematiken des 16. und 17. Jahrhunderts' (115–66), which analyses several kinds of dedication attached to individual emblems within a range of published collections, two of which were compiled in the early 17th c. by Jacob von Bruck. One of these S. categorizes as an *album amicorum* (some emblems are left undedicated, to be 'claimed' by a reader's friends); the second, published on the eve of the Thirty Years' War, he sees as a political instruction manual (emblems remind named rulers and politicians of their duty to pursue policies of appeasement). R. Jacobsen, 'Fürstenfreundschaft. Landgraf Ludwig VI. von Hessen-Darmstadt und Herzog Friedrich I. von Sachsen Gotha und Altenburg' (475–502), which bases discussion of the friendship between these two princes on unpublished material from their correspondence and from F.'s 'Schreibkalender'. *Chloe*, 27, 1997, is a 'Gedenkschrift' for Gerhard Spellerberg (1937–1996). Most contributions are on individual authors and are discussed under their names, below. A. Martino, 'Von den Wegen und Umwegen der Verbreitung spanischer Literatur im deutschen Sprachraum (1550–1750)', *ib.*, 285–344, outlines the confessional, cultural, political, and economic routes taken by Spanish literature into early modern Germany; discusses the spread of printed works in Latin, in Spanish and in translation; traces the circulation of manuscript material and the integration of extracts from Spanish sources into dramatic and narrative texts; and discusses the oral reflection of Spanish literature in German drama and sermons. M. draws attention to the fact that this article is to be augmented by another, forthcoming in *Daphnis*, on the reception of *Lazarillo de Tormes* in early modern Germany. Garber, *Stadt*, contains the proceedings of an interdisciplinary conference on literature in early modern German towns which was held in Osnabrück in June 1990. The time separating the event from the appearance of these two volumes is not seriously detrimental to the original innovatory intention, which was to treat literature as part of the urban cultures which nurtured it. K. Garber, 'Stadt und Literatur im alten deutschen Sprachraum. Umrisse der Forschung — Regionale Literaturgeschichte und kommunale Ikonologie — Nürnberg als Paradigma', *ib.*, 3–90, takes account of changes in research since 1990, especially of the impact of reunification, in an outline of the problems, resources and rewards facing this multidisciplinary approach. G. takes *Die Nymphe Noris* (1650) by Johann Helwig, doctor and member of the Pegnesischer Blumenorden, as a paradigm, arguing that H. departs from the pastoral conventions followed by Harsdörffer and Klaj in order to air social, political, religious, and scientific ideas which reflect his own status and profession in Nuremberg but aim, above all, at promoting civic health in the city and lasting peace in Europe. W. Adam, 'Urbanität und poetische Form. Überlegungen zum Gattungsspektrum städtischer Literatur in der Frühen Neuzeit', *ib.*, 90–111, and M. Schilling, 'Stadt und Publizistik in der Frühen Neuzeit' *ib.*, 112–41, complete the general introduction to the volumes by outlining the genres, from occasional poetry to newspapers, and the categories of author, such as 'Stadtschreiber' or travelling 'Pritschmeister', which fall outside the scope of the accepted literary canon yet offer revealing insights into literary activity within the complex networks of urban life. The remaining six sections cover towns in various regions: (*ib.*, 145–278) in areas under the reformed confession; (*ib.*, 281–546) southern German imperial free cities and territorial capitals; (*ib.*, 549–634) the central German Lutheran area; (*ib.*, 637–896) the northern area of the Hanseatic League; (*ib.*, 899–1029) the central European areas of Silesia and Bohemia, and, finally (*ib.*, 1033–1113) Catholic towns (Ingolstadt, Munich, Lucerne). Many articles provide useful historical surveys of urban literary activity. Literary production is related to music, the visual arts and 'Sprachgesellschaften', to universities, schools, libraries, or printers, and to cross currents of political, confessional, commercial or scholarly interests either within or between regions. Recurrent topics are tensions between the confessions, and between town and court. Several articles encourage further research by describing untapped source material or offering specialized bibliographies. Articles on individual authors are discussed under their names, below. Neil Kenny, *'Curiosity' in Early Modern Europe. Word Histories* (WoF, 81), 215 pp., is a contribution to European intellectual history. K. shows that the concept of 'curiosity' underwent a general transformation around 1650, when Renaissance connotations of 'sinful inquisitiveness' gave ground to the less pejorative meaning of 'desire for knowledge'; the term might now refer to new scientific enquiry or even attach itself to objects in a collector's cabinet: 'the cravings of "curiosity" could be sated by "curiosities" '. He discusses the genealogy (pp. 41–43) and 18th-c. dictionary definitions (pp. 90–102) of words used in German for 'curiosity', pointing out that in 17th-c. Germany such words were seen as exotic implants and treated accordingly by divergent cultural trends, either as undesirable linguistic impurities or as fashionable marks of sophistication. He suggests that these and other details will provoke readers to reconsider words related to 'curiosity' which appear, for example, in the titles of works by Christian Weise and Christian Friedrich Hunold. S. Heissler, 'Christine Charlotte von Ostfriesland (1645–1699) und ihre Bücher oder lesen Frauen Anderes?', *Daphnis*, 27:335–418, extends the hitherto scant research into women's private libraries by analysing C. C.'s collection of some 500 books. Their subject-matter is predominantly devotional, political-historical or fictional; in this last category, C. C. shows a preference for recent French novels either by women, or about women who were *not* passive heroines. H. finds, in fact, that the entire library reflects the duchess's interest in women's place in society and connects this with her own political activities as regent during her son's minority. A catalogue of the library is appended. R. Breymayer, 'Städtisches und literarisches Leben in Stuttgart im 17. Jahrhundert. Ein bibliographischer Versuch mit besonderer Berücksichtigung der Prinzessin Antonia von Württemberg und ihrer Bibliothek', Garber, *Stadt*, 308–83, includes discussion of cabbalic tables which were commissioned by Princess Antonia (1613–1679) and depict the heavenly bride Shulamith on their covers, with 77 identifiable female figures from the Old and New Testaments in the bridal procession. B. suggests that Johann Valentin Andreae was one of the collaborators in this project. The appended bibliography includes a commented inventory of the princess's library. D. Peil, 'Emblematik zwischen Memoria und Geographie. *Der Thesaurus Philo-Politicus. Das ist: Politisches Schatzkästlein*', Peil, *Erkennen*, 351–82, classifies this collection (1623–31) of over 800 emblems as multi-functional, but concentrates on how the depiction of a different town in each emblem relates to travel itineraries and how a sub-set of emblems dominated by planetary images also serve to commemorate a circle of friends. P. M. Daly, 'Emblem und Enigma. Erkennen und Verkennen im Emblem', *ib.*, 325–49, rejects the still current notion that the image in an emblem presents an enigma which the motto solves, demonstrating that the compilers of emblem-books could and would assume that their intended readers had sufficient relevant knowledge to be visually literate. A. Simon, 'Product, packaging and purpose: the recycling of the *Reyßbuch*', *OGS*, 26, 1997:73–100, compares the prefaces to the editions of the *Reyßbuch* of 1584, 1609, 1629, and 1659, viewing them as examples of canny 'packaging':

under Sigmund Feyerabend, the first preface introduces much earlier pilgrimage accounts with a call for a new crusade against the Turks; the three 17th-c. publishers then change or recycle it in turn, angling the compendium towards the more secular needs of the would-be politicians or travellers who represented promising contemporary markets.

2. POETRY

INDIVIDUAL AUTHORS

BIRKEN. H. Laufhütte, 'Programmatik und Funktionen der allegorischen Verwendung antiker Mythenmotive bei Sigmund von Birken (1626–1681)', Horn, *Allegorese*, 287–310, explains a discrepancy between B.'s theory and practice, noting how he, unlike Opitz, urges in *Teutsche Redebind- und Dichtkunst* (1679) that allegorical figures from classical myth should be replaced by Biblical figures. L. uses the religious drama *Psyche* (1652) and the secular pastoral *Der Norische Föbus* (1677) to demonstrate that B. followed his own theoretical dictum in religious poetry but not in secular poetry, and goes on to suggest that this dictum and B.'s increasing concentration on religious work in later life were due to the influence of his friendship with Greiffenberg. H. Laufhütte, 'Philologisches Detektivspiel. Der Nürnberger Birken-Nachlaß als Materialfundus und Stimulus für die Erforschung der Literatur des 17. Jahrhunderts', Garber, *Stadt*, 491–508, describes the Birken archive in considerable detail as potential source material on urban literary production; it contains, for instance, the hitherto completely unexplored papers of minor literary figures such as Johann Gabriel Maier (1639–99), a member of the Pegnesischer Blumenorden.

DACH. J. A. Steiger, 'Der Mensch in der Druckerei Gottes und die Imago Dei. Zur Theologie des Dichters Simon Dach (1605–1659)', *Daphnis*, 27:263–90, relates D.'s office as occasional poet to the 'priesthood of all believers', interpreting an epicedium addressed to his printer in the light of Lutheran doctrine. This approach reassesses D.'s lingering reputation for simple piety and lack of intellectual interest in theological matters.

FABRICIUS. D. Seeber, ' "In Officin und Bett: GOtt laß den Druck gelingen." Buchdrucker und -händler im Spiegel der Gelegenheitsdichtung des Stettiner Pastors Friedrich Fabricius', Garber, *Stadt*, 752–68, selects 15 poems addressed to printers in Stettin and nearby towns from the two-volume collection of F.'s occasional poetry (1691). She detects intriguing examples of an author's familiarity with printing processes in S.'s analogies, and finds the high social status which generally set printers apart from other urban craftsmen to be clearly reflected in the interdependent relationship between S. and his addressees.

FLEMING. Blake Lee Spahr, 'Fleming's Friendship', *Chloe*, 28:271–93, presents a descriptive commentary on F.'s *Manes Glogoriana*, a poetic monument to his close friend and mentor Georg Gloger which is so substantial as to be unique in 17th-c. literature. S. translates some poems and illustrates the often touchingly witty mannerism of F.'s neo-Latin style.

GRYPHIUS. B. Becker-Cantarino, ' "Die edlen Rosen leben so kurtze Zeit": Zur Rosen-Metaphorik bei Gryphius, Gongora und den Quellen', *Chloe*, 27, 1997:11–33, examines rose metaphors in work by Gryphius and Gongora, tracing nuances of meaning back to sources in the Bible, in Horace and other classical poets, in the *carpe diem* treatment by Ausonius (*c*.310) and in medieval mystical writings. B.-C. concludes that Gryphius concentrates on the thorns of suffering to strengthen faith in redemption while Gongora, in contrast, conveys a sense of lonely entrapment in the beauty and transience of life. E. Bonfatti, 'Andreas Gryphius Abschiedssonett an Johann Friedrich von Sack (1636 und 1643)', *Chloe*, 28: 245–52, looks at G.'s friendship poetry in general, but focuses on two versions of a sonnet which exploit the rich connotations of '(an)binden' and related words.

HOFMANNSWALDAU. Marie-Thérèse Mourey, *Poésie et éthique au XVIIe siècle. Les Traductions et poèmes allemands de Christian Hoffmann von Hoffmannswaldau (1616–1679)* (WAB, 30), x + 536 pp., 26 illus., is a slightly revised version of an outstanding doctoral thesis. M. addresses the still current view of Hofmannswaldau as morally suspect, first suggested by the division of his work into 'official' and 'unofficial' editions: *Deutsche Übersetzungen und Getichte* (1679), authorized by H. himself, and Neukirch's anthology (1695/7), containing erotic poetry omitted in 1679. H.'s ethical beliefs are therefore central to M.'s study, which is organized into sections dealing with his poetic theory, links between theory and practice, and textual analysis, firstly of the ethical concepts embedded in H.'s treatments of heroism, and then of the moral beliefs reflected in his approach to statecraft, the affects and satire on 'anti-heroes'. The result is a detailed survey which throws new light on H. and emphasizes the coherence of his work. L. Noack, 'Die Gelegenheitsdichtung Hoffmannswaldaus. Anmerkungen zu Adressatenkreis und Produktionsmotivationen', Garber, *Stadt*, 973–87, yields insights into both Breslau's cultural history and Hoffmannswaldau's work. N. demonstrates in detail that the addressees of H.'s few funeral poems belonged to the town's patriciate, like H. himself, and that several were his close friends; on this basis he argues that the poems are motivated by real grief, not

merely by a conventional sense of duty, and may be read as H.'s own
personal views on mortality.

KUHLMANN. W. Schmidt-Biggemann, 'Erlösung durch Philologie.
Der poetische Messianismus Quirinus Kuhlmanns (1651–1689)',
Chloe, 27, 1997:243–84, expounds K.'s political theology in some
detail, building a framework which forms the basis for interpretation
of a poem from the final, most apocalyptic part of the *Kühlpsalter*. S.-
B. outlines K.'s life and travels, and the formative influence on his
thought of Böhme, Comenius, and nearer contemporaries, then sets
these in the rich context of 17th-c. apocalyptic beliefs in Germany,
England, and Holland. S.-B. notes that K. was the only messianic
figure of his time to voice his prophecies in verse, and stresses his faith
in the power of the word to instate the millennium. J. N. Schneider,
'Kuhlmanns Kalkül. Kompositionsprinzipien, sprachtheoretischer
Standort und Sprechpraxis in Quirinus Kuhlmanns Kühlpsalter',
Daphnis, 27:93–140, fortuitously complements the above article by
presenting a detailed analysis of K.'s compositional principles, both
in relation to the *Kühlpsalter* as a whole and in relation to individual
poems. S. argues above all against the tendency to criticise K.'s style
from a rhetorical point of view, as the epitome of mannered excess;
massed repetition of the word 'Triumf', for example, was meant not
simply to persuade readers, but to actualize spiritual triumph in their
minds through the acoustics of the word.

MAUERSBERGER. E. Pietrzak, ' "Ich singe diese Stadt/ zu mehren
Jhren Ruhm". Stadt und städtische Literatur in Johann Andreas
Mauersbergers Lobgedicht auf Breslau (1679)', Garber, *Stadt*,
899–922, views this work by a little-known pastor with literary
ambitions as a realistic topography of Breslau in 1679, which glorifies
its institutions, buildings, and inhabitants by presenting them as
sources of utility and pleasure (*prodesse* and *delectare*). P. appends the
extensive passage on Breslau's literary figures, including
Hoffmannswaldau, Lohenstein, and Heinrich Mühlpfort.

PEUCKER. K. Kiesant, 'Berliner Gelegenheitsdichtung im Spannungsfeld von Stadt und Hof: Nicolaus Peucker (um 1620–1674)',
Garber, *Stadt*, 260–78, redresses entrenched misconceptions of P.'s
poetic standing in Berlin in a comparative analysis of two cradle
songs, one for a pastor's daughter and one for a son of the Great
Elector. K. links them in detail to the different contexts of bourgeois
life and court politics and finds P. subscribing to the belief that the
function of literature is to stabilize social and political norms.

RIST. G. Dammann, 'Das Hamburger Friedensfest von 1650. Die
Rollen von Predigt, Feuerwerk und einem Gelegenheitsgedicht
Johann Rists in einem Beispielfall städtischer Repräsentation',
Garber, *Stadt*, 697–728, contrasts three texts related to the 1650

peace celebrations in Hamburg, showing how their imagery conveys different political angles on the war, the peace and the town, but focuses on how R. asserts his own brand of irenicism by manipulating the significance of images in the firework display during his poetic account of it.

SPEE. Andrea Rösler, *Von Gotteslob zum Gottesdank: Bedeutungswandel in der Lyrik von Friedrich Spee zu Joseph von Eichendorff und Annette von Droste-Hülshoff*, Paderborn, Schöningh, 1997, 368 pp., sets out to trace the change of emphasis from praise to thankfulness which she sees occuring in the historical range of religious poetry represented by these three authors. R. finds (pp. 1–95) that the poems of praise in Spee's *Trutznachtigall* exclude expressions of thankfulness; but her method here consists largely in categorizing the symbolic motifs that are the vehicles of praise and regrettably conveys little sense of S.'s religious beliefs or of his unique poetic voice.

ZEIDLER. Cornelia Niekus Moore, '"Wer innig Freundschaft kennt". Declarations of friendship among German women authors in the seventeenth century', *Chloe*, 28: 223–43, concentrates on poems by Catharina Regina von Greiffenberg and Susanna Elisabeth Zeidler, demonstrating that women could appropriate both the traditions of male friendship and the conventions of occasional poetry to commemorate their friendships with other women.

OTHER WORK

W. Segebrecht, '"Was ist die Welt? — Ein ewiges Gedicht." Nachzeichnung einer Traditionslinie', Peil, *Erkennen*, 437–54, interprets a sonnet by Hugo von Hofmannsthal and traces fascinating connections and disconnections of both formal and thematic kinds between it and several 17th-c. poems on the same perennial query. G. Braungart, 'Barocke Grabschriften: Zu Begriff und Typologie', *Chloe*, 27, 1997:425–87, provides a valuable definitive description of the baroque epitaph, demarcating the often very fine line between it and the related forms of the inscription and epigram. B. works with baroque concepts, making especial use of a hitherto unnoticed poetics of the epitaph by Johannes Bonifacius (1629) and referring to Hoffmannswaldau's 'Grabschriften' (1662/3). He appends an extensive list of sources which includes both works on poetics and collections of epitaphs. A. Carrdus, 'Consolatory dialogue in devotional writings by men and women of early modern Germany', *MLR*, 93:411–27, examines poems on occasions of bereavement by little-known authors, male and female, showing how various dialogue forms shape writings intended for self-consolation and for the consolation of others, and how the arts of poetry, rhetoric and music help relatively ordinary people to come to terms with grief.

3. PROSE

INDIVIDUAL AUTHORS

BEER. A. Solbach, 'Poetik und erzählerisches Verfahren in Johann Beers *Teutsche Winternächte* (1682)', *Simpliciana*, 20:229–53, addresses a neglected area of research into B.'s work. S. takes the discrepancy created in this novel between the main protagonist's lustful puruit of women and his moralizing reflections on such behaviour as a starting point for rhetorical analysis of B.'s narrative poetics, detecting four layers of compositional procedure within the text and illustrating them with the help of tabular diagrams.

BIRKEN. H. Laufhütte, 'Freundschaften. Ihre Spuren im Briefarchiv Sigmund von Birkens', *Chloe*, 28:309–29, explores the friendships B. cultivated over a lifetime. Bearing in mind the variables of age and status that determine the conventions of 17th-c. friendship, L. sees varying degrees of intimacy in the correspondence: utilitarian politeness in business requests, ritualistic formalities exchanged with fellow 'Pegnitzschäfer', intense spirituality shared with Greiffenberg, and spontaneous sympathy on both sides of a friendship dating from childhood. The implication is that B.'s correspondence spans almost all the many forms of literary friendship prevalent in the 17th-c.

GREIFFENBERG. Kathleen Foley-Beining, *The Body and Eucharistic Devotion in Catharina Regina von Greiffenberg's "Meditations"*, Columbia, Camden House, 1997, ix + 154 pp., takes a feminist approach to G.'s meditations on the 'Menschwerdung' (1678) and the 'Abendmahls-Andachten' (1693). F.-B. concentrates on the corporeality of G.'s meditations, paying particular attention to this aspect of her work in commentary on 'Von der Heiligen JEsus-Mutter Schwangergehen', where G. meditates in physical terms not only on Mary's sensations of pregnancy but on the details of fetal growth. This volume promises to be especially valuable to students: it introduces G. by placing her in a tradition of mystical writing by women, and makes her linguistically challenging prose accessible to native English-speakers by supplying carefully judged translations alongside quotations. However, translation is not always reliable; 'Beruf', for instance, referring to G.'s poetic calling, is misleadingly rendered as 'profession'.

GRIMMELSHAUSEN. S. S. Tschopp, 'Zum Verhältnis von Bildpublizistik und Literatur am Beispiel von Hans Jacob Christoffel von Grimmelshausens *Simplicissimus Teutsch*', Peil, *Erkennen*, 419–36, demonstrates that certain episodes and major themes in *Simplicissimus* echo images familiar from contemporary broadsheets, and suggests that drawing on popular material of this kind enabled G. to appeal to a readership not confined, as hitherto supposed, to noble and learned levels of society. *Simpliciana*, 20, includes the proceedings of a conference held in Zurich in 1998 on the theme 'Fabula und Historia in der Frühen Neuzeit'. Most contributions examine tensions between fiction and history in relation to G.'s work. I. M. Battafarano, 'Paolo Grillando, François de Rosset, Martin Zeiller, Grimmelshausen: Die Literarisierung von Hexenprozeßakten in der frühen Neuzeit', *ib.*, 13–24, considers the citations from records of witch trial proceedings which G. incorporates into the account of a witches' sabbath in the second book of *Simplicissimus*. B. argues that by embedding such citations in patently fictional narrative, G. not only questions their verity, but, in a general sense, releases the imagination from suspicion of influence by the devil (witch trials made imaginings of devilish intercourse as culpable as 'real' intercourse), thus freeing it in an artistic sense for the concoction and enjoyment of literature. S. Streller, ' "um wieder auf meine Histori zu kommen." Die Verwendung der Begriffe Histori und Fabula bei Grimmelshausen', *ib.*, 25–36, explores G.'s concept and usage of the terms 'Histori' and 'Fabula', and of the somewhat more idiosyncratic term 'Stücklein', surveying his work chronologically. D. Breuer, 'Der Erzähler Grimmelshausen als Historiker und die *Vollkommenheit der Histori*', *ib.*, 37–46, examines G.'s view of himself as a historian by looking at four works which he claimed to have compiled from historical sources: *Keuscher Joseph, Musai, Dietwalt und Amelinde* and *Proximus und Lympida*. R. Zeller, '*Fabula* und *Historia* im Kontext der Gattungspoetik', *ib.*, 49–58, shows how 17th.-c. theoretical discussion of prose genres in, for example, work by Harsdörffer and Birken, was dominated by the question of whether fiction held pride of place over history or *vice versa*, and relates this discussion to G.'s practice. S. Trappen, 'Fiktionsvorstellungen der Frühen Neuzeit. Über den Gegensatz zwischen "fabula" und "historia" und seine Bedeutung für die Poetik', *ib.*, 137–63, extends theoretical discussion of these concepts through reference to a wide selection of sources stretching from Quintilian to Dubos. R. Wimmer, 'Historia und Fabula in Drama und Roman der Frühen Neuzeit', *ib.*, 63–76, continues discussion of genre, but links the concepts of 'Historia' and 'Fabula' to both dramatic and narrative contexts, focusing on Bible comedy as well as on work by Grimmelshausen. F. Gaede, 'Janusköpfiger Ratio Status. Grimmelshausen's Beitrag zum Thema: Chaos wird Geschichte', *ib.*, 77–91, relates episodes from a number of G.'s novels to early modern concepts of history as the 'school of life', and as a constant repetition of events characterized by double-faced patternings such as pride and downfall. G. Weydt, '*Springinsfeld*. Hintergründe einer simplicianische Gestalt', *ib.*, 93–103, approaches tensions between fiction and history more playfully than many other contributions to this volume and presents intriguing implications, detecting a 'real' person behind the frontispiece portrait of Springinsfeld, and speculating on evidence from church registers of two historical people who bore this name and may well have been known to Grimmelshausen. J.-J. Berns, 'Erzählte und erzählende Bilder. Porträttechniken im Simplicianischen Zyklus', *ib.*, 105–22, inspects scenes of portraiture embedded in the narrative of the Simplician cycle, concentrating on portraits of male figures from chapters 6–24 of the first book of *Simplicissimus*, and on portraits of female figures from throughout the cycle (noting, incidentally, that all female figures are portrayed through a male gaze). B. analyses the dynamics of this narrative portraiture — for example, it always serves to characterize both portraitee and portraitist — and compares it with the graphic portraits in the frontispieces to the novels, concluding that narrative and graphic portraits interact and help bind the novels into a cycle. P. Hesselmann, 'Fiktion und Wahrheit. Poetologische und hermeneutische Reflexe in Grimmelshausens Baldanders-Episode', *ib.*, 165–88, accepts the view that this blatantly fictional episode from the 'Continuatio' to *Simplicissimus* is crucial to understanding of the truths conveyed by the novel as a whole, and uses it as a focal point for discussion of hermeneutics in relation to G.'s work.

HARSDÖRFFER.   M. Reinhart, 'Battle of the Tapestries: A war-time Debate in Anhalt-Köthen. Georg Philipp Harsdörffer's *Peristromata Turcica* and *Aulaea Romana*, 1641–1642', *Daphnis*, 27: 291–333, details the political and literary links between two Latin pamphlets from H.'s early career, after he was a member of the Fruchtbringende Gesellschaft but before he founded the Pegnesischer Blumenorden. In this context, R. highlights Prince Ludwig's influence on H.'s development. E. Locher, ' "Vor Augenstellen" als Enargeia/Energeia und Hypotypose im Spannungsfeld von Fabula und Historia bei Georg Philipp Harsdörffer', *Simpliciana*, 20: 189–209, traces the overlap between the many rhetorical terms in classical sources (Aristotle, Cicero, Quintilian) for the literary presentation of subject matter 'before the mind's eye', and makes a fundamental distinction between terms referring to factual narration and terms referring to fictional *mimesis*. L. then examines H.'s theoretical dicussion of such techniques in the *Frauenzimmer-Gesprächsspiele* and relates it to his narrative treatment of tapestries in the same work. K. Gajek, 'Georg Philipp Harsdörffers Brief vom 30. Mai 1652 an Abraham von Frankenberg', *Chloe*, 27, 1997: 403–12, accounts for the rediscovery of this 'lost' letter, and appends a facsimile with a commentated transcription.

HORTENSIA VON SALIS. R. Zeller, 'Konversation und Freundschaft. Die *Conversations Gespräche* der Hortensia von Salis', *Chloe*, 28:331–42, examines a 1696 novel by a Swiss noblewoman loosely modelled on M. de Scudéry's *Nouvelles Conversations* (also 1696). Characters in the novel embody French concepts of friendship and social discourse, and discuss these topics — along with others such as theology, medicine, and women's place in society — in the setting of a spa.

MOSCHEROSCH. W. E. Schäfer, 'Zwischen Freier Reichsstadt und Absolutistischem Hof. Lebensräume Moscheroschs', Garber, *Stadt*, 293–307, is a revised version of an essay first published in 1982 which sees M.'s official career in Strasbourg and at court in Hanau as united by his belief in a divinely ordained social order. S. refines the notion that M. was unrelentingly hostile to court life by arguing, with reference to M.'s own comment, especially in *Insomnis Cura Parentum*, that he thrived better as an author not while fitting himself into absolutist strictures in Hanau but while exercising civic responsibilities in the free imperial city.

SPIZEL. D. Blaufuss, '*Commercium epistolicum* in der Reichsstadt. Gottlieb Spizel/Augsburg (1639–1691) und seine Briefwechselsammlung im Umkreis von Orthodoxie und Pietismus', Garber, *Stadt*, 411–24, explores a substantial collection of 'Polyhistor-Korrespondenz' mostly addressed to Spizel, an Augsburg pastor, and including letters from such luminaries as Philipp Jakob Spener, Christian Scriver and Leibniz. B. discusses August Hermann Francke's transcription of the correspondence for his archive in Halle, but also shows that it offers rich source material on less well-known clerics or scholars and on intellectual life in 17th-c. Augsburg.

WEISE. W. Neuber, '"Jch habe mich fast in keiner Sache so sehr bemühet, als in den Episteln": Christian Weises Brieftheorie und die Tradition', *Daphnis*, 27, 419–442, surveys 17th-c. letter-writing manuals, showing how their emphasis shifts over the course of the century from the judicial tradition, where style is determined in relation to subject-matter, towards a social orientation where style seeks to match or alter the individual recipient's affects. W.'s political orientation is then seen as developing out of of this trend.

OTHER WORK

I. Breuer, 'Überlegungen zur Gattungstypologie frühneuzeitlicher Erzählliteratur am Beispiel des "Schäfferromans"', *Simpliciana*, 20:255–82, seeks to redress inadequate current categorizations of early modern narrative genres and sub-genres. B. suggests, for example, that the 'Schäfferroman' is not, strictly speaking, a type of novel, and can be more accurately categorized as 'pastorale Liebeserzählung', a term which would usefully allow it to be classified alongside other sub-genres that are related to the 'Historia' and distinct from the novel, such as the 'historische Erzählung' (a term applied by Rosmarie Zeller to Grimmelshausen's 'Legendenromane') and the so-called 'satirischer Roman' of the late 17th c.; but B. concludes provocatively by questioning whether the concept 'Historia' proves, in fact, to be a wholly reliable criterion in matters of genre definition.

4. DRAMA
INDIVIDUAL AUTHORS

GRYPHIUS. Nicola Kaminski, *Andreas Gryphius*, Stuttgart, Reclam, 264 pp., concentrates on aesthetic aspects of G.'s work. His drama receives the fullest treatment. K. sees the tragedies as a unified project emerging from G.'s preoccupation with the concept of life as *theatrum mundi*, interpreting each as a variation on the issues of how humans recognize the transcendental and of how to represent the transcendental on stage. She perceives the device of 'a play within a play' in each of G.'s three main comedies, examines it as a means of allowing the comic to approach tragic patterns, and discusses comic structures such as 'doubling'. She takes a broad view of G.'s poetry, but focuses in particular on the structuring of the books of sonnets according to a symbolic numerical system. A biography and a welcome section on G.'s much neglected funeral speeches are included. E. Mannack, 'Schwarze Magie in Gryphs *Cardenio und Celinde*', *Chloe*, 27, 1997:35–44, is a detailed commentary on G.'s discussion of black magic and ghostly apparitions in the 'Vorrede' to *Cardenio und Celinde*, and on events in the play around the figure of Tyche (a 'Zauberin'). M. stresses the relevance of the play to a society where witch trials were still current and the temptation to resort to the black arts was not uncommon. F. van Ingen, 'Andreas Gryphius' *Catharina von Georgien*. Märtyrertheologie und Luthertum', *ib.*, 45–70, refutes views of this drama as a Protestant 'Kontrafaktur' of Jesuit martyr plays or as an instance of anti-Habsburg polemic, analysing its structure, argumentation and imagery as vehicles for orthodox Lutheran teachings on trial by suffering, *imitatio Christi*, bridal union with Christ and the Last Judgement, and arguing that performers and audience would have absorbed these teachings by becoming eye-witnesses to Catharina's recognition and exemplification of them. H. Feger, 'Zeit und Angst. Gryphius' *Catharina von Georgien* und die Weltbejahung bei

Luther', *ib.*, 71–100, also relates this play to Lutheran doctrine, but focuses in particular on the issues of rulership and conscience which G. highlights in the dynamic contrast between Chach Abas as tyrant and Catharina as martyr. L. Bornscheuer, 'Diskurs-Synkretismus im Zerfall der Politischen Theologie. Zur Tragödienpoetik des Gryphschen Trauerspiele', *ib.*, 489–529, re-examines G.'s four so-called 'martyr tragedies', focusing on what B. treats as their most striking common factor: the interlocking of discourse on religious-ethical and historical-political issues. B. argues that G.'s tragedy is driven by concern at the gulf between these two spheres that was widening to the point of crisis in 17th-c. Europe. He sees G. as problematizing the loss of harmony between the transcendental and secular realms (embodied in the ideal of the anointed ruler), and views his tragedies as disputations on this topic rather than as purely religious-ethical teachings. E. A. Metzger and M. M. Metzger, 'Die Heilung des *Schwermenden Schäfers* durch das Wunderbare', *ib.*, 159–78, compare Corneille's *Le berger extravagant* with G.'s translations (1660 and 1663), demonstrating that this pastoral comedy presented G. not only with the opportunity of portraying a character suffering from an extreme form of delusion (the 'schwärmende Schäfer' abandons bourgeois reality to inhabit pastoral fantasy), but also of examining the causes and cures of delusion in far greater detail than in his own *Horribilicribrifax* and *Peter Squentz*.

HALLMANN. J. P. Aikin, 'What happens when opera meets drama, and vice versa? J. C. Hallmann's Experiments and their Significance', *Chloe*, 27, 1997:137–58, looks at the overlap between drama and opera in work by H. from the early 1670s which includes translations of Italian libretti into texts resembling the 'Heldenspiel', a serious but non-tragic form characterized by rapid action, spectacle, and comic elements as well as episodes of music and song; and a 'musikalisches Trauer-Spiel', *Catharina Königin in Engelland*. A. claims that such works seek a realism otherwise absent from Silesian 'Kunstdrama', and sees in them the seeds of 18th-c. German-language oratorio. B. Neuge-bauer, ' "Wir dienen GOtt' und uns/ und was dem Nachbarn nützt/ Jst unser höchstes Ziel" — Ein Beitrag zu Johann Christian Hallmanns Schäferspielen', *ib.*, 179–202, discusses H.'s adaptation of pastoral conventions in *Urania* (1666) and *Rosibella* (1671–73). N. claims that the two plays resemble tragedy, both in their seriousness of purpose and in certain formal aspects, and shows how they thematize love, the derangement of the affects and the stabilizing role of reason, thus departing from the idyllic world of pastoral to encourage self-control in the political interactions of public life. A. Solbach, 'Vorsehung und freier Wille in Hallmanns *Theodoricus Veronensis*', *ib.*, 203–242, looks at an early (pre-1666) tyrant/martyr drama by H. which has attracted little critical attention, perhaps, S. notes, because it closely resembles Gryphius's *Leo Armenius* and *Papinian*, or because the formal innovation characteristic of H.'s somewhat later work is lacking. S. treats the play as an opportunity to distinguish between the different notions of providence and free will subscribed to by Gryphius, Lohenstein and H., with reference to the *De consolatione philosophiae* of Boethius (the martyr figure in the play) and Lipsius's *De constantia*.

LOHENSTEIN. S. Colvin, 'Eine Warnung vor dem Weiblichen? Die Venus-Allegorese in den Frauendramen D. C. von Lohensteins', Horn, *Allegorese*, 267–85, views the destructive force ascribed to the allegorical figure of Venus in the myth of the Judgement of Paris as the basis for Lohenstein's *Cleopatra*, *Agrippina*, and *Sophonisbe*. C. claims, however, that L. is intent on warning the schoolboys performing these plays not against female sexuality as such — the female protagonists, after all, do not lack positive qualities — but against the male urges which it excites and which cloud political judgement: a ruler who succumbs to his own lustful desires is weak, the efficient ruler can control such desires by subordinating them to the power of reason.

OTHER WORK

Christiane Caemmerer, *Siegender Cupido oder Triumphierende Keuschheit. Deutsche Schäferspiele des 17. Jahrhunderts* (Arbeiten und Editionen zur Mittleren Deutschen Literatur, 2), Stuttgart–Bad Cannstatt, Frommann-Holzboog, 526 pp., is a thorough and illuminating examination of the 'Schäferspiel'. After identifying the formal and thematic conventions established in two Italian prototypes, Tasso's *Aminta* (1573) and Guarini's *Pastor Fido* (1590), C. takes them as a basis for analysis of 14 of the approximately 50 pastoral plays published in Germany during the 17th c. She approaches these texts in eight classificatory groupings, starting with Dach's *Cleomedes* (1635–36) and ending with Hallmann's *Urania* (1666) and *Rosibella* (1671–73) and Jacob Reich's *Der unbeglückte Schäffer Corydon* (1686). She thus traces both the development and the variety of the genre, which after 1648 took on increasing importance as a mode of celebration among familial circles at court centres; in such a setting a prologue frequently defined the Arcadia of the play as the prince's territory (antithetical tension between arcadian and courtly life is not a defining characteristic of the 'Schäferspiel'). C. shows that although the theme of love is constant on the literal level, authors treat it very differently according to their immediate purpose; it may, for example, represent the chaste foundation of Lutheran marriage in a bourgeois context or, on a distinctly allegorical level and in a courtly context, the ruler's power over his people. R. Tarot, 'Der Alexandriner als Sprachvers im Barocken Trauerspiel', *Chloe*, 27, 1997:377–401, takes a new look at the much-maligned alexandrine, observing it as a *spoken* metre and demonstrating that its general reputation for monotony is undeserved. T. bases his analysis on a huge sample consisting of six tragedies by Gryphius and Lohenstein (representing *c.*12,000 lines). He concentrates in greatest detail on the productive disruption of the regular iambic metre by emphatic speech rhythms, but also systematically examines the use of stichomythia and of features inextricably linked with the alexandrine since Opitz first introduced it into German, such as enjambement and the caesura.

THE CLASSICAL ERA

By JEFFREY MORRISON, *Lecturer in German, National University of Ireland Maynooth*

1. GENERAL

BIBLIOGRAPHY, REFERENCE. The extraordinary undertaking *Die Deutsche Literatur: Biographisches und bibliographisches Lexikon*, ed. Hans-Gert Roloff et al., Stuttgart–Bad Cannstatt, Frommann–Holzboog, continues with *Die Deutsche Literatur zwischen 1720 und 1830*, Abt. A (Autorenlexikon), I, Lieferung 1–3, ed. Gerhard Pail et al., 260 pp. In 62 contributions it covers authors with surnames beginning with 'A' as far as 'Adolphi, Marie'. In each case there is a biographical sketch, a characterization of the author's work, and a primary bibliography (with locations, and including reviews, editorial, and journalistic work). The series is clearly developing into a major resource, particularly for colleagues dealing with more marginal areas of literature. *The Oxford Companion to German Literature*, ed. Henry Garland and Mary Garland, 3rd edn, OUP, 1997, 951 pp., is an expanded and revised edition of this valuable work.

PERIODS: AUFKLÄRUNG. *Der sympathetische Arzt: Texte zur Medizin im 18. Jahrhundert*, ed. Heinz Schott (Bibliothek des 18. Jahrhunderts), Munich, Beck, 397 pp., is an extremely useful resource in the context of Enlightenment studies. The assumption that medicine was uniformly a progressive science is qualified by some of the evidence of less enlightened practice collected here. An extremely valuable series of texts is being produced under the series title *Volksaufklärung: Ausgewählte Schriften*, ed. Holger Böning and Reinhart Siegert. The aim of the series is to illustrate how Enlightenment ideas were transferred into the realm of the *Volk*, often by figures (teachers, doctors, priests) who would not be part of the literary/philosophical mainstream. In each volume we are provided with a text in its original form and a *Nachwort* to introduce us to the author and the *Gedankengut* which he was seeking to popularize. With this enterprise the editors have helped to reclaim a number of authors from history, or at least make them much more accessible, and remind us of the scope of the Enlightenment. The latest publications are volumes 5–7, in order: Johann Georg Schlosser, *Katechismus der Sittenlehre für das Landvolk* (repr. of 1st edn, Frankfurt am Main, 1771), ed. Reinhart Siegert, Stuttgart–Bad Cannstadt, Frommann–Holzboog, 176 pp.; Hans Caspar Hirzel, *Die Wirtschaft eines philosophischen Bauers* (repr. of the updated edn, Zurich, 1774), ed. Holger Böning, Stuttgart–Bad Cannstadt, Frommann–Holzboog, 493 pp.; Johann Friedrich Mayer,

Maximen in dem Lebenslaufe eines Bauern (repr. of the journal edition in *Beyträge und Abhandlungen*, Frankfurt am Main, 1776), ed. Holger Böning, Stuttgart–Bad Cannstadt, Frommann–Holzboog, 281 pp. Peter Schünemann, *Wiederholte Spiegelungen: Elf Essays um Goethe & Andere* (Promenade 11), Tübingen, Klöpfer & Meyer, 142 pp., brings together a number of essays (some republications) on a variety of subjects, although there is a substantial focus on the Enlightenment period. New/revised articles of interest include: ' "Die elementa speculieren": Die "Mütter" im *Faust*, noch einmal' (23–32); 'Phantasie eines Urbilds: Zu einer Kindgestalt bei Goethe und Thomas Mann' (33–42); ' "Ein Weltgarten hatte sich aufgetan": Goethes Begegnung mit Friedlieb Ferdinand Runge' (43–56); ' "Das wundersamste aller Heldenleben": Heinrich Luden und Goethes Napoleon' (57–72); 'Humboldt's Paradies' (81–88); ' "To bäh or not to bäh" — Voß und Lichtenberg: Ein Kapitel zur Streitkultur des 18. Jahrhunderts' (97–114); 'Gebrochener Horizont: Johann Heinrich Voß in der deutschen Aufklärung' (115–26); ' "Citoyens, la liberté est morte": Zur Geschichte der Persönlichkeit in der deutschen Aufklärung am Beispiel Johann Gottfried Seume' (127–40). The articles lack conventional academic apparatus but that perhaps adds to the readability of the short contributions.

Aufklärung als Form: Beiträge zu einem historischen und aktuellen Problem, ed. Helmut Schmiedt and Helmut J. Schneider, Würzburg, Königshausen & Neumann, 203 pp., contains a collection of essays which range widely in subject matter (from literature to information technology) and historical scope (from the 18th c. to the present day). Enlightenment is understood as more than an historical movement — it is almost a state of mind, and so on this basis the inner form or essence of the Enlightenment could be preserved (with its complexities) long after the 18th c. There is a strong emphasis upon the role of literature within the project of Enlightenment. Contributions include: T. J. Reed, 'Das Volk der Dichter oder Denker: Auch ein Lessingsches Erbe' (15–28); D. von Mücke, 'Vor dem Spiegel des Dichters: Biographie und Autorfunktion in der Aufklärung' (29–45); H. J. Schneider, 'Aufklärung und Fiktion in Lessings Ringparabel' (46–63); J. Fohrmann, 'Aufklärung als Doppelpunkt (:)' (64–79); L. Pikulik, 'Der Traum der Vernunft: Die andere Aufklärung — Über ein romantisches Modell und seine Variationen in der Moderne' (80–105); G. Neumann, 'Romantische Aufklärung: Zu E. T. A. Hoffmanns Wissenschaftspoetik' (106–48); B. von Wolff-Metternich, 'Formen des Schönen in der Natur: Kant und Adorno' (149–60); D. E. Wellbery, 'Die Strategie des Paradoxons: Nietzsches Verhältnis zur Aufklärung' (161–72); B. Sorg, 'Kaspar im Elfenbeinturm: Zur Ambivalenz der Form in den frühen Texten Peter Handkes' (173–80);

E. Lämmert, 'Wissensexplosion und Bildung' (181–200). Harro Segeberg, *Literatur im technischen Zeitalter: Von der Frühzeit der deutschen Aufklärung bis zum Beginn des Ersten Weltkriegs*, WBG, 1997, viii + 437 pp., covers in its first part (pp. 19–95) the impact of developments in science and technology upon contemporary literature in the period 1680 to 1830. In brief treatments S. covers the adoption of ideas from science into literature (e.g. automatons/ the idea of flight/ optics); in some cases (Goethe) there is a high level of interdependence of scientific thinking and literary production. Scientific progress is shown to demand a revision of the individual's perception of himself, of nature and the world in general. This section serves largely as an introduction to the treatment of the 19th and 20th cs. Thomas P. Saine, *The Problem of Being Modern — Or: The German Pursuit of Enlightenment from Leibniz to the French Revolution*, Detroit, Wayne State U.P., 1997, 370 pp., is a revised and expanded version of the German original *Von der Kopernikanischen bis zur Französischen Revolution: Die Auseinandersetzung der deutschen Frühaufklärung mit der neuen Zeit*, Berlin, Erich Schmidt, 1987. The English version makes accessible to a wider public a very lucid account of German thought, specifically pre-Kantian philosophy. The text is particularly good at illuminating the ways in which thought is shaped by cultural and political pressures and at examining the contemporary tensions between secular and religious world views. Literary texts are used to illustrate important shifts in outlook, and works of cultural theory by literary figures (esp. Lessing) are at the core of S.'s argument. Gabriele Dürbeck, *Einbildungskraft: Perspektiven der Philosophie, Anthropologie und Ästhetik um 1750* (SDL, 148), vii + 357 pp., is a highly interesting study of the varying perceptions of the nature, value and function of imagination. It is divided into two sections covering respectively theories of imagination from around 1700 and 1750; this enables productive comparisons to be made within and across sections. The evidence is drawn together from a large number of sources — from e.g. the fields of lexicography, psychological theory, aesthetics, medecine, and anthropology. In each context the imagination is shown to be reassuringly elusive. *Aufklärung* 10.1 is a special number: *Die deutsche Aufklärung im Spiegel der neueren französischen Aufklärungsforschung*, ed. Robert Theis. The emphasis is philosophical; literary-critical contributions are detailed in the relevant sections. *StV*, 346/7/8 (published as a single volume), 1996[1997] contains the 'Transactions of the Ninth International Congress on the Enlightenment'. The range of material presented is gigantic with over 1600 pages of short contributions. Sections with a specific German interest include: 1.2 'Germany' (203–21); 1.6 'Moses Mendelssohn: Enlightenment and modernity' (293–312); 2.6 'German literature' (459–88).

There are, however, innumerable papers with some bearing on German studies. *Das Achtzehnte Jahrhundert*, 22.1, Göttingen, Wallstein, 151 pp., is a special number entitled *Enzyklopädien, Lexika und Wörterbücher im 18. Jahrhundert*. U. Hebekus, ' "Practicus des Indecori": Die Zeichen der Melancholie in Aufklärung und Empfindsamkeit', *DVLG*, 72:56–80. P. A. Alt, 'Kopernikanische Lektionen. Zur Topik des Himmels in der Literatur der Aufklärung', *GRM*, 48:141–64. W. Albrecht, 'Literaturkritik und Öffentlichkeit im Kontext der Aufklärungsdebatte: Fünf Thesen zu einem vernachlässigten Thema', *Lenz-Jahrbuch*, 7, 1997:163–84.

PERIODS: EMPFINDSAMKEIT, STURM UND DRANG. Inka Mülder-Bach, *Im Zeichen Pygmalions: Das Modell der Statue und die Entdeckung der 'Darstellung' im 18. Jahrhundert*, Munich, Wilhelm Fink, 254 pp., deals with a broader range of material than that usually suggested by the term *Empfindsamkeit* but is concerned with brands of sensibility characteristically associated with the period. The author is centrally concerned with instances of 'pygmalionische Ekphrasis' which contrast with the prevailing rationalizing aesthetics. The live, sensual exchange between art and the observer is shown to be at the core of writing on art by Winckelmann, Herder, Lessing and Klopstock (among others) who each contribute in different ways to 'ein ästhetisches Animationsprogramm' rather than a static aesthetic.

PERIODS: CLASSICISM. Friederike Schmidt-Möbus and Frank Möbus, *Kleine Kulturgeschichte Weimars*, Cologne–Weimar–Vienna, Böhlau, 352 pp. + 43 pls, covers much more than the period of Weimar Classicism. It ranges from the beginnings of the settlement to the present day and covers a huge range of themes. The section on our period (pp. 94–212 only) provides a useful introduction to the Weimar scene, aided by marginal headings which identify the particular themes/personalities being discussed. *Weimar: Lexikon zur Stadtgeschichte*, ed. Gitta Günther, Wolfram Huschke and Walter Steiner, Weimar, Hermann Böhlaus Nachfolger, 549 pp., covers an even wider range of material in a more compact form. It is a useful first port of call and has been significantly improved since its first publication (1993). Astrid Köhler, 'Redouten und Maskenzüge im klassischen Weimar: Variationen zum Thema Chaos und Ordnung', *IASL*, 23:30–47. A. Costazza, 'Das "Charakteristische" als ästhetische Kategorie der deutschen Klassik: Eine Diskussion zwischen Hirt, Fernow und Goethe nach 200 Jahren', *JDGS*, 42:64–94. Y.-G. Mix, 'Mit Goethe und Diderot gegen die Pächter des klassischen Erbes: U. Plenzdorfs *Die neuen Leiden des jungen W.*, V. Brauns Texte zu *Hinze und Kunze* und die Kontrolle der literarischen Kommunikation in der DDR', *ib.*, 401–20.

GENRES. *Abgerissene Einfälle: Deutsche Aphorismen des 18. Jahrhunderts*, ed. Harald Fricke and Urs Meyer (Bibliothek des 18. Jahrhunderts), Munich, Beck, 273 pp., presents a selection of aphorisms, or texts with something of the character of aphorisms, to show the emergence of a characteristic German aphorism from the shadow of a French precursor. Authors represented include: A. Bohse, N. H. Gundling, J. C. Nemeitz, A. G. Kästner, F. G. Klopstock, J. C. Lavater, A. von Knigge, Jean Paul, M. Ehrmann, J. G. Heinzmann, S. Mutschelle, J. W. von Goethe, J. G. Seume, F. Schlegel, F. von Hardenberg, A. W. Schlegel, F. Schleiermacher, G. C. Lichtenberg. *Briefe an junge Dichter*, ed. Helmut Göbel et al., Göttingen, Wallstein, 239 pp., is of only limited relevance to scholars of our period. The collection of letters (with commentary and brief *Nachwort*) to young poets from more experienced colleagues contains some examples from our period (pp. 7–48) involving G. E. Lessing, W. von Gerstenberg, G. A. Bürger, P. Gatterer, C. M. Wieland, F. Schiller, S. Mereau, J. W. Goethe. Jörg Krämer, *Deutschspachiges Musiktheater im späten 18. Jahrhundert: Typologie, Dramaturgie und Anthropologie einer populären Gattung* (SDL, 149), 2 vols, xi + 596 pp., xi + 597–933 pp., covers exhaustively each of the areas suggested in its title and it will clearly become a central reference work for and critical guide to these neglected dramas. Whilst it ranges widely, the core interest in the treatment of the texts is clearly anthropological; more specifically it is concerned with philosophical anthropology and the historical construction of the *Subjekt* and such matters as the reconciliation of body and soul. These plays allow a new perspective upon the anthropological debates as represented in literature. After all, we have here a brand of popular literature which depends to a high degree upon the senses and yet is particularly important during the Age of Reason. The broad sweep of the anthropological argument is compelling as is the treatment of the detail; this is equally true of the treatment of the intrinsic properties of the dramas. Jürgen Hein, *Das Wiener Volkstheater*, 3rd edn, WBG, viii + 262 pp., is a revised edition. A substantial part of the text deals with the development of this brand of theatre in the 18th c. The treatment of the economic and political circumstances (including the problem of censorship) which determined the emergence of *Volkstheater* is perhaps the most important feature of the text. In this connection: *ASt*, 9 is a special number on 'The Austrian Comic Tradition', ed. John R.P. McKenzie and Lesley Sharpe. Articles of interest include: L. Adey Huish, 'An Austrian comic tradition?' (3–23); R. Robertson, 'Heroes in their underclothes: Aloys Blumauer's travesty of Virgil's *Aeneid*' (24–40); P. Branscombe, 'Nestroy and Schiller' (58–70). Susanne Kord, 'All's well that ends well?

Marriage, madness and other happy endings in eighteenth-century women's comedies', *LY*, 28, 1996 [1997]: 181–98.

THEMES. Two important texts have appeared which deal with European reception of Asia and which throw considerable light upon that process as it develops during our period. Jürgen Osterhammel, *Die Entzauberung Asiens: Europa und die asiatischen Reiche im 18. Jahrhundert*, Munich, Beck, 560 pp., is a wide-ranging volume. The text covers the broad political/historical relationship between Europe and Asia, the perception of Asian culture in Europe, and the literary processing of the perception and experience of Asia. Whilst reference to literature/cultural theory inevitably abounds (on a European rather than specifically German basis) one chapter exclusively concerned with *Reiseberichte* (pp. 176–210) is particularly interesting; it is perhaps more direct in its analysis of the ideology informing contemporary travel literature than many similar treatments from dedicated literary scholars. Adrian Hsia, *Chinesia: The European Construction of China in the Literature of the 17th and 18th Centuries* (Communicatio: Studien zur europäischen Literatur- und Kulturgeschichte, 16), Tübingen, Niemeyer, 144 pp., has three chapters of specific interest to German scholars. 'The transplanted *Chinese Orphan* in England, France, Germany, Italy and his repatriation to Hong Kong' (75–98) deals with the possibility of transcultural transfer of themes and motifs in literature using German examples from Lessing and Goethe. Also included: 'Sinism within a despotic oriental utopia: From Montesquieu's *L'Esprit des lois* to Albrecht von Haller's political novel *Usong*' (99–114); 'Chinesia in Weimar: The transition from J. G. Herder's Sinophobia to S. von Seckendorff's Sino-Romanticism' (115–30).

Catriona MacLeod, *Embodying Ambiguity: Androgny and Aesthetics from Winckelmann to Keller*, Detroit, Wayne State U.P., 302 pp., investigates the lasting attraction of the myth of the androgyne. The fascination with such figures (in literature and aesthetic theory) derives from the fact that they appear to offer the prospect of reconciliation between assumed polar opposites, and so 'an explosion of categories'. They allow revision of categories of gender and sexuality; they also come to be identified with 'the aesthetic', that problematic territory which is neither entirely of the senses nor of the intellect and so another difficult intermediate state. The liberating associations of these figures are shown to have a very positive effect in the writing of Winckelmann, but Humboldt, Schiller, and Goethe (and various 19th-c. authors) find them more difficult to accommodate. M. identifies a powerful counter-current to their liberating potential, particularly well detailed in G. (*Wilhelm Meisters Lehrjahre*). The androgynous characters represented tend ultimately to be defeated; their intermediate/ambivalent status is, as it were, resolved in favour of one of the poles. The prospect of wholeness can only be maintained briefly, and the androgynous characters have to be removed to assure the survival of the status quo. Eva Horn, *Trauer schreiben: Die Toten im Text der Goethezeit* (TGLSK, n.s. 95/A/11), 266 pp., covers rather more than the title suggests since it reaches back into the Baroque period and deals with texts published in the late 19th c. Nonetheless core chapters have a direct bearing on our period and the investigation of Baroque representations of death is important in providing a benchmark against which to measure later treatments. The text elucidates the increasingly complex relationship between life and death in the advancing 18th c. where death is seen increasingly as a threat to the enlightened *Subjekt*. There is a corresponding difficulty in writing about death, particularly in confronting its unaesthetic aspects. H. deals with works from our period by Lessing, Herder, Schiller, and Goethe. The section on *Die Wahlverwandtschaften* (pp. 130–64) could usefully be read in combination with Elisabeth Herrmann's treatment of the same topic (detailed under 'Goethe' below). Gesa von Essen, *Hermannsschlachten: Germanen- und Römerbilder in der Literatur des 18. und 19. Jahrhunderts* (Internationalität nationaler Literaturen, B/2), Göttingen, Wallstein, 288 pp., investigates the tendency of literature on this theme to reproduce established prejudice about either or both groups which is not rooted in experience. The author shows how the transmission of prejudice develops its own dynamic; it depends upon the fact that each stereotype is driven on by the existence of its opposite. Two 18th-c. examples of Hermann-literature are featured, J. E. Schlegel's and Klopstock's. In focusing on the Germanic they are seen as differing reactions to French cultural hegemony — appropriate since Hermann was, of course, a 'decolonizer' himself. Neither author notes the irony in the fact that their image of Hermann is derived from foreign models. Articles dealing primarily with themes include: H. Benning, 'Die "himmlische Schrift" und das "heilige Gedicht": Theologische und ästhetische Fassetten der spannungsreichen Beziehung von Kunst und Religion im 18. Jahrhundert', *DUS*, 50.5 : 14–24; D. Schöttker, 'Metamorphosen der Freude: Darstellung und Reflexion der Heiterkeit in der Literatur des 18. Jahrhunderts', *DVLG*, 72 : 354–75, details the gradual suppression of the merry in favour of the melancholy, the moral or the philosophical; C. Benthen, 'Hand und Haut: Zur historischen Anthropologie von Tasten und Berührung', *ZGer*, n.F., 8 : 335–48; I. M. Krüger-Fürhoff, 'Der vervollständigte Torso und die verstümmelte Venus: Zur Rezeption antiker Plastik und plastischer Anatomie in Ästhetik und Reiseliteratur des 18. Jahrhunderts', *ib.*, 361–74; B. Damerau, 'Horaz oder Die Wahrheit der Literatur: Eine

Anmerkung zum Umgang mit Horaz im 18. Jahrhundert', *ib.*, 649–54.

2. GOETHE

EDITIONS. Access to G.' s work has been made considerably easier by the appearance of two CD-ROMs. The first, a selection entitled *Johann Wolfgang Goethe: Werke*, ed. Mathias Bertram et al., Reinbek, Rowohlt, contains some 12,400 pages of text and so a massive range of G.'s literary, scientific, philosophical, and autobiographical writing. The innovation is not to be found in the editing, which relies upon standard editions and employs sensible principles detailed in the accompanying leaflet, but rather in the programming which allows a whole new and speedy way of approaching the text. A variety of search modes are available, notes can be made and collated, and pieces of text marked. In all it is a very useful tool for research and teaching; particularly useful in the latter context are the collections of images, the presence of the *Hörtext* version of *Werther* and the digital version of Peter Boerner's *rororo* monograph *Johann Wolfgang von Goethe*. The CD-ROM *Johann Wolfgang von Goethe: Briefe, Tagebücher, Gespräche*, ed. Mathias Bertram et al., Reinbek, Rowohlt, is similarly useful. The letter collection is based upon the full Weimar edition including *Nachträge*, as are the diaries. Only subtle changes have been made for purposes of editorial clarity, e.g. in the chronological ordering of letters. The third section of the CD-ROM brings together reported conversations with Goethe including those from Eckermann, Riemer, and Müller following Woldemar von Biedermann's concept. The *Personenverzeichnis* which makes up the fourth section of the disk is a particularly useful supplement to the already powerful search capability of the program. The first volume (of 10) of a freshly and marvellously edited collection of G.'s diaries has just appeared and one cannot help but think how useful it would have been for these to have appeared simultaneously in digital form. As it is, the hard editions are a magnificent research tool. *Johann Wolfgang Goethe: Tagebücher*. I. *(1775–1787)*, ed. Wolfgang Albrecht and Andreas Döhler, Stuttgart, Metzler, xvi + 911 pp., is subdivided for practical purposes into two vols, 1.1 *Text* (pp. 1–351), 1.2 *Kommentar* (pp. 352–911). Taken together they constitute an outstanding piece of textual scholarship, already subjected to peer review in a pre-publication run, and they are likely to establish and retain a dominant position for scholars in this field. The presentation of the text in vol. 1.1 is meticulous. The basis is provided by the available manuscripts, reproduced in an unsanitized form, rather than published editions; authorial mistakes and omissions as well as subsequent editorial variants are recorded in footnotes. The commentary in vol. I.2 is most exhaustive, even including as an *Anhang* (pp. 627–784) the relevant parts of Volkmann's *Historisch-Kritische Nachrichten von Italien* which were an important source for Goethe in Italy. Heinz Hamm, *Goethe und die Zeitschrift 'Le Globe': Eine Lektüre im Zeichen der 'Weltliteratur'*, Weimar, Hermann Böhlaus Nachfolger, 500 pp., is included here amongst the primary literature because it consists substantially of the collection and analysis of some of Goethe's largely unknown marginalia. H. records all of the marked parts of *Le Globe* and further collects all other tangible references to this journal which was a favourite of G.'s between 1826–30. This enables the reader to follow e.g. G.'s wide range of literary and scientific interests during this period, the reception of his and Schiller's work abroad, and to monitor his responses to political and social change. On this basis it is a very useful resource book and it is very well organized to allow access to the material.

GENERAL STUDIES AND ESSAY COLLECTIONS. Gero von Wilpert, *Goethe-Lexikon*, Stuttgart, Kröner, 1227 pp., is a practical volume which fulfils its own ambitions in providing pertinent and compact treatments of people, places, and topics connected with G. as well as compact treatment of his works. Whilst the range of material treated brings with it inevitable economies in the treatment of individual matters, the text will find a useful space on bookshelves. The publication of the *Goethe-Handbuch*, ed. Bernd Witte et al., 4 vols, Stuttgart, Metzler, is completed with the publication of *Goethe-Handbuch*, IV/2 *(Personen, Sachen, Begriffe L-Z)*, ed. Hans-Dietrich Dahnke and Regine Otto, Stuttgart, Metzler, xvii + 645–1270 pp. Many of the entries are short essays by experts in the particular field (with brief bibliography) and this has the effect of making this volume an exceptionally useful work of reference and point of access to themes or individuals. Christoph Perels, *Goethe in seiner Epoche: Zwölf Versuche*, Tübingen, Niemeyer, 253 pp., brings together a number of papers produced by the author, largely in the context of his work for *Das Freie Deutsche Hochstift* or the Frankfurt Goethe-Museum. Included: 'Die Mächtigen und die Musen: Zum Auftrag der Kultur im aufgeklärten Staat des 18. Jahrhunderts' (1–24); 'Die Sturm und Drang-Jahre 1770–1776 in Straßburg' (25–48); 'Auf der Suche nach dem verlorenem Vater: Das *Werther*-Evangelium, noch einmal' (49–64); 'Die Faust-Legende in Deutschland: Eine Skizze' (65–82); 'Herder und die junge Dichtergeneration um Goethe' (83–96); ' "Ich begreife, daß Goethe sich so ganz an sie attachiert hat": Über Charlotte von Stein' (97–118) (previously unpublished); 'Maler Müllers *Iphigenia*: Zum Spielraum der Antike-Rezeption in der Goethezeit' (119–58); 'Goethes Weg zu *Wilhelm Meisters Lehrjahren*:

Italienische Erfahrungen und klassischer Erzählstil' (159–76) (previously unpublished); 'Der Begriff der Begebenheit in Goethes Bemerkungen zur Erzählkunst' (177–90); 'Unmut, Übermut und Geheimnis: Versuch über Goethes *West-östlichen Divan*' (191–218); 'Goethes *Divan*-Gedicht *Es geht eins nach dem andern hin*: Zur Entstehung und Überlieferung' (219–38); 'Der Autor und sein Werk: Goethes Einschätzung seiner Sturm und Drang-Lyrik in den verschiedenen Epochen seines Lebens' (239–52) (previously unpublished).

Jochen K. Schütze, *Goethe-Reisen*, Wien, Passagen, 108 pp., is not a conventional critical study but is none the less interesting for the light it casts upon G.'s travels. G. has a different perspective on travel because 'Goethe war nie weg. Das Wegsein ist der Entzug der Örtlichkeit schlechthin, man ist weder hier noch dort [. . .] Goethe dagegen fühlte sich, wohin er auch kam, zu Hause'. There is interesting treatment of G.'s 'Inszenierung' of his journeys, his prediction of experiences which only needed to be acted out — e.g. the rebirth in Rome — and also a new angle on the development of G.'s 'eye'. Hans-J. Weitz, *Der einzelne Fall: Funde und Erkundungen zu Goethe* (Schriften der Goethe-Gesellschaft, 66), Weimar, Hermann Böhlaus Nachfolger, 365 pp + 6 pls, brings together a large number of mostly short articles, the majority of which were previously published elsewhere: 'Über die Interpunktion im *Divan*-Band der Welt-Goethe-Ausgabe' (13–55) (previously unpublished); 'Zum Goethe-Text' (56–63); 'Das göttliche Wunder: Ein unerkannter Beitrag von Goethe' (64–78); 'Goethe über die Deutschen' (79–89); 'Goethe-Studien' (90–101); 'Eine Parodie von Marianne Willemer?' (102–09); 'Goethes Briefwechsel mit Marianne und Johann Jakob Willemer' (110–27); 'Goethes Gedicht *Die Weisen und die Leute*' (128–70); 'Des Pindus Adler' (171–72); 'Unerkannte Grüße Goethes an Marianne Willemer' (173–227); '"Prüft das Geschick dich [. . .]": Ein Spruch im *West-östlichen Divan*' (228–30); 'Das früheste Gedicht im *West-östlichen Divan*' (231–58); 'Ein Motiv in den *Wanderjahren*: Der Fingerschnitt' (259–67); 'Aus dem *West-östlichen Divan* auszuschließen' (268–79); 'Ein Schweizer Maler bei Goethe' (280–313); 'Bemerkungen zum frühen *West-östlichen Divan* (314–39); 'Goethe als Bühnenfigur auf dem zeitgenössischen Theater' (340–48); '"Weltliteratur" zuerst bei Wieland' (349–52); 'Zwei Paralipomena zum Faust' (353–55); 'Der Doctor Marianus' (previously unpublished) (356–58).

GJb, 113, 1996, contains the usual extraordinary range of articles on G.: J. Baur, 'Martin Luther im Urteil Goethes' (11–22); W. Woesler, 'Möser und Goethe' (23–36); K. Dedecius, 'Goethe und Mickiewicz — zwei Sterne auf getrennten Bahnen' (37–50); A. Smirnow, 'Das Symbol in der Lyrik Lermontows im Verhältnis zur Symbolik Goethes' (51–66); H. Reiss, 'Sozialer Wandel in Goethes

Werk' (67–84); U. Lorenz, 'Sprache als wissenschaftshistorischer Faktor: Eine wissenschaftssoziologische und sprachrezeptive Untersuchung zu Goethes Aufsatz über den Zwischenkieferknochen' (85–104); K. Gerth, ' "Das Wechselspiel des Lebens" ': Ein Versuch, *Wilhelm Meisters Lehrjahre* (wieder) einmal anders zu lesen' (105–20); E. Seitz, 'Die Vernunft des Menschen und die Verführung durch das Leben: Eine Studie zu den *Lehrjahren*' (121–38); P. Michelsen, 'Wie frei ist der Mensch? Über Notwendigkeit und Freiheit in Goethes *Wahlverwandtschaften*' (139–60); K. Mommsen, 'Ein Gedicht Goethes zu Ehren von Johann Sebastian Bach? Plädoyer für seine Echtheit' (161–78); A. Anglet, 'Die lyrische Bewegung in Goethes *Chinesisch-Deutschen Jahres- und Tageszeiten*' (179–98); G. Schulz, 'Goethe für den Hausgebrauch: Spruchdichtung als Nationalerziehung?' (199–216); G. Schnitzler, 'Interpretation von Kunst durch Kunst? Goethes *Heidenröslein* und Beethovens Vertonungsfragmente' (217–32); W. D. Wilson, 'Fürstenbund oder Überwachung? Noch einmal zu Goethes Beitritt in den Illuminatenorden: Eine Replik' (233–52); B. Leistner, 'Goethe uns Gegenwärtige betreffend?' (253–58); H. Fuhrmann, 'Klassiker oder Computer?' (259–72); W. von Engelhardt and Dorothea Kuhn, 'Nicht von Goethe: *Der Dynamismus in der Geologie*' (273–76); F. Satta and R. Zapperi, 'Goethes Faustine: Die Geschichte einer Fälschung' (277–80); J. Kost, 'Die Fortschrittlichkeit des scheinbar Konventionellen: Das Motive der Liebesheirat in Goethes *Hermann und Dorothea*' (281–86); M. Pütz, 'Goethes *Des Epimenides Erwachen* — politisch betrachtet' (287–90); T. Richter, 'Doris Zelters Briefe nach Weimar, 1818–1834: Teil 1: Die Briefe an Goethe' (291–308); R. Wartusch, 'Neue Spuren der ersten Aufführungen von Szenen aus dem *Faust*' (309–14); I. Jahn, 'Die Leopoldina-Ausgabe von Goethes Schriften zur Naturwissenschaft im Urteil eines Benutzers' (315–22). The same applies to the following volume, *GJb*, 114, 1997, which includes: W. Frühwald, 'Goethes Spätwerk: Die Erfahrung, sich selbst historisch zu werden' (23–34); D. Blondeau, 'Goethes Naturbegriff in den *Wahlverwandtschaften*' (35–48); P. Øhrgaard, 'Analogische Feldforschung: Überlegungen zu Wilhelm Meisters *Wanderjahren*' (49–62); H. Segeberg, 'Diagnose und Prognose des technischen Zeitalters im Schlußakt von *Faust II*' (63–74); P. Boerner, 'Zeitbezug und testamentarische Absicht in Goethes späten Briefen' (75–88); J. Golz, 'Geschichtliche Welt und gedeutetes Ich in Goethes Autobiographik' (89–100); R. H. Stephenson, 'Die ästhetische Gegenwärtigkeit des Vergangenen: Goethes *Maximen und Reflexionen* über Geschichte und Gesellschaft, Erkenntnis und Erziehung' (101–12); H. Birius, 'Begegnungsformen des Westlichen und Östlichen in Goethes *West-östlichem Divan*' (113–32); R. Wild, 'Natur und Subjekt in Goethes später Lyrik' (133–46); W. M. Fues, 'Goethes *Novelle*:

Utopie einer befriedeten Welt?' (147–62); J. Neubauer, '"Ich lehre nicht, ich erzähle": Geschichte und Geschichten in Goethes naturwissenschaftlichen Schriften' (163–74); D. Kuhn, '"In Naturerscheinungen verstrickt": Goethes morphologisches Spätwerk und seine Wirkung' (175–84); N. Kimura, 'Goethes Alterspoetik' (185–98); A. Bohnenkamp, 'Goethes Arbeit am *Faust*' (199–218); D. Liewerscheidt, 'Selbsthelferin ohne Autonomie: Goethes *Iphigenie*' (219–30); O. Hildebrand, 'Sinnliche Seligkeit: Goethes heidenischer Sensualismus und seine Beziehung zu Heine' (231–52); I. Egger, '"[. . .] ihre große Mäßigkeit": Diätetik und Askese in Goethes Roman *Die Wahlverwandtschaften*' (253–64); E. Lippert-Adelberger, 'Die Platanen in Goethes *Wahlverwandtschaften*: Versuch einer mariologischen Deutung' (265–76); G. Debon, '"Nur nicht mit Creuzer und Schorn!": Zur Datierung einer "Invective"' (335–40); T. Zabka, 'Überlagerte Gespräche: Goethes Reaktion auf die Julirevolution und den französischen Akademiestreit 1830' (341–46); W. I. Sacharow, 'Iwan Wassiljewitsch über Goethe' (347–50).

POETRY. Rudolf Brandmeyer, *Die Gedichte des jungen Goethe: Eine gattungsgeschichtliche Einführung* (Uni-Taschenbücher, 2062), Göttingen, Vandenhoeck und Ruprecht, 236 pp., is a very useful tool, as well as being interesting in its own right. The approach to the poetry is indicated in the subtitle. In focusing on *Gattungsgeschichte* B. is able to indicate the development in the use of poetic forms by G., often employing illuminating comparisons with contemporary poems by other authors. B. does not aim at rigid, absolute characterizations of the individual poems but wishes to reveal the dynamic choices which the poet makes in selecting from and adapting the available repertoire of forms, structures, styles, tones, and themes. In this context there is also very interesting discussion of the tension between *Satz* and *Vers*, perhaps the first difficulty which the new student of poetry encounters. Smaller studies include: H. Birus, '"ich möcht nicht gern vergessen sein": Goethes Stammbuchverse', Peil, *Erkennen*, 487–515; A. Fineron, 'Goethe, Schelling's theology and the genesis of *Prooemion*', *DVLG*, 72:81–114, concerns G.'s engagement with the increasingly theological Schelling around 1810 (e.g. in debate with Jacobi). The poem is seen in part as a response to this; T. Buck, 'Goethes *Ginkgo biloba*', *EG*, 53:277–90; H. Rölleke, 'Goethes letzte Verse', *Euphorion*, 92:130–34; M. Titzmann, 'Vom "Sturm und Drang" zur "Klassik": *Grenzen der Menschheit* und *Das Göttliche* — Lyrik als Schnittpunkt der Diskurse', *JDSG*, 42:42–63; G. Kaiser, 'Französische Revolution und deutsche Hexameter: Goethes *Hermann und Dorothea* nach 200 Jahren — Ein Vortrag', *Poetica*, 30:81–97; T. J. Reed, 'Rhyme and reason: Enlightenment by other means', *PEGS(NS)*, 67, 1997 [1998]:1–16.

DRAMA. Thomas Frantzke, *Goethes Schauspiele mit Gesang und Singspiele 1773–1782* (EH, I, 1671), 308 pp., serves as a useful reminder of these neglected texts. We are reminded of the contemporary popularity of the genre and of the fact that they now only ever appear in collected works and are rarely selected by editors. The treatment of the reasons for the popularity of the genre is enlightening, but since this popularity seems to have depended upon external circumstances (the structure of theatre troops, the financing of theatre, the emergence of a *bürgerlich* audience with corresponding tastes) we do rather fear for the intrinsic qualities of the plays. Whilst F. points out the range of themes etc which they offer he does not suggest that there is more than the occasional glimpse of high quality work. Above all the existence of these texts seems to indicate G.'s ambition to be popular at that time and so his need to adopt the genre. There is no treatment of the music itself (beyond the lyrics), although we are pointed in the direction of recent work in that area. Alexander Weiszflog, *Zeiterfahrung und Sprachkunst: Goethes 'Torquato Tasso' im Kontext der Ästhetik Schillers und Schlegels* (Ep, Reihe Literaturwissenschaft, 226), 1997, 156 pp., reveals the problematic nature of time in *Tasso*. Whilst the text is known for its classical features, including unity of time, it is simultaneously 'ein Schauplatz eines Wechsels von Erwartung und Enttäuschung, Erinnerung und Antizipation, Augenblicksemphase und Beständigkeitsstreben', i.e. a text where time is experienced as highly unstable. This tension between 'innere- und äußere Zeit' is seen as a key element of the modernity of the text. The difficulty with time is reflected in difficulty in expression since the act of expression fixes a statement, makes it endure in words, even when the speaking character is in a state of flux. Hence individual statements and conversations are always subject to revision. The effective 'Unvorhersehbarkeit kommunikativer Prozesse' is seen as an essential determinant of the structure of the play. W. provides interesting comparisons with the 'bürgerliches Trauerspiel' and the plays of Schiller, indicating an historical move away from essentially simple plot-driven drama towards more complex psychological drama more appropriate to modern man. Schiller and Schlegel provide the theoretical elucidation of the nature of modernity. R. Hillebrand, 'Cophtisches bei Goethe', *Neophilologus*, 82 : 259–78.

FAUST. Andreas Kosir, *Denkende Dichtung: Hermeneutik und Mantik zu Goethes 'Faust I'*, Frankfurt, Lang, 1997, 474 pp., is a treatment of morality, mysticism, and religion in *Faust*, viewed through the filter of Hegelian philosophy. This reviewer is not competent to deal with the text. Soon-He Oh, *Ontologie und Geschichte in Goethes 'Faust'* (EH, I, 1689), 184 pp., is *Faust* seen through the filter of reception theory (also in G.'s embryonic version). The starting-point for the discussion is G.'s awareness of the gaps in the last part of his text and his confidence that the *Verstand* of the reader will enable him to read it as a *Ganzes*. A discussion of the basic structural problem of the text — the contradiction between its identification as a tragedy and the apparent happy ending — develops through a treatment (amongst others) of the character Mephistopheles and the introduction of illustrative material from Platonic and Neoplatonic philosophy into a debate about the tension between history and ontology. A prospect of hope for the resolution of the tensions generated by the text is seen in the act of reading itself in which the 'historical' work of art becomes 'actual' once more. Smaller studies include: T. Zabka, 'Dialektik des Bösen: Warum es in Goethes "Walpurgisnacht" keinen Satan gibt', *DVLG*, 72:201–26; H. Rölleke, '"Sie ist die Erste nicht" und "Geschehen ist leider nun geschehen": Zu zwei Sentenzen in Goethes *Faust*-Dichtung', *Euphorion*, 92:125–29; F. Möbus, 'Die Meyrink-Hypothese: Zur aktuellen Verwendung geflügelter Worte — das Beispiel *Faust*', *Muttersprache*, 108:232–51; L. P. Koepnick, 'Simulating simulation: Art and modernity in *Faust II*', *Seminar*, 34:1–25; H. Rölleke, '"Im Deutschen lügt man": Ein *Faust*-Splitter', *WW*, 48:1–2.

NARRATIVE. Elisabeth Herrmann, *Die Todesproblematik in Goethes Roman 'Die Wahlverwandtschaften'* (PSQ, 147), 291 pp., is a most interesting volume. In the introductory sections H. locates G.'s treatment of death in the novel in a literary-historical context in which a process of aestheticization of death is at work, e.g. in the 'Beschönigung des Todes' to be found in Lessing or in the 'Todessehnsucht' of the Romantic period. It is shown that death can be used in literature to carry more than its contemporary cultural-historical meaning or confirm some philosophical category; it can have a symbolic function. H. moves on to indicate how G., the man, responded to death, usually rather cooly with 'Distanz, Abwehr'. This apparent coolness extends even to the death of his wife, and H. indicates an apparent contradiction with his apparent belief in the immortality of the soul. *Die Wahlverwandtschaften* is then shown to reflect G.'s complex and ambivalent understanding of death or death-like states. By the latter H. understands the tendency in the text for characters to stagnate, return to old ways, appear lifeless, reject the present. In part this is seen as *Zeitkritik* reflecting the state of the contemporary aristocracy. But it is more than this since: 'Der Tod in den *Wahlverwandtschaften* symbolisiert nicht ein abruptes Ende, sondern nicht stattgefundenes Leben, Stagnation, Wiederholung, Entbehrung und Scheitern' — a fear of living death. G.'s personal difficulty in dealing with the reality of death is also reflected in the text. Deaths or near-deaths in the text are presented undramatically, without horror. Or death is mediated aesthetically, as H. indicates most interestingly in her treatment e.g. of the *Kirchhof* scenes, the *tableaux vivants*, and other visual images. *Leidenschaften literarisch*, ed. Reingard M. Nischik (Texte zur Weltliteratur, 1), Konstanz U.P., 302 pp., contains: E. Horn, 'Chemie der Leidenschaft: Johann Wolfgang von Goethes *Die Wahlverwandtschaften*' (163–82), an examination of the text as 'poetische Versuchsanordnung'. In its treatment of death and the *Jenseits* it could usefully be read together with Hermann's text (above). Other smaller studies include: J. Adler, ' "Kein wissenschaftlicher Gärtner [. . .]": Werther's letter of 10 May and his reading of Hirschfeld's *Landleben*', *London Ger. St. VI*, 71–119; C. Liebrand, 'Briefromane und ihre "Lektüreanweisungen": Richardsons *Clarissa*, Goethes *Die Leiden des jungen Werthers*, Laclos' *Les Liasons dangereuses*', *Arcadia*, 32, 1997:342–64; H. Koopmann, 'Goethes Werther — der Roman einer Krise und ihrer Bewältigung', *Aurora*, 58:1–17; C. Tang, 'Two German deaths: Nature, body and text in Goethe's *Werther* and Theodor Storm's *Der Schimmelreiter*', *OL*, 53:105–16; G. Sasse, ' "Der Abschied aus diesem Paradies": Die Überwindung der Sehnsucht durch die Kunst in der Lago Maggiore-Episode in Goethes *Wanderjahren*', *JDSG*, 42:95–119; D. Blondeau, 'La figure d'Ottilie dans les *Wahlverwandtschaften*: Le Discours de l'inconscient', *RG*, 27, 1997:37–73; F. Schöbler, 'Mechanische Uhr und Sonnenwende: Zeit und Gesellschaft in Goethes Roman *Wilhelm Meister's (sic) Wanderjahre*', *ib.*, 75–92.

THEMES. Wolfgang Rothe, *Der politische Goethe: Dichter und Staatsdiener im deutschen Spätabsolutismus* (Sammlung Vandenhoeck), Göttingen, Vandenhoeck & Ruprecht, 239 pp., provides a punchy treatment of G.'s responses to contemporary political developments. R. focuses on correspondence and spontaneous observations from G. rather than e.g. *Dichtung und Wahrheit* where observations would necessarily be mediated by hindsight. R. notes in this context the rather surprising lack of political-theoretical publication on G.'s part given the times he lived in. Broadly, Goethe emerges as a defender of late absolutist aristocratic/reactionary principles rather than an embodiment of *Bürgerlichkeit*. Chapter 1 examines the tensions between his roles as *Staatsdichter* in Weimar and as *Künstlergenie*, a tension resolved in favour of the state; this is seen as all rather ironic given that his employment was essentially a young aristocrat's whim. R. spends much time on contradictions in G.'s attitudes — his statements on 'class loyalty' and his own change of rank, his social awareness and political conservatism, his awareness of social problems and his creation of rural idylls in literature, his criticism of aristocrats in general (and his employer in particular) and his loyalty to Weimar. From Chapter 2 onwards the canvas is broader, dealing with G.'s similarly ambivalent attitudes towards political change and revolution. Wolfgang Rothe, *Goethe, der Pazifist: Zwischen Kriegsfurcht und Friedenshoffnung* (Kleine Reihe V & R), Göttingen, Vandenhoeck & Ruprecht, 142 pp., clearly deals with similar material to the previous title by the same author. R. examines G.'s lifelong fascination with war despite its sinister presence as an historical fact in his life. He identifies numerous statements on negative aspects of war and an equal number of expressions of fascination with it. In a reported conversation with J.-Ch. Lobe about the profession of soldiery G. typically indicates that he is both attracted and repelled by the idea. The text covers three areas of source material: G.'s life (and so correspondence and conversation), his reading, and his writing. Barbara Naumann, *Philosophie und Poetik des Symbols: Cassirer und Goethe*, Munich, Wilhelm Fink, 218 pp., makes a link between C.'s philosophy of symbolic forms and G.'s symbolic praxis. The link is justified by the interest of both parties in Kantian philosophy and C.'s lifelong interest in G. (Chapter 2). From our perspective Chapter 3 is the most illuminating; it deals with the *Bildlichkeit* of G.'s late fiction, particularly *Wilhelm Meisters Wanderjahre* and G.'s *Symboltheorie*, in as far as it can be reconstructed. The subtitle to Angelika Jacobs, *Goethe und die Renaissance: Studien zum Connex von historischem Bewußtsein und ästhetischer Identitätskonstruktion* (TGLSK, 94, n.F. C/14), 1997, 439 pp., compactly identifies the subject-matter of this highly interesting text. J. offers a new perspective upon what she acknowledges as well-trodden territory, namely G.'s relationship with history. She examines how the historical, often in the form of individual historical figures, when processed aesthetically in the production of fictional and other texts, can become a means for the individual to locate himself in an unstable present — or at least to come to terms with his own instability. But it is not a matter of the Renaissance providing models for modern life: as Goethe's historical consciousness and sense of self develop we see in fact rather the opposite. J. offers very compactly formulated treatments of the Renaissance in itself, of Enlightenment Renaissance reception and of specifically Goethean Renaissance reception. The treatment of G. ranges widely, from drama (especially *Egmont* and *Tasso*) to biography (Winckelmann, Cardano) and autobiography.

    Goethe und die Verzeitlichung der Natur, ed. Peter Matussek, Munich, Beck, 571 pp., brings together 21 varied and interdisciplinary contributions on this subject, organized into three sections 'Historisierung' (pp. 15–232), 'Wirkungsgechichte' (pp. 233–344), and 'Aktualisierung' (pp. 345–476). The editor provides an introduction to the theme and to the individual contributions (pp. 7–14) entitled 'Transformation der Naturgeschichte: Thema und Kompositionsprinzip'. Other contributions include: H. B. Nisbet, 'Naturgeschichte und Humangeschichte bei Goethe, Herder und Kant' (15–43); D. Kuhn, 'Geschichte, begriffen als Beschreibung, als Biographie und als Historie: Goethes Konzepte' (44–57); D. von Engelhardt, 'Natur und Geist, Evolution und Geschichte: Goethe in seiner Beziehung zur romantischen Naturforschung und metaphysischen Naturphilosophie' (58–74); J. Barkhoff, 'Tag- und Nachtseiten des animalischen Magnetismus: Zur Polarität von Wissenschaft und Dichtung bei Goethe' (75–100); U. Pörksen, 'Raumzeit: Goethes Zeitbegriff aufgrund seiner sprachlichen Darstellung geologischer Ideen und ihrer Visualisierung' (101–27); F. Fehrenbach, '"Das lebendige Ganze, das zu allen unsern geistigen und sinnlichen Kräften spricht": Goethe und das Zeichnen' (128–56); T. Zabka, 'Ordnung, Willkür und die "wahre Vermittlerin": Goethes ästhetische Integration von Natur- und Gesellschaftsidee' (157–77); H. Böhme, 'Fetisch und Idol: Die Temporalität von Erinnerungsformen in Goethes *Wilhelm Meister, Faust* und *Der Sammler und die Seinigen* (178–202); P. Matussek, 'Formen der Verzeitlichung: Der Wandel des Faustschen Naturbildes und seine historischen Hintergründe' (202–32); K. R. Mandelkow, 'Natur und Geschichte bei Goethe im Spiegel seiner wissenschaftlichen und kulturtheoretischen Rezeption' (233–58); H. W. Ingensiep, 'Metamorphosen der Metamorphosenlehre: Zur Goethe-Rezeption in der Biologie von der Romantik bis in die Gegenwart' (259–75); R. Hoppe-Sailer, 'Genesis und Prozeß: Elemente der Goethe-Rezeption bei Carl Gustav Carus, Paul Klee und Joseph Beuys' (276–300); H. Danuser, 'Natur-Zeiten in transzendenter Landschaft: Gustav Mahlers Faust-Komposition der *Achten Symphonie*' (301–25); A. Abel, 'Natur als Klangphänomen: Zur Umsetzung von Goethes Methodik der Farbenlehre in der Dodekaphonie Weberns' (326–44); W. Schad, 'Zeitgestalten der Natur: Goethe und die Evolutionsbiologie' (345–82); F. Schweitzer, 'Naturwissenschaft und Selbsterkenntnis' (383–98); W. Krohn, 'Goethes Versuch über den Versuch' (399–413); H. Schmitz, 'Das Ganz-Andere: Goethe und das Ungeheure' (414–35); G. Böhme, 'Phänomenologie der Natur: Eine Perspektive' (436–61); K. M. Meyer-Abich, 'Der Atem der Natur: Goethes Kritik der industriellen Wirtschaft' (462–76).

Gerhard Schulz, *Exotik der Gefühle: Goethe und seine Deutschen*, Munich, Beck, 223 pp., is substantially a republication of essays on Goethe, united by the themes of travel in space or time (Faust) and the opposite notion of home or home culture. Includes: 'Goethe und seine Deutschen: Über die Schwierigkeiten, ein Klassiker zu sein' (7–31); 'Wann und wo entsteht ein klassischer Nationalautor? Zur *Italienischen Reise*' (32–47); '"Es wandelt niemand ungestraft unter Palmen": Über Goethe, Alexander von Humboldt und einen Satz aus den *Wahlverwandtschaften*' (48–74); '"Dichten selbst ist schon Verrat": Parameter des *West-östlichen Divan*' (75–104); 'Exotik der Gefühle: Goethes *Novelle*' (105–28); 'Gesellschaftsbild und Romanform: Zum Deutschen in Goethes *Wanderjahren*' (129–54); 'Faust und der Fortschritt: Anmerkungen zum *Faust*' (155–71); 'Goethe für den Hausgebrauch: Spruchdichtung als Nationalerziehung' (172–93). Luz-María Linder, *Goethes Bibelrezeption: Hermeneutische Reflexion, fiktionale Darstellung, historisch-kritische Bearbeitung* (EH, 1, 1691), 210 pp., details the dynamic process of Bible reception in Goethe, dynamic because of 'Die Signifikanz, die Goethe dem Leseakt als lebendigen Dialog beimißt'. Because reading is a live process it produces variation and so we are asked to see 'Goethes variierende Positionen als natürliches Oszillieren'. The range of analysis to which it is exposed, and the creative use to which the Bible is put are extraordinary; most interesting is the treatment of use of motifs and images and the rewriting or paraphrasing of biblical episodes. Broadly, L. identifies an increasing tendency to aestheticize the Bible in the process of reception, particularly as its theological impact is reduced. Its fascination remains because it can never be grasped as a whole and so the conversation suggested above need never come to an end.

Other themes covered in smaller contributions include: B. Kuhn, 'Natural history and the history of the self: botany, geology, and autobiography in the works of Goethe and Rousseau', *ColH*, 25, 1997:41–62, which investigates the use of the language of natural history as an antidote to outworn poetic language and makes a connection in G. between the search for the 'Urpflanze' and his notions of 'Selbstbildung'; J.-Ch. Bürgel, 'Hafiz, Zarathustra, Goethe: Intuition, influence, intertextualité', *ColH*, 26, 1997:51–70, which deals with the development and derivation of G.'s notion of 'Reinheit' from the named sources with particular reference to the *West-östlicher Divan*; W. Hogrebe, 'Ahnung und Erinnerung: Bemerkungen zur Funktion der Ahnung bei einigen Dichtern von Goethe bis Musil', Peil, *Erkennen*, 517–26; H. Müller-Dietz, 'Goethe und die Todesstrafe', *JDSG*, 42:120–45; H. Ammerlahn, 'Produktive und destruktive Einbildungskraft: Goethes Tasso, Harfner und Wilhelm Meister', *OL*, 53:83–104; R. Cardinal, 'The passionate traveller: Goethe in Italy', *PEGS(NS)*, 67, 1997 [1998]:17–32; G.-L. Fink, 'L'image du peuple chez Goethe', *RG*, 27, 1997:33–55; S. Bertho, 'Les Anciens et les Modernes: la question de l'ekphrasis chez Goethe et chez Proust', *RLC*, 72:53–62; U. Schödlbauer, 'Der "schreckliche Zug": Lesarten des Irrationalen bei Goethe', *ZDP*, 117:497–515.

INFLUENCE. RECEPTION.   Gregor Eisenhauer, *Antipoden*, Tübingen, Niemeyer, 109 pp., contains a section 'Ernst Jünger und Johann

Wolfgang von Goethe' (pp. 1–43). Here E. responds to the rather personal, moralizing tone of much criticism of Jünger and proceeds by dealing in parallel with aspects of J. and of the perhaps less problematic figure of Goethe. He covers briefly elements of their biographies, their writing and reading; in the most interesting final section he analyses their contrasting attitudes to death. Gerlinde Röder-Bolton, *George Eliot and Goethe: An Elective Affinity* (Studies in Comparative Literature, 13), Amsterdam–Atlanta, Rodopi, 290 pp., is substantially a study of Eliot, dealing in depth with her reception of German culture and of Goethe in particular. Whilst this interest in things German is shown to be typical of the period, E.'s interest is revealed as so profound that aspects of G.'s work emerge as a key to understanding hers. Awareness of *Die Wahlverwandtschaften* is shown as vital to an understanding of the moral scheme and narrative structure of the latter part of *The Mill on the Floss*. *Faust I* and *Wilhelm Meisters Lehrjahre* impact in turn upon the moral scheme and understanding of the idea of *Bildung* in *Daniel Deronda*. An amusing and irreverent modern look at Goethe, often using his words wilfully or even attributing new words to him, is provided by Stammtisch unser Huhn, *Goethe von hinten: Als Kunstblume und Mensch*, Tübingen, Klöpfer und Meyer, 142 pp. Daniel J. Farrelly, *Goethe in East Germany 1949–1989: Toward a History of Goethe Reception in the GDR*, Columbia, Camden House, x + 168 pp., is divided into two parts. The first (pp. 3–39) deals with the historical development of literary-critical method in the GDR, detailing the complex interactions between the most important intellectual/political circles. No single method emerges but rather a differentiated group of related methods. F. also investigates how and why G. became such a cornerstone of GDR criticism. The second part deals with the methods in action as applied to core Goethe texts with the aim of illustrating (as becomes clear in Chapter 12) that there was never (or only briefly) a monolithic brand of orthodox GDR criticism.

BIOGRAPHY. John R. Williams, *The Life of Goethe: A Critical Biography* (Blackwell Critical Biogaphies, 10), Oxford, Blackwell, xiv + 318 pp., provides a very accessible and readable biography as well as necessarily brief treatments of G.'s work (including his scientific work but not other areas of theory) which locate it primarily in terms of literary history and the author's biography. It is notable that 'pure' biography only accounts for 52 pages of the text and because life and work (with the German translated) are skilfully interwoven in the rest of the volume it invites less experienced G. readers towards further study. To this extent the text successfully fulfils its own declared aim, to provide an undaunting introduction to G. for students and lay readers. Similarly accessible, but perhaps less useful is the highly readable biography by Klaus Seehafer, *Mein Leben ein einzig Abenteuer: Johann Wolfgang Goethe*, Berlin, Aufbau, 496 pp. The text attempts to bring us nearer to Goethe 'the man' and breach the historical divide which leads to a dynamic narrative but a less useful academic tool. The text has an interesting structure. The biographical narrative is punctuated and re-energized by so-called *Reise-Intermezzi*. Fritz Ebner, *Goethe: Aus seinem Leben. Reden, Vorträge, Zeitbilder*, Darmstadt, Roether, 1997, 271 pp., brings together a number of E.'s papers on Goethean themes (largely from the 1980s) and a series of biographical sketches. The latter (pp. 7–79) provide snapshots of G.'s life with treatments of his work as supporting evidence. *Unwandelbar G.: Ein Lesebuch zu Goethes Leben*, ed. Peter Schünemann (Beck'sche Reihe, 1279), Munich, Beck, 352 pp., strings together all sorts of material (letters, diaries, literary excerpts etc) from G. and contemporaries to provide an entertaining but uncritical jog through Goethe's life and times. A. Dusini, ' "Leere und Todtenstille in und außer mir": Goethes Tagebuch zum 6. Juni 1816', *GRM*, 48:165–78, deals with his apparently shocking and undifferentiated treatment of his wife's death as one of many events on this day.

3. SCHILLER

EDITIONS. The extraordinary academic enterprise which is the publication of the *Nationalausgabe* of Schiller's works continues with the *Briefwechsel: Briefe an Schiller 1.3.1790–24.5.1794 (Anmerkungen)*, *Nationalausgabe* 34/2, ed. Ursula Naumann, Weimar, Böhlau, 1997, 707 pp. These notes are exhaustive and particularly strong in providing a sense of the literary and biographical context in which the letters were produced, even drawing in parallel (literary) evidence where it will illuminate a point.

LITERARY WORKS. Karla Reinhart, *Jene Lilien von Valois: Eine spanische Königin in der Geschichte des 16. Jahrhunderts, in Schillers 'Don Karlos' und in Verdis 'Don Carlos'*, Frankfurt, Lang, 376 pp., provides a relatively light and accessible treatment of the reception of this historical figure with a central chapter (pp. 39–168) devoted to Schiller's work. It covers S.'s sources, the process of adaptation and the textual history. Barthold Pelzer, *Tragische Nemesis und historischer Sinn in Schillers Wallenstein-Trilogie: Eine rekonstruierende Lektüre* (FLK, 60), 1997, 399 pp., is an attempt to come to terms with rather than explain away the complexity of the trilogy. The text is based upon detailed analysis of *Die Geschichte des Abfalls der vereinigten Niederlande* [. . .] and the *Geschichte des Dreißigjährigen Krieges*, as well as of the plays and of Schiller's aesthetics and moral philosophy. This is understood as a kind of 'rekonstruierende Hermeneutik'. It reveals that it is precisely the tension between his understanding of different layers of history, the requirements of dramatic form and his sense of what is right which generates the unresolved complexity of *Wallenstein*. Walter Hinderer, *Von der Idee des Menschen: Über Friedrich Schiller*, Würzburg, Königshausen & Neumann, 351 pp., consists largely of republication of material available elsewhere. Nonetheless it provides in this form a very useful and compact treatment of S.'s biography and theoretical and practical literary (dramatic) work. The sections on the genesis of his aesthetic theory (pp. 41–144) are particularly useful; the treatment of the dramas emphasizes the theoretical input. U. Martin, 'Im Zweifel für die Freiheit: Zu Schillers Lied *An die Freude*', *GRM*, 48:47–59, discusses the idea that the poem was originally addressed to freedom and that the subsequent change makes for a less successful poem. *JDSG*, 42, contains the following relevant articles: T. Nutz, 'Vergeltung oder Versöhnung? Strafvollzug und Ehre in Schillers *Verbrecher aus Infamie*' (146–64); A. Sergl, 'Das Problem des Chors im deutschen Klassizismus: Schillers Verständnis der *Iphigenie auf Tauris* und seine *Braut von Messina*' (165–94).

THEMES.   E. Baker, 'Fables of the Sublime: Kant, Schiller, Kleist', *MLN*, 113:524–36. F. J. Lamport, 'Schiller and the "European Community": "Universal History" in theory and practice', *MLR*, 93:428–40. K. F. Gille, ' "Ein angenehmer Traum eines guten Kopfs": Friedrich Nicolai und Schillers Briefe über die ästhetische Erziehung', *WB*, 44:190–206.

INFLUENCE, RECEPTION.   *Schiller-Handbuch*, ed. Helmut Koopmann, Stuttgart, Alfred Kröner, xviii + 966 pp., delivers rather more than the title might suggest. The text consists of a large range of essays by established scholars in the field (too numerous to mention), divided into five subject-areas: 1. 'Schiller in seiner Zeit'(1–90); 2. 'Schiller und die kulturelle Tradition' (91–215); 3. 'Ästhetik' (216–302); 4. 'Das Werk' (303–757); 5. 'Schiller und seine Wirkung' (758–932). Whilst it was clearly intended as a broad introduction it has emerged as much more than this and will become one of the primary routes to the study of Schiller. P. Bishop, 'Über die Rolle des Ästhetischen in der Tiefenpsychologie: Zur Schillerrezeption in der analytischen Psychologie C. G. Jungs', *JDSG*, 42:358–400.

4.   INDIVIDUAL AUTHORS
(EXCLUDING GOETHE AND SCHILLER)

BÖTTIGER.   Karl August Böttiger, *Literarische Zustände und Zeitgenossen: Begegnungen und Gespräche im klassischen Weimar*, ed. Klaus Gerlach and René Sternke, Berlin, Aufbau, 601 pp., provides a full, critical publication of these observations which provide an interesting perspective upon the Weimar scene and its central figures.

BÜRGER. *LitL*, 1, is a Bürger special number containing: M. Anders-Sailer, 'Das Thema Kindsmord und G. A. Bürgers Ballade *Des Pfarrers Tochter von Taubenhain*: Ein Angebot mit mehreren Diskursebenen' (1–13); H. Ritter, 'Gottfried August Bürgers Liebeslyrik: Literarisches Muster und lebendige Erfahrung' (14–28); H.-J. Kertscher, 'Vom "Nutzen der Silbenstecherei": Bürgers Arbeiten an seiner *Nachtfeier der Venus*' (29–49); W. Braungart, ' "Veredelte, lebendige, darstellende Volkspoesie": Bürgers Ballade *Die Entführung*, oder *Ritter Karl von Eichenhorst und Fräulein Gertrude von Hochburg*' (50–68).

CAMPE. The first volume (*Briefe von 1766–1788*) of *Briefe von und an Joachim Heinrich Campe*, ed. Hanno Schmidt (WoF, 71), 2 vols, 1996, 592 pp., has appeared. It offers a critical edition of letters which for the most part were previously unpublished, or published without commentary. The letters are preceded by a substantial introduction (pp. 23–72) to the man, his work, the literary context and the edition itself.

FORSTER. J. Schneider, 'Literatur und Wissenschaft bei Georg Forster', *EG*, 53:673–86. H. Pietsch, 'French and German masses in the Revolution: Images and concepts in Georg Forsters 1793 writing on Paris and Mainz', *HY*, 1996[1997]:19–36. J. Gomsu, 'Georg Forsters Wahrnehmung Neuer Welten', *ZGer*, n.F., 8:538–50.

HAMANN. J. E. Antonsen, 'Das Motto als Anzeiger von Intertextualität: Hamann und Horaz', *ColH*, 26, 1997:19–33, is an interesting study. The mottoes at the head of the *Aesthetica in nuce* (1762), one from the Bible, one from Horace, are taken, in the author's terms, as an exemplary site of intertextuality. B. Jacobs, 'Self-incurrence, incapacity, and guilt: Kant and Hammann on Enlightenment guardianship (with an annotated translation of Hammann's letter to C. J. Kraus)', *LY*, 28, 1996[1997]:147–62.

HERDER. *Herder und die Philosophie des deutschen Idealismus*, ed. Marion Heinz (Fichte-Studien-Supplementa, 8), Amsterdam–Atlanta, Rodopi, 345 pp., contains: H. D. Irmscher, 'Aspekte der Geschichtsphilosophie Johann Gottfried Herders' (5–47); K. Huizing, 'Morphologischer Idealismus: Herder als Gestalthermeneut' (48–64); G. L. Schiewer, 'Das Konzept einer Integration von "Körper" und "Geist" in Herders Metakritik' (65–88); M. Heinz, 'Herders Metakritik' (89–106); J. H. Zammito, 'Herder, Kant, Spinoza und die Ursprünge des deutschen Idealismus' (107–44); P. H. Reill, ' "Doch die Metaphysik bleibe beiseite, wir wollen Analogien betrachten": Das Verhältnis zwischen Herders und Humboldts Formulierung einer Wissenschaft der Menschheit' (145–65);

K. Hammacher, 'Herders Stellung im Spinozastreit' (166–88); G. Arnold, 'Herder und die Philosophen des deutschen Idealismus nach den biographischen Quellen' (189–202); M. Bondeli, 'Von Herder zu Kant, zwischen Kant und Herder, mit Herder gegen Kant — Karl Leonard Reinhold' (203–34); W. Düsing, 'Der Nemesisbegriff bei Herder und Schiller' (235–55); P. Rohs, 'Fichte und Herder' (256–68); S. Lampenscherf, 'Excentrische Bahnen: Hölderlin — Herder' (269–95); S. Dietzsch, 'Differenzierungen im Begriff des Geschichtlichen: Herder und Schelling' (296–309); R. Hofmann, 'Das Theodizeeproblem bei Herder und Schelling' (310–27); K. M. Meyer-Abich, 'Herders Naturphilosophie in der Naturkrise der Industriegesellschaft' (328–41). R. Hartmann, 'Denkmale der Vorzeit: Zur Herder-Rezeption im Schaffen von Ludwig Theobul Kosegarten', *Euphorion*, 92:273–92 provides an example of regional reception of Herder in Swedish Pomerania. *HY*, 3, 1996 [1997] contains the following articles with a bearing on H.: A. Bohm, 'Mixing Church and State: Herder's sermons on the birth of Carl Friedrich' (1–17); C. Moser, 'Der "Traum der schreibenden Person von ihr selbst": Autobiographie und Subjektkonzeption bei Johann Gottfried Herder' (37–56); H. Clairmont, ' " [. . .] un tableau vivant": Herders physiologisch fundierte Psychologie, Lavaters Physiognomik und ein Disput in der Berliner Akademie der Wissenschaften' (57–80); A. Corkhill, 'Herder and the misuse of language' (81–92); R. S. Leventhal, 'The critique of the concept: Lessing, Herder, and the semiology of historical semantics' (93–110). *HY*, 4 contains: J. H. Zammito, ' "Method" versus "manner"'? Kant's critique of Herder's *Ideen* in the light of the epoch of science, 1790–1820' (1–26); R. Simon, 'Apokalyptische Hermeneutik: Johann Gottfried Herder: *Maran Atha*, Geschichtsphilosophie, *Adrastea*' (27–52); V. Spencer, 'Beyond either/or: The pluralist alternative in Herder's thought' (53–70); J. Johanssen, 'Vom Zeitigen in der Geschichte: Revolution, Zeiterfahrung und historische Sinnbildung beim späten Herder' (71–96); H. P. Herrmann, ' "Mutter Vaterland": Herders Historisierung des Germanenmythos und die Widersprüchlichkeit des Vaterlandsdiskurses im 18. Jahrhundert' (97–122); S. B. Knoll, 'Europe in the history of humanity: Herder, Kurt Breysig, and the discourse on eurocentrism in the study of world history' (123–42); U. Zeuch, '*Sentio, Ergo Sum*: Herder's concept of "feeling" versus Kant's concept of "consciousness" ' (143–56); K. Menges, ' "Sinn" und "Besonnenheit": The meaning of "meaning" in Herder' (157–76). Articles appearing individually include: H. Adler, 'Monumentalfragment und Totalität: Johann Gottfried Herders Stellung zum diskursiven Konstrukt der Geschichtsphilosophie', *MDU*,

90:5–16; A. Sow, 'Johann Gottfried Herders Volks- und Nationsver-
ständnis im Lichte der afrikanischen Entwicklungskonstellationen',
ZGer, n.F., 8:551–66.

HÖLTY. Ludwig Christoph Heinrich Hölty, *Gesammelte Werke und
Briefe: Kritische Studienausgabe*, ed. Walter Hettche, Göttingen,
Wallstein, 598 pp., is exactly what its subtitle suggests. Most important
is the editorial treatment of the poetry which where possible goes
back to the original manuscripts whilst still taking account of later
published editions. The commentary provided deals with textual
history and difficulties but does not offer interpretations. The volume
also covers his prose translations and adaptations from other
literatures, his letters and various relevant documents (biographical
sketches/tributes).

JACOBI. The publication of J.'s correspondence in an outstanding
complete critical edition continues with the publication of Friedrich
Heinrich Jacobi, *Briefwechsel 1775–1781 (Nr. 381–750): Kommentar*, II/
2, ed. Michael Brüggen et al., Stuttgart, Frommann-Holzboog,
xxv + 444 pp. As one would expect it offers full treatment of
manuscript transmission, extensive commentary and four useful
indices.

KLOPSTOCK. M. Nenon, 'Women as objects of imagination for
Klopstock and Wieland', *LY*, 28, 1996 [1997]:199–212.

KNIGGE. *Wirkungen und Wertungen: Adolph Freiherr Knigge im Urteil der
Nachwelt (1796–1994) — Eine Dokumentensammlung*, ed. Michael Schlott
(Das Knigge-Archiv: Schriftenreihe zur Knigge-Forschung, 1), Göttingen, Wallstein, lxxxviii + 582 pp., will prove an extremely valuable
resource for scholars in the field. The massive selection of material
shows in great detail the variations in Knigge reception and enables
synchronic and diachronic comparisons to be made. The selection is
restricted to materials concerned with Knigge's place in literary
history which maintains a high degree of focus in an already very
substantial body of text. The introduction covers editorial principles
but also provides us with important orientation in the complex matter
of Knigge reception.

LA ROCHE. P. Arnds, 'Sophie von La Roche's *Geschichte des
Fräuleins von Sternheim* as an answer to Samuel Richardson's *Clarissa*',
LY, 29, 1997[1998]:87–106. C. Swanson, 'Textual transgression in
the epistolary mode: Sophie von La Roche's *Geschichte des Fräuleins von
Sternheim*', *MGS*, 22, 1996[1997]:144–61.

LAVATER. J. P. Heins, ' "Es ist ja kein Geschriebnes": The parody
of Lavater's physiognomics in Musäus's *Physiognomische Reisen*', *LY*, 29,
1997[1998]:107–30.

LENZ. *Lenz-Jahrbuch*, 7, 1997, contains the following articles
specifically concerned with L.: E. Faul and C. Weiss, 'Ferdinand von

Ecksteins Aufsatz *Œuvres dramatiques de Lenz* in der Zeitschrift *Le Catholique* (1828): Ein unbekanntes Zeugnis zur Lenz-Rezeption im 19. Jahrhundert' (51–88); W. H. Preuss, 'Aus den Memoiren des "Verwundeten Bräutigams": Reinhold Johann von Igelström (1740–1799)' (89–100). Other articles include: R. Krebs, 'Lenz' Beitrag zur Werther-Debatte: die *Briefe über die Moralität der Leiden des jungen Werthers*', *Aufklärung*, 10.1:67–80; H. Madland, 'J. M. R. Lenz: Poetry as communication', *LY*, 29, 1997[1998]:151–74; M. Kagel, 'Bewaffnete Augen: Anschauende Erkenntnis und militärischer Standpunkt in J.M.R. Lenz' *Anmerkungen über das Theater*', *ColGer*, 31:1–19, which emphasizes L.'s exposure to military thinking in its broadest sense but also, on a more profound psychological level shows how his mindset/perception may have been shaped by it; U. Profitlich, 'Zur Deutung von J. M. R. Lenz' Komödientheorie', *DVLG*, 72:411–32, which investigates the relative importance of plot and character in Lenz, as well as his views on the contemporary theatre-going public.

LESSING. Gotthold Ephraim Lessing, *Tagebuch der italienischen Reise*, ed. Wolfgang Milde (Wolfenbüttler Schriften zur Geschichte des Buchwesens, 28), Wiesbaden, Harrassowitz, 1997, 143 pp., is a handsome fascimile edition of the manuscript held in the Berliner Staatsbibliothek with parallel printed version of the text (without commentary). It also features four handsome plates (in body of text) and a brief *Nachwort* by the editor. The Goethe CD-ROMs discussed above are joined in the Rowohlt series by Gotthold Ephraim Lessing, *Werke*, ed. Mathias Bertram et al., Reinbek, Rowohlt, which includes a massive selection from L.'s creative and critical writing, as well as a *Hörtext* version of the *Fabeln* (read by Achim Hübner), and the previously published *rororo Monographie* on Lessing by Wolfgang Drews. As with the Goethe disk, the substantial advantage of the edition is in the programming, in particular in the powerful search functions available. *LY*, 28, 1996[1997] contains the following articles with a direct bearing on L.: K. S. Guthke, 'Lessing und die Exoten: Aspekte einer Berührungsangst und –lust' (1–34); E. Schaefer, ' "Charles Guichard nommé Quinctus Icilius" — ein commensalis Friedrichs II. Von Preußen' (35–50); W. Mauser, 'Kein Fackelzug für Lessing' (51–52); M. Bell, 'Psychological conceptions in Lessing's dramas' (53–82); L. C. Roetzel, 'Aesthetic experience as imaginary experience: Masculinity and the regulation of sentiments in *Emilia Galotti*' (83–104); W. Goetschel, 'Negotiating truth: on Nathan's business' (105–24); E. M. Knodt, 'Herder and Lessing on truth: toward an ethic of incommunicability' (125–46). *LY*, 29, 1997 [1998], contains the following articles on L.: S. Gustafson, 'Abject fathers and suicidal sons: G. E. Lessing's *Philotas* and Kristeva's *Black Sun*' (1–30);

S. Matuschek, 'Undogmatische Anschauung: Diderots Tempel- und Lessings Palast-Parabel' (31–40); J. Daiber, ' "Der Dichtern nöthge Geist, der Möglichkeiten dichtet": Lessing und das naturwissenschaftliche Experiment' (41–56); B. Allert, 'About a burning building in Eco and Lessing, or: How to process messages' (57–86). *Neues zur Lessing-Forschung: Ingrid Strohschneider-Kohrs zu Ehren am 26. August 1997*, ed. Eva J. Engel and Claus Ritterhoff, Tübingen, Niemeyer, viii + 184 pp., contains: D. Döring, 'Die Fürstenschule in Meißen zur Zeit des jungen Lessing' (1–30); S.-A. Jørgensen, 'Versuch über die *Jungen Gelehrten* um 1750' (31–42); E. J. Engel, 'Ad se ipsum? — "Werde ich denn niemals des Vorwurfs los werden können, den sie mir wegen M. machten?" ' (43–58); E. Bonfatti, 'Vom Fechter zum Spartacus: Überlegungen zu Lessings *Spartacus*-Fragment' (59–68); A. Schmitt, ' "Die Wahrheit rühret unter mehr als einer Gestalt": Versuch einer Deutung der Ringparabel in Lessings *Nathan der Weise* — "more rabbinico" ' (69–104); D. M. Nielaba, ' "Die arme Recha, die indes verbrannte": Zur Kombustibilität der Bedeutung in Lessings *Nathan der Weise*' (105–26); J. von Lüpke, 'Der fromme Ketzer: Lessings Idee eines Trauerspiels *Der fromme Samariter nach der Erfindung des Herrn Jesu Christi*' (127–52); G. Gawlick, ' "Von Duldung der Deisten": Zu einem Thema der Lessing-Zeit' (153–68); W. G. Jacobs, ' "Der garstige breite Graben": Lessing, Kant und Schelling zum Verhältnis von Vernunft und Tatsachen' (169–80). Other articles of interest include: M. Rohwasser, 'Lessing, Gleim und der nationale Diskurs', *Lenz-Jahrbuch*, 7, 1997:137–62; G. H. Wolf, 'Lessing's *Philotas*: A problematization of selfsacrifice within the context of duty and honor', *MGS*, 22, 1996[1997]:1–21; K. Niklaus, 'Die "poetische Moral" in Lessings bürgerlichen Trauerspielen und der zeitgenössischen Trivialdramatik: Ein Strukturvergleich', *ZDP*, 117:481–96.

LICHTENBERG. *'Ihre Hand, Ihren Mund, nächstens mehr': Lichtenbergs Briefe 1765–1799*, ed. Ulrich Joost (Bibliothek des 18. Jahrhunderts), Munich, Beck, 476 pp., although a substantial volume, consists only of a selection of the thousands of Lichtenberg letters preserved. It is a very useful critical selection with appropriate indices and a short critical essay by the editor. Lichtenberg offers a valuable perspective upon the literary, social and political environment of the period and the letters serve as a reminder of the central position of correspondence in the literary life of the age. Hans-Georg von Arburg, *Kunst-Wissenschaft um 1800: Studien zu Georg Christoph Lichtenbergs Hogarth-Kommentaren* (Lichtenberg-Studien, 11), Göttingen, Wallstein, 434 pp. + 29 pls, also serves to locate Lichtenberg at the heart of contemporary debate. The dedicated analysis of L.'s treatment of Hogarth is highly illuminating. However, the text's main purpose is to locate L. in the context of contemporary aesthetic theory. And it is aesthetic theory broadly understood since the text ranges over related aspects of natural science and physiognomy and relates aesthetic debates to the whole question of Enlightenment hermeneutics and modern understanding of aesthetic reception. Frank Schäfer, *Lichtenberg und das Judentum* (Lichtenberg-Studien, x), Göttingen, Wallstein, 175 pp., also explores L.'s relationship to Enlightenment thought. S. is, however, concerned with the more limited but equally complex issue of his attitude towards Jews and Jewish emancipation. L. emerges as 'einigermaßen typischer Repräsentant aufgeklärter Judenfeindschaft' — like many others he e.g. mocks Jewish religious codes whilst maintaining an enlightened understanding of the need for religious tolerance. The text offers particularly powerful treatment of his hardening views on Jewish emancipation. It covers his responses to Jewish questions in general and to specific Jews (e.g. Mendelssohn) and investigates the genesis of those responses.

MENDELSSOHN. The *Jubiläumsausgabe* of Mendelssohn's *Gessammelte Schriften* continues with vol. 23, *Dokumente*. II. Die frühen Mendelssohn-Biographien, ed. Michael Albrecht, Stuttgart, Frommann-Holzboog, xxvi + 444 pp. A substantial biography by I. A. Euchel (pp. 102–63) is provided in a translation (with *Nachschrift*) by Reuven Michael. The collection of biographical material is exhaustive (44 sources in all). In each case detail of the source/author is provided and in all cases where some original material is presented we are offered the text itself. The editorial procedure does not involve correcting errors of fact or interpretation made by any of the biographers, the motive being to preserve the process of M. reception in its original form. A summary of the findings is found in the introduction (pp. i-xxvi). This will clearly be an extremely valuable resource for scholars in the field and it maintains the high level of scholarship and the high production values of earlier volumes.

MORITZ. J.-M. Paul, 'Karl Philipp Moritz: Die unmögliche Aufklärung', *Aufklärung* 10.1 : 81–98. E. M. Batley, 'Masonic thought in the work of Karl Philipp Moritz: Sheen or substance?', *London Ger. St. VI*, 121–46.

MÜLLER. U. Leuschner, 'Aus Maler Müllers Werkstatt: *Auszüge* — Ein unbekanntes Fragment zu seinen Faust-Dichtungen', *Lenz-Jahrbuch*, 7, 1997 : 101–20.

REIMARUS. *Hermann Samuel Reimarus 1694–1786: Beiträge zur Reimarus-Renaissance in der Gegenwart*, ed. Wolfgang Walter (Veröffentlichung der Joachim Jungius-Gesellschaft der Wissenschaften, 85), Göttingen, Vandenhoeck & Ruprecht, 52 pp., includes: F. Kopitzsch, 'Heinrich Samuel Reimarus als Gelehrter und Aufklärer in Hamburg' (14–22); W. Schmidt-Biggemann, 'Erbauliche versus rationale

Hermeneutik: Heinrich Samuel Reimarus' Bearbeitung von Johann Adolf Hoffmanns *Neue Erklärung des Buchs Hiob'* (23–52).

STEIN. The series *Frühe Frauenliteratur in Deutschland* continues with Charlotte von Stein, *Dramen (Gesamtausgabe)*, ed. Susanne Kord, Hildesheim, Olms, xxxiv + original mixed pagination from 18th-c. editions reproduced. K. introduces all four plays, making explicit the link to Goethe but at the same time making clear the fact that S. introduced a wider range of female characters than many male contemporaries; not all were 'schöne Seelen'. The texts themselves are photographically reproduced versions from the 18th c. without modern commentary.

VULPIUS. Roberto Simanowski, *Die Verwaltung des Abenteuers: Massenkultur um 1800 am Beispiel Christian August Vulpius* (Palaestra, 302), Göttingen, Vandenhoeck & Ruprecht, 403 pp., is another text which marks the increasing tendency to look at marginal literary forms/writers. This text provides penetrating analyses of individual texts by V. and also (pp. 19–79) offers substantial theoretical justification of engagement with trivial literature. It also offers specific methodological guidelines for the treatment of such texts in the context of the Enlightenment (pp. 80–171). S. examines the limitations of *Aufklärung* in the specific social context and reveals a corresponding lack of literary ambition. The analysis of the texts shows them to be, in a social sense, experimental works, testing the possibility and sustainability of asocial behaviour. The fundamentally conservative texts suggest that asocial behaviour has to be normalized — but at least *Abenteuer* is experienced for a short while.

WEIDMANN. Paul Weidmann, *Der Eroberer: Eine Parodie der Macht*, ed. Leslie Bodi and Friedrich Voit (RS, Germ. Abt., 6), 1997, pp. 1–95 (introd. and comm.) surround separately paginated text (pp. 1–192). The text is a facsimile of the 1786 Vienna/Leipzig edition. The commentary is substantial but the editors admit to the impossibility of covering the high degree of parodistic reference to contemporary events etc. which is a feature of the text. Interestingly they do offer a glossary of literary terminology employed by W. to aid understanding of this little-known text.

WIELAND. Jan Cölln, *Philologie und Roman: Zu Wielands erzählerischer Rekonstruktion griechischer Antike im 'Aristipp'* (Palaestra, 303), Göttingen, Vandenhoeck & Ruprecht, 344 pp., deals with the process of dismantling the ideal of Greek antiquity. The epistolary structure of the novel means an inevitable range of perspective and so relativization of the subject matter. Detailed analysis further reveals how the text covers political and philosophical debates specific to the period of the novel's production and how philological scholarship can inform literary production. The end-product of the three tendencies within the novel is systematic demystification of Greek antiquity. Michael Hofmann, *Reine Seelen und komische Ritter: Aspekte literarischer Aufklärung in Christoph Martin Wielands Versepik*, Stuttgart, Metzler, 373 pp., provides compelling analysis of the tendency towards 'komisch-kritische Selbstreflexion aufklärerischer Subjektivität' in W.'s verse epics after 1760. The use of intertextuality, parody, and comedy as deconstructive tools indicate the (post-) modernity of this enterprise, particularly when compared with W.'s own more naïve earlier work. M. Hofmann, 'Ironische Arbeit am Mythos und kritische Selbstreflexion der Aufklärung: Christoph Martin Wielands *Comische Erzählungen* (1765)', *JDSG*, 42:23–41.

WINCKELMANN. W. Lange, 'Watteau und Winckelmann oder Klassizismus als antik drapiertes Rokoko', *DVLG*, 72:376–410. T. P. Bonfiglio, 'Winckelmann and the aesthetics of Eros', *GR*, 73:132–44.

THE ROMANTIC ERA

By LAURA MARTIN, *Lecturer in German, University of Glasgow*

1. GENERAL STUDIES

This year's publications have concentrated on early Romanticism and there has been a great deal of attention paid to distinguishing the *Frühromantik* either from Classicism or from later Romanticism, or conversely to seeing the movement as part of a continuous process. Both general studies and works on particular authors disagree about the optimism or pessimism of the writers. In Vietta, *Moderne*, we have a truly general study, which explodes any temporal or geographical boundaries. Yet European Modernity, in terms of aesthetics, despite its own origins in antiquity and its more immediate impetus from the Enlightenment, has its beginnings in the German *Frühromantik*, say S. Vietta and D. Kemper, 'Einleitung' (1–55). An historical view is given in W. Demel, 'Der Prozess der Modernisierung der Gesellschaft: Französische Revolution, Industrialisierung und sozialer Wandel' (71–95). He shows that while there are much earlier expressions of a consciousness that one's own age is 'modern', it is only with Schiller's *Über die naive und sentimentalische Dichtung* that the 'modern' is defined as essentially and irrevocably different from the 'ancient'. E. Behler, 'Von der romantischen Kunstkritik zur modernen Hermeneutik' (127–50), also finds the beginnings of modern aesthetics in Romantic theory, this time in F. Schlegel's concept of open-ended, processual art, the *progressive Universalpoesie*. Having lost its roots in myth and religion, this new aesthetic bases itself on theory. For I. Oesterle, 'Innovation und Selbstüberbietung: Temporalität der ästhetischen Moderne' (151–78), consciousness of time is what makes the difference between ancient and modern. Progressive thinking and nostalgia are opposite sides of the same coin; various aspects of the pre-modern (as well as the extra-European) become elements to 'quote' in modern fashions which are discarded as quickly as they are picked up. Novalis was the real futurist, according to J. H. Petersen, 'Grundzüge einer Ästhetik des Inkohärenten in Romantik und Moderne' (179–95), for he described an aesthetics that was very much in advance of its time, including a literary aesthetics that left the meaning for the reader to complete and a visual art aesthetics which defied representation. These plans for an experimental writing and art could only be realized much later in French Symbolist poetry and in 20th-c. abstract painting. C. Zelle, 'Ästhetik des Häßlichen: Friedrich Schlegels Theorie und die Schock- und Ekelstrategien der ästhetischen Moderne' (197–233), gives a brief history of the ugly in art, including comments on Schlegel (and many others) and focusing on 20th-c. expressions of the ugly and disgusting. Ugliness or dissonance in music is the topic of W. Keil, ' "O wundervoller Kapellmeister, der solcher Dissonanzen mächtig!" — Romantische Musikästhetik und die Frankfurter Schule. Von E. T. A. Hoffmanns *Kreisler* zu Th. W. Adornos *Dissonanzen*' (235–58). E. T. A. H. , like Adorno, reacted to the man-made catastrophes around him (namely, the Napoleonic Wars) in an increased artistic production conceived as a kind of resistance to the inhumanity he witnessed. Unlike depictions of insanity before the Romantic Era which held on to the possibility of reason (*Vernunft*) that could be returned to, S. Sanna, 'Im gesprungenen Spiegel des Wahnsinns: Die Moderne und ihre Bewußtseinskrise' (287–319), finds in Tieck, Bonaventura, and E. T. A. Hoffmann the depiction of the bottomless abyss of modern subjectivity. A. von Arnim, on the other hand, depicts a subjectivity that renews itself, and Novalis suggests the possibility of travelling through the insanity 'in full consciousness' in order to create new modalities of language. Again, Novalis is seen to anticipate much more recent writing (here, Surrealism) as suggested by Petersen (see p. 673 above). N. Saul, 'Experimentelle Selbsterfahrung und Selbsde-struktion: Anatomie des Ichs in der literarischen Moderne' (321–42), investigates the creation of a self through the act of writing, which is paradoxically enabled precisely by the disillusionment and threats to the integrity of the self. Examples are taken from a series of authors, including Novalis and E. T. A. Hoffmann. Creation of feminine rather than masculine selfhood is the subject of G. Horn, ' "Vorgänger ihr, Blut im Schuh" — Autonomie der Lebensentwürfe schreibender Frauen. Anmerkungen zur Romantikrezeption in der DDR-Literatur' (343–60). The particular difficulties facing women is traced for the Romantic Era through to the 20th c.; Christa Wolf's rehabilitation of Romantic women writers is seen in a context of a *DDR-Germanistik* more interested in emancipatory thoughts than doubts about the possibility of constructing a self. P. Seibert, 'Ästhetischer Geselligkeitsraum: Romantischer Salon, Literaten-café, Cyber-Kommunikation' (361–80), discusses the supposedly *freie Gesel-ligkeit* of the salons and its more recent manifestations. According to U. Barth, 'Schleiermachers *Reden* als religionstheoretisches Modernis-ierungsprogramm' (441–74), S. saved Christian religion by removing the focus from church and doctrine and placing it instead on the (modern) subject. Yet L. Zagari, 'Säkularisation und Privatreligion: Novalis — Heine — Benn — Brecht', shows how the experience of the divine becomes problematic already in early Romanticism, as soon as the Romantic, secularized re-mythologizing of the world begins. He traces this impossibility through three other authors, surprisingly including Brecht. J.-M. Paul, 'Von der romantischen Desillusion zur Dekonstruktion' (509–30), traces the origins of Deconstruction all the way back to the Middle Ages, but finds the passage from the late Enlightenment to early Romanticism (here exemplified in K. P. Moritz) a defining moment because of the radical criticism of ideology which occurs then. Thomas Bernhard is the final stage in a centuries-old development. Lastly, S. Vietta, 'Die Moderne-kritik der ästhetischen Moderne' (531–49), follows metaphors of coldness through Modernity, and of Modernity's critical attitude as a cold spot in history. In Modernity, utopia still seems possible, and yet a drastic disillusionment has already set in. Several studies demand a re-assessment of the field and of the term 'Romantic'. Peer, *Romanticisms*, comprises three sections: on power, on gender and on subjectivity, and it covers British, French, German, Russian, and American Romanticism. In their introduction to the volume, 'A lens for comparative Romanticisms' (1–8), Larry H. Peer and Diane Long Hoeveler call for a comparative Romanticism in the style of René Wellek, which should avoid the pitfalls both of absolutism and of relativism. Otto F. Best, *Die blaue Blume im englischen Garten*, Frankfurt, Fischer, 262 pp., is a continuation of Best's 1994 book *Volk ohne Witz*. The author argues that it is necessary to consider the *Frühromantik* as a completely different movement than the *Hochromantik* and *Spätromantik* successors, and in fact that the *Frühromantiker* did not break with the Enlightenment tradition, but rather carried it further, in that they tried to unite German *Genie* with French *esprit* or *Witz*. The book is written in a style that approaches a stream-of-consciousness technique, which can make it difficult to follow. It concentrates on the Jena Romantics, especially Novalis and Friedrich Schlegel, and there is a long section on *Heinrich von Ofterdingen*. Every Romanticist will want a copy of Theodor Ziolkowski, *Das Wunderjahre in Jena*, Stuttgart, Klett-Cotta, 354 pp., a synchronistic study of the *annus mirabilis*, 1794–95, in Jena. Defying categories we would now use to describe the era, such as *Klassik* and *Romantik*, Ziolkowski endeavours to depict a slice of literary, artistic, and academic life in order to show how the spatial and temporal conjunction of so many brilliant minds and historical occurrences allowed the especially fertile year to come about. The book is written with a wit and ease that make it a very pleasant read, yet it has ample material to interest the scholar. Somewhat disappointing is Gerhart Söhn, *Frauen der Aufklärung und Romantik. Von der Karschin bis zur Droste*, Düsseldorf, Grupello, 334 pp. The article on Luise Gottsched, for example, has as much on her husband as on the ostensible subject of the chapter. The one on Christiane Vulpius is longer than many on women who certainly had more impact on the two eras mentioned in the title, and a look at the chapter reveals that the length is due to the space spent justifying concubinage. The Charlotte von Stein chapter is in essence a paean to Goethe's love of women. One chapter is named in the table of contents simply 'Caroline', and it is only by opening to the chapter itself that the reader can discover that it is, indeed, about C. Schlegel-Schelling, not Günderode, Herder, etc. Disappointing, if less so, for the opposite reason is Carol Diethe, *Towards German Women Writers of the Nineteenth Century*, NY–Oxford, Berghahn, x + 214 pp., which does provide biographies of 20 19th-c. women, some of which it would be difficult to find elsewhere. The rather random selection of women from the Romantic Era includes Henriette Herz, Rahel Varnhagen, Caroline de la Motte Fouqué, and Bettina von Arnim. There is also a brief introduction to the historical background, unfortunately so brief as to be of little use. Furthermore, Diethe deteriorates at times into platitudes about the victimization of women. Nevertheless, the book could serve as handy background reference for undergraduates. Carl Schmitt, *Politische Romantik*, Berlin, Dunker & Humblot, 174 pp., originally published in 1919, receives a welcome new edition. S. still has many things to say to the modern Romanticist concerning the interpretation of the late 18th c. and early 19th c. Thoroughly grounding his interpretation in the contingencies of time and place, S. eschews both the tendency to generalize the concept of Romanticism to include all related phenomena throughout history, and the tendency to reduce the phenomenon to psychoanalytical or materialist explanations. Also noted: Charles Rosen, *Romantic Poets, Critics and Other Madmen*, Cambridge, Mass., Harvard U.P., xi + 257 pp.

THEMES. Mary R. Strand, *I/You. Paradoxical Constructions of Self and Other in Early German Romanticism* (SMGL, 87), viii + 130 pp., focuses on Novalis and Friedrich Schlegel, early Romantics who broke with the Enlightenment tradition of seeing the sameness of all human beings and instead posited differences between the sexes as well as between European and Oriental cultures. Dorothea Veit-Schlegel criticizes their idealization of the feminine Other, but paradoxically also reconfirms their notions. Lacan and Irigaray are invoked, not to interpret the Romantics retrospectively, but rather in order to show that modern post-structuralist, psychoanalytical, and feminist theories are grounded in the Romantic era, while the very real differences between them are acknowledged. A volume of conference proceedings on Romantic dreams includes M. Engel, 'The dream theory of Romantic anthropology', Dickson, *Dreams*, 1–15, which provides a clear and succinct account of scientific thought on sleep and dreaming during the Enlightenment and Romantic Eras. He concludes that it is the literary dream which becomes the best representative of Romantic thought, for it is here that conscious and unconscious elements meet in an artistic production, and that the connection of the individual will to the universal *Weltseele* is made manifest. There is a useful bibliography of Romantic writings on the dream, from Schubert (1808) to Schopenhauer (1851). Other references to this volume will be found under the individual authors' names. T. Wirtz, ' "Vom Geiste der Spekulation": Hermeneutik und ökonomischer Kredit in Weimar', *Athenäum*: 9–32, uses Adam Müller's economics, G. M. Meier's hermeneutics, the poetic practice of Goethe and Jean Paul, and the letters of Charlotte von Kalb in order to discuss the division of 'labour' on the literary market into the gendered roles of female reader and male writer. A. Kilcher, 'Aesthetik des Magnets. Zu einem physikalischem Modell der Kunst in der Frühromantik', *DVLG*, 72:463–511, discusses not animal magnetism, which became a popular topic in later Romanticism, but rather (physical) magnetism *per se*, which in Early Romanticism could be used symbolically in discourses on natural philosophy and philosophy of art without the anxiety of the loss of self that Mesmerism entailed for later generations. Jörg Paulus, *Der Enthusiast und sein Schatten. Literarische Schwärmer- und Philisterkritik um 1800*, Berlin–NY, de Gruyter, x + 382 pp., traces the development of the relationship of the physical and moral worlds as expressed in various forms of writing around 1800. He wishes to draw a sharp distinction between the Romantics and their precursors in the irrationalism of the 18th c. There are long chapters on Jean Paul, Tieck, and Novalis. Despite its very promising-sounding title, Christoph E. Schweitzer's *Men Viewing Women as Art Objects* (SGLLC), xiv + 103 pp., limits itself to describing male characters' use of paintings or silhouettes of women to inspire them. The selection of texts is seemingly random and the analysis is simplistic in the extreme, because Schweitzer avoids any contact with feminist, psychoanalytical, materialist, sociological, or any other type of critical discourse with which he might have given some weight to his argument. For a published master's thesis, Johanna J. S. Aulich, *Orphische Weltanschauung der Antike und ihr Erbe bei den Dichtern Nietzsche, Hölderlin, Novalis und Rilke* (GSC, 10), 204 pp., exhibits a truly impressive breadth. Aulich traces the beginnings of Orphism in antiquity through its renewal in the Renaissance (with the beginnings of opera) to the present, with longer studies on the four authors. Unfortunately, the book reads very much like a thesis, written to prove acquisition of knowledge rather than to further the field for fellow scholars. The style is so simple in places as to be naive; the chapters themselves are little more than lists of citations and the work is sprinkled with unnecessary exhortations to the reader to change the world by means of a greater attention to art. Also noted: M Wenzel, 'Reizbarkeit — Bildungstrieb — Seelenorgan. Aspekte der Medizingeschichte der

Goethezeit, *Hölderlin-Jb.*: 83–101. K. Braun, 'Nerventheorie um 1800, *ib.*, 119–24. Peter Lentwojt, **Die Lorley in ihrer Landschaft: romantische Dichtungsallegorie und Klischee: ein literarisches Sujet bei Brentano, Eichendorff, Heine und anderen* (EH, 1, 1664), 503 pp.

GENRES. A welcome contribution to the study of women's writing is Margaret Mary Daley, *Women of Letters. A Study of Self and Genre in the Personal Writing of Caroline Schlegel-Schelling, Rahel Varnhagen, and Bettina von Arnim*, Columbia, Camden House, xii + 135 pp. D. argues for continued and deepened study of women's published correspondence, not as history, sociology or biography of important men's lives, but rather as art. Letter writing is not a cop-out by women writers, nor is it a consolation prize granted them to compensate for their exclusion from other genres; rather it is uniquely suited to the needs of women who were trying to create an artistic, fictional self. The three writers studied had different levels of commitment to publication, and differing levels of attainment of a literary self; yet all three produced work that should be taken seriously as art and Daley would like to motivate scholars to come to terms with the problematic relationship of gender and genre. There have been several studies of Märchen and related genres. *Erzählungen der deutschen Romantik*, ed. and comm. Albert Meier, Walter Schmitz, Sibylle von Steinsdorff, and Ernst Weber, DTV, 463 pp., is a handy collection of 11 stories and Märchen which would be eminently suitable for undergraduate teaching. For each author there is a chronological table, information about the particular work and an interpretation of it, plus references for further reading. Gabriela Brunner Ungericht, *Die Mensch-Tier-Verwandlung. Eine Motivgeschichte unter besonderer Berücksichtigung des deutschen Märchens in der ersten Hälfte des 19. Jahrhunderts* (EH, 1, 1676), 337 pp., provides a refreshing relief from the usual turgidity of published dissertations. The outline plan is very straightforward, the prose is crystal-clear, and the breadth of the volume is admirable. The early chapters have no new material for the scholar, but do provide a concise and eminently readable summary of previous research. The phenomena of totemism and animal magic and the literary motif of metamorphosis are traced from earliest times, and there follows a succinct account of the differences between the related genres of saga and legend and a brief history of fairy-tale collecting since the French Baroque. Only then does Ungericht begin her own work proper, namely a study of *Volks- und Kunstmärchen* (Grimm, Hauff, Hoffmann, Brentano, and others). Max Lüthi, *Es war einmal [. . .]. Vom Wesen des Volksmärchens*, Göttingen, Vandenhoeck & Ruprecht, 127 pp., originally published in 1962, is a new edition of a well-known classic, and can still provide an insightful view into the phenomenon of the Märchen. Lüthi brings psychology, anthropology, history, and aesthetics into his study, but they are seen as handmaidens to his fundamental topic; they do not overwhelm it. Lutz Röhrlich has written a short introduction to this edition which places Lüthi's work into the context of the 20th-c. revival of interest in the Märchen. Another new edition is Walther Killy, *Wandlungen des lyrischen Bildes*, Göttingen, Vandenhoeck & Ruprecht, 160 pp., first published in 1956. This classic work covers the lyric from Goethe to Brecht and has a brief introduction by Dieter Lamping, where the limitations of Killy's *werkimmanent* interpretation are recognized but minimized. Hartmut Steinecke, *Unterhaltsamkeit und Artistik. Neue Schreibarten in der deutschen Literatur von Hoffmann bis Heine*, Berlin, Schmidt, 226 pp. This impressive study describes the history of the division of artistic production into high art and low art which, S. says, was more rigidly adhered to in 19th-c. Germany than in Great Britain or France. Two writers, however, managed to bridge the divide between popular and artistic production, namely E. T. A. Hoffmann and Heinrich Heine, and they were thus seen as disseminators of dangerous ideas by contemporaries who held power. There are long chapters on the two, as well as shorter thematic chapters on the historical novel, travel literature, literary criticism, and on the concept of *Weltliteratur* among the *Jungdeutsche*. A volume has appeared on the genre of autobiography, although in the widest, least literary sense of the word: Fohrmann, *Lebensläufe*. Included in the collection is an article by G. Geitner, 'Soviel wie nichts? Weiblicher Lebenslauf, weibliche Autorschaft um 1800' (29–50), which discusses the difficulties in finding the material for women's biographies from a time when women were not expected to develop a life-story, taking Friderika Baldinger and Sophie von la Roche as negative examples before showing a different solution as found by Maria Anna Sagar. M. Kraul, 'Erziehungsgeschichten und Lebensgeschichten in der Pädagogik des ausgehenden 18. Jahrhunderts' (11–28), investigates the connection between life-stories and the new science of pedagogy, taking Moritz's *Anton Reiser* as a kind of case-study. Also included in the volume: U.-K. Ketelsen, 'Narrative Form und Präsenz der Figur. "Lebensläufe" im Drama um 1800 oder: Warum gab es kein Bildungsdrama?' (105–120); H.-M. Kruckis, 'Charakteristik Friedrich Ludwig Jahns' (177–202), about the gymnast; F. Nies, 'Bilder von Bildung und Verbildung durch Lesen' (203–22), which includes illustrations; K. Dörner, 'Die implizite Vorstellung von biographischer Normalität im psychologischen Diskurs um 1800' (235–39); and W. Vosskamp, 'Individualität — Biographie — Roman' (257–61). There are also articles on Jean Paul and Hoffmann; see pp. 684, 691 below.

2. INDIVIDUAL AUTHORS

ARNIM, BETTINA VON. Gisela Dischner, *B. v. A. Eine Biographie aus dem 19. Jahrhundert*, Bodenheim, Philo, 191 pp., is a reprint of a ground-breaking biography-cum-*Lesebuch* (originally published in 1977). Von Arnim, with her mixture of absolute idealism and concrete political goals, is shown to have connections both to the Frühromantik and to Jungdeutschland, rather than to the sentimental Spätromantik or Biedermeier, as has often been assumed. H. Härtle, 'Bettinas Salon der "edlen Weltverbesser"', *Internationales Jb. der B.-v.-A.-Gesellschaft*, 8–9, 1996–97:163–76, grounds A.'s Berlin salon in an idea of the early Romantic *Geselligkeit*, which she acquired through her reading of Novalis and correspondence with Schleiermacher. The article is, however, mostly a description of the salon and the people who came there, as well as an account of its political character. In the same volume, U. Landfester, 'Von Frau zu Frau? Einige Bemerkungen über historische und ahistorische Weiblichkeitsdiskurse in der Rezeption B. v. As' (201–19), gives an interesting overview of B. v. A. reception, from her contemporaries to the *Brigitte-Zeitschrift* in the 1990s, and it exposes thereby the dangers of an over-strong sense of identification on the part of some readers which makes the historical author disappear from view. Also in this volume: H. Härtle, 'Zur Ausgabe des Briefwechsels B. v. As mit Philipp Hössli' (223–28).

ARNIM, L.A. VON. Holger Schwinn, *Kommunikationsmedium Freundschaft. Der Briefwechsel zwischen L. A. v. A. und Clemens Brentano in den Jahren 1801 bis 1818* (EH, I, 1635), 221 pp. The letter is taken seriously as an art form, as a vehicle of communication and as an important historical document of intellectual history (which points in the direction of much recent work on women writers). The correspondence documents an episode in the cult of friendship of the late 18th and early 19th c. In the absence of a commentated edition of this correspondence, the bibliography provides much useful information. S. Dickson, 'Making dreams come true in the works of A. v. A.', Dickson, *Dreams*, 127–38, discusses the narrative function of dreams. A character's dreams and his/her willingness and ability to interpret the dreams are an indication of depth, insight, and ability to live well. J. Knaack, 'Ein Aufsatz A. v. As in der Hamburger Zeitschrift *Originalien*', *Internationales Jahrbuch der Bettina-von-Arnim-Gesellschaft*, 8–9:11–36, speculates on the possibility that an anti-censorship article which appeared in 1819 may have been written by A. v. A.

BRENTANO, CLEMENS. J. Barth, 'Schlange und Fisch. Zu Bs Ballade Großmutter Schlangenköchin', *Euphorion*, 92:135–38, discusses likely folk and biblical sources for the fish (in some sources a snake or an eel) in the ballad from *Des Knaben Wunderhorn* which also appears in a different version in *Godwi*.

BROSSE, FRIEDRICH CHRISTIAN. M. Bergengruen, 'Das Buch als Zwiebel und die Wiederbelebung des Begriffsleichnams. Eine zu Unrecht vergessene Satire: F. C. Bs *Antipseudo-Kantiade*', *Athenäum*: 57–73, rediscovers a satire on Kantian philosophy and sets it into the context of the new philosophical trend in satire at the end of the 18th c.

CHAMISSO. E. Mornin, ' "[. . .] viele Städte der Menschen gesehen und Sitten gelernt": observations on Chamisso's cosmopolitan verse', *ColGer*, 31:55–65.

EICHENDORFF, JOSEPH VON. J. v. E., *Historische-kritische Ausgabe*, ed. Hermann Kunisch and Helmut Koopmann, vol. 5/4 *Erzählungen*, part 3 *Autobiographische Fragmente, Text und Kommentar*, ed. Dietmar Kunisch, Tübingen, Niemeyer, xx + 530 pp., comes complete with an editorial apparatus and an extensive bibliography. In Harry Fröhlich, *Dramatik des Unbewußten. Zur Autonomieproblematik von Ich und Nation in Es 'historischen' Dramen*, Tübingen, Niemeyer, viii + 224 pp., several much-ignored dramas and drama fragments are analysed. Fröhlich bases his study on Lacanian psychoanalysis, not to put the author on the couch, but rather because the texts themselves are systems of language within an historical setting. E. both problematizes the construction of a self in these dramas and falls into rigid concepts of the self, a problem which plays itself out on the level of national identity as well. J. Purver, 'Dreams and dreaming in the works of J. v. E.', Dickson, *Dreams*, 139–54, finds the starting point for E.'s literary use of dreams in Schubert.

FICHTE. J.-G. F., *Gesamtausgabe der Bayrischen Akademie der Wissenschaften*, ed. Reinhard Lauth, Hans Gliwitzky, series II, vol. 11, *Nachgelassene Schriften 1807–1810*, ed. Reinhard Lauth, Hans Gliwitzky, Erich Fuchs, and Peter K. Schneider, Stuttgart–Bad Canstatt, Frommann-Holzboog, x + 467 pp., contains posthumous material from F.'s later years in Berlin, including 'Spekulation zu Koppenhagen' and 'Seit dem 1. April', and it continues the editing and documenting of F.'s work.

FOUQUÉ. K. Baumgartner, 'Through the eyes of fashion: political aspects of fashion and C. d. l. F. 's *Geschichte der Moden, vom Jahre 1785 bis 1829: als Beytrag zur Geschichte der Zeit*', *GR*, 72, 1997:215–30.

GRIMM, JACOB AND WILHELM. J. G. and W. G., *Kinder- und Hausmärchen gesammelt durch die Brüder Grimm. Vollständige Ausgabe auf der Grundlage der dritten Auflage (1837)*, ed. Heinz Rölleke, DKV, 1304 pp., comes complete with notes and commentary. Craig Monk, *Parody as an Interpretative Response to Gs' 'Kinder- und Hausmärchen'* (Otago German Studies, 10), Dunedin, University of Otago German Department,

135 pp., argues for a literary interpretation of the *KH*, as even despite the (possible) oral origins of the tales, they have undoubtedly been preserved by literary men writing in a literary context. Although the bulk of the book focuses on matters not of immediate relevance to the Romanticist (there is a long discussion of various humorous genres, wherein parody is rehabilitated as a genre with serious implications, and there are several chapters on recent parodies of *Rotkäppchen*) there is a useful chapter on the background of the Gs' collection as well as a short chapter on the their version of *Rotkäppchen*. H. Rölleke, ' "Das ihm bei jedem Wort, das es spricht, eine Kröte aus dem Mund springt." Die Brüder Grimm und Perraults Märchen', *ZDP*, 117 : 616–18. A new discovery of a copy of Perrault's 1697 first edition once owned by the Gs invites speculation about whether they were influenced by it to change their original version, which had had an oral source. Also noted: W. Rankin, 'G. allusions to Gottfried von Strassburg's *Tristan*', *GN*, 29 : 31–35. S. Gessner, *'Märchenhochzeit oder Realität? Die Hochzeit in den Kinder- und Hausmärchen der Brüder G. aus kulturhistorischen Sicht', *Fabula*, 39 : 38–52. H. H. Baumann, *' "Es sei denn, es singt einer." Verrat und Geständnis im Märchen "Der singende Knochen" (KHM 28) und anderswo', *ib.*, 21–37.

HAUFF. J. S. Chase, 'The wandering court Jew and the land of God: W. H.'s "Jud Süss" as historical fiction', *MLR*, 93 : 724–40.

HEINSE. Werner Keil, **Das Mass des Bacchanten: W.Hs Überlebenskunst*, Munich, Fink, 319 pp.

HOFFMANN, E. T. A. In Nikolai Vogel, *E. T. A. Hs Erzählung 'Der Sandmann' als Interpretation der Interpretation* (MSLKD, 28), 131 pp., communication theory is used to show that *Der Sandmann* can be interpreted as precisely about the impossibility of communicating; thus it becomes a meta-interpretation. Vogel's point is well-made, but the complication caused by the theoretical language only obscures what we already know about the story. The analysis is, however, thorough, and it does provide an overview of scholarship on the subject. H. D. Schäfer, 'H. am Fenster', *Athenäum*: 33–35, is a biographical account of H.'s last years in Berlin, which, as 'Des Vetters Eckfenster' proves, were not unproductive, despite his ill health. The style, content, and length of Detlef Kremer, *E. T. A. H. zur Einführung*, Hamburg, Junius, 197 pp., make it suitable for an undergraduate library. There is a short biography (*c.* 30 pp.) plus chapters on some of H.'s themes and works. The bibliography is general rather than specifically relevant to H., and there is little on his musical activity. In this year's *E. T. A. H.-Jb.*, N. Werber, 'Gestalten des Unheimlichen. Seine Struktur und Funktion bei Eichendorff und H.' (7–27), discusses the transformation of the

Unheimlich from an experiential category to a literary one, as city dwellers are no longer faced with the real or imagined dangers of the natural world. In two Märchen, Eichendorff's *Die Zauberei im Herbste* and H.'s *Ignaz Denner*, the *Unheimlich* is not overcome, as it is in a *Volksmärchen*, but instead it becomes the site of a sexualized curiosity and adventurousness. U. H. Gerlach, 'E. T. A. Hs *Spielerglück*' (28–38), loses persuasiveness due to his constant avowals that the story is still relevant today, as if this needed to be argued in the context of a yearbook dedicated to the author! H.'s late stories, according to A. Dunker, 'Der "preßhafte Autor". Biedermeier als Verfahren in E. T. A. Hs späten Almanach-Erzählungen' (39–49), have been unfairly dismissed as *Trivialliteratur*. Two stories, *Datura fastuosa* and *Meister Johannes Wacht*, are shown instead to take on popular forms in order that these might be parodied. The concept of artistic originality is in this way radically undermined, and H. also deals with his own illness and concomitant pain through an artistic handling of them. See also in this volume A. Olbrich, ' "Um aller Wunden willen." E. T. A. Hs *Datura fastuosa* — einige neue Quellen zur zeitgenössischen Rezeption' (113–16). Several short articles in the volume address the 20th-c. reception of H.: K. Kanzog, 'E. T. A. H. in der "Höchstbegabtensammlung Adela Juda" ' (117–19), writes of genealogical and psychiatric investigations of H.; T. Molzahn, ' "Ein Märchen ist ein Träumen der holden Phantasie [. . .]." Der "Gespenster-Hoffmann" als Figur einer Operette von Eduard Künneke' (120–22); and W. Olma, 'E. T. A. H. auf der documenta X in Kassel 1997' (123–28), write about adaptations in opera and film, respectively. S. Sirc, ' "Bottom, thou art translated": Schlegel's *Sommernachtstraum*, the German Romantics and E. T. A. H. 's *Der goldene Topf*, Dickson, *Dreams*, 53–76. This wide-ranging essay convincingly links the Shakespearean and H. texts directly (via Schlegel's translation) and indirectly through common sources in folk-myth, the Bible, and most importantly the alchemical tradition. Intertextual transformation of received art by a writer in a dream-like state resembles alchemical transformation, and this functions as a subject of both Shakespeare's play and H.'s story. In another article in the same volume, E. T. A. H. 's 'Die Abenteuer der Sylvester-Nacht' is read by R. Schmidt, 'Karnavelesque Mesalliancen oder der Autor als Bauchredner der Sprache', *ib.*, 77–98, as a warning to the artist to keep his ideals, but to refrain from expecting them to be incorporated in any concrete woman. The story's many references to actual paintings have been traced, and copies of most them are included in the volume. The warning against seductive femininity and the belief in the possibility of transcendence both speak against Bakhtinian interpretations. S. thus takes to task two critics who give such interpretations for their wilful misunderstanding of H.'s text. And finally in this volume, S. Neuhaus, 'The dream as motif in E. T. A. H. 's works', *ib.*, 99–126, gives an account of the various types of dreams in H.'s works. He traces H.'s source of dream knowledge back solely to Schubert and no further, and he reads the dreams as close precursors to Freud's concept of wish-fulfilment. Unlike Schmidt, he sees H. as beyond Romanticism, not part of it. The conclusions N. draws are at times simplistic, and the English is sometimes difficult to follow. Also noted: E. Lämmert, 'Lebens-Ansichten einer Katers. Anomalien eines Künstlerlebens nach 1800', Fohrmann, *Lebensläufe*, 157–75; A. R. Becker, '*Die Elixiere des Teufels*: E. T. A. H. 's house of mirrors', *Journal of the Fantastic in the Arts*, 9:117–30; B. Neymeyr, *'Narzissistische Destruktion: zum Stellenwert von Realitätsverlust und Selbstentfremdung in E.T.A.Hs Nachtstück "Der Sandmann"', *Poetica*, 29:499–531.

HÖLDERLIN, F. H. The *Internationale H.-Bibliographie (IHB) auf der Grundlage der Neuerwerbungen des Hölderlin-Archivs der Württembergischen Landesbibliothek 1995–1996. Quellen und Sekundärliteratur, Rezeption und Rezensionen*, ed. Werner Paul Sohnle and Marianne Schütz (H.-Archiv), Stuttgart, Frommann-Holzboog, vol. 1, *Erschließungsband*, xxxiv + 384 pp., vol. 2, *Materialband*, viii + 520 pp., is of course an invaluable source for H. scholars. Charlie Louth, *Hölderlin and the Dynamics of Translation* (Studies in Comparative Literature, 2), Oxford, Legenda, x + 270 pp., claims that H. merely took to the extreme what was common practice among Romantics, namely to view translation as a means of rejuvenating one's own language and national literature as well as being itself a creative process closely akin to writing poetry. Translation incorporates the other into the self. The book contains excerpts from various 18th-c. and 19th-c. translations. There is a long chapter on H.'s Pindar translations, and reference is also made to his poetic output. English translations are provided throughout. Ingeborg Joppien, *F. H. Eine Psychobiographie*, Stuttgart, Kohlhammer, 230 pp., is a biography, not a literary study, and thus there is very little reference to the actual poetic output. Written by a psychologist, it does bring a refreshing view from outside the field, though it is an admittedly speculative account of H.'s insanity. Most of the book consists of traditional biography with sections on themes ('Psychiatry in Württemburg around 1800' for example) and the overtly psychological sections take up only very little space at the end of each chapter. For readers ready for rougher play, two very confrontational books have appeared this year. Flemming Roland-Jensen, *Vernünftige Gedanken über Die Nymphe Mnemosyne — wider die autoritären Methoden in der Hölderlinforschung*, Würzburg, Königshausen & Neumann, 257 pp., takes traditional H. scholarship to task (namely Friedrich Beissner and Jochen Schmidt) for what Roland-Jensen terms its 'authoritarian' refusal of self-criticism. Unfortunately, the argument is tortured and repetitious, and the purpose of the criticism gets lost. The reader ends up feeling a bit bruised, as if having been caught in the middle of a fist-fight of no immediate interest to himself. Yahya A. Elsaghe, *Untersuchungen zur Funktion des Mythos in Hs Feiertagshymne*, Tübingen, Francke, 230 pp., seems anodyne by comparison, although again the critical tradition is chastised in the introduction. The main body of the text is more interesting: here the Semele myth is taken to be the crux of the poem, and the reason the poem comes to grief is because H. fails to integrate the impregnation/fertility myth with that of fathering and paternity. Therefore the issues the poem raises — of gendered social roles, the use of the literary tradition, the existence of the numinous, the social function of literature — all remain unanswered. Elsaghe has also addressed this topic in ' "Süßer als Gebären": Matriarchale und patriarchale Metaphern in Hs Feiertagshymne', *GR*, 72, 1997:119–29. J. Lyon, ' "Was nemlich mehr sei, das Ganze oder das Einzelne": Hs *Hyperion* as an unresolved crisis', *GLL*, 51:1–14, takes issue with Lawrence Ryan's and Gerhard Kurz's interpretations, which claim a resolution of particular and whole in *Hyperion*. Yet it is precisely in the unsettling lack of closure that H.'s later works are here foreshadowed. A. Thomasberger, 'Erinnerungsbilder. Das Konzept Hs und eine Applikation auf Storm', Peil, *Erkennen*, 527–41. This year's *Hölderlin-Jahrbuch* has articles dealing with H. and nature. U. Hölscher, 'Vom Ursprung der Naturphilosophie' (1–14); A. Bennholdt-Thomsen, 'Dissonanzen in der späten Naturauffassung Hs' (15–41); J. Söring, ' "Die göttlichgegenwärtige Natur bedarf der Rede nicht." Wozu also die Dichter?' (58–82). Other articles include S. Oehler-Klein, 'Der "Trieb in uns, das Ungebildete zu bilden": Der Begriff "Bildungstrieb" bei Blumenbach und H.' (102–18); J. Link, 'Rousseaus "Naturgeschichte der menschlichen Gattung" und Hs Dichtung nach 1800' (125–45); V. Waibel, 'Hs Rezeption von Fichtes *Grundlage des Naturrechts*' (146–72); D. Bremer, ' "Versöhnung ist mitten im Streit": Hs Entdeckung Heraklits' (173–99); T. Birkenhauer, ' "Natur" in Hs Trauerspiel *Der Tod des Empedokles*' (207–25); H. Bothe, 'Jovialität. Anmerkungen zu Hs Ode "Natur und Kunst oder Saturn und Jupiter" ' (226–34).

HÜLSEN, AUGUST LUDWIG.   G. Naschert, 'A. G. Hs erster Beitrag zur philosophischen Frühromantik', *Athenäum*: 111–35, continues his investigation (begun in *Athenäum*, 1997:11–36) into the mostly forgotten H., whom Friedrich Schlegel had praised inordinately, perhaps because H. helped him develop beyond Fichte.

HUMBOLDT, WILHELM VON. Hans-Ernst Schiller, *Die Sprache der realen Freiheit. Sprache und Sozialphilisophie bei W. v. H.*, Würzburg, Königshausen & Neumann, 307 pp., is a very broad study including chapters on politics, philosophy, education, and of course language and the rise of the individual.

KLEIST. *Interpretationen. Ks Erzählungen*, ed. Walter Hinderer, Stuttgart, Reclam, 258 pp., has helpful articles on all the stories. Contributors include Kurt Wölfel, Dirk Grathoff, Jochen Schmidt, Norbert Oellers, Hans Peter Herrmann, Ulrike Landfester, Günter Oesterle, Walter Hinderer, and Gerhard Neumann. Doris Claudia Borelbach, *Mythos-Rezeption in H. v. Ks Dramen*, Würzburg, Königshausen & Neumann, 241 pp. Four plays (*Die Familie Schroffenstein, Penthesilea, Amphitryon*, and *Der zerbrochene Krug*) are studied in relation to his use and reception of myths, i.e. those of antiquity, the Christian myth of a fall from grace, and the concept of tragedy. K. neither rejected myth as superstition, as a neo-Classical writer might have done, nor did he give it favoured status as the truth, as some of his contemporary Romantic counterparts did. Rather, he shows how received notions (including myth) structure our only partial perception of the world. An especial emphasis is placed on the relations between the sexes. K.'s 'alienating glance' shows both the archetypal foundation of these relations as well as their basis in violence; idealization and prescriptive divisions into sexual roles are both revealed to be results of repression (*Verdrängung*). Peter Staengele, *H. v. K.* (dtv Portrait), Munich, DTV, 159 pp., will prove a useful addition to the undergraduate library. The text is clear and straightforward, the polychromatic formatting will please the modern student. Interspersed throughout the biographical narrative are illustrations (some of K. and his associates, some of a more general nature) as well as excerpts of contemporary commentary on K., letters to and from K., and historical background. D. Brüggemann, 'Babylonische Musik. Die heilige Cäcilie als Paradigma für Ks Hermetik', *DVLG*, 72:592–636, finds in the textual inconsistencies of the story and in the many reversals of biblical material evidence of a hermetic meaning. The alchemical interpretation explains the apparently blasphemous tendencies in K.'s work. Conceptions of the sublime are traced in E. Baker, 'Fables of the Sublime: Kant, Schiller, K.', *MLN*, 113:524–36, which is mostly about Kant and Schiller and only briefly addresses K.'s 'Fabel ohne Moral'. For Kant, the sublime is ineffable, for Schiller it can be expressed through metaphor, but for K. the didactic function of the fable — which could lead man to the sublime through *Bildung* — is no longer a possibility, as all sense of a moral of the story is lost. G. Kluge 'Die mißlungene Apotheose des Prinzen vom Homburg', *Neophilologus*, 82:279–90, argues against a happy ending the play. When the prince accepts the Kurfürst's judgement of him, he is ready to die; the consequent amnesty cannot but be unwelcome.

A common theme in K. studies was the attempt to account for the number of factual errors, inconsistencies and anachronisms in his work. M. Heggestad, 'Pedagogical performances in K.'s shorter essays', *Seminar*, 34:26–44, looks at two short essays where K. performs a contradiction of what the essay ostensibly sets out to do. In 'Allerneuester Erziehungsplan', a fictional character, Levanus, claims that pedagogy works best by way of negative example, by making the student disagree. Since the 'editor' disagrees, has Levanus's method worked, or is the fictional editor simply correct? It is impossible to decide. Similarly, in 'Über die allmähliche Verfertigung der Gedanken beim Reden', a highly self-conscious rhetorical structure is used ostensibly to prove that thought is expressed unconsciously and spontaneously. One should therefore not look to these or other Kleistian texts for straightforward examples of his intention, but should let them persist in all their contradictions. K. Müller-Salget, 'August und die Mestize. Zu einigen Kontroversen um Ks Verlobung in San Domingo', *Euphorion*, 92:103–13, answers questions raised by Roland Reuss concerning two puzzles in the play. 'Mestize' meant for K. simply racially mixed and did not have our narrower modern meaning of half white, half Native American. The problem of the name change from Gustav to August is less satisfactorily accounted for. J. Hibberd, 'H. v. K.'s report on Heligoland', *GLL*, 51:431–42, claims that K. cleverly subverted Franco-Prussian censorship in order to give a subtly positive account of the smuggling operation based on this island during the Napoleonic blockade. Factual errors or exaggerations in the report are seen as intentional. Various aspects of K.'s portrayal of duels, both literal and figurative, are the theme of this year's *KlJb*, but the theme could just as well have been 'violence' or 'power'. Factual errors and inconsistencies are again considered. J.-D. Müller, 'Ks Mittelalter-Phantasma. Zur Erzählung *Der Zweikampf* (1811)' (3–20), says that the medieval setting (full of anachronisms and incorrect or hazy detail) forms not a local colouring nor a veiled reference to the contemporary fashion for duelling, but rather a background for K.'s obsession with the impossibility of deciphering truth from signs in the natural world. I. M. Krüger-Fürhoff, 'Den verwundeten Körper lesen. Zur Hermeneutik physischer und ästhetischer Grenzverletzungen im Kontext von Ks *Zweikampf* (21–36), eschews moral or epistemological interpretations. A comparison with Lessing's *Laokoon* and the autopsy report on K.'s and Henriette Vogel's double-suicide show the aesthetic, medical, and literary aspects of interpreting the body through its wounds, where only the latter (K.'s story) indicates the difficulty of such interpretations. Language, power, and politics form a common interest of some of the contributors to this volume. B. J. Dotzler, ' "Federkrieg." K. und die Autorschaft des Produzenten' (37–61), discusses K.'s decision to enter the public fray as a journalist at the moment of his highest confidence in himself as a writer. Writing journalistic prose is not simply a public service, but also the exercising of power. W. Kittler, 'K. und Clausewitz' (62–79), sets *Prinz Friedrich von Homburg* into the context of war, politics, and the violence of language, using Freud's *fort-da* game and Clausewitz's statements about war as a background. Politics and power are the subject of another story in H. Bay, ' "Als die Schwarzen die Weißen ermordeten." Nachbeben einer Erschütterung des europäischen Diskurses in Ks *Verlobung in St. Domingo*' (80–108). Racial relations and the overthrow of the white French regime are an integral part of the story, not supplementary to the love-story aspects. Violence is at the very root of language for B. Hansen, 'Gewaltige Performanz. Tödliche Sprechakte in Ks *Penthesilea*' (109–26). Language, which establishes taboos and laws, not only fails to control violence, but actually calls it into being. Even in death there is no reconciliation, no coming to an understanding, in K.'s cultural pessimism. A more optimistic reading of *Penthesilea* is given in M. Chaouli, 'Die Verschlingung der Metapher. Geschmack und Ekel in der *Penthesilea*' (127–49). The language of the play performs a double movement of making metaphors literal, while at the same time making the metaphors possible to begin with by representing them graphically. The beautiful and the disgusting, or the metaphorical and the literal, are the two pillars which mutually support each other (in Chaouli's play on K.'s recurrent metaphor of the arch.) The opposites, which Classical aesthetics seeks to keep apart, are inextricably bound together in Kleist. Another deconstruction of Classical aesthetics occurs in *Über das Marionettentheater*, where there is a literal staging of the self, according to H. J. Schneider, 'Dekonstruktion des hermeneutischen Körpers. Ks Aufsatz *Über das Marionettentheater* und der Diskurs der klassischen Ästhetik' (153–75). Body and language are once more foregrounded in the discussion, and the inconsistencies of the text have become its most interesting aspect. Both B. Greiner, ' "Die neueste Philosophie in dieses [. . .] Land verpflanzen." Ks literarische Experimente mit Kant' (176–208), and M. Schneider, 'Die Gewalt von Raum und Zeit. Ks optische Medien und das Kriegstheater' (209–26), investigate K.'s 'Kant-Krise'. Greiner sets out not to determine the origins of K.'s crisis nor to evaluate the validity of his reading of Kant, but rather simply to trace the thoughts that K. develops at this time. Letters, essays, and fictional works are brought to bear on the argument. Schneider, like

Kittler (see p. 688 above), investigates K. together with Clausewitz. A third essay on Clausewitz and K. in the volume is H.-C. von Herrmann, 'Beweglicher Heere. Zur Kalkulation des Irregulären bei K. und Clausewitz' (227–43). Both men use a hermeneutics of improbability in their depictions of partisan warfare. There is little here directly about K., but instead about Clausewitz and more generally about contemporary science. In U. Abraham, 'Kohlhaas und der Kanon, oder: Was hat K. in der Schule verloren?' (244–63), the concept of the duel must be understood in a more figurative sense. Abraham discusses *Michael Kohlhaas* and its (and K.'s) status in the 'canon', bringing up the debate about what the canon is, should be and might be. Also in the *KJb* volume: H. F. Weiss, 'Gerüchte vom Heldentod des Dichters. Unbekannte Zeugnisse von K. vom Jahre 1809' (267–83); K. Müller-Salget, '"Anything goes?" Reinhard Pabst und die "Würzburger Reise"' (317–21); B. J. Dotzler, 'K. mit Ballhorn' (322–24). W. Jordan and S. Feuchert, 'Philosophische Implikate im Werk H. v. Ks oder der sichere Weg, das Glück zu verfehlen', *BKF*, 1997: 16–43, seek to trace K.'s development of a personal (not systematic) philosophy (his attempt to find 'a way to happiness') through his reception of Leibniz, Spinoza, Fichte, and Rousseau (and of course, Kant), for which they investigate his fictional as well as non-fictional output. Two further articles of *BKF*, 1997, deal very differently with *Penthesilea*, though both from a feminist perspective. R. M. Schell, 'The eye of the beholder: female subjectivity in K.'s *Penthesilea*' (44–59), reads the play as 'the relation between war-time sexuality and the construction of female subjectivity'. As the founding of the Amazon state remains subject to the male gaze (as evidenced in the fear of male mockery), so Penthesilea remains bound to a self-definition through Achilles's eyes. Her suicide parallels Tanaïs's self-mutilation: both are acts of sacrifice (in a Girardian sense) that allow the Amazon state first to be established and later to overcome a crisis. C. Köhler, 'Aktive Penthesilea — passiver Achill. Das Aufbrechen traditioneller Geschlechterrollen in H. v. Ks *Penthesilea*' (60–74), on the other hand, sees the play as a silencing of strong women which parallels the silencing of politically active women some years before in revolutionary France. The exchange of gendered roles is experimented with, but found an inadequate solution, and since neither party will accept the passive role, the end must be a tragic one. Also in this volume, R. Loch, 'Stammbücher aus der Lausitz — Fingerzeige zu K.' (75–116) looks to archival material in the home-town of K.'s mother's family for evidence of his childhood, that *terra incognita*. Parts of two letters by C. L. Fernow with negative judgements of *Phöbus* are printed in R. Wartusch, 'Spuren der *Phöbus*-Rezeption im klassischen Weimar'

(117–27), adding evidence about classical Weimar's rejection of K.'s and Adam Müller's journal. H. Weiss, 'Neues zu zwei *Abendblätter*-Anekdoten' (128–42), has found two anecdotes similar to ones by K. in a collection of anecdotes published in 1809. A connection seems clear, though the exact history is impossible to trace. A sad and disconcerting document to K. reception is provided by H. Häker, 'Arthur Eloessers K-Studie von 1903 — Dokument eines tragischen Irrtums' (143–46). A turn of the century German-Jewish academic wrote a biography which praises K. in a way that could have been later quoted by a Goebbels. C. Kaiser, 'Der eine und ein anderer K., wobei auch von G. und einem anderen G. die Rede sein wird' (147–62), discusses several works (an essay, a radio play, a story, and a poem) by Günter Kunert which imply a relationship of censor to censored between Peter Goldammer and himself which parallels one between Goethe and Kleist 200 years previously. Kaiser makes an interesting contribution to our understanding of the reception history of K. (and to a lesser extent, of Goethe) in the former German Democratic Republic. P. Goldammer, 'Ein Wort in eigener Sache' (163–64), writes a brief but pithy defence of himself against what he sees as Kaiser's accusations of collaboration with the repressive government. (The reply is to a different essay than the one published here.) Also in the *BKF*, 1997, volume: S. Herrath, K. Jeziorkowski et al., 'Textraum K.' (168–81), and R. Wartusch, 'H. v. Ks Aufenthalt in Dresden 1807–1809' (182–90). Also noted: K. Jeziorkowski, 'Traum-Raum und Text-Höhle. Beobachtungen an dramatischen Szenen H. v. Ks', *Fest. Geith*, 215–24; A. Plotnitsky, 'A dancing arch: formalization and singularity in K., Shelley and de Man', *ERR*, 9.2:161–76; R. Herzinger, 'The squalor of the times and the poet's tendency toward the bizarre. A new edition of the *Berliner Abendblätter* reveals H. v. K. as a practical journalist and a patriotic missionary', *Theater Heute*, 7:34–39; N. Nobile, 'Charting the body politic. H. v. K.'s "Charite-Vorfall"', *ColGer*, 30:1–24. J. Plug, 'The borders of a lip: K., language and politics', *StRom*, 36:391–425.

MEREAU, SOPHIE. B. Guenther, 'Letters exchanged across borders: Mme de Stael's *Delphine* and the epistolary novels of Juliane von Krudener and Sophie Mereau', *Comparatist*, 22:78–90.

NOVALIS. M. Frank, 'Von der Grundsatz-Kritik zur freien Erfindung. Die ästhetische Wende in den *Fichte Studien* und ihr konstellatorischer Kontext', *Athenäum*: 75–95, investigates N.'s so-called *Fichte-Studien* in order to trace his development as a philosopher. The early fragments discussed in O. Wilhelm, 'Denkfiguren in N' Fragmenten *Vermischte Bemerkungen* (Urfassung vom *Blüthenstaub*) und ihr Zusammenhang mit Fichtes *Wissenschaftslehre*. Überlegungen zur frühromantischen Aphoristik', *DVLG*, 72:227–42, show N.'s interest in Fichte's philosophy, but also his first attempts to move beyond it. H. F. Weiss, 'Friedrich von Hardenberg und Johann Gottfried Langermann', *ZDP*, 117 : 173–88, rediscovers a psychiatrist (still known in the fields of medical and social history as a founder of German psychiatry) who exercised a tangible influence on N.'s development. R. Littlejohns, 'Romantic eschatology: Novalis and dreams', Dickson, *Dreams*, 43–52, discusses N.'s *Hymnen an die Nacht* and *Heinrich von Ofterdingen*, where the dream points to a visionary window to a utopian future. In the same volume, R. A. Davis, 'Moneta's daughters: The representation of the female in some Romantic and Post-Romantic dream texts' (169–94), after a quick look at Fichte and N., gives an interpretation of British Romantics (mostly Keats) and Post-Romantics that is strongly influenced by Freud. Also noted: D. F. Krell, *'Eating out: Voluptuosity for dessert' pp. 76–88 of *Eating Culture*, ed. Ron Scapp and Brian Seitz, Albany NY, State of NY Press, vii + 303 pp.; L. Johnson, ' "Wozu überhaupt ein Anfang?" Memory and history in *Heinrich von Ofterdingen*', *ColGer* 31.1 : 21–35; W. Fromm, *'Inspirierte Ähnlichkeit. Überlegungen zu einen ästhetischen Verfahren des N.', *DVLG*, 71, 1997:559–88.

RICHTER, JEAN PAUL. J. P., *J. Ps Sämtliche Werke. Historisch-kritische Ausgabe*, section 2, vol. 7, *Philosophische, ästhetische und politische Untersuchungen*, ed. Götz Müller and Janina Knab (Deutsche Schillergesellschaft), Weimar, Böhlau, 737 pp., continues work begun near the beginning of this century to create a critical edition of J.-P.'s work. These posthumous writings are from notebooks he kept and are a source for much of his published work. T. Wirtz, 'Liebe und Verstehen. J. P. im Briefwechsel mit Charlotte Kalb und Esther Grad', *DVLG*, 72 : 175–200. J. P.'s sentimental writing appropriates women's feelings as a stylistic form, and also controls the feelings of the woman reader. T. Schestag, 'Bibliographie für J. P.', *MLN*, 113 : 465–523, investigates the function of the book in western religion and literature, with J. P. as an example. The style of the article will put off all but the most intrepid. Also noted: S. Mosès, 'Aporien des Subjektivität in J. Ps *Titan*', Fohrmann, *Lebensläufe*, 141–56.

SCHELLING. A. Fineron, 'Goethe, S.'s theology and the genesis of Prooemion', *DVLG*, 72 : 81–114. W. Schmidt-Biggemann, 'Geistige Prozeßnatur. Ss spirituelle Naturphilosophie zwischen 1800 und 1810', *Hölderlin-Jb.*: 42–57. M. Franz, 'Die Natur des Geistes. Ss Interpretation des Platonischen *Timaios* in Tübingen 1794', *ib.*, 237–38.

SCHLEGEL, FRIEDRICH. J. Costello, 'Aesthetic discourses and maternal subjects: Enlightenment roots, Schlegelian revisions,' Peer, *Romanticisms*, 171–88, argues that S. does not fear the maternal body, as do Enlightenment figures such as Kant and Hume, but rather recognizes in it the inevitable disruption of self and other. Costello relates ideas of the maternal body to the body politic: whereas Kant sought to destroy political particularism in unified duty to the common good, S. sees the benefits of disunity and particularism. Thus in *Lucinde*, despite its faults, S. does allow a certain articulation of woman's voice. P. Kösling, 'Die Wohnungen der Gebrüder Schlegel in Jena', *Athenäum*: 97–110, sets the record straight about where the Schlegels really lived in Jena, for the markers on the houses have long been incorrect. Schlegel scholars will be interested in E. Behler's account of the *Kritische Friedrich Schlegel Ausgabe*, a project which Behler came close to completing before his death in 1997 (*Athenäum*: 211–300). Elke-Barbara Schmeier, *Zur politischen Philosophie im Spätwerk F. Ss* (EH, XXXI, 330), 1997, 242 pp., is a welcome investigation into the later philosophy of S., considering the imbalance of attention to the earlier, more radical S. The style is refreshing, in that the author is clearly convinced of the importance of rehabilitating the late S., but this also often leads her to solecisms, and it is disturbing that the most recent sources she cites are from 1989. C. Schärf, 'Artistische Ironie und die Fremdheit der Seele. Zur ästhetischen Disposition in der Frühromantik bei F. S. und Karoline Günderode', *DVLG*, 72:433–62, traces a similarity of impulses between the two authors, both of whom aestheticize experience and idealize the opposite sex in their writings. It is encouraging to see the woman writer incorporated into a discussion of an established, 'canonical' writer.

SCHLEIERMACHER, FRIEDRICH. A very welcome new book is Andre Bowie's translation of F. S., *Hermeneutics and Criticism and Other Writings*, ed. Andrew Bowie, CUP, xl + 284 pp. There is an informative introduction and useful footnotes as well as ample documentation to explain the problematic terms in the translation. More texts on the New Testament are included than in the most recent (German) edition, and there are paraphrases of some passages which have been left out. Bowie hopes with this book to make S. more available to an English-speaking audience and to correct what he sees as misconceptions which have been propagated in this century (primarily by Gadamer).

TIECK, LUDWIG. The Foucauldian concept of the paradigm shift is utilized by R. Borgards, 'Die Schrift, das Rätsel, der Mensch. L. Ts *William Lovell*', *Athenäum*: 231–52, in order to discuss the modernity of T.'s novel.

VARNHAGEN, RAHEL LEVIN. B. Wägenbauer, '"Ich denke mir es sehr möglich, daß wir einander verstehen." Der Briefwechsel zwischen R. L. V. und Karoline von Fouqué', *ZDP*, 117:189–209. A detailed analysis of the correspondence between these two very different women shows that the early end to their friendship had as much to do with their modes of writing as with their politics. V. wrote in a dialogic fashion, while even K. v. F.'s novels, now almost unknown, are self-contained monologues.

WACKENRODER. H. I. Sullivan, 'The postponed narratives of desire in L. T.'s Novel *Franz Sternbalds Wanderungen*', Peer, *Romanticisms*, 223–34, relates Franz Sternbald's frustrated attempts to narrate his own story to the creation of art. Just as Franz's story is intermingled with others' stories, the work of art also has meaning only within a context. Franz's story must remain forever incomplete, as a story of a living being can never reach ultimate meaning. J. Schneider, 'Autonomie, Heteronomie und Literarizität in dem *Herzensergießungen eines kunstliebenden Klosterbruders* und den *Phantasien über die Kunst*', *ZDP*, 117 : 161–72, reads W. and Tieck's two works not as many critics do, either as an apology for a pragmatic (religious) function of art nor as the opposite, a functionless flight into ineffable music. Rather, through literature itself (and not through art or music) a compromise between the general and the particular is found.

LITERATURE, 1830–1880

By BOYD MULLAN, *Senior Lecturer in German in the University of St Andrews*

1. GENERAL

REFERENCE WORKS AND GENERAL STUDIES. Two similar publications this year which invite comparison are Jost Hermand, *Die deutschen Dichterbünde: Von den Meistersingern bis zum PEN-Club*, Cologne, Böhlau, viii + 383 pp., and the *Handbuch literarisch-kultureller Vereine 1825–1933*, ed. W. Wülfing et al. (Repertorien zur deutschen Literaturgeschichte, 18), Stuttgart, Metzler, xviii + 597 pp. Both aim successfully to fill an important gap, both are attractively illustrated and both are well indexed and easy to use. But whereas Hermand's book is the work of one scholar and takes the form of an historical survey covering 500 years of German literature, the Metzler *Handbuch* is the result of a collaborative effort by a team of researchers and is encyclopaedic in style. For 19th-c. specialists most of the advantages lie with the Metzler publication. Not only has it more space to cover a significantly shorter period, but it also benefits from the much more detailed research that a collaborative venture makes possible. Although Hermand gives good accounts each about five pages long of such important groups as the Viennese *Ludlamshöhle*, the *Tunnel über der Spree*, the *Rütli* circle and the *Münchner Dichterkreis*, he cannot match the density of information that the Metzler *Handbuch* provides about the dates and circumstances of foundation, the aims and history, the structure and organization, and the membership of no less than 132 associations. The third, revised and enlarged edition of the *Quellenlexikon zur deutschen Literaturgeschichte: Personal- und Einzelwerkbibliographien der internationalen Sekundärliteratur 1945–1990 zur deutschen Literatur von den Anfängen bis zur Gegenwart*, ed. Heiner Schmidt et al., has reached the letter K with the appearance of vols 14–17, Duisburg, Vlg für pädagogische Dokumentation, 512 pp. per volume. The new Goedeke, *Deutsches Schriftsteller-Lexikon 1830–1880: Goedekes Grundriß zur Geschichte der deutschen Dichtung. Fortführung* (see *YWMLS*, 60:805), has added vols 2, 1, and 2, 2, ed. H. and M. Jacob, Berlin, Akademie, 427 pp. and 489 pp. The two new vols cover writers whose names begin with C–D and E–F. The three vols that have so far appeared contain no less than 3,500 entries and are an invaluable resource for 19th-c. specialists. *Zwischen Restauration und Revolution 1815–1848*, ed. Gert Sautermeister et al. (Hansers Sozialgeschichte der deutschen Literatur, 5), Munich, Hanser, 760 pp., maintains the impressive quality that one has come to expect from this outstanding set. As the title implies, the book consistently emphasizes the tension between the reactionary and the progressive forces at work in the *Restaurations-zeit* and brings out clearly the 'Übergangscharakter' of the period. The literature of the time, both canonical and popular, is reviewed in the light of the radical and often rapid developments that were taking place. The main part of the book's 23 chapters is arranged by genre, with extensive treatments of the narrative forms, the lyric and the drama. The first part of the volume is however of a general nature and has chapters by P. Stein on the impact of industrial, economic, social, and political change; G. Goetzinger on the position of authors in society (problems confronting women writers, censorship, relations with publishers); U. Schmid on the condition of the book market (rapidly expanding readership, technical innovations in book production, role of colporters and lending libraries); S. Weigel on the populist writers and pamphleteers who emerged in 1848 (Albert Hopf, F. W. A. Held); and G. Sautermeister on travel literature. There then follow chapters by M. Heigenmoser, W. Beutin and H. Adler (195–209) on the various types of novel (*Bildungsroman,* historical novel, social novel); R. McNicholl and K. Wilhelms on women's fiction: R. Meyer, W. Lukas and H. Böning on the shorter narrative forms (Novelle, *Dorfgeschichte*); H. Plaul and U. Schmid on popular literature; O. Beishart on children's reading; R. Meyer and G. M. Rösch on drama and theatre; and H.-W. Jäger, G. Sautermeister and P. Stein on aspects of the lyric (workers' verse, political verse). Finally, J. Jokl contributes a chapter devoted entirely to Heine, and G. Frank one on Büchner. Effective cross-referencing, full indexes of names and titles, and a detailed table of contents make the book easy to use. The decision to keep the bibliography short was a wise one since so much material quickly becomes dated. The *Geschichte der deutschen Literatur von den Anfängen bis zur Gegenwart,* ed. de Boor and Newald, Munich, Beck, has added vol. IX, 1, Peter Sprengel's excellent *Geschichte der deutschsprachigen Literatur 1870–1900: Von der Reichsgründung zur Jahrhundertwende,* xix + 825 pp. Michael Patterson, *German Theatre: A Bibliography from the Beginning to 1945,* Leicester, Motley, 1996, 887 pp., is the third volume to be published in a series of bibliographies that is planned to encompass 'the whole of the world's theatrical and dramatic publications in every culture and most languages'. It is the first to be devoted to a language other than English. It contains a great deal of useful information and deserves a place in every institutional library. Gerd Müller, *Deutsche Literatur im 19. Jahrhundert,* II, Berne, Lang, 1997, 186 pp., covers the period 1848–1880 and is concerned with the effect of changing market conditions on literary production after 1848 and the development of a Realist style suited to the needs of the times. Elke P. Frederiksen and Elizabeth G. Ametsbichler, *Women Writers in German-Speaking*

Countries: A Bio-biographical Critical Sourcebook, Westport, Connecticut–London, Greenwood Press, xv + 561 pp., has articles on 54 writers including Louise Aston, Birch-Pfeiffer, Droste-Hülshoff, Ebner-Eschenbach, Ida Hahn-Hahn, Fanny Lewald, Louise Otto-Peters, Gabriele Reuter and Johanna Schopenhauer. The articles are typically eight to ten pages long and divided into four parts covering 'biography', 'major themes and narrative/poetic strategies', 'survey of criticism', and 'bibliography'. There is a full index of names and titles treated and, very helpfully, of subjects (e.g. abortion, anti-Semitism, marriage).

THEMES. *Text into Image: Image into Text. Proceedings of the Interdisciplinary Bicentenary Conference held at St Patrick's College Maynooth (The National University of Ireland) in September 1995*, ed. Jeff Morrison et al. (Internationale Forschungen zur Allgemeinen und Vergleichenden Literaturwissenschaft, 20), Amsterdam, Rodopi, 1997, 353 pp., is concerned with the relationship between the visual arts and French and German literature. Four of the contributions fall into our period: F. Krobb, 'Marginal daubings: On Wilhelm Raabe's graphic œuvre' (57–65); D. Müller, 'Self-portraits of the poet as a painter: Narratives on artists and the bounds between the arts (Hoffmann–Balzac–Stifter' (169–74); H. Bonnlander, 'The fictional tourist: The limits of the picturesque in the travel writings of Prince Hermann Pückler-Muskau (175–81); A. S. Coulson, 'Veit Harlan's *Immensee*: A study in the perversion of a literary classic' (277–86). Carol Diethe, *Towards Emancipation: German Women Writers of the Nineteenth Century*, NY–Oxford, Berghahn, x + 214 pp., provides brief introductions to the lives and works of 20 female writers seen against the backdrop of the changing political and social landscape of 19th-c. Germany. Some of them are well-known figures (A. v. Droste-Hülshoff, F. Lewald, E. Marlitt), but there are useful treatments of a number of less familiar names too (Henriette Herz, Caroline de la Motte Fouqué, Franziska zu Reventlow). The decision to opt for 'the biographical, historical and cultural approach' rather than 'the application of feminist theory' was a sound one, for straightforward factual accounts of the history of women's writing are still rare enough. Diethe's critical method is not ambitious; she gives us a brief biographical sketch of each of the women, and this is followed by plot summaries of their main works with a minimum of interpretative comment. She does however bring out well the irony that these women tended to accept the disadvantages that were forced upon them and in their novels and stories portrayed characters who conformed to the norms of society. Despite its limitations the book will be a useful source of factual information for future researchers in the field of women's writing. *Bildung und Konfession: Politik, Religion und literarische Identitätsbildung 1850–1918*, ed. M. Huber et al. (STSL, 59), 1996, v + 175 pp., publishes ten papers given at a colloquium held in Augsburg in 1995 to explore the role of German (and German-Swiss) literature and of religion in the formation of national identity and social class. Of the six contributions that are relevant to our period the most interesting are those of L. Forte, 'Lob der Faulheit: Muße und Müßiggang im 19. Jahrhundert' (79–93), who discusses texts of Büchner, Eichendorff and Stifter; and E. Sagarra, 'Fürsorgliche Obrigkeit und Lebenswirklichkeit: Die katholischen Dienstbotenzeitschriften Deutschlands 1832–1918' (95–106), who shows that the effort to control the minds of young Catholic servant girls through literature ironically had the effect of making them aware of their rights. The other four articles are: R. Paulin, ' "Shakespeare's allmähliches Bekanntwerden in Deutschland": Aspekte der Institutionalisierung Shakespeares 1840–1875' (9–20); M. Böhler, 'Nationalisierungsprozesse von Literatur im deutschsprachigen Raum: Verwerfungen und Brüche — vom Rande betrachtet' (21–38), on the Swiss and Austrian experience; J. Schönert, 'Die "bürgerlichen Tugenden" auf dem Prüfstand der Literatur: Zu Gottfried Kellers *Der grüne Heinrich*, *Die Leute von Seldwyla* und *Martin Salander*' (39–51); W. Hahl, 'Zur immanenten Theorie und Ästhetik des Erlebens in Gottfried Kellers *Der grüne Heinrich* (erste Fassung 1854/55)' (53–78). Harro Segeberg, *Literatur im technischen Zeitalter: Von der Aufklärung bis zum Beginn des Ersten Weltkriegs*, WBG, 1997, ix + 437 pp., is based on a lecture course first given by the author in Hamburg university in the early 1990s and on various of his publications since the late 1980s. The aim is to examine the way in which literature has both reflected and interacted with advances in technology from the late 17th c. up to 1914. The book is divided into three sections which reflect broadly different stages that Segeberg sees in the development of technological change and attitudes to it. The first section (17–95) covers the early period 1680–1830, and the third one (205–324) the modern age 1880–1914. The period 1830–1880 is treated in the second section (99–201). Here Segeberg underlines the ambivalence of the age, in which the hostility to technology that we encounter in the conservative Biedermeier novel contrasts with the adoption of 'panoramic' and 'photographic' techniques of presenting reality in literature (Gutzkow, Heine) and an enthusiastic welcome for such innovations as railways. Much is made of the damage done to book sales by the advent of illustrated magazines like the *Gartenlaube*. There is an index of names and one of motifs ('Bergbau', 'Eisenbahn', 'Photographie'). Segeberg has undoubtedly chosen an interesting topic to explore, but his book is not easy to read, partly because of the sheer bulk and complexity of the material (of which he is himself painfully aware) and partly because his style tends to the opaque. *Berliner Universität und deutsche Literaturgeschichte: Studien im Dreiländereck von Wissenschaft, Literatur und Publizistik*, ed. Gesine Bey (Berliner Beiträge zur Wissenschaftsgeschichte, 1), Frankfurt, Lang, 261 pp., studies the complex relationships between *Germanistik*, literary life and the press in Berlin in the period 1871–1945. Peter Lentwojt, *Die Loreley in ihrer Landschaft. Romantische Dichtungsallegorie und Klischee: Ein literarisches Sujet bei Brentano, Eichendorff, Heine und anderen* (EH, 1, 1664), 502 pp. *Beruf: Schriftstellerin. Schreibende Frauen im 18. und 19. Jahrhundert*, ed. K. Tebben, Göttingen, Vandenhoeck & Ruprecht, 340 pp., has the twofold aim of tracing the development of market conditions in Germany which made it possible for growing numbers of women to make a living from their writing instead of treating it as a mere hobby, and of providing profiles of ten leading female writers of prose fiction born in the 18th and 19th centuries. The editor contributes the introductory chapter on the social and cultural background, and there then follow ten generally good chapters by G. Loster-Schneider on Sophie von La Roche; E. Ramm on Isabella von Wallenrodt; A. Hahn on Therese Huber; K. v. Hammerstein on Sophie Mereau-Brentano; B. Wägenbaur on Fanny Tarnow; G. Schneider on Fanny Lewald; C. Tönnesen on Luise Mühlbach; C. Hobohm on Eugenie Marlitt; K. Tebben on Gabriele Reuter; and B. Balzer on Ricarda Huch. *Der Text im musikalischen Werk: Editionsprobleme aus musikwissenschaftlicher und literaturwissenschaftlicher Sicht*, ed. Walther Dürr et al. (Beihefte zur *ZDP*, 8), 416 pp., includes: J. Hein and D. Zumbusch-Beisteiner, 'Probleme der Edition "musikalischer Texte" im Wiener Dialekt, dargestellt am Beispiel Johann Nestroys' (212–32); J. Deathridge, 'Vollzugsbeamte oder Interpreten?: Zur Kritik der Quellenforschung bei Byron und Wagner' (263–74, on *Parsifal*); Ulrich Wyss, 'Die Inszenierung des Operntexts im Libretto' (275–83, on *Götterdämmerung*); W. Breig, 'Überlegungen zur Edition von Richard Wagners musikdramatischen Texten' (284–311). Jost Hermand, *Judentum und deutsche Kultur: Beispiele einer schmerzhaften Symbiose*, Cologne, Böhlau, 1996, 266 pp., republishes a number of articles by the author including: 'Unerwiderte Sympathie: Heinrich Heine und die Burschenschaften' (6–24); ' "Was ist des Deutschen Vaterland?": Ludwig Börne contra Wolfgang Menzel' (25–39); 'Zweierlei Geschichtsauffassung: Heines *Rabbi von Bacherach*' (40–50); 'Eine Geschichte aus dem Osten: *Der Pojaz* von Karl Emil Franzos' (51–70). *Kunstbefragung: 30 Jahre psychoanalytische Werkinterpretation am Berliner Psychoanalytischen Institut*, ed. G. Greve, Tübingen, Diskord, 1996, 320 pp., includes E. Lürssen, 'Büchners *Lenz*: Der psychotische Bruch mit der Realität oder das Scheitern an der Welt' (105–34); J. Matzner-Eicke,

'Eduard Mörike, "Um Mitternacht": Psychoanalytisches Deuten aus dem Zusammenspiel von metrisch-rhythmischer Form und Gehalt' (75–103); J. Wessel, 'Deichbau gegen den Untergang: Zur Abwehr von Todesangst in T. Storms Novelle *Der Schimmelreiter*' (155–76). Walter Grab, *Jakobinismus und Demokratie in Geschichte und Literatur: 14 Abhandlungen* (Forschungen zum Junghegelianismus, 2), Frankfurt, Lang, 267 pp., has 14 essays, including one each on Büchner and Freiligrath. Susanne Zantop, **Colonial Fantasies: Conquest, Family and Nation in Precolonial Germany, 1770–1870*, Duke U.P., 1997, 292 pp., has some discussion of popular literature. *Themes and Structures: Studies in German Literature from Goethe to the Present. A Fest. for Theodore Ziolkowski*, ed. A. Stephan, Columbia, SC, Camden House, 1997, viii + 332 pp., has: Ellis Finger, 'The poetry of Friedrich Rückert in the songs of Schubert, Schumann, and Mahler' (114–34); Otto W. Johnston, 'Chromatic symbolism in Gottfried Keller's *Romeo und Julia auf dem Dorfe*' (149–63). Paul Michael Lützeler, *Europäische Identität und Multikultur: Fallstudien zur deutschsprachigen Literatur seit der Romantik* (Stauffenburg Diskussion, 8), Tübingen, Stauffenburg, 1997, 198 pp., has a chapter on 'Jackson vs. Metternich: Karl Postls frühe Amerika- und Europa-Essays' (63–85). O. Briese, 'Der abgeleitete Blitz: Metapherngeschichte als Mentalitätsgeschichte', *Euphorion*, 92:413–35, investigates the metaphorical significance of lightning in a wide range of 18th-c. and 19th-c. authors including Heine, Wienbarg, Alexis, Droste-Hülshoff, and Auerbach. J. Pizer, 'The disintegration of Libussa', *GR*, 73:145–60, compares the treatment of the Libussa theme by Grillparzer, Brentano, J. K. A. Musäus and the Czech novelist Libuše Moníková. M. Zens, 'Die "Cathegorie der halb verbotenen Artikel [...]": Das Handlungsfeld Zensur im realistischen Paradigma' *WW*, 48:3–30, considers the role of censorship in the period 1850–1870. E. Lindner, 'Die Buchhändler und Verleger in der Paulskirche 1848–49', *Buchhandelsgeschichte*: B2–B12. M. Feldt, 'Die Stadt Berlin im Lyrikdiskurs: Überlegungen zur Genese und zu den drei Schwellenzeiten im 19. Jahrhundert', *DB*, 101:25–34.

MOVEMENTS AND PERIODS. *Forum Vormärz Forschung*, 3, 1997[1998], *1848 und der deutsche Vormärz*, is devoted in this year which marks the 150th anniversary of the *annus mirabilis* of 1848 entirely to literary reactions to the Revolution and has: P. Stein and F. Vassen, 'Dialog über eine Revolution: 1848 zwischen Vormärz und Nachmärz' (9–26); O. Briese, '"Jleechgültigkeit und rochen im Thierjarten": Tabak und Ekstase in den Rebellionen 1830 und 1848 (27–42); P. Hartmann, 'Geschichtsschreibung für die Gegenwart: Theodor Mundt und Ludolf Wienbarg' (43–54); L. Calvié, 'Karl Gutzkow et la révolution de 1848' (55–65); L. Lambrecht, 'À la recherche de la démocratie perdue: Eine Dokumentation am Beispiel von Karl Nauwerck' (67–84); W. Schmidt, 'Wilhelm Wolffs Artikel "Aus dem Reich" in der *Neuen Rheinischen Zeitung*' (85–115); M. Freund, '"Wenn die Zeiten gewaltsam laut werden [. . .] so kann es niemals fehlen, daß auch die Frauen ihre Stimme vernehmen und ihr gehorchen": Schriftstellerinnen und die Revolution von 1848–49' (117–42); K. Wilhelms, '"Sie schien ein Mann worden": Phantastische Frauen in Romanen der Revolution von 1848–49' (143–60); I. Fellrath, 'Georg Herwegh und das Spritzleder: Zur Genese eines Rufmordes und seine Folgen' (161–75); N. Gatter, '"1848. Vorsichtig!": Die "Sammlung Varnhagen" und die *Tageblätter* von Karl Varnhagen von Ense als Revolutionschronik. Mit einer ungedruckten diaristischen Beilage vom 20. März 1848' (177–205); C. Liedtke, '"Ich kann ertragen kaum den Duft der Sieger": Zur politischen Dichtung Heinrich Heines nach 1848' (207–23); T. Spreckelsen, '"Ist nicht der Karneval schon längst vorbei?": Der badische Aufstand in Carl Spindlers Roman *Putsch & Comp*' (225–35); M. Perraudin, 'Mörikes *Mozart auf der Reise nach Prag*, die französische Revolution und die Revolution von 1848' (237–57); H. Lengauer, 'Katalinarische Existenz: Mühen und Mutationen eines alten Achtundvierzigers im Nachmärz. Dargestellt an Ferdinand Kürnberger' (259–80); W. Beutin, 'Eines ungeratenen Vaters wohlgeratener Sohn schreibt die Geschichte des Jahres 1848–49' (281–96). *Vormärzliteratur in europäischer Perspektive*, II. *Politische Revolution — Industrielle Revolution — Ästhetische Revolution*, ed. Martina Lauster et al. (Studien zur Literatur des Vormärz, 2), Bielefeld, Aisthesis, 332 pp., is the second of three planned volumes on aspects of the *Vormärz* (for the first volume see *YWMLS*, 58:858–59). The originally stated intention of the project, which was to examine European — not only German literature — of the period from an interdisciplinary and comparative viewpoint, seems to have been changed because the focus of this volume is overwhelmingly on the German scene. The book is divided into three parts, dealing with political (especially Jewish) thought, the impact of industrialization, and the aesthetic revolution that followed the end of the 'Kunstperiode'. Each part opens with a helpful summary by Lauster of the main points covered by the papers that it contains, and access to the material is further improved by a full index of names and titles. The contributions are of mixed quality and too numerous to list in their entirety. Those likely to be of special interest to Germanists are: M. Perraudin, 'Heine und das revolutionäre Volk: Eine Frage der Identität' (41–55); E. Bourke, 'Carl Schurz und seine Radikalisierung durch die Ereignisse von 1848 bis 1851' (93–102, on a now almost forgotten figure); I. Hilton, 'Robert Prutz and the writer's crisis of conscience' (123–30); I. Oesterle, 'Bewegung und

Metropole: Ludwig Börne, "der gegenwärtigste aller Menschen, die sich je in den Straßen von Paris herumgetrieben haben"?' (179–206); H. Schmidt, 'Jungdeutsche Publizistik als "Ideenzirkulation": Ludwig Börnes *Ankündigung der Wage* und Theodor Mundts Essay *Zeitperspektive*' (207–28); T. Bremer, 'Revolution in der Kunst, Revolution in der Politik: Hugos Dramen, Büchner's Übersetzung und das Periodisierungsproblem in der Literaturgeschichte' (229–50), on Büchner's translations of Victor Hugo's *Marie Tudor* and *Lucrèce Borgia*); and M. Lauster, 'A cultural revolutionary: George Eliot's and Matthew Arnold's appreciation of Heinrich Heine' (281–313). A useful publication in the 150th anniversary year of the 1848 Revolution is Walter Grab, *Die Revolution von 1848/49: Eine Dokumentation* (UB, 9699), 279 pp., which reprints a selection of the most important manifestos, decrees, pamphlets, speeches and political poems of the time. J. Paech, '"Filmisches Schreiben" im Poetischen Realismus', *Mediengeschichte des Films*, ed. Harro Segeberg, Munich, Fink, 1, *Die Mobilisierung des Sehens: Zur Vor- und Frühgeschichte des Films in Literatur und Kunst*, 1996, 237–60. T. C. Kontje, 'Gender-bending in the Biedermeier', *WGY*, 12, 1996:53–69. G. Butzer and M. Günter, 'Der Wille zum Schönen: Deutscher Realismus und die Wirklichkeit der Literatur', *SLWU*, 79, 1997:54–77. R. Wolff, ' "[. . .] Kein Geistlicher hat ihn begleitet": Über Peinlichkeitsgefühle, Kitsch, Trivialität, Wunscherfüllungsphantasien und die Roman-Ästhetik des Realismus', *ib.*, 78–107. L. Calvié, 'Les travaux français sur le *Vormärz* de 1986 à 1996', *TI*, 11, 1996:226–49.

JOURNALS AND OTHER MEDIA. *Die Rundschau-Debatte 1877: Paul Lindaus Zeitschrift 'Nord und Süd' und Julius Rodenbergs 'Deutsche Rundschau'. Dokumentation*, ed. R. Berbig et al., Berne, Lang, 450 pp., gives an intriguing insight into the conflict that was sparked off in 1877 when Rodenberg, editor of the *Rundschau* which he had founded in 1874, suddenly discovered to his shock that Lindau was planning to start a rival literary journal to complement the more politically orientated *Die Gegenwart* which he had founded in 1872. Rodenberg feared there was not room for two directly competing literary journals and was determined to preserve the position of the *Rundschau* which had quickly established itself as the leading organ of its kind in the German-speaking world. The commercial rivalry was sharpened by the temperamental difference between the 'frivolous' Lindau and the circumspect Rodenberg. Both of them attempted to buttress their positions by recruiting the support of leading writers (Storm, Heyse, Auerbach) and academics (W. Scherer). The book falls into two main parts, the first of which is the introduction by the editor (17–75), who gives an account of the careers of the two protagonists, the history of the journals they edited, and the attitudes of those from whom they sought help. Interestingly, the writers, who depended on the editors to publish their work, tended to be cautious (Storm refused to become involved at all and Heyse tried to offend neither side), while the academics, with less to lose, proved more willing to enter the fray. The main part of the book is the *Dokumentation* (79–409) which reprints letters, diary-entries, and newspaper articles by a large number of people who were involved one way or another in the debate. Hildegard Kernmayer, *Judentum im Wiener Feuilleton (1848–1903): Exemplarische Untersuchungen zum literarischen und politischen Diskurs der Moderne* (CJ, 24), ix + 326 pp., has a lengthy theoretical introduction followed by detailed analyses of feuilleton texts by, among others, Moritz Gottlieb Saphir, Ferdinand Kürnberger, Friedrich Schlögl, Betty Paoli, Daniel Spitzer and Theodor Herzl. J. Schöberl, ' "Verzierende und erklärende Abbildungen": Wort und Bild in der illustrierten Familienzeitschrift des 19. Jahrhunderts am Beispiel der *Gartenlaube*', *Mediengeschichte des Films*, ed. Harro Segeberg, Munich, Fink, 1, *Die Mobilisierung des Sehens: Zur Vor- und Frühgeschichte des Films in Literatur und Kunst*, 1996, 209–36. A. Harnisch, 'Der Harem in Familienblättern des 19. Jahrhunderts: Koloniale Phantasien und nationale Identität', *GLL*, 51:325–41, examines how aspects of oriental life were portrayed in the pages of the *Gartenlaube* and *Daheim* during the *Gründerzeit* as a means of helping forge a German national identity. M. Günter and G. Butzer, 'Deutsch-schweizerische Literaturbeziehungen nach 1848 im Spiegel der Zeitschriften: Ein Beitrag zur interkulturellen Germanistik', *JDSG*, 42:214–41.

LYRIC. *Frankfurter Anthologie: Gedichte und Interpretationen*, xx, ed. M. Reich-Ranicki, Frankfurt–Leipzig, Insel, 1997, 293 pp., is a collection of interpretations by various critics all previously published in the *Frankfurter Allgemeine Zeitung*; it includes interpretations of poems by Droste-Hülshoff, Heine, and Meyer. Nicole Ahlers, *Das deutsche Versepos zwischen 1848 und 1914* (HBG, 26), 435 pp., discusses verse epics by Carl Spitteler, Robert Hamerlin, and Wilhelm Jordan. Heinrich Lassak, **Von Bonaparte bis Bismarck: Verfassungskämpfe im Spiegel politischer Lyrik*, Göttingen, Cuvillier, 1996, 224 pp. Günter Häntzschel, *Die deutschsprachigen Lyrikanthologien 1840 bis 1914: Sozialgeschichte der Lyrik des 19. Jahrhunderts* (Buchwissenschaftliche Beiträge aus dem Deutschen Bucharchiv München, 58), Wiesbaden, Harrassowitz, 1997, x + 471 pp.

NARRATIVE PROSE. Michael Minden, *The German Bildungsroman: Incest and Inheritance*, CUP, 1997, xi + 291 pp., is 'a study of the German *Bildungsroman* as a series of variations on Goethe's *Wilhelm Meisters Lehrjahre*'. The book is considerably influenced by late–20th-c. literary theory (Lacan, Derrida, Foucault) and Freudian psychoanalysis. The two texts which, in addition to Goethe's novel, play a pivotal part in the work are Keller's *Der grüne Heinrich*, and Stifter's *Der Nachsommer*; the other texts discussed are Wieland's *Agathon*, Moritz's *Anton Reiser*, Hölderlin's *Hyperion*, and Thomas Mann's *Der Zauberberg*. Minden's thesis, outlined in his Introduction, is that although the idea of *Bildung* is basically 'linear' the novels that he has selected for study are all in fact 'circular' in the sense that in each case the hero's journey of maturation and discovery leads him in the famous phrase of Novalis 'immer nach Hause'. The circularity of this return has both a feminine and a masculine aspect — feminine in that the protagonists' desire is embodied in women figures in whom Minden perceives 'a fundamental orientation upon the mother', and masculine in that they draw their material or spiritual inheritance from fathers or father figures. This thesis remains frankly rather puzzling to the present reviewer (which of course may merely reveal a personal limitation), but the interpretations of the individual novels follow more familiar paths and contain stimulating comment. Claudia Streit, *(Re-)Konstruktion von Familie im sozialen Roman des 19. Jahrhunderts* (MSLKD, 27), 1997, 247 pp., examines the portrayal of the family as the primary social unit in 16 novels, including works of L. Otto-Peters, Robert Prutz, F. Spielhagen and E. Wichert. Luc Herman, **Concepts of Realism* (SGLLC), 1996, x + 240 pp. Christine Anton, **Selbstreflexivität der Kunsttheorie in den Künstlernovellen des Realismus* (NASNCGL, 23), 227 pp. Claus-Michael Ort, *Zeichen und Zeit: Probleme des literarischen Realismus* (STSL, 64), vi + 252 pp., is concerned with the increasingly self-referential nature of Realist writing between 1840 and 1910. There are detailed analyses of texts by Storm, Fontane, and Sacher-Masoch among others. Winfried Freund, *Novelle* (UB, 17607), 348 pp., has an introductory first part, some 50 pages long, on the theory of the Novelle, followed by a much longer second part which surveys the historical development of the genre in a series of chapters covering all the major periods of German literature (e.g. Romanticism, *Restaurationszeit*, Poetic Realism). There are good, brief accounts of selected texts by all the important authors and also by not a few less well-known ones. The book should easily establish itself as a handy reference work. S. Weing, 'Aristotelian foundations of German novella theory', *Seminar*, 34:45–62, traces Aristotelian influence in the ideas of, among others, Feuchtersleben, Wilhelm Heinrich Riehl, Heyse, Storm and Spielhagen. C. Brecht, 'Die Muse der Geschichtsklitterung: Historismus, Realismus und literarische Moderne', *GR*, 73:203–19, revisits texts of Sir Walter Scott, Felix Dahn, Freytag, Alexis, Scheffel, and Raabe.

DRAMA. Manfred Brauneck, *Die Welt als Bühne: Geschichte des europäischen Theaters*, Stuttgart, Metzler, has added vol. II, *Zwischen Renaissance und Aufklärung — 18. Jahrhundert — Von der Romantik bis zum*

Beginn des Realismus, 1996, xviii + 1009 pp. + 107 coloured and 597 monochrome pls. The book is principally concerned with the 17th and 18th cs but also considers the changes in attitude and theatrical practice brought about by the advent of the industrial era in later 19th-c. Europe. Herbert Herzmann, *Tradition und Subversion: Das Volksstück und das epische Theater* (Stauffenburg Colloquium, 41), Tübingen, Stauffenburg, 1997, 214 pp., proposes the thought-provoking thesis that there is a continuous line of development which runs from Baroque theatre through Austrian popular theatre of the 18th and 19th centuries to Brecht's epic theatre and the new Austrian *Volksstück* of the 20th c. The *Altwiener Volkskomödie* is, he argues, a late offshoot of the Baroque age and in matters of form and technique more conservative than German Classical drama. And yet, because it is less abstract than Classical drama, it points the way to the future and, along with Büchner's plays, represents the only serious opposition to the aesthetic of German Idealism and its epigones. Its spirit reappears in the 20th c. in the work of Brecht and Austrian playwrights like Horváth, Felix Mitterer, and others. The thesis is a daring one and Herzmann drives the argument hard at times. A weakness in his case — one that he himself acknowledges — is that Brecht never once mentions the Viennese *Volkskomödie* among the predecessors of his epic theatre. Nevertheless, this is a stimulating, well-written and highly readable book. Part of its charm lies in the fact that Herzmann is not afraid to express unorthodox views, as when he claims that *Minna von Barnhelm*, *Der zerbrochene Krug*, and *Weh dem, der lügt* are far from being funny or comic in the way that Molière is. As so often, one regrets the lack of an index. H.-P. Bayerdörfer, 'Einakter mit Hilfe des Würfels? Zur Theatergeschichte der *Kleinen Formen* seit dem 18. Jahrhundert', *Kurzformen des Dramas: Gattungspoetische, epochenspezifische und funktionale Horizonte*, ed. W. Herget et al. (MFDT, 16), 1996, 31–57. Bettina Theben, *Maximilian Robespierre als literarische Figur im deutschen Drama zwischen Vormärz und Kaiserreich* (EH, 1, 1683), 277 pp., examines the portrayal of Robespierre in a large number of German dramas including Büchner's *Dantons Tod*. '*Und jedermann erwartet sich ein Fest': Fest Theater, Festspiele. Gesammelte Vorträge des Salzburger symposions 1995*, ed. P. Csobádi et al. (Wort und Musik, 31), Anif–Salzburg, Müller-Speiser, 1996, x + 765 pp., has three contributions relevant to our period: S. Vill, 'Kunstreligion und Lebenskunst: Zur Aktualität von Richard Wagners Bühnenweihfestspiel' (137–49); H. Thomke, 'Das nationale Festspiel in der Schweiz des 19. und 20. Jahrhunderts' (719–30 with comment on Keller's *Am Mythenstein*); S. B. Würffel, 'Festspiele und nationale Identität: Zur Geschichte der Festspielidee im bürgerlichen Zeitalter' (753–65 with some treatment of Heine and Wagner). Zhang, Yuan Zhi, *Der*

Legendenstoff des heiligen Genevova in dramatischen Bearbeitungen vom Barock bis zum Realismus (EH, 1, 1697), 230 pp., discusses among others the dramatizations of F. ('Maler') Müller, Tieck, Hebbel and Ludwig. Andrea Hofmann-Wellenhof, '[. . .] *das Stück scheint für die Darstellung auf dieser Bühne nicht geeignet': Schriftsteller und ihre am Burgtheater eingereichten Theaterstücke 1850–1870*, Vienna, Praesens, 1996, 296 pp. Dorothee Grill, **Tristan-Dramen des 19. Jahrhunderts* (GAG, 642), 1997, vi + 250 pp., is a 1995 Berlin dissertation. H. Thomé, 'Römertragödien des 19. Jahrhunderts: Ein vorläufiger Bericht', *Konflikt, Grenze, Dialog: Kulturkonstrastive und interdisziplinäre Textzugänge. Fest. für Horst Turk zum 60. Geburtstag*, ed. J. Lehmann, Frankfurt, Lang, 1997, 157–72.

REGIONAL LITERATURE. *The Austrian Comic Tradition: Essays in Honour of W. E. Yates*, ed. J. R. P. McKenzie et al. (*ASt*, 9), xviii + 279 pp., contains 15 articles of which the following ten are relevant to our period: L. A. Huish, 'An Austrian comic tradition?' (3–23); R. Robertson, 'Heroes in their underclothes: Alois Blumauer's travesty of Virgil's *Aeneid*' (24–40); I. F. Roe, 'The comedies of Johanna von Weissenthurn' (41–57); P. Branscombe, 'Nestroy and Schiller' (58–70); D. Zumbusch-Beisteiner, 'Music in Nestroy's plays (71–85); J. Hein, 'Nestroy's "epic" theatre' (86–101); W. Obermaier, 'Nestroy and slavery' (102–17); F. Walla, '"Crying out loud in silence": Social inequality in Nestroy's *Die Gleichheit der Jahre*' (118–29); J. R. P. McKenzie, 'Nestroy's *Zwey ewige Juden und Keiner*: A tale of three cities' (130–34); P. Skrine, 'Friedrich Halm and the comic muse' (145–59). Stefan Koslowski, *Stadttheater contra Schaubuden: Zur Basler Theatergeschichte des 19. Jahrhunderts* (Theatrum Helveticum, 3), Zurich, Chronos, 271 pp., provides an interesting insight into important aspects of Swiss theatre history, mainly the struggle to establish a serious theatre in competition with popular forms of entertainment such as the circus. Patricia K. Calkins, *Wo das Pulver liegt: Biedermeier Berlin as Reflected in Adolf Glassbrenner's 'Berliner Don Quixote'* (STML, 23), x + 219 pp., considers the light that Glassbrenner's short-lived journal (1832–33) throws on the cultural, political, and social concerns of Berlin's non-aristocratic classes. Joseph P. Strelka, *Mitte, Maß und Mitgefühl: Werke und Autoren der österreichischen Literaturlandschaft* (Literatur und Leben, 49), Vienna, Böhlau, 1997, 224 pp., devotes six of his 14 chapters to literature of our period. 'Die Sonderstellung der österreichischen innerhalb der gesamtdeutschsprachigen Literatur' (11–26) contrasts Stifter's *Der Nachsommer* with Fontane's *Der Stechlin*, while 'Ein österreichischer Exilroman des Jahres 1842: Ein Beitrag zum Problem des Josephinismus' (49–61) is concerned with F. E. Pipitz's novel *Der Jakobiner in Wien* (1842). Other chapters are: 'Die bukowinaösterreichische Literatur von 1848 bis zur Gegenwart' (27–48); 'Buddhistische Religiosität in der österreichischen Literatur von 1848 bis 1955' (61–73); '*Kishogues Fluch*: Zur Sprachkunst und Romankonzeption von Sealsfields *Kajütenbuch*' (75–85); and 'Altösterreichischer Erzähler zwischen Ost und West: Karl Emil Franzos' (87–98). Id., *Austroslavica: Die Slaven und Österreich in ihrer literarischen Wechselwirkung* (Edition Orpheus, 12), Tübingen, Stauffenburg, 1996, 257 pp., contains one essay relevant to our period, 'Eine breite Skala: Zum Bild der slavischen Menschen im Werk von Karl Emil Franzos' (15–33) with comment on various of F.'s novels and *Aus Halb-Asien*. Richard Reutner, *Lexikalische Studien zum Dialekt im Wiener Volksstück vor Nestroy* (Schriften zur deutschen Sprache in Österreich, 15), Frankfurt, Lang, 454 pp., analyses the use of Viennese dialect vocabulary in the works of N.'s predecessors Kringsteiner, Gleich, Meisl, and Bäuerle, and shows the originality that N.'s language brought to the tradition. *Geehrter Herr — lieber Freund: Schweizer Autoren und ihre deutschen Verleger*, ed. R. Luck et al., Basle–Frankfurt, Stroemfeld, 392 pp., was published to accompany an exhibition 'Lieber Herr und Freund': Schweizer Autorinnen und Autoren und ihre Deutschen Verleger' held in the Deutsche Bibliothek, Frankfurt, September 1998–January 1999. It contains four articles relevant to our period: H.-P. Holl, 'Jeremias Gotthelf und Julius Springer' (99–114); W. Morgenthaler, 'Gottfried Kellers Verleger — in 20 unveröffentlichten Briefen' (115–45); H. and R. Zeller, ' "Das wirklich bestehende Verhältnis eines Dichters zu seinem Verleger": C. F. Meyer und Hermann Haessel' (147–68); J. Villain, 'Johanna Spyri und ihre Verleger' (169–83). Rudolf Becker, *Ernst Elias Niebergall: Bilder aus einem unauffälligen Leben*, Darmstadt, Roether, 219 pp., gives a nicely illustrated account of the life and work of this minor Darmstadt writer of the *Restaurationszeit* who lived 1815–1843. Although he wrote a number of Novellen he is chiefly remembered for his dialect farce *Datterich: Localposse in der Mundart der Darmstädter* (1841). K. Habitzel, 'Die Wahrnehmung des "österreichischen" historischen Romans im Literatursystem des Vormärz', Daviau, *Literatur*, 640–51. H.-L. Worm, ' "Polnisch Blut" in der hessischen Trivialliteratur des 19. Jahrhunderts', *Orbis linguarum*, 6, 1997:305–12. J. Dewitz, 'Le *Volkstheater* de Munich: Symbole de l'identité bavaroise après 1848', *RG*, 28:33–53. M. Ritter, ' "Nichts als Wien!" Die Wiener Lokalskizze im Zeitalter des Biedermeier. Vom Alltagsbild (Franz Gräffer) zur Alltagssprache (Johann G. Seidel)', *Lenau-Jb.*, 24:49–66. S. P. Scheichl, 'Bissige Literatur — zahnloser Kanon: Zu Fragen der literarischen Tradition in Österreich', *Sprachkunst*, 28, 1997:247–74, looks again at the troublesome problem of a separate Austrian literary tradition and its canon.

K. Lipinski, 'Grenzgänger Gottes: Die Literatur und Kultur Galiziens', *JIG*, 29, 2, 1997[1998]:76–92, discusses a number of Jewish authors including K. E. Franzos and Joseph Roth.

2. INDIVIDUAL AUTHORS

AUERBACH. Regine Kress-Fricke, '*Wer mich einen Fremden heißt': Berthold Auerbachs Jahre in Karlsruhe*, Eggingen, Isele, 1996, 39 pp. W. Seidenspinner, 'Oralisierte Schriftlichkeit als Stil: Das literarische Genre Dorfgeschichte und die Kategorie Mündlichkeit', *IASL*, 22, 1997:36–51, has some discussion of A.'s *Schwarzwälder Dorfgeschichten*.

BIRCH-PFEIFFER. Birgit Pargner, *Zwischen Tränen und Kommerz: Das Rührtheater Charlotte Birch-Pfeiffers (1800–1868) in seiner künstlerischen und kommerziellen Verwertung*, Bielefeld, Aisthesis, 510 pp.

BÖRNE. B. Budde, 'Das literarische Ich als Seismograph oder von der Objektivität der Subjektivität: Zu Bs früher vormärzlicher Erzählprosa', *ZDP*, 117:210–28.

BÜCHNER. G. B. and F. L. Weidig, *Der hessische Landbote: Studienausgabe*, ed. G. Schaub (UB, 9486), 1996, 213 pp. *Ein Haus für Georg Büchner*, ed. H. Boehnke et al., Marburg, Jonas, 1997, 93 pp., has: B. Dedner, 'G. B. aus Goddelau' (7–22); L. Leonhard, 'Radierungen zum *Hessischen Landboten*' (30–39); G. Kummer, 'Von den Schwierigkeiten der Politik mit G. B. und seiner Geburtsstätte' (40–46); L. Leonard, 'Farbholzschnitte zu *Leonce und Lena*' (55–63); '"Ein Jahrtausendgenie": Wolf Biermann, Adolf Muschg, Peter Schneider und Karl Corino im Gespräch über G. B.' (64–70); K. Berg, 'G. B. ein hessischer Autor' (71–73); L. Leonhard, 'Zeichnungen zu *Dantons Tod*' (74–81). Jürgen Schwann, *Georg Büchners implizite Ästhetik: Rekonstruktion und Situierung im ästhetischen Diskurs* (MBSL, 35), 1997, 339 pp., explores the philosophical and political context of B.'s 'implicit' asthetic and establishes links with Goethe, Lenz, Wieland, Diderot, and Ovid; a new interpretation of *Lenz* is also offered. Andreas Erb, *Georg Büchner, 'Lenz': Eine Erzählung*, Munich, Oldenbourg, 1997, 135 pp., publishes the text using the new orthography and adds an interpretation of it. James Crighton, *Büchner and Madness: Schizophrenia in Georg Büchner's 'Lenz' and 'Woyzeck'* (Bristol German Studies, 9), Lewiston, NY, Mellen, 318 pp., examines the text as both Germanist and experienced medical practitioner. Hubert Gersch, **Der Text, der (produktive) Unverstand des Abschreibers und die Literaturgeschichte: Johann Friedrich Oberlins Bericht 'Herr L . . .' und die Textüberlieferung bis zu Georg Büchners 'Lenz'-Entwurf* (Büchner-Studien, 7), Tübingen, Niemeyer, ix + 198 pp. John Walker, 'The tradition of Enlightment and the tradition of Empathy: Büchner and the legacy of classical German drama', *London Ger. St. VI*, 147–64, is concerned principally with *Dantons Tod*. H. Knoll, 'Schwermütige Revolten: Melancholie bei G. B.', *Protomoderne: Künstlerische Formen überlieferter Gegenwart*, ed. C. Hilmes et al., Bielefeld, Aisthesis, 1996, 99–112. B. Dedner, 'Die Darstellung von Quellenabhängigkeiten anhand von Beispielen', *Editio*, 11, 1997:97–115, uses illustrative examples from *Dantons Tod* and *Lenz*. K. Sanada, 'Solipsistisches Mitleid und Märchenmotive: G. Bs *Lenz* im Vergleich mit Ludwig Tiecks *Der blonde Eckbert*', *DB*, 100:142–49. L. Ginters, 'G. B.'s *Dantons Tod*: History and her story on the stage', *ModD*, 39, 1996:650–67. T. Kamio, 'Hieroglyphen des Körpers: Zu den "Maschinen" in Bs *Lenz*', *Literatur und Kulturhermeneutik: Beiträge des Tateshina-Symposien 1994 und 1995*, Munich, Iudicium, 1996, 227–49. H. Schmidt, 'Die Apokalypse des melancholischen Bewußtseins im Gebirge: Zur Verschränkung psychotischen Weltuntergangserlebens und katastrophischer Natur in G. Bs *Lenz*', *Apokalytische Visionen in der deutschen Literatur*, ed. J. Jabłowska, Łódź U.P., 1996, 152–69. H. Knoll, 'Schwermütige Revolten: Melancholie bei G. B.', *Protomoderne: Künstlerische Formen überlieferter Gegenwart*, ed. C. Hilmes et al., Bielefeld, Aisthesis, 1996, 99–112. C. Pornschlegel, 'Das Drama des Souffleurs: Zur Dekonstitution des Volks in den Texten G. Bs', *Poststrukturalismus: Herausforderung an die Literaturwissenschaft. DFG-Symposium 1995*, ed. G. Neumann (Germanistische Symposien, Berichtsbände, 17), Stuttgart, Metzler, 1997, 557–74. F. Cercignani, 'G. B. e l'incubo della follia', *Studia Theodisca*, IV, ed. F. Cercignani, Milan, Edizioni Minute, 1997, 207–34. T. Elm, 'G. B. und Leopold Ranke: Poetische und historische Erkenntnis der Geschichte', *Hermenautik – Hermeneutik: Literarische und geisteswissenschaftliche Beiträge zu Ehren von Peter Horst Neumann*, ed. H. Helbig et al., Würzburg, Königshausen & Neumann, 1996, 163–78. H.-P. Nowitzki, ' "Halt, ist der Schluß logisch?": Zu Bs anamorphotischer Poesiekonzeption', *Euphorion*, 92:309–30. H. Schmidt, 'Schizophrenie oder Melancholie? Zur Differentialdiagnostik in G. Bs *Lenz*', *ZDP*, 117:516–42. D. Goltschnigg, 'Briefe Hofmannsthals, Alfred Rollers und Eugen Kilians zur Uraufführung von Bs *Wozzeck* am Münchener Residenztheater 1913', *Hofmannsthal-Jb.*, 6:117–27. K. Sanada, 'Solipsistisches Mitleid und Märchenmotive: G. Bs *Lenz* im Vergleich mit Tiecks *Der blonde Eckbert*', *DB*, 100:142–49.

BURCKHARDT. J. Grosse, 'Die Verteidigung der Vergangenheit: J. Bs anderer Geschichtsmoralismus,' *DVLG*, 72:637–81.

BUSCH. W. B., *Der Schmetterling*, ed. C. Jenny-Ebeling, Zurich, Manesse, 1997[1998], 114 pp., reprints the text of B.'s last prose work, the symbolic and allegorical tale of 1895, and his accompanying illustrations. Gottfried Willems, *Abschied vom Wahren — Schönen — Guten: Wilhelm Busch und die Anfänge der ästhetischen Moderne* (Jenaer

Germanistische Forschungen, n.F., 3), Heidelberg, Winter, iv + 257 pp.

DIEPENBROCK, CONRAD JOSEPH. Werner Schneider, *Leben und Werk des Revolutionärs und Schriftstellers Conrad Joseph Diefenbrock* (HKADL, 21), 732 pp.

DROSTE-HÜLSHOFF. A. v. D.-H., *Historisch-kritische Ausgabe. Werke, Briefwechsel*, ed. Winfried Woesler, Tübingen, Niemeyer, has added 1, 2, *Gedichte zu Lebzeiten. Dokumentation. Erster Teil*, ed. W. Theiss, 1997, ix + 927 pp.; 1, 3, *Gedichte zu Lebzeiten. Dokumentation. Zweiter Teil*, ed. W. Theiss, viii + 752 pp.; II, 2, *Gedichte aus dem Nachlaß. Dokumentation*, ed. B. Kortländer, xi + 685 pp.; VII, *Literarische Mitarbeit, Aufzeichnungen, Biographisches*, ed. Ortrun Niethammer, xiii + 839 pp.; IX, 2, *Briefe 1839–42. Kommentar*, ed. J. Grywatsch, 1997, ix + 989 pp. A. v. D.-H., *Sämtliche Gedichte*, ed. Karl S. Kemminghausen, Frankfurt, Insel, 721 pp. Annette von Droste-Hülshoff. *Der Distel mystische Rose: Ein Lesebuch. Gedichte und Briefe*, ed. W. Fritsch (IT, 2193), 170 pp. Winfried Freund, *Annette von Droste-Hülshoff* (DTV, 31002), 159 pp. Ingrid Kessl, **Zauberwelt im eigenen Kopf: Das Leben der Dichterin Annette von Droste-Hülshoff* (Frieling Biographie), Berlin, Frieling, 1996, 112 pp. W. Gödden, **Annette von Droste-Hülshoff unterwegs: Auf den Spuren der Dichterin durch Westfalen*, Münster, Ardey, 1996, 188 pp. Wilderich Freiherr Droste zu Hülshoff, **Annette von Droste-Hülshoff im Spannungsfeld ihrer Familie* (Aus dem Deutschen Adelsarchiv, 16), Limburg, Starke, 296 pp. Andrea Rösler, *Vom Gotteslob zum Gottesdank: Bedeutungswandel in der Lyrik von Friedrich Spee zu Joseph von Eichendorff und Annette von Droste-Hülshoff*, Paderborn, Schöningh, 1997, 368 pp., traces a strand of religious thought through the Biblical *Book of Psalms*, the *Confessions* of St Augustine, the *Trutznachtigall* of Spee, the *Geistliche Gedichte* of Eichendorff, and A. v. D.-H.'s *Das Geistliche Jahr*. Considerable emphasis is placed on the morbid awareness of suffering and sense of guilt in Droste's cycle. *Dialoge mit der Droste: Kolloquium zum 200. Geburtstag von Annette von Droste-Hülshoff*, ed. Ernst Ribbat, Paderborn–Munich, Schöningh, 318 pp., publishes the papers given at an interdisciplinary colloquium held in Münster in January 1997 to mark the bicentenary of D.-H.'s birth (and the 150th anniversary of her death in 1998). The 13 contributions, which represent the disciplines of history and theology as well as *Germanistik* and are of generally good quality, are: B. Kortländer, 'Vergleiche im Unvergleichlichen: A. v. D.-H. und Heinrich Heine' (9–24): M. Botzenhart, 'Westfalen in der ersten Hälfte des 19. Jahrhunderts' (25–37, on the political, economic, and social background to *Die Judenbuche*); P. Dollinger, 'Literarische Salons der Biedermeier- und Vormärzzeit: Beteiligung und Distanzierung der A. v. D.-H.' (39–69, on her preference for small, informal gatherings with like-minded female friends); L. Köhn, ' "Was ist die Liebe?" Ein problemgeschichtliches Rätsel in der Prosa der Restaurationszeit und im Werk der D.' (71–93, on the for the time unusually bleak view of love in *Die Judenbuche*); J. Werbick, ' "Ist denn der Glaube nur dein Gotteshauch? Theologische Bemerkungen zum Glaubensverständnis der A. v. D.-H. im *Geistlichen Jahr*' (95–111); M. Schumacher, 'A. v. D.-H. und die Tradition: Das *Geistliche Jahr* in literarhistorischer Sicht' (113–45); M. Wagner-Egelhaaf, 'Grenz-Rede: A. v. D.-Hs "Klänge aus dem Orient" ' (147–64); W. Rohe, 'Schiffbruch und Moral: A. v. D.-Hs "Die Vergeltung" ' (165–83); H. Heselhaus, ' "Hier möcht' ich Haidebilder schreiben": A. v. D.-Hs Poetisierung der Naturgeschichte' (185–208); R. v. Heydebrandt, 'Geschichte vom Schreiben: A. v. D.-Hs *Bey uns zu Lande auf dem Lande*' (209–29); E. Ribbat, 'Stimmen und Schriften: Zum Sprachbewußtsein in den *Haidebildern* und in der *Judenbuche*' (231–47); A. Kilcher and D. Kremer, 'Romantische Korrespondenzen und jüdische Schriftmagie in Ds *Judenbuche*' (249–61, on links between the Novelle and traditions of Jewish thought); W. Gödden, ' "Das Jahr geht um/ [. . .] Ich harre stumm": Bilanz eines D.-Jahres' (263–91, on events of the anniversary year). *Annette von Droste-Hülshoff (1797–1848): 'aber nach hundert Jahren möcht ich gelesen werden'*, ed. Bodo Plachta (Schriften der Universitäts- und Landesbibliothek Münster, 16 — Staatsbibliothek zu Berlin, Preußischer Kulturbesitz, Ausstellungskataloge, n.F., 23), Wiesbaden, Reichert, 1997, 316 pp., has: R. Schneider, 'Das künstlerische Selbtverständnis der D. im Horizont ihrer Zeit' (3–11); H. Brandes, ' "Dichter, Verleger, und Blaustrümpfe": Über A. v. D.-Hs Lustspiel *Perdu!*' (12–19); H. Kraft, 'Ein Leben mit Zillah' (20–23); M. Zywietz, ' "Wer nie sein Brod in Thränen aß ": Anmerkungen zur Liedästhetik A. v. D.-Hs' (24–31); W. Jung, 'Timo im Moor: A. v. D.-Hs "Der Knabe im Moor" und "Die Moorgeister" von Angela Sommer-Bodenburg: Überlegungen zu einem produktionsorientierten Deutschunterricht' (32–40); R. Nutt-Kofoth, 'Werkrepräsentation und Autorbild: Die postumen Ausgaben der Werke A. v. D.-Hs' (41–52); W. Woesler, 'Droste-Forschung in Münster' (53–56); J. Thamer, 'Bildnis und Bild der A. v. D.-H.' (57–71); H.-G. Koch, ' "Nicht fröhnen mag ich kurzem Ruhme . . .": Kollegialer Nachruhm einer Dichterin "von Gottes Gnaden" ' (72–76); U. Willer, 'Illustrationen zur *Judenbuche* A. v. D.-Hs' (77–82). *Annette von Droste-Hülshoff zum 200. Geburtstag: Katalog zur Ausstellung von 170 Künstlerarbeiten zu Person, Leben und Werk der Dichterin*, ed. L. Folkerts, Münster, Burlage, 1996, 256 pp. G. Sautermeister, 'Die Lyrik A. v. D.-Hs: Eine sozialgeschichtliche Skizze', *Literaturtheorie und Geschichte: Zur Diskussion materialistischer Literaturwissenschaft*, ed. R. Scholz et al., Opladen, Westdeutscher Vlg, 1996, 310–31. Hannes Fricke, '*Niemand wird lesen, was ich hier schreibe':* Über den Niemand in der Literatur, Göttingen, Wallstein, 560 pp., has some discussion of *Die Judenbuche.* C. Rieb, ' "Ich kann nichts davon oder dazu tun": Zur Fiktion der Berichterstattung in A. v. D.-Hs *Judenbuche', Erzähler, Erzählen, Erzähltes: Fest. der Marbacher Arbeitsgruppe Narrativik für Rudolf Freudenberg zum 65. Geburtstag,* ed. W. Brandt, Stuttgart, Steiner, 1996, 47–65. W. Woesler, 'Eine Claudius-Reminiszenz der Droste', *Jahresschriften Claudius-Ges.,* 6, 1997:5–9. B. Bianchi, 'L'esclusione e il trionfo: Scrittura del limite nel *Geistliches Jahr* della Droste', *Studia Theodisca,* IV, ed. F. Cercignani, Milan, Edizioni Minute, 1997, 59–104.

EBNER-ESCHENBACH. M. v. E.-E., *Tagebücher,* VI, *1906–1916,* ed. K. K. Polheim et al., Tübingen, Niemeyer, 1997, 412 pp., covers the last years of E.-E.'s life. There is to be a supplementary vol. containing a commentary and index to the set. Edith Toegel, *Marie von Ebner-Eschenbach: Leben und Werk* (Austrian Culture, 25), NY, Lang, 1997, vii + 150 pp., is a straightforward but competent critical biography by an experienced student of E.-E. It covers E.-E.'s life, her early literary attempts, her unsuccessful struggles with the dramatic form, her subsequent success with prose fiction, and her aphorisms and autobiographical writings. Doris M. Klostermaier, *Marie von Ebner-Eschenbach: The Victory of a Tenacious Will* (Studies in Austrian Culture and Thought), Riverside, Ariadne, 1997, xvi + 348 pp., is a naive, chatty, and over-long attempt at a biography of E.-E., made fully redundant by Toegel's book. Sybil von Schönfeldt, **Marie von Ebner-Eschenbach: Dichterin mit dem Scharfblick des Herzens,* Stuttgart, Quell, 1997, 311 pp. *Des Mitleids tiefe Liebesfähigkeit: Zum Werk der Marie von Ebner-Eschenbach,* ed. J. Strelka (New Yorker Beiträge zur Österreichischen Literaturgeschichte, 7), Berne, Lang, 1997, 265 pp., has: F. Schüppen, 'Bürgerlicher Realismus in E.-Es *Božena* (1876)' (13–55); G. Brokoph-Mauch, ' "Die Frauen haben nichts als die Liebe": Variationen zum Thema Liebe in den Erzählungen der M. v. E.-E.' (57–76); N. Gabriel, ' "[. . .] daß die Frauen in Deutschland durchaus Kinder bleiben müssen [. . .]": Die Tagebücher der M. v. E.-E.' (77–95); A. Meštan, 'M. v. E.-E. und die Tschechen' (97–109); H. Zeman, 'Ethos und Wirklichkeitsdarstellung: Gedanken zur literaturgeschichtlichen Position M. v. E.-Es' (111–18); W. Bauer, 'Falsche Analogie: Vermenschlichung und Säkularisation in den Tiergeschichten der M. v. E.-E.' (121–42, on *Krambambuli);* B. Bittrich, ' "Uneröffnet zu verbrennen": Ein spätes Meisterwerk der E.-E.' (143–54); N. S. Pavlova, 'Der Konflikt als Grundstruktur in der Novellistik von M. v. E.-E. und Jeremias Gotthelf' (155–61); L. Roberts, '*Unsühnbar* und Hawthornes *The Scarlet Letter*' (163–79); G. Marahrens, 'Über den Werte-Kosmos der *Aphorismen* von M. v.

E.-E.' (183–217); A. Stillmark, 'E.-E. und Turgenjew: Eine Begegnung im Prosagedicht' (219–37); K. Weissenberger, '*Meine Kinderjahre. M. v. E.*-Es Autobiographie als literarisches Kunstwerk' (239–65). C. Girardi, ' "Alte Schlösser lieb ich [. . .]": Mährische Salonkultur am Beginn der literarischen Moderne. Briefe von M. v. E.-E. und Richard Smekal', *Beiträge zu Komparatistik und Sozialgeschichte der Literatur: Fest. für Alberto Martino*, ed. N. Bachleitner et al. (*Chloe*, 26), Amsterdam, Rodopi, 1997, 741–78.

FONTANE. The Munich edition of F.'s *Werke, Schriften und Briefe*, ed. W. Keitel et al., Munich, Hanser, has added Abt. III, 3, *Reiseberichte und Tagebücher*. 2. *Halbband, Tagebücher*, ed. H. Nürnberger et al., 1997, 772 pp. T. F., *Wanderungen durch die Mark Brandenburg*, ed. G. Erler et al., Berlin, Aufbau, has been completed by the addition of vol. 8, *Personenregister, geographisches Register*, ed. R. Reuter, 1997, 448 pp. T. F., *Von Zwanzig bis Dreißig: Autobiographisches*, ed. O. Drude, Frankfurt, Insel, 1997, 467 pp. T. F., *Briefe: Ausgabe in fünf Bänden*, ed. H. Nürnberger et al. (DTV, 59037), 4240 pp. T. F., *Gedichte in einem Band*, ed. O. Drude, Frankfurt, Insel, 751 pp. T. F., *Gedichte*, ed. K. Richter (UB, 6956), 211 pp. T. F., *Gedichte*, ed. R. Görner (IT, 2221), 208 pp. *Theodor Fontane und Friedrich Eggers: Der Briefwechsel. Mit Fontanes Briefen an Karl Eggers und der Korrespondenz von Friedrich Eggers mit Emilie Fontane*, ed. Roland Berbig (Schriften der Theodor Fontane Gesellschaft, 2), Berlin–NY, de Gruyter, 1997, xi + 521 pp. + 20 pls., fills an important gap in our picture of the literary and cultural world of 19th-c. Germany. The scholarship here is meticulous and the book very nicely printed and illustrated, as one would expect from this leading F. expert and this respected publisher. Berbig's introduction (1–65) gives an account of the life and career of Friedrich Eggers as art historian, man of letters, and editor. There then follow the correspondence between F. and Eggers with 99 letters written over a period of half a century; the 79 letters and postcards sent by F. to Eggers's younger brother Karl between 1871 and 1898; and the 14 letters exchanged by Eggers and F.'s wife Emilie between 1854 and 1870. By far the most important of the correspondences is that between F. and Friedrich Eggers which occupies half the book and which is here published in full and reliable form for the first time; 17 of the letters have not been printed before and many corrections have been made to those which have. Berbig has added numerous explanatory footnotes throughout. The book also contains F.'s articles on the Eggers brothers in the *Vossische Zeitung*, occasional poems by F. and Eggers, useful time charts and lists of publications by and about the two Eggers brothers, and an annotated index of persons and journals mentioned in the texts.

H. Nürnberger, *Fontanes Welt*, Berlin, Siedler, 1997, 446 pp.
Wolfgang Hädecke, *Theodor Fontane: Biographie*, Munich, Hanser,
445 pp. T. F., *Die Saison hat glänzend begonnen: Theaterkritiken*, ed.
P. Goldammer, Berlin, Aufbau, 207 pp., reprints 50 of the total of
over 600 reviews that F. wrote as theatre critic for the *Vossische Zeitung*.
Gisela Heller, **'Geliebter Herzensmann [. . .]': Emilie und Theodor Fontane*,
Berlin, Nicolai, 351 pp. Cord Beintmann, *Theodor Fontane* (DTV,
31003), 155 pp. Otto Drude, **Fontane und sein Berlin: Personen, Häuser,
Straßen*, Frankfurt, Insel, 415 pp. *Mit Fontane durch die Mark Brandenburg*,
ed. O. Drude (IT, 1798), 219 pp. *Mit Fontane durch England und
Schottland*, ed. O. Drude (IT, 2222), 115 pp. Heinz Ohff, **Theodor
Fontane: Leben und Werk* (SPi, 2657), 462 pp. Hanjo Kesting, **Theodor
Fontane: Bürgerlichkeit und Lebensmusik* (Göttinger Sudelblätter), Göt-
tingen, Wallstein, 62 pp. Hans Blumenberg, **Gerade noch Klassiker:
Glossen zu Fontane*, Munich–Vienna, Hanser, 159 pp. Christian Grawe,
Fontane-Chronik (UB, 9721), 313 pp., traces the day-to-day course of
F.'s life from his birth on 30 December 1819 to his death on 20
September 1898. Grawe draws extensively on the letters and diaries
so that it is as far as possible F.'s own voice that is heard. The book
replaces H. Fricke's *Theodor Fontane: Chronik seines Lebens* of 1960. It will
be warmly welcomed by all F. scholars as a useful and reliable source
of factual information. Marion Doebeling, **Theodor Fontane im Gegen-
licht: ein Beitrag zur Essay- und Romantheorie*, Würzburg, Königshausen
& Neumann, 1997, 204 pp. Hugo Aust, *Theodor Fontane: Ein Studienbuch*
(UTB, 1988), Tübingen, Francke, 250 pp., provides a rapid and
convenient means of orientation in F. studies. Michael Scheffel,
**Formen selbstreflexiven Erzählens: Eine Typologie und sechs exemplarische
Analysen* (SDL, 145), 1997, vi +285 pp., is a Göttingen *Habilitationsschrift* with a theoretical first part which attempts a typology of
various forms of self-reflection in narrative fiction. The second part
then offers analyses of six German texts from the 18th c. to the present
day; it includes a chapter on Fontane. Agni Daffa, **Frauenbilder in den
Romanen 'Stine' und 'Mathilde Möhring': Untersuchungen zu Fontane*
(GANDLL, 19), 309 pp. Julia Encke, **Bürgerliche Zitierkultur in den
späten Romanen Fontanes und Flauberts* (MSLKD, 29), 120 pp., investigates the influence of the increasingly popular 19th-c. dictionaries of
quotations on F.'s novels, especially *Der Stechlin*. Roman Paul,
**Fontanes Wortkunst: Von 'Angstmeierschaft' bis 'Zivil-Wallenstein' — ein
blinder Fleck der Realismusforschung* (Frankfurter Forschungen zur Kul-
tur- und Sprachwissenschaft, 2), Frankfurt, Lang, 180 pp., is concerned with F.'s numerous neologisms. Susan Wansink, *Female Victims
and Oppressors in Novels by Theodor Fontane and François Mauriac* (Currents
in Comparative Romance Languages and Literatures, 53), NY, Lang,
139 pp., focuses on the parallels between *Effi Briest* and *Thérèse*

Desqueyroux, and *Frau Jenny Treibel* and *Genitrix*. Rudolf Helmstetter, *Die Geburt des Realismus aus dem Dunst des Familienblattes: Fontane und die öffentlichkeitsgeschichtlichen Rahmenbedinungen des Poetischen Realismus*, Munich, Fink, 295 pp. Christine Kretschmer, *Der ästhetische Gegenstand und das ästhetische Urteil in den Romanen Theodor Fontanes* (EH, I, 1637), 1997, 256 pp. Harald Tanzer, *Theodor Fontanes Berliner Doppelroman: 'Die Poggenpuhls' und 'Mathilde Möhring'. Ein Erzählkunstwerk zwischen Tradition und Moderation*, Paderborn, Igel, 1997, 304 pp., is a 1996 Regensburg dissertation. Ulrike Hanraths, *Bilderfluchten: Weiblichkeitsbilder in Fontanes Romanen und im wissenschaftlichen Diskurs seiner Zeit*, Aachen, Shaker, 1997, 231 pp., is a Düsseldorf dissertation. Sylvain Guarda, *Schach von Wuthenow, Die Poggenpuhls und Der Stechlin: Fontanes innere Reisen in die Unterwelt*, Würzburg, Königshausen & Neumann, 1997, 113 pp. Birgit A. Jensen, *Auf der morschen Gartenschaukel: Kindheit als Problem beit Theodor Fontane* (APSL, 132), 178 pp.

Fontane-Blätter, 65–66, is chiefly concerned with biographical and autobiographical elements in F.'s writing and has: R. Berbig, '*Der Dichter Firdusi* — "sehr gut": Zu T. Fs Lektüre des *Romanzero* von Heine. Begleitumstände mit einem detektivischen Diskurs' (10–53); C. Hehle, ' "Der Altmoabiter hat Recht, aber auch Unrecht": Ein unbekannter Brief Fs aus dem *Berliner Tageblatt*' (54–56); P. Wruck, 'Die "wunden Punkte" in Fs Biographie und ihre autobiographische Euphemisierung' (61–71); W. Wülfing, ' "Aber nur dem Auge des Geweihten sichtbar": Mythisierende Strukturen in Fs Narrationen' (72–86); M. Masanetz, 'Vom Ur-Sprung des Pegasus: *Meine Kinderjahre* oder die schwere Geburt des Genies' (87–124); R. Dieterle, 'Die "Insel der Seligen": Stationen einer Vater-Tochter-Beziehung" (125–137); C. Grawe, ' "Die wahre hohe Schule der Zweideutigkeit": Frivolität und ihre autobiographische Komponente in Fs Erzählwerk' (138–62); H. Fischer, 'T. Fs *Achtzehnter März*: Neues zu einem alten Thema' (163–87); S. Neuhaus, 'Und nichts als die Wahrheit? Wie der Journalist F. Erlebtes wiedergab' (188–213); R. Berbig, 'Kein Ort für ein Ich? Zum autobiographischen Diskurs in Fs England-Tagebüchern 1852 bis 1858' (214–33); J. Osborne, 'Autobiographisches als Nebenprodukt zu Fs Kriegsbüchern' (234–45); R. Muhs, 'F., Marx und Freiligrath: Überlegungen zu ihrer Beziehungslosigkeit' (246–65); M. Thuret, 'Bedenkliche Nachrufe: F. als Biograph seines *Tunnel*-Kreises' (266–84); S. Greif, 'Tunnelfahrt mit Lichtblick; Fs anekdotische Künstlerbiographien' (285–99); P. I. Anderson, 'Von "Selbstgesprächen" zu "Text-Paradigma": Über den Status von Fs Versteckspielen' (300–17); H. Streiter-Buscher, 'Das letzte Wort: Autobiographische Spiegelungen im *Stechlin*' (318–45); M. Scheffel, 'Auto(r)reflexionen in T. Fs *Die Poggenpuhls*' (346–63); L. Berg-Ehlers, ' "Um neun Uhr ist alles aus": Nachrufe und Gedenkartikel für T. F.

in deutschen Zeitungen' (366–417); P. Schaefer, 'Auswahlbibliographie: Neuerscheinungen und -erwerbungen des F.-Archivs bis Mai 1998' (426–48). *Theodor Fontane und Thomas Mann: Die Vorträge Des Internationalen Kolloquiums in Lübeck 1997*, ed. Eckhart Heftrich et al. (TMS, 18), 291 pp., is an important publication containing 12 articles by leading experts on F. and Mann of which 11 are relevant to F.: E. Heftrich, 'T. F. und T. M.: Legitimation eines Vergleichs' (9–23); E. Sagarra, 'Intertextualität als Zeitkommentar: T. F., Gustav Freytag und T. M. oder: Juden und Jesuiten' (25–47); H. Nürnberger, '"Hohenzollernwetter" oder Fünf Monarchen suchen einen Autor: Überlegungen zu Fs politischer und literarischer Biographie' (49–76); P. Pütz, '"Der Geist der Erzählung": Zur Poetik Fs und T. Ms' (99–111); R. Wimmer, 'T. F. und T. M. im Dialog' (112–34); M. Swales, '"Nimm doch vorher eine Tasse Tee [. . .]": Humor und Ironie bei T. F. und T. M.' (135–48); M. Neumann, 'Eine Frage des Stils: Keller — F. — T. M.' (149–67); M. Dierks, 'Reisen in die eigene Tiefe — nach Kessin, Altershausen und Pompeij' (169–86); H. Aust, 'Künstlerisch betreute Privatheit: T. Fs und T. Ms Briefe an Frau, Tochter und Freundin' (187–216); D. Borchmeyer, 'F., T. M. und das "Dreigestirn" Schopenhauer — Wagner — Nietzsche' (217–48); H. R. Vaget, 'F., Wagner, T. M: Zu den Anfängen des modernen Romans in Deutschland' (249–74). Michael Scheffel, 'Drama und Theater im Erzählwerk T. Fs', *Aspekte des politischen Theaters und Dramas von Calderón bis Georg Seidel: Deutsch-französische Perspektiven (JIB, A, Kongreßberichte, 40)*, ed. H. Turk et al., Berne, Lang, 1996, 221–27. K. Haberkamm, 'Links und rechts: Nochmals zur Symbolik der "Verführungsszene" in Fs *Effi Briest*', *Eros, Ehe, Ehebruch* (Spektrum Literatur. Literarische Abende zu menschlichen Themen, 2), Münster, Regensberg–Münster U.P., 1997, 58–75. B. Holbeche, 'Mother and daughter: A key relationship in F.'s *Effi Briest*', *Fest. Marson*, 37–56. D. Krohn, 'Wer hat eigentlich Mitleid mit Innstetten in Fs *Effi Briest*', *Fest. Härd*, 157–64. R. Lotz, 'Opfer der Ehe: Eine vergleichende Untersuchung zu Form und Wirksamkeit von ethischen Konzepten in T. Fs *Effi Briest* und Premchands *Nirmala*', *Kulturelle Identität: Deutsch-indische Kulturkontakte in Literatur, Religion und Politik*, ed. H. Turk et al., Berlin, Schmidt, 1997, 191–208. J. Wertheimer, 'Hierarchien des Lachens: Machtstrukturen der Affektäußerung im Roman des 19. Jahrhunderts', *Semiotik, Rhetorik und Soziologie des Lachens: Vergleichende Studien zum Funktionswandel des Lachens vom Mittelalter zur Gegenwart*, ed. L. Fietz et al., Tübingen, Niemeyer, 1996, 312–24, is principally concerned with *Effi Briest* and *L'Adultera*. P.-P. Sagave, 'T. F. und die Pariser Kommune: Von der Reportage zum Dichtwerk', *Konkurrierende Diskurse: Studien zur französischen Literatur des 19. Jahrhunderts zu Ehren von Winfried Engler*, ed. G. Wehinger (*ZFSL*, Beihefte, n.F., 24), 1997, 11–20. H. Rohse, ' "Arme Effi": Widersprüche geschlechtlicher Identität in Fs *Effi Briest*', *Widersprüche geschlechtlicher Identität*, ed. J. Cremerius (*FLG*, 17), 203–16. B. Stolt, 'Von Maria zu Eva: Innstettens Anteil an Effis Entwicklung. Eine Gesprächsanalyse', *Sozusagen: Eine Fest. für Helmut Müssener*, ed. E. Biedermann, Stockholm U.P., 1996, 231–45.

DUS, 50, has one number (4) entirely devoted to Fontane. It contains the following articles: K. Sollimann, 'F., Schüler, Texte' (4–15); H. O. Horch, 'Arabesken zur Prosa: Über zwei politische Gedichte T. Fs' on 'Die zehn Gebote' and 'Britannia an ihren Sohn John Bull' (16–24); H. Scheuer, 'Der Realist und die Naturalisten: T. F. als Theaterkritiker' (25–33); H. Tanzer, 'Das Spiel mit dem Tabu: T. Fs erotische Kriminalgeschichte *Ellernklipp*' (34–45); S. Greif, ' "Neid macht glücklich": Fs *Mathilde Möhring* als wilhelminische Satire' (46–57); M. Grisko, 'F. im DDR-Fernsehen: Historische Lesart oder ideologische Adaption' (58–68). I. Knoll, ' "Aber wer kann alles? Nur sehr wenige": Der "Kriminalautor" Fontane', *Berliner Lesezeichen*, 4.5, 1996: 24–30. G. Brandstetter and G. Neumann, ' "Le laid c'est le beau": Liebesdiskurs und Geschlechterrolle in Fs Roman *Schach von Wuthenow*', *DVLG*, 72: 243–67. K. Kauffmann, 'Plaudern oder verstehen? T. Fs Roman *Graf Petöfy*', *GRM*, 48: 61–89. H. V. Geppert, ' "A cluster of signs": Semiotic micrologies in nineteenth-century Realism. *Madame Bovary*, *Middlemarch*, *Effi Briest*', *GR*, 73: 239–50. E. Miller, 'Der Stechlinsee: Symbol und Struktur in Fs Altersroman', *JEGP*, 97: 352–70. E. Kaiser, ' "Butterstullen statt Kanonen": Zur Entstehung eines F.-Gedichts', *WW*, 48: 173–91, is concerned with F.'s poem 'Butterstullenwerfen'. J. Nelles, 'Bedeutungsdimensionen zwischen dem Gesagten und dem Ungesagten: Intertextuelle Korrespondenz in Fs *Effi Briest* und Goethes *Faust*', *WW*, 48: 192–214. B. W. Seiler, 'T. Fs uneheliche Kinder und ihre Spuren in seinem Werk', *WW*, 48: 215–33, reveals the fact that F. probably had two illegitimate children. K. Kaufmann, 'Plaudern oder Verstehen? T. Fs Roman *Graf Petöfy*', *GRM*, 48: 61–90. S. Neuhaus, 'Warum sich Herz zum Herzen find't: Die Bedeutung eines Schiller-Zitats für die Interpretation von Fs *Frau Jenny Treibel*', *LWU*, 31: 189–95.

FRANZOS. W. Kraus, 'Von "Halb-Asien" nach Thüringen: K. E. Fs' ironisch-edle Reisebilder', *Palmbaum*, 5, 1997: 117–25.

FREILIGRATH. *'Trotz alledem und alledem': Ferdinand Freiligraths Briefe an Karl Heinzen (1845–1848). Mit einem Verzeichnis der Schriften Heinzens*, ed. G. Friesen (Vormärz-Studien, 3), Bielefeld, Aisthesis, 167 pp., publishes for the first time the complete correspondence between

F. and his politically like-minded German-American friend. *Grabbe-Jb.*, 17, 1997, in conformity with the recent editorial decision to cover Grabbe, Freiligrath and Weerth, is devoted mainly to Freiligrath and contains: G. Gadek, 'F. F. und die Wende in der DDR' (11–14); V. Giel, 'F. F.: Eine poetische Biographie' (15–54); G. Schmitz, 'Deutschland ist *Hamlet*: F. Fs 'Hamlet'-Gedicht in parodistischem Kontext' (55–66); K. Hutzelmann, 'F. F. — Unbekanntes und Vergessenes' (84–105); K. Roessler, 'Eine unbekannte Übersetzung des Gedichts "The Death of the Flowers" von William Cullen Bryant durch F. F.' (106–12); A. Ewald-Bouillon and K. Roessler, 'Eine Vertonung des Gedichts "Ruhe in der Geliebten" von F. F. durch Ferdinand Hiller' (113–26); K. Roessler, 'F. als Volksliedsammler in Menzenberg: "Guten Abend, liebes Kind!"' (127–37); G. Gadek, 'F., Weerth und Krummacher in Kettwig: Eine Bestandsaufnahme und Zusammenschau' (143–59); K. Roessler, 'Ein unbekanntes Porträt Fs von Carl Schlickum' (191–99); M. Walz, 'F.Fs Lebensabend in Cannstatt und Stuttgart (1867–1876). 1. Teil: Stätten der Erinnerung an F.' (200–20); F. Takaki, 'F. F. in Japan' (221–25); W. Broer, 'Neues zu Levin Schücking, Katharina Busch und Louise von Gall' (226–28); K. Nellner, 'Grabbe-Bibliographie 1996 — mit Nachträgen' (232–39)'; Id., Freiligrath-Bibliographie 1996 — mit Nachträgen' (240–42); Id., Weerth-Bibliographie 1996 — mit Nachträgen' (243–45).

FREYTAG. D. Brockmeyer, 'Über den Antisemitismus in G. Fs Roman *Soll und Haben*', *Antisemitismus — Zionismus — Antizionismus 1850–1940*, ed. R. Heuer et al. (Campus Judaica, 10), Frankfurt, Campus, 1997, 54–65. E.J. Krzywon, 'G. Fs Lyrik und Versdichtung: Anmerkungen zu seiner Metrik und Poetik', *Orbis linguarum*, 4, 1997:5–26. H. D. Tschörtner, 'G. F. und Gerhart Hauptmann', *ib.*, 27–34. J. Matoni, 'G. F. — der "verkannte" Gegner', *ib.*, 35–41. M. Jaroszewski, 'Das Erbe der Aufklärung in G. Fs *Soll und Haben*', *GeW*, 114, 1996:259–68.

GOTTHELF. Pierre Cimaz, *Jeremias Gotthelf (1797–1854): Der Romancier und seine Zeit*, trans. from the French by H. P. Holl, Tübingen, Francke, 572 pp. '[. . .] *zu schreien in die Zeit hinein [. . .]*': *Beiträge zu Jeremias Gotthelf / Albert Bitzius (1797–1854)*, ed. H. Holl (Schriften der Burgerbibliothek Bern), Stämpfli, 1997, 284 pp., has eight contributions on aspects of G. *SchwM*, 77.10, 1997, has several articles on G.: W. Stauffacher, 'Christlicher Widerspruch: J. Gs Widerstand gegen das radikaldemokratische Staatsmodell von 1848' (19–23); M. Andermatt, 'J. G. als Volksschriftsteller: "Dialektik der Aufklärung"' (24–28); R. Nef, 'G. — zwischen Zeitgeist und Aktualität' (29–31); M. Wirth, 'G. im Gurnigel' (33–34); P. Niederhauser, '"Fassen": Der Radiostreit um J. G. 1954' (35–36).

GRABBE. Roy C. Cowen, *Christian Dietrich Grabbe: Dramatiker ungelöster Widersprüche*, Bielefeld, Aisthesis, 278 pp. P. Langemayer, 'Geschichte als Natur: Die Mythisierung historischer Zeit und ihre Relativierung in Gs Drama *Napoleon oder die hundert Tage*', *Aspekte des politischen Theaters und Dramas von Calderón bis Georg Seidel: Deutschfranzösische Perspektiven*, ed. H. Turk et al. (*JIB*, A, Kongreßberichte, 40), Berne, Lang, 1996, 181–200. G. Scheilin, 'Gs drei letzte Stücke: *Napoleon oder die hundert Tage*, *Hannibal* und *Die Hermannsschlacht*, als Modelle zur Umformung des politischen Theaters im 19. Jahrhundert', *ib.*, 159–79. J. Kost, 'Probleme der Tragödiendramaturgie in Gs *Napoleon*', *Aspekte des Geschichtsdramas: Von Aischylos vis Volker Braun*, ed. W. Düsing (MFDT, 19), 95–110, examines the function of the grotesque element in G.'s play.

GRILLPARZER. *Autobiographien in der österreichischen Literatur: Von Franz Grillparzer bis Thomas Bernhard*, ed. Klaus Amann et al. (Schriftenreihe Literatur des Instituts für Österreichkunde, 3), Innsbruck, Studien Vlg, 272 pp., takes account of G. and Franz Michael Felder among others. G. Fieguth, 'Möglichkeiten der Aphoristik: G. — Hofmannsthal — Kraus', *Geschichte der österreichischen Literatur*, Daviau, *Literatur*, 285–95. O. Gutjahr, 'Iphigenie — Penthesilea — Medea: Zur Klassizität weiblicher Mythen bei Goethe, Kleist und G.', *Frauen: MitSprechen, MitSchreiben. Beiträge zur literatur- und sprachwissenschaftlichen Frauenforschung* (SAG, 349), 1997, 223–43. M. Ritzer, 'Von Weimar nach Habsburg: Zur Entwicklung eines österreichischen Nationalbewußtseins bei F.G.', *JIG*, 29.1, 1997[1998]:105–31. F. Genton, '*La Juive de Tolède*: G. et Feuchtwanger', *ChrA*, 6, 1997:61–72. A. Schininà, 'Das Bild F.Gs in der italienischen Literaturkritik', *Jura Soyfer*, 6.3, 1997:6–9. W. C. Reeve, '"in the beginning [...]": The opening scene of G.'s *Die Jüdin von Toledo*', *MAL*, 31:1–19. W. Schaller, 'Historischer Kontext, Plastizität und Publikumswirkung: Dramenlektüre und programmatische Reflexion in den Tagebüchern Franz Grillparzers', *Lenau-Jb.*, 22, 1996:39–50. U. Tanzer, '"Was soll mit mir? Wo leitet man mich hin?": Identität als Illusion in F.Gs Dramenfragment *Esther*', *Sprachkunst*, 29:1–16.

GROTH. *Quickborn*, ed. Ulf Bichel, Heide, Boyens, 416 pp., makes available once more the anthology for which G. is best remembered. The book is essentially a reprint of the text contained in vol. 2 of the 1956 edition of the *Sämtliche Werke* by Braak and Mehlem, but with a new introduction and notes and an alphabetical index of titles and first lines. The handsome illustrations of Otto Speckter prepared for the fourth edition of *Quickborn* in 1856 and Mehlem's glossary from the 1956 *SW* are retained. *Jahresgabe der K.-G.-Gesellschaft*, 40, has only two articles on G. himself: J. Hartig, 'Die Übersetzung von K.Gs

Werken ins Dänische' (9–24); and Id., 'Vor hundert Jahren: K.G. im Jahre 1898' (25–52).

GUTZKOW. *Bibliographie Karl Gutzkow (1829–1880)*, ed. W. Rasch (Bibliographien zur deutschen Literaturgeschichte, 5), 2 vols, Bielefeld, Aisthesis, 1199 pp. *Der Briefwechsel zwischen Karl Gutzkow und Levin Schücking 1838–1876*, ed. W. Rasch, Bielefeld, Aisthesis, 278 pp. G. K. Friesen, ' "Wir können alle gar nicht Respect genug vor Ihnen haben": Der Briefwechsel zwischen K.G. und Luise Büchner 1859–76', *Jb. der Bettina-von-Arnim Gesellschaft*, 8–9, 1996–97:75–138.

HACKLÄNDER. *Friedrich Wilhelm Hackländer 1816–1877*, ed. J. Dendt et al. (*MaM*, 81), 96 pp., was written to accompany the Hackländer exhibition held in the Schiller-Nationalmuseum in Marbach January–May 1998.

HEBBEL. Thomas Neumann, *Völkisch-nationale Hebbelrezeption: Adolf Bartels und die Weimarer Nationalfestspiele*, Bielefeld, Aisthesis, 1997, 271 pp., is a 1997 Kiel dissertation which examines the life and ideas of the minor writer and popularizing literary historian Adolf Bartels, an energetic proponent of *Heimatkunst* and notorious for introducing the canon of 'race' into the writing of literary history. The book focuses on his influence on both Hebbel-reception and the development of the Weimar *Nationalfestspiele*. Although he was actively involved in the organization of the *Festspiele* only briefly in the years 1909–13, the 'völkisch-national' ideas which he had developed in the 1890s in his journalistic work and his monographs on German literature, not least in his numerous publications on Hebbel, continued to exercise a powerful influence on the Weimar celebrations right up to the catastrophe of 1945. The strongest chapters of the book are those in which Neumann traces the development of Bartels's theory and his use of such loaded terms as 'Volkstum', 'Stamm', 'Staat', 'Reich', and 'Rasse'. There are also some interesting statistical tables relating to the *Festspiele*. An index of names aids access to the material. Andrea Stumpf, *Literarische Genealogien: Untersuchungen zum Werk Friedrich Hebbels* (Ep, 229), 1997, 167 pp. *Hebbel-Jb.*, 53, has: O. Ehrismann, 'Der schöne Schein des sozialen Friedens — Hs *Mutter und Kind*: Das Epos und Aspekte seiner Rezeption' (7–34); G. Marci-Boehncke, 'Unterhaltung oder Propaganda? Hs *Mutter und Kind* im Dritten Reich' (35–56); H. Detering, 'Lemurenschlottern: Hans Christian Andersen in Hs Zeit' (57–79); V. Nölle, ' "Repräsentation" und restringierte Zeitdimension in Hs Tragödie *Herodes und Mariamne*' (81–93); C Scholz, 'Der fremde Vater: F. Hs Erinnerungen als Zeugnisse mentalitätsgeschichtlichen Wandels' (95–130); C. M. Lewis, 'Verzeichnis der Vertonungen von F. Hs Gedichten' (131–69); T. Neumann, ' "Die Dichter im feurigen Ofen der Nachwelt!" oder "Daß ich nicht nach Weimar gehe, werden Sie schon wissen": F. Hs

Nachlaß im Goethe- und Schiller-Archiv Weimar' (171–204); H. Thomsen, 'Theaterbericht' (205–13).

J. Milewski, *Frank-Peter Steckels Bilder von Deutschland: Eine 'Deutsche Trilogie': Hs 'Die Nibelungen', Bechers 'Winterschlacht' und Müllers 'Germania Tod in Berlin' am Bochumer Schauspielhaus*, Herne, Vlg für Wiss. und Kunst, 1997, 117 pp.

C. D. Conter, 'Zwischen Geschlechterkampf und verweigerter Interkulturalität: Zur Brunhild-Figur in den Nibelungenbearbeitungen von F. H. und Emanuel Geibel', *GerLux*, 11, 1997:11–49. E. Frenzel, 'Der Haustyrann und seine Opponenten: Wandlung von Rollenbildern zwischen Hebbel und Gerhart Hauptmann', *Familienbindung als Schicksal: Wandlungen eines Motivbereichs in der neueren Literatur. Bericht über Kolloquien der Kommission für Literaturwissenschaftliche Motiv- und Themenforschung 1991–1994*, ed. T. Wolpers (Abh. d. Akad. d. Wiss. in Göttingen, phil.-hist. Kl., ser. 3, 219), 99–122.

HEINE.   The *Säkularausgabe* of H.'s *Werke, Briefwechsel, Lebenszeugnisse* has added vol. 2K, II, *Gedichte 1827–1844 und Versepen: Atta Troll. Ein Sommernachtstraum. Kommentar*, ed. Irmgard Möller, 525 pp.; vol. 2K, III, *Gedichte 1827–1844 und Versepen: Deutschland. Ein Wintermärchen. Kommentar*, ed. Hans Böhm, 345 pp.; and vol. 10/11, 1.1 and 1.2, *Pariser Berichte 1840–1848 und Lutezia. Kommentar*, ed. Christa Stöcker, 1248 pp. H. H., *Ich hab im Traum geweinet: 44 Gedichte mit Interpretationen*, ed. M. Reich-Ranicki, Frankfurt, Insel, 1997, 211 pp. H. H., *Memoiren und Geständnisse*, ed. W. Zimorski et al., Düsseldorf, Artemis & Winkler, 1997, 214 pp. H. H., *Mit scharfer Zunge: 999 Aperçus und Bonmots*, ed. J.-C. Hauschild, Frankfurt, Büchergilde Gutenberg, 1997, 219 pp. H. H., *Neue Melodien spiel ich: Gedichte*, ed. K. Briegleb, Frankfurt–Leipzig, Insel, 1997, 118 pp. Christian Liedtke, *Heinrich Heine* (RoM, 50535), 1997, 174 pp. K.-I. Voigt, **Ich habe hier bloß mit den Bäumen Bekanntschaft gemacht [. . .] Heinrich Heine in Lüneburg*, Hamburg, Lit, 1997, 52 pp.

Heine-Bibliographie 1983–1995, ed. E. von Wilamowitz-Moellendorff et al. (Personalbibliographien zur neueren deutschen Literatur, 2), Stuttgart–Weimar, Metzler, xiv + 396 pp., carries on the bibliographical work of E. Galley (1960) and S. Seifert (1968 and 1986) and lists almost 2,400 titles published in the short space of 12 years. Renate Stauf, *Der problematische Europäer: Heinrich Heine im Konflikt zwischen Nationenkritik und gesellschaftlicher Utopie* (BNL, 154), 1997, vi + 517 pp., is a 1996 Berlin *Habilitationsschrift* by an established H. expert. In it she returns to the thesis that she first put forward in an article published in *GRM* in 1993 (see *YWMLS*, 55:880–81) and challenges the conventional view of H. as a politically-committed and progessively-minded supporter of the European ideal, an early enthusiast for the kind of thinking that led to the creation of today's

European Union. In reality, she argues, H.'s vision of a unified
Europe was more a cultural than a political one. His thinking was
rooted in the Utopian ideals of the 18th. c and at a considerable
remove from the constitutional preoccupations of the men of 1848.
He was in fact sceptical of institutional politics and disappointed by
the course of political developments both before and after 1848.
Furthermore, although he dreamt of a close cultural alliance between
Germany and France, his European vision conspicuously excluded
Britain. Stauf's thesis is certainly an interesting one and she sustains
it with a massive amount of documentation and clear argument,
though it cannot be said too often that a book of this length and
complexity really needs to be properly indexed. With the aid of
modern technology this should not be a huge task, and it would
significantly enhance the value of a book that deserves to be widely
read. Bodo Morawe, *Heines 'Französische Zustände': Über die Fortschritte
des Republikanismus und die anmarschierende Weltliteratur* (Beihefte zum
Euphorion, 28), Heidelberg, Winter, 1997, 109 pp., examines this
controversial text in the light of its contemporary French sources and
argues that, far from being a constitutional monarchist as is usually
believed, H. was in fact a convinced republican. Manfred Windfuhr,
Rätsel Heine: Autorenprofil — Werk — Wirkung (RS, 133), 1997, 439 pp.,
contains 14 essays on H. written by the author over a period of almost
40 years; 13 of them have been published before though all have been
revised, some of them extensively. As in Windfuhr's 1969 monograph
Heinrich Heine: Revolution und Reflexion, considerable attention is paid to
the political aspects of H.'s thought and writing, though account is
taken of more recent developments in critical methodology such as
reception history and intertextuality. The book opens with a long and
interesting new essay, 'Heine privat: Aus der Innensicht eines
Schriftstellerlebens' (15–72). This deals with H.'s living arrangements
(the constant changes of address caused by his hatred of noise); his
working habits; his fragile health; his relationships with family (chiefly
his mother and uncle Salomon), with friends and with Mathilde and
other women; the unusually open though always stylized way in
which he portrayed these relationships; and the impression that he
made on others (August Lewald, Rahel Varnhagen von Ense) in
private conversation. *Die französische Heine-Kritik: Rezensionen und
Notizen zu Heines Werken aus den Jahren 1830–1834*, 1, ed. H. Hörling,
Stuttgart, Metzler, 1996, 338 pp., is the first of three planned volumes
which will reprint French reviews of H.'s writings during the period
1830–1856. The editor's introduction (5–42) is followed by 109
reviews varying in length from a few lines to several pages. Analysis
of them reveals much about the rapid growth of his reputation in
France after his arrival there in 1830, and about the reasons for the

French interest in him. He was chiefly seen as a political writer; the great majority of the reviews were published in the political press while comparatively few appeared in the leading literary journal *Revue des deux mondes*. The political organs had of course widely differing allegiances and this is reflected in the views that they took of H., though Hörling points out that in general about 80% of the reviews were positive and only some 20% negative. An interesting incidental point that emerges is that H. is the German writer most often translated into French; by the year 1930 there were about 350 translations of his works, compared with 264 for Goethe. The book has an index of reviewers (Sainte-Beuve being the leading name in this early period), of H.'s works discussed, and of the French journals represented. There are however no annotations of any kind. M. Espagne, *Les Juifs allemands de Paris à l'époque de Heine: La translation ashkénase* (Perspectives Germaniques), PUF, 1996, vi + 260 pp., deals with the advent of large numbers of German-speaking Jews in France, especially in Paris, in the 19th c. and their impact on the intellectual and cultural life of the city. There are chapters on their contribution to the academic world, music, politics, and economics. For Germanists however the most interesting parts of the book will be chapter 3, 'La littérature et le ghetto' (57–83), and chapter 7, 'Femmes juives' (157–72, on the literary salons run by Jewish women).

Camille Selden, *Heinrich Heines letzte Tage*, Bodenheim, Philo, 1997, 106 pp. The book was first published in 1884 with the title *Les derniers jours de Henri Heine*. The author was H.'s last lover. Jürgen Fohrmann, *Schiffbruch mit Strandrecht: Der ästhetische Imperativ in der 'Kunstperiode'*, Munich, Fink, 202 pp., includes some discussion of Heine. Thomas Gutmann, **Im Namen Heinrich Heines: Der Streit um die Benennung der Universität Düsseldorf 1965–88*, Düsseldorf, Droste, 1997, viii + 216 pp. Burkhard Gutleben, **Die deutsch-deutsche Heine-Forschung: Kontroversen und Konvergenzen 1949–1990*, Frankfurt, Rita Fischer, 1997, 151 pp. Diana L. Justis, **The Feminine in Heines's Life and Œuvre: Self and Other* (NASNCGL, 19), 1997, vi + 247 pp. Jochanaan C. Trilse-Finkelstein, **Gelebter Widerspruch: Heinrich-Heine-Biographie*, Berlin, Aufbau, 1997, 420 pp. Klaus Briegleb, **Bei den Wassern Babels: Heinrich Heine. Jüdischer Schriftsteller in der Moderne*, Munich (DTV, 30648), 1997, 439 pp. Christian Höpfner, **Romantik und Religion: Heinrich Heines Suche nach Identität*, Stuttgart, Metzler 1997, 319 pp., is a 1995 Bamberg dissertation. Ortwin Lämke, **Heines Begriff der Geschichte: Der Journalist Heinrich Heine und die Julimonarchie*, Stuttgart, Metzler, 1997, x + 180 pp., is a 1996 Hamburg dissertation. Matthias Starke, *Heinrich Heines Auffassungen von der Geschichte und der Revolution als impulsgebenden Elementen des Prosaschaffens im französischen Exil (1831–1848)*, Aachen, Shaker, 1997, 291 pp., is a 1992 Leipzig dissertation. Petra Ziech, *Entlarven und Heucheln: Formen des Zynischen und ihre Wirkung im Werk Heinrich Heines*, Aachen, Shaker, 1997, ix + 211 pp., is a 1997 Berlin dissertation. Erzsébet von Gaál Gyulai, *Heinrich Heine — Dichter, Philosoph und Europäer: Eine Studie zum weltanschaulich-philosophischen Strukturprinzip seiner Pariser Schriften* (EH, 1, 1658), 199 pp. Kwang-Bok Lee, *Rezeption — Vermittlung — Reflexion: Ein literaturdidaktisches Konzept für die Vermittlung Heinrich Heines in Korea* (EH, 1, 1669), ix + 214 pp.

Heine-Jb., 37, contains: L. Jordan, 'Von der Subversität zur Repräsentativität: Über Hs Schwierigkeiten, ein kritischer Schriftsteller zu bleiben' (1–21); K. Abels, ' "Waisenkinder des Ruhms": Grenadiere, Tamboure und andere Soldaten im Werk Hs' (22–58); M. Gamper, 'Übersetzung oder Interpretation? H. Hs Gemäldekommentare und ihre Auseinandersetzung mit der romantischen Kunsttheorie' (59–86); J. Schneider, 'Widersprüche in Hs Werk und Inkonsequenzen in der H.-Forschung: Methodologische Überlegungen am Beispiel von *Über Polen* und "Zwei Ritter" ' (87–106); R. Kleinertz, ' "Wie sehr ich auch Liszt liebe, so wirkt doch seine Musik nicht angenehm auf mein Gemüt": Freundschaft und Entfremdung zwischen H. und Liszt' (107–39); J. L. Sammons, 'Charles Godfrey Leland and the English-language Heine edition' (140–67); G.-J. Berendse, 'H. im Kalten Krieg: Wolf Biermanns selektive Rezeption des *Wintermärchens*' (168–81); H. Tölle, 'Der kranke H.' (211–22); F. Paul, 'Plagiat, *imitatio* oder writing back? Hans Christian Andersen auf Hs Spuren im Harz' (225–37); I. Fellrath, 'Von der Deutschen Demokratischen Gesellschaft zur Deutschen demokratischen Legion (Paris, März-Juni 1848)'; P. Wapnewski, 'Aber ist das eine Antwort [. . .]? Fragen von und an H.' (281–94); T.-R. Feuerhake, 'H.-Literatur 1996–97 mit Nachträgen' (331–63).

Heine: Ein Bildermärchen, ed. Gabriele Henkel, Cologne, Dumont, 1997, 277 pp., has: J. M. Morley, 'Harry H.: Ein englisches Fragment' (143–52); J. Willms, ' "Der Zukunft fröhliche Kavallerie": Anmerkungen zu Hs *Deutschland. Ein Wintermärchen*' (169–90); and G. Knapp, ' "In Düsseldorf wird mir dann wohl ein Monument gesetzt werden": warum Denkmäler für H. H. in Deutschland immer mißlingen müssen' (241–48). J. Jané, 'Hs ewiger Verstoß gegen jede Norm', *Norm und Transgression in deutscher Sprache und Literatur: Kolloquium in Santiago de Compostela, 4.–7. Oktober 1995*, ed. V. Millet, Munich, Iudicium, 1996, 181–93. Lech Kolago, *Musikalische Formen und Strukturen in der deutschsprachigen Literatur des 20. Jahrhunderts* (Wort und Musik, 32), Anif–Salzburg, Müller-Speiser, 1997, 331 pp., has a chapter on H., 'Zum "Dialog" zwischen sprachlichen und musikalischen Strukturen in der Lyrik am Beispiel von Gedichten H. Hs' (58–74). G. Neumann, 'Der Abbruch des Festes: Gedächtnis und

Verdrängung in Hs Legende *Der Rabbi von Bacherach*', Peil, *Erkennen*, 583–619. Karl Kröhnke, 'Signum ex avibus? Joseph Roths Harzreise und seine Reise durch die Harzreisen anderer Harzreisender', *Neophilologus*, 82 : 107–24, examines the links between Roth's text and Heine's *Harzreise*. R. Berbig, 'Das Heine-Jahr vorbei — alles vorbei? Eine Revue der neuesten Literatur über H. H. 1997', *ZGer*, n.F. 8 : 627–40, gives an astute critical account of the major publications of the H. year. G. Sautermeister, 'H. H.: Zur Wahrheit entstellt. Drei Traumgebilde Hs', *CEtGer*, 33, 1997 : 87–104. M. Werner, 'La réception de H. en France: Éléments pour un dossier', *CEtGer*, 34, 11–25. L. Calvié, 'Que nous dit H. aujourd'hui?', *ib.*, 27–40. D. P. Meier-Lenz, 'Hs Modernität: Aspekte zu Hs Denkmethode', *ib.*, 41–53. H. Jauregui, 'La blessure de H.', *ib.*, 57–65. D. Harth, '"Literatur, das sind wir und unsere Feinde": Vier Variationen über einen Satz von H.', *ib.*, 67–82. F. Salvan-Renucci, 'Sprache als Musik und in der Musik: H. und das Lied', *ib.*, 85–104. A. Betz, ' "Aus meinen großen Schmerzen/Mach ich die kleinen Lieder": H. H und die Musik', *ib.*, 105–17. M.-O. Blum, 'Les tropes dans la poésie de H.', *ib.*, 119–28. C. Geitner, 'Un art de la fausse citation et de la fausse répétition?: Les apaisements inquiétants et contradictoires dans le lyrisme de H.', *ib.*, 129–45. J.-P. Lefebvre, 'Le ton de H.', *ib.*, 147–65. B. Kortländer, ' "[. . .] in der Kunst wie im Leben ist die Freyheit das Höchste": H. H. — Politik und Poesie', *ib.*, 169–86. K. H. Götze, 'Heurs et malheurs de l'amour: La poésie amoureuse de H. dans l'histoire de la sensibilité', *ib.*, 187–202. P. Peters, '*Ergriffenheit* and *Kritik*: Or, decolonizing H.', *MDU*, 89, 1997 : 285–306. L. A. Rainwater van Suntum, 'Hiding behind literary analysis: H. H.'s *Shakespeares Mädchen und Frauen* and Lou Andreas-Salomés *Henrik Ibsens Frauengestalten*', *ib.*, 307–23. K. Fall, 'H. Hs Inszenierung des Ammenmärchens vom Kaiser Rotbart in seinem Versepos *Deutschland. Ein Wintermärchen*, *Andere Blicke: Habilitationsvorträge afrikanischer Germanisten an der Universität Hannover*, ed. L. Kreutzer, Hanover, Revonnah, 1996, 89–108. H.-J. Schrader, '*Fichtenbaums Palmentraum*: Ein Heine-Gedicht als Chiffre deutsch-jüdischer Identitätssuche', *The Jewish Self-Portrait in European and American Literature*, ed. H.-J. Schrader (CJ, 15), 1996, 5–44. E. Platen, 'H. Hs *Harzreise* als Bild der kulturellen Restauration am "Ende der Kunstperiode" ', *Poesie und Technik: Interpretationen zum Fragehorizont*, ed. E. Platen, Frankfurt, Lang, 1997, 119–45. K. Sauerland, 'Das Spiel mit dem abgeschlagenen Haupt oder: Der Salome-Stoff bei Heine, Flaubert, Oscar Wilde und Jan Kasprowicz', *Konflikt, Grenze, Dialog: Kulturkontrastive und interdisziplinäre Textzugänge. Fest. für Horst Turk zum 60. Geburtstag*, ed. J. Lehmann, Frankfurt, Lang, 1997, 249–62, deals with

H.'s 'Romanzero'. D. Arendt, 'H. — ein Tribun mit der Schellenkappe oder: Ein politischer Don Quichote', *SLWU*, 80, 1997:3–20. C. Hohoff, 'H. Hs religiöse Varianten: Zum zweihundertsten Geburtstag am 13 Dezember 1997', *Internationale katholische Zeitschrift 'Communio'*, 26, 1997:466–74. B. Leistner, 'Der Humorist und die Späße des Allmächtigen', *NDL*, 45.5, 1997:24–35. H. Urbahn de Jauregui, 'Von der Freiheit eines Dichtergeistes', *NDL*, 45.6, 1997:37–50. L. Quattrocchi, 'Orazio nel giudizio di H. H.', *Epigrafi, Documenti e Ricerche: Studi in Memoria di Giovanni Forni*, ed. M. L. C. Pierotti (Studi e Ricerche dell'Istituto di Storia della Facoltà di Magistero dell'Università di Perugia, 14), Naples, Edizioni Scientifiche Italiane, 1996, 381–96. A. Böhn, 'Neinsagen zur Geschichte: Emblematik als Zitat bei H.', *Widersprüche im Widersprechen: Historische und aktuelle Ansichten der Verneinung. Festgabe für Horst Meixner zum 60. Geburtstag*, ed. P. Rau, Frankfurt, Lang, 1996, 50–65. H. Mojem, 'Als Cottascher Musquetir: Zu einem neu aufgefundenen Brief an H. H.' *JDSG*, 42:5–20. J. Hermand, 'Franz Mehrings H.-Bild' *MDU*, 89, 1997:324–34. R. Stauf, '"Und Gott ist alles was da ist/Er ist in unseren Küssen": H. Hs Traum von der Menschengöttlichkeit', *DUS*, 50:25–37, takes as the starting point of her argument the seventh poem of the *Seraphine* cycle of the *Neue Gedichte*. C. Schärf, 'Die Selbstinszenierung des modernen Autors: H. Hs *Ideen. Das Buch Legrand*', *LitL*, 21:301–11.

HERWEGH. H. Kircher, '"Der Freiheit Priester, ein Vasall des Schönen": Anmerkungen zu Stilwandel und Formgestaltung in G. Hs politischen Sonetten', *Stil und Stilwandel: Bernhard Sowinski zum 65. Geburtstag gewidmet*, ed. U. Fix et al. (Leipziger Arbeiten zur Sprach- und Kommunikationsgeschichte, 3), Frankfurt, Lang, 1996, 237–54. I. Pepperle, 'Georg Herwegh: Korrespondenzen aus Paris 1848 in Arnold Ruges Zeitung *Die Reform*', *Heine-Jb.*, 37:182–210.

HEYSE. Rainer Hillenbrand has excelled himself in H. studies this year with no less than three major publications to his name. The first is an edition of a selection of the prose fiction under the title P. H., *Novellen*, Zurich, Manesse, 669 pp. This is a handsomely produced little volume which reprints the text of nine Novellen together with a brief *Nachwort* and ten pages of explanatory notes. The Novellen are presented in the chronological order of composition and the selection is designed to reveal H.'s artistic development and the range and variety of his work over four decades. The chosen texts are: *L'Arrabbiata, Andrea Delfin, Die Stickerin von Treviso, Der letzte Zentaur, Siechentrost, Himmlische und irdische Liebe, F.V.R.I.A., Das Haus 'Zum ungläubigen Thomas' oder Des Spirits Rache*, and *Die Nixe*. The volume is particularly welcome since it represents the only substantial and readily accessible selection of H.'s work currently in print, the expensive Olms reprint of the *GW* being strictly for the specialist. Given Manesse's admirable record in keeping material in print, this attractive edition is likely to remain available for the foreseeable future unlike most of the H. publications of recent years. The second of Hillenbrand's contributions is an edition of a hitherto unpublished correspondence, *Paul Heyses Briefe an Wilhelm Petersen. Mit Heyses Briefen an Anna Petersen, vier Briefen Petersens an Heyse und einigen ergänzenden Schreiben aus dem Familienkreis*, Frankfurt, Lang, 469 pp., which makes available for the first time a total of nearly 200 letters written by H. in the years 1876–1900 to the Schleswig government official who was also a friend and correspondent of Storm and Keller. It was in fact through Storm that the first contact between Petersen (1835–1900) and H. was made. Unfortunately the correspondence is incomplete for all but four of Petersen's letters to H. have been lost. Nevertheless there is a great deal of interesting material in the numerous letters of H. that have survived; apart from anything else they complement his correspondences with Storm and Keller and theirs with Petersen and each other. Hillenbrand has done an excellent editorial job, providing nearly 200 pages of expert notes which draw extensively on H.'s still unpublished diaries. Full indexes of titles and names make the book easy to use. The publication represents a significant advance in H. scholarship. The third of Hillenbrand's books is entitled *Heyses Novellen: Ein literarischer Führer*, Frankfurt, Lang, 991 pp. It is by any measure a monumental achievement which will be of enormous value not just to H. specialists but to all researchers into German prose fiction of the second half of the 19th c. What Hillenbrand has done is to provide a synopsis and a brief, but extremely informative, *apparatus criticus* for every single one of H.'s 177 (!) stories (the novels, dramas, and *Novellen in Versen* are not included). Each article follows the same pattern: the title is followed by details of the date of composition and publication history; a summary of the content; a short interpretation; comments on the text made by H. in his letters and diaries and by contemporaries like Storm, Keller, and Fontane; and finally a reference to any secondary literature that exists. There is an excellent 26–page introduction which is notable not least for its lucid explanation of H.'s conception of the Novelle form and the meaning of the terms 'Idealismus' and 'Realismus' as applied to him. A 10–page bibliography updates W. Martin's 1978 *H.-Bibliographie* as far as 1995, and the work is rounded off by a number of indexes, including one of themes and key words ('Aberglaube', 'Ehebruch', 'Standesunter-schied'), and another of places where the action is set (towns, rivers, mountains). For scholars working on Fontane, Storm, and Keller, who know how necessary some knowledge of H.'s work is and how difficult it has until now been to acquire it easily and quickly, the book will be an inestimable boon. Fastidious readers will be pained by the caustic tone in which the author refers to secondary literature with which he disagrees — and he disagrees frequently. G. Kroes-Tillmann certainly deserves better treatment than she receives here. Nevertheless, despite this blemish, Hillenbrand's book is one of the outstanding publications of the year and without any doubt the most significant contribution to H. scholarship so far produced. H. Rasche, '*Die Pfälzer in Irland*: Anmerkungen zu einem dramatischen Frühwerk Paul Heyses', *Schein und Widerschein: Festschrift für T. J. Casey*, ed. Eoin Bourke et al., Galway U.P., 1997, 169–86. N. Nelhiebel, 'Versepik in der zweiten Hälfte des 19. Jahrhunderts, vor allem bei Paul Heyse: Ein Arbeitsbericht', *SGGed*, 4, 1997:37–47. B. Burns, 'H. and Storm on the slippery slope: Two different approaches to euthanasia', *GLL*, 51:28–42.

HOFFMANN VON FALLERSLEBEN.   R. Ehnert, 'Das Deutschlandlied als Gegenstand des Deutsch-als-Fremdsprachenunterrichts', *DUSA*, 27, 1996:54–64.

IMMERMANN.   *Epigonentum und Originalität: Immermann und seine Zeit — Immermann und die Folgen*, ed. Peter Hasubek, Frankfurt, Lang, 1997, 345 pp., publishes the proceedings of an interdisciplinary conference held in I.'s home town of Magdeburg in 1996 to mark the bicentenary of his birth. The aim of the volume is to examine I. in the cultural context of his time, to look at his links with other writers, artists, and thinkers, and to review his reception in Germany and abroad. Of special interest for the present reviewer were the contributions of M. Richter (141–68, on the *Alexis*-trilogy, I.'s best-known historical tragedy); T. Spreckelsen (191–210, on I.'s often difficult relations with his numerous publishers); G. Oesterle (235–52, on the originality of *Tulifäntchen*); and P. Hasubek (267–95, on the reception of *Münchhausen*). The other contributions, all of good quality, are: L. Ehrlich, 'I. und die Klassik' (19–34); W. Maierhofer, '"Heilsamer Stachel": Goethe und I.' (35–58); H. H. Marks, ' "Mein Ich ist mir gestohlen": Liebhabertheater und inszeniertes Glück im Lustspiel von I. und Büchner' (59–77); H. Steinecke, ' "Keine neue Gemüthslage oder Denkweise": Notiz zu I. und Lenau' (79–84); J. A. Kruse, ' "Weil ich ein Garnichts bin,/Geb ich mich selber her": I. und die Frauen' (85–110); H. Karge, ' "Denn die Kunst ist selbst nichts Absolutes [. . .]": K. I., K. Schnaase und die Theorie der Düsseldorfer Malerschule' (111–40); H. Lück, 'Mythos und Realität: Klassische Themen der deutschen Rechtsgeschichte in Is *Münchhausen*' (169–90); M. Fauser, 'Imaginäre Subjektivität: Das Leben nach der Literatur in den Briefen Is' (211–34); E. McInnes, 'Gestörte Idylle: Zur Tradition des Bauernromans im 18. und 19. Jahrhundert' (253–65); S. Itoda, 'Is Theaterreform und die Modernisierung des

japanischen Theaters: I. und Ogai Mori' (297–317); H. Richter,
'Eideshelfer und Gewährsmann: Vorstudien, Texte und Thesen zu
einer künftigen Darstellung der Rezeption Is' (343–41). As so often
with collective volumes one regrets only the lack of an index.
B. Bauer, 'Richtige und falsche Naturdeutung: K. Is *Waldmärchen Die
Wunder im Spessart*, magischer Idealismus und Renaissancephiloso-
phie', Peil, *Erkennen*, 543–82.

KELLER. This year has seen the publication of the first volume of
a major new HKA of K.'s *Sämtliche Werke*, ed. Walter Morgenthaler,
Basle–Frankfurt, Stroemfeld. The first volume to appear is *Abteilung
A, Gesammelte Werke*, 7, *Das Sinngedicht. Sieben Legenden*, ed. W. Morgenthaler, 432 pp. In all, 32 volumes are planned. The edition is to
be a multi-media publication with CD-ROMs accompanying the
printed volumes. Richard R. Ruppel, *Gottfried Keller and His Critics: A
Case Study in Scholarly Criticism* (SGLLC), xi + 214 pp., is a carefully
researched and well-written addition to the Camden House series. It
succeeds admirably in its aim of giving a representative picture of the
best of K. scholarship in each of the successive stages of its
development. The first chapter provides a valuable introduction to
K.'s main themes and interests and an insight into the rigorous
literary market-place which sorely tested the endurance of the
wayward author and the patience of his publishers. Chapter 2 is
concerned with his correspondence with his publishers (Vieweg,
Rodenberg), contemporary literary historians and critics (F. T.
Vischer, E. Kuh), and his friends (Storm, Heyse). Chapter 3 covers
the early years of scholarship up to the centennial year 1919, while
chapter 4 gives an account of the great tide of academic criticism
which began in the 1920s and has never receded. Here there are
useful discussions of the research done on K.'s realism, his humour,
and his religious and political views. Chapter 5 examines the notable
contribution of Anglo-Saxon scholars to the critical literature, and
chapter 6 traces the developments which have taken place over the
past 25 years culminating in the publication of the DKV edition
completed in 1996. Diana Schilling, *Kellers Prosa* (HKADL, 27),
279 pp., attempts new readings of K.'s novels and Novellen from an
historical perspective. Christian Stotz, *Das Motiv des Geldes in der Prosa
Gottfried Kellers* (EH, 1, 1684), x + 250 pp., sees close parallels between
K.'s own economic situation and the treatment of money in his
fiction. Dominik Müller, '"Wo, ungestört und ungekannt, ich
Schweizer darf *und* Deutscher sein!" G. K. im Spannungsraum
zwischen der Schweiz und Deutschland', *JIG*, 29.1,
1997[1998]:85–104. J. Gomsu, 'G.Ks Novelle *Das verlorne Lachen* als
Unterrichtsversuch an der Universität Yaoundé', *Andere Blicke: Habilitationsvorträge afrikanischer Germanisten an der Universität Hannover*, ed.

L. Kreutzer, Hanover, Revonnah, 1996, 109–25. M. Böhler, 'Die falsch besetzte zweite Herzkammer: Innere und äußere Fremde in G. Ks *Pankraz der Schmoller*', *Figuren des Fremden in der Schweizer Literatur*, ed. C. Caduff, Zurich, Limmat, 1997, 36–61. G. Neumann, 'Der Körper des Menschen und die belebte Statue: Zu einer Grundformel in G. Ks *Sinngedicht*', *Pygmalion: Die Geschichte des Mythos in der abendländischen Kultur*, ed. M. Mayer et al. (Rombach Wissenschaften, Reihe Litterae, 45), Freiburg, Rombach, 1997, 555–91. L. B. Jennings, 'Virgin, knight, and devil: G. K.'s legends as fantasy', *Visions of the Fantastic: Selected Essays from the Fifteenth International Conference on the Fantastic in the Arts*, ed. A. R. Becker (Contributions to the Study of Science Fiction and Fantasy, 68), Westport, CT, Greenwood Press, 1996, 51–55. F. Berndt, '*Das Meretlein*: Zur Ikonographie der Novelle in G. Ks *Der grüne Heinrich*', *Historismus und Moderne*, ed. H. Tausch (Literatura, 1), Würzburg, Ergon, 1996, 161–80. E. Downing, 'Double takes: Genre and gender in K.'s *Sieben Legenden*', *GR*, 73:221–38. F. Schössler, ' "Fleißige Tätigkeit in lebendigem Menschenstoffe": Die Vision körperlicher Kunst und ihre immanente Poetik in G. Ks *Der Grüne Heinrich*', *Sprachkunst*, 28, 1997:181–98.

KOMPERT. Maria Theresia Wittemann, *Draußen vor dem Ghetto: Leopold Kompert und die 'Schilderung jüdischen Volkslebens' in Böhmen und Mähren* (CJ, 22), vi + 399 pp., is a 1997 Munich dissertation. J. Golec, 'Jüdische Identitätssuche in Aaron Bernsteins Ghettogeschichten und Leopold Komperts Roman *Am Pfluge*', *Convivium*, 1997:167–79.

LASSALLE. A. Seemann, 'Nur kein Skandal, arrangiere dich bitte! F. L. und Sophie von Hatzfeldt', *Berühmte Liebespaare: Von Johann Wolfgang Goethe und Christiane Vulpius bis Simone Signoret und Yves Montand*, ed. T. Schröder, Frankfurt, Insel, 1997, 102–16.

LENAU. The HKA of L.'s *Werke und Briefe*, ed. Norbert Oellers et al., Stuttgart, Klett-Cotta, has added vol. 3, *Versepen, Teil* I, 371 pp. The old *Lenau Forum* has been known since 1996 under the new title *Lenau-Jahrbuch*. *Lenau-Jb.*, 22, 1996, contains: M. Ritter, ' "Es war ein völliger Parnaß": Die junge Dichtergeneration um N. L. im "silbernen Kaffeehaus". Ein Stück Wiener literarischer Kaffeehaustradition aus den zwanziger und frühen dreißiger Jahren des 19. Jahrhunderts' (7–38). *Lenau-Jb.*, 23, 1997, takes as its theme 'Nikolaus Lenau und der europäische Weltschmerz' and has: H. Zeman, 'Vom Weltschmerz zum Vormärz in Österreich: Literarhistorische Notizen als Vorwort' (11–15); H. Steinecke, ' "L. und der europäische Weltschmerz": Schlüssel zum Werk oder Leerformel?' (17–26); D.-R. Moser, ' "Wonne der Wehmut": Weltschmerz in der Lieddichtung der Biedermeierzeit' (29–43); W. Kriegleder, 'Weltschmerz und Romantik in Österreich' (45–57); B. Schöckl, 'Die österreichische

Dichtung von der Neo-Empfindsamkeit zum Weltschmerz: Konturen einer Entwicklung' (59–80); R. Schmier, 'Der Weltschmerz und die Neue Welt: L., Byron und Goldsmith' (125–46); M. Ritter, 'Die amerikanische Enttäuschung: Biographische Realität und fiktionale Reminiszenz (L. und Kürnberger)' (147–72); A. Mádl, 'Ein unbekanntes L.-Gedicht' (201–13); H.-G. Werner, 'Neuere Einsichten in die Entstehungsgeschichte von Ls *Faust*' (223–31); Z. Konstantinović, 'Der Schmerz an der Welt: aktuelle L.-Reminiszenzen in Werken mitteleuropäischer Schriftsteller' (233–44); J. Lukuszuk and M. Ritter, 'L.-Bibliographie: Erscheinungen aus den Jahren 1995 und 1996 mit Nachträgen aus früheren Jahren' (245–47). *Lenau-Jb.*, 24, has: I. Dürhammer, ' "Zerflossen in ein immer schmachtend Sehnen" — "Wo man ewig zwecklos leidet": Österreichischer Weltschmerz abseits von L.' (81–95); G. Haika, 'Ls "Herbst", Schuberts *Andantino* und der Freitod des *Schülers Gerber*: Beobachtungen über die stimmige Zusammenführung unterschiedlicher Kunstgattungen im Medium des Films' (97–114); K. Harer, 'N. L. und der "Brief eines russischen Literaten and H. Koenig" (1840)' (115–47); M. Ritter and J. Lukuszuk, 'L.-Bibliographie: Erscheinungen aus den Jahren 1996 und 1997 mit Nachträgen aus früheren Jahren' (149–51).

LEWALD. Gabriele Schneider, *Fanny Lewald* (RoM 553), 1996, 154 pp. Gudrun Marci-Boehncke, *Fanny Lewald: Jüdin, Preußin, Schriftstellerin. Studien zu autobiographischem Werk und Kontext* (SAG, 337) 364 pp., is a 1994 Giessen dissertation. Sabine Buchal, **Magdphantasien: Zum Motiv des weiblichen Dienens in Prosatexten des 19. und 20. Jahrhunderts*, Osnabrück, Rasch, 1997, 139 pp., is an Osnabrück dissertation with some treatment of L. W. Albrecht, 'Mobilität und Wahrnehmung: Über ein Reflexionsgefüge reisender Frauen (Johanna Schopenhauer und F. L.) in der ersten Hälfte des 19. Jahrhunderts', *Frauen: MitSprechen, MitSchreiben. Beiträge zur literatur- und sprachwissenschaftlichen Frauenforschung* (SAG, 349), 1997, 107–17. Robert C. Fuhrmann, 'Masculine form/feminine writing: The autobiography of Fanny Lewald', *Transforming the Center, Eroding the Margins: Essays on Ethnic and Cultural Boundaries in German-speaking Countries*, ed. Dagmar C. G. Lorenz et al. (SGLLC), 103–14. G. Schneider, ' "Meine Mutter paßt auf, daß mir Keiner was thut!": F. L. privat. Familienbriefe F. Ls aus Privatbesitz im Heinrich-Heine-Institut (Stiftung Gurlitt)', *Heine-Jb.*, 37:252–71.

MARLITT. *Ich kann nicht lachen, wenn ich weinen möchte: Die unveröffentlichten Briefe der E. M.*, ed. C. Hobohm, Wandersleben, Gleichen-Vlg, 1996, 175 pp.

MEYER. C. F. M., *Sämtliche Erzählungen*, ed. W. Schafarschik (UB, 6947), 850 pp. Andrea Jäger, *Die historischen Erzählungen von Conrad*

Ferdinand Meyer: Zur poetischen Auflösung des historischen Sinns im 19. Jahrhundert, Tübingen, Francke, 323 pp., is a Bochum *Habilitationsschrift.* By the same author is the short work *Conrad Ferdinand Meyer zur Einführung* (Zur Einführung, 179), Hamburg, Junius, 168 pp. Theodor Pelster, *Conrad Ferdinand Meyer* (UB, 15216), 118 pp. Christof Laumont, **Jeder Gedanke als sichtbare Gestalt: Formen und Funktionen der Allegorie in der Erzähldichtung Conrad Ferdinand Meyers,* Göttingen, Wallstein, 1997, 351 pp. Gunter H. Hertling, 'Mißhandlung, *Leiden und Tod zweier Knaben:* C. F. Ms Julian Boufflers und Hermann Hesses Hans Giebenrath *Unterm Rad* des Lebens', *Gingkobaum,* 15, 1997:308–24. P. Sprengel, 'Epilog(e): Zum Abschluß der historisch-kritischen M.-Ausgabe', *ZDP,* 117:229–38. M. Fauser, 'Anthropologie der Geschichte: Jacob Burckhardt und die historische Lyrik von C. F. M.', *Euphorion,* 92:331–59.

MEYSENBUG. S. Arndt, ' "[...] so war es ein Götterleben u. eine wahre Colonie": Malwida von Ms Versuche, in Italien einen Kreis Gleichgesinnter zu versammeln', *Lippische Mitteilungen aus Geschichte und Landeskunde,* 65, 1996:269–91.

MÖLLHAUSEN, BALDUIN. A reprint of M.'s *Ausgewählte Werke* in 19 vols has begun with the publication of *Abteilung* I, *Erzählungen,* I, *Palmblätter und Schneeflocken,* and II, *Erzählungen aus dem fernen Westen* (2 vols in one), ed. A. Graf, Hildesheim, Olms, 512 pp.

MÖRIKE. *'Der Sonnenblume gleich steht mein Gemüthe offen': Neue Studien zum Werk Eduard Mörikes,* ed. R. Wild (Mannheimer Studien zur Literatur- und Kulturwissenschaft, 14), St Ingbert, Röhrig, 1997, 189 pp., contains seven essays by different contributors on M.'s lyric and narrative work. Ulrich Hötzer, **Mörikes heimliche Modernität,* Tübingen, Niemeyer, x + 314 pp. Mathias Mayer, *Eduard Mörike* (UB, 17611), 160 pp. Christa Linsenmaier-Wolf, *'[...] *zu Dreien in Ruhe und Frieden geborgen': Eduard Mörike in Fellbach* (Spuren, 37), Marbach, Dt. Schiller-Ges., 1997, 15 pp.

MÜHLBACH. L. Tatlock, 'Recollections of a small-town girl: Regional identity, nation, and the flux of history in L.M.'s *Erinnerungen aus der Jugend* (1870)', *WGY,* 13, 1997:49–65.

NESTROY. The HKA of N.'s *Sämtliche Werke,* ed. Jürgen Hein et al., Vienna, Deuticke (formerly Jugend und Volk), has added *Stücke,* 17, 2, *Das Mädl aus der Vorstadt,* ed. W. E. Yates, xviii + 382 pp.; *Stücke,* 26, 2, *Lady und Schneider. Judith und Holofernes,* ed. J. R. P. McKenzie, xviii + 494 pp.; *Stücke,* 35, *Umsonst,* ed. P. Branscombe, xvi + 238 pp. *Prinz Friedrich von Corsica: Historisch-romantisches Drama in fünf Acten. Nach van der Veldes Erzählung von Johann Nestroy. Mit einem Fundbericht von Oskar Pausch,* ed. F. Walla (Mimundus, 6), Vienna–Cologne, Böhlau, 1997, 116 pp., publishes the text of a manuscript missing since 1937 and found again by Pausch in the theatre collection of the Austrian

National Library in the 1980s, but only after the appearance of Walla's edition of the corrupt and unreliable prose version of N.'s first play in *Stücke*, 1 of the HKA in 1979. Walla has now edited the rediscovered blank-verse version according to the principles of the HKA so that his new edition of the play effectively replaces his earlier edition in *Stücke*, 1. F. Walla, 'London–Vienna–New York–London: From N.'s Vienna to *Hello, Dolly*', *Culture in Context: A Selection of Papers Presented at Inter-Cultural Studies '96, The University of Newcastle, May 23 & 24, 1996*, ed. G. Squires, Newcastle (NSW) U.P., 1996, pp. 49–64. Johannes Braun, *Das Närrische bei Nestroy*, Bielefeld, Aisthesis, 204 pp., is a 1998 Freiburg dissertation.

Nestroyana, 18, has: S. P. Scheichl, 'Der "Kanon" der Nestroy-Stücke' (5–16); F. Walla, ' "Cantu dignoscitur ales": Der Kritiker Nr 23 entlarvt. Franz (Wiest) hieß die Kanaille' (17–27); D. Zumbusch-Beisteiner, 'M. Hebenstreits Partiturhandschrift zu Ns *Der alte Mann mit der jungen Frau*: Bericht über eine Neuentdeckung in der Österreichischen Nationalbibliothek' (28–30); F. Schüppen, 'Ein N. für Paris: Gérard de Nervals Reminiszenzen eines Wiener Theaterabends' (30–38); S. P. Scheichl, 'Hieronymus Lorm über N.' (39); J. R. P. McKenzie, 'Zur Entstehungs- und Überlieferungsge-schichte von Ns vorrevolutionären Possen *Zwei ewige Juden und Keiner* und *Der Schützling*' (40–49); R. Theobald, 'Ns *Meister der Täuschung* in Berlin' (50–52); P. Gruber, 'Ein brillanter Ausgang? Überlegungen zu *Mein Freund*' (53–58); G. Magenheim, 'Bäuerles Namensgebung, seine "Flucht" und das spurlose Verschwinden seiner sterblichen Überreste' (77–82); S. P. Scheichl, 'Wie wir Noblen uns ausdrücken . . .: Hochdeutsch-Sprechen bei N.' (83–95); U. Tanzer, 'Die Demontage des Patriarchats: Vaterbilder und Vater-Tochter-Bezie-hung bei J. N.' (96–105); H. J. Koning, ' "Ihr' Frau könnt' auch was anders tun; auf d' Wirtschaft schaun, was nähen, wär g'scheiter als Bücher lesen": Leihbibliothek und Lektüre in Ns *Mein Freund* (106–14); J. Hein, 'N. und die Autographensammler' (115–16); G. and W. Schlögl, 'Nonverbale Lazzi: *Der böse Geist Lumpacivagabundus oder Das liederliche Kleeblatt*' (117–18); J. Holzner, 'Theater-Teufeleien: J. N. und Franz Kranewitter' (119–26); H. Aust, 'Das "Körperliche" und das "Geistige": Kampf bei N. und Brecht' (127–37). P. Bran-scombe, 'Die frühe Offenbach-Rezeption in Wien und Ns Anteil daran', *Austriaca*, 46:41–51.

NIETZSCHE. Manfred Riedel, *Nietzsche in Weimar: Ein deutsches Drama*, Leipzig, Reclam, 1997, 357 pp. Erkme Joseph, *Nietzsche im 'Zauberberg'* (Thomas-Mann-Studien, 14), Frankfurt, Klostermann, 1996, viii + 388 pp., is a 1993 Marburg dissertation which traces in great detail the influence and presence of N. in Mann's novel. Carol Diethe, **Nietzsche's Women: Beyond the Whip* (MTNF, 31), 1996, xiv + 178 pp. Horst Dieter Rauh, *Heilige Wildnis: Naturästhetik von Hölderlin bis Beuys*, Munich, Fink, 367 pp., includes some discussion of N. Reinhard Gasser, *Nietzsche und Freud* (MTNF, 38), 1997, xxi + 746 pp., is a massive and imposing volume, though only marginally relevant to Germanists. *Vom Nutzen und Nachteil der Historie fürs Leben: Nietzsche und die Erinnerung in der Moderne*, ed. D. Borchmeyer (STW, 1261), 1996, 234 pp., contains 12 contributions, four of them by leading Germanists. *Jüdischer Nietzscheanismus*, ed. W. Stegmaier et al. (MTNF, 36), 1997, xxxi + 476 pp., is a collection of essays which trace the influence on N.'s thought on Jewish writers and thinkers of the early 20th c. Martin Stingelin, '*Unsere ganze Philosophie ist Berichtigung des Sprachgebrauchs': Friedrich Nietzsches Lichtenberg-Rezeption im Spannungsfeld zwischen Sprachkritik (Rhetorik) und historischer Kritik (Genealogie)* (Figuren, 3), Munich, Fink, 1996, 255 pp. Stanley Corngold, *Complex Pleasure: Forms of Feeling in German Literature*, Stanford U.P., xxvx + 243 pp., has a chapter on 'Nietzsche's moods' (79–102) which deals mainly with *Die Geburt der Tragödie*. Rüdiger Braun, **Quellmund der Geschichte: Nietzsches poetische Rede in 'Also sprach Zarathustra'* (Heidelberger Beiträge zur deutschen Literatur, 2), Frankfurt, Lang, 358 pp., is concerned with the function of literary parody in N.'s text. Susan von Rohr Scaff, *History, Myth, and Music: Thomas Mann's Timely Fiction* (SGLLC), viii + 85 pp., considers the influence of Nietzsche and Wagner on Mann's *Dr Faustus*. Johanna J. S. Aulich, **Orphische Weltanschauung der Antike und ihr Erbe bei den Dichtern Nietzsche, Hölderlin, Novalis und Rilke* (GSC, 10), 204 pp. Vivetta Vivarelli, **Nietzsche und die Masken des freien Geistes: Montaigne, Pascal und Sterne* (Nietzsche in der Diskussion), Würzburg, Königshausen & Neumann, 164 pp. Aaron Ridley, **Nietzsche's Conscience: Six Character Studies from the 'Genealogy'*, Cornell U.P., 163 pp. Detlef Otto, **Wendungen der Metapher: Zur Übertragung in poetologischer, rhetorischer und erkenntnistheoretischer Hinsicht bei Aristoteles und Nietzsche*, Munich, Fink, 503 pp., is a 1996 Berlin dissertation. Hays A. Steilberg, **Die amerikanische Nietzsche-Rezeption von 1896 bis 1950* (MTNF, 35), 1996, xiii + 438 pp. G. Bauer, 'Vom Entzücken an gut gebauten Sätzen: N. als klassisch/unklassischer Philologe', *Wechsel der Orte: Studien zum Wandel des literarischen Geschichtsbewußtseins. Fest. für Anke Bennholdt-Thomsen*, ed. I. von der Lühe et al., Göttingen, Wallstein, 1997, 107–19; H. Schmidt, 'Zerbrechen am Wort: Epilegomena zu Zarathustras Untergang', *ib.*, 120–28. E. Behler, 'Ns Sprachtheorie und die literarische Übersetzung als Kunst', *Zwiesprache: Beiträge zur Theorie und Geschichte des Übersetzens*, ed. U. Stadler et al., Stuttgart, Metzler, 1996, 64–76. M. Riedel, 'Ns Philosophie der Tragödie', *Hermenautik — Hermeneutik: Literarische und geisteswissenschaftliche Beiträge zu Ehren von Peter Horst Neumann*, ed. H. Helbig et al., Würzburg, Königshausen &

Neumann, 1996, pp. 191–202. N. Bolz, 'Das Verschwinden der Rhetorik in ihrer Allgegenwart', *Die Aktualität der Rhetorik*, ed. H. F. Plett (Figuren, 5), Munich, Fink, 1996, 67–76. M. Crépon, 'L'histoire et la géographie des corps: N. et la question des races', *RGI*, 10:161–72. K. Mishima, 'Wieweit hat sich der Virtuose der Moralistik verstiegen? Zur Symbiose von Ethnozentrismuskritik und Machtapotheose beim späten N.', *ZGer*, n.F., 7, 1997:38–48. J. Undusk, 'Zur Anatomie des Epigonentums: Altenberg, N. und Louis Berlandt' *Gingkobaum*, 15, 1997:339–60. F. Hickel, '*Freund Hain', die erotische Süßigkeit und die Stille des Nirvanas: Thomas Manns Rezeption der Erlösungsthematik zwischen Schopenhauer, N. und Wagner* (Poetica, 24), Hamburg, Kovač, 1997, 310 pp. Karl Pestalozzi, ' "Aus des Dionysos, der Venus Sippe": Reflexe von Nietzsches *Geburt der Tragödie aus dem Geiste der Musik* in der deutschen Literatur der Jahrhundertwende', *London Ger. St. VI*, 223–50. M. Schröder-Augustin, 'Décadence und Lebenswille: Tonio Kröger im Kontext von Schopenhauer, Wagner und Nietzsche', *WW*, 48:255–74, analyses the 19th-c. philosophical influences on *Tonio Kröger* and their place in Mann's life. H. Detering, ' "Das Ich wird zum Wortspiel": N., Ibsen, Strindberg und das Drama der Abstraktion', *Hofmannsthal-Jb.*, 6:229–56. F. B. Parkes-Perret, 'N.'s "Glück" and Thomas Mann's *Enttäuschung*', *Seminar*, 34:235–55.

OTTO-PETERS, LOUISE. L. O.-P., *Schloß und Fabrik: Roman. Erste vollständige Ausgabe des 1846 zensierten Romans*, ed. J. Ludwig, Leipzig, LKG, 1996, 366 pp., publishes the recently rediscovered original text of the novel as it was before the censors cut out the passages deemed sympathetic to communism. '*Mit den Muth'gen will ich's halten': Zur 150jährigen aufregenden Geschichte des Romans 'Schloß und Fabrik' von Louise Otto-Peters. Mit der 1994 wiederaufgefundenen vollständigen Zensurakte*, ed. J. L. Rothenburg et al. (Louiseum, 4), Beucha, Sax, 1996, 48 pp.

PLATEN. A. v. P., *Memorandum meines Lebens: Eine Auswahl aus den Tagebüchern*, ed. G. Mattenklott et al. (IT, 1857), 1996, 244 pp. A. v. P., *Wer wußte je das Leben? Ausgewählte Gedichte*, ed. R. Görner (IT, 1713), 1996, 60 pp.

PÜCKLER-MUSKAU. Mounir Fendri, *Kulturmensch in 'barbarischer' Fremde: Deutsche Reisende im Tunesien des 19. Jahrhunderts*, Munich, Iudicium, 1996, 491 pp., is a Karlsruhe *Habilitationsschrift* which includes some treatment of P.-M.'s experiences.

RAABE. W. R., *Meistererzählungen*, ed. R. Görner, Zurich, Manesse, 659 pp., expressly avoids reprinting the best-known of R.'s works such as *Der Hungerpastor* or *Die Chronik der Sperlingsgasse*. Instead the editor has chosen six rather less well-known but still significant stories by an author whom he sees as one of the three leading prose writers of the late 19th c. Like Storm and Fontane, he belongs to the tradition of German Realism, but Görner stresses the greater modernity of his themes and narrative technique. Pessimism, irony, and humour are seen as the essential elements of his style. The informative 15-page *Nachwort* is followed by a dozen pages of useful explanatory notes on the individual texts. The selected titles are *Holunderblüte, Zum wilden Mann, Horacker, Frau Salome, Im Siegeskranze,* and *Die Hämelschen Kinder.* Friedhelm Henrich, **Wilhelm Raabe und die deutsche Einheit: Die Tagebuchdokumentation der Jahre 1860–1863*, Munich, Fink, 198 pp. Ulla Heine, *Psychopathologische Phänomene im Kunstspiegel der Literatur des Realismus — dargestelt an Werken von Wilhelm Raabe*, Marburg, Tectum, 1996, 216 pp.

Raabe-Jb., 39, has: J. Hieber, 'W. R., der bürgerliche Held: Wirkung und Werk eines aufrechten Erzählers' (1–10); P. Sprengel, 'Herr German Fell und seine Brüder: Darwinismus-Phantasien von R. bis Canetti' (11–31); O. Schwarz, '"[...] das Entsetzliche im ganzen und vollen": Zur "Modernität" von Rs *Deutscher Mondschein*' (32–49); G. Cremer, 'Das Odfeld als Wille und Vorstellung: Zur Schopenhauer-Affinität in Rs *Das Odfeld*' (50–65); H. Rölleke, 'Beim Wiederlesen von W. Rs *Stopfkuchen*' (66–69); H.-J. Schrader, 'Das Klobige der Irdenware und die Zartheit des Porzellans: Vor hundert Jahren *Hastenbeck*' (70–98); J. Graf, '"Der in doppelter Hinsicht verschlagene Reisende": Joachim Heinrich Campe in Rs Werk' (99–114); J. Pizer, 'Auf der Suche nach der verlorenen Totalität: Rs *Pfisters Mühle* und Storms *Psyche*' (115–25); W. Dittrich, 'R.-Bibliographie 1998' (199–204). N. Jückstock, 'Zitierend die Welt deuten: W. Rs *Akten des Vogelsangs*', *Hermenautik — Hermeneutik: Literarische und geisteswissenschaftliche Beiträge zu Ehren von Peter Horst Neumann*, ed. H. Helbig et al., Würzburg, Königshausen & Neumann, 1996, pp. 179–98. H.-J. Schrader, 'Luftiges Geträume: Zum Reigen der Nachtgesichte in W. Rs *Das Odfeld*', *Fest. Geith*, 225–44. Gerald Opie, 'Having the last word, or, home thoughts from abroad: The reliable narrator in W. R.'s *Unruhige Gäste*', *Neophilologus*, 82:97–105. W. Hanson, 'Any old iron? Aspects of R.'s realism in *Im alten Eisen*', *Seminar*, 34:63–73. K. Grätz, 'Alte und neue Knochen in W. Rs *Stopfkuchen*: Zum Problem historischer Relativität und seiner narrativen Bewältigung' *JDSG*, 42:242–64. E. Joseph, 'Thomas Manns *Doktor Faustus*: Variationen über ein Thema von W. R.' *Thomas-Mann-Jb.*, 11:155–70, argues on the basis of circumstantial evidence that R.'s *Die Akten des Vogelsangs* was a major source for Mann's novel. R. G. Czapla, 'Der Rattenfänger unter dem Regenbogen: Zur sozial- und literaturkritischen Adaption eines Sagenstoffes in W. Rs Novelle *Die Hämelschen Kinder*', *Fabula*, 39:1–20. P. Arnds, 'The boy with the old face: Thomas Hardy's Antibildungsroman and W. R.'s Bildungsroman *Prinzessin Fisch*', *GSR*, 21:221–40. H. Richter, 'Regionale

Literatur und nationaler Gehalt: Eine Stimme aus dem Süddeutsch-
land des Jahres 1866 zur Literatur in der Mark Brandenburg', *WB*,
44:165–89, is concerned with the reaction of various writers,
including R. and Wilhelm Jensen, to the Prussian victories of 1866
and the end of the *Bund*.

RAIMUND. D. Tureček, 'F. R. in Prag', *Germanoslavica*, 4,
1997:15–25.

REUTER, F. F. F. F. R., *Meine Vaterstadt Stavenhagen*, ed. C. Nenz,
Rostock, Reich, 1997, 176 pp. H.-D. Dahnke, 'F. Rs Aufstieg in die
deutsche Nationalliteratur: Zur Stellung niederdeutscher Dichtung
in der deutschen Literatur in der zweiten Hälfte des 19. Jahrhunderts',
JIG, 29.1, 1997[1998]:157–73. G. Schmidt-Henkel, 'Wie F. R.
"Feigen von den Disteln pflückte": Einige Beobachtungen zu Texten
und Rezeptionsstufen', *NdJb*, 120, 1997:117–34. H. Krosenbrink,
'F. R. en Nederland', *Driemaandelijkse bladen*, 48, 1996:65–78.

REUTER, GABRIELE. G. Rahaman, ' "Aber was einem gefiel, dem
mußte man mißtrauen" (Gabriele Reuter) — a female perspective on
Bismarck's Germany', *London Ger. St. VI*, 210–22, reads Reuter's
novel *Aus guter Familie* as a devastating critique of Wilhelmine society
and the restrictions it placed on rights and needs of women.

RÜCKERT. I. Forssmann, 'Tagebuch der Luise Rückert', *Rückert-
Studien*, 10, 1996:119–83, prints the text of the diary of R.'s wife with
a short introduction. *Rückert-Studien*, 11, 1997, has: H. Wollschläger,
' "[. . .] der Welt abhanden gekommen": F. R. in Neuseß. Rede zur
Neu-Eröffnung des R.-Hauses am 16. Mai 1997' (7–21); A. S.
Bakalow, 'Friedrich Rückert und Theodor Storm' (47–96). H. Helbig,
'Vergängliches Bewahren: Zu F. Rs *Kindertodtenliedern*', *Hermenautik —
Hermeneutik: Literarische und geisteswissenschaftliche Beiträge zu Ehren von
Peter Horst Neumann*, ed. H. Helbig et al., Würzburg, Königshausen &
Neumann, 1996, pp. 153–62.

SAAR. F. v. S., *Novellen aus Österreich*, ed. Karl Wagner, 2 vols,
Vienna–Munich, Deuticke, 272, 319 pp., is an attractively produced
yet moderately priced bibliophile edition of S.'s most famous cycle of
Novellen, a companion piece to Wagner's edition of the *Wiener Elegien*
issued by Deuticke in 1997 (see *YWMLS*, 59:813). It reprints in
chronological order the 14 stories that were published under this
collective title in 1897 during S.'s own lifetime, beginning with
Innocens (1866) and ending with *Schloß Kostenitz* (1893). The succinct
and lucid *Nachwort* in vol. 2 explains the place of the collection in S.'s
troubled career and also situates it in the wider context of Austrian
culture and society in the later 19th c. The edition is rounded off with
a brief publication history of the texts and a select bibliography.
R. Gamziukaite-Mažiuliene, 'Das Entsagungsmotiv in F. v. Ss und

Theodor Storms Werk', *Mitteleuropa: Mitten in Europa*, ed. G. Gimpl, Helsinki U.P., 1996 (*Der Gingko-Baum*, 14), 150–60.

SACHER-MASOCH. Svetlana Milojevic, *Die Poesie des Dilettantismus: Zur Rezeption und Wirkung Leopold von Sacher-Masochs* (GSC, 11), 282 pp., argues that the real reason for the decline in S.-M.'s reputation was not his non-conformist eroticism or lack of literary talent, but his espousal of socio-political and philosophical views towards which conservative 19th-c. critics were unsympathetic. **Wanda und Leopold von Sacher-Masoch: Szenen einer Ehe. Eine kontroversielle Biographie. Eine Collage*, ed. A. Opel, Vienna, Wiener Frauenverlag, 1996, 304 pp. A. Opel, 'L. v. S.-M.: Ein "österreichischer Turgeniew"'. Ein Kapitel österreichischer Literaturgeschichte ist neu zu schreiben', Daviau, *Literatur*, 448–54. B. Hyams, 'The whip and the lamp: L. v. S.-M., the woman question, and the Jewish question', *WGY*, 13, 1997:67–79. A. del Caro, 'Nietzsche, S.-M., and the whip', *GSR*, 21:241–61. K. Gerstenberger, 'Her (per)version: *The Confessions of Wanda von Sacher-Masoch*', *WGY* 13, 1997:81–99.

SCHOPENHAUER, ADELE. G. Büch, 'A. S.: Ein Leben zwischen Anspruch und Resignation', *Palmbaum*, 5, 1997:92–101.

SCHWAB, GUSTAV. M. Hałub, '"Meine Wege gehen auf Ihre Straße": Über die Wechselbeziehungen der Brüder Grimm mit schwäbischen Romantikern', *GeW*, 116, 1996:99–117.

SEALSFIELD. *Österreich wie es ist oder: Skizzen von Fürstenhöfen des Kontinents*, ed. P.-H. Kucher, Vienna, Böhlau, 1997, 167 pp., is an abridged *Leseausgabe* of Kucher's edition of 1994. A. Ritter, 'Natchez in the fiction of three centuries: Variations of literary regionalism in Chateaubriand, Sealsfield and Welty', *Southern Quarterly*, 35, 1996–97:13–28, is concerned with *Das Kajütenbuch*. P.-H. Kucher, 'Polyphonie und paradoxe Diskursstrukturen: Zur Romanpoetik bei C. S. (Karl Postl) am Beispiel des *Virey*', Daviau, *Literatur*, 383–96.

STIFTER. The HKA of S.'s *Werke und Briefe*, ed. A. Doppler et al., Stuttgart, Kohlhammer, has added 1.9, *Studien. Kommentar*, ed. H. Bergner et al., 1997, 442 pp.; IV.1, *Der Nachsommer*, ed. W. Frühwald et al., 1997, 312 pp. Muriel Honhon, '*da ich stets die Kinder als Knospen der Menschheit außerordentlich geliebt habe': Studie zu den Kinderprotagonisten im Werk Adalbert Stifters* (EH, 1, 1678), 208 pp., investigates the formative experience of childhood in *Mein Leben*, *Bunte Steine* and *Der Nachsommer*. Karl Pörnbacher, *Adalbert Stifter* (UB, 15217), 144 pp. *JASI*, 3, 1996, has: M. Mayer, 'Gedächtniskunst: Ss *Studien-Mappe*' (7–23); U. Dittmann, '*Brigitta* und kein Ende: Kommentierte Randbemerkungen' (24–28); R. Simon, 'Eine strukturale Lektüre von Ss *Granit*' (29–36); W. Wittkowski, 'Zeitgenossen: S., Hebbel, Grillparzer' (37–58); K. Bonn, 'Initiation des Blicks: Zur

Erzählung der *Nachkommenschaften*' (59–69); M. Beckmann, 'Ss Erzählung *Der fromme Spruch*: Die Verdoppelung der Wirklichkeit' (70–92); C.-P. Berger, '"[...] dann suchte ich den Jupiter, die Vesta und andere [...]": Hat A. S. den Kleinplaneten Vesta beobachtet?' (93–109); R. Selbmann, 'Späte "bunte Steine": Die Denkmäler für A. S.' (110–28); F. van Ingen, 'Ss Modernität: Bemerkungen zur Eröffnung der S.-Ausstellung in Amsterdam' (129–32); H. Grundmann, 'Wozu S. im Deutschunterricht? Ein paar grundsätzliche Anmerkungen zur Legitimation vergangener Werke generell und der Werke Ss insbesondere als Gegenstand des Literaturunterrichts' (133–43); A. Doppler, 'Spurenlesen in Texten A. Ss' (144–51); H. Bleckwenn, 'Annäherung an einen toten Dichter: Überlegungen zur Beschäftigung mit A. S. im Literaturunterricht' (152–63); I. Stahlová, 'A. S. im Literaturseminar der Preßburger Germanistik' (164–66); C. Schacherreiter, 'S. light — S. heavy' (167–80).

R. Block, 'Stone deaf: The gentleness of law in S.'s *Brigitta*', *MDU*, 90 : 17–33, reads the text as a political allegory of the fate of Hungary. D. Lányi, 'Die Faszination des Lesens: Ss *Der Kondor*', *Die Unzulänglichkeit aller philosophischen Engel: Fest. für Ž. Széll*, ed. I. Kurdi et al. (Budapester Beiträge zur Germanistik, 28), Budapest, ELTE, Germanistisches Inst., 1996, 61–66. D. Lányi, 'Konrad und Sanna an der Baumgrenze: Stifter mit Bernhard gelesen', '[...] als hätte die Erde ein wenig die Lippen geöffnet [...]': Topoi der Heimat und Identität*, ed. P. Plener et al. (Budapester Beiträge zur Germanistik, 31), Budapest, ELTE, Germanistisches Inst., 1997, 169–74. Mark Bailey, 'Stifter and the revolution of 1848', *London Ger. St. VI*, 165–200. J. H. Reid, 'Silvio Blatters Romantrilogie *Tage im Freiamt*: Der Öko-Roman zwischen Heinrich Böll und Adalbert Stifter', ABNG, 44 : 161–75, contains a brief reference to the *Vorrede* to *Bunte Steine*. A. Dusini, 'Wald. Weiße Finsternis: Zu Ss Briefen und Erzählung *Aus dem bairischen Walde*', *Euphorion*, 92 : 437–55. S. Halse, 'Strategies for dealing with nature in A. S.'s *Bunte Steine*', *OL*, 53 : 117–28. E. Geulen, 'Depicting description: Lukács and Stifter', *GR*, 73 : 267–79, is concerned with the notorious attack launched by Lukács in his 1936 essay 'Erzählen oder Beschreiben' on the discursiveness of S.'s descriptive style as exemplified in the 'Eisgeschichte' in *Die Mappe meines Urgroßvaters*. U. Stadler, 'Wirklichkeitserkundung und Geschlechterkonkurrenz in A. Ss Erzählung *Der Condor*', *GeW*, 121 : 1–11. H. Achenbach, '"Komme! Der Stiftende führet dich ein": Das mineralogische Titelprinzip in A. Ss *Bunte Steine* und ein Privatscherz Goethes', *Sprachkunst*, 29 : 241–48. B. Menke, 'Rahmen und Disintegration: Die Ordnung der Sichtbarkeit, der Bilder und der Geschlechter: Zu Ss *Der Condor*', *WB*, 44 : 325–63.

STORM. T. S., *Immensee: Texte (1. und 2. Fassung), Entstehungsge-schichte, Aufnahme und Kritik, Schauplätze und Illustrationen*, ed. G. Eversberg (Editionen aus dem Storm-Haus, 9), Heide, Boyens, 143 pp., reprints both the heavily revised book version of the Novelle published in the *Sommergeschichten und Lieder* of 1851 and the until now almost unknown original text that had appeared in Biernatzski's *Volksbuch* in 1849. The editor's commentary includes useful accounts of the genesis and critical reception of the story, but the most valuable part of the book comes on page 95 ff. with the reproduction of the famous illustrations by Edmund Kanold and Wilhelm Hasemann (1887) and the earlier ones by Ludwig Pietsch (1857). Karl Ernst Laage, *Theodor Storms letzte Reise und seine 'Sylter Novelle'*, Heide, Boyens, 76 pp. + 38 b/w pls, is an attractive little publication in which, with the aid of old photographs, maps and drawings, Laage provides a fascinating insight into S.'s (only) journey to Sylt in 1887 and the sources and genesis of the fragmentary *Sylter Novelle* which was drafted during the ten days he spent in Westerland. The text of the fragment is also reproduced. E. S. Poluda, 'Sie war doch ein wildes Blut [. . .] Einbruch und Aufbruch in der weiblichen Adoleszenz', *Adoleszenz*, ed. J. Cremerius (*FLG*, 16), 1997, 9–25. A. Thomasberger, 'Erin-nerungsbilder: Das Konzept Hölderlins und eine Applikation auf Storm', Peil, *Erkennen*, 527–41. A. Schwarz, 'Social subjects and tragic legacies: The uncanny in T. S.'s *Der Schimmelreiter*', *GR*, 73:251–56. C. Tang, 'Two German deaths: Nature, body and text in Goethe's *Werther* and T. S.'s *Der Schimmelreiter*', *OL*, 53:105–16. S. Schröder, 'Von Feen und Nixen: T. Ss *Zur Wald- und Wasserfreude*', *ZDP*, 117:543–63, explores the mythological and fantastic elements of S.'s story and argues that it is a more substantial text than critical opinion has generally acknowledged. D. Plöschberger, ' "[. . .] und Nieman-dem . . .] durfte er davon reden!": Zur Problematik der Überlieferung in T. Ss *Der Schimmelreiter*', *Sprachkunst*, 29:249–68.

Schriften der T.-S.-Ges., 47, contains: I. Roebling, 'Marienphanta-sien des Poetischen Realismus: Keller, Storm, Fontane' (7–24); D. Jackson, 'Getarnt aber deutlich: Kritik am preußischen Adel in T. Ss Novelle *Der Herr Etatsrat*' (25–39); C. E. Schweitzer, 'Die Bedeutung des "Familienbildes" für die Interpretation von T. Ss Novelle *Carsten Curator*' (41–46); L. Gerreckens ' "Und hier ist es" — die verwirrende Fiktion erzählerischer Objektivität in Ss Novelle *Zur Chronik von Grieshuus*' (47–72); G. Eversberg, 'Zu einigen Bildern des Malers Nicolaes Peters im Husumer Storm-Haus' (73–81); P. Gold-ammer, ' "Du gottbegnadeter Sänger": Ein Nachtrag zum Briefwech-sel zwischen T. S. und Heinrich Schleiden' (83–85); G. Ciemnyjewski, 'Offener Brief an Robert Leroy und Eckart Pastor' (86); E. Jacobsen,

'S.-Bibliographie' (87–94); G. Eversberg, 'S.-Forschung und S.-Gesellschaft' (95–104). *Storm-Blätter aus Heiligenstadt,* includes: P. Goldammer, ' "Ein großer bärtiger Mann": T. S. und sein Bruder Otto' (10–20); G. Jaritz, ' "Hätte ich doch nur einen meiner Jugendfreunde in der Nähe!": Freude und Wehmut Ss beim Besuch ferner Freunde' (40–46).

UHLAND. D. Till, 'Vom "Stilistikum" zum "Creative Writing": L. U. (1787–1862) und die "Rhetorik des Schreibens" in Tübingen', *500 Jahre Tübinger Rhetorik, 30 Jahre Rhetorisches Seminar: Katalog zur Ausstellung im Bonatzbau der Universitätsbibliothek Tübingen vom 12. Mai bis 31. Juli 1997,* ed. J. Knape, Tübingen, Seminar für Allgemeine Rhetorik, 1997, 198 pp.

WAGNER. Annette Hein, **Es ist viel "Hitler" in Wagner': Rassismus und antisemitische Deutschtumsideologie in den 'Bayreuther Blättern' (1878–1938)* (CJ, 13), 1996, vii + 551 pp. Christine Emig, **Arbeit am Inzest: Richard Wagner und Thomas Mann* (Heidelberger Beiträge zur deutschen Literatur, 1), Frankfurt, Lang, 283 pp. James M. McGlathery, *Wagner's Operas and Desire* (NASNCGL, 22), 312 pp. J. Krämer, 'Wagners Rhetorik: Zur Gestaltung von Erinnern und Erkennen in *Tristan und Isolde*', Peil, *Erkennen,* 621–52. J. Langeveld, 'Im Banne des Ringes? Ideologische Ingredienzen im Werk Ws', *DK,* 47, 1997:117–32. S. Bub, 'Künstlerrache: R. Ws Umprägung germanischer Sagenstoffe am Beispiel von *Wieland der Schmied*', *ASNS,* 235:32–47. A. Krämer, ' "Die Wunde ist's, die nie sich schließen will": Zu einem Motiv in R. Ws *Parsifal* und Hans Henny Jahnns *Die Nacht aus Blei*', *Juni,* 25, 1996:49–58. A. Reck, 'Friedrich Theodor Vischer und R. W. Mit dem unveröffentlichten Entwurf der Wagner-Satire *Ricciardini Carradowsky der edle Viehmensch im Gletscherwald Patagoniens oder die Genesis des Dicht-Tondichters: Räuber- und Schauder-Roman*', *Euphorion,* 92:375–93.

WIDMANN. *Carl Spitteler — Joseph Viktor Widmann: Briefwechsel,* ed. W. Stauffacher (Schweizer Texte, n.F., 11), Berne, Haupt, 782 pp., publishes for the first time Spitteler's correspondence with his lifelong friend, the now almost forgotten minor writer and journalist Joseph Widmann (1842–1911). Interestingly, they were both pupils of Jacob Burckhardt at the Basler Pädagogikum. Most of the letters written by Widmann have been lost and they take up much less space in the book (589–732) than those of Spitteler (35–588). The main topics of discussion are personal matters (Spitteler's infatuation with Widmann's sister), literary plans (most importantly Spitteler's *Olympischer Frühling*), and the two men's reaction to Elisabeth Förster-Nietzsche's revelation that her brother had had no great opinion of their work. There are some references to Keller and Meyer, but they contain nothing of consequence. The editor has added a short introduction, extensive explanatory footnotes, a time chart, and indexes of persons mentioned and of works of Spitteler and Widmann discussed in the correspondence.

ZSCHOKKE. Werner Ort, *'Die Zeit ist kein Sumpf, sie ist Strom': Heinrich Zschokke als Zeitschriftenmacher in der Schweiz* (Geist und Werk der Zeiten, 91), Berne, Lang, 496 pp., analyses the content and reception of the various liberal German-language journals published by Z. in Switzerland.

LITERATURE, 1880–1945

By D. H. R. JONES, *Lecturer in German in the University of Keele*

1. GENERAL

LITERARY HISTORIES AND SURVEYS. *A Companion to German Literature: from 1500 to the Present*, ed. Eda Sagarra and Peter Skrine, Oxford, Blackwell, 1997, xiv + 380 pp., has two chapters on the period, characterized by a catholicity which does not neglect almost forgotten but nevertheless fascinating writers such as Eduard von Keyserling, and which uses imaginative sub-headings, e.g. 'The Sanatorium, the Desert Island and the Hotel', which testify to the fresh thinking and interpretative originality which the authors bring to their survey. With its impressive breadth and its sound scholarship this is a work for both the general reader and the serious student, and is one to keep and to cherish.

MOVEMENTS AND PERIODS. G. Weiss-Sussex, 'Two literary representatives of maidservant life in early 20th-c. Berlin: Clara Viebig's *Das tägliche Brot* (1901) and Georg Hermann's *Kubinke* (1910)', *GLL*, 51:342–59. Sven Arnold, *Das Spektrum des literarischen Expressionismus in den Zeitschriften 'Der Sturm' und 'Die Weissen Blätter'*, Frankfurt, Lang, 341 pp., considers the aesthetic theory propounded by these central Expressionist journals, together with their statements on contemporary political and theological issues. A. then examines, in relation to the theoretical context, two anthologies published in 1918 but consisting of poems which had appeared solely in the journals during the course of the war: 'Sturm-Abende', published in the May 1918 number of *Der Sturm*, and 'Menschliche Gedichte im Krieg', a collection of poems which had featured in *Die Weissen Blätter* between January 1915 and August 1917, during the editorship of René Schickele. Klaus-Dieter Bergner, *Natur und Technik in der Literatur des frühen Expressionismus*, Frankfurt, Lang, 348 pp., offers close examination of selected prose texts by Alfred Döblin, Gottfried Benn, and Carl Einstein. The author's aim is to investigate to what extent the early Expressionist texts of these writers foreshadow aspects of the environmental debate at the end of the 20th c., particularly in respect of the relationship between nature and technological progress. G. Streim, 'Das neue Pathos und seine Vorläufer. Beobachtungen zum Verhältnis von Frühexpressionismus und Symbolismus', *ZDP*, 117:239–54. H. Esselborn, 'Die "verrückte" Perspektive. Der Wahn in Literatur und Film des Expressionismus', *WW*, 48:91–108. M. Brady, '*Entrückung* and *Bilderverbot*. Arnold Schoenberg and film', *London Ger. St. VI*, 251–85. B. Niven, 'The procreative male: male images of masculinity and femininity in right-wing German literature of the 1918–1945 period', *FMLS*, 34:226–36. Olaf Peters, *Neue Sachlichkeit und Nationalsozialismus: Affirmation und Kritik 1931–1947*, Berlin, Reimer, 351 pp. *Keine Klage über England?: deutsche und österreichische Exilerfahrungen in Großbritannien 1933–1945*, ed. Charmian Brinson, München, Iudicium, 333 pp. Id., 'The Gestapo and the German political exiles in Britain during the 1930s: the case of Hans Wesemann — and others', *GLL*, 51:43–64. Id., 'A woman's place [. . .]?': German-speaking women in exile in Britain, 1933–1945', *ib.*, 204–24. A. Grenville, 'The earliest reception of the Holocaust: Ernst Sommer's *Revolte der Heiligen*', *ib.*, 250–65. D. C. G. Lorenz, 'Jewish women authors and the exile experience: Claire Goll, Veza Canetti, Else Lasker-Schüler, Nelly Sachs, Cordelia Edvardson', *ib.*, 225–39. H. Müssener, 'Deutschsprachiges Exil in Skandinavien: "im Abseits [. . .]" — Die Gastländer Dänemark, Norwegen, Schweden', *ib.*, 302–23. H. Reiss, 'Victor Klemperer (1881–1960): reflections on his "Third Reich" diaries', *ib.*, 65–92. J. M. Ritchie, 'Kurt Hiller — a "Stänkerer" in exile 1934–1955', *ib.*, 266–86. Guy Stern, *Literarische Kultur im Exil: gesammelte Beiträge zur Exilforschung (1989–1997)* (Philologica/Reihe A: 1), Dresden U.P., 426 pp. Dirk Wiemann, *Exilliteratur in Großbritannien 1933–1945*, Opladen, Westdeutscher Vlg, 377 pp.

AUSTRIA, PRAGUE AND SWITZERLAND. W. Schmidt-Dengler, 'Dionysos im Wien der Jahrhundertwende', *EG*, 53:313–25. J. Stewart, 'Talking of modernity: the Viennese "Vortrag" as form', *GLL*, 51:455–69.

2. POETRY

A reprint of *Gedichte des Expressionismus*, Stuttgart, Reclam, 260 pp., first published 1966, is to be welcomed, although it is unfortunate that the opportunity has not been taken to provide a revised introduction which acknowledges the changes in the perception of the movement which have taken place over the past 30 years. A. C. Plaenitz, 'Handschriftliche Sammlungen geistlicher Lieder der Rußlanddeutschen', Gottzmann, *Osteuropa*, 169–84.

3. PROSE

C. L. Gottzmann, 'Siegfried von Vegesack: Die baltische Tragödie in Aurel von Heidenkamp', Gottzmann, *Osteuropa*, 185–204.

4. INDIVIDUAL AUTHORS

BENJAMIN, WALTER. M. Katz, 'Rendezvous in Berlin: Benjamin and Kierkegaard on the architecture of repetition', *GQ*, 71:1–13. D. B.

McBride, 'Romantic phantasms: Benjamin and Adorno on the subject of critique', *MDU*, 90:465–87. Patrick Primavesi, *Kommentar, Übersetzung, Theater in Walter Benjamins frühen Schriften*, Basel, Stroemfeld, 384 pp. G. Richter, 'Fall-Off', *ib.*, 90:411–44. U. Steiner, 'Kapitalismus als Religion. Anmerkungen zu einem Fragment Walter Benjamins', *DVLG*, 72:147–71. M. Swales, '"Mind the gap". Reflections on the importance of allegory in Benjamin, Kafka, and Brecht', *London Ger. St. VI*, 315–36.

BRECHT, BERTOLT.　*Bertolt Brecht: Centenary Essays*, ed. Steve Giles and Rodney Livingstone (*GMon*, 41), Amsterdam, Rodopi, 260 pp. The Spring issue of *MDU*, 90, contains the following articles on B.: R. Cohen, 'B. in Goldbach' (300–06); T. Eickhoff, 'Keuner und Karajan im "Kalten Krieg" — Die Versuche des Komponisten Gottfried von Einem, B. B. für die Salzburger Festspiele zu gewinnen' (317–38); H. Peitsch, '"In den Zeiten der Schwäche [. . .]": Zu Spuren Bs in der europäischen Debatte über engagierte Literatur' (358–72); K. L. Schultz, 'Utopias from hell: B.'s *Mahagonny* and Adorno's *Treasure of Indian Joe*' (307–16); E. Schuhmacher, '"Die Verurteilung der Roten Armee nach B. B.": Eine Retrouvaille' (339–57). E. Lichter, '"Nichts ist also der Tod [. . .]" Östliche und westliche Elemente in Bs Denken über Tod und Identität', *Neophilologus*, 82:435–62.

BROCH, HERMANN.　J. Heizmann, 'Neuer Mythos oder Spiel der Zeichen? Hermann Brochs literarästhetische Auseinandersetzung mit James Joyce', *DVLG*, 72:512–30. G. Sanberg, 'Hermann Broch and Hermann Cohen: Jewish Messianism and the Golden Age', *MAL*, 31:71–80. K. Yamaguchi, 'Zu Hermann Brochs *Die Verzauberung. Massenwahn und Mythos*', *DB*, 100:150–57. Jörg Zeller, *Die Zeitdarstellung bei Hermann Broch*, München, Fink, 147 pp.

CELAN, PAUL.　G. Bevilacqua, 'Erotische Metaphorik beim frühen Celan', *EG*, 53:471–80. B. Böschenstein, 'Die Bedeutung Stefan Georges und Conrad Ferdinand Meyers für Paul Celans Frühwerk', *ib.*, 481–92. S. Mosès, 'P. Celan als Übersetzer Apollinaires *L'Adieu / Der Abschied*', *ib.*, 493–503. L. Naiditsch, 'Paul Celans Gedicht *Eine Gauner- und Ganovenweise* im Blick auf die Frage "Celan-Mandelstam"', *ib.*, 687–700. Uta Werner, *Textgräber: Paul Celans geologische Lyrik*, München, Fink, 210 pp.

DODERER, HEIMITO VON.　H.-A. Koch, '"Wurzelbärte von Bedeutung": Zur Sprache in Heimito von Doderers *Dämonen*', *MAL*, 31:84–97.

DÖBLIN, ALFRED.　R. Geissler, 'Alfred Döblins Apokalypse des Wachstums. Überlegungen zum Roman *Berge Meere und Giganten*',

LitL, 98.2:154–70. S.-H. Jang, 'Chaotic diversity and secret connection in *Berlin Alexanderplatz*: an interpretation in the light of Döblin's philosophy of existence', *Neophilologus*, 82:607–16.

EINSTEIN, CARL. *EG*, 53, is devoted to E. and contains the following articles: J.-M. Valentin, 'Parler de C. E. aujourd'hui' (5–12); L. Meffre, 'Théorie et experience de l'art chez C. E.' (13–27); G. Didi-Huberman, 'L'anachronisme fabrique l'histoire: sur l'inactualité de C. E.' (29–54); C. W. Haxthausen, 'Reproduktion und Wiederholung. Benjamin und E.: eine kritische Gegenüberstellung' (55–76); I. Sokologorsky, 'C. E.: la "vision autonome" des peintres cubistes' (77–98); E. Bassani, 'Les oevres illustrées dans *Negerplastik* (1915) et dans *Afrikanische Plastik* (1921)' (99–121); W. E. Drewes, 'Max Raphael und C. E.. Konstellation des Aufbruchs in die "Klassische Moderne" im Zeichen der Zeit' (123–58); J. Heusinger von Waldegg, 'Von der Geometrie des Lebens zur Kultur der Massen. C. E. und Fernand Léger' (159–70); G. Hoffmann, 'Sehen und Wahrnehmen in der Kunsttheorie von C. E.' (171–86); M.-V. Howlett, 'C. E.: réévaluation du concept de mimesis' (187–99); L. Stéphan, 'Théorie de la sculpture et arts nègres chez C. E.' (201–22); D. Chateau, 'Le développement de l'idée de plasticité en relation avec l'art nègre et l'art moderne chez C. E.' (223–36); C. Lichtenstern, 'Es Begriff der "metamorphotischen Identifikation" und seine Beobachtungen zur surrealistischen Kunst' (237–49).

FALLADA, HANS. G. Müller-Waldeck, 'Neues zu Romain Rolland, Hans Fallada und Ada Ditzen', *EG*, 53:719–32. Cecilia von Studnitz, *Es war wie ein Rausch. Fallada und sein Leben*, Düsseldorf, Droste, 450 pp., is a welcome addition to the relatively modest critical literature on F. Considering F.'s novels as 'seismographische Darstellungen der Zeit', S., biographer of Wilhelm Raabe and Maxim Gorki, provides a soundly-researched account of the apparent contradictions presented by F. as man and writer. The use of the present tense in her narrative, although occasionally irritating, creates an immediacy which is reminiscent of that of the novels themselves. The detailed chronological account of F.'s life and the comprehensive bibliography are particularly useful and help to render the work an excellent introduction to F. and one which one hopes may inspire further critical attention to this neglected writer.

FEUCHTWANGER, LION. P. Levesque,' Mapping the Other: Lion Feuchtwanger's topographies of the Orient', *GQ*, 71:145–65. John M. Spalek, *Lion Feuchtwanger: a Bibliographic Handbook*, München, Saur, 392 pp.

GEORGE, STEFAN. B. Böschenstein, 'Georges widersprüchliche Mittelalter-Bilder und sein Traum der Zukunft', *Fest. Geith*, 207–13.

GRAF, OSKAR MARIA.   J. Margetts, 'Oskar Maria Graf: the centenary of a "Bavarian Balzac"(?)', *London Ger. St. VI*, 337–66.

GUMPERT, MARTIN.   Jutta Ittner, *Augenzeuge im Dienst der Wahrheit: Leben und literarisches Werk Martin Gumperts (1891–1955)*, Bielefeld, Aisthesis, 508 pp.

HOFMANNSTHAL, HUGO VON.   D. Iehl, 'Reprise et modification. Aspects de la temporalité dans *L'Homme difficile* de Hugo von Hofmannsthal', *EG*, 53:425–34. G. Neumann, '"Tourbillon." Wahrnehmungskrise und Poetologie bei Hofmannsthal und Valéry', *ib.*, 397–424. J.-M. Valentin, ' "Der Theodor ist kein Dienstbote, sondern eben der Theodor". Types comiques et vision du monde dans *Der Unbestechliche* de Hugo von Hofmannsthal', *ib.*, 435–53. T. Wirtz, 'Abenteuer Ehe. Anmerkungen zu einem Dualismus in Hofmannsthals späten Komödien', *ColGer*, 31:155–72.

HORVÁTH, ÖDÖN VON.   *Ödön von Horváth: Kind seiner Zeit*, Berlin, Ullstein, 336 pp., is a reprint of the excellent monograph by the late Traugott Krischke, first published in 1980. E. Tworek, 'Verlassene Jugend. Zur Aktualität von Ödön von Horváths Roman *Jugend ohne Gott*', *LiB*, 53:49–61.

HUCH, RICARDA.   S. Anderson, 'The insider as outsider: Ricarda Huch's autobiographical texts', *GLL*, 51:470–82. *Du, mein Dämon, meine Schlange [. . .]: Briefe an Richard Huch: 1887–1897*, ed. Anne Gabrisch, Göttingen, Wallstein, 871 pp.

JAHNN, HANS HENNY.   Kai Stalmann, *Geschlecht und Macht: maskuline Identität und künstlerischer Anspruch im Werk Hans Henny Jahnns*, Vienna, Böhlau, 288 pp.

JÜNGER, ERNST.   Paul Noack, *Ernst Jünger. Eine Biographie*, Berlin, Alexander Fest, 368 pp., attempts to reconcile the paradoxes in the reputation of J. and to see this controversial figure in the light, not merely of German but of 20th-c. European history. Although N. pays close attention to J.'s private life, especially the crucial role of J.'s father in his development, and does not neglect to highlight J.'s inherent shyness and tendency to melancholy, at the forefront of this work is a commentary on the political history of Germany and Europe in the 20th c. The many black and white photographs subtly underline the linking of the private and the political sphere which is the strength of the biography. Since critical attention to J. is in its infancy, other monographs will doubtless follow, some of which will be more robust in their judgements. N.'s work does not purport to be a critical appraisal, especially where J.'s literary reputation is concerned, but it sets high standards in political judgement and narrative clarity.

KAFKA, FRANZ. J.-L. Bandet, ' "Si la roue n'avait pas grincé [. . .]" ' Imitation et parodie chez Franz Kafka', *EG*, 53:339–64. A. Geisenhanslüke, 'Vor dem Gesetz der Dichtung: Hebel und Kafka', *GR*, 73:299–308. R.J. Goebel, 'Paris, capital of modernity: Kafka and Benjamin', *MDU*, 90:445–64. Axel Hecker, *An den Rändern des Lesbaren: dekonstruktive Lektüren zu Franz Kafka: Die Verwandlung, In der Strafkolonie und Das Urteil*, Vienna, Passagen, 181 pp. H. Rudloff, 'Franz Kafkas "Arme-Seelen-Sagen". Anmerkungen zur Textzusammenstellung *Ein Landarzt. Kleine Erzählungen*', *WW*, 48:31–53. H. Vollmer, 'Die Verzweiflung des Artisten. Franz Kafkas *Erstes Leid* — eine Parabel künstlerischer Grenzerfahrungen', *DVLG*, 72:126–46. Id., 'Die verlorene Heimat in der Fremde. Franz Kafkas "Ernst-Liman" Fragment', *ZDP*, 117:255–73. N. Werber, 'Bürokratische Kommunikation: Franz Kafkas Roman *Der Proceß*', *GR*, 73:309–26.

KOLMAR, GERTRUD. Gudrun Jäger, *Gertrud Kolmar. Publikations- und Rezeptionsgeschichte*, Frankfurt, Campus, 297 pp., is in two parts. The first examines K.'s publications during her lifetime and her connections to contemporary literary figures, including Walter Benjamin, Elisabeth Langgässer and Ida Seidel. The second part focuses on the publication and reception of her work after 1945, and includes an evaluation of her work by fellow-Jews and the GDR view of her as an 'antifaschistische Widerstandskämpferin'. J.'s subtle and sensitive approach serves as a constant reminder that such facile stereotyping leads to a distortion of our understanding of this fascinating and relatively neglected poet. A comprehensive bibliography, which includes details of reviews and radio discussions of K.'s poetry, completes this important monograph.

MANN, HEINRICH. K. Schröter, 'Heinrich Manns *Der Untertan* als Roman der Epoche', *Marginalien*, 150:26–39.

MANN, KLAUS. A. Stephan, 'Überwacht und ausgebürgert: Klaus Mann und Erika Mann in den Akten des Dritten Reiches', *GLL*, 51:185–203.

MANN, THOMAS. *Thomas Mann Jb.*, 11, ed. Eckhard Heftrich and Thomas Sprecher, Frankfurt, Klostermann, 280 pp., presents the following papers given at the May 1998 meeting of the Thomas-Mann-Gesellschaft on the topic 'Mythos und Religion': D. Borchmeyer, ' "Zurück zum Anfang aller Dinge". Mythos und Religion in T. Ms *Joseph*romanen' (9–29); W.-D. Hartwich, 'Prediger und Erzähler. Die Rhetorik des Heiligen im Werk T. Ms' (31–50); F. Marx, 'Künstler, Propheten, Heilige. T. M. und die Kunstreligion der Jahrhundertwende' (51–60); A. U. Sommer, 'Der mythoskritische "Erasmusblick". *Doktor Faustus*, Nietzsche und die Theologen' (61–71); K. Hübner, 'Höllenfahrt. Versuch einer Deutung von T. Ms

Vorspiel zu seinen *Josephs*-Romanen' (73–90); R. Wimmer, 'Der sehr
große Papst. Mythos und Religion im *Erwählten*' (91–107); A. Martin,
'Schiwegersohn und Schriftsteller. T. M. in den Briefen Hedwig
Pringheims an Maximilian Harden' (127–52); E. Joseph, 'T. Ms
Doktor Faustus. "Variationen über ein Thema von Wilhelm Raabe"'
(155–70); W. Frizen, ' "Wiedersehen — ein klein Kapitel". Zu *Lotte
in Weimar*' (171–202); E. Heftrich, ' "In my beginning is my end."
Vom *Kleinen Herrn Friedemann* und *Buddenbrooks* zum *Doktor Faustus*'
(203–15). *Thomas-Mann-Studien*, 18, Frankfurt, Klostermann, 292 pp.,
is devoted to the connections between M. and Fontane and contains
the following: E. Heftrich, 'T. F. und T. M.. Legitimation eines
Vergleichs' (9–23); E. Sagarra, 'Intertextualität als Zeitkommentar.
T. F., Gustav Freytag und T. M.: oder Juden und Jesuiten' (25–47);
H. Nürnberger, ' "Hohenzollernwetter" oder Fünf Monarchen
suchen einen Autor. Überlegungen zu Fs politischer und literarischer
Biographie' (49–76); H. Lehnert, 'T. Ms Politikverständnis,
1893–1914' (77–97); P. Pütz, ' "Der Geist der Erzählung". Zur
Poetik Fs und T. Ms' (99–111); R. Wimmer, 'T. F. und T. M. im
Dialog' (113–34); M. Swales, ' "Nimm doch vorher eine Tasse Tee
[. . .]". Humor und Ironie bei T. F. und T. M.' (135–48); M. Neu-
mann, 'Eine Frage des Stils. Keller — F. — T. M.' (149–67);
M. Dierks, 'Reisen in die eigene Tiefe — nach Kessin, Altershausen
und Pompeij' (169–86); H. Aust, 'Künstlerisch betreute Privatheit.
T. Fs und T. Ms Briefe an Frau, Tochter und Freundin' (187–215);
D. Borchmeyer, 'F., T. M. und das "Dreigestirn" Schopenhauer —
Wagner — Nietzsche' (217–48); H. R. Vaget, 'F., Wagner, T. M. Zu
den Anfängen des modernen Romans in Deutschland' (249–74).
E. Heftrich, 'T. Ms *Doktor Faustus* und die "innere Emigration" ', *EG*,
53:455–69. S. Ireton, 'Die Transformation zweier Gregors. T. Ms
Der Erwählte und Kafkas *Die Verwandlung*', *MDU*, 90:34–48. S.-H.
Jang, 'Dichtung und Wahrheit bei T. M.: Ms "letzte Liebe" und ihre
Verarbeitung im *Felix Krull* in doppelter Form', *GLL*, 51:372–82.
I. Jens, ' "Über das Falsche, Schädliche und Kompromittierende des
Tagebuch-Schreibens, das ich unter dem Choc des Exils wieder
begann und fortführte [. . .]" (Thomas Mann, *Tagebuch*, 8. Februar
1942)', *GLL*, 51:287–301. A. Levenson, 'Christian author, Jewish
book? Methods and sources in T. M.'s *Joseph*', *GQ*, 71:166–78. *Erika
Mann: mein Vater, der Zauberer*, ed. Irmela von der Lühe and Uwe
Naumann, Hamburg, Rowohlt Taschenbuch, 559 pp., is a comprehensive documentation of the relationship between father and
daughter, comprising the correspondence from 1919 to 1955 together
with essays, statements and newspaper articles by Erika M. on the
subject of her father, his work and the filming of the novels.
C. Rauseo, 'Die Erwählten: T. Ms Gregorius und André Gide's

Theseus', *ASNS*, 235:18–31. Edo Reents, *Zu Thomas Manns Schopen-hauer-Rezeption* (Studien zur Literatur- und Kulturgeschichte, 12), Würzburg, Königshausen & Neumann, 521 pp., is a major contribution to the critical literature on M.'s interpretation of and indebtedness to Schopenhauer. The first part is devoted to an assessment of the influence of S., with initial emphasis on the evidence of the non-fictional texts before attention is turned to *Buddenbrooks*, *Der Zauberberg*, the *Joseph* novels, and *Doktor Faustus*. The second part of the study comprises a detailed commentary on the different stages of the critical literature on this theme. This particularly illuminating section is characterized by impressive research and a willingness to take issue with established opinions. Within a wide-ranging and commentated bibliography, the theme-based section is especially useful. M. Schröder-Augustin, 'Décadence und Lebenswille. Tonio Kröger im Kontext von Schopenhauer, Wagner und Nietzsche', *WW*, 48:255–74. T. Sprecher, 'Bürger Krull', *Blätter der Thomas-Mann-Gesellschaft*, 27:5–25.

MUSIL, ROBERT. S. Arndal, '"Illusionistische Kunst." Zur Jacobsen-Rezeption Robert Musils', *OL*, 53:358–78. Thomas Hake, *"Gefühlserkenntnisse und Denkerschütterungen": Robert Musils Nachlaß zu Lebzeiten*, Bielefeld, Aisthesis, 481 pp. A. Kramer, 'Language and desire in Musil's *Törless*', *London Ger. St. VI*, 287–314. A. Schwartz, 'Vom Aktivismus zum Taoismus: Robert Musils utopisches Wirkungs-konzept', *Seminar*, 34:347–63.

NIETZSCHE, FRIEDRICH. A. Del Caro, 'Nietzsche, Sacher-Masoch, and the Whip', *GSR*, 21:241–61. F. B. Parkes-Perret, 'Nietzsche's "Glück" and Thomas Mann's "Enttäuschung"', *Seminar*, 34:235–55. K. Pestalozzi, '"Aus des Dionysos, der Venus Sippe". Reflexe von Nietzsches *Geburt der Tragödie aus dem Geiste der Musik* in der deutschen Literatur der Jahrhundertwende', *London Ger. St. VI*, 223–50.

REUTER, GABRIELE. G. Rahaman, '"Aber was einem gefiel, dem musste man misstrauen": a female perspective on Bismarck's Germany', *London Ger. St. VI*, 201–22.

RILKE, RAINER MARIA. K. Asadowski, 'Sur les traces du Vieil Enthousiaste: A. Volynski, L. Andreas-Salomé, R.M. Rilke', *EG*, 53:291–311. K. S. Calhoon, 'Personal effects: Rilke, Barthes, and the matter of photography', *MLN*, 113:612–34. P. Por, '"Hyperbel [des] Weges" und "Inschrift [des] Daseins": *Die Aufzeichnungen des Malte Laurids Brigge*', *ColGer*, 31:117–53. Stefan Schank, *Rainer Maria Rilke*, Munich, DTV, 159 pp., is a concise yet academically sound introduction to R. A chronological survey of his life and the places where he lived and worked provides the background to a number of perceptive interpretative observations. The text is attractively illustrated and includes useful footnotes on the social and political background and on R.'s friends and contemporaries. A. Stevens, '*Das maltesche Paris in seiner ganzen Vollzähligkeit*: Rilke, Cézanne und Baudelaire', *EG*, 53:365–96.

ROTH, JOSEPH. K. Kröhnke, 'Signum ex avibus? Joseph Roths "Harzreise" und seine Reise durch die Harzreisen anderer Harzreisender', *Neophilologus*, 82:107–24. A. Wirthensohn, 'Die "Skepsis der metaphysischen Weisheit" als Programm. Das Fragment *Der stumme Prophet* im Lichte von Joseph Roths Romanpoetik', *DVLG*, 72:268–315.

SCHNITZLER, ARTHUR. R. Bauer, 'Arthur Schnitzler et la décadence', *EG*, 53:327–38. C. Morris, 'Der vollständige innere Monolog: eine erzählerlose Erzählung? Eine Untersuchung am Beispiel von *Leutnant Gustl* und *Fräulein Else*', *MAL*, 31:30–51. P. Plener, 'Arthur Schnitzlers Tagebücher 1879–1931. Vom Verschwinden zum Tod', *ÖGL*, 42:99–114. Felix W. Tweraser, *Political Dimensions of Arthur Schnitzler's Late Fiction*, Columbia SC, Camden House, 1997, 163 pp. M. L. Wandruszka, 'Die Liebe und das Erzählen. Zu Schnitzlers *Casanovas Heimfahrt*', *MAL*, 31:1–29.

TOLLER, ERNST. K. Leydecker, 'The laughter of Karl Thomas: madness and politics in the first version of Ernst Toller's *Hoppla, wir leben!*', *MLR*, 93:121–32.

TRAKL, GEORG. Three articles on Trakl appear in the *MBA*, 16:1997; L. Cheie, 'Sprachgebärden und Gebärdensprache in der Lyrik G. Ts. Glossen zur Bewegungskultur der Jahrhundertwende und des Frühexpressionismus' (8–20); H. Zwerschina, 'G. Ts "Psalm(I)": genetische Interpretation' (21–30); and E. Sauermann, 'Eine unbekannte Rezeption Ts aus dem Ersten Weltkrieg' (31–40).

WALSER, ROBERT. Peter Utz, *Tanz auf den Rändern: Robert Walsers 'Jetztzeitstil'*, Frankfurt, Suhrkamp, 527 pp.

WASSERMANN, JAKOB. R. Koester, 'Jakob Wassermann, antisemitism and German politics', *OL*, 53:179–90.

WEISS, ERNST. H.-H. Müller and A. Tatzel, ' "Das Klarste ist das Gesetz. Es sagt sich nicht in Worten." Ernst Weiß' Roman *Die Feuerprobe*. Eine Interpretation im Kontext von Weiß' Kritik an Kafkas *Proceß*', *Euphorion*, 92:1–23.

WERFEL, FRANZ. Volker Hartmann, *Religiosität als Intertextualität: Studien zum Problem der literarischen Typologie im Werk Franz Werfels*, Tübingen, Narr, 351 pp.

ZUCKMAYER, CARL. *Briefwechsel/Carl Zuckmayer: Paul Hindemith*, ed. Gunther Nickel and Giselher Schubert, St. Ingbert, Röhrig, 122 pp.

ZWEIG, ARNOLD. J. Hermand, 'The Rohme episode in Arnold Zweig's *Das Beil von Wandsbek*', *GLL*, 51:240–49.

LITERATURE FROM 1945 TO THE PRESENT DAY

By OWEN EVANS, *Lecturer in German, University of Wales, Bangor*

1. GENERAL

Zwischen Distanz und Nähe. Eine Autorinnengeneration in den 80er Jahren, ed. Helga Abret and Ilse Nagelschmidt (Convergences, 6), Berne, Lang, x + 242 pp. K. Adam, 'Années nazies — années d'après-guerre: le prisme de la mille-et-unième année dans les regards autobiographiques', *Germanica*, 20, 1997:111–24. *Schreiben im heutigen Deutschland. Fragen an die Vergangenheit*, ed. Ursula E. Beitter (Contemporary German Literature and Society, 2), NY, Lang, 280 pp. *In der Sprache der Täter. Neue Lektüren deutschsprachiger Nachkriegs- und Gegenwartsliteratur*, ed. Stephan Braese, Opladen–Wiesbaden, Westdeutscher Vlg, 257 pp. Günter Butzer, *Fehlende Trauer. Verfahren epischen Erinnerns in der deutschsprachigen Gegenwartsliteratur*, Munich, Fink, 370 pp. Anna Chiarloni, *Germania '89. Cronache letterarie della riunificazione tedesca*, Mi, FrancoAngeli, 138 pp. Anne-Marie Corbin-Schuffels, *La Force de la Parole. Les intellectuels face à la RDA et à l'unification allemande (1945–1990)*, Villeneuve-d'Ascq, Septentrion U.P., 279 pp. *Baustelle Gegenwartsliteratur. Die neunziger Jahre*, ed. Andreas Erb, Opladen–Wiesbaden, Westdeutscher Vlg, 1997, 236 pp. K. Fuji, 'Körper und Gedächtnis der Stadt. Berlin in der Literatur der 90er Jahre', *DB*, 101:76–86. D. Gutzen, 'Vom Fremdwerden des Vertrauten. Die Vereinigung im Spiegel der Literatur oder: "Ein weites Feld"', *EG*, 53:619–34. G. Henckmann, 'Doppelgängerinnen in der zeitgenössischen Frauenliteratur', *JDSG*, 62:421–53. Ewa Hendryk, *Hinterpommern als Weltmodell in der deutschen Literatur nach 1945* (EH, I, 1701), 215 pp. *Maulhelden und Königskinder. Zur Debatte über die deutschsprachige Gegenwartsliteratur*, ed. Andrea Köhler and Rainer Moritz, Leipzig, Reclam, 266 pp. H. Kreuzer, 'Zur literarisch-kulturellen Situation in der Mitte der 90er Jahre', *Orbis linguarum*, 4, 1996:5–14. Dieter Lamping, *Von Kafka bis Celan. Jüdischer Diskurs in der deutschen Literatur des 20. Jahrhunderts*, Göttingen, Vandenhoek & Ruprecht, 206 pp. *Gendering German Studies. New Perpectives on German Literature and Culture*, ed. Margaret Littler, Oxford, Blackwell, 1997, 216 pp., is another text which seeks to underline 'a general recognition of the contribution of Women's Studies towards the continuing diversification of *Germanistik* in Britain'. The variety of eras and topics presented here do, indeed, point up this diversity, and all but three of the articles fall beyond the remit of this review, as the study embraces linguistics, contemporary studies and film alongside literature of all eras. M. Puw

Davies's exploration of the 'Blaubartmärchen' in Karen Struck's *Blaubarts Schatten* and Elisabeth Reichart's 'Die Kammer' uncovers how the fairy tale operates as a 'nexus of associations' in the texts. Davies argues convincingly that both authors manipulate the source material to engineer an interweaving of private experience, in both cases male oppression of women, with the collective trauma of the Holocaust. J. Leal's lucid exploration of Struck's *Klassenliebe* and Verena Stefan's *Häutungen* reveals a tension at the heart of both which militates against their seamless inclusion in the feminist canon. Both texts have been perceived as significant for the Women's Movement, but Leal stresses that the feminist critical reception accorded them has been far from unanimous in its praise. Both protagonists express political resignation and seek to achieve self-fulfilment through literature. However, Leal identifies a paradox at work, inasmuch as the solution is an intensely private one effected in solitude: 'Writing promotes an end to alienation *within* society only by providing the narrators with a means to distance themselves *from* society'. Finally, A. Phipps provides an overview of 'Naturtheater' in southern Germany and its systemic marginalization of women. In terms of text, performance and organization, 'Naturtheater' remains a predominantly male preserve with women strait-jacketed in stereotypical roles, with the notable exception of the work of Martin Schleker and productions in Hayingen. P. proves an eloquent champion of this particular brand of popular culture, and her conclusion, with reference to her extensive research in this field, indicates that signs of greater equality are on the horizon. *Schriftsteller und 'Dritte Welt'. Studien zum postkolonialen Blick*, ed. Paul Michael Lützeler, Tübingen, Stauffenburg, 306 pp. A. M. Magnani, 'Ostalgie. Aspetti della letteratura tedesca dopo la riunificazione: Volker Braun, Jurek Becker, Günter Grass', *Cultura tedesca*, 8, 1997 : 193–206. Helgard Mahrdt, *Öffentlichkeit, Gender und Moral. Von der Aufklärung zu Ingeborg Bachmann*, Göttingen, Vandenhoek & Ruprecht, 295 pp. Hans-Christoph Graf von Nayhauss, *Einsichten und Ordnungsversuche. Studien zur Gegenwartsliteratur und Literatur-Rezeption in der Gegenwart* (FEK, 11), 530 pp. *Deutschlands 'innere Einheit'. Traum oder Alptraum, Ziel oder Zwangsvorstellung?*, ed. Ernst-Ulrich Pinkert (Text & Kontext, Sonderreihe 40), Copenhagen–Munich, Fink, 213 pp. Andrew Plowman, *The Radical Subject. Social Change and the Self in Recent German Autobiography* (Britische und Irische Studien zur deutschen Sprache und Literatur, 13), Berne, Lang, 168 pp., is a concise study of five recent autobiographical texts which strives for 'an approach [. . .] that overcomes both the aesthetic limitations of the debates about New Subjectivity and the social and historical blind spots of many accounts of the autobiography of the period'. To this end, P. runs the rule in his introduction over certain key contributions to the debate about autobiographical discourse, indicating that much German theory is overshadowed by the Goethean model established by *Dichtung und Wahrheit*. The most striking lacuna, in P.'s view, is that little attention has been paid to the discourses of the student and feminist movements themselves, despite the interest in New Subjectivity following events in 1968. P.'s approach, therefore, is to situate the subjects of his scrutiny, Bernward Vesper's *Die Reise*, Rolf Dieter Brinkmann's *Erkundungen für die Präzisierung des 'Gefühls' für einen Aufstand*, Karin Struck's *Klassenliebe*, Inga Buhmann's *Ich habe mir eine Geschichte geschrieben*, and Verena Stefan's *Häutungen*, firmly in their historical context, in addition to exploring the aesthetic features. He does not seek to provide his own contribution to myriad conflicting theories of autobiography, opting to pick his way through existing positions. Turning his attention to Vesper's text, P. argues that an attempted revolutionary case history is undermined by the autobiographical act itself, a tension which appears built into the text's subtitle, 'Romanessay'. A similar tension underpins Brinkmann's text, which swings between Herbert Marcuse's views of the destructive force of mass media and its manipulation of the subject, and Marshall McLuhan's conflicting belief in the media's capacity to transform the subject, to form an extension to man; both positions strike one as having retained their currency. For P., these conflicting forces in the *Erkundungen* signal the 'rift that opened up after 1968 between the political currents of anti-authoritarianism and its cultural and subcultural streams'. The three feminist texts are treated together, permitting a contrastive approach, which teases out the problems facing women autobiographical writers and explores the different strategies open to them in rendering the self. Struck's text is interesting in this regard; although designated as a 'Roman', it has widely been perceived as a *Schlüsselroman* and critics have pursued the author therein. The novel's diary form, however, has attracted little attention until now. Buhmann's text, a blend of autobiography and diary, is a more successful representation of self-actualization, although P. argues that, of the three feminist texts, *Häutungen* achieves the most effective dialectic of feminism and autobiography. Indeed, P. offers a compelling defence of the text's much criticized essentialism, suggesting that it reflects the quest for a voice at the heart of a work of fiction 'in which the rallying cry of a call to essence was combined with a more complex grasp of the self as an open-ended nexus of possibilities, and of self-invention as a process dependent upon seizing those possibilities'. Despite its rather perfunctory conclusion, the volume provides a stimulating appraisal of autobiographical writing produced after 1968, but may not be comprehensive enough in its coverage to convince fully that its interdisciplinary approach can close the gap identified at the outset. *Les littératures de langue allemande en Europe central. Des lumières à nos jours*, ed. Jacques le Rider and Fridrun Rinner, PUF, 263 pp. *Green Thought in German Culture. Historical and Contemporary Perspectives*, ed. Colin Riordan, Cardiff, Univ. of Wales Press, 1997, xv + 317 pp., represents an engagingly eclectic introduction to the intersection of Green ideas and culture in its widest possible form. Although a large number of the key chapters sadly fall outside the parameters of the present review, it is nevertheless worth stressing the value of contributions on Gustav Landauer, Green thought under National Socialism, ecological thought and critical theory, and Green ideas and right-wing politics, to name but a few, which provide a rich tapestry against which the more directly cultural aspects of the volume are examined. Indeed, R.'s opening chapter is an instructive exploration of the origins of Green ideas which isolates the key coordinates underpinning the movement; the extensive endnotes attest to the painstaking manner in which the survey has been compiled. A. Ricken explores Irmtraud Morgner's ecofeminist agenda in *Amanda*, with particular reference to her appropriation of mythology as a critical tool. A. Goodbody presents an engaging overview of catastrophism in literature after 1945, leaning especially on work by Günter Grass and Christa Wolf, and signals the moments which gave rise to flurries of apocalyptic texts. Goodbody points to the inherent paradox that some critics view as a flaw in some texts on this theme: should such writing allow itself to be considered entertaining? Goodbody's piece is neatly supplemented by articles on the GDR and Swiss literature. M. Kane provides an informative insight into the ecological situation in the GDR with reference to Monika Maron's *Flugasche*, as one might expect, but opts to concentrate primarily on two novels, Werner Bräunig's *Rummelplatz* and Martin Viertel's *Sankt Urban*. Both focus on uranium mining, but whereas the latter text eulogizes the enterprise, which Kane clearly finds unpalatable in the face of the 'calamitous situation' in the GDR, the former is a more differentiated depiction, highlighting the tension between what Bräunig's 'eye as a writer saw, and what his heart as a socialist wanted to see'. J. Barkhoff's contribution forms a welcome counterpoint, indicating that a commitment to the environment is an essential element of a Swiss writer's ethos. The chapter succeeds not only in describing the differing ways in which authors such as Adolf Muschg and Max Frisch reflect ecological themes in their work, but also in garnering space for Swiss literature in general in a study of this kind. The literary section is completed with two more specific chapters. J. Siemon explores Grass's *Die Rättin*, perceiving hope in the face of world annihilation, whilst B. Niven takes three texts as

examples of 'The Green *Bildungsroman*' and argues that they represent an inversion of the traditional pattern of such novels, in that individuals are withdrawn from society and seek new values. Niven asserts that these new values are ecological, and although his argument is sound, his choice of title is, perhaps, a little misleading. The final section rounds the volume off by looking at art and popular culture, with contributions on Joseph Beuys, the *Öko-Krimi*, and Werner Herzog's controversial production of *Fitzcarraldo*. A. Phipps's introduction to Swabian *Naturtheater* is especially interesting. A form of open-air popular theatre which embraces a broad repertoire, P. indicates that it reflects how green-conscious German society has become, and focuses on one of its key creative exponents, Martin Schleker. The necessarily brief scope of this review cannot do justice to this fine volume, which is certain to form the cornerstone for any new exploration in this field. It reflects the complex, and often shifting, opinions and stances associated with Green issues, which can share common threads and yet cut across one another too.
G. Schneilin, 'Avant-Propos — Sieben Vorlesungen zur Wiedervereinigung', *EG*, 53:521–23. U. C. Steiner, ' "Abseits vom Abseits". Randgänge der neueren deutschsprachigen Stadt-Literatur', *Manuskripte*, 139:91–97. H. Wetzel, 'Begegnungen mit der "Dritten Welt" in der deutschen Literatur der achtziger Jahre', *WW*, 47, 1997:228–48. D. Wrobel, 'Postmoderne Augen-Blicke. Das Sehen in der jüngsten Literatur', *WB*, 43, 1997:520–37.

WEST GERMANY, AUSTRIA,SWITZERLAND. *Autobiographien in der österreichischen Literatur. Von Franz Grillparzer bis Thomas Bernhard*, ed. Klaus Amann and Karl Wagner, Innsbruck-Vienna, Studien Vlg, 272 pp. *Literatur in der Schweiz*, ed. Heinz Ludwig Arnold (TK, Sonderband), 262 pp. *Hier spricht der DichterIn. Wer? Wo? Zur Konstitution des dichtenden Subjekts in der neueren österreichischen Literatur*, ed. Friedbert Aspetsberger, Innsbruck-Bozen, Studien Vlg, 224 pp. J. Bouveresse, 'Infelix Austria. L'Autriche ou les infortunes de la vertu philosophique', *Austriaca*, 22, 1997:7–21. Stefan Busch, *Und gestern, da hörte uns Deutschland. NS-Autoren in der Bundesrepublik. Kontinuität und Diskontinuität bei Friedrich Giese, Werner Beumelberg, Eberhard Wolfgang Möller und Kurt Ziesel*, Würzburg, Königshausen & Neumann, 352 pp. A. Czeglédy, 'Der problematisierte Heimatroman in der österreichischen Prosaliteratur der 60er und 70er Jahre', *Jb. der ungarischen Germanistik*, 1997:149–60. *Other Austrians. Post-1945 Austrian Women's Writing*, ed. Allyson Fiddler, Berne, Lang, 247 pp., serves as a corrective to those studies of Austrian postwar literature and culture which have tended to concentrate on Handke and Bernhard and neglected the output of the country's 'other' writers. Indeed, a glance down the table of contents reflects the breadth and variety of post–1945 women's writing in Austria, and there is insufficient scope in the present review to do justice to the full range of subjects. As one would expect, there are contributions here devoted to Bachmann, Jelinek, and Aichinger, but it is pleasing that other women are also featured that one might not have expected. There are two contributions on Christine Nöstlinger's children's fiction, for example, although, as G. Steinke points out, the author 'understands most of her books as literature proper'. The theme of childhood is amplified in two further articles with H. Lengauer's examination of three collections of short stories by Margit Schreiner and P. Bagley's comparative study of the literary treatment of Catholic schooling in Austria, with reference to Barbara Frischmuth's *Die Klosterschule* amongst other texts. Bagley outlines the contours of subordination inculcated into schoolgirls with a resultant suppression of self, a lack of freedom and the guilt felt at trying to break these confines. Bagley's citation of the Bible as a paradigm of patriarchal authority is echoed in J. Wigmore's article comparing the depiction of abuse in texts by Marlen Haushofer and Elisabeth Reichart, one of two guest writers at the conference held in April 1996, upon which this volume is based. Wigmore concurs with an earlier interpretation of Haushofer's 'Wir töten Stella' that abuse might be viewed as a 'metaphor for the morality of fleeing from political responsibility in the time following the Anschluß'. The second guest author, Anna Mitgutsch, is handled as part of a series of chapters on Austria as multicultural society. M. Stone runs the rule over the novel *Abschied von Jerusalem*, in which the author's attachment to the city in question is addressed as well as the dualities which underpin the novel. Conversely, P. Günther explores Mitgutsch's use of the 'Grenze' motif in her work. With Jörg Haider's popularity on the rise in Austria, the contributions on ethnicity enjoy a particular resonance here. A. Hammel argues in her essay on Hilde Spiel that the author herself embodied multicultural attitudes and an inherent optimism about its possibilities. S. Tebbutt's article on Ceija Stojka, the Roma author, and her autobiographical writing is the most compelling contribution here, insofar as it reflects most clearly the breadth of Austrian post–1945 literature as a whole; the likes of Handke and Bachmann may rank amongst the dominant figures, but, in the context of Haider's recent success, Stojka might arguably be the more significant now: 'Stojka is breaking new ground in the history of Austrian literature in that she offers insights not only into the Roma culture and perspective, but also into the border areas where experiences of minority and majority community overlap'. Tebbutt underlines the harrowing frankness to Stojka's descriptions of suffering in the concentration camps, and yet her very articulation of these experiences in German, in itself unusual as Roma tend not to use language in written form, let alone German, echoes what Hammel sees as Hilde Spiel's belief in the role of 'communication and the ability to face up to personal and historical past as the ultimate prerequisites for a possible multicultural society'. Fiddler's marshalling of the contributions thematically works very effectively, lending the volume a neat coherence to which the present review can barely do justice. It is to be hoped that the volume will indeed stimulate further interest in the writers presented here. C. Gürtler, 'Scharf von Erkenntnis und bitter von Sehnsucht — österreichische Literatur von Frauen seit 1945', *JFinL*, 29, 1997:50–54. S. Haupt, 'Wie reimt sich Hermetik auf Helvetik? Streifzug durch die "experimentelle" Literatur der Schweiz', *NDL*, 46.5:107–19. H. Hofreiter, 'Österreich — ein gutes und weites Land: vielgerühmt, vielgeprüft, vielgeliebt?', *MAL*, 30.3/4, 1997:111–29. M. Konzett, 'The politics of recognition in contemporary Austrian Jewish literature', *MDU*, 90:71–88. Gerhard Melzer, **Die verschwiegenen Engel. Aufsätze zur österreichischen Literatur*, Graz, Droschl, 208 pp. E. Müller, 'Lo real maravilloso. Österreichische Literatur in Kuba', *LK*, 323–24:11–14. Josef Rattner and Gerhard Danzer, **Österreichische Literatur und Psychoanalyse*, Würzburg, Königshausen & Neumann, 365 pp. **Von Qualtinger bis Bernhard. Satire und Satiriker in Österreich seit 1945*, ed. Paul Sigurd Scheichl, Innsbruck-Bozen, Studien Vlg, 196 pp. K. Wagner, 'Wie gegenwärtig ist die österreichische Gegenwartsliteratur? Ein Vortrag vor niederländischen Germanisten', *DeutB*, 27, 1997:249–62. Astrid Wallner, **Österreichische Literatur 1996. Ein Pressespiegel*, Vienna, Dokumentationsstelle für neuere österreichische Literatur, 1997, 118 pp.

GDR. **Retrospect and Review. Aspects of the Literature of the GDR 1976–1990*, ed. Robert Atkins and Martin Kane, Amsterdam, Rodopi, 1997, iii + 348 pp. H. Bulmahn, 'Ideology, family policy, production, and (re)education: literary treatment of abortion in the GDR of the early 1980s', *STCL*, 21, 1997:315–35. Kerstin Dietrich, **'DDR-Literatur' im Spiegel der deutsch-deutschen Literaturdebatte. 'DDR-Autorinnen' neu bewertet* (EH, 1, 1698), 370 pp. Karsten Dümmel, *Identitätsproblematik in der DDR-Literatur der siebziger und achtziger Jahre*, Frankfurt, Lang, 1997, 261 pp., tackles a topos of GDR literature, which has been the subject of previous studies. After outlining the theoretical and methodological parameters of his survey, D. selects a number of texts by authors whom he describes as purveyors of 'kritische Literatur' and who build on the foundations of subjective authenticity laid by Christa Wolf in *Nachdenken über Christa T.* D.'s selection incorporates seminal GDR works, such as Volker Braun's *Unvollendete Geschichte* and Monika Maron's *Flugasche*, alongside less well-known texts by established authors such as Ulrich Plenzdorf,

Klaus Schlesinger, Joachim Walter, and Thomas Brasch. D. investigates 'Identitätsproblematik' from the different perspectives of children, teenagers, adults and the elderly, choosing a representative text in each case. To facilitate his study, D. explores the use of various themes and motifs in the works in question, in particular the Icarus myth and the Romeo and Juliet motif, and the variety of ways in which these aspects are manipulated and applied by the authors. The study charts familiar territory, namely the interweaving of private and public in the GDR, but D.'s approach does succeed in teasing out the way in which individual identity was 'behindert, gesteuert oder kanalisiert' from childhood. Indeed, the dimension which makes this study compelling is D.'s own GDR background. His insight into aspects of the GDR education system and the detailed planning behind syllabi is valuable. It is a shock, for instance, to learn that teachers were encouraged to identify potential recruits for the *Stasi* amongst schoolchildren as young as twelve and that hitherto 17,000 pupils are known to have worked as *Inoffizielle Mitarbeiter* at school. A significant weakness to the study is D.'s use of excursi in each chapter, which briefly introduce a second text to the discussion. For example, the chapter exploring *Flugasche* concludes with reference to Christoph Hein's *Der fremde Freund*. The resultant imbalance caused makes one question why D. did not simply adopt a contrastive approach in the first place, instead of introducing such digressions which sometimes dilute, rather than sustain, the thrust of his argument. Nevertheless, the study has a great deal to commend it. S. Faust, 'Von der Vogelfreiheit des Geistes. Beispiele oppositioneller Lyrik in der DDR', *LWU*, 4:377–85. Wilhelm Frank, **Literarische Satire in der SBZ/DDR 1945–1961. Autoren, institutionelle Rahmenbedingungen und kulturpolitische Leitlinien*, Hamburg, J. Kovač, 261 pp. H. Fuhrmann, 'Vorausgeworfene Schatten. Lyrik in der DDR — DDR in der Lyrik', *WW*, 46, 1996:454–81. Dorothea Germer, **Von Genossen und Gangstern. Zum Gesellschaftsbild in der Kriminalliteratur der DDR und Ostdeutschlands von 1974 bis 1994*, Essen, Die Blaue Eule, 448 pp. **Contentious Memories. Looking Back at the GDR*, ed. Jost Hermand and Marc Silbermann (GLC, 24), x + 251 pp. T. Jung, 'Nicht-Darstellung und Selbst-Darstellung: der Umgang mit der "Judenfrage" in der SBZ und der frühen DDR und dessen Niederschlag in Literatur und Film', *Monatshefte*, 90:49–70. Brigitte Kehrberg, **Der Kriminalroman der DDR 1970–1990*, Hamburg, J. Kovač, 218 pp. B. Lönne, ' "Als ich noch in meinen Träumen lag [. . .]". Erinnerungen an subjektive Wahrnehmungen einer vergangenen Welt. Zur Jugendkultur in der DDR der achtziger Jahre', *CEtGer*, 32, 1997:303–14. Alexandra Schichtel, **Zwischen Zwang und Freiwilligkeit. Das Phänomen Anpassung in der Prosaliteratur der DDR*, Opladen–Wiesbaden, Westdeutscher Vlg,

255 pp. Jürgen Serke, **Zu Hause im Exil. Dichter, die eigenmächtig blieben in der DDR*, Munich, Piper, 464 pp. D. M. Sweet, 'A literature of "truth": writing by gay men in East Germany', *STCL*, 22:205–25. Klaus Welzel, **Utopieverlust — die deutsche Einheit im Spiegel ostdeutscher Autoren* (Ep, 242), 262 pp.

MINORITY LITERATURE. Hiltrud Arens, **'Kulturelle Hybridität' in der deutschen Minoritätenliteratur der achtziger Jahre* (Discussion, 12), Tübingen, Stauffenburg, x + 244 pp. H. Henderson, 'Re-thinking and re-writing *Heimat*: Turkish women writers in Germany', *WGY*, 13, 1997:225–43. Thomas Krause, **'Die Fremde rast durchs Gehirn, das Nichts [. . .]' Deutschlandbilder in den Texten der Banater Autorengruppe (1969–1991)* (Studien zur Reiseliteratur- und Imagologieforschung, 3), Frankfurt, Lang, 296 pp. Claude Meintz, **Bibliographie courante de la littérature luxembourgeoise 1997 (10e année) et compléments des années précédentes*, Mersch, Centre national de littérature, 202 pp. C. Tuk, ' "Meine Heimat ist die Fremde meines Vaters, die Fremde meines Vaters ist meine Heimat." Gedichte türkischer Migranten im DaF-Unterricht', *Info DaF*, 25:702–11.

2. Lyric Poetry

*Das verlorene Alphabet. Deutschsprachige Lyrik der neunziger Jahre, ed. Michael Braun and Hans Thill, Heidelberg, Wunderhorn, 256 pp. **Jahrbuch der Lyrik 1998/99. Ausreichend lichte Erklärung*, ed. Christoph Buchwald and Marcel Beyer, Munich, Beck, 143 pp. Dieter Hoffmann, **Arbeitsbuch Deutschsprachige Lyrik seit 1945*, Tübingen, Francke/UTB, 410 pp. J. Larrige, 'La poésie autrichienne depuis 1945: orientation bibliographique', *Austriaca*, 22, 1997:157–78. C. Riccabona, 'Konvention und Experiment in der Lyrik der frühen sechziger Jahre in Nordtirol', *MBA*, 16, 1997:74–81.

3. Prose

Elvira Armbröster-Groh, **Der moderne realistische Kinderroman. Themenkreise, Erzählstrukturen, Entwicklungstendenzen, didaktische Perspektiven* (KASL, 21), 1997, 296 pp. Jörg Bernig, **Eingekesselt. Die Schlacht um Stalingrad im deutschsprachigen Roman nach 1945* (GLC, 23), 1997, 376 pp. Karina Gómez-Montero, **Sinnverlust und Sinnsuche. Literarischer Nihilismus im deutschsprachigen Roman nach 1945* (KGS, 40), viii + 231 pp. W. Mieder, '(Un)sinnige Phrasendrescherei. Sprichwörtliche Prosatexte von Elias Canetti bis Marie Luise Kaschnitz', *Ginkgobaum*, 15, 1997:201–28. H. C. von Nayhauss, 'Von der Kulturrevolte zur Postmoderne. Aspekttypische Erzählungen und Romane deutschsprachiger Literatur der Gegenwart', *Orbis linguarum*, 6, 1997:121–43.

Yoriko Nishitani, *Literarische Auseinandersetzung mit der zerstörten Mutter/ Tochter-Beziehung in autobiographischen Prosawerken deutschsprachiger und japanischer Autorinnen* (EH, 1, 1663), 272 pp. I. Scheitler, 'Musik als Thema und Struktur in deutscher Gegenwartsprosa', *Euphorion*, 92:79–102.

4. INDIVIDUAL AUTHORS

ADLER, H. G.   F. Hocheneder, 'Aufzeichnungen einer Displaced person. Werk und Nachlaß H.G.As (1910–1988)', *LK*, 329–30:50–56.

AICHINGER, ILSE.   G. Melzer, 'Tanzende Kirschbäume. Kinder und Kindheit im Werk I.As', *Manuskripte*, 141:141–45. Catherine Purdie, *'Wenn ihr nicht werdet wie die Kinder'. The Significance of the Child in the World-View of I.A.* (EH, 1, 1681), 127 pp. I. Rabenstein-Michel, 'Entre réalité et imaginaire. *Die größere Hoffnung* d'I.A.', *CEtGer*, 32, 1997:131–42. Nicole Rosenberger, *Poetik des Ungefügten* (Untersuchungen zur österreichischen Literatur des 20. Jahrhunderts, 13), Vienna, W. Braumüller, x + 190 pp.

ANDERSCH, ALFRED.   R. Kolk, ' "Du willst nur nicht." Zu A.As *Der Vater eines Mörders*', *Euphorion*, 92:69–77. See also FRISCH, MAX.

ANDRES, STEFAN.   John Klapper, *S.A. Der christliche Humanist als Kritiker seiner Zeit*, Berne, Lang, 21 pp.

ARENDT, ERICH.   R. Zekert, 'Natur und Mythos. Bemerkungen zu E.A. und Rudolf Bahro', *SGG*, 4, 1997:71–78.

ARMER, KARL MICHAEL.   J. Rzeszotnik, 'Zeitkritik im Zukunftsgewand. Zum Kurzgeschichtenwerk von K.M.A.', *Orbis linguarum*, 5, 1996:133–48.

ARTMANN, HANS CARL.   Maria Fialik, *'Strohkoffer'-Gespräche. H.C.A. und die Literatur aus dem Keller*, Vienna, Zsolnay, 256 pp. J. Lajarrige, 'Routes et déroutes exotiques dans la poésie de H.C.A.', *Austriaca*, 22, 1997:119–36. H. Röbl, 'H.C.A.: *die fahrt zur insel nantucket*. Une pièce sans contenu? — Une pièce sans signification?', *CEtGer*, 32, 1997:117–29.

BACHMANN, INGEBORG.   *Über die Zeit schreiben. Literatur- und kulturwissenschaftliche Essays zu I.Bs 'Todesarten'-Projekt*, ed. Monika Albrecht and Dirk Göttsche, Würzburg, Königshausen & Neumann, 254 pp. Klaus Amann, *'Denn ich habe zu schreiben. Und über den Rest hat man zu schweigen.' I.B. und die literarische Öffentlichkeit*, Klagenfurt-Celovec, Drava Vlg, 1997, 79 pp. Edith Bauer, *Drei Mordgeschichten. Intertextuelle Referenzen in I.Bs 'Malina'* (EH, 1, 1668), 237 pp. *I.B. und Paul Celan. Poetische Korrespondenzen. Vierzehn Beiträge*, ed. Bernhard Böschenstein and Sigrid Weigel, Frankfurt, Suhrkamp, 1997, 269 pp. Corinna Caduff, *'dadim dadam.' Figuren der Musik in der Literatur I.Bs*

(Literatur-Kultur-Geschlecht, 12), Cologne–Weimar, Böhlau, 259 pp. M. Moustapha Diallo, **Exotisme et conscience culturelle dans l'œuvre d'I.B.*, Frankfurt, IKO, 226 pp. **'Text-Tollhaus für Bachmann-Süchtige?' Lesarten zur Kritischen Ausgabe von I.Bs 'Todesarten'-Projekt*, ed. I. Heidelberger-Leonard, Opladen–Wiesbaden, Westdeutscher Vlg, 197 pp. I. Meyer, '"Ein Schandgesetz erkennt man, nach dem alles angerichtet ist": Täter-Opfer-Konstellationen in I.Bs Erzählung "Unter Mördern und Irren"', *MAL*, 31.1:39–55. H. L. Ott, 'L'impossible généalogie féminine chez I.B.', *Germanica*, 22:123–34. Ursula Töller, **Erinnern und Erzählen. Studie zu I.Bs Erzählband 'Das dreißigte Jahr'* (PSQ, 151), 167 pp. F. de Vecchi, 'Ein Ich im Kontext des Schreibens. Überlegungen zu *Malina* von I.B.', *Script*, 15:16–21. See also HAUSHOFER, MARLEN.

BECHER, JOHANNES R. Jens-Fietje Dwars, **Abgrund des Widerspruchs. Das Leben des J.R.B.'*, Berlin, Aufbau, 861 pp. See also JÜNGER, ERNST.

BECKER, JUREK. Thomas Jung, **'Widerstandskämpfer oder Schriftsteller sein [. . .]' J.B. — Schreiben zwischen Sozialismus und Judentum. Eine Interpretation der Holocaust-Texte und deren Verfilmungen im Kontext* (Osloer Beiträge zur Germanistik, 20), Frankfurt, Lang, 255 pp. *J.B.*, ed. Colin Riordan, Cardiff, Univ. of Wales Press, xii + 154 pp., is an exception in this fine series in that it does not contain a literary contribution from B. due to his death in March 1997. Instead, a personal tribute from Peter Schneider is included. In the interview which follows, B. gives very full answers to questions pertaining to the dearth of female characters in his fiction, relations between Germany and Israel and especially to his attitude to the GDR, its literature and his role therein: 'Ich bezweifle, ob ich je DDR-Schriftsteller gewesen bin'. D. Rock argues that B.'s work on the holocaust and Jewish efforts to come to terms with it constitute an attempt to retrieve memories of his own childhood, or even to create some in the first place: 'Seine jüdischen Werke stellen also eine Art Identitätssuche mittels sprachlicher Konstruktionen dar, den Versuch, gleichsam die verschlossene Tür der Vergangenheit mit einem sprachlichen Schlüssel aufzumachen'. When B. learnt German after 1945, his experiences from the time he spoke Polish were lost; his father refused to fill in the gaps and was unable even to remember his son's birthday. P. O'Doherty builds on Rock's contribution by refuting B.'s claim that his Jewishness only became an issue on settling in West Berlin. In truth, the author's first three novels touched on Jewish assimilation. O'Doherty argues that *Bronsteins Kinder* provocatively indicates that only by eschewing the role of victims can the Jewish community establish 'an individual identity that is self-sufficient and self-perpetuating'. H. Helbig changes tack in his examination of *Amanda herzlos* and shifts attention back onto B. as a GDR author. In his survey, Helbig is especially interested in the depiction of the GDR *Alltag* and the censorship issue. Censorship also featured in B.'s Frankfurt lectures in 1989, which are scrutinized by R. Williams. For any reader unfamiliar with B., Williams reveals the charm and the challenge that awaits. A cultural pessimism is located at the heart of the lectures which compare the role of the writer in West and East Germany, a comparison that B. was able to make with great clarity. Although the general tenor of the lectures suggests the impotence of literature, Williams warns us to beware of B.'s cunning and sophistic-ated powers of argument. The volume would be incomplete without an analysis of B.'s work for television, for which he is probably most famous, and so it is that M. McGowan examines *Wir sind auch nur ein Volk*, B.'s screenplay dealing with the *Wende* and its aftermath. Here too light is cast upon the author's playful sophistication as evinced by the screenplay's subtle use of self-referential devices to subvert the very genre in question. As a result, the finished product cannot be dismissed purely as one-dimensional entertainment. The depiction of a series being created within the series draws attention to *Wessi* prejudices and the *Ossis*' capacity to exaggerate and fabricate stories for the camera. A full bibliography compiled by P. O'Doherty rounds off the volume. It is hard to read the contributions to this enlightening monograph and not to feel a sense of frustration at the tragic loss of an innovative, playful, provocative, and perceptive author. See also WOLF, CHRISTA.

BERNHARD, THOMAS. L. Cassagnau, 'Entre Vergile et Eliot: le sens des références poétiques de T.B. dans *Ave Vergil*', *Austriaca*, 22, 1997:67–84. Herbert Grieshop, **Rhetorik des Augenblicks. Studien zu T.B., Heiner Müller, Peter Handke and Botho Strauss* (Ep, 221), 266 pp. Y. Hoffmann, ' "Les mots du jour pour les images de la nuit." Récits de cauchemars comme rêves manqués chez T.B.', *CEtGer*, 33, 1997:161–69. Johannes Frederik G. Podszun, **Untersuchungen zum Prosawerk T.Bs 'Die Studie und der Geistesmensch'. Entwicklungstendenzen in der literarischen Verarbeitung eines Grundmotivs* (GANDLL, 20), 175 pp. S. Rieger, 'Ohrenzucht und Hörgymnastik. Zu T.Bs Roman *Das Kalkwerk*', *WB*, 44:411–33. Eun-Hee Ryu, **Auflösung und Auslöschung. Genese von T.Bs Prosa im Hinblick auf die 'Studie'* (EH, 1, 1647), 300 pp. C. Wulf, 'La hantise de la question chez T.B.', *Germanica*, 22:135–44. See also WEISS, PETER.

BIERMANN, WOLF. Veit Sorge, **Literarische Länderbilder in Liedern W.Bs und Wladimir Wyssozkis* (Studien zur Reiseliteratur- und Imago-logieforschung, 2), Frankfurt, Lang, 135 pp.

BLOCH, ERNST. G. Kleinschmidt, 'Der zweimal verschwindende Rahmen — eine Geschichte von E.B. oder : Was man tut, wenn man liest', *WW*, 48:109–22.

BOBROWSKI, JOHANNES. J. von der Thüsen, 'Flußmythen, Strombilder. Zur Lyrik J.Bs', *Euphorion*, 92:47–67.

BÖLL, HEINRICH. W. Bellmann, 'B. und Benn. Zu zwei Texten H.Bs aus den Jahren 1959/60', *WW*, 47, 1997:221–27. Id., 'Wort und Wörtlichkeit. Zu einer Shaw-Übersetzung und einem Essay von Annemarie und H.B.', *Euphorion*, 92:483–91. G. de Bruyn, 'Über B., das Geschwätz und das Schweigen', *NDL*, 46.2:31–43. Leszek Żyliński, **H.Bs Poetik der Zeitgenossenschaft*, Toruń, Univ. Mikolaja Kopernika, 1997, 166pp.

BRANDSTETTER, ALOIS. P. Firchow, 'Who done it?: narrative gamesmanship in A.B's *Die Abtei*', *MAL*, 31.1:98–114. **Vom Manne aus Pichl. Über A.B.*, ed. Egyd Gstättner, Vienna, Residenz, 160 pp. G. U. Sandford, '*Bernhardsland*. Zum Österreichbild A.Bs', *MAL*, 30.3–4, 1997:222–38.

BRINKMANN, ROLF DIETER. Michael Strauch, **R.D.B. Studie zur Text-Bild-Montagetechnik* (Colloquium, 48), Tübingen, Stauffenburg, 204 pp.

BROCH, HERMANN. **H.B. Perspektiven interdisziplinärer Forschung*, ed. Bernáth Arpád, Michael Kessler and Endre Kiss (Colloquium, 42), Tübingen, Stauffenburg, vii + 344 pp. J. Heizmann, 'Neuer Mythos oder Spiel der Zeichen. H.Bs literarästhetische Auseinandersetzung mit James Joyce', *DVLG*, 72:512–30. G. Sandberg, 'H.B. and Hermann Cohen: Jewish messianism and the Golden Age', *MAL*, 31.2:71–80. Jörg Zeller, **Die Zeitdarstellung bei H.B.* (Text und Kontext, Sonderreihe, 41), Copenhagen–Munich, Fink, 148 pp.

DE BRUYN, GÜNTER. Owen Evans, '*Ein Training im Ich-Sagen': Personal Authenticity in the Prose Work of G.d.B.* (EH, I, 1580), 1996, 344 pp, represents the first full study of de B. in English and charts the course of his career up to 1995. Special attention is paid to the long, and troubled, genesis of his first novel, *Der Hohlweg* (1963), which fell prey to the tenets of Socialist Realism. The planned autobiographical reckoning with his wartime experiences became a sprawling GDR epic so typical of the period. By the time of its publication, de B. could not bear it. The present study argues that de B. subsequently embarked upon a period of literary experimentation and consolidation in the search for his own voice, whilst simultaneously drawing on personal experience to colour his fiction. Even de B.'s extensive work on Germany's literary heritage, such as his biography of Jean Paul, is shot through with autobiographical features. Thus, the study concludes that *Zwischenbilanz* (1992), the first volume of de B.'s highly acclaimed autobiography, represents not only a literary milestone for the author, but also the salvation of personal material abused by early literary practices in the GDR, and feared lost and irretrievable.

BURMEISTER, BRIGITTE. M. Gebauer, 'Vom "Abenteuer des Berichtens" zum "Bericht eines Abenteuers". Eine poetologische "Wende" im Schreiben von B.B.', *WB*, 44:538–53.

CANETTI, ELIAS. E. L. du Cardonnoy, 'Le judéo-espagnol de C.: une crypto-langue', *ChrA*, 6, 1997:107–16. Id.,'Crises des rapports interpersonnels dans le roman *Auto-da-fé* d'E.C. Apocalypse et phobie du bleu', *Germanica*, 22:79–91. W. C. Donahue, ' "Eigentlich bist du eine Frau. Du bestehst aus Sensationen." Misogyny as cultural critique in E.Cs *Die Blendung*', *DVLG*, 71, 1997:668–70. E. W. Schaufler, 'Wohin mit Canetti? Versuch einer Zu- und Einordnung innerhalb der österreichischen Literatur', *Jb. der ungarischen Germanistik*, 1997:191–208. R. Wintermeyer, '*Flüssige Geständnisse*? Zu E.Cs Autobiographie', *Germanica*, 20, 1997:47–76.

CELAN, PAUL. Stephan Bleier, **Körperlichkeit und Sexualität in der späten Lyrik P.Cs* (BBL, 21), 228 pp. S. Bogumil, 'P.C. De passage à Vienne', *Austriaca*, 22, 1997:43–65. E. Dzikowska, '*Schwarze Flocken*. Zum Kosakenbild in der frühen Lyrik P.Cs', *Orbis linguarum*, 7, 1997:113–18. Jean Firges, **Den Acheron durchquert ich'. Eine Einführung in die Lyrik P.Cs*, Tübingen, Stauffenburg, 322 pp. E. van der Knaap, ' "Dein Gesang, was weiß er?" C.-Vertonungen in den Niederländen', *DK*, 47, 1997:99–116. Sabine Markis, **'mit lesendem Aug'. Prinzipien der Textorganisation in P.Cs 'Niemandsrose'*, Bielefeld, Aisthesis, 128 pp. E. Mulder, 'Bemerkungen zu P.Cs "Todesfuge"', *DK*, 47, 1997:89–98. C. Parry, 'Übersetzung als poetische Begegnung. P.C. als Übersetzer und als Gegenstand von Übersetzung', *JDF*, 24:159–84. Otto Pöggeler, **Lyrik als Sprache unserer Zeit? P.Cs Gedichtbände*, Opladen–Wiesbaden, Westdeutscher Vlg, 45 pp. H. Sekiguchi, 'Cs Körperpoetik', *DB*, 100:168–78. Peter Waterhouse, **Im Genesis-Gelände. Versuch über einige Gedichte von P.C. und Andrea Zanzotto*, Weil am Rhein, Engeler, 96 pp. Uta Werner, **Textgräber. P.Cs geologische Lyrik*, Munich, Fink, 210 pp. See also BACHMANN, INGEBORG.

CZERNIN, FRANZ JOSEF. A. Puff-Trojan, 'Form — Natur — Esse. Bemerkungen zu F.J.Cs "kunst des dichtens" ', *Austriaca*, 22, 1997:137–56.

DELIUS, FRIEDRICH CHRISTIAN. **F.C.D. Studien über sein literarisches Werk*, ed. Manfred Durzak and Hartmut Steinecke, Tübingen, Stauffenburg, 1997, xii + 258 pp.

DODERER, HEIMITO VON. Hubert Kerscher, **Zweite Wirklichkeit. Formen der grotesken Bewußtseinsverengung im Werk H.v.Ds* (RBDSL, 68), 557 pp. H.-A. Koch, ' "Wurzelbärte von Bedeutungen". Zur Sprache in H.v.Ds *Dämonen*', *MAL*, 31.1:84–97. R. Kray, 'Über "Revolution" im Roman. Last, Belastung, Elastik eines historischen Schlüsselbegriffs in Ds *Die Dämonen*', *WB*, 44:364–91. **Excentrische Einsätze'. Studien und Essays zum Werk H.v.Ds*, ed. Kai Luehrs, Berlin–NY, de

Gruyter, xvi + 355 pp. Michael Vrüsch, *Wirklichkeit und Existenz. Ds Wirklichkeits- und Literaturverständnis zwischen Ideologie und Erfahrung* (EH, I, 1685), 206 pp.

DOMIN, HILDE. Birgit Lermen and Michael Braun, *H.D. Hand in Hand mit der Sprache*, Bonn, Bouvier, 1997, 199 pp.

DRACH, ALBERT. R. Kowalski, 'Zum Leben und Schaffen von A.B.', *SGG*, 4, 1997:59–69.

DRAWERT, KURT. R. Prachtl, 'Zu K.D. Festrede', *Internationales Johnson-Forum*, 6, 1997:161–65.

DUDEN, ANNE. S. Bird, 'Desire and complicity in A.D's *Das Judasschaf*', *MLR*, 93:741–53. A. Meusinger, 'The wired mouth: on the possibility of perception in A.D's *Opening of the Mouth* and *Das Judasschaf*', *WGY*, 13, 1997:189–203. See also HAUSHOFER, MARLEN.

DÜRRENMATT, FRIEDRICH. Heinz Ludwig Arnold, *Querfahrt mit F.D.*, Zurich, Diogenes, 208 pp. Walter Bossard, 'Der Kaiser als Hühnerzüchter. Eine neue Quelle bringt Licht in die Entstehungsgeschichte von Ds Komödie *Romulus der Große*', *SchwM*, 78.2:49–53. Christoph Vratz, 'Kontrapunktik als Strukturprinzip in F.Ds *Der Richter und sein Henker* und *Der Verdacht*', *WW*, 48:367–75.

EICH, GÜNTER. *G.E.*, ed. Karl Karst, Frankfurt, Suhrkamp, 350 pp. S. Reb, 'De l'acceptation du monde à l'anarchie: langage, pouvoir et quête d'identité personnelle dans la poésie et la réflexion poétologique de G.E.', *Germanica*, 22:161–80.

ENZENSBERGER, HANS MAGNUS. A. Descomps, 'H.M.E. et la traduction', *NCA*, 15, 1997:401–04. Monika Kilian, *Modern and Postmodern Strategie. Gaming and the Question of Morality: Adorno, Rorty, Lyotard, and E.* (Studies in Literary Criticism and Theory, 11), NY, Lang, 240 pp. R. Luckscheiter, 'Die Masse massakriert ihre Agenten. Über den hellhörigen H.M.E.', *Merkur*, 52:736–40. See also WEISS, PETER.

ERB, ELKE. B. Dahlke, 'Avant-gardist, mediator, and [...] mentor? E.E.', *WGY*, 13, 1997:123–32. Id., 'Not "man or woman", but rather "what kind of power structure is this?": E.E. in conversation', *ib.*, 133–50.

FICHTE, HUBERT. Silke Cramer, *Reisen und Identität. Autogeographie und Werk H.Fs*, Bielefeld, Aisthesis, 116 pp.

FORTE, DIETER. *Vom Verdichten der Welt. Zum Werk von D.F.*, ed. Holger Hof, Frankfurt, Fischer, 238 pp.

FRIED, ERICH. Steven Lawrie, '"Das große Turnierfeld, auf dem sie sich versuchen." E.F.'s work for German radio', *GLL*, 51:121–46. Katrin Schäfer, *Die andere Seite: E.Fs Prosawerk. Motive und Motivationen seines Schreibens*, Vienna, Praesens, 420 pp. Klaus Schuhmann, 'Brecht bei Fried. Zeitalterdialog im Gedicht', *WB*, 44:118–32.

FRISCH, MAX. A.-M. Baranowski, 'Mein Name sei Gantenbein de M.F.: Les visages de la comédie et du refus', *Germanica*, 22:65–77. Iris Block, *'Daß der Mensch allein nicht das Ganze ist!'. Versuche menschlicher Zweisamkeit im Werk M.Fs* (BLL, 17), 368 pp. Id., '"Das Ausmaß der Trauer." Negativdarstellung und Engagement bei M.F.', *LWU*, 3:231–49. Liette Bohler, *Der Mythos der Weiblichkeit im Werke M.Fs* (STML, 36), 248 pp. Romanita Constantinescu, *Selbstvermöglichungs-strategien des Erzählers im modernen Roman. Von ästhetischer Selbstaufsplit-terung bis zu ethischer Selbstsetzung über mehrfache Rollendistanzen im Erzählen Robert Musil — M.F. — Martin Walser — Alfred Andersch* (EH, 1, 1700), 302 pp. Kyung-Og Lee, *Antagonismen in den Dramen von M.F.* (EH, 1, 1661), 166 pp. E. Poulain, '"Que faites-vous? De l'amour?" Les désarrois amoureux dans le roman *Stiller* de M.F.', *Germanica*, 22:53–64.

FÜHMANN, FRANZ. Barbara Heinze, *F.F. Eine Biographie in Bildern, Dokumenten und Briefen*, Rostock, Hinstorff, 400 pp. *'Jeder hat seinen F.' Herkunft — Prägung — Habitus. Potsdamer Literaturwissenschaftliche Studien und Konferenzberichte. Zugänge zu Poetologie und Werk F.Fs*, ed. Brigitte Krüger, Margid Bircken and Helmut John, Frankfurt, Lang, 339 pp. A. Lagny, 'L'autobiographie comme "exécution de soi-même": F.F.: *Zweiundzwanzig Tage oder die Hälfte des Lebens*', *Germanica*, 20, 1997:95–109.

GAPPMAYR, HEINZ. P. Garnier, 'La poésie spatiale en Autriche: l'exemple de H.G.', *Austriaca*, 22, 1997:85–91.

GRASS, GÜNTER. *Warum Einmischung not tut. Die Kontroverse um G.G. und die Laudatio auf Yasar Kemal in der Paulskirche*, ed. Manfred Bissinger and Daniela Hermes, Göttingen, Steidl, 208 pp. Iris Heilmann, *G.G. und John Irving. Eine transatlantische Intertextualitätsstudie* (KSL, 11), 267 pp. U. Matthäus, 'G.G. und die deutsche Frage', *Ginkgobaum*, 15, 1997:398–418. F. Szász, 'Der entdämonisierte Künstler und sein entteufelter Teufel. Eine Interpretation von G.Gs *Ein weites Feld*', *Jb. der ungarischen Germanistik*, 1996[1997]:13–32. S. Taberner, 'Feigning the anaesthetisation of literary inventiveness: G.G.'s *örtlich betäubt* and the public responsibility of the politically engaged author', *FMLS*, 34:69–81. H. Wetzel, 'G.G.: Annäherung an Calcutta', *WB*, 44:5–26. H. Winkel, 'Nicht von der Bank der Sieger aus. Gespräch mit G.G.', *NDL*, 46.2:6–24.

GRÜNBEIN, DURS. E. Sturm-Trigonakis, 'Formen der Alterität in der neuen deutschen Dichtung: José A. Oliver und D.G.', *WW*, 48:376–407.

HANDKE, PETER. L. Bluhm, '"Schon lange [...] hatte ich vorge-habt, nach Serbien zu fahren." P.Hs Reisebücher', *WW*, 48:68–90. K. Buchheister, 'Elfenbeintürme — leerstehend. Zum Dementi von Subjektivität bei P.H. und Botho Strauss', *JIG*, 29.2, 1997:94–122.

B. Desbrière-Nicolas, 'Le style de l'autobiographie chez P.H. (1967–1972)', *Germanica*, 20, 1997:77–94. Id., 'P.H. *La femme gauchère*: du récit aux images', *Germanica*, 22:145–59. Volker Michel, **Verlustgeschichten. P.Hs Poetik der Erinnerung* (Ep, 245), 233 pp. H. Moysich, 'Von luftigen Hütten und Pantoffeln im Kopf. Lese-Aufblicke zu P.H., Joseph Beuys, Goffredo Parise u.a.', *Manuskripte*, 141:153–55. Eleonora Pascu, **Unterwegs zum Ungesagten. Zu P.Hs Theaterstücken 'Das Spiel vom Fragen' und 'Die Stunde da wir nichts voneinander wußten', mit Blick über die Postmoderne*, Frankfurt, Lang, 226 pp. S Yoshimochi, 'P.Hs Serbien-Reiseberichte oder die Entstehung der Bilder', *DB*, 101:117–26. See also BERNHARD, THOMAS.

HARIG, LUDWIG. W. Jung, 'Erinnerung, Ordnung, Spiel. Zur Poetik von L.H.', *Orbis linguarum*, 4, 1997:31–40.

HAUSHOFER, MARLEN. Franziska Frei Gerlach, **Schrift und Geschlecht. Feministische Entwürfe und Lektüren von M.H.*, Ingeborg Bachmann und Anne Duden (Geschlechterdifferenz und Literatur, 8), Berlin, Erich Schmidt, 448 pp.

HEIN, CHRISTOPH. Hélène Guibert-Yèche, **C.H. — L'œuvre romanesque des années 80. De la provocation au dialogue* (Contacts, III, Études et documents, 39), Berne, Lang, xii + 402 pp. G. Jackman, '"Unverhofftes Wiedersehen": narrative paradigms in C.H's *Nachtfahrt und früher Morgen* and *Exekution eines Kalbes*', *GLL*, 51:398–414.

HERMLIN, STEPHAN. M. Feldt, 'Nachruf auf S.H.', *DB*, 99, 1997:168–71. G. Seibt, 'Kann eine Biographie ein Werk zerstören? Bemerkungen zu de Man, Jauß, Schwerte und H.', *Merkur*, 3:215–26.

HEYM, STEFAN. B. Hocke, 'S.H.: *Nachruf* — eine moderne Autobiographie?', *Germanica*, 20, 1997:151–76. M. Tait, 'S.H.'s *Radek*: the conscience of a revolutionary', *GLL*, 51:496–508.

HILSENRATH, EDGAR. M. Marko, 'Die Verteidigung des Erinnerns. Laudatio auf den Hans-Sahl-Preisträger E.H.', *Europäische Ideen*, 112:12–18.

HOCHHUTH, ROLF. R. Kolk, '"Nemesis aus Gütersloh". Anmerkungen zur Dramatik R.Hs', *WW*, 48:54–67.

HOFFER, KLAUS. Madeleine Napetschnig, **K.H.*, Graz, Droschl, 200 pp.

HUCHEL, PETER. Cornelia Freytag, **Weltsituationen in der Lyrik P.Hs* (EH, I, 1665), xii + 256 pp. J. Joachimsthaler, 'Nachträgliche Politisierung. P.Hs "Späte Zeit"', *Convivium*, 1997:241–66. S. H. Kaszyński, 'P.H. in Polen. Die Geschichte einer komplizierten Rezeption', *ib.*, 267–91. Hub Nijssen, **Der heimliche König. Leben und Werk von P.H.*, Würzburg, Königshausen & Neumann, 625 pp. Stephen Parker, **P.H. A Literary Life in 20th-Century Germany* (British and Irish Studies in German Language and Literature, 15), Berne, Lang, 617 pp.

HÜRLIMANN, THOMAS. **Verleihung des Literaturpreises der Konrad-Adenauer-Stiftung e. V. an T.H., Weimar, 3. Juni 1997. Dokumentation*, ed. Günther Rüther, Wesseling, Konrad-Adenauer-Stiftung, 1997, 38 pp.

JAHNN, HANS HENNY. Uwe Kai Stalmann, **Geschlecht und Macht. Maskuline Identität und künstlerischer Anspruch im Werk H.H.Js*, Cologne-Weimar-Vienna, Böhlau, vii + 288 pp.

JELINEK, ELFRIEDE. Heidi Strobel, **Gewalt von Jugendlichen als Symptom gesellschaftlicher Krisen. Literarische Gewaltdarstellungen in E.Js 'Die Ausgesperrten' und in ausgewählten Jugendromanen der neunziger Jahre* (EH, 1, 1655), 306 pp. Monika Szczepaniak, **Dekonstruktion des Mythos in ausgewählten Prosawerken von E.J.* (EH, 1, 1695), 225 pp. S. Treude, 'Die Kontextualität des Gespenstischen in E.Js Roman *Die Kinder der Toten*', *Script*, 15:9–15. Veronika Vis, **Darstellung und Manifestation von Weiblichkeit in der Prosa E.Js* (EH, 1, 1690), 454 pp.

JIRGL, REINHARD. W. Jung, 'Material muß gekühlt werden. Gespräch mit R.J.', *NDL*, 46.3:124–40.

JOHNSON, UWE. J. Brummack, 'Ein Traum Gesines. Über Traum, Bild, Erzählung in U. Js *Jahrestage*', *CEtGer*, 33, 1997:147–59. Corinna Bürgerhausen, **Variante des verfehlten Lebens. U. Js 'Skizze eines Verunglückten'* (LU, 33), 158 pp. A.-M. Lohmeier, 'Jerichow in New York. Provinz und Welt in U. Js *Jahrestagen*', *JIG*, 29.2, 1997:62–75. M. Maron, 'Verspätete Lektüre. Über U. J.', *NDL*, 46.2:158–70. Barbara Scheuermann, **Zur Funktion des Niederdeutschen im Werk U. Js. '[. . .] in all de annin Saokn büssu hie nich me-i to Hus'* (Johnson-Studien, 2), Göttingen, Vandenhoeck & Ruprecht, 474 pp.

JÜNGER, ERNST. J.-F. Dwars, 'E.J. und Johannes R. Becher. Anmerkungen zu einer Nicht-Debatte in den *Weimarer Beiträgen*', *WB*, 44:242–64. Paul Noack, **E.J. Eine Biographie*, Berlin, Alexander Fest Vlg, 368 pp. See also MAYRÖCKER, FRIEDERIKE.

KAISER, REINHARD. A. Nuber, 'Gespräch mit R.K.', *DeutB*, 28:1–9.

KIPPHARDT, HEINAR. Elin Nesje Vestli, **Die Figur zwischen Faktizität und Poetizität. Zur Figurenkonzeption im dokumentarischen Drama H.Ks, Peter Weiss' und Tankred Dorsts* (Osloer Beiträge zur Germanistik, 22), Frankfurt, Lang, 459 pp.

KLEMPERER, VICTOR. H. Reiss, 'V.K. (1881–1960): reflections on his "Third Reich" diaries', *GLL*, 51:65–92. R. H. Watt, 'V.K's "Sprache des vierten Reiches": LTI = LQ1?', *GLL*, 51:360–71.

KLÜGER, RUTH. J. Rau, 'Laudatio auf R.K.', *Heine Jb.*, 36, 1997:255–61.

KOEPPEN, WOLFGANG. D. Linck, ' "Solidarisieren wollte ich mich nämlich eigentlich nie." Zum Tod W.Ks', *Forum Homosexualität und Literatur*, 25, 1996:133–38. S. Matuschek, 'Bonn allegorisch und die

Aktualität der fünfziger Jahre. Ks Roman *Das Treibhaus*', *DUS*, 50.5:92–96. Marcel Reich-Ranicki, **W.K. Aufsätze und Reden*, Frankfurt, Fischer, 171 pp.

KRONAUER, BRIGITTE. J. Illner, 'Jigsaw puzzles: female perception and self in B.K's "A Day that Didn't End Hopelessly After All"', *WGY*, 13, 1997:11–87. **Die Sichtbarkeit der Dinge. Über B.K.*, ed. Heinz Schafroth, Stuttgart, Klett-Cotta, 191 pp.

KRUSCHE, DIETRICH. A. Wierlacher, 'D.Ks *Stimmen im Rücken* oder: der Streuselkuchen. Hommage für einen Schriftsteller und langjährigen Mitherausgeber des Jahrbuchs *Deutsch als Fremdsprache*', *JDF*, 23, 1997:13–24.

KUCKART, JUDITH. H. Mörchen, 'Spurensuche. Anmerkungen zur Verarbeitung von NS-Vergangenheit in zwei deutschen Romanen der neunziger Jahre: J.K. *Die schöne Frau* und Jens Sparschuh *Der Schneemensch*', *LiLi*, 28:160–72.

KUNERT, GÜNTER. Yu Gu, **Strukturen und Denkweisen in G.Ks Dichtung. Eine Untersuchung zu den Werken 'Fremd daheim' und 'Im toten Winkel'* (Schriften zur Europa- und Deutschlandforschung, 6), Frankfurt, Lang, 243 pp.

KUNZE, REINER. **'Mit dem Wort am Leben hängen[. . .]' R.K. zum 65. Geburtstag*, ed. Marek Zybura (BNL, 162), 176 pp.

LANDER, JEANNETTE. M. Shafi, '"Between worlds": reading J.L's *Jahrhundert der Herren* as a postcolonial novel', *WGY*, 13, 1997:205–24.

LANGGÄSSER, ELISABETH. C. Gelbin, '"Es war zwar mein Kind, aber die Rassenschranke fiel zwischen uns": E.L. und die Mutter-Tochter-Beziehung', *ZDP*, 117:565–96.

LASKER-SCHÜLER, ELSE. Vivian Liska, **Die Dichterin und das schelmische Erhabene. E. L.-Ss 'Die Nächte Tino von Baghdads'*, Tübingen, Francke, 172 pp. Ulrike Müller, **Auch wider dem Verbote. E.L.-S. Und ihr eigensinniger Umgang mit Weiblichkeit, Judentum und Mystik* (EH, 1, 1493), 1997, 471 pp. **E.L.-S. Ansichten und Perspektiven / Views and Reviews*, ed. Ernst Schürer and Sonja Hedgepeth, Tübingen-Basel, Francke, 250 pp.

LAVANT, CHRISTINE. Veronika Schlör, **Hermeneutik der Mimesis. Phänomene. Begriffliche Entwicklungen. Schöpferische Verdichtung in der Lyrik C.Ls*, Düsseldorf, Parerga, 258 pp. A. Steinsiek, 'Stirne an Stirne. Zu zwei Briefen C.Ls an Hermann Lienhard', *MBA*, 16, 1997:58–67.

LEBERT, HANS. Jürgen Egyptien, **Der 'Anschluß' als Sündenfall. H.Ls literarisches Werk und intellektuelle Gestalt*, Vienna, Sonderzahl, 301 pp. **H.L.*, ed. G. Fuchs and G. A. Höfler (Dossiers über österreichische Autoren, 12), Graz, Droschl, 1997, 387 pp. S. Ganzer, 'Die Toten haben Hunger. Zu H.Ls Roman *Die Wolfshaut*', *CEtGer*, 32, 1997:143–58.

LENZ, HERMANN. Daniel Hoffmann, *Stille Lebensmeister. Dienende Menschen bei H.L.* (Colloquium, 46), Tübingen, Stauffenburg, 118 pp.

LOBE, JOCHEN JOACHIM. E. J. Krzywon, 'Auf der Gegenspur zwischen Hochdeutsch und Mundart. Zur literarischen Zweisprachigkeit des Lyrikers J.L.', *Orbis linguarum*, 7, 1997:43–49.

LOEST, ERICH. Sabine Brandt, *Vom Schwarzmarkt nach St. Nikolai. E.L. und seine Romane*, Leipzig, Linden, 192 pp.

MANDER, MATTHIAS. R. G. Weigel, 'Vom Marchfeld zur Welt. M.Ms universalistisches Österreichbild', *MAL*, 30.3–4, 1997:200–12.

MANN, THOMAS. S.-H. Jang, 'Dichtung und Wahrheit bei T.Ms "letzte Liebe" und ihre Verarbeitung in *Felix Krull* in doppelter Form', *GLL*, 51:372–82.

MARON, MONIKA. A. Lewis, 'Remembering the barbarian: memory and repression in M.M.'s *Animal Triste*', *GQ*, 71:30–46.

MAUTHNER, FRITZ. H. Miesbacher, 'Alles Sprache. Versuch über den Sprachbegriff bei F.M. und Werner Schwab', *Manuskripte*, 139:126–33.

MAYRÖCKER, FRIEDERIKE. U. Krechel, 'Vom Gießen und Fließen. Zur Pfingstlichkeit von F.M.', *Manuskripte*, 141:146–49. F. Lartillot, 'Les choix de F.M. et Ernst Jandl: tierce voix de la poétologie. Quand le syndrôme fait rage en Autriche?', *Austriaca*, 22, 1997:93–118.

MEISTER, ERNST. Françoise Lartillot, *Le lieu commun du moi. Identité poétique dans l'œuvre d'E.M. (1911–1979)* (Contacts, III, Études et documents, 42), Berne, Lang, xx + 490 pp.

MERKEL, INGE. A. Kunne, 'Die "Wiener Apokalypse" in I.Ms Roman *Das andere Gesicht*', *MAL*, 31.1:56–83.

MERZ, KLAUS. A. Nuber, ' "daß das wahre Glück wortlos ist und nur von kurzer Dauer": Zu K.Ms Erzähltext *Jakob erzählt. Eigentlich ein Roman*', *DeutB*, 28:83–91.

MONÍKOVÁ, LIBUŠE. H. G. Braunbeck, 'The body of the nation: the texts of L.M.', *MDU*, 89, 1997:489–506. S. Gross, 'Einleitung: Sprache, Ort, Heimat', *ib.*, 441–51. U. Vedder, ' "Mit schiefem Mund auch *Heimat*" — Heimat und Nation in L.Ms Texten', *ib.*, 477–88.

MORGNER, IRMTRAUD. H. Bridge, 'Myth and history in I.M.'s *Amanda*', *GLL*, 51:483–95. Martina Elisabeth Eidecker, *Sinnversuche und Trauerarbeit. Funktionen von Schreiben in I.Ms Gesamtwerk*, Hildesheim, Olms-Weidmann, vi + 256 pp. Doris Janssen, *Blue-Note-Akrobatik. I.M. im kulturellen Kontext der sechziger Jahre* (Edition Wissenschaft, 49), Marburg, Tectum, 670 pp. Beth V. Linklater, *'Und immer zügelloser wird die Lust'. Constructions of Sexuality in East German Literatures. With Special Reference to I.M. and Gabriele Stötzer-Kachold*, Berne, Lang, 248 pp. Id., ' "Unbeschreiblich köstlich wie die Liebe selber": food and sex in the work of I.M.', *MLR*, 93 : 1045–57. C. Wolf, 'Heroischer Entwurf', *NDL*, 46.6 : 5–7.

MÜLLER, HEINER. David Barnett, *Literature versus Theatre. Textual Problems and Theatrical Realization in the Later Plays of H.M.* (Britische und Irische Studien zur deutschen Sprache und Literatur, 14), Berne, Lang, 289 pp., represents a detailed and engaging exploration of a selection of M.'s later dramatic work and documents the inherent challenge facing reader, actor, and director alike. In his introduction, B. suggests that no extensive study of M.'s dramaturgical aproach has been undertaken hitherto and, thus, the current volume selects the most technically complex of the playwright's works to lay bare the precise nature of the challenge. Although a fine introduction to M. in its own right, B.'s study devotes time to the practicalities of staging the plays, dividing his material into discrete chapters which focus on three specific issues: acting, the attribution of characters and voices, and plot and structure. These themes are illuminated with reference to specific plays, and textual analysis is underpinned by detailed comparisons of theatrical productions of the plays in question. The detailed technical exploration of these various performances may be of more interest to the theatrical expert than the literary scholar, although they indeed reflect just how much the original texts resist staging. Indeed, as B. amply demonstrates, M.'s texts 'attempt to terrorize the theatre as much as the audience'; one need only cite one of the texts under scrutiny here, *Die Hamletmaschine*, as an example of quite bewildering complexity. The contrast in the productions of this play are arguably the most interesting here, by virtue of its hermetic nature as dramatic text; the account of M.'s own staging is especially fascinating. We learn that it is the one of his own plays he directed the most, indicating, perhaps best of all, M.'s own view that texts resist the authority of the playwright, and thus offer myriad possibilities to the director. B. argues that perception of M. changed following the *Wende* with the demise of Eastern bloc socialism, inasmuch as he has since been perceived as a 'great dramatic poet', rather than as a 'political dramatist'. If his popularity with theatre producers and directors has waned, B. asserts nonetheless that there is a robustness to M.'s work which ensures it has retained its provocative nature. Even if the subject matter of some plays may no longer seem relevant or has lost its power to shock through repeated productions, B. argues convincingly that the form of much of M.'s work militates against it being assimilated into the mainstream: 'The blistering diversity of the realizations of Müller at his most provocative bear witness to the strength of a dramaturgy that cannot be apprehended'. In eschewing the jargon of literary theory, B. presents an accessible, and stimulating, appraisal of M.'s achievements and fills the lacuna he identifies in his introduction. Horst Domdey, *Produktivkraft Tod. Das Drama H.Ms*, Cologne, Bohläu, xi + 350 pp. Katharina Keim, *Theatralität in den späten Dramen H.Ms* (Theatron, 23), Tübingen, Niemeyer, viii + 291 pp. M. Krajenbrink, 'Der Fall H.M.', *DeutB*, 28:237–41. I. Kurdi, 'Gemeinplätze zu einer Schlüsselfigur. H.M. (1929–1995)', *Jb. der ungarischen Germanistik*, 1996:33–41. Peter W. Marx, *H.M.: 'Bildbeschreibung'. Eine Analyse aus dem Blickwinkel der Greimas'schen Semiotik* (Studien zur deutschen und europäischen Literatur des 19. und 20. Jahrhunderts, 37), Frankfurt, Lang, 178 pp. C. Rochow and A. Schalk, 'On heroes and hero-worship. Anmerkungen zu H.Ms *Germania 3*', *IASL*, 22.2, 1997:52–65. M Schneider, 'Bertolt Brecht und sein illegitimer Erbe H.M.', *NDL*, 46.3:124–40. Fernando Suárez Sánchez, *Individuum und Gesellschaft. Die Antike in H.Ms Werk* (Helicon, Beiträge zur deutschen Literatur, 23), Frankfurt, Lang, 307 pp. See also BERNHARD, THOMAS.

MÜLLER, HERTA.   V. Glajar, 'Banat-Swabian, Romanian, and German: conflicting identities in H.M.'s *Herztier*', *MDU*, 89, 1997:521–40. *H.M.*, ed. Brigid Haines, Cardiff, Univ. of Wales Press, xi + 157 pp., continues the stimulating series of monographs on contemporary German writers and features currently one of the most celebrated. The volume follows the now familiar pattern and includes ten short texts by M. herself, an outline biography, an interview, an up-to-date bibliography and a selection of essays on aspects of the author's canon. The interview is extremely revealing, with M. answering candidly and fully about features of her work, many of which are explored later in the volume. For instance, M. admits to being drawn to authors who conflate biography and literature, conceding that her own texts might best be described as 'autofiktional'. M.'s comments on the interplay between her two languages, German and Romanian, and its effect primarily on her use of metaphor and idiom is especially fascinating. D. Midgley pursues M.'s use of motifs in *Der Mensch ist ein großer Fasan auf der Welt*, exploring how objects become the spur for memories, but also how the attention to the minutiae of Romanian life undercuts the totality prescribed by Socialist Realism. M. Littler contrasts the depiction of the city in the novels of M. and Libuše Moníková and finds that, for M., the metropolis affords sanctuary and anonymity, in contrast to the state oppression that permeates claustrophobic village life. R. Schmidt reveals the intricacy and subtlety of M.'s application of metaphor and metonymy in a careful, well observed guide to *Herztier*. S. postulates that the aesthetic device exposes the dehumanizing effects of dictatorship on the individual, but concedes the difficulty in pinning anything down in the novel, not least the image of the title. J. White corroborates the findings of both Midgley and Schmidt in his survey of how totalitarianism is depicted in M.'s work as a whole. The article blends an analysis of the importance of fragmentary 'Einzelheiten' and intense subjectivity for M. with an informative account of the political issues which have shaped post–1945 Romania. D. Hoff's contribution is the weakest here, locating M.'s resistance to the state in the moral stance of her work. Despite raising a number of interesting points, such as M.'s belief in the value of poetry as a means of survival for writers, it is a shame that they were not explored more fully. B. Haines's closing chapter revisits many of the aspects explored by the other contributors, such as M.'s use of attention to small details, which Haines neatly terms 'anti-systematic poetics', but returns in particular to the alleged 'autofiktional' quality of the work. The subjective authenticity of M.'s fiction lays bare the destructive impact of the public violation of the private sphere. Haines remarks that the further away Ceauşescu's Romania slides, the more bleak become M.'s depictions of life at that time, but concludes with a compelling defence of the author against the charge that her work has stagnated: '[. . .] As long as there exists a single country which can be described as a "prison without bars" [. . .], writing which investigates and celebrates resistance through the God of Small Things will demand our urgent attention'. It is hoped that this volume will promote further interest in a challenging, yet fascinating, writer. A. Harnisch, ' "Ausländerin im Ausland": H.Ms *Reisende auf einem Bein*', *MDU*, 89, 1997:507–20. W. Müller, ' "Poesie ist ja nichts Angenehmes": Gespräch mit H.M.', *ib.*, 468–76.

MÜLLER, INGE. B. Vanderbeke, 'Über I.M.', *NDL*, 46.2:58–77.

MUSCHG, ADOLF. Anabel Niermann, **Frauengestalten in den Parzival-romanen A.Ms und Wolframs von Eschenbach. Eine kontrastive Analyse anhand der Frauengestalten Herzeloyde und Sigûne* (Edition Wissenschaft, 44), Marburg, Tectum, 130 pp. S. Obermaier, ' "Die Geschichte erzählt uns" — Zum Verhältnis von Mittelalter und Neuzeit in A.Ms Roman *Der Rote Ritter. Eine Geschichte von Parzivâl*', *Euphorion*, 91, 1997:467–88.

NADOLNY, STEN. Angela Fitz, **'Wir blicken in ein ersonnenes Sehen'. Wirklichkeits- und Selbstkonstruktion in zeitgenössischen Romanen. S.N. — Christoph Ransmayr — Ulrich Woelk*, St. Ingbert, Röhrig, 384 pp.

NEUMANN, GERT. J. Lehmann, 'Die Suche nach dem Gespräch. Überlegungen zu den Texten G.Ns', *Orbis linguarum*, 8:21–36.

PASTIOR, OSKAR. H. Müller, 'Die ungewohnte Gewöhnlichkeit bei O.P.', *Wespennest*, 110:80–86.

PLENZDORF, ULRICH. Y.-G. Mix, 'Mit Goethe und Diderot gegen die Pächter des klassischen Erbes. U.Ps *Die neuen Leiden des jungen W.*, Volker Brauns Texte zu *Hinze und Kunze* und die Kontrolle der literarischen Kommunikation in der DDR', *JDSG*, 62:401–20.

RANSMAYR, CHRISTOPH.   Esther F. Gehlhoff, *Wirklichkeit hat ihren eigenen Ort. Lesearten und Aspekte zum Verständnis des Romans 'Die letzte Welt'* von C.R., Paderborn, Schöningh, 156 pp. J. Landa, 'Fractured vision in C.R's *Morbus Kitahara*', *GQ*, 71 : 136–44. Barbara Vollstedt, **Ovids 'Metamorphoses', 'Tristia' and 'Epistulae ex Ponto' in C.Rs Roman 'Die letzte Welt'*, Paderborn, Schöningh, 201 pp. See also NADOLNY, STEN.

REIMANN, BRIGITTE.   H. L. Jones, 'Narrative structure and the search for self in B.R.'s *Franziska Linkerhand'*, *GLL*, 51 : 383–97.

REZZORI, GREGOR VON.   E. Konradt, 'Schlawiner, Salonlöwe, Lebenskünstler. Die deutschen Nachrufe auf G.v.R. Eine Bilanz', *LK*, 327–28 : 9–11. G. Köpf, 'Die Vorzüge der Windhunde. G.v.R. "auf der Spur" ', *NDL*, 46.2 : 181–89.

RICHTER, HANS WERNER.   G. Holzheimer, 'Immer nach vorne [. . .] Neue Literatur zu H.W.R. und der "Gruppe 47" ', *LiB*, 52 : 22–24.

ROSENLÖCHER, THOMAS.   J. Engler, 'Der eigene Ton oder Das langsame Heraufkommen von Dampfschiffen aus der Flußbiegung. Gespräch mit T.R.', *NDL*, 46.6 : 26–43.

ROTH, GERHARD.   Uwe Schütte, **Auf der Spur der Vergessenen. G.R. und seine Archive des Schweigens* (Literatur und Leben, 50), Vienna, Böhlau, 1997, 335 pp.

SACHS, NELLY.   **N.S. An letzter Atemspitze des Lebens*, ed. Birgit Lermen and Michael Braun, Bonn, Bouvier, 308 pp.

SCHIRMBECK, HEINRICH.   Cynthia L. Appl, **H.S. and the Two Cultures. A Post-War German Writer's Approach to Science and Literature* (STML, 34), viii + 160 pp.

SCHMIDT, ARNO.   Guido Graf, **Über den Briefwechsel zwischen A.S. und Hans Wollschläger*, Wiesenbach, Bangert, 1997, 287 pp. C. Hein, 'A.S. Elitär? Allerdings! oder Der kahle Mongolenschädel über uns', *NDL*, 46.2 : 104–30. Henning Hermann-Trentepohl, **Dialoge. Polyphonie und Karneval im Spätwerk A.Ss* (Cursus, Texte und Studien zur deutschen Literatur, 13), Munich, Iudicium, 249 pp. Kurt Jauslin, **Der magersüchtige Leviathan. Essen und Trinken im Werk A.Ss — ein Versuch zur Mythologie des Alltagslebens*, Wiesenbach, Bangert, 275 pp. Thomas Körber, **A.Ss Romantik-Rezeption*, Heidelberg, C. Winter, viii + 353 pp. Timm Menke, **Die Goethe-Rezeption A.Ss*, Bielefeld, Aisthesis, 138 pp.

SCHNEIDER, PETER.   S. Machocki, 'Liebe in den Zeiten der Individualisierung. Zur Darstellung der Liebe in P.Ss *Paarungen*', *Convivium*, 1997 : 293–329.

SCHUBERT, HELGA.   Alessandro Bigarelli, **Ethik und Diskurs im weiblichen Schreiben am Beispiel von H.Ss Geschichten. Eine interdisziplinäre Untersuchung: Literatur, Philosophie, Psychologie* (EH, 1, 1693), 281 pp.

SEBALD, W. G.   H. Detering, 'Schnee und Asche, Flut und Feuer. Über den Elementardichter W.G.S.', *Neue Rundschau*, 2:147–58. Gerhard Köpf, *Mitteilungen über Max. Marginalien zu W.G.S.*, Oberhausen, Laufen, 100 pp.

SEGHERS, ANNA.   Marie Haller-Nevermann, *Jude und Judentum im Werk A.Ss. Untersuchungen zur Bedeutung jüdischer Traditionen und zur Thematisierung des Antisemitismus in den Romanen und Erzählungen von A.S.* (EH, I, 1612), 1997, 279 pp. L. Rinser, 'Hoffnung und Glaube der A.S.', *NDL*, 46.2:131–43. *A.S. in Perspective*, ed. Ian Wallace (GM, 43), Amsterdam–Atlanta, Rodopi, 212 pp. W. Wende, '*Überfahrt* von A.S. Liebesgeschichte, Zeitporträt und Erzählung über das Erzählen', *Euphorion*, 92:25–46.

SPERBER, MANÈS.   A.-M. Corbin-Schuffels, 'Le messager d'un monde disparu', *Germanica*, 20, 1997:177–91. M. Stancic, 'M.S. und die Linke. Der historische, politische und literarische Kontext', *WB*, 44:392–410. G. Stieg, 'Le philosophe comme héros: le *Socrate* de M.S.', *Austriaca*, 22, 1997:125–37.

SPIEL, HILDE.   Bettina Krammer, *Wer ist Lisa L. Curtis? Manifestation der hysterischen Charakterstruktur sowie der Emigrations- und Suchtproblematik bei Lisa Leitner Curtis in 'Lisas Zimmer' von H.S.* (EH, I, 1686), 221 pp. Marcel Reich-Ranicki, *Über Hilde Spiel*, Munich, DTV, 126 pp.

STÖTZER-KACHOLD, GABRIELE.   B. Linklater, 'Erotic provocations: G.S.-K.'s reclaiming of the female body?', *WGY*, 13, 1997:151–70. See also MORGNER, IRMTRAUD.

STRAUSS, BOTHO.   J. Born and M. Nakamasa, 'Der *Bockgesang* von B.S. — Provokation oder Gelegenheit zur Reflexion über divergierende Blickwinkel in "West" und "Ost"? Ein Beitrag zum Problem kulturdifferenter Lektüren', *JDF*, 24:47–81. W. Braungart, 'Ästhetik der Präsenz. Zu B.S. mit Blick auf "Kalldewey, Farce"', *DUS*, 50.5:80–89. J. Daimer, 'Berührungspunkte zwischen Wissen und Poesie. Die Analogie als Erkenntnisform bei B.S.', *WB*, 44:276–82. Steffen Damm, *Die Archäologie der Zeit. Geschichtsbegriff und Mythosrezeption in den jüngeren Texten von B.S.*, Opladen–Wiesbaden, Westdeutscher Vlg, 231 p. See also BERNHARD, THOMAS; HANDKE, PETER; WEISS, PETER.

STREERUWUTZ, MARLENE.   W. Riemer and S. Berka, '"Ich schreibe vor allem gegen, nicht für etwas." Ein Gespräch mit M.S., Bränerhof, 15.Januar 1997', *GQ*, 71:47–60.

STRITTMATTER, ERWIN.   M. von der Grün, 'S., der poetische Realist', *NDL*, 46.2:44–57.

WALLNER, PETER.   A. Unterkirchner, 'Erinnerung an P.W. (1950–1987)', *MBA*, 16, 1997:68–73.

WALSER, MARTIN.   D. Lenz, 'Lesen und Schreiben. Gespräch mit M.W.', *NDL*, 46.1:8–22. Franz Oswald, *The Political Psychology of the*

White Collar Worker in M.W.'s Novels. The Impact of Work Ideology on the Reception of M.W.'s Novels 1957–1978, Frankfurt, Lang, 238 pp. W. Schaller, 'Überdeutlich Herr Walser. Beobachtungen an der Textoberfläche der Prosa-Arbeiten der achtziger Jahre sowie der Vorschlag, *Ein fliehendes Pferd* rückblickend neu zu bewerten', *Orbis linguarum*, 7, 1997:101–12. J. Schlosser, 'Die Entwicklung der Kleinbürgerthematik in M.Ws Prosawerken', *Augias*, 51, 1997:3–46. Hi-Young Song, **Poetologische Reflexion und realistische Schreibweise bei M.W. Realismuskonzeption und Interpretation von vier ausgewählten Erzählwerken M.Ws aus den 70er Jahren* (FLK, 63), 211 pp. See also FRISCH, MAX.

WALTER, OTTO F.   F. A. Lubich, ' "Das Ewig Weibliche" *Up to Date*: Gegenkultur und Mutterrecht in O.F.Ws Roman *Die Verwilderung*', *GQ,* 71:14–29.

WEISS, PETER.   V. Braun, 'Ein Ort für Peter Weiss', *NDL*, 46.2:171–80. C. Rodiek, 'Écriture et vérité. Renn, W. et Enzensberger sur l'anarchisme et la guerre d'Espagne', *ChrA*, 6, 1997:95–106. Laura Sormani, **Semiotik und Hermeneutik im interkulturellen Rahmen. Interpretationen zu Werken von P.W., Rainer Werner Fassbinder, Thomas Bernhard und Botho Strauss*, Frankfurt, Lang, ix + 345 pp. See also KIPPHARDT, HEINAR.

WELLERSHOFF, DIETER.   W. Jung, 'Literatur als Probebühne. Der Schriftsteller D.W.', *Orbis linguarum*, 7, 1997:91–100. G. Laudin, 'Innenansichten des Krieges: historie et autobiographie chez D.W.', *Germanica*, 20, 1997:137–50.

WIDMER, URS.   **U.W.*, ed. Heinz Ludwig Arnold (TK, 140), 90 pp.

WOLF, CHRISTA.   **C.Ws 'Medea'. Voraussetzungen zu einem Text. Mythos und Bild*, ed. Marianne Hochgeschurz, Berlin, Janus, 190 pp. Suzanne Legg, **Zwischen Echos leben. C.Ws Prosa im Licht weiblicher Ästhetikdebatten*, Essen, Die Blaue Eule, 208 pp. A. Palej, 'Im Angesicht des Nationalsozialismus: Kinder und NS-Zeit in C.Ws *Kindheitsmuster*, Ödön von Horváths *Jugend ohne Gott* und Jurek Beckers *Bronsteins Kinder*', *Convivium*, 1997:219–40. Monika Papenfuss, **Die Literaturkritik zu C.Ws Werk im Feuilleton. Eine kritische Studie vor dem Hintergrund des Literaturstreits um den Text 'Was bleibt'*, Berlin, wvb Wiss. Vlg, 206 pp. **Prospettive zu C.W. Dalle Sponde del Mito*, ed. Giulio Schiavoni, Mi, FrancoAngeli, 134 pp. R. Schmidt, 'Ein doppelter Kater? C.Ws *Neue Lebensansichten eines Katers* und E. T. A. Hoffmanns *Lebens-Ansichten des Katers Murr*', *Hoffmann Jb.*, 4, 1996:41–53.

ZUCKMAYER, CARL.   **Zuckmayer-Jahrbuch*, 1, ed. Gunther Nickel, Erwin Rotermund and Hans Wagener, St. Ingbert, Röhrig, 333 pp.

ZWEIG, ARNOLD.   J. Hermand, 'The Rohme episode in A.Z.'s *Das Beil von Wandsbek*', *GLL*, 51:240–49.

II. DUTCH STUDIES

LANGUAGE

POSTPONED

LITERATURE

By WIM HÜSKEN, *Lecturer in Dutch, University of Auckland*

1. GENERAL

200 years after the establishing, in 1797, of the first chair in Dutch language and literature at the University of Leiden a symposium was held in commemoration of this event. **'Eene bedenkelijke nieuwigheid': Twee eeuwen neerlandistiek*, ed. Jan W. de Vries, Hilversum, Verloren, 1997, 128 pp., contains articles on the works of some of the best known scholars of Dutch language and literature in the Netherlands during the past two centuries. Frits van Oostrom, 'Van toen en nu en straks: De studie van de Middelnederlandse letterkunde' (54–68), reviews the contributions made to the study of medieval Dutch literature by W. G. Hellinga, J. van Mierlo, and W. P. Gerritsen. Marijke Spies, 'Van "vaderlandsch gevoel" tot Europees perspectief: De studie van de 17e- en 18e-eeuwse literatuur in de 19e en 20e eeuw: En hoe verder?' (69–83) concentrates on how 17th-c. and 18th-c. Dutch literary research changed over the two centuries, paying special attention to the works of Jan te Winkel. Ton Anbeek, 'Liaisons dangereuses: Literatuurstudie tussen kunst en wetenschap' (84–97), deals with the topic of value judgement in the critical approaches of, among others, Albert Verwey, Frank C. Maatje, J. J. Oversteegen, and Teun A. van Dijk. **Nederlands 200 jaar later*, ed. Hugo Brems et al., Woubrugge, IVN–Münster, Nodus, 575 pp., publishes the acts of a colloquium, held between 24 and 30 August, 1997, on the occasion of the same commemoration. Problems and potentials of a future 'Council for Netherlandic Studies' (Raad voor de Neerlandistiek) are reflected upon in a numbers of essays edited by E. Viskil in *Wat unbidan we nu: Naar een raad voor de neerlandistiek*, The Hague, SDU, 127 pp.

L. H. Maas, *Pro Patria: Werken, leven en streven van de literatuurhistoricus Gerrit Kalff (1856–1923)* (Publicaties van de Faculteit der Historische en Kunstwetenschappen, 28), Hilversum, Verloren, 317 pp., dedicates a monograph to the literary historian, Gerrit Kalff. Appointed as professor of literature at the University of Leiden in 1901, Kalff published as his principal work a 7–vol. history of Dutch literature, *Geschiedenis der Nederlandsche letterkunde* (1906–12). Personal aesthetic feelings and the degree to which liberally inspired nationalism was present in an author's works were two of Kalff's main criteria to give or deny a writer his appreciation. The Golden Age, viewed by so many as the most glorious period in Dutch history, both from an historical and a literary perspective, did not pass without being criticized in his *Geschiedenis*. Religious intolerance, materialism, cowardice in civic and state dignitaries, and cruelty in merchants making their fortune in the East Indies, were among the issues Kalff strongly attacked, Maas notes. But above all, the literary historian felt an abhorrence for the oligarchic structures of authority, the bad relations between different social groups, and the social injustice of the times. A further aspect of Kalff's academic aspirations was to give greater publicity to Dutch literature abroad. In 1913, he established the Queen Wilhelmina Lectureship at the University of Columbia, New York, which was converted to a full professorship in 1921. In Maas's opinion, Kalff was particularly important as a pioneer of Dutch literary studies, bringing out many books and articles on topics few had ever written about before.

A very useful reference book on the history, evolution, locations, variations, and cultural background of fairy tales is Ton Dekker, Jurjen van der Kooi, and Theo Meder, *Van Aladdin tot Zwaan kleef aan: Lexicon van sprookjes. Ontstaan, ontwikkeling, variaties*, Nijmegen, SUN, 1997, 478 pp. A previously published volume in the same series, *Van Aiol tot de Zwaanridder* (1993), is now available in English translation: *A Dictionary of Medieval Heroes: Characters in Medieval Narrative Traditions and their Afterlife in Literature, Theatre, and the Visual Arts*, ed. Willem P. Gerritsen and Anthony G. van Melle, Woodbridge, Boydell, vii + 336 pp.

**Naar hoger honing? Plato en Platonisme in de Nederlandse literatuur*, ed. Marcel F. Fresco and Rudi van der Paardt, Groningen, Historische Uitgeverij, 266 pp., studies Plato's reception in the Netherlands and Platonism in Dutch literary texts. In his opening essay, 'Platonisme: Naar hoger honing?' (9–51), Fresco assesses the influence of Plato on modern Dutch poets, notably in P. C. Boutens, J. C. Bloem, Martinus Nijhoff and Jan Hanlo. F. continues with observations on the 16th-c. ethic publicist, Dirck Volckertszoon Coornhert, in 'Coornhert en zijn transformatie van een platonische dialoog' (52–71). Annemarie van Toorn concentrates on Hendrik Spieghel's ethic manual *Hart-spieghel* (1615) in 'Belering en bekering rond Plato's grot: De ethica van H. L. Spiegel' (72–93). J. D. Meerwaldt, 'Vondel platoniserend' (94–100), discusses Joost van den Vondel's poem 'De koningklijcke idea'. Wim van den Berg returns to Jacob Geel's *Gesprek op den Drachenfels* (1835) in 'Een nieuw species der kunst: Jacob Geel en de platonische dialoog' (123–40). Further contributions include P. Kralt, 'Invloed of spel? Plato bij Kloos' (141–52); J. de Gier, 'De dichter als paria: Geerten Gossaert en Plato' (153–68); C. Rutenfrans, 'De lijn de volmaakte ontwikkeling: De invloed van Plato op Bordewijk' (169–86); R. van der Paardt, 'Het schone en het goede: Platonisme in het vroege werk van B. Rijdes' (187–98); M. Koenen, 'Die Eroos in het hart bleef dragen: Plato in het dichtwerk van Ida Gerhardt' (199–219); and H. Bekkering, 'Ons leren is niets anders dan herinnering: Plato en Ovidius in *Het volgende verhaal* van Nooteboom' (220–38). Finally, Arnold Heumakers discusses Geerten Meijsing's novel *De ongeschreven leer* (1995) in 'De filosofie op reis naar Syracuse' (239–43).

*De stijl van de burger: over Nederlandse burgerlijke cultuur vanaf de middeleeuwen, ed. Remieg Aerts and Henk te Velde, Kampen, Kok Agora, 304 pp., reviews bourgeois culture between the Middle Ages and the present. C. Santing, 'Tegen ledigheid en potverteren: De habitus van de laatmiddeleeuwse stadsburger' (28–59) focuses on thoughts regarding moral behaviour of late-medieval citizens as found in treatises by Jan van Boendale and Dirc Potter. W. Velema, 'Beschaafde republikeinen: Burgers in de achttiende eeuw' (80–99) pays special attention to Justus van Effen, the 18th-c. author of the periodical *De Hollandsche Spectator*. J. Kloek, 'Burgerdeugd of burgermansdeugd? Het beeld van Jacob Cats als nationaal zedenmeester' (100–22) returns to one of Holland's most influential 17th-c. moralists whose fame lasted until well into the 19th c. H. te Velde, 'Herenstijl en burgerzin: Nederlandse burgerlijke cultuur in de negentiende eeuw' (157–85) discusses contributions to 19th-c. bourgeois culture by the novelist Lodewijk van Deyssel and the linguist Matthias de Vries. Y. Kuiper, 'Aristocraten contra burgers: Couperus' *Boeken der kleine zielen* en het beschavingsdefensief rond 1900' (186–217) concentrates on the impressive four-vol. saga written by one of the most prolific early 20th-c. novelists in the Netherlands, Louis Couperus. Political songs are central to H. Wedman's, 'Hoeden en petten: Socialisme en burgerlijke cultuur in Nederland' (218–45).

E. M. Beekman, *Paradijzen van weleer: Koloniale literatuur uit Nederlands-Indië, 1600–1950*, Amsterdam, Prometheus, 735 pp., is the Dutch translation by Maarten van der Marel and René Wezel of Beekman's previously published book, *Troubled Pleasures: Dutch Colonial Literature from the East Indies, 1600–1950*, Oxford–NY, Clarendon, 1996, x + 654 pp. (see *YWMLS*, 58:925).

In her introduction to *Dutch and Flemish Feminist Poetry from the Middle Ages to the Present: A Bilingual Anthology*, ed. Maaike Meijer, Erica Eijsker, Ankie Peypers, and Yopie Prins, NY, Feminist Press at the City Univ. of NY, xi + 194 pp., Meijer defines the expression 'feminist poetry' as 'woman-identified works, poems with telling glimpses into women's lives, poems that resist mainstream hetero-sexual pressures and the social and erotic confinement that often accompany them'. At the risk of using the term anachronistically, this collection of poems, given in the original and in English translation, offers more than 100 texts in which women are shown in their struggle to conquer their own position in a male-dominated society. Consequently, many of them do not belong to the canon of literary texts as established by 19th-c. male scholars. Hence the presence in this anthology of authors such as Katharina Questiers, Juliana Cornelia de Lannoy, and Katharina Wilhelmina Bilderdijk-Schweickhardt. In the area of 20th-c. poetry the editors' choice is somewhat more traditional, although here too there are some less familiar names such as Loes Nobel and Chawwa Wijnberg. By showing the distinct impact of immigrant authors on present-day Dutch poetry, this anthology reveals a remarkable aspect of modern female authorship in the Netherlands. Compared to this collection of poems, *Kaleidoscope: Dutch Poetry in Translation from Medieval Times to the Present*, ed. Martijn Zwart and Ethel Grene, Wilmette, Fairfield Books, x + 256 pp., supplies a slightly more comprehensive selection of Dutch poetry, given in the original language and in translation. It contains poems by some 80 authors, less than a dozen of them female. In *In liefde bloeyende: De Nederlandse poëzie van de twaalfde tot en met de twintigste eeuw in honderd en enige gedichten*, Amsterdam, Bert Bakker, 378 pp., the poet and literary critic Gerrit Komrij displays his personal views on 100 of the best poems in Dutch literature.

2. THE MIDDLE AGES

Did the literature of the Low Countries have an identity of its own as early as the Middle Ages? Frits van Oostrom attempts to answer this question in *Medieval Dutch Literature and Netherlandic Cultural Identity* (Uhlenbeck Lecture, 15), Wassenaar, NIAS, 18 pp. Eventually he arrives at the conclusion that moralizing was as distinctive for medieval Dutch literature as it was between the 17th and early 20th c. Wim van Anrooij, *Helden van weleer: De Negen Besten in de Nederlanden (1300–1700), Amsterdam U.P., 1997, 328 pp., traces the Nine Worthies in Dutch literature from the Middle Ages until the end of the 17th c. In *Boethius in the Middle Ages: Latin and Vernacular Traditions of the 'Consolatio philosophiae', ed. Maarten J. F. M. Hoenen and Lodi Nauta, Leiden, Brill, 1997, P. Wackers reviews 'Latinitas' in Middle Dutch literature (89–106); T. Mertens discusses 'Consolation in late medieval Dutch literature' (107–20); M. Goris and W. Wissink study 'The medieval Dutch tradition of Boethius' *Consolatio philosophiae*'

(121–65); M. J. F. M. Hoenen reviews 'The transition of academic knowledge: scholasticism in the Ghent Boethius (1485) and other commentaries on the *Consolatio*' (167–214); B. van Dommelen and D.-J. Dekker present an excerpt of 'Boethius' edition of the Ghent Boethius, book v, prose 3: Latin text, Middle Dutch translation and commentary' (305–25).

Jozef D. Janssens et al., *Op avontuur: Middeleeuwse epiek in de Lage Landen* (Nederlandse literatuur en cultuur in de Middeleeuwen, 18), Amsterdam, Prometheus, 389 pp., focuses on medieval Dutch epic literature. In his introductory essay Janssens claims that today's specialists in epic literature should be pleased with the situation in which they find themselves. There seem to be hardly any problems as to what texts belong to the genre, a wide range of studies on various aspects have been published, and many editions are available though most of them slightly out of date. On closer inspection, however, many things remain unresolved. How, for instance, to draw a borderline between epic and didactic literature? Or between epic texts and historiography? J. pleads for a re-examination of the concept of the genre, not in aesthetic terms but in a historical-functional sense. Intertextuality, or rather the lack of it, is another problem in Dutch epic texts. If we concentrate on the authors, this is, in various degrees, easy to describe and explain. But to what extent did intertextuality play a role for the readers of and listeners to epic stories? According to J. and others it is possible to discriminate between an intended audience and the epics' intended intertextual reception. In most cases this audience would consist of the nobles in whose service the authors were, but a wider audience consisting of people the authors did not know needs to be included as well. The latter category of people would often fall back on their familiarity with the genre and, hence, make use of a different kind of intertextuality. The majority of the fourteen essays in this collection deal with the questions raised by J. in his introduction. Some of the other topics discussed are the absence of certain popular names, such as Galahad and Percival, from everyday nomenclature in the province of Brabant, the use of linguistic methods in determining a text's provenance and the implications of double authorship in the *Grimbergsche oorlog*.

After Frits van Oostrom published, in 1996, his prize-winning book *Maerlants wereld*, scholars' interest in Jacob van Maerlant and his works has strengthened. Raymond Alan Harper, *Als God met ons is [. . .]: Jacob van Maerlant en de 'vijanden van het christelijke geloof'*, [n.pl.], 236 pp., discusses Maerlant's views on the enemies of Christian faith, the Saracens in particular. Jos Biemans, *Onsen Speghele Ystoriale in Vlaemsche: Codicologisch onderzoek naar de overlevering van de Spiegel historiael*

(Schrift en schriftdragers in de Nederlanden in de middeleeuwen, 2), Leuven, Peeters, 1997, 2 vols., 548 + 100 pp., studies the *Spieghel historiael*, a history of the world written by Van Maerlant and completed by Philips Utenbroeke and Lodewijk van Velthem. *Maerlants werk: Juweeltjes van zijn hand*, ed. Ingrid Biesheuvel (Delta-reeks), Baarn, Ambo–Amsterdam U.P., 597 pp., presents a generous anthology of the works of this 13th-c. author, both in the original language and in modern Dutch. Karina van Dalen-Oskam, *Studies over Jacob van Maerlants Rijmbijbel* (Middeleeuwse studies en bronnen, 37), Hilversum, Verloren, 1997, 269 pp., focuses on his rhymed version of the Bible.

Dirk Kinable, *Facetten van Boendale: Literair-historische verkenningen van 'Jans Teesteye' en de 'Lekenspiegel'* (Leidse opstellen, 31), Leiden, Dimensie, ix + 240 pp., contains six essays on the 14th-c. author Jan Boendale, his dialogue 'Jans teesteye' (Jan's conviction) and his treatise *Lekenspiegel* (Layman's Mirror) in particular. K. concentrates on Boendale's courtly and urban reception, the audience of his works, which mainly consisted of lay people, and its structural and ethical aspects. In a final chapter the author discusses the religious background of the audience and the way in which Boendale helps them to establish their personal relationship with the Christian faith.

De Noordnederlandse historiebijbel: Een kritische editie met inleiding en aantekeningen van Hs. Ltk 231 uit de Leidse Universiteitsbibliotheek, ed. M. K. A. van den Berg (Middeleeuwse studies en bronnen, 56), Hilversum, Verloren, 845 pp., presents a critical edition of a northern Dutch 'history-bible', copied in 1458 by an unknown scribe. Adapted from the Vulgate it was supplemented with a translation of Petrus Comestor's *Historia scholastica* and Van Maerlant's *Rijmbijbel*. The term 'history-bible' refers to the free prose translations of selected narrative passages from the Bible, popular among wealthy merchants and the nobility. Kristina Freienhagen-Baumgardt, *Hendrik Herps 'Spieghel der volcomenheit' in oberdeutscher Überlieferung: Ein Beitrag zur Rezeptionsgeschichte niederländischer Mystik im oberdeutschen Raum* (Miscellanea Neerlandica, 17), Leuven, Peeters, xi + 177 pp., reviews the High German reception of Hendrik Herp's influential 15th-c. treatise on Catholic asceticism and mysticism, *Spieghel der volcomenheit*.

New editions of the popular story of Charlemagne going out on a foray with one of his cast-off vassals were published by A. M. Duinhoven and Karel Eykman, *Karel ende Elegast* (Nederlandse klassieken, 14), Amsterdam, Prometheus–Bakker, 111 pp., and in *Karel ende Elegast*, ed. Hubert Slings, Amsterdam U.P., 1997, 96 pp. *Lanceloet: De Middelnederlandse vertaling van de Lancelot en prose overgeleverd in de Lancelotcompilatie*, ed. Ada Postma (Middelnederlandse Lancelot-romans, 7), Hilversum, Verloren, vii + 518 pp., is the fourth volume in the integral edition of the 'Lancelotcompilatie', the Middle Dutch adaptation of the French *Lancelot en prose*, comprising lines 16,264 to 26,636.

Het leven van de zalige maagd Sint Clara: De Middelnederlandse bewerking van de Legenda Sanctae Clarae Virginis, ed. Ludo Jongen, Herman de Groot et al. (San Damianoreeks, 11), Megen, Werkgroep San Damianoreeks, 240 pp., is an edition of a Middle Dutch translation of a Latin hagiography of St Clara of Assisi. *Den duytschen Cathoen, naar de Antwerpse druk van Henrick Eckert van Homberch: Met als bijlage de andere redacties van de vroegst bekende Middelnederlandse vertaling der Dicta Catonis*, ed. A. M. J. van Buuren, O. S. H. Lie and A. P. Orbán (Middelnederlandse tekstedities, 5), Hilversum, Verloren, 207 pp., presents an edition of a collection of proverbial aphorisms attributed to the Roman statesman Cato. The editors decided to give both the early 16th-c. chapbook version printed by the Antwerp printer Henrick Eckert van Homberch and, as an appendix, the incomplete earlier versions going back to the 13th c.

3. THE RHETORICIANS' PERIOD

Johan Verberckmoes, *Schertsen, schimpen en schateren: Geschiedenis van het lachen in de Zuidelijke Nederlanden, zestiende en zeventiende eeuw* (SUN Memoria), Nijmegen, SUN, 287 pp., sketches a history of laughter in an early-modern Southern Low Countries' society. The author observes that present-day historical, literary, and anthropological research invariably see laughter as a tool in a post-medieval process of civilization. In early-modern times people bursting out in laughter were regarded as highly suspect because they were not capable of controlling their emotions and, above all, their bodies. V. discriminates between three types of laughter. Jesting (*schertsen*) implies a breach of hierarchical conditions under which it is appropriate to laugh, scoffing (*schimpen*) directly aims at people who, consequently, will feel ridiculed by it, and roaring (*schateren*) refers to unrestrained and autonomous laughter. To the international debate on the social function of laughter the author adds his claim that laughter escapes the laws of social control as much as it is determined by it. In the first part of his book V. deals with the historical anthropology of laughter. In it he reviews 16th- and 17th-c. philosophical and medical treatises, as well as iconographical sources, manuals of etiquette, and travel stories. Bodily aspects receive special treatment in an iconographical study of laughter between smiling and uncontrolled roaring. The second part of the book focuses on the Southern Low Countries. Observations are based on comic chapbooks (*facetiae*), diaries, memoirs, chronicles, and other sources. In a last chapter the author tries to answer the difficult question to what extent the Counter-Reformation influenced attitudes towards laughter.

Karel Bostoen, *Bonis in bonum: Johan Radermacher de Oude (1538–1617), humanist en koopman* (Zeven Provinciënreeks, 15), Hilversum, Verloren, 80 pp., is a short monograph on one of the lesser known merchants and men of letters, living in Antwerp and Vlissingen, author of the oldest grammar-book in Dutch. Central to Johan Koppenol, *Leids heelal: Het Loterijspel (1596) van Jan van Hout*, Hilversum, Verloren, 511 pp., is a play by the Leiden town clerk Jan van Hout, performed on 27 May 1596 on the occasion of a lottery held to raise money for the transformation of a vacated convent into ·an asylum for plague sufferers and the mentally ill. In a lively style K. depicts the world in which Van Hout lived, Leiden's poor relief, Van Hout's literary environment and the poetic principles behind his works. He meticulously analyses the text of the play and comments on topical references, discusses its literary style and Van Hout's method of structuring his text and reconstructs the social and ideological concepts on which the play's argument is based. In an appendix K. publishes editions of the two versions of the *Loterijspel*, the longer of the two including a *Ruyt bewerp*, a rough outline of the play in prose.

Between 1481 and 1485, the Ghent nobleman Joos van Ghistele travelled to the Mediterranean and countries in the Middle East. R. Gaspar presents a new edition of the account of this journey, entrusted to a certain Ambrosius Zeebout, *Tvoyage van Mher Joos van Ghistele* (Middeleeuwse studies en bronnen, 58), Hilversum, Verloren, lvii + 448 pp. The edition is based on two MS versions of the text which was printed for the first time in 1557. *Van die becooringe des duvels hoe hij crijstus becoorden: Zestiende-eeuws rederijkersstuk van Jan Tömisz*, ed. Herman van Iperen et al. (Uitgaven Stichting Neerlandistiek VU, 23), Amsterdam, Stichting Neerlandistiek VU–Münster, Nodus, 106 pp., is an edition of a Rhetoricians' play on the Temptation of Christ (Luke 4:2–13). The editors present the text, found in a MS in the Haarlem Chamber of Rhetoric, 'Trou moet blijcken', in the original language as well as in modern adaptation. The edition of the entire play collection of the Chamber has been completed in *Trou Moet Blijcken: Bronnenuitgave van de boeken der Haarlemse rederijkerskamer 'de Pellicanisten'*, VIII: *De boeken I, N, M en R*, ed. W. N. M. Hüsken, B. A. M. Ramakers, and F. A. M. Schaars, Slingenberg, Quarto, 838 pp. *Mariken van Nieumeghen & Elckerlijc: Zonde, hoop en verlossing in de late Middeleeuwen*, ed. Bart Ramakers and Willem Wilmink (Klassieken van de Nederlandse Letterkunde, 13), Amsterdam, Prometheus–Bert Bakker, 1997, 241 pp., is the latest edition of two of the best-known plays from the early 16th c. Both texts are given in the original and in modern Dutch.

4. THE SEVENTEENTH CENTURY

Ingrid M. Weekhout, *Boekencensuur in de Noordelijke Nederlanden: Een verkennend onderzoek naar de vrijheid van drukpers gedurende de zeventiende eeuw* (Nederlandse cultuur in Europese context, 11), The Hague, SDU, xii + 580 pp., is a detailed study of book censorship in the Dutch Republic. The author concentrates on four sets of nine-year periods, starting in the year 1617, with a two-decade interval between each of the periods, thus covering the time-span between 1617 and 1695. Aspects of censorship reviewed are the legislation and its enforcement by the States-General and the Court of Holland as well as by the Dutch and French Reformed Churches. W. then turns to censorship in three different towns, Rotterdam, Deventer, and 's-Hertogenbosch. Eventually she arrives at the conclusion that, contrary to general opinion, there was no unlimited freedom of the press in the Netherlands. For various reasons some printers were persecuted and punished. Every now and then ordinances were issued but their observance was poor. During the 17th c. Dutch presses were certainly censored, in some cases entire editions were even impounded or publicly burnt.

In 1997, the 350th anniversary of P. C. Hooft's death, on 21 May 1647, was widely commemorated. *Zeven maal Hooft: Lezingen ter gelegenheid van de 350ste sterfdag van P. C. Hooft, uitgesproken op het herdenkingscongres in de Amsterdamse Agnietenkapel op 21 mei 1997*, ed. Jeroen Jansen, Amsterdam, A D & L, 138 pp., is a collection of essays on Hooft's life and works. J. Konst, ' "Ick had wat in den zin": Het handelingsinitiatief in de ernstige spelen van Pieter Cornelisz Hooft' (13–33) analyses the dramatic structure of Hooft's tragedies, the unity of action in particular and the extent to which actions are motivated internally or externally. T. ter Meer, 'Stijlmiddelen in de brieven van Hooft aan Huygens en Barlaeus' (35–44) scrutinizes matters of style in the correspondences between Hooft and two of the most famous intellectuals of his time, Constantijn Huygens and Caspar Barlaeus. K. Porteman, 'Van beeld naar lied: Een terugblik op Hoofts *Emblemata amatoria* (45–59) reiterates the question of whether Hooft's collection of emblems, published in 1611, was ever meant for publication. B. Hartlieb, 'Geen kleen deel der burgerlyke wysheit': Fürstliche Herrschaft in Hoofts Dramen' (61–77) reviews various ideas about the concept of monarchy in Hooft's plays. In them she observes a distinct influence of the works of the humanist scholar, Justus Lipsius. P. J. Verkruijsse, 'P. C. Hooft, een toontje lager: Over liedbundels, lettertypes en lezers' (79–97) concentrates on the different typefaces used in the various editions of Hooft's songbooks as an indication of the type of audience they were intended for. H. Duits, 'De biograaf aan het werk: Enkele historiografische aspecten van Hoofts *Henrik de Gróte*' (99–121) studies the author's biography of the French king, Henry IV, and his use of Plutarch's *Alexander* as a model. The final contribution by M. J. van der Wal, 'Richtlijnen voor het nageslacht? Hoofts taal en taalreflectie na 1647' (122–32) discusses Hooft's influence on the development of Dutch language and linguistics until the beginning of the 18th c. in scholars such as David van Hoogstraten, Jacobus Nyloë, Arnold Moonen, and Lambert ten Kate.

Willemien B. de Vries, *Wandeling en verhandeling: De ontwikkeling van het Nederlandse hofdicht in de zeventiende eeuw (1613–1710)*, Hilversum, Verloren, 319 pp., is a study of a subgenre in Dutch Renaissance poetry called *hofdicht* or country-house poem. The first representative in this type of poetry in which the joys of well-to-do people's lives on their estates in the country are described is Philibert van Borsselen's *Den Binckhorst* (1613), the country-house of one of Van Borsselen's friends, Jacob Snouckaert. The Dutch version of this Renaissance subgenre differs from that of its European peers in that the Dutch poems are explicitly addressed to the owners of the estates praised. In 1710, when the genre had passed its prime, the first scholarly treatise on this type of poetry was published by Jan Baptista Wellekens. Ultimately country-house poetry goes back to country-life poetry, a subgenre in classical literature which Renaissance authors had used as a model for imitation. Vergil's *Georgics* and Horace's 'Beatus ille' (*Epod.* 2,1) are the best-known examples in this area. The most famous example in the Netherlands of country-house poetry is Constantijn Huygens' poem *Hofwijck* (1653). De Vries believes that Calvinist authors, such as Van Borsselen and Huygens, expressed religious ideas about nature in their country-house poems much more explicitly than their remonstrant, Roman Catholic, or Mennonite colleagues.

Een lezer aan het woord: Studies van L. Strengholt over zeventiende-eeuwse Nederlandse letterkunde, ed. H. Duits et al. (Uitgaven Stichting Neerlandistiek VU, 26), Amsterdam, Stichting Neerlandistiek VU–Münster, Nodus, xv + 339 pp., is a collection of essays written by a former professor of the Free University of Amsterdam who died in 1989. *Leven in mijn dicht: Historisch-kritische uitgave van Constantijn Huygens' Nederlandse gedichten (1614–1625)*, ed. Ad Leerintveld, [n.pl.], 1997, 2 parts in 3 vols, presents an edition of Constantijn Huygens' earliest Dutch poetry. P. C. Hooft, *Granida*, ed. Lia van Gemert (Alfa), Amsterdam U.P., vii + 116 pp., is the latest edition of Hooft's pastoral drama *Granida* (1605). In an appendix to the introduction of this edition Louis Peter Grijp pays special attention to the melodies of the eleven songs included in this play. *Buyten gaets: Twee burleske reisbrieven van Aernout van Overbeke*, ed. Marijke Barend-van Haeften and Arie Jan Gelderblom (Egodocumenten, 15), Hilversum, Verloren, 125 pp., publishes two burlesque letters by Aernout van Overbeke, an explorer employed by the United East Indies Company.

5. THE EIGHTEENTH CENTURY

Gender and emotional culture as reflected in spectatorial papers are reviewed by Dorothée Sturkenboom, *Spectators van Hartstocht: Sekse en emotionele cultuur in de achttiende eeuw*, Hilversum, Verloren, 421 pp. In her first chapter S. presents an outline of 'spectators' as they developed in the Netherlands, obviously related to the Enlightenment, scrutinizing its emotional culture in particular. The latter aspect is made visible through a study of a typically spectatorial vocabulary expressing emotions. But to what extent is it possible to judge the historical implications of utterances voiced in fictional texts? This problem is dealt with in the second chapter. The concept of gender is not restricted to male and female relationships but applies to a wider social phenomenon. S. observes that various groups of people, both men and women, are criticized by spectatorial authors for lacking ability to control their emotions. They include, among others, pietistic zealots, libertines, onanists, and blubbering vicars. Why these groups in particular? In contemporary psychological and philosophical theories, elaborated upon in the next two chapters, they would have been blamed for their intemperance. By the mid-18th c., attitudes towards passion and emotions change in that a certain appreciation of them is developed, yet only on condition that they be channeled through charity. Sensitivity becomes a virtue mainly in women, men having to show that they are sturdy, rational human beings.

Jan Oosterholt, *De ware dichter: De vaderlandse poëticale discussie in de periode 1775–1825*, Assen, Van Gorcum, x + 222 pp., concentrates on a poetic discussion in the Netherlands, between the end of the 18th and the beginning of the 19th c., on what is required to be regarded a true poet. In this context, Annemieke Meijer, *The Pure Language of the Heart: Sentimentalism in the Netherlands, 1775–1800* (Textxet, 14), Amsterdam, Rodopi, 197 pp., deserves a special mention. G. J. Johannes, *De lof der aalbessen: Over (Noord-)Nederlandse literatuurtheorie, literatuur en de consequenties van kleinschaligheid 1770–1830* (Nederlandse cultuur in Europese context, 10), The Hague, SDU, 1997, xi + 128 pp., discusses the concept of 'small scale dimensions' in Dutch literary theories written between 1770 and 1830. Once people had come to the conclusion that it is impossible to return to the Golden Age of the 17th c., thinking in small scale dimensions was turned into a virtue, and it remains so to this very day.

Uncharted waters of classicist theatrical poetics in the Netherlands, related to the genre of tragedy in particular, have for the first time been mapped by Anna de Haas, *De wetten van het treurspel: Over ernstig toneel in Nederlands, 1700–1772*, Hilversum, Verloren, xvi + 350 pp. Compared to what happened on the 17th-c. Dutch stage, 18th-c. drama has the odium of not being very exciting, innovating, or original. Dutch dramatists had adopted theories developed by French authors like Corneille of how to model plays according to classicist principles. Champions of this new trend were the members of a poetic society called *Nil volentibus arduum*, established in 1669, consisting of a number of prominent Amsterdam citizens who, by the end of the 17th c., completely dominated the capital's theatrical life. Andries Pels in particular became important as the circle's codifier, writing, in 1681, *Gebruik én misbruik des tooneels*. In it he presented an outline of *Nil*'s poetic credo. In her book, De Haas focuses on prefaces to editions of plays. She reviews the classicist theory in chapters each devoted to a particular rule such as the doctrines of the three unities, poetic justice, and the principles of *bienséance* and *vraisemblance*. Authors had to obey these rules in order to avoid being mocked by fellow playwrights. By the time the Amsterdam playhouse was burnt to the ground, in 1772, classicism had passed its apogee. Alternatives were, *inter alia*, a return to Greek tragedy, and a more realistic type of drama with ordinary people as stage-characters who no longer spoke in verse but in prose. Throughout the 19th c. playwrights continued to search for a new form of drama which only emerged at the end of the century with the introduction of realism and naturalism.

Commemorating 750 years of town-rights, Aad Meinderts, Saskia Petit, and Dick Welsing, *Den Haag, je tikt er tegen en het zingt: Literair Den Haag vanaf 1750* (Schrijversprentenboek, 41), The Hague, SDU, 168 pp., review literary life in The Hague between 1750 and the present.

Poems by Hiëronymus van Alphen, intended for children yet without being nursery rhymes, were edited by P. J. Buijnsters in *Kleine Gedigten voor Kinderen* (Deltareeks), Amsterdam, Athenaeum–Polak & Van Gennep, 233 pp. Published in three volumes (1778–82), Van Alphen's poems were enormously popular. In the 19th c. they were seriously criticized by anti-moralist authors. In his afterword B. restores their ideological and aesthetic value by showing how they were tied to Van Alphen's enlightened pedagogical philosophy. *De Bataafsche Republiek, zo als zij behoord te zijn, en zo als zij weezen kan: Of revolutionaire droom in 1798: Wegens toekomstige gebeurtenissen tot 1998*, ed. Peter Altena and Mireille Oostindië, Nijmegen, Vantilt, 120 pp., presents an edition of a remarkable futuristic story by the Dutch patriotic author, Gerrit Paape. In this pamphlet Paape reflected on how the Dutch Republic would look like in 200 years' time, while in fact commenting on political issues related to the Dutch Republic, as ruled by the French, in 1798.

6. THE NINETEENTH CENTURY

Toos Streng, *Geschapen om te scheppen? Opvattingen over vrouwen en schrijverschap in Nederland, 1815–1860*, Amsterdam U.P., viii + 140 pp., discusses opinions held on women and female authorship in the first half of the 19th c. Joris van Eijnatten, *Hogere sferen: De ideeënwereld van Willem Bilderdijk (1756–1831)*, Hilversum, Verloren, 768 pp., studies the ideas of one of the most brilliant thinkers and poets at the turn of the 19th c. Four questions are central to its argument: what concepts does B. discuss in his works ranging from treatises, letters and poems to notes in manuscript; how do they relate to his philosophy; what sources did he use; and how does one interpret his ideas from their cultural-historical background? Special attention is paid to B.'s ethical system, his theology, theosophy, philosophy, sociology, and psychology as well as to his erotic, political, linguistic, aesthetic, and scientific ideas.

Rondom Daum, ed. Gerard Termorshuizen, Amsterdam, Nijgh & Van Ditmar, 1997, 136 pp., unites half a dozen essays on the novelist P. A. Daum, who spent most of his life in the Dutch East Indies. Daum's works are currently enjoying a revival, witness the reprint of his Dutch and Malay novels and short stories. Theo D'haen and Gerard Termorshuizen edited a collection of essays on censorious voices in literary texts related to the Dutch colonies, both the former and the present ones, in *De geest van Multatuli: Proteststemmen in vroegere Europese koloniën* (Semaian, 17), Leiden, Vakgroep Talen en Culturen van Zuidoost-Azië en Oceanië, 248 pp. The book contains articles by P. van Zonneveld, 'Een echte antikoloniaal: Jacob Haafner (1754–1809)' (19–29); B. Paasman, 'Het onvolmaakte paradijs: Over Dirk van Hogendorp en Indië' (30–51); and G. Termorshuizen, 'De bittere waarheden van Henri Lion: Het *Bataviaasch Handelsblad* als eerste politieke krant van Indië' (81–100). These are followed by an essay on Multatuli's *Max Havelaar* (1860), politically the most influential book on the social situation in the Dutch East Indies, in H. van den Bergh, 'Een revolutionair boek?' (101–09). In most of the other contributions to this book, Multatuli remains the central focus of attention: T. Anbeek, 'In de huid van een ander' (110–22); K. Snoek,

' "Omkeeren is mijn metier": E. du Perron, de geest van Multatuli en die van Setiabuddhi' (123–41); and L. Dolk, 'Gebruik en misbruik in de Gordel van Smaragd: Multatuli als merknaam' (142–50). In his essay W. Rutgers turns to the Dutch Antilles in 'Frank Martinus Arion: "Over het schijnbare overwigt der westersche beschaving"' (151–65); M. van Kempen addresses Multatuli's influence in Surinam in 'Wat verwaait er op de passaat? Of hoe de geest van Multatuli de krabben in de Surinaamse ton weerstond' (184–213). The involvement with the Congo in two novelists, Henri van Booven and Cyriel Buysse, one Dutch the other Belgian, is reviewed by L. Renders in 'De Congo-Vrijstaat op de korrel' (214–32). D. Kolff concludes this volume by wondering why there has never been a Multatuli in British India, 'Waarom was er geen Multatuli in Brits-Indië?' (233–44).

Holländer und Deutsche: Beiträge zur Multatuli-Forschung, ed. Bernd Schenk and Hans-Jürgen Fuchs (Mitteilungen der Internationalen Multatuli-Gesellschaft Ingelheim, 6), Fernwald, Litblockin, 186 pp., also focuses on Multatuli. A new edition of his famous novel *Max Havelaar* (1860) has been published: *Max Havelaar, of De koffiveilingen der Nederlandsche Handelmaatschappy,* ed. Annemarie Kets-Vree (Nederlandse klassieken, 15), Amsterdam, Prometheus–Bakker, 418 pp.

Camera Obscura, ed. Willem van den Berg, Henk Eijssens, Joost Kloek, and Peter van Zonneveld (Delta), 2 vols, Amsterdam, Athenaeum–Polak & Van Gennep, 390, 399 pp., presents a new edition of Hildebrand's collection of witty realistic short stories. In the second part of this edition the editors discuss matters such as the realization of the collection, its international context and reception.

7.   1880 TO 1945

Extra muros, langs de wegen: Opstellen voor Marcel Janssens ter gelegenheid van zijn afscheid als hoogleraar Nederlandse en Europese letterkunde aan de Katholieke Universiteit Leuven, ed. Dirk de Geest and Hendrik van Gorp (Symbolae: Facultatis Litterarum Lovaniensis, A, 23), Leuven U.P., 1997, 183 pp., is a collection of articles on 19th-c. and 20th-c. literature in honour of Marcel Janssens, former professor at the University of Leuven.

Ruth Beijert, *Van tachtiger tot modernist: Het Gezellebeeld in de Nederlandse kritiek, 1897–1940,* Groningen, Passage, 1997, 271 pp. discusses the reception of the works of the Flemish poet Guido Gezelle in Dutch literary criticism during the first four decades of the 20th c. *Met Louis Couperus op tournee: Voordrachten uit eigen werk 1915–1923 in recensies, brieven en andere documenten,* ed. H. T. M. van Vliet et al. (Achter het boek, 30), The Hague, Letterkundig Museum–Amsterdam, Lubberhuizen, 241 pp., contains a number of Louis Couperus's lectures of 1915 to 1923 on his numerous tours through the Netherlands. John Irons, *The Development of Imagery in the Poetry of P. C. Boutens*, Odense, 1997, 98 + xlv pp., concentrates on the symbolist poet P. C. Boutens.

In *De eenheid in de tegendelen: De psychomachische verhaalwereld van F. Bordewijk (1884–1965) en de mythe van de hermafrodiet: Een interpretatie*, Amsterdam U.P., 301 pp., Dorian Cumps deals with psychomachic aspects of the non-mimetic stories written by Bordewijk, texts in which the author does not attempt to recreate a tangible, extra-literary society but in which he evokes a world governed by psychological processes. His early realist novels, *Blokken* (1931), *Bint* (1934), and *Karakter* (1937), have been studied widely whereas large quantities of his other works have never received much attention. According to C., B.'s complicated hermetic style of narration is to be blamed for that. The stories he wrote should be seen as metaphors for the in-depth psychological developments the author lived through rather than expressions of philosophical or social-critical observa-tions. In his final chapter, C. attempts to prove that an analysis of thematic as well as formal aspects of B.'s non-realist stories reveals a *mythe personnel*, traceable in his other works as well, of a subconscious fear of hermaphrodites.

Both Wim Wennekes, *Het Nederland van Nescio: 'Schrijft u over mij maar nix' (Nescio 1882–1961)*, Baarn, Kasteel Groeneveld, 95 pp., and *Is u Amsterdammer? Ja, Goddank: Een literaire wandeling door het Amsterdam van Nescio*, ed. Maurits Verhoeff (Nescio-cahier, 3), Amsterdam, Lubberhuizen, 1997, 102 pp., focus on Nescio (pseudonym of J. H. F. Grönloh), author of a number of short stories famous for their bohemian setting and unique style. Anna C. N. van Beusekom, *Film als kunst: Reacties op een nieuw medium in Nederland, 1895–1940*, [n.pl.], 336 pp., offers a survey of film criticism by, among others, I. K. Bonset (pseudonym of Theo van Doesburg), and Menno ter Braak.

P. J. Buijnsters, *Het Nederlandse antiquariaat tijdens de Tweede Wereldoor-log* (Bert van Selm-lezing, 6), Amsterdam, De Buitenkant, 1997, 46 pp., presents a review of the antiquarian book trade during the Second World War. One of the sad observations in this study is that many Jewish booksellers did not return from the German concentra-tion camps. After 1945, antiquarian booksellers moved to an English style of book trade. They also introduced the 'new bibliography' method and displayed a larger degree of professionalism in their approach. New-style antiquarian booksellers changed from buyers of old paper into specialists in rare books. René Marres, *Zogenaamde politieke incorrectheid in Nederlandse literatuur: Ideologiekritiek in analyse* (Leidse opstellen, 30), Leiden, Internationaal Forum voor Afrikaanse en Nederlandse Taal en Letteren, Dimensie, 127 pp., concentrates on political and social (in)correctness in a number of 20th-c. authors.

With the exception of Frans Kellendonk, the greater majority of authors discussed lived before the Second World War, Eduard Du Perron, Albert Helman, Madelon Székely-Lulofs, Nescio, and P. C. Boutens receiving special attention.

Literair landschap: Dichters en schrijvers over Nederland, ed. Peter van Zonneveld, Alphen aan den Rijn, Atrium, 128 pp., presents an anthology of modern Dutch poetry on the Dutch landscape. A similar selection of poems by authors reflecting on the landscape which they grew up in is given by *Daar waar ik leefde: Nederlandstalige dichters over het landschap van hun jeugd*, ed. Henk van Zuiden, Utrecht, Kwadraat, 94 pp.

8. 1945 TO THE PRESENT DAY

Martje Breedt Bruyn, *Tijdloze ogenblikken: Een biografie van Marianne Philips*, [The Hague], Stichting Ex Libris–Utrecht, Prestige, 110 pp., is a biography of one of the *dii minores* in modern Dutch literature, Marianne Philips (pseudonym of M. Goudeket-Philips). One of her best-known works is her collection of short stories, *Tussen hemel en aarde* (1947). Mirjam Rotenstreich, *Over den titel dienen wij ons geen zorgen te maken: Het slot van 'De Avonden' in het licht van Tolstoi*, Amsterdam, De Bezige Bij, 1997, 76 pp., assesses Tolstoy's influence on Gerard Reve's novel *De Avonden* (1947). Oek de Jong, *Zijn muze was een harpij: Over het wereldbeeld van W. F. Hermans*, Nijmegen, Uitgeverij KU Nijmegen, 31 pp., reviews the 'world-picture' of one of the most important Dutch post-Second World War authors, Willem Frederik Hermans, who died in 1995. Carel Peeters, *Pakhuis 'De tandeloze tijd': Over de romancyclus van A. F. Th. van der Heijden*, Amsterdam, De Harmonie, 68 pp., discusses the as yet unfinished popular cycle of novels, *De tandeloze tijd*, the first volumes of which were published in 1983. Jan Brands, *A. F. Th. van der Heijden: Gemankeerd leven omgesmeed tot heldendicht* (De school van de literatuur), Nijmegen, SUN, 1997, 126 pp., is a more general introduction to the works of this author. Hans Renders, *Zo meen ik dat ook jij bent: Biografie van Jan Hanlo* (Open domein, 34), Amsterdam, De Arbeiderspers, 679 + 24 pp., presents a biography of one of the experimental poets of the 1950s, Jan Hanlo.

The acclaimed poet Rutger Kopland questioned a number of young poets about their poetic activities. He published these interviews in *Mooi, maar dat is het woord niet: Geschreven gesprekken met Esther Jansma, Frank Koenegracht, K. Michel, Tonnus Oosterhoff, Martin Reints*, Amsterdam, Van Oorschot, 183 pp. Rob Schouten, *Hoe laat is 't aan den tijd: Essays*, Amsterdam, De Bezige Bij, 218 pp., reviews post-war modern Dutch poetry. Schouten thinks it reveals a change in that, some time during the 1980s, authors such as Gerrit Komrij, Jules

Deelder, and Jean Pierre Rawie developed a distinct interest in the boundaries of poetry. Other essays in this collection concentrate on poetry by the 1950s poets, Hans Lodeizen, Hans Andreus, and Hugo Claus. A. L. Sötemann, *Verzen als leeftocht: Over Gerrit Kouwenaar*, Groningen, Historisch Uitgeverij, 159 pp., is a reprint of six essays on the poet and translator, Gerrit Kouwenaar, by a former professor of modern Dutch literature at the University of Utrecht, previously published in various literary periodicals. Sötemann analyses Kouwenaar's poetry, he discusses his poetics and attitude towards life and compares the author to the late 19th-c. poet, P. C. Boutens. Stella Irene Linn, **Dichterlijkheid of letterlijkheid? Prioriteiten in de Spaanse vertalingen van Nederlandstalige poëzie*, Amsterdam, Thesis, 288 pp., attempts to offer an explanation for the reasons behind the choices made by Spanish translators of Dutch poetry. Based on his diary, the young poet Rogi Wieg supplies personal impressions of the year 1997 in **Liefde is een zwaar beroep: Persoonlijke kroniek 1997* (Privé-domein, 221), Amsterdam, De Arbeiderspers, 331 pp.

Complete with a key map drawn by Jan Hiersch, Wim Huijser depicts a literary topography of Dordrecht, the hometown of Cees Buddingh', in **'Een stad is een boek': Het Dordrecht van C. Buddingh'*, Zutphen, Walburg Pers, 1997, 160 pp. Evert van der Starre, **Vestdijk over Frankrijk*, Zutphen, Walburg Pers, 207 pp., studies V.'s opinion on France as reflected in his works, the novels *De hôtelier doet niet meer mee* (1968) and *De filosoof en de sluipmoordenaar* (1961) in particular. Van der Starre reviews V.'s frequent references to the French authors, Stendhal and Proust, and his relationship to Eduard Du Perron and Menno ter Braak as two of the best-known pre-War Dutch Francophiles.

Jos Wuijts, **Serieuze poging tot een volledige bibliografie van de zelfstandige en verspreide geschriften van Arnon Grunberg: Waarin opgenomen diens 'Interview met mijn bibliograaf' & 'In ieder mens schuilt een maniak'*, Amsterdam, Nijgh & Van Ditmar, 96 pp., emphatically stresses the fact that his bibliography of Arnon Grunberg's works should be taken seriously. Grunberg, who enjoys a tremendous popularity amongst his younger readers, is an author who manages to marry melancholy and irony to carefully structured stories in which erotic excitement serves as one of the driving forces in his novels' male characters. Two interviews with Grunberg are included to supplement the list of titles.

*Wien, Wien, nur du allein [. . .]? Niederländische und flämische Autorinnen über Wien, ed. Herbert van Uffelen and Matthias Hüning (Wiener Broschüren zur niederländischen und flämischen Kultur, 5), Vienna, Institut für Germanistik/Niederlandistik, 190 pp., is an anthology of Dutch literary texts on Vienna, with translations by Ulrike Vogl. Tom van Deel offers a selection of 100 of the best poems written in 1997 in

his edition *De 100 beste gedichten van 1997*, Amsterdam, De Arbeiderspers, 136 pp.

Two of Gerard Walschap's children, Carla and Bruno, have edited
the first volume of their father's collection of letters, *Brieven*,
Amsterdam, Nijgh & Van Ditmar, 1462 pp. In these letters, the
Flemish novelist Walschap is shown to be a man never tired of
fighting for his artistic freedom, especially against the omnipresent
Roman Catholic Church. Erik Verstraete and Edwin Truyens
commemorate the 100th birthday of Wies Moens, poet and fervent
supporter of the Flemish movement, in *Wies Moens (1898–1998): Van
celbrieven tot politiek vluchteling*, Kontich, Vormingsinstituut Wies Moens,
139 pp. This is the catalogue of an exhibition in the author's honour,
held in Antwerp between 3 and 30 October, 1998. Moens died in
1982. Aad Meinderts and Erna Staal, *Ogen in je achterhoofd: Over Miep
Diekmann* (Schrijversprentenboek, 42), The Hague, Letterkundig
Museum–Amsterdam, Leopold, 128 pp., publish their catalogue of
an exhibition on Miep Diekmann, held at the 'Letterkundig Museum',
The Hague, from 1 October 1998 to 9 May 1999. Charlotte de Cloet,
Tilly Hermans, and Aad Meinderts, *'Oprecht veinzen': Over Frans
Kellendonk* (Schrijversprentenboek, 43), The Hague, Letterkundig
Museum–Amsterdam, Meulenhoff, 144 pp., catalogues another
exhibition in the same museum on Frans Kellendonk, author of
novels, short stories and essays, from 24 October 1998 to 29 March
1999. Kellendonk died in 1990, a mere 38 years old.

III. DANISH STUDIES*

LANGUAGE

By TOM LUNDSKÆR-NIELSEN, *Queen Alexandra Lecturer in Danish,
Department of Scandinavian Studies, University College London*

1. GENERAL

Det vigtigste fag, Modersmål-Selskabets årbog 1997, C.A. Reitzel,
1997, 127 pp., contains a number of articles by educationalists,
industrialists, linguists, and politicians about Danish as a subject in
the Danish 'Folkeskole'. The following year's volume, *Det sproglige
kunstværk*, Modersmål-Selskabets årbog 1998, C.A. Reitzel, 127 pp., is
chiefly concerned with approaches to literature, but a number of the
articles make interesting comments about language, too. *Det er korrekt.
Dansk retskrivning 1948–98*, ed. Erik Hansen and Jørn Lund, *Dansk
Sprognævns skrifter*, 27, Hans Reitzel, 156 pp., celebrates the half
centenary since the important spelling reform of 1948 with a number
of contributions by leading experts in the field. The book contains:
H. Galberg Jacobsen, '1948–reformen — og før og efter' (9–45);
A. Hamburger, 'Å på sin rette plads' (46–56); B. Jørgensen, 'Stednavne og personnavne under retskrivningsreformen' (57–68);
E. Hansen, 'Uløste og uløselige retskrivningsproblemer' (69–78);
N. Davidsen-Nielsen, 'Fordanskning af engelske låneord — Kan det
nytte?' (79–93); A. Karker, 'Det nordiske argument i dansk retskrivning' (94–103); J. Lund, 'Efter 1948' (104–15); L. Brink, 'Onomato-
poietika — når udtalen maler betydningen' (116–40); and J. E.
Mogensen, 'Ballade hos naboen' (141–55). Among the other books
and articles on spelling and punctuation are the following. T. Andersson, 'Aa's plads i alfabetet', *Nyt fra Sprognævnet*, no.1 : 9–10. N. Elf et
al., 'Nyt komma—en situationsrapport fra Det Flyvende Kom-
makorps', *Mål & Mæle*, no.4 : 22–27. Erik Hansen and Kirsten Rask,
Sætning, komma — kommasætning (Dansk Sprognævns skrifter, 26), Hans
Reitzel, 47 pp., with useful exercises and a disk. E. Hansen, 'Stor
reform — små bogstaver', *Mål & Mæle*, no.2 : 18–22. **Hermes.
Tidsskrift for Sprogforskning*, 21, Handelshøjskolen i Århus, 237 pp., has
contributions from H. Bergenholtz, 'Variantangivelser i en dansk
produktionsordbog ud fra eksempler med flektionsangivelser i Ret-
skrivningsordbogen' (95–119), and H. Eskesen and H. Fuglsang,
'Kolon: den oversete konnektor' (151–79). T. Hoel, 'Valgfrihed i

---

* The place of publication of books is Copenhagen unless otherwise indicated.

skriftnormalene — en fordel eller en ulempe?', *NyS*, 23, ed. Anne Holmen et al., Dansklærerforeningen, 1997, 25–34. **Sprog og Samfund*, Nyt fra Modersmåls-Selskabet, 16.4, 16 pp., contains K. Rask, 'Kommaet og den danske folkesjæl' (4–5), and J. Brogård, 'Det nye komma — ulovligt indført og uden saglig argumentation?' (6–7). One article even looks forward to the next spelling reform, viz. H. Galberg Jacobsen, 'Den næste retskrivningsreform', *Mål & Mæle*, no.4: 17–21. A brief survey of the functionalist paradigm is found in L. Falster Jakobsen, 'Funktionalism — et sprogvidenskabeligt paradigme', *Mål & Mæle*, no.3: 21–29. A general linguistic perspective is also presented in J. Rischel, 'Feltarbejde blandt ånder', *Mål & Mæle*, no.2: 24–31. *NyS*, 24, ed. Peter Juel Henrichsen et al., Dansklærerforeningen, 130 pp., is devoted to the theme of language and gender; its four major contributions are: Inge Lise Pedersen, 'Sprog og køn' (9–40); B.-L. Gunnarsson, 'Spelet om den akademiska kunskapen' (41–72); M. Ohlsson, '"Om vi tar motorsåg då ska dom ha förbandslåda"' (73–95); and J. Scheuer, 'På catwalk med 3x3 matrix' (97–122). Language and gender are also the main themes of a conference report with many valuable contributions from Nordic scholars: *Sprog, køn — og kommunikation. Rapport fra 3. Nordiske Konference om Sprog og Køn, København, 11.–13. oktober 1997*, ed. Inge Lise Pedersen and Jann Scheuer, C.A. Reitzel, 250 pp. **Tidsskrift for Sprogpsykologi*, 4.1, ed. Marie Louise Quist, 72 pp. A short analysis of political correctness in language appears in P. Frost, 'Halvfemsernes sprogstrid — om politisk korrekthed', *Nyt fra Sprognævnet*, no.3: 1–10.

2. History of the Language, Phonology, Morphology, Lexis, Syntax, and Semantics

J. Bendix, 'Hvor dansk er det danske sprog?' *Mål & Mæle*, no.1: 9–13. H.F. Nielsen, 'Det ældste sprog i Danmark', **Humaniora*, 13.2: 4–7. H. Basbøll, 'Nyt om stødet i moderne rigsdansk — om samspillet mellem lydstrukturer og ordgrammatik', *DSt*: 33–86. B. Ege, 'Lyd og bogstav', **Læsepædagogen*, 46.3: 145–48. Nina Grønnum, *Fonetik og Fonologi. Almen og Dansk*, Akademisk Forlag, 391 pp., falls into two sections, the first one dealing with general phonetics and phonology and the second one specifically with Danish phonology. Peter Lykke-Olesen and Peter Schmidt, *Den lille sproglære(r) — en bog om sprog for dansklærere og lærerstuderende*, Dansklærerforeningen, 152 pp. *Studies in Valency*. IV. *Valency and Verb Typology*, ed. Karen van Durme and Lene Schøsler (RASK Supplement, 8), Odense U.P., contains a number of interesting articles on these two topics. Of special interest for Danish are: K. T. Thomsen, 'A typology of Danish simplex verb constructions' (33–52); I. Baron and M. Herslund, 'Verbo-nominal predicates and the object relation' (89–112); P. A. Jensen and C. Vikner, 'The double nature of the verb HAVE' (113–27); and L. Lokshtanova, 'Halbgrammatikalisierte biverbiale Verbindungen im Dänischen' (129–45). *Acta linguistica Hafniensia*, 30, features three articles on Danish sentence structure: J. A. Hawkins, 'A processing approach to word order in Danish' (63–101); L. Heltoft, 'Analogy, weight and content' (103–28); and O. Nedergaard Thomsen, 'Syntactic processing and word order in Danish' (129–66). Some articles on words and word classes and related issues appear in *Mål & Mæle*: C. Elbro, 'Valte, se skalte. Om stærke ordpar', no.4:28–31; E. Hansen, 'Skulle vi ikke være Des?', no.1:19–22; Id., 'Glæden ved grammatik', no.4:6–10; S. Hedegård Nielsen, 'Adstantiver: en ny ordklasse i dansk?', no.1:23–25; K. T. Thomsen, 'Ordet *i* for tredje gang', no.1:14–18. Other relevant articles occur in *Nyt fra Sprognævnet*, including E. Bojsen, 'Godt ord igen!', no.1:1–5; A. Karker, 'Historien om et ord — Endsige', no.1:5–9; E. Hansen, 'Ingen logik?', no.2:1–5; M. Heidemann Andersen, 'Lidt om bandeord, eder og kraftudtryk', no.2:7–9; A.M. Ågerup, '*Andel i* eller *andel af*?', no.3:10–12; V. Sandersen, 'Om -s eller ingenting i toleddede navne', no.4:1–6. H. Korzen, 'Se storken på cykel. Noget om frie prædikativer o.l. på dansk og fransk', *Sprint*, no.2:11–32, Handelshøjskolen i København. J. Schack, 'Betydning og reference. Om varemærker og deres relation til kategorierne proprium og appellativ', *DSt*:87–102. T. Thrane, 'Nominaler, nominaliseringer og semantisk kompleksitet', *Hermes. Tidsskrift for Sprogforskning*, 21, Handelshøjskolen i Århus. *From Words to Utterances in LSP*, ed. Dorrit Faber and Finn Sørensen (Copenhagen Studies in Language, 20), Samfundslitteratur, Handelshøjskolen i København, 1997, 148 pp., has two relevant articles: I. Baron and M. Herslund, 'Place and sub-place: locative specifications in *have*-clauses' (5–21), and E. Engdahl, 'Scandinavian relatives revisited' (59–86). E. Skafte Jensen, 'Modalitet og dansk', *NyS*, 23, ed. Anne Holmen et al., Dansklærerforeningen, 1997:9–24. P. H. Traustedt, *Sproghjørnet. Aschehougs store bog om sjove ord og udtryk*, Aschehoug, 338 pp.

3. DIALECTOLOGY, CONTRASTIVE LINGUISTICS, AND BILINGUALISM

Danske Folkemål, 40, C.A. Reitzel, 112 pp., contains three dialect studies: F. Køster, 'Da jokket vi med Fyns Tidende' (25–49), which argues that the 'new' past tense form in the Funen dialect may be somewhat older; B. Jul Nielsen, 'Talesprogsvariationen i Århus' (51–78), is a sociolinguistic study of the spoken language in Århus and a comparison with the situation in Odder; and K. M. Pedersen,

'Metaforer som identitetsmarkører' (79–104), shows that maritime metaphors are used on Langeland to identify people as sailors and fishermen and that in general dialect functions as a marker of occupation on the surrounding islands also. *Ord & Sag*, 18, includes P. Michaelsen, 'Somme trak også tavl — om et gammelt tidsfordriv og dets navne' (11–44), and a story in the Djursland dialect by Aa. Sørensen, 'En ståkel' (47–64), with a standard Danish parallel translation. *Elefant — se også myg. Festskrift til Jens Axelsen*, ed. Anna Garde et al., Gyldendal, 220 pp., includes P. Harder, 'Lidt om *få* og *blive* i dansk' (34–42); V. Hjørnager Pedersen, 'Nye ord i 10. udgave af Dansk-Engelsk Ordbog sammenlignet med 3. udgave af Vinterberg og Bodelsen' (43–47); A. Hamburger, 'Vågne ordbøger fra og til dansk' (66–71); J. Rasmussen, 'Artikelstruktur for præpositioner' (133–41); P. Jarvad, 'Pseudolån fra engelsk' (164–71); J. Lund, 'Sprogørets velsignelser' (172–79); and B. and H. Holmberg, 'Chatté, simre, surfe–og andre engelske verber i dansk' (180–85). *Nominal Determination*, ed. Gyde Hansen (Copenhagen Studies in Language, 21), Samfundslitteratur, Handelshøjskolen i København, 158 pp., features two comparative studies: G. Hansen, 'Studies on the use of articles in Danish and German' (9–66), and I. Korzen, 'On nominal determination — with special reference to Italian and comparisons with Danish' (67–132). So does the following volume in the series, *Clause Combining and Text Structure*, ed. Iørn Korzen and Michael Herslund (Copenhagen Studies in Language, 22), Samfundslitteratur, Handelshøjskolen i København, 158 pp., with L. Jansen, 'On text structure in Russian and Danish. A comparative study of Russian and Danish Frog-stories' (43–64), and I. Korzen, 'On the grammaticalisation of rhetorical satellites. A comparative study on Italian and Danish' (65–86). N. Møller Andersen, 'Finners svenske misforståelser i dansk', *NyS*, 23, ed. Anne Holmen et al., Dansklærerforeningen, 1997, 35–47. H. Obertin Bertelsen, 'Dansk med accent — en torn i øjet', *Sprogforum*, 3.11:55–59. R. Brodersen, 'Leksikalsk akkommodation blandt 11 danskere i Norge', *Ord etter ord. Heiderskrift til Oddvar Nes*, ed. Gunnstein Akselberg and Jarle Bondevik, Norsk Bokreidingslag, Bergen, 57–78. Christian Hougaard, *Slangdannelsens Principper. Polsk overfor dansk (med norsk)*, Odense U.P., 1997, 131 pp. H. Hartvig Jepsen, 'Gengivelse af ukrainske navne på dansk', *Svantevit*, 19.2:67–82. K. Lomholt, 'Lettiske og danske lumske ligheder. Betydningsmæssigt venskab og stilistisk lumskeri', *Mål & Mæle*, no.3:14–20. B. Preisler, 'Om biskoppen og arvesynden: debatten om det engelske sprogs indflydelse på dansk', *Sprogforum*, 3.11:3–6. S. Rimmer, 'Sprogstimulering af tosprogede småbørn', *Sygeplejersken*, 39:36–38. *Portraits — Denmark and its Linguistic Minorities Seen in an International Perspective with Special Emphasis on Grade School Education of*

Bilingual Children, ed. Jørgen Gimbel et al. (Copenhagen Studies in Bilingualism, 28), Royal Danish School of Educational Studies, 1997, 120 pp. *Modersmålsundervisning i mindretalssprog i Danmark*, ed. Anne Holmen and Jens Normann Jørgensen (Copenhagen Studies in Bilingualism, 29), Royal Danish School of Educational Studies. **Nordiske sprog som andetsprog*, ed. Anne Holmen and Jens Normann Jørgensen (Copenhagen Studies in Bilingualism, 30), Royal Danish School of Educational Studies. Anne Holmen and Jens Normann Jørgensen, **Tosproget udvikling*, vol. K4, Royal Danish School of Educational Studies. Pia Quist, *Ind i gruppen, ind i sproget*, vol. K5, Royal Danish School of Educational Studies.

4. LEXICOGRAPHY, GRAMMARS, AND RHETORIC

The two classic dictionaries for Danish and English have both appeared in new revised editions. They are B. Kjærulff Nielsen, *Engelsk-Dansk Ordbog*, 6th edn, Gyldendal, 1817 pp., and Hermann Vinterberg and C. A. Bodelsen, *Dansk-Engelsk Ordbog*, 4th edn by Viggo Hjørnager Pedersen, Gyldendal, 2610 pp. The same is true of two other important foreign language dictionaries, viz. Andreas Blinkenberg and Poul Høybye, *Fransk-dansk ordbog*, 2 vols, 3rd rev. edn by Jens Rasmussen et al., Nyt Nordisk Forlag Arnold Busck, 1997, 2058 pp., and Giovanni Màfera et al., *Dansk-italiensk ordbog*, 2nd edn, Gyldendal, 887 pp. New foreign language dictionaries include: Abdulahi Mukhtar et al., **Dansk-somali ordbog*, Special-pædagogisk forlag, Herning, 460 pp., and Fereydun Vahman and Claus V. Pedersen, **Persisk-dansk ordbog*, Gyldendal, 915 pp. Two dictionaries of Danish idioms have emerged. Stig Toftgaard Andersen, *Talemåder i dansk. Ordbog over idiomer*, Munksgaard, 419 pp., provides explanations of the idioms listed and information on origin, style, subject area, variants, and synonymous phrases, plus English, German, and French equivalents, and has a long theoretical postscript; while Allan Røder, *Danske talemåder*, Gad, 616 pp., in addition to explanations and brief information about style and century of origin, supplies contextual material in the form of quotes from the sources. Bertil Molde, **Norstedts dansk-svenska ordbok*, 3rd rev. edn, Norstedts ordbok, Stockholm, xiv + 726 pp., contains 50,000 words and phrases. Georg C. Brun, **Modsætninger i sproget. En begrebsordbog*, Frydenlund, 168 pp. Knud Sørensen, **A Dictionary of Anglicisms in Danish*, Historisk-Filosofiske Skrifter 18, Det Kongelige Danske Videnskabernes Selskab, Munksgaard, 1997. *Ømålsordbogen. En sproglig-saglig ordbog over dialekterne på Sjælland, Lolland-Falster, Fyn og omliggende øer*, IV *(faldbarm-forornet)* (Institut for Dansk Dialektforskning, Københavns Universitet, Universitets-Jubilæets danske Samfunds skrifter, 546), C. A. Reitzel,

473 pp. *Retorik Studier*, 11, C. A. Reitzel, 81, contains three articles on rhetoric: J. Fafner, 'Retorik og rytme' (7–23); M. Onsberg, 'En mand er en mand og et ord er et ord — men hvis ord er mandens? Om nogle problemer ved den politiske taleskrivning' (24–61); and P. Steensbech, 'På ministerens vegne. Om taleskrivning i et dansk ministerium' (62–81). Leif Becker Jensen, *Kancellistil eller Anders And-sprog?*, Roskilde Universitetsforlag, 2nd edn, 165 pp., examines modern administrative language. M. Cristofoli, G. Dyrberg, and L. Stage, 'En festival af gode historier? Om metaforernes liv og færden', *Sprint*, no.1:1–14, Handelshøjskolen. B. Henriksen, 'At lære i helheder', *Sprogforum*, 3.10:24–31. K. Kabel, 'Metaforer i EU-debatten', *Mål & Mæle*, no.3:6–13. S. Lundgaard Rasmussen, 'Nogle semiotiske overvejelser om metaforer i kunst og kommunikation' (49–64), and K. Sode, 'Konflikt på et personalemøde — to analysetilgange' (65–89), are both in *NyS*, 23, ed. Anne Holmen et al., Dansklærerfor-eningen, 1997. Jann Scheuer, *Den Umulige Samtale — sprog, køn og magt i jobsamtaler*, Akademisk Forlag, 295 pp., analyses the language and speech acts used in job interviews and also looks at the relationship between language and gender. A shorter version of this is found in his own article, 'En kritisk oversigt over diskursanalyser af interview', *Danske Folkemål*, 40, C. A. Reitzel, 3–23. *Sprog i Norden 1998*, Nordisk Sprogråd, includes C. Jørgensen, 'Politisk debat i tv-demokratiet' (19–30), and K. Brix, 'Moders mål — faders tale' (62–68). Gert Smistrup, *At skrive godt. Få øje på dit eget sprog — og de andres*, Gyldendal, 190 pp.

5. ONOMASTICS

Byens navne: Stednavne i urbaniserede områder, ed. Vibeke Dalberg and Bent Jørgensen (NORNA-rapporter, 64), 1997, 197 pp., contains B. Christensen, 'Nyere gadenavne i Tønder' (49–61); G. Fellows-Jensen, 'Byer i vikingetidens England. Dansk indflydelse på deres udformning' (77–89); and B. Jørgensen, 'Storbyens dele' (113–22). J. Bendix, 'Et godt dansk navn', *Mål & Mæle*, no.4:11–16. G. Sønder-gaard, 'Personnavnets stilfunktion', *Mål & Mæle*, no.2:11–17, deals specifically with the stylistics of personal names.

LITERATURE

POSTPONED

IV. NORWEGIAN STUDIES*

LANGUAGE

By ARNE KRUSE, *Lecturer in Norwegian at Department of Scandinavian Studies, University of Edinburgh*

1. GENERAL

Price, *Encyclopedia*, includes introductory but informative accounts of Old Norse (M. P. Barnes, 332–35) and of Norwegian (S. J. Walton, 335–43). Kurt Braunmüller, *De nordiske språk*, Novus, 248 pp., is a systematic and structuralist description of the current six North Germanic languages, meant as a handbook and textbook for students of Scandinavian. A separate chapter deals with Scandinavian intercommunication. Along the same line is Arne Torp, *Nordiske språk i nordisk og germansk perspektiv*, Novus, 123 pp., where the emphasis is put on similarities and differences among modern Danish, Norwegian and Swedish, but there are also references to Icelandic and Faroese. There is a separate chapter discussing the relationship between the dialects of Scandinavia. *Minority languages in Scandinavia, Britain and Ireland*, ed. Ailbhe Ó Córrain and Séamus Mac Mathuna (Studia Celtica Upsaliensia, 3), Uppsala, 220 pp., includes articles on the Sami and Finnish languages in Norway.

Innføring i språkvitenskap, ed. Torbjørn Nordgård, Ad Notam–Gyldendal, 293 pp., is a course in general linguistics, aiming at students starting language studies at university level. K. L. Berge, M. Halliday, and J. Martin, *Å skape mening med språk*, Cappelen, 500 pp., is another introductory course in new grammatical theory with translated articles by H. and M. and newly written contributions by B. and E. Maagerø. Ragnhild Willumsen, *The Language of Very Low Birthweight 5-Year-Olds. A Conversational Analysis*, Kristiansand, Høgskoleforlaget, 203 pp., suggests that premature birth is linked to developmental speech and language difficulties and might imply increased probability of cognitive, social, and physical problems. Finn-Erik Vinje, *Bedre norsk. Språkråd fra A til Å*, Fagbokforlaget, 171 pp., is part of V.'s handbook series on how to write better Norwegian. Professor Oddvar Nes has been honoured with an impressive Festschrift *Ord etter ord*, ed. Gunnstein Akselberg and Jarle Bondevik, Bergen, Norsk Bokreidingslag, 280 pp., with contributions covering all the topics of Nes's special interests: etymology, onomastics, dialectology, and language history.

---

* The place of publication of books is Oslo unless otherwise indicated.

PERIODICALS AND JOURNALS. In *Språk i Norden 1998*, ed. Birgitta Lindgren et al., Nordic Language Board, Novus, 232 pp., D. Gundersen (5–18) shares his experience of his meeting with the language used in the various media, and M. Hovdenak (76–81) finds that gender equality is reflected in linguistic changes which have taken place within a generation but that there are still many problems ahead for a language which has both articles and pronouns reflecting gender — H. is presenting the leaflet *Kjønn, språk, likestilling* (Norwegian Language Board, 1997); and finally, G. Wiggen, 'Det nordiske språkfellesskapet: språksosiologiske vilkår og framtidsutsikter' (120–64), outlines the current situation and reflects on the future of Scandinavian linguistic unity. W. is very critical of the decision made by the Nordic Council of Ministers to close down the Nordic Language Secretariat and the Nordic Language Information Centre. W. also discusses the consequences of linguistic and socio-economic internationalization on the Norwegian language in *Språklig samling*, no.1 : 5–22. In *Syn og Segn*, no.3, J. Myking (242–49) describes how the development of a Norwegian oil terminology was regarded as part of a national will to get national control over the oil resources, and R. M. Blakar (276–83) shows how male perspectives are still reflected in modern Norwegian. In *Syn og Segn*, no.4 : 322–27, J. T. Faarlund argues for allowing more modern spoken forms into the Nynorsk written standard.

2. HISTORY OF THE LANGUAGE AND TEXTUAL STUDIES

Aslak Bolts jordebok, ed. J. G. Jørgensen and T. Ulset, Riksarkivet, 1997, xl + 320 pp., is the first modern translation of this medieval cadaster covering the middle part of Norway. An introduction by J. covers the history of the manuscript (and how it ended up in Munich); there then follows a parallel edition of the original text alongside a translation into modern Norwegian (Bokmål), done by T. Ulset. This is a most useful source book for historians, linguists, and name researchers. The textbook on Old Norse, Odd Einar Haugen, *Grunnbok i norrønt språk*, AdNotam–Gyldendal, 320 pp., is already now in its third edition and includes a CD-ROM with texts and exercises. Martin Syrett, 'On Sievers' Law, and its converse, in North Germanic', *NOWELE*, 34 : 75–98, finds the 'converse' of Sievers's law an economical way to account for phonological and morphological features of late proto-Germanic and in particular some features in North Germanic. In *NOWELE* 33, Karl-Heinz Mottausch has the article 'Die reduplizerenden Verben im Nord- und Westgermanischen: Versuch eines Raum-Zeitmodells'. There are three articles in English in *MM*, no.1, where L. Motz (11–19)

discusses the designation *blindi* — one of the many names of Óðinn —
and argues for a meaning 'concealment', attached to the hidden,
mysterious side of the god; I. Matiushina, 'The emergence of lyrical
self-expression in scaldic love poetry' (21–33), gives a textual analysis
of the so-called *mansǫngr*; and K. E. Gade (41–60) utilizes the
chronology of the names *Kaupangr* — *Þrándheimr* — *Niðaróss* as a
criterion for establishing the dates of the earliest kings' sagas.
B. Mæhlum sums up the linguistic effects of the Black Plague in *Norsk
Lingvistisk Tidsskrift*, no.1:3–32. F.-E. Vinje outlines the thorough
work behind Henrik Ibsen's representation of the Norwegian language on stage, in *Ordet*, no. 3:15–19. There are new publications
from the Ivar Aasen Institute: a new edition of Ivar Aasen's *Norsk
Navnebog* of 1878, ed. Kristoffer Kruken and Terje Aarset, and a
collection of articles from the international Ivar Aasen conference at
the University of Oslo, November 1996: *Language Contact and Language
Conflict. Proceedings of the International Ivar Aasen Conference, Oslo 1996*, ed.
Unn Røyneland, Volda College, 320 pp. In *MM*, no.2, M. Myhren
(131–50) and H. Baklid (151–64) investigate Ivar Aasen's work as a
folklorist, how he treated this material linguistically, and how he saw
it as useful for building national identity.

3. RUNOLOGY

In *MM*, no.1:35–40, O. Grønvik returns to the inscription on the
Tune stone and argues for the interpretation 'WiwaR conducted a
religious sermon after Wodurid', and in 'Runeinnskriften på
doppskoen fra Thorsbjerg i Sønderjylland', *MM*, no.2:113–30, he
suggests a new interpretation of this very early inscription. In
Runeinschriften als Quellen interdiziplinärer Forschung, ed. Klaus Düwel
(Ergänzungsbände zum Reallexikon der Germanischen Altertumskunde, 15), Berlin–NY, de Gruyter, K. F. Seim has the article 'Runes
and Latin script: runic syllables', and J. R. Hagland has 'Runes as
sources for the Middle Ages' (619–28). *Innskrifter og datering. Dating
Inscriptions*, ed. Audun Dybdahl and Jan Ragnar Hagland,
Trondheim, Tapir, 147 pp., includes an article by H. and R. I. Page,
'Runica manuscripta and runic dating: the expansion of the younger
Fuþark (55–72). H. also writes about the use of runes and letters in
medieval Trondheim, pp. 171–83 of *Myter og humaniora*, ed. K. E.
Haug and B. Mæhlum, Sypress, 285 pp.

4. DIALECTOLOGY AND PHONOLOGY

In *Talatrosten*, 32, J. A. Schulze (8–13) investigates an anonymous
word collection from Østfold, and J. Øverby (15–98) gives an

extraordinarily long and detailed review of T. E. Jenstad and
A. Dalen, *Trønderordboka* (see *YWMLS*, 59:886). Olaf Husby and
Marit Helene Kløve, *Andrespråksfonologi. Teori og metodikk*, AdNotam–Gyldendal, 202 pp., is an introduction to the theory and
methodology of teaching the phonology of Norwegian as a second
language. The first part of the book presents various theories on the
subject and then compares the sound systems of Norwegian and a
number of other languages. The second part outlines a method in the
teaching of the subject. A very useful book for all teachers of
Norwegian as a second language. A. Dalen, 'Contributing factors in
the making of the post-medieval urban dialect of Trondheim',
Language Change. Advances in Historical Sociolinguistics, ed. Ernst Håkon
Jahr, Berlin–NY, de Gruyter, pp. 291–304. In *Nordic Prosody. Proceedings of the VIIth Conference, Joensuu 1996*, ed. S. Werner, Frankfurt,
Lang, W. van Dommelen, T. Fretheim, and R. A. Nilsen have the
article 'The perception of boundary tone in East Norwegian' (73–86).
E. Papazian, *MM*, no.2: 165–92, discusses length as a distinctive
factor in the Scandinavian languages (except Danish), and suggests
that rather than seeing the length of the vowel as distinctive and the
length of the consonant as redundant there is an opposition between
sequences of vowel + consonant.

5. ONOMASTICS

Byens navne. Stednavne i urbaniserede områder, ed. Vibeke Dalberg and
Bent Jørgensen (*NORNA*-Rapporter, 64), Uppsala, NORNA, 1997,
208 pp., is from a conference in Copenhagen on names in urban
areas. Here G. Akselberg (9–35) analyses the public naming practice
in the municipality of Voss, I. Lund (123–33) does the same for
Halden, O. Stemshaug (135–46) discusses street-naming in relation
to Norwegian language politics, and F. F. Thorp (147–58) shows how
names of smallholdings in the region of Aker survive today as the
names of other localities.

Margit Harsson, *Skiptvet*, Solum, 1997, is vol. 2 in the series on
settlement names in Østfold. In *MM*, no.1, F. Korslund (61–65)
argues against the traditional interpretation of the name *Oslo* as 'the
meadow of the god' and would rather see 'the meadow under the
hill', and K. Bakken (67–83) discusses onomastics as a field of study
in Norway and its relationship to modern linguistics. B. shows that
Norwegian onomastics is rather out of pace with current developments in linguistics and that it is deeply rooted in new-grammarian
tradition, but she is hopeful for the future as modern linguistics regain
an interest in diachronic studies. K. Bakken also has an article in *You
Name it. Perspectives on Onomastic Research*, ed. Ritva Liisa Pitkänen and

Kaija Mallat (Studia Fennica. Linguistica, 7), Helsinki, Finnish Literature Society, 1997, 297 pp. The article, in English, is called 'Form and meaning. The basis for name-specific phonological development' (21–30), and B. here argues that name-specific phonological changes are to be interpreted as concomitants of an extreme degree of lexicalization, not as an inherent aspect of the category of proper names. In *Proceedings of the XIXth International Congress of Onomastic Sciences, Aberdeen, August 4–11, 1996*, II, ed. W. F. H. Nicolaisen, Aberdeen U.P., 402 pp., are G. Akselberg, 'Street names: norms and forms' (3–8), R. Cox, 'Old Norse *berg* in Hebridean place-nomenclature' (59–65), J. Ellingsve, 'Naming the unseen: theoretical problems and pragmatic solutions concerning the naming of Norwegian oil and gas fields in the North Sea' (90–96), G. Fellows-Jensen, 'Little Thwaite, who made thee?' (101–06), P. Hallaråker, 'Names and ethnicity: the triple identity of the Norwegian Americans indicated by their choice and spelling of surnames and place names' (152–62), Å. S. Hansen, 'Noms de lieu normands d'origine scandinave: Quelle dimensions et perspectives offre l'étude des noms de lieu dans le domain plurilinguistique?' (163–68), and B. Helleland, 'Place-names, a source used in the study of religious activity in pre-Christian society: some methodological aspects' (169–77); *ib.*, III, 405 pp., contains G. Alhaug, 'Name, status and gender: on the use of initial letter instead of full first name in Norway in the 19th century' (3–10). In *Namn och Bygd*, 86, L. Elmevik (31–39) analyses the name *Lærdal* in the county of Sogn og Fjordane and leans towards an etymology based on the river name with the meaning 'the river flowing in a gully (hollow) in the terrain, through a ravine' or possibly simply 'the clay valley', while B. Sandnes (41–63) writes about her investigation of Orkney names, mostly field-names, from the parish of Harray, especially seen from the perspective of linguistic interference between Norse and Scots-English, and J. Sandnes (81–90) discusses if we should regard widespread names like *Uppsala/Oppsal* as name transfers or 'autonomous names'. In *Namn og Nemne*, 15, I. Særheim (7–19) presents a newly found collection of names made by schoolchildren in the 1930s, A. Kruse (21–31) writes about the names of the mountains fishermen use in order to find their fishing grounds, K. Flokenes (37–44) analyses four place-names in Askvoll, West Norway, T. Eskeland (45–60) discusses the spelling of Finnish place-names in Finnskogene, East Norway, F. Myrvang (61–74) continues the discussion of a possible Sami stratum in the place-names of Lofoten, Northern Norway, V. Haslum (75–92) outlines the strategies of a cartographer in his meeting with the name material to be included on a map, and K. Sæther (93–102) presents the personal names of the 18th and 19th cs in Sunndal, West Norway. The *Annual*

Report from the Section for Name Research, ed. B. Helleland, Oslo U.P., includes articles by K. Bakken (17–39), analysing the name *Langlim*, Telemark, and Å. Wetås (79–89) on the reconstruction of place-names using medieval sources. The Section's publication *Nytt om namn* is an excellent source of information on onomastics research in Norway and Scandinavia.

6. SYNTAX, MORPHOLOGY

Jarle Rønhovd, *Norsk morfologi*, AdNotam–Gyldendal, 1997, 177 pp., is the second edition of the text-book on modern Norwegian (Bokmål and Nynorsk) morphology. A new chapter on compound words is written by O.-J. Johannesen. T. A. Åfarli, 'The basic combination: the verb and its subject', *Papers from the 16th Conference of Linguistics*, ed. T. Haukioja, Turku U.P., pp. 485–96; Id. and T. Nordgård, 'Syntactic change in generative syntax', *ib.*, pp. 497–508. J. Haugan writes about the passive subject in Old Norse double object construc-tions in *Norsk lingvistisk tidsskrift*, no.2 : 157–84, and he has the article 'Right dislocated "subjects" in Old Norse', in *Working Papers in Scandinavian Syntax*, 62 : 37–60. Jon Erik Hagen, *Norsk grammatikk for andrespråklærere*, AdNotam–Gyldendal, 418 pp., aims at teachers of Norwegian as a second language and presents grammatical subjects from the perspective of a non-Norwegian. The book is part of a distance learning course in Norwegian as a foreign language, run by the University of Bergen. The comparative aspect is consequently important and this makes the book useful and different from most other grammars. For a similar audience is Anne Golden, *Ordforråd, ordbruk og ordlaging i et andrespråkperspektiv*, AdNotam–Gyldendal, 171 pp. Lars Anders Kulbrandstad, *Språkets mønstre. Grammatiske begreper og metoder*, 282 pp., is an introduction to grammar in a wide sense, including pronounciation and orthography. This second edition is changed in several ways, e.g. it now includes a separate chapter on sentence analysis. The target purchaser is the student in the teacher-training college, and there is also, by the same author, *Inn i Språkets mønstre. Oppgavesamling*, 152 pp., a collection of exercises linked to the grammar book. In *MM*, no.2 : 193–206, H.-O. Enger explores the limits between the s-forms of the present tense and the infinitive. K. E. Kristoffersen, 'Forholdet mellom tematiske roller og syntaktiske funksjonar i norrønt, jamført med tysk og islandsk', *ANF*, 113 : 97–149, analyses transitive verbs in three languages. In *Norsk lingvistisk tidsskrift*, 15.1, 1997, the doctoral thesis by A. L. Graedler, *Morphological, Semantic and Functional Aspects of English Lexical Borrowings in Norwegian* is discussed by the two opponents M. Ljung (83–89) and K. Venås (90–99).

7. LEXICOGRAPHY AND DICTIONARIES

Normer og regler. Festskrift til Dag Gundersen 15. januar 1998, ed. R. V. Fjeld and B. Wangensteen, Nordic Society for Lexicography, 367 pp., celebrates the highly respected lexicographer Dag Gundersen with 26 contributions from scholars and colleagues covering most aspects within the theory and practice of lexical norms. Anne-Lise Graedler and Stig Johansson, *Anglisismeordboka*, Norwegian U.P., 1997, 466 pp., is the first dictionary concerned with English loans in Norwegian, how these behave, pronunciation, declination, compounds, etc. *Password — English Dictionary for Speakers of Norwegian*, ed. Nancy L. Coleman, Kunnskapsforlaget, 955 pp., is a 'semi-bilingual dictionary', meaning that all entries are translated into Norwegian, but all examples of usage are in English. Arild and Kjell Raaheim, *Psykologiske fagord. Fra engelsk til norsk*, Fagbokforlaget, 219 pp., is useful for students who find their reading list is mainly English but their examination is in Norwegian. Audun Øyri, *Norsk medisinsk ordbok*, Samlaget, 875 pp., is a thorough revision of the dictionary that first appeared ten years ago, and it now even includes Web-addresses for further readings. In *Det Kgl Norske Videnskabers Selskabs Forhandlinger 1997*, Trondheim, A. Dalen (1–20) writes about Scandinavian terminology relating to skis and skiing, and D. does the same in French in the article 'Les origines et la terminologie du ski en Scandinavie', *Proxima Thulé*, Paris, 3:49–77. Terminology is the topic for the report from the symposium *Terminologi — system og kontekst*, ed. J. Myking, R. Sæbø, and B. Toft, Norwegian Council for Research, 300 pp. *Norskrift*, 97, Scandinavian Studies, Oslo U.P., 1997, is dedicated to lexicography.

LITERATURE SINCE THE REFORMATION

By ØYSTEIN ROTTEM, *Cand. phil., Copenhagen*
(This survey covers the years 1997 and 1998)

1. GENERAL

In most literary histories works of non-fiction are allotted but small place. In order to give this kind of writing more attention, a research programme was initiated some years ago, the outcome of which is the publication of *Norsk litteraturhistorie. Sakprosa fra 1750 til 1995*, ed. T. B. Eriksen and E. B. Johnsen. I. *1750–1920*, 770 pp.; II. *1920 til 1995*, 749 pp., Universitetsforlaget. A large number of scholars have contributed to the work, covering all kinds of non-fiction — cookery books as well as doctoral theses in physics, text books on linguistics as well as biographies and prayer-books. Altogether the two volumes give a broad, but salient survey of the subject matter. The idea behind it is to stimulate and help future literary historians to include non-fiction in their works. Per T. Andersen, *Fra Petter Dass til Jan Kjærstad. Studier i diktekunst og komposisjon*, LNU/Cappelen Akademiske Forlag, 1997, 333 pp., offers a varied selection of interesting studies of works by e.g. H. Wergeland, H. Ibsen, B. Bjørnson, A. Garborg, K. Hamsun, R. Jacobsen, and J. Kjærstad. In *Diktet natur. Natur og landskap hos Andreas Munch, Vilhelm Krag og Hans Børli*, Aschehoug, 1997, 478 pp., Henning H. Wærp sets out to investigate the history of the changing modes and forms of poetry of nature; he presents penetrating readings of separate poems by three widely different poets. *Hugbod. Heidersskrift til Leif Mæhle på 70-årsdagen*, ed. L. Bliksrud and V. Ystad, Samlaget, 1997, 312 pp., contains articles about O. Aukrust (by T. Modalsli), A. Garborg (by L. Bliksrud and I. Hauge), H. Garborg (by G. Bøe), A. Hauge (by I. Kongslien), H. M. Vesaas (by J. Hareide), T. Vesaas (by D. G. Myhren). L. A. Vaage (by H. Skei), and I. Aasen (by M. Myhren). T. Birkeland, G. Risa, and K. B. Vold, *Norsk barnelitteraturhistorie*, Samlaget, 1997, 477 pp., constitutes the first lengthy and comprehensive study of children's literature in N. and thus bears witness to the growing interest in this type of literature during the last 20 years. The book is a 'must' for all students of children's literature. Of special interest are the presentation and evaluation of the formal and thematic innovations in the literature of the 1980s. A sample of interesting studies on a wide range of topics concerning the present status of children's literature is presented in *Nye veier til barneboka*, ed. Harald Bache-Wiig, LNU/Cappelen Akademiske Forlag, 1997, 277 pp. The volume includes articles on e.g. the problems of defining children's literature as genre (by P. Nodelman), the theory of adaptation (by T. Weinreich), and the relation of children's literature to modernism, postmodernism, and fantasy (by Z. Shavit, R. Romøren, M. Nikolajeva, and S. Gilead), and feminist approaches to children's literature are discussed by L. Paul. The first volume of what is planned to be an annual publication, *Litteratur for barn og unge*, ed. P. O. Kaldestad and K. B. Vold, Samlaget, 207 pp., contains interviews with and introductions to several writers, as well as a bibliography, which includes both belletristic and scholarly work in the field, information about literary prizes, etc. I. Mjør, 'Kan små tøydyr gråta? Tøydyrmytologi i den postmoderne barneboka', *NLÅ*, 1997:175–96. *Religiøsitet og litteratur i regionalt perspektiv*, ed. T. Maistad (KULTs skriftserie, 68), Norges forskningsråd, 1997, 276 pp. Oddmund Hjelde, *Det indre lys. Religiøs mystikk i norsk litteratur og åndsliv*, Solum, 1997, 248 pp. J. I. Sørebø, 'Hjartespråk og bibelspråk i litteraturen', *Mål og makt*, 27, 1997:52–75. The editor's investigation into the theoretical problems and historical development of fantasy literature in *Litterære skygger. Norsk fantastisk litteratur*, ed. T. Haugen, LNU/ Cappelen Akademiske Forlag, 252 pp., is most useful and stimulating. Furthermore the volume includes analysis of authors such as L. Holberg (by N. Dalgaard), M. Hansen (by Å. Svensen), R. Jølsen (by H. H. Wærp), T. Andersen (by H. Bache-Wiig), F. Carling (by I. Johansen), T. Å. Bringsværd (by G. Vestad), K. Fløgstad (by N. Dalgaard), and J. Kjærstad (by G. Mose). Martin Nag, *Turgenjev i norsk åndsliv*, Solum, 1997, 352 pp. Steinar Gimnes, *Sjølvbiografiar. Skrift, fiksjon og liv*, Samlaget, 352 pp., is the first extensive study of autobiography as genre in Norwegian. G. is mainly concerned with the relations between writing and reality and between roles and identity, indicating that the writers' self-presentations are ruled by a need for coherence. The relevance and benefit of theoretical and historical considerations are shown in penetrating studies of three autobiographies (C. Collett, *I de lange Nætter*, N. C. Vogt, *Fra gutt til mann*, and K. Hamsun, *På gjengrodde stier*). Leif Longum, *På fallrepet. Artikler, essays, innlegg 1962–1997*, Bergen U.P., 341 pp. H. H. Wærp, 'The poetry of the Romantic garden', *Norlit*, Tromsø U.P., 1997, no.1:85–98. O. Grepstad, 'Same gamle historia? Krøniken som litteratur- og kulturhistorie', *NLÅ*: 232–51. Henning Hagerup, *Vinternotater*, Tiden, 344 pp., includes essays on e.g. G. Hofmo, S. Mjelve, D. Solstad, and T. Å. Bringsværd.

2. THE SIXTEENTH TO NINETEENTH CENTURIES

GENERAL

Laila Akslen: *Norsk barokk. Dorothe Engelbretsdatter og Petter Dass i retorisk tradisjon*, LNU/Cappelen Akademiske Forlag, 1997, 231 pp. *Herr Petter 350 år. Et festskrift fra Universitetet i Tromsø*, ed. S. Nesset,

Universitetsbiblioteket i Tromsø, 1997, 235 pp. *Digternes paryk. Studier i 1700–tallet. Festskrift til Thomas Bredsdorff*, ed. M. Alenius et al., Copenhagen, Museum Tusculanum, 373 pp.

INDIVIDUAL AUTHORS

BRUN, J.N.   *Den firfoldige fader. Allegori og sjølvframstilling i spenning mellom klassisisme og romantikk med særlig vekt på Johan Nordahl Brun (1745–1816)*. doct. diss., Faculty of Theology, Oslo University, 1997, 368 pp.

DASS, P.   P. J. Haarberg, 'Filologien som utfordring til litteraturvitenskapen: Momenter til en lesning av Petter Dass' "Herre Gud, ditt dyre navn og ære" ', *Norsk Litteraturvitenskapelig Tidsskrift*, no.1:79–92. Odd Rattsø, *Petter Dass. Leilighetsdikter i en barokktid*, Sandnessjøen, 1997, 111 pp. About 60 pages are devoted to the memory of Petter Dass's authorship in *Hymnologiske meddelser*, 26, 1997, Copenhagen. The contributors are Ø. Danielsen, J. Haarberg, L. Akslen, and T. Aurdal. L. Akslen, ' "[. . .] En skøn lystig oc besynderlig nyttig histori [. . .]" Petter Dass' *Ruths Bog* i retorisk perspektiv', *Edda*, 1997:331–45.

FASTING, C.   B. K. Nicolaysen, 'Claus Fasting og småsjangrane på 1700–talet. Fragment av eit oppløyst univers, byggjesteinar til eit nytt', *Nordica Bergensia*, 18:9–32.

3.   THE NINETEENTH CENTURY
GENERAL

K. B. Gilje, 'Profeter, geiter og kokebokforfattere. Norsk essayistikk på 1800–tallet', *NLÅ*, 1997:24–41.

INDIVIDUAL AUTHORS

BJØRNSON, B.   Øystein Sørensen, *Bjørnstjerne Bjørnson og nasjonalismen*, Cappelen, 1997, 266 pp. B. K. Nicolaysen, 'Frelselære og lagnadstru: Bjørnsons "Faderen" som nasjonal allegori', *Omvegar fører lengst. Stykkevise essay om forståing*, Samlaget, 1997, 246–74.

COLLETT, C.   P. M. Brudal, 'Metonymisk selvrepresentasjon i Camilla Colletts memoireverk *I de lange nætter*', *Bøygen*, 1997, no.3:6–10.

FLATABØ, J.   Kåre Glette, *Jon Flatabø og Vestfold. Om opphaldet i Jarlsberg og populærforteljingane Aagot og Vebjørn Tangen*, Skibladner forlag, 1997, 161 pp.

GARBORG, A.   K. Glette, 'Ei regionalistisk lesing av *Fred, Læraren* og *Den burtkomne Faderen* av Arne Garborg', *Nordica Bergensia*, 16, 1997:163–80. A. Skjervøy, 'Revolusjon med Arne Garborg som fadder, Ivar Mortenson som prest og Rasmus Steinsvik som dåpsbarn', *Syn og Segn*, 1997, no.2 : 143–55.

GARBORG, H. Sønnøv S. Borse, *Hulda Garborg og miljøet i Asker*, Asker, Forskningsstiftelsen Bics, 1997, 84 pp. S. S. Borse, *Hulda Garborgs liv og forfatterskap*, Asker, Forskningsstiftelsen Bics, 1997, 40 pp.

HAMSUN, K. Finn Aarsæther, *Om Pan av Knut Hamsun* (Veier til verket), Ad Notam Gyldendal, 1997, 116 pp. Amongst the contributions in *De røde jærn. 7 foredrag fra Hamsun-dagene på Hamarøy 1996*, ed. N. M. Knutsen, Tromsø, Hamsun-Selskapet, 1997, 155 pp., are articles on H. and Brandes (H. P. Thøgersen), H. and Ibsen (B. Hemmer), H. and D. Solstad (Ø. Rottem), and H. and the small town (A. Kittang). *Hamsun in Edinburgh. Papers Read at the Conference in Edinburgh 1997*, ed. P. Graves and A. Kruse, Tromsø, Hamsun-Selskapet, 1997, 124 pp. *Film, religion, kjærlighet. 8 foredrag fra Hamsun-dagene på Hamarøy 1998*, ed. N. M. Knutsen, Tromsø, Hamsun-Selskapet, 159 pp. Ø. Rottem, 'Nirvanas bulder. Schopenhauer, Hamsun og viljens selvopphevelse', *Kritik*, 129, 1997 : 42–49. K. Bale, 'Hamsuns hvite hest. Om *Victoria*', *Edda*, 1997 : 292–302. M. Zagar, 'Knut Hamsun's black man or lament for paternalist society. A reading of Hamsun's play *Livet ivold* through *Fra det moderne Amerikas aandsliv*', *Edda*, 1997 : 364–79. M. Humpál, 'Editing and interpreting. Two editions of Hamsun's *Pan* and the question of the fictional authorship of "Glahns død"', *Edda*: 20–29. S. Dingstad, 'Om *Sult* (1890) — og andre tekster med samme tittel', *Edda*: 30–38. L. H. Nesby, 'Ironi og metafiksjonalitet i Knut Hamsuns *Siste Kapitel*', *Norlit*, Tromsø University, no.3 : 285–318. D. Buttry, 'Pursuit and confrontation. The short stories of Knut Hamsun', *ScSt*, 70 : 233–50. M. Zagar, 'Knut Hamsun's Taming of the Shrew', *ib.*, 337–58. *Hamsuns polemiske skrifter*, ed. G. Hermundstad, Gyldendal, 287 pp. Walter Baumgartner, *Den modernistiske Hamsun. Medrivende og frastøtende*, Gyldendal, 205 pp. Martin Nag, *Geniet Knut Hamsun — en norsk Dostojevskij*, Solum, 242 pp. Knut Brynhildsvoll, *Sult, sprell og Altmulig. Alte und neue Studien zu Knut Hamsuns antipsychologischer Romankunst* (TUGS), 151 pp. Lars F. Larsen's doctoral thesis, *Den unge Hamsun (1859–1888)*, Schibsted, 607 pp., is the first academic biography about H. It offers an overwhelming amount of new and interesting information about the writer's life as a young man, and L. convincingly argues that much that has been previously written about these years is based on myths. His main point of view is that the young H. sympathized with democratic ideas and the left wing party of that time.

IBSEN, H. The 9th volume of *Contemporary Approaches to Ibsen*, ed. B. Hemmer and V. Ystad, Scandinavian University Press, 1997, provides a large number of interesting articles, written by international Ibsen experts. To be mentioned are C. Collin, 'Henrik Ibsen's dramatic construction technique'; J. W. Dietrichson, 'The theatrical ideas of Henrik Ibsen'; E. Eide, 'Henrik Ibsen and reforms in Chinese drama'; I.-S. Ewbank, ' "Spiritual Property": intertextuality and influence in Ibsen's texts'; F. Paul, 'Metaphysical landscapes in Ibsen's late plays'; E. Durbach, 'The modernist malaise: "nichts og ingenting" at the core of Ibsen's onion'; E. Hartman, '*The Lady from the Sea* in a mythologic and psychoanalytic perspective'; A. M. V. Stanton-Ife, ' "Lykke" as contemporary fiction in *Bygmester Solness*'; J. Templeton, 'Ibsen early and late. *Little Eyolf*, female selfhood and Ibsenian triangles'; and J. D. Johansen, 'Art is (not) a woman's body: art and sexuality in Ibsen's *When We Dead Awaken*'. *Garborg, Ibsen, Johannesen, Munch, Uppdal. A Contribution to the Ibsen Conference 1997*, ed. F. Delle Cave and H. Mehren, Vienna, 1997, 104 pp. *Lørdagsforum høst 1993: Ibsen i fokus*, Senter for Ibsenstudier, 1997, 117 pp., offers a varied selection of lectures about Ibsen. Amongst the lecturers are well-known Ibsen scholars such as I.-S. Ewbank, V. Ystad, H. Rønning, A. Aarseth and S. Saari. *Den optiske fordring. Pejlinger i den visuelle kultur omkring Henrik Ibsens forfatterskab*, ed. E. Østerud, Aarhus U.P., 1997, 226 pp. Gunhild Hoem, *Under forvandlingens lov. En studie i Henrik Ibsens dramatikk*, Solum, 1997, 53 pp. Sverre Mørkhagen, *Peer Gynt. Historie, sagn og dikt*, Cappelen, 1997, 208 pp. Atle Næss, *Ibsens Italia*, Gyldendal, 1997, 125 pp. Norman Rhodes, *Ibsen and the Greeks. The Classical Greek Dimension in Selected Works of Henrik Ibsen as Mediated by German and Scandinavian Culture*, Lewisburg–London, Bucknell U.P.–Associated U.P. 1995, 209 pp. Kiersten Shepherd-Barr, *Ibsen and Early Modernist Theatre 1890–1900*, Westport, Conn., Greenwood Press, 1997, 200 pp. Joan Templeton, *Ibsen's Women*, CUP, 1997, 386 pp. M. Wells, 'Ibsen's personal myth', *Edda*, 1997:3–13. G. Bø, 'Historismen i Ibsens nasjonalromantiske dramatikk', *ib.*, 20–27. K. Madsen, 'Tanken om Det tredje rike. En "positiv verdensanskuelse" fra Ibsens hånd?', *ib.*, 28–36. L. P. Wærp, 'Historie og retorikk, historiens retorikk. Keiser Julians historiske frafall som litterært forbilde?', *ib.*, 37–46. J. L. Levy, 'Dobbeltmennesket Julian og Maximos. *Kejser og galilæer* i æstetisk og religionshistorisk perspektiv', *ib.*, 47–53. V. Ystad, '*John Gabriel Borkman*. Historisk analyse eller tidløs tragedie?', *ib.*, 54–64. H. Skaar, '*Brand* som epos og dram', *ib.*, 65–74. W. Solheim, 'At crossroads and cross purposes. The resolution of *Samfundets støtter*', *ib.*, 75–87. T. Selboe, 'Maskerade — kvinnelighet — frihet. Perspektiver på Henrik Ibsens *Et dukkehjem*', *ib.*, 88–98. B. Wicklund, 'Ibsens kvener og havfruer. Myter, samfunnskritikk og overføring i *Fruen fra havet*', *ib.*, 99–110. M. G. Lokrantz, 'Ibsen och det italienska renässansmåleriet, En möjlig inspirataionskälla till

Hedda Gabler', *ib.*, 118–25. A. Nærø, 'Realisme som tidløs tragedie? En kritikk av Daniel Haakonsens Ibsen-fortolking', *ib.*, 126–36. J. Templeton, 'New light on the Bardach Diary. Eight unpublished letters from Ibsen's Gossensass Princess', *ScSt*, 69, 1997:147–70. R. Shindler, 'Ibsen and the Name-of-the-Father', *ib.*, 227–95. S. R. Medbøen, 'Maktforhold og bruken av det sceniske rommet i *Hedda Gabler* av Henrik Ibsen', *Nordica Bergensia*, 16, 1997:61–81. L. Kallek-lev, 'Replikkunst og retorikk i *Fruen fra havet* av Henrik Ibsen', *ib.*, 83–100. A. Hydle, 'Ironi i Ibsens *Gengangere*', *ib.*, 101–20. T. A. Dyrerud, 'Den Kierkegaardske "Relex" i Ibsens dramatikk', *Bøygen*, 1997, 4:17–22. Trond B. Eriksen, *Egne veier. Essays og foredrag*, Universitetsforlaget, 1997, contains an essay on Ibsen's *Brand*, 'Ibsens *Brand* — en klassisk tragedie'. A. Hoel, 'Det provoserende svangerska-pet i Henrik Ibsens *Hedda Gabler*', *Norlit*, Tromsø U.P., no.3:267–84. V. Ystad, 'Ibsen, Drachman and *The Lady of the Sea*', *Scandinavica*, 37:185–96. M. Wells, 'Ghosts and white horses. Ibsen's *Gengangere* and *Rosmersholm* revisited', *ib.*, 197–214. Terje Johansen, *Om Gengangere av Henrik Ibsen* (Veier til verket), Karnov, 1997, 96 pp. Id., *Om Vildanden av Henrik Ibsen* (Veier til verket), Ad Notam Gyldendal, 1997, 97 pp. P. E. Larson and B. Elbrønd-Bek, 'A selection of Henrik Ibsen's letters', *Edda*:58–87. E. B. Hagen, 'Ibsens forsoning eller hvorfor *Rosmersholm* egentlig er en politisk komedie', *ib.*, 245–58. Brita Pollan, *Peer Gynt og Carl Gustav Jung. Med sjelen som følgesvenn*, Aschehoug, 332 pp. E. Østerud, *Theatrical and narrative space. Studies in Strindberg, Ibsen and J. P. Jacobsen*, Aarhus U.P., 152 pp., is mainly concerned with the modernity of I. *Livet på likstrå. Henrik Ibsens Når vi døde vågner*, ed. L. P. Wærp, LNU/Cappelen Akademiske Forlag, 287 pp., contains old and new articles about I.'s last play. Of special interest are F. Paul, 'Scenelandskapene i *John Gabriel Borkman* og *Når vi døde vågner*'; H. Detering, ' "Pax vobiscum." Allegorisering og metafysikk i Ibsens *Når i døde vågner*'; L. P. Wærp, 'Oppstandelsen som forførerisk morder. Personifikasjon, allegori, parodi og ironi i *Når vi døde vågner*'; F. Helland, 'Irene: objekt eller subjekt?'; S. G. Ottesen, 'Melodrama som skepticisme i Ibsens *Når vi døde vågner*'; P. Buvik, 'Kunsten, kjønnet og kvinnen. Om Ibsens *Når vi døde vågner*'; and B. Wicklund, 'Kjønnskampens kunst, kunsten som kjønnskamp. En feministisk lesning av Ibsens *Når vi døde vågner*'.

KIELLAND, A. Hilde Sejersted, *Om Garman & Worse av Alexander Kielland*, Karnov, 1997, 154 pp.

MUNCH, A. S. Aa. Aarnes, 'Inn og ut av kanon — Andreas Munch som eksempel', *Nordica Bergensia*, 17:168–87.

OBSTFELDER, S. Britt Holgersen, ... *på en feil klode. Sigbjørn Obstfelder — mennesket og dikteren*, Stavanger, Dreyer, 1997, 96 pp. *Obstfelder. Fjorten essays*, ed. Asbj. Aarnes, Aschehoug, 1997, 265 pp.

SKRAM, A. *Amalie Skraam — 150 år. Nye perspektiver på Amalie Skram-forskningen*, ed. P. Bjørby and Elisabeth Aasen, Bergen U.P., 1997, 131 pp. E. Aasen, *Om Sjur Gabriel av Amalie Skram*, Karnov, 1997, 95 pp. S. Ødegaard, ' "Min længsel går mod andre kloder." Tvetydig seksualitet i Amalie Skrams liv og diktning', *NLÅ*: 72–96.

WERGELAND, H. Odd A. Storsveen, *Henrik Wergelands norske historie. Et bidrag til nasjonalhistoriens mythos* (KULTs skriftserie), Norges forskningsråd, 369 pp. M. Egeland, 'Biografisk kritikkløshet. Wergelands *Hassel-Nødder* og overleveringer', *Nytt norsk tidsskrift*, 1997:161–71. A. Dvergsdal, 'Hvor ille var de? Henrik Wergelands tidligste lyrikk belyst ved Liége-gruppens *Rhetorique générale*', *Edda*, 1997:270–91. A.-L. Langfeldt, 'Melodrama og sekularisering. En lesning av Henrik Wergelands *Barnemordersken*', *NLÅ*: 32–56.

4. THE TWENTIETH CENTURY

GENERAL

The two last volumes of Ø. Rottem, *Norges litteraturhistorie. Etterkrigslitteraturen.* II. *Inn i medietidsalderen 1965–1980*, Cappelen, 1997, 738 pp., and III. *Vår egen tid 1980–98*, Cappelen, 893 pp., provide a comprehensive presentation of literary tendencies up until the present day, as well as portraits of all the main writers. The work is aimed at scholars and students as well as at a broader audience. The chapter on children's literature from 1945 to 1980 is written by Tordis Ørjasæter, vol. II, 571–736. *Nordisk kvindelitteraturhistorie.* IV. *På jorden 1960–1990*, ed. E. M. Jensen, Copenhagen, Munksgaard–Rosinante, 1997, 597 pp.; and V. *Liv og værk*, 456 pp. Petter Aaslestad, *Pasienten som tekst. Fortellerrollen i psykiatriske journaler. Gaustad 1890–1990*, Tano Aschehoug, 1997, 205 pp. In addition to contributions about individual authors, *Folia Scandinavica Posnaniensia*, 3, 1996, contains articles on trends in contemporary N. writing (by W. Baumgartner and E. Wojciechowska). M. Riber, 'Mellem Karin Moe og Sissel Lie — om norsk kvindelitteratur i 1980'erne og 1990'erne', *Nordica Bergensia*, 16, 1997:121–43. H. O. Andersen, 'Lyrikken etterpå. Nedslag og trender i nyere dansk og norsk lyrikk, med et sidesprang til Sverige', *NLÅ*, 1997:153–74. In a posthumously published volume of *Essays*, ed. H. Hagerup and M. Moi, Gyldendal, 1997, 200 pp., the poet and author Tor Ulven deals with several N. writers in a personal and compelling way, e.g. S. Obstfelder, T. Andersen, T. Vesaas, E. Boyson, K. Heggelund, and Ø. Berg. Geir Gulliksen, *Virkelighet og andre essays*, Oktober, 1996, 251 pp. I. T. Hjelmervik, 'Jagten på den nordiske bog. Litterære vurderinger i Nordisk Råds litteraturpris', *NLÅ*:15–31. W. Larsen, 'Kvinner, sex og samtid. Noen sørgelige fortellinger fra den nordiske kvinnelitteraturhistorien', *ib.*, 211–31.

INDIVIDUAL AUTHORS

ANDERSEN, A. H.   K. Skjeldal, 'Det jeg sier er ikke det jeg mener. Et forsøk på å beskrive Astrid Hjertenæs Andersens paradoksale poetikk', *NLÅ*, 1997:88–96.

BAKKAN, E.   *Vegen til regnbogen. Av og om Engvald Bakkan til 100-årsjubileet i 1997*, Komiteen for Engvald Bakkan-jubileet, Åmli, 1997, 210 pp., covers several aspects of B.'s authorship, but only a small number of the contributors have academic aspirations. Amongst these are T. Thorsen and B. Hemmer. A useful bibliography to the writings of this rather unknown author is also included.

BANG, K.   Kåre Glette, *Vestfold og Karin Bangs forfatterskap. Ein regionalistisk studie*, Tano Aschehoug, 426 pp., is one of the first theses in N. scholarship where an author is studied from a regionalistic point of view. The work demonstrates the relevance of such a method in a convincing way.

BELSVIK, R.   H. H. Skei, 'Den vanskelege kjærleiken. Om Rune Belsviks: *Kjærleiken er eit filmtriks*', *NLÅ*: 199–210. S. Slettan, 'Mellom lys og mørke. Ironi og poesi i Rune Belsviks bøker om Arne Bu', *Syn og Segn*, 1997, no.2:159–70.

BJØRNEBOE, J.   Joe Martin, *Keeper of the Protocols. The Works of Jens Bjørneboe in the Crosscurrents of Western Literature*, NY, Lang, 1996, 188 pp. Laila Aase, *Om Haiene av Jens Bjørneboe* (Veier til verket), Karnovs Forlag, 1997, 119 pp.

BORGEN, J.   Kåre Folkedal, *Om Lillelord av Johan Borgen* (Veier til verket), Ad Notam Gylendal, 1997, 180 pp.

BOYSON, E.   The contributions to *En vandrer på jorden. Om Emil Boysons liv og diktning*, ed. S. Blandhol, H. Holtsmark, and J. J. Tønseth, Aschehoug, 1997, 204 pp., differ with respect to length and quality, and as a whole the book gives a varied and penetrating picture of this outstanding, but unfortunately rather marginalized poet. Special attention should be paid to the following articles: V. Ystad, 'Kullmeisens vekkende rop: Emil Boysons epifasier'; H. Holtsmark, 'Poesiens glassmalerier. Den poetiske akt i Emil Boysons diktning'; M. Nygård, 'Emil Boysons *Vandring mot havet* — en "lærebok" i fenomenologi'; and S. Blandhol, 'Severin og det romantiske'. Of great interest is moreover A. Aarne's introduction to the correspondence between Boyson and Alf Larsen.

BULL, O.   Andreas G. Lombnæs, *Natur — subjekt — språk. Lesninger i Olaf Bulls forfatterskap* (Acta humaniora, 15), Oslo U.P., 1997, 395 pp.

BØRLI, H.   In *Svarttrost-strupen så hvit av toner. Om Hans Børlis forfatterskap*, ed. O. Karlsen, a wide variety of themes is treated. Amongst the contributors are O. Røsbak, T. Gjefsen, H. H. Wærp, Ø. Rottem, E. Steen, T. Seiler, Ø. T. Gulliksen, and S. Gimnes.

Truls Gjefsen, *Syng liv i ditt liv! Hans Børlis liv og diktning*, Aschehoug, 310 pp., is a well-documented biography focusing on the life of the poet.

CHRISTENSEN, L. S.   L. E. Lorentzen, 'Resirkulert havfrue. Intertekstualiteten i Lars Saabye Christensens roman *Jubel*', *NLÅ*, 1997:119–34.

CHRISTIANSEN, S.   Tor Bomann-Larsen, *Det usynlige blekk. Sigurd Christiansens liv*, Cappelen, 1997, 335 pp., is an extremely well-written biography in which the roots of the main themes of C.'s work are traced to a secret love affair.

DUUN, O.   K. Bang-Hansen, 'Duun og teatret', *NLÅ*, 1997:197–206. L. Groven, 'Mellom Namdalen og verda. Olav Duun og det nasjonale', *ib.*, 60–70. Id., 'Det er både lang og kort veg mellom Juvika og Bunese', *Syn og Segn*, 1997, no.1:73–79. O. A. Kvamme, 'Teodicéproblemets oppløsning. Om fiendskap og forsoning i Olav Duuns roman *Menneske og maktene*', *NLÅ*:115–25.

EIDSLOTT, A.   Jan Inge Sørbø, ' "*Høstet på himlens skråninger.*" *Sju essay om Arnold Eidslott*, Gyldendal, 105 pp.

EINAN, E.   C. I. Armstrong, 'The sacrifices of Ellen Einan', *ScSt*, 69, 1997:212–42.

FANGEN, R.   J. I. Sørbø, 'Ronald Fangen og det litterære hegemoniet. Kulturradikalisme, modernisme og "den annen front" ', *Nytt norsk tidsskrift*, 14, 1997:297–309.

FLØGSTAD, K.   O. E. Ystanes, 'Metafiksjon med holrom i språket. Om Kjartan Fløgstads *Det 7. klima*', *Nordica Bergensia*, 17:113–31.

FOSSE, J.   R. Nøtvik Jakobsen, 'Det namnlause. Litteratur og mystikk. Med utgangspunkt i dramatiske tekster av Jon Fosse', *NLÅ*, 1997:225–38. U. Langås, 'Intet er hans stoff. Om Jon Fosses dramatikk', *Edda*:197–211.

FRICH, Ø. R.   Christopher Hals Gylseth, . . . *seg selv til det ytterste. Øvre Richter Frich og hans forfatterskap*, Cappelen, 1997, 298 pp.

GULBRANSSEN, T.   Tore Hoel and Ragna Gulbranssen, *Manns plikt. En biografisk dokumentar om forfatteren Trygve Gubransson og Veslas egen beretning*, Aschehoug, 1997, 327 pp. T. Hoel, 'Trygve Gulbranssen og kulturradikalerne', *NLÅ*, 1997:72–87.

HAUGE, O. H.   O. Karlsen, 'Sonetten som aritmetisk og arkitektonisk struktur. En intertekstuell lesning av Olav H. Hauges "Gullhanen" ', *Norlit*, Tromsø U.P., no.3:121–41.

HAUGEN, P.-H.   A. B. Storm-Larsen, 'Paal-Helge Haugen og musikkdramatikken', *Nordica Bergensia*, 17:57–72.

HIIDE, L.   H. O. Andersen, 'Den kvinnelige teksten. Refleksjoner omkring forholdet mellom kjønn, kropp og skrift i nyere kvinnelitteratu, med utgangspunkt i tekster av Lisbeth Hiide', *Norsklæraren*, 1997, no.1:14–19.

HOEM, E.   Bente Aamotsbakken, *Tekst og intertekst. En studie i intertekstualitetens betydning i tre åttitallsromaner av Edvard Hoem*, Oslo U.P., 1997, 311 pp. (doctoral thesis). Mette Elisabeth Nergård, *Om Heimlandet barndom av Edvard Hoem* (Veier til verket), Ad Notam Gyldendal, 1997, 87 pp.

HOFMO, G.   I. Havnevik, 'Etterkrigslyrikerens gjennombrudd. Gunvor Hofmos *Fra en annen virkelighet*', *NLÅ*:144–64. A. Utnes, 'Meditasjoner over ensomheten. Ekfrasiske dikt som G. Hofmos epilog', *Nordlit*, Tromsø U.P., no.3:59–78.

HOLTH, A.   R. Brenden, 'Sterke kvinner og svake menn? Åsta Holths novelle "Tomasdagen" i gynokritisk perspektiv', *NLÅ*:165–173.

HOVLAND, R.   I. Stegane, 'Junior og dotter til Jellinek. Ungdomsromanen *Mercedes* av Ragnar Hovland', *Nordica Bergensia*, 17:132–47. R. Jåstad, 'Intertekstualitet og karnevalisme i Ragnar Hovlands *Ein motorsykkel i natta*', *ib.*, 148–59.

JACOBSEN, R.   Ove Røsbak, *Rolf Jacobsen. En dikter og hans skygge*, Gyldendal, 464 pp., is an excellent biography and a challenge to the established picture of J. Røsbak was a friend of J., and the presentation is marked by his affection for the man and his admiration for his poetry. At the same time he uncovers J.'s sympathies for the Nazis during the war. Hanne Lillebo, *Ord må en omvei. En biografi om Rolf Jacobsen*, Aschehoug, 515 pp., is more concerned with the poetry of J., and thus the two biographies supplement each other in a fine way. A. Grydeland, 'Regnet som motiv i Rolf Jacobsens lyrikk', *Nordlit*, Tromsø U.P., no.3:79–85.

KINCK, H.   E. Arntzen, 'Modernitet og tekstualitet i femte akt av Hans E. Kincks drama *Driftekaren*', *Nordlit*, Tromsø U.P., 1997, no.2:57–97. R. Gaasland, 'Ekspresjonisme i Hans E. Kincks romaner', *NLÅ*, 1997:42–59.

KØLTZOW, L.   U. Langås, 'Den produktive vegring. En lesning av Liv Køltzows novelle "Nå"', *Edda*, 1997:221–30.

LØNN, Ø.   A. Fosvold, 'Er vi alene nå? En tematisk analyse av *Thranes metode* av Øystein Lønn', *NLÅ*, 1997:97–111.

LØVEID, C.   W. Larsen, 'Kvinnekroppen i visjonskiosken. En analyse av kroppen som tegn i skuespillet *Rhindøtrene* av Cecilie Løveid', *Sosiologi i dag*, 26, 1996:111–35. *Klangen av knust språk. Cecilie Løveids prosa og lyrikk*, ed. B. Eyde, LNU/Cappelen Akademiske Forlag, 211 pp. *Livsritualer. En bok om Cecilie Løveids dramatikk*, ed. Merete M. Andersen, Gyldendal, 204 pp.

MEHREN, S.   I. Økland, 'Natur og bevissthet i Stein Mehrens kjærlighetsdiktning — noen utviklingslinjer', *Edda*, 1997:183–94.

MYKLE, A.   Jahn Thon, *Om Lasso rundt fru Luna av Agnar Mykle* (Veier til verket), Karnov, 1997, 134 pp. R. Isaksen, 'Den religiøse Mykle',

Vinduet, 1997, no.2:44–53. T. Pedersen, 'Den dømte romanen. Om resepsjonen av Agnar Mykles *Lasso rundt fru Luna* (1954) og *Sangen om den røde rubin* (1956)', *NLÅ*: 174–90.

NORMANN, R.   Liv H. Willumsen, *Havmannens datter. Regine Normann — et livsløp*, Aschehoug, 1997, 307 pp.

NYGAARD, O.   *Nordica Bergensia*, 15, 1997, 205 pp., is a special issue dedicated to the poet Olav Nygaard. The contributors examine themes, forms of language and style as well as literary influences and provide much useful information about the author. The book is based on lectures given at a seminar, amongst which the following deserve to be mentioned: I. Stegane, 'Olav Nygaard og den litterære tradisjonen'; A. Aarseth, 'Den vanskeleggjorde forma. Linjer og verkemiddel i Olav Nygards lyrikk'; and M. Tveisme, 'Ikkje berre himmelsyner. Nærværet i Olav Nygard si dikting'.

PRØYSEN, A.   T. B. Haugstveit, 'Blant stugujinter, kokker og sladrekjærringer. Kvinnesyn og kvinnekjebner i et utvalg noveller av Alf Prøysen', *Norskrift*, 94, 1997:46–63.

RASMUSSEN, E.   R. Engelskjøn, 'Barndommens bøker i menns verden. *Guttene fra Gokkohjørnet* av Egil Rasmussen', *Norlit*, Tromsø U.P., no.3:181–207.

SANDEL, C.   E. Rees, 'På spor av modernismen i Cora Sandels Alberte-trilogi', *Edda*, 1997:209–20. B. Aamotsbakken, 'Cora Sandel: *Dyr jeg har kjent*. Genreproblem og tematikk', *NLÅ*:97–114.

SANDEMOSE, A.   *Nytt lys på Aksel Sandemose*, ed. T. Nilsson, Aschehoug, 287 pp. Jens Andersen, *Vildmanden. Sandemose og animalismen i mellemkrigstidens litteratur*, Copenhagen, Gyldendal, 117 pp.

SCOTT, G.   S. Slettan: '"Som et dyr paa bare marken." Om det motbydelige i Gabriel Scotts *Stien og Josefa*', *NLÅ*: 124–43.

SOLSTAD, D.   E. B. Hagen, 'Dag Solstad og det sublime. Om litteraturens rystelser i *Professor Andersens natt* og noen av estetikkens klassikere', *Skrift*, 1997, no.2:63–82. H. Hagerup, 'Og det ble natt. Om Dag Solstads roman *Professor Andersens natt*', *Vagant*, 1997, no.1:10–16. A. Krogstad, 'Snøværet i Vilnius. Om det "nærværende" og det "fjerne" i Dag Solstads *Ellevte roman, bok atten*', *NLÅ*, 1997:135–52. M. Zagar, 'Å kvitte seg med mor? "Invaliden" av Dag Solstad', *NLÅ*: 191–98. G. Hjorthol, 'Mimesis, metafiksjon og melodrama. Dag Solstads *Forsøk på å beskrive det ugjennomtrengelige*', *Edda*: 129–146. 'Disputas. Anne Heith: *Kontrapunktik. En studie i Dag Solstads Roman 1987 och Medaljens forside. En roman om Aker*. Universitetet i Bergen, 10. januar 1997. Førsteopponent professor dr. philos. Petter Aaslestad, NTNU. Andreopponent docent Urpu-Liisa Karahka, Stockholms universitet', *Edda*: 147–74.

SVERDRUP, H.   Tom Lotherington, *Med solen ytterst i nebbet. En bok om Harald Sverdrup*, Aschehoug, 229 pp.

UDNÆS, S. H. H. Wærp, 'Sverre Udnæs' dramatikk', *NLÅ*, 1997:207–24.

UNDSET, S. Olav Solberg, *Tekst møter tekst. Kristin Lavransdatter og mellomalderen*, Aschehoug, 1997, 245 pp. Liv Bliksrud, *Sigrid Undset* (Ariadne-serien), Gyldendal, 1997, 158 pp. Mette E. Nergård, *Om Kransen av Sigrid Undset* (Veier til verket), Karnov, 1997, 109 pp. Kristin Johansen, *Hvis kvinner ville være kvinner. Sigrid Undset, hennes samtid og kvinnespørsmålet*, Aschehoug, 256 pp.

VESAAS, T. O. M. Høystad, 'Bildebruken til Tarjei Vesaas. Natur og kultur i *Leiken og lynet*', *Syn og Segn*, 1997, no.4:351–64. L. Nylander, 'Omniscience and phallocentrism in Vesaas, Tarjei *The Bridges*', *Literature and Psychology*, 42, 1996:41–64. Sverre Wiland, *Om Fuglane av Tarjei Vesaas* (Veier til verket), Ad Notam Gyldendal, 1997, 182 pp.

VAAGE, L. A. A. Kittang, 'Tankar om tid og forteljing under lesinga av Lars Amund Vaages *Rubato*', *Vinduet*, 1996, no.1:10–16.

WASSMO, H. Karin E. Ellefsen, *Om Huset med den blinde glassveranda av Herbjørg Wassmo* (Veier til verket), Karnov, 1997, 137 pp.

ØKLAND, E. *Ein orm i eit auge. Om Einar Øklands forfatterskap*, ed. O. Karslen, LNU/Cappelen Akademiske Forlag, 1997, 277 pp.

V. SWEDISH STUDIES

LANGUAGE

By GUNILLA HALSIUS, *Lector in Swedish, University of Edinburgh*

1. GENERAL

P. Holmes, Price, *Encyclopedia*, 461–68, surveys the historical development and current state of the Swedish language. *Språk i Norden 1998*, ed. Birgitta Lindgren et al., 231 pp., the yearly issue published by the Nordic Language Council, contains articles on language (cultivation) and the media, including M. Reuter and E. Sommerdahl, 'Erfarenhet av språkvård för massmedierna' (31–42), and C. Grünbaum, 'Språkvård på en dagstidning' (43–51). Lars Melin, *Vett och etikett i språket*, Norstedts ordbok, 224 pp., is an unorthodox book on what is the right, wrong, and politically correct usage of Swedish — and why. Pär Segerdahl, *Språkteorier och språkspel*, Lund, Studentlitteratur, 221 pp., is a welcome work for anyone interested in the philosophy of language. *Folkmålsstudier* (Meddelanden från föreningen för nordisk filologi, 38), 162 pp., contains articles on Swedish as written and spoken in Finland. *Mummenskans: masker i den språkliga interaktionen*, ed. Erik Andersson and Hannele Oksanen (Skrifter från svenska institutionen vid Åbo Akademi, 4), 89 pp., contains five essays on different aspects of language as 'mask'. *Samtalsstudier*, ed. Ann-Marie Ivars and Mirja Saari (Meddelanden från Institutionen för nordiska språk och nordisk litteratur vid Helsingfors universitet, B:19), 254 pp., is an enjoyable volume of essays highlighting the great variety of topics in this field of research; for instance, V. Adelswärd, 'Skrattets funktion i gruppsamtal' (11–20), M. Eriksson, 'Dialog i drama och verklighet: en sekvens hos Norén och i ett vardagssamtal' (43–70) and A.-M. Ivars, 'Om konsten att svära' (105–19). *Språket i tiden*, ed. Jerker Blomquist and Gösta Bruce, 1997, Lund U.P., 141 pp., is a selection of papers given at the Humanist days at Lund University (1997) on different aspects of 'language and time', including language change, language continuity, and language learning as a process over time.

2. PHONETICS AND METRICS

Gösta Bruce, *Allmän och svensk prosodi* (Praktisk lingvistik, 16), Lund, Institutionen för lingvistik, 213 pp., includes an overview of recent research in the field. Peter E. Czigler, *Timing in Swedish VC(C) Sequences* (Phonum, 5), Umeå, Department of Phonetics, 175 pp., diss., describes the temporal behaviour of consonant clusters in standard

Swedish and argues that the phonological long-short dichotomy is only partly maintained in postvocalic consonant clusters. Eva Gårding and Olle Kjellin, *Vårt tal*, Uppsala, Hallgren & Fallgren, 105 pp., is a useful introduction to the production and perception of human speech, to the structure of speech and to contemporary research on speech, which also includes a comprehensive bibliography to related areas. **Proceedings of FONETIK 98*, ed. Peter Branderund and Hartmut Traunmüller, Stockholm U.P., 203 pp., is a collection of 50 papers given at the Eleventh Swedish Phonetics Conference at Stockholm University, 27–29 May 1998. Gun Widmark, *Stora vokaldansen: om kvantitativa och kvalitativa förändringar i fornsvenskans vokalsystem* (Acta Academiae Regiae Gustavi Adolphi, 65), Uppsala, Gustav Adolfs akademien, 105 pp., with a summary in English, examines the quantitative and qualitative changes in the vowel system of Old Swedish. An interesting discussion on metric from an actor's point of view is M. Kurténs, 'Metern som regissör', pp. 37–51 of *Meter, Mål, Medel. Studier framlagda vid Sjätte nordiska metrikkonferensen med temat 'Metrik och dramatik' Vasa 25–27.9.1997*, ed. Marianne Nordman (Vaasan Yliopiston Julkaisuja Selvityksiä ja Raportteja, 30), 183 pp.

3. Morphology, Syntax, Semantics

Ebba Lindberg, *När voro blev var: så skapades den moderna svenskan*, Norstedt, 167 pp., is a study of the generalized use of the singular verb form 1900–65 and the discussions surrounding it. Kersti Börjars, *Feature Distribution in Swedish Noun Phrases* (Publications of the Philological Society, 32), Oxford, Blackwell, 290 pp., is a detailed study of various aspects of the structure of Swedish noun phrases. Christer Platzack, *Svenskans inre grammatik — det minimalistiska programmet*, Lund, Studentlitteratur, 307 pp., aims to introduce into Swedish the most recent developments in generative grammar, and it shows how the minimalist programme can be used and how this inner grammar combines other cognitive processes to form Swedish. Ulla Stroh-Wollin, *Koncentrerad nusvensk formlära och syntax*, Lund, Studentlitteratur, 69 pp. (also workbook with key, 128 pp.), is an introduction for university students to the study of grammar. *Working papers in Scandinavian Syntax*, 61, Lund, Institutionen för nordiska språk, 126 pp., includes V. Egerland, 'On verb-second violations in Swedish and the hierarchical ordering of adverbs (1–22), G. Josefsson and C. Platzack, 'Short raising of V and N in mainland Scandinavia' (23–52), C. Platzack, 'A visibility condition for the C-domain' (53–99), and G. Josefsson, 'On the licensing and identification of (optionally) null heads in Swedish' (101–26). Sofia Tingsell, *Han bad henne städa sin väska. Pragmatiska infallsvinklar på reflexivering i svenska och isländska* (Meddelanden från Institutionen för svenska språket vid Göteborgs universitet, 24), 33 pp. Ann Lindvall, *Transitivity in Discourse. A Comparison of Greek, Polish and Swedish* (TILL, 37), 222 pp., discusses how various linguistic forms in different languages can be related to common cognitive functions and semantic properties. Hans Rignell, *Komma åt och ta upp: en undersökning av svenskinlärares förståelse av partikelverb* (Meddelanden från Institutionen för svenska språket vid Göteborgs universitet, 22), 38 pp. Peter Schlesier, *Deutsch-skandinavische Wortsemantik* (EH, XXI, 197), 339 pp., diss.

4. RHETORIC, STYLISTICS, DISCOURSE ANALYSIS, AND TEXT LINGUISTICS

Among the many books on rhetoric are the following: Göran Hägg, *Praktisk retorik: med klassiska och moderna exempel*, Wahlström och Widstrand, 253 pp., describes how to use classical rhetoric in modern situations. Kurt Johannesson, Olle Josephson, and Erik Åsard, *Ordet är en makt: Svenska tal från Torgny Lagman till Carl Bildt och Mona Sahlin: en antologi*, 2nd edn, Norstedt, 314 pp., includes speeches from different epochs with an introduction of the speakers, the period and the effect of the speeches on the historical development. Maria Karlberg and Brigitte Mral, *Heder och påverkan: att analysera modern retorik* (Studier i kommunikation och medier, 11), Natur och Kultur, 193 pp., Swedish and English text. Göran Stenberg, *Döden dikterar: En studie av likpredikningar och gravtal från 1600- och 1700-talen*, Atlantis, 444 pp., diss., with a summary in German. This is a genre study of sepulchral rhetoric, whose aim is to identify and define the two genres of funeral sermons and funeral speeches. *Form — innehåll — effekt. Stilistiska och retoriska studier tillägnade Peter Cassirer på 65-årsdagen*, ed. Aina Lundqvist et al., Gothenburg U.P., Institutionen för svenska språket, 364 pp., is a *Festschrift* in honour of Peter Cassirer. Thorwald Lorentzon, *Marx med mervärde möter moderna miljömål. En studie av emotiva och ideologiska ord i Vänsterpartiets och Ung Vänsters parti- och principprogram* (Meddelanden från Institutionen för svenska språket vid Göteborgs universitet, 23), 59 pp. H. Perridon, 'Translating pronouns of power and solidarity: forms of address in Strindberg's *Miss Julie*', pp. 161–75 of *Strindberg, Ibsen & Bergman*, ed. Harry Perridon, Maastricht, Shaker. Håkan Åbrink, '*Gomorron Stockholm' Radioprat som stil, genre och samtal med lyssnaren* (Acta Universitatis Tamperensis, 632), diss., 475 pp., describes the language and performance of the radio disc jockey in the 1990s. Natascha Karolija, *Episodes in Talk. Constructing Coherence in Multiparty Conversation* (Linköping Studies in Arts and Sciences, 171), 277 pp., diss. Ulla Melander Marttala, *Medicinska fackord i läkare — patientsamtal: analysmodell, klassificering, frekvenser* (FUMS rapport 189),

Uppsala, Institutionen för nordiska språk, 58 pp., is the first part of a study of the use of medical terms and expressions in authentic medical encounters. Ulla Moberg, *Språkbruk och interaktion i en svensk pingstförsamling. En kommunikationsetnografisk studie* (SINSU, 45), 227 pp. Catrin Norrby, **Vardagligt berättande. Form, funktion och förekomst* (NG, 21), 361 pp. Kerstin Nordenstam, *Skvaller. Om samtalsstrategier hos kvinnor och män* (Ord och stil, 29), 172 pp., examines the different functions of gossip. The aim of the interdisciplinary research project 'Svensk sakprosa' is to throw light on the development of Swedish factual prose from 1750 to the present day and a number of interesting reports have appeared, including the following. Viktor Lundberg, *Högervind och sossetvång: en textanalys av två partiers valbroschyrer 1928, 1958 och 1988* (Svensk sakprosa, 22), Lund, Institutionen för nordiska språk, 78 pp., uses the theory of critical discourse analysis to study political propaganda texts and how they have changed during this century. Gunilla Byrman, *Tidningsnotisen i förändring: 1746–1997* (Svensk sakprosa, 15), 137 pp., deals with the changes in subject areas, content, textual structure and language in newspaper items over the past 250 years. In Karin Mårdsjö, *Maten, metoderna och livet: svenska husliga handböcker 1750–1900* (Svensk sakprosa, 21), 81 pp., cookery books and the transition from an oral to a written culture are discussed. Björn Melander, *'Det är Husqvarna': om språket i tre upplagor av Läsebok för folkskolan* (Svensk sakprosa, 17), 78 pp. Ingegerd Bäcklund, *Metatext in Professional Writing: a Contrastive Study of English, German and Swedish* (Texts in European Writing Communities 3; TeFa, 25), Uppsala U.P., 43 pp., is part of a larger project examining how texts are influenced by the cultural context in which they are produced. The report focuses on the frequency and function of metatexts in a variety of texts from four professional fields in three countries. Kristina Jämtelid, *Flerspråkig textproduktion. Det internationella företaget och översättningen,* 1 (TeFa, 26), Uppsala U.P., 40 pp., presents the first study of a project on multilingual text production and language use at Electrolux with a discussion of different models adopted by the company. *Nation och individ i fackspråk. Forskning i Norden,* ed. Christer Laurén and Marianne Nordman (Vaasan yliopiston julkaisuja, Selvityksiä ja raportteja, 34), 116 pp., is the first report from the Nordic research project 'Språk i Norden som vetenskapsspråk'.

5. FIRST AND SECOND LANGUAGE ACQUISITION, BILINGUALISM, LANGUAGES IN CONTACT

Marianne Gullberg, *Gesture as a Communication Strategy in Second Language Discourse: A Study of Learners of French and Swedish* (TILL, 35), 253 pp., diss., suggests a method by which gesture is integrated into a theory of Communication Strategies. Sinikka Lahtinen, **Genuskongruens och genus i finska gymnasisters inlärarsvenska* (Studia philologica Jyväskyläensia, 47), diss., 260 pp., with summaries in English and Finnish. Monica Reichenberg Carlström, *Koherens i röst och läsning på ett andraspråk: ett pilotförsök med olika textversioner i historia i åk, 7* (ROSA. Rapporter om svenska som andraspråk, 2), Göteborg, Institutionen för svenska språket, 59 pp., is a study of the importance of coherence and voice in textbook texts for reading comprehension. Ellen Bijvoet, *Sverigefinnar tycker och talar: om språkattityder och stilistisk känslighet hos två generationer Sverige-finnar* (SINSU, 44), 279 pp., diss., with an English summary, examines bilingual Sweden-Finns' attitudes towards different varieties of Swedish and Finnish and their perception of stylistic nuances of lexical items. M. Tandefelt, 'Swedish in Finland', pp. 103–18 of *Minority Languages in Scandinavia, Britain and Ireland*, ed. Áilbhe Ó Corráin and Séamus Mac Mathúna (Studia Celtica Upsaliensia, 3), 220 pp., outlines when, how and by whom the Swedish language can be used in Finland and describes the particular features of Finland-Swedish compared with Swedish in Sweden. Maria Wingstedt, **Language Ideology and Minority Language Politics in Sweden. Historical and Contemporary Perspectives*, Centre for Research on Bilingualism, 376 pp., diss.

6. RUNOLOGY, HISTORY OF LANGUAGE, TEXTUAL STUDIES

Lars Magnar Enoksen, **Runor: historia, tydning, tolkning*, Lund, Historiska media, 240 pp., illus. Magnus Källström, *Järfällas runstenar*, Järfälla hembygdsförening, 72 pp. **Runeninschriften als Quellen interdisziplinärer Forschung: Abhandlungen des Vierten Internationalen Symposiums über Runen und Runeninschriften in Göttingen vom 4.–9. August 1995*, ed. Klaus Düwel (Ergänzungsbände zum Reallexikon der germanischen Altertumkunde, 15), Berlin, Mouton de Gruyter, xiv + 812 pp. In *ANF*, 113, B. Sigurd (151–73) describes a computer programme called RUNE which interprets typical rune stone texts and translates them into modern Swedish, or vice versa, by means of a generative phrase structure grammar. L. Wollin (175–97) provides a penetrating critical examination and review of Bo-A. Wendt's thesis, *Landslagsspråk och stadslagsspråk. Stilhistoriska undersökningar i Kristoffers landslag*. Rakel Johnson, *De svenska medeltidsbrevens form, funktion och tillkomstsituation* (Meddelanden från Institutionen för svenska språket vid Göteborgs universitet, 21), 98 pp. I. Shimizu, 'Presentation av referenslitteratur över svensk språkhistoria', pp. 89–111 of *Idun*, 13, Osaka, Department of Danish and Swedish, 263 pp. An historical overview of Swedish as a translation language is given by L. Wollin, 'Svenskan —

ett översättningsspråk?', *Språkbruk*, 4:6–14. *Dagboken över Linnés resa på Öland 1741* (Skrifter utgivna av Institutionen för nordiska språk vid Umeå universitet, 10), 90 pp., illus., is a reprint of Linnaeus's diary from the Sigurd Fries manuscript with philological notes.

7. DIALECTOLOGY, ONOMASTICS

Ordbok över folkmålen i övre Dalarna, ed. Lars Levander (SDFU, ser. D, Dialektordböcker från Dalarna, Gotland och andra landskap, 1), has reached IV.35, *Snod-Spitkanna*, pp. 2455–2534. *Mål i norr. Två artiklar om nutida dialektförhållanden i norra Sverige* (Kulturens frontlinjer, 11), Umeå, 118 pp., contains two articles on the state of dialects in the north of Sweden: L. Eriksson, '"Man pratar inte dialekt med kungen i alla fall." En presentation av ett antal studentuppsatser om dialekt samt en diskussion om fortsatt forskning på området' (11–59), and G. Flodell, '"Det lilla språket" som gränsmarkör: Rapport från en pilotundersökning i Bjurholm, Västerbotten' (61–118), where the discussion focuses on the question of dialect boundaries — are they still maintained or subject to levelling? *Från Pyttis till Nedervetil: tjugonio prov på dialekter i Nyland, Åboland, Åland och Österbotten*, ed. Gunilla Harling-Kranck (SSLF, 610), 196 pp., illus., two CDs and two audio cassettes. In *Svenska landsmål och svenskt folkliv*, ed. Maj Reinhammar, Uppsala, Gustav Adolfs Akademien, 204 pp., G. Eklund (7–18) describes the thinking behind the design of the Swedish Dialect Alphabet, and G. Söderberg (29–75), using a computer font designed especially for broad transcriptions, draws attention to a phenomenon referred to as 'vocalic ending' in a Västergötland dialect.

In *SASc*, 16, L. Peterson sets out to determine whether the stem vowel in Hedinn or Hidinn was /e/ or /i/ in Runic Swedish (5–14); T. Andersson discusses the use of words for gods as final elements in Old Scandinavian personal names (21–25); an uninterpreted man's name on the Viggeby Stone (U 428) is discussed by M. Källström (27–34); R. Valtavuo-Pfeifer presents a research project on the family names of the Swedish-speaking community in Finland which aims to provide an overview of the surname stock (89–108); and T. Andersson and E. Brylla discuss how the surname law is being interpreted (109–11). A new instalment of the dictionary of medieval personal names has appeared: *Sveriges medeltida personnamn: ordbok: förnamn* (Arkivet för ordbok över Sveriges medeltida personnamn). III.13. *Henrik — Holger*, cols 321–480. *Byens navne: Stednavne i urbaniserede områder. Rapport fra Nornas 24. symposium i København 25.–27.4. 1996*, ed. Vibeke Dalberg and Bent Jørgensen (NORNA-rapporter, 64), Copenhagen, 1997, 197 pp., is a report of a symposium on place names in an urban context in which J. Ferenius (91–101) discusses current problems with naming in Stockholm and describes some of the principles according to which the committee for naming (Namnberedningen) carries out its work; G. Harling-Kranck (103–12) gives some examples of new generics adopted for use in street names in Helsinki; and M. Wahlberg (185–97) discusses Swedish street-names as a historical source and a mirror of contemporary ideas. Eberhard Löfvendahl, *Post- och järnvägsstationernas namn i Götaland 1860–1940. Namngivning i spänningsfältet mellan allmänna och enskilda intressen* (Acta Academiae Regiae Gustavi Adolphi, 67), Uppsala, 330 pp., diss., argues that the expansion of the rail network and the network of sub-post offices helped to preserve and consolidate important components of the existing agrarian nomenclature. Ritva Valtavuo-Pfeifer, **Terrängnamn i Svenskfinland* (SSLF, 615), 263 pp., maps, illus., is a comprehensive study of the naming of terrain formations in Åland, Åboland, Nyland and Österbotten. *Namn och bygd*, 86, includes articles by S. Fridell, 'Hulundsfarahult, Hulingsryd och Hultsfred' (2–24), and T. Andersson, 'Ununge' (25–29). Bengt Pamp, *Från Gödelöv till Östen Undéns gata: en uppslagsbok över ortnamn i Lund under tvåtusen år*, Lund, Gamla Lund, 208 pp. A popular study of place names in Närke is found in Karin Calissendorff and Anna Larsson, *Ortnamn i Närke* (Humanistica Oerebroensia. Artes et linguae), AWE/GEBERS ortnamnserie, 180 pp.

8. Lexicography

Svenska akademiens ordlista, Svenska Akademien, Norstedts ordbok, 12th edn, xxxvi + 1066 pp., also available on CD, includes a comprehensive introduction to the new layout. For further discussion of the new edition see also M. Gellerstam, 'Ordlista i nya kläder — om tolfte upplagan av SAOL', *Språkbruk*, 3:3–10. *Bonniers svenska ordbok*, ed. Sten Malmström, Bonniers, 695 pp., illus. Ulla-Britt Kotsinas. *Norstedts svenska slangordbok*, Norstedts ordbok, 367 pp., is a useful complement to standard dictionaries containing 10,000 contemporary slang words. Ralf Svenblad, *Norstedts förkortningsordbok*, Norstedts ordbok, xviii + 249 pp., offers abbreviations from many different areas, for instance, law, computing, international organizations, and the EU. Bertil Molde, *Norstedts dansk-svenska ordbok*, 3rd rev. edn, Norstedts ordbok, xiv + 726 pp., contains 50,000 words and phrases. *Stora finsk-svenska ordboken*, ed. Birgitta Romppanen, Helsinki, WSOY [Werner Söderström Osakeytitiö], has now become available on CD and has been supplemented with more terms in the areas of computer technology and the environment. **Svenskt lagspråk i Finland*, ed. Henrik Bruun, Esbo, Schildts, 342 pp., is a revised and enlarged edition. Anna Helga Hannisdóttir, *Lexikografihistorisk spegel — Den* *enspråkiga svenska lexikografins utveckling ur den tvåspråkiga* (Meijerbergs arkiv för svensk ordforskning, 23), Gothenburg Univ., 541 pp., diss., with an English summary, describes some of the most important dictionaries of the 18th and early 19th cs and shows the development from bilingual to monolingual Swedish lexicography. Lena Rogström, *Jacob Serenius lexikografiska insats* (Meijerbergs institut för svensk ordforskning, 22), Gothenburg U.P., 412 pp., with an English summary, examines the lexicographical technique of Jacob Serenius in three dictionaries and shows the dependency of parts of the Swedish vocabulary, as it appears in the dictionaries, on the English material. Christer Laurén, Johan Myking, and Heribert Picht, *Terminologie unter der Lupe. Vom Grenzgebiet zum Wissenschaftszweig* (Internationales Institut für Terminologieforschung, IITF Ser. 9), Vienna, TermNet, 353 pp.

LITERATURE

By BIRGITTA THOMPSON, *Lecturer in Swedish, University of Wales, Lampeter*

1. GENERAL

A History of Finland's Literature, ed. George C. Schoolfield (Histories of Scandinavian Literature, 4), Nebraska U.P., Lincoln–London, The American-Scandinavian Foundation, xxxiv + 877 pp., is the fourth volume in this series of the history of Scandinavian literature under the general editorship of Sven H. Rossel. The literary history of Finland, which is here taken up to 1990, immediately presents a problem to its chronicler with its roots in the history of the country and two distinct bodies of literature. Predictably the work consists of two main parts of five chapters each, 'Finnish-language literature' (1–272) and 'Finland-Swedish literature' (273–726), plus a third, M. Lehtonen, 'Children's literature in Finland' (727–51), summarizing the overall picture of children's literature, even if individual authors such as Zacharias Topelius and Tove Jansson have been treated elsewhere. In addition to being the editor of the whole work and co-operating with K. Laitinen for one of the Finnish-language chapters, George Schoolfield is the sole contributor to the whole section on Finland-Swedish literature, a rather impressive performance. There is no separate chapter on women writers; like their male colleagues they are treated in sub-sections of the main chapters. Under the sub-heading 'Women writers: Ostrobothnia and elsewhere' in chapter 10, it simply states that 'an effort to create a separate history of women writers in Finland is futile; women have long been major voices in both literatures of the country, on an equal footing with men'; then follows a presentation of the appearance in the 1970s of a group of women writers in Ostrobothnia. Schoolfield closes his work on a positive note by saying that what is startling about 'Swedish Finland's' cultural fate is the vigour of its literature, during a time when the proportional representation of Swedish-speakers in Finland's populace has steadily decreased. Å. Bertenstam, 'Svensk litteraturhistorisk bibliografi 114 (1995); med tillägg och rättelser för tidigare år', *Samlaren*, 118, 1997[1998].2:1–125. *Parnass*, no. 6, is a special issue on Svenska Vitterhetssamfundet, the literary society for all Swedish classic writers; its latest publications include Haquin Spegel, Jacob Wallenberg, and the collected works of C. J. L. Almqvist. Lars Furuland, *Bergslagen i litteraturen. Kommenterad bibliografi med en inledande litteratursociologisk uppsats* (Avdelningen för litteratursociologi, 37, SLIUU), Hedemora, Gidlunds, 264 pp., covers publications in book form from the 17th c. in the Bergslagen mining and forestry district of central Sweden. Its ten separate sections include both fiction and non-fiction: novels and short stories, poetry, literature for children and young people, memoirs, books of travels, and picture books, together with a selection of specialist literature and bibliographies. *Litteraturvetenskap — en inledning*, ed. Staffan Bergsten, Lund, Studentlitteratur, 190 pp., is an anthology of essays dealing with various theoretical approaches to the study of literature. The overwhelming impression is the great diversity of approaches in reading and interpreting a literary text. Anders Palm's essay 'Att tolka texten' (155–69) stands out as the main summary of the possibilities inherent in the study of literature, not least in his warning that each so-called theory also entails its own limitation in interpreting the text.

Perspektiv på litteraturvetenskapen, ed. Roger Holmström and John Sundholm (MLIÅA, 25), 175 pp., includes 13 papers based on a series of lectures during the academic session 1997–98, some of which make specific references to Swedish studies: R. Holmström, on literary scholarship and criticism exemplified by various contemporary scholars (7–17); F. Hertzberg, on Peter Weiss, Gunnar Björling, and hypertext (47–56); A. Westerlund, on Hans Ruin (73–84); A. T. Pedersen, on preconceived ideas formed by models such as the classical review by H. Neiglick of K. A. Tavaststjerna's *Barndomsvänner* and Lagercrantz's 1958 biography of Stig Dagerman (95–109); M. Österlund, on feministic readings (135–49); C. Zilliacus, on his own approaches to short texts and to documentarism (151–58). Anders Cullhed, *Minnesord. Litterära essäer*, Eslöv, Symposion, 208 pp., spans a wide area, both in time and geographically. The section 'Svensk barock' includes three essays: 'Det svenska 1600-talsdramat', originally a paper given in Ghent in 1997 (45–56); all other relevant essays have been previously published in journals or newspapers; 'Samuel Columbus' (57–61); 'Skogekär Bergbos Wenerid' (62–66). The section 'Svenska gestalter' includes more recent writers: 'Rikslikaren Levertin' (69–73); 'En melankoliker i Arkadien' (74–78), on Artur Lundkvist's poetry in *Vit man*, 1932; 'Vennberg längtar till Egypten' (79–84). Fredrik Böök, *Under stjärnorna. Ett ofullbordat självporträtt av Fredrik Böök*, ed. Nathan Shachar, Atlantis, 277 pp., is the unfinished autobiography of this leading literary scholar and critic, providing insight into his contradictory personality and his pro-German attitude up to the end of the Second World War. I. Algulin, 'Litteraturteori — tradition och utveckling', Algulin, *Traditioner*, 12–25. A. Pettersson, 'En teori om litteratur och litteraturupplevelse', *Edda*: 116–28. J. Svedjedal, 'Kritiska tankar. Om litteraturkritiken och det litterära systemet', *TidLit*, 27.1:49–61. T. Forser, 'Tabloidiseringen av det litterära samtalet — om kritiken, dess villkor och former', *ib.*, 62–86, on the current position of literary criticism in the daily press. *TidLit*, 27.3–4, is a special issue on 'Canon, criticism, and writing literary history', and includes: E. Adolfsson, 'Kritik, litteratur och journalistikens tvång. Några kommentarer vid ett seminarium' (3–9); P. Rydén, 'Även Gud kan recenseras. Om kritikens paradoxala betydelse' (11–19); B. Holm, 'Litteraturhistoria, litteraturvetenskap, litteraturkritik — likhet eller särart?' (30–34); L. Lönnroth, 'Särart och korsbefruktning. Svar till Birgitta Holm' (35–38); A. Nordlund, 'En skola utan kanon? Litteraturarv och litteraturundervisning i förändring' (59–78); T. Olsson, 'Kritikern som konstnär — konstnären som kritiker' (121–32); M. Karlsson, 'Vad tycks om *Nordisk kvinnolitteraturhistoria*? De fyra första banden recenseras ur ett mottagarperspektiv' (139–51). *Litteratursociologi. Texter om litteratur och samhälle*, ed. Lars Furuland and Johan Svedjedal, Lund, Studentlitteratur, 1997, 572 pp., is an anthology of essays on sociological aspects of literature. It contains central essays and extracts from major works published earlier, abroad as well as in Sweden, including two general surveys by the editors, and a wide range of relevant articles of specific Swedish interest with introductory notes about the authors: K. Aspelin, on C. J. L. Almqvist (330–43); B. Bennich-Björkman, on professional writers and the function of literature 1640–1809 (346–54); D. Broady and M. Palme, on recent literary criticism and its impact in national quality newspapers (356–73); G. Hansson, 'Läsarnas litteraturhistoria — när, hur och varför?' (376–87); S. Hansson, 'En ny litteratursociologi?' (390–98); Y. Hirdman, on the gender system (400–18); B. Holm, on Fredrika Bremer's novel *Famillen H**** (420–38); L. Lönnroth, on Erik Lindegren's 'Arioso' (440–70); S. Mählqvist, on the book market in the late 1980s (472–89); M. von Platen, 'Romanföraktet. En genres väg till prestige' (492–505), which also deals with Swedish novels; L. Thorsell, 'Den svenska parnassens "demokratisering" och de folkliga bildningsvägarna' (520–52).

Böcker och bibliotek. Bokhistoriska texter, ed. Margareta Björkman, Lund, Studentlitteratur, 447 pp., includes several essays relevant to Swedish literature: H. Schück, 'Från vår bokhandels barndom (54–65); M. Björkman, 'Svensk bokhistoria. En forskningsöversikt' (66–95); E. Heggestad, 'Eva Brags *Sjelfviskhetens offer*. Följetongsberättelsen som fick raritetsstämpel' (112–30); B. Peterson, 'Förlag och förläggare — en historisk bakgrund' (147–80); B. Bennich-Björkman, 'Förutsättningar för kort fiktionsprosa på den litterära marknaden i Sverige 1850–1914' (202–07); S. Hansson, ' "Afsatt på Swensko." 1600–talets tryckta översättningslitteratur' (208–16); J. Svedjedal, 'Almqvists *Det går an* och konsten att överleva' (229–65), on the various editions of the novel; L. Furuland, 'Jan Fridegårds bildningsgång och bibliotek' (371–92), on the struggle for culture of the autodidact. *Med andra ord. Texter om litterär översättning*, ed. Lars Kleberg, Natur och Kultur, 344 pp., is an anthology of essays dealing with the art and problems of literary translations; it includes references to Birgitta, and opposing views expressed by Johan Henrik Kellgren and Thomas Thorild. E. Tegelberg, 'Några reflektioner kring nordisk litteratur i fransk översättning', *FT*: 189–202. Göte Klingberg, *Den tidiga barnboken i Sverige. Litterära strömningar, marknad, bildproduktion* (SSBI, 64), Natur och Kultur, 240 pp. + 16 pls, gives an introductory description of the historical, largely general European background, to children's books in the 19th c., examining literary movements from the 16th c. to 1900, the book market, production, and graphic techniques for illustrations on the basis of two recent bibliographies (1988, 1996) compiled by Ingar Bratt and Klingberg that between them cover the period 1840–99; the period before 1840 had already been examined by Klingberg in a dissertation and a subsequent bibliography (1964, 1967). Three books from the 1620s stand out as the first children's books in Swedish, while the spirit of Enlightenment dominated this literature from the 1750s to the 1820s, first introduced by two teachers of the future King Gustav III, Carl Gustaf Tessin and Olof von Dalin. The German Romantic influence played an important role in the early 19th c., while English took over as the main source language in the latter half of the century. *Barnens rum*, ed. Gunnar Berefelt (SCB, 28), 176 pp., includes essays on 'children's rooms and space', the theme of the Centre's annual symposium in the spring of 1997, among them: T. Lengborn, 'Ellen Key och barnets rum. Några pedagogiska och estetiska betraktelser' (107–18); B. Werkmäster, 'Barnkammaren och det egna rummet — historia, ideologi och estetik' (119–33). Sven-Gustaf Edqvist and Inga Söderblom, *Svenska författare genom tiderna*, Almqvist & Wiksell, 432 pp., focuses on selected writers through the ages, and is a useful general handbook. It includes introductions to literary periods and fairly comprehensive coverage of the writers selected, i.e. the classics and a wide range of modern writers. In addition to the more comprehensive articles there are brief mentions of other writers, especially in the chapter on the latter half of the 20th c. Tom Hedlund and Ulrika Palme, *På diktens vägar genom Sverige*, Ordfront, 288 pp., was never intended as a comprehensive literary atlas of Sweden, but is a sensitive advocate for a geographical approach to literature in its description of landscape as a literary experience. It is a rather rhapsodic volume containing text and photographs of the Swedish landscape immortalized by authors through the ages; even so it manages to include quite a number of literary figures with the stress on writers of the modern age. It looks at runestones, touches on the origins of nature poetry, examines the provinces linked to various writers, such as Verner von Heidenstam, Hjalmar Gullberg, and Sara Lidman, and discusses travelling and travelogues by Almqvist, for instance. *Öppna dörrar. Guide till 44 författares hus och miljöer*, ed. Marianne Enge Swartz, Carlssons, 125 pp. + 3 maps, presents in alphabetical order the homes and regions of 44 writers, ranging in time from Linnæus to Artur Lundkvist; it provides additional information on the possibility of visits to these former homes, and details about the literary societies devoted to individual writers. *Naturen som livsrum. Ekologiska perspektiv i modern litteratur och bildkonst*, ed. Hans Henrik Brummer and Allan Ellenius, Natur och Kultur, 138 pp. + 8 pls, includes lectures given at a symposium in connection with the Bruno Liljefors exhibition in the autumn of 1996, and makes reference to Linnæus, Selma Lagerlöf, and Sven Rosendahl among others. *Staden mellan pärmarna. Litterära friluftsessäer i Stockholm*, ed. Magnus Bergh, Bonniers, 176 pp., contains eight essays with valuable cross-references, examining the picture of Stockholm presented by a number of writers: B. Torsson, on C. J. L. Almqvist (8–27); M. Florin, on Strindberg (28–53); Å. Beckman, on Agnes von Krusenstjerna (54–63); B. Munkhammar, on Eyvind Johnson's Krilon novels (64–105); T. Ekbom, on the city of the blue trams in Gösta Oswald and Gunnar Ekelöf (106–19); M. Bergh, on Peter Weiss's Stockholm in his novel *Motståndets estetik* (120–31); S. Danius, on the southern parts of the city in Tomas Tranströmer (132–49); M. Peterson, on suburbia and how it features in a number of modern writers (150–65). *SBR*, supp., ed. B. Thompson, is a special issue on Stockholm in literature.

2. THE MIDDLE AGES

BIRGITTA.   M. Andrews, 'St Birgitta — wise woman or witch? Emilia Fogelklou's Birgitta studies', *BASS 11*, 71–81.

3. FROM THE RENAISSANCE TO THE GUSTAVIAN AGE

A. Cullhed, 'Det svenska 1600–talsdramat', *TsSk*, 19.1 : 149–62. D. Hedman, 'Kampen på det gustavianska litterära fältet. Om Kellgrens problematiska förhållande till Bellman och Thorild', *Samlaren*, 118, 1997[1998] : 14–39, discusses Kellgren's animosity as an aspect of the writers' rivalry in currying favour with the king, rather than the result of differing aesthetic norms. Uecker, *Opplysning*, on Enlightenment in Scandinavia, includes: A. Jarrick, 'Visst fanns det en upplysning i Sverige!' (43–57); M. von Platen, 'Svensk rokokodiktning' (75–84); K. Bak, 'Romantikens upplysningstid' (121–26); A. Cullhed, 'Professorer och poesi. Om den akademiska poetiken i sent 1700–tal' (167–73); B. Lewan, 'Ett herdespel i upplysningens tecken' (311–15); V. Lindgärde, 'Andaktslitteratur och svenskt 1700–tal' (317–24); H. Lindkjølen, 1700–talets litteratur om Nordkalotten' (325–31), includes references to Olof Rudbeck the elder and the younger, and to Carl von Linné (or Linnæus); P. E. Ljung, 'Kant och Swedenborg — i Vilhelm Ekelunds optik' (333–39), discusses the importance of Swedenborg and Kant's criticism of him for the writing of Ekelund in the early 20th c.; S. Ljungquist, ' "Mappa Geographica Scelestina" som den kända världens spegelbild. Om en 1700–talsutopi' (341–49), discusses the work by Carl Nyrén published in 1786; M. Malm, 'Bildspråket mellan klassicism och romantik' (365–72); I. Ridder, 'Überlegungen zur Rezeption des mittelalterlichen deutschen Volksbuches "König Salomon und Markolfus" in Carl Nyréns "Mappa Geographica Scelestinae" ' (439–44); I. Selander, 'Carl Serlachius' psalmbok "Christeliga Fägne-Timmar" prövad mot pietistisk estetik och teologi' (461–70). H. Tandefelt, 'Husets heder, värn och sämja. Om rojalistisk retorik under Gustaf III:s ryska krig', *HLS*, 73:31–90 (SSLF, 614), in particular on Carl Gustaf Leopold's poetic account of 'Öfver Segren vid Hogland 1788'.

BELLMAN, CARL MICHAEL. *Bellmansstudier*, ed. Olof Holm (Bellmanssällskapet, 20), Proprius, 202 pp., includes contents lists and indexes of all the B. studies in the series 1924–98 compiled by the editor (137–202). This would seem to belie effectively the complaint made in the preface that B. is not given the scholarly attention his popularity would demand. Other articles include A. Ringblom, on food and stimulus of the senses (9–38); M.-L. Sibbmark explains how the star and sun engravings on drinking glasses made at the Kungsholmen glassworks have led to various symbolic interpretations of a line in *Fredmans Epistlar* (39–53); S. Östergren, on a hitherto unknown MS of *Gustafs skål* (54–68); L. Bohn, on diseases and medicine at the time (69–105); S. Opitz, on B.'s usage of German in *Fredmans Epistlar* (109–35). L. Braude, 'Bellmans enastående plats i svensk litteratur — Bellman i Ryssland', Uecker, *Opplysning*, 143–47. A. Dvergsdal, 'Den senklassistiske teksten. Med eksempler fra Ewald, Bellman og Wessel', *ib.*, 183–95.

LENNGREN, ANNA MARIA. G. Printz-Påhlson, ' "Innocence" and "Nature". Two concepts of Romanticism: American, European, Scandinavian perspectives', *Glienke Vol.*, 289–300, analyses L.'s poem 'Pojkarne', first published in 1797, stressing that with its description of games and plays it clearly belongs to the Rousseauist (and revolutionary) emphasis of the age as part of an 'invisible' culture; thus he argues against the claim of the historiography of Western culture that childhood is a modern invention from, say, the latter half of the eighteenth century. A. Swanson, 'Mamsell Malmstedt går på operan', Uecker, *Opplysning*, 477–83, discusses L.'s translations of opera librettos on the basis of her first, Lucile by Jean-François Marmontel, stressing her professional competence.

LINNÆUS, CARL. E. Zillén, 'Linné i en balkonglåda. Om 1700-tal och historicitet i Magnus Florins "Trädgården" (1995)', Uecker, *Opplysning*, 493–98.

LIDNER, BENGT. J. Balbierz, ' "På Nova Zemblas Fjäll." Utopi och antiutopi i Bengt Lidners "Grevinnan Spastaras Död" ', Uecker, *Opplysning*, 127–31.

OXENSTIERNA, JOHAN GABRIEL. S. Göransson, 'Klassikern som försvann — Johan Gabriel Oxenstiernas "Skördarne" (1796)', Uecker, *Opplysning*, 249–54.

SCHMIDT, JOHAN ALBRECHT. B. Ståhle Sjönell, 'Johan Albrecht Schmidts Landt-Nöjet — vår första svenska Decamerone', *Samlaren*, 118, 1997[1998]:5–13, discusses this little-known writer and official and his early collection of short stories published in 1772, a pioneer work of significance for the development of the Romantic 'novell' almost fifty years later.

SPEGEL, HAQUIN. *Haquin Spegel, Samlade skrifter.* 1. *Guds Werk och Hwila*, ed. Bernt Olsson and Barbro Nilsson (Svenska författare, 25), 2 vols, Svenska Vitterhetssamfundet, xxxii + 405, 592 pp., is the first part in two volumes of a planned text-critical edition of S.'s collected works; the first volume includes an introduction and the text itself, S.'s most ambitious work about the creation of the world and simultaneously a description of the contemporary one; the second volume includes variant readings, a meticulous commentary, word and name lists. B. Olsson, 'Inledning', pp. vii-xxxii, the authority in the field since his doctoral dissertation in 1963, explores the work in exemplary scholarly fashion with a wealth of information, such as the provenance of the existing manuscripts, i.e. the printer's copy and two transcripts of an earlier version; there are possible indications of yet another version dating back to the 1670s. There are also relevant references to theology, literary models, and contemporary history of ideas; the introduction also deals with language, prosody, and reception. The work was first published in 1685 and again in 1705 in revised form; the current edition is based on that of 1685; variant readings are listed throughout in the commentary volume.

STIERNHIELM, GEORG. Rune Pär Olofsson, *Georg Stiernhielm — diktare, domare, duellant. En levnadsteckning*, Hedemora, Gidlunds, 222 pp., is both a popular and an informative biography of the 'father of Swedish verse', published to celebrate the 400th anniversary of his birth. Here the reader meets the most learned man of his day, not merely the author of *Hercules*, but a jurist, a scientist, a moralist, a linguist, a philosopher, a teacher, a diplomat, a humorist, a politician, a courtier; the list is endless, and rightly so, according to Samuel Columbus, his early biographer who knew him well.

THORILD, THOMAS. K. Hoff, 'Freiheit und Disziplin: Die Ambivalenz der Aufklärung in Thomas Thorilds "En critik öfver critiker"', Uecker, *Opplysning*, 255–64.

WALLENBERG, JACOB. Jacob Wallenberg, *Samlade skrifter*. I. *Dikter. Fragment ur Wiborgska Smällen. Sannfärdig resebeskrifning. Korrespondensartiklar. Brev*, ed. and comm. Torkel Stålmarck (Svenska författare. Ny serie), Svenska Vitterhetssamfundet, 318 pp., is the first of a planned text-critical edition comprising three volumes, and includes W.'s poetry, European travel book, and letters. The editing and exhaustive commentary is a first-class scholarly achievement by W.'s biographer. The first two volumes, although revised and extended, are based on the earlier two-volume scholarly edition published in the years 1928–41 by Nils Afzelius, now out of print; some previously unknown letters are published for the first time, and W.'s verse letters in Latin also appear in a Swedish translation. The third volume will include W.'s sermons from the years 1770–78, never published before.

4. ROMANTICISM AND LIBERALISM

Sara Rönn, *Årstafrun och hennes böcker* (Litteratur och Samhälle, 33.1), MLIUU, 146 pp., examines the reading habits of the famous 'Årstafrun', Märta Helena Reenstierna (1753–1841), from the evidence in her diaries; simultaneously it throws light on the introduction of light reading at the turn of the 18th c.

ALMQVIST, CARL JONAS LOVE. Lars Burman, *Tre fruar och en mamsell. Om C.J.L. Almqvists tidiga 1840-talsromaner* (Almqviststudier, 2), Hedemora, Gidlunds, 254 pp., is a study in six independent chapters based on diverse approaches to A.'s two novels from the early 1840s, *Amalia Hillner* and *Tre fruar i Småland*; Burman has also edited and annotated the scholarly editions of these two novels in the *Collected Works*, currently being published by Svenska Vitterhetssamfundet in 51 volumes since 1993. The study tries to unveil certain 'constant perceptions' common throughout A.'s writings, such as his Swedenborgianism and his view of women with its mixture of extreme political radicalism and conservative romanticism. Id., 'Inledning', pp. vii–xxv of C. J. L. Almqvist, *Tre fruar i Småland*, ed. and comm. Lars Burman (Samlade Verk, 25), Svenska Vitterhetssamfundet–Almqvistsamfundet, xxv + 545 pp., considers the work as a novel of social protest, and provides a background survey of its origin, reception and A.'s own views on his work, together with a summary of research to date. B. Romberg, 'Inledning', pp. vii–xxxii of C. J. L.

Almqvist, *Törnrosens bok. Duodesupplagan.* v-vii, ed. and comm. Bertil Romberg (Samlade Verk, 7), Svenska Vitterhetssamfundet–Almqvistsamfundet, xxxii + 436 pp., discusses the various works in the volume, originally published in 1834–35, followed by a survey of contemporary reception and research to date. G. Hermansson, 'Almqvist og Mytepoesien. En analyse af de 3 Mythopoiesis-tekster, *Guldfågel, Rosaura* og *Arctura,* samt Skönhetens tårar og Sviavigamal med udgangspunkt i Almqvists definitioner og opfattelser af det mytiske', *Samlaren,* 118, 1997[1998]: 40–90. K. Müller-Wille, ' "En af verldens största gåtor." Zur Reflexion von monetärer und literarischer Repräsentation bei C. J. L. Almqvist', *Glienke Vol.,* 35–61, discusses the text 'Hvad är Penningen?' in *Törnrosens bok,* which has been neglected hitherto. A. Cavallin, 'Androgynens kön — en feministisk läsning av C. J. L. Almqvists *Drottningens juvelsmycke*', *TidLit,* 27.1:3–24.

ATTERBOM, PER DANIEL AMADEUS. Otto Fischer, *Tecknets tragedi. Symbol och allegori i P.D.A. Atterboms sagospel Lycksalighetens ö* (AUU, SLIUU, 36), 246 pp., is a doctoral dissertation dealing with the aesthetic concepts of symbol and allegory applied to one of the main works of Swedish Romanticism, A.'s *Lycksalighetens ö.* A.'s aesthetic writings, based on the theories of F. W. J. Schelling and Karl Philipp Moritz, are analysed, as is the contemporary polemic that followed the publication of the play, discussing whether it was a work of allegory or symbolism. According to A.'s intentions his play depicts the history as well as the tragedy of poetry. It is argued that the play is structured as a dialectic progression between a symbolical and an allegorical aesthetic principle, or between the real and the ideal. On the basis of a simple folk-tale A. was able to compose a complex drama about his own aesthetic theories, about the tragedy and the apotheosis of poetry.

BREMER, FREDRIKA. Å. Arping, 'Hushållet som romanverkstad — Fredrika Bremers *Famillen H**** och 1830–talets litterära debatt', *Samlaren,* 118,1997[1998]:91–111.

RUNEBERG, JOHAN LUDVIG. *Johan Ludvig Runeberg, Dikter,* introd. Lars Forssell (ix-xxiii), ed. and comm. Lars Huldén (Svenska klassiker), Svenska Akademien–Atlantis, xxiii + 325 pp., includes R.'s three collections of poetry from 1830, 1833, and 1843. The text is according to the Svenska Vitterhetssamfundet R. edition (Svenska författare, 16), but in modern spelling; the commentary is also based on this edition, but the emphasis is on the explanation of words.

STAGNELIUS, ERIK JOHAN. Louise Vinge, *'Med dolken i hand'. Kvinnoroller i Stagnelius' dramatiska författarskap* [Borgholm], Sällskapet Erik Johan Stagnelii Vänner, 12 pp., is a previously unpublished paper from 1993; the S. Society also publishes *Stagneliusbladet* since 1998.

TEGNÉR, ESAIAS. Ragnar Thoursie, *Kyrkomakt och irrfärder*, Lund, Tegnérsamfundet, 30 pp., the winner of the T. prize in 1997 follows in the footsteps of T., the bishop, and looks at the implications of some of his newly-built churches.

TOPELIUS, ZACHARIAS. Nils Erik Forsgård, *I det femte inseglets tecken. En studie i den åldrande Zacharias Topelius livs- och historiefilosofi* (SSLF, 616), Helsinki, 264 pp., is a doctoral dissertation which examines the last few decades of the life of T. and his increasingly pessimistic and conservative, or anti-modernistic, outlook on life, based on strong religious convictions. T. was in many ways a typical product of his own time and in the mainstream of 19th-c. European thinking. Well-known in Scandinavia as the writer of tales for children and *Fältskärns berättelser*, he was a tireless advocate for the Finnish nation under Russia as a journalist, historian, and writer. To him, the mission of the chosen people of Finland was to spread Western civilization as far north and east as possible. He saw the final solution in a collective Jewish conversion to the Christian faith according to the Bible and its prophecies; only then would the Jews be the people to lead the world towards 'the fulfilment of the prophecy', i.e. the future renewal of mankind and of the earth, a recurring theme in T.'s late writing. M. Lehtonen, 'Topelius reser i Europa. Föredrag vid Svenska litteratursällskapets i Finland årshögtid den 5 februari 1998', *HLS*, 73:7–30 (SSLF, 614), on T.'s travelogues as an important part of his journalism. N. E. Forsgård, 'Topelius, Orienten och islam', *ib.*, 143–56, on T.'s negative view of Islam. M. Lehtonen, 'Tant Mirabeau', *ib.*, 157–83, on the best-known of T.'s short stories that depicts a journey on the first railway between Helsinki and Tavastehus. M. Lehtonen, 'Topeli änglar', *Horisont*, 45.2:4–15. N.-E. Forsgård, 'Historien om ett brev', *FT*: 220–23. C. Nordlund, ' "Huru Gud skapade Finland". Om Topelius och landhöjningens kulturpolitiska betydelse', *ib.*, 349–59. The journal of Svenska litteratursällskapet i Finland, *Källan*, no. 2, is a special issue on T. and his family.

5. THE LATER NINETEENTH CENTURY

Bakom maskerna. Det dolda budskapet hos kvinnliga 1880-talsförfattare, ed. Yvonne Leffler, Karlstad U.P., 133 pp., concentrates on the narrative strategies of the three main female writers of the Modern Breakthrough, namely Victoria Benedictsson, Anne Charlotte Leffler, and Alfhild Agrell; in addition to Y. Leffler's introduction (9–17), it includes four relevant articles: A. Williams, on the treatment of female writers in literary histories and handbooks (19–46); Y. Leffler, on Benedictsson's *Pengar* and the prose version of *Den bergtagna* (47–67); A. Uddenberg, on Leffler's novel *En sommarsaga* (69–93); J. Rahm, on a reinterpretation of Agrell's novel *Guds drömmare* (95–120). Benedikt Jager, *Sollizitation und Sehnsucht nach Parusie. Literarischer Diskurs in Skandinavien zwischen 1880 und 1900* (TUGS, 41), 265 pp., is a doctoral dissertation; on the basis of a few representative Scandinavian texts and postmodern theories, it discusses distinctive features of the period within the parameters of the chosen opposite poles. The Swedish texts include Ola Hansson's *Sensitiva Amorosa* and Strindberg's *I havsbandet* and *Inferno*; other leading Scandinavian writers are J. P. Jacobsen, Knut Hamsun, Arne Garborg, and Sigbjørn Obstfelder. K. Naumann, 'Bergverzaubert: Die Lungenmetropole Davos und ihre skandinavischen Dichter', pp. 245–66 of *Schweiz 1998. Beiträge zur Sprache und Literatur der deutschen Schweiz*, ed. Gérard Krebs (Der Ginkgo-Baum, Germanistisches Jahrbuch für Nordeuropa, 16), Helsinki, Finn Lectura, on Verner von Heidenstam, Oscar Levertin, and Edith Södergran.

ENGSTRÖM, ALBERT. *Årsbok 1998*, ed. Esse Jansson (Albert Engström Sällskapet, 17), Grisslehamn, 157 pp., includes: H. Lång, on Dan Andersson and Kolingen (28); R. S. Samuelsson, on E. and Henrik Ibsen (41–48); H. Lönegren, on food in E. (49–66); L. Jansson, compares hexameter verse by Strindberg and E. (71–80). *Årsbok 1997*, ed. Esse Jansson (Albert Engström Sällskapet, 16), Grisslehamn, 1997, 157 pp., includes: H. Lång, on *Strix* (11–26), Kolingen 1897 (27–38); P.-Å. Berg, on an analysis of Karlfeldt's poem 'Svarta Rudolf' (91–100). *Årsbok 1996*, ed. Birgit Tyréus (Albert Engström Sällskapet, 15), Grisslehamn, 1996, 160 pp. H. Lönegren, on the clergy (15–23); T. Hagström, on landscape and shooting (43–49); H. Lång, on gender roles in E. (50–63).

FRÖDING, GUSTAF. Ove Moberg, *Gustaf Fröding och Karlstad* (Gustaf Fröding-sällskapet, 30), Karlstad, 166 pp., is a facsimile of the 1957 edition, and examines the many connections F. had with this Värmland city and its importance for his writing, from his school days to his career as a journalist on *Karlstads-Tidningen* which he abandoned in 1894; F.'s intended satirical small-town epic on Karlstad never materialized. *Parnass*, 4–5, is a special issue on F.

KARLFELDT, ERIK AXEL. *Mellan myrten och rönn. Tolv texter om Erik Axel Karlfeldt*, ed. Hans Landberg (Karlfeldtsamfundets skriftserie, 30), Wahlström & Widstrand, 219 pp., is an anthology of papers given at colloquia arranged by the K. Society. The title reflects the scope of K.'s writing, spanning the myrtles of Hellas and the rowan-trees of his Pungmakarbo, and includes: K.-G. Hildebrand (9–21) and I. Fries (22–36), on K.'s religious beliefs; L. Falk (37–50), on the meaning of K.'s bookplate; V. Edström (51–71), on comparing Fridolin and

Gösta Berling — Karlfeldt and Lagerlöf; I. Algulin (72–99), on K. as the foremost poetical virtuoso in Swedish literature; O. Nordenfors (100–17), on K.'s poetry set to music; S. Delblanc (118–35), on K.'s oral and singable poetry, contrasted with Tranströmer's; B. Olsson (124–35), on a comparison of K.'s style with that of the Baroque, and in particular Haquin Spegel's *Guds Werk och Hwila*; S. Björkman (136–64), on K., Italian writers, and the Nobel Prize for literature; G. Michanek, 'Karlfeldt i skämtpressen' (165–83), on caricatures of K. in contemporary satirical and humorous journals; J. Stenström (184–97), on K.'s memoir to Carl Fredrik Dahlgren; J. Myrdal (198–212), on K. and country life. I. Algulin, ' "Drifven och lärd i mitt sångarekall". Några anteckningar om Karlfeldt som virtuos poet', Algulin, *Traditioner*, 86–97.

LAGERLÖF, SELMA. *Mammas Selma. Selma Lagerlöfs brev till modern*, ed. Ying Toijer-Nilsson, Bonniers, 291 pp., includes all the 201 letters in the Stockholm Royal Library archives from L. to her mother Louise from 1879 to 1915, the year her mother died. The letters are presented together with a running commentary and detailed notes. They charter L.'s life as an unknown teacher in southern Sweden, her breakthrough as a writer and later journeys abroad which throw light on her writing. Although writing to one's mother would almost invariably imply some elements of restraint and self-censorship, these letters are nevertheless an invaluable source of information, such as L.'s first-hand impressions of meeting the Nås families in Jerusalem which she then incorporated in her novel *Jerusalem*. Isabelle Desmidt, **Bilden av Nils Holgerssons underbara resa genom Sverige i ett urval av Selma Lagerlöfs brev till Sophie Elkan* (SGG, 41), Ghent U.P., 1997, 143 pp. David Anthin, Jenny Bergenmar, and Birgitta Johansson, *Om Lagerlöf* (MLIGU, 23), 174 pp., includes three essays: D. Anthin, 'Landskapets upplösning. En studie av landskapets och platsens betydelse i Selma Lagerlöfs roman *Bannlyst*' (7–59), on the dangers of narrow-mindedness in bourgeois provincialism; J. Bergenmar, 'Parodin som strategi. En studie av det parodiska i Selma Lagerlöfs romaner *Charlotte Löwensköld* och *Anna Svärd*' (61–120), on the play with literary conventions through parody which helps to undermine the patri-archal structures of the text; B. Johansson, 'Kritikens sagoberätterska. En receptionsstudie av Selma Lagerlöfs 90-talsverk' (121–74), dis-cusses how attitudes towards L.'s works changed, from bewilderment concerning literary tradition and genre to positive acceptance of her writings as fairy-tales and legends. J. Bergenmar, 'Bortom kvinnligh-eten. Kön och identitet i Selma Lagerlöfs självbiografi', *TidLit*, 27.2:3–30, on the construction of the self in *Mårbacka, Ett barns memoarer* and *Dagbok för Selma Ottilia Lovisa Lagerlöf*, based on current ideas of gender identity. K. Munck, 'Makt, sexualitet och gränsöver-skridanden hos Selma Lagerlöf', *ib.*, 31–38, discusses 'that which she does not dare to mention by name', i.e. forbidden love, on the basis of the short story 'Dunungen', and advocates a new reading of L. after the publication of the letters to her two female friends. *Selma Lagerlöf Seen from Abroad — Selma Lagerlöf i utlandsperspektiv*, ed. Louise Vinge (Konferenser, 44), Kungl. Vitterhets Historie och Antikvitets Akade-mien–Almqvist & Wiksell International, 156 + [3] pp., includes a number of relevant studies given as papers by non-Swedish scholars at a Stockholm colloquium in September, 1997: P. Graves, on reception in Britain (9–18); I. Desmidt, on translations and adapta-tions into Dutch and German of *Nils Holgerssons underbara resa genom Sverige* (19–32); M. Zitny, on Slovakian reception (33–40); N. Thun-man, on translations and translators into Japanese (41–59); S. Death, on the challenges of translating 'Dunungen' (61–71); S. L. Beckett, on *Nils Holgersson* as the perfect text for the French author Michel Tournier (73–85); J. Watson Madler, on *Herr Arnes penningar* and Gerhart Hauptmann (87–103); E. Segerberg, on the importance of the storyteller in the literary work and in Mauritz Stiller's film adaptations of *Gösta Berlings saga* and *En herrgårdssägen* (105–19); M. Giordano Lokrantz, on the legend 'Fiskarringen' (121–30); B. Thorup Thomsen, on a comparative study of the significance of place in *Jerusalem*, part 2, and *Nils Holgersson* (131–42); H. Forsås-Scott, on text and identity in *Dagbok* (143–53). Birgitte Rahbek and Mogens Bähncke, *Tro og skaebne i Jerusalem. Virkeligheden bag Selma Lagerlöfs roman Jerusalem*, Copenhagen, Gyldendals, 1996, 180 pp., examines the reality behind S.'s novel, in particular revivalism in the farming families from Nås, Dalarna, and in the Jerusalem American colony. B. Thorup Thomsen, 'Destruction or construction in Selma Lagerlöf's *Jerusalem*, vol. II', *BASS* 11, 82–98.

LEVERTIN, OSCAR. A. Krummacher, ' "Ett enda stort tillslutet och förstenadt Babylon". Oscar Levertins *Lifvets fiender* (1891) als Groß-stadtroman', *Glienke Vol.*, 215–30.

STRINDBERG, AUGUST. Germund Michanek, *Strindberg i karikatyr och skämtbild. Hur vår störste författare hyllades och smädades i sin samtids skämtpress*, Wahlström & Widstrand, 142 pp., is precisely as the title indicates an illustrated examination of how S. was reproduced in contemporary satirical and humorous journals and magazines. The decades round the turn of the century a hundred years ago represented the golden age for a number of brilliant and ingenious cartoonists. What is portrayed in this work is Swedish history, such as the *Giftas* prosecution and the infamous so-called 'S. feud' in 1910–11. Michael Robinson, *Studies in Strindberg*, Norwich, Norvik Press, 244 pp., is a welcome and relevant work in its attempt to redress the neglect S. has suffered in Britain, a task which Robinson has been fulfilling over the years, and most recently with his translation of S., *Selected Essays*, 1996. The current work is concerned with facilitating a re-evaluation of S. in the English-speaking world. It considers a number of subjects rarely addressed in English before, such as his painting and thoughts on acting and directing, his interest in historical drama as reflecting his own life and his new aesthetic direction as a writer after the Inferno crisis of the mid-1890s. The focus in all these essays is on S. the writer and his artistry and not his biography, even when his attention turns to his own autobiographical image. Björn Meidal et al., *August Strindbergs kokbok*, Rabén Prisma, 240 pp.; and Catharina Söderbergh et al., *Till bords med Strindberg*, Bonniers, 160 pp., are two very similar, lavishly illustrated works about food and drink in contemporary settings. Meidal justifies his title on the fact that S. was planning to write a cookery book, and traces the importance of food and drink throughout his life and their symbolic overtones in his writing. Söderbergh starts by pointing out how much S. enjoyed good food and drink together with his friends, and how this interest runs all through his life and work. With a generous number of extracts from S.'s works, it is made abundantly clear by both writers that the strange thing is not the simultaneous publication, but rather the fact that the importance of food and drink has not been properly discussed earlier. The descriptions of various meals in *Giftas* alone capture in a nutshell the bliss or hell of being married; to S. food and eating are connected with the fragile balance of body and soul, with sexuality and joie de vivre. Boel Westin, *Strindberg, sagan och skriften*, Eslöv, Symposion, 310 pp. + 8 pls, provides new and stimulating aspects of S. which have so far been largely ignored, namely his interest in fairy-tales and their importance for his works, be they inspired by the Arabian Nights, Hans Christian Andersen, or Nordic folk-tales. Although Harry Carlson has dealt with myths in the dramas, this book focuses more specifically on fairy-tale motifs in S.'s 'sagospel' and *Sagor*. The previous neglect might well be due to the fact that the fairy-tale was considered a 'lower' literary form for women and children and therefore unsuitable for a writer like S. who, however, looked upon the genre in a different way; the fairy-tale was in fact one of the universal forms to which he continually returned. It takes a scholar specializing in literature for children and young people like Westin to reveal this exciting perspective. *Strindberg. The Moscow Papers*, ed. Michael Robinson, Strindbergssällskapet, 224 pp., includes twenty-five essays by Russian and Western scholars which were originally papers presented at the XII International Strindberg Conference in Moscow in June 1994. It is a varied collection, which on the one hand investigates S. and Russia, on the other his consanguinity with symbolism, while a third part deals with new readings of individual works, including a number of less familiar ones, and includes among other essays: M. Robinson, 'Towards a new language: Strindberg and symbolism' (15–26); T. Bredsdorff, ' "Give us a sign!" Allegory and symbol in Strindberg's *Inferno*' (69–76); B. Meidal, 'Strindberg's Russia — cultural history, nihilism, historical metaphysics and antimilitarism' (95–104); M. Nikolajeva, 'Strindberg through the eyes of the Russian critics' (113–20); B. Ståhle Sjönell, ' "Sådant skräp som ger mig bröd": Strindberg's short stories' (173–79); B. Westin, 'The butterfly and the gold: symbolist elements in Strindberg's fairy-tale, "Blåvinge finner Guldpudran" ' (181–86); B. Nolin, 'Symbolism and the making of a fairy-tale play: *Svanevit* at the Intimate theatre'. *Strindbergiana*, ed. Birgitta Steene (Strindbergs-sällskapet, 13), Atlantis, 160 pp., includes essays by both Swedish and foreign writers, concentrating on S.'s last years and the view of posterity: H. von Born, 'Strindberg och Gustaf Falkvinge' (10–13); A. Lalander, 'Strindbergs Gersau-kamera återfunnen' (14–15); P. Hemmingsson, 'Strindbergs "blixtkamera" ' (16–20); B. Steene, 'Med Strindberg i Österrike' (21–36), reports from the 13th international S. conference in Linz in October, 1997; E. Szalczer, 'Strindberg och Georg Ljungström. En teosofisk bekantskap' (37–48); J. Austin, ' "En reform? Falck har verkat!" Intima teaterns betydelse i Stockholms teaterliv' (49–77); B. Meidal, 'Strindbergscensur 1908. Anna Branting recenserar *Svanevit* på Intima teatern' (78–81); B. Lide, 'Strindberg på scenen i dag. Postmoderna parodier' (82–91); H. F. Königsgarten, ' "Romeo och Julia." Den strindbergska versionen' (92–94); B. Nolin, 'Strindberg och Moderniteten. Den faustiske sökaren och det ondas triumf' (95–103); L. Gavel Adams, 'Strindbergs Paris' (104–26); B. Sundberg, ' "Silverträsket" och *Taklagsöl* — två prosastycken från sekelskiftet' (127–38); U. Olsson, 'Den andra rösten. Strindbergs galenskap och litteraturhistorien' (139–58). G. Syréhn, ' "Den starkare" och "Persona". Några jämförelsepunkter', *Fenix*, 13.4, 1997 : 114–123, compares S.'s one-act play and Ingmar Bergman's film. The *Törnqvist Vol.* includes several relevant essays which reflect Egil Törnqvist's interest in Scandinavian film and drama: T. Bredsdorff, 'Give us a sign! Allegory and symbol in Strindberg's infernal usage' (23–34); A.-C. Hanes Harvey, 'Strindberg and scenography' (61–83); B. Jacobs, 'Strindberg's *Miss Julie* and the decadent spirit: waiting for the barbarians' (95–111); H. Perridon, 'Translating pronouns of power and solidarity. Forms of address in Strindberg's *Miss Julie*' (161–75); E. Sprinchorn, '*Fanny and Alexander* and Strindberg and Ibsen and — ' (177–87); B. Steene, 'Fire rekindled: Strindberg and Ingmar Bergman' (189–203). F. Paul,

' "Den stora oredan och det oändliga sammanhanget". Zur komposi-
torischen Funktion orientalischer Motive in Strindbergs *Ett drömspel*,
Glienke Vol., 121–33, concludes that these can be seen as 'innovatively
effective functional elements of modern drama'. A. Melberg, 'Strindberg stiger ner: *Inferno*', *ib.*, 231–41, investigates the theme of descent
and its connection with conversion, the turning-point which produces
S.'s modernism. *TsSk*, 19.1, is a special issue on transposing Scandinavian drama, and includes: E. Törnqvist, 'Translating Strindbergian
imagery for the stage' (7–23); A.-C. Hanes Harvey, 'Translating
Scandinavian drama — for whom?'(25–49); B. Jacobs, 'Translating
for the stage — the case of Strindberg' (75–101); J. F. Evelein,
'Drama turning inward: Strindberg's station play and its Expressionist
continuum' (163–84). S. Flühmann, 'Der Doppelgänger als strukturie-
rendes Motiv in August Strindbergs *Inferno*,' *Edda*: 39–50. T. Forslid,
'Berättande och minne i Strindbergs "Ett halvt ark papper" ', *ib.*,
51–56. P. Stounbjerg, 'Position og positur. Om mandigheden i
Strindbergs roman *En dåres forsvarstale*', *ib.*, 209–15. E. Szalczer,
'Spectator, spectacle, and the modern self: the cosmic theatre of
Strindberg's prose works', *Scandinavica*, 37:5–44. E. Törnqvist,
'Strindberg som fornisländare', *TsSk*, 17.2, 1996:7–19.

TAVASTSTJERNA, KARL AUGUST. C. Appelberg, 'Tavaststjernas
ofullbordade', *FT*:211–19.

6. THE TWENTIETH CENTURY

Läs mig — sluka mig. En bok om barnböcker, ed. Kristin Hallberg, Natur
och Kultur, 404 pp., is an anthology dealing with how views on
children's books and Swedish research in the genre have developed
and changed during the last few decades; the essays cover four main
groups: nursery rhymes, songs and poetry, picture books, and
literature for children and young people. Most of the essays have
been published in earlier collective works, while others listed here are
newly written: K. Hallberg, 'Änglaprinsessa och flickbyting. Några
svenska flickskildringar' (99–150), deals with girls in works by Astrid
Lindgren, Barbro Lindgren, Margareta Strömstedt, and Inger Edel-
feldt in a feminstic and psychoanalytical perspective; B. Hedén, 'Det
jämlika tilltalet — ungdomsboken från 40-tal till 90-tal' (161–80), is
an updated and revised version of an earlier essay; L. Kåreland,
'1990-talets svenska bilderbok. Några exempel' (277–95). Maria
Nikolajeva, *Barnbokens byggklossar*, Lund, Studentlitteratur, 201 pp., is
a study of the narrative techniques used in the 'Swedish canon of
children's literature'; examples are from a selection of modern and
older works, both originally Swedish and literature in translation. On
the basis of modern narratology it examines the characters, the

narrative perspective, and the setting to establish if and how children's literature is different from adult literature. *Modernity, Modernism and Children's Literature*, ed. Ulf Boëthius (SCB, 29), 128 pp., includes papers given at an international symposium in early 1998 in connection with the current research project at Stockholm University, 'Modernism and children's literature'. *Från flygdröm till swingscen. Ungdom och modernitet på 1930-talet*, ed. Matz Franzén, Lund, Arkiv, 352 pp., is an anthology that examines various genres, media, and leisure activities for young people, and includes: U. Boëthius, 'Mot gryningen! Ungdom och modernitet i Alvar Zackes flygböcker' (58–111), on Alvar Zacke's action-packed aviation books for boys, characterized by the particular youth-culture built round the current interest in modern aviation, and a sign of new man and the different society of the future; M. Czaplicka, 'Yrhättor, backfischar och unga damer — ett flickboksgalleri' (112–98), on the popular genre of books for girls in the 1930s when a new title was published every ten days, including both Swedish originals and translations, concluding that as early as this period there was an abundance of such books dealing with modern themes. Maj Asplund Carlsson, *The Doorkeeper and the Beast. The Experience of Literary Narratives in Educational Contexts* (SLIGU, 33), 108 pp., is a doctoral dissertation based on four separate research projects about children's reader responses in various educational settings; the primary texts include works by Astrid Lindgren and Tove Jansson. B. Fransson, 'Swedish books for young adults: living in the present', *SBR*, 1:56–59. Mats Jansson, *Kritisk tidsspegel. Studier i 1940-talets svenska litteraturkritik*, Eslöv, Symposion, 430 pp., examines the significance of literary criticism in the 1940s for the breakthrough of Modernism. Many of the leading new critics were in fact themselves writers of prose and verse, such as Stig Dagerman and Karl Vennberg; the latter's contributions in particular are central to the new literary climate. The study focuses primarily on critics connected with leading avant-garde journals, such as *40-tal* and *Utsikt*, and deals comprehensively with the important role of Stig Ahlgren and emerging modernist critics that have not been studied previously in scholarly depth, namely Stig Carlson, Allan Fagerström, Lennart Göthberg, Viveka Heyman, and Axel Liffner. *Sammanhang. Elva essäer om text och läsning tillägnade Anders Ringblom*, ed. Christina Angelfors, Margareta Petersson, and Elisabeth Stenborg (Rapporter Humaniora, 1998.4), Växjö U.P., 135 pp., includes, in addition to I. Nettervik, on Vilhelm Moberg's novel *A. P. Rosell, bankdirektör* (71–80), essays of a more general nature: A. Höglund, 'Att bryta tankens bojor' (44–57), on fiction and reality; M. Nilsson, 'Den självbespeglande spegeln' (81–94), on Göran Printz-Påhlson's essay 'Solen i spegeln' and metapoetry (81–94); E. Stenborg, 'Gudsbilden i litteraturen. Tre exempel från svenskt 1900-tal' (110–21), on Sven Delblanc's *Livets ax*, Pär Lagerkvist, and Harriet Löwenhjelm. *Jung och litteraturen*, ed. Kurt Almqvist, Natur och Kultur, 208 pp., is a collective work of nine essays on Jung's importance in the works of various individual writers, and includes: A. Pleijel, 'Världen är en. Om jag, värld och medvetande i Tomas Tranströmers lyrik' (76–97); M. Schottenius, 'Den kvinnliga hemligheten. Om Kerstin Ekmans berättarkonst' (132–64); E. Ekselius, 'Kapten Nemo och Jona i valfiskens buk. Om initiationsmyten som struktur hos Jules Verne och Per Olov Enquist' (165–84). Bo Strömstedt, *Den tjugonionde bokstaven. Blad ur en ABC-bok*, Bonniers, 187 pp., includes essays on Gustaf Fröding, Birger Sjöberg, Anders Österling, and Werner Aspenström. L. Ekelund, 'Ett Bauerskt författartorp. Om Baddaren och en gästbok', *Horisont*, 45.3:71–79, includes references to Elin Wägner, Pär Lagerkvist, and Johannes Edfelt. E.-K. Josefson, 'Unanimismen i Sverige', *Samlaren*, 118, 1997[1998]:112–21, discusses the influence of Jules Romains. Algulin, *Traditioner*, includes: I. Algulin, 'Att tolka dikt — att tolka musik' (26–44); 'Nyklassicism som litterär tradition: en historisk överblick' (67–84), both on modern poetry; 'Karlfeldt, Lars Forssell och det lyriska femtitalet' (98–114). A. Born, 'New Swedish poetry from the 1990s', *SBR*, no. 1:37–55.

Gabriele Beyer-Jordan, *Literarische Labyrinthe. Über die Bewegungen des skandinavischen Romans der 1980er Jahre zwischen Ich und Welt, Wirklichkeit und Fiktion, Mythos und Aufklärung* (TUGS, 38), 1997, 194 pp., originally a doctoral dissertation in 1996, includes essays on Stig Larsson, *Nyår* (43–70), Klas Östergren, *Plåster* (71–97), and Lars Gustafsson, *En kakelsättares eftermiddag* (98–123). *Fragmente einer skandinavischen Poetikgeschichte*, ed. Heiko Uecker (TUGS, 39), 1997, 357 pp., includes K. B. Adam, on Lars Ahlin (53–69); M. Wasilewska-Chmura, on relations between music and poetry (71–86); E. Zillén, on concrete poetry (103–11); K. Bak, on Birgitta Trotzig's poetological strategies (119–28); J. Trinkwitz, on Gunnar Ekelöf's short essay 'Ett fotografi' (157–78); P. Berf, on Lars Gustafsson (191–211); B. Jager, on Stig Larsson, *Nyår* (221–32); A. Heitmann, on Göran Palm and Katarina Frostensson (233–47); P. E. Ljung, on Jesper Svenbro (263–76); K. Hoff, on Lars Jacobsson and Ola Larsmo (323–35). *Försök om litteratur*, ed. Daniel Birnbaum and Leif Zern, Bonniers, 123 pp., includes: S. Danius, 'Litteraturens död 1–6' (5–28), on the stifling effect on art of literary criticism; B. Munkhammar, on a defence of literary critics (29–74); A. Olsson, 'Poesins plats' (75–117), dicusses the thesis in Göran Printz-Påhlson's essay 'Platsens poesi, satsens poesi'. *Bo-lövens sorl. Romantisk modernism och estetisk funktionalism i femtitalets poesi*, ed. Eva Lilja and Jan Magnusson (SLIGU, 32), 214 pp., is an anthology of papers given at a colloquium in the spring of 1997; it examines the poetry of the fifties both as a reaction to the modernism of the 1940s and as a preparation for the socially committed literature of the 1960s. It includes: J. Magnusson, on neo-romanticism and theories discussed in the journal *Femtital* by authors such as Bo Setterlind (17–43); R. Schönström, on the early literary criticism of Göran Palm and Göran Printz-Påhlson (45–63); C. Wahlin, on Lars Forssell and Ezra Pound (67–81); E. Lilja, on Majken Johansson (127–39); J. Bankier, on Tomas Tranströmer (141–56). The anthology closes with a series of analyses of individual poems by Tranströmer, Paul Andersson, Sandro Key-Åberg, and Folke Isaksson. H. A. Barton, 'From Swede to Swedish American, or vice versa. The conversion motif in the literature of Swedish America', *ScSt*, 70:26–38. Houe, *Documentarism*, based on papers given at a conference in 1994, considers documentarism in Scandinavian literature, and includes: S. H. Rossel, 'Scandinavian documentary fiction' (1–23), outlines the theoretical background to documentary literature, and highlights the dilemma of traditional literary criticism on how to classify the genre, with reference to Josef Kjellgren's collective novel *Människor kring en bro*, Per Olof Sundman's *Ingenjör Andrées luftfärd*, Sven Delblanc's *Åsnebrygga*, Per Olov Enquist's *Legionärerna*, Jan Myrdal's *Rapport från kinesisk by*, and Sara Lidman's *Samtal i Hanoi*; R. Yrlid, 'The elusive documentary: the Swedish documentary movement with an attempt at a definition' (24–35), examines documentarism and attempts to define key concepts; B. Agrell, 'Documentarism and theory of literature' (36–76), is a comprehensive study of the topic; J. Ingvarsson, 'Media and the documentary strategies' (77–89); C. Zilliacus, 'The act of quotation: motives in report literature' (90–100); P. Bouquet, 'The Swedish "report-school" and the renewal of working-class literature' (101–06), is a detailed review of a specific school of documentary writing, i.e. the working-class version of documentarism; G. Anderman, '*The Night of the Tribades*: fact and fiction in Grez-sur-Loing' (148–54), on Per Olov Enquist's *Tribadernas natt*, a play that uses gender relations around 1890 as a mirror for those of the 1970s, with Strindberg as a fitting central character; E. Törnqvist, 'Playwright on playwright: Per Olov Enquist's Strindberg and Lars Norén's O'Neill' (155–64), on Enquist's *Tribadernas natt*, 1975, and Norén's *Och ge oss skuggorna*, 1991. B. Agrell, 'Genreteori och genrehistoria. Eva Hættner Aurelius & Thomas Götselius (red.), *Genreteori*, Lund, Studentlitteratur, 1997', *TidLit*, 27.2:95–114, discusses the theory of genres on the basis of a recently published anthology of central essays by international scholars in Swedish translation. M. Persson, 'Värdefrågan i nyare litteratur- och kulturforskning', *ib.*, 3–4:40–58. E. Heggestad, 'Petitesser om grossesser? Kön och kritik i *Ord och Bilds* litterära trettiotal', *ib.*, 79–95; T. Forser, 'Dagspress och tidspress I. Kritikerns roll, exemplet Knut Jaensson', *ib.*, 133–34; S.-E. Liedman, 'Dagspress och tidspress II. Förstadagsrecensionens dilemma', *ib.*, 135–37. B. Karlsson, '"Och så bröt kriget ut."' Svenska Teatern under spelåren 1939–1944', *HLS*, 73:185–213 (SSLF, 614), discusses the repertoire and activity of the Swedish Theatre in Helsinki during the Second World War. R. Holmström, 'Några russin i den finlandssvenska 1900-talsprosans klassikerkaka', *Horisont*, 45.5:17–21, includes references to five works by Mikael Lybeck, Sigrid Backman, Hagar Olsson, R. R. Eklund, and Anna Bondestam. *Leva skrivande. Finlandssvenska författare samtalar*, ed. Monika Fagerholm, Helsinki, Söderströms, 268 pp., brings together a number of contemporary Finland-Swedish writers in an exchange of ideas and thoughts. Bo G. Jansson, *Nedslag i 1990-talets svenska prosa. Om 90-talets svenska roman och novell i postmodernt perspektiv* (Kultur och Lärande, 1998.2), Högskolan Dalarna U.P., 127 pp., deals with the prose of the 1990s, the decade of Swedish post-modernist literature, even if the discussion on postmodernism took place a decade earlier. By no means all the works discussed can be labelled post-modernist; several are realistic or modernist. The distinctions between these three concepts are central for the work, as are the terms intertext and metafiction. The study opens up interesting perspectives for the most recent prose fiction. There are useful analyses of novels by authors such as Carina Burman, Kerstin Ekman, and P. C. Jersild. Magnus Florin's novel *Trädgården* on Linnæus is labelled a genuinely post-modernist work, as are books by Göran Tunström, Björn Ranelid, and Carl-Johan Vallgren. *Femton poeter ur 90-talet*, ed. Helena Eriksson and Maria Gummesson (FIB:s Lyrikklubbs bibliotek, 272), FIB:s Lyrikklubb, 214 pp., is an anthology of fifteen current poets, edited and introduced by two fellow poets. C. G. Widén, 'Bland änglar och smugglare. Finlandssvensk litteratur 1997', *NT*, 74:245–50. B. Widegren, 'Inget stort litterärt år. Svensk litteratur 1997', *ib.*, 279–88. B. Gunnarsson, 'Prosadebutanter', *BLM*, 67.4:70–72. B. Wallén, 'Det upplösta nuet. Finlandssvensk poesiöversikt anno 1997', *FT*:166–78. A.-C. Snickars, 'Sibirien, soporna, pappa. Några teman i och kring fjolårets skönlitteratur', *ib.*, 179–88. Bo Lundin, *Studier om mord från Trenter till Mankell*, Utbildningsförlaget Brevskolan, 176 pp., is a useful introduction to the detective-story genre from about 1945 to the present day with individual chapters on some of its foremost writers. It examines the works of Stieg Trenter, followed by Ulla Trenter, starting with the 'first modern Swedish detective novel' in 1944, *Farlig fåfänga*. The novels of the internationally successful duo Maj Sjöwall and Per Wahlöö attempt to analyse what effect the political and ideological doctrine of the welfare state might have on the crime rate, while

Gösta Unefäldt's small-town policeman is firmly rooted on the west coast. Henning Mankell's highly popular recent novels are characterized by hard-hitting action and a good grasp of contemporary problems. O. Wijnbladh, 'Var stod *BLM?*', *BLM*, 67.3 : 54–56, on *BLM* and Nazism 1932–38.

AHLIN, LARS.　Helen Andersson, *Det etiska projektet och det estetiska. Tvärvetenskapliga perspektiv på Lars Ahlins författarskap*, Eslöv, Symposion, 520 pp., a doctoral dissertation, is a study of interdisciplinary aspects of A.; it concentrates on 'the ethics of A.'s aesthetics and the aesthetics of ethics, the ethics of narration and the narration of ethics, with particular attention to the self and its relations'. Although a close analysis of A.'s late novel *Din livsfrukt*, 1987, is the main focus of the study, it also provides considerable insight into his works in general.

ANDERSSON, DAN.　*Parnass*, no. 3, is devoted to A.

ARONSON, STINA.　P. Broomans, 'En litterär delinkvent. Stina Aronson och litteraturhistorikerna', *TidLit*, 27.3–4 : 20–29. **Röster om Stina Aronson*, ed. Martin Aagård and Birgitta Holm, Uppsala U.P., 1996, 41 pp.

BECKMAN, ERIK.　*Av Jordbeckman är du kommen*, ed. Peter Grönborg (Erik Beckman-sällskapet, 1), Borås, 1996, 48 pp., includes a presentation of the B. Society which was founded in order to further interest in B. and his writings; H. Engdal, on B. and his writing (6–9); B., *Dardanellerna* (10–20), never published before; Nisse Larsson, an interview with B. (22–27); five obituaries from various daily newspapers on B.'s death in 1995 (28–39); L. Hagström, on B.'s early novel *Hertigens kartonger*, 1961 (40–46). Christer Ekholm, *Tilltalets paradox. Om Erik Beckmans roman Hertigens kartonger* (Erik Beckman-sällskapet, 2), Borås, 1997, 28 pp., is a draft plan of a coming doctoral dissertation, University of Gothenburg. *Känner vi igen oss*, ed. Lars Hagström (Erik Beckman-sällskapet, 3), Borås, 48 pp., includes S. Hansell, on the novel *Jag känner igen mej*, 1977 (39–44).

BENGTSSON, FRANS G.　Lennart Ploman, *Frans G. Bengtsson, poet och prosaist. Två föredrag* (Frans G. Bengtsson-sällskapet, 7), Lund, 16 pp., on B. as a poet and prose writer. Frans G. Bengtsson, *Myt och medeltid*, ed. Jonas Ellerström (Frans G. Bengtsson-sällskapet, 8), Lund, 64 pp., includes a number of rare essays and articles by B. as well as an introduction by the editor. Ingrid Sällryd, *Frans G. Bengtssons människosyn och konstsyn* (Scripta minora, 33), Växjö U.P., 1996, 71 pp., tries to modify the generally accepted picture of B. and to clarify his aesthetic views.

BERGMAN, INGMAR.　B. Steene, 'The transpositions of a filmmaker — Ingmar Bergman at home and abroad', *TsSk*, 19.1 : 103–28. I. Holmqvist, 'Ingmar Bergman's winter journey —

intertextuality in "Larmar och gör sig till"', *ib.*, 2:79–94, on B.'s *Femte akten*, 1994.

BURMAN, CARINA. S. Death, 'Carina Burman'; 'An interview with Carina Burman, March 1998', *SBR*, no.1:2–6. C. Burman, 'Faking the 18th century', *ib.*, 17–24.

CARPELAN, BO. Roger Holmström, *Vindfartsvägar. Strövtåg i Bo Carpelans Urwind*, Helsinki, Schildts, 200 pp., is not only a well-informed and captivating week-by-week excursion into C.'s novel, but also opens up new and exciting perspectives on C.'s writing as a whole through the eyes of this dedicated scholar. 'Femtio år av nyfiken noggrannhet. Samtal med Bo Carpelan', ed. M. Westö (SSLF, 614), *HLS*, 73:243–68, on literary influences, the modernism of the 1940s, writer colleagues through the years, in particular Gunnar Björling, writing as a trade, and the role of the writer. A shortened version of the conversations, which took place in the autumn of 1996, is also published in *Leva skrivande* (see p. 847 above).

DAGERMAN, STIG. Claes Ahlund, *Fallets lag och jagets stjärna. En studie i Stig Dagermans författarskap*, Hedemora, Gidlunds, 420 pp., considers central structural themes in D.'s works. The first part deals with the motion of falling, the spatialization of consciousness (often in the form of a building), and the interrupted meeting; the second part focuses on the interaction between the conscious and the unconscious in a number of short stories and the novel *De dömdas ö* to demonstrate the decisive importance of the unconscious, and the third analyses the novel *Bröllopsbesvär* with reference to Ahlin's novel *Min död är min*, in addition to poems and the late radio drama *Den yttersta dagen*. The aim has been to integrate two different perspectives and to balance the non-reflexive themes analysed in the first part with the more reflexive psychic interaction between conscious and unconscious in the analyses of the second part and the late works of the third. Georges Ueberschlag, *Stig Dagerman ou l'innocence préservée. Une biographie*, Nantes, L'Élan, 1996, 303 pp., is a useful biography for the French reader, providing information about the writer, his life, work, and cultural environment. *Stig Dagerman et L'Europe. Perspectives analytiques et comparatives*, ed. Georges Périlleux, Paris, Didier Érudition, 153 pp., includes 17 papers in English and French on various themes by a number of international and Swedish scholars. There is no indication that these papers were given at a colloquium in Brussels in April 1990; it is a pity that bibliographical references have not been updated before publication. For instance, it might not be totally irrelevant that in the meantime two further novels have been translated into English. C. Ahlund, 'Förklaringsögonblickets förvandlingar. Om Dagermans transformation av en ahlinsk epifanimodell', *TidLit*, 27.1:25–48, on technical similarities in D. and Lars Ahlin. L. Lotass, 'Disharmonins dialektik — Stig Dagerman och samfärdselns problem', *ib.*, 2 : 39–60, discusses writing as communication and D.'s gradual questioning of this. C. Ahlund, 'Om Kristussymboliken i Stig Dagermans *Bröllopsbesvär*', *Horisont*, 45.1 : 59–66.

DAHL, TORA. *Parnass*, no. 2, is devoted to the married couple D. and Knut Jaensson, the critic.

EDVARDSON, CORDELIA. A. Ohlsson, 'Vår outtröttliga strävan att laga världen. Förintelsen och Cordelia Edvardsons författarskap', *Horisont*, 45.4 : 3–17.

EKELÖF, GUNNAR. Bengt Landgren, *Polyederns gåta. En introduktion till Gunnar Ekelöfs Färjesång* (AUU, Historia litterarum, 20), Uppsala U.P., 233 pp., is the first comprehensive scholarly monograph on E.'s fifth collection of poetry from September 1941, is Landgren's third published book on E. and will be indispensable for future research. It examines the background to the work and its origins in the late thirties, and discusses the negative and indifferent first reception of what is now regarded as possibly the most important and influential poetry to be published in Sweden during the Second World War; the main bulk of the study analyses the poetic structures in close readings of central texts, such as the suites 'Tag och skriv' and 'Etyder', and the two separate, antithetical poems in the concluding epilogue 'Fuga', namely 'Melancholia', and 'Eufori'. Two lines in the introductory poem of the collection, 'Jag sjunger om det enda som försonar, / det enda praktiska, för alla lika', might be a programme declaration for *Färjesång* as a whole, the more so as they are repeated separately as a coda at the very end, after the final poem itself; it is convincingly suggested that this emphasis signals the very theme of the work and hints at its musical composition. Olof Lagercrantz, *Ekelöf, Proust och Conrad. Tre valfränder*, Wahlström & Widstrand, 224 + 210 + 194 pp., includes *Jag bor i en annan värld men du bor ju i samma. Gunnar Ekelöf betraktad av Olof Lagercrantz*, pp. [1]1–224; originally published in 1994; it assesses E. on the basis of personal notes, letters, and years of friendship going back to the 1930s. O. Widhe, 'Att se Dagen. Skuggans figurativa språk i Gunnar Ekelöfs diktning', *TidLit*, 27.2 : 75–94. P. Talme, 'Litteraturkritik och kanonisering — nedslag i debatten kring Ekelöfs Skrifter (1991–93)', *ib.*, 3–4 : 96–120. J. Lundbo Levy, 'Om ting der går i stykker — Gunnar Ekelöf og H. C. Andersen', *Edda* : 259–68.

EKMAN, KERSTIN. L. H. Rugg, 'Revenge of the rats. The Cartesian body in Kerstin Ekman's *Rövarna i Skuleskogen*', *ScSt*, 70 : 425–39. P. Binding, 'From house with five windows', *SBR*, no.2 : 54–67, an extract from a forthcoming book, is an interview with E.

ELGSTRÖM, ANNA LENAH. Catrine Brödje, *Ett annat tiotal. En studie i Anna Lenah Elgströms tiotalsprosa*, Eslöv, Gondolin, 293 pp., is a doctoral dissertation which examines the largely forgotten woman writer E. She was, however, a leading personality in the cultural and social life in the years between 1910 and 1920. Elin Wägner, Marika Stiernstedt and E. were three contemporary women writers, all friends, feminists, and pacifists. But while the other two are still current in Swedish literary history, E. has been almost completely marginalized. On the basis of E.'s works, a perspective of literature in the decade up to 1920 emerges which is different from that of most literary handbooks; there are important points of contact between E. and Vilhelm Ekelund and Pär Lagerkvist on the one hand, and Hagar Olsson and Edith Södergran on the other, in their radical and avant-garde modernism. By stressing E.'s affinity with Swedish and Finland-Swedish early modernism and German Expressionism as well as her position on the contemporary feministic literary and political scene, early modernism in the second decade of the twentieth century appears in a somewhat new light.

ENQUIST, PER OLOV. Houe, *Documentarism*, includes several relevant essays. H. Fricke, 'Unausweichlichkeit der projektion in Per Olov Enquists *Kapten Nemos bibliotek*', *Skandinavistik*, 27, 1997:98–113. E. Törnqvist, 'Translating docudrama. Per Olov Enquist's *Tribadernas natt* in English and French', *TsSk*, 19.1:129–48.

ERIKSSON, ULF. P. Nilsson, 'En sinnlig tillägnelse av staden. Samtal med Ulf Eriksson', *BLM*, 67.2:45–52, on E.'s Stockholm novels.

FAHLSTRÖM, ÖYVIND. *OB*, nos 1–2 + CD, is a special issue on F. and concrete poetry.

FERLIN, NILS. Jenny Westerström, *Nils Ferlin. Ett diktarliv*, Bonniers, 477 pp., is a comprehensive biography of F. by the scholar who published a dissertation on F., 'our saddest and most popular poet', in 1990. The publication commemorates the 100th anniversary of the poet's birth; simultaneously, Bonniers has also issued a volume of F.'s collected poetry 1930–62, *Får jag lämna några blommor. Dikter*, 412 pp. (2nd edn.; 1st edn. 1991). The current life-and-letters monograph is aimed at a wide readership; much to its advantage, although it has a bibliography and index, it lacks footnotes and other trappings of an academic nature. This is an eminently readable and well-written work in which commentaries on poems form an integral and indispensable part. Karl-Olof Andersson, *Nils Ferlin — poet i livets villervalla*, Utbildningsförlaget Brevskolan, 189 pp., is a smaller, yet compact and informative biography in which individual poems are used as focal points for each chapter to illuminate various periods in the poet's life.

FOGELSTRÖM, PER ANDERS. Arne Reberg, *Per Anders Fogelström. Stockholms förste älskare*, Utbildningsförlaget Brevskolan, 1997, 224 pp., is a biographical account with somewhat ideological overtones of this genuine and popular writer on Stockholm and everyday, ordinary life in the capital; it appeared the year before F.'s death in 1998. His novels about the early days of industrialization are the story of the origins of the welfare state; history, F. maintains, is active in the present.

FRIDEGÅRD, JAN. Erik Peurell, *En författares väg. Jan Fridegård i det litterära fältet* (Avdelningen för litteratursociologi, 39, SLIUU), Hedemora, Gidlunds, 320 pp., is a doctoral dissertation which examines this proletarian writer's progress, or lack of it, on the basis of Pierre Bourdieu's theory of social fields; in other words, playing in accordance with the rules of the game in order to achieve success. F.'s rather ambivalent relationship to the game in the 'literary field', his reluctance to take part at all, i.e. what is termed his insufficient *illusio*, goes some way in explaining why it took so long for him to establish himself and also why his position weakened in later years, although he still reached large groups of readers.

GULLBERG, HJALMAR. I. Algulin, 'Naturmotiv i den unge Gullbergs lyrik', Algulin, *Traditioner*, 115–26.

GUSTAFSSON, LARS. Ulrike-Christine Sander, *Ichverlust und fiktionaler Selbstentwurf. Die Romane Lars Gustafssons* (Palaestra, 305), Göttingen, Vandenhoeck & Ruprecht, 424 pp., is a doctoral dissertation and, in spite of his popularity in German-speaking countries, the first exhaustive work in German on G., in which the focus is on the fifteen novels published between 1957 and 1993. It identifies and interprets G.'s preoccupation with the nature of personal identity in three main chronological phases, the first characterized by scepticism and pessimism, the second by overcoming the isolation of the self, and the third by increasingly metaphysical, religious, and ethical ideas regarding the problem of identity. L. G. Andersson and P. Svensson, 'Något som gör isarna allt blankare. Vårtecknens semiotik i Lars Gustafssons poesi', *Horisont*, 45.1 : 4–10.

HILLARP, RUT. Annelie Bränström Öhman, *Kärlekens ödeland. Rut Hillarp och kvinnornas fyrtiotalsmodernism*, Eslöv, Symposion, 341 pp., is a doctoral dissertation that examines the modernism of the 1940s with its marginalization of women writers; it discusses how and why the canonized image of poetic modernism has become an exclusively male affair. A similar impression is given through literary critics of the period: contributions by women modernists have been largely ignored. The study tries to rectify this marginalization by emphasizing in particular H.'s love poetry and its important role at the time, not least in its affinity with Erik Lindegren, and as a main genre of the 1940s.

JERSILD, PER CHRISTIAN. R. Shideler, 'Zola and the problem of the objective narrator in Per Olov Enquist and Per Christian Jersild', Houe, *Documentarism*, 120–34.

JOHNSON, EYVIND. U. Linde, 'Själens polyfoni', pp. vii-xvii of Eyvind Johnson, *Herr Clerk Vår Mästare*, ed. Örjan Lindberger (Svenska klassiker), Svenska Akademien–Atlantis, xvii + 351 pp., the year-book of the J. Society, is the first publication of the novel *Minnas*, 1928, in its original and unabbreviated form. F. Strauss, 'Eyvind Johnsons Stad i ljus. Eine semio-narratologische Lektüre', *Glienke Vol.*, 243–64.

JÄNDEL, RAGNAR. Bengt Jändel, *Ragnar Jändel. En levnadsskildring*, Jämjö, Jändelsällskapet, 334 pp., is a son's biography of his father written as early as 1949 and only recently edited by the author's widow and published. J., who belongs to the first generation of working-class writers, is today largely forgotten; possibly this unique and well-informed biography might help to reawaken interest in him, the more so as it includes numerous quotations from J.'s works together with knowledgeable and objective analyses. This might well prove to be a positive asset today when his poetry is largely unknown, but in 1949 it was a disadvantage for the publishing house; it consequently turned down the biography with a request for a shorter version which never materialized.

KOCH, MARTIN. I. Algulin, 'Berättaren Martin Koch', Algulin, *Traditioner*, 233–53.

KYRKLUND, WILLY. Paul Norlén, '*Textens villkor': a Study of Willy Kyrklund's Prose Fiction* (AUS, Stockholm Studies in History of Literature, 38), Almqvist & Wiksell International, 1997, vi + 240 pp., is a doctoral dissertation focusing on the construction of K.'s texts, primarily the short texts that make up the bulk of his production; it is K.'s 'novels' that have received the most critical attention to date. K.'s persistent 'genre-bending' is analysed, as is the element of intertextuality and the construction of the texts in terms of genre, conventions, and reader expectations, not to mention their humour. The concluding chapter deals with *Polyfem förvandlad*, 1964, 'a book which might well serve as a model of the author's entire œuvre'. J. van Luxemburg, 'Medea's murders: stories for children and literates', *Törnqvist Vol.*, 137–59, on K.'s *Medea från Mbongo* and P. Lysander and S. Osten, *Medeas barn*.

LAGERKVIST, PÄR. I. Algulin, 'Pär Lagerkvists kortprosa', Algulin, *Traditioner*, 254–65. *Parnass*, no. 1, is devoted to L.

LARSSON, BJÖRN. L. Thompson, 'Björn Larsson', *SBR*. no.2:2. T. Geddes, 'Björn Larsson's *Long John Silver*', *ib.*, 10–13; the issue includes several translations of L.'s works.

LIDMAN, SARA. Birgitta Holm, *Sara Lidman — i liv och text,* Bonniers, 472 pp., is the first exhaustive monograph on L. and her works. L.'s first novel, published in 1953, revealed her deep affinity for her native northern Sweden and the village in which she has her roots. Holm shows how L. went on to be not only a significant literary figure, but also a person to be reckoned with in the international political arena, protesting against nuclear weapons, colonialism and racial prejudice, and the Vietnam War. When L. returns to portraying her home village in the late 1970s she is able to view it from a global perspective, and her five-volume suite describing the arrival of the railway in that part of Sweden at the end of the 19th c. can be read as an account of the development of modern Sweden. Holm has had unique access to L.'s private archive and letters, and has interviewed her at length. The result is an important life-and-letters monograph which will benefit future research. T. Tchesnokova, 'Sara Lidman and the art of narration in *The Tar Valley*', Houe, *Documentarism,* 174–78.

LINDEGREN, ERIK. I. Algulin, 'Ung man utan väg', Algulin, *Traditioner,* 117–39; 'Modernism som medvetet känsloliv', *ib.,* 140–48.

LINDGREN, ASTRID. Gabriele Cromme, *Astrid Lindgren und die Autarkie der Weiblichkeit. Literarische Darstellung von Frauen und Mädchen in ihrem Gesamtwerk,* Hamburg, Kovac, 1996, 375 pp., is a doctoral dissertation; it concludes that there are no stereotype heroines, and that the untypical girl is the rule in L. Although adult females are often traditional wives and mothers, there are also magically powerful figures, such as Pippi, the witch, and Ronia's mother who rules her menfolk supremely. As a thoroughly modern writer, L. portrays unquestionable equality between girls and boys, men and women, balanced by equally natural female qualities. Werner Fischer-Nielsen, *Astrid Lindgren og kristendommen — set gennem Pippi, Emil og Grynet,* Valby, Unitas, 117 pp., is a Danish book which examines Christian background, traditions and faith in L.'s works; it is less convincing when it traces parallels between the stories and the Bible.

LINDGREN, TORGNY. Magnus Nilsson, *Sanningen som vilja och föreställning. En studie av Torgny Lindgrens roman Till sanningens lov och dess förhållande till Arthur Schopenhauers filosofi* (Scripta minora, 32), Växjö U.P., 1996, 38 pp., examines the importance of Schopenhauer for L.'s novel, not only on a textual level, but also as a polemic against his pessimism.

LJUNGQUIST, WALTER. Bo Georgii-Hemming, *Träd. Ett försök till lacansk läsning av Walter Ljungquists berättelser särskilt Jerk Dandelinsviten* (SLIUU, 33), Almquist & Wiksell International, 1997, 412 pp., is a doctoral dissertation which focuses on L.'s works in order to illustrate Jacques Lacan's psychoanalytical models, and makes use of his understanding of man as linguistically created and defined. It attempts to show that literature can help to bring psychoanalytical insight, and that the series resembles the psychoanalytical process. The methodological basis is mainly two of Lacan's texts in *Écrits*, 'Fonction et champ de la parole et du langage en psychanalyse' (1953) and 'L'instance de la lettre dans l'inconscient ou la raison depuis Freud' (1957).

LO-JOHANSSON, IVAR. Ola Holmgren, *Ivar Lo-Johansson — Frihetens väg* (Litterära profiler), Natur och Kultur, 403 pp., is a comprehensive study of L. and his works over more than 60 years, a prominent figure not only in the literary history, but also the social history of Sweden. Usually the emphasis is on L., the social reformer, the 'ombudsman' for the impoverished agricultural proletariat in the 1930s, and the spokesman for more humane care of the elderly in the early 1950s; he has always been closely identified with decisive social and cultural changes in modern Swedish history. Holmgren focuses his interest on other aspects, using psychology to understand and interpret L.'s struggle to break free from his background and become a writer, and stressing the recurring conflicts: realism versus romance, the individual versus the collective, dream versus reality.

LUNDKVIST, ARTUR. SALV, the L. Society Sällskapet Artur Lundkvists vänner, together with the publishing house Aiolos, has launched a journal devoted to L. (four issues per year). The first issue includes: I. Algulin, 'Artur Lundkvist och Afrika', *Vindrosor & moteld*, no. 1–2 : 2–16.

MARTINSON, HARRY. K. Olsoni, 'En vandring i förnedring och försoning', pp. 329–61 of Harry Martinson, *Vägen till Klockrike*, ed. Stefan Sandelin, Harry Martinson-sällskapet–Bonniers, 374 pp., the third volume of the collected works currently being published in ten volumes; the afterword stresses M.'s early concern with environmental and ecological issues, something which led to accusations of him being a reactionary and grumbler; now time has finally caught up with him. More than ever before, his way of thinking is needed, based as it is on respect for all living creatures, and a warning not to let technology take over both man and nature. S. Sandelin, 'Ett livsspråk i vinden', pp. 311–43 of Harry Martinson, *Dikter 1953–1973*, ed. Stefan Sandelin, Harry Martinson-sällskapet–Bonniers, 371 pp.; the fourth volume of this welcome and excellent new ten-volume edition of the collected works includes the five collections of poetry in their original form as published by M. from the 1950s onwards. In his informative concluding remarks, Sandelin discusses their reception, condemns the rather unjustified negative criticism of the three later works, and analyses individual poems at length. I. Algulin, 'Gestalterna i Aniara', Algulin, *Traditioner*, 186–93.

MYRDAL, JAN.   Cecilia Cervin, *Det illojala barnets uppror. Studier kring Jan Myrdals självbiografiska texter*, Hägglunds, 1997, 631 pp., is a doctoral dissertation.

NORÉN, LARS.   C. Sjöholm, 'Nytt om Norén', *TidLit*, 27.2:115–26, discusses recent works on N. by Lars Nylander and Mikael van Reis (see *YWMLS*, 59:922).

PARLAND, HENRY.   Per Stam, *Krapula. Henry Parland och romanprojektet Sönder* (SSLF, 612 and SLIUU, 35), Helsinki — Stockholm, Almqvist & Wiksell International, 408 pp., is a doctoral dissertation on 'the most modern of modernists', which makes use of previously overlooked archive material, such as letters to and from Gunnar Björling and Rabbe Enckell. The focus of interest is on the unfinished novel project which P. started in Lithuania a year before his early death from scarlet fever. The dissertation emphasizes the importance of Finland-Swedish Modernism, Proust, and Russian Formalism for the conception of this metafiction which deals with the writing of a novel of the same name.

ROSENDAHL, SVEN.   Bengt Emil Johnson and Staffan Söderblom, *Legohjon åt alltet. En bok om Sven Rosendahl*, Bonniers, 343 pp., attempts to rehabilitate this marginalized and largely forgotten regional writer whose primary achievement was to make remote parts of Värmland and Lappland his universe. He wrote about their flora and fauna and accelerating environmental destruction, topics that did not help to improve his reputation among critics, in spite of his considerable literary qualities worthy of more recognition. A bibliography with listed source material would have been welcome.

SJÖBERG, BIRGER.   *Musik och lyrik*, ed. Eva Hættner Aurelius, Johan Svedjedal, and Lars Helge Tunving, Vänersborg, Birger Sjöbergsällskapet, 193 pp., is an anthology of essays on S.'s career as a journalist as well as articles and texts by S., among them three reconstructed texts by G. Axberger with comments, and includes: B. Lindberg, '"alla damhandskar som sprucko vid applåderna". Birger Sjöberg och musiklivet i Helsingborg' (9–55); J. Svedjedal, '"Tomtebolycka önskas Mälardrottningen". Birger Sjöberg och invigningen av Stockholms stadshus' (116–21), an extract from his coming S. biography *Skrivaredans*; Id., 'August Peterson och Birger Sjöberg' (169–81), on S.'s first biographer.

STRANDBERG, INGELA.   L. Sjögren, 'Fast naknare nu. Om Ingela Strandbergs poesi', *BLM*, 67.3:24–28.

STRÖM, EVA.   E.-B. Ståhl, 'Åkra. Eva Ström om det bortvända fadersansiktet, utblottelsen och språktillåtelsen', *Samlaren*, 118, 1997[1998]:122–51.

SUND, LARS. K. Saranpa, 'Att leka med historien. Lars Sunds *Colorado Avenue*', *HLS*, 73:267–79 (SSLF, 614), explores the novel as a complement to a traditionally historical narrative.

SUNDMAN, PER OLOF. Per Svensson, *Frostviken. Ett reportage om Per Olof Sundman, nazismen och tigandet*, Bonniers, 224 pp., is a biographical account by an investigative journalist of S.'s involvement in Swedish Nazi organizations in his youth. Not surprisingly, it leaves unanswered the main questions it raises: did S.'s own secrecy about the affair turn him into a writer? Did the secret itself gradually kill off his talent as a writer? Ö. Lindberger, 'Per Olof Sundman och Frostviken', *NT*, 74:313–22, questions the almost symbolic overtones that Svensson attaches to the name of the place where S. lived, Frostviken, and his frozen silence; instead he stresses that it was here S. managed successfully to combine his literary and political careers in local government, and write his most important works. L. Jacobsson, 'Översten kom tillbaka från Ingenting-alls', *OB*, 6:85–116, argues that Svensson's analysis in Frostviken is prejudiced and unsatisfactory; rather than guilt for earlier Nazi sympathies, he suggests more mundane and obvious reasons for S.'s silence as a writer towards the end of his life, such as overwork and writer's block. R. McGregor, 'The silence of Per Olof Sundman: a Swedish novelist's guilty secret', *SBR*, 1:25–31, argues that S. chose to use the lessons he had learnt from his mistaken early political beliefs in his writing, and finds it is gratifying that the recent revelations about S.'s past have stimulated a renewal of interest in his works. The *SBR* issue includes a translation of S.'s short story 'Lek', 32–36, his first half-hearted attempt to break his silence in 1957. L. Bäckström, 'Lek', *BLM*, 67.1:15–19, expands on his earlier theme that the story reveals something essential about the trauma which became S.'s most important asset as a writer, and his insuperable problem. W. Butt, '"Ett stort och märkligt moraliskt botgöringsdrama"? Zu P.O. Sundmans *Berättelsen om Såm*', *Glienke Vol.*, 181–91, disputes the view that the novel is a showdown in disguise with the Nazism of S.'s youth, and argues convincingly that instead it challenges the political correctness of the early 1970s, the ideas of social engineering and the welfare state model. P. Houe, 'Per Olof Sundman's documentarism: knowledgeable representation of unknowable man', Houe, *Documentarism*, 165–73.

SÄFVE, TORBJÖRN. J.-C. Hussais, 'Lapplands svarta får. Intervju med Torbjörn Säfve', *BLM*, 67.3:37–40.

SÖDERGRAN, EDITH. J. Hedberg, 'Edith Södergrans anknytning till finlandssvensk poesi', *Horisont*, 45.3:13–27. H. O. Andersen, 'Nietzsche og Södergran', *ib.*, 28–37. B. Rönnholm, 'Forskarens klassiker — och läsarens. I marginalen till en recension', *ib.*, 5:13–16.

SÖDERHJELM, ALMA.   M. Engman, 'Fersens sista älskarinna',
FT: 305–13, on S.'s research of the period.

TAUBE, EVERT.   Mikael Timm, *Evert Taube. Livet som konst, konsten
som liv*, Bonniers, 617 pp., is the first comprehensive biography of T.,
the troubadour and Swedish national poet, an impressive, amply
illustrated work. T., larger than life and a myth in his own lifetime,
dramatized his life in poetry and prose. Most of what he wrote is
autobiographical, but at the same time also very unreliable; this must
be problematic for any biographer, and the very title indicates the
difficulty of separating life and work. The biography is obviously
intended mainly for the general public and not primarily for literary
scholars; however, it would have been helpful for future research if
the bibliography and footnotes had been much more comprehensive,
even if this book is only a 'stroll in the fragrant gardens of the text'.
Den Gyldene Fredens skål! Texter om Taube och om Freden, ed. Leif Bergman,
Evert Taube-sällskapet–Proprius, 240 pp., is the T. Society year-book
for 1998 and includes texts by and on T., and also on the famous
18th-c. tavern Freden and its many associations with various writers
and other cultural personalities over the centuries, not least its
resurrection thanks to Anders Zorn and others. A lot of its fame is
associated with Bellman; in fact it seems it has less to do with the poet
himself than with the origin of the society Bellmans Minne.

THORVALL, KERSTIN.   P. Nilson, 'Kontakten som försvann.
Intervju med Kerstin Thorvall', *BLM*, 67.3:5–14. J.-H. Swahn, 'Det
mest kvinnliga', *ib.*, 2–4, on Cora Sandel's influence on T., Anna-
Karin Palm, and Mirjam Tuominen.

TIDHOLM, THOMAS.   G. Berggren, 'Thomas Tidholm', *SBR*,
no.2:33; the issue includes a number of translations.

TIKKANEN, HENRIK.   'Henrik Tikkanen om vägen till författarska-
pet. "Därför denna underliga aforistiska stil . . ."', ed. I.-B. Wik,
HLS, 73:215–42 (SSLF, 614), is an interview dating from June, 1976
with T., who talks about his literary models and claims that he
became a writer by first being an artist.

TROTZIG, BIRGITTA.   I. Armin and C. Ekholm, 'Trotzigs humor.
Essä om *Sjukdomen*', *BLM*, 67.4:58–63.

VÄRING, ASTRID.   Karin Edlund, 'Länge ville man förmena oss
rätten att ha en historia'. *Studier i Astrid Värings biografi och författarskap
fram till andra världskriget*, Umeå U.P., 133 pp., is a dissertation and an
attempt to rejuvenate general interest in a forgotten local Västerbotten writer from the unfamiliar Norrland region that was marginalized as a colony even as late as the 1920s. This is reflected not
only in the literature of Norrland at the turn of the century, but also
in V.'s novels from the 1920s and her four-volume family chronicle
from the 1930s set in the 19th c.

WÄGNER, ELIN. *Flory Gate 1904–1998* (Elin Wägner-sällskapet, 9), Växjö, 32 pp., includes tributes in memory of W.'s friend Flory Gate by E. H. Linder, H. Forsås-Scott, L. Trojer, E. Hermodsson, and K. Sahlström. Ria Wägner, *Faster* (Elin Wägner-sällskapet, 2), Växjö, 15 pp., is a reprint from 1991.

5

SLAVONIC LANGUAGES*

I. CZECH STUDIES

LANGUAGE**

By Marie Nováková and Jana Papcunová,
Ústav pro jazyk český Akademie věd České republiky, Prague

1. General and Bibliographies

A significant topic of current Czech linguistics is the Czech National Corpus compiled and processed by lexicographers from the Czech Language Institute and from the Faculty of Arts of Charles University. The introductory paper by F. Čermák in *Procs* (Brno), 9–14, sums up the theoretical and methodical fundamentals which the Czech National Corpus is built on. The monograph *Český jazyk* is a result of taking part in a large international project on Slavonic languages and focuses on the functioning and development of Czech in the last 50 years. J. Kořenský writes on the language situation (15–20), on the functional stratification of Czech (61–94), on language law and politics (95–101), and M. Krčmová (117–42), on the care of Czech. O. Uličný, *Práce z dějin slavistiky*, 20 : 129–34, presents interesting ideas concerning contemporary codificatory conceptions in Czech. Furthermore, several other volumes covering a wide spectrum of themes are to be noted here: *Česká slavistika. České přednášky pro 12. mezinárodní sjezd slavistů. Krakov 27.8.–2.9. 1998*, ed. Emilie Bláhová, Eva Šlaufová, Slavomír Wollman, and Miloš Zelenka, Prague, Euroslavica, 288 pp., includes Czech papers from the International Slavist Congress in Cracow (the same essays have also been published in *Slavia*, 67, with the same pagination); *Dialoganalyse 6. Referate der 6. Arbeitstagung Prag 1996*, 2 vols, ed. Světla Čmejrková, Jana Hoffmannová, Olga Müllerová, and Jindra Světlá, Tübingen, Niemeyer, 558, 473 pp.; *Pocta 650*; and two festschrifts: *Panevová Vol*; and *Jelínek Vol.*

A remarkable book by Václav Jamek, *O patřičnosti v jazyce*, Prague, Nakladatelství Franze Kafky, 204 pp., is a collection of brilliant essays

* For languages using the Cyrillic alphabet names are transliterated according to the Library of Congress system, omitting diacritics and ligatures.
** This contribution has been written thanks to the support of programme 28, Language Data Processing, Nr. K 3083603.

devoted to Czech language culture and correctness, offering a different view on these questions.

BIBLIOGRAPHIES. Ludmila Stěpanovová, *Historie a etymologie českých rčení. Bibliografie pramenů*, Prague, Karolinum, 132 pp., is an interesting bibliographic contribution to the history and etymology of Czech set phrases and idioms. Marie Nováková, *Bibliografie české onomastiky 1993–1994*, Prague, Ústav pro jazyk český AV ČR, 72 pp., compiles entries on Czech onomastics (536 items). Zdeňka Rachůnková and Michaela Řeháčková, **11. mezinárodní sjezd slavistů. Bratislava 1993. Bibliografie*, Prague, Národní knihovna ČR, 365 pp., record given papers, proceedings, books, and journals published on this occasion. Finally, two personal bibliographies should be mentioned: J. Hasil, *PLS*, 41:74–79, submits a selective bibliography of the dialectal works of Jaromír Bělič; bibliographies of Milan Jelínek and Jarmila Panevová appear in *Jelínek Vol.*, 15–39, covering 1947–97, and in *Panevová Vol.*, 293–307, covering 1961–97, respectively.

2. HISTORY OF THE LANGUAGE

An erudite study by J. Pečírková, *Interpretation of the Bible*, ed. Jože Krašovec, Ljubljana, Slovenska akademija znanosti in umetnosti, 1167–1200, follows the development of Czech translations of the Bible from the Old Czech until the present ones. A collection, *Jazyk a literatura v historické perspektivě*, ed. Dobrava Moldanová, Ústí nad Labem, Univ. J. E. Purkyně, 149 pp., comprises several interesting articles: J. Krtková (92–95) writes on the preposition *ot/od* in the Old Czech Chronicle of the so-called Dalimil; Z. Millerová (96–99) analyses names of female characters in ethical pamphlets at the beginning of the 16th c.; K. Kamiš (60–91) is a diachronic description of the Old Czech locative. *K jazyku a stylu českých barokních textů*, ed. Milan David, České Budějovice, Jihočeská univ., 127 pp., includes essays by A. Jaklová (8–41), Z. Holub (42–62), J. Alexová (78–89), M. Janečková (90–109), (117–27), and B. Junková (110–16), on the language and style of Czech Baroque authors. P. Kosek, *SPFFBU — řada jazykovědná*, A46, 131–41, sketches the development of linking expressions derived from the word *brže* (based on material of Baroque literary documents); S. Romportl, *ib.*, 95–100, gives information on the development of the imperative in Czech. J. Skutil, *Vlastivědný věstník moravský*, 50:69–72, comments on the language and stylistic features of Czech Jesuit documents from 1573–1773. J. Hubáček, *NŘ*, 81 : 92–99, studies comparisons in the prose works of Jan Amos Komenský; Id., *ČL*, 46:339–69, is a syntactic and stylistic analysis of Komenský's works. R. Adam, *SaS*, 59 : 200–06, presents a phonological and morphological analysis and, 249–55, a syntactic and lexical analysis of a Czech Baroque play from the 1680s. J. Kraus, *Jelínek Vol.*, 91–95, elucidates the roots and development of Czech and European purism.

3. PHONETICS AND PHONOLOGY

Z. Palková, *Dialoganalyse*, 6.1 : 527–34, deals with the phonetic form of spoken dialogues; L. Lízalová, *ib.*, 535–41, investigates the intonation of Czech and Russian dialogues; T. Dickins, *SEER*, 76 : 201–33, analyses vocalization of prepositions (*k/ke, ku, s/se, v/ve, nad/nade*, etc.) in both spoken and written Czech. O. Martincová, *Slavia*, 67 : 143–48, describes the repertoire of neologic variants from the phonological and morphological point of view and deals with the conditions of the integration of loan words (especially from English) into Czech. Jiřina Hůrková, *Próza versus poezie*, Prostějov, Ipos artama, 41 pp., analyses the acoustic structure (intonation and rhythm) of prose works by Karel Čapek, Vladislav Vančura and Bohumil Hrabal.

4. MORPHOLOGY AND WORD FORMATION

A detailed monograph by Zbyněk Šiška, *Bázový morfematický slovník češtiny*, Olomouc, Univ. Palackého, 191 pp., describes the morphemic segmentation of the word in Czech and compiles a dictionary of root morphemes and of segmental words and forms. M. Krčmová, *Český jazyk*, 164–77, is basic information on Czech morphology; P. Karlík and N. Nübler, *SaS*, 59 : 105–12, discuss the substantivization of verbs by suffixes, while mathematical linguists K. Osolsobě and K. Pala, *ib.*, 265–77, treat the frequency of verb paradigms and, *SPFFBU — řada jazykovědná*, A 46, 77–94, of substantive paradigms. P. Karlík, *ib.*, 77–94, classifies the Czech adnominal genitive case. J. Vondráček, *NŘ*, 81 : 29–37, tries to elucidate the boundaries of particles and interjections, the distinguishing of which is rather problematic in Czech; J. Obdržálek, *ib.*, 124–28, focuses on the declension of names of physical units. K. Šenkeřík, *Pocta 650*, 165–79, examines verbal aspect in Czech and compares it to German.

5. SYNTAX AND TEXT

A major work in this section is an extended treatise by Miroslav Grepl and Petr Karlík, *Skladba češtiny*, Olomouc, Votobia, 503 pp. The authors expound syntactic phenomena, standard and substandard, from today's Czech. P. Sgall, *ČMF*, 80 : 1–11, writes a study on Czech word order, discussing specifically the impact of context and topic-focus articulation on word order and comparing Czech, English and German. Theoretical problems of Czech syntax and methods of its processing for the Czech National Corpus are the topic of an article by J. Hajič, E. Hajičová, J. Panevová, and P. Sgall, *SaS*, 59 : 168–77. They pay attention both to dependency and analytical syntax and to questions of valency. They deal with valency independently, too: J. Panevová, *ib.*, 1–13, applies the theory of valency to the phenomena of non-central character and the other word classes; P. Sgall, *ib.*, 15–29, sketches the formal treatment of valency; A. Horák, *Procs* (Brno), 61–66, presents a semantic classification of Czech verbs according to their valency; J. Hajič, *Panevová Vol.*, 106–32, reports on building a syntactically annotated corpus and the Prague dependency treebank; S. Čmejrková, *ib.*, 75–87, is on the reflexive pronoun *svůj* from the syntactic point of view. F. Štícha, *LPr*, 8 : 73–80, examines yes-no questions and their forms and meaning in Czech, English, French, and German; P. Karlík, *NŘ*, 81 : 232–39, writes on complex sentences with *když už*, *tak už* following the question of phrasemization of this linking expression; P. Adamec, *PLS*, 41 : 55–58, is on semantics of the so-called 'small words' (e.g. *to*) and implies four variants of syntactic use of these expressions.

6. ORTHOGRAPHY

Description of changes in the efficiency and complexity of the Czech writing system over more than seven centuries is the topic of an essay by K. Kučera, *SaS*, 59 : 178–99; M. Sedláček, on the contrary, *Český jazyk*, 152–63, concentrates only on changes in orthography in the last period (since 1945). O. Uličný, *Jelínek Vol.* 101–06, studies two cases of codificatory suppression of morphemic principle in Czech orthography (suffixes -*ismus*/-*izmus* and prefixes *des-*, *dis-*, *dyz-*, *trans-*) and shows some ways of solving theoretical questions of the graphic adaptation of loan words into Czech.

7. LEXICOLOGY AND PHRASEOLOGY

1998 has been a fruitful year for both Czech diachronic and synchronic lexicography. Olga Martincová et al., *Nová slova v češtině. Slovník neologizmů*, Prague, Academia, 356 pp., compile a necessary dictionary based on material from 1985–95. The authors cover the newest Czech vocabulary, loan words and those words, the meaning of which has changed recently. The work on another important dictionary continues, too. The team of authors, led by J. Pečírková, has published further the 22nd issue of the *Old Czech Dictionary*,

prazápis — *pronésti sě,* ed. Igor Němec, Prague, Academia, 112 pp.
Olga Martincová and Radoslava Brabcová, *Malý slovník jazykovědných termínů,* Prague, Charles Univ., 118 pp., compile a useful dictionary of linguistic terms.

K. Pala and P. Rychlý, *Procs* (Brno), 97–102, is on the first results of work with the corpus ESO (containing 61,001,371 Czech word forms) for lexicographic research into Czech; J. Filipec, *Český jazyk,* 180–96, discusses the dynamics of Czech vocabulary in the 20th c.; R. Brabcová, *Slavia,* 67 : 107–12, documents social-political changes and their reflection in the lexicon; P. Klötzerová, *SaS,* 59 : 277–80, writes on lexical phrasemes in Czech; Z. Rusínová, *SPFFBU — řada jazykovědná,* A46, 101–06, on diminutives in phraseology and she, *Jelínek Vol.,* 113–19, on diminutives in phraseological comparisons. A paper entitled 'Srovnávací studium sémantických modelů a lexikografický popis' by I. Němec and M. Homolková, *Slavia,* 67 : 93–98, exploits the explanatory method of description of Czech synsemantic words and defines the meaning of lexical units in the function of a preposition, conjunction and particle. Moreover, M. Homolková, *NŘ,* 81 : 70–79, informs on the methodology of diachronic lexicography and shows the semantic structure of a headword using a headword from the Old Czech Dictionary (adjective *prostý*) as an example. As far as etymology is concerned, M. Vajdlová, *Varia 7. Zborník zo 7. kolokvia mladých jazykovedcov,* ed. Mira Nábělková, Bratislava, Slovenská jazykovedná spoločnosť, 139–47, refers to substantivized adjectives denoting charges, fees, taxes, and wages in Old Czech, and A. Černá, *NŘ,* 81 : 189–96, analyses the oldest Czech names for fingers.

8. SEMANTICS AND PRAGMATICS

From a great number of studies devoted to these questions we note here the most important ones: Petr Fidelius, *Řeč komunistické moci,* Prague, Triáda, 216 pp., is a semantic analysis of the language in the Czech Communist era. The study is based on detailed material from *Rudé právo* in the 1970s and its aim is to show the functions of language in that political situation and the language deformation of that time. K. Trost, *Jazyk a kultura vyjadřování,* 135–43, submits a semantic classification of abstract nouns in Czech; M. Friš, *SaS,* 59 : 113–20, follows semantic classes in a Czech scientific (mathematical) text.

M. Hrdlička, *SaS,* 59 : 96–104, describes factors which impact upon the choice of prepositions in Czech; I. Kolářová, *NŘ,* 81 : 118–23, deals with the meaning and functions of the word *tedy (teda)* in discourse. H. Donátová, *Čeština,* 9 : 33–47, examines the structure of shopping dialogues; O. Müllerová, *Człowiek—dzieło—sacrum,* ed.

Stanisław Gajda, Opole, Uniwersytet Opolski, 301–08, focuses on dialogic features of a Mass; then, she, *Dialoganalyse*, 6.2 : 59–63, deals with communication breakdowns in dialogue between institutions and the public. Furthermore, the author and J. Hoffmannová, *Slavia*, 67 : 129–36, also treat institutional communication: doctor-patient dialogue and discourses in old people's homes; similarly, J. Světlá, *Dialoganalyse*, 6.2 : 203–08, analyses phone dialogues with the fire brigade; J. Holšánová, *ib.*, 253–60, studies the use of quotations in dialogue about ethnicity; S. Čmejrková, *ib.*, 281–89, gives the results of some questionnaire research among students of Prague grammar schools concerning the strategies of the mass media in addressing teenagers. Finally, J. Hoffmannová, *Słowo i czas*, ed. Stanisław Gajda and Anna Pietryga, Opole, Uniwersytet Opolski, 151–58, analyses the discourse of elderly people.

9. SOCIOLINGUISTICS AND DIALECTOLOGY

Jarmila Bachmannová, *Podkrkonošský slovník*, Prague, Academia, 265 pp., records the Northeast Bohemian dialect in the region of Železný Brod and compiles a great number of technical glass terms. Jiří Běl, *Jak se mluvilo na Přešticku. Z pozůstalosti přeštického učitele Václava Vacka*, Přeštice, Základní škola, 517 pp., publishes a dictionary of the West Bohemian dialect in the environs of Přeštice. J. Balhar, *Jelínek Vol*, 193–98, follows unification in dialectal declension; Z. Hladká, *SPFFBU — řada jazykovědná*, A46, 107–12, on formal diminution in folk plant names; J. Siatkowski, *Pocta 650*, 131–37, reports on Czech dialects in Poland.

SOCIOLINGUISTICS AND SLANG. A. Rangelová, *Slavia*, 67 :149–54, writes on sociolinguistic aspects of new lexical units from the sphere of drug addiction (in comparison with Bulgarian); E. Věšínová, *NŘ*, 81 : 21–28, misses 'woman's sexual slang' in Czech, which could express nuances of modern American texts (from the viewpoint of a translator of American literature). Kryštof Bajger et al., *Šestijazyčný slovník vulgarismů*, Český Těšín, Gabi, 189 pp., is a list of Czech vulgarisms with English, German, French, Spanish, Slovak, and Polish equivalents. *Sborník přednášek z 6. konference o slangu a argotu v Plzni 15.-16. září 1998*, ed. Lumír Klimeš, Plzeň, Západočeská univ., 154 pp., includes: Z. Tichá (9–13), on the lexicographical approach to slang materials; M. Nováková (14–20), on slang and text corpus; R. Blatná (33–39), on slang in newspaper texts; M. Krčmová (54–59), on family slang; Z. Suda (65–69), on football slang; M. Grygerková (83–86), on ecclesiastical slang; J. Málková (103–09), on mountaineering slang; K. Kamiš (126–31), on Romany argot expressions in

Czech; and M. David (145–50), on the discourse of Czech political prisoners in the 1950s.

10. STYLISTICS

Hana Srpová, *K aktualizaci a automatizaci v současné psané publicistice*, Ostrava, Ostravská univ., 168 pp., elucidates functional styles, specifically the journalistic style and its specific devices. Jiří Homoláč, *A ta černá kronika!*, Brno, Doplněk, 171 pp., analyses the language and style of reports on criminality. E. Minářová, *Jelínek Vol.*, 57–62, writes on the stylistic form of present-day advertising; J. Hoffmannová, *ib.*, 49–55, presents characteristics of the conversational style of Czech students and she, *NŘ*, 81 : 100–11, focuses on the language and style of players of computer games; V. Staněk, *ib.*, 13–20, on the language and style of radio reports.

ASPECTS OF THE LANGUAGE OF INDIVIDUAL WRITERS. P. Mareš, *PLS*, 41 : 101–12, deals with multilingualism in Czech prose works of the 19th c.; Id., *ČL*, 46 : 498–517, on multilingualism in a novel by Josef Škvorecký. J. Kraus, *ib.*, 269–73, compares polemics by František Xaver Šalda and Tomáš Garrigue Masaryk; K. Sgallová, *ib.*, 79–85, analyses the rhyme of Vítězslav Nezval; Z. Hladká, *Jelínek Vol.*, 81–90, follows dialectisms in the poems of Jan Skácel; O. Hausenblas, *ČL*, 46 : 518–36, deals with substandard language in a short novel by Jan Trefulka; and J. Hoffmanová, *Człowiek—dzieło—sacrum*, 389–95, concentrates on the language and multilingualism in Czech post-modern poetry. F. Štícha, *NŘ*, 81 : 1–12, analyses and compares three Czech translations of a novel by Franz Werfel; A. Schwabiková, *Souvislosti*, 2 : 95–102, follows the development of translations from English into Czech by comparing three translations of 'Babbit' by Sinclair Lewis.

11. ONOMASTICS

It is necessary to mention three monographs dealing with anthroponyms in this section: Jana Pleskalová, *Tvoření nejstarších českých osobních jmen*, Brno, Masaryk Univ., 158 pp., dwells on word-formative analysis of the oldest Czech anthroponyms in written documents from the 9th till the first half of the 13th c. Josef Beneš, *Německá příjmení u Čechů*, 2 vols, ed. Marie Nováková, Ústí nad Labem, Univ. J. E. Purkyně, 359, 242 pp., compiles extensive material of German surnames of Czechs, analyses and explains them. Jiří Kučera and Jiří Zeman, *Výslovnost a skloňování cizích osobních jmen v češtině. Anglická osobní jména*, Hradec Králové, Gaudeamus, 141 pp., deal with the pronunciation and declension of foreign first names and with their adaptation into Czech.

AOn, 38, includes: J. Malenínská (28–31), on the toponym *Opyš* and synonymous common nouns; L. Olivová-Nezbedová (43–68), on street names in the cadastre of the city of Choceň; J. Panáček (69–82), on Czech and German names of castles in the region of Česká Lípa; the editors of the journal publish the third chapter of the dissertation by V. Šmilauer (87–150), on the formation of place names from common nouns. *Najnowsze przemiany nazewnicze*, ed. Ewa Jakus-Borkowa and Krystyna Nowik, Wa, Energeia, 433 pp., includes: L. Olivová-Nezbedová (175–80), on changes in minor place names in the Czech Republic after 1945; J. Malenínská (385–400) is a survey of German dialectal common nouns used in Czech oronyms. *13. slovenská onomastická konferencia Modra-Piesok 2.-4. októbra 1997. Zborník materiálov*, ed. Milan Majtán and Pavol Žigo, Bratislava, Univ. Komenského, 195 pp., includes: L. Olivová-Nezbedová (79–90), on Czech minor place names derived from the names of vegetation; J. Malenínská (99–103), on the hydronymic root morpheme **brl-* in minor place names; M. Knappová (139–43), on diachronic and synchronic research of anthroponyms; and N. Bayerová (187–90), on Slovak surnames in the region of Ostrava. L. Olivová-Nezbedová, *Slavia*, 67 : 87–92, reports on the processing of the prepared dictionary of Czech minor place names on computer; A. Erhart, *ib.*, 289–94, contributes on the etymology of the ethnonym *Čech*; M. Knappová, *PLS*, 41 : 47–53, on nicknames in present-day Czech; M. Harvalík, *SaS*, 59 : 259–65, on the classification of exonyms.

12. LANGUAGE IN CONTACT AND COMPARATIVE STUDIES

Helena Běličová, *Nástin porovnávací morfologie spisovných jazyků slovanských*, Prague, Karolinum, 222 pp., is actually a comparison of Czech and other Slavonic languages. She, *PLS*, 41 : 5–16, confronts the grammatical structure of Czech and Slovak against the background of standard Slavonic languages; J. Anderš, *Slavia*, 67 : 19–23, discusses Czech-Bulgarian language contacts; E. Lotko, *Český jazyk*, 33–43, compares Czech with Polish, while K. Oliva, *Slavia*, 67 : 57–60, compares Czech and Polish vocabulary; M. Nábělková, *Pocta 650*, 93–101, comments on the state of Czech and Slovak after 1993; C. Avramová, *SPFFBU — řada jazykovědná*, A46, 143–50, writes on the word formation of new nouns denoting persons in Czech and Bulgarian.

E. Skála, *PLS*, 41 : 213–27, sums up the history and the present of Czech-German language contacts; M. Malinovský, *ČMF*, 80 : 65–75, focuses on sentence adverbials in Czech and English; J. Povejšil, *Český jazyk*, 43–51, is on the confrontation of Czech and German; K. Kamiš, *ib.*, 51–60, compares Czech and Romany.

13. CZECH ABROAD

A series of studies on Czech in Texas has been augmented by E. Eckert, *NŘ*, 81 : 38–49, who investigates inscriptions of Moravian origin on tombstones in Texas and the impact of English on Moravian dialects, which becomes evident in diacritics and in the form of names; S. Kloferová, *ib.*, 80–91, 169–78, examines the speech of young Viennese Czechs from the phonological, morphological and lexical point of view; N. Valášková, *Český lid*, 85 : 161–70, reports on the language situation of Czechs in Kazakhstan.

14. BILINGUAL DICTIONARIES

Nikolaj Savický, *Česko-ruský slovník neologismů*, Prague, Academia, 300 pp., records new expressions in Czech and Russian. Karel Kraft, *Česko-esperantský slovník*, Dobřichovice, Kava-Pech, 495 pp., is an extensive Czech-Esperanto dictionary. Slavko Krtalič, *Chorvatsko-český, česko-chorvatský slovník s nejpoužívanějšími konverzačními frázemi*, Ostrava, Montana, 231 pp., is the first Croat-Czech and Czech-Croat dictionary.

LITERATURE

POSTPONED

II. SLOVAK STUDIES

POSTPONED

III. POLISH STUDIES

LANGUAGE

By Nigel Gotteri, *University of Sheffield*

1. Appreciations and Surveys

M. Balowski, 'Theodor Bešta (5.02.1920–6.03.1996)', *PJ*, 1997, no. 8: 1–3, surveys the work of a Polonist at the Charles University in Prague. Z. Gałecki, 'O profesorze Tadeuszu Brajerskim wspomnienie', *PJ*, 1997, no. 7: 1–7; Z. Leszczyński, 'Profesor Tadeusz Brajerski (14 XI 1913–24 VII 1997)', *JPol*, 78: 161–64. E. Siatkowska, 'Wanda Budziszewska (1925–1995)', *SFPS*, 33, 1996: 15–20. H. Schaller, 'Erwin Koschmieder', *Slavia*, 1997: 51–57. E. Smułkowa, 'Antonina Obrębska-Jabłońska (1901–1994)', *SFPS*, 33, 1996: 21–26. K. Rymut, 'Witold Taszycki — w setną rocznicę urodzin', *Onomastica*, 42, 1997[1998]: 5–10. In addition to Taszycki, M. Kucała, 'O tych, co odeszli, wspomnienia rocznicowe', *JPol*, 78: 165–70, covers Lucjan Malinowski, Jan Łoś, Stanisław Szober, Kazimierz Nitsch, Stanisław Pigoń, Jerzy Kuryłowicz, Mikołaj Rudnicki, Alfred Zaręba, and Józef Reczek.

Polish linguists will be disappointed but not surprised by 'Slavistique belge — Bibliographie 1988–1997', *SlaG*, 25: 207–37, which is dominated by literature and history, and by Russian; it contains nothing on the Polish language. As valuable as ever, by contrast, is Z. Gałecki et al., 'Przegląd polskich prac językowych ogłoszonych drukiem w roku 1997', *PJ*, nos 1–2: 72–101. E. Teodorowicz-Hellman, 'O liście podpisanym "ręką własną" Mikołaja Reja z nagłowic, czyli o nie zbadanych zbiorach polskich w Riksarkivet w Sztokholmie', *JPol*, 78: 107–10, includes valuable bibliographical information.

2. Phonetics and Phonology

B. Chrząstowska et al., 'Defekty mowy', *Polonistyka*, 51: 67. K. Dobrogowska, 'Połączenia głoskowe w języku polskim', *Polonica*, 47, 1995: 5–36; and her, 'Grupy spółgłoskowe w krótkich tekstach języka polskiego', *ib.*, 67–74. K. Dobrogowska and A. Dobrogowski, 'Asymetria rozkładu długości sylab jako przejaw działania prawa Menzeratha', *Polonica*, 48, 1997: 209–24. J. Górka, 'Phonetische Probleme polnischer Deutschlernender', *ZNUJ*, 1210: 21–29, argues for an approach based on contrastive analysis, and draws attention to specific details of Polish pronunciation. J. Mędelska, 'Wymowa kowieńska w zwierciadle słownikowym (na podstawie *Słownika litewsko-polsko-rosyjskiego* z 1992 r.)', *PJ*, 1997, no. 7 : 27–39. J. Roman, 'Przywróćmy ćwiczenia ortofoniczne', *Polonistyka*, 51 : 85–89, is particularly useful for its section on the spoken language of young people (85–87). E. Stadnik, 'Phonemtypologie der slawischen Sprachen und ihre Bedeutung für die Erforschung der diachronen Phonologie', *ZSl*, 48 : 377–400, includes a clear statement of two coexisting norms of Polish pronunciation, with and without palatalization. Speakers adhere to one or the other, and the choice is not conditioned regionally. M. Wolan, 'O poprawną wymowę w szkole', *Polonistyka*, 51 : 79–84.

3. Morphology and Syntax

I. Bobrowski, 'Eksplicytność jako jedno z kryteriów opisów gramatycznych', *Polonica*, 48, 1997 : 5–10. R. Genis, '*Prze-* meaning and aspect, variant and invariant meaning. Some remarks on "pure" perfectivization; *prze-* as empty prefix', *ib.*, 191–208. B. Kreja, 'Glosy do "Słowotwórstwa języka doby staropolskiej..." pod red. K. Kleszczowej', *JPol*, 78 : 188–95. M. Krupa, 'Dopełniacz liczby mnogiej rzeczowników męskich miękkotematowych — norma a uzus', *PJ*, 1997, no. 9 : 31–43. H. S[atkiewicz], 'Z wahań w wyborze form słowotwórczych przymiotników', *ib.*, 72–73, deals with *przeciwśnieżny*, *przeciwśniegowy*, *obcojęzyczny*, and *obcojęzykowy*. M. Urban, 'O podzielności na temat słowotwórczy i formant w związku z wielomotywacyjnością przymiotników', *PJ*, 1998, nos 4–5 : 23–32. K. Waszakowa, 'Problem produktywności formantów obcych', *SFPS*, 33, 1996 : 75–83.

I. Bobrowski, 'O pewnych arbitralnych decyzjach ściśle gramatycznych przy wyznaczaniu zbioru zdań lingwistycznych', *Polonica*, 47, 1995 : 75–80. K. Kallas, 'Składnia zdań porównawczych. Uwagi o zdaniach zespolonych spójnikiem *niż*', *ib.*, 48, 1997 : 11–28. I. Kosek, 'Człony zdania odpowiadające na pytania *gdzie*? i *dokąd*? w języku polskim', *PJ*, 1997, no. 7 : 23–26, notes the inconsistencies of usage with *wieszać*, *siadać* and *kłaść*. B. Milewska, 'Co to są przyimki wtórne?', *JPol*, 78 : 179–87, identifies and exemplifies seven groups of secondary prepositions. A. Moroz, 'Wstępne założenia formalnego opisu konstrukcji składniowych zawierających zerowy wykładnik składnika użytego w kontekście', *PJ*, no. 3 : 9–21. Jerzy Podracki, **Składnia polska. Książka dla nauczycieli, studentów i uczniów*, Wa, Wyd. Szkolne i Pedagogiczne, 1997, 248 pp. A. Przepiórkowski, 'Transmisja wymagań składniowych', *Polonica*, 48, 1997 : 29–50. I. Szczepankowska, 'Adiektywne formacje dewerbalne w funkcji przydawki atrybutywnej (na materiale gwar północno-wschodniopolskich)', *SFPS*, 33, 1996:67–73. M. Szupryczyńska, 'Jeszcze o tzw. "predykatywach przysłówkowych"', *Polonica*, 47, 1995:173–88. E. Walusiak, 'Właściwości składniowe jednostek o postaci *byle*', *ib.*, 48, 1997:147–62. K. Węgrzynek, 'Wpływ informacji składniowej na rozpoznawanie kategorii gramatycznych i form fleksyjnych w tekście (na przykładzie analizy składniowej słowoformy *rad*)', *ib.*, 65–76. P. Żmigrodzki, 'Model gramatyki generatywnej a fakt językowy (na wybranym przykładzie)', *ib.*, 77–94.

4. Lexicology and Phraseology

S. Bąba, '*Oddać (wyświadczyć, wyrządzić) niedźwiedzią przysługę — niedźwiedzia przysługa*', *JPol*, 78:278–80. S. Bąba, '*Koniec kropka* czy *koniec, kropka*?', *ib.*, 280–81. V. Blažek, 'Slavic **kresati/*kresiti* "to strike a spark/to bring to life"', *RoczSl*, 50, 1997:25–44. Maria Borejszo, '*Syndyk* w historii języka polskiego', *JPol*, 78:57–61. B. Cooper, 'Russian *kukuruza* and its cognates: a possible new etymology', *Slavonica*, 4, 1997–98:46–63. K. Cyra, 'Frekwentatywne użycia przysłówka *zawsze*', *PJ*, nos 1–2:43–49. I. Czerwińska, 'O łączliwości i znaczeniu przyimka *za pośrednictwem*', *PJ*, 1997, no. 10:34–42. W. J. Darasz, 'O paronomazji', *JPol*, 78:238–45. R. Dulian, 'O definiowaniu czasowników *czynić, robić*', *Polonica*, 47, 1995:205–08. H. Grochola Szczepanek, 'O sposobach definiowania i klasyfikacji compositów w polskich pracach językoznawczych XX wieku', *PJ*, 1997, no. 7:40–52. Kwiryna Handke et al, **Nie dajmy zginąć słowom. Rzecz o odchodzącym słownictwie*, Wa, Slawistyczny Ośrodek Wydawniczy, 1996, 370 pp. M. Karpluk, 'O Słowniku staropolskiej terminologii chrześciańskiej (do r. 1500)', *JPol*, 78:91–97. C. Kosyl, 'Kynonimy literackie na tle zoonimii uzualnej (Część I)', *Onomastica*, 41, 1996:153–211. C. Kosyl, 'Kynonimy literackie na tle zoonimii uzualnej (Część II)', *ib.*, 42, 1997[1998]:251–70. B. Kreja, 'Jakie mogą być *kserografy*?', *JPol*, 78:282–83. *Słownik synonimów polskich*, ed. Zofia Kurzowa, Wa, PWN, 530 pp. M. Mycawka, 'Na tropach nowych zapożyczeń: *image*', *Polonica*, 47, 1995:189–204. R. Ociepa, 'Parę uwag na temat anglicyzmu *burger*', *PJ*, no. 3:32–36. M. Piela, 'Glosa do *Módł się za nami*', *JPol*, 78:269. Id., 'Jeszcze w sprawie wyrażenia *błogosławionej pamięci*', *ib.*, 270. J. Rusek, 'O nazwach kapusty (Brassica oleracea) w językach słowiańskich', *RoczSl*, 50, 1997:53–61. H. S[atkiewicz], 'O granicach równoważności znaczeniowej przymiotników *społeczny* i *socjalny*', *PJ*, 1997, no. 7:73–75. H. S[atkiewicz], 'Źle usytuowany dom ludzi dobrze sytuowanych', *ib.*, no. 8:80–81. K. Siekierska, 'Słownik języka polskiego XVII i 1. połowy XVIII wieku. Historia przedsięwzięcia, założenia teoretyczne, plan prac, prognozy na przyszłość', *JPol*, 78:82–90. R. S[inielnikoff], 'Nowe czasowniki', *PJ*, nos 4–5, 52–57, deals with *klonować, zadzwonić — oddzwonić, zatelefonować — odtelefonować, zakłamać — odkłamać, załamać się — odłamać się, zawiesić — odwiesić, ukoławiać się, stepować* and *piwkować*. R. S[inielnikoff], 'Aferzysta i paparazzo', *PJ*, nos 1–2:102–06. R. S[inielnikoff], 'Polityczna poprawność', *ib.*, no. 3:57–62, identifies a general euphemistic tendency. Sinielnikoff classifies phenomena broadly into political correctness, delicacy, and status-elevation (*stróż* becomes *dozorca, służąca* becomes *pomoc domowa*, etc.). The paper can now be read in conjunction with the introductory material in Anna Dąbrowska, *Słownik eufemizmów polskich czyli w rzeczy mocno, w sposobie łagodnie*, Wa, PWN, 323 pp.; the dictionary is arranged thematically, with sections devoted to categories such as body parts, illness, death, religion, and politics. F. Sławski, '*Matka, mać, macica, macierz, maciora, mama*', *JPol*, 78:6–15. L. Styrcz-Przebinda, 'Parę uwag o możliwościach klasyfikacji wykrzykników', *Polonica*, 48, 1997:163–68. H. Synowiec, 'Z badań nad frazeologią uczniów', *Polonistyka*, 51:68–74. M. Szupryczyńska, 'Funkcje leksykalne jednostki *super* we współczesnym języku polskim', *Polonica*, 47, 1995:167–72. J. Wawrzyńczyk, 'Z życia wyrazu *składnica*', *PJ*, no. 3:63–65, argues that the word considered by Doroszewski to be an interwar euphemism in fact dates back to before 1917. A. Zajda, 'Über altpolnische juristische Terminologie', *ZNUJ*, 1210:137–52; Id., *JPol*, 78:260–53, reviews two limited-edition reprints of Latin–German–Polish dictionaries dating from 1518. P. Żmigrodzki, *Mały słownik synonimów*, Kw-Wa, 1997, 458 pp. Discussions of a dictionary edited by H. Zgółkowa include: K. Handke, 'O Praktycznym słowniku współczesnej polszczyzny', *SFPS*, 33, 1996:307–14; M. Jurkowski, 'O praktyczności "Praktycznego słownika współczesnej polszczyzny"', *ib.*, 315–20; and J. Puzynina, 'Krytycznie o nowym słowniku języka polskiego', *ib.*, 321–46.

5. SEMANTICS AND PRAGMATICS

H. Běličová, 'Imperativ a výzvové věty v současných slovanských jazycích,' *Slavia*, 1997:127–41; and her 'Sekundární funkce komunikativních typů vět a výzva v současných slovanských jazycích,' *ib.*, 385–400. M. Bera, 'Jednostki z wyrażeniami *cholera* i *diabeł*. Próba analizy semantycznej', *Polonica*, 48, 1997:125–40. A. Czamara, 'Wartościujący akt illokucyjny', *ib.*, 169–74. B. Hansen, 'Powstanie i rozwój wyrazów modalnych w języku polskim', *PJ*, nos 1–2:25–41. M. Grochowski, 'O strukturze semantycznej zdań z zaimkiem *ktokolwiek*', *Polonica*, 48, 1997:103–14. K. Herej-Szymańska, 'Słowiańskie **golъ* — rozwój semantyczny', *RoczSl*, 50, 1997:63–66. A. Holvoet, 'O semantyce polskich czasowników typu *nałowić, nałowić się*', *SFPS*, 33, 1996:39–46. I. Iwanowa, 'Próba eksplikacji semantycznej spójnika *wobec tego*', *Polonica*, 47, 1995:135–46. M. Kawka, '*Co się dzieje na pierwszym obrazku?* O roli implikatur konwersacyjncyh i presupozycji w kształceniu sprawności językowej uczniów', *ib.*, 147–54. A. Janczak, 'Akty mowy wprowadzające prośbę', *PJ*, 1997, no. 10:24–33. R. Lebda, 'Semantičko-pragmatička analiza i interpretacija izabranih reklama na srpskom i poljskom jeziku,' *Slavia*, 1997:153–57. J. Lizak, 'Sposoby wartościowania w reklamie telewizyjnej skierowanej do dzieci', *PJ*, 1997, no. 8:43–49. K. Mosiołek-Kłosińska, 'Metafora w tekście użytkowym — charakterystyka, próba oceny normatywnej', *ib.*, no. 10:1–23. N. Nübler, 'Terminitivität und Telizität beim polnischen Verbum', *ASP*, 25, 1997:65–78. Irena Putka, 'Rola kontekstu w interpretacji znaczenia zaimka *nasz*', *PJ*, 1997, no. 7:8–13. J. Reszka, 'Potępianie a krytyka i wytykanie — analiza semantyczna', *Polonica*, 48, 1997:115–24. B. Szumińska, 'Relacje semantyczne między *ledwie* i *omal nie*', *ib.*, 141–46. H. K. Ulatowska et al., 'Zmiany formy i znaczenia przysłów (na materiale wypowiedzi osób z afazją)', *PJ*, 1997, no. 9:22–30. M. Urban, 'Słowotwórcza zależność motywacji semantycznej przymiotników od kontekstu rzeczownikowego', *PJ*, nos 1–2:50–56. M. Witucka, 'Jak opisuje się zapachy w reklamie perfum', *PJ*, no. 3:1–8.

V. Orel, '"Freedom" in Slavic', *JSL*, 5, Winter-Spring 1997:144–49, examines the etymology of **sveboda*, possibly traceable to an adjective **sve-bodъ* with a semantic development similar to that of **sverěpъ* 'wildly growing'. Thus **svebodъ* 'having thorns of its own' would be related to Polish *świeboda* and *swoboda*. Also relevant here, if so, is F. Sławski, 'Gdzie bursztynowy *świerzop*', *JPol*, 78:329–36. The concept of freedom features in Anna Wierzbicka, *Understanding Cultures through their Key Words*, OUP, 1997, 317 pp., which book is discussed at length by K. Pisarkowa, in *JPol*, 78:121–31.

6. SOCIOLINGUISTICS AND DIALECTOLOGY

*Język polski czasu drugiej wojny światowej (1939–45), ed. Irena Bajerowa, Wa, 1996, 507+xix pp. M. Brzezina, 'Polszczyzna Żydów jako derywat socjolingwistyczny i stylistyczny oraz stylizacja żydowska', *ZNUJ*, 1210:7–20. N. Chmielewska, 'Graffiti — osobliwa technika językowa', *Polonica*, 47, 1995:121–34. W. Czekmonas, J. Konickaja, and M. Krupowies, 'Między Niemczynem a Molatami (z badań nad polszczyzną ludową na Wileńszczyźnie)', *JP*, 78:382–88. W. Decyk, 'Kształtowanie się świadomości językowej w XVI wieku', *PJ*, 1997,

no. 9:11–21. K. Depta, 'Struktura narracji mówionej', *JPol*, 78:223–30. Ewa Dzięgiel, 'On two isolated Polish dialects in the Ukraine', *ZSl*, 43:101–08, studies the dialects of Zielona, and of Stary Skałat and Połupanówka. T. Karpowicz, 'Stan świadomości normatywnej w kwestii posługiwania się liczebnikami zbiorowymi', *PJ*, nos 4–5:12–22. W. Kędzierski, 'Sposoby tworzenia neosemantyzmów w gwarach środowisk dewiacyjnych', *JPol*, 78:231–37. B. Klebanowska, 'Czy to dobre wzory?', *PJ*, 1997, no. 10:43–56, is a review article based on *Korespondencja służbowa i prywatna — wzory listów i pism*, Wa, Wyd. Informacji Zawodowej Alfa-WEKA, itself apparently a Polish version (but not translation) of Ulrich Schoënwald, *Erfolgreiche Musterbriefe für alle geschäftlichen und privaten Vorgänge* [no publication details available]. Ewa Kołodziejek, 'Uwagi do projektu *Ustawy o języku polskim*', *PJ*, 1998, nos 4–5:34–37. E. Kraskowska, 'Feminizm w nauce i literaturze', *Polonistyka*, 51:352–58, is concerned not with language at all, but with feminist literature and literary criticism. On the other hand, issue 9 (pp. 579–638) of *Polonistyka*, 51, is mostly concerned with language. W. Lubaś, 'Czy powstanie śląski język literacki?', *JPol*, 78:49–56. J. Maćkiewicz, 'Jak mówimy o mówieniu, czyli językowy model komunikacji werbalnej', *PJ*, nos 1–2:1–12. E. Michow, 'Polskie graffiti', *Polonica*, 47, 1995:109–20. A. Małyski, 'Formy adresatywne w wypowiedziach parlamentarzystów polskich', *PJ*, no. 3:22–31. M. Marcjanik, 'Opisywanie etykiety językowej. Problemy metodologiczne', *Polonica*, 47, 1995:99–108. Her **Polska grzeczność językowa*, Kielce, Wyd. WSP im. Jana Kochanowskiego w Kielcach, 1997, 295 pp. K. Ożóg and S. Suszylo, 'Teksty gwarowe 87. Z Grodziska Dolnego w województwie rzeszowskim', *JPol*, 78:115–20. W. Pisarek, '*Ustawa o języku*', *PJ*, nos 4–5:33, follows from J. Saloni, 'Szkodzić — albo nie szkodzić', *PJ*, 1997, no. 6:65–70. A 64-page supplement to issue 5 of *Polonistyka*, with its own pagination, is devoted to reform in Polish teaching in Polish schools. Issue 5 itself of *Polonistyka* is devoted to *Małe ojczyzny*; of particular interest is H. Synowiec, 'Gwara w edukacji regionalnej', *Polonistyka*, 51:276–82. Renata Makarewicz, 'Gdy w klasie jest dyslektyk...', *ib.*, 75–79. J. Puzynina, 'Uwagi dyskusyjne do *Podstawy programowej języka polskiego w szkole*', *PJ*, 1997, no. 9:44–48. K. Ożóg, 'Język kampanii wyborczej z 1997 r. na tle polszczyzny lat dziewięćdziesiątych', *JPol*, 78:171–78. From the Polish Language Council of the PAN Presidium: '*Nie* z imiesłowami przymiotnikowymi (z zasadzie) zawsze razem', *PJ*, nos 1–2:107–09, and reports in 'III posiedzenie Rady Języka Polskiego', *ib.*, 109–10, and 'Stanowisko Rady Języka Polskiego w sprawie "Edukacji Polonistycznej" w *Podstawach programowych obowiązkowych przedmiotów ogólnokształcących* wprowadzonych zarządzaniem Ministra Edukacji Narodowej z 15 v 1997 r. (ze szczególnym uwzględnieniem kształcenia językowego)', *ib.*, 110–11. R. S[inielni-koff], 'Przyczyny wulgaryzacji języka polskiego', *PJ*, 1997, no. 8 : 75–79. Z. Saloni, 'O sytuacji w polskiej ortografii', *PJ*, 1998, nos 4–5 : 37–41, is generally sceptical. M. Wingender, 'Standardsprach-lichkeit in der Slavia: Eine Überprüfung des Begriffsapparates', *ZSl*, 43 : 127–39.

7. INDIVIDUALS, WORKS, STYLISTICS

ACTING. M. Steffen-Batogowa, 'Międzyosobnicze zróżnicowanie sposobów wyrażania emocji w mowie aktorów', *Polonica*, 47, 1995 : 37–66.

ANNA KATARZYNA. J. Wronicz, 'Korespondencja królewny Anny Katarzyny Konstancji', *JPol*, 78 : 111–14.

BAROQUE POETRY. J. Senderska, 'O pewnym rodzaju inwersji w polskiej poezji barokowej', *Polonica*, 48, 1997 : 183–90.

BORROW. The emphasis of G. Hyde, '"Language is first of all a foreign one": George Borrow as a translator from Polish', *SEER*, 77 : 74–92, is mainly literary.

BUDNY. I. Kwilecka, 'Problem autorstwa przekłady Apokryfów w Biblii Szymona Budnego z 1572 roku', *SFPS*, 33, 1996 : 47–66.

CHMIELEWSKI. E. Makowska, 'Słowotwórcze neologizmy Henryka Jerzego Chmielewskiego', *ZNUJ*, 1210 : 77–86.

FAUST. A. Czesak, 'O nowym przekładzie fragmentu Fausta. Zagadnienia językowej stylizacji gwarowej', *JPol*, 78 : 196–203.

GOMBROWICZ. M. Wojtak, 'Wielostylowość w utworze drama-tycznym na przykładzie *Ślubu* Witolda Gombrowicza', *PJ*, nos 1–2 : 13–24.

HERBERT AND SZYMBORSKA. M. Nowotna, 'Quelques remarques sur la nature de l'énonciation dans deux poèmes de W. Szymborska et de Z. Herbert', *RSl*, 70 : 215–27, draws on linguistics.

KOCHANOWSKI. J. Senderska, 'Pozycja przymiotnika w strukturze wyjściowej grupy nominalnej (na przykładzie poezji Jana Kocha-nowskiego)', *Polonica*, 47, 1995 : 155–66.

KONWICKI. H. Wszeborowska, 'Stylizacja na język potoczny w powieści Tadeusza Konwickiego *Rzeka podziemna, podziemne ptaki*', *PJ*, 1997, no. 10 : 57–68.

LINDE. B. Matuszczyk, 'W sprawie koncepcji Słownika języka polskiego Samuela Bogumiła Lindego', *JPol*, 78 : 98–103; M. Ptaszyk, 'Kopczyński a Słownik Lindego', *ib.*, 104–06.

MICKIEWICZ. S. Bąba, 'O jednym ze skrzydlatych słów Mickie-wicza. Komentarz leksykograficzny do frazy *bania się (z kimś) rozbiła*', *JPol*, 78 : 362–65; M. Białoskórska, 'Pole leksykalno-stylistyczne *wiatru* w utworach Adama Mickiewicza', *ib.*, 321–28; Z. Bukowcowa,

'Bibliografia artykułów o języku Adama Mickiewicza drukowanych w Języku Polskim R. XXXV (1955) - LXXVIII (1998)', *ib.*, 389–92, contains 54 items. W. J. Darasz, 'Z mickiewiczowskich tradycji polskiej wersyfikacji: anapest', *ib.*, 366–72. S. Kania, 'Językowy obraz flory w *Panu Tadeuszu* Adama Mickiewicza', *ib.*, 337–46. A. Krupianka, 'Synonimy *gwedzkać* / / *gwazdać* / / *bazgrać* w języku Mickiewicza', *ib.*, 357–61. B. Kułak, 'Formy długie i krótkie zaimków dzierżawczych w języku Adama Mickiewicza', *ib.*, 372–81. Z. Kurzowa, 'O języku Adama Mickiewicza', *ib.*, 290–302. T. Skubalanka, 'Uwagi o stylu wiersza Adama Mickiewicza "Wsłuchać się w szum wód głuchy', *ib.*, 303–08. E. Stachurski, 'Słownictwo *Epilogu Pana Tadeusza* na tle tekstu ksiąg Mickiewiczowej epopei', *ib.*, 347–56. B. Walczak, 'Język Mickiewicza a regionalne zróżnicowanie polszczyzny', *Polonistyka*, 51 : 395–402. W. Witkowski, 'Elementy białoruskie w języku Adama Mickiewicza', *RoczSl*, 50, 1997 : 115–20. M. Zarębina, 'Wartościowanie związane ze *słońcem* w *Panu Tadeuszu* Adama Mickiewicza', *JPol*, 78 : 309–20.

NIZIURSKI. J. Głowacki, 'O nazwach autentycznych w dziele literackim (na materiale z utworów Edmunda Niziurskiego)', *Onomastica*, 42, 1997[1998] : 239–49.

ORKAN. Józefa Kobylińska, **Świat językowy Władysława Orkana. Słowa i stereotypy*, Kw, Wyd. Edukacyjne, 1997, 212 pp.

PASSIONS. E. Stryjniak-Sztankó, 'Sposoby realizowania compassio w XV- i XVI-wiecznych prozatorskich pasjach polskich', *SSH*, 42, 1997 : 117–22.

PSALTER. S. Koziara, 'O szyku zaimkowej przydawki dzierżawczej w polskich przekładach Psałterza (na przykładzie psalmu Miserere)', *JPol*, 78 : 62–69.

RAMUŁT. J. Treder, 'Ocena drugiej części "Słownika" Stefana Ramułta w opracowaniu Haliny Horodyskiej"', *SFPS*, 33, 1996 : 347–67, treats a dictionary of Pomeranian whose first part was published in 1893, but whose second part was not published until 1993, despite having won a prize from the Polish Academy of Arts (PAU) in 1893.

RZEWUSKI. B. Bartnicka, 'Frazeologia w powieściach Henryka Rzewuskiego', *PJ*, 1997, no. 8 : 4–17; and her 'Frazeologia w powieściach Henryka Rzewuskiego (cd.)', *PJ*, 1997, no. 9 : 1–10.

SALES LETTERS. M. Wolny, 'List motywacyjny jako nowy gatunek językowy', *PJ*, nos 4–5 : 1–11, regards the advertising letter as a distinct genre.

SAMOZWANIEC. M. Ruszkowski, 'Językowe wykładniki parodii (na przykładzie powieści Magdaleny Samozwaniec *Na ustach grzechu*', *PJ*, 1997, no. 7 : 14–22. A. Wojciechowska, 'Obraz artystów w tekstach Magdaleny Samozwaniec', *ib.*, no. 8 : 30–42.

SLOGANS. B. Lenkiewicz, 'Sztuka precyzyjnego mówienia. Slogan', *Polonistyka*, 51 : 190, suggests lessons based on the advertising slogan as a genre.

STASZIC. M. Drzazgowski, 'Terminy oroграficzne i góralszczyzna w języku Stanisława Staszica', *SFPS*, 33, 1996 : 27–38.

TECHNICAL TEXTS FOR TRANSLATION. D. Zielińska, 'Tekst naukowy, który się łatwo tłumaczy', *JPol*, 78 : 204–07.

TRANSLATION OF NAMES. M. Perek, 'Literacki przekład nazw własnych, cz. I', *Onomastica*, 42, 1997[1998] : 215–37.

8. POLISH AND OTHER LANGUAGES

T. Bergen, 'Äußere Einflüsse und interne Faktoren bei der Herausbildung der slavischen Anredesysteme', *WSl*, 43 : 307–22. J. Besters-Dilger, 'Модальность в польском и русском языках. Историческое развитие выражения необходимости и возможности как резчльтат вне- и межславянского влцяния', *WSJ*, 43, 1997 : 17–31. H. Birnbaum, 'Common Slavic in time and space,' *ScSl*, 44 : 131–45. H. Galton, 'Gedanken über den Ursprung des slavischen Verbalaspekts', *WSJ*, 43, 1997 : 67–76. R. L. Górski, 'O pewnym sposobie opisu czasu i trybu zdania podrzędnego w języku polskim i łacinie', *Polonica*, 48, 1997 : 95–102. Z. Greń, 'Struktura pola semantycznego mówienia w języku polskim i czeskim (na podstawie analizy reprezentacji czasownikowej)', *SFPS*, 33, 1996 : 85–110, uses componential and cognitive methods. M. Guiraud-Weber, 'La préfixation des emprunts verbaux en russe et en polonais', *RSl*, 70 : 67–75. B. Hansen, 'Modalauxiliare in den slavischen Sprachen', *ZSl*, 43 : 249–72. H. Karlíková, 'Typy a původ semantických změn výrazů pro pojmenování citových stavů a jejich projevů ve slovanských jazycích,' *Slavia* : 49–56. J. Kořenský, 'Metodologické problémy porovnávání vývoje a synchronní dynamiky současných slovanských jazyků', *ib.*, 99–106. M. Korytkowska, 'Imperceptywność w języku bułgarskim i polskim a struktura tekstu', *SFPS*, 33, 1996 : 131–45. B. Kunzmann-Müller, 'Spezialfälle der Diathese in den slavischen Sprachen', *ZSl*, 43 : 273–79. E. Lotko, *Synchronní konfrontace češtiny a polštiny (Soubor statí)*, Olomouc, Palacký UP, 1997, 153 pp. A. Lubecka, 'La notion de la mi-formalité dans les titres d'addresse en français et en polonais', *ZNUJ*, 1210 : 69–75. Polish remains well hidden in C. Mouton, 'Étude contrastive de la notion temps/aspect dans les langues indo-européennes,' *SlaG* : 29–42. V. E. Moiseenko, 'Из истории славянского диакритического правописания', *SSH*, 42, 1997 : 99–108. D. Müller-Ott, 'Neue englische Fremd- und Lehnwörter in der polnischen Wirtschaftsterminologie', *WSJ*, 43, 1997 : 141–48.

K. Oliwa, 'Zarys konfrontacji zasobów słownych języka polskiego i czeskiego,' *Slavia*: 57–60. T. Z. Orłoś, 'Zapożyczenia polskie w słowackiej terminologii botanicznej. Część I — Nazwy botaniczne pochodzenia polskiego w tzw. słowniku Hadbavnego', *RoczSl*, 50, 1997:87–92. B. Ostrowski, 'O kilku przykładach wykorzystania materiału języka polskiego przy rekonstrukcji leksyki prasłowiańskiej', *ib.*, 45–51. A. Otwinowska-Kasztelanic, 'Wpływ języka angielskiego na polszczyznę (wyniki badania ankietowego świadomości językowej młodego pokolenia Polaków)', *PJ*, nos 1–2:57–65. R. Pawelec, 'Polskie nazwy *artysta* i *sztukmistrz* oraz niemieckie *der Künstler* na tle pola nazw twórcy dzieła sztuki w obu językach', *PJ*, 1997, no. 8:18–29. W. Pianka, 'Typologia partycypiów słowiańskich', *WSJ*, 43, 1997:161–71. Tadeusz Piotrowski, 'O anglicyzmach — a może germanizmach? — w języku polskim', *JPol*, 78:271–73. J. Reinhart, 'Zwischenslavische Übersetzungen im Mittelalter', *WSJ*, 43, 1997:189–203. J. Rejzek, 'Initial *sk-(šk-)/ch-* doublets in the Slavonic languages', *SEER*, 76:234–40. J. Rieger, 'O polskich wpływach leksykalnych na gwary ukraińskie (na przykładzie gwar bojkowskich)', *SFPS*, 33, 1996:181–92. S. Schmidt, 'Rozwój stereotypów oraz wzajemnych ocen Niemców i Polaków', *JPol*, 78:70–81. I. Sěrakowa, 'Werbalny substantiw wot refleksiwneho werba w zapadnosłowjanskich rěčach (z wosebitym wobkedźbowanjom serbšćiny)', *SFPS*, 33, 1996:213–24. O. Tsaruk, 'До проблеми засад генеалогічної класифікації слов'янских мов', *Slavia*, 1997:331–36. J. Waniakowa, 'Derywaty z ps. rdzeniem *tuch* i *tęch* w języku polskim i innych językach słowiańskich na tle indoeuropejskim', *SFPS*, 33, 1996:225–43. K. Weyssenhoff-Brożkowa, 'Frazeologia staropolska w szacie łacińskiej', *Polonica*, 48, 1997:175–82. H. Włodarczyk, 'Wykładniki wartości informacyjnej wypowiedzenia w języku polskim i francuskim (aspekt, określoność, modalność)', *RSl*, 70:53–66. A. Zielińska, 'Język rosyjski, polski i niemiecki w mowie staroobrzędowców polskich', *SFPS*, 33, 1996:297–305.

9. ONOMASTICS

M. Biolik, 'Przezwiska nauczycieli i uczniów o przejrzystej motywacji semantycznej', *Onomastica*, 42, 1997[1998]:195–210. I. Bily, 'Zur Typologie der ältesten Belege slawischer Ortsnamen im Mittelgebiet', *ib.*, 81–93. E. Breza, 'Kaszubskie nazwiska *Mudlaf(f)* i *Mycław* oraz ich warianty', *JPol*, 78:208–11. E. Breza, 'Nazwiska *Kuik*, *Kujk* i podobne', *PJ*, no. 3:37–43. A. Cieślikowa, 'Prasłowiańskie apelatywy antroponimiczne', *Onomastica*, 42, 1997[1998]:129–40. K. Długosz, 'Współczesne hybrydalne composita przezwiskowe', *ib.*, 171–94. E. Eichler, 'Zum Problem der historischen Sprachlandschaften im deutsche-slavischen Berührungsgebiet', *ib.*, 71–80. I. Janyšková, 'Etymologicko-onomaziologická analýza slovanských názvů dřevin,' *Slavia*: 39–48. Z. Kaleta, 'Nazwisko w kulturze Słowian', *JPol*, 78:29–38. Zygmunt Klimek, **Słownik etymologiczno-motywacyjny staropolskich nazw osobowych, część 5: Nazwy osobowe pochodzenia niemieckiego*, Kw, 1997, 300+xxiii pp. D. Kopertowska, 'Słowiańska antroponimia i toponimia we wzajemnych relacjach', *Onomastica*, 42, 1997[1998]:141–47. Bogusław Kreja, **Księga nazwisk ziemi gdańskiej*, Gdańsk, 1998, 301 pp. Id., 'Geografia nazwisk a zasięgi cech gwarowych', *JPol*, 78:39–48. H. Leeming, 'Jak brzmiało i skąd pochodzi imię wielkomorawskiego księcia Rościsława?', *ib.*, 16–20. J. Malicki, 'Dyskusja o nazwie państwa czeskiego', *PJ*, nos 1–2:66–71, is concerned with the Czech, not the Polish, name of the Czech state. E. Mrhačová, 'Složená osobní jména slovanského původu v češtině, slovenštině a polštině,' *Slavia*, 1997:269–84. J. Nalepa, 'Nazwy geograficzne Tatr i Beskidów', *JPol*, 78:21–28, treats Lepietnica and Salatyn (Salatün); Id., 'Nazwy geograficzne Tatr i Beskidów 3. Chocz (Choč)', *ib.*, 212–17. A. Pisowicz, 'Polskie formy nazwy stolicy Armenii', *JPol*, 78:218–22, expresses a preference for *Erywań*. K. Rymut, 'Onomastyka prasłowiańska. Zakres i możliwości badawcze', *Onomastica*, 42, 1997[1998]:11–19. J. Udolph, 'Alteuropäische Hydronimie und urslavische Gewässernamen', *ib.*, 21–70. P. Valčaková, 'Nazvy koření ve slovanských jazycích,' *Slavia*: 73–80. E. Wolnicz-Pawłowska, 'Łemkowskie imiona kobiece', *SFPS*, 33, 1996:275–95.

10.   POLISH AND THE COMPUTER

K. Szafran, 'Automatyczne hasłowanie tekstu polskiego', *Polonica*, 48, 1997:51–64.

LITERATURE

By JOHN BATES, *University of Glasgow*

(This survey covers the years 1996–98)

1. GENERAL

Wiedza o literaturze i edukacji. Księga referatów Zjazdu Polonistów, ed. Teresa Michałowska, Zbigniew Goliński, and Zbigniew Jarosiński, Wa, Wyd. IBL, 1996, 984 pp., is a collection of general overviews. Tomasz Milkowski, *Leksykon dzieł i tematów literatury polskiej dla szkół podstawowych i średnich*, Wa, KiW, 687 pp. In 1997, the Cracow publisher Universitas launched an important new initiative, 'Klasycy współczesnej polskiej myśli humanistycznej', which has thus far reprinted the major theoretical works of M. Głowiński, H. Markiewicz, and J. Sławiński, each in five volumes. These are works which largely appeared during the Communist period in often miniscule print runs. The series appears under the general editorship of A. Nowakowski, and individual volumes and editors are listed below. *Postać literacka. Teoria i historia*, ed. Edward Kasperski and Brygida Pawlikowska-Jądrzyk, Wa, Wyd. Uniwersytetu Warszawskiego, 261 pp. *Retoryka i badania literackie. Rekonesans*, ed. Jakub Z. Lichański, Wa, Wyd. Uniwersytetu Warszawskiego, 254 pp., is a collection of essays chiefly devoted to popular literature. Janusz Maciejewski, *Obszary i konteksty literatury*, Wa, Wyd. DiG, 236 pp. *Autor tekst cenzura*, ed. Janusz Pelc and Marek Prejs, Wa, Wyd. Uniwersytetu Warszawskiego, 291 pp., covers censorship and editorship from the Middle Ages to the present. R. Nycz, 'Literatura polska w cieniu cenzury (Wykład)', *TD*, no. 2:5–27, is an overview of developments throughout Polish history with some interesting new theoretical propositions for the subject. Lucylla Pszczołowska, *Wiersz polski. Zarys historyczny*, Ww, Leopoldinum, 434 pp. Andrzej Stoff, *Studia z teorii literatury i poetyki historycznej*, Lublin, Towarzystwo Naukowe KUL, 1997, 235 pp., contains chapters on the narrative strategy of Sienkiewicz's *Potop* and Lem, amongst others. Tadeusz Ulewicz, *Konterefekty, sylwetki, cienie. (Z dziejów filologii w Polsce)*, Kw, Universitas, 1997, 354 pp., is devoted to Polish 19th–20th-c. literary scholarship, as influenced by Aleksander Brückner and Stanisław Pigoń. *TD*, no. 3, contains two essays on émigré literature: K. Dybciak, 'Systemy komunikacji literackiej wielkich literatur emigracyjnych' (29–41) and H. Filipowicz, 'Polska literatura emigracyjna — próba teorii' (43–62), whose article 'Beginning to theorize Polish émigré literature', *Periphery*, 1997, 89–93, is an earlier version of the same.

Lidia Burska, *Kłopotliwe dziedzictwo*, Wyd. IBL, Wa, 244 pp., concerns the function of history and its relations to the present in Polish literature from the 19th c. to recent times as exemplified by the works of H. Sienkiewicz, W. Berent, S. Żeromski, J. Iwaszkiewicz, H. Malewska, and T. Parnicki. Stanisław Eile, *Modernist Trends in 20th-Century Polish Fiction*, London, SSEES, 1996, 226 pp., is an analysis of developments in Polish prose since the end of the 19th c. consisting of three parts: the origins of modern fiction, the interwar period, and since World War II. *Engendering Slavic Literatures*, ed. Pamela Chester and Sibelan Forrester, Bloomington and Indianapolis, Indiana U. P., 1996, 249 pp., contains two excellent essays on Polish subjects: H. Filipowicz, 'The daughters of Emilia Plater' (34–58) and M. Zaborowska, 'Writing the virgin, writing the crone' (174–200), which deal respectively with accounts of Plater's life, including on stage, and Maria Kuncewicz's work. Danuta Danek, *Sztuka rozumienia. Literatura i psychoanaliza*, Wa, Wyd. IBL, 1997, 536 pp., considers, *inter alia*, Gombrowicz's *Operetka* and the significance of dreams in 19th-c. Polish literature. Andrzej Mencwel, *Przedwiośnie czy potop. Studium postaw polskich w XX wieku*, Wa, Czytelnik, 1997, 542 pp., is an important collection of essays on 20th-c. Polish intellectuals and their attitudes towards the contemporary Polish situation, including M. Dąbrowska, S. Żeromski, L. Kołakowski, S. Żółkiewski, Paris *Kultura*, etc. Władysław Parnas, *Pismo i rana. Szkice o problematyce żydowskiej w literaturze polskiej*, Lublin, Wyd. Dabar, 1996, 155 pp., covers the period from the latter half of the 19th c. to the present. *Kobieta i kultura, tom IV*, ed. Anna Żarnowska and Andrzej Szwarc, Wa, Wyd. PiG, 1996, 315 pp., contains essays devoted to sociological issues as well as Borkowska on female genius in the 19th and 20th c. Marek Zaleski, *Formy pamięci. O przedstawianiu przeszłości w polskiej literaturze współczesnej*, Wa, Wyd. IBL, 1996, 239 pp., examines the impact of a number of issues on Polish postwar literature, including the 1939 invasion, Poland's multicultural past and the Holocaust, in relation to, particularly, Huelle's *Weiser Dawidek*, Miłosz's poetry, H. Grynberg's prose works, and the trend of works on the pre-1939 borderlands.

Maria Janion, *Płacz generała. Eseje o wojnie*, Wa, Wyd. Sic !, 307 pp., is a volume of previously published essays covering K. Wyka, J. J. Szczepański, and the Romantics, amongst others. *Literacka symbolika roślin*, ed. Anna Martuszewska, Gd, Wyd. Uniwersytetu Gdańskiego, 1997, 231 pp., a collection of essays by important critics, addresses the subject as exemplified in works of authors from the early Baroque onwards. *Dzieciństwo i sacrum. Studia i szkice literackie*, ed. Joanna Papuzińska and Grzegorz Leszczyński, Wa, Stowarzyszenie Przyjaciół Książki dla Młodych — Polska Sekcja IBBY, 317 pp., is a very wide-ranging collection of essays, dealing with, for instance, Irzykowski's *Pałuba* and K. Filipowicz's prose. Ryszard Przybylski, *Baśń zimowa. Esej o starości*, Wa, Wyd. Sic!, 125 pp., contains reflections on old age as depicted in the works of J. Iwaszkiewicz and T. Różewicz, amongst others. *Szybko i szybciej. Eseje o pośpiechu w kulturze*, ed. Dorota Siwicka, Marek Bieńczyk, and Aleksander Nawarecki, Wa, Wyd. IBL, 1996, 228 pp., is an often intriguing collection of essays by prominent critics on speed in European culture with specific treatments of M. Białoszewski's poetry, K. Bielecki's novels, and the announcement of Mickiewicz's death. Wojnowska, *Literatura*, is a collection of papers on literature's relations with the state from a conference held in December 1994; individual items are dealt with below. *Kłamstwo w literaturze*, ed. Zofia Wójcicka and Piotr Urbański, Kielce, Szuhmacher, 1996, 270 pp., discusses lying, misrepresentation and delusion in relation to the portrayal of Jews in Polish literature, Mickiewicz's *Zdania i uwagi*, and the work of Norwid, A. Nowaczyński, and T. Kantor.

Lektury polonistyczne. Oświecenie-Romantyzm, ed. Andrzej Borowski and Juliusz S. Gruchała, Kw, Universitas, 1997, 335 pp., covers writers from Krasicki to Norwid. *Innowiercy odszczepieńcy herezje* (Poznańskie studia polonistyczne. Seria literacka 3 [23]), ed. Barbara Judkowiak, Elżbieta Nowicka, and Barbara Sienkiewicz, Pń, Abedik, 1996, 361 pp. + 1 p. of errata, includes D. Ratajczakowa on Różewicz, and individual essays on M. Rej, B. Schulz, A. Wat, and J. Pilch. Wojciech Owczarski, **Diabeł w dramacie polskim. Z dziejów motywu*, Gd, Wyd. Uniwersytetu Gdańskiego, 1996, 114 pp., contains three sketches on Romantic, Modernist, and postmodernist drama, as well as on Gombrowicz's plays. Marek Tomaszewski, *Od chaosu do kosmosu. Szkice o literaturze polskiej i francuskiej XX wieku* (Badania Polonistyczne za Granicą, 2), Wa, Wyd. IBL, 237 pp., has rather more on Polish writers: Schulz, Gombrowicz, Odojewski, Konwicki, Andrzejewski, and Żakiewicz. *Świat jeden, ale nie jednolity*, ed. Lidia Wiśniewska, WSP, Bydgoszcz, 137 pp., is an eclectic collection of essays by young academics on writers as diverse as O. Tokarczuk, Gombrowicz, T. Słobodzianek, T. Parnicki, and B. Leśmian.

M. Inglot, 'Poetyckie testamenty liryczne. (Uwagi wokół wiersza 'Testament mój' Juliusza Słowackiego)', *ZRL*, 40.1–2, 1997:101–19, is an analysis of mainly 20th-c. examples of the genre by Z. Herbert, M. Białoszewski, A. Słonimski, and S. I. Witkiewicz. K. Jakowska, 'Metafizyka i religia w cyklu opowiadań', *RoczH*, 45.1, 1997:37–48, reflects on short story cycles by E. Orzeszkowa, J. Andrzejewski, B. Schulz, and A. Stasiuk. J. Z. Lichański, 'Przemilczenie i niedomówienie: technika narracyjna oraz figura myśli. Niejasności teorii retorycznej', *PrzH*, 42.4:37–46, concludes, on the basis of an analysis of works by S. H. Lubomirski, A. Mickiewicz, J. Słowacki, J. Parandowski, and others, that it is impossible to define either entirely satisfactorily. P. Michałowski, '*Cisza*, miejsca niedookreślenia i graniczne stany słowa', *TD*, no.6:47–67, considers the poetry of W. Szymborska, and the prose of P. Grzesik, E. Stachura, and W. Broniewski. R. Nycz, 'Poetyka epifanii a modernizm (od Norwida do Leśmiana)', *TD*, 1996, no. 4:20–38. E. Rybicka, 'Labirynt: temat i model konstrukcyjny. Od Berenta do młodej prozy', *PL(W)*, 88.3, 1997:67–90.

2. FROM THE MIDDLE AGES UP TO ROMANTICISM

Pisarze staropolscy, ed. Stanisław Grzeszczuk, Wa, Wiedza Powszechna, 1997, 611 pp., the second volume of an edition begun in 1991, contains substantial essays on writers from Ł. Górnicki through J. Kochanowski, M. Sęp Szarzyński, and P. Skarga, to J. Jurkowski. *Cały świat nie pomieściłby ksiąg. Staropolskie opowieści i przekazy apokryficzne*, ed. Maria Adamczyk, Wojciech R. Rzepka, and Wiesław Wydra, Wa-Pń, Wyd. Naukowe PWN, 1996, 364 pp., is an anthology of texts with a useful introduction by Adamczyk. *Lektury polonistyczne, Średniowiecze-renesans-barok. Tom drugi*, ed. Andrzej Borowski and Janusz S. Gruchała, Kw, Universitas, 1997, 317 pp. Janusz K. Goliński, *Okolice trwogi. Lęk w literaturze i kulturze dawnej Polski*, Bydgoszcz, WSP, 271 pp. Teresa Michałowska, *Mediaevalia i inne*, Wa, PWN, 343 pp., is a collection of essays on, amongst other matters, the pilgrim *topos* in Polish medieval literature and Gall Anonim. Dorota Szostek, *Exemplum w polskim średniowieczu*, Wa, Wyd. IBL, 1997, 198 pp., deals with the device's range and status in the Middle Ages. Luigi Marinelli, *Polski Adon. O poetyce i retoryce przekładu*, Izabelin, Świat Literacki, 1997, 256 pp., compares Giambattisto Marino's *L'Adone* with its anonymous Polish translation. Dariusz Śnieżko, *Mit wieku złotego w literaturze polskiego renesansu. Wzory — warianty — zastosowania*, Wa, Semper, 1996, 176 pp., appears to be the first monograph devoted extensively to the subject.

D. Chemperek, '*Descriptio gentium* Macieja Kazimierza Sarbiewskiego i Daniela Naborowskiego. Zagadki powstania, translacji i recepcji utworu', *PrzH*, 41.5, 1997:95–104. A. Czyż, ' "Zdrów bądź, Krolu anielski" — najdawniejsza kolęda polska', *PL(W)*, 87.1, 1996:5–17. M. Elżanowska, '*Pieśni łysogórskie*. Prologomena filologiczne', *ib.*, 88.3, 1997:131–59. J. Godyń, 'Retoryka w pieśni pasyjnej Władysława z Gielniowa, *Psałterzu Floriańskim* i *Kazaniach tzw. Świętokrzyskich*. (Funkcje średniowiecznej interpunkcji)', *RuLit*, 37, 1996:669–83. J. Kolbuszewski, 'Eschatologia i megalomania. O polskiej barokowej wierszowanej epigrafice nagrobnej', *PrzH*, 41.5,

1997:63–81. N. Korniłłowicz, 'Płacz i śmiech w poezji polskiej XVII wieku', *RuLit*, 37, 1996:151–61, analyses the work of Kochanowski, J. A. Morsztyn, and Kochowski. R. Mazurkiewicz, 'Matka Boska Kwietna. O średniowiecznej pieśni maryjnej "Kwiatek czysty, smutnego serca ucieszenie"', *PL(W)*, 89.4:149–64. A. Nowicka-Jeżowa, 'Sonet polski od Kochanowskiego do Morsztyna — zarysy dróg twórczych', *RuLit*, 38, 1997:435–50. J. Partyka, 'Angielskie "commonplace books" a polskie "sylwy". Z dziejów rękopisów domowych w Europie', *PL(W)*, 88.2, 1997:173–82. J. Pelc, ' "Rycerz" — "pasterz" — "ziemianin"', *PrzH*, 40.1, 1996:111–19, examines the use of these figures during the Renaissance and early Baroque. P. Buchwald-Pelcowa, 'Autorzy polscy w indeksach ksiąg zakazanych', *ib.*, 121–29. M. and M. Skwarowie, 'Melancholia — głupota — pycha — szaleństwo. O motywach polskiej literatury XVII wieku', *PL(W)*, 88.3, 1997:35–65. Paweł Stępień, 'Chaos i ład. *Lament Świętokrzyski* w świetle tradycji teologicznej', *ib.*, 89.1:69–94. A. Wilkoń, 'Kategorie stylistyczne w poezji barokowej', *ZRL*, 41.1–2:119–32, is a highly theoretical article examining the overlapping and contrastive stylistic categories in Polish verse of the 17th c. in terms of syncretism, excess, amplification, dynamicism, autotelicism, ambiguity, and conceptuality, in relation to the work of J. A. Morsztyn and S. Twardowski. K. Ziemba, 'Klemens Janicjusz — Jan Kochanowski. Dwie koncepcje elegii neołacińskiej', *PL(W)*, 89.4:125–37.

Mieczysław Klimowicz, *Polsko-niemieckie pogranicza literackie w XVIII wieku. Problemy uczestnictwa w dwu kulturach*, Ww, Ossolineum, 235 pp., assesses the reception of Polish Enlightenment works in German culture of the time. Stanisław Kukurowski, *Racjonalna, radykalna, antyklerykalna. Literatura Oświecenia w publikacjach lat 1944–1956*, Ww, WUW, 211 pp., deals with the reception of Enlightenment authors and works in literary histories, journalism, and school programmes of the Stalinist era. J. IJ. van der Meer, 'The early authors of the Stanisław age and their attitude toward the later developments of the literary field', *ZSP*, 57.2:415–35; Id., 'Zur Konstruktion der vom Autor intendierten Rezeption in Bohomolec' *Monitor* und Gogol's *Revizor*', *ZSl*, 41.4, 1996:464–85.

INDIVIDUAL WRITERS

DEMBOŁĘCKI. R. Sztyber, 'Zróżnicowanie gatunkowe *Przewag elearów polskich* Wojciecha Dembołęckiego', *PL(W)*, 88.4, 1997:109–22.

GAŁKA. K. Biliński, 'Biblijne konteksty *Pieśni o Wiklefie* Jędrzeja Gałki z Dobczyna', *PL(W)*, 88.4, 1997:139–44.

KALLIMACH.   T. Ulewicz, 'Przełom humanistyczny w Polsce i jego sprawca. W pięćsetlecie zgonu Filipa Kallimacha', *RuLit*, 38, 1997:159–71.

KOCHANOWSKI.   Jacek Sokolski, *Lipa, Charon i Labyrint. Esej o 'Fraszkach'*, Ww, Ossolineum, 120 pp. A. Fulińska, 'Erotyk dla kobiety uczonej. O *Pieśni II Ksiąg wtórych* Jana Kochanowskiego', *RuLit*, 38, 1997:565–72. N. Korniłłowicz, 'Melancholia w *Pieśni XXIV* Jana Kochanowskiego', *ib.*, 883–92. J. Sokolski, 'Nad *Fraszkami* Jana Kochanowskiego', *PL(W)*, 88.2:161–72. T. Ulewicz, 'Niespodzianka humanistyczna: *Fraszki* Kochanowskiego w przekładzie włoskim', *RuLit*, 37, 1996:389–96.

KORCZYŃSKI.   R. Grześkowiak, 'Poeta z logogryfu. O *Wizerunku złocistej przyjaźnią zdrady* Adama Korczyńskiego', *TD*, 1997, no. 4:51–67.

KRASICKI.   Teresa Kostkiewiczowa, *Studia o Krasickim*, Wa, IBL, 1997, 231 pp., comprises seven articles, of which two are published for the first time and the rest are revised and expanded versions of pieces published previously. They include studies of the poetics of his lyrical poetry (61–83) and his poetic language (163–222), as well as his relationship to the Enlightenment (135–62). J. IJ. van der Meer, 'Die Theatertheorien Ignacy Krasickis im Kontext der europäischen Aufklärungsästhetik', *ŽSl*, 41.1, 1996:34–49. M. Parkitny, 'O genezie *Myszeidy* Ignacego Krasickiego', *PL(W)*, 89.1:51–67.

LUBOMIRSKI.   G. Raubo, 'O łasce, predestynacji i Bogu ukrytym. Wątki jansenistyczne w twórczości Stanisława Herakliusza Lubomirskiego', *PL(W)*, 88.4, 1997:3–22.

MORSZTYŃ.   J. S. Gruchała, 'Jan Andrzeja Morsztyna gry z czytelnikiem (O pewnym typie wiersza enumeracyjnego)', *TD*, 1997, no. 4:29–40.

NABOROWSKI.   Dariusz Chemperek, *Umysł przecię z swojego toru nie wybiega. O poezji medytacyjnej Daniela Naborowskiego*, Lublin, Wyd. UMCS, 146 pp. His '*Umysł przecię z swojego toru nie wybiega*. Poetycki dialog Daniela Naborowskiego z tradycją filozoficzną', *RuLit*, 38, 1997:311–36, detects the influence of Stoicism on N. in a comparison with works by Kochanowski, the Gdańsk philosopher Bartłomiej Keckermann (17th c.), and, ultimately, Cartesian rationalism. K. Mrowcewicz, 'Żółw, orzeł i łysa kalwińska głowa (W wileńskim kręgu poezji Daniela Naborowskiego)', *TD*, 1997, no. 4:17–27. M. Włodarski, 'O poezjach łacińskich Daniela Naborowskiego', *RuLit*, 38, 1997:465–75.

PAWEŁ Z KROSNA.   A. Gorzkowski, 'Paweł z Krosna i jego twórczość w świetle dotychczasowych badań', *PL(W)*, 89.3:143–54.

POTOCKI.   **Wokół Wacława Potockiego. Studia i szkice staropolskie w 300 rocznicę śmierci poety*, ed. Jan Malicki and Dariusz Rott, Katowice,

Wyd. Uniwersytetu Śląskiego, 1997, 147 pp. J. Kotarska, '*Dignitas humana* w twórczości Wacława Potockiego', *RuLit*, 38, 1997:27–39. K. Obremski, ' "Głupi się trochę uczą, a mędrszy głupieją". Wacław Potocki i polski spór o obrazy', *PL(W)*, 87.3, 1996:3–16. *PL(W)*, 89.2, contains two essays on P.: K. Obremski, 'Myśl antropologiczna i wyobraźnia. *Ogród fraszek* i *Moralia* Wacława Potockiego' (5–16) and J. K. Goliński, ' "Via purgativa". O religijności Wacława Potockiego i jej świadectwach poetyckich' (17–28). H. Wiśniewska, 'Wartościowanie Turków w *Wojnie chocimskiej* Wacława Potockiego', *PrzH*, 41.1, 1997:45–62.

REJ. *Mikołaj Rej z Nagłowic: sylwetka, twórczość, epoka*, ed. Maria Garbaczowa, Kielce, Kieleckie Towarzystwo Naukowe, 1997, 222 pp. D. Dybek, 'Muzy Mikołaja Reja. O samoświadomości twórczej', *PL(W)*, 87.2, 1996:21–31.

SARBIEWSKI. Aleksander Wojciech Mikołajczak, *Studia Sarbieviana*, Gniezno, Tum, 159 pp.

ZIMOROWIC R. Grześkowiak, 'Z tekstologicznej problematyki *Roksolanek*. Przyczynek krytyczny', *PL(W)*, 89.2:147–64. P. Stępień, ' "Amarant" znaczy "nie więdnący". Tajemnice neoplatońskiej architektury *Roksolanek* Szymona Zimorowica', *ib.*, 87.1, 1996:19–38.

3. ROMANTICISM

Alina Witkowska and Ryszard Przybylski, *Romantyzm*, Wyd. Naukowe PWN, 1997, 743 pp., consists of two parts: 1) Przybylski on Classicism and Sentimentalism, 1795–1830, 2) Witkowska on Romanticism, with chapters on the 'four bards' and then specific genres. Hieronim Chojnacki, *Polska 'poezja północy'*, Gd, Wyd. Uniwersytetu Gdańskiego, 202 pp., discusses *Maria, Irydion* and *Lilla Weneda*. *Trzynaście arcydzieł romantycznych*, ed. Elżbieta Kiślak and Marek Gumkowski, Wa, Wyd. IBL, 1996, 208 pp., contains essays by leading critics on Romantic masterpieces. Alina Kowalczykowa, *Dramat i teatr romantyczny*, Wa, Wyd. IBL, 1997, 268 pp., is a study of European Romantic drama from a Polish perspective, comparing French dramatists such as Dumas and Hugo with Mickiewicz and Słowacki. Charles S. Kraszewski, *The Romantic Hero and Contemporary Anti-Hero in Polish and Czech Literature. Great Souls and Grey Men*, Lewiston-Queenston-Lampeter, The Edwin Mellen Press, 325 pp., contains chapters on Mickiewicz's *Dziady*, Słowacki's *Król-Duch* and *Kordian*, Krasiński's *Nie-Boska komedia*, Norwid's *Quidam*, as well as such post-World War II authors as Herbert and Barańczak. *Góry literatura kultura*, 2 vols, ed. Jacek Kolbuszewski, WUW, Wrocław, 1996, 132 and 144 pp., is a collection of articles on mountains in Polish and other literatures. Michał Masłowski, *Gest, symbol i rytuały polskiego teatru romantycznego*,

Wa, PWN, 219 pp. + 40 pp. of plates, is an anthropological approach to the significance of the great Romantic dramas in Polish cultural life from the time of their publication to postwar Poland. Ewa Nawrocka, *W imię władzy i przeciwko władzy*, Kw, Universitas, 195 pp., contrasts Argentinian and Polish writing on the basis of Mickiewicz, Słowacki and Łoziński's writings. Anna Opacka, *Trwanie i zmienność. Romantyczne ślady oralności*, Katowice, Wyd. Uniwersytetu Śląskiego, 129 pp., discusses Dunin-Borkowski, Mickiewicz's *Pan Tadeusz* and Kraszewski's *Anafielas*. Teresa Skubalanka, *Mickiewicz, Słowacki, Norwid: Studia nad językiem i stylem*, Lublin, Wyd. UMCS, 1997, 245 pp., is a stylistic/linguistic analysis of their prose and poetry. Władysław Stabryla, *Wernyhora w literaturze polskiej*, Kw, Universitas, 1996, 144 pp., examines the origins of the legend in folk traditions, its subsequent treatment in Polish Romantic literature (Goszczyński, Zaleski, Czajkowski, and Mickiewicz), its place in Słowacki's work, and in that of later writers such as Wyspiański. Marek Stawisz, *Wczesnoromantyczne spory o poezję*, Kw, Universitas, 318 pp. Zdzisław Szeląg, *Romantyzm i polityka. Materiały i szkice*, Grójec, Towarzystwo Literackie im. Adama Mickiewicza, 1996, 161 pp., contains essays on the censorship, distribution, and reception of Mickiewicz's writings in the Russian Partition in the first half of the 19th c. as well as on studies published in the underground press between 1980 and 1989. Marian Śliwiński, *Czytając romantyków*, Zielona Góra, WSP, 1997, 148 pp., discusses *Sonety krymskie, Irydion, Dziady kowieńsko-wileńskie* and Wincenty Pola's *Pieśń o ziemi naszej*. Marta Zielińska, *Polacy, rosjanie, romantyzm*, Wa, Wyd. IBL, 187 pp., discusses the Russian contexts of Mickiewicz's 'Ustęp' and Kraszewski's *Poeta i świat*. S. Chwin, 'Romantyzm i poszukiwanie "trzeciej drogi"', *TD*, no. 5:79–101. M. Inglot, 'Uwspółcześnianie Golema. Postać człowieka-maszyny w literaturze polskiej lat 1817–1867', *PL(W)*, 88.1, 1997:25–34.

INDIVIDUAL WRITERS

GODEBSKI. G. Zając, 'Dziennik podróży czy prawdziwa powieść? O *Grenadierze-filozofie* Cypriana Godebskiego', *RuLit*, 37, 1996:685–98, sees the travelogue as a novel of ideas and precursor of novels of the latter half of the 19th c.

KOŹMIAN. S. Kufel, 'Dydaktyka i parenetyka. Uwagi o elementach świata przedstawionego w *Ziemiaństwie polskim* Kajetana Koźmiana', *PL(W)*, 89.3:5–14. M. Mycielski, '*O duchu publicznym* Kajetana Koźmiana', *ib.*, 88.1, 1997:5–24.

KRASIŃSKI. Zbigniew Sudolski, *Krasiński. Opowieść biograficzna*, Wa, Ancher, 1997, 586 pp. M. L. Dixon, 'Maria beyond marriage in Zygmunt Krasiński's *Nie-Boska komedia*', *SEEJ*, 41, 1997:442–57.

Z. Miedziński, 'Wokół *Legendy* Zygmunta Krasińskiego', *RuLit*, 37, 1996:541–51. M. Śliwiński, 'Tradycja antyczno-chrześcijańska w *'Irydionie'*, *PL(W)*, 87.2, 1996:33–52. B. Zwolińska, 'Frenetyczny obraz śmierci w *Agaj-Hanie* Krasińskiego', *RuLit*, 38, 1997:173–87.

MALCZEWSKI. Elżbieta Feliksiak, *"Maria" Malczewskiego. Duch dawnej Polski w stepowym teatrze świata*, Białystok, Towarzystwo Literackie im. Adama Mickiewicza, 1997, 255 pp. *PrzH*, 40.2, contains three essays relating to M.: B. Dopart, *'Maria* Antoniego Malczewskiego i wczesnoromantyczne konwencje literackie' (61–70), on Byronism; W. Sturc, *'Maria* Malczewskiego. Od vanitas ku nihilizmowi' (71–83); and S. Makowski, 'Słowacki — kontynuator Malczewskiego' (85–99).

MICKIEWICZ. The 200th anniversary of M.'s birth has generated an extensive amount of new studies as well as reprints of old critical works, and has necessarily involved a reappraisal of M.'s continuing relevance in today's Poland. Rolf Fieguth, *Verzweignungen. Zyklische und assoziative Kompositionsformen bei AM (1798–1855)*, Freiburg UP, 326 pp., analyses the poetic cycles *Ballady i romanse, Sonety*, and *Zdania i uwagi*, together with Parts II and IV of *Dziady* and the 'Ustęp'. Maria T. Lizisowa, *Prawem sądzić czyli o języku Statutów Litewskich w 'Panie Tadeuszu'*, Kw, Wyd. Naukowe WSP, 164 pp., is a highly original legalistic approach to the quarrel between the families in M.'s masterpiece. Jacek Łukasiewicz, *Mickiewicz*, Ww, Wyd. Dolnośląskie, 248 pp., is rather a popular account. Zbigniew Majchrowski, *Cela Konrada. Powracając do Mickiewicza*, Gd, Wyd. słowo/obraz terytoria, 347 pp., is a major new study of the significance of the 'Improwizacja' and responses in the work of Różewicz, Mrożek, Gombrowicz, and considers some celebrated stagings. **Adam Mickiewicz — Leben und Werk*, ed. Bonifacy Miązek, Frankfurt/M, Lang, 414 pp., is a collection of essays by contributors old and new, covering different aspects of M.'s creative work and his reception in Germany. Arnoldas Piroczkinas, *Litewskie lata Adama Mickiewicza*, Iskry, Wa, 442 pp. Józef Półturzycki, *Adam Mickiewicz jako nauczyciel i pedagog*, Toruń, Wyd. Adam Marszałek, 174 pp. Stanisław Rosiek, *Zwłoki Mickiewicza. Próba nekrografii poety*, Gd, Wyd. słowo/obraz terytoria, 1997, 336 pp. Krzysztof Rudnicki, *Mistrz. Widowisko*, Gd, Wyd. słowo/obraz terytoria, 1996, 199 pp. Janusz Ruszkowski, *Adam Mickiewicz i ostatnia krucjata. Studium romantycznego millenaryzmu*, Ww, Leopoldinum, 1997, 275 pp. Alina Witkowska, *Rówieśnicy Mickiewicza*, Wa, Oficyna Wydawnicza RYTM, 391 pp. Bogdan Zakrzewski has written two monographs on M.: *Dwaj wieszcze: Mickiewicz i Wernyhora*, Ww, Towarzystwo Przyjaciół Polonistyki Wrocławskiej, 1996, 257 pp., and *O 'Panie Tadeuszu' inaczej*, Ww, Ossolineum, 222 pp. *Tajemnice Mickiewicza*, ed. Marta Zielińska, Wa, Wyd. IBL, 232 pp., is a collection of essays by leading critics on relatively underexposed aspects of M's creative work. *PL(W)*, 89.1, contains six essays on M. including: Z. Mitosek, 'Mickiewicz, Napoleon i Francuzi' (13–25); L. Zwierzyński, 'Motyw łez w poezji Mickiewicza. Symbolika oczyszczenia i regeneracji' (39–50); Z. Sudolski, ' "Narodowej sprawy męczennicy". O adresatach dedykacji *Dziadów części III*' (95–102); and M. Inglot, 'Przypowieść o Marszałkowiczu. Literackie konteksty pierszej wersji księgi I *Pana Tadeusza*' (103–15). *TD*, no. 5, contains the views of certain contemporary writers on M. (159–91) as well as a number of essays: B. Kuczera-Chachulska, 'Uwagi o kształcie gatunkowym IV części *Dziadów*' (5–29); M. Prussak, 'Kto napisał *Odę do młodości?*' (31–39); and M. Zielińska, 'Puszkin i Mickiewicz wobec wolnościowych zrywów swoich rówieśników' (41–51). *RPN*, nos 7–8, contains two considerable essays on M.: M. Rudaś-Grodzka, 'Gustaw mierzył zbyt wysoko' (55–62) and P. Śliwiński, 'Na co komu Mickiewicz' (81–87), who holds out hope for the continuing relevance of M.'s legacy for young poets.

D. Balašaitienė 'Ksiąžki litewskie o Mickiewiczu', *RuLit*, 39:449–60, is a useful overview of Lithuanian works on Mickiewicz from the start of the 20th c. K. Biliński, 'Swedenborg a *Zdania i uwagi* Adama Mickiewicza', *PrzH*, 41.4, 1997:65–71. M. Cieśla-Korytowska, 'O wzniosłości *Dziadów*', *TD*, 1996, nos 2–3:24–49. B. Dopart, 'Rosja w twórczości poetyckiej Adama Mickiewicza', *RuLit*, 39:357–65. R. Fieguth, 'Kilka uwag o stylu *Grażyny*,' *PL(W)*, 87.1, 1996:127–40. R. Koropeckyj, 'Narrative and social drama in Adam Mickiewicz's *Pan Tadeusz*', *SEER*, 76:467–83, is a highly interesting and partly anthropological reading of Wojski's narrative in Book XII, which he sees as exemplifying in miniature the larger social drama. B. Shallcross, 'Intimations of intimacy: Adam Mickiewicz's *On the Grecian Room*', *SEEJ*, 42:216–30, sees M.'s conceptions of domesticity as being in the Classical vein of A. Naruszewicz and J. P. Woronicz. Z. Stefanowska, 'Pan Tadeusz — i co dalej?', *TD*, 1997, nos 1–2:5–17. A. Stępniewska, 'Rola kategorii *anagnorismós* w strukturze homeryckiej *Pana Tadeusza* Adama Mickiewicza', *RoczH*, 44 (3. Filologia klasyczna), 1996:285–313. P. Żbikowski, 'Oświeceniowe antecedencje Wielkiej Improwizacji', *RuL*, 37, 1996:699–711, sees antecedents for the 'Great Improvization' in Leibniz, the Book of Job, Kołłątaj's *Hymn II*, Koźmian's *Modlitwa o pokój*, A. J. Czartoryski's 'Starzec' from *Bard polski*, Józef Morelowski, and Niemcewicz.

NORWID. Elżbieta Dąbrowicz, *Cyprian Norwid. Osoby i listy*, Lublin, Towarzystwo Naukowe KUL, 1997, 235 pp. *Nie tylko o Norwidzie* (Prace komisji filologicznej, 38), ed. Jolanta Czarnomorska, Zbigniew Przychodniak, and Krzysztof Trybuś, Pń, Poznańskie Towarzystwo

Przyjaciół Nauk, 1997, 314 pp., includes essays on Fredro, Mickiewicz, and Wyspiański by critics such as Głowiński, Barańczak, and Ratajczakowa. Mariusz Śliwiński, *Szkice o Norwidzie* (Rozprawy literackie), Wa, Wyd. IBL, 107 pp. Kryszak, *Polonistyka*, contains three essays on N.'s work: G. Halkiewicz-Sojak, 'Interpretacja *Snu* Cypriana Norwida' (117–24), Z. Mocarska-Tycowa, '*Na zgon poezji* — niewydarzona polemika Asnyka z Norwidem. Z problematyki przemian języka poezji pozytywistycznej' (125–32), and M. Kalinowska, '*Zwolon* Cypriana Norwida wobec stereotypów polskiego romantyzmu' (133–44). A. Kuciak, 'Norwid wobec Dantego. Kilka przybliżeń', *PL(W)*, 87.3, 1996:33–59. S. Sawicki, 'Pawłowy prorok. O obrazie autora w *Promethidionie* Cypriana Norwida', *RoczH*, 45.1:111–16. M. Śliwiński, 'Synkretyzm religijno-filozoficzny Norwida', *PrzH*, 41.4, 1997:53–64. D. Uffelmann, 'Der Antizipationstopos (Am Beispiel der Rezeption Cyprian K. Norwids)', *ZSP*, 56.1, 1997:55–89, is a highly theoretical approach to the history of Norwid's reception by, in particular, Przesmycki and Przyboś.

SŁOWACKI.   Krzysztof Biliński, *Biblia i historiozofia. Kordian jako synteza wczesnej twórczości Juliusza Słowackiego*, Ww, WUW, 214 pp. Dorota Kudelska, *Juliusz Słowacki i sztuki plastyczne*, Lublin, Towarzystwo Naukowe KUL, 1997, 338 pp., is an interesting study of portraits of the poet and illustrations for his plays by Wyspiański, amongst others, as well as an examination of S.'s own aesthetic views and tastes. Magdalena Siwiec, *Sen w twórczości Juliusza Słowackiego i Gérarda de Nerval*, Kw, Universitas, 1997, 132 pp. *PP*, 52, 1997, is devoted exclusively to S. and contains articles on a variety of themes, particularly his imagery, including: J. Ławski, 'Teatr śmierci w *Balladynie*. Glosy do rozważań o wyobraźni poetyckiej Juliusza Słowackiego' (45–98); D. Kudelska, 'Veronese i czas przeszły u Słowackiego' (99–122); M. Inglot, ' "Rzym" — elegia dramatyczna Juliusza Słowackiego' (165–77); K. Biliński, 'Motyw papieża w *Kordianie* na tle biblijnej historiozofii dramatu' (179–90); O. Krysowski, 'Chrystus solarny w lirykach genezyjskich Słowackiego. Ikonograficzne źródła symboliki' (191–212); and S. Makowski, 'Wizja ognista Juliusza Słowackiego' (213–42). M. Janion and M. Żmigrodzka, 'Gorzkie arcydzieło', *TD*, 1996, nos 2–3:14–23, deals with the plays *Kordian* and *Horsztyński* against the background of Romantic concepts of the sublime. E. Kasperski, 'Wyznaczniki i kryteria mistyki. O wierszach liryczno-mistycznych Juliusza Słowackiego', *PrzH*, 41.4, 1997:39–52. A. Kowalczykowa, 'Dramatów Słowackiego, na szczęście, w romantycznym teatrze nie wystawiono...', *RuLit*, 37, 1996:523–39, considers it a blessing that S.'s plays were not staged at their time of writing, given the fiasco of stagings of Hugo's plays on similar themes. S. Makowski, '*Król-Duch* — czyli tajemnica początku i

końca', *PrzH*, 40.4, 1996:41–50. A. Ziołowicz, 'Ja — chór. O roli
chóru w mistycznej dramaturgii Juliusza Słowackiego', *PL(W)*, 88.4,
1997:23–35.

STARZYŃSKI. D. Kowalewska, 'Spuścizna dramatyczna Stanisława Starzyńskiego', Kryszak, *Polonistyka*, 87–94.

ZAN. Z. Sudolski, 'Zapomniane wartości prozy Tomasza Zana',
RoczH (1. Literatura polska), 45, 1997:85–98, recalls Z.'s fascination
with Sterne and his visual sensitivity.

ŻMICHOWSKA. M. Woźniakiewicz-Dziadosz, '*Pisma Gabrielli* —
romantyczna formuła dyskursu powieściowego', *PL(W)*, 88.4,
1997:37–52.

4. From Realism to Neo-Realism

Grażyna Borkowska, *Cudzoziemki*, Wa, Wyd. IBL, 1996, 268 pp., is a
pioneering feminist study of 19th-c. Polish women's writing and
includes chapters on Orzeszkowa, Żmichowska, Konopnicka as well
as the diaries of Dąbrowska and Nałkowska. Her *Pozytywiści i inni*
(Mała Historia Literatury Polskiej), Wa, PWN, 1996, 215 pp., deals
with similar subjects in a more general and concise manner, as befits
that series: the 'others' are Dąbrowska, Nałkowska, and early
modernist writers. A . Martuszewska, 'Jak bada prozę kobiecą polska
"córka Miltona"? (O *Cudzoziemkach* Grażyny Borkowskiej)', *RuLit*, 38,
1997:593–606, provides a stimulating critique of Borkowska's
approach. Anna Czabanowska-Wróbel, *Baśń w literaturze Młodej Polski*,
Kw, Universitas, 1996, 268 pp., examines the fairy tale in Młoda
Polska prose, poetry, and drama before turning her attention to its
place in Tadeusz Miciński and Leśmian's work. Anna Gemra, '*Kwiaty
zła' na miejskim bruku. O powieści zeszytowej XIX i XX wieku*, Ww, WUW,
153 pp. Michał Głowiński, *Ekspresja i empatia. Studia o młodopolskiej
krytyce literackiej*, Kw, WL, 1997, 408 pp., is an important study of
Młoda Polska literary criticism. His *Powieść Młodopolska* (Prace wybrane 1), Kw, Universitas, 1997, 335 pp., is a reprint of the famous
1969 treatise, with an introduction by R. Nycz. *Pisarze Młodej Polski i
Warszawa*, ed. Danuta Knysz-Tomaszewska, Roman Taborski, and
Jadwiga Zacharska, Wa, Uniwersytet Warszawski, 385 pp. Leszek
Pułka, *Hołota, masa, tłum. Bohater zbiorowy w prozie polskiej 1890–1918*,
Ww, WUW, 1996, 251 pp., examines the collective hero in fables,
stories, and social fiction of the time. *Stara i młoda prasa. Przyczynek do
historii literatury ojczystej 1866–1872*, ed. Dobrosława Świerczyńska,
Wa, Wyd. IBL, 209 pp., is an edition of critical texts probably written
by W. Przyborowski and J. Kaliszewski.

M. Podraza-Kwiatkowska, 'Ibsenowska "prawda" w literaturze
Młodej Polski', *RuLit*, 37, 1996:137–50, considers the response to

Ibsen's dictum on the part of Young Poland writers; her 'Obraz Boga wśród światopoglądowych przemian Młodej Polski (Na przykładzie poezji)', *ib.*, 38, 1997:777–98. A. Romanowski, '*Banda — Żórawce*. Z dziejów grup literacko-artystycznych w Wilnie okresu Młodej Polski', *ib.*, 37, 1996:713–28, provides an overview of a little-known offshoot of the movement in the years 1908–15.

INDIVIDUAL WRITERS

BERENT. M. Okulicz-Kozaryn, '*Żywe kamienie* Berenta: źródła i ujścia europejskości', *PL(W)*, 88.4, 1997:75–90.

KASPROWICZ. Irena Pereszczako, *W kręgu ballad Jana Kasprowicza*, Olsztyń, WSP, 1996, 168 pp.

KOMORNICKA. Edward Boniecki, *Modernistyczny dramat ciała. Maria Komornicka*, Wa, Wyd. IBL, 206 pp. + 12 pl.

KONOPNICKA. B. Bobrowska, 'Z dziejów motywu prometejskiego w literaturze polskiej. *Prometeusz i Syzyf* Konopnickiej', *RuLit*, 37, 1996:553–76. E. Teodorowicz-Hellman, 'Epos dziecięcy *Na jagody* Marii Konopnickiej a książka obrazkowa Elsy Beskow', *ib.*, 38, 1997:643–52.

KRASZEWSKI. Bogumiła Kosmanowa, *Kraszewski mniej znany*, Bydgoszcz, WSP, 219 pp.

T. MICIŃSKI. J. Wróbel, 'Podwójna architektonika świtu w "Bazilissie Teofanu" T. Micińskiego', *RuLit*, 37, 1996:173–81.

OSTROWSKA. Anna Wydrycka, . . . *Rymów gałążeczki skrzydlate. W świecie poetyckim Bronisławy Ostrowskiej*, Białystok, Wyd. Uniwersytetu w Białymstoku, 211 pp., includes an anthology of works published in newspapers but not in her volumes of poetry.

PRUS. C. Kasparek, 'Prus' *Pharoah* and the Wieliczka Salt Mine', *PolR*, 42, 1997:349–55. W. Klemm, ' "Panna Leokadia widzi cały garnitur". O ubraniach w *Lalce* Bolesława Prusa', *PL(W)*, 88.4, 1997:53–74.

PRZYBYSZEWSKA. Kazimiera Ingdahl, *A Gnostic Tragedy. A Study in Stanisława Przybyszewska's Aesthetics and Works* (Stockholm Slavic Studies, 26), Stockholm, Acta Universitatis Stockholmiensis, 1997, 217 pp. + 24 illus., is a major new study of P.

PRZYBYSZEWSKI. A. Moskwin, 'Dzieje sceniczne dramatu *Śnieg* Stanisława Przybyszewskiego w Rosji początku XX wieku', *PrzH*, 42.3:133–47, and 'Twórczość Stanisława Przybyszewskiego przez pryzmat cenzury rosyjskiej końca XIX i początku XX wieku', *PL(W)*, 89.2:165–73. M. Popiel, 'Laokoon, czyli o granicach wzniosłości w prozie Stanisława Przybyszewskiego', *TD*, 1996, nos 2–3:50–71, and 'Wzniosłość — retoryka cierpienia. (O prozie Stanisława Przybyszewskiego)', *RuLit*, 37, 1996:37–49.

REYMONT. B. Fert, 'Reymont wobec spraw nie z tego świata', *RuLit*, 38, 1997:387–401.

SIENKIEWICZ. Tadeusz Bujnicki, *Sienkiewicza 'Powieści z lat dawnych'*, Kw, Universitas, 1996, 236 pp. Tadeusz Żabski, *Sienkiewicz*, Ww, Wyd. Dolnośląskie, 321 pp. The whole of *PrzH*, 40.6, 1996, is devoted to S. and includes: J. Kulczycka-Saloni, 'Literaci i literatura w publicystyce Henryka Sienkiewicza' (57–63) and J. Zacharska, 'Sienkiewiczowski ideał kobiety — Marynia Połaniecka' (71–82). A. Stoff, 'Zbaraż i jego obrońcy. Funkcjonowanie pamięci wewnątrzpowieśiowej w *Trylogii* Henryka Sienkiewicza', *RuLit*, 38, 1997:629–42. *PL(W)*, 87.4, 1996, contains several essays on S., including: K. Stępnik, 'O Sienkiewiczu: mowy, kazania, wiersze' (15–48) and R. Koziołek, 'O przedstawieniu ciąży i macierzyństwa w *Trylogii* Henryka Sienkiewicza. Próba lektury feministycznej' (49–63). *RoczH*, 45.1, 1997, contains two essays on S.: S. Fita, 'Przeoczona młodzieńcza korespondencja Henryka Sienkiewicza' (131–37), concerning the often overlooked *Listy z Podlasia. W kwestii reformy wychowania kobiet*, and A. Stoff, 'Sienkiewiczowskie studium zemsty. Wątek Adama Nowowiejskiego w *Panu Wołodyjowskim*' (139–50).

WYSPIAŃSKI. M. Prussak, ' "Społeczeństwo! Oto tortury najsroższe" ', *TD*, 1996, nos 2–3:139–48, deals with *Wesele*. S. Wrzosek, '*Warszawianka* inaczej', *RuLit*, 38, 1997:41–54, indicates the classical Greek tragic elements in the play.

ŻEROMSKI. *The Literature of Nationalism. Essays on East European Identity*, ed. Robert P. Pynsent, Houndmill, Basingstoke and London, Macmillan, 1996, 282 pp., contains a chapter by S. Eile, 'Stefan Żeromski and the Crisis of Polish Nationalism' (66–82). Zbigniew Lisowski, *Nowelistyka Stefana Żeromskiego*, Kielce, Wyd. Szumacher, n.d., 284 pp. M. Popiel, 'Próba tragizmu epickiego — *Ludzie bezdomni* Stefana Żeromskiego', *PL(W)*, 89.2:59–92. *PrzH*, 40.4, 1996, contains two essays on Ż.: Z. Przybyła, 'Żeromski wobec malarstwa polskiego (na podstawie *Dzienników*)' (79–90) and J. Zacharska, 'Stefana Żeromskiego Prometeusz polski' (91–103), which deals with *Rozdziobią nas kruki, wrony*.

5. FROM 1918 TO 1945

Stulecie Skamandrytów, ed. K. Biedrzycki, Kw, Universitas, 1996, 215 pp., is a collection of papers from a conference at Cracow University in December 1994, which covers all the major figures of the group, and M. Pawlikowska-Jasnorzewska. Przemysław Czapliński, *Poetyka manifestu literackiego 1918–1939*, Wa, Wyd. IBL, 1997, 216 pp. Oskar S. Czarnik, *Ideowe i literackie wybory 'Robotnika' w latach 1918–1939*, Wa, Biblioteka Narodowa, 1996, 450 pp., includes chapters on the literary preferences and cultural debates carried on in the columns of the famous socialist newspaper. Ryszard Nycz, *Język modernizmu. Prologomena historycznoliterackie*, Ww, Leopoldinum, 1997, 330 pp. Ireneusz Opacki, *Król-Duch, Herostates i codzienność*, Katowice, Agencja Artystyczna PARA, 1997, 361 pp., contains essays on J. Lechoń, J. Tuwim and others, published over the past 30 years. J. Sławiński, *Koncepcja języka poetyckiego awangardy krakowskiej* (Prace wybrane, 1), Kw, Universitas, 1998, 293 pp., is a corrected and slightly stylistically altered reprint of the 1965 classic, with a lengthy introduction by W. Bolecki. Jagoda Hernik-Spalińska, *Wileńskie Środy literackie (1927–1939)*, Wa, Wyd. IBL, 339 pp. + 12 pp. of illus. Kazimierz Świegocki, *Światopogląd poetów ziemi*, Siedlce, Wyższa Szkoła Rolniczo-Pedagogiczna, 1996, 147 pp., deals with the 'autentyzm' movement of the 1930s in relation to the poetry of Czernik and Ożóg. Maria Tarnogórska, *Poemat międzywojenny*, Ww, Towarzystwo Przyjaciół Polonistyki Wrocławskiej, 1997, 326 pp., contains chapters on T. Peiper and A. Ważyk. Maciej Urbanowski, *Nacjonalistyczna krytyka literacka. Próba rekonstrukcji i opisu nurtu w II Rzeczypospolitej*, Kw, Arcana, 1997, 167 pp. Krzysztof Woźniakowski, *W kręgu jawnego piśmiennictwa literackiego Generalnego Gubernatorstwa (1939–1945)*, Kw, WSP, 1997, 474 pp., is a novel and monumental analysis of the Polish publications which appeared legally during the German occupation.

M. Delaperrière, 'La modernité et l'avant-gardisme polonais dans le contexte européen', *RSl*, 70.1:201–13. M. Urbanowski, 'Jawne piśmiennictwo Generalnego Gubernatorstwa (1939–1945) wobec tradycji literatury polskiej', *RuLit*, 37, 1996:51–69. M. Wierczyński, 'Dwudziestolecie z felerami', *ib.*, 91–95, contains useful corrections to Andrzej Zawada's volume *Dwudziestolecie literackie* from the 'A to Polska właśnie' series (Ww, 1995). A. Kluba, 'Referencyjność i autoteliczność w twórczości Tadeusza Peipera i Juliana Przybosia', *PL(W)*, 89.4:37–71. E. Pogonowska, 'Moskal i bolszewik. Szkic o polskiej antybolszewickiej twórczości poetyckiej po 1917 roku', *PrzH*, 42.1:103–21, is largely devoted to the anti-Bolshevik poems which appeared in Polish newspapers during the 1920 campaign.

INDIVIDUAL WRITERS

BOGUSZEWSKA. E. Kraskowska, 'Świat według Boguszewskiej i po kobiecemu', *PL(W)*, 88.3, 1997:91–105.

CZECHOWICZ. G. Grochowski, '*Eros i Psyche*. Dyskurs miłosny Czechowicza', *PL(W)*, 88.2, 1997:113–29. D. Kobylska, 'Między współczesnością a pragnieniem Boga. O poezji Józefa Czechowicza', *PP*, 51, 1996:163–85.

CZYŻEWSKI. J. Krzysztoforska-Doschek, 'Reflexe urslawischer Dichtung in der futuristischen Lyrik Tytus Czyżewskis', *WSJ*, 42, 1996:123–27, is largely linguistic.

GOMBROWICZ. Michał Legierski, *Modernizm Witolda Gombrowicza. Wybrane zagadnienia* (Stockholm Slavic Studies, 25), Stockholm, Acta Universitatis Stockholmiensis, 1996, 460 pp. +4 pp. errata. Krzysztof Łęcki, *Zinstytucjonalizowane formy komunikowania o literaturze. Socjologia analiza zjawiska Św. Gombrowicza*, Katowice, 'Śląsk', 1997, 215 pp. *Gombrowicz's Grimaces. Modernism, Gender, Nationality*, ed. Ewa Plonowska Ziarek, Albany, State University of New York Press, 327 pp., is an important collection of essays on different aspects of G.'s creative work, including the less-discussed issue of his homosexuality. *Periphery*, 1997, contains three essays on G.: J. Jarzębski, 'Gombrowicz and Wittlin — two conspirators' (94–99); E. Ziarek, 'Nationality as form in Gombrowicz's *Trans-Atlantyk*' (100–05); and A. J. Kuharski, 'Gombrowicz's tragedy of dispossession' (106–09). *TD*, 1996, no. 4, contains two essays on G.: J. Jarzębski, 'Kicz jest w nas (Gombrowicza romans z kiczem' (52–70), and D. Korwin-Piotrowska, 'PĘTA *Opętanych*' (135–53). R. Fieguth, 'Słowo, *sacrum* i władza. Komentarze do *Ślubu* Gombrowicza i jego tradycji romantycznych', Wojnowska, *Literatura*, 177–93. M. Głowiński, 'Gombrowicz a Brzozowski', *TD*, 1997, nos 1–2:47–62. G. Langer, 'Witold Gombrowiczs Erzählung *Zdarzenia na brygu Banbury* als homoerotischer Maskentext', *ZSl*, 42, 1997:290–99. O. Kühl, 'Ciało i jego maskowanie u Gombrowicza', *TD*, 1996, no. 1:59–68.

IRZYKOWSKI. H. Markiewicz, 'Strategie krytycznoliterackie Karola Irzykowskiego', *RuLit*, 39:475–92.

IWASZKIEWICZ. German Ritz, *Jarosław Iwaszkiewicz. Ein Grenzgänger der Moderne* (Slavica Helvetica, 47), Berne, Lang, 1996, 290 pp., deals with the development of I.'s prose work from before World War II to the late travel literature. '*Panny z Wilka' Jarosława Iwaszkiewicza*, ed. Inga Iwasiów and Jan Madejski, Szczecin, Uniwersytet Szczeciński, 1996, 175 pp. Elżbieta Tyseczka-Grygorowicz, *Poetyka krótkich form narracyjnych Jarosława Iwaszkiewicz*, Łódź, Wyd. ASTRA, 1996, 127 pp. Z. Chojnowski, 'Antyk, wojna i propaganda. O kilku *odach* Jarosława Iwaszkiewicza', *PL(W)*, 89.4:73–97. B. Gryszkiewicz, '*Panny z Wilka* Jarosława Iwaszkiewicza jako opowieść o postrzeganiu świata', *RuLit*, 38, 1997:373–85. A. Pawłowska, 'Metamorfozy koła w poezji Jarosława Iwaszkiewicza', *PrzH*, 40.5, 1996:95–107. G. Ritz, 'Stosunek niejednoznaczy, czyli Jarosław Iwaszkiewicz wobec władzy', Wojnowska, *Literatura*, 195–206, examines I.'s flirtation with the Communist authorities in People's Poland as a kind of 'third way'. S. Stabro, 'Późna liryka Jarosława Iwaszkiewicza', *RuLit*, 37, 1996:309–25. S. Wysłouch, '*Bitwa na równinie*

Sedgemoor Jarosława Iwaszkiewicza, czyli o klęsce fundamentalizmu', *RoczH*, 55.1, 1997:165–72.

JASIEŃSKI. K. Jaworski, '*Morze* Brunona Jasieńskiego przykładem poezji wizualnej, *PP*, 51, 1996:249–55.

KORCZAK. *Janusz Korczak. Pisarz — wychowawca — myśliciel*, ed. Hanna Kirschner, Wa, Wyd. IBL, 1997, 282 pp., comprises 12 articles by experts on various aspects of K.'s creative activity, his thinking about pedagogy, and his professional and personal life.

LECHOŃ. R. Korepyckyj, 'Konstrukcje homoseksualizmu w *Dzienniku* Jana Lechonia (Próba innej lektury)', *TD*, 1996, no. 4:154–68.

LEŚMIAN. P. Dybel, 'Lacan i Leśmian — dwa zwierciadła', *TD*, nos 1–2:19–36. A. Kluba, 'Niezrozumiałe — nienazwane —nowoczesne. Leśmian i Iwaszkiewicz — dwa modele poetyckiej niewyrażalności', Bolecki, *Literatura*, 249–66.

B. MICIŃSKI. R. Kwiecień, 'Bolesław Miciński i psychoanaliza', *TD*, nos 1–2:85–108.

MNISZEK. M. Bujnicka, 'Feministki czytają *Gehennę* Heleny Mniszek', *RuLit*, 39:55–64, is an exemplary feminist critique.

NAŁKOWSKA. E. Kraskowska, 'Niebezpieczne związki. Jeszcze raz o prozie Zofii Nałkowskiej', *TD*, 1996, no. 4:71–91.

PAWLIKOWSKA. M. Semczuk, 'Anna Achmatowa — Maria Pawlikowska-Jasnorzewska. Paralele nie tylko poetyckie', *PrzH*, 41.2, 1997:69–78.

PEIPER. H. Konicka, 'Czy konstruktywizm był konstruktywny? Uwagi o teorii sztuki Tadeusza Peipera', *TD*, 1996, no. 6:17–30.

PIGOŃ. *Non omnis moriar. Studia i szkice o Stanisławie Pigoniu*, ed. Czesław Kłak, Rzeszów, WSP, 1997, 235 pp.

PRZYBOŚ. Z. Zarębianka, 'Widzieć znaczy wiedzieć. Motyw katedry w twórczości Juliana Przybosia', *RoczH* (1. Literatura polska), 45, 1997:173–79.

SCHULZ. Władysław Panas, *Księga blasku. Traktat o kabale w prozie Brunona Schulza*, Lublin, Towarzystwo Naukowe KUL, 1997, 229 pp. *Periphery*, 1997, contains four interesting essays on S.: J. Jarzębski, 'Reading Schulz' (70–74); S. Chwin, ' "Sinful manipulations": the history of art and the history of medicine' (75–78); T. S. Robertson, 'Imagery and history in the stories of Bruno Schulz: the case of the railroad' (79–83); E. Prokop-Janiec, 'Schulz and the Galician melting pot of cultures' (84–88). F. M. Cataluccio, 'Niema samotność w zwierciadle. Mit i przemiany u Brunona Schulza', *TD*, 1996, no. 1:148–53. D. Głowacka, 'Wzniosła tandeta i *simulacrum*: Bruno Schulz w postmodernistycznych zaułkach', *ib.*, 1996, nos 2–3:72–91. W. Kośny, ' "Bo czymże jest wiosna, jeśli nie zmartwychwstaniem historyj." (Zu Bruno Schulz' Erzählung *Wiosna*)', *ZSP*, 55, 1995–96:313–22. D. Kuprel, 'Errant events on the branch tracks of time: Bruno Schulz and mythical consciousness', *SEEJ*, 40, 1996:100–17. A. Schönle, 'Of sublimity, shrinkage, and selfhood in the works of Bruno Schulz', *ib.*, 42:467–82, places S.'s stories in the context of Western notions of sublimity from Kant through the Romantics, Freudian psychoanalysis and Lyotard.

TUWIM. G. Gazda, 'Tuwim i awangarda', *PP*, 51, 1996:21–34. A. Kowalczykowa, 'Tuwim — poetyckie wizje Łodzi', *ib.*, 7–19. P. Michałowski, 'Bukiet, wiecheć, ikebana. Uwagi o kompozycji *Kwiatów polskich* Juliana Tuwima', *TD*, 1996, no. 6:113–31, and '*Za stachetami gęstych jambów*. O wersyfikacji *Kwiatów polskich* Juliana Tuwima', *RuLit*, 38, 1997:55–69.

WAT. Jarosław Borowski, '*Między bluźniercą a wyznawcą*'. *Doświadczenie sacrum w poezji Aleksandra Wata*, Lublin, Towarzystwo Naukowe KUL, 249 pp. Tomas Venclova, *Aleksander Wat*, Kw, Wyd. Literackie, 1997, 513 pp., is the Polish version of *Aleksander Wat. Life and Art of an Iconoclast*, New Haven, Yale UP, 1996, xiii + 369 pp., the first major study of W.'s life and work. W. Bolecki, 'Czy nazism może być parabolą? (O *Ucieczce Lotha* Aleksandra Wata)', Wojnowska, *Literatura*, 31–63, suggests that Wat's failure to complete the novel stemmed from an inability to apply his experience of the Soviet system.

WIERZYŃSKI. A. Hutnikiewicz, ' "Na Placu Bastylii" Kazimierza Wierzyńskiego', Kryszak, *Polonistyka*, 155–60. A Nasiłowska, 'Wierzyński i ideologia sanacji', Wojnowska, *Literatura*, 207–19.

WITKIEWICZ. Jan Błoński, *Od Stasia do Witkacego*, Kw, WL, 1996/97, 159 pp. + 16 pl. Wiesław Rzońca, *Witkacy — Norwid. Projekt komparatystyki dekonstrukcjonistycznej*, Wa, Semper, 238 pp., an innovative study, concludes that N. is a more modern (i.e. postmodern) writer than Witkiewicz. J. Błoński, 'I cóż dalej, dziwna monado? Witkacy u progu niepodległości', *TD*, 1996, no. 4:39–51. G. Grochowski, 'Trudna sztuka mówienia głupstw. O *Narkotykach* Stanisława Ignacego Witkiewicza', *PL(W)*, 89.3:115–41. E. Łubieniewska, 'Uwikłani w moc ... (O *Gyubalu Wahazarze* Witkacego)', *RuLit*, 38, 1997:671–93. B. Schultze, 'Upadek władcy. Temat, motywy i polskie toposy w scenicznej paraboli St. I. Witkiewicza *Gyubal Wahazar* (1921)', *TD*, no. 3:91–105.

WOLICA. K. Woźniakowski, ' "Człowiek jest zawsze sam ze swoją męką i cierpieniem" (nad nieznanym dramatem Andrzeja Wolicy)', *PrzH*, 41.5, 1997:167–72, discusses *Mężczyzna publiczna*, set in the years 1936–38.

6. 1945 TO THE PRESENT DAY

The first part of the third and final volume of *Literatura polska 1918–1975*, ed. Alina Brodzka and Tadeusz Bujnicki, Wa, Wiedza

Powszechna, 1996, 432 pp., covers the literary culture, periodicals, essays, and scholarship produced during the years 1945–75. The massive undertaking *Słownik pseudonimów pisarzy polskich* reaches completion with vol. IV (*XV w.-1970. Nazwiska*), ed. Edmund Jankowski, Ww, Ossolineum, 1996, 820 pp., an index of surnames, which is complemented by vol. V (*1971–1995*), ed. Dobrosława Świerczyńska, Ww, Ossolineum, 1067 pp., which contains corrections and additional information. *Współczesne polscy pisarze i badacze literatury*, ed. Jadwiga Czachowska and Alicja Szałagan, Wa, WSiP, has now reached vols 4, 1996, 535 pp., covering the letter 'K', and 5, 1997, 534 pp., covering the letters 'L–M'. Władysław Chojacki, *Bibliografia polskich publikacji podziemnych wydanych pod rządami komunistycznymi w latach 1939–1941 i 1944–1953: czasopisma, druki zwarte, druki lotne*, Wa, Literackie Towarzystwo Wydawnicze, 1996, 352 pp. Zbigniew Andres, *W stronę współczesności. Studia i szkice o literaturze polskiej po 1939 roku*, Rzeszów, WSP, 1996, 352 pp., contains essays on Odojewski, Wierzyński, Kamieńska, Stachura, Wirpsza, Kuśniewicz, Pietrkiewicz, and Łobodowski. Stanisław Burkot, *Literatura polska w latach 1986–1995*, Kw, Wyd. Edukacyjne, 1996, 147 pp., deals with recent poetry, prose, and drama, and contains tables juxtaposing the most significant works by year. Mieczysław Dąbrowski, *Literatura polska 1945–1995. Główne zjawiska*, Wa, Wyd. TRIO, 1997, 282 pp., is an overview of the period. Zbigniew Jarosiński, *Literatura lat 1945–1975* (Mała Historia Literatury Polskiej), Wa, Wyd. Naukowe PWN, 1996, 203 pp., describes developments (i) up to 1949, (ii) during the Socialist Realist period, and (iii) from 1956 to 1975 and the rise of independent publishing. Marian Stępień, *Pięćdziesiąt lat literatury polskiej (1939–1989)*, Kw, Oficyny wydawnicze Impuls and Text, 1996, 236 pp. *Sporne postaci polskiej literatury współczesnej*, ed. Alina Brodzka and Lidia Burska, Wa, Wyd. IBL, 1996, 245 pp., is a collection of essays by leading critics dealing with such figures as P. Huelle, K. Brandys, L. Tyrmand, G. Herling-Grudziński, Z. Herbert, and M. Świetlicki, amongst others. Edward Balcerzan, *Śmiech pokoleń — płacz pokoleń*, Kw, Universitas, 1997, 195 pp., discusses the poetry of Szymborska, Różewicz, Białoszewski, Maiakovskii, and Przyboś. Maria Delaperrière, *Dialog z dystansem*, Kw, Universitas, 277 pp., considers the influence of the Baroque on contemporary Polish literature, as well as devoting specific essays to S. Grochowiak and A. Kuśniewicz. *Postmodernism in Literature and Culture of Central and Eastern Europe*, ed. Halina Janaszek-Ivaničková and Douwe Fokkema, Katowice, Śląsk, 1996, 339 pp., examines postmodernism across all Slavic cultures, but includes essays on J. Andrzejewski's *Miazga*, the plays of M. Pankowski, W. Gombrowicz, as well as general essays on postmodernist tendencies in Polish poetry up to 1980. *Pogranicza*

wrażliwości w literaturze dawnej oraz współczesnej. Cz. I. Miłość (Materiały.
Konferencje, 32), ed. Inga Iwasiów and Piotr Urbański, Szczecin,
Uniwersytet Szczeciński, 217 pp., is principally about 20th-c. Polish
writers and contains essays by leading scholars on J. Andrzejewski,
T. Różewicz, and A. Stasiuk. Maria Janion, *Kobiety i duch inności*, Wa,
Wyd. Sic !, 1996, 351 pp., is extremely wide-ranging and contains
mostly previously published essays on female figures in Polish
literature and specific writers, such as M. Komornicka,
S. Przybyszewska, and I. Filipiak. Anna Legeżyńska, *Dom i poetycka
bezdomność w liryce współczesnej*, Wa, PWN, 1996, 192 pp., deals with
the theme in the poetry of Herbert, Różewicz, and Barańczak,
amongst others. Tadeusz Nycz, *Sylwy współczesne*, Kw, Universitas,
1996, 222 pp., is a reprint of the 1984 edition with an additional two
sketches on Buczkowski. Tadeusz Nyczek, *Plus nieskończoność. Trzy
tercety krytyczne na poezję, teatr i malarstwo oraz solo na głosy mieszane*, Kw,
WL, 1997, 240 pp., discusses the poetry of A. Zagajewski, Z. Bieńkow-
ski, and K. Miłobędzka. *Enttabuisierung: Essays zur russischen und
polnischen Gegenwartsliteratur*, ed. Jochen-Ulrich Peters and German
Ritz, Bern, Lang, 1996, 176 pp., leans rather more towards the
Russian than Polish, but contains essays on Konwicki, Holocaust
literature (H. Grynberg), *bruLion*, and sexual deviation in the prose of
J. Iwaszkiewicz, M. Nowakowski, and G. Musiał. Jerzy Skarbowski,
Literacki koncert polski, Rzeszów, Fosze, 1997, 200 pp., discusses
particular authors' relationships with music, including S. Kisielewski,
M. Dąbrowska, J. Lechoń, M. Kuncewiczowa, and J. Tuwim. Waleria
Szydłowska, *Egzystencja-LIZM w kontekstach polskich. Szkic o doświad-
czeniu, myśleniu i pisaniu powojennym*, Wa, Wyd. IFiS PAN, 1997, 145
pp., discusses such classics as *Kartoteka*, *Popiół i diament*, *Mała apokalipsa*
and *Tango*. *Ja, autor. Sytuacja podmiotu w polskiej literaturze współczesnej*,
ed. Dariusz Śnieżko, Wa, Semper, 1996, 216 pp., contains general
theoretical articles by R. Nycz, J. Abramowska, A. Stoff and others,
as well as two devoted to S. Lem and T. Karpowicz. Jan Tomkowski,
Dwadzieścia lat z literaturą, 1977–1995, Wa, PIW, 202 pp. Andrzej
Werner, *Krew i atrament*, Wa, Wyd. PWN, 1997, 216 pp.

The issue of émigré writing has been dealt with by a number of
specialists. The most geographically specific is *Poetycki krąg 'Kontynen-
tów'*, ed. Zbigniew Andres and Jan Wolski, WSP, Rzeszów, 1997, 274
pp., devoted to the poetry of Polish poets based in London and
elsewhere from the 1950s onwards. Jerzy Jarzębski, *Pożegnanie z
emigracją. O powojennej prozie polskiej*, Kw, WL, 257 pp., is a collection of
recently published pieces, devoted not only to émigré writers, but also
figures such as Lem, Schulz, and Konwicki, as well as historical
overviews. *Szkice o polskich pisarzach emigracyjnych*, ed. Marian Kisiel
and Włodzimierz Wójcik, Katowice, Towarzystwo Zachęty Kultury,

132 pp., contains pieces on Z. Haupt, A. Bobkowski, J. Mackiewicz, C. Miłosz, Wat, and M. Pankowski. Wojciech Ligęza, *Jerozolima i Babilon. Miasta poetów emigracyjnych*, Kw, Wyd. Baran i Suszczyński, 288 pp., examines the theme of exile in the works of Mrożek, Wat, Szymborska, Herbert, and Obertyńska. Elżbieta Sawicka, *Przystanek Europa. Rozmowy nie tylko o literaturze*, Wa, MOST, 1996, 231 pp., is a series of interviews on cultural and political topics with Russian and Polish writers and artists who have lived in emigration, such as Mrożek, Miłosz, K. Brandys, Herling-Grudziński, and Barańczak. Piotr Wilczek, *Ślady egzystencji. Szkice o polskich pisarzach emigracyjnych*, Katowice, 'Śląsk', 1997, 107 pp., gives brief introductions to the work of Miłosz, Lechoń, Gombrowicz, and A. Czerniawski. M. Kłosińska-Duszczyk, 'Funkcjonalizacja przestrzeni w prozie Zygmunta Haupta i Czesława Miłosza. Kresy — Ameryka', *PrzH*, 42.3: 111–22. H.-C. Trepte, 'Tematy żydowskie w polskiej literaturze emigracyjnej w USA po roku 1945', *ib.*, 40.3, 1996:97–105, provides a typology of themes in, principally, Miłosz and Grynberg's work.

There have been a number of works relating to the politicization of literature under the Communists. Tadeusz Drewnowski, *Próba scalenia. Obiegi — wzorce — style*, Wa, Wyd. Naukowe PWN, 1997, 543 pp., is a balanced, summative assessment of Polish literature from World War II to 1989. Devoted to an earlier period and more biased is Jacek Trznadel, *Kolaboranci. Tadeusz Boy-Żeleński i grupa komunistycznych pisarzy we Lwowie 1939–1941*, Komorów, Wyd. Antyk Marcin Dybowski, 551 pp., a part-essay, part-anthology of literary works and journalism from the first stage of the Communist experiment in Soviet-occupied Lvov (1939–41). Jan Prokop continues his trenchant exploration of the immediate postwar period with *Sowietyzacja i jej maski*, Kw, Viridis, 1997, 160 pp., which examines such issues as the role of IBL in promoting the Socialist Realist agenda in schools and universities, Maria Dąbrowska's diaries, and Polish historical amnesia regarding the wrongs done to the German inhabitants of the 'Regained Territories' after the war. His *Lata niby-Polski*, Kw, Viridis, 146 pp., contains wider-ranging essays on the literary canon and current Polish myths about Russia. Specifically devoted to the early 1950s are the following: Z. Jarosiński, ' "Człowiek radziecki" w polskiej poezji socrealistycznej', *PrzH*, 42.4:55–63, and 'Socrealizm dla dzieci', *TD*, no. 6:69–86; J. Smulski, 'Epizod z dziejów przedpaździernikowej "odwilży". Wokół *Pamiętnika uczennicy*', Kryszak, *Polonistyka*, 171–79, revisits a minor episode of the pre-Thaw liberalization, while his 'Jak niewyrażalne staje się wyrażalne? O języku ezopowej w prozie polskiej lat pięćdziesiątych', Bolecki, *Literatura*, 144–64, analyses the phenomenon of Aesopic language in relation to Andrzejewski's *Ciemności kryją ziemię*, Malewska's *Sir Thomas*

More odmawia and Szczepański's _Pojedynek._ Dorota Tubielewicz Matt-
son, _Polska socrealistyczna krytyka literacka jako narzędzie władzy_, Uppsala
UP, 1997, 202 pp., an important first extensive study on the subject,
examines the place of literary criticism and critics in the official
promotion and supervision of Socialist Realism. On the later period
are Krzysztof Łabędź, *_Spory wokół zagadnień programowych w publikacjach
opozycji politycznej w Polsce w latach 1981–1989_, Kw, Księgarnia
Akademicka, 1997, 298 pp., and Małgorzata Anna Szulc Packalén,
Pokolenie 68. Studium o poezji polskiej lat siedemdziesiątych, Wa, Wyd. IBL,
262 pp., the first in a new series of reprints of works, entitled 'Badania
Polonistyczne za Granicą' (see Tomaszewski above), by experts based
outwith Poland. T. Witkowski, 'Between poetry and politics: two
generations', _Periphery_, 1996, 38–43, examines the legacy of the 'Nowa
Fala' in today's poetry; his 'Politics for Art's Sake', _ib._, 1997, 62–68, is
an assessment of the same movement's aesthetics. On the subject of
censorship and resistance to it are: W. Bolecki, 'The totalitarian urge
vs. literature: the origins and achievements of the Polish Independent
Publishing Movement', _CanSP_, 39.1–2, 1997: 47–62; and two good
essays about the practices and effects of postwar censorship in _TD_,
no. 3: J. Hobot, '"Trzeci obieg" literatury: Cenzor jako odbiorca
poezji nowofalowej' (107–24); and J. Czachowska, 'Literatura emigracyjna w krajowych bibliografiach literackich' (129–44), which is
based on the author's own experience of many years. A more general
essay on censorship in People's Poland is M. Fik, 'Cenzor jako
współautor', Wojnowska, _Literatura_, 131–47. K. Braun, 'Religious
theater in Poland under totalitarianism', _PolR_, 42, 1997: 297–315, is
a sketchy overview with consideration, _inter alia_, of K. Wojtyła and
J. Zawieyski's work. M. Sugiera, 'Szwajcarscy Dioskurowie rozdzie-
leni. Recepcja sztuk Dürrenmatta i Frischa w polskim dramacie po
1956', _RuLit_, 38, 1997: 695–708, considers Dürrenmatt's influence on
Mrożek, Broszkiewicz, Grochowiak up to 1965 to have been greater
than Frisch's at least partly for 'extra-literary' reasons.

Przemysław Czapliński, _Ślady przełomu: o prozie polskiej 1976–1995_,
Kw, Wyd. Literackie, 1996, 267 pp., examines the development of
Polish prose to the present day in terms of the end of collective
political concerns and the recovery of an individual perspective. Jan
Galant, _Polska proza lingwistyczną. Debiuty lat siedemdziesiątych_ (Poznańskie studia polonistyczne, 12), Pń, Biblioteka Literacka, 171 pp.,
discusses writers such as J. Łoziński and T. Siejak. Rafał Grupiński
and Izolda Kiec, _Niebawem spadnie błoto czyli kilka uwag o literaturze
nieprzyjemnej_, Pń, Obserwator, 1997, 166 pp., considers the journals
Czas kultury and _bruLion_, and the influence of Różewicz and Miłosz on
young writers. Jarosław Klejnocki and Jerzy Sosnowski, _Chwilowe
zawieszenie broni_, Wa, Wyd. Sic!, 1996, 190 pp., is the first monograph

on the work of the so-called 'bruLion' generation (1986–96). B. Owczarek, 'Współczesna polska niefabularna proza powieściowa. Próba opisu', *PL(W)*, 87.3, 1996:61–82, contrasts the work of T. Parnicki, L. Buczkowski, Białoszewski, and J. Bocheński. Leszek Szaruga, *Dochodzenie do siebie. Wybrane wątki literatury po roku 1989*, Sejny, Pogranicze, 1997, 224 pp. *TD*, 1996, no. 5, is devoted exclusively to young (post-1989) writers. Essays on individuals are dealt with below, but general articles include: J. Jarzębski, 'Trzecia epoka (o prozie lat dziewięćdziesiątych)' (5–19); G. Borkowska, ' "Wyskrobać starą zaprawę z pomnika polskiej literatury..." O "młodej" prozie kobiecej' (55–67); P. Czapliński, 'Nieepicki model prozy w literaturze najnowszej' (68–84); and I. Iwasiów, 'Siostry — szkic o prozie (młodej) kobiet' (84–100). *CanSP*, 39.1–2, 1997, contains two essays on literature since the fall of communism: M. Czermińska, 'On the turning point: Polish prose, 1989–1995' (109–22); and B. Tokarz, 'After the Fall: a new beginning. A trial characterization of new Polish poetry' (153–66). I. Iwasiów, 'Słownik nieświadomości. Sny literackie po psychoanalizie', *TD*, nos 1–2:55–83, deals largely with Polish writers who have come to the fore since the late 1970s: K. Kofta, M. Saramonowicz, J. Łukosz, and A. Burzyńska. A. Legeżyńska, 'Jaka zmiana warty? Problem pokolenia w dzisiejszej literaturze', *TD*, 1997, no. 5:41–52.

INDIVIDUAL WRITERS

ANDRZEJEWSKI. Anna Synoradzka, *Jerzy Andrzejewski*, Kw, WL, 1997, 243 pp. + 16 pl., is the rather disappointing first monograph on A., although based on access to family archives. P. Coates, 'Forms of the Polish intellectual's self-criticism: revisiting *Ashes and Diamonds* with Andrzejewski and Wajda', *CanSP*, 38, 1996.3–4:287–303. J. Smulski, 'Kilka uwag o genezie *Miazgi* Jerzego Andrzejewskiego', *RuLit*, 37, 1996:217–21, traces A.'s original conception of the novel back to 1961.

BARAŃCZAK. M. Sukienni, 'Między "papierowym" a rzeczywistym światem (Jeszcze jeden głos o *Podróży zimowej* Stanisława Barańczaka), *TD*, 1997, no. 3:131–55.

BEREZA. A. Skrendo, 'Krytyka literacka wobec niewyrażalnego. Przykład Henryka Berezy', Bolecki, *Literatura*, 219–31.

BIAŁOSZEWSKI. Jacek Kopciński, *Gramatyka i mistyka. Wprowadzenie w teatralną osobność MB*, Wa, Wyd. IBL, 1997, 395 pp., is a major new study of B.'s dramatic work. J. Fazan, 'Fizjologia i metafizyka, czyli o "nudnociekawym byciu" jako temacie poezji Mirona Białoszewskiego', *RuLit*, 38, 1997:203–13; id., 'Teatr i kontemplacja. Rekonstrukcja poezji po katastrofie', *PL(W)*, 87.4, 1996:127–42.

J. Grądziel, 'Miron Białoszewski: "Prawo smaku rzeczy nieobecnych"', Bolecki, *Literatura*, 267–77. Grzegorz Grochowski, '"którędy wyjść ze słowa?" — *Transy* Mirona Białoszewskiego a poetyka monologu wewnętrznego', *PL(W)*, 87.3, 1996:113–32. H. Konicka, 'Kulturowy sens gatunkowych decyzji Mirona Białoszewskiego', *TD*, 1997, nos 1–2:63–80. A. Makowski, 'Papierowy Mahomet i inne figury niezdeterminowania', *TD*, 1997, no. 3:157–64.

BOROWSKI. S. Buryla, 'Na antypodach tradycji literackiej. Wokół "sprawy Borowskiego"', *PL(W)*, 89.4:99–123.

BUCZKOWSKI. A. Weidemann, 'Miejsce i rola muzyki w twórczości Leopolda Buczkowskiego', *TD*, 1997, nos 1–2:233–44.

BURSA. Ewa Dunaj-Kozakow, *Bursa*, Kw, WL, 1996, 248 pp. + 16 pl.

CZAPSKI. Jan Zieliński, *Józef Czapski. Krótki przewodnik po długim życiu*, Wa, Wyd. IBL, 1997, 106 pp. + 12 pl.

FIK. *Pośród spraw publicznych i teatralnych*, ed. Maria Napiotkowa and Joanna Krakowska-Narożniak, Wa, Errata, 352 pp., is a collection of essays on various themes by prominent critics and scholars.

FILIPIAK. *Od kobiety do mężczyzny i z powrotem. Rozważania o płci w kulturze*, ed. Jolanta Brach-Czaina, Białystok, Transhumana, 1997, 352 pp., contains A. Górnicka-Boratyńska, 'Odwrotna strona rzeczy, czyli dlaczego Izabela Filipiak jest pisarką feministyczną' (330–52).

FILIPOWICZ. S. Burkot, '"Co jest w człowieku?" — czyli o opowiadaniach Kornela Filipowicza', *RuLit*, 39: 595–609.

GAŁCZYŃSKI. Kira Gałczyńska, *Gałczyński*, Ww, Wyd. Dolnośląskie, 237 pp.

GOŁUBIEW. Aleksandra Chomiuk, *Antoniego Gołubiewa powieść o Bolesławie Chrobrym*, Lublin, Wyd. UMCS, 224 pp.

GRETKOWSKA. *TD*, no. 6, contains two essays on G.: M. Miszczak, 'Manueli Gretkowskiej zabawy (z) kiczem' (135–53), and H. Pułaczewska, 'Postmodernizm i polskość w powieściach Manueli Gretkowskiej' (155–69). A. Nacher, 'W labiryncie nowej wrażliwości. (Na marginesie *Podręcznika do ludzi* Manueli Gretkowskiej)', *RuLit*, 39: 101–11.

HAUPT. Aleksander Madyda, **Zygmunt Haupt. Życie i twórczość literacka*, Toruń, Wyd. Uniwersytetu Mikołaja Kopernika, 174 pp.

HERBERT. *Poznanie Herberta*, ed. Andrzej Franaszek, Kw, WL, 442 pp., is a collection by leading critics. J. Dudek, '"Wierny niepewnej jasności". O poezji Zbigniewa Herberta: część II', *RuLit*, 37, 1996:729–42, is the concluding part of an article whose first part appeared in *RuLit*, 12, 1971. A. Franaszek, '"a pod każdym liściem rozpacz"', *TD*, 1997, no. 1:245–68, discusses the religious elements in H.'s work. C. S. Kraszewski, 'Now the hungry dogs come out: Zbigniew Herbert's *Lalek* and the question: who is my brother?', *PolR*, 42, 1997:277–96.

HERLING-GRUDZIŃSKI. Zdzisław Kudelski, *Studia o Herlingu-Grudzińskim. Twórczość — recepcja — biografia*, Lublin, Towarzystwo Naukowe KUL, 532 pp. + 32 pp. of illus., is a major study. S. Buryła, 'Herlinga-Grudzińskiego spór z Borowskim wokół koncepcji rzeczywistości koncentracyjnej', *RuLit*, 38, 1997:65–81, details H.-G.'s criticisms of the moral dangers inherent in Borowski's treatment of concentration camp reality.

JANION. K. Chlipalski, 'Historia literatury jako forma zbawienia. (Glosa do portretu Marii Janion)', *RPN*, nos 7–8, 1997:43–49. B. Helbig-Mischewski, 'Guru przełomu tysiąclecia. Dyskurs Nowej Ery w pracach Marii Janion', *TD*, 1997, nos 1–2: 165–92.

KAPUŚCIŃSKI. E. Rybicka, ' "Znikający punkt" (O *Lapidariach* Ryszarda Kapuścińskiego)', *RuLit*, 39:545–53.

KISIELEWSKI. Mariusz Urbanek, *Kisiel*, Ww, Wyd. Dolnośląskie, 1997, 271 pp.

KONWICKI. Judith Arlt, *Tadeusz Konwickis Prosawerk von 'Rojsty' bis 'Bohiń'. Zur Entwicklung von Motivbestand und Erzählstruktur* (Slavica Helvetica, 55), Berne, Lang, 1997, 620 pp., is a major study of Konwicki's novels, with an excellent bibliography and short biography. M. Bury, 'Porównania utarte i indywidualne w twórczości T. Konwickiego', *RoczH* (6. Językoznawstwo), 44, 1996:37–58, is a linguistic analysis of K.'s similes in the novels up to *Czytadło* (1992). J. Z. Maciejewski, 'Widok z Wieży Babel (O powieści *Wniebostąpienie* T. Konwickiego)', Kryszak, *Polonistyka*, 189–97. J. Smulski, 'Trzy redakcje *Władzy* Tadeusza Konwickiego. Przyczynek do dziejów realizmu socjalistycznego w Polsce', *PL(W)*, 88.4, 1997:171–81.

KOTT. R. Szczerbakiewicz, 'Doświadczenie historii. Eseje Jana Kotta i tragedii antycznej', *PL(W)*, 88.4, 1997:91–107.

KRALL. I. Mandziej, 'Między reportażem a mikropowieścią: o *Sublokatorce* Hanny Krall', *PL(W)*, 89.3:85–97.

KRYNICKI. M. Sukiennik, 'Świat "niedoistnień" Ryszarda Krynickiego', *RuLit*, 37, 1996:455–66.

KUNCEWICZOWA. *O twórczości Marii Kuncewiczowej*, ed. Lech Ludorowski, Lublin, Wyd. UMCS, 1997, 183 pp. + 6 pp. of illus., contains essays on the novels *Tristan 1946*, *Cudzoziemka* and *Fantomy* by various hands.

LEM. Mariusz M. Leś, *Stanisław Lem wobec utopii*, Białystok, Towarzystwo Literackie im. Adama Mickiewicza, 189 pp.

LIPSKA. A. Legeżyńska, 'Dom i bezdomność w poezji Ewy Lipskiej', *PL(W)*, 87.1, 1996:39–57.

LIPSKI. H. Gosk, **Jesteś sam w swojej drodze. O twórczości Leo Lipskiego*, Izabelin, Świat Literacki, 188 pp., and her 'Juwenelia Leo Lipskiego', *PrzH*, 42.1:123–35. B. Zielińska, 'W kloace świata. O *Piotrusiu* Leo Lipskiego', *TD*, nos 1–2:37–54.

MACKIEWICZ. Adam Fitas, *Model powieści Józefa Mackiewicza*, Lublin, Towarzystwo Naukowe KUL, 1996, 231 pp., is the first significant stylistic study of the émigré writer.

MALEWSKA. E. Czuchro, 'Imperium i katedra — w stronę historiozofii Hanny Malewskiej', *PP*, 51, 1996:219–35.

MIŁOSZ. Beata Tarnowska, *Geografia poetycka w powojennej twórczości Czesława Miłosza*, WSP, Olsztyń, 1996, 172 pp.+40 pl. Andrzej Zawada, *Miłosz*, Wyd. Dolnośląskie, 1997, 274 pp. P-A. Bodin, 'Miłosz i Rosja. Z perspektywy szwedzkiej', *TD*, 1997, no. 5:5–23. A Fiut, 'Powroty Miłosza', *Periphery*, 1996:60–64. E. Kiślak, 'Druga emigracja Czesława Miłosza', *TD*, 1997, no. 5:103–23.

MROŻEK. Barbara Gutkowska, **O 'Tangu' i 'Emigrantach' Sławomira Mrożka*, Katowice, Książnica, 106 pp. Halina Stephan, *Mrożek*, Kw, WL, 1996, 283 pp. + 16 pl. Her *Transcending the Absurd. Drama and Prose of Sławomir Mrożek*, Amsterdam-Atlanta, GA, Rodopi, 1997, 276 pp., is essentially the same work. Małgorzata Sugiera, *Dramaturgia Sławomira Mrożka*, Kw, Universitas, 1996, 295 pp., represents a major contribution to studies of Mrożek. A. Kurnik, 'W pułapkach "zewnętrzności" i "wewnętrzności". Sławomira Mrożka opowieść o Kogucie, Lisie i sobie', *RuLit*, 37, 1996:467–73.

MUSIAŁ. J. Bates, 'Introduction', pp. 17–54 of *Poems of Grzegorz Musiał*, Madison, Fairleigh Dickenson U.P., 163 pp.

MYŚLIWSKI. Z. Ziątek, 'Nowy widnokrąg (Z okazji czwartej powieści Wiesława Myśliwskiego)', *TD*, 1997, no. 5: 153–68.

PARNICKI. S. Szymutko, 'Parnicki: między historią a literaturą. Od *Aecjusza ostatniego rzymianina* do *Słowa i ciała*', *PL(W)*, 88.1, 1997:79–94.

RÓŻEWICZ. R. Fieguth, 'Toter Dichter, in die Bewegung verliebt. Tadeusz Różewiczs Gedichtzyklus *Twarz* (1964)', *ZSP*, 56.2, 1997:360–413. T. Kłak, 'Liryka Sodalisa. O juwenaliach poetyckich Tadeusza Różewicza', *RoczH* (1. Literatura polska), 45, 1997:199–211. T. Kunz, 'Tadeusza Różewicza poetyka negatywna', Bolecki, *Literatura*, 293–99; id., 'Próba lektury wiersza Tadeusza Różewicza *Der Tod ist ein Meister aus Deutschland*', *RuLit*, 37, 1996:327–43. A. Ściepuro, 'Wobec stalinizmu. Wiersze Różewicza z lat 1949–1956', *PL(W)*, 88.2, 1997:33–49.

RYMKIEWICZ. A. Poprawa, 'Samowiedza w samych wierszach. Autotematyzm w poezji Jarosława Marka Rymkiewicza', *TD*, 1997, no. 5: 100–14.

STASIUK. L. Burska, 'Sprawy męskie i nie', *TD*, 1996, no. 5:34-43.

STRYJKOWSKI. Wiesław Kot, **Julian Stryjkowski* (Czytani Dzisiaj), Pń, Rebis, 1997, 170 pp., is intended for school pupils. J. Smulski, 'Juliana Stryjkowskiego "Tragedia optymistyczna". Rozważania o *Biegu do Fragala*', *PL(W)*, 88.1, 1997:61-78.

SZCZEPAŃSKI. S. Gawliński, ' "Antypaństwowe" książki Jana Józefa Szczepańskiego', *RuLit*, 37, 1996: 195-209.

SZYMBORSKA. A vast amount of works of very variable quality has appeared to mark the award of the Nobel Prize to the author in 1996, who, to that point, had not been the subject of a critical monograph. There is some overlap in the best collections, which also invariably contain excerpts from the best monographs. Michał Głowiński's article in *TD*, no. 4 (177-99), is a sober guide to the quality of a majority of the works. Amongst the best are: Stanisław Balbus, *Świat ze wszystkich stron. O Wisławie Szymborskiej*, Kw, WL, 1996, 250 pp., including an annex with 21 poems by the poet, index of works written on the poet, poems and collections of the poet herself; Tadeusz Nyczek, *22x Szymborska*, Wyd. a5, Poznań, 1997, 171 pp., is a close reading of twenty-two poems by Sz., generally of a very high quality; Dorota Wojda, *Milczenie słowa. O poezji Wisławy Szymborskiej*, Kw., Universitas, 1996, 137 pp., is an original reading of the dimension of silence in Sz.'s works; Dörte Lütvogt, *Untersuchungen zur Poetik der Wisława Szymborska* (Opera Slavica, Neue Folge 33), Wiesbaden, Harrassowitz, 317 pp., analyses individual poems under the general thematic headings of (i) the feminine experience of reality, (ii) philosophical observations and metaphysical fantasies, (iii) Man and his surroundings, and (iv) Art. Her bibliography of secondary literature is sparser than Polish collections but includes some non-Polish contributions. In order of increasing eccentricity/personalism are: Małgorzata Baranowska, *Tak lekko było nic o tym nie wiedzieć. Szymborska i świat*, Ww, Wyd. Dolnośląskie, 1996, 134 pp.; Marta Fox, *Zdarzyć się mogło, zdarzyć się musiało. Z. Wisławą Szymborską spotkanie w wierszu*, Katowice, Towarzystwo Zachęty Kultury, 1996, 158 pp., a so-called drama which assembles the responses of leading critics and writers to the question of their favourite poem by Sz.; Malgorzata Antoszewska-Tuora, *Niektórzy lubią Szymborską. Mały przewodnik po twórczości*, Wa, STENTOR, 1996, 127 pp., a variable interpretation of S.'s verse; and Ewa and Stanisław Krajscy, *Dwie twarze Wisławy Szymborskiej*, Wa, Wyd. św. Tomasza z Akwinu, 1996, 144 pp., who seek to bring Sz. to book for her 'Stalinist' past. Displaying greater balance are: Anna Bikont and Joanna Szczęsna, *Pamiątkowe rupiecie. Przyjaciele i sny Wisławy Szymborskiej*, Wa, Prószyński i S-ka, 1997, 256 pp., part-reminiscence/biography, part-picture album of the poet's life up to the Nobel Prize; Jan Majda, *Świat poetycki Wisławy Szymborskiej*, Kw, 'Impuls' and 'Text', 1996, 60 pp., a more popular work; Aneta Wiatr, *Syzyf poezji w piekle współczesności. Rzecz o Wisławie Szymborskiej*, Wa, Wyd. Kram, 1996, 186 pp., which examines Sz.'s poetry under the rubrics of (i) gender, (ii) literature and history, (iii) literature's 'correction' of the historical process, and (iv) essence; Bogdan Zeler, *O poezji Wisławy Szymborskiej*, Katowice, Wyd. Książnica, 1997, 121 pp., is intended for school pupils.

Good collections are: *Radość czytania Szymborskiej*, ed. Stanisław Balbus and Dorota Wojda, Kw, Wyd. Znak, 1996, 381 pp., which contains 32 pieces by major critics and writers on the poet from different periods, and includes an excellent bibliography of articles on Sz. published in Polish; *O wierszach Wisławy Szymborskiej*, ed. Jacek Brzozowski, Łódź, Wyd. Uniwersytetu Łódzkiego, 1996, 130 pp., a collection of essays/interpretations of eight of Sz.'s poems by different academics; *Szymborska. Szkice*, Wa, OPEN, 1996, 104 pp., containing essays by eminent critics and writers, such as Jarzębski, L. Neuger, and Miłosz; and *Wokół Szymborskiej* (Poznańskie studia polonistyczne. Seria literacka), Pń, Wyd. WiS, 1996, 143 pp., ed. Barbara Judkowiak, Elżbieta Nowicka, and Barbara Nowicka, containing essays by major critics, which is a special, shorter reprint of the 1995 volume. Another (corrected) reprint, Anna Legeżyńska, *Szymborska* (Czytani Dzisiaj), Pń, Rebis, 127 pp., is a popular account.

PL(W), 87.2, 1996, has two essays on Sz.'s work: J. Grądziel, 'Świat sztuki w poezji Wisławy Szymborskiej' (85–102), and P. Michałowski, 'Wisławy Szymborskiej poetyka zaprzeczeń' (123–43). S. Balbus, 'Eros w Rzece Heraklita. Miłość w poezji Szymborskiej', *TD*, 1996, no. 6: 5–16. E. M. Bojanowska, 'Wisława Szymborska: naturalist and humanist', *SEEJ*, 41, 1997: 199–223. C. Cavanagh, 'Wisława Szymborska and the political age', *Periphery*, 1997: 44–49. M. Nowotna, 'Quelques remarques sur la nature du sujet de l'énonciation dans deux poèmes de W. Szymborska i Z. Herbert', *RSl*, 70.1: 215–27, is a mainly linguistic analysis based on H.'s 'Rovigo' and Sz.'s 'Może być bez tytułu' and 'Jacyś ludzie'. D. Wojda, ' "Spisane na wodzie Babel". Przemilczenie a strategie retoryczne Wisławy Szymborskiej', Bolecki, *Literatura*, 279–92.

TRYZNA. M. Masłowski, 'Ból nie-istnienia. O "postmodern-istycznej" powieści Tomka Tryzny', *TD*, 1997, no. 5: 53–67.

TWARDOWSKI. S. Cieślak, 'Bóg, święci i świętość w poezji Jana Twardowskiego', *PP*, 51, 1996: 187–218. A. Sulikowski, *Na początku był wiersz, czyli 13 nowych odczytań poezji Jana Twardowskiego*, Kw, Znak, 138 pp., and his 'Dwa wiersze ks. Jana Twardowskiego', *RoczH* (1. Literatura polska), 45, 1997: 213–21, analyses 'Pan Jezus niewierzą-cych' and 'O spacerze po cmentarzu wojskowym'.

VINCENZ. Mirosława Ołdakowska-Kuflowa, *Stanisław Vincenz wobec dziedzictwa kultury*, Lublin, Wyd. KUL, 1997, 208 pp. Her 'Żywe słowo Stanisława Vincenza', *RoczH* (1. Literatura polska), 45, 1997:181–97, discusses the tetralogy *Na wysokiej połoninie*.

WOJTYŁA. Waldemar Smaszcz, *Słowo poetyckie Karola Wojtyły*, Wa, PAX, 169 pp. *Twórczość Karola Wojtyły*, ed. Zbigniew W. Solski, Ww, WUW, 143 pp., is concerned with W.'s last published play, *Promieniowanie ojcostwa. Misterium*. J. Majda, 'Dramat Karola Wojtyły o miłości', *RuLit*, 38, 1997:9–25, examines *Przed sklepem jubilera* in conjunction with the philosophical tract *Miłość i odpowiedzialność*.

ZAGAJEWSKI. U. Klatka, 'Podmiot w lyrice Adama Zagajewskiego', *RuL*, 39:205–15.

IV. RUSSIAN STUDIES
POSTPONED

V. UKRAINIAN STUDIES
POSTPONED

VI. BELARUSIAN STUDIES
POSTPONED

VII. SERBO-CROAT STUDIES
POSTPONED

VIII. BULGARIAN STUDIES
POSTPONED

ABBREVIATIONS

I. ACTA, FESTSCHRIFTEN AND OTHER COLLECTIVE AND GENERAL WORKS

Actas (Birmingham), I: *Actas del XII Congreso Internacional de Hispanistas (Birmingham, 21–26 de agosto de 1995)*. I. *Medieval y lingüística*, ed. Aengus Ward, Birmingham, Department of Hispanic Studies, xiii + 359 pp.

Actas (Birmingham), IV: *Actas del XII Congreso Internacional de Hispanistas (Birmingham, 21–26 de agosto de 1995)*. IV. *Del romantismo a la guerra civil*, ed. Derek Flitter, Birmingham, Department of Hispanic Studies, xiii + 301 pp.

Actas (Lisbon): *Actas das primeiras xornadas das Letras Galegas en Lisboa* ed. Luis Alonso Girgado, Santiago de Compostela, Xunta de Galicia.

Actes (Bloomington): *Actes del Vuitè Col·loqui d'Estudis Catalans a Nord-Amèrica. Bloomington, 1995*, ed. J. M. Sobrer (Biblioteca Abat Oliva, 194), Montserrat, Abadia de Montserrat, 334 pp.

Actes (Caen): *Lectures d'une oeuvre. 'Laberinto de Fortuna' de Juan de Mena. Actes du colloque international des 16 et 17 janvier organisé à l'Université de Caen*, ed. Françoise Maurizi, Paris, Klincksieck, 175 pp.

Actes (Palma): *Actes del l'Onzè Col·loqui Internacional de Llengua i Literatura Catalanes. Palma de Mallorca, 1997*, I, ed. J. Mas Vives, J. Miralles Montserrat, and P. Rossellò Bover (Biblioteca Abat Oliva, 201), Montserrat, Abadia de Montserrat, 497 pp.

Actes (Rambures): *Château et société castrale au moyen âge. Actes du Colloque des 7–8–9 mars 1997*, ed. Jean-Marc Pastré (Publications de l'Université de Rouen, 239), Presses de l'Université de Rouen, 366 pp.

Aertsen, *Individuum: Individuum und Individualität im Mittelalter*, ed. Jan A. Aertsen and Andreas Speer (Miscellanea Mediaevalia, 24), Berlin, de Gruyter, 1996, xxiii + 878 pp.

AIEO 1995: Le rayonnement des troubadours. Actes du colloque de l'Association Internationale d'Études Occitanes, Amsterdam, 16–18 octobre 1995, ed. Anton Touber (Internationale Forschungen zur Allgemeinen und Vergleichenden Literaturwissenschaft), Amsterdam–Atlanta, Rodopi, 1997, 400 pp.

AIEO 5: Toulouse à la croisée des cultures. Actes du Ve colloque international de l'AIEO, août 1996, ed. J. Gourc and F. Pic, 2 vols, Pau, AIEO, 1–385, 386–789 pp.

AIL 5: Actas do Quinto Congresso da Associação Internacional de Lusitanistas, Universidade de Oxford, 1 a 8 de Setembro de 1996, 3 vols, ed. T. F. Earle, Oxford–Coimbra, Associação Internacional de Lusitanistas, 1–655, 657–1304, 1305–1946 pp.

Algulin, *Traditioner:* Ingemar Algulin, *Traditioner i förvandling*, ed. Anders Cullhed and Barbro Ståhle Sjönell, Stockholm, Norstedts, 286 pp.

APL 13: Actas do XIII Encontro Nacional da Associação Portuguesa de Linguística, ed. Maria Antónia Mota and Rita Marquilhas, 2 vols, Lisbon, Colibri–APL, 384, 378 pp.

Atti (AISLLI 15): *Letteratura e industria. Atti del XV Congresso dell'Associazione Internazionale per gli Studi di Lingua e Letteratura Italiana (Torino, 15–19 maggio 1994)*, ed. Giorgio Bárberi Squarotti and Carlo Ossola, 2 vols, Florence, Olschki, 1997, xviii + 1288 pp + 76 pls.

Atti (Palermo), I: *Atti del XXI Congresso Internazionale di Linguistica e Filologia Romanza (Palermo, 18–24 settembre 1995)*, I, ed. Giovanni Ruffino, Tübingen, Niemeyer, xviii + 494 pp.

Atti (Palermo), II: *Atti del XXI Congresso Internazionale di Linguistica e Filologia Romanza (Palermo, 18–24 settembre 1995)*, II, ed. Giovanni Ruffino, Tübingen, Niemeyer, xxii + 940 pp.

Atti (Palermo), III: *Atti del XXI Congresso Internazionale di Linguistica e Filologia Romanza (Palermo, 18–24 settembre 1995)*, III. *Lessicologia e semantica delle lingue romanze*, ed. Giovanni Ruffino, Tübingen, Niemeyer, xii + 1032 pp.

Atti (Palermo), IV: *Atti del XXI Congresso Internazionale di Linguistica e Filologia Romanza (Palermo, 18–24 settembre 1995)*, IV. *Le strutture del parlato - Storia linguistica e culturale del Mediterraneo*, ed. Giovanni Ruffino, Tübingen, Niemeyer, xi + 627 pp.

Atti (Palermo), V: *Atti del XXI Congresso Internazionale di Linguistica e Filologia Romanza (Palermo, 18–24 settembre 1995)*, V. *Dialettologia, geolinguistica, sociolinguistica*, ed. Giovanni Ruffino, Tübingen, Niemeyer, xi + 813 pp.

Atti (Palermo), VI: *Atti del XXI Congresso Internazionale di Linguistica e Filologia Romanza (Palermo, 18–24 settembre 1995)*, VI. *Edizione e analisi linguistica dei testi letterari e documentari del Medioevo - Paradigmi interpretativi della cultura medievale*, ed. Giovanni Ruffino, Tübingen, Niemeyer, xi + 825 pp.

Auwera, *Adverbial Constructions: Adverbial Constructions in the Languages of Europe*, ed. Johan van der Auwera and Dónall P. Ó Baoill (Eurotyp, 20–3), Berlin, Mouton de Gruyter, xviii + 825 pp.

Baker, *Encyclopedia: Routledge Encyclopedia of Translation Studies*, ed. Mona Baker and Kirsten Malmkjaer, London–New York, Routledge, xxx + 654 pp.

Balari, *Romance: Romance in HPSG*, ed. Sergio Balari and Luca Dini, Stanford, Center for the Study of Language and Information, xxxi + 402 pp.

BASS 11: Proceedings of the Eleventh Biennial Conference of the British Association of Scandinavian Studies held at the University of Hull 23–26 March 1997, ed. Charlotte Whittingham and Phil Holmes, Hull U.P., 1997, 212 pp.

Beer, *Saggi:* Marina Beer, *L'ozio onorato. Saggi sulla letteratura italiana del Rinascimento*, Rome, Bulzoni, 1996, 309 pp.

Beltrán, *Caballerías: Literatura de caballerías y orígenes de la novela*, ed. R. Beltrán, Valencia U.P., 341 pp.

Benincà, *Romance Syntax: Romance Syntax. A Reader*, ed. Paola Benincà and Giampaolo Salvi, Budapest, L. Eötvös University, 225 pp.

Beniscelli, *Naturale: Naturale ed artificiale in scena nel secondo Settecento*, ed. Alberto Beniscelli, Rome, Bulzoni, 1997, 287 pp.

Bertinetto, *Unità: Unità fonetiche e fonologiche: produzione e percezione. Atti delle 8e giornate di studio del Gruppo di Fonetica Sperimentale (A.I.A.), Pisa, 17–19 dicembre 1997*, ed. Pier Marco Bertinetto and Lorenzo Cioni (Collana degli Atti dell'Associazione Italiana di Acustica), Pisa, Scuola Normale Superiore.

Bertrand, *Geste: Le Geste et les gestes au moyen âge*, ed. Margaret Bertrand and Christian Hory (Sénéfiance, 41), Aix-en-Provence, CUER MA, 626 pp.

Beutin, *Mystik: Europäische Mystik vom Hochmittelalter zum Barock. Eine Schlüsselepoche in der europäischen Mentalitäts-, Spiritualitäts- und Individuationsentwicklung. Beiträge der Tagungen 1996 und 1997 der Evangelischen Akademie Nordelbien in Bad Segeberg*, ed. Wolfgang Beutin and Thomas Bütow (Bremer Beiträge zur Literatur- und Ideengeschichte, 21), Frankfurt, Lang, 249 pp.

Blanche-Benveniste Vol.: Analyse linguistique et approches de l'oral. Recueil d'études offert en hommage à Claire Blanche-Benveniste, ed. Mireille Bilger, Karel van den Eynde, and Françoise Gadet (*Orbis*, Supplementa, 10), Louvain–Paris, Peeters, vii + 385 pp.

Bolecki, *Literatura: Literatura wobec niewyrażalnego*, ed. Włodzimierz Bolecki and Erazm Kuźma (Z dziejów Form Artystycznych w Literaturze Polskiej, 79), Wydawnictwo IBL, n. pl. [Warsaw], ii + 366 pp.

Borillo, *Aspect: Regards sur l'aspect*, ed. Andrée Borillo, Carl Vetters, and Marcel Vuillaume (Cahiers Chronos, 2), Amsterdam–Atlanta, Rodopi, ix + 266 pp.

Borillo, *Variations: Variations sur la référence verbale*, ed. Andrée Borillo, Carl Vetters, and Marcel Vuillaume (Cahiers Chronos, 3), Amsterdam–Atlanta, Rodopi, viii + 345 pp.

Bräuer, *Kontext: Die deutsche Literatur des Mittelalters im europäischen Kontext. Tagung Greifswald, 11.–15. September 1995*, ed. Rolf Bräuer (Göppinger Arbeiten zur Germanistik, 651), Göppingen, Kümmerle, 174 pp.

Brault, *Vol.: Echoes of the Epic: Studies in Honor of Gerald J. Brault*, ed. David P. Schenk and Mary Jane Schenk, Birmingham, Alabama, Summa, xxiv + 257 pp.

Camps, *Languedoc: Languedoc - Roussillon - Catalogne. État, nation, identité culturelle régionale (des origines à 1659). (Actes du colloque 20–22 mars 1997)*, ed. Christian Camps and Carlos Heusch, Montpellier, Université Paul-Valéry, 385 pp.

Český jazyk: Český jazyk, ed. Jan Kořenský, Opole, Uniwersitet Opolski, 216 pp.

Chant et Enchantement: Chant et Enchantement au Moyen Age. Travaux du Groupe de Recherches 'Lectures Médiévales', Université de Toulouse II (Collection Moyen Age), Toulouse, Éditions Universitaires du Sud, 1997, 235 pp.

Chiarini Vol.: Echi di memoria. Scritti di varia filologia, critica e linguistica in ricordo di Giorgio Chiarini, Florence, Alinea.

Coleman Vol.: The Art of Reading: Essays in Memory of Dorothy Gabe Coleman, ed. Philip Ford and Gillian Jondorf, Cambridge, Cambridge French Colloquia, xv + 199 pp.

CRISIMA 3: Felonie, trahison, reniements au moyen âge. Actes du troisième colloque international de Montpellier Université Paul-Valery (24–26 novembre 1995), ed. Marcel Faure (Les Cahiers du CRISIMA, 3), 1997, 631 pp.

Croce Vol.: Studi di filologia e letteratura offerti a Franco Croce, pref. Vittorio Coletti, Rome, Bulzoni, 1997, xlix + 719 pp.

Daviau, *Literatur: Geschichte der österreichischen Literatur*, ed. Donald G. Daviau and Herbert Arlt, 2 vols, St. Ingbert, Röhrig, 1996, 758 pp.

Debatin, *Metaphor: Metaphor and Rational Discourse*, ed. Bernhard Debatin, Timothy R. Jackson, and Daniel Steuer, Tübingen, Niemeyer, 1997, viii + 264 pp.

De Lorenzi Vol.: Sequenze novecentesche per Antonio de Lorenzi, Modena, Mucchi, 1996, 262 pp.

Demarolle Vol.: Mélanges de langue et de littérature françaises du moyen âge offerts à Pierre Demarolle, ed. Charles Brucker, Paris, Champion — Geneva, Slatkine, 381 pp.

Desportes, *Semantik: Semantik der syntaktischen Beziehungen. Akten des Pariser Kolloquiums zur Erforschung des Althochdeutschen 1994*, ed. Yvon Desportes (Germanische Bibliothek, ser. 3, n. F., 27), Heidelberg, Winter, 1997, 252 pp.

Dickson, *Dreams: Romantic Dreams. Proceedings of the Glasgow Conference, April 1997*, ed. Sheila Dickson and Mark Ward, Glasgow, University of Glasgow French and German Publications, vi + 222 pp.

Dionisotti, *Ricordi:* Carlo Dionisotti, *Ricordi della scuola italiana*, Rome, Edizioni di Storia e Letteratura, 620 pp.

Dolfi, *Terza generazione:* Anna Dolfi, *Terza generazione. Ermetismo e oltre*, Rome, Bulzoni, 1997, 457 pp.

Duffy, *Transgression: Les Lieux Interdits. Transgression and French Literature*, ed. Larry Duffy and Adrian Tudor, Hull U.P., vi + 323 pp.

Dutton Vol.: Nunca fue pena mayor (Estudios de Literatura Española en homenaje a Brian Dutton), ed. Ana Menendez Collera and Victoriano Roncero Lopez, Cuenca, Universidad de Castilla-La Mancha, 1996, 693 pp.

Fabre Vol.: Hommage à Paul Fabre, ed. Teddy Arnavielle and Jeanne-Marie Barbéris, Montpellier, Univ. Paul-Valéry, 1997, 189 pp.

Fest. Birkhan: Ir sult sprechen willekomen. Grenzlose Mediävistik. Festschrift für Helmut Birkhan zum 60. Geburtstag, ed. Christa Tuczay, Ulrike Hirhager, and Karin Lichtblau, Berne, Lang, 863 pp.

Fest. Emden: Reading Around the Epic: A Festschrift in Honour of Professor Wolfgang von Emden, ed. Marianne Ailes, Philip E. Bennett, and Karen Pratt (King's College London Medieval Studies, 15), London, King's College London Centre for Late Antique and Medieval Studies, xx + 340 pp.

Fest. Ertzdorff: Chevaliers errants, demoiselles et l'Autre: höfische und nachhöfische Literatur im europäischen Mittelalter. Festschrift für Xenja von Ertzdorff zum 65. Geburtstag, ed. Trude Ehlert (Göppinger Arbeiten zur Germanistik, 644), Göppingen, Kümmerle, xiii + 430 pp.

Fest. Fleischer: Nominationsforschung im Deutschen. Festschrift für Wolfgang Fleischer zum 75. Geburtstag, ed. Irmhild Barz and Marianne Schröder, Frankfurt, Lang, 1997, 499 pp.

Fest. Geith: 'Ist mir getroumet mîn leben?' Vom Träumen und vom Anderssein. Festschrift für Karl-Ernst Geith zum 65. Geburtstag, ed. André Schnyder, Claudia Bartholemy-Teusch, Barbara Fleith, and René Wetzel (Göppinger Arbeiten zur Germanistik, 632), Göppingen, Kümmerle, vi + 354 pp.

Fest. Härd: Kleine Beiträge zur Germanistik. Festschrift für John Evert Härd, ed. Bo Andersson and Gernot Müller (Acta Universitatis Upsaliensis. Studia Germanistica Upsaliensia, 37), Uppsala U.P., 1997, 314 pp.

Fest. Kremnitz: Lo Gai Saber. Zum Umgang mit sprachlicher Vielfalt. Georg Kremnitz zum 50. Geburtstag, ed. Peter Cichon, Karl Ille, and Robert Tanzmeister, Vienna, Braumüller, 1995, xi + 320 pp.

Fest. Marson: Unravelling the Labyrinth. Decoding Text and Language. Festschrift for Eric Lowson Marson, ed. Kerry Dunne and Ian R. Campbell, Frankfurt, Lang, 1997, 174 pp.

Fest. Molk: Literature, Geschichte und Verstehen, Festschrift für Ulrich Molk zum 60. Geburstag, ed. Heinrich Hudde, Udo Schoning, and Friedrich Wolfzettel, Heidelberg, Winter, 1997, 555 pp.

Fest. Pfister: Italica et Romanica: Festschrift für Max Pfister zum 65. Geburtstag, ed. Günter Holtus, Johannes Kramer, and Wolfgang Schweickard, I. *Historische Lexikologie und Lexicographie;* II. *Morphologie, Syntax, Wortbildung. Sprachkontakte und Sprachvergleich*, 3 vols, Tübingen, Niemeyer, 1997, xl + 487, vi + 367, vi + 513 pp.

Fest. Schmidt-Wiegand: Alles was Recht war. Rechtsliteratur und literarisches Recht. Festschrift für Ruth Schmidt-Wiegand zum 70. Geburtstag, ed. Hans Höfinghoff (Item mediävistische Studien, 3), Essen, Item, 1996, 258 pp.

Fest. Tatzreiter: Beharrsamkeit und Wandel. Festschrift für Herbert Tatzreiter zum 60. Geburtstag, ed. Werner Bauer and Hermann Scheuringer, Vienna, Praesens, 355 pp.

Fest. Vater: Sprache im Fokus. Festschrift für Heinz Vater zum 65. Geburtstag, ed. Christa Dürscheid, Karl Heinz Ramers, and Monika Schwarz, Tübingen, Niemeyer, 1997, xiv + 502 pp.

Fest. Wiesinger: Deutsche Sprache in Raum und Zeit. Festschrift für Peter Wiesinger zum 60. Geburtstag, ed. Peter Ernst and Franz Patocka, Vienna, Praesens, 714 pp.

Fest. Wimmel: Candide iudex: Beiträge zur augusteischen Dichtung. Festschrift für Walter Wimmel zum 75. Geburtstag, ed. Anna E. Radke, Stuttgart, Steiner, 406 pp.

Fest. Woll: Lusitanica et Romanica. Festschrift für Dieter Woll, ed. Martin Hummel and Christina Ossenkop, Hamburg, Buske, xxviii + 407 pp.

Feu et Lumière: Feu et lumière au moyen âge. Travaux du Groupe de Recherche 'Lectures Médiévales', Université de Toulouse II (Collection Moyen Age), Toulouse, Editions Universitaires du Sud.

Feuillet, *Actance: Actance et valence dans les langues de l'Europe*, ed. Jack Feuillet (Eurotyp, 20–2), Berlin, Mouton de Gruyter, 1997[1998], xiv + 975 pp.

Flitter, *Ondas: Ondas do Mar de Vigo. Actas do Simposio Internacional sobre a Lírica Medieval Galego-Portuguesa, Birmingham, 1998*, ed. Derek W. Flitter and Patricia Odber de Baubeta, Birmingham, Seminario de Estudios Galegos, University of Birmingham, vii + 173 pp.

Fohrmann, *Lebensläufe: Lebensläufe um 1800*, ed. Jürgen Fohrmann, Tübingen, Niemeyer, 262 pp.

Fónagy Vol.: Polyphonie pour Iván Fónagy. Mélanges offerts en hommage à Iván Fónagy par un groupe de disciples, collègues et admirateurs, ed. and introd. Jean Perrot, Paris, L'Harmattan, 1997, 529 pp.

Fullana, *Central Romance: Studies on the Syntax of Central Romance Languages. Proceedings of the III Symposium on the Syntax of Central Romance Languages*, ed. Olga Fullana and Francesc Roca, Girona U.P., 255 pp.

Garber, *Stadt:* Klaus Garber, *Stadt und Literatur im deutschen Sprachraum der fruehen Neuzeit* (Fruehe Neuzeit, 39), 2 vols, Tübingen, Niemeyer, xvii + 1–546, x + 547–1144 pp.

Garcia, *Formes fixes: Les formes fixes dans la poésie du moyen âge roman (1180–1500)*, ed. Michel Garcia (*Atalaya*, 8), 1997[1998], 192 pp.

García Gómez Vol.: Lírica popular / lírica tradicional. Lecciones en homenaje a Don Emilio García Gómez, ed. Pedro M. Piñero, Seville U.P., 298 pp.

Gardy, *Mistral: Frédéric Mistral et 'Lou Pouèmo dóu Rose'. Actes du colloque de Villeneuve-lès-Avignon (10–11 mai 1996)*, ed. and introd. Philippe Gardy and Claire Torreilles, Bordes, CELO — Bordeaux, William Blake, 295 pp.

Géographie: La Géographie au moyen âge: espaces pensés, espaces vécus, espaces rêvés. Arras, journée d'études, 30 janvier 1998 (Perspectives médiévales, supp. to no. 24), Paris, Société de langue et littératures médiévales d'oc et d'oïl, 124 pp.

Gerli, *Poetry: Poetry at Court in Trastamaran Spain: From the 'Cancionero de Baena' to the 'Cancionero general'*, ed. Michael E. Gerli and Julian Weiss, Tempe, Arizona State U.P., 297 pp.

Glienke *Vol.: Ästhetik der skandinavischen Moderne. Bernhard Glienke zum Gedenken*, ed. Annegret Heitmann and Karin Hoff (Beiträge zur Skandinavistik, 14), Frankfurt, Lang, 370 pp.

Goebl, *Kontaktlinguistik: Kontaktlinguistik/Contact Linguistics/Linguistique de contact*, ed. Hans Goebl, Peter Nelde, Zdenek Stary, and Wolfgang Wölck, Berlin–New York, de Gruyter, 1997.

Goetz, *Geschichtsbewußtsein: Hochmittelalterliches Geschichtsbewußtsein im Spiegel nichthistoriographischer Quellen*, ed. Hans-Werner Goetz, Berlin, Akademie, 416 pp.

Gottzmann, *Osteuropa: Studien zu Forschungsproblemen der deutschen Literatur in Mittel- und Osteuropa*, ed. Carola L. Gottzmann and Petra Hörner (Deutsche Literatur in Mittel- und Osteuropa. Mittelalter und Neuzeit, 1), Frankfurt, Lang, 218 pp.

Gould, *Post-colonial Subjects: Post-colonial Subjects: Francophone Women Writers*, ed. Karen Gould et al., Minneapolis, University of Minnesota Press, 1996, 359 pp.

Grosse, *Wörterbücher: Bedeutungserfassung und Bedeutungsbeschreibung in historischen und dialektologischen Wörterbüchern. Beiträge zu einer Arbeitstagung der deutschsprachigen Wörterbücher, Projekte an Akademien und Universitäten vom 7. bis 9. März 1996 anläßlich des 150jährigen Jubiläums der Sächsischen Akademie der Wissenschaften zu Leipzig*, ed. Siegfried Grosse (Abhandlungen der Sächsischen Akademie der Wissenschaften zu Leipzig. Philologisch-historische Klasse, 75, no. 1), Leipzig, Hirzel, 278 pp.

Haegemann, *Comparative Syntax: The New Comparative Syntax*, ed. Liliane Haegeman, London, Longman, 1997, x + 294 pp.

Holtus, *Lexikon*, VII: *Lexikon der Romanistischen Linguistik*, VII. *Kontakt, Migration und Kunstsprachen. Kontrastivität, Klassifikation und Typologie. Langues en contact, langues des migrants et langues artificielles. Analyses contrastives, classification et typologie des langues romanes*, ed. Gunter Holtus, Michael Metzeltin, and Christian Schmitt, Tübingen, Niemeyer, xliii + 1085 pp.

Horn, *Allegorese: Die Allegorese des antiken Mythos*, ed. Hans-Jürgen Horn and Hermann Walter (Wolfenbütteler Forschungen, 75), Wiesbaden, Harrassowitz, 1997, 447 pp.

Hörner, *Hartmann: Hartmann von Aue. Mit einer Bibliographie 1976–1997*, ed. Petra Hörner (Information und Interpretation, 8), Frankfurt, Lang, 283 pp.

Houe, *Documentarism: Documentarism in Scandinavian Literature*, ed. Poul Houe and Sven Hakon Rossel (Internationale forschungen zur allgemeinen und vergleichenden Literaturwissenschaft, 18) Amsterdam–Atlanta, GA, Rodopi, 1997, 230 pp.

ICHL 13: Historical Linguistics 1997. Selected Papers from the 13th International Conference on Historical Linguistics, Düsseldorf, 10–17 August 1997, ed. Monika S. Schmid, Jennifer R. Austin, and Dieter Stein (CILT, 164), Amsterdam, Benjamins, x + 409 pp.

ICOS 19: Proceedings of the XIXth International Congress of Onomastic Sciences, Aberdeen, August 4–11, 1996, ed. W. F. H. Nicolaisen, 3 vols, Department of English, University of Aberdeen, xviii + 356, vi + 402, vi + 405 pp.

Jelínek *Vol.: Jazyk a kultura vyjadřovaní. Milanu Jelínkovi k pětasedmdesátinám*, ed. Petr Karlík and Marie Krčmová, Brno, Masaryk Univ., 212 pp.

Jung *Vol.: Ensi firent li ancessor: Mélanges de philologie médiévale offerts à Marc-René Jung*, ed. Luciano Rossi, Christine Jacob-Hugon, and Ursula Bahler, Alessandria, Edizioni dell'Orso, 1996, xxiv + 463, vii + 465 pp.

Kolloquium (Meissen): *Autor und Autorschaft im Mittelalter. Kolloquium Meißen 1995*, ed. Elizabeth Andersen, Jens Haustein, Anne Simon, and Peter Strohschneider, Tübingen, Niemeyer, vii + 415 pp.

Korzen, *Clause Combining: Clause Combining and Text Structure*, ed. I. Korzen and Michael Herslund (Copenhagen Studies in Language, 22), Federiksberg, Samfundslitteratur, 158 pp.

Kryszak, *Polonistyka: Polonistyka Toruńska uniwersytetowi w 50. rocznicę utworzenia UMK: literatura*, ed. Janusz Kryszak, Toruń, Wydawnictwo UMK, 1996.

Lagrée, *Parlers: Les Parlers de la foi: Religion et langues régionales (Actes de la journée d'études de Lyon, 11 dec. 1993)*, ed. Michel Lagrée, Rennes U.P., 1995, 165 pp.

Lauretta, *Pirandello: Pirandello e la sua opera. Atti del XXXIII Convegno di studi pirandelliani, Agrigento, 1996*, ed. Enzo Lauretta and John C. Barnes, Palermo, Palumbo, 1997, 212 pp.

Lepschy Vol.: In amicizia. Essays in honour of Giulio Lepschy, ed. Zygmunt Barański et al. (*The Italianist* 17, special supp.), 1997, 536 pp.

London Ger. St. VI: London German Studies VI, ed. Edward M. Batley (Publications of the Institute of Germanic Studies, 73), London, University of London School of Advanced Study–Institute of Germanic Studies, ix + 423 pp.

Lorenzo Vol.: Homenaxe a Ramón Lorenzo, ed. Dieter Kremer, Vigo, Galaxia, 2 vols, xxxvi + 547, 555–1138 pp.

LSRL 26: Theoretical Analyses on Romance Languages. Selected Papers from the 26th Linguistic Symposium on Romance Languages (LSRL XXVI), Mexico City, 28–30 March 1996, ed. José Lema and Esthela Treviño (Current Issues in Linguistic Theory, 157), Amsterdam, Benjamins, viii + 379 pp.

LSRL 27: Romance Linguistics. Theoretical Perspectives. Selected Papers from the 27th Linguistic Symposium on Romance Languages (LSRL XXVII), Irvine, 20–22 February 1997, ed. Armin Schwegler, Bernard Tranel, and Myriam Uribe-Etxebarria (Current Issues in Linguistic Theory, 160), Amsterdam–Philadelphia, Benjamins, viii + 349 pp.

Lutzeier, *Challenges: German Studies: Old and New Challenges. Undergraduate Programmes in the United Kingdom and the Republic of Ireland*, ed. Peter Rolf Lutzeier (German Linguistic and Cultural Studies, 1), Berne, Lang, 250 pp.

Macpherson Vol.: Cancionero Studies in Honour of Ian Macpherson, ed. Alan Deyermond, London, Queen Mary and Westfield College, 219 pp.

Mandach Vol.: De l'aventure épique à l'aventure romanesque. Mélanges offerts à André de Mandach, ed. Jacques Chocheyras, Berlin, Lang, 1997, 307 pp.

Maninchedda, *Sardegna: La Sardegna e la presenza catalana nel Mediterraneo. Atti del VI congresso (III Internazionale) dell'Associazione Italiana di Studi Catalani*, ed. P. Maninchedda, Cooperativa Universitaria Editrice Cagliaritana.

Mar das cantigas: Actas do Congreso 'Mar das cantigas', Santiago de Compostela, Xunta de Galicia, 364 pp.

Marcato, *Donna: Donna e linguaggio. Atti del Convegno Donna e Linguaggio, Sappada/Plodn, 26–30 giugno 1995*, ed. Gianna Marcato, Padova, CLEUP, 1995, 632 pp.

Masciandaro, *Letture:* Franco Masciandaro, *La conoscenza viva. Letture fenomenologiche da Dante a Machiavelli*, Ravenna, Longo, 129 pp.

Mathieu, *Francophonie: Littératures autobiographiques de la francophonie*, ed. Martine Mathieu, Paris, L'Harmattan, 1996, 351 pp.

Melli Vol.: Filologia romanza e cultura medievale. Studi in onore di Elio Melli, ed. Andrea Fassò, Luciano Formisano, and Mario Mancini, 2 vols, Alessandria, Edizioni dell'Orso, xxi + 449, vii + 451–915 pp.

Ménard Vol.: Miscellanea Mediaevalia. Mélanges offerts à Philippe Ménard, ed. J. Claude Faucon, Alain Labbé, and Danielle Queruel, 2 vols, Paris, Champion, 1–757, 759–1530 pp.

Merschini Vol.: Do-ra-qe pe-re. Studi in memoria di Adriana Quattorio Merschini, ed. Luciano Agostiniani et al., Pisa–Rome, Istituti Editoriali e Poligrafici Internazionali.

Mildonian, *Parodia: Parodia, pastiche, mimetismo. Atti del Convegno Internazionale di Letterature Comparate, Venezia 13–15 Ottobre 1993*, ed. Paola Mildonian, Venice, Bulzoni, 1997, 458 pp.

Mioni, *Dialetti: Dialetti, cultura e società. Quarta raccolta di saggi dialettologici*, ed. Alberto M. Mioni, M. Teresa Vigolo, and Enzo Croatto, Padua, CSDI–CNR, vii + 345 pp.

Monfrin Vol.: Autour de Jacques Monfrin. Néologie et création verbale. Actes du Colloque international Université McGill, Montréal, 7–8–9 octobre 1996, ed. Giuseppe Di Stefano and Rose M. Bidler (*MoyFr*, 39–40–41), Éditions CERES, Montreal, 1997, 680 pp.

Mujica, *Premio Nóbel: Premio Nóbel: once grandes escritores del mundo hispánico. Antología con introducciones críticas*, ed. Bárbara Mujica, Georgetown U.P., 1997, vii + 359 pp.

Müller, *Sprachnormen: Sprachnormen und Sprachnormwandel in gegenwärtigen europäischen Sprachen*, ed. Oskar Müller (Rostocker Beiträge zur Sprachwissenschaft, 1), Rostock U.P., 1995, 258 pp.

Nació secreta: La Nació secreta, Barcelona, Vers un Nou Congrés de Cultura — Llibres de l'Index.

Panevová Vol.: Issues of Valency and Meaning. Studies in Honour of Jarmila Panevová, ed. Eva Hajičová, Prague, Charles Univ., 307 pp.

Papers (ICLS 8): *The Court and Cultural Diversity. Selected Papers from the Eighth Triennial Congress of the International Courtly Literature Society, The Queen's University of Belfast, 26 July–1 August 1995*, ed. Evelyn Mullally and John Thompson, Cambridge, Brewer, 1997, x + 426 pp.

Paredes, *Formas breves: Hacia una tipología de las formas breves medievales*, ed. Juan Paredes and Paloma Gracia, Granada, U.P., 381 pp.

Paxton, *Desiring Discourse: Desiring Discourse: The Literature of Love, Ovid through Chaucer*, ed. James Paxton and Cynthia Gravlee, Selinsgrove, PA, Susquehanna U.P., 239 pp.

Peer, *Romanticisms: Comparative Romanticisms: Power, Gender, Subjectivity*, ed. Larry H. Peer and Diane Long Hoeveler, Columbia, S.C., Camden House, 243 pp.

Peil, *Erkennen: Erkennen und Erinnern in Kunst und Literatur. Kolloquium Reisensburg, 4.–7. Januar 1996*, ed. Dietmar Peil, Michael Schilling, Peter Strohschneider, and Wolfgang Frühwald, Tübingen, Niemeyer, ix + 675 pp.

Pocta 650: Pocta 650. výročí založení Univerzity Karlovy v Praze. Sborník příspěvků přednesených zahraničnimi bohemisty na mezinárodním sympoziu v Praze 20.–26. srpna 1998, ed. Alexandr Stich, Prague, Charles Univ., 307 pp.

Português falado, II-III, V-VI: *Gramática do Português falado*, II: *Níveis de análise lingüística* ed. Rodolfo Ilari, III: *As abordagens*, ed. Ataliba Teixeira de Castilho, introd. Margarida Basílio, V: *Convergências*, ed. Mary A. Kato, VI: *Desenvolvimentos*, ed. Ingedore G. Villaça Koch, Campinas, UNICAMP, 1996, 447, 440, 366, 526 pp.

Price, *Encyclopedia: Encyclopedia of the Languages of Europe*, ed. Glanville Price, Oxford, Blackwell, xviii + 499 pp.

Procs (Brno): *Text, Speech, Dialogue. Proceedings of the First Workshop on Text, Speech, Dialogue — TSD '98, Brno, September 23–26, 1998*, Brno, Masaryk Univ.

Procs (Harvard), 14: *Proceedings of the Harvard Celtic Colloquium (April 29–May 1, 1994)*, ed. P. Hopkins, L. Maney, and D. Wong, vol. 14, 1994[1997], ix + 218 pp.

Pryce, *Literacy: Literacy in Medieval Celtic Societies*, ed. Huw Pryce, CUP, xiii + 297 pp.

Ramat, *Grammaticalization: The Limits of Grammaticalization*, ed. Anna Giacalone Ramat and Paul J. Hopper (TSL, 37), Amsterdam, Benjamins, vi + 302 pp.

Ramat, *Indo-European: The Indo-European Languages*, ed. Anna Giacalone Ramat and Paolo Ramat, London, Routledge, xxiv + 526 pp.

Ramat Vol.: Ars linguistica. Studi offerti a Paolo Ramat, ed. Giuliano Bernini, Pierluigi Cuzzolin, and Piera Molinelli, Rome, Bulzoni, 544 pp.

Rinaldi, *Studi:* Rinaldo Rinaldi, *Le imperfette imprese. Studi sul Rinascimento*, Turin, Tirrenia, 1997, 339 pp.

RK 11: Neuer Beschreibungsmethoden der Syntax romanischer Sprachen. Romanistisches Kolloquium XI, ed. Wolfgang Dahmen et al. (TBL, 423), Tübingen, Narr, 494 pp.

Rothwell Vol.: De Mot en Mot: Aspects of Medieval Linguistics. Essays in Honour of William Rothwell, ed. Stewart Gregory and D. A. Trotter, Cardiff, University of Wales Press - MHRA, 1997, xxii + 282 pp.

Scheible, *Melanchthon: Melanchthon in seinen Schülern*, ed. Heinz Scheible (Wolfenbütteler Forschungen, 73), Wiesbaden, Harrassowitz, 1997, 587 pp.

Shimmura Vol.: Mélanges in memoriam Takeshi Shimmura, offerts par ses amis, ses collègues et ses élèves, Tokyo, i + 358 pp.

Siewierska, *Order: Constituent Order in the Languages of Europe*, ed. Anna Siewierska (Eurotyp, 20–1), Berlin, Mouton de Gruyter, xvi + 829 pp.

SLI 29: La 'lingua d'Italia': usi pubblici e istituzionali. Atti del XXIX Congresso della Società di Linguistica Italiana, Malta, 3–5 novembre 1995, ed. Gabriella Alfieri and Arnold Cassold (Publicazioni della Società di Linguistica Italiana, 40), Rome, Bulzoni, 504 pp.

SLI 30: Sintassi storica. Atti del XXX Congresso internazionale della Società di Linguistica Italiana, Pavia, 26–28 settembre 1996, ed. Paolo Ramat and Elisa Roma (Publicazioni della Società di Linguistica Italiana, 39), Rome, Bulzoni, iii + 716 pp.

Taylor, *Place-names: The Uses of Place-names*, ed. Simon Taylor (St John's House Papers, 7), Edinburgh, Scottish Cultural Press–St Andrews Scottish Studies Institute, xiv + 190 pp.

Tomasch and Gilles, *Text and Territory: Text and Territory. Geographical Imagination in the European Middle Ages*, ed. Sylvia Tomasch and Sealy Gilles, Philadelphia, University of Pennsylvania Press, ix + 330 pp.

Törnqvist Vol.: Strindberg, Ibsen and Bergman. Essays on Scandinavian Film and Drama Offered to Egil Törnqvist on the Occasion of his 65th Birthday, ed. Harry Perridon, Maastricht, Shaker, 238 pp.

Uecker, *Opplysning: Opplysning i Norden. Foredrag på den XXI. studiekonferanse i International Association for Scandinavian Studies (IASS) arrangert av Skandinavistiche Abteilung, Germanistisches Seminar, Universität Bonn 5.–11. august 1996*, ed. Heido Uecker (TUGS, 40), Frankfurt, Lang, 519 pp.

Veny Vol. II: Estudis de llengua i literatura en honor de Joan Veny, ed. J. Massot Muntaner, vol. II (Biblioteca Abat Oliva, 188), Montserrat, Abadia de Montserrat, 1998, 684 pp.

Vietta, *Moderne: Ästhetische Moderne in Europa: Grundzüge und Problemzusammenhänge seit der Romantik*, ed. Silvio Vietta and Dirk Kemperer, Munich, Fink, 572 pp.

Villari Vol.: Sguardi sull'Italia. Miscellanea dedicata a Francesco Villari dalla Society for Italian Studies, ed. Gino Bedani, Zygmunt Barański, Anna Laura Lepschy, and Brian Richardson (The Society for Italian Studies Occasional Papers, 3), Leeds, Maney, 1997, 259 pp.

Wilmet Vol.: La Ligne claire de la linguistique à la grammaire. Mélanges offerts à Marc Wilmet à l'occasion de sa 60e anniversaire, ed. Annick Engelbert et al., Paris–Brussels, Duculot, 398 pp.

Wojnowska, *Literatura: Literatura i władza*, ed. Bożena Wojnowska, Warsaw, Wydawnictwo IBL, 1996.

WS XV: Wolfram-Studien XV. Neue Wege der Mittelalter-Philologie. Landshuter Kolloquium 1996, ed. Joachim Heinzle, L. Peter Johnson, and Gisela Vollmann-Profe, Berlin, Schmidt, 525 pp. + 27 pls.

Ygaunin, *Pindare*, III: Jean Ygaunin, *Pindare et les poètes de la célébration*, III: *Ronsard et les poètes de la monarchie*, Fleury-sur-Orne, Minard, 1997, v + 421 + xix pp.

Ygaunin, *Pindare*, VII: Jean Ygaunin, *Pindare et les poètes de la célébration*, VII: *Le Symbolisme au bord de la Méditerranée, Valéry*, Fleury-sur-Orne, Minard, 1997, vi + 118 + xxii pp.

Ygaunin, *Pindare*, VIII: Jean Ygaunin, *Pindare et les poètes de la célébration*, VIII: *La Mystique et l'Art, Claudel. Montherlant et la renaissance des Jeux Olympiques*, Fleury-sur-Orne, Minard, 1997, vi + 108 + xxii pp.

Zink, *Art d'Aimer: L'Art d'aimer au Moyen Age*, ed. Michel Zink, Daniel Poirion et al., Paris, Éditions du Felin–Philippe Lebaud, 1997.

Ziolkowski, *Obscenity: Obscenity: Social Control and Artistic Creation in the European Middle Ages*, ed. Jan M. Ziolkowski (Cultures, Beliefs and Traditions, 4), Leiden–Boston–Cologne, Brill, x + 359 pp.

II. GENERAL

abbrev.	abbreviation, abbreviated to
Acad., Akad.	Academy, Academia, etc.
acc.	accusative
ann.	annotated (by)
anon.	anonymous
appx	appendix
Arg.	Argentinian (and foreign equivalents)
Assoc.	Association (and foreign equivalents)
Auv.	Auvergnat
Bel.	Belarusian
BL	British Library
BM	British Museum
BN	Bibliothèque Nationale, Biblioteka Narodowa, etc.
BPtg.	Brazilian Portuguese
bull.	bulletin
c.	century
c.	circa
Cat.	Catalan
ch.	chapter
col.	column
comm.	commentary (by)
comp.	compiler, compiled (by)
Cz.	Czech
diss.	dissertation
ed.	edited (by), editor (and foreign equivalents)
edn	edition
EPtg.	European Portuguese
fac.	facsimile
fasc.	fascicle
Fest.	Festschrift, Festskrift
Fin.	Finnish
Fr.	France, French, Français
Gal.-Ptg.	Galician-Portuguese (and equivalents)
Gasc.	Gascon
Ger.	German(y)
Gk	Greek
Gmc	Germanic
IE	Indo-European
illus.	illustrated, illustration(s)
impr.	impression
incl.	including, include(s)
Inst.	Institute (and foreign equivalents)
introd.	introduction, introduced by, introductory
It.	Italian
izd.	издание
izd-vo	издательство
Jb.	Jahrbuch
Jg	Jahrgang
Jh.	Jahrhundert
Lang.	Languedocien
Lat.	Latin
Lim.	Limousin

lit.	literature
med.	medieval
MHG	Middle High German
Mid. Ir.	Middle Irish
Mil.	Milanese
MS	manuscript
n.d.	no date
n.F.	neue Folge
no.	number (and foreign equivalents)
nom.	nominative
n.p.	no place
n.s.	new series
O Auv.	Old Auvergnat
Occ.	Occitan
OE	Old English
OF	Old French
O Gasc.	Old Gascon
OHG	Old High German
O Ir.	Old Irish
O Lim.	Old Limousin
O Occ.	Old Occitan
O Pr.	Old Provençal
O Ptg.	Old Portuguese
OS	Old Saxon
OW	Old Welsh
part.	participle
ped.	педагогический, etc.
PIE	Proto-Indo-European
Pied.	Piedmontese
PGmc	Primitive Germanic
pl.	plate
plur.	plural
Pol.	Polish
p.p.	privately published
Pr.	Provençal
pref.	preface (by)
Procs	Proceedings
Ptg.	Portuguese
publ.	publication, published (by)
Ren.	Renaissance
repr.	reprint(ed)
Rev.	Review, Revista, Revue
rev.	revised (by)
Russ.	Russian
s.	siècle
ser.	series
sg.	singular
Slg	Sammlung
Soc.	Society (and foreign equivalents)
Sp.	Spanish
supp.	supplement
Sw.	Swedish
Trans.	Transactions
trans.	translated (by), translation

Ukr.	Ukrainian
Univ.	University (and foreign equivalents)
unpubl.	unpublished
U.P.	University Press (and foreign equivalents)
Vlg	Verlag
vol.	volume
vs	versus
W.	Welsh
wyd.	wydawnictwo

* before a publication signifies that it has not been seen by the contributor.

III. PLACE NAMES

B	Barcelona		Na	Naples
BA	Buenos Aires		NY	New York
Be	Belgrade		O	Oporto
Bo	Bologna		Pń	Poznań
C	Coimbra		R	Rio de Janeiro
F	Florence		Ro	Rome
Gd	Gdańsk		SPo	São Paulo
Kw	Kraków, Cracow		StP	St Petersburg
L	Lisbon		T	Turin
Ld	Leningrad		V	Valencia
M	Madrid		Wa	Warsaw
Mi	Milan		Ww	Wrocław
Mw	Moscow		Z	Zagreb

IV. PERIODICALS, INSTITUTIONS, PUBLISHERS

AA, Antike und Abendland

AAA, Ardis Publishers, Ann Arbor, Michigan

AAA, Archivio per l'Alto Adige

AAASS, American Association for the Advancement of Slavic Studies

AABC, Anuari de l'Agrupació Borrianenca de Cultura

AAC, Atti dell'Accademia Clementina

AAL, Atti dell'Accademia dei Lincei

AALP, L'Arvista dl'Academia dla Lenga Piemontèisa

AAM, Association des Amis de Maynard

AAPH, Anais da Academia Portuguesa da História

AAPN, Atti dell'Accademia Pontaniana di Napoli

AAPP, Atti Accademia Peloritana dei Pericolanti. Classe di Lettere Filosofia e Belle Arti

AARA, Atti della Accademia Roveretana degli Agiati

AASB, Atti dell'Accademia delle Scienze dell'Istituto di Bologna

AASF, Annales Academiae Scientiarum Fennicae

AASLAP, Atti dell'Accademia di Scienze, Lettere ed Arti di Palermo

AASLAU, Atti dell'Accademia di Scienze, Lettere e Arti di Udine

AASN, Atti dell'Accademia di Scienze Morali e Politiche di Napoli

AAST, Atti dell'Accademia delle Scienze di Torino

AAVM, Atti e Memorie dell'Accademia Virgiliana di Mantova

AAWG, Abhandlungen der Akademie der Wissenschaften in Göttingen, phil.-hist. Kl., 3rd ser., Göttingen, Vandenhoeck & Ruprecht

AB, Analecta Bollandiana

ABa, L'Année Balzacienne

ABÄG, Amsterdamer Beiträge zur älteren Germanistik

ABB, Archives et Bibliothèques de Belgique — Archief- en Bibliotheekswezen in België

ABDB, Aus dem Antiquariat. Beiträge zum Börsenblatt für den deutschen Buchhandel

ABDO, Association Bourguignonne de Dialectologie et d'Onomastique, Fontaine lès Dijon

ABHL, Annual Bulletin of Historical Literature

ABI, Accademie e Biblioteche d'Italia

ABN, Anais da Biblioteca Nacional, Rio de Janeiro

ABNG, Amsterdamer Beiträge zur neueren Germanistik, Amsterdam, Rodopi

ABor, Acta Borussica

ABP, Arquivo de Bibliografia Portuguesa

ABR, American Benedictine Review

ABr, Annales de Bretagne et des Pays de l'Ouest

ABS, Acta Baltico-Slavica

AC, Analecta Cisterciensa, Rome

ACCT, Agence de Coopération Culturelle et Technique

ACer, Anales Cervantinos, Madrid

ACIS, Association for Contemporary Iberian Studies

ACo, Acta Comeniana, Prague

AColl, Actes et Colloques

Acme, Annali della Facoltà di Filosofia e Lettere dell'Università Statale di Milano

ACP, L'Amitié Charles Péguy

ACUA, Anales del Colegio Universitario de Almería

AD, Analysen und Dokumente. Beiträge zur Neueren Literatur, Berne, Lang

ADEVA, Akademische Druck- und Verlagsanstalt, Graz

AE, Artemis Einführungen, Munich, Artemis

AE, L'Autre Europe

AEA, Anuario de Estudios Atlánticos, Las Palmas

AECI, Agencia Española de Cooperación Internacional

AEd, Arbeiten zur Editionswissenschaft, Frankfurt, Lang

AEF, Anuario de Estudios Filológicos, Cáceres

AEL, Anuario de la Escuela de Letras, Mérida, Venezuela

AELG, Anuario de Literarios Galegos

AEM, Anuario de Estudios Medievales

AF, Anuario de Filología, Barcelona

AFA, Archivo de Filología Aragonesa

AfAf, African Affairs

AfC, Afrique Contemporaine

AFe, L'Armana di Felibre

AFF, Anali Filološkog fakulteta, Belgrade

AFH, Archivum Franciscanum Historicum

AFHis, Anales de Filología Hispánica

AfHR, Afro-Hispanic Review

AfL, L'Afrique Littéraire

AFLE, Annali della Fondazione Luigi Einaudi

AFLFUB, Annali della Facoltà di Lettere e Filosofia dell'Università di Bari

AFLFUC, Annali della Facoltà di Lettere e Filosofia dell'Università di Cagliari

AFLFUG, Annali della Facoltà di Lettere e Filosofia dell'Università degli Studi di Genova

AFLFUM, Annali della Facoltà di Lettere e Filosofia dell'Università di Macerata

AFLFUN, Annali della Facoltà di Lettere e Filosofia dell'Università di Napoli

AFLFUP(SF), Annali dellà Facoltà di Lettere e Filosofia dell'Università di Perugia. 1. Studi Filosofici

AFLFUP(SLL), Annali della Facoltà di Lettere e Filosofia dell'Università di Perugia. 3. Studi Linguistici-Letterari

AFLFUS, Annali della Facoltà di Lettere e Filosofia dell'Università di Siena

AFLLS, Annali della Facoltà di Lingua e Letterature Straniere di Ca' Foscari, Venice

AFLN, Annales de la Faculté des Lettres et Sciences Humaines de Nice

AFLS, Association for French Language Studies

AFP, Archivum Fratrum Praedicatorum

AFrP, Athlone French Poets, London, The Athlone Press

AG, Anales Galdosianos

AGB, Archiv für Geschichte des Buchwesens

AGF, Anuario Galego de Filoloxia

AGI, Archivio Glottologico Italiano

AGJSG, Acta Germanica. Jahrbuch des Südafrikanischen Germanistenverbandes

AGP, Archiv für Geschichte der Philosophie

AH, Archivo Hispalense

AHAW, Abhandlungen der Heidelberger Akademie der Wissenschaften, phil.-hist. Kl

AHCP, Arquivos de História de Cultura Portuguesa

AHDLMA, Archives d'Histoire Doctrinale et Littéraire du Moyen Âge

AHF, Archiwum Historii Filozofii i Myśli Społecznej

AHP, Archivum Historiae Pontificae

AHPr, Annales de Haute-Provence, Digne-les-Bains

AHR, American Historical Review

AHRF, Annales Historiques de la Révolution Française

AHRou, Archives historiques du Rouergue

AHSJ, Archivum Historicum Societatis Jesu

AHSS, Annales: Histoire — Science Sociales

AI, Almanacco Italiano

AIB, Annali dell'Istituto Banfi

AIBL, Académie des Inscriptions et Belles-Lettres, Comptes Rendus

AIEM, Anales del Instituto de Estudios Madrileños

AIEO, Association Internationale d'Études Occitanes

AIFMUR, Annali dell'Istituto di Filologia Moderna dell'Università di Roma

AIFUF, Annali dell'Istituto di Filosofia dell'Università di Firenze

AIHI, Archives Internationales d'Histoire des Idées, The Hague, Nijhoff

AIHS, Archives Internationales d'Histoire des Sciences

AIL, Associação Internacional de Lusitanistas

AILLC, Associació Internacional de Llengua i Literatura Catalanes

AISIGT, Annali dell'Istituto Storico Italo-Germanico di Trento

AION(FG), Annali dell'Istituto Universitario Orientale, Naples: Sezione Germanica. Filologia Germanica

AION(SF), Annali dell'Istituto Universitario Orientale, Naples: Studi Filosofici

AION(SL), Annali dell'Istituto Universitario Orientale, Naples: Sezione Linguistica

AION(SR), Annali dell'Istituto Universitario Orientale, Naples: Sezione Romanza

AION(SS), Annali dell'Istituto Universitario Orientale, Naples: Sezione Slava

AION(ST), Annali dell'Istituto Universitario Orientale, Naples: Sezione Germanica. Studi Tedeschi

AIPHS, Annuaire de l'Institut de Philologie et de l'Histoire Orientales et Slaves

AIPS, Annales Instituti Philologiae Slavica Universitatis Debreceniensis de Ludovico Kossuth Nominatae — Slavica

AITCA, Arxiu informatizat de textos catalans antics

AIV, Atti dell'Istituto Veneto

AJ, Alemannisches Jahrbuch

AJCAI, Actas de las Jornadas de Cultura Arabe e Islámica

AJFS, Australian Journal of French Studies

AJGLL, American Journal of Germanic Linguistics and Literatures

AJL, Australian Journal of Linguistics

AJP, American Journal of Philology

AKG, Archiv für Kulturgeschichte

AKML, Abhandlungen zur Kunst-, Musik- und Literaturwissenschaft, Bonn, Bouvier

AL, Anuario de Letras, Mexico

AlAm, Alba de América

ALB, Annales de la Faculté des Lettres de Besançon

ALC, African Languages and Cultures

ALE, Anales de Literatura Española, Alicante

ALEC, Anales de Literatura Española Contemporánea

ALet, Armas y Letras, Universidad de Nuevo León

ALEUA, Anales de Literatura Española de la Universidad de Alicante

ALFL, Actes de Langue Française et de Linguistique

ALH, Acta Linguistica Hungaricae

ALHA, Anales de la Literatura Hispanoamericana

ALHa, Acta Linguistica Hafniensia

ALHisp, Anuario de Lingüística Hispánica

ALHist, Annales: Littérature et Histoire

ALit, Acta Literaria, Chile

ALitH, Acta Litteraria Hungarica

ALLI, Atlante Linguistico dei Laghi Italiani

ALM, Archives des Lettres Modernes

ALMA, Archivum Latinitatis Medii Aevi (Bulletin du Cange)

ALo, Armanac de Louzero

ALP, Atlas linguistique et ethnographique de Provence, CNRS, 1975–86

AlS, Almanac Setòri

ALT, African Literature Today

ALUB, Annales Littéraires de l'Université de Besançon

AM, Analecta Musicologica

AMAA, Atti e Memorie dell'Accademia d'Arcadia

AMAASLV, Atti e Memorie dell'Accademia di Agricoltura, Scienze e Lettere di Verona

AMal, Analecta Malacitana

AMAP, Atti e Memorie dell'Accademia Patavina di Scienze, Lettere ed Arti

AMAPet, Atti e Memorie dell'Accademia Petrarca di Lettere, Arti e Scienze, Arezzo

AMAT, Atti e Memorie dell'Accademia Toscana di Scienze e Lettere, La Colombaria

AMDLS, Arbeiten zur Mittleren Deutschen Literatur und Sprache, Berne, Lang

AMDSPAPM, Atti e Memorie della Deputazione di Storia Patria per le Antiche Province Modenesi

AMGG, Abhandlungen der Marburger Gelehrten Gesellschaft, Munich, Fink

AmH, American Hispanist

AMid, Annales du Midi

AML, Main Monographien Literaturwissenschaft, Frankfurt, Main

AmIn, América Indígena, Mexico

AMSSSP, Atti e Memorie della Società Savonese di Storia Patria

AN, Академия наук

AN, Americana Norvegica

ANABA, Asociación Nacional de Bibliotecarios, Arquiveros y Arqueólogos

AnAlf, Annali Alfieriani

AnEA, Anaquel de Estudios Arabes

ANeo, Acta Neophilologica, Ljubljana

ANF, Arkiv för nordisk filologi

AnI, Annali d'Italianistica

AnL, Anthropological Linguistics

AnM, Anuario Medieval

AnN, Annales de Normandie

AnnM, Annuale Medievale

ANPOLL, Associação Nacional de Pós-graduação e Pesquisa em Letras e Lingüística, São Paulo

ANQ, American Notes and Queries

ANTS, Anglo-Norman Text Society

AnVi, Antologia Vieusseux

ANZSGLL, Australian and New Zealand Studies in German Language and Literature, Berne, Lang

AO, Almanac occitan, Foix

AÖAW, Anzeiger der Österreichischen Akademie der Wissenschaften

AOn, Acta Onomastica

AP, Aurea Parma

APIFN, Актуальные проблемы истории философии народов СССР.

APK, Aufsätze zur portugiesischen Kulturgeschichte, Görres-Gesellschaft, Münster

ApL, Applied Linguistics

APL, Associação Portuguesa de Linguística

APPP, Abhandlungen zur Philosophie, Psychologie und Pädagogik, Bonn, Bouvier

APr, Analecta Praemonstratensia

AProu, Armana Prouvençau, Marseilles

APS, Acta Philologica Scandinavica

APSL, Amsterdamer Publikationen zur Sprache und Literatur, Amsterdam, Rodopi

APUCF, Association des Publications de la Faculté des Lettres et Sciences Humaines de l'Université de Clermont-Ferrand II, Nouvelle Série

AQ, Arizona Quarterly

AqAq, Aquò d'aquí, Gap

AR, Archiv für Reformationsgeschichte

ARAJ, American Romanian Academy Journal

ARAL, Australian Review of Applied Linguistics

ARCA, ARCA: Papers of the Liverpool Latin Seminar

ArCCP, Arquivos do Centro Cultural Português, Paris

ArEM, Aragón en la Edad Media

ArFil, Archivio di Filosofia

ArI, Arthurian Interpretations

ARI, Архив русской истории

ARL, Athlone Renaissance Library

ArL, Archivum Linguisticum

ArLit, Arthurian Literature

ArP, Археографски прилози

ArSP, Archivio Storico Pugliese

ArSPr, Archivio Storico Pratese

ArSt, Archivi per la Storia

ART, Atelier Reproduction des Thèses, Univ. de Lille III, Paris, Champion

AS, The American Scholar

ASAvS, Annuaire de la Société des Amis du vieux-Strasbourg

ASB, Archivio Storico Bergamasco

ASCALF, Association for the Study of Caribbean and African Literature in French

ASCALFB, ASCALF Bulletin

ASCALFY, ASCALF Yearbook

ASE, Annali di Storia dell'Esegesi

ASEES, Australian Slavonic and East European Studies

ASELGC, 1616. Anuario de la Sociedad Española de Literatura General y Comparada

ASGM, Atti del Sodalizio Glottologico Milanese

ASI, Archivio Storico Italiano

ASJ, Acta Slavonica Japonica

ASL, Archivio Storico Lombardo

ASLSP, Atti della Società Ligure di Storia Patria

ASMC, Annali di Storia Moderna e Contemporanea

ASNP, Annali della Scuola Normale Superiore di Pisa

ASNS, Archiv für das Studium der Neueren Sprachen und Literaturen

ASocRous, Annales de la Société J.-J. Rousseau

ASolP, A Sol Post, Editorial Marfil, Alcoi

ASP, Anzeiger für slavische Philologie

AsP, L'Astrado prouvençalo. Revisto Bilengo de Prouvenço/Revue Bilingue de Provence, Berre L'Etang.

ASPN, Archivio Storico per le Province Napoletane

ASPP, Archivio Storico per le Province Parmensi

ASR, Annalas de la Società Retorumantscha

ASRSP, Archivio della Società Romana di Storia Patria

ASSO, Archivio Storico per la Sicilia Orientale

ASSUL, Annali del Dipartimento di Scienze Storiche e Sociali dell'Università di Lecce

AST, Analecta Sacra Tarraconensia

ASt, Austrian Studies

ASTic, Archivio Storico Ticinese

AŞUI, (e), (f), Analele Ştiinţifice ale Universităţii 'Al. I. Cuza' din Iaşi, secţ. e, Lingvistică, secţ. f, Literatură

AT, Athenäums Taschenbücher, Frankfurt, Athenäum

ATB, Altdeutsche Textbibliothek, Tübingen, Niemeyer

ATCA, Arxiu de Textos Catalans Antics, IEC, Barcelona

Ate, Nueva Atenea, Universidad de Concepción, Chile

ATO, A Trabe de Ouro

ATS, Arbeiten und Texte zur Slavistik, Munich, Sagner

ATV, Aufbau Taschenbuch Verlag, Berlin, Aufbau

AtV, Ateneo Veneto

AUBLLR, Analele Universităţii Bucureşti, Limba şi literatura română

AUBLLS, Analele Universităţii Bucureşti, Limbi şi literaturi străine

AUC, Anales de la Universidad de Cuenca

AUCP, Acta Universitatis Carolinae Pragensis

AuE, Arbeiten und Editionen zur Mittleren Deutschen Literatur, Stuttgart–Bad Cannstatt, Frommann-Holzboog

AUL, Acta Universitatis Lodziensis

AUL, Annali della Facoltà di Lettere e Filosofia dell'Università di Lecce

AUMCS, Annales Uniwersytetu Marii Curie-Skłodowskiej, Lublin

AUML, Anales de la Universidad de Murcia: Letras

AUMLA, Journal of the Australasian Universities Modern Language Association

AUN, Annali della Facoltà di Lettere e Filosofia dell'Università di Napoli

AUNCFP, Acta Universitatis Nicolai Copernici. Filologia Polska, Toruń

AUPO, Acta Universitatis Palackianae Olomucensis

AUS, American University Studies, Berne — New York, Lang

AUSP, Annali dell'Università per Stranieri di Perugia

AUSSR, Acta Universitatis Stockholmiensis. Stockholm Studies in Russian Literature

AUSSSS, Acta Universitatis Stockholmiensis. Stockholm Slavic Studies

AUTŞF, Analele Universităţii din Timişoara, Ştiinţe Filologice

AUUSRU, Acta Universitatis Upsaliensis. Studia Romanica Upsaliensia

AUUUSH, Acta Universitatis Umensis, Umeå Studies in the Humanities, Umeå U.P.

AUW, Acta Universitatis Wratislaviensis

AVen, Archivio Veneto

AVEP, Assouciacien vareso pèr l'ensignamen dòu prouvençou, La Farlède

AVEPB, Bulletin AVEP, La Farlède

AvT, L'Avant-Scène Théâtre

AWR, Anglo-Welsh Review

BA, Bollettino d'Arte

BAAA, Bulletin de l'Association des Amis d'Alain

BAAG, Bulletin des Amis d'André Gide

BAAJG, Bulletin de l'Association des Amis de Jean Giono

BAAL, Boletín de la Academia Argentina de Letras

BaB, Bargfelder Bote

BAC, Biblioteca de Autores Cristianos

BACol, Boletín de la Academia Colombiana

BÄDL, Beiträge zur Älteren Deutschen Literaturgeschichte, Berne, Lang

BADLit, Bonner Arbeiten zur deutschen Literatur, Bonn, Bouvier

BAE, Biblioteca de Autores Españoles

BAEO, Boletín de la Asociación Española de Orientalistas

BAFJ, Bulletin de l'Association Francis Jammes

BAG, Boletín de la Academia Gallega

BAIEO, Bulletins de l'Association Internationale d'Études Occitanes

BAJR, Bulletin des Amis de Jules Romains

BAJRAF, Bulletin des Amis de Jacques Rivière et d'Alain-Fournier

BALI, Bollettino dell'Atlante Linguistico Italiano

BALM, Bollettino dell'Atlante Linguistico Mediterraneo

BalS, Balkan Studies, Institute for Balkan Studies, Thessaloniki

BAN, Българска Академия на Науките, София

BAO, Biblioteca Abat Oliva, Publicacions de l'Abadia de Montserrat, Barcelona

BAPC, Bulletin de l'Association Paul Claudel

BAPRLE, Boletín de la Academia Puertorrigueña de la Lengua Española

BAR, Biblioteca dell'Archivum Romanicum

BARLLF, Bulletin de l'Académie Royale de Langues et de Littératures Françaises de Bruxelles

BAWA, Bayerische Akademie der Wissenschaften. Phil.-hist. Kl. Abhandlungen, n.F.

BB, Biblioteca Breve, Lisbon

BB, Bulletin of Bibliography

BBAHLM, Boletín Bibliografico de la Asociación Hispánica de Literatura Medieval

BBB, Berner Beiträge zur Barockgermanistik, Berne, Lang

BBGN, Brünner Beiträge zur Germanistik und Nordistik

BBib, Bulletin du Bibliophile

BBL, Bayreuther Beiträge zur Literaturwissenschaft, Frankfurt, Lang

BBLI, Bremer Beiträge zur Literatur- und Ideengeschichte, Frankfurt, Lang

BBMP, Boletín de la Biblioteca de Menéndez Pelayo

BBN, Bibliotheca Bibliographica Neerlandica, Nieuwkoop, De Graaf

BBNDL, Berliner Beiträge zur neueren deutschen Literaturgeschichte, Berne, Lang

BBSANZ, Bulletin of the Bibliographical Society of Australia and New Zealand

BBSIA, Bulletin Bibliographique de la Société Internationale Arthurienne

BBSMES, Bulletin of the British Society for Middle Eastern Studies

BBUC, Boletim da Biblioteca da Universidade de Coimbra

BC, Bulletin of the 'Comediantes', University of Wisconsin

BCB, Boletín Cultural y Bibliográfico, Bogatá

BCEC, Bwletin Cymdeithas Emynwyr Cymru

BCél, Bulletin Célinien

BCh, Болдинские чтения

BCLSMP, Académie Royale de Belgique: Bulletin de la Classe des Lettres et des Sciences Morales et Politiques

BCMV, Bollettino Civici Musei Veneziani

BCRLT, Bulletin du Centre de Romanistique et de Latinité Tardive

BCS, Bulletin of Canadian Studies

BCSM, Bulletin of the Cantigueiros de Santa Maria

BCSS, Bollettino del Centro di Studi Filologici e Linguistici Siciliani

BCSV, Bollettino del Centro di Studi Vichiani

BCZG, Blätter der Carl Zuckmayer Gesellschaft

BD, Беларуская думка

BDADA, Bulletin de documentation des Archives départementales de l'Aveyron, Rodez

BDB, Börsenblatt für den deutschen Buchhandel

BDBA, Bien Dire et Bien Aprandre

BDP, Beiträge zur Deutschen Philologie, Giessen, Schmitz

BEA, Bulletin des Études Africaines

BEC, Bibliothèque de l'École des Chartes

BelE, Беларуская энцыклапедыя

BelL, Беларуская лінгвістыка

BelS, Беларускі сьвет

BEP, Bulletin des Études Portugaises

BEPar, Bulletin des Études Parnassiennes et Symbolistes

BEzLit, Български език и литература

BF, Boletim de Filologia

BFA, Bulletin of Francophone Africa

BFC, Boletín de Filología, Univ. de Chile

BFE, Boletín de Filología Española

BFF, Bulletin Francophone de Finlande

BFFGL, Boletín de la Fundación Federico García Lorca

BFi, Bollettino Filosofico

BFLS, Bulletin de la Faculté des Lettres de Strasbourg

BFo, Biuletyn Fonograficzny

BFPLUL, Bibliothèque de la Faculté de Philosophie et Lettres de l'Université de Liège

BFR, Bibliothèque Française et Romane, Paris, Klincksieck

BFR, Bulletin of the Fondation C.F. Ramuz

BFr, Börsenblatt Frankfurt

BG, Bibliotheca Germanica, Tübingen, Francke

BGB, Bulletin de l'Association Guillaume Budé

BGDSL, Beiträge zur Geschichte der deutschen Sprache und Literatur, Tübingen

BGKT, Беларускае грамадска-культуральнае таварыства

BGL, Boletin Galego de Literatura

BGLKAJ, Beiträge zur Geschichte der Literatur und Kunst des 18. Jahrhunderts, Heidelberg, Winter

BGP, Bristol German Publications, Bristol U.P

BGREC, Bulletin du Groupe de Recherches et d'Études du Clermontais, Clermont-l'Hérault

BGS, Beiträge zur Geschichte der Sprachwissenschaft

BGS, Beiträge zur germanistischen Sprachwissenschaft, Hamburg, Buske

BGT, Blackwell German Texts, Oxford, Blackwell

BH, Bulletin Hispanique

BHR, Bibliothèque d'Humanisme et Renaissance

BHS(G), Bulletin of Hispanic Studies, Glasgow

BHS(L), Bulletin of Hispanic Studies, Liverpool

BI, Bibliographisches Institut, Leipzig

BibAN, Библиотека Академии наук СССР

BIDS, Bulletin of the International Dostoevsky Society, Klagenfurt

BIEA, Boletín del Instituto de Estudios Asturianos

BIHBR, Bulletin de l'Institut Historique Belge de Rome

BIHR, Bulletin of the Institute of Historical Research

BJA, British Journal of Aesthetics

BJCS, British Journal for Canadian Studies

BJECS, The British Journal for Eighteenth-Century Studies

BJHP, British Journal of the History of Philosophy

BJHS, British Journal of the History of Science

BJL, Belgian Journal of Linguistics

BJR, Bulletin of the John Rylands University Library of Manchester

BKF, Beiträge zur Kleist-Forschung

BL, Brain and Language

BLAR, Bulletin of Latin American Research

BLBI, Bulletin des Leo Baeck Instituts

BLe, Börsenblatt Leipzig

BLFCUP, Bibliothèque de
Littérature Française
Contemporaine de l'Université
Paris 7
BLI, Beiträge zur Linguistik und
Informationsverarbeitung
BLi, Беларуская літаратура.
Міжвузаўскі зборнік.
BLJ, British Library Journal
BLL, Beiträge zur Literatur und
Literaturwissenschaft des 20.
Jahrhunderts, Berne, Lang
BLM, Bonniers Litterära Magasin
BLR, Bibliothèque Littéraire de la
Renaissance, Geneva,
Slatkine–Paris, Champion
BLR, Bodleian Library Record
BLVS, Bibliothek des Literarischen
Vereins, Stuttgart, Hiersemann
BM, Bibliothek Metzier, Stuttgart
BMBP, Bollettino del Museo
Bodoniano di Parma
BMCP, Bollettino del Museo Civico
di Padova
BML, Беларуская мова і
літаратура ў школе
BMo, Беларуская мова.
Міжвузаўкі зборнік
BNE, Beiträge zur neueren
Epochenforschung, Berne, Lang
BNF, Beiträge zur Namenforschung
BNL, Beiträge zur neueren
Literaturgeschichte, 3rd ser.,
Heidelberg, Winter
BNP, Beiträge zur nordischen
Philologie, Basel, Helbing &
Lichtenhahn
BO, Biblioteca Orientalis
BOCES, Boletín del Centro de
Estudios del Siglo XVIII, Oviedo
BOP, Bradford Occasional Papers
BP, Български писател
BP, Lo Bornat dau Perigòrd
BPTJ, Biuletyn Polskiego
Towarzystwa Językoznawczego
BR, Болгарская русистика.
BRA, Bonner Romanistische
Arbeiten, Berne, Lang
BRABLB, Boletín de la Real
Academia de Buenas Letras de
Barcelona
BRAC, Boletín de la Real Academia
de Córdoba de Ciencias, Bellas
Letras, y Nobles Artes

BRAE, Boletín de la Real Academia
Española
BRAH, Boletín de la Real Academia
de la Historia
BrC, Bruniana & Campanelliana
BRIES, Bibliothèque Russe de
l'Institut d'Études Slaves, Paris,
Institut d'Études Slaves
BRJL, Bulletin ruského jazyka a
literatury
BrL, La Bretagne Linguistique
BRP, Beiträge zur romanischen
Philologie
BS, Biuletyn slawistyczny, Łódź
BSAHH, Bulletin de la Société
archéologique et historique des
hauts cantons de l'Hérault,
Bédarieux
BSAHL, Bulletin de la Société
archéologique et historique du
Limousin, Limoges
BSAHLSG, Bulletin de la Société
Archéologique, Historique,
Littéraire et Scientifique du Gers
BSAM, Bulletin de la Société des
Amis de Montaigne
BSAMPAC, Bulletin de la Société des
Amis de Marcel Proust et des
Amis de Combray
BSASLB, Bulletin de la Société
Archéologique, Scientifique et
Littéraire de Béziers
BSATG, Bulletin de la Société
Archéologique de Tarn-et-
Garonne
BSBS, Bollettino Storico–
Bibliografico Subalpino
BSCC, Boletín de la Sociedad
Castellonense de Cultura
BSD, Bithell Series of
Dissertations — MHRA Texts
and Dissertations, London,
Modern Humanities Research
Association
BSD, Bulletin de la Société de
Borda, Dax
BSDL, Bochumer Schriften zur
deutschen Literatur, Berne, Lang
BSDSL, Basler Studien zur
deutschen Sprache und Literatur,
Tübingen, Francke
BSE, Галоўная рэдакцыя
Беларускай савеюкай
энцыклапедыі

BSEHA, Bulletin de la Société
d'Études des Hautes-Alpes, Gap

BSEHTD, Bulletin de la Société
d'Études Historiques du texte
dialectal

BSELSAL, Bulletin de la Société des
Études Littéraires, Scientifiques
et Artistiques du Lot

BSF, Bollettino di Storia della
Filosofia

BSG, Berliner Studien zur
Germanistik, Frankfurt, Lang

BSHAP, Bulletin de la Société
Historique et Archéologique du
Périgord, Périgueux

BSHPF, Bulletin de la Société de
l'Histoire du Protestantisme
Français

BSIH, Brill's Studies in Intellectual
History, Leiden, Brill

BSIS, Bulletin of the Society for
Italian Studies

BSLLW, Bulletin de la Société de
Langue et Littérature Wallonnes

BSLP, Bulletin de la Société de
Linguistique de Paris

BSLV, Bollettino della Società
Letteraria di Verona

BSM, Birmingham Slavonic
Monographs, University of
Birmingham

BSOAS, Bulletin of the School of
Oriental and African Studies

BSP, Bollettino Storico Pisano

BSPC, Bulletin de la Société Paul
Claudel

BSPia, Bollettino Storico Piacentino

BSPN, Bollettino Storico per le
Province di Novara

BSPSP, Bollettino della Società
Pavese di Storia Patria

BsR, Beck'sche Reihe, Munich,
Beck

BSRS, Bulletin of the Society for
Renaissance Studies

BSSAAPC, Bollettino della Società
per gli Studi Storici, Archeologici
ed Artistici della Provincia di
Cuneo

BSSCLE, Bulletin of the Society for
the Study of the Crusades and the
Latin East

BSSP, Bullettino Senese di Storia
Patria

BSSPin, Bollettino della Società
Storica Pinerolese, Pinerolo,
Piemonte, Italy.

BSSPHS, Bulletin of the Society for
Spanish and Portuguese
Historical Studies

BSSV, Bollettino della Società
Storica Valtellinese

BSZJPS, Bałtosłowiańskie związki
językowe. Prace Slawistyczne

BT, Богословские труды, Moscow

BTe, Biblioteca Teatrale

BTH, Boletim de Trabalhos
Historicos

BulEz, Български език

BW, Bibliothek und Wissenschaft

BySt, Byzantine Studies

CA, Cuadernos Americanos

CAAM, Cahiers de l'Association Les
Amis de Milosz

CAB, Commentari dell'Ateneo di
Brescia

CAC, Les Cahiers de l'Abbaye de
Créteil

CadL, Cadernos da Lingua

CAG, Cahiers André Gide

CAIEF, Cahiers de l'Association
Internationale des Études
Françaises

CalLet, Calabria Letteraria

CAm, Casa de las Américas,
Havana

CAm, Casa de las Américas, Havana

CanJL, Canadian Journal of
Linguistics

CanL, Canadian Literature

CanSP, Canadian Slavonic Papers

CanSS, Canadian–American Slavic
Studies

CARB, Cahiers des Amis de Robert
Brasillach

CarQ, Caribbean Quarterly

CAT, Cahiers d'Analyse Textuelle,
Liège, Les Belles Lettres

CatR, Catalan Review

CAVL, Cahiers des Amis de Valery
Larbaud

CB, Cuadernos Bibliográficos

CC, Comparative Criticism

CCe, Cahiers du Cerf XX

CCend, Continent Cendrars

CCF, Cuadernos de la Cátedra Feijoo

CCMe, Cahiers de Civilisation Médiévale

CCol, Cahiers Colette

CCU, Cuadernos de la Cátedra M. de Unamuno

CD, Cuadernos para el Diálogo

CdA, Camp de l'Arpa

CDA, Christliche deutsche Autoren des 20. Jahrhunderts, Berne, Lang

CDB, Coleção Documentos Brasileiros

CDr, Comparative Drama

ČDS, Čeština doma a ve světě

CDs, Cahiers du Dix-septième, Athens, Georgia

CDU, Centre de Documentation Universitaire

CduC, Cahiers de CERES. Série littéraire, Tunis

CE, Cahiers Élisabéthains

CEA, Cahiers d'Études Africaines

CEAL, Centro Editor de América Latina

CEC, Cahiers d'Études Cathares, Narbonne

CEC, Conselho Estadual de Cultura, Comissão de Literatura, São Paulo

CECAES, Centre d'Études des Cultures d'Aquitaine et d'Europe du Sud, Université de Bordeaux III

CEcr, Corps Écrit

CEDAM, Casa Editrice Dott. A. Milani

CEG, Cuadernos de Estudios Gallegos

CEL, Cadernos de Estudos Lingüísticos, Campinas, Brazil

CELO, Centre d'Etude de la Littérature Occitane, Bordes.

CEM, Cahiers d'Études Médiévales, Univ. of Montreal

CEMa, Cahiers d'Études Maghrebines, Cologne

CEMed, Cuadernos de Estudios Medievales

CEPL, Centre d'Étude et de Promotion de la Lecture, Paris

CEPON, Centre per l'estudi e la promocion de l'Occitan normat.

CEPONB, CEPON Bulletin d'échange.

CER, Cahiers d'Études Romanes

CERCLiD, Cahiers d'Études Romanes, Centre de Linguistique et de Dialectologie, Toulouse

CERoum, Cahiers d'Études Roumaines

CeS, Cultura e Scuola

CESCM, Centre d'Études Supérieures de Civilisation Médiévale, Poitiers

CET, Centro Editoriale Toscano

CEtGer, Cahiers d'Études Germaniques

CF, Les Cahiers de Fontenay

CFC, Contemporary French Civilization

CFI, Cuadernos de Filologia Italiana

CFLA, Cuadernos de Filología. Literaturas: Análisis, Valencia

CFM, Cahiers François Mauriac

CFMA, Collection des Classiques Français du Moyen Âge

CFol, Classical Folia

CFS, Cahiers Ferdinand de Saussure

CFSLH, Cuadernos de Filología: Studia Linguistica Hispanica

CFTM, Classiques Français des Temps Modernes, Paris, Champion

CG, Cahiers de Grammaire

CGD, Cahiers Georges Duhamel

CGFT, Critical Guides to French Texts, London, Grant & Cutler

CGGT, Critical Guides to German Texts, London, Grant & Cutler

CGP, Carleton Germanic Papers

CGS, Colloquia Germanica Stetinensia

CGST, Critical Guides to Spanish Texts, London, Támesis, Grant & Cutler

CH, Crítica Hispánica

CHA, Cuadernos Hispano-Americanos

CHAC, Cuadernos Hispano-Americanos. Los complementarios

CHB, Cahiers Henri Bosco

ChC, Chemins Critiques

ChR, The Chesterton Review

ChRev, Chaucer Review

ChrA, Chroniques Allemandes
ChrI, Chroniques Italiennes
ChrL, Christianity and Literature
ChrN, Chronica Nova
ChS, Champs du Signe
CHum, Computers and the Humanities
CHLR, Cahiers d'Histoire des Littératures Romanes
CHP, Cahiers Henri Pourrat
CI, Critical Inquiry
CiD, La Ciudad de Dios
CIDO, Centre International de Documentation Occitane, Béziers
CIEL, Centre International de l'Écrit en Langue d'Òc, Berre
CIEM, Comité International d'Études Morisques
CIF, Cuadernos de Investigación Filológica
CIH, Cuadernos de Investigación Historica
CILF, Conseil International de la Langue Française
CILH, Cuadernos para Investigación de la Literatura Hispanica
CILL, Cahiers de l'Institut de Linguistique de l'Université de Louvain
CIMAGL, Cahiers de l'Institut du Moyen Âge Grec et Latin, Copenhagen
CIn, Cahiers Intersignes
CIRDOC, Centre Inter-Régional de Développement de l'Occitan, Béziers
CIRVI, Centro Interuniversitario di Ricerche sul 'Viaggio in Italia', Moncalieri
CISAM, Centro Italiano di Studi sull'Alto Medioevo
CIt, Carte Italiane
CIUS, Canadian Institute of Ukrainian Studies Edmonton
CivC, Civiltà Cattolica
CJ, Conditio Judaica, Tübingen, Niemeyer
CJb, Celan-Jahrbuch
CJC, Cahiers Jacques Chardonne
CJG, Cahiers Jean Giraudoux
CJIS, Canadian Journal of Italian Studies
ČJL, Český jazyk a literatura

CJNS, Canadian Journal of Netherlandic Studies
CJP, Cahiers Jean Paulhan
CJR, Cahiers Jules Romains
CL, Cuadernos de Leiden
CL, Comparative Literature
ČL, Česká literatura
CLA, Cahiers du LACITO
CLAJ, College Language Association Journal
CLCC, Cahiers de Littérature Canadienne Comparée
CLE, Comunicaciones de Literatura Española, Buenos Aires
CLe, Cahiers de Lexicologie
CLEAM, Coleción de Literatura Española Aljamiado–Morisca, Madrid, Gredos
CLESP, Cooperativa Libraria Editrice degli Studenti dell'Università di Padova, Padua
CLett, Critica Letteraria
CLEUP, Cooperativa Libraria Editrice, Università di Padova
CLF, Cahiers de Linguistique Française
CLHM, Cahiers de Linguistique Hispanique Médiévale
CLin, Cercetări de Lingvistica
CLit, Cadernos de Literatura, Coimbra
CllL, La Clau lemosina
CLO, Cahiers Linguistiques d'Ottawa
ClP, Classical Philology
CLS, Comparative Literature Studies
CLSl, Cahiers de Linguistique Slave
CLTA, Cahiers de Linguistique Théorique et Appliquée
CLTL, Cadernos de Lingüística e Teoria da Literatura
CLUEB, Cooperativa Libraria Universitaria Editrice Bologna
CLus, Convergência Lusíada, Rio de Janeiro
CM, Classica et Mediaevalia
CMA, Cahier Marcel Aymé
CMar, Cuadernos de Marcha
CMCS, Cambrian Medieval Celtic Studies
CMERSA, Center for Medieval and Early Renaissance Studies, State

University of New York at Binghamton. Acta

ČMF (PhP), Časopis pro moderni filologii: Philologica Pragensia

CMHLB, Cahiers du Monde Hispanique et Luso-Brésilien

CMi, Cultura Milano

CML, Classical and Modern Literature

ČMM, Časopis Matice Moravské

CMon, Communication Monographs

CMP, Cahiers Marcel Proust

CMRS, Cahiers du Monde Russe et Soviétique

CN, Cultura Neolatina

CNat, Les Cahiers Naturalistes

CNCDP, Comissão Nacional para a Comemoração dos Descobrimentos Portugueses, Lisbon

CNor, Los Cuadernos del Norte

CNR, Consiglio Nazionale delle Ricerche

CNRS, Centre National de la Recherche Scientifique

CO, Camera Obscura

CoF, Collectanea Franciscana

COJ, Cambridge Opera Journal

COK, Centralny Ośrodek Kultury, Warsaw

CoL, Compás de Letras

ColA, Colóquio Artes

ColGer, Colloquia Germanica

ColH, Colloquium Helveticum

ColL, Colóquio Letras

ComB, Communications of the International Brecht Society

ComGer, Comunicaciones Germánicas

CompL, Computational Linguistics

ConL, Contrastive Linguistics

ConLet, Il Confronto Letterario

ConLit, Contemporary Literature

ConS, Condorcet Studies

CORDAE, Centre Occitan de Recèrca, de Documentacion e d'Animacion Etnografica, Cordes

CP, Castrum Peregrini

CPE, Cahiers Prévost d'Exiles, Grenoble

CPL, Cahiers Paul Léautand

CPr, Cahiers de Praxématique

CPR, Chroniques de Port-Royal

CPUC, Cadernos PUC, São Paulo

CQ, Critical Quarterly

CR, Contemporary Review

CRAC, Cahiers Roucher — André Chénier

CRCL, Canadian Review of Comparative Literature

CREL, Cahiers Roumains d'Études Littéraires

CRev, Centennial Review

CRI, Cuadernos de Ruedo Ibérico

CRIAR, Cahiers du Centre de Recherches Ibériques et Ibéro-Américains de l'Université de Rouen

CRIN, Cahiers de Recherches des Instituts Néerlandais de Langue et Littérature Françaises

CRLN, Comparative Romance Linguistics Newsletter

CRQ, Cahiers Raymond Queneau

CRR, Cincinnati Romance Review

CRRI, Centre de Recherche sur la Renaissance Italienne, Paris

CS, Cornish Studies

CSAM, Centro di Studi sull'Alto Medioevo, Spoleto

ČSAV, Československá akademie věd

CSDI, Centro di Studio per la Dialettologia Italiana

CSem, Caiete de Semiotică

CSFLS, Centro di Studi Filologici e Linguistici Siciliani, Palermo

CSG, Cambridge Studies in German, Cambridge U.P.

CSGLL, Canadian Studies in German Language and Literature, Berne — New York — Frankfurt, Lang

CSH, Cahiers des Sciences Humaines

CSIC, Consejo Superior de Investigaciones Científicas, Madrid

CSJP, Cahiers Saint-John Perse

CSl, Critica Slovia, Florence

CSM, Les Cahiers de Saint-Martin

ČSp, Československý spisovatel

CSS, California Slavic Studies

CSSH, Comparative Studies in Society and History

CST, Cahiers de Sémiotique Textuelle

CSt, Critica Storica

CT, Christianity Today
CTC, Cuadernos de Teatro Clásico
CTE, Cuadernos de Traducción e
  Interpretación
CTe, Cuadernos de Teología
CTex, Cahiers Textuels
CTH, Cahiers Tristan l'Hermite
CTh, Ciencia Tomista
CTL, Current Trends in Linguistics
CTLin, Commissione per i Testi di
  Lingua, Bologna
CUECM, Cooperativa
  Universitaria Editrice Catanese
  Magistero
CUER MA, Centre Universitaire
  d'Études et de Recherches
  Médiévales d'Aix, Université de
  Provence, Aix-en-Provence
CUP, Cambridge University Press
CUUCV, Cultura Universitaria de la
  Universidad Central de
  Venezuela
CV, Città di Vita
CWPL, Catalan Working Papers in
  Linguistics
CWPWL, Cardiff Working Papers in
  Welsh Linguistics

DAEM, Deutsches Archiv für
  Erforschung des Mittelalters
DaF, Deutsch als Fremdsprache
DAG, Dictionnaire onomasiologique
  de l'ancien gascon, Tübingen,
  Niemeyer
DalR, Dalhousie Review
DanU, Dansk Udsyn
DAO, Dictionnaire onomasiologique
  de l'ancien occitan, Tübingen,
  Niemeyer
DaSt, Dante Studies
DB, Дзяржаўная бібліятэка
  БССР
DB, Doitsu Bungaku
DBl, Driemaandelijkse Bladen
DBO, Deutsche Bibliothek des
  Ostens, Berlin, Nicolai
DBR, Les Dialectes Belgo-Romans
DBr, Doitsu Bungakoranko
DCFH, Dicenda. Cuadernos de
  Filología Hispánica
DD, Diskussion Deutsch
DDG, Deutsche Dialektgeographie,
  Marburg, Elwert

DDJ, Deutsches Dante-Jahrbuch
DegSec, Degré Second
DELTA, Revista de Documentação
  de Estudos em Lingüística
  Teórica e Aplicada, Šao Paulo
DESB, Delta Epsilon Sigma
  Bulletin, Dubuque, Iowa
DeutB, Deutsche Bücher
DeutUB, Deutschungarische
  Beiträge
DFC, Durham French Colloquies
DFS, Dalhousie French Studies
DGF, Dokumentation
  germanistischer Forschung,
  Frankfurt, Lang
DgF, Danmarks gamle Folkeviser
DHA, Diálogos Hispánicos de
  Amsterdam, Rodopi
DHR, Duquesne Hispanic Review
DhS, Dix-huitième Siècle
DI, Deutscher Idealismus, Stuttgart,
  Klett-Cotta Verlag
DI, Декоративное искусство
DIAS, Dublin Institute for
  Advanced Studies
DiL, Dictionnairique et
  Lexicographie
DiS, Dickinson Studies
DisA, Dissertation Abstracts
DisSlSHL, Dissertationes Slavicae:
  Sectio Historiae Litterarum
DisSlSL, Dissertationes Slavicae:
  Sectio Linguistica
DK, Duitse Kroniek
DkJb, Deutschkanadisches Jahrbuch
DKV, Deutscher Klassiker Verlag,
  Frankfurt
DL, Детская литература
DLA, Deutsche Literatur von den
  Anfängen bis 1700, Berne —
  Frankfurt — Paris — New York,
  Lang
DLit, Discurso Literario
DLM, Deutsche Literatur des
  Mittelalters (Wissenschaftliche
  Beiträge der Ernst-Moritz-Arndt-
  Universität Greifswald)
DLR, Deutsche Literatur in
  Reprints, Munich, Fink
DLRECL, Diálogo de la Lengua.
  Revista de Estudio y Creación
  Literaria, Cuenca
DM, Dirassat Masrahiyyat

DMRPH, De Montfort Research Papers in the Humanities, De Montfort University, Leicester

DMTS, Davis Medieval Texts and Studies, Leiden, Brill

DN, Дружба народов

DNT, De Nieuwe Taalgids

DOLMA, Documenta Onomastica Litteralia Medii Aevi, Hildesheim, Olms

DOM, Dictionnaire de l'occitan médiéval, Tübingen, Niemeyer, 1996–

DosS, Dostoevsky Studies

DoV, Дошкольное воспитание

DPA, Documents pour servir à l'histoire du département des Pyrénées-Atlantiques, Pau

DPL, De Proprietatibus Litterarum, The Hague, Mouton

DpL, День поэзии, Leningrad

DpM, День поэзии, Moscow

DR, Drama Review

DRev, Downside Review

DRLAV, DRLAV, Revue de Linguistique

DS, Diderot Studies

DSEÜ, Deutsche Sprache in Europa und Übersee, Stuttgart, Steiner

DSL, Det danske Sprog- og Litteraturselskab

DSp, Deutsche Sprache

DSRPD, Documenta et Scripta. Rubrica Paleographica et Diplomatica, Barcelona

DSS, XVIIe Siècle

DSt, Deutsche Studien, Meisenheim, Hain

DSt, Danske Studier

DT, Deutsche Texte, Tübingen, Niemeyer

DteolT, Dansk teologisk Tidsskrift

DtL, Die deutsche Literatur

DTM, Deutsche Texte des Mittelalters, Berlin, Akademie

DTV, Deutscher Taschenbuch Verlag, Munich

DUB, Deutschunterricht, East Berlin

DUJ, Durham University Journal (New Series)

DUS, Der Deutschunterricht, Stuttgart

DUSA, Deutschunterricht in Südafrika

DV, Дальний Восток

DVA, Deutsche Verlags-Anstalt, Stuttgart

DVLG, Deutsche Vierteljahresschrift für Literaturwissenschaft und Geistesgeschichte

E, Verlag Enzyklopädie, Leipzig

EAL, Early American Literature

EALS, Europäische Aufklärung in Literatur und Sprache, Frankfurt, Lang

EAS, Europe-Asia Studies

EB, Estudos Brasileiros

EBal, Etudes Balkaniques

EBM, Era Bouts dera mountanho, Aurignac

EBTch, Études Balkaniques Tchécoslovaques

EC, El Escritor y la Crítica, Colección Persiles, Madrid, Taurus

EC, Études Celtiques

ECan, Études Canadiennes

ECar, Espace Caraïbe

ECent, The Eighteenth Century, Lubbock, Texas

ECentF, Eighteenth-Century Fiction

ECF, Écrits du Canada Français

ECI, Eighteenth-Century Ireland

ECIG, Edizioni Culturali Internazionali Genova

ECla, Les Études Classiques

ECon, España Contemporánea

EconH, Économie et Humanisme

EcR, Echo de Rabastens. Les Veillées Rabastinoises, Rabastens (Tarn)

ECr, Essays in Criticism

ECS, Eighteenth Century Studies

EdCat, Ediciones Cátedra, Madrid

EDESA, Ediciones Españolas S.A.

EDHS, Études sur le XVIIIe Siècle

EDL, Études de Lettres

EDT, Edizioni di Torino

EE, Erasmus in English

EEM, East European Monographs

EEQ, East European Quarterly

EF, Erträge der Forschung, Darmstadt, Wissenschaftliche Buchgesellschaft

EF, Études Françaises

EFAA, Échanges Franco-Allemands sur l'Afrique

EFE, Estudios de Fonética Experimental

EFF, Ergebnisse der Frauenforschung, Stuttgart, Metzler

EFil, Estudios Filológicos, Valdivia, Chile

EFL, Essays in French Literature, Univ. of Western Australia

EFR, Éditeurs Français Réunis

EG, Études Germaniques

EH, Europäische Hochschulschriften, Berne–Frankfurt, Lang

EH, Estudios Humanísticos

EHF, Estudios Humanísticos. Filología

EHN, Estudios de Historia Novohispana

EHQ, European History Quarterly

EHR, English Historical Review

EHS, Estudios de Historia Social

EHT, Exeter Hispanic Texts, Exeter

EIA, Estudos Ibero-Americanos

EIP, Estudos Italiano em Portugal

EL, Esperienze Letterarie

El, Elementa, Würzburg, Königshausen & Neumann –Amsterdam, Rodopi

ELA, Études de Linguistique Appliquée

ELF, Études Littéraires Françaises, Paris, J.-M. Place — Tübingen, Narr

ELH, English Literary History

El'H, Études sur l'Hérault, Pézenas

ELit, Essays in Literature

ELL, Estudos Lingüísticos e Literários, Bahia

ELLC, Estudis de Llengua i Literatura Catalanes

ELLF, Études de Langue et Littérature Françaises, Tokyo

ELM, Études littéraires maghrebines

ELR, English Literary Renaissance

EMarg, Els Marges

EMH, Early Music History

EMus, Early Music

ENC, Els Nostres Clàssics, Barcelona, Barcino

ENSJF, École Nationale Supérieure de Jeunes Filles

EO, Edition Orpheus, Tübingen, Francke

EO, Europa Orientalis

EOc, Estudis Occitans

EP, Études Philosophiques

Ep, Epistemata, Würzburg, Königshausen & Neumann

EPESA, Ediciones y Publicaciones Españolas S.A.

EPoet, Essays in Poetics

ER, Estudis Romànics

ERab, Études Rabelaisiennes

ERB, Études Romanes de Brno

ER(BSRLR), Études Romanes (Bulletin de la Société Roumaine de Linguistique Romane)

ERL, Études Romanes de Lund

ErlF, Erlanger Forschungen

ERLIMA, Équipe de recherche sur la littérature d'imagination du moyen âge, Centre d'Études Supérieures de Civilisation Médiévale/Faculté des Lettres et des Langues, Université de Poitiers.

EROPD, Ежегодник рукописного отдела Пушкинского дома

ERR, European Romantic Review

ES, Erlanger Studien, Erlangen, Palm & Enke

ES, Estudios Segovianos

EsC, L'Esprit Créateur

ESGP, Early Studies in Germanic Philology, Amsterdam, Rodopi

ESI, Edizioni Scientifiche Italiane

ESk, Edition Suhrkamp, Frankfurt, Suhrkamp

ESor, Études sorguaises

EspA, Español Actual

ESt, English Studies

EstE, Estudios Escénicos

EstG, Estudi General

EstH, Estudios Hispánicos

EstL, Estudios de Lingüística, Alicante

EstR, Estudios Románticos

EStud, Essays and Studies

ET, L'Écrit du Temps

EtCan, Études Canadiennes

ETF, Espacio, Tiempo y Forma, Revista de la Facultad de Geografía e Historia, UNED
EtF, Etudes francophones
EtH, Études sur l'Hérault, Pézenas
EthS, Ethnologia Slavica
ETJ, Educational Theatre Journal
ETL, Explicación de Textos Literarios
EtLitt, Études Littéraires, Quebec
EUDEBA, Editorial Universitaria de Buenos Aires
EUNSA, Ediciones Universidad de Navarra, Pamplona
EUS, European University Studies, Berne, Lang
ExP, Excerpta Philologica
EzLit, Език и литература

FAL, Forum Academicum Literaturwissenschaft, Königstein, Hain
FAM, Filologia Antica e Moderna
FAPESP, Fundação de Amparo à Pesquisa do Estado de São Paulo
FAR, French-American Review
FAS, Frankfurter Abhandlungen zur Slavistik, Giessen, Schmitz
FBAN, Фундаментальная бібліятэка Акадэміі навук БССР
FBG, Frankfurter Beiträge zur Germanistik, Heidelberg, Winter
FBS, Franco-British Studies
FC, Filologia e Critica
FCE, Fondo de Cultura Económica, Mexico
FCG — CCP, Fondation Calouste Gulbenkian — Centre Culturel Portugais, Paris
FCS, Fifteenth Century Studies
FD, Fonetică şi Dialectologie
FDL, Facetten deutscher Literatur, Berne, Haupt
FEI, Faites entrer l'infini. Journal de la Société des Amis de Louis Aragon et Elsa Triolet
FEK, Forschungen zur europäischen Kultur, Berne, Lang
FemSt, Feministische Studien
FF, Forma y Función

FF, Forum für Fachsprachenforschung, Tübingen, Narr
FFM, French Forum Monographs, Lexington, Kentucky
FGÄDL, Forschungen zur Geschichte der älteren deutschen Literatur, Munich, Fink
FH, Fundamenta Historica, Stuttgart-Bad Cannstatt, Frommann-Holzboog
FH, Frankfurter Hefte
FHL, Forum Homosexualität und Literatur
FHS, French Historical Studies
FIDS, Forschungsberichte des Instituts für Deutsche Sprache, Tübingen, Narr
FilM, Filologia Mediolatina
FilMod, Filologia Moderna, Udine –Pisa
FilN, Филологические науки
FilR, Filologia Romanza
FilS, Filologické studie
FilZ, Filologija, Zagreb
FiM, Filologia Moderna, Facultad de Filosofía y Letras, Madrid
FinS, Fin de Siglo
FIRL, Forum at Iowa on Russian Literature
FL, La France Latine
FLa, Faits de Langues
FLG, Freiburger literaturpsychologische Gespräche
FLin, Folia Linguistica
FLinHist, Folia Linguistica Historica
FLK, Forschungen zur Literatur- und Kulturgeschichte. Beiträge zur Sprach- und Literaturwissenschaft, Berne, Lang
FLP, Filologia e linguística portuguesa
FLS, French Literature Series
FLV, Fontes Linguae Vasconum
FM, Le Français Moderne
FMADIUR, FM: Annali del Dipartimento di Italianistica, Università di Roma 'La Sapienza'
FMDA, Forschungen und Materialen zur deutschen Aufklärung, Stuttgart — Bad Cannstatt, Frommann-Holzboog

FMLS, Forum for Modern Language Studies
FmSt, Frühmittelalterliche Studien
FMT, Forum Modernes Theater
FN, Frühe Neuzeit, Tübingen, Niemeyer
FNDIR, Fédération nationale des déportés et internés résistants
FNS, Frühneuzeit-Studien, Frankfurt, Lang
FoH, Foro Hispánico, Amsterdam
FNT, Foilseacháin Náisiúnta Tta
FoI, Forum Italicum
FoS, Le Forme e la Storia
FP, Folia Phonetica
FPub, First Publications
FR, French Review
FrA, Le Français Aujourd'hui
FranS, Franciscan Studies
FrCS, French Cultural Studies
FrF, French Forum
FrH, Französisch Heute
FrP Le Français Préclassique
FS, Forum Slavicum, Munich, Fink
FS, French Studies
FSB, French Studies Bulletin
FSlav, Folia Slavica
FSSA, French Studies in Southern Africa
FT, Fischer Taschenbuch, Frankfurt, Fischer
FT, Finsk Tidskrift
FTCG, 'La Talanquere': Folklore, Tradition, Culture Gasconne, Nogano
FUE, Fundación Universitaria Española
FV, Fortuna Vitrea, Tübingen, Niemeyer
FZPT, Freiburger Zeitschrift für Philosophie und Theologie

GA, Germanistische Arbeitshefte, Tübingen, Niemeyer
GAB, Göppinger Akademische Beiträge, Lauterburg, Kümmerle
GAG, Göppinger Arbeiten zur Germanistik, Lauterburg, Kümmerle
GAKS, Gesammelte Aufsätze zur Kulturgeschichte Spaniens
GalR, Galician Review, Birmingham

GANDLL, Giessener Arbeiten zur neueren deutschen Literatur und Literaturwissenschaft, Berne, Lang
GAS, German-Australian Studies, Berne, Lang
GASK, Germanistische Arbeiten zu Sprache und Kulturgeschichte, Frankfurt, Lang
GB, Germanistische Bibliothek, Heidelberg, Winter
GBA, Gazette des Beaux-Arts
GBE, Germanistik in der Blauen Eule
GC, Generalitat de Catalunya
GCFI, Giornale Critico della Filosofia Italiana
GEMP, Groupement d'Ethnomusicologie en Midi-Pyrénées, La Talvèra
GerAb, Germanistische Abhandlungen, Stuttgart, Metzler
GerLux, Germanistik Luxembourg
GermL, Germanistische Linguistik
GeW, Germanica Wratislaviensia
GF, Giornale di Fisica
GFFNS, Godišnjak Filozofskog fakulteta u Novom Sadu
GG, Geschichte und Gesellschaft
GGF, Göteborger Germanistische Forschungen, University of Gothenburg
GGVD, Grundlagen und Gedanken zum Verständnis des Dramas, Frankfurt, Diesterweg
GGF, Greifswalder Germanistische Forschungen
GGVEL, Grundlagen und Gedanken zum Verständnis erzählender Literatur, Frankfurt, Diesterweg
GIDILOc, Grop d'Iniciativa per un Diccionari Informatizat de la Lenga Occitana, Montpellier
GIF, Giornale Italiano di Filologia
GIGFL, Glasgow Introductory Guides to French Literature
GIGGL, Glasgow Introductory Guides to German Literature
GJ, Gutenberg-Jahrbuch
GJb, Goethe Jahrbuch
GJLL, The Georgetown Journal of Language and Linguistics

GK, Goldmann Klassiker, Munich, Goldmann

GL, Germanistische Lehrbuchsammlung, Berne, Lang

GL, General Linguistics

GLC, German Life and Civilisation, Berne, Lang

GLL, German Life and Letters

GLML, The Garland Library of Medieval Literature, New York –London, Garland

GLR, García Lorca Review

GLS, Grazer Linguistische Studien

Glyph, Glyph: Johns Hopkins Textual Studies, Baltimore

GM, Germanistische Mitteilungen

GML, Gothenburg Monographs in Linguistics

GMon, German Monitor

GN, Germanic Notes and Reviews

GPB, Гос. публичная библиотека им. М. Е. Салтыкова-Щедрина

GPI, Государственный педагогический институт

GPSR, Glossaire des Patois de la Suisse Romande

GQ, German Quarterly

GR, Germanic Review

GREC, Groupe de Recherches et d'Études du Clermontais, Clermont-l'Hérault

GREHAM, Groupe de REcherche d'Histoire de l'Anthroponymie Médiévale, Tours, Université François-Rabelais

GRELCA, Groupe de Recherche sur les Littératures de la Caraïbe, Université Laval

GRLH, Garland Reference Library of the Humanities, New York — London, Garland

GRLM, Grundriss der romanischen Literaturen des Mittelalters

GRM, Germanisch-Romanische Monatsschrift

GrSt, Grundtvig Studier

GS, Lo Gai Saber, Toulouse

GSA, Germanic Studies in America, Berne–Frankfurt, Lang

GSC, German Studies in Canada, Frankfurt, Lang

GSI, German Studies in India

GSl, Germano-Slavica, Ontario

GSLI, Giornale Storico della Letteratura Italiana

GSR, German Studies Review

GSSL, Göttinger Schriften zur Sprach– und Literaturwissenschaft, Göttingen, Herodot

GTN, Gdańskie Towarzystwo Naukowe

GTS, Germanistische Texte und Studien, Hildesheim, Olms

GV, Generalitat Valenciana

GY, Goethe Yearbook

H, Hochschulschriften, Cologne, Pahl-Rugenstein

HAHR, Hispanic American Historical Review

HB, Horváth Blätter

HBA, Historiografía y Bibliografía Americanistas, Seville

HBG, Hamburger Beiträge zur Germanistik, Frankfurt, Lang

HDG, Huis aan de Drie Grachten, Amsterdam

HEI, History of European Ideas

HEL, Histoire, Epistemologie, Language

Her(A), Hermes, Århus

HES, Histoire, Économie et Société

HeyJ, Heythrop Journal

HF, Heidelberger Forschungen, Heidelberg, Winter

HHS, History of the Human Sciences

HI, Historica Ibérica

HIAR, Hamburger Ibero-Amerikanische Reihe

HICL, Histoire des Idées et Critique Littéraire, Geneva, Droz

HIGL, Holland Institute for Generative Linguistics, Leiden

HisJ, Hispanic Journal, Indiana–Pennsylvania

HisL, Hispanic Linguistics

HistL, Historiographia Linguistica

HistS, History of Science

His(US), Hispania, Los Angeles

HJ, Historical Journal

HJb, Heidelberger Jahrbücher

HJBS, Hispanic Journal of Behavioural Sciences

HKADL, Historisch-kritische Arbeiten zur deutschen Literatur, Frankfurt, Lang

HKZMTLG, Handelingen van de Koninklijke Zuidnederlandse Maatschappij voor Taalen, Letterkunde en Geschiedenis

HL, Hochschulschriften Literaturwissenschaft, Königstein, Hain

HL, Humanistica Lovaniensia

HLB, Harvard Library Bulletin

HLQ, Huntington Library Quarterly

HLS, Historiska och litteraturhistoriska studier

HM, Hommes et Migrations

HMJb, Heinrich Mann Jahrbuch

HP, History of Psychiatry

HPh, Historical Philology

HPos, Hispanica Posnaniensia

HPS, Hamburger Philologische Studien, Hamburg, Buske

HPSl, Heidelberger Publikationen zur Slavistik, Frankfurt, Lang

HPT, History of Political Thought

HR, Hispanic Review

HRel, History of Religions

HRev, Hrvatska revija

HRSHM, Heresis, revue semestrielle d'hérésiologie médiévale

HS, Helfant Studien, Stuttgart, Helfant

HS, Hispania Sacra

HSLA, Hebrew University Studies in Literature and the Arts

HSlav, Hungaro-Slavica

HSMS, Hispanic Seminary of Medieval Studies, Madison

HSp, Historische Sprachforschung (Historical Linguistics)

HSSL, Harvard Studies in Slavic Linguistics

HSt, Hispanische Studien

HSWSL, Hallesche Studien zur Wirkung von Sprache und Literatur

HT, Helfant Texte, Stuttgart, Helfant

HT, History Today

HTh, History and Theory

HTR, Harvard Theological Review

HUS, Harvard Ukrainian Studies

HY, Herder Yearbook

HZ, Historische Zeitschrift

IÅ, Ibsen-Årbok, Oslo

IAP, Ibero-Americana Pragensia

IAr, Iberoamerikanisches Archiv

IARB, Inter-American Review of Bibliography

IASL, Internationales Archiv für Sozialgeschichte der deutschen Literatur

IASLS, Internationales Archiv für Sozialgeschichte der deutschen Literatur: Sonderheft

IB, Insel-Bücherei, Frankfurt, Insel

IBKG, Innsbrucker Beiträge zur Kulturwissenschaft. Germanistische Reihe

IBL, Instytut Badań Literackich PAN, Warsaw

IBLA, Institut des Belles Lettres Arabes

IBLe, Insel-Bücherei, Leipzig, Insel

IBS, Innsbrücker Beiträge zur Sprachwissenschaft

IC, Index on Censorship

ICALP, Instituto de Cultura e Língua Portuguesa, Lisbon

ICALPR, Instituto de Cultura e Língua Portuguesa. Revista

ICC, Instituto Caro y Cuervo, Bogotà

ICMA, Instituto de Cooperación con el Mundo Árabe

ID, Italia Dialettale

IDF, Informationen Deutsch als Fremdsprache

IDL, Indices zur deutschen Literatur, Tübingen, Niemeyer

IdLit, Ideologies and Literature

IEC, Institut d'Estudis Catalans

IEI, Istituto dell'Enciclopedia Italiana

IEO, Institut d'Estudis Occitans

IES, Institut d'Études Slaves, Paris

IF, Impulse der Forschung, Darmstadt, Wissenschaftliche Buchgesellschaft

IF, Indogermanische Forschungen

IFC, Institución Fernando el Católico

IFEE, Investigación Franco-Española. Estudios

IFiS, Instytut Filozofii i Socjologii PAN, Warsaw

IFOTT, Institut voor Functioneel Onderzoek naar Taal en Taalgebruik, Amsterdam

IFR, International Fiction Review

IG, Informations Grammaticales

IHC, Italian History and Culture

IHE, Índice Histórico Español

IHS, Irish Historical Studies

II, Information und Interpretation, Frankfurt, Lang

IIa, Институт языкознания

III, Институт истории искусств

IIFV, Institut Interuniversitari de Filologia Valenciana, Valencia

IJ, Italian Journal

IJAL, International Journal of American Linguistics

IJBAG, Internationales Jahrbuch der Bettina-von-Arnim Gesellschaft

IJCS, International Journal of Canadian Studies

IJFS, International Journal of Francophone Studies, Leeds

IJHL, Indiana Journal of Hispanic Literatures

IJL, International Journal of Lexicography

IJP, International Journal of Psycholinguistics

IJSL, International Journal for the Sociology of Language

IJSLP, International Journal of Slavic Linguistics and Poetics

IK, Искусство кино

IKU, Institut za književnost i umetnost, Belgrade

IL, L'Information Littéraire

ILASLR, Istituto Lombardo. Accademia di Scienze e Lettere. Rendiconti

ILen, Искусство Ленинграда

ILing, Incontri Linguistici

ILTEC, Instituto de Linguistica Teórica e Computacional, Lisbon

IMN, Irisleabhar Mhá Nuad

IMR, International Migration Review

IMU, Italia Medioevale e Umanistica

INCM, Imprensa Nacional, Casa da Moeda, Lisbon

InfD, Informationen und Didaktik

INLF, Institut National de la Langue Française

INIC, Instituto Nacional de Investigação Científica

InL, Иностранная литература

INLE, Instituto Nacional del Libro Español

InstEB, Inst. de Estudos Brasileiros

InstNL, Inst. Nacional do Livro, Brasilia

IO, Italiano e Oltre

IPL, Istituto di Propaganda Libraria

IPZS, Istituto Poligrafico e Zecca dello Stato, Rome

IR, L'Immagine Riflessa

IRAL, International Review of Applied Linguistics

IRIa, Институт русского языка Российской Академии Наук

IrR, The Irish Review

IRSH, International Review of Social History

IRSL, International Review of Slavic Linguistics

ISC, Institut de Sociolingüística Catalana

ISI, Institute for Scientific Information, U.S.A.

ISIEMC, Istituto Storico Italiano per l'Età Moderna e Contemporanea, Rome

ISLIa, Известия Академии наук СССР. Серия литературы и языка

ISOAN, Известия сибирского отделения АН СССР, Novosibirsk

ISP, International Studies in Philosophy

ISPS, International Studies in the Philosophy of Science

ISS, Irish Slavonic Studies

IsS, Islamic Studies, Islamabad

ISSA, Studi d'Italianistica nell'Africa Australe: Italian Studies in Southern Africa

ISt, Italian Studies

ISV, Informazioni e Studi Vivaldiani

IT, Insel Taschenbuch, Frankfurt, Insel

ItC, Italian Culture

ITL, ITL. Review of Applied Linguistics, Instituut voor Toegepaste Linguistiek, Leuven

ItQ, Italian Quarterly

ItStudien, Italienische Studien

IUJF, Internationales Uwe-Johnson-Forum

IULA, Institut Universitari de Lingüística Aplicada, Universitat Pompeu Fabra, Barcelona

IUP, Irish University Press

IUR, Irish University Review

IV, Istituto Veneto di Scienze, Lettere ed Arti

IVAS, Indices Verborum zum altdeutschen Schrifttum, Amsterdam, Rodopi

IVN, Internationale Vereniging voor Nederlandistiek

JAAC, Journal of Aesthetics and Art Criticism

JACIS, Journal of the Association for Contemporary Iberian Studies

JAE, Journal of Aesthetic Education

JAIS, Journal of Anglo-Italian Studies, Malta

JAMS, Journal of the American Musicological Society

JAOS, Journal of the American Oriental Society

JanL., Janua Linguarum, The Hague, Mouton

JAPLA, Journal of the Atlantic Provinces Linguistic Association

JARA, Journal of the American Romanian Academy of Arts and Sciences

JAS, The Journal of Algerian Studies

JASI, Jahrbuch des Adalbert-Stifter-Instituts

JATI, Association of Teachers of Italian Journal

JazA, Jazykovědné aktuality

JazŠ, Jazykovedné štúdie

JAZU, Jugoslavenska akademija znanosti i umjetnosti

JBSP, Journal of the British Society for Phenomenology

JČ, Jazykovedný časopis, Bratislava

JCanS, Journal of Canadian Studies

JCHAS, Journal of the Cork Historical and Archaeological Society

JCL, Journal of Child Language

JCLin, Journal of Celtic Linguistics

JCS, Journal of Celtic Studies

JDASD, Deutsche Akademie für Sprache und Dichtung: Jahrbuch

JDF, Jahrbuch Deutsch als Fremdsprache

JDSG, Jahrbuch der Deutschen Schiller-Gesellschaft

JEA, Lou Journalet de l'Escandihado Aubagnenco

JEGP, Journal of English and Germanic Philology

JEH, Journal of Ecclesiastical History

JEL, Journal of English Linguistics

JES, Journal of European Studies

JF, Južnoslovenski filolog

JFDH, Jahrbuch des Freien Deutschen Hochstifts

JFinL, Jahrbuch für finnisch-deutsche Literaturbeziehungen

JFL, Jahrbuch für fränkische Landesforschung

JFLS, Journal of French Language Studies

JFR, Journal of Folklore Research

JG, Jahrbuch für Geschichte, Berlin, Akademie

JGO, Jahrbücher für die Geschichte Osteuropas

JHA, Journal for the History of Astronomy

JHI, Journal of the History of Ideas

JHispP, Journal of Hispanic Philology

JHP, Journal of the History of Philosophy

JHR, Journal of Hispanic Research

JHS, Journal of the History of Sexuality

JIAS, Journal of Inter-American Studies

JIES, Journal of Indo-European Studies

JIG, Jahrbuch für Internationale Germanistik

JIL, Journal of Italian Linguistics

JILAS, Journal of Iberian and Latin American Studies (formerly *Tesserae*)

JILS, Journal of Interdisciplinary Literary Studies

JIPA, Journal of the International Phonetic Association

JIRS, Journal of the Institute of Romance Studies

JJQ, James Joyce Quarterly

JJS, Journal of Jewish Studies

JL, Journal of Linguistics

JLACS, Journal of Latin American Cultural Studies

JLAL, Journal of Latin American Lore

JLAS, Journal of Latin American Studies

JLH, Journal of Library History

JLS, Journal of Literary Semantics

JLSP, Journal of Language and Social Psychology

JMemL, Journal of Memory and Language

JMEMS, Journal of Medieval and Early Modern Studies

JMH, Journal of Medieval History

JML, Journal of Modern Literature

JMLat, Journal of Medieval Latin

JMMD, Journal of Multilingual and Multicultural Development

JMMLA, Journal of the Midwest Modern Language Association

JModH, Journal of Modern History

JMP, Journal of Medicine and Philosophy

JMRS, Journal of Medieval and Renaissance Studies

JMS, Journal of Maghrebi Studies

JNT, Journal of Narrative Technique

JONVL, Een Jaarboek: Overzicht van de Nederlandse en Vlaamse Literatuur

JOWG, Jahrbuch der Oswald von Wolkenstein Gesellschaft

JP, Journal of Pragmatics

JPC, Journal of Popular Culture

JPCL, Journal of Pidgin and Creole Languages

JPh, Journal of Phonetics

JPol, Język Polski

JPR, Journal of Psycholinguistic Research

JQ, Jacques e i suoi Quaderni

JRA, Journal of Religion in Africa

JRG, Jahrbücher der Reineke-Gesellschaft

JRH, Journal of Religious History

JRIC, Journal of the Royal Institution of Cornwall

JŘJR, Jazyk a řeč jihočeského regionu. České Budéjovice, Pedagogická fakulta Jihočeské univerzity

JRMA, Journal of the Royal Musical Association

JRMMRA, Journal of the Rocky Mountain Medieval and Renaissance Association

JRS, Journal of Romance Studies

JRUL, Journal of the Rutgers University Libraries

JS, Journal des Savants

JSEES, Japanese Slavic and East European Studies

JSem, Journal of Semantics

JSFWUB, Jahrbuch der Schlesischen Friedrich-Wilhelms-Universität zu Breslau

JSH, Jihočeský sborník historický

JSHR, Journal of Speech and Hearing Research

JSL, Journal of Slavic Linguistics

JSS, Journal of Spanish Studies: Twentieth Century

JTS, Journal of Theological Studies

JU, Judentum und Umwelt, Berne, Lang.

JUS, Journal of Ukrainian Studies

JV, Jahrbuch für Volkskunde

JVF, Jahrbuch für Volksliedforschung

JVLVB, Journal of Verbal Learning and Verbal Behavior

JWBS, Journal of the Welsh Bibliographical Society

JWCI, Journal of the Warburg and Courtauld Institutes

JWGV, Jahrbuch des Wiener Goethe-Vereins, Neue Folge

JWH, Journal of World History

JWIL, Journal of West Indian Literature

JZ, Jazykovedný zborník

KANTL, Koninklijke Akademie voor Nederlandse Taal- en Letterkunde

KASL, Kasseler Arbeiten zur
Sprache und Literatur, Frankfurt,
Lang
KAW, Krajowa Agencja
Wydawnicza
KAWLSK, Koninklijke Academie
voor Wetenschappen, Letteren en
Schone Kunsten van België,
Brussels
KB, Književni barok
KBGL, Kopenhagener Beiträge zur
germanistischen Linguistik
Kbl, Korrespondenzblatt des
Vereins für niederdeutsche
Sprachforschung
KDPM, Kleine deutsche
Prosadenkmäler des Mittelalters,
Munich, Fink
KGOS, Kultur- und
geistesgeschichtliche
Ostmitteleuropa-Studien,
Marburg, Elwert
KGS, Kölner germanistische
Studien, Cologne, Böhlau
KGS, Kairoer germanistische
Studien
KH, Komparatistische Hefte
KhL, Художественная
литература
KI, Književna istorija
KiW, Książka i Wiedza
KJ, Književnost i jezik
KK, Kirke og Kultur
KlJb, Kleist-Jahrbuch
KLWL, Krieg und Literatur: War
and Literature
Klage, Klage: Kölner linguistische
Arbeiten. Germanistik, Hürth-
Efferen, Gabel
KN, Kwartalnik Neofilologiczny
KnK, Kniževna kritika
KO, Университетско
издателство
'Климент Охридски'
KO, Книжное обозрение
КР, Книжная палата
KRA, Kölner Romanistische
Arbeiten, Geneva, Droz
KS, Kúltura slova
KSDL, Kieler Studien zur
deutschen Literaturgeschichte,
Neumünster, Wachholtz

KSL, Kölner Studien zur
Literaturwissenschaft, Frankfurt,
Lang
KSt, Kant Studien
KTA, Kröners Taschenausgabe,
Stuttgart, Kröner
KTRM, Klassische Texte des
romanischen Mittelalters,
Munich, Fink
KU, Konstanzer Universitäts-
reden
KUL, Katolicki Uniwersytet
Lubelski, Lublin
KuSDL, Kulturwissenschaftliche
Studien zur deutschen Literatur,
Opladen, Westdeutscher Verlag
KZG, Koreanische Zeitschrift für
Germanistik
KZMTLG, Koninklijke
Zuidnederlandse Maatschappij
voor Taal- en Letterkunde en
Geschiedenis, Brussels
KZMTLGH, Koninklijke
Zuidnederlandse Maatschaapij
voor Taal- en Letterkunde en
Geschiedenis. Handelingen

LA, Linguistische Arbeiten,
Tübingen, Niemeyer
LA, Linguistic Analysis
LaA, Language Acquisition
LAbs, Linguistics Abstracts
LaF, Langue Française
LAILJ, Latin American Indian
Literatures Journal
LaLi, Langues et Linguistique
LALIES, LALIES. Actes des sessions
de linguistique et de littérature.
Institut d'Etudes linguistiques et
phonétiques. Sessions de
linguistique. Ecole Normale
Supérieure Paris, Sorbonne
nouvelle
LALR, Latin-American Literary
Review
LaM, Les Langues Modernes
LangH, Le Langage et l'Homme
LArb, Linguistische Arbeitsberichte
LARR, Latin-American Research
Review
LaS, Langage et Société
LATR, Latin-American Theatre
Review

LatT, Latin Teaching, Shrewsbury
LB, Leuvense Bijdragen
LBer, Linguistische Berichte
LBIYB, Leo Baeck Institute Year Book
LBR, Luso-Brazilian Review
LC, Letture Classensi
LCC, Léachtaí Cholm Cille
LCh, Literatura Chilena
LCP, Language and Cognitive Processes
LCrit, Lavoro Critico
LCUTA, Library Chronicle of the University of Texas at Austin
LD, Libri e Documenti
LdA, Linha d'Agua
LDan, Lectura Dantis
LDanN, Lectura Dantis Newberryana
LDGM, Ligam-DiGaM. Quadèrn de lingüistica e lexicografía gasconas, Fontenay aux Roses
LE, Language and Education
LEA, Lingüística Española Actual
LebS, Lebende Sprachen
LEMIR, Literatura Española Medieval y del Renacimiento, Valencia U.P.; http:// www.uv.es/ ~lemir/Revista.html
Leng(M), Lengas, Montpellier
Leng(T), Lengas, Toulouse
LenP, Ленинградская панорама
LetA, Letterature d'America
LetD, Letras de Deusto
LETHB, Laboratoires d'Études Théâtrales de l'Université de Haute-Bretagne. Études et Documents, Rennes
LetL, Letras e Letras, Departmento de Línguas Estrangeiras Modernas, Universidade Federal de Uberlândia, Brazil
LetMS, Letopis Matice srpske, Novi Sad
LetP, Il Lettore di Provincia
LetS, Letras Soltas
LevT, Levende Talen
Lex(L), Lexique, Lille
LF, Letras Femeninas
LFil, Listy filologické
LFQ, Literature and Film Quarterly
LGF, Lunder Germanistische Forschungen, Stockholm, Almqvist & Wiksell

LGGL, Literatur in der Geschichte, Geschichte in der Literatur, Cologne–Vienna, Böhlau
LGL, Langs Germanistische Lehrbuchsammlung, Berne, Lang
LGP, Leicester German Poets, Leicester U.P.
LGW, Literaturwissenschaft — Gesellschaftswissenschaft, Stuttgart, Klett
LH, Lingüística Hispánica
LHum, Litteraria Humanitas, Brno
LI, Linguistic Inquiry
LIÅA, Litteraturvetenskapliga institutionen vid Åbo Akademi, Åbo Akademi U.P.
LiB, Literatur in Bayern
LIC, Letteratura Italiana Contemporanea
LiCC, Lien des chercheurs cévenols
LIE, Lessico Intellettuale Europeo, Rome, Ateneo
LiL, Limbă şi Literatură
LiLi, Zeitschrift für Literaturwissenschaft und Linguistik
LingAk, Linguistik Aktuell, Amsterdam, Benjamins
LingBal, Галканско езикознание – Linguistique Balkanique
LingCon, Lingua e Contesto
LingFil, Linguistica e Filologia, Dipartimento di Linguistica e Letterature Comparate, Bergamo
LingLett, Linguistica e Letteratura
LíngLit, Língua e Literatura, São Paulo
LinLit, Lingüística y Literatura
LINQ, Linq [Literature in North Queensland]
LInv, Linguisticae Investigationes
LiR, Limba Română
LIT, Literature Interpretation Theory
LIt, Lettera dall'Italia
LitAP, Literární archív Památníku národního písemnictví
LItal, Lettere Italiane
LitB, Literatura, Budapest
LitC, Littératures Classiques
LitG, Литературная газета, Moscow
LitH, Literature and History

LItL, Letteratura Italiana Laterza, Bari, Laterza

LitL, Literatur für Leser

LitLing, Literatura y Lingüística

LitM, Literární měsíčník

LitMis, Литературна мисъл

LitP, Literature and Psychology

LitR, The Literary Review

LittB, Litteraria, Bratislava

LittK, Litterae, Lauterburg, Kümmerle

LittS, Litteratur og Samfund

LittW, Litteraria, Wrocław

LiU, Література Україна

LJb, Literaturwissenschaftliches Jahrbuch der Görres–Gesellschaft

LK, Literatur-Kommentare, Munich, Hanser

LK, Literatur und Kritik

LKol, Loccumer Kolloquium

LL, Langues et Littératures, Rabat

LlA, Lletres Asturianes

LLC, Literary and Linguistic Computing

LlC, Llên Cymru

LlLi, Llengua i Literatura

LLS, Lenguas, Literaturas, Sociedades. Cuadernos Hispánicos

LLSEE, Linguistic and Literary Studies in Eastern Europe, Amsterdam, Benjamins

LM, Le Lingue del Mondo

LN, Lingua Nostra

LNB, Leipziger namenkundliche Beiträge

LNL, Les Langues Néo-Latines

LNouv, Les Lettres Nouvelles

LoP, Loccumer Protokolle

LOS, Literary Onomastic Studies

LP, Le Livre de Poche, Librairie Générale Française

LP, Lingua Posnaniensis

LPen, Letras Peninsulares

LPh, Linguistics and Philosophy

LPLP, Language Problems and Language Planning

LPO, Lenga e Païs d'Oc, Montpellier

LPr, Linguistica Pragensia

LQ, Language Quarterly, University of S. Florida

LR, Linguistische Reihe, Munich, Hueber

LR, Les Lettres Romanes

LRev, Linguistic Review

LRI, Libri e Riviste d'Italia

LS, Literatur als Sprache, Münster, Aschendorff

LS, Lingua e Stile

LSa, Lusitania Sacra

LSc, Language Sciences

LSil, Linguistica Silesiana

LSNS, Lundastudier i Nordisk Språkvetenskap

LSo, Language in Society

LSp, Language and Speech

LSPS, Lou Sourgentin/La Petite Source. Revue culturelle bilingue nissart-français, Nice

LSty, Language and Style

LSW, Ludowa Spółdzielnia Wydawnicza

LTG, Literaturwissenschaft, Theorie und Geschichte, Frankfurt, Lang

ŁTN, Łódzkie Towarzystwo Naukowe

LTP, Laval Théologique et Philosophique

LU, Literarhistorische Untersuchungen, Berne, Lang

LVC, Language Variation and Change

LW, Literatur und Wirklichkeit, Bonn, Bouvier

LWU, Literatur in Wissenschaft und Unterricht

LY, Lessing Yearbook

MA, Moyen Âge

MAASC, Mémoires de l'Académie des Arts et des Sciences de Carcassonne

MACL, Memórias da Academia de Ciências de Lisboa, Classe de Letras

MAe, Medium Aevum

MAKDDR, Mitteilungen der Akademie der Künste der DDR

MAL, Modern Austrian Literature

MaL, Le Maghreb Littéraire – Revue Canadienne des Littératures Maghrébines, Toronto

MaM, Marbacher Magazin

MAPS, Medium Aevum.
Philologische Studien, Munich,
Fink
MAST, Memorie dell'Accademia
delle Scienze di Torino
MatSl, Matica Slovenská
MBA, Mitteilungen aus dem
Brenner-Archiv
MBAV, Miscellanea Bibliothecae
Apostolicae Vaticanae
MBMRF, Münchener Beiträge zur
Mediävistik und Renaissance-
Forschung, Bachenhausen, Arbeo
MBRP, Münstersche Beiträge zur
romanischen Philologie, Münster,
Kleinheinrich
MBSL, Mannheimer Beiträge zur
Sprach- und
Literaturwissenschaft, Tübingen,
Narr
MC, Misure Critiche
MCV, Mélanges de la Casa de
Velázquez
MD, Musica Disciplina
MDan, Meddelser fra
Dansklærerforeningen.
MDG, Mitteilungen des deutschen
Germanistenverbandes
MDL, Mittlere Deutsche Literatur
in Neu- und Nachdrucken,
Berne, Lang
MDr, Momentum Dramaticum
MDU, Monatshefte für deutschen
Unterricht, deutsche Sprache und
Literatur
MEC, Ministerio de Educação e
Cultura, Rio de Janeiro
MedC, La Méditerranée et ses
Cultures
MedH, Medioevo e Umanesimo
MedLR, Mediterranean Language
Review
MedRom, Medioevo Romanzo
MedS, Medieval Studies
MEFR, Mélanges de l'École
Française de Rome, Moyen Age
MerP, Mercurio Peruano
MF, Mercure de France
MFDT, Mainzer Forschungen zu
Drama und Theater, Tübingen,
Francke
MFS, Modern Fiction Studies
MG, Молодая гвардия
MG, Молодая гвардия

MGB, Münchner Germanistische
Beiträge, Munich, Fink
MGG, Mystik in Geschichte und
Gegenwart, Stuttgart-Bad
Cannstatt, Frommann-Holzboog
MGS, Marburger Germanistische
Studien, Frankfurt, Lang
MGS, Michigan Germanic Studies
MGSL, Minas Gerais, Suplemento
Literário
MH, Medievalia et Humanistica
MHLS, Mid-Hudson Language
Studies
MHRA, Modern Humanities
Research Association
MichRS, Michigan Romance Studies
MILUS, Meddelanden från
Institutionen i Lingvistik vid
Universitetet i Stockholm
MINS, Meddelanden från
institutionen för nordiska språk
vid Stockholms universiteit,
Stockholm U.P.
MiscBarc, Miscellanea
Barcinonensia
MiscEB, Miscel·lània d'Estudis
Bagencs
MiscP, Miscel·lània Penedesenca
MJ, Mittellateinisches Jahrbuch
MK, Maske und Kothurn
MKH, Deutsche
Forschungsgemeinschaft:
Mitteilung der Kommission für
Humanismusforschung,
Weinheim, Acta Humaniora
MKNAWL, Mededelingen der
Koninklijke Nederlandse
Akademie van Wetenschappen,
Afd. Letterkunde, Amsterdam
ML, Mediaevalia Lovaniensia,
Leuven U.P.
ML, Modern Languages
MLAIntBibl, Modern Language
Association International
Bibliography
MLIÅA, Meddelanden utgivna av
Litteraturvetenskapliga
institutionen vid Åbo Akademi,
Åbo Akademi U.P.
MLIGU, Meddelanden utgivna av
Litteraturvetenskapliga
institutionen vid Göteborgs
universitet, Gothenburg U.P.
MLit, Мастацкая літаратура

MLit, Miesięcznik Literacki

MLIUU, Meddelanden utgivna av Litteraturvetenskapliga institutionen vid Uppsala universitet, Gothenburg U.P.

MLJ, Modern Language Journal

MLN, Modern Language Notes

MLQ, Modern Language Quarterly

MLR, Modern Language Review

MLS, Modern Language Studies

MM, Maal og Minne

MMS, Münstersche Mittelalter-Schriften, Munich, Fink

MN, Man and Nature. L'Homme et la Nature

MNGT, Manchester New German Texts, Manchester U.P.

ModD, Modern Drama

ModS, Modern Schoolman

MoL, Modellanalysen: Literatur, Paderborn, Schöningh–Munich, Fink

MON, Ministerstwo Obrony Narodowej, Warsaw

MosR, Московский рабочий

MoyFr, Le Moyen Français

MP, Modern Philology

MQ, Mississippi Quarterly

MQR, Michigan Quarterly Review

MR, Die Mainzer Reihe, Mainz, Hase & Koehler

MR, Medioevo e Rinascimento

MRev, Maghreb Review

MRo, Marche Romane

MRS, Medieval and Renaissance Studies

MRTS, Medieval and Renaissance Texts and Studies, Tempe, Arizona, Arizona State University

MS, Marbacher Schriften, Stuttgart, Cotta

MS, Moderna Språk

MSC, Medjunarodni slavistički centar, Belgrade

MSG, Marburger Studien zur Germanistik, Marburg, Hitzeroth

MSISS, Materiali della Società Italiana di Studi sul Secolo XVIII

MSL, Marburger Studien zur Literatur, Marburg, Hitzeroth

MSLKD, Münchener Studien zur literarischen Kultur in Deutschland, Frankfurt, Lang

MSMS, Middeleeuse Studies — Medieval Studies, Johannesburg

MSNH, Mémoires de la Société Néophilologique de Helsinki

MSp, Moderne Sprachen (Zeitschrift des Verbandes der österreichischen Neuphilologen)

MSSp, Münchener Studien zur Sprachwissenschaft, Munich

MTCGT, Methuen's Twentieth-Century German Texts, London, Methuen

MTG, Mitteilungen zur Theatergeschichte der Goethezeit, Bonn, Bouvier

MTNF, Monographien und Texte zur Nietzsche-Forschung, Berlin — New York, de Gruyter

MTU, Münchener Texte und Untersuchungen zur deutschen Literatur des Mittelalters, Tübingen, Niemeyer

MTUB, Mitteilungen der T. U. Braunschweig

MUP, Manchester University Press

MusL, Music and Letters

MusP, Museum Patavinum

MyQ, Mystics Quarterly

NA, Nuova Antologia

NAFMUM, Nuovi Annali della Facoltà di Magistero dell'Università di Messina

NArg, Nuovi Argomenti

NAS, Nouveaux Actes Sémiotiques, PULIM, Université de Limoges

NASNCGL, North American Studies in Nineteenth-Century German Literature, Berne, Lang

NASSAB, Nuovi Annali della Scuola Speciale per Archivisti e Bibliotecari

NAWG, Nachrichten der Akademie der Wissenschaften zu Göttingen, phil.-hist. Kl., Göttingen, Vandenhoeck & Ruprecht

NBGF, Neue Beiträge zur George-Forschung

NC, New Criterion

NCA, Nouveaux Cahiers d'Allemand

NCEFRW, Nouvelles du Centre
d'études francoprovençales 'René
Willien'
NCF, Nineteenth-Century Fiction
NCFS, Nineteenth-Century French
Studies
NCo, New Comparison
NCSRLL, North Carolina Studies
in the Romance Languages and
Literatures, Chapel Hill
ND, Наукова думка
NDH, Neue deutsche Hefte
NdJb, Niederdeutsches Jahrbuch
NDL, Nachdrucke deutscher
Literatur des 17. Jahrhunderts,
Berne, Lang
NDL, Neue deutsche Literatur
NdS, Niederdeutsche Studien,
Cologne, Böhlau
NDSK, Nydanske Studier og almen
kommunikationsteori
NdW, Niederdeutsches Wort
NE, Nueva Estafeta
NEL, Nouvelles Éditions Latines,
Paris
NFF, Novel: A Forum in Fiction
NFS, Nottingham French Studies
NFT, Német Filológiai
Tanulmányok. Arbeiten zur
deutschen Philologie
NG, Nordistica Gothoburgensia
NGC, New German Critique
NGFH, Die Neue Gesellschaft/
Frankfurter Hefte
NGR, New German Review
NGS, New German Studies, Hull
NH, Nuevo Hispanismo
NHi, Nice Historique
NHLS, North Holland Linguistic
Series, Amsterdam
NHVKSG, Neujahrsblatt des
Historischen Vereins des Kantons
St Gallen
NI, Наука и изкуство
NIMLA, NIMLA. Journal of the
Modern Language Association of
Northern Ireland
NJ, Naš jezik
NJL, Nordic Journal of Linguistics
NKT, Norske klassiker-tekster,
Bergen, Eide
NL, Nouvelles Littéraires
NLÅ, Norsk Litterær Årbok
NLD, Nuove Letture Dantesche

NLe, Nuove Lettere
NLH, New Literary History
NLi, Notre Librairie
NLLT, Natural Language and
Linguistic Theory
NLN, Neo-Latin News
NLT, Norsk Lingvistisk Tidsskrift
NLWJ, National Library of Wales
Journal
NM, Народна младеж
NMi, Neuphilologische
Mitteilungen
NMS, Nottingham Medieval Studies
NN, Наше наследие
NNH, Nueva Narrativa Hispano-
americana
NNR, New Novel Review
NOR, New Orleans Review
NORNA, Nordiska
samarbetskommittén för
namnforskning, Uppsala
NovE, Novos Estudos (CEBRAP)
NovM, Новый мир
NovR, Nova Renascenza
NOWELE, North-Western
European Language Evolution.
Nowele
NP, Народна просвета
NP, Nouvello de Prouvènço (Li),
Avignon, Parlaren Païs
d'Avignoun
NQ, Notes and Queries
NR, New Review
NŘ, Naše řeč
NRe, New Readings, School of
European Studies, University of
Wales, College of Cardiff
NRE, Nuova Rivista Europea
NRF, Nouvelle Revue Française
NRFH, Nueva Revista de Filología
Hispánica
NRL, Neue russische Literatur.
Almanach, Salzburg
NRLett, Nouvelles de la République
des Lettres
NRLI, Nuova Rivista di Letteratura
Italiana
NRMI, Nuova Rivista Musicale
Italiana
NRO, Nouvelle Revue
d'Onomastique
NRP, Nouvelle Revue de
Psychanalyse
NRS, Nuova Rivista Storica

NRSS, Nouvelle Revue du Seizième Siècle
NRu, Die Neue Rundschau
NS, Die Neueren Sprachen
NSc, New Scholar
NSh, Начальная школа
NSL, Det Norske Språk- og Litteraturselskap
NSlg, Neue Sammlung
NSo, Наш современник . . . Альманах
NSP, Nuovi Studi Politici
NSS, Nysvenska Studier
NSt, Naše stvaranje
NT, Навука і тэхніка
NT, Nordisk Tidskrift
NTBB, Nordisk Tidskrift för Bok- och Biblioteksväsen
NTC, Nuevo Texto Crítico
NTE, Народна творчість та етнографія
NTg, Nieuwe Taalgids
NTQ, New Theatre Quarterly
NTSh, Наукове товариство ім. Шевченка
NTW, News from the Top of the World: Norwegian Literature Today
NU, Narodna umjetnost
NV, Новое время
NVS, New Vico Studies
NWIG, Niewe West-Indische Gids
NyS, Nydanske Studier/Almen Kommunikationsteori
NYSNDL, New Yorker Studien zur neueren deutschen Literaturgeschichte, Berne, Lang
NYUOS, New York University Ottendorfer Series, Berne, Lang
NZh, Новый журнал
NZh (StP), Новый журнал, St Petersburg
NZJFS, New Zealand Journal of French Studies
NZSJ, New Zealand Slavonic Journal

OA, Отечественные архивы
OB, Ord och Bild

OBS, Osnabrücker Beiträge zur Sprachtheorie, Oldenbourg, OBST
OBTUP, Universitetsforlaget Oslo–Bergen–Tromsø
ÖBV, Österreichischer Bundesverlag, Vienna
OC, Œuvres et Critiques
OcL, Oceanic Linguistics
Oc(N), Oc, Nice
OCP, Orientalia Christiana Periodica, Rome
OCS, Occitan/Catalan Studies
ÖGL, Österreich in Geschichte und Literatur
OGS, Oxford German Studies
OH, Ottawa Hispánica
OIU, Oldenbourg Interpretationen mit Unterrichtshilfen, Munich, Oldenbourg
OL, Orbis Litterarum
OLR, Oxford Literary Review
OLSI, Osservatorio Linguistico della Svizzera italiana
OM, L'Oc Médiéval
ON, Otto/Novecento
OPBS, Occasional Papers in Belarusian Studies
OPEN, Oficyna Polska Encyklopedia Nezależna
OPI, Overseas Publications Interchange, London
OPL, Osservatore Politico Letterario
OPM, 'Ou Païs Mentounasc': Bulletin de la Société d'Art et d'Histoire du Mentonnais, Menton
OPRPNZ, Общество по распространению политических и научных знаний
OPSLL, Occasional Papers in Slavic Languages and Literatures
OR, Odrodzenie i Reformacja w Polsce
ORP, Oriental Research Partners, Cambridge
OS, 'Oc Sulpic': Bulletin de l'Association Occitane du Québec, Montreal
OSP, Oxford Slavonic Papers
OT, Oral Tradition
OTS, Onderzoeksinstituut voor Taal en Spraak, Utrecht
OUP, Oxford University Press

OUSL, Odense University Studies in Literature

OUSSLL, Odense University Studies in Scandinavian Languages and Literatures, Odense U.P.

OWPLC, Odense Working Papers in Language and Communication

PA, Présence Africaine

PAf, Politique Africaine

PAGS, Proceedings of the Australian Goethe Society

Pal, Palaeobulgarica — Старобългаристика

PAM, Publicacions de l'Abadia de Montserrat, Barcelona

PAN, Polska Akademia Nauk, Warsaw

PaP, Past and Present

PapBSA, Papers of the Bibliographical Society of America

PAPhS, Proceedings of the American Philosophical Society

PapL, Papiere zur Linguistik

ParL, Paragone Letteratura

PartR, Partisan Review

PaS, Pamiętnik Słowiański

PASJ, Pictish Arts Society Journal

PAX, Instytut Wydawniczy PAX, Warsaw

PB, Д-р Петър Берон

PBA, Proceedings of the British Academy

PBib, Philosophische Bibliothek, Hamburg, Meiner

PBLS, Proceedings of the Annual Meeting of the Berkeley Linguistic Society

PBML, Prague Bulletin of Mathematical Linguistics

PBSA, Publications of the Bibliographical Society of America

PC, Problems of Communism

PCLS, Proceedings of the Chicago Linguistic Society

PCP, Pacific Coast Philology

PD, Probleme der Dichtung, Heidelberg, Winter

PDA, Pagine della Dante

PdO, Paraula d'oc, Centre International de Recerca i Documentació d'Oc, Valencia

PE, Poesía Española

PEGS(NS), Publications of the English Goethe Society (New Series)

PenP, Il Pensiero Politico

PerM, Perspectives Médiévales

PEs, Lou Prouvençau à l'Escolo

PF, Présences Francophones

PFil, Prace Filologiczne

PFPS, Z problemów frazeologii polskiej i słowiańskiej, ZNiO

PFSCL, Papers on French Seventeenth Century Literature

PG, Païs gascons

PGA, Lo pais gascon/Lou pais gascoun, Anglet

PGIG, Publikationen der Gesellschaft für interkulturelle Germanistik, Munich, Iudicium

PH, La Palabra y El Hombre

PhilosQ, Philosophical Quarterly

PhilP, Philological Papers, West Virginia University

PhilR, Philosophy and Rhetoric

PhilRev, Philosophical Review

PhLC, Phréatique, Langage et Création

PHol, Le Pauvre Holterling

PhonPr, Phonetica Pragensia

PhP, Philologica Pragensia

PhR, Phoenix Review

PHSL, Proceedings of the Huguenot Society of London

PI, педагогическиб институт

PId, Le Parole e le Idee

PIGS, Publications of the Institute of Germanic Studies, University of London

PiH, Il Piccolo Hans

PIMA, Proceedings of the Illinois Medieval Association

PIMS, Publications of the Institute for Medieval Studies, Toronto

PIW, Państwowy Instytut Wydawniczy, Warsaw

PJ, Poradnik Językowy

PLing, Papers in Linguistics

PLit, Philosophy and Literature

PLL, Papers on Language and Literature

PL(L), Pamiętnik Literacki, London

PLRL, Patio de Letras/La Rosa als Llavis

PLS, Přednášky z běhu Letní školy slovanských studií

PL(W), Pamiętnik Literacki, Warsaw

PM, Pleine Marge

PMH, Portugaliae Monumenta Historica

PMHRS, Papers of the Medieval Hispanic Research Seminar, London, Department of Hispanic Studies, Queen Mary and Westfield College

PMLA, Publications of the Modern Language Association of America

PMPA, Publications of the Missouri Philological Association

P.N, Paraulas de novelum, Périgueux

P.NCIP, Plurilinguismo. Notizario del Centro Internazionale sul Plurilinguismo

P.NR, Poetry and Nation Review

P.NUS, Prace Naukowe Uniwersytetu Śląskiego, Katowice

PoetT, Poetics Today

PolR, Polish Review

PortSt, Portuguese Studies

PP, Prace Polonistyczne

PP.NCFL, Proceedings of the Pacific Northwest Conference on Foreign Languages

PPr, Papers in Pragmatics

PPU, Promociones y Publicaciones Universitarias, S.A., Barcelona

PQ, The Philological Quarterly

PR, Podravska Revija

PrA, Prouvenço aro, Marseilles

PraRu, Prace Rusycystyczne

PRev, Poetry Review

PRF, Publications Romanes et Françaises, Geneva, Droz

PRH, Pahl-Rugenstein Hochschulschriften, Cologne, Pahl–Rugenstein

PrH, Provence Historique

PrHlit, Prace Historycznoliterackie

PrHum, Prace Humanistyczne

PRIA, Proceedings of the Royal Irish Academy

PrIJP, Prace Instytutu Języka Polskiego

Prilozi, Prilozi za književnost, jezik, istoriju i folklor, Belgrade

PrilPJ, Prilozi proučavanju jezika

PRIS-MA, Bulletin de liaison de l'ERLIMA, Université de Poitiers

PrLit, Prace Literackie

PRom, Papers in Romance

PrRu, Przegląd Rusycystyczny

PrzH, Przegląd Humanistyczny

PrzW, Przegląd Wschodni

PS, Проблеми слов'янознавства

PSCL, Papers and Studies in Contrastive Linguistics

PSE, Prague Studies in English

PSGAS, Politics and Society in Germany, Austria and Switzerland

PSLu, Pagine Storiche Luganesi

PSML, Prague Studies in Mathematical Linguistics

PSQ, Philologische Studien und Quellen, Berlin, Schmidt

PSR, Portuguese Studies Review

PSRL, Полное собрание русских летописей

PSS, Z polskich studiów slawistycznych, Warsaw, PWN

PSSLSAA, Procès-verbaux des séances de la Société des Lettres, Sciences et Arts de l'Aveyron

PSV, Polono-Slavica Varsoviensia

PT, Pamiętnik Teatralny

PUC, Pontifícia Universidade Católica, São Paulo

PUE, Publications Universitaires, Européennes, NY–Berne–Frankfurt, Lang

PUF, Presses Universitaires de France, Paris

PUG Pontificia Università Gregoriana

PUMRL, Purdue University Monographs in Romance Languages, Amsterdam — Philadelphia, Benjamins

PUStE, Publications de l'Université de St Étienne

PW, Poetry Wales

PWN, Państwowe Wydawnictwo Naukowe, Warsaw, etc

QA, Quaderni de Archivio

QALT, Quaderni dell'Atlante Lessicale Toscano

QASIS, Quaderni di lavoro dell'ASIS (Atlante Sintattico dell'Italia Settentrionale), Centro di Studio per la Dialettologia Italiana 'O. Parlangèli', Università degli Studi di Padova

QCFLP, Quaderni del Circolo Filologico Linguistico Padovano

QDLC, Quaderni del Dipartimento di Linguistica, Università della Calabria

QDLF, Quaderni del Dipartimento di Linguistica, Università degli Studi, Firenze

QDLLSMG, Quaderni del Dipartimento di Lingue e Letterature Straniere Moderne, Università di Genova

QDSL, Quellen zur deutschen Sprach- und Literaturgeschichte, Heidelberg, Winter

QFCC, Quaderni della Fondazione Camillo Caetani, Rome

QFESM, Quellen und Forschungen zur Erbauungsliteratur des späten Mittelalters und der frühen Neuzeit, Amsterdam, Rodopi

QFGB, Quaderni di Filologia Germanica della Facoltà di Lettere e Filosofia dell'Università di Bologna

QFIAB, Quellen und Forschungen aus italienischen Archiven und Bibliotheken

QFLK, Quellen und Forschungen zur Literatur- und Kulturgeschichte, Berlin, de Gruyter

QFLR, Quaderni di Filologia e Lingua Romanze, Università di Macerata

QFSK, Quellen und Forschungen zur Sprach- und Kulturgeschichte der germanischen Völker, Berlin, de Gruyter

QI, Quaderni d'Italianistica

QIA, Quaderni Ibero-Americani

QIGC, Quaderni dell'Istituto di Glottologia, Università degli Studi 'G. D'Annunzio' di Chieti, Facoltà di Lettere e Filosofia

QIICM, Quaderni dell'Istituto Italiano de Cultura, Melbourne

QILLSB, Quaderni dell'Istituto di Lingue e Letterature Straniere della Facoltà di Magistero dell'Università degli Studi di Bari

QILUU, Quaderni dell'Istituto di Linguistica dell'Università di Urbino

QINSRM, Quaderni dell'Istituto Nazionale di Studi sul Rinascimento Meridionale

QJMFL, A Quarterly Journal in Modern Foreign Literatures

QJS, Quarterly Journal of Speech, Speech Association of America

QLII, Quaderni di Letterature Iberiche e Iberoamericane

QLL, Quaderni di Lingue e Letterature, Verona

QLLP, Quaderni del Laboratorio di Linguistica, Scuola Normale Superiore, Pisa

QLLSP, Quaderni di Lingua e Letteratura Straniere, Facoltà di Magistero, Università degli Studi di Palermo

QLO, Quasèrns de Lingüistica Occitana

QM, Quaderni Milanesi

QMed, Quaderni Medievali

QP, Quaderns de Ponent

QPet, Quaderni Petrarcheschi

QPL, Quaderni Patavini di Linguistica

QQ, Queen's Quarterly, Kingston, Ontario

QR, Quercy Recherche, Cahors

QRCDLIM, Quaderni di Ricerca, Centro di Dialettologia e Linguistica Italiana di Manchester

QRP, Quaderni di Retorica e Poetica

QS, Quaderni di Semantica

QSF, Quaderni del Seicento Francese

QSGLL, Queensland Studies in German Language and Literature, Berne, Francke

QSt, Quaderni Storici

QStef, Quaderni Stefaniani

QSUP, Quaderni per la Storia dell'Università di Padova

QT, Quaderni di Teatro

QuF, Québec français

QuS, Quebec Studies
QV, Quaderni del Vittoriale
QVen, Quaderni Veneti
QVer, Quaderni Veronesi di
 Filologia, Lingua e Letteratura
 Italiana
QVR, Quo vadis Romania?, Vienna

RA, Romanistische Arbeitshefte,
 Tübingen, Niemeyer
RA, Revista Agustiniana
RAA, Rendiconti dell'Accademia di
 Archeologia, Lettere e Belle Arti
RABM, Revista de Archivos,
 Bibliotecas y Museos
RAct, Regards sur l'Actualité
Rad, Rad Jugoslavenske akademije
 znanosti i umjetnosti
RAE, Real Academia Española
RAfL, Research in African
 Literatures
RAL, Revista Argentina de
 Lingüística
RAN, Regards sur l'Afrique du Nord
RANL, Rendiconti dell'Accademia
 Nazionale dei Lincei, Classe di
 scienze morali, storiche e
 filologiche, serie IX
RANPOLL, Revista ANPOLL,
 Faculdade de Filosofia, Letras e
 Ciências Humanas, Univ. de São
 Paulo.
RAPL, Revista da Academia
 Paulista de Letras, São Paulo
RAR, Renaissance and Reformation
RAS, Rassegna degli Archivi di
 Stato
RB, Revue Bénédictine
RBC, Research Bibliographies and
 Checklists, London, Grant &
 Cutler
RBDSL, Regensburger Beiträge zur
 deutschen Sprach- und
 Literaturwissenschaft, Frankfurt–
 Berne, Lang
RBG, Reclams de Bearn et
 Gasconha
RBGd, Rocznik Biblioteki Gdańskiej
 PAN (Libri Gedanenses)
RBKr, Rocznik Biblioteki PAN w
 Krakowie
RBL, Revista Brasileira de
 Lingüística

RBLL, Revista Brasileira de Lingua
 e Literatura
RBN, Revista da Biblioteca
 Nacional
RBPH, Revue Belge de Philologie et
 d'Histoire
RC, Le Ragioni Critiche
RCat, Revista de Catalunya
RČAV, Rozpravy Československé
 akademie věd, Prague, ČSAV
RCB, Revista de Cultura Brasileña
RCCM, Rivista di Cultura Classica e
 Medioevale
RCEH, Revista Canadiense de
 Estudios Hispánicos
RCEN, Revue Canadienne d'Études
 Néerlandaises
RCF, Review of Contemporary
 Fiction
RCL, Revista Chilena de Literatura
RCLL, Revista de Crítica Literaria
 Latino-Americana
RCo, Revue de Comminges
RCSF, Rivista Critica di Storia della
 Filosofia
RCVS, Rassegna di Cultura e Vita
 Scolastica
RD, Revue drômoise: archéologie,
 histoire, géographie
RDE, Recherches sur Diderot et sur
 l''Encyclopédie'
RDM, Revue des Deux Mondes
RDsS, Recherches sur le XVIIe
 Siècle
RDTP, Revista de Dialectología y
 Tradiciones Populares
RE, Revista de Espiritualidad
REC, Revista de Estudios del Caribe
RECat, Revue d'Études Catalanes
RedLet, Red Letters
REE, Revista de Estudios
 Extremeños
REEI, Revista del Instituto Egipcio
 de Estudios Islámicos, Madrid
REH, Revista de Estudios
 Hispánicos, Washington
 University, St Louis
REHisp, Revista de Estudios
 Hispánicos, Puerto Rico
REI, Revue des Études Italiennes
REJ, Revista de Estudios de
 Juventud
REJui, Revue des Études Juives,
 Paris

REL, Revue des Études Latines
RELA, Revista Española de Lingüística Aplicada
RelCL, Religion in Communist Lands
RELI, Rassegna Europea di Letteratura Italiana
RELing, Revista Española de Lingüística, Madrid
RelLit, Religious Literature
ReMS, Renaissance and Modern Studies
RenD, Renaissance Drama
RenP, Renaissance Papers
RenR, Renaissance and Reformation
RenS, Renaissance Studies
RES, Review of English Studies
RESEE, Revue des Études Sud-Est Européennes
RESS, Revue Européenne des Sciences Sociales et Cahiers Vilfredo Pareto
RevA, Revue d'Allemagne
RevAl, Revista de l'Alguer
RevAR, Revue des Amis de Ronsard
RevAuv, Revue d'Auvergne, Clermont-Ferrand
RevEL, Revista de Estudos da Linguagem, Faculdade de Letras, Universidade Federal de Minas Gerais
RevF, Revista de Filología
RevHA, Revue de la Haute-Auvergne
RevG, Revista de Girona
RevIb, Revista Iberoamericana
RevL, Revista Lusitana
RevLM, Revista de Literatura Medieval
RevLR, Revista do Livro
RevO, La Revista occitana, Montpellier
RevP, Revue PArole, Université de Mons-Hainault
RevPF, Revista Portuguesa de Filosofia
RevR, Revue Romane
RF, Romanische Forschungen
RFe, Razón y Fe
RFE, Revista de Filología Española
RFHL, Revue Française d'Histoire du Livre

RFLSJ, Revista de Filosofia y Lingüística de San José, Costa Rica
RFLUL, Revista da Faculdade de Letras da Universidade de Lisboa
RFLUP, Revista da Faculdade de Letras da Universidade do Porto
RFN, Rivisti di Filosofia Neoscolastica
RFo, Ricerca Folklorica
RFP, Recherches sur le Français Parlé
RFR, Revista de Filología Románica
RFr, Revue Frontenac
RG, Recherches Germaniques
RGand, Romanica Gandensia
RGCC, Revue du Gévaudan, des Causses et des Cévennes
RGG, Rivista di Grammatica Generativa
RGI, Revue Germanique Internationale
RGL, Reihe Germanistische Linguistik, Tübingen, Niemeyer
RGo, Romanica Gothoburgensia
RGT, Revista Galega de Teatro
RH, Reihe Hanser, Munich, Hanser
RH, Revue Hebdomadaire
RHA, Revista de Historia de America
RHAM, Revue Historique et Archéologique du Maine
RHCS, Rocznik Historii Czasopiśmiennictwa Polskiego
RHDFE, Revue Historique de Droit Français et Étranger
RHE, Revue d'Histoire Ecclésiastique
RHEF, Revue d'Histoire de l'Église de France
RHel, Romanica Helvetica, Tübingen and Basle, Francke
RHFB, Rapports — Het Franse Boek
RHI, Revista da Historia das Ideias
RHis, Revue Historique
RHL, Reihe Hanser Literaturkommentare, Munich, Hanser
RHLF, Revue d'Histoire Littéraire de la France
RHLP, Revista de História Literária de Portugal

RHM, Revista Hispánica Moderna

RHMag, Revue d'Histoire Maghrébine

RHMC, Revue d'Histoire Moderne et Contemporaine

RHPR, Revue d'Histoire et de Philosophie Religieuses

RHR, Réforme, Humanisme, Renaissance

RHRel, Revue de l'Histoire des Religions

RHS, Revue Historique de la Spiritualité

RHSc, Revue d'Histoire des Sciences

RHSt, Ricarda Huch. Studien zu ihrem Leben und Werk

RHT, Revue d'Histoire du Théâtre

RHTe, Revue d'Histoire des Textes

RI, Rassegna Iberistica

RIA, Rivista Italiana di Acustica

RIa, Русский язык

RIAB, Revista Interamericana de Bibliografía

RIaR, Русский язык за рубежом

RICC, Revue Itinéraires et Contacts de Culture

RICP, Revista del Instituto de Cultura Puertorriqueña

RicSl, Ricerche Slavistiche

RID, Rivista Italiana di Dialettologia

RIE, Revista de Ideas Estéticas

RIEB, Revista do Instituto de Estudos Brasileiros

RIL, Rendiconti dell'Istituto Lombardo

RILA, Rassegna Italiana di Linguistica Applicata

RILCE, Revista del Instituto de Lengua y Cultura Españoles

RILP, Revista Internacional da Língua Portuguesa

RIM, Rivista Italiana di Musicologia

RIndM, Revista de Indias

RInv, Revista de Investigación

RIO, Revue Internationale d'Onomastique

RIOn, Rivista Italiana di Onomastica

RIP, Revue Internationale de Philosophie

RIS, Revue de l'Institute de Sociologie, Université Libre, Brussels

RiS, Ricerche Storiche

RITL, Revista de Istorie și Teorie Literară, Bucharest

RivF, Rivista di Filosofia

RivL, Rivista di Linguistica

RJ, Romanistisches Jahrbuch

RKHlit, Rocznik Komisji Historycznoliterackiej PAN

RKJŁ, Rozprawy Komisji Językowej Łódzkiego Towarzystwa Naukowego

RKJW, Rozprawy Komisji Językowej Wrocławskiego Towarzystwa Naukowego

RLA, Romance Languages Annual

RLaR, Revue des Langues Romanes

RLB, Recueil Linguistique de Bratislava

RLC, Revue de Littérature Comparée

RLD, Revista de Llengua i Dret

RLet, Revista de Letras

RLettI, Rivista di Letteratura Italiana

RLF, Revista de Literatura Fantástica

RLFRU, Recherches de Linguistique Française et Romane d'Utrecht

RLH, Revista de Literatura Hispanoamericana

RLI, Rassegna della Letteratura Italiana

RLib, Rivista dei Libri

RLing, Russian Linguistics

RLiR, Revue de Linguistique Romane

RLit, Revista de Literatura

RLJ, Russian Language Journal

RLLCGV, Revista de Lengua y Literatura Catalana, Gallega y Vasca, Madrid

RLLR, Romance Literature and Linguistics Review

RLM, Revista de Literaturas Modernas, Cuyo

RLMC, Rivista di Letterature Moderne e Comparate

RLMed, Revista de Literatura Medieval

RLMod, Revue des Lettres Modernes

RLModCB, Revue des Lettres
Modernes. Carnets
Bibliographiques
RLSer, Revista de Literatura Ser,
Puerto Rico
RLSL, Revista de Lingvisticä şi
Ştiinţä Literarä
RLT, Russian Literature
Triquarterly
RLTA, Revista de Lingüística
Teórica y Aplicada
RLV, Revue des Langues Vivantes
RLVin, Recherches Linguistiques de
Vincennes
RM, Romance Monograph Series,
University, Mississippi
RM, Remate de Males
RMAL, Revue du Moyen Âge Latin
RMar, Revue Marivaux
RMC, Roma Moderna e
Contemporanea
RMEH, Revista Marroquí de
Estudios Hispánicos
RMH, Recherches sur le Monde
Hispanique au XIXe Siècle
RMM, Revue de Métaphysique et
de Morale
RMon, Revue Montesquieu
RMRLL, Rocky Mountain Review
of Language and Literature
RMS, Reading Medieval Studies
RNC, Revista Nacional de Cultura,
Carácas
RNDWSPK, Rocznik Naukowo-
Dydaktyczny WSP w Krakowie
RO, Revista de Occidente
RoczH, Roczniki Humanistyczne
Katolickiego Uniw. Lubelskiego
RoczSl, Rocznik Slawistyczny
ROl, Rossica Olomucensia
RoM, Rowohlts Monographien,
Reinbek, Rowohlt
RomGG, Romanistik in Geschichte
und Gegenwart
ROMM, Revue de L'Occident
Musulman et de la Méditerranée
RoN, Romance Notes
RoQ, Romance Quarterly
RORD, Research Opportunities in
Renaissance Drama
RoS, Romance Studies
RoSl, Роднае слова
RP, Радянський письменник
RP, Revista de Portugal

RPA, Revue de Phonétique
Appliquée
RPac, Revue du Pacifique
RPC, Revue Pédagogique et
Culturelle de l'AVEP
RPF, Revista Portuguesa de
Filologia
RPFE, Revue Philosophique de la
France et de l'Étranger
RPh, Romance Philology
RPL, Revue Philosophique de
Louvain
RPl, Río de la Plata
RPLit, Res Publica Litterarum
RPN, Res Publica nowa, Warsaw
RPP, Romanticism Past and Present
RPr, Raison Présente
RPS, Revista Paraguaya de
Sociologia
RPyr, Recherches pyrénéennes,
Toulouse
RQ, Renaissance Quarterly
RQL, Revue Québécoise de
Linguistique
RR, Romanic Review
RRe, Русская речь
RRL, Revue Roumaine de
Linguistique
RRou, Revue du Rouergue
RS, Reihe Siegen, Heidelberg,
Winter
RS, Revue de Synthèse
RSC, Rivista di Studi Canadesi
RSCI, Rivista di Storia della Chiesa
in Italia
RSEAV, Revue de la Société des
enfants et amis de Villeneuve-de-
Berg
RSF, Rivista di Storia della Filosofia
RSH, Revue des Sciences Humaines
RSh, Радянська школа
RSI, Rivista Storica Italiana
RSJb, Reinhold Schneider Jahrbuch
RSL, Rusycystyczne Studia
Literaturoznawcze
RSl, Revue des Études Slaves
RSLR, Rivista di Storia e
Letteratura Religiose
RSPT, Revue des Sciences
Philosophiques et Théologiques
RSR, Rassegna Storica del
Risorgimento
RSSR, Rivista di Storia Sociale e
Religiosa

RST, Rassegna Storica Toscana
RSt, Research Studies
RStI, Rivista di Studi Italiani
RT, Revue du Tarn
RTAM, Recherches de Théologie Ancienne et Médiévale
RTLiM, Rocznik Towarzystwa Literackiego im. Adama Mickiewicza
RTr, Recherches et Travaux, Université de Grenoble
RTUG, Recherches et Travaux de l'Université de Grenoble III
RUB, Revue de l'Université de Bruxelles
RUC, Revista de la Universidad Complutense
RuLit, Ruch Literacki
RUM, Revista de la Universidad de Madrid
RUMex, Revista de la Universidad de México
RUOt, Revue de l'Université d'Ottawa
RUS, Rice University Studies
RusH, Russian History
RusL, Русская литература, ПД, Leningrad
RusM, Русская мысль
RusMed, Russia Medievalis
RusR, Russian Review
RUW, Rozprawy Uniwersytetu Warsawskiego, Warsaw
RVB, Rheinische Vierteljahrsblätter
RVF, Revista Valenciana de Filología
RVi, Revue du Vivarais
RVQ, Romanica Vulgaria Quaderni
RVV, Romanische Versuche und Vorarbeiten, Bonn U.P.
RVVig, Reihe der Villa Vigoni, Tübingen, Niemeyer
RyF, Razón y Fe
RZLG, Romanistische Zeitschrift für Literaturgeschichte
RZSF, Radovi Zavoda za slavensku filologiju

SA, Studien zum Althochdeutschen, Göttingen, Vandenhoeck & Ruprecht
SAB, South Atlantic Bulletin
Sac, Sacris Eruditi

SAG, Stuttgarter Arbeiten zur Germanistik, Stuttgart, Heinz
SAH, Studies in American Humour
SANU, Srpska akademija nauka i umetnosti
SAOB, Svenska Akademiens Ordbok
SAQ, South Atlantic Quarterly
SAR, South Atlantic Review
SAS, Studia Academica Slovaca
SaS, Slovo a slovesnost
SASc, Studia Anthroponymica Scandinavica
SATF, Société des Anciens Textes Français
SAV, Slovenská akadémia vied
SAVL, Studien zur allgemeinen und vergleichenden Literaturwissenschaft, Stuttgart, Metzler
SB, Slavistische Beiträge, Munich, Sagner
SB, Studies in Bibliography
SBAW, Sitzungsberichte der Bayerischen Akad. der Wissenschaften, phil.-hist. Kl., Munich, Beck
SBL, Saarbrücker Beiträge zur Literaturwissenschaft, St. Ingbert, Röhrig
SBL, Старобългарска литература
SBR, Swedish Book Review
SBVS, Saga-Book of the Viking Society
SC, Studia Celtica, The Bulletin of the Board of Celtic Studies
SCB, Skrifter utgivna av Centrum för barnkulturforskning, Stockholm U.P.
SCC, Studies in Comparative Communism
SCen, The Seventeenth Century
SCES, Sixteenth Century Essays and Studies, Kirksville, Missouri, Sixteenth Century Journal
SCFS, Seventeenth-Century French Studies
SchG, Schriftsteller der Gegenwart, Berlin, Volk & Wissen
SchSch, Schlern-Schriften, Innsbruck, Wagner
SchwM, Schweizer Monatshefte
SCJ, Sixteenth Century Journal
SCL, Studii şi Cercetări Lingvistice

SCl, Stendhal Club

ScL, Scottish Language

ScM, Scripta Mediterranea

SCN, Seventeenth Century News

SCO, Studii şi Cercetări de Onomasticä

ScO, Scriptoralia, Tübingen, Narr

SCR, Studies in Comparative Religion

ScRev, Scandinavian Review

ScSl, Scando-Slavica

ScSt, Scandinavian Studies

SD, Sprache und Dichtung, n.F., Berne, Haupt

SD, Современная драматургия.

SdA, Storia dell'Arte

SDFU, Skrifter utgivna genom Dialekt- och folkminnesarkivet i Uppsala

SDG, Studien zur deutschen Grammatik, Tübingen, Narr

SDL, Studien zur deutschen Literatur, Tübingen, Niemeyer

SDLNZ, Studien zur deutschen Literatur des 19. und 20. Jahrhunderts, Berne, Lang

SdO, Serra d'Or

SDOFU, Skrifter utgivna av Dialekt-, ortnamns- och folkminnesarkivet i Umeå

SDS, Studien zur Dialektologie in Südwestdeutschland, Marburg, Elwert

SDSp, Studien zur deutschen Sprache, Tübingen, Narr

SDv, Sprache und Datenverarbeitung

SE, Série Esludos Uberaba

SeC, Scrittura e Civiltà

SECC, Studies in Eighteenth-Century Culture

SEDES, Société d'Éditions d'Enseignement Supérieur

SEEA, Slavic and East European Arts

SEEJ, The Slavic and East European Journal

SEER, Slavonic and East European Review

SEES, Slavic and East European Studies

SEI, Società Editrice Internazionale, Turin

SELA, South Eastern Latin Americanist

SemL, Seminarios de Lingüística, Universidade do Algarve, Faro

SEN, Società Editrice Napoletana, Naples

SEP, Secretaría de Educación Pública, Mexico

SeS, Serbian Studies

SEz, Съпоставително езикознание

SF, Slavistische Forschungen, Cologne — Vienna, Böhlau

SFAIEO, Section Française de l'Association Internationale d'Études Occitanes, Montpellier

SFI, Studi di Filologia Italiana

SFIS, Stanford French and Italian Studies

SFKG, Schriftenreihe der Franz–Kafka–Gesellschaft, Vienna, Braumüller

SFL, Studies in French Literature, London, Arnold

SFL, Studi di Filologia e Letteratura

SFPS, Studia z Filologii Polskiej i Słowiańskiej PAN

SFR, Stanford French Review

SFr, Studi Francesi

SFRS, Studia z Filologii Rosyjskiej i Slowiańskiej, Warsaw

SFS, Swiss-French Studies

SFUŠ, Sborník Filozofickej Fakulty Univerzity P. J. Šafárika, Prešov

SG, Sprache der Gegenwart, Düsseldorf, Schwann

SGAK, Studien zu Germanistik, Anglistik und Komparatistik, Bonn, Bouvier

SGECRN, Study Group on Eighteenth-Century Russia Newsletter

SGEL, Sociedad General Española de Librería

SGesch, Sprache und Geschichte, Stuttgart, Klett-Cotta

SGF, Stockholmer Germanistische Forschungen, Stockholm, Almqvist & Wiksell

SGG, Studia Germanica Gandensia

SGGed, Studia Germanica Gedanensia

SGI, Studi di Grammatica Italiana

SGLL, Studies in German
Language and Literature,
Lewiston-Queenston-Lampeter

SGLLC, Studies in German
Literature, Linguistics, and
Culture, Columbia, S.C.,
Camden House, Woodbridge,
Boydell & Brewer

SGP, Studia Germanica
Posnaniensia

SGS, Stanford German Studies,
Berne, Lang

SGS, Scottish Gaelic Studies

SGU, Studia Germanistica
Upsaliensia, Stockholm, Almqvist
& Wiksell

SH, Slavica Helvetica, Berne, Lang

SH, Studia Hibernica

ShAn, Sharq al-Andalus

SHAW, Sitzungsberichte der
Heidelberger Akademie der
Wissenschaften, phil.-hist. Klasse,
Heidelberg, Winter

SHCT, Studies in the History of
Christian Thought, Leiden, Brill

SHPF, Société de l'Histoire du
Protestantisme Français

SHPS, Studies in History and
Philosophy of Science

SHR, The Scottish Historical
Review

SI, Sprache und Information,
Tübingen, Niemeyer

SIAA, Studi di Italianistica
nell'Africa Australe

SiCh, Слово і час

SIDES, Société Internationale de
Diffusion et d'Édition
Scientifiques, Antony

SIDS, Schriften des Instituts für
deutsche Sprache, Berlin, de
Gruyter

Siglo XX, Siglo XX / 20th Century

SILTA, Studi Italiani di Linguistica
Teorica ed Applicata

SiN, Sin Nombre

SINSU, Skrifter utgivna av
institutionen för nordiska språk
vid Uppsala universitet, Uppsala
U.P.

SIR, Stanford Italian Review

SIsp, Studi Ispanici

SISSD, Società Italiana di Studi sul
Secolo XVIII

SJLŠ, Slovenský jazyk a literatúra v
škole

SkSt, Skandinavistische Studien

SKZ, Srpska Književna Zadruga,
Belgrade

SL, Sammlung Luchterhand,
Darmstadt, Luchterhand

SL, Studia Linguistica

SLÅ, Svensk Lärarföreningens
Årsskrift

SlaG, Slavica Gandensia

SlaH, Slavica Helsingensia

SlaL, Slavica Lundensia

SlavFil, Славянска филология,
Sofia

SlavH, Slavica Hierosolymitana

SlavLit, Славянските литератури
в България

SlavRev, Slavistična revija

SlaW, Slavica Wratislaviensia

SLeg, Studium Legionense

SLeI, Studi di Lessicografia Italiana

SLESPO, Suplemento Literário do
Estado de São Paulo

SLF, Studi di Letteratura Francese

SLG, Studia Linguistica
Germanica, Berlin, de Gruyter

SLI, Società di Linguistica Italiana

SLI, Studi Linguistici Italiani

SLIGU, Skrifter utgivna av
Litteraturvetenskapliga
institutionen vid Göteborgs
universitet, Gothenburg U.P.

SLILU, Skrifter utgivna av
Litteraturvetenskapliga
institutionen vid Lunds
universitet, Lund U.P.

SLit, Schriften zur
Literaturwissenschaft, Berlin,
Dunckler & Humblot

SLit, Slovenská literatúra

SLitR, Stanford Literature Review

SLIUU, Skrifter utgivna av
Litteraturvetenskapliga
institutionen vid Uppsala
universitet, Uppsala U.P.

SLK, Schwerpunkte Linguistik und
Kommunikationswissenschaft

SLL, Skrifter utg. genom
Landsmålsarkivet i Lund

SLM, Studien zur Literatur der
Moderne, Bonn, Bouvier

SlN, Slovenský národopis

SLO, Slavica Lublinensia et
  Olomucensia
SlO, Slavia Orientalis
SlOc, Slavia Occidentalis
SlOth, Slavica Othinensia
SlPN, Slovenské pedagogické
  nakladateľstvo
SlPoh, Slovenské pohľady
SlPr, Slavica Pragensia
SLPS, Studia Linguistica Polono-
  Slovaca
SLR, Second Language Research
SLS, Studies in the Linguistic
  Sciences
SlSb, Slezský sborník
SlSl, Slavica Slovaca
SlSp, Slovenský spisovateľ
SLRev, Southern Literary Review
SLu, Studia Lulliana
SLWU, Sprach und Literatur in
  Wissenschaft und Unterricht
SM, Sammlung Metzler, Stuttgart,
  Metzler
SM, Studi Medievali
SMC, Studies in Medieval Culture
SME, Schöninghs mediävistische
  Editionen, Paderborn, Schöningh
SMer, Студенческий меридиан
SMGL, Studies in Modern German
  Literature, Berne – Frankfurt –
  New York, Lang
SMLS, Strathclyde Modern
  Language Studies
SMRT, Studies in Medieval and
  Reformation Thought, Leiden,
  Brill
SMS, Sewanee Medieval Studies
SMu, Советский музей
SMV, Studi Mediolatini e Volgari
SN, Studia Neophilologica
SNL, Sveučilišna naklada Liber,
  Zagreb
SNM, Sborník Národního muzea
SNov, Seara Nova
SNTL, Státní nakladatelství
  technické literatury
SÖAW, Sitzungsberichte der
  Österreichischen Akademie der
  Wissenschaften, phil.-hist. Klasse
SoCR, South Central Review
SOH, Studia Onomastica
  Helvetica, Arbon, Eurotext:
  Historisch-Archäologischer
  Verlag

SoK, Sprog og Kultur
SopL, Sophia Linguistica, Tokyo
SoRA, Southern Review, Adelaide
SoRL, Southern Review, Louisiana
SOU, Skrifter utgivna genom
  Ortnamnsarkivet i Uppsala
SP, Sammlung Profile, Bonn,
  Bouvier
SP, Studies in Philology
SPat, Studi Patavini
SpC, Speech Communication
SPCT, Studi e Problemi di Critica
  Testuale
SPES, Studio per Edizioni Scelte,
  Florence
SPFB, Sborník Pedagogické fakulty
  v Brně
SPFFBU, Sborník prací Filosofické
  fakulty Brněnské Univerzity
SPFHK, Sborník Pedagogické
  fakulty, Hradec Králové
SPFO, Sborník Pedagogické fakulty,
  Ostrava
SPFOl, Sborník Pedagogické fakulty,
  Olomouc
SPFUK, Sborník Pedagogické
  fakulty Univerzity Karlovy,
  Prague
SPGS, Scottish Papers in Germanic
  Studies, Glasgow
SPh, Studia philologica, Olomouc
SPi, Serie Piper, Munich, Piper
SPIEL, Siegener Periodicum zur
  Internationalen Empirischen
  Literaturwissenschaft
SPK, Studia nad polszczyzną
  kresową, Wrocław
SpLit, Sprache und Literatur
SpMod, Spicilegio Moderno, Pisa
SPN, Státní pedagogické
  nakladatelství
SPol, Studia Polonistyczne
SPR, Slavistic Printings and
  Reprintings, The Hague, Mouton
SpR, Spunti e Ricerche
SPRF, Société de Publications
  Romanes et Françaises, Geneva,
  Droz
SPS, Specimina Philologiae
  Slavicae, Munich, Otto Sagner
SPS, Studia Philologica
  Salmanticensia
SPSO, Studia Polono–Slavica–
  Orientalia. Acta Litteraria

SpSt, Spanish Studies
SPUAM, Studia Polonistyczna
 Uniwersytetu Adama
 Mickiewicza, Poznań
SR, Slovenská reč
SRAZ, Studia Romanica et Anglica
 Zagrabiensia
SRev, Slavic Review
SRF, Studi e Ricerche Francescane
SRL, Studia Romanica et
 Linguistica, Frankfurt, Lang
SRLF, Saggi e Ricerche di
 Letteratura Francese
SRo, Studi Romanzi
SRom, Studi Romeni
SRoP, Studia Romanica
 Posnaniensia
SRP, Studia Rossica Posnaniensia
SRU, Studia Romanica Upsaliensia
SS, Symbolae Slavicae,
 Frankfurt–Berne–Cirencester,
 Lang
SS, Syn og Segn
SSBI, Skrifter utgivna av Svenska
 barnboksinstitutet
SSB, Strenna Storica Bolognese
SSCJ, Southern Speech
 Communication Journal
SSDSP, Società Savonese di Storia
 Patria
SSE, Studi di Storia dell'Educazione
SSF, Studies in Short Fiction
SSFin, Studia Slavica Finlandensia
SSGL, Studies in Slavic and
 General Linguistics, Amsterdam,
 Rodopi
SSH, Studia Slavica Academiae
 Scientiarum Hungaricae
SSL, Studi e Saggi Linguistici
SSLF, Skrifter utgivna av Svenska
 Litteratursällskapet i Finland
SSLP, Studies in Slavic Literature
 and Poetics, Amsterdam, Rodopi
SSLS, Studi Storici Luigi Simeoni
SSMP, Stockholm Studies in
 Modern Philology
SSPHS, Society for Spanish and
 Portuguese Historical Studies,
 Millersville
SSS, Stanford Slavic Studies
SSSAS, Society of Spanish and
 Spanish-American Studies,
 Boulder, Colorado

SSSlg, Sagners Slavistische
 Sammlung, Munich, Sagner
SSSN, Skrifter utgivna av Svenska
 språknämnden
SSSP, Stockholm Studies in
 Scandinavian Philology
SST, Sprache — System und
 Tätigkeit, Frankfurt, Lang
SSt, Slavic Studies, Hokkaido
ST, Suhrkamp Taschenbuch,
 Frankfurt, Suhrkamp
ST, Studi Testuali, Alessandria,
 Edizioni dell'Orso
StB, Studi sul Boccaccio
STC, Studies in the Twentieth
 Century
StCJ, Studia Celtica Japonica
STCL, Studies in Twentieth
 Century Literature
StCL, Studies in Canadian
 Literature
StCrit, Strumenti Critici
StD, Studi Danteschi
StF, Studie Francescani
StFil, Studia Filozoficzne
STFM, Société des Textes Français
 Modernes
StG, Studi Germanici
StGol, Studi Goldoniani
StH, Studies in the Humanities
StI, Studi Italici, Kyoto
StIt, Studi Italiani
StL, Studium Linguistik
StLa, Studies in Language,
 Amsterdam
StLi, Stauffenburg Linguistik,
 Tübingen, Stauffenburg
StLI, Studi di Letteratura Ispano-
 Americana
StLIt, Studi Latini e Italiani
StLM, Studies in the Literary
 Imagination
StLo, Studia Logica
StM, Studies in Medievalism
STM, Suhrkamp Taschenbuch
 Materialien, Frankfurt,
 Suhrkamp
STML, Studies on Themes and
 Motifs in Literature, New York,
 Lang
StMon, Studia Monastica
StMus, Studi Musicali
StMy, Studia Mystica
StN, Studi Novecenteschi

StNF, Studier i Nordisk Filologi

StO, Studium Ovetense

StP, Studi Piemontesi

StPet, Studi Petrarcheschi

StR, Studie o rukopisech

StRLLF, Studi e Ricerche di Letteratura e Linguistica Francese

StRmgn, Studi Romagnoli

StRo, Studi Romani

StRom, Studies in Romanticism

StRu, Studia Russica, Budapest

StS, Studi Storici

StSec, Studi Secenteschi

StSk, Studia Skandinavica

StSet, Studi Settecenteschi

STSL, Studien und Texte zur Sozialgeschichte der Literatur, Tübingen, Niemeyer

StT, Studi Tassiani

STUF, Sprachtypologie und Universalienforschung

StV, Studies on Voltaire and the 18th Century

STW, Suhrkamp Taschenbücher Wissenschaft, Frankfurt, Suhrkamp

StZ, Sprache im technischen Zeitalter

SU, Studi Urbinati

SUBBP, Studia Universitatis Babeş-Bolyai, Philologia, Cluj

SUDAM, Editorial Sudamericana, Buenos Aires

SuF, Sinn und Form

SUm, Schede Umanistiche

SUP, Spisy University J. E. Purkyně, Brno

SupEz, Съпоставително езикознание, Sofia

SV, Studi Veneziani

SZ, Studia Zamorensia

TAL, Travaux d'Archéologie Limousine, Limoges

TAm, The Americas, Bethesda

TAPS, Transactions of the American Philosophical Society

TB, Tempo Brasileiro

TBL, Tübinger Beiträge zur Linguistik, Tübingen, Narr

TC, Texto Critico

TCBS, Transactions of the Cambridge Bibliographical Society

TCERFM, Travaux du Centre d'Études et de Recherches sur François Mauriac, Bordeaux

TCL, Twentieth-Century Literature

TCLN, Travaux du Cercle Linguistique de Nice

TCWAAS, Transactions of the Cumberland and Westmorland Antiquarian and Archaeological Society

TD, Teksty Drugie

TDC, Textes et Documents pour la Classe

TEC, Teresiunum Ephemerides Carmeliticae

TECC, Textos i Estudis de Cultura Catalana, Curial — Publicacions de l'Abadia de Montserrat, Barcelona

TeK, Text und Kontext

TELK, Trouvaillen — Editionen zur Literatur- und Kulturgeschichte, Berne, Lang

TeN, Terminologies Nouvelles

TeSt, Teatro e Storia

TE(XVIII), Textos y Estudios del Siglo XVIII

TF, Texte zur Forschung, Darmstadt, Wissenschaftliche Buchgesellschaft

TFN, Texte der Frühen Neuzeit, Frankfurt am Main, Keip

TGLSK, Theorie und Geschichte der Literatur und der Schönen Künste, Munich, Fink

TGSI, Transactions of the Gaelic Society of Inverness

THESOC, Thesaurus Occitan

THL, Theory and History of Literature, Manchester U.P.

THM, Textos Hispánicos Modernos, Barcelona, Labor

THR, Travaux d'Humanisme et Renaissance, Geneva, Droz

THSC, Transactions of the Honourable Society of Cymmrodorion

TI, Le Texte et l'Idée

TidLit, Tidskrift för Litteraturvetenskap

TILAS, Travaux de l'Institut d'Études Latino-Américaines de l'Université de Strasbourg

TILL, Travaux de l'Institut de Linguistique de Lund

TJ, Theatre Journal

TK, Text und Kritik, Munich

TKS, Търновска книжевна школа, Sofia

TL, Theoretical Linguistics

TLF, Textes Littéraires Français, Geneva, Droz

TLit, Travaux de Littérature

TLP, Travaux de Linguistique et de Philologie

TLQ, Travaux de Linguistique Québécoise

TLTL, Teaching Language Through Literature

TM, Les Temps Modernes

TMJb, Thomas Mann-Jahrbuch

TMo, O Tempo e o Modo

TMS, Thomas-Mann Studien, Frankfurt, Klostermann

TN, Theatre Notebook

TNA, Tijdschrift voor Nederlands en Afrikaans

TNT, Towarzystwo Naukowe w Toruniu

TOc, Tèxtes Occitans, Bordeaux

TODL, Труды Отдела древнерусской литературы Института русской литературы АН СССР

TP, Textual Practice

TPa, Torre de Papel

TPS, Transactions of the Philological Society

TQ, Theatre Quarterly

TR, Телевидение и радиовещание

TravL, Travaux de Linguistique, Luxembourg

TRCTL, Texte-Revue de Critique et de Théorie Littéraire

TRI, Theatre Research International

TrK, Трезвость и культура

TrL, Travaux de Linguistique

TrLit, Translation and Literature

TRS, The Transactions of the Radnorshire Society

TS, Theatre Survey

TSC, Treballs de Sociolingüística Catalana

TSDL, Tübinger Studien zur deutschen Literatur, Frankfurt, Lang

TSJ, Tolstoy Studies Journal

TSL, Trierer Studien zur Literatur, Frankfurt, Lang

TSLL, Texas Studies in Literature and Language

TSM, Texte des späten Mittelalters und der frühen Neuzeit, Berlin, Schmidt

TsNTL, Tijdschrift voor Nederlandse Taal- en Letterkunde

TSRLL, Tulane Studies in Romance Languages and Literature

TsSk, Tijdschrift voor Skandinavistiek

TsSV, Tijdschrift voor de Studie van de Verlichting

TSWL, Tulsa Studies in Women's Literature

TT, Tekst en Tijd, Nijmegen, Alfa

TT, Travail Théâtral

TTAS, Twayne Theatrical Arts Series, Boston–New York

TTG, Texte und Textgeschichte, Tübingen, Niemeyer

TTr, Terminologie et Traduction

TUGS, Texte und Untersuchungen zur Germanistik und Skandinavistik, Frankfurt, Lang

TVS, Theorie und Vermittlung der Sprache, Frankfurt, Lang

TWAS, Twayne's World Authors Series, Boston–New York

TWQ, Third World Quarterly

UAB, Universitat Autònoma de Barcelona

UAC, Universidad de Antioquia, Colombia

UAM, Uniwersytet Adama Mickiewicza, Poznań

UB, Universal-Bibliothek, Stuttgart, Reclam

UBL, Universal-Bibliothek, Leipzig, Reclam

UCLWPL, UCL Working Papers in Linguistics

UCPL, University of California
Publications in Linguistics

UCPMP, University of California
Publications in Modern Philology

UDL, Untersuchungen zur
deutschen Literaturgeschichte,
Tübingen, Niemeyer

UDR, University of Dayton Review

UFPB, Universidade Federal da
Paraiba

UFRGS, Univ. Federal do Rio
Grande do Sul (Brazil)

UFRJ, Universidade Federal do Rio
de Janeiro

UFSC, Universidade Federal de
Santa Catarina

UGE, Union Générale d'Éditions

UGFGP, University of Glasgow
French and German Publications

UL, Українське
літературознавство, Lvov U.P.

UM, Українська мова і література
в школі

UMCS, Uniwersytet Marii Curie-
Skłodowskiej, Lublin

UMov, Українське мовазнавство

UNAM, Universidad Nacional
Autónoma de Mexico

UNC, Univ. of North Carolina

UNCSGL, University of North
Carolina Studies in Germanic
Languages and Literatures,
Chapel Hill

UNED, Universidad Nacional de
Enseñanza a Distancia

UNESP, Universidade Estadual de
São Paulo

UNMH, University of Nottingham
Monographs in the Humanities

UPP, University of Pennsylvania
Press, Philadelphia

UQ, Ukrainian Quarterly

UR, Umjetnost riječi

USCFLS, University of South
Carolina French Literature Series

USFLQ, University of South Florida
Language Quarterly

USH, Umeå Studies in the
Humanities, Stockholm, Almqvist
& Wiksell International

USLL, Utah Studies in Literature
and Linguistics, Berne, Lang

USP, Universidade de São Paulo

UTB, Uni-Taschenbücher

UTET, Unione Tipografico-
Editrice Torinese

UTPLF, Università di Torino,
Pubblicazioni della Facoltà di
Lettere e Filosofia

UTQ, University of Toronto
Quarterly

UVAN, Українська Вільна
Академія Наук, Winnipeg

UVWPL, University of Venice
Working Papers in Linguistics

UWCASWC, The University of
Wales Centre for Advanced
Studies in Welsh and Celtic

UZLU, Ученые записки
Ленинградского университета

VAM, Vergessene Autoren der
Moderne, Siegen U.P.

VAS, Vorträge und Abhandlungen
zur Slavistik, Giessen, Schmitz

VASSLOI, Veröffentlichungen der
Abteilung für Slavische Sprachen
und Literaturen des Osteuropa–
Instituts (Slavistiches Seminar) an
der Freien Universität Berlin

VB, Vestigia Bibliae

VBDU, Веснік Беларускага
дзяржаўнага ўніверсітэта імя
У. І. Леніна. Серыя IV

VCT, Les Voies de la Création
Théâtrale

VDASD, Veröffentlichungen der
Deutschen Akademie für Sprache
und Dichtung, Darmstadt,
Luchterhand

VF, Вопросы философии

VGBIL, Всесоюзная
государственная библиотека
иностранной литературы

VH, Vida Hispánica,
Wolverhampton

VHis, Verba Hispanica

VI, Военно издателство

VI, Voix et Images

VIa, Вопросы языкознания

VIN, Veröffentlichungen des
Instituts für niederländische
Philologie, Erftstadt, Lukassen

ViSH, Вища школа

VIst, Вопросы истории

Vit, Вітчизна

VKP, Всесоюзная книжная палата

VL, Вопросы литературы

VLet, Voz y Letras

VM, Время и мы, New York — Paris — Jerusalem

VMKA, Verslagen en Mededelingen, Koninklijke Academie voor Nederlandse Taal- en Letterkunde

VMUF, Вестник Московского университета. Серия IX, филология

VMUFil, Вестник Московского университета. Серия VII, философия

VÖAW, Verlag der Österreichischen Akademie der Wissenschaften, Vienna

Voz, Возрождение

VP, Встречи с прошлым, Moscow

VPen, Vita e Pensiero

VR, Vox Romanica

VRKhD, Вестник Русского христианского движения

VRL, Вопросы русской литературы

VRM, Volkskultur am Rhein und Maas

VS, Вопросы семантики

VSAV, Vydavateľstvo Slovenskej akadémie vied

VSh, Вышэйшая школа

VSh, Визвольний шлях

VSPU, Вестник Санкт-Петербургского университета

VSSH, Вечерняя средняя школа

VV, Византийский временник

VVM, Vlastivědný věstník moravský

VVSh, Вестник высшей школы

VWGÖ, Verband der wissenschaftlichen Gesellschaften Österreichs

VySh, Вища школа

VysSh, Высшая школа

VyV, Verdad y Vida

VZ, Vukova zadužbina, Belgrade

WAB, Wolfenbütteler Arbeiten zur Barockforschung, Wiesbaden, Harrassowitz

WADL, Wiener Arbeiten zur deutschen Literatur, Vienna, Braumüller

WAGAPH, Wiener Arbeiten zur germanischen Altertumskunde und Philologie, Vienna, Halosar

WAiF, Wydawnictwa Artystyczne i Filmowe, Warsaw

WaT, Wagenbachs Taschenbücherei, Berlin, Wagenbach

WB, Weimarer Beiträge

WBDP, Würzburger Beiträge zur deutschen Philologie, Würzburg, Königshausen & Neumann

WBG, Wissenschaftliche Buchgesellschaft, Darmstadt

WBN, Wolfenbütteler Barock-Nachrichten

WF, Wege der Forschung, Darmstadt, Wissenschaftliche Buchgesellschaft

WGCR, West Georgia College Review

WGY, Women in German Yearbook

WHNDL, Würzburger Hochschulschriften zur neueren Deutschen Literaturgeschichte, Frankfurt, Lang

WHR, The Welsh History Review

WIFS, Women in French Studies

WKJb, Wissenschaftskolleg. Institute for Advanced Study, Berlin. Jahrbuch

WL, Wydawnictwo Literackie, Cracow

WŁ, Wydawnictwo Łódzkie

WLub, Wydawnictwo Lubelskie

WLT, World Literature Today

WM, Wissensliteratur im Mittelalter, Wiesbaden, Reichert

WNB, Wolfenbütteler Notizen zur Buchgeschichte

WNT, Wydawnictwa Naukowo-Techniczne

WoB, Wolfenbütteler Beiträge

WoF, Wolfenbütteler Forschungen, Wiesbaden, Harrassowitz

WP, Wiedza Powszechna, Warsaw

WPEL, Working Papers in Educational Linguistics

WPFG, Working Papers in Functional Grammar, Amsterdam U.P.

WRM, Wolfenbütteler Renaissance
Mitteilungen
WS, Wort und Sinn
WSA, Wolfenbütteler Studien zur
Aufklärung, Tübingen, Niemeyer
WSiP, Wydawnictwa Szkolne i
Pedagogiczne, Warsaw
WSJ, Wiener Slavistisches Jahrbuch
WSl, Die Welt der Slaven
WSlA, Wiener Slawistischer
Almanach
WSP, Wyższa Szkoła Pedagogiczna
WSp, Word and Spirit
WSPRRNDFP, Wyższa Szkoła
Pedagogiczna w Rzeszowie.
Rocznik Naukowo-Dydaktyczny.
Filologia Polska
WuW, Welt und Wort
WUW, Wydawnictwo Uniwersytetu
Wrocławskiego
WW, Wirkendes Wort
WWAG, Woman Writers in the Age
of Goethe
WWE, Welsh Writing in English. A
Yearbook of Critical Essays
WZHUB, Wissenschaftliche
Zeitschrift der Humboldt-
Universität, Berlin: gesellschafts-
und sprachwissenschaftliche
Reihe
WZPHP, Wissenschaftliche
Zeitschrift der pädagogischen
Hochschule Potsdam.
Gesellschafts- und
sprachwissenschaftliche Reihe
WZUG, Wissenschaftliche
Zeitschrift der Ernst-Moritz-
Arndt- Universität Greifswald
WZUH, Wissenschaftliche
Zeitschrift der Martin-Luther-
Universität Halle-Wittenberg:
gesellschafts- und
sprachwissenschaftliche Reihe
WZUJ, Wissenschaftliche
Zeitschrift der Friedrich-Schiller-
Universität Jena/Thüringen:
gesellschafts-und
sprachwissenschaftliche Reihe
WZUL, Wissenschaftliche
Zeitschrift der Karl Marx
Universität Leipzig: gesellschafts-
und sprachwissenschaftliche
Reihe

WZUR, Wissenschaftliche
Zeitschrift der Universität
Rostock: gesellschafts- und
sprachwissenschaftliche Reihe

YaIS, Yale Italian Studies
YB, Ysgrifau Beirniadol
YCC, Yearbook of Comparative
Criticism
YCGL, Yearbook of Comparative
and General Literature
YDAMEIS, Yearbook of the Dutch
Association for Middle Eastern
and Islamic Studies
YEEP, Yale Russian and East
European Publications, New
Haven, Yale Center for
International and Area Studies
YES, Yearbook of English Studies
YFS, Yale French Studies
YIP, Yale Italian Poetry
YIS, Yearbook of Italian Studies
YJC, Yale Journal of Criticism
YM, Yearbook of Morphology
YPL, York Papers in Linguistics
YR, Yale Review
YSGP, Yearbook. Seminar for
Germanic Philology
YSPS, The Yearbook of the Society
of Pirandello Studies
YWMLS, The Year's Work in
Modern Language Studies

ZÄAK, Zeitschrift für Ästhetik und
allgemeine Kunstwissenschaft
ZB, Zeitschrift für Balkanologie
ZBL, Zeitschrift für bayerische
Landesgeschichte
ZbS, Zbornik za slavistiku
ZCP, Zeitschrift für celtische
Philologie
ZD, Zielsprache Deutsch
ZDA, Zeitschrift für deutsches
Altertum und deutsche Literatur
ZDL, Zeitschrift für Dialektologie
und Linguistik
ZDNÖL, Zirkular.
Dokumentationsstelle für neuere
österreichische Literatur
ZDP, Zeitschrift für deutsche
Philologie

ZFKPhil, Zborník Filozofickej
    fakulty Univerzity Komenského.
    Philologica
ZFL, Zbornik za filologiju i
    lingvistiku
ZFSL, Zeitschrift für französische
    Sprache und Literatur
ZGB, Zagreber germanistische
    Beiträge
ZGer, Zeitschrift für Germanistik
ZGKS, Zeitschrift der Gesellschaft
    für Kanada-Studien
ZGL, Zeitschrift für germanistische
    Linguistik
ZGS, Zürcher germanistische
    Studien, Berne, Lang
ZK, Zeitschrift für Katalanistik
ZL, Zeszyty Literackie, Paris
ZMS(FL), Zbornik Matice srpske za
    filologiju i lingvistiku
ZMS(KJ), Zbornik Matice srpske za
    književnost i jezik
ZMS(Sl), Zbornik Matice srpske za
    slavistiku
ZNiO, Zakład Narodowy im.
    Ossolińskich, Wrocław
ZnS, Знание — сила
ZNTSh, Записки Наукового
    товариства ім. Шевченка
ZNUG, Zeszyty Naukowe Uniw.
    Gdańskiego, Gdańsk
ZNUJ, Zeszyty Naukowe Uniw.
    Jagiellońskiego, Cracow
ZNWHFR, Zeszyty Naukowe
    Wydziału Humanistycznego.
    Filologia Rosyjska

ZNWSPO, Zeszyty Naukowe
    Wyższej Szkoly Pedagogicznej w
    Opolu
ZO$_x$ Zeitschrift für Ostforschung
ZPSSlav, Zborník Pedagogickej
    fakulty v Prešove Univerzity
    Pavla Jozefa Šafárika v
    Košiciach-Slavistika, Bratislava
ZR, Zadarska revija
ZRAG, Записки русской
    академической группы в США
ZRBI, Зборник радова
    бизантолошког института,
    Belgrade
ZRL, Zagadnienia Rodzajów
    Literackich
ZRP, Zeitschrift für romanische
    Philologie
ZS, Zeitschrift für
    Sprachwissenschaft
ZSJ, Zápisnik slovenského
    jazykovedca
ZSK, Ze Skarbca Kultury
ZSL, Zeitschrift für siebenbürgische
    Landeskunde
ZSl, Zeitschrift für Slawistik
ZSP, Zeitschrift für slavische
    Philologie
ZSVS, Zborník Spolku
    vojvodinských slovakistov, Novi
    Sad
ZT, Здесь и теперь
ZV, Zeitschrift für Volkskunde
ZvV, Звезда востока
ZWL, Zeitschrift für
    württembergische
    Landesgeschichte

NAME INDEX

Monti, S., 281
Monti, V., 460, 462
Monticelli, T., 449
Montoliu, C. de, 298
Montoro, A. de, 217
Montoro, J. de, 217
Montoro, S. A. de, 217
Montoya, J., 209
Montoya Ramírez, M. I., 221
Montreuil, J.-P., 45
Montseny, F., 268
Monville-Burston, M., 48
Monzó, Q., 301
Moonen, A., 786
Moore, C. N., 635
Moos, P. von, 570
Mora, F., 61
Mora, J. L., 243
Mora Guarnido, J., 257
Moracchini, G., 367
Moraes, J., 305, 306
Moraes, M. A., 305
Moral, J. del., 236
Morales, C. J., 280
Morales, L., 333
Moran, B. T., 625
Moran Ocenrinjauregui, J., 293
Morand, P., 148
Morandini, G., 467, 472
Morante, E., 472, 493
Morasso, M., 472
Morata, O. F., 412
Moravia, A., 493
Morawe, B., 721
Mörchen, H., 769
More, T., 619
Moreira, B., 308
Moreira, L. F., 342, 344
Moreiro, J., 249
Morejón, N., 334
Morel, R., 117
Moreland, J., 574
Morell, C.-M., 246
Morell, C. R., 242
Morell, H. R., 331
Morelli, G., 253, 256
Morelli Timpanaro, M. A., 452
Morelo, A., 458
Morelowski, J., 890
Moreno, A., 308
Moreno Cabrera, J. C., 25
Moreno Hernández, C., 247
Moreno Martínez, M., 241
Moreno Villa, J., 254, 256, 261
Moretti, G., 504
Moretti, M., 471
Morgan, D. Ll., 530, 532
Morgan, G., 521
Morgana, S., 421
Morgenthaler, W., 706, 728

Morgner, I., 754, 770–71
Mori, M., 273
Mori, O., 728
Mori, R., 52
Mörike, E., 699, 700, 731
Moritz (*Duke of Saxony*), 616
Moritz, K. P., 670, 675, 679, 703, 836
Moritz, R., 751
Moriuht, 4
Mørkhagen, S., 812
Morley, J. M., 723
Mormando, F., 10
Mornin, E., 681
Moro, A., 22, 362
Moro, C., 400
Morotti, S., 482
Moroz, A., 871
Morpurgo Davies, A., 15
Morrall, E. J., 595
Morrás, M., 217
Morris, C., 750
Morris, H., 330
Morris, L., 530
Morrison, I., 106
Morrison, J., 696
Morselli, G., 493
Morsztyn, J. A., 885, 886
Mortara Garavelli, B., 473
Mortenson, I., 811
Morvan, F., 537
Moscardelli, N., 470
Moscherosch, J. P., 639
Mose, G., 809
Moser, C., 666
Moser, D.-R., 595, 729
Möser, J., 653
Mosès, F., 59
Mosès, S., 691, 744
Mosetti Casaretto, F., 3
Mosiołek-Kłosińska, K., 874
Moskwin, A., 893
Moss, A., 89, 95, 623, 624
Mota, C., 212
Mota, J., 311
Mota, M. A. C., 308, 911
Mothu, A., 139, 142
Motta, U., 429, 508
Mottausch, K.-H., 549, 802
Motz, L., 580, 802
Moulakis, A., 169
Moulis, A., 198
Mourão, E., 307
Mouret, F., 94
Mourey, M.-T., 633
Mourin, Y.-C., 44
Mouton, C., 878
Moutote, D., 158
Moyà, Ll., 300
Moysich, H., 767

Mozarska-Tycowa, Z., 891
Mozzarelli, C., 431
Mral, M., 822
Mrhačová, E., 880
Mrowcewicz, K., 886
Mrożek, S., 889, 901, 902, 906
Mrozowicz, W., 606
Mücke, D. von, 645
Mudersbach, K., 548
Mudimbe-Boyi, E., 184
Mufwene, S., 26
Múgica, D., 270
Mühlbach, L., 698, 731
Mühlethaler, J. C., 109
Mühlpfort, H., 634
Muhr, R., 544
Muhs, R., 714
Muir, E., 618
Mujdei, C., 24
Mujica, B., 916
Mukhtar, A., 799
Mulch, R., 563
Mulder, E., 764
Mülder-Bach, I., 647
Muljačić, Ž., 14, 26
Mullally, E., 917
Mullen, E. J., 334
Müller, A., 677
Müller, A. L., 308
Müller, B., 24
Muller, C., 21, 35
Müller, D., 696, 728
Müller, E., 757
Müller, F., 651, 652, 670, 705
Müller, G., 560, 691, 695, 913
Müller, H., 720, 762, 771–72, 772–73
Müller, H.-H., 750
Müller, I., 773
Müller, J., 561
Müller, J.-D., 588, 621, 625, 68
Müller, M. G., 615
Müller, O., 916
Müller, P. O., 549, 622
Müller, U., 581, 597, 604, 618, 769
Müller, W., 571, 618, 773
Müller-Dietz, H., 661
Müller-Jahncke, W.-D., 624
Müller-Ott, D., 878
Müllerová, O., 861, 865
Müller-Salget, K., 687, 689
Müller-Waldeck, G., 745
Müller-Wille, K., 836
Multatuli, 789, 790
Munaro, N., 364, 367
Munch, A., 808, 812, 813
Münchberg, K., 392
Munck, K., 840
Mundhenk, C., 7